The International Legal Status and Protection of Environmentally-Displaced Persons: A European Perspective

International Refugee Law Series

Editor-in-Chief

David James Cantor

Editorial Board

Deborah Anker
Bhupinder Chimni
Geoff Gilbert
Guy S. Goodwin-Gill
Liliana Jubilut
Susan Kneebone
Hélène Lambert
Bonaventure Rutinwa
Volker Türk

VOLUME 8

The titles published in this series are listed at *brill.com/irls*

The International Legal Status and Protection of Environmentally-Displaced Persons: A European Perspective

By

Hélène Ragheboom

BRILL
NIJHOFF

LEIDEN | BOSTON

Library of Congress Cataloging-in-Publication Data

Names: Ragheboom, Hélène, author.
Title: The international legal status and protection of
   environmentally-displaced persons : a European perspective / By Hélène
   Ragheboom.
Description: Leiden : Brill Nijhoff, 2017. | Series: International refugee
   law series ; 8 | Includes bibliographical references and index.
Identifiers: LCCN 2017018353 (print) | LCCN 2017022710 (ebook) | ISBN
   9789004317420 (E-book) | ISBN 9789004317413 (hardback : alk. paper)
Subjects: LCSH: Environmental refugees--Legal status, laws, etc.--European
   Union countries. | Human rights--European Union countries. | Forced
   migration. | International law. | Climatic changes--Social aspects.
Classification: LCC KJE6057 (ebook) | LCC KJE6057 .R34 2017 (print) | DDC
   342.2408/3--dc23
LC record available at https://lccn.loc.gov/2017018353

Typeface for the Latin, Greek, and Cyrillic scripts: "Brill". See and download: brill.com/brill-typeface.

ISSN 2213-3836
ISBN 978-90-04-31741-3 (hardback)
ISBN 978-90-04-31742-0 (e-book)

Copyright 2017 by Koninklijke Brill NV, Leiden, The Netherlands.
Koninklijke Brill NV incorporates the imprints Brill, Brill Hes & De Graaf, Brill Nijhoff, Brill Rodopi and Hotei Publishing.
All rights reserved. No part of this publication may be reproduced, translated, stored in a retrieval system, or transmitted in any form or by any means, electronic, mechanical, photocopying, recording or otherwise, without prior written permission from the publisher.
Authorization to photocopy items for internal or personal use is granted by Koninklijke Brill NV provided that the appropriate fees are paid directly to The Copyright Clearance Center, 222 Rosewood Drive, Suite 910, Danvers, MA 01923, USA. Fees are subject to change.

This book is printed on acid-free paper and produced in a sustainable manner.

Contents

Acknowledgements VII
List of Abbreviations IX

Introduction 1

PART 1
Protecting People Fleeing Indiscriminate Threats: Law and Practice within the European Union

Introduction to Part 1 21

1 Preliminary Remark: Member States' Obligations under International Human Rights Law are Unaltered by EU Membership 23

2 European Union Law Relevant to Asylum 33

3 Relevant Provisions of International Human Rights Law 182

4 Member States' Non-harmonised Protection Responses 268

5 Conclusions of Part 1 277

PART 2
Testing Existing Refugee Law, Human Rights Law and Practices through the Prism of Environmental Disasters

Introduction to Part 2 281

6 Environmentally-Displaced Persons as Beneficiaries of International Protection under Refugee Law? 293

7 Under International Human Rights Law 358

8 State Practice in Response to Disasters and Other Humanitarian Crises 399

9 Conclusions of Part 2 422

PART 3
Exploring Means of Protecting "environmental refugees" in International Law

Introduction to Part 3   427

10   Solutions Based on Existing Asylum Law and Relevant Norms International Human Rights Law   429

11   Can (and Should) States be Held Responsible for Environmental Displacement?   489

12   A *Sui Generis* Framework to Address Environmental Displacement and Migration   505

13   Conclusion of Part 3   571

General Conclusion   572

Annex   577
Bibliography   589
Index   668

Acknowledgements

This book is based on my doctoral thesis, written at the Faculty of Law of the University of Luxembourg between 2008 and 2012. The content has been updated since, to take account of recent development. In particular, it was truly inspirational and stimulating to note that the outcome of my work was being corroborated by the findings of the Nansen Initiative. Throughout the process of writing my doctoral dissertation, I have received support and encouragement from numerous people. I wish to express my sincere gratitude to all those who contributed from near or far to this adventure, and will name below but a few of them.

I am grateful to the Luxemburgish *Fonds National de la Recherche* (FNR) for the generous and indispensable funding I received for the duration of my PhD studies, and to the University of Luxembourg. Within the University, I thank my PhD supervisor, Jörg Gerkrath, as well as the other members of my PhD committee, Patrick Kinsch and Rusen Ergec, for their guidance but also for the autonomy they entrusted me with. Furthermore, I am indebted to those, colleagues and friends, who facilitated my work and provided me with precious advice, comments and company. Anne-Marie Vesdrevanis, Katya Islentyeva, Marie Marty, Christian Deprez, Lawrence and Chris Siry, Martin Petschko, and Wessel Vermeulen, thank you for your unaltered faith in my work. Lawrence, thank you again, for reading and commenting on my dissertation.

A few months working at UNHCR Regional Representation for the Benelux and European Institutions in Brussels constituted a very useful introduction to my PhD work, providing me with invaluable insight in the field of asylum law and policies, at the national, European and global levels.

I was delighted to return to Lund, Sweden, where I could research and discuss with professors, former colleagues and friends at the Raoul Wallenberg Institute (RWI) and the Faculty of Law. It was, as always, a great source of motivation and inspiration. In particular, I wish to thank Gregor Noll, Olof Beckman and Nina-Louisa Arold for stimulating discussions, Rolf Ring for his friendship and help in organising my stay, and Lena Olsson, as a friend and as the fairy godmother of the RWI plentiful library.

I also had the privilege and pleasure of spending some time researching in Montreal, at McGill Centre for Human Rights & Legal Pluralism (McGill University, Faculty of Law). I am immensely grateful to Nandini Ramanujam and François Crépeau, who made this research stay possible. I reiterate my thanks to François Crépeau in particular, for his genuine interest in my work and for his availability, unaltered by his otherwise busy schedule.

Additionally, a number of persons, working in various institutions, kindly shared with me useful publications, information and explanations. Liv Feijen and Nabil Benbekhti (UNHCR), and Barbara Derain (OFPRA) were among them.

Many thanks to my dissertation defense committee, Jörg Gerkrath and Rusen Ergec (University of Luxembourg), Laura Westra (York University, Canada), Walter Kälin (University of Bern, Switzerland and Envoy of the Chairmanship of the Nansen Initiative) and Jean-Pierre Marguénaud (University of Limoges, France). It was an honour and a true pleasure to discuss my work with them.

I would also like to thank Jane McAdam (University of New South Wales) and David James Cantor (University of London), who have been decisive in convincing me to publish this book.

Lastly, I thank the Ministry of Foreign and European Affairs of Luxembourg. As legal adviser and human rights desk officer within the Directorate for Political Affairs, I was given the opportunity to participate in discussions on climate change, human rights and displacement, notably within the UN Human Rights Council, the EU Working Party on Human Rights (COHOM), and the Nansen Initiative.

Above all, I am greatly indebted to those, family and friends, who have been a true source of motivation going forth and an infallible safety net. My mother, father and brother, my cousins Camille, Claire, Nicolas and Rémy, Eszter, Jonas and Vreni, Emilie and Philippe.

Maman, tu as été parfaite.

List of Abbreviations

1933 Convention	Convention Relating to the International Status of Refugees of 28 October 1933, *LNTS* Vol. CLIX, p. 199
1951 Convention	Convention Relating to the Status of Refugees, adopted 28 July 1951, entered into force 22 April 1954, *UNTS* Vol. 189, p. 137
AALCO	Asian-African Legal Consultative Organization
ACHPR	African Charter on Human and Peoples' Rights
ACHR	American Convention on Human Rights
ACnHPR	African Commission on Human and Peoples' Rights
Amsterdam Treaty	Treaty of Amsterdam Amending the Treaty on European Union, the Treaties Establishing the European Communities and Related Acts [10 November 1997] *OJ* C 340/1
APG	Asylum process guidance (published by the UK Home Office Border Agency)
API	Asylum Policy Instruction (published by the UK Home Office Border Agency)
Arab Charter	League of Arab States, Arab Charter on Human Rights, adopted 15 September 1994, entered into force 15 March 2008, reprinted in *International Human Rights Report* Vol. 12, p. 893 [2005]
AU	African Union
AU Convention	African Union Convention Governing the Specific Aspects of Refugee Problems in Africa, 10 September 1969, *UNTS* Vol. 1001, p. 45
AU Convention	African Union Convention Governing the Specific Aspects of Refugee Problems in Africa, 10 September 1969, *UNTS* Vol. 1001, p. 45
Bangkok Principles	Asian-African Legal Consultative Organization (AALCO) Bangkok Principles on the Status and Treatment of Refugees, 31 December 1966
BVerwG	Germany: *Bundesverwaltungsgericht* (Federal Administrative Court)
Cairo Declaration	UN GAOR, Cairo Declaration on Human Rights in Islam, 5 August 1990, World Conference on Human Rights, 4th Sess., Agenda Item 5, UN Doc A/CONF.157/PC/62/Add.18, [1993]

Cartagena Declaration	Cartagena Declaration on Refugees, 22 November 1984, Colloquium on the International Protection of Refugees in Central America, Mexico and Panama
CAT	Convention against Torture and Other Cruel, Inhuman or Degrading Treatment or Punishment, 10 December 1984, entered into force 26 June 1987, UNTS Vol. 1465, p. 85
CE	French highest administrative court: *Conseil d'État* (Council of State)
CEDAW	Convention on the Elimination of All Forms of Discrimination against Women
CERD	Committee on the Elimination of Racial Discrimination
CESCR	Committee on Economic, Social and Cultural Rights
CESEDA	France: *Code de l'entrée et du séjour des étrangers et du droit d'asile* (French code on immigration and asylum)
Charter of Fundamental Rights	Charter of Fundamental Rights of the European Union [14/12/2007] OJ C 303/01
CJ	Court of Justice (commonly referred to as European Court of Justice – ECJ)
CJEU	Court of Justice of the European Union (including the Court of Justice, the General Court and specialised courts)
CNDA	France: *Cour nationale du droit d'asile* (National Court of Asylum), ex Commission des recours des réfugiés – CRR
CoE	Council of Europe
CRDP	Centre de recherche sur les droits de la personne (University of Limoges, France)
CRIDEAU	Centre de recherches interdisciplinaires en droit de l'environnement de l'aménagement et de l'urbanisme (University of Limoges, France)
Dublin Regulation	EU, Council Regulation (EC) No 343/2003 of 18 February 2003 Establishing the Criteria and Mechanisms for Determining the Member State Responsible for Examining an Asylum Application Lodged in One of the Member States by a Third-Country National [25/02/2003] OJ L 50/1, pp. 1–10, consolidated version of 04/12/2008
EC	European Community
ECnHR	European Commission of Human Rights
ECOSOC	United Nations Economic and Social Council
ECRE	European Council on Refugees and Exiles
ECtHR	European Court of Human Rights
EEC	European Economic Community

ELENA	ECRE's European Legal Network on Asylum
EMN	European Migration Network
ETS	European Treaty Series
EU	European Union
EU Charter	Charter of Fundamental Rights of the European Union [14/12/2007] OJ C 303/01
Euratom	Treaty Establishing the European Atomic Energy Community, 25 March 1957, UNTS Vol. 298, p. 167
EWCA	England and Wales Court of Appeal
ExCom	Executive Committee of the High Commissioner's Programme (UNHCR)
FRA	European Union Agency for Fundamental Rights
GAOR	General Assembly Official Records
GARR	Groupe d'Appui aux Rapatriés et Réfugiés
GC	General Court (ex Court of First Instance – CFI)
Gisti	Groupe d'information et de soutien des immigrés
HRC	Human Rights Committee
IACHR	Inter-American Court of Human Rights
IASC	Inter-Agency Standing Committee
ICCPR	International Covenant on Civil and Political Rights
ICERD	International Convention on the Elimination of All Forms of Racial Discrimination
ICESCR	International Covenant on Economic, Social and Cultural Rights
IDMC	Internal Displacement Monitoring Centre
IFRC	International Federation of Red Cross and Red Crescent Societies
IGO	Intergovernmental organization
ILC	International Law Commission
ILC Articles RIO	International Law Commission, Articles on the Responsibility of International Organizations, with Commentaries, adopted by the ILC at its sixty-third session, in 2011, [2011] *Yearbook of the International Law Commission* Vol. II, Part 2
ILM	International Legal Materials
IOM	International Organization for Migration
IPCC	Intergovernmental Panel on Climate Change
Lisbon Treaty	Treaty of Lisbon Amending the Treaty on European Union and the Treaty Establishing the European Community, 13 December 2007, entered into force 1 December 2009, [17 December 2007] OJ C 306/50

LNTS	League of Nations Treaty Series
OCHA	Office for the Coordination of Humantiarian Affairs
OFPRA	France: *Office français de protection des réfugiés et apatrides* (Office for the Protection of Refugees and Stateless Persons)
OHCHR	Office of the United Nations High Commissioner for Human Rights
OJ	Official Journal
PACE	Parliamentary Assembly of the Council of Europe
Procedures Directive	European Union, Council Directive 2005/85/EC of 1 December 2005 on Minimum Standards on Procedures in Member States for Granting and Withdrawing Refugee Status [13/12/2005] *OJ* L 326/13
QD	Qualification Directive
Qualification Directive	EU, Directive 2011/95/EU of the European Parliament and of the Council of 13 December 2011 on Standards for the Qualification of Third-Country Nationals or Stateless Persons as Beneficiaries of International Protection, for a Uniform Status for Refugees or for Persons Eligible for Subsidiary Protection, and for the Content of the Protection Granted [20/12/2011] *OJ* L 337/09, pp. 9–26
Qualification Directive (2004)	EU Council of the European Union, Council Directive 2004/83/EC of 29 April 2004 on Minimum Standards for the Qualification and Status of Third Country Nationals or Stateless Persons as Refugees or as Persons Who Otherwise Need International Protection and the Content of the Protection Granted, 2004/83/EC, [30 September 2004] *OJ* L 304/12
Reception Conditions Directive	European Union, Council Directive 2003/9/EC of 27 January 2003 Laying Down Minimum Standards for the Reception of Asylum Seeker [06/02/2003] *OJ* L 31/18
Refugee Convention	Convention Relating to the Status of Refugees, adopted 28 July 1951, entered into force 22 April 1954, UNTS Vol. 189, p. 137
TEC (1997)	Treaties Establishing the European Community, Consolidated Amsterdam version [10 November 1997] OJ C 340/03
Temporary Protection Directive	Council Directive 2001/55/EC of 20 July 2001 on Minimum Standards for Giving Temporary Protection in the Event of a Mass Influx of Displaced Persons, 2001/55/EC, [7 August 2001] *OJ* L 212/12
TEU	Treaty on European Union

LIST OF ABBREVIATIONS

TEU (1992)	Treaty on European Union, signed in Maastricht, 29 July 1992, [1992] *OJ* C 191/01
TEU (1997)	Treaty on European Union, Consolidated Amsterdam version [10 November 1997] OJ C 340/02
TFEU	Treaty on the Functioning of the European Union
Treaty of Rome	Treaty Establishing the European Economic Community, 25 March 1957, *UNTS* Vol. 298, p. 3
UDHR	UN General Assembly, Universal Declaration of Human Rights, 10 December 1948, UNGA Res. 217 A (III)
UKAIT	United Kingdom Asylum and Immigration Tribunal
UKHL	United Kingdom House of Lords
UKIAT	United Kingdom Immigration Appeal Tribunal
UKUT	United Kingdom Upper Tribunal
UN	United Nations
UN Charter	Charter of the United Nations, 24 October 1945, *UNTS* Vol. 1 p. XVI
UNEP	United Nations Environment Programme
UNFCCC	United Nations Framework Convention on Climate Change, 9 May 1992 [1992] UNTS Vol. 1771, p. 107
UNGA	United Nations General Assembly
UNHCR	Office of the United Nations High Commissioner for Refugees
UNHRC	United Nations Human Rights Council
UNSC	United Nations Security Council
UNTS	United Nations Treaty Series
VCLT	United Nations, Vienna Convention on the Law of Treaties, 23 May 1969, entered into force 27 January 1980, *UNTS* Vol. 1155, p. 331
WHO	World Health Organization

Introduction

The present work originates in an intriguing observation. Let A, B and C be nationals of State A, State B and State C respectively. A, B and C reach the territory of a Member State of the European Union where they claim asylum. Each argues that return to his country of origin would expose him to indiscriminate threats to his life or person against which his national State authorities would fail to protect him. None of them claims to be specifically targeted or denied protection by reason of factors particular to his personal circumstances. State A is in the grip of an internal armed conflict. State B was hit by a devastating earthquake that made many victims in every section of the population and destroyed housings and infrastructures, including hospitals and governmental buildings. State C was the scene of a disastrous nuclear power plant accident that exposes the population to accumulated radiation exposures, and caused long-term contamination of soils, waters and food. The three claims, albeit similar, will lead to different conclusions. Neither A, B or C qualifies for refugee status but other forms of protection exist, that complement refugee status. In fact, under European Union legislation on asylum, the receiving Member State's authorities may recognise A as beneficiary of "subsidiary protection" but deny this status to B and C. The authorities may however choose, for compassionate reasons, to allow B and, or C to remain on the territory of the Member State, for a given period of time. The logic behind such distinction between individuals invoking similarly distressing situations does not forthrightly present itself.

In recent decades and years, the world has witnessed a growing number of events, of increasing intensity, causing the environment to deteriorate and, incidentally, the affected populations to move either within their own country or across its international border.[1] Natural disasters have always in human history triggered population movements.[2] Migration is indeed a traditional "human coping mechanism" for populations confronted with catastrophic changes in their environment;[3] it is however anticipated that the impacts of

---

[1] To be sure, suffice is to glance through disaster reports published by ReliefWeb and continuously updated. See Annex Table 4.

[2] UNHCR, "Chapter 1: Safeguarding Human Security", in *The State of the World's Refugees: A Humanitarian Agenda* (Geneva: UNHCR, 1997), Box 1.2, p. 28.

[3] J.R. Smith, "Human Adaptation to Climate Change in the Archaeological Past", presentation made during the Radcliffe Institute for Advanced Study's science symposium on "Something in the Air: Climate Change, Science and Policy", organised in Cambridge, Harvard University, on 15 April 2011.

climate change on the environment (sea-level rise, increase in intensity and frequency of severe weather events, desertification, etc.) will considerably intensify the phenomenon in the near and further future. The case of low-lying South-Pacific island States doomed to sink under rising sea level is particularly illustrative. It therefore appeared necessary and all the more topical to ponder on the issue of the international protection of persons forced to flee abroad by reason of the degradation of the environment, be it sudden or progressive, in their country of origin.

Why address climate change and environmentally-induced displacement from an international protection perspective? Some rather suggest that population movements triggered by environmental disasters are a matter of national concern or, concerning slow-onset disasters especially, at best pertain to immigration law. Proponents of such an approach will argue that this environment-related displacement will occur mainly within the national territory of States. Accordingly, populations affected by environmental degradation being internally displaced, they remain within the jurisdiction of their national State (or State of residence), the authorities of which are solely responsible for their protection and well-being. The persons concerned are entitled to the full range of human rights guaranteed by the State to all individuals within its jurisdiction. In practice however, the affected State is sometimes unable – or unwilling – to assist its internally-displaced populations. In such cases, support from the international community, in the form of a provision of humanitarian aid by States, individually or collectively through the organs of an international organisation (*e.g.* UNICEF or UNHCR for the UN) is sometimes called for. To ensure that the persons concerned are effectively protected, be it by their national State only or with the support of the international community, the adoption of a binding instrument, addressing the needs of internally-displaced persons (IDPS) is proposed.

Discussions on the adoption of a convention to this end are on-going but to date, no universally-binding instrument exists. Two progressive developments have nevertheless occurred. In 1998 were adopted the United Nations Guiding Principles on Internal Displacement.[4] They compile provisions and principles of human rights and humanitarian law relevant to the issue of internal displacement. They identify the protection needs of internally-displaced persons and urge States to adopt a number of recommended measures to address those needs. They have since been praised and often referred to, not least

---

4   UN Commission on Human Rights, *Report of the Representative of the Secretary-General, Mr. Francis M. Deng, submitted pursuant to Commission resolution 1997/39. Addendum: Guiding Principles on Internal Displacement*, 11 February 1998, E/CN.4/1998/53/Add.2.

in the context of discussions on environmentally-related displacement.⁵ At the regional level, the African Union went a step further in 2009 by adopting a legally-binding instrument: the African Union Convention for the Protection and Assistance of Internally Displaced Persons in Africa ("Kampala Convention") refers to the UN Guiding Principles.⁶

It has been repeatedly observed and denounced by international organisations and civil society mainly that internally-displaced persons are in dire straits. The adoption of an instrument of international law binding its Contracting States, in all regions of the world, to implement the rules (or similar) enshrined in the Guiding Principles would safeguard the rights and freedoms of internally-displaced persons. From the point of view of environment-related displacement however, it would fail to comprehensively address the needs of all the persons concerned. As observed by the Council of Europe:

> The *majority* of migratory movements prompted by climate change and environmental degradation are expected to occur within countries, although increased cross-border movement of people will also occur. The Assembly maintains that all the affected persons, whether or not they leave their country, need to be properly protected as regards their human, social and economic rights. Furthermore, this protection should include reliance on effective support from the international community if national support is lacking or insufficient.⁷

In certain circumstances, environmental degradation prompts populations to try and resettle in a different region within their own country or to cross their national border and seek relocation abroad.⁸ If internal displacement is likely

---

5 Participants in the 2011 Nansen Conference on climate change and displacement agreed on ten principles which should guide responses to the challenges raised by displacement in the context of environmental hazards, including the effects of climate change. The Guiding Principles on Internal Displacement were referred to and said to provide "a sound legal framework to address protection concerns arising from climate- and other environmentally-related internal displacement". Nansen Conference, *The Nansen Principles on Cross-Border Displacement*, The Nansen Conference on "Climate Change and Displacement in the 21st Century", Oslo, 5–7 June 2011, Principle VIII.
6 African Union Convention for the Protection and Assistance of Internally Displaced Persons in Africa – Kampala Convention ("AU Convention on IDPS"), 22 October 2009, entered into force 6 December 2012.
7 Council of Europe (2009), *Resolution 1655 on Environmentally Induced Migration and Displacement: A 21st Century Challenge*, § 11 [emphasis added].
8 O. Brown, *Migration and Climate Change*, No. 31 (Geneva: IOM, 2008), pp. 23–24.

to represent the majority of environmentally-induced migratory movements, the Council of Europe however notes that the amount of people moving across border is expected to increase. Some cross-border movements are in fact already observed. Projections vary but most studies yet concur on the substance: in the next decades, environmental degradation – mainly caused by climate change – will affect millions of persons, possibly hundreds of millions.

Environmental "refugees" have come to the fore, hand in hand with the controversial issue of climate change. Society growing more aware of the impacts of global warming on the planet environment, theories flourished on future floods of "climate refugees" fleeing their homes and seeking protection in third countries, less prone to disasters. In the debate on the accuracy of the model and scale of the phenomenon, a maximalist – if not alarmist[9] – school of thought opposed a minimalist one[10] and, in parallel categories it seems, natural scientists opposed social scientists.[11] On this controversial issue, which has many unknowns, the anticipated number of persons displaced by climate change varies immensely: from 25 million to one billion people could be displaced by 2050.[12] If predictions are manifestly an uneasy task, imbued with uncertainty, looking at the retrospective estimates of the global number of persons internally displaced annually by natural hazard-induced disasters offers a tangible picture of the impact of environmental change on forced displacement. The Internal Displacement Monitoring Centre (IDMC) assesses that, between 2008 and 2015, an average of 26,4 million people were uprooted by disasters brought on by natural hazards each year – *i.e.*, as tellingly pointed out by the IDMC, the equivalent of one person every second.[13] In 2014, the vast majority of them (91 percent of the 19,3 million people concerned) were displaced due to weather-related hazards, such as storms and

---

9 N. Myers and J. Kent, *Environmental Exodus: An Emergent Crisis in the Global Arena* (Washington DC: Climate Institute, June 1995); N. Stern, *The Economics of Climate Change: The Stern Review* (Cambridge: Cambridge University Press, January 2007).

10 W. Kälin and N. Schrepfer, *Protecting People Crossing Borders in the Context of Climate Change Normative Gaps and Possible Approaches*, No. PPLA/2012/01 (Geneva: UNHCR, February 2012), pp. 11–13; F. Gemenne, "Migrations et environnement : État des savoirs sur une relation méconnue", *in* Gisti (Ed.), *Quel Statut Pour Les Réfugiés Environnementaux ? Actes de La Journée Du 14 Décembre 2007* (Paris: Gisti, Juin 2008), pp. 6–7.

11 E. Piguet, *et al.*, *Migration and Climate Change* (Cambridge, New York: Cambridge University Press, UNESCO Publishing, 2011), pp. 2–6.

12 UNHCR, *The State of the World's Refugees 2012: In Search of Solidarity* (Oxford, New York: Oxford University Press, 2012), p. 171. See also references cited above notes 9 and 10.

13 M. Yonetani and IDMC, *Global Estimates 2015: People Displaced by Disasters* (Geneva: IDMC – NRC, July 2015), p. 11.

floods.[14] Scientific studies anticipate that the rise in the average temperature of the Earth's atmosphere and oceans will cause environmental changes and increase the frequency and intensity of weather-related disasters. Logic suggests that displacement triggered by environmental degradations will follow a similar pattern (logical as it may be, this deduction however overlooks the positive impact adaptation, resilience-building, resettlement and other measures may have on mitigating the impacts of disasters on the environment and populations). The above estimates, although they concern internal displacement specifically, are pertinent insofar as they illustrate beyond doubt the impact of environmental change on forced displacement.[15] There is only one short step to conclude that, even if international displacement will only represent a minority of environmentally-induced migratory movements, the number of persons concerned will nevertheless be significant and displacement therefore affect not only States of origin but also destination States. Addressing the situation of those who are often referred to as "environmental refugees" is therefore a necessity, in legal as well as in moral terms.

Moreover and as mentioned earlier, the entry point in the topic was not migration but forced displacement. The idea behind this work was spurred on by the apparent gap, not to say inconsistency, in European Union asylum law, which grants a protective status to individuals who flee certain life-threatening situations (generalised violence) but not others (severe environmental degradation). It is commonly noted by humanitarian agencies and non-governmental organisations that individuals forced to leave their home will only do so after all efforts to adapt have been exhausted. In most cases, they will first seek to relocate within their country. Cross-border displacement is often a secondary movement: it generally occurs only as a last resort, after internal migration has failed to provide them with safe conditions of living.[16] It can be deduced from this observation that people who move across borders are those who have no other option. They flee uninhabitable regions; in that sense, they are compelled to leave and are therefore in genuine need of international protection.

14   Ibid., pp. 19–20.
15   On the correlation between environmental degradation and subsequent movements of population, see: A. Lopez, "The Protection of Environmentally-Displaced Persons in International Law", Environmental Law Review, Vol. 37, No. 2 (2007), pp. 365–409, pp. 369–377.
16   See in that sense the findings of a recent research conducted by the United Nations University (UNU), the UN High Commissioner for Refugees, the London School of Economics (LSE) and the University of Bonn. T. Afifi, et al., Climate Change, Vulnerability and Human Mobility: Perspectives of Refugees from the East and Horn of Africa (Bonn: United Nations University Institute for Environment and Human Security – UNU-EHS, June 2012), pp. 12–13.

Cross-border displacement triggered by environmental degradation – whether it is linked or not to climate change – has in fact been identified as a normative gap in the international legal protection regime.[17] With a view to addressing this gap in the most comprehensive manner possible, it is important to bear in mind that the international protection regime is a "holistic"[18] one. It emanates from various sources:

> If the concept of international protection might once have been perceived as merely another form of consular or diplomatic protection, limited to one closely confined category of border crossers, today its roots are securely locked into an international law framework which is still evolving. This encompasses refugee law, human rights law, aspects of international humanitarian law, and elementary considerations of humanity.[19]

The aim of the research undertaken and presented here was to understand whether persons who, being outside their country of origin, are unable or unwilling to return due to the severe degradation of their living environment in that country could or, in the negative, should receive international protection in Europe. To this end, the different branches of the concept of international protection were considered. I therefore analysed refugee law – in particular, the 1951 Refugee Convention, the European Union Qualification Directive and asylum law and practice in EU Member States but also relevant norms of international human rights law as well as elements of international humanitarian law.

Concerned with addressing and overcoming the initially identified stumbling block, I sought, in the first Part, to better apprehend how and to what extent the different forms of complementary protection, available in the European Union, protect individuals fleeing indiscriminate threats to their

---

17 UNHCR, "High Commissioner's Dialogue on Protection Challenges: Breakout Session 1: Gaps in the International Protection Framework and its Implementation: Report by the Co-Chairs" (8–9 December 2010), 3; António Guterres, "Statement by António Guterres, United Nations High Commissioner for Refugees", *Nansen Conference on Climate Change and Displacement in the 21st Century, Oslo, 6–7 June 2011* (6 June 2011), 4; M. Wahlström, "Chairperson's Summary", Nansen Conference on Climate Change and Displacement in the 21st Century, organised in Oslo, on 6–7 June 2011 § 23.
18 J. McAdam, *Complementary Protection in International Refugee Law* (New York: Oxford University Press Inc., 2007), p. 29.
19 Guy Goodwin-Gill, High Commissioner's Dialogue on Protection Challenges, December 2, 2010. Statement cited by Erika Feller, in: UN High Commissioner for Refugees, *"The Refugee Convention at 60: Still fit for its Purpose?" – Protection Tools for Protection Needs Statement by Erika Feller, Assistant High Commissioner (Protection)*, UNHCR, 2 May 2011, p. 8.

lives or persons (Part 1). The second Part analyses the existing international protection regime as it is implemented within the European Union through the prism of environmentally-related displacement. Are asylum law and human rights law fit to address the protection needs of environmentally-displaced persons? In other words, *de lege lata*, could environmentally-displaced persons who apply for international protection in an EU Member State benefit refugee status or any form of complementary protection (Part 2)? I conclude from this analysis that, as it currently reads and is interpreted, law does not provide suitable solutions, if any, to persons forced to move by reason of threats to their lives or persons emanating from a degraded or deteriorating environment. This unfortunate conclusion, together with the scientific consensus on the impacts of climate change on the Earth environment, hurriedly calls for the development of international law. A number of means can be explored to tackle the issue of displacement caused by environmental factors, ranging from constructive interpretations of existing norms to the preferable creation of a *sui generis* framework (Part 3).

Throughout this work, reference will be made to environmental "disasters" and "degradations" rather than to environmental "catastrophes". This terminological choice best reflects the ambit of this work. Environmentally-triggered displacement is therein considered generally and includes displacement linked with sudden as well as slow-onset environmental changes. The terms disaster and degradation both convey the idea of a detrimental change to the environment but do not presume their pace. Disaster will be the term generally used; in certain cases, degradation – which can be defined as a condition or as a process – will be used to connote a slower-onset environmental change. The definition of disaster endorsed in the present work is that proposed by the International Law Commission:

> "disaster" means a calamitous event or series of events resulting in widespread loss of life, great human suffering and distress, mass displacement, or large-scale material or environmental damage, thereby seriously disrupting the functioning of society.[20]

Moreover, reference will be made to "environmental" disasters broadly rather than to "climate", "climatic", "climate change-related" (or any of the like)

---

20   ILC, "Report of the Drafting Committee on the 68th Session of the International Law Commission (2016) – Draft Articles on the Protection of Persons in the Event of Disasters" ("Draft Articles on the Protection of persons in the event of disasters"), A/CN.4/L.871, 27 May 2016 [2016], Draft article 3, para (a).

disasters since this work will address the issue of the international protection of persons displaced by environmental disasters, including but not limited to those triggered or amplified by the effects of climate change. For that reason, disasters and correlative displacements will not be categorised according to their climatic source; instead, the typology proposed and developed since by W. Kälin and endorsed by the UN Human Rights Council[21] will be followed. The typology identifies five main scenarios, initially devised as climate change-related displacement scenarios, each defined by its specific push-factor for displacement; they can be expanded to environmental disasters in general:

- Sudden-onset disasters;
- Slow-onset environmental degradation;
- Low lying small island states;
- Areas prohibited for human habitation;
- Unrest seriously disturbing public order, violence or even armed conflict.[22]

For the purpose of this work, technological accidents are also included.

There might be some objections to an approach whereby all five categories of disaster are addressed jointly; it can be argued that displacement triggered by slow-onset environmental changes pertains to immigration rather than to international protection. It can also be argued that population movements triggered by climate change-related disasters should be addressed on their own in view of the specificity of the issue of climate change, and of the level of State responsibility involved in its causation in particular. The choice for a broad understanding of the term and corresponding phenomenon of "environmental displacement" was mainly motivated by pragmatism, logic, and what could be described as a concern for fairness. Warnings about the difficulties arising from the fragmentation of international law persuaded me that considering a protection regime applicable not to displacement caused by environmental degradation in general but to displacement caused by climate change-related environmental degradation only, or to either sudden or slow-onset degradations,

---

21   OHCHR, "Annual Report of the United Nations High Commissioner for Human Rights and Reports of the Office of the High Commissioner and the Secretary-General: Report of the Office of the United Nations High Commissioner for Human Rights on the Relationship between Climate Change and Human Rights" ("Report on the relationship between climate change and human rights"), A/HRC/10/61, 15 January 2009, § 56.

22   W. Kälin and N. Schrepfer, *Protecting People Crossing Borders in the Context of Climate Change Normative Gaps and Possible Approaches* (February 2012), *op. cit.*, pp. 15–16.

or to "natural" disasters only by opposition to man-made disasters or vice versa, might lead to incoherence in the international protection regime.

> Fragmentation puts to question the coherence of international law. Coherence is valued positively owing to the connection it has with predictability and legal security. Moreover, only a coherent legal system treats legal subjects equally.[23]

A justification for such distinction between environmentally-displaced persons on the basis of a distinction between environmental degradations appears hardly conceivable.

As mentioned above, some invoke the notion of State responsibility to justify a differential treatment of climate change-related displacement. The reasoning is as follows. Under the 1951 Refugee Convention, refugees are protected by reason of the risk of persecution they are exposed to in their country of origin, whether persecution emanates from State authorities or from the unwillingness or inability of those authorities to effectively prevent persecution from occurring. Let us infer therefrom that, under the Convention, protection is justified only in cases where a degree of State responsibility is involved in the causation of forced displacement. Climate change being explained in part by anthropogenic emissions of greenhouse gases, displacement triggered by climate change involves a level of State responsibility and the persons displaced would therefore be entitled to protection. It further implies that those States which are identified as the main contributors to climate change should bear a larger part of responsibility in climate change-related displacement.

A number of arguments run counter this approach. They will be discussed in the third and last Part, when avenues of reflection are proposed for the protection of environmentally-displaced persons. For the sake of justifying the terminological choice made, suffice is to note that distinguishing between victims of earthquakes or tsunamis (geologic hazards) and victims of technological accidents or weather events have no justification in law or morals. Moreover, the example of recent disasters is telling: in 2011, Japan was struck by a powerful earthquake which was followed by the devastating tsunami it had caused, and the combination of the two triggered an accident in the Fukushima Daiichi nuclear power plant and radiation releases. In the aggregate, the

---

23 M. Koskenniemi, ILC, "Fragmentation of International Law: Difficulties Arising from the Diversification and Expansion of International Law, Report of the Study Group of the International Law Commission", A/CN.4/L.682, 13 April 2006, § 491.

disasters caused human casualties[24] and major structural damage, including heavy damage to infrastructures (such as roads, railways and a dam). In Haiti, the 2010 earthquake caused unprecedented devastation, killing over 220,000 persons and injuring 300,000.[25] A cholera epidemic which broke out in the aftermath of the earthquake – possibly after the strain of cholera was accidentally introduced in Haiti by peacekeepers[26] – adds to the death toll. It also caused severe damage to infrastructures, including official buildings (government, police, prison, etc.), hospitals, schools, roads, and dwellings. The devastating impact was amplified by the numerous landslides triggered by the earthquake. The widespread deforestation of Haiti[27] also contributed to those landslides.

Those are just two examples drawn from recent years but they illustrate the complexity of causes and consequences of environmental disasters and harm. Attempting to disentangle them to identify which disaster is purely natural or instead man-made or both, to distinguish between sudden and slow-onset disasters, and to identify the State or actor responsible risks diverting decision makers' focus away from the reality of the risks to which the population is or may be exposed, and of their needs for international protection (and assistance). For these reasons, environmental displacement and the possibility to grant international protection, not least against return, to the persons concerned is addressed at large, whichever the causes of the environmental degradation, its pace and duration. Causes, pace and duration will however be

---

24 Information published by the National Police Agency of Japan has confirmed 15,867 deaths, 6,109 injured, and 2,909 people missing. Information translated from Japanese and reported in "2011 Tōhoku Earthquake and Tsunami" (Wikipedia, 2012), last updated 11 September 2012, retrieved from: <http://en.wikipedia.org/wiki/2011_T%C5%8Dhoku _earthquake_and_tsunami#cite_note-21> [12/09/2012].

25 Government of the Republic of Haiti, "Annex: Haiti Earthquake Post-Disaster Needs Assessment: Assessment of Damage, Losses, General and Sectoral Needs", *in Action Plan for National Recovery and Development of Haiti: Immediate Key Initiatives for the Future* (n/a: Government of the Republic of Haiti, March 2010), p. 5.

26 "Haiti Cholera: UN Peacekeepers to Blame, Report Says", *BBC News, Latin America & Caribbean* (BBC, 2012), 8 December 2010, retrieved from: <http://www.bbc.co.uk/news/world-latin-america-11943902> [12/09/2011]; M. Doyle, "UN 'Should Take Blame for Haiti Cholera' – US House Members", *BBC News, Latin America & Caribbean* (BBC, 2012), 20 July 2012, retrieved from: <http://www.bbc.co.uk/news/world-africa-18928405> [11/09/2012].

27 N. Myers and J. Kent, *Environmental Exodus: An Emergent Crisis in the Global Arena* (June 1995), *op. cit.*, pp. 34–36; A. Suhrke, "Environmental Degradation and Population flows", *Journal of International Affairs*, Vol. 47 (1994), pp. 473–496, p. 479.

occasionally considered, in particular when they have a bearing on the type of protection which ought to be granted.

Lastly, before entering the legal sphere, it appears worth making a detour in climate science to have a more general picture of a discussion which often lingers in the realm of climate change.

It may be tempting – but simplistic and undoubtedly misguided – to stigmatise science, and climate science in particular, as a troublemaker. Scientific publications based on data collection and analysis, probability theory, and diverse calculations periodically formulate more or less alarming projections of the impacts of climate change on the environment and population movements. Although figures may vary from on publication to the other, the reality of anthropogenic climate change is undisputed within the international scientific community. The reports produced by the Intergovernmental Panel on Climate Change (IPCC) are an essential source of information on the issue. The United Nations Environment Programme (UNEP) and the World Meteorological Organization (WMO) jointly established the IPCC in 1988 as a scientific body endowed with the missions of "assessing the scientific information that is related to the various components of the climate change issue such as emissions of major greenhouse gases and modification of the Earth's radiation balance resulting therefrom, and that needed to enable the environmental and socio-economic consequences of climate change to be evaluated", and "formulating realistic response strategies for the management of the climate change issue".[28] Its creation was soon endorsed by the UN General Assembly.[29] The IPCC does not itself conduct research but makes, on an "objective, open and transparent basis",[30] a comprehensive review and assessment of the state of scientific, technical and socio-economic knowledge available worldwide and relevant to the understanding of climate change.[31] The findings of the hundreds of experts participating in the work of the IPCC as authors, contributors or reviewers are published in a series of reports, the most important of which are the IPCC Assessment Reports. Since the inception of the IPCC, five Assessment Reports have been published. Already in the First Assessment

---

28 World Meteorological Organization, "40th Session of the WMO Executive Council: Intergovernmental Panel on Climate Change", Res. 4 (EC-XL), 1988.

29 UNGA, "Resolution 43/53: Protection of Global Climate for Present and Future Generations of Mankind", A/RES/43/53, 6 December 1988.

30 Principles Governing IPCC Work Approved at the Fourteenth Session (Vienna, 1–3 October 1998) on 1 October 1998, amended at the 21st Session (Vienna, 3 and 6–7 November 2003) and at the 25th Session (Mauritius, 26–28 April 2006).

31 *See* information on the organisation of the IPCC provided by the IPCC website and available at: <http://www.ipcc.ch/organization/organization.shtml> [accessed 04/06/2012].

Report, the international scientific community stated their common certitude that the Earth global mean surface air temperature had already increased[32] and that anthropogenic emissions of greenhouse gases would contribute to additional global warming.[33] Subsequent Assessment Reports consistently confirmed the consensual scientific opinion that the Earth's temperature is increasing and will continue doing so, causing various changes in the environment. The latest and Fifth Assessment Report confirms previous reports' findings and mentions a number of observed changes in the climate: snow and ice extents have decreased whereas sea level has risen. Precipitation has increased in some regions (such as eastern parts of North and South America, northern Europe and northern and central Asia) but declined in others (such as the Sahel, the Mediterranean, southern Africa and parts of southern Asia). Additionally, an increase in intensity and frequency of some extreme weather and climate events has been observed over the past seven decades, including intense tropical cyclone activity in the North Atlantic since 1970 especially, heat waves and heavy precipitations.[34] Parallel to the experts acquiring broader knowledge and understanding of ongoing and anticipated climate changes, their opinion that more than half of the increase in global average temperatures, observed since the 1951, was mainly caused by the increase in anthropogenic greenhouse gas concentrations. The causal link between the two phenomena is, according to the IPCC Report, "extremely likely".[35]

Climate experts are increasingly capable of analysing climate changes and of anticipating their impacts on the environment, ecosystems and societies. For example, the climate models they have produced and used since the First Assessment Report issued in 1990 by the Intergovernmental Panel on Climate Change (IPCC) have already demonstrated their ability to accurately simulate future climate changes and related environmental phenomena. The 2007 Fourth IPCC Assessment Report thus highlighted that the observed increase in global average temperature of about 0.2 °C per decade for 1990 to 2005 was

---

32   J.T. Houghton, et al., *First Assessment Report, Climate Change: The IPCC Scientific Assessment, Report Prepared for Intergovernmental Panel on Climate Change by Working Group I: Policymakers Summary* (*IPCC AR1 – WG I: SPM*) (Cambridge: Cambridge University Press, 1990), p. xii.
33   *Ibid.*, p. xi.
34   IPCC: Core Writing Team, *et al.* (Eds.), *Climate Change 2014: Synthesis Report Contribution of Working Groups I, II and III to the Fifth Assessment Report of the Intergovernmental Panel on Climate Change*, Contribution of Working Groups I, II and III to the Fifth Assessment Report of the Intergovernmental Panel on Climate Change (Geneva: IPCC, 2014), pp. 40–41 and 53.
35   *Ibid.*, p. 48.

coherent with the projections made since IPCC's first report according to which global average temperature would increase by about 0.15 °C to 0.3 °C per decade for 1990 to 2005.[36] The demonstrated performance of some of the existing (and continuously developing) climate models further strengthens the level of scientific confidence[37] in their ability to provide useful projections of future climate.[38] It is thus reasonable to expect that the projected climate changes and attached effects on the environment and populations will indeed materialise, including environmental displacement.

Examinations of archaeological records and contemporary observations indicate that "migration is and has always been an adaptive response"[39] to climate and environmental change. Numerous reports are published by specialists, be they statisticians, environmentalists, political scientists, sociologists or lawyers, on the impacts of climate change on the world and its populations. They all reach the conclusion that climate change will impact on the environment worldwide. Different countries will be affected to different degrees and in different ways but all will be affected. It is therefore anticipated that population movements will increase.[40] What commentators disagree upon is numbers: when precisely will climate change trigger these population movements? How many people will move? The same questions are in fact pending

---

36 IPCC, "2007: Summary for Policymakers", *in* S. Solomon, *et al.* (Eds.), *Climate Change 2007: The Physical Science Basis. Contribution of Working Group I to the Fourth Assessment Report of the Intergovernmental Panel on Climate Change* (New York: Cambridge University Press, 2007), p. 12.

37 *Ibid.*, p. 8 (Table SPM 2).

38 IPCC, "Summary for Policymakers", *in* J.T. Houghton, *et al.* (Eds.), *Climate Change 2001: The Scientific Basis. Contribution of Working Group I to the Third Assessment Report of the Intergovernmental Panel on Climate Change* (Cambridge: Cambridge University Press, 2001), p. 9; D.A. Randall, *et al.*, "2007: Climate Models and Their Evaluation", *in* S. Solomon, *et al.* (Eds.), *Climate Change 2007: The Physical Science Basis. Contribution of Working Group I to the Fourth Assessment Report of the Intergovernmental Panel on Climate Change* (New York: Cambridge University Press, 2007), pp. 591–596 in particular.

39 Jennifer R. Smith, "Human Adaptation to Climate Change in the Archaeological Past", presentation made during the Radcliffe Institute for Advanced Study's science symposium "Something in the Air: Climate Change, Science and Policy", held at Harvard University in Cambridge, 15 April 2011.

40 The Intergovernmental Panel on Climate Change anticipates that climate change and its exposure to its impacts (*e.g.* floods, droughts and other extreme weather events) will increase population movements, be it in the form of planned migration or displacement. IPCC: Core Writing Team, *et al.* (Eds.), *Climate Change 2014: Synthesis Report* (2014), *op. cit.*, p. 73.

concerning any environmentally-induced migration: nuclear accidents[41] or other industrial catastrophes[42] for instance constitute sudden, typically unforeseen, severe disruptions of the environment, and the number of persons displaced in their aftermath is hardly predictable. A decision to migrate is the approximate solution of an equation with multiple variables. Ecological and human adaptive capacity, socio-economic and political context, security situation in the country, personal circumstances and availability of natural resources are but a few of those variables.

Recent years bear witness of the growing awareness in the international community of the necessity to effectively address climate change. This is done in various fora concerned with either the causes or the effects of climate change on the world, its environment and populations. The causes of climate change are the main focus of the UN Framework Convention on Climate Change (UNFCCC) and its Kyoto Protocol.[43] Parties to those binding instruments (the European Union and 196 respectively 192 States have ratified the UNFCCC and its Protocol[44]) have undertaken to endeavour to curb climate change and, in the meantime, to mitigate its effects. To this end, they committed themselves to adopting and implementing mitigating measures to reduce their emission of greenhouse gases. If addressing the causes of climate-related disasters is essential, it is however not sufficient. Scientific publications conclude that even if all heat-trapping greenhouse gases emissions were to stop overnight, the planetary mean surface temperature would still increase in the decades and centuries to come due to the high concentrations of greenhouse gases already accumulated in the atmosphere.[45] As mentioned, science fails to

---

41   2011 Fukushima Daiichi nuclear disaster for example.
42   Bhopal disaster for example, where toxic gas and chemicals were accidently released, killing and injuring thousands of people.
43   United Nations Framework Convention on Climate Change ("UNFCCC"), 9 May 1992 [1992] UNTS Vol. 1771, p. 107; Kyoto Protocol to the United Nations Framework Convention on Climate Change ("Kyoto Protocol"), 11 December 1997, entered into force 16 February 2005, U.N. Doc FCCC/CP/1997/7/Add.1 [1998] ILM Vol. 37, p. 22.
44   "Status of Ratification of the UNFCCC", retrieved from: <http://unfccc.int/essential_background/convention/status_of_ratification/items/2631.php> [07/11/2016]; "Status of Ratification of the Kyoto Protocol", retrieved from: <http://unfccc.int/kyoto_protocol/status_of_ratification/items/2613.php> [07/11/2016].
45   *See* for example: Susan Solomon, G.K. Platter, R. Knutti, and P. Friedlingstein, "Irreversible climate change due to carbon dioxide emissions", *Proceedings of the National Academy of Sciences*, No.106 (2009), pp. 1704–1709; G.H. Roe and K.C. Armour, "How sensitive is climate sensitivity?", *Geophysical Research Letters*, *38*, L14708 (2011); and Marcia B. Baker, Gerard H. Roe, "The Shape of Things to Come: Why Is Climate Change So Predictable?", *Journal*

provide exact figures: the number of degrees by which the global surface temperature will increase remains unknown. Uncertainty also prevails concerning the pace of increase in temperature:

> Another result that carries some important policy implications is that the larger the temperature change that is being contemplated, the more uncertain is the timing of when that temperature will be reached.[46]

A major drawback for scientists in their attempts to make climate projections is the number of unknown variables in the climate change equation. Anthropogenic emissions of greenhouse gases contribute to the increase in concentrations of such gases in the atmosphere which, in turn, affects the radiation balance of the Earth system. Specifically, it produces a positive radiative forcing characterised by its warming effect on the average temperature of Earth's atmosphere and oceans. This change in the planetary climate will, itself, further affect the climate; this phenomenon is known as "climate change feedback". For instance, it is anticipated that the permafrost, thawing as the global temperature increases, is likely to release large quantities of methane in the atmosphere, which will further exacerbate global warming, methane being a greenhouse gas.[47]

> ... importantly for future climate projections, the uncertainties in climate feedbacks are dwarfed by the uncertainty in future climate forcing, primarily due to uncertainty in anthropogenic emissions[48]

States, at least those parties to the UNFCCC, are in the process of limiting their emissions of greenhouse gases. However, to date, the exact terms and pace of greenhouse gas emission reduction by the different States remain unclear. This

---

of Climate, Vol.22, Issue 17 (2009), pp. 4574–4589. For a popularised version of the findings of G.H. Roe and K.C. Armour, *see*: University of Washington, "If greenhouse gas emissions stopped now, Earth would still likely get warmer, new research shows", *ScienceDaily*, 15 February 2011, available at: <http://www.sciencedaily.com/releases/2011/02/110215150845.htm> [accessed 30/04/2012].

46 M.B. Baker and G.H. Roe, "The Shape of Things to Come: Why Is Climate Change So Predictable?", *Journal of Climate*, Vol. 22, No. 17 (2009), p. 4587.

47 *See* for example S.A. Zimov, E.A.G. Schuur, and F.S. Chapin III, "Climate change: Permafrost and the global carbon budget", *Science* Vol.312, No.5780 (June 2006), pp. 1612–1613.

48 M.B. Baker and G.H. Roe (2009), *op. cit.*

together with the complexity of the physical processes involved render climate change projections "inherently probabilistic".[49]

Policymakers should however not let themselves be distracted by these uncertainties in numbers. The scientific community unanimously observes that the Earth's climate is warming. Climate change already causes and will continue causing major changes in the planet ecosystem, with disastrous consequences for human populations. The Intergovernmental Panel on Climate Change (IPCC) predicts that the climate will be significantly changed in every part of the world with a continued increase in global surface temperature by 2100.[50] Increases in severe droughts and heavy rains, flooding, seasonally higher or lower temperatures are some of the anticipated impacts of climate change; the extent to and way in which they will affect the Earth ecosystem will vary from one region to the other.[51]

On a geologic time scale, climate naturally fluctuates but science shows that the pattern and rapid pace in which climate change is currently occurring are not entirely "natural" but affected by human activity. Climate researchers point at anthropogenic greenhouse gas emissions as a crucial factor in global warming and find that emission reduction can be an effective means of curbing the increase in surface temperature. This is however but a (very) long-term solution. The greenhouse gases already emitted are expected to persist in the atmosphere, presumably for a thousand years, and decline only slowly due to the long atmospheric retention time of gases (*e.g.* carbon dioxide).[52]

Global warming is therefore inevitable: striving to mitigate it by addressing its causes is essential but taking steps to reduce its effects and address its consequences is a pressing necessity.

---

49   *Ibid*, p. 4574.
50   M. Collins, *et al.*, "2013: Long-Term Climate Change: Projections, Commitments and Irreversibility", in T.F. Stocker, *et al.* (Eds.), *Climate Change 2013: The Physical Science Basis. Contribution of Working Group I to the Fifth Assessment Report of the Intergovernmental Panel on Climate Change* (Cambridge, New York: Cambridge University Press, 2013).
51   IPCC, 2012: *Summary for Policymakers*, in: C.B. Field, V. Barros, T.F. Stocker, D. Qin, D.J. Dokken, K.L. Ebi, M.D. Mastrandrea, K.J. Mach, G.-K. Plattner, S.K. Allen, M. Tignor, and P.M. Midgley (eds.), *Managing the Risks of Extreme Events and Disasters to Advance Climate Change Adaptation: A Special Report of Working Groups I and II of the Intergovernmental Panel on Climate Change* (Cambridge and New York: Cambridge University Press, 2012), pp. 9–14.
52   Susan Solomon, "Understanding Climate Change, Irreversibility, and the Societal Challenge", presentation made during the *9th annual Radcliffe Institute for Advanced Study science symposium*, "Something in the Air: Climate Change, Science and Policy", Harvard University, Cambridge, 15 April 2011.

The foundation of the present work being laid, the first Part will examine the norms and practice relevant to the protection of persons displaced by non-targeted or indiscriminate threats and seeking protection within the European Union. As said, the second Part will envisage the applicability of existing norms of asylum law and human rights law, including those identified in the first Part, to cases of displacement triggered by environmental disaster. It appears that if environmentally-displaced persons are not automatically excluded from the scope of asylum law or human rights law and are sometimes considered in State practice, existing law, as it is implemented, will in most cases fail to protect persons displaced by environmental disasters. It is however argued that the principle of *non-refoulement*, as it derives from international human rights law, is theoretically fully applicable to cases of environmental displacement but provided decision-makers do not give in to restrictive interpretations of its scope and terms. The third Part, drawing on the rather pessimistic conclusion of the second Part will turn to consider developments of the law intended to protect environmentally-displaced persons. After a consideration of possible developments in each of the respective areas of law studied in the first two Parts, and after pondering on the question of State responsibility for environmentally-triggered displacement, the third Part will identify some key elements of a *sui generis* framework.

PART 1

*Protecting People Fleeing Indiscriminate Threats:
Law and Practice within the European Union*

∴

Introduction to Part 1

The existence of international protection needs, outside those covered by refugee status, has long been acknowledged by States. Originally, the refugee definition as it appeared in international refugee instruments consisted in exhaustive lists of national categories, extended on an ad hoc basis. The 1951 Refugee Convention parted ways with the category-based approach, prevailing at the time.[1] Universal in that it applies to all asylum-seekers irrespective of their nationalities (or absence thereof), its benefit is however circumscribed to those who fulfil all three criteria: refugees are outside their country of origin and can demonstrate a well-founded fear of persecution as well as a causal link between the alleged persecution and their race, religion, nationality, political opinion or membership of a particular social group.[2] Inherent to the identification of definitional criteria is the exclusion of others. Operating the rule can reveal that the definitional choice was fit for the aim pursued; it can also identify the limits, if not the shortcomings, of the adopted definition. States have long recognised that some persons who did not fit in the refugee definition were nevertheless in need of international protection and granted them some form of protection, thus supplementing the 1951 Refugee Convention; the practice is described as "complementary protection". Typically, it is used to protect persons who flee generalised violence or a danger of torture, inhuman or degrading treatment or punishment, and who cannot establish a causal link between those risks and any of the five Refugee Convention grounds for persecution. It is granted by States in compliance with their "protection obligations arising from international legal instruments and custom" and is "in effect, a shorthand term for the widened scope of non-refoulement under international law".[3] Complementary protection as a "legal concept"[4] whose content is informed by States' obligations under international law is to be distinguished

---

1   The historical development of the refugee definition will be further elaborated upon in Chapter 3, Part 1 where the possibility to extend the scope of the Refugee Convention will be considered. *See* also J. McAdam, *Complementary Protection in International Refugee Law* (2007), *op. cit.*, Chapter 1, pp. 19s.
2   UN General Assembly, Convention Relating to the Status of Refugees ("Refugee Convention"), 28 July 1951 [1954] *UNTS* Vol. 189, p. 137, Article 1(A)2.
3   G.S. Goodwin-Gill and J. McAdam, *The Refugee in International Law*, 3rd ed. (New York: Oxford University Press, 2007), p. 285.
4   *Ibid.*, p. 286.

from other forms of protection, granted on a discretionary basis by States, on humanitarian or compassionate grounds.⁵

Intended to provide a comprehensive overview of the protection available in the European Union to persons who do not qualify for refugee status, because the risk they incur is indiscriminate, the present Part will examine the forms of protection available under European Union law (Chapter 2), international human rights law (both conventional and customary) (Chapter 3) and at the national level (Chapter 4). A preliminary remark will be made on the status of EU Member States' obligations deriving from the treaties they are Parties to, besides the EU Treaties (Chapter 1).

---

5 *Ibid.* The distinction to be made is also highlighted in the EU Qualification Directive: Directive 2011/95/EU of the European Parliament and of the Council of 13 December 2011 on Standards for the Qualification of Third-Country Nationals or Stateless Persons as Beneficiaries of International Protection, for a Uniform Status for Refugees or for Persons Eligible for Subsidiary Protection, and for the Content of the Protection Granted ("Qualification Directive") [20/12/2011] *OJ L 337/09*, pp. 9–26, Preamble, Recital 15.

CHAPTER 1

Preliminary Remark: Member States' Obligations under International Human Rights Law are Unaltered by EU Membership

Besides European Union law, international treaties also create obligations that are incumbent upon EU Member States and relevant in the field of asylum. Are they still binding upon States despite them becoming Members of the European Union (I)? In the affirmative, what does it imply concerning treaties relevant in the field of asylum (II)?

I   The Impact of EU Membership on States' Pre-existing International Human Rights Obligations: The General Rule

Upon joining the European Union (EU), States express their consent to be bound by obligations arising out of Union's Treaties[1] and resulting from the acts of its institutions.[2] Since 1992, when Member States agreed in Maastricht to cooperate in the fields of justice and home affairs, and in particular recognised asylum policy as a matter of "common interest",[3] the competence of the Union in the area of asylum has significantly grown,[4] so much so that Member States are now bound by a substantial body of norms of EU asylum law. These

---

1   The term "Treaties" is used to designate primary Union law. They include the founding Treaties and the instruments amending and supplementing them (*i.e.* to date essentially the Treaties of Maastricht, 1992; Amsterdam, 1997; Nice, 2001; and Lisbon, 2007), and the various Accession Treaties. This terminology is used by the European Union. *See*: "The legal order of the EU", retrieved from the EUR-Lex website: © European Union, <http://eur-lex.europa.eu> [accessed on 07/07/2012].
2   Consolidated version of the Treaty on European Union ("TEU") [2010] *OJ C 83/13*, Article 4(3), §2.
3   Treaty on European Union ("TEU (1992)"), signed in Maastricht, 29 July 1992 [1992] *OJ C 191/01*, Article K.1(1) and Declaration 31 on Asylum.
4   I gave a more detailed account of the gradual development of European Union's competence in the area of asylum in: H. Ragheboom, "Le paquet asile", *in* J. Gerkrath (Ed.), *Droit d'asile au Grand-Duché de Luxembourg et en Europe : développements récents*, Collection de la Faculté de Droit, d'Economie et de Finance de l'Université de Luxembourg (Bruxelles: Larcier, 2009), 189–193.

norms, and more generally the Common European Asylum System,[5] are based on "the full and inclusive application" of the Refugee Convention.[6]

The international protection regime, however, emanates from a variety of sources:[7] if refugee law is an essential part of it, international human rights law and the principle of *non-refoulement* in particular are also key components of the regime. All EU Member States are parties to a number of international human rights law treaties that have a bearing in the context of international protection; they include the 1950 European Convention on Human Rights (ECHR),[8] the 1966 International Covenant on Civil and Political Rights (ICCPR),[9] the 1966 International Covenant on Economic, Social and Cultural Rights (ICESCR)[10] and the 1984 Convention against Torture (CAT)[11] among others. It is important to consider those instruments in the present Chapter, insofar as they impose obligations on State Parties to protect individuals who were forced to leave their countries of origin and cannot be returned there, and it is possible to do so since EU Membership does not affect Member States' rights and obligations under those instruments of international law.

The 1997 Amsterdam Treaty gave competence to the Union in the field of asylum.[12] The incidence of this transfer of powers on Member States' obligations

---

5   The establishment of a "Common European Asylum System" (CEAS) was initiated by the European Council in Tampere. EU Council, "Presidency Conclusions: Tampere European Council, 15 and 16 October 1999" ("Tampere Conclusions"), 16 October 1999, SN 200/99, §§ 13–17.
6   *Ibid.*, § 13.
7   Guy Goodwin-Gill, High Commissioner's Dialogue on Protection Challenges, December 2, 2010. Statement cited by Erika Feller, in: UN High Commissioner for Refugees, *"The Refugee Convention at 60: Still fit for its Purpose?" – Protection Tools for Protection Needs Statement by Erika Feller, Assistant High Commissioner (Protection)*, UNHCR, 2 May 2011, p. 8.
8   Council of Europe, European Convention for the Protection of Human Rights and Fundamental Freedoms ("ECHR"), 4 November 1950, in force 3 September 1953 ETS Vol. 5.
9   UN General Assembly, International Covenant on Civil and Political Rights ("ICCPR"), 16 December 1966, in force 23 September 1976 [1976] UNTS Vol. 999, p. 171.
10 UN General Assembly, International Covenant on Economic, Social and Cultural Rights ("ICESCR"), 16 December 1966, in force 23 March 1976 [1976] UNTS Vol. 993, p. 3.
11 UN General Assembly, Convention against Torture and Other Cruel, Inhuman or Degrading Treatment or Punishment ("CAT"), 10 December 1984, in force 26 June 1987 [1987] UNTS Vol. 1465, p. 85.
12 Article 2 of the Treaty of Amsterdam introduced into the then "Treaty establishing the European Community" ("TEC") a new title headed "Visas, asylum, immigration and other policies related to free movement of persons" thereby giving competence to the Union in the field of asylum. Since the entry into force of the Lisbon Treaty on 1 December 2009, the provisions on asylum are now included in Chapter 2 ("Policies on border checks,

under international refugee law was elaborated upon by, among other authors, H. Battjes. Relying on the customary rules of the international law of treaties that are *pacta sunt servanda* and *pacta tertiis nec nocent nec prosunt*, crystallised in Articles 26 and 34 respectively of the Vienna Convention on the Law of Treaties,[13] Battjes finds that "[r]elevant international law suggests that the Member States' obligations under international law remained unaltered after the conclusion or entry into force of the Treaty of Amsterdam".[14] Since the entry into force of the Amsterdam Treaty, the European Union is competent, in its internal legal order, to adopt legislation on asylum and hence create obligations for EU Member States in that field but, in so doing, it cannot create obligations for non-EU Member States insofar as, as third States *vis-à-vis* the TEU, they have not consented to those obligations.[15] The EU cannot either alter relevant existing international treaties; a modification of those treaties would indeed require that all State Parties be involved in the process.[16] It can

    asylum and immigration") of Title V ("Area of Freedom, Security and Justice") of the Treaty on the Functioning of the European Union (TFEU). Treaty of Amsterdam Amending the Treaty on European Union, the Treaties Establishing the European Communities and Related Acts ("Amsterdam Treaty") [10 November 1997] *OJ C 340/1*, Article 2; Treaty of Lisbon Amending the Treaty on European Union and the Treaty Establishing the European Community ("Lisbon Treaty"), 13 December 2007, entered into force 1 December 2009 [17 December 2007] *OJ C 306/50*, Article 2, Points 63–65; Consolidated version of the Treaty on the Functioning of the European Union ("TFEU") [2010] *OJ C 83/47*, Art. 77–80.

13   United Nations, Vienna Convention on the Law of Treaties ("VCLT"), 23 May 1969, entered into force 27 January 1980 [1980] *UNTS* Vol. 1155, p. 331.

14   H. Battjes, *European Asylum Law and International Law* (Leiden: Brill Academic Publishers, 2006), 59–61.

15   VCLT, Art. 34; and H. Battjes, *European Asylum Law and International Law* (2006), *op. cit.*, 60.

16   Revision of the Refugee Convention is addressed under its Article 45. States may request revision of the Convention by a notification to the UN Secretary-General. The General Assembly subsequently recommends the procedure to be followed (UN, Convention Relating to the Status of Refugees ("Refugee Convention"), 28 July 1951, entered into force 22 April 1954 [1954] UNTS Vol. 189, p. 137, Art.45.) As for the ICCPR, its amendment procedure is rather lengthy. Firstly, it requires that a third of ICCPR's State Parties consent to convene a conference for this purpose. Proposed amendments, if any, must then be adopted by a majority of the present and voting States so that they can be submitted to the General Assembly. Only those draft amendments that have been approved by the General Assembly and accepted by a two-third majority of ICCPR's Sate Parties will enter into force but even then, only *vis-à-vis* those States Parties which have accepted them (ICCPR, Art.51.) The CAT Convention's procedure for revision consists in a notification to the Secretary-General who will convene a conference of States Parties if at least one third of them favour it, within four months after the notification. Any draft amendment must be approved by a majority of the States present and voting at the said conference so

be concluded that EU Membership (or membership in any other intergovernmental organisation for that matter[17]) does not alter Member States' obligations deriving from international treaties, including human rights treaties.[18]

This principle is in fact well recognised. As far back as 1958, the Council of Europe's Commission of Human Rights asserted that States were answerable for any breach of their obligations under a treaty resulting from their performing obligations deriving from a later treaty.[19] The Commission stressed that the same was all the more true of a breach of obligations under the ECHR, the Convention being a treaty whose guarantees concern "the Public order of Europe".[20] The European Court of Human Rights has since endorsed the Commission's reasoning and repeatedly stated, in the same way, that:

> Where States establish international organisations, or *mutatis mutandis* international agreements, to pursue co-operation in certain fields of activities, there may be implications for the protection of fundamental rights. It would be incompatible with the purpose and object of the Convention if Contracting States were thereby absolved from their responsibility under the Convention in relation to the field of activity covered by such attribution.[21]

---

that it is submitted to the vote of all States Parties. A majority of two-third of the States Parties to the CAT Convention is then required for the amendment to enter into force but only *vis-à-vis* those States Parties which have accepted them (CAT, Art.29.). The European Convention on Human Rights does not provide for an amendment procedure; the general rules of the international law of treaties shall therefore apply. As clarified by VCLT Articles 39–41, all States Parties must be informed of and have the right to take part in the amendment process and only those which have consented to the said amendment will be bound by it (VCLT, Art. 39–41.).

17 T. Ahmed and I.D.J. Butler, "The European Union and Human Rights: An International Law Perspective", *The European Journal of International Law*, Vol. 17, No. 4 (2006), 781–783.

18 According to H. Battjes, this holds true "not only in situations where third States are involved (...) but also if individuals invoke their rights under international asylum law". H. Battjes, *European Asylum Law and International Law* (2006), op. cit., endnote no. 3 (text of the note p. 123).

19 European Commission of Human Rights, *Decision of 10 June 1958*, no. 235/56 *Yearbook 2*, p. 256.

20 European Commission of Human Rights, *Austria v. Italy* ("*Austria v. Italy*"), no. 788/60 (11 January 1961) *Yearbook 4*, p. 116.

21 ECtHR, *T.I. v. the United Kingdom* ("*T.I. v. UK*"), Application no. 43844/98 (07 March 2000) *Reports of Judgments and Decisions 2000-III*, p. 15; ECtHR, *Case of Capital Bank Ad v. Bulgaria*, No. 49429/99 (24 November 2005), §111; ECtHR, *Case of Waite and Kennedy v. Germany*, Application no. 26083/94 (18 February 1999) *Reports of Judgments and Decisions 1999-I*, § 67.

The Court rules alike in cases involving legal obligations flowing from EU membership specifically where it reiterates that a finding of the contrary would deprive the European Convention on Human Rights of its "peremptory character" and undermine the practical and effective nature of its safeguards since it would permit States Parties to the Convention to limit or exclude its guarantees "at will".[22]

In like manner, it is understood that the UN Human Rights Committee has expressed its readiness to hold States Parties accountable for breaches of the ICCPR caused by national measures they adopted in order to implement their obligations under other instruments of law.[23] This can be inferred from the following statement by the Human Rights Committee:

> While the Committee could not consider alleged violations of other instruments such as the UN Charter (…), the Committee was competent to admit a communication alleging that a State party had violated rights set forth in the Covenant regardless of the source of the obligations implemented by the State party.[24]

It can be deduced that EU Membership, as a source of legal obligations for EU Member States, does not absolve States from their responsibility to comply with and implement the ICCPR.

As a matter of fact, at the European Union level, the rule is the same. Article 351 of the Treaty on the Functioning of the EU preserves and clarifies the status of EU Member States' pre-existing international obligations, whether they pre-date the creation of the European Union or States' accession to the EU. The first paragraph of Article 351 provides that the "rights and obligations arising from agreements concluded before 1 January 1958 or, for acceding States, before the date of their accession, between one or more Member States on the one hand, and one or more third countries on the other, shall not be affected by the provisions of the Treaties".[25] According to the Court of Justice (CJ)[26] ruling in 1972, this provision of the Treaty discloses that it was not the

---

22 ECtHR, *Case of Bosphorus Hava Yollari Turizm Ve Ticaret Anonim Sirketi v Ireland* ("Bosphorus"), No. 45036/98 (30/06/2005), § 154.
23 I.D.J. Butler, "The EU and International Human Rights Law", *in* (Geneva: OHCHR, Regional Office for Europe, date unknown), p. 25, retrieved from: <http://www.europe.ohchr.org/EN/Publications/Pages/publications.aspx> [10/07/2012].
24 Human Rights Committee, *Sayadi v. Belgium*, Communication No. 1472/2006 (22 October 2008), § 7.2.
25 TFEU, Article 351(1).
26 With the entry into force of the Lisbon Treaty in 2009, the judicial arm of the European Union was renamed "Court of Justice of the European Union". According to the Treaty

intention of Member States to "withdraw from their obligations to third countries" by establishing the European Economic Community.[27] In 1980, in *Burgoa*, the Court made clear that the provisions in Article 351 of the TFEU applied "to any international agreement, irrespective of its subject-matter".[28] Parting ways with a rigid interpretation of Article 351 of the TFEU,[29] the Court found that the "rights" deriving from international agreements anterior to States' EU membership mentioned in Article 351 referred not only to third States' rights but also to "the rights which individuals may derive from such an agreement".[30] The Court later drew from this 1980 finding to confirm in 2000 that:

> [a]s is clear from *Burgoa* (...) the purpose of the first paragraph of Article 234 of the Treaty [now Art. 351 TFEU] is to make it clear, in accordance with the principles of international law (...), that application of the EC

---

on the Functioning of the European Union, this EU institution comprises the Court of Justice (formerly and still commonly referred to as "European Court of Justice" or "ECJ"), the General Court (ex "Court of First Instance" or "CFI") and specialised courts (*TFEU*, Arts. 13, 19 and 251–281, and Protocol No. 3 on the statute of the Court of Justice of the European Union). As a consequence and in line with the practice of the European Union Agency for Fundamental Rights and the Office of the UN High Commissioner for Human Rights notably, the new terminology will be used in the present work. The terms "Court of Justice of the European Union" and "CJEU" will be used to designate the EU institution, which comprises the Court of Justice, the General Court and, the EU's sole "specialised court" as of now, the Civil Service Tribunal. The upper tier will be referred to as "Court of Justice" (or "EU Court of Justice" or "the Court" in context) and "CJ"; those terms will be used interchangeably to designate this Court, throughout its history. In like manner, "General Court" or "GC" will be used to designate this court, formerly known as Court of First Instance, throughout its history. This is in fact also the terminology used in the United Kingdom, by the House of Lords: House of Lords – European Union Committee, *The Workload of the Court of Justice of the European Union: 14th Report of Session 2010–11*, HL Papers 128 (London: The Stationery Office, 2011), p. 9.

27 CJ, Joined cases 21 to 24–72, *International Fruit Company Case v. Produktschap Voor Groenten En Fruit* ("*International Fruit Company*") (12 December 1972) [1972] ECR 1219, §§ 11–13.

28 CJ, Case 812/79, *Attorney General v Juan C. Burgoa* ("*Burgoa*") (14 October 1980) [1980] ECR 2787, § 6; CJ, Case C-158/91, *Criminal Proceedings against Jean-Claude Levy (Levy)* ("*Levy*") (2 August 1993) [1993] ECR I-4287, § 11; CJ, Case C-84/98, *Commission of the European Communities v. Portuguese Republic* ("*Commission v. Portugal*") (4 July 2000) [2000] ECR I-05215, § 52.

29 J. Klabbers analyses the development of the ECJ doctrine in that regard in: J. Klabbers, "Moribund on the Fourth of July? The Court of Justice on Prior Agreements of the Member States", *European law review* (Sweet & Maxwell), Vol. 26, No. 2 (2001), pp. 187–197.

30 CJ, *Burgoa*, § 10.

Treaty is not to affect the duty of the Member State concerned to respect the rights of third countries under a prior agreement and to perform its obligations thereunder.[31]

If the Court does refer to "the rights of third countries" deriving from prior agreements, it also and most importantly mentions Member States' "obligations" under the same agreements. In this regard, it is worth noting that human rights treaties are peculiar instruments of international law. Their idiosyncrasy is well-known: they create norms of international origin but whose object is "internal".[32] They endow individuals with opposable rights and are designed to protect those rights from infringement by any State Party "rather than to create subjective and reciprocal rights"[33] for the States themselves. In other words, they are not merely a "web of inter-State exchanges of mutual obligations"[34] but in fact create "over and above" this network, "objective obligations".[35] State Party obligations they create are not only directed towards other contracting States[36] but also and chiefly towards individuals; the use by the CJEU in the above-cited decision of the term "obligations" therefore permits that, by a "ricochet-effect",[37] the rights of individuals are not affected by EU membership. Thanks to this interpretation by the Court of Article 351 TFEU, individuals

---

31 CJ, *Commision v. Portugal*, § 53; without referring to Burgoa, the Court had already concluded similarly that third States' rights and Member States' obligations under pre-existing international treaties were not affected by EU Membership in CJ, Case C-124/95, *R. v. H.M. Treasury and Bank of England, Ex Parte. Centro-Com Srl* ("*Centro-COM*") (14 January 1997) [1997] ECR I-00081, § 56.

32 J. Combacau and S. Sur, *Droit International Public*, 6th ed. (Paris: Montchrestien, 2004), 388–389.

33 ECnHR, *Austria v. Italy*, pp. 138–140.

34 HRC, "General Comment No. 24: Issues Relating to Reservations Made Upon Ratification or Accession to the Covenant or the Optional Protocols Thereto, or in Relation to Declarations under Article 41 of the Covenant" ("General Comment No. 24"), CCPR/C/21/Rev.1/Add.6, 04/11/1994, § 17.

35 ECtHR (Plenary), *Ireland v. The United Kingdom*, Application no. 5310/71, Series A Vol. 25 (18 January 1978), § 239.

36 Concerning the ICCPR in particular, see M. Nowak, *U.N. Covenant on Civil and Political Rights: CCPR Commentary*, 2nd ed. (Kehl: N.P. Engel, Publisher, 2005), XXIV at 13.

37 The notion is borrowed from Lawson and translated in English (from Dutch) by Klabbers. See J. Klabbers (2001), *op. cit.*, fn. 51; and R.A. Lawson, *Het EVRM en de Europese Gemeenschappen: Bouwstenen voor een aansprakelijkheidsregime voor het optreden van internationale organisaties*, 1999, Doctoral thesis (Leiden: Kluwer – Europese Monografieën, 1999), at 487.

are entitled to the same level of protection in all the States Parties to a given human rights treaty, including those States that are Members of the European Union. The Court has since reiterated this assertion[38] so that the rule is now well-established: joining the EU does not affect pre-existing legal obligations States bear under international human rights treaties. How does this general rule apply to those treaties that are relevant in the field of asylum?

II 1 May 1999, the EU Acquires Competence in the Field of Asylum: A Decisive Date

One must ponder on the time limit set in Article 351 and which may seem problematic regarding those treaties that are relevant to asylum. Article 351 refers to "agreements concluded before 1 January 1958 or, for acceding States, before the date of their accession". Article 351 is clearly applicable to the European Convention on Human Rights and the Refugee Convention as they both fulfil all the criteria set therein (they are international agreement between States, and were adopted in 1950 and 1951 respectively) but doubts arise concerning other norms pertaining to international protection. Should January 1958 be the decisive date, as far as the six original Member States only are concerned, Article 351 would apply neither to the 1966 International Covenant on Civil and Political Rights (ICCPR) nor to the 1984 Convention Against Torture (CAT). For those six States, Parties to the Treaty establishing the European Economic Community since it entered into force in 1958, EU law would take precedence over the ICCPR and the CAT Convention. This interpretation would however be unreasonable: it would create an "odd asymmetry"[39] between the six original Member States and the twenty-one others.

Battjes argues that where asylum is concerned, the relevant date should be the date the Treaty of Amsterdam entered into force, *i.e.* 1 May 1999, or, for States who acceded to the EU later, their date of accession. It can indeed be deduced from the letter of Article 351 and from its purpose[40] that the decisive

---

38 CJ, Case C-216/01, *Budějovický Budvar National Corporation v Rudolf Ammersin Gmbh* ("*Budějovický Budvar*") (18 November 2003) [2003] ECR I-13617, §§ 144–145; CJ (Grand Chamber), Case C-205/06, *Commission of the European Communities v. Republic of Austria* ("*Commission v Austria*") (3 March 2009) [2009] ECR I-01301, § 33; CJ, Case C-118/07, *Commission of the European Communities v. Republic of Finland* (19 November 2009) [2009] ECR I-10889, § 27.

39 H. Battjes, *European Asylum Law and International Law* (2006), op. cit., p. 64.

40 The purpose of Article 351 of the TFEU is clarified in: CJ, *Commission v. Portugal*, § 53.

moment is not the date of birth of the EU but the moment of transfer of competence to it on the "subject matter" that is relevant to the international treaty at issue.[41] The EU gained competence to act in the field of asylum with the entry into force of the Treaty of Amsterdam:[42] as from 1 May 1999, the Union was competent to create asylum law obligations for its Member States. So to speak, EU asylum law and resulting State obligations were created at a time EU Member States were already Parties to the treaties forming part of the international protection regime. As mentioned above, it is well-established that EU Member States did not intend to and, as a matter of fact, could not legally exonerate themselves from their obligations under prior international conventions by adopting later agreements between them on the same subject-matter. As a consequence, in the area of asylum specifically, Article 351 must be applied as follows: it gives precedence to international human rights and refugee law treaties to which EU Member States became Parties before 1 May 1999 or, for States who joined the Union after that date, before their accession date.

Article 61 of the International Law Commission (ILC) Articles on the Responsibility of International Organizations reinforces this interpretation:

> A State member of an international organization incurs international responsibility if, by taking advantage of the fact that the organization has competence in relation to the subject-matter of one of the State's international obligations, it circumvents that obligation by causing the organization to commit an act that, if committed by the State, would have constituted a breach of the obligation.[43]

The ILC does not refer to the *creation* of an international organisation as a means States may potentially use to the end of bypassing their obligations under prior treaties. Whether States create an organisation *ad hoc* or use an existing organisation has no bearing: what matters is that they transfer to this organisation the *competence* to act in relation to the *subject-matter* of the legal obligation they seek to exonerate themselves from.[44] In other words, States

---

41   H. Battjes, *European Asylum Law and International Law* (2006), op. cit., pp. 64–66.
42   See Part I, p. 23.
43   ILC, Articles on the Responsibility of International Organizations, with Commentaries ("ILC Articles RIO"), adopted by the ILC at its sixty-third session, in 2011, [2011] *Yearbook of the International Law Commission* Vol. II, Part Two, Art. 61. The UN General Assembly took note of the articles in its Resolution 66/100 of 2011: UNGA, "Resolution 66/100 on the Responsibility of International Organizations", A/RES/66/100, 9 December 2011.
44   See also the Commentary of Article 61: ILC, ILC Articles RIO, Commentary para. 6.

cannot use international organisations as veils behind which they could hide to perform actions in breach of their international obligations. The wording of the ILC draft article connotes intention on the part of the States.[45] Ian Brownlie formulates the prohibition in broader terms and finds that a State:

> ...cannot by delegation (even if this be genuine) avoid responsibility for breaches of its duties under international law.[46]

From the foregoing, it can be concluded that in addition to their obligations under EU asylum law, Member States remain bound by the treaties they are Parties to, including those that form parts of the international protection regime.

As a matter of fact, Article 351, paragraph 2, of the Treaty on the Functioning of the EU, referring to Member States' obligations under international treaties, states that:

> To the extent that such agreements are not compatible with the Treaties, the Member State or States concerned shall take all appropriate steps to eliminate the incompatibilities established.[47]

Pursuant to this provision of the TFEU, and as interpreted by the Court of Justice, not only are EU Member States still bound by the treaties they are parties to, but they are even allowed to disregard an obligation they have under EU law, including under the TEU,[48] if performance of their prior obligations under international treaties to which they are parties so requires.[49]

---

45   In its Commentary on Article 61, the ILC explains that international responsibility will not arise when the breach of an international obligation by the international organisation was not intentionally caused by the State. The ILC however subsequently refers to the jurisprudence of the European Court of Human Rights in cases where the Court did not actually require that States intentionally cause the international organisation to act in breach of their own international obligations, in order to circumvent them. The ECtHR instead, and as the ILC mentions, requires that States, upon transferring competences to an international organisation, ensure that this organisation provides a level of human rights protection "equivalent" to that ensured by the ECHR. See also *ibid.*, Commentary para. 2.

46   I. Brownlie, "State Responsibility: The Problem of Delegation", *in* K. Ginther, *et al.* (Eds.), *Völkerrecht Zwischen Normativem Anspruch Und Politischer Realität: Festschrift Für Karl Zemanek Zum 65. Geburtstag* (Berlin: Duncker & Humblot GmbH, 1994), pp. 300–301.

47   TFEU, Article 351(2).

48   CJ, *Centro-COM*, §§ 56–61.

49   *Ibid.*, § 61; see also T. Ahmed and I.D.J. Butler (2006), *op. cit.*, pp. 785–786.

CHAPTER 2

European Union Law Relevant to Asylum

A number of factors contributed to the development of the European Union; they include the establishment and liberalisation of the internal market, through the realisation of the four fundamental freedoms, the affirmation of the primacy and direct effect of EU law, and the enhancement of the competences of the Union. In this context, States expressed their concerns that, in the absence of any human rights guarantee in the founding Treaties, acts of the Community institutions might infringe fundamental rights, as they are enshrined in particular in national Constitutions. To allay States' concerns and as a counterpart to growing European integration, the Court of Justice, followed by the European legislator, progressively incorporated fundamental rights into the EU legal order. Human rights norms form part of the international protection regime and their introduction into and current status within the European Union will therefore be accounted for (1).

Parallel to the development of the European Union as an area devoid of internal borders but sharing a common external border, cooperation between Member States has increased in the fields of immigration, police, judicial cooperation and asylum and was eventually incorporated into the Treaties as "matters of common interest".[1] The role of the EU institutions in that field grew, especially with the adoption of the Amsterdam Treaty following which asylum – among other policy areas – was governed by the Community method. A consequence of the empowerment of the institutions in the field of asylum was the adoption from 2000 of a series of measures including, in 2001, the "Council Directive on Minimum Standards for Giving Temporary Protection in the Event of a Mass Influx of Displaced Persons"[2] and in 2004, the "Council Directive on Minimum Standards for the Qualification and Status of Third Country Nationals or Stateless Persons as Refugees or as Persons Who Otherwise Need International Protection and the Content of the Protection Granted" ("Qualification Directive").[3] Temporary protection must be distinguished from refugee status

---

1   TEU (1992), Article K.1.
2   Council Directive 2001/55/EC of 20 July 2001 on Minimum Standards for Giving Temporary Protection in the Event of a Mass Influx of Displaced Persons ("Temporary Protection Directive") 2001/55/EC [7 August 2001] *OJ L* 212/12.
3   Council Directive 2004/83/EC of 29 April 2004 on Minimum Standards for the Qualification and Status of Third Country Nationals or Stateless Persons as Refugees or as Persons Who

and subsidiary protection: it is a "short-term emergency response to a significant influx of asylum seekers"[4] devised to protect individuals arriving *en masse* against *refoulement* pending national asylum authorities' examination of their claim for international protection on a case-by-case basis. Originally excluded from the scope of this study for the above reason, it will nevertheless be mentioned briefly in this Chapter insofar as it does provide some (non-negligible) protection to persons displaced by indiscriminate threats: protection against *refoulement* (II). The Qualification Directive is in turn the key instrument of EU asylum law, in that it defines who can benefit international protection in EU Member States. In particular, it incorporates a new form of international protection that supplements – or complements – refugee status: subsidiary protection. This *lex specialis* instrument of EU asylum law will be elaborated upon, in particular in that it can provide (subsidiary) protection to persons who do not qualify for refugee status because they flee indiscriminate threats (III).

I Fundamental Rights and European Union Law

The Lisbon Treaty, in force since 1 December 2009, clearly articulates the status of fundamental rights within the European Union. Their anchorage in the EU legal order is threefold: they are enshrined in General Principles of EU law as well as in the legally-binding Charter of Fundamental Rights but also in the European Convention on Human Rights to which the EU is to accede.[5] This solemn and unequivocal affirmation of the human rights foundation of the European Union was initiated by the pioneering jurisprudence of the Court of Justice. The Court's analysis of fundamental rights as general principles of EU law was endorsed by the EU legislator (A) who went one step further by adopting the binding Charter of Fundamental Rights and recommending the adhesion of the EU to the European Convention of Human Rights (B). In this corpus of fundamental rights, which ones are relevant in the field of asylum (C)?

A *Fundamental Rights as General Principles of Community Law*

The development of fundamental rights protection within the European Union legal order was initiated by the Court of Justice who progressively elaborated

---

 Otherwise Need International Protection and the Content of the Protection Granted ("Qualification Directive (2004)") 2004/83/EC [30 September 2004] *OJ L 304/12*. A recast Qualification Directive has since been adopted: *see* Qualification Directive, *op. cit.*, note 52.

4 R. Mandal, *Protection Mechanisms Outside of the 1951 Convention ("Complementary Protection")*, No. PPLA/2005/02 (Geneva: UNHCR, June 2005), p. 3.

5 TEU, Article 6, §§ 3, 1 and 2 respectively.

a "fundamental rights doctrine", thereby including fundamental rights norms among the general principles of law it protects (A). Following the Court's lead, the Treaties also incorporated fundamental rights as sources of general principles of EU law (2).

1   A Principle Affirmed by the Court of Justice...

The development of the European Union including the realisation of the internal market and the changes that accompanied them (growing powers of the institutions as well as the primacy and direct effect of Union law) called for the inclusion of fundamental rights, as a counterpart. The CJEU developed its doctrine progressively, since the 1960s (a) and recently entrenched fundamental rights even more firmly in the EU legal order with the rulings of the General Court and of the Court of Justice in the *Kadi* case (b).

(a)   *Development of a Fundamental Rights Doctrine*

It is well known that the treaties on the basis of which the European Union was built originally did not refer to human rights (or to "fundamental rights"[6]).[7] However and as it is recalled in the Preamble of the Treaty on the European Union in its current consolidated version, the initial purpose of the Communities was not actually purely economic; it was in fact "the ending of the division of the European continent".[8] The founding Treaties were drafted as a means to this end: their authors and signatories had the hope that the development of common interests among States within the region would bring nations of Europe together and lay "firm bases for the construction of the future Europe".[9] This theory, which has since been borne out by the facts, was formulated by Robert Schuman in 1950: Europe, he asserted, would be built "through concrete achievements which first create a *de facto* solidarity".[10] Accordingly, the European venture was launched on the basis of a "sectoral and functionalist

---

6   There is no conceptual or legal difference between the two terminologies although "fundamental rights" is the one favoured by the EU. "The EU and International Human Rights Law", *op. cit.* p. 9.
7   T. Ahmed and I.D.J. Butler (2006), *op. cit.* pp. 772–773 and references cited.
8   TEU, Preamble, Recital 3.
9   *Ibid.*, Preamble, Recital 3.
10 R. Schuman, Déclaration du 9 mai 1950, issued in Paris (translation available on the website of the European Union) at: <http://europa.eu/about-eu/basic-information/symbols/europe-day/schuman-declaration/index_en.htm> [09/07/2012].

approach".[11] Three Communities were created, each concerned solely with one well-defined economic sector: coal and steel industries for the ECSC, atomic energy for the Euratom, and the establishment of a common market for the EEC. The first was the European Coal and Steel Community, in 1951.[12] The attempts made in 1952 and 1954 to depart from this approach through the creation of political entities (the European Defence Community – EDC, and the European Political Community – EPC respectively) both failed,[13] which encouraged the drafters of the Treaties of Rome to aim at economic integration rather than political integration: the two other economic communities were hence created.[14]

The founding Treaties were mainly of a market-oriented nature and each was chiefly concerned with endowing the European Community it established with the necessary competences and means to act in the economic sector it was devised to regulate. In this context, a solemn declaration on fundamental rights did not find its place in the Treaties, which were hence distinguishable

---

11   "Fundamental Rights and Non-Discrimination", *in The Amsterdam treaty: a comprehensive guide* (n/a: European Union, 1995–2012), retrieved from: <http://europa.eu/legislation_summaries/institutional_affairs/treaties/amsterdam_treaty/index_en.htm> [03/08/2010].

12   Treaty Establishing the European Coal and Steel Community, 18 April 1951, expired 23 July 2002 [1957] *UNTS* Vol. 261, p. 140.

13   Both projects failed due to the opposition of the French National Assembly to the ratification of the European Defence Community ("EDC") Treaty – the EDC being the institutional corollary of the European Political Community ("The European Political Community" (Centre Virtuel de la Connaissance sur l'Europe – CVCE, 2004–2012), 11 August 2011, retrieved from: <www.cvce.eu> [19/07/2012].) For an account of the reasons behind France's reservations about the establishment of the EDC, which eventually led the French National Assembly to reject the EDC and the loss of national sovereignty (*"aliénations nécessaires mais importantes de souveraineté"*) it implied, see: "Verbatim Record of the 22nd Meeting of the Council Held on Friday, 24th April, 1953 at 11 a.m. at the Palais de Chaillot, Paris XVIe." *NATO Secret Verbatim Record C-VR(53)2* (*unclassified and public disclosed*), pp. 6, 21–22 and 24–25 in particular; Pierre Mendès-France, then President of the French Republic, elaborated on the reasons of the rejection of the EDC Treaty by French Parliament in Statement by Mr Mendes-France, Chairman of the North Atlantic Council, at the Meeting of the North Atlantic Council Held on 9th September 1954 C-M(54)71 (unclassified an public disclosed) [10 September 1954] *NATO Secret doc.*, p. 2; see also J. van der Harst, "The European Defence Community and Nato: A Classic Case of Franco-Dutch Controversy", *in* M. Drent, *et al.* (Eds.), *Nato's Retirement? Essays in Honour of Peter Volten*, Greenwood Paper 26 (Groningen: Centre of European Security Studies, 2011), pp. 83–94.

14   Treaty Establishing the European Economic Community ("Treaty of Rome (EEC)"), 25 March 1957 [1958] *UNTS* Vol. 298, p. 3; Treaty Establishing the European Atomic Energy Community ("Euratom"), 25 March 1957 [1958] *UNTS* Vol. 298, p. 167.

from norms of constitutional character.[15] The need to incorporate a bill of rights in the founding Treaties did not in fact manifest itself as critical at the time since the protection human rights was already elsewhere secured. Firstly, in the Universal Declaration of Human Rights, adopted in 1948 by the United Nations General Assembly,[16] States proclaimed a catalogue of inalienable human rights. Secondly, the European Convention on Human Rights, adopted in 1950 by the Council of Europe, already established a binding framework for the protection of fundamental rights in Europe. As a consequence, the inclusion of a "separate human rights foundation" in the structure of the nascent European Communities appeared all the less topical.[17]

Human rights nevertheless progressively entered the Community legal order. Their development is closely related to the growing role given by the Court of Justice to the four fundamental freedoms. The freedoms of movement of goods and of persons, the freedom of establishment and the freedom to provide services, now perceived as foundation of the Community,[18] were initially enshrined in the Treaty Establishing the European Economic Community[19] as "abstract objectives"[20] to be achieved by the institutions for the purpose of establishing a common market between Member States. The Court of Justice, who perceived the necessity to secure those fundamental freedoms, essential to the realisation and liberalisation of the internal market,[21] dubbed them

---

15 Europa, "Fundamental Rights and Non-Discrimination", *op. cit.*; *see* also a contrario I. Pernice who argues that the newly adopted EU Charter of Fundamental Rights is indeed evidence of the constitutional character of current European Union Primary lawI. Pernice, "The Treaty of Lisbon and Fundamental Rights", *in* S. Griller and J. Ziller (Eds.), *The Lisbon Treaty: EU Constitutionalism without a Constitutional Treaty?* (Wien, New York: Springer, 2008), pp. 236–239 and 252 in particular.

16 UN General Assembly, Universal Declaration of Human Rights ("UDHR"), 10 December 1948 UNGA Res. 217 A (III).

17 P. Alston and J.H.H. Weiler, "An 'Ever Closer Union' in Need of a Human Rights Policy", *European Journal of International Law* (Oxford University Press / USA), Vol. 9, No. 4 (1998), pp. 658s, 659.

18 ECJ judgment of 3 June 1986, *R.H. Kempf v Staatssecretaris van Justitie*, Case 139/85, [1986] ECR I-1741, §13; ECJ judgements of 29 April 2004, Joined Cases C-482/01 and C-493/01, *Georgios Orfanopoulos and Others* and *Raffaele Oliveri v Land Baden-Württemberg*, [2004] ECR I-5257, § 62.

19 *Treaty of Rome (EEC)*, Articles 2, 3 and *passim*.

20 V. Skouris, "Fundamental Rights and Fundamental Freedoms: The Challenge of Striking a Delicate Balance", *European business law review*, Vol. 17, No. 2 (2006), pp. 225–239, p. 227.

21 In 1992, Article 7a of the then Treaty establishing the European Community (now Article 26 TFEU) already made clear that the goal of the Community was the progressive establishment of an "internal market" which "shall comprise an area without internal frontiers in which the free movement of goods, persons, services and capital is ensured in

fundamental principles that confer rights upon individuals.[22] In other words, from being the sole responsibility of the Community institutions, they became directly applicable and could thus be invoked by individuals.[23] Through its jurisprudence, the Court of Justice tremendously contributed to the materialisation of the four freedoms and hence to the realisation of the internal market and the advancement of European integration.[24] Incidentally, concerns spread among Member States that the seeming unabated expansion of those economic freedoms might be to the detriment of fundamental rights, which from part of their Constitutional traditions. Another element nourished the concerns of States, pertaining to the status of Community law *vis-à-vis* national law.

In the course of the development of the Communities, the European Court of Justice specified the nature of Community law and its relation to Member State national law. In particular, the Court developed the doctrines of "direct effect"[25] and supremacy of Community law. In its landmark 1964 decision in the *Costa v. Enel* case, the Court established the primacy of Community law over the law of the Member States:

---

accordance with the provisions of the Treaties". TFEU, Article 26 (originally Article 7a TEC (1992), then 14 TEC (1997)).

22 On the freedom of movement, for instance, the ECJ ruled in the 2005 *Oulane* case: "According to settled case-law, the right of nationals of a Member State to enter the territory of another Member State and reside there for the purposes intended by the Treaty is a right conferred directly by the Treaty or, as the case may be, by the provisions adopted for its implementation". CJ, Case C-215/03, *Salah Oulane v Minister Voor Vreemdelingenzaken En Integratie* ("*Oulane*") (17 February 2005) ECR I-1215, § 17; see also CJ, Case 48–75, *Jean Noël Royer* ("*Royer*") (8 April 1976) [1976] ECR 497, § 31; CJ, Case C-376/89, *Panagiotis Giagounidis v Stadt Reutlingen* (5 March 1991) [1991] ECR I-1069, § 12.

23 Concerning the freedom of etablishment, CJ, Case 2/74, *Reyners v Belgium* (21 June 1974) [1974] ECR 631, §§ 25s; and concerning the free movement of services CJ, Case 33/74, *Van Binsbergen v Bestuur Van de Bedrijfsvereniging Voor de Metaalnijverheid* ("*Van Binsbergen*") (3 December 1974) [1974] ECR 1299, § 27.

24 V. Skouris (2006), *op. cit.*, pp. 226–230.

25 In the *Van Gend en Loos* case, the Court affirmed the direct effect of Community law when it ruled as follows: "Independently of the legislation of member states, community law not only imposes obligations on individuals but is also intended to confer upon them rights which become part of their legal heritage. These rights arise not only where they are expressly granted by the treaty but also by reason of obligations which the treaty imposes in a clearly defined way upon individuals as well as upon the member states and upon the institutions of the community". CJ, Case 26–62, *Nv Algemene Transport- En Expeditie Onderneming Van Gend & Loos v. Netherlands Inland Revenue Administration* ("*Van Gend en Loos*") (5 February 1963) [1963] ECR 1. *See* also CJ, Case 2/74, *Gabrielle Defrenne v. Société Anonyme Belge de Navigation Aérienne Sabena* (8 April 1976) [1974] ECR 631.

[the] law stemming from the treaty, an independent source of law, could not, because of its special and original nature, be overridden by domestic legal provisions, however framed, without being deprived of its character as community law and without the legal basis of the community itself being called into question.[26]

The two doctrines together imply that individuals may invoke their rights deriving from Community law before national courts to seek the non-application of national legal provisions. A further step was taken by the Court that reinforced its doctrines and the prominence of Community law. The Court of Justice, in *Simmenthal*, stated that Treaty provisions and measures adopted by the institutions not only rendered conflicting national law automatically inapplicable but also, prospectively, precluded the adoption of incompatible national legislative measures.[27] Those principles asserted by the Court implied, among other consequences, that Member States could not escape their obligations under Community law by enacting conflicting domestic law. Given the absence of any reference to human rights in the founding treaties, it could also adversely lead to Community measures taking precedence over domestic law albeit infringing on the human rights protection therein enshrined.

The above-mentioned features of the development of the European Community, *i.e.* the absence from the Treaties of human rights provisions, the advancing liberalisation of the internal market through the affirmation of the four economic freedoms, the enlargement of the competences of the Community, combined with the affirmed principles of supremacy and direct effect of Community law were received with mitigated enthusiasm by Member States who perceived them as threats to the protection of human rights:

> To them, the Community's sphere of operation increasingly resembled a gaping fundamental rights loophole: given the absence of provisions of basic rights from the Treaties, Community institutions appeared to be exercising public power unsullied by rights norms.[28]

---

26   CJ, Case 6/64, *Flaminio Costa v. Enel* (15 July 1964) [1964] ECR 585.
27   CJ, Case 106/77, *Amministrazione Delle Finanze Dello Stato v. Simmenthal Spa* ("*Simmenthal*") [1978] ECR 629, §§ 17 and 21.
28   N.T. Isiksel, "Fundamental Rights in the EU after Kadi and Al Barakaat", *European Law Journal*, Vol. 16, No. 5 (September 2010), pp. 551–577, p. 553; see similarly J.H.H. Weiler, "Fundamental Rights and Fundamental Boundaries: On Standards and Values in the Protection of Human Rights", *in* N.A. Neuwahl and A. Rosas (Eds.), *The European Union and Human Rights* (The Hague: Kluwer Law International, 1995), pp. 51–76, pp. 56–57.

This belief led some Member States to occasionally challenge the applicability of Community measures which they perceived were incompatible with their constitutional law. This was particularly true in Italy and Germany. In Germany, case law and literature at the time both contended that Community law could not infringe the fundamental rights protected under Member States' constitutional laws.[29] The case law of the Italian and German Constitutional Courts is particularly indicative of some Member States' reluctance to recognising the supremacy of Community law over national norms of Constitutional nature inasmuch as they enshrine fundamental rights. Both Constitutional Courts repeatedly and firmly asserted that Member States' national courts possessed jurisdiction to review the acts of Community institutions to ensure that Community law did not impinge on the fundamental rights enshrined in their respective national Constitutions.[30]

Faced with this reticence of the Italian and German Constitutional Courts chiefly to fully abide by the principle of supremacy of Community law over national law, the EU Court of Justice (CJ), in order to preserve this principle and the normative hierarchy it had devised, had to respond to Member States' calls and take a stand on the place occupied by human rights protection within this hierarchy.[31] Because recognition that obligations deriving from fundamental right provisions in international treaties or national Constitutional laws outranked obligations of Community law would have undermined the system it had built up, based on the supremacy of Community law, the CJ decided instead to ground the protection of fundamental rights "in the Community legal order itself".[32] The Court of Justice had the opportunity to address Member States' concerns in 1969, in the case of *Stauder v. City of Ulm*,[33] referred by a German administrative tribunal (*Verwaltungsgericht*) for preliminary ruling. The impugned Community act was a decision of the Commission to set up a

---

29 H.G. Schermers and "The European Communities Bound by Fundamental Human Rights", *Common Market Law Review*, Vol. 27, No. 2 (1990), 253–254.

30 The topic has been addressed many times in literature, see for example P. Craig and G.D. Búrca, *EU Law: Text, Cases, and Materials*, 4th ed. (Oxford: Oxford University Press, 2008), pp. 357–365; N.T. Isiksel (September 2010), *op. cit.*, pp. 553–556; T. Ahmed and I.D.J. Butler (2006), *op. cit.*, p. 775 (n. 20 in particular).

31 The necessary compromise made by the CJEU in order to safeguard the supremacy of EC/EU law is oft mentioned in literature. See for example: S. Peers, "Chapter 5: Human Rights in the EU Legal Order: Practical Relevance for EC Immigration and Asylum Law", *in* S. Peers and N. Rogers (Eds.), *EU Immigration and Asylum Law: Text and Commentary*, Series: Immigration and Asylum Law and Policy in Europe, Vol. 12 (Leiden: Koninklijke Brill NV, 2006), pp. 115–137, p. 116.

32 T. Ahmed and I.D.J. Butler (2006), *op. cit.*, 775.

33 CJ, Case 29/69, *Erich Stauder v. City of Ulm* ("*Stauder*") (12 November 1969) [1969] ECR 419.

Community scheme for the retail of surplus butter at reduced price in return for a coupon in the beneficiaries' names.³⁴ The German court found that the publication of the name, required by the Commission, raised justifiable doubts as to the legality of the Commission decision in view of Germany's constitutional rights.³⁵ Ruling in this case, the Court of Justice set the first stone of its doctrine of fundamental rights protection: the Court safeguarded the supremacy of Community law by "lifting" fundamental rights up to the level of Community law, as "general principles".³⁶ Notwithstanding the fact that the founding Treaties contained no reference to fundamental rights, the CJ creatively confirmed the existence of fundamental rights in the Community legal order and thus referred for the first time to "the fundamental human rights enshrined in the General Principles of Community Law and protected by the court".³⁷

This statement was reinforced and developed a year later by the CJ in yet another German case: *Internationale Handelsgesellschaft*.³⁸ A German administrative tribunal refused to accept the validity of two regulations, one issued by the Council and one by the Commission,³⁹ on the ground that the system of deposits they provided was contrary to certain structural principles of national constitutional law which had to be protected within the framework of Community law. In the German court's view, the primacy of Community law had to yield before the fundamental principles of the German Basic Law.⁴⁰ The

---

34   It is worth noting that the requirement that the names of the beneficiaries of the measures appears on the coupon was a specificity of the German version of the Commission's decision (*"auf ihren Namen ausgestellten"*). Other versions merely required that the coupons be individualised (*"bon individualisé"* in the French version). *Décision de la Commission, du 12 février 1969, relative aux mesures permettant à certaines catégories de consommateurs d'acheter du beurre à prix réduit*, 12 February 1969 [03/03/1969] JO L 52, pp. 9–10.

35   The decision of the Verwaltungsgericht is cited by Advocate General Karl Roemer in his Submissions in the case: Opinion of Adv. Gen. Karl Roemer, CMLR 112, delivered on 12 November 1969, *Case 29/69 Stauder v. City of Ulm* [1970] CMLR 112, p. 113.

36   CJ, *Stauder*, § 7.

37   *Ibid.*, § 7.

38   CJ, Case 11–70, *Internationale Handelsgesellschaft Mbh v Einfuhr- Und Vorratsstelle Für Getreide Und Futtermittel* (*"Internationale Handelsgesellschaft"*) (17 December 1970) [1970] ECR 1125.

39   *Regulation no 120/67/EEC of the Council of 13 June 1967 on the Common Organization of the Market in Cereals*, OJ English special edition: Series I Chapter 1967, p. 33 and *Regulation no 473/67/EEC of the Commission of 21 August 1967 on Import and Export Licences*, [24/08/1967] OJ 204, p. 16. The two regulations concerned the system of export licences and the deposit attaching to them (the "system of deposits").

40   The German administrative tribunal was referring in particular to the German constitutional principles of freedom of action and of disposition, of economic liberty, and of proportionality.

Court of Justice rejected the argument. Assessing the validity of Community measures by the yardstick of national law, be it principles of constitutional law, the Court found, would jeopardise the uniformity and efficacy of Community law. Conversely, the Court asserted that Community law was the only yardstick by which Community measures could be judged.[41] The Court hence first recalled the supremacy of Community law before adding:

> However, an examination should be made as to whether or not any analogous guarantee inherent in Community law has been disregarded. In fact, respect for fundamental rights forms an integral part of the general principles of law protected by the Court of Justice. The protection of such rights, whilst inspired by the constitutional traditions common to the Member States, must be ensured within the framework of the structure and objectives of the Community.[42]

The Court thus confirmed the supremacy of Community law, reiterated that fundamental rights formed an integral part of the Community legal order, as general principles of law, and, in what looks like an endeavour to secure the support of sceptical Constitutional Courts, asserted that Member State Constitutions were the primary source of those general principles of Community law. In *Nold v. Commission*,[43] the Court of Justice made it clear that it would not uphold Community measures which were incompatible with the fundamental rights established and guaranteed by the Constitutions of Member States, from which it draws inspiration.[44] In the same decision, the Court went one step further and mentioned international human rights treaties as an additional source of fundamental rights:

> Similarly, international treaties for the protection of human rights, on which the Member States have collaborated or of which they are signatories, can supply guidelines which should be followed within the framework of Community law.[45]

---

41   CJ, *Internationale Handelsgesellschaft*, §§ 3.
42   *Ibid.*, §§ 4.
43   CJ, Case 4–73, *J. Nold, Kohlen- Und Baustoffgroßhandlung v Commission of the European Communities* ("*Nold*") (14 May 1974) [1974] ECR 491.
44   *Ibid.*, § 13.
45   CJ, Case 4–73, *J. Nold, Kohlen- Und Baustoffgroßhandlung v. Commission* ("*Nold*") (14 May 1974) [1974] ECR 491 § 13.

The Court has since reiterated that international human rights treaties were sources of general principles of Community law.⁴⁶ In that respect, the Court has made clear that fundamental rights, the observance of which it ensures, derive in part from the European Convention on Human Rights (ECHR).⁴⁷ The Court in fact oft cites the ECHR which, it finds, has "special significance".⁴⁸ References to other human rights treaties also made their way, although in sparse manner, in CJ case-law. The Court has had the opportunity to mention the International Covenant on Civil and Political Rights⁴⁹ as well as the Convention on the Rights of the Child.⁵⁰

The European Union is not – yet⁵¹ – party to those international human rights treaties that are relevant in asylum cases and the Court of Justice can therefore not directly apply them as elements of EU law. Nevertheless, in recognising them as sources of general principles of law common to EU Member States, principles which the CJ applies, the Court in practice does apply them, "by the back-door".⁵² The Court in fact occasionally went beyond the standards set by the ECHR – as interpreted by the European Court of Human

---

46 CJ (Grand Chamber), Case C-540/03, *European Parliament v. Council* ("*Parliament v. Council*") (27 June 2006) [2006] ECR I-5769, § 35.

47 CJ, Case C-260/89, *Elliniki Radiophonia Tiléorassi Ae and Panellinia Omospondia Syllogon Prossopikou v. Dimotiki Etairia Pliroforissis and Sotirios Kouvelas and Nicolaos Avdellas and Others* ("*ERT V. DEP*") (18 June 1991) [1991] ECR I-2925, § 42.

48 CJ, Case C-222/84, *Johnston v. Chief Constable of the Royal Ulster Constabulary* (15 May 1986) [1986] ECR 1651, § 18; CJ, *ERT V. DEP*, § 41; CJ, Case C-112/00, *Eugen Schmidberger, Internationale Transporte Und Planzüge v. Republik Österreich* ("*Schmidberger*") (12 June 2003) [2003] ECR I-05659, § 71; CJ (First Chamber), Case C-36/02, *Omega Spielhallen- Und Automatenaufstellungs Gmbh v. Oberbürgermeisterin Der Bundesstadt Bonn* ("*Omega*") (14 October 2004) [2004] ECR I-09609, § 33.

49 CJ, Case 374/87, *Orkem v. Commission* ("*Orkem*") (18 October 1989) [1989] ECR 3283, § 31; CJ, Joined Cases C-297/88 and C-197/89, *Massam Dzodzi v. Belgian State* ("*Dzodzi*") (18 October 1990) [1990] ECR I-3763, § 68; CJ, Case C-249/96, *Lisa Jacqueline Grant v. South-West Trains Ltd.* ("*Grant*") (17 February 1998) [1998] ECR I-621, § 44; CJ, *Parliament v. Council*, § 37.

50 CJ, *Parliament v. Council*, § 37.

51 As discussed, Article 6(2) of the Lisbon Treaty provides for the formal accession of the European Union to the European Convention on Human Rights.

52 H. Schermers, "Remarks on Human Rights Protection in Europe", *in* R. Lefeber (Ed.), *Contemporary International Law Issues: Opportunities at a Time of Momentous Change, Proceedings of the Second Joint Conference of the American Society of International Law and the Nederlandse Vereniging Voor Internationaal Recht Held in the Hague, the Netherlands, 22–24 July 1993* (Dordrecht: Martinus Nijhoff Publishers, 1994), pp. 22–24, 22.

Rights – and by the ICCPR.[53] In the *Orkem* case, the Court was asked whether legal persons could invoke the right not to give evidence against oneself in relation to infringements in the economic sphere, in particular infringements of competition law. The Court found that this right, as guaranteed by national laws and the ICCPR, was only granted to natural persons charged with an offence in criminal proceedings and found no evidence, neither in the wording of the ECHR nor in the case-law of the European Court of Human Rights (ECtHR), that ECHR Article 6 right to a fair trial could be upheld in such a way. Notwithstanding these observations, the Court of Justice found that certain limitations on the Commission's powers of investigation were indeed implied by the need to safeguard the rights of the defence which the Court had held to be a fundamental principle of the Community legal order.[54]

The CJ thus progressively developed its doctrine pursuant to which Community institutions were bound to respect fundamental rights. It was in fact determining in convincing Member States and their national courts in particular to accept the supremacy of EU law.[55] The Court has gone further and found that Member States themselves were also bound by those general principles when acting in the field of EU law:[56] national measures adopted to implement Community law[57] as well as national rules entering the scope of Community law[58] are concerned.[59]

(b)   *The Kadi Case: A Strong Commitment to Fundamental Rights*
In two recent cases, joined before the Court of Justice, the CJEU firmly reasserted the central role fundamental rights play within the EU legal order. The decisions of the Court of Justice and of the General Court (then "Court of First

---

53   CJ, *Orkem*, §§ 29–35.
54   *Ibid.*, §§ 29–35.
55   J.H.H. Weiler, "The Transformation of Europe", *The Yale Law Journal* (The Yale Law Journal Company, Inc.), Vol. 100, No. 8 (1991), pp. 2403–2483, p. 2418.
56   F. Jacobs, "Remarks on Human Rights Protection in Europe", *in* R. Lefeber (Ed.), *Contemporary International Law Issues: Opportunities at a Time of Momentous Change, Proceedings of the Second Joint Conference of the American Society of International Law and the Nederlandse Vereniging Voor Internationaal Recht Held in the Hague, the Netherlands, 22–24 July 1993* (Dordrecht: Martinus Nijhoff Publishers, 1994), pp. 26–29, 27.
57   CJ, Case 5/88, *Wachauf v. Bundesamt Für Ernährung Und Forstwirtschaft* (13 July 1989) [1989] ECR 2609, § 19.
58   CJ, *ERT v. DEP*, § 42.
59   C.L. Kline, "EU Inconsistencies Regarding Human Rights Treatment: Can the EU Require Czech Action as a Criterion for Accession", *Boston College International and Comparative Law Review*, Vol. 23 (1999–2000), pp. 35–55, p. 41.

Instance")[60] before are particularly interesting on two aspects: they elaborate on the hierarchy of norms within the EU legal order and place the protection of human rights at the top of it. The two cases will be commented below as they are particularly instructive.

In the *Ysuf* and *Kadi* cases the General Court (GC) first dismissed the plaintiffs' actions[61] before the Court of Justice eventually ruled in their favour.[62] The following developments will focus on the elements of the decisions that are pertinent to the question of the continuation of States' obligations deriving from the international human rights treaties to which they are parties, despite their European Union membership (the substance of the claims, on alleged breaches of fundamental rights by the contested EU regulations will therefore not be addressed here). The background to the dispute is similar in the two cases. From 1999 to 2003 when the General Court heard the cases, the UN Security Council adopted a series of resolution urging States to freeze funds and other financial resources of, or benefiting, Taliban entities and persons identified in a regularly updated list.[63] Following their adoptions and in order to implement them, the Council of the European Union and the Commission of the European Communities enacted Common Positions or Regulations[64]

---

60 Above note 78. The Lisbon Treaty has renamed the Court of First Instance (CFI) "General Court". The new terminology will be used in the work to refer to the General Court (or "GC") throughout its history.

61 GC, Case T-315/01, *Yassin Abdullah Kadi v. Council and Commission* ("*Kadi*") (21 September 2005) [2005] ECR II-3649; GC, Case T-306/01 *Ahmed Ali Yusuf and Al Barakaat International Foundation v. Council and Commission* ("*Yusuf*") (21 September 2005) [2005] ECR II-03533.

62 CJ (Grand Chamber), Joined cases C-402/05 P and C-415/05 P, *Kadi and Al Barakaat International Foundation v. Council and Commission* ("*Kadi*") (3 September 2008) [2008] ECR I-06351.

63 UN Security Council, Resolution 1452 (2002): Threats to International Peace and Security Caused by Terrorist Acts, 20 December 2002 S/RES/1452 (2002); UN Security Council, Resolution 1267 (1999): Establishes Security Council Committee; Imposes Limited Air Embargo and Funds and Financial Assets Embargo on the Taliban, 15 October 1999 S/RES/1267 (1999); UN Security Council, Resolution 1333 (2000): Air and Arms Embargo, Restricted Travel Sanctions, Freezing of Funds of Usama Bin Laden and Associates, 19 December 2000 S/RES/1333 (2000); UN Security Council, Resolution 1390 (2002): Modifies the Sanctions Regime Originally Imposed in Resolutions 1267 (1999) and 1333 (2000), 16 January 2002 S/RES/1390 (2002).

64 Council Common Position of 15 November 1999 Concerning Restrictive Measures against the Taliban 1999/727/CFSP [16/11/1999] *OJ* Vol. L 294, p. 1; Council Common Position of 27 May 2002 Concerning Restrictive Measures against Usama Bin Laden, Members of the Al-Qaida Organisation and the Taliban and Other Individuals, Groups, Undertakings

translating the language of the resolutions into binding EU law, directly applicable in all Member States.[65] The applicants in the two cases at hand, whose names appeared on the above-mentioned list, sought annulment of a specific regulation, arguing that the restrictive measures imposed by it infringed their fundamental rights (*i.e.* their right to respect for property, to effective judicial review and to be heard).[66] The General Court, taking into consideration Article 351 of the TFEU[67] and Article 103 of the 1945 UN Charter[68] (stating that State Parties' obligations created under the Charter prevail over other international obligations) stated the primacy of EU Member States' obligations under the UN Charter *vis-à-vis* their obligations under EU law:

> From the standpoint of international law, the obligations of the Member States of the United Nations under the Charter of the United Nations

and Entities Associated with Them and Repealing Common Positions 96/746/CFSP, 1999/727/CFSP, 2001/154/CFSP and 2001/771/CFSP [29/05/2002] *OJ* Vol. L 139, pp. 4–5; Council Regulation (EC) No 337/2000 of 14 February 2000 Concerning a Flight Ban and a Freeze of Funds and Other Financial Resources in Respect of the Taliban of Afghanistan, 16/02/2000 *OJ L* Vol. 43, p. 1; Council Common Position of 26 February 2001 Concerning Additional Restrictive Measures against the Taliban and Amending Common Position 96/746/CFSP, 27/02/2001 *OJ L* Vol. 57, pp. 1–2; Council Regulation (EC) No 467/2001 of 6 March 2001 Prohibiting the Export of Certain Goods and Services to Afghanistan, Strengthening the Flight Ban and Extending the Freeze of Funds and Other Financial Resources in Respect of the Taliban of Afghanistan, and Repealing Regulation (EC) No 337/2000 [09/03/2001] *OJ L* Vol. 67, p. 1; Commission Regulation (EC) No 2062/2001 of 19 October 2001 Amending, for the Third Time, Council Regulation (EC) No 467/2001 Prohibiting the Export of Certain Goods and Services to Afghanistan, Strengthening the Flight Ban and Extending the Freeze of Funds Andother Financial Resources in Respect of the Taliban of Afghanistan and Repealing Regulation (EC) No 337/2000 [20/10/2001] *OJ* Vol. L 277, p. 25; Council Regulation (EC) No 881/2002 of 27 May 2002 Imposing Certain Specific Restrictive Measures Directed against Certain Persons and Entities Associated with Usama Bin Laden, the Al-Qaida Network and the Taliban, and Repealing Council Regulation (EC) No 467/2001 Prohibiting the Export of Certain Goods and Services to Afghanistan, Strengthening the Flight Ban and Extending the Freeze of Funds and Other Financial Resources in Respect of the Taliban of Afghanistan [29/05/2002] *OJ* Vol. L 139, p. 9; Council Regulation (EC) No 561/2003 of 27 March 2003 Amending, as Regards Exceptions to the Freezing of Funds and Economic Resources, Regulation (EC) No 881/2002 Imposing Certain Specific Restrictive Measures Directed against Certain Persons and Entities Associated with Usama Bin Laden, the Al-Qaida Network and the Taliban [29/03/2003] *OJ* Vol. L 82, p. 1.

65 TFEU, Art. 288.
66 GC, *Kadi*, §§ 37 and 59; GC, *Yusuf*, § 284.
67 Former Article 307 of the TEC.
68 Charter of the United Nations ("UN Charter"), 24 October 1945 [1946–1947] *UNTS* Vol. 1 p. XVI.

clearly prevail over every other obligation of domestic law or of international treaty law including, for those of them that are members of the Council of Europe, their obligations under the ECHR and, for those that are also members of the Community, their obligations under the EC Treaty.[69]

This primacy, the General Court finds, necessarily extends to obligations created under Security Council resolutions since, under Article 25 of the UN Charter, Member States of the United Nations undertake to accept and carry out the decisions of the Security Council.[70] It is suggested that this approach "could logically be extended to the obligation to promote respect for human rights established by the UN Charter"[71] and imply the supremacy of EU Member States' obligations deriving from applicable human rights instruments. Human rights are indeed at the core of the UN Charter: not only does the Charter present them as a prerequisite to the realisation and maintenance of a stable international order,[72] it also gave impetus to the development of international and regional human rights law.[73] The UN General Assembly and Human Rights Council have in fact consistently stated and reaffirmed in numerous resolutions that, under the UN Charter, "all Member States have an obligation to promote and protect human rights and fundamental freedoms, as stated in the Charter of the United Nations and elaborated in the Universal Declaration of Human Rights, the International Covenants on Human Rights, and other applicable human rights instruments".[74]

---

69   GC, *Kadi*, § 181; GC, *Yusuf*, § 231.
70   GC, *Kadi*, § 184; GC, *Yusuf*, § 234.
71   T. Ahmed and I.D.J. Butler (2006), *op. cit.*, 787.
72   I. Brownlie and G.S. Goodwin-Gill (Eds.), *Basic Documents on Human Rights*, 6th ed. (New York: Oxford University Press, 2010), p. 1.
73   C. Beyani, "The Legal Premises for the International Protection of Human Rights", *in The Reality of International Law: Essays in Honour of Ian Brownlie* (New York: Oxford University Press, 1999), p. 24.
74   UNGA, "Resolution 51/113 on the Situation of Human Rights in Cuba", A/RES/51/113, 7 March 1997, Preamble. *See* also: HRC, "Resolution 16/24: Situation of Human Rights in Myanmar", A/HRC/RES/16/24, 12 April 2011, Preamble, Recital 5; UNHRC, "Resolution 16/31: Israeli Settlements in the Occupied Palestinian Territory, Including East Jerusalem, and in the Occupied Syrian Golan", A/HRC/RES/16/31, 13 April 2011, Preamble, Recital 2; the General Assembly also elaborated on UN Member States' obligation to promote and protect human rights, as elaborated in international human rights instruments, in Resolution 60/251 whereby it established the Human Rights Council, see UNGA, "Resolution 60/251: Human Rights Council", A/RES/60/251, 3 April 2006.

The General Court in fact took a first step in that direction. Taking into consideration the purposes and principles of the United Nations, as enshrined in the Charter,[75] the General Court noted that the UN Charter considered the protection of fundamental rights as a "mandatory principle of international law", binding upon the Members and bodies of the United Nations.[76] As a consequence, the Court inferred, Security Council resolutions have binding force only insofar as they observe "the fundamental peremptory provisions of *jus cogens*".[77] The Court concluded that it could therefore, in connection with an action for annulment of a Community act implementing Security Council resolutions, carry out an "indirect judicial review" of the lawfulness of the Security Council resolutions in question with regard to *jus cogens*.[78] The General Court eventually dismissed both actions on the ground that there was no violation of *jus cogens*.[79] The aspect of the decision concerning the status of Member States' international treaty obligations is problematic and will be discussed below. Let us first address the question of fundamental rights protection.

By accepting to assess the validity of Member States obligations under the UN Charter by the yardstick of fundamental rights norms, the General Court affirmed that it considered the protection of fundamental rights as the upper layer[80] of the hierarchy of norms. By referring to *jus cogens* norms specifically however, the General Court appears to narrow the scope of its conclusion: only those human rights that are "accepted and recognized by the international community of States as a whole" as rights "from which no derogation is permitted"[81] could prevail over conflicting acts of EU institutions and Member States. Such was apparently not the intention of the General Court who

---

75 UN *Charter*, Article 1.
76 GC, *Kadi*, §§ 228–229; GC, *Yusuf*, §§ 279–280.
77 GC, *Kadi*, § 230; GC, *Yusuf*, § 281.
78 GC, *Kadi*, §§ 226 and 231; GC, *Yusuf*, §§ 277 and 282.
79 GC, *Kadi*, §§ 251–252, 275 and 290–291; GC, *Yusuf*, §§ 302–303, 330–331 and 345–346.
80 The theory of a hierarchy of norms or of the "layered structure" (*Stufenbaulehre*) of the legal order was initially formulated by Adolf Merkl and popularised by Kelsen, in his *Pure Theory of Law*. See H. Kelsen, *Pure Theory of Law*, 2nd ed., Translated by M. Knight (Berkeley, Los Angeles: University of California Press, 1967); A. Merkl, "Das Doppelte Rechtsantlitz", *Juristische Blätter*, Vol. 47 (1918). See also, for a critical analysis of the Pure Theory of Law, A. Jakab, who argues that the Stufenbaulehre, central to Kelsen's Theory, is flawed because it is erroneously premised on the thought that norms derive their validity from other norms: A. Jakab, "Problèmes de la Stufenbaulehre: L'échec de l'idée d'inférence et les perspectives de la théorie pure du droit", *Droit et société*, Vol. 2, No. 66 (2007), pp. 411–447.
81 Article 53 of the Vienna Convention on the Law of Treaties (1969).

instead seems to consider all human rights to be part of *jus cogens*[82] including those from which derogations are permitted. In fact, the Court appears to confer *jus cogens* status to a fundamental right as long and as soon as it is enshrined in an international instrument.[83] For example, the judgment acknowledged that the right of access to court is not absolute but nevertheless considered that "the limitation of the applicant's right of access to a court (...) is inherent in that right as it is guaranteed by *jus cogens*".[84] If it is erroneous in law and "over-generous"[85] to adopt such a construction of the concept of *jus cogens* norms, it however makes the General Court's doctrine clear: the protection of human rights constitutes a yardstick of legality against which EU law must be assessed.

The decision of the General Court was particularly problematic insofar as it allowed the CJEU to review the legality of acts deriving from international treaties to which the EU itself is not party. By its judgment, the General Court undermined the well-established principle that Member States' prior obligations under international treaties to which they are Parties prevail over EU law. The decision of the General Court was overruled by the Court of Justice on this point.

The Court of Justice restated the primacy of international law and, more specifically, of obligations under the UN Charter.[86] It is highlighted that the CJ is not competent to review the lawfulness of resolutions adopted by an international body, not even if that review "were to be limited to examination of the compatibility of that resolution with *jus cogens*"[87]; "the existing hierarchy of norms within the international legal order" is therefore unchallenged by the Court.[88] The Court however makes clear the distinction between a review of the lawfulness of an international agreement – which the Court is not competent to conduct – and that of the lawfulness of EU acts intended to

---

82 T. Ahmed and I.D.J. Butler (2006), *op. cit.*, 780.
83 Specifically, the General Court cites the right to property and the right of access to courts, recognised by the Universal Declaration of Human Rights (GC, *Kadi*, § 241; GC, *Yusuf*, § 292.) and/or the International Covenant on Civil and Political Rights (GC, *Kadi*, § 287; GC, *Yusuf*, § 342.).
84 GC, *Kadi*, § 288; GC, *Yusuf*, § 343.
85 T. Ahmed and I.D.J. Butler (2006), *op. cit.*, 780.
86 See for example paragraph 288 of the judgment where the Court mentions "the primacy of [UN Security Council resolutions] in international law". CJ, *Kadi*, § 288.
87 *Ibid.*, § 287.
88 A. Posch, "The Kadi Case: Rethinking the Relationship between EU Law and International Law?", *Columbia Journal of European Law Online*, Vol. 15 (2009), pp. 1–5, p. 4.

give effect to the international agreement at issue:[89] a finding by the CJEU of the unlawfulness of an EU act does not carry with it a judgment of the lawfulness of the international agreement the EU act implements.[90] Therefore, in contradiction with the General Court, the Court of Justice states that, unlike the UN Security Council Resolution itself, the Community measure intended to implement the Resolution is not immune from jurisdiction.[91]

According to the settled case-law of the CJEU, respect for human rights is a condition of the lawfulness of EU acts and no obligation imposed by an international agreement can "have the effect of prejudicing the constitutional principles of the EC Treaty, which include the principle that all Community acts must respect fundamental rights".[92] In *Kadi*, the Court of Justice takes note of Article 351 of the TFEU (then Article 307 EC), which states that Member States remain bound despite their EU Membership by pre-existing international treaty obligations, can allow for derogations from EU law, including EU Primary law, where the performance of Member States' obligations under international law so requires.[93] The Court however reinforces the approach it had adopted in its earlier case-law and stresses that Article 351 of the TFEU:

> ... may in no circumstances permit any challenge to the principles that form part of the very foundations of the Community legal order, one of which is the protection of fundamental rights, including the review by the Community judicature of the lawfulness of Community measures as regards their consistency with those fundamental rights.[94]

The Court thereby indicates that, in the EU legal order, fundamental rights constitute "a higher rule of law",[95] from which derogation is not allowed, not even pursuant to international obligations deriving from the UN Charter.

In this respect, and to a limited extent only, the decision Court of Justice appears to concur with the prior judgments of the General Court: both courts locate human rights norms at the top of the hierarchy of norms whose observance they each ensure. The differences highlighted above between the two

---

89 CJ, *Kadi*, § 286.
90 *Ibid.*, § 288.
91 *Ibid.*, § 305.
92 *Ibid.*, §§ 283–285.
93 *Ibid.*, § 301. *See* also "Preliminary remark: Member States' obligations under international human rights law are unaltered by EU membership", pp. 23s.
94 *Ibid.*, § 304.
95 *Ibid.*, § 288.

courts' reasoning must however be kept in mind to put this apparent confluence of views into perspective.

An additional difference pertains to how each court defines those fundamental rights norms. The General Court referred to norms of *jus cogens*, albeit partly erroneously, and in fact to all human rights enshrined in instruments of international law.[96] The General Court hence identified within the international legal order norms of higher rank *vis-à-vis* which it could review the lawfulness of obligations of international law. The Court of Justice on the other hand declined to review the lawfulness of international obligations (UN Security Council Resolutions) but asserted its competence to consider the *internal* lawfulness of acts of EU law intended to give effects to the latter. Logically therefore, it situated a "higher rule"[97] of human rights law within the European Union legal order itself, in the general principles of EU law.[98] Unlike the General Court, the Court of Justice relinquished a justification based on *jus cogens* and instead chose to refer broadly to "respect for human rights" as a condition of lawfulness of any measure within the Union.[99] As to the sources of the general principles of fundamental rights, in line with its settled case-law, the Court recalls that they derive from:

> ... the constitutional traditions common to the Member States and from the guidelines supplied by international instruments for the protection of human rights on which the Member States have collaborated or to which they are signatories.[100]

In the same paragraph of the judgment, the Court mentions the ECHR as a source of fundamental rights of "special significance".[101]

---

96   Above, n. 83.
97   Above, n. 95.
98   CJ, *Kadi*, § 283.
99   *Ibid.*, § 284. See also the Opinion of Advocate General Maduro who had, anticipatorily it seems, recalled the judgment of the Court of Justice issued in *Schmidberger* where the Court stated that "measures which are incompatible with the observance of human rights (…) are not acceptable in the Community". The same case was quoted by the Court of Justice in the *Kadi* judgment (*ibid.*, § 284.) Opinion of Adv. Gen. Poiares Maduro, Case C-402/05 P *Yassin Abdullah Kadi v. Council of the European Union and Commission of the European Communities* (16 January 2008), § 31. The Advocate General quoted: Court of Justice, Case C-112/00, *Eugen Schmidberger Internationale Transporte Planzuge v. Austria* [2003] ECR I-5659, § 73.
100 CJ, *Kadi*, § 283.
101 *Ibid.*, § 283.

For the above reasons, the Court of Justice finds that the General Court erred in law when it declared itself incompetent to review the lawfulness of the impugned Community measure and concludes:

> It follows from the foregoing that the Community judicature must, in accordance with the powers conferred on it by the EC Treaty, ensure the review, in principle the full review, of the lawfulness of all Community acts in the light of the fundamental rights forming an integral part of the general principles of Community law, including review of Community measures which, like the contested regulation, are designed to give effect to the resolutions adopted by the Security Council under Chapter 7 of the Charter of the United Nations.[102]

Where an EU act is intended to implement an international obligation, whichever status this obligation has within the international legal order (*i.e.* be it a resolution adopted by the Security Council under Chapter 7 of the UN Charter),[103] the Court of Justice has in any case the power to review the internal lawfulness of the EU acts concerned in the light of EU general principles of fundamental rights.

It has been argued in literature that the Court of Justice in *Kadi* in fact demonstrated little or no jurisdictional deference towards the UN Security Council.[104] For de Búrca, the Court erroneously analyses the international legal space as "horizontal and segregated" where the EU legal order would exist parallel to other "constitutional systems", including the United Nations legal

---

102 *Ibid.*, § 326.
103 The Court refers to the principle of the primacy at the level of international law of obligations under the UN Charter, "especially those relating to the implementation of resolutions of the Security Council adopted under Chapter VII of the Charter". *Ibid.*, § 300.
104 G. de Búrca compares the different positions adopted by the Court of First Instance in *Kadi* and *Yusuf*, by the Court of Justice in *Kadi* and by the European Court of Human Rights (ECtHR) in a similar case (*Behrami*). De Búrca analyses that the Court of Justice is the court that shows less deference towards the UN Security Council whereas the ECtHR demonstrates "strong substantive deference" towards it, insofar as, taking into consideration the scope and importance of the United Nations' mission, it declined all jurisdiction to rule on a claim of violation of human rights by acts of the UN Security Council. Conversely, de Búrca concudes that from a human rights perspective, it is the Court of Justice that offers the most generous approach. G. de Búrca, "The European Court of Justice and the International Legal Order after *Kadi*", *Harvard International Law Journal*, Vol. 51, No. 1 (Winter 2010), pp. 1–49, pp. 27–31; the ECtHR case the article refers to is ECtHR (Grand Chamber), *Agim Behrami and Bekir Behrami v. France, Ruzhdi Saramati v. France, Germany and Norway* ("*Behrami*"), Nos. 71412/01 and 78166/01 (2 May 2007).

order. According to this author, in *Kadi*, the Court emphasised that "*no international treaty could affect the autonomy of the EC legal system, and that even if the Charter were to be ranked as part of EC law it would be ranked below the normative level of the EC treaties themselves and lower than the general principles of EC law*".[105] As a matter of fact, nowhere in the judgment does the Court affirms the supremacy of the Treaties over the UN Charter. *Au contraire*, the Court confirms its settled case-law: if the performance of an obligation deriving from an international treaty so requires, it is possible to derogate from EU law, including EU Primary law.[106] Moreover, concerning Security Council Resolutions specifically, the Court insistently recalls that the European Union must observe the undertakings given in the context of the United Nations and all the more carefully so when those undertakings pertain to the maintenance of international peace and security, for which the Security Council is primary responsible.[107] The Court hence rigorously circumscribes the exception to the principle of supremacy of international law: it is only those provisions of the Treaties that pertain to fundamental rights protection that can take precedence over international legal obligations.[108] The very fact that the Court takes such good care in narrowing the exception to the principle of supremacy of international law to a limited subset of cases actually reinforces the principle: the narrowest the exception, the strongest the rule.[109]

In *Kadi*, the Court of Justice reaffirms the primacy of international obligations but prioritise fundamental rights protection as the superior norm to which any rule of international law and EU law must bow. Just like the Court had established that Member States could not hide behind the European Union to avoid responsibility for breaches of their international law obligations, the

---

105   De Búrca refers here in particular to paragraph 305 of the judgment. G. de Búrca (Winter 2010), *op. cit.*, p. 27.
106   Above, n. 194.
107   CJ, *Kadi*, §§ 291–297.
108   *Ibid.*, §§ 303–305 and 326.
109   This argument draws from a reasoning made by J. Allain in the context of the discussion on the *jus cogens* status of the principle of *non-refoulement* in international law. Allain argues, on the basis of a paragraph of the ruling of the International Court of Justice (ICJ) on the merits of the Nicaragua case, that violations of a recognised rule can in fact strengthen the said rule. In Nicaragua the ICJ observed that when States acting in violation of a rule defend themselves by appealing to exceptions or justifications to that rule, "the significance of that attitude is to confirm rather than to weaken the rule". J. Allain, "The Jus Cogens Nature of Non-Refoulement", *International Journal of Refugee Law*, Vol. 13, No. 4 (2001), pp. 533–558, pp. 540–541; ICJ, *Case Concerning the Military and Paramilitary Activities in and against Nicaragua (Nicaragua v. United States of America), Merits, Judgment* ("*Nicaragua (Merits)*") (27 June 1986) *ICJ Reports 1986*, p. 14, § 186.

Court now finds that the European Union and Member States alike cannot hide behind their international law obligations to infringe general principles of EU human rights law. It is therefore possible to conclude that the judgment of the Court of Justice in *Kadi* "represents a strong commitment to fundamental rights".[110] N.T. Isiksel welcomes the judgment and finds that the Court's decision to uphold human rights at the expense of a norm of international law as high in the hierarchy of norms as a UN Security Council Resolution is to be construed as an act of "civil disobedience" on the part of the Court of Justice:[111]

> Departing from international law in order to protect basic rights, therefore, can *only* be classified as civil disobedience, as breaking with international law to uphold its basic principles.[112]

This judgment, Isiksel adds, is a "sure step in the long journey beyond the market constitutionalism of the Treaty of Rome system towards a European constitutionalism of basic rights".[113]

The place given to fundamental rights in Community law has considerably changed since the European venture was first launched and the credit for this evolution is to be attributed to the Court of Justice.[114] Through its constructive case-law, the Court has incorporated fundamental rights principles in the Community legal order which, being originally purely market-oriented, contained none. As highlighted by Vassilios Skouris, President of the Court of Justice since 2003, the protection of fundamental rights is "an indispensable prerequisite for any national or supranational legal order based on the rule of law".[115]

The well-established case-law of the CJ was confirmed, with growing binding force, by the other Community institutions so that the recognition of fundamental rights as general principles of Community law, evolved from being a judicial development to forming part of the Treaties.

---

110   Albert Posch, "The Kadi Case: Rethinking the Relationship Between EU Law and International Law?", *Columbia Journal of European Law*, Vol.15, F. 1 (2009).
111   N.T. Isiksel (September 2010), *op. cit.*, pp. 563–569.
112   *Ibid.*, p. 569.
113   *Ibid.*, p. 569.
114   J.H.H. Weiler (1991), *op. cit.*, 2417–2419; F. Jacobs (1994), *op. cit.*, 26; T. v. Danwitz, "The Charter of Fundamental Rights of the European Union between Political Symbolism and Legal Realism", *Denver Journal of International Law and Policy*, Vol. 29 (Summer/Fall 2001), pp. 289–304, p. 293.
115   V. Skouris, "Fundamental Rights and Fundamental Freedoms: The Challenge of Striking a Delicate Balance", *European Business Law Review* (2006) 225–239, p. 225.

2   A Principle Confirmed by the Treaties

As already mentioned and often rehearsed in literature, the founding Treaties contained no specific provisions on fundamental rights. However, parallel to the evolution of the Court's fundamental rights doctrine, Community legislation also developed in the same direction. A first step taken by the institutions was a 1977 joint declaration by the European Parliament, the Council and the Commission.[116] After they had recalled the fundamental rights jurisprudence of the Court of Justice, the three Community institutions stressed the prime importance they attached to the protection of fundamental rights, as derived among other sources from the Member States' Constitutions and the ECHR, and committed to continue respecting them in the exercise of their powers.[117] This statement made jointly by the three institutions, albeit significant, was deprived of any binding force. Therefore, a further step needed be and was indeed taken in 1986, with the adoption of the Single European Act[118] whose preamble included an express reference to the promotion of "democracy on the basis of the fundamental rights recognised in the constitutions and laws of the Member States, in the Convention for the Protection of Human Rights and Fundamental Freedoms and the European Social Charter".[119]

It is worth noting that the growing commitment of the European Community towards human rights protection also shows through in its external policy: since the early 1990s[120] the Community has put emphasis upon human rights in its relations with third countries. This is even truer after May 1995 when, in a Communication addressed to the Council and Parliament, the European Commission spelled out a standard human rights clause to be included in subsequent trade and cooperation agreements with third countries.[121] The European Community could invoke this clause to suspend or terminate an agreement when it found that its co-contracting State did not respect human rights.[122] The paradox

---

116   Joint Declaration by the European Parliament, the Council and the Commission Concerning the Protection of Fundamental Rights and the European Convention for the Protection of Human Rights and Fundamental Freedoms, *Official Journal C 103*, 27/04/1977 pp. 0001–0002.

117   *Ibid.*, §§1–2.

118   Single European Act, 17 February 1986 [29/06/1987] *OJ L* Vol. 169/1.

119   *Ibid.*, Preamble, Recital 3.

120   EU Commission, "Communication from the Commission on the Inclusion of Respect for Democratic Principles and Human Rights in Agreements between the Community and Third Countries", COM (95) 216 final, 23 May 1995, pp. 5–11 and Annex 3 especially.

121   *Ibid.*, Annex 1 (standard human rights clause).

122   A. Rosas, "Human Rights and the External Relations of the European Community: A Conceptual Perspective", *in* J.H.H. Weiler and M. Kocjan (Eds.), *Principles of Constitutions Law: The Protection of Human Rights*, The Law of the European Union: Teaching Material, Unit 7

has not gone unnoticed in literature: the European Community appeared to be "preaching democracy to others"[123] although it itself lacked any internal human rights policy.[124] The Community human rights policy was eloquently depicted as an implementation of the adage "don't do what I do, do what I tell you to do".[125] The paradox was however soon corrected.

The legislative consecration of the Court of Justice's doctrine of fundamental rights became increasingly visible through subsequent amendments to the Treaties. In 1992, the Treaty of Maastricht,[126] establishing the European Union, included a reference to fundamental rights and to the European Convention on Human Rights in the operative part of the Treaty on European Union ("TEU"). Article F(2) of the TEU (1992) read as follows:

> The Union shall respect fundamental rights, as guaranteed by the European Convention for the Protection of Human Rights and Fundamental Freedoms signed in Rome on 4 November 1950 and as they result from the constitutional traditions common to the Member States, as *general principles* of Community law.[127]

In 1997, the Treaty of Amsterdam[128] enriched the abovementioned article and added a new paragraph thereto that stated unequivocally:

> The Union is founded on the principles of liberty, democracy, respect for human rights and fundamental freedoms, and the rule of law, principles which are common to the Member States.[129]

(New York, Florence: NYU School of Law, EUI, 2004/05), pp. 88–89; a similar article was published earlier as B. Brandtner and A. Rosas, "Article. Human Rights and the External Relations of the European Community: An Analysis of Doctrine and Practice", *European Journal of International Law* (Oxford University Press / USA), Vol. 9, No. 3 (1998), p. 468.

123 J.H.H. Weiler and S.C. Fries, "A Human Rights Policy for the European Community and Union: The Question of Competences", *in* P. Alston (Ed.), *The EU and Human Rights* (Oxford, New York: OUP, 1999), pp. 147–166.

124 P. Alston and J.H.H. Weiler (1998), *op. cit.*, pp. 662–663; P. Leino, "When Every Picture Tells a Story: The European Court of Justice and the Jigsaw Puzzle of External Human Rights Competence", *in* J. Petman and J. Klabbers (Eds.), *Nordic Cosmopolitanism: Essays in International Law for Martti Koskenniemi* (Leiden: Brill Academic Publishers, 2003), pp. 261–290.

125 J.H.H. Weiler and S.C. Fries (1999), *op. cit.*

126 TEU (1992).

127 *Ibid.*, Article F(2) [emphasis added].

128 Treaty of Amsterdam Amending the Treaty on European Union, the Treaties Establishing the European Communities and Related Acts, *Official Journal C 340, 10 November 1997.*

129 Treaty on European Union, Consolidated Amsterdam version ("TEU (1997)") [10 November 1997] *OJ C 340/02*, Article 6(1).

Additionally, the Treaty of Amsterdam amended the preamble of the Treaty on European Union to reaffirm Member States' attachment to fundamental social rights as defined in the European Social Charter of 1961 and the Community Charter of the Fundamental Social Rights of Workers of 1989.[130]

In addition to clarifying the place of fundamental rights within the European Union legal order, the Amsterdam Treaty enhanced their enforceability. Firstly, the powers of the European Court of Justice were expanded. Under Article L of the EU Treaty, concerning the powers of the Court of Justice, the Court had no power regarding fundamental rights provisions.[131] In its amended version however, Article L (Article 46 of the TEU in its consolidated Amsterdam version) provides that the Court is competent to decide on Article 6 issues.[132] It follows from this amendment that the Court of Justice is empowered to ensure that the EU institutions respect fundamental rights when they interpret and apply the Treaties: the scope of fundamental rights provisions is hence increased.

Secondly, the Treaty of Amsterdam acknowledged the risk that Member States infringe on the principles founding the Union and therefore laid down a procedure which the Union should follow in dealing with any serious and persistent breach by a Member State of Article 6(1) principles, *i.e.* including the principle of respect for human rights.[133] The procedure can lead to the voting rights of the Member State's representative of the government in the Council being suspended.[134]

The Treaty of Amsterdam has brought in the EU Treaty a number of fundamental rights guarantees. Those guarantees are oft analysed as the necessary counterpart to European integration.[135] Member States, determined to speak

---

130   *Ibid.*, Preamble, § 4.
131   Under Article L(c), the powers of the Court did not apply to Article F provisions. TEU (1992), Articles L(c) and F(2).
132   Article 46 of the EU Treaty as amended by the Treaty of Amsterdam stipulates that the provisions of the Treaties establishing the European Communities concerning the powers of the Court of Justice of the European Communities and the exercise of those powers "shall apply only to the following provisions of this Treaty: (...) (d) Article 6(2) with regard to action of the institutions, insofar as the Court has jurisdiction under the Treaties establishing the European Communities and under this Treaty". TEU (1997), Article 46.
133   *Ibid.*, Article 7(1).
134   *Ibid.*, Article 7.
135   Ingolf Pernice, commenting on the Treaty of Lisbon, in particular insofar as it incorporates into EU Primary law the European Charter for Fundamental Rights, observes that fundamental rights can operate as a "moderation of an executive power or government" and, in the specific context of the European Union, as a counterpart to the principle of primacy of EU law over national law. I. Pernice, "The Treaty of Lisbon and Fundamental Rights", *in* S. Griller and J. Ziller (Eds.), *The Lisbon Treaty: EU Constitutionalism without a*

with one voice in areas such as internal security and the fight against racism and xenophobia, which were traditionally national preserves, have agreed in Amsterdam to transfer new competences to the European Union in those fields. In technical terms, this transfer of competences found expression in the partial communautarisation of Justice and Home Affairs: "visas, asylum, immigration and other policies related to free movement of persons"[136] are shifted from intergovernmental cooperation between Member States to the co-decision procedure.[137] As summarised by the European Commission commenting on those changes brought by the Treaty of Amsterdam:

> In view of these changes, which necessarily go beyond the sectoral context of the Community's early days and impinge on the daily life of European citizens, there is a need for clear legal texts which proclaim respect for fundamental rights as a basic principle of the European Union. The Treaty of Amsterdam meets this need.[138]

The Lisbon Treaty[139] brought fundamental rights even more to the fore. Fundamental rights are mentioned in a new paragraph, added to the Preamble of the EU Treaty, that refers to the "cultural, religious and humanist inheritance of Europe, from which have developed the universal values of the inviolable and inalienable rights of the human person, freedom, democracy, equality and the rule of law".[140] This provision is reinforced by the text of Article 2 of the Treaty, which reproduces in part former Article 6(1) and reads as follows:

> The Union is founded on the values of respect for human dignity, freedom, democracy, equality, the rule of law and respect for human rights, including the rights of persons belonging to minorities. These values are common to the Member States in a society in which pluralism,

---

Constitutional Treaty?, Schriftenreihe Der Österreichischen Gesellschaft Für Europaforschung (Ecsa Austria), Vol. 11 (Wien, New York: Springer, 2008), pp. 235–256, pp. 236–240 in particular.

136   Treaties Establishing the European Community, Consolidated Amsterdam version ("TEC (1997)") [10 November 1997] *OJ C 340/03*, Title IV.
137   See for example, with a particular focus on asylum: S. Da Lomba, *The Right to Seek Refugee Status in the European Union* (Antwerp, Oxford, New York: Intersentia, 2004), pp. 21–46.
138   Europa, "Fundamental Rights and Non-Discrimination", *op. cit.*
139   Treaty of Lisbon Amending the Treaty on European Union and the Treaty Establishing the European Community *Official Journal C 306, 17 December 2007.*
140   TEU, Preamble, § 2.

non-discrimination, tolerance, justice, solidarity and equality between women and men prevail.[141]

Article 6 of the EU Treaty, in its consolidated Lisbon version identifies more specifically the sources of fundamental rights within the EU legal order. Not only does it confirm that fundamental rights are general principles of EU law, it further adds two new dimensions to the EU system of fundamental rights protection: the Charter, and a provision for the future adhesion of the EU to the European Convention on Human Rights (those two new "pillars"[142] of fundamental rights will be discussed below[143]). The Lisbon Treaty confirms the settled case-law of the Court of Justice of the European Union and reiterates that:

> [f]undamental rights, as guaranteed by the European Convention for the Protection of Human Rights and Fundamental Freedoms and as they result from the constitutional traditions common to the Member States, shall constitute general principles of the Union's law.[144]

The Treaties have endorsed the fundamental rights doctrine developed by the Court of Justice who construed fundamental rights as parts of the EU legal order and derived them from Member States' constitutional traditions and from the international treaties to which Member States are parties. The Lisbon Treaty in fact goes beyond merely reiterating the Court's doctrine.

B   Fundamental Rights in the European Union: Beyond General Principles of EU Law

The Lisbon Treaty endorses the Court of Justice fundamental rights doctrine. It also goes beyond and creates two additional "pillars"[145] to the EU fundamental rights system: the adoption of the European Charter of Fundamental Rights and the future adhesion of the European Union to the European Convention of Human Rights anchor fundamental rights even more firmly in the EU legal order.

The three pillars of the newly designed EU fundamental rights system are described in Article 6 of the EU Treaty.

---

141   *Ibid.*, Article 2.
142   I. Pernice (2008), *op. cit.*, p. 240.
143   See below, "2. Fundamental rights in the European Union: beyond general principles of EU law", pp. 58s.
144   TEU, Article 6(3).
145   *Ibid.*, p. 240.

1   On the Accession of the European Union to the ECHR

Article 6(2) reflects the idea, which was rejected by the Court of Justice in 1996, of the accession of the European Union to the ECHR.[146] Upon being asked its Opinion by the Council, the Court of Justice then held that, as Community law stood at that time, the Community was not competent to accede to the ECHR[147] and added that the "modification of the system for the protection of human rights in the Community" the accession would require an amendment to the Treaty.[148] In 2007, the drafters of the Lisbon Treaty chose to amend the EU Treaty in the following terms:

> The Union shall accede to the European Convention for the Protection of Human Rights and Fundamental Freedoms. Such accession shall not affect the Union's competences as defined in the Treaties.[149]

The inclusion of the above provision in the EU Treaty transforms the accession of the EU to the ECHR into a legal obligation. The accession of the European Union to the ECHR will empower the European Court of Human Rights, who already monitors fundamental rights protection in every EU Member State, to review European Union acts. The EU will be obligated to guarantee a level of human rights protection at least equivalent to that of the ECHR. As provided in Protocol 8 to the Treaty on the European Union, accession requires that the Council of Europe and the EU elaborate a legal instrument to this end.[150]

---

146   CJ, Opinion 2/94, *Accession by the Community to the European Convention for the Protection of Human Rights and Fundamental Freedoms* ("*Opinion 2/94*") (28 March 1996) [1996] ECR I-1759.

147   *Ibid.*, § 36. The reasons which motivated the Court's conclusion are formulated in paragraphs 34 and 35 of the Opinion and are the following: "[r]espect for human rights is therefore a condition of the lawfulness of Community acts. Accession to the Convention would, however, entail a substantial change in the present Community system for the protection of human rights in that it would entail the entry of the Community into a distinct international institutional system as well as integration of all the provisions of the Convention into the Community legal order. (...) Such a modification of the system for the protection of human rights in the Community, with equally fundamental institutional implications for the Community and for the Member States, would be of constitutional significance and would therefore be such as to go beyond the scope of Article 235. It could be brought about only by way of Treaty amendment".

148   *Ibid.*, §35.

149   Consolidated versions of the Treaty on European Union, *Official Journal C 83 of 30 March 2010*, p. 13, Article 6(2).

150   Protocol (No. 8) Relating to Article 6(2) of the Treaty on European Union on the Accession of the Union to the European Convention on the Protection of Human Rights and Fundamental Freedoms ("Protocol 8 – Accession of the Union to the ECHR") [2010] *OJ C 83/273*.

The agreement will enter into force if it is ratified by all States Parties to the ECHR as well as by the EU itself. In 2011, a Draft Agreement on the Accession of the European Union to the Convention for the Protection of Human Rights and Fundamental Freedoms was elaborated;[151] it provides in particular that a delegation of Members of the European Parliament will participate, with a right to vote, in the election of judges of the European Court of Human Rights. Additionally, and as for any other Contracting Party to the ECHR, a judge will be elected in respect of the European Union.[152] To date however, accession cannot proceed, in part due to the opposition of France and the United Kingdom.[153]

2   On the Charter of Fundamental Rights of the European Union

The second adjustment to the wording of Article 6 of the Treaty on European Union concerns the Charter of Fundamental Rights of the European Union.[154] Article 6(A) TEU gives binding force to the Charter while clarifying its status and role within the Union:

> The Union recognises the rights, freedoms and principles set out in the Charter of Fundamental Rights of the European Union of 7 December 2000, as adopted at Strasbourg, on 12 December 2007, which shall have the same legal value as the Treaties.[155]

---

151   Council of Europe Steering Committee for Human Rights, "Draft Legal Instruments on the Accession of the Union to the European Convention on Human Rights, Appendix I to the Report to the Committee of Ministers on the Elaboration of Legal Instruments for the Accession of the European Union to the European Convention on Human Rights", CDDH (2011)009 [14 October 2011]; for a discussion of the Draft Agreement, see X. Groussot, *et al.*, "EU Accession to the European Convention on Human rights: A Legal Assessment Of the Draft Accession Agreement of 14th October 2011", *Fondation Robert Schuman, European Issues*, No. 218 (7 November 2011).
152   CDDH, [14 October 2011], *op. cit.*, Article 6, para. 67–69.
153   "MEPs Clash over EU Accession to ECHR", *Democracy Live* (BBC, 2012), last updated 19 April 2012, retrieved from: <http://news.bbc.co.uk/democracylive/hi/europe/news-id_9709000/9709051.stm> [23/07/2012]; a discussion on the Draft Agreement took place on 19 April 2012 within the European Parliament where Members of Parliaments expressed their diverging views again, European Parliament, "EU Accession to the European Convention on Human Rights (Debate)", 19 April 2012, © European Union [2012], see in particular the statement made by British Member of Parliament Ashley Fox, retrieved from the website of European Parliament at: <www.europarl.europa.eu> [23/07/2012].
154   Charter of Fundamental Rights of the European Union ("EU Charter"), 12 December 2007, entered into force 1 December 2009 [14/12/2007] *OJ C 303/01*.
155   TEU, Article 6(1).

As illustrated above, the Court of Justice and General Court have developed through their case-law a catalogue of general principles of fundamental rights. The Charter reflects those general principles but in fact does more than that. Firstly, it is in fact broader than general principles of EU law: it includes the rights that the Court of Justice of the European Union has construed as general principles of law and complements them with fundamental rights deriving from other legal sources. The European Commission describes the Charter as an "innovative instrument" that "brings together in one text all the fundamental rights protected in the Union, spelling them out in detail and making them visible and predictable".[156] More than a catalogue of the existing general principles of EU law, it is indeed an all-encompassing instrument of EU fundamental rights protection. The Preamble of the text makes clear that the Charter *reaffirms* (the term itself suggests that the Charter is intended to give visibility to existing rights):

> ... the rights as they result, in particular, from the constitutional traditions and international obligations common to the Member States, the European Convention for the Protection of Human Rights and Fundamental Freedoms, the Social Charters adopted by the Union and by the Council of Europe and the case-law of the Court of Justice of the European Union and of the European Court of Human Rights.[157]

Although general principles are not explicitly mentioned in the Charter, the wording, similar to that used by the Court of Justice and General Court to identify general principles (the constitutional traditions and international obligations common to the Member States, including the ECHR[158]) and the reference to the case-law of the CJEU make clear that the Charter derives fundamental rights in part from the general principles set out by the Court. The Charter further refers to the case-law of the European Court of Human Rights and to "Social Charters" adopted by the EU and the Council of Europe as other

---

156 EU Commission, "Communication from the Commission: Strategy for the Effective Implementation of the Charter of Fundamental Rights by the European Union", COM (2010) 573 final, 19/10/2010, p. 3.
157 EU Charter, Preamble, § 5.
158 *See* above "(ii) The Kadi case: a strong commitment to fundamental rights", pp. 44s and, for example: GC, Joined Cases T-213/95 and T-18/96, *Stichting Certificatie Kraanverhuurbedrijf (Sck) and Federatie Van Nederlandse Kraanverhuurbedrijven (Fnk) v. Commission of the European Communities* ("*SCK and FNK v. Commission*") (22 October 1997) [1997] ECR II-01739, § 53.

sources of fundamental rights in the EU. The array of rights enshrined in the Charter confirms that its drafters did not draw only from the general principles developed by the CJEU: although it did not invent any new right, the Charter "certainly smuggled into the Union some that had not been previously contemplated as Union rights per se".[159] In other words, the Charter looks for fundamental rights in the same place as the CJEU did but derives therefrom a number of rights that the Court had not (yet?) identified as general principle of EU law. In the words of Craig and de Búrca: the Charter can be described as "a creative distillation of the rights contained in the various European and international agreements and national constitutions on which the ECJ had for some years already been drawing".[160] In that sense, the Charter may boast of honouring its commitment: it indeed "reaffirms"[161] existing rights, only some of those rights were in fact in existence outside the EU legal order, in international human rights law.

A second essential feature of the Charter is its binding force: with the entry into force of the Lisbon Treaty on 1 December 2009, the Charter has acquired the same legal status as the Treaties. As a consequence, those rights the protection of which the CJEU has progressively ensured by setting out a catalogue of general principles of EU law now sit at the top of the hierarchy of norms in the EU, next to the Treaties, and above general principles of law.[162] Where they incorporate general principles of EU law, Charter provisions, as norms of higher legal force, can be viewed as superseding the corresponding general principles: the Charter becomes the "criterion" for assessing claims pertaining to rights otherwise recognised as general principles of EU law,[163] and there is no need to look into constitutional traditions or international obligations common to the Member States to confirm its existence. In that sense, the Charter indeed gives more "visibility"[164] to existing rights: it can be described as "an optimal arsenal

---

159 F. Fontanelli, "The European Union's Charter of Fundamental Rights Two Years Later", *Perspectives on Federalism*, Vol. 3, No. 3 (2011), pp. 22–47, p. 24.
160 P. Craig and G.D. Búrca, *EU Law: Text, Cases, and Materials*, 3rd ed. (Oxford: Oxford University Press, 2003), p. 359.
161 EU Charter, Preamble, § 5.
162 P. Craig and G.D. Búrca, *EU Law: Text, Cases, and Materials*, 5th ed. (Oxford: Oxford University Press, 2011), pp. 108–112.
163 Advocate General Kokott stated so concerning the principle of effective judicial protection, a principle recognised by the Court of Justice as general principle of EU law and now enshrined in the Charter of Fundamental Rights. Opinion of Adv. Gen. Kokott, delivered on 29 April 2010, *Case C-550/07 P Akzo Nobel Chemicals Ltd and Akcros Chemicals Ltd v. European Commission*, § 42.
164 EU Charter, Preamble, § 4.

of ready-made general principles".¹⁶⁵ The decision of the Court of Justice in *Test-Achats* reinforces this perception: the Court, was referred a question for preliminary ruling on an alleged breach of the general principle of prohibition of discrimination on grounds of sex by a Council Directive that allowed insurance providers to exceptionally use gender-related statistical data to calculate insurance premiums and benefits.¹⁶⁶ The Court set the question back in the context of the newly devised system of fundamental rights. The Court stated:

> Article 6(2) EU, to which the national court refers in its questions (...) provides that the European Union is to respect fundamental rights as guaranteed by the European Convention for the Protection of Human Rights and Fundamental Freedoms and as they result from the constitutional traditions common to the Member States, as general principles of Community law. Those fundamental rights are incorporated in the Charter, which, with effect from 1 December 2009, has the same legal status as the Treaties.¹⁶⁷

Accordingly, it is on the legal basis of Charter Articles 21 (non-discrimination) and 23 (equality between men and women) that the Court of Justice ruled in the case.

It is worth recalling at this point that Article 6 of the Treaty on European Union mentions the Charter as one of three sources of fundamental rights in the EU; the two others being the ECHR – which will be binding upon the EU once it has acceded to it – and general principles of EU law.¹⁶⁸ In other words, the incorporation in the Charter of the language of the CJEU fundamental rights doctrine does not deprive the CJEU of its power to continue developing general principles.¹⁶⁹ General principles sit below the Treaties but may be used to interpret them; they are, on the other hand, above EU secondary law which must be in conformity with them.¹⁷⁰ The Charter applies to European institutions and to Member States when they implement EU law.¹⁷¹ The CJEU, as an EU institution, is therefore bound by the provisions of the Charter. Fundamental

---

165   F. Fontanelli (2011), *op. cit.*, p. 28.
166   CJ (Grand Chamber), Case C-236/09, *Association Belge Des Consommateurs Test-Achats Asbl and Others v Conseil Des Ministres* ("*Test-Achats*") (1 March 2011) [2011].
167   *Ibid.*, § 16.
168   TEU, Article 6 (2) and (3).
169   I. Pernice (2008), *op. cit.*, p. 249.
170   P. Craig and G.D. Búrca, *EU Law: Text, Cases, and Materials* (2011), *op. cit.*, p. 109.
171   EU Charter, Article 51(1).

rights guarantees are however but minimum standards; the Court could therefore set higher standards of protection. As said, Article 6(3) of the EU Treaty allows the Court to pursue its soft-law-making work and hence identify additional general principles of EU law that derive from Member States' Constitutional traditions and international treaty obligations and are binding upon EU institutions and Member States acting in the scope of EU law. In so doing, the Court could impose on EU institutions and Member States a higher level of human rights protection than that provided in the Charter. It remains for the future case-law of the CJEU to confirm or infirm this. General principles' existence outside the Charter has the potential of ensuring that fundamental rights protection in the EU is dynamic and evolves in time, independent of any formal revision of the Charter.[172]

The Charter itself instils some flexibility in the EU fundamental rights system. Instrument of same legal value as the Treaties, a modification of its text would require that all EU Member States agree on the proposed amendment. It can nevertheless be inferred from several provisions of the Charter that it is intended as a living instrument of human rights protection. Firstly, the Preamble of the Charter refers to the case-law of the European Court of Human Rights as a source of fundamental rights[173] and Article 52(3) provides that in areas where both legal instruments overlap, the Charter provisions should be given the same (at least) meaning and scope as the corresponding ECHR guarantees.[174] The European Court of Human Rights, through its case-law, constantly interprets the provisions of the ECHR therefore, for the Charter to provide at least the same level of protection as the ECHR, its interpretation will have to keep the pace of the European Court of Human Rights case-law.[175] Secondly, Article 52(3) of the Charter clarifies that EU law, if it must be in conformity with the ECHR, can in any case provide more extensive protection;[176] the European Convention of Human Rights and the guarantees it provides are construed as

---

172   *See* in that sense: S. Peers, "Human Rights in the EU Legal Order: Practical Relevance for EC Immigration and Asylum Law", *in* S. Peers and N. Rogers (Eds.), *EU Immigration and Asylum Law: Text and Commentary*, Immigration and Asylum Law and Policy in Europe (Leiden: Brill Academic Publishers, 2006), pp. 115–137, at 3.3.

173   EU Charter, Preamble, § 5.

174   *Ibid.*, Article 52(3).

175   Advocate General Trstenjak notes that "the reference to the ECHR contained in Article 52(3) of the Charter of Fundamental Rights is to be construed as an essentially dynamic reference which, in principle, covers the case-law of the European Court of Human Rights". Opinion of Adv. Gen. Trstenjak, delivered on 22 September 2011, *Case C-411/10 N. S. v. Secretary of State for the Home Department* ("*Opinion AG Trstenjak in NS*"), § 145.

176   EU Charter, Article 52(3).

minimum standards of protection. The EU legislator is hence invited to use the Charter together with the ECHR to develop more generous standards of protection. A third element of flexibility is the inclusion, in the Charter of an "evolutionary" clause. Human rights protection, the Charter observes, must be adequate to existing and evolving protection needs:

> ... it is necessary to strengthen the protection of fundamental rights in the light of changes in society, social progress and scientific and technological developments by making those rights more visible in a Charter.[177]

Accordingly, the Charter was adopted as a means to ensure the adequacy of human rights protection to modern-day challenges. The same concern for the appropriateness of human rights protection must guide the interpretation of the Charter, in the light of new, contemporary challenges.

A last remark concerns the rights recognised in the Charter. The Charter structure itself appears dynamic: it does not reproduce the classical dichotomy between civil and political rights on the one hand and economic, social and cultural rights on the other. The provisions are instead divided into seven titles: Dignity,[178] Freedoms,[179] Equality,[180] Solidarity,[181] Citizen's Rights,[182] Justice[183] and General Provisions.[184] Citizen's rights being addressed in a specific title, it is to be understood that the rights enshrined under the other titles of the Charter are rights to which anyone is entitled within the jurisdiction of the Union, not solely Member States' nationals.[185] Although the Charter does not appear on its face to reproduce the above-mentioned dichotomy, in effect, two categories of guarantees are identified, of different legal force: "rights" shall be respected whereas "principles" shall be observed.[186] The Explanations to the Charter articulate the distinction between rights and principles under the Charter: only rights "give rise to direct claims for positive action by the Union's institutions

---

177 *Ibid.*, Preamble, § 3.
178 *Ibid.*, Articles 1–5.
179 *Ibid.*, Articles 6–19.
180 *Ibid.*, Articles 20–26.
181 *Ibid.*, Articles 27–38.
182 *Ibid.*, Articles 39–46.
183 *Ibid.*, Articles 47–50.
184 *Ibid.*, Articles 51–54.
185 See similarly: S. Peers, "Immigration, Asylum and the European Union Charter of Fundamental Rights", *European Journal of Migration and Law*, Vol. 3 (2001), pp. 141–169, pp. 146–149.
186 EU Charter, Article 51(5).

or Member States authorities",[187] principles do not. The Explanation cites among others "integration of persons with disabilities"[188] and "environmental protection"[189] as examples of principles.[190] The division between rights and principles is in fact understood as similar to the traditional distinction between first and second generation rights, or between "directly enforceable and programmatic rights":[191] under the Charter, and although the text is not explicit and is in fact ambiguous, economic, social and cultural rights are mainly seen as "principles" whereas "rights" are principally civil and political rights.[192] This observation leads to the conclusion that, under the Charter, the seeming indivisibility of human rights truly is a "mirage".[193]

The fact remains that the Charter gathers in a single, binding, instrument both economic, social and cultural rights, and civil and political rights which are traditionally addressed separately – particularly illustrative of this is the example of the two separate human rights covenants: the International Covenant on Civil and Political Rights (ICCPR)[194] on the one hand and the International Covenant on Economic, Social and Cultural Rights (ICESCR)[195] on the other. Although the indivisibility of fundamental rights appears to be but an illusion in the current Charter, the symbolism of the adoption of a single instrument of human rights law combining both "generations" of rights cannot be ignored; it could be an indication of a "shift in ethic" following which so-called second generation rights would be "recognised as inherently valuable" and

---

187 "Explanations Relating to the Charter of Fundamental Rights" ("Explanations to the Charter") [14/12/2007] *OJ C 303/17*, p. 35.
188 EU Charter, Article 26.
189 *Ibid.*, Article 37. On the protection of the environment in the Charter of Fundamental Rights. Alexandre Kiss deplores that the EU Charter classifies the protection of the environment as a "pure policy principle" and does not use instead a stronger language capable of ensuring a high level of environmental protection in the EU. A. Kiss, "Environmental and Consumer Protection", *in* S. Peers and A. Ward (Eds.), *The European Union Charter of Fundamental Rights: Politics, Law and Policy* (Portland: Hart Publishing, 2004), pp. 247–268.
190 "Explanations to the Charter", [14/12/2007], *op. cit.*, p. 35.
191 X. Groussot and L. Pech, "Fundamental Rights Protection in the European Union Post Lisbon Treaty", *Fondation Robert Schuman, European Issues*, No. 173 (14 June 2010), p. 7.
192 J. Kenner, "Economic and Social Rights in the EU Legal Order: The Mirage of Indivisibility", *in* T.K. Hervey and J. Kenner (Eds.), *Economic and Social Rights under the EU Charter of Fundamental Rights: A Legal Perspective* (Portland: Hart Publishing, 2003), pp. 1–24.
193 *Ibid.*, p. 24.
194 ICCPR, *op. cit.*
195 ICESCR, *op. cit.*

would be granted "as ends not means".[196] In other words, it is anticipated that the Charter could contribute to the progressive recognition of human rights as being indivisible (within the EU legal order to begin with). Charter "principles" might not be directly enforceable, they must nevertheless be "observed";[197] in particular, EU institutions and Member States implementing EU law will implement them through legislative and executive acts[198] and henceforth contribute to improving the protection of economic, social and cultural "principles" within the Union. In brief, the Charter may well "serve to raise the status of economic and social rights in the EU's legal order".[199]

From the foregoing observations pertaining to the sources of fundamental rights in the EU legal order as it was redefined by the Lisbon Treaty and, in particular in view of the relationship between the Charter guarantees and other instruments of international human rights law, it is possible to conclude that the newly devised European system for the protection of fundamental rights inherently provides for its "necessary openness and dynamic development".[200]

The adoption and entry into force of the Charter as a binding instrument of European human rights law, separate from the Treaty on the European Union but of "same legal value"[201] redresses what had been described as a paradox:

> On the one hand, the Union is a staunch defender of human rights in both its internal and external affairs. On the other hand, it lacks a comprehensive or coherent policy at either level and fundamental doubts persist as to whether the institutions of the Union possess adequate legal competence in relation to a wide range of human rights issues arising within the framework of Community policies.[202]

The Charter of Fundamental Rights of the European Union asserts that the EU places the individual "at the heart of its activities" by establishing "the citizenship of the Union and by creating an area of freedom, security and justice".[203] On the latter point, it must be recalled that the Charter, an instrument of

---

196 J. Hunt, "Fair and Just Working Conditions", *in* T.K. Hervey and J. Kenner (Eds.), *Economic and Social Rights under the EU Charter of Fundamental Rights: A Legal Perspective* (Portland: Hart Publishing, 2003), pp. 45–66.
197 EU Charter, Article 51(1).
198 "Explanations to the Charter", [14/12/2007], *op. cit.*, p. 35.
199 J. Kenner (2003), *op. cit.*
200 I. Pernice (2008), *op. cit.*, 240.
201 TEU, Article 6(1), §1.
202 P. Alston and J.H.H. Weiler (1998), *op. cit.*, 661.
203 EU Charter, Preamble, § 2.

Primary EU law, is binding upon EU institutions and Member States when they are implementing EU law.[204] It follows from this, the Union being competent to act in the field of asylum, that secondary legislation on asylum as well as, pursuant to the principle of primacy of EU law, Member States' law and decisions on international protection claims all fall within the scope of the Charter.[205]

From the original market-oriented sectoral Communities to the European Union, with a legally-binding and comprehensive "Bill of Rights", the place awarded to fundamental rights in Community then Union law has considerably changed. The evolution clearly shows a growing concern for human rights on the part of the EU institutions and, incidentally, of the Member States. The Lisbon Treaty together with the Charter of Fundamental Rights significantly shifts the focus of the Union on individuals:

> By addressing the citizens of the EU directly as individuals especially concerning their personal freedom and security [the new Treaties] merge (at least within the reach of the Union powers) the national societies into a European society of free people and thus hold the political powers on the Union level directly responsible for their rights and freedoms. [206]

The transformation of the European Union in fact manifests itself clearly from the combined reading of Article 2 of the TEU, in its consolidated Amsterdam version (TEU 1997),[207] with Article 3 TEU (ex Article 2), in its current version[208] (TEU). Whereas the internal market was in 1997 the first-mentioned objective of the Union, the new provision refers instead in its first paragraph to the Union's aim to "promote peace, its values and the well-being of its peoples".[209] The establishment of the internal market only appears in the third paragraph of the new Article 3 TEU. Conversely, the realisation of an area of freedom, security and justice, which includes inter alia the adoption of a common asylum policy, was previously mentioned fourth in the TEU (1997) but now appears already in the second paragraph of Article 3 TEU. Lastly, human rights protection is markedly expanded: current Article 3 TEU dispenses with

---

204 *Ibid.*, Article 51(1). *See also*: European Commission, "Report from the Commission to the European Parliament, the Council, the European Economic and Social Committee and the Committee of the Regions: 2013 Report on the Application of the EU Charter of Fundamental Rights", SWD (2014) 224 final, 14 April 2014.
205 S. Peers (2006), *op. cit.*, p. 133 and 137.
206 I. Pernice (2008), *op. cit.*, p. 238.
207 TEU (1997), Article 2.
208 TEU, Article 3.
209 Compare TEU (1997) Article 2, first paragraph, with TEU Article 3(1).

the reference to the rights of the sole "nationals of [EU] Member States"[210] and instead intimates the principles of non-discrimination and equality.[211] Those formal modifications of the Treaty are clear signs of the shift from a market-oriented organisation to a Union with affirmed "values",[212] whose actions chiefly centre around the individual. Moreover, not only does the EU commit to ensure that fundamental rights are respected within its territory – and to some extent, beyond it, with the introduction of a human rights clause in its agreements with third countries – but the range of protected fundamental rights is broad: social and economic rights as well as civil and political rights are all enshrined in the Charter of Fundamental Rights of the European Union,[213] which constitutes a comprehensive catalogue of the rights protected by the EU. It is noteworthy that two asylum rights have found their way in the Charter of Fundamental Rights: Article 18 enshrines a "right to asylum" and Article 19 reaffirms the principle of *non-refoulement*. What are EU asylum rights and where can they be derived from will be the object of the following developments.

C   Asylum Rights

As shown above, fundamental rights have acquired an important place within the EU legal order. The Court of Justice, followed by Treaty provisions, have identified their sources as the constitutional traditions common the EU Member States and international treaties to which Member States are signatories, which include in particular the ECHR.[214] The Charter of Fundamental Rights incorporates those rights which the Court of Justice had already identified as forming part of the general principles of EU law and complemented the protection they provided by enshrining a number of other fundamental rights, derived from national and international law.[215]

The focus of the present work being the eligibility to or, in EU language, the criteria for the "qualification"[216] for international protection, the following develop will address the rights that are pertinent to trigger international protection within the European Union. Asylum rights in the EU legal order

---

210   TEU (1997), Article 2, § 3.
211   TEU, Article 3(3) §2.
212   *Ibid.*, Article 3(1).
213   EU Charter.
214   *See* above, "1. Fundamental Rights as General Principles of Community Law", pp. 35s. and "2. Fundamental rights in the European Union: beyond general principles of EU law", pp. 58s.
215   EU Charter, Preamble, § 5 and Article 53.
216   *See* Qualification Directive.

however also include a broad range of rights, civil, political, economic, social and cultural, to which asylum-seekers (including those whose claim has been rejected) and beneficiaries of international protection (*i.e.* in the context of EU law: refugees and subsidiary protection beneficiaries) are entitled.[217]

For the purpose of this work, it is particularly relevant to note the inclusion in the Charter of Fundamental Rights of the right to asylum (Article 18), the prohibition of torture and inhuman or degrading treatment or punishment (Article 4) and the principle of *non-refoulement* as well as the prohibition of collective expulsions (Article 19). Those rights however are enshrined in general terms and it is therefore necessary to ponder on the interpretation they ought to be given.

An illustration of the question concerns the principle of *non-refoulement*. Often referred to as the cornerstone of international protection, which is considered part of customary international law,[218] was codified in 1951 in the Refugee Convention and defined as the obligation for States not to expel or return (*"refouler"*) a refugee, in any manner whatsoever, to the frontiers of territories where his life or freedom would be threatened on account of his race, religion, nationality, membership of a particular social group or particular opinion. The principle has since been defined in a number of subsequent instruments of

---

217 *Ibid.*, Articles 20, 22–35; Council Directive 2005/85/EC of 1 December 2005 on Minimum Standards on Procedures in Member States for Granting and Withdrawing Refugee Status ("Procedures Directive") [13/12/2005] *OJ L 326/13*; Council of the European Union, Council Directive 2003/9/EC of 27 January 2003 Laying Down Minimum Standards for the Reception of Asylum Seeker ("Reception Conditions Directive") [06/02/2003] *OJ L 31/18*; Council Regulation (EC) No 343/2003 of 18 February 2003 Establishing the Criteria and Mechanisms for Determining the Member State Responsible for Examining an Asylum Application Lodged in One of the Member States by a Third-Country National ("Dublin Regulation") [25/02/2003] *OJ L 50/1*, pp. 1–10, consolidated version of 04/12/2008, Article 4 in particular grants to the individual concerned with a "Dublin transfer" the right to be effectively informed of the procedure and of decisions concerning him or her. Note: for the Procedures Directive, Reception Conditions Directive and the Dublin Regulation, discussions on recast are ongoing.

218 E. Lauterpacht and D. Bethlehem, "The Scope and Content of the Principle of Non-Refoulement: Opinion", *in* E. Feller, *et al.* (Eds.), *Refugee Protection in International Law: UNHCR's Global Consultations on International Protection* (Cambridge: Cambridge University Press, 2003), pp. 87–177; G.S. Goodwin-Gill and J. McAdam, *The Refugee in International Law* (2007), *op. cit.*, pp. 345–354; UNHCR, "The Principle of Non-Refoulement as a Norm of Customary International Law: Response to the Questions Posed to UNHCR by the Federal Constitutional Court of the Federal Republic of Germany in Cases 2 Bvr 1938/93, 2 Bvr 1953/93, 2 Bvr 1954/93", 31 January 1994.

international refugee law adopted at the universal[219] and regional[220] levels. It also found its way in international human rights law, either explicitly, as in the 1984 Convention Against Torture[221] or implicitly, chiefly in the European Convention on Human Rights and the International Covenant on Civil and Political Rights. The European Court of Human Rights and the Human Rights Committee and the Committee Against Torture in particular have indeed deduced the principle of *non-refoulement* from the ECHR and the ICCPR respectively although neither of those instruments expressly mentioned it. Specifically, they have interpreted the prohibition of torture and other inhuman or degrading treatment or punishment as well as the right to life as necessarily carrying with them the obligation for States to refrain from expelling individuals to a territory where those rights would risk be violated.[222] The principle, now enshrined in the Charter of Fundamental Rights had hence been long developed and interpreted in international law before; will EU law conform with the principle as it is understood and implemented in international law? The same question can be asked concerning all the other rights that now form part of EU Primary law, since the entry into force of the Charter.

1   International Treaties as Sources of EU Fundamental Rights

Even a cursory glance of European Union law suffices to hint the importance of the European Convention of Human Rights and of the rights enshrined therein within the European Union: the Treaties, EU legislation and the Court of Justice all repeatedly refer to the European Convention of Human Rights and commit to ensure respect for the rights it enshrines. The omnipresence of the ECHR in European Union law could have casted doubts as to the status

---

219 UNGA, "Declaration on Territorial Asylum", A/RES/2312(XXII) [14 December 1967], Article 3(1).

220 Convention Governing the Specific Aspects of Refugee Problems in Africa ("AU Refugee Convention"), 10 September 1969 [1976] *UNTS* Vol. 1001, p. 45, Article II(3); Asian-African Legal Consultative Organization (AALCO) Bangkok Principles on the Status and Treatment of Refugees ("Bangkok Principles"), 31 December 1966, Article III. Cartagena Declaration on Refugees, 22 November 1984, Colloquium on the International Protection of Refugees in Central America, Mexico and Panama, § 5; EU, European Parliament and Council, Directive 2011/95/EU of the European Parliament and of the Council of 13 December 2011 on Standards for the Qualification of Third-Country Nationals or Stateless Persons as Beneficiaries of International Protection, for a Uniform Status for Refugees or for Persons Eligible for Subsidiary Protection, and for the Content of the Protection Granted ("Qualification Directive") [20/12/2011] *OJ L 337/09*, pp. 9–26, Article 21.

221 CAT, Article 3.

222 This will be further developed under Part II.A.

of other instruments of international law, including those relevant in the field of asylum. Three observations could alleviate these concerns; the entry into force of the Lisbon Treaty and Charter of Fundamental Rights of the European Union further dispels them.

(a)   *Pre Lisbon*

In its earlier version, before the Lisbon Treaty had amended it, the Treaty on European Union stated the obligation of the Union to respect "fundamental rights, as guaranteed by the European Convention for the Protection of Human Rights and Fundamental Freedoms ... and as they result from the constitutional traditions common to the Member States, as general principles of Community law".[223] This provision of the EU Treaty reflected the development by the Court of Justice of fundamental rights as general principles of law but it did not reproduce the Court's doctrine in its entirety. Prior to the Maastricht Treaty when the first reference to general principles of fundamental rights was introduced in the Treaties,[224] the Court of Justice had already referred to international human rights treaties as sources of general principles.[225] A first argument that tempers the finding of a dissention between the Treaties and the case-law of the Court on the sources of general principles of fundamental rights could be that the various relevant international treaties offer similar guarantees. With regards to asylum in particular, a parallel can be drawn between Article 33 of the Refugee Convention, Article 3 of the CAT Convention, Article 3 of the ECHR and Article 7 of the ICCPR, which all contain or were interpreted as containing the prohibition of *refoulement* to torture, worded in similar terms.[226]

Secondly, it is worth noting that the ECHR is not the only instrument of international law the Treaties refer to. In the area of Freedom, Security and Justice, Article 78 of the Treaty on the Functioning of the European Union (former Article 63 TEC), although it does not refer to the Refugee Convention specifically as a source of the fundamental rights the Union shall respect, nevertheless calls upon the Union to develop a common policy on asylum, subsidiary protection and temporary protection "in accordance with the Geneva Convention of 28 July 1951 and the Protocol of 31 January 1967 relating to the status

---

223   TEU (1997), Article 6(2).
224   See above, note 228 and corresponding text.
225   See above, note 144 and corresponding text.
226   However, even assuming that those various instruments of international law contained the same catalogue of protected rights, the scope and meaning of their respective provisions do vary. The principle of *non-refoulement*, absolute in human rights law but qualified in the Refugee Convention confirms it. See below II.

of refugees, and other relevant treaties".[227] The reference made in the Treaty (TFEU) to the Refugee Convention and its Protocol, together with the fact that all Member States have ratified those instruments of international refugee law, suggests that those international instruments too must be accepted as a source of general principle of EC law.[228] This interpretation was confirmed in 2010 by the CJEU, as will be discussed below.

A third argument could put into perspective the potential impact of a partial reproduction of the Court of Justice's doctrine into the Treaties; it draws on an observation of the practice of the Court. Despite the incomplete transposition of its doctrine into the EU Treaty, the Court indeed kept referring to "the guidelines supplied by international instruments for the protection of human rights on which the Member States have collaborated or to which they are signatories"[229] and occasionally drew upon the ICCPR,[230] the Convention on the Rights of the Child[231] or the Refugee Convention,[232] besides the ECHR, as sources of EC human rights protection.[233] Concerning the Refugee Convention in particular and as mentioned above, the Court of Justice confirmed in 2010 that it is a source of general principles of EU law. The Court was asked to pronounce on the interpretation of the Qualification Directive[234] in three references for preliminary rulings.[235] The Court clearly elaborated on the place and role of the Refugee Convention within the EU legal order following a three-step reasoning, unaltered through its judgments. The Court of Justice first

---

227 Consolidated version of the Treaty on European Union, *Official Journal C 83 of 30 March 2010*, p. 47s, Article 78(1).
228 Steve Peers, "Human Rights, Asylum and European Community Law", UNHCR *Refugee Survey Quarterly*, 2005, Vol. 24, Issue 2, p. 29.
229 CJ, *Kadi*, § 283.
230 The decision of the Court in *Grant* affirms that that "the Covenant is one of the international instruments relating to the protection of human rights of which the Court takes account in applying the fundamental principles of Community law". CJ, *Grant*, § 44.
231 CJ, *Parliament v. Council*, § 37.
232 CJ, Joined Cases C-175/08, C-176/08, C-178/08 & C-179/08, *Salahadin Abdulla and Others v. Bundesrepublik Deutschland* ("*Salahadin*") (2 March 2010), §§ 51–54; CJ, Case C-31/09, *Bolbol v. Bevándorlási És Állampolgársági Hivatal* ("*Bolbol*") (17 June 2010), §§ 36–38; CJ, Joined cases C-57/09 and C-101/09, *Bundesrepublik Deutschland v. B and D* ("*B and D*") (9 November 2010), §§ 76–78.
233 S. Peers (2001), *op. cit.*, p. 142.
234 Qualification Directive (2004).
235 The questions asked to the Court concerned Article 3 of the Qualification Directive, under which Member States may introduce or retain more favourable standards than those set in Directive, Article 11, on the cessation of refugee status, and Article 12(2)(a),(b) and (c) concerning exclusion from refugee status. CJ, *Salahadin*; CJ, *Bolbol*; CJ, *B and D*.

recalls that one of the legal bases for the adoption of the Qualification Directive was Article 63 TEC (now Article 78 TFEU), under which, as mentioned above, the Council was required to adopt measures on asylum, in accordance with, among others, the 1951 Geneva Convention.[236] The Court then cites Recitals 3[237] to the Directive which describes the Geneva Convention as the "cornerstone of the international legal regime for the protection of refugees" as well as recitals 16 and 17 which state that the aim of the Directive and of the minimum standards and common criteria it laid down was to guide Member States' competent authorities in the application of the Convention.[238] In view of the above, the Court concludes:

> Directive 2004/83 must for that reason be interpreted in the light of its general scheme and purpose, and in a manner consistent with the 1951 Geneva Convention and the other relevant treaties referred to in point (1) of the first paragraph of Article 63 EC, now Article 78(1) TFEU.[239]

According to the Court of Justice, the Refugee Convention, together with its additional Protocol, are among the international treaties in consistence with which EU law must be interpreted and applied. It is, as such, a source of general principles of EU human rights law. The Lisbon Treaty and the Charter of Fundamental Rights have since confirmed that international treaties to which Member States are parties are sources of fundamental rights in the EU.

(b)   *Clarifications Brought by the Lisbon Treaty and Charter*
The Lisbon Treaty and the Charter of Fundamental Rights provide guidance on the role of international treaties as sources of EU fundamental rights. With the entry into force of the Lisbon Treaty, neither has the express mention of the ECHR disappeared from the text of Article 6 TEU, nor was a broader reference to international treaties introduced in this article; nevertheless, Article 6 TEU now provides that, in addition to the rights protected as general principles

---

236   CJ, *B and D*, § 76.
237   Mistakenly, the English translation of the judgments in the *Salahadin* and *B and D* cases, paragraphs 52 and 77 respectively, referred to Recital 13 to the Qualification Directive instead of Recital 3 which is where the Refugee Convention is described as the cornerstone of the international legal regime for the protection of refugees. The French versions are, on the other hand, correct and refer to the third ("*troisième*") Recital of the Directive. Upon being notified of this mistake, the Registry of the CJEU has since corrected it.
238   CJ, *B and D*, § 77.
239   *Ibid.*, § 78.

of EU law,[240] the Union also "recognises the rights, freedoms and principles set out in the Charter of Fundamental Rights of the European Union".[241] Looking at the Preamble of the Charter in turn informs us that the Charter reaffirms the rights "as they result, in particular, from the constitutional traditions and international obligations common to the Member States, the European Convention for the Protection of Human Rights and Fundamental Freedoms, the Social Charters adopted by the Union and by the Council of Europe and the case-law of the Court of Justice of the European Union and of the European Court of Human Rights". This wording of the Charter resembles the well-established fundamental rights doctrine of the Court of Justice pursuant to which the European Convention on Human Rights is but one, albeit of "special significance",[242] international agreement common to all EU Member States and whose provisions serve as guidelines for the interpretation and development of EU law.

A combined reading of Article 6(1) of the EU Treaty and of the Preamble of the Charter shows that the European Union now recognises not only those rights that are enshrined in the European Convention on Human Rights but more generally, the rights that emanate from other international treaties to which EU Member States are parties. The large catalogue of rights enshrined in the Charter indeed confirms that it is all-encompassing and apparently reflects all the rights which are guaranteed in one or the other international human rights treaty.

2 Examples of Rights Imported from International Human Rights Law into the EU Legal Order

At a time when fundamental rights were not protected by the Primary law of the Union, the Court of Justice developed, through its case-law, a number of general principles deduced in particular from the constitutional traditions or international treaties common to Member States.

A search in the case-law of the Court[243] indicate that occurrences of the right to life and of the prohibition of torture and inhuman or degrading treatment or punishment can be found but they are only few. In the *Schmidberger* case for instance,[244] the Court had to determine whether a fair balance had

---

240 The provision reproduces Article 6(2) of the TEU in its Amsterdam consolidated version. TEU, Article 6(3).
241 *Ibid.*, Article 6(1).
242 CJ, § 18; CJ, *ERT v. DEP*, § 41; CJ, *Schmidberger*, § 71; CJ, *Omega*, § 33.
243 Information retrieved from the website of the CJEU, at: <http://curia.europa.eu> [20/07/2012].
244 CJ, *Schmidberger*.

been struck between the fundamental freedom of movement and the fundamental rights to freedom of expression and assembly. In doing so, the Court highlighted that the latter rights were not absolute, unlike, the Court noted incidentally, "other fundamental rights enshrined in [the ECHR], such as the right to life or the prohibition of torture and inhuman or degrading treatment or punishment, which admit of no restriction".[245]

Steve Peers notes that since the Court has affirmed the "special significance"[246] of the ECHR as a source of general principles of EU law, all the rights set out in the ECHR ought to be recognised as part of the general principles of Community law, including in particular the right to life and freedom from torture.[247] This position was backed up in the 2009 *Elgafaji* case. In this decision, the first concerning substantive EU asylum law, the Court had the opportunity to note that the fundamental right not to be subjected to torture or to inhuman or degrading treatment or punishment contained in Article 3 of the ECHR formed "part of the general principles of Community law, observance of which is ensured by the Court".[248] Most recently, the General Court acknowledged that EU institutions (the Commission in the case at hand) must "comply with mandatory rules of international law" and referred in that respect to the prohibition of torture.[249]

It clearly follows that European Union institutions drew from rules of international human rights law, such as the right to life and the prohibition of torture, inhuman or degrading treatment or punishment, to define the corpus of fundamental rights protected under EU law. Fundamental rights of the European Union have gained significant visibility with the entry into force of the Charter of fundamental rights of the European Union. Although it is a comprehensive catalogue of rights, the Charter however provides very little clarification as to the content of those rights. Charter provisions are concise and worded in general terms. As a consequence, interpretation will be essential to flesh out those rights in practice. Should EU fundamental rights be interpreted in conformity with the rules of international law from which they derive?

---

245 *Ibid.*, § 80. Confirmed, incidentally again in CJ, Case C-548/09 P, *Bank Melli Iran v Council* (16 November 2011) [2011], § 89.

246 CJ, § 18; CJ, *ERT v. DEP*, § 41; CJ, *Schmidberger*, § 71; CJ, *Omega*, § 33.

247 S. Peers, "Human Rights, Asylum and European Community Law", *UNHCR Refugee Survey Quarterly*, Vol. 24, No. 2 (2005), p. 28.

248 CJ, C-465/07, *Meki Elgafaji and Noor Elgafaji v. Staatssecretaris Van Justitie* ("*Elgafaji*") (17 February 2009) ECR I-921, § 28.

249 More specifically, the General Court was referring to the prohibition to accept evidence obtained under torture. GC (Second Chamber), Case T-527/09, *Ayadi v. Commission* ("*Ayadi*") (31 January 2012).

3 The Meaning and Scope of EU Asylum Rights, Reflective of International Human Rights Law

Before turning to more specific observations on the different sources available for the interpretation of EU rights relevant in the field of asylum, a remark can be made on the interpretation of rights enshrined in the Charter. A particularity of the EU Charter of Fundamental Rights lies in its Article 52 concerning the scope and interpretation of Charter rights and principles. Typically, human rights instruments emphasise that certain human rights are non-derogable; the right to life and the prohibition of torture are classical examples. The Charter does not do so. All the rights recognised in the Charter are granted in general terms: "no one shall...", "everyone has the right...", "the Union recognises...", "the Union shall..." are just so many examples of strong language used to define the rights of individuals and corresponding obligations of the Union under the Charter. Article 52 of the Charter however hampers this observation. It states:

> Any limitation on the exercise of the rights and freedoms recognised by this Charter must be provided for by law and respect the essence of those rights and freedoms. Subject to the principle of proportionality, limitations may be made only if they are necessary and genuinely meet objectives of general interest recognised by the Union or the need to protect the rights and freedoms of others.[250]

The significance of this provision for the rights traditionally perceived as non-derogable must in turn be nuanced: the same Article points to the fact that where Charter rights are also guaranteed under the ECHR or Member States' constitutional traditions, those rights must be interpreted in conformity with the latter instruments.[251] Additionally, Article 53 makes clear the level of protection provided by the Charter: it shall be at least equivalent to that guaranteed "by Union law and international law and by international agreements to which the Union or all the Member States are parties".[252] As a consequence, it can be inferred from the foregoing that those rights from which no derogation is possible under international human rights law should also be absolute under EU fundamental rights law.[253]

---

250 EU Charter, Article 52(1).
251 *Ibid.*, Article 52(3) and (4).
252 *Ibid.*, Article 53.
253 Steve Peers reaches a similar conclusion: he finds that Article 52(1) should be construed as a "residual derogation clause". The derogation clause would only apply to those rights that are not enshrined elsewhere (in international treaties, in the case-law of the European

Let us consider now more specifically which sources could be used as guidance for the interpretation of EU fundamental rights. In that context and in view of the major role played by Treaty-monitoring bodies in defining the meaning and scope of fundamental rights enshrined in international law, it must be considered whether the interpretation of fundamental rights within the EU should be in conformity with that provided in the international legal order by the European Court of Human Rights and the Human Rights Committee in particular. The well-known inference by the European Court of Human Rights and the UN Human Rights Committee of the principle of *non-refoulement* from the prohibition of torture and inhuman or degrading treatment or punishment is but one telling example of the fundamental role played by Treaty-body interpretation in advancing human rights protection: monitoring bodies, through their decisions, comments or recommendations, clarify the scope of the provisions of the treaties they monitor. The question thus arises whether or not EU law, drawing on Member States' obligations under international treaties to identify EU fundamental rights, shall also take account of the corresponding interpretations provided by the respective treaty monitoring bodies. As far as ECHR provisions are concerned, the question calls for a positive answer (a); this will be illustrated by the judgment of the Court of Justice in the *NS & ME* case where the Court interpreted Charter provisions in direct line with the case-law of the European Court of Human Rights and in particular, with the ECtHR judgment in the *MSS v. Belgium and Greece* case (b). If the pertinence of the ECtHR's case-law for the interpretation of EU fundamental rights is unquestionable, *quid* of clarifications issued by other treaty-monitoring bodies? Should EU fundamental rights also take account of the interpretation provided by the Human Rights Committee or UNHCR in particular? (c)

Besides treaty law, customary international law also includes rules that are relevant in the field of asylum. Chiefly, it sanctions the principle of *non-refoulement*. Should EU fundamental rights also be interpreted in conformity with customary international law? (d)

(a) *The ECtHR Case Law: A Key Source of Interpretation of EU Fundamental Rights*

The case-law of the European Court of Human Rights is indeed a key source of interpretation of EU fundamental rights. Two main reasons account for this. Firstly, rulings of the European Court of Human Rights (ECtHR) being binding upon

---

Court of Human Rights or in Member States' constitutional traditions for example) but not to the others, for which the Union must safeguard a level of protection equivalent to that guaranteed under the relevant instrument. S. Peers (2001), *op. cit.*, pp. 152–155.

State Parties,[254] for the latter to fully comply with their obligations under the ECHR, they must ensure respect for the rights and freedoms not merely as they are enshrined in the letter of the ECHR but also as they are interpreted by the ECtHR. Every obligation State Parties to the ECHR have under the Convention is twofold: they are made of the Convention provision itself and of the relevant jurisprudence of the European Court of Human Rights. As a consequence and in the light of Article 351 of the Treaty on the Functioning of the European Union which implies "duty" on the part of the institutions of the European Union "not to impede the performance of the obligations of Member States which stem from a prior agreement",[255] the case-law of the European Court of Human Rights must be given due consideration by EU institutions when they refer to provisions of the ECHR.

Secondly, the practice of the EU institutions and subsequently, Primary law, as amended by the Lisbon Treaty confirm this analysis. The indivisibility of ECHR provision from their jurisprudential interpretation by the European Court of Human Rights was first acknowledged by the Court of Justice, who repeatedly referred to ECtHR case-law in its own decisions.[256] The entry into force of the Lisbon Treaty and the adoption of the EU Charter of Fundamental Rights further confirmed the bearing of ECtHR case-law in cases where ECHR rights or freedoms are at issue. The Preamble of the Charter indeed makes clear that the Charter reaffirms existing rights, as they result from a variety of sources including, in particular, the case-law of the European Court of Human Rights.[257] Additionally, the prohibition of *refoulement* enshrined in Article 19 of the Charter of Fundamental Rights[258] mirrors the well-established case-law of the European Court of Human Rights that inferred it from the prohibition of the death penalty, torture or other inhuman or degrading treatment or punishment.[259] The Explanations to the Charter achieve to make it unquestionable that ECtHR case-law contributes to defining the content of Charter rights. The Explanation on Article 52(3) makes it clear:

> The meaning and the scope of the guaranteed rights are determined not only by the text of those instruments [*i.e.* the ECHR and its Protocols],

---

254   ECHR, Article 53.
255   CJ, *Burgoa*, §§ 9–11.
256   *See* for example Judgment of 14 February 2008, *Varec SA v État belge*, Case C-450/06, [2008] ECR I-581, §§46 and 48.
257   Charter of Fundamental Rights of the European Union, *Official Journal C 364 of 18 December 2000*, p. 8, Preamble §5.
258   EU Charter, Article 19.
259   *See* developments below, Chapter 3, pp. 177s.

but also by the case-law of the European Court of Human Rights and by the Court of Justice of the European Union.[260]

Furthermore, the Explanation on Article 19(2) of the Charter confirms that paragraph 2 "incorporates the relevant case-law from the European Court of Human Rights regarding Article 3 of the ECHR".[261] Similarly, the Explanation on Article 4 of the Charter clarifies that the prohibition of torture, inhuman or degrading treatment or punishment "has the same meaning and the same scope as the ECHR Article 3".[262]

Following the entry into force of the Charter, the Court of Justice recently had the opportunity to highlight the importance of ECtHR case-law. In 2010, in a case concerning specifically the right to private and family life (Article 7 Charter, Article 8 ECHR), the Court of Justice stated:

> Article 7 [of the Charter] contains rights corresponding to those guaranteed by Article 8(1) of the ECHR. Article 7 of the Charter must therefore be given the same meaning and the same scope as Article 8(1) of the ECHR, as interpreted by the case-law of the European Court of Human Rights.[263]

The principle that rights enshrined in the Charter be given the same meaning and scope as corresponding rights under the ECHR, as interpreted by the European Court of Human Rights, is of utmost importance in the field of asylum: it ensures in particular that the principle of *non-refoulement* is protected in the legal order of the European Union in the same terms as under the European Convention of Human Rights and related case-law of the ECtHR.

(b) *The Court of Justice Interprets Charter Rights in Line with ECtHR Case Law: The NS & ME Case*

A recent decision of the EU Court of Justice in the field of asylum clearly illustrates that the case-law of the European Court of Human Rights penetrates EU fundamental rights law. In August 2008, the Court of Justice was referred questions for preliminary rulings concerning the interpretation of fundamental rights set out in the Charter, in the context Dublin transfers from

---

260 "Explanations to the Charter", [14/12/2007], *op. cit.*, Explanation on Article 52 Paragraph 3, p. 33.
261 *Ibid.*, on Article 19 (2).
262 *Ibid.*, on Article 4.
263 CJ, Case C-400/10 PPU, *J. Mcb. v. L. E.* ("*J. McB. v. L. E.*") (5 October 2010) [2010] *OJ C 328/10*, § 53.

Ireland and the United Kingdom to Greece.[264] It is well-known, the operation of the Dublin system[265] puts increased pressure on the asylum systems of those Member States that are at the external borders of the European Union.[266] In that respect, Greece, as a major point of entry of asylum seekers in the EU,[267] is tragically famous for failing to provide asylum seekers with the adequate standards of treatment. Reception conditions are outrageous,[268] procedures lengthy and examinations of asylum claims, when they eventually take place, expeditious.[269] As a consequence, asylum seekers facing "Dublin" removal to Greece, have sought to halt their transfer and lodged appeals against the decision ordering it.

In January 2011, court litigation gained marked momentum with the Grand Chamber judgment of the European Court of Human Rights (ECtHR) in the *M.M.S.* case.[270] The ECtHR confirms its earlier case-law and analyses the

---

264 CJ (Grand Chamber), Joined Cases C-411/10 and C-493/10, *N.S. v. Secretary of State for the Home Department and M.E., A.S.M., M.T., K.P., E.H. v. Refugee Applications Commissioner, Minister for Justice, Equality and Law Reform* ("*NS & ME*") (21 December 2011).

265 Four legal instruments constitute the so-called Dublin system: Dublin Regulation; Council Regulation (EC) No 2725/2000 of 11 December 2000 Concerning the Establishment of 'Eurodac' for the Comparison of Fingerprints for the Effective Application of the Dublin Convention ("Eurodac Regulation") [15/12/2000] *OJ L 316/1*; Commission Regulation (EC) No 1560/2003 of 2 September 2003 Laying Down Detailed Rules for the Application of Council Regulation (EC) No 343/2003 Establishing the Criteria and Mechanisms for Determining the Member State Responsible for Examining an Asylum Application Lodged in One of the Member States by a Third-Country National ("Regulation – Dublin detailed rules") [05/09/2003] *OJ L 222/3*; Council Regulation (EC) No 407/2002 of 28 February 2002 Laying Down Certain Rules to Implement Regulation (EC) No 2725/2000 Concerning the Establishment of "Eurodac" for the Comparison of Fingerprints for the Effective Application of the Dublin Convention [05/03/2002] *OJ L 62/1*.

266 R. Byrne, "Harmonization and Burden Redistribution in the Two Europes", *Journal of Refugee Studies*, Vol. 16, No. 3 (2003), pp. 336–358; ECRE, "Sharing Responsibility for Refugee Protection in Europe: Dublin Reconsidered" (March 2008); UNHCR, *The Dublin II Regulation: A UNHCR Discussion Paper* (Brussels: UNHCR, April 2006).

267 CJ, *NS & ME*, § 87.

268 In H. Labayle's words, the whole European Union is perfectly aware of the fact that the situation of asylum seekers in Greece is *"parfaitement scandaleuse"*. H. Labayle, "Le droit européen de l'asile devant ses juges : précisions ou remise en question ?", *RFDA*, No. 2 (March–April 2011), pp. 273–290, p. 280.

269 Human Rights Watch, "European Union", *in World Report 2012: Events of 2011* (New York: January 2012), pp. 441–458, and particularly pp. 447–448; B. Frelick, "Sharing Greece's Asylum Shame", *The European Voice*, 29 September 2011.

270 ECtHR (Grand Chamber), *M.S.S. v. Belgium and Greece* ("*M.S.S.*"), Application No. 30696/09 (21 January 2011) *Reports of Judgments and Decisions 2011*.

conditions of detention awaiting asylum seekers in Greece as "unacceptable:"[271] those conditions, the Court finds, amount to degrading treatment within the meaning of Article 3.[272] Greece is therefore in violation of Article 3 ECHR because of asylum seekers' conditions of detention and living conditions in the country. Furthermore, of utmost importance for the EU asylum system was the Court's finding that Belgium, because of its decision to transfer the applicant back to Greece, also infringed Article 3 ECHR. Firstly, the Court notes that Belgian asylum authorities "knew or ought to have known"[273] the "real and individual" risks[274] the applicant would face upon return to Greece. Belgium's decision to transfer the applicant to Greece, insofar as it exposed the applicant to the notorious risks arising from the deficiencies in the asylum procedure in Greece, gave rise to a violation of Article 3 ECHR.[275] Secondly, the applicant having been sent back to Greece and subjected there to degrading conditions of detention and living conditions, Belgium also violated Article 3 ECHR on account of the treatment actually suffered by the applicant in Greece. On this point, the Court unequivocally stated:

> Based on these conclusions and on the obligations incumbent on the States under Article 3 of the Convention in terms of expulsion, the Court considers that by transferring the applicant to Greece the Belgian authorities knowingly exposed him to conditions of detention and living conditions that amounted to degrading treatment.[276]

The ruling of the European Court of Human Rights clearly challenged the premise of the EU Dublin system. In particular, it can be extrapolated from the Court's decision that EU national asylum authorities shall not merely assume that the applicant would be treated in conformity with the Convention standards upon being removed to another EU Member States. On the contrary, the authorities of the returning States shall first verify how asylum legislation is applied in practice in the destination State before deciding whether or not to return asylum seekers there.[277] Rejecting the concept of mutual trust

---

271 *Ibid.*, § 222.
272 *Ibid.*, § 233.
273 *Ibid.*, § 358.
274 *Ibid.*, § 359.
275 *Ibid.*, §§ 344–361.
276 *Ibid.*, § 367.
277 Those two sentences draw on § 359 of the *M.S.S.* judgment.

underpinning the EU asylum system, the ECtHR instead formulates a "quasi-obligation of mistrust".[278]

Before the ECtHR delivered its judgment in the *M.S.S.* case, a number of States participating in the Dublin system[279] had already announced that they would temporarily suspend transfers to Greece and assume responsibility for examining the claims.[280] Since the Court's *M.S.S.* judgment, more States have done so, either on their own initiative, or upon request from the ECtHR.[281]

It is against this backdrop that in December 2011 the Court of Justice gave its judgment in the *NS & ME* cases. The Court of Justice first notes that the Common European Asylum System Member, which States agreed to establish, is based on the full and inclusive application of the Geneva Convention and the guarantee that nobody will be sent back to a place where they again risk being persecuted,[282] and that all the relevant asylum regulations and directives state that they respect the fundamental rights and observe the principles recognised, in particular, in the EU Charter.[283] On this basis, the Court finds, it was possible for the EU legislator to assume "that the treatment of asylum seekers in all Member States complies with the requirements of the Charter, the Geneva Convention and the ECHR" and devise the Dublin system accordingly.[284] The Court however nuances this principle of "mutual confidence" by acknowledging that a given Member State may experience "major operational problems (...), meaning that there is a substantial risk that asylum seekers may, when transferred to that Member State, be treated in a manner incompatible with their fundamental rights". Only in certain extreme cases would those operational problems obligate States not to carry out Dublin transfers. Specifically, the Court clarifies that in cases where those "major operational problems" reach the threshold of:

> ... systemic flaws in the asylum procedure and reception conditions for asylum applicants in the Member State responsible, resulting in inhuman

---

278 "*Loin de la confiance mutuelle qui sous-tend toute la réglementation communautaire en la matière, la CEDH instaure ainsi une quasi-obligation de méfiance entre Etats membres*". M. Aubert, et al., "Chronique de jurisprudence de la CJUE", *AJDA*, No. 6 (20/02/2012), pp. 306–316, pp. 309–310.
279 This includes EU Member States and Iceland, Norway and Switzerland.
280 UNHCR, *The Dublin II Regulation: A UNHCR Discussion Paper* (April 2006), *op. cit.*, pp. 47–48.
281 UNHCR, "Updated UNHCR Information Note on National Practice in the Application of Article 3(2) of the Dublin II Regulation in Particular in the Context of Intended Transfers to Greece" (31 January 2011); T. Vogel, "Greek Asylum System in Disarray", *European Voice*.
282 CJ, *NS & ME*, § 75.
283 *Ibid.*, § 15.
284 *Ibid.*, § 80.

or degrading treatment, within the meaning of Article 4 of the Charter, of asylum seekers transferred to the territory of that Member State, the transfer would be incompatible with that provision.[285]

In the *NS & ME* judgment, the Court of Justice appears to engage in a balancing act between reaffirming the validity of EU law and ensuring respect for fundamental rights in the EU.[286] The Court is not unfamiliar with the exercise. After all, it is it who already constructively interpreted fundamental rights as general principles of the EU legal order which originally did not appear to devote much attention to them.[287] It is also the Court who endeavoured to safeguard the *effet utile* of subsidiary protection by offering to disentangle the obscure language of the Qualification Directive conditioning the grant of subsidiary protection in situations of indiscriminate violence upon the alleged threat being "individual".[288] In the *NS & ME* case, the Court of Justice, careful not to discard the premise of the Dublin system instead reaffirms its validity while providing for exceptions to it, for the sake of human rights protection. The underlying presumption, the Court finds, is not conclusive but rebuttable.[289]

The rest of the Court of Justice's judgment is very similar to the ECtHR's decision in the *M.S.S.* case; in particular, the interpretation of Article 4 of the Charter of Fundamental Rights is in direct line with ECtHR's interpretation of Article 3 of the European Convention of Human Rights:

> Article 4 of the Charter of Fundamental Rights of the European Union must be interpreted as meaning that the Member States, including the national courts, may not transfer an asylum seeker to the 'Member State responsible' within the meaning of Regulation No 343/2003 where they *cannot be unaware* that systemic deficiencies in the asylum procedure and in the reception conditions of asylum seekers in that Member State amount to *substantial grounds for believing* that the asylum seeker would

---

285 *Ibid.*, § 86.
286 M. Aubert, E. Broussy and F. Donnat reach a similar conclusion: "*la Cour a voulu donner une solution équilibrée qui, sans saper le bon fonctionnement d'un règlement essentiel à l'existence même d'un système européen commun d'asile, concilie le respect des droits fondamentaux avec à la fois l'esprit d'une législation et les spécificités de l'Union européenne, basée sur la confiance mutuelle entre Etats membres*". M. Aubert, *et al.* (20/02/2012), *op. cit.*, p. 310.
287 *See* above, "1. Fundamental Rights as General Principles of Community Law", p. 35.
288 The judgment of the Court of Justice in *Elgafaji* case, which I am alluding to too here, will be discussed below in "B. 3. A controversial innovation in EU law: Article 15(c)", pp. 124s.
289 CJ, *NS & ME*, §§ 103–104.

face a *real risk of being subjected to inhuman or degrading treatment* within the meaning of that provision.²⁹⁰

In other words, and in accord with the European Court of Human Rights, the Court of Justice concludes that when Member States know or ought to know that removing an asylum seeker to another State, including an EU Member State, would expose him or her to inhuman or degrading treatment there, they have the obligation to suspend the transfer of the person concerned. This interpretation of the prohibition of torture and inhuman or degrading treatment or punishment laid down in Article 4 of the Charter is called for in order "to ensure compliance by the European Union and its Member States with their obligations concerning the protection of the fundamental rights of asylum seekers".²⁹¹

Going one step further, the Court adds that not only should States refrain from returning the asylum seeker to the Member State identified as primarily responsible, they also must either identify another Member State responsible for examining the asylum claim, in accordance with the other criteria set out in Chapter 3 of the Dublin Regulation²⁹² or themselves proceed with the examination of the claim, in particular if the first option would result in unreasonably delaying the treatment of the asylum seekers' claim.²⁹³ The Court of Justice finds that, in exceptional circumstances, the rights of each Member States to examine an asylum claim although it is not the State responsible for the assessment of the claim pursuant to the Dublin Regulation, can, in exceptional circumstances, be a duty of the State and not merely a right.²⁹⁴

Four concluding remarks can be made on this case.

Firstly, it is symptomatic of the "ECHR-ification"²⁹⁵ of the Charter, which the Explanation to the Charter had anticipated: the prohibition of torture and inhuman or degrading treatment or punishment set out in Article 4 of the Charter is given a scope and meaning that call to mind ECtHR *non-refoulement* jurisprudence.²⁹⁶ In particular, the Court of Justice, like the ECtHR before

---

290 *Ibid.*, § 106 [emphases added].
291 *Ibid.*, § 99.
292 Dublin Regulation, Chapter III.
293 CJ, *NS & ME*, §§ 107–108.
294 *Ibid.*, § 107.
295 F. Fontanelli (2011), *op. cit.*, p. 39.
296 This is in line with the Explanation on Article 4: the Explanation states that the right protected in Article 4 of the Charter is the right guaranteed by Article 3 of the ECHR, which has the same wording. The Explanation adds that by virtue of Article 52(3) of the Charter, Article 4 of the Charter therefore has the same meaning and the same scope as the ECHR. "Explanations to the Charter", [14/12/2007], *op. cit.*, Explanation on Article 4.

it,[297] sanctions the extraterritoriality of Member States' obligation deriving from Article 4 of the Charter.

Secondly, the case brings some light on Article 18 of the Charter, enshrining the "right to asylum". The provision is rather sibylline; its sole paragraph reads as follows:

> The right to asylum shall be guaranteed with due respect for the rules of the Geneva Convention of 28 July 1951 and the Protocol of 31 January 1967 relating to the status of refugees and in accordance with the Treaty on European Union and the Treaty on the Functioning of the European Union.[298]

Not much can be inferred from this provision concerning this right's meaning and scope. The Explanation on Article 18 adds little tenor to the provision although, on the substance, it does clarify that the Article is "in line with the Protocol on Asylum annexed to the Treaties", which limits the right to lodge an application for asylum to third-country nationals.[299] A cross-reading of the decision of the Court of Justice in *NS & ME*[300] with the corresponding Opinions of Advocate General Trstenjak[301] informs that the right to asylum protected under Article 18 of the Charter essentially is the right of refugees not to be expelled or returned, directly or indirectly (chain deportation[302]), to a risk of persecution. Otherwise stated, this means that the right in Article 18 Charter is the right to *non-refoulement* guaranteed by Article 33 of the Refugee Convention to any person who satisfies the refugee definition criteria, whether or not he or she has been formally recognised as refugee pursuant to a municipal law process (*i.e.* "refugee" for the purposes of the 1951 Convention and the 1967 Protocol[303]). Thus understood, it differs from Article 19(2), which incorporates

---

297 See below, under "III. A. 1 (b), Territoriality of the ill-treatment: an immaterial consideration" pp. 184s.
298 EU Charter, Article 18.
299 "Explanations to the Charter", [14/12/2007], *op. cit.*, Explanation on Article 18 and TFEU, Protocol (no 24) on asylum for nationals of Member States of the European Union.
300 CJ, *NS & ME*, § 75.
301 Opinion AG Trstenjak in NS, §§ 113–115; and Opinion of Adv. Gen. Trstenjak, delivered on 22 September 2011, *Case C-493/10 M. E. And Others v. Refugee Applications Commissioner and Minister for Justice, Equality and Law Reform* ("Opinion AG Trstenjak in ME"), §§ 61–62. On this point, the two opinions are similar. Hereafter, reference will be made to Advocate General Trstenjak's Opinion in the NS case only.
302 Opinion AG Trstenjak in *NS*, § 114.
303 E. Lauterpacht and D. Bethlehem (2003), *op. cit.*, § 90.

the international human rights law prohibition of *refoulement*.³⁰⁴ The difference between the two articles therefore is significant: whereas Article 18 of the Charter read together with Protocol 24 TFEU only applies to third-country nationals who fulfil the 1951 Convention refugee definition, Article 19(2) instead applies to *anyone*³⁰⁵ who risks be subjected to the death penalty, torture or other inhuman or degrading treatment or punishment. In that sense, it is clear from Advocate General Trstenjak's Opinion that the Charter prohibits transfers of asylum seekers when they are incompatible with the Refugee Convention (under Article 18 of the Charter) or with Article 3 of the ECHR (under Articles 1, 4 and 19(2) of the Charter).³⁰⁶

Thirdly, the Court of Justice had and took the opportunity to adjust the procedure for determining the Member State responsible for examining an asylum claim in the EU, devised by the Dublin Regulation.³⁰⁷ The Court addressed the concerns voiced in international protection circles that the Dublin system was built on the faulty presumption that the same level of rights was available throughout the European Union at all times.³⁰⁸ In particular, the Court's decision directly it seems responds to commentators' concerns: the Court indeed concurs with the critics and stresses that "the mere ratification of conventions by a Member State cannot result in the application of a conclusive presumption that that State observes those conventions. The same principle is applicable both to Member States and third countries".³⁰⁹ Incidentally, although the Court of Justice was not asked to pronounce on the interpretation of Protocol 24 of the TFEU, on asylum for nationals of Member States of the European Union (or for that matter on Article 2 of the Qualification Directive, based on Protocol 24 and limiting the benefit of refugee status and subsidiary protection to third-country nationals), logic would suggest that the Court's judgment in *NS & ME* also impacts the interpretation of the Protocol. Under Protocol 24,

---

304   The Explanation on Article 19 indicates that paragraph 2 "incorporates the relevant case-law from the European Court of Human Rights regarding Article 3 of the ECHR". "Explanations to the Charter", [14/12/2007], *op. cit.*, Explanation on Article 19, Paragraph 2.
305   Charter Article 19(2) states: "*No one* may be removed, expelled or extradited, ..." [emphasis added].
306   Opinion AG Trstenjak in *NS*, §§ 153–158. A similar view was expressed by the German Government in the case: see § 66 of the Opinion where the German Government's view is cited.
307   *Op. cit.* Dublin Regulation.
308   At the time the Treaty of Amsterdam was adopted, commentators already firmly criticised this idea, that underpinned the Protocol on asylum for nationals of Member States of the European Union. *See* below note 528.
309   CJ, *NS & ME*, § 103.

nationals of EU Member States may submit asylum claims within the European Union only in a well-circumscribed subset of cases. It is founded on the presumption that the level of protection of fundamental rights and freedoms is equivalent across the European Union and provides that, as a consequence, all EU Member States "shall be regarded as constituting safe countries of origin in respect of each other for all legal and practical purposes in relation to asylum matters".[310] If the Protocol, annexed to the Treaty on the Functioning of the European Union forms part of primary law, so does the Charter of Fundamental Rights since the entry into force of the Lisbon Treaty and the Protocol, as any Treaty provision must indeed be interpreted in light of the Charter.[311]

Fourthly and lastly, the judgment is a further step on the path the Court had engaged in in the 1970s by developing its fundamental rights. It is clear from the settled case-law of the Court of Justice that respect for fundamental rights is a condition of the lawfulness of EU measures[312] and that measures which are incompatible with respect for human rights are not acceptable within the European Union.[313] In line with its doctrine, the Court reviews the lawfulness of the Dublin Regulation in the light of fundamental rights enshrined in the EU Charter. Although the Court takes obvious pain not to fully discard the underlying premise of the Dublin system, the firm language used unambiguously attests to the supremacy of fundamental rights within the EU legal order: EU law must yield to fundamental rights. The judgment of the Court of Justice in *NS & ME* might in fact reach beyond the sole Dublin Regulation. Among other questions, the Court was asked whether the extent of the protection conferred by the rights set out in Articles 1 (human dignity), 18 (right to asylum) and 47 (right to an effective remedy) of the Charter was wider than the protection conferred by Article 3 of the ECHR. The Advocate General Opinion mainly refers to Article 52(3) of the Charter to conclude, in brief, that the protection deriving from Articles 1, 18 and 47 of the Charter must be at least equivalent to the protection granted by corresponding ECHR provisions and the relevant case-law of the ECtHR.[314] The Court answers the question quite concisely too. It notes that a Member State would infringe Article 4 of the Charter if it carried out a Dublin transfer to a Member State where there are substantial grounds for believing that the asylum seeker would face a real risk of being subjected to inhuman or degrading treatment. The Court of Justice then concludes without

---

310 TFEU, Protocol No. 24, Sole Article.
311 P. Craig and G.D. Búrca, *EU Law: Text, Cases, and Materials* (2011), op. cit., p. 109.
312 CJ, *Opinion 2/94*, § 34.
313 CJ, *Schmidberger*, §§ 71–73.
314 Opinion AG Trstenjak in *NS*, §§ 137–148.

much ado that Articles 1, 18 and 47 of the Charter "do not lead to a different answer". In other words, in cases where the operation of the Dublin system jeopardises asylum seekers' right to human dignity, to asylum, or to an effective remedy and to fair trial, Member States must also suspend the transfer.

Incidentally, it can be noted that recognition of the extraterritoriality of the right to human dignity might substantially extend the scope of the prohibition of *non-refoulement*. The concept however is still fuzzy so that it is unsure as of yet how human dignity can effectively contribute to an increased level of protection for asylum seekers. The Explanation on Article 1 clarifies that human dignity is not only a fundamental right in itself, recognized by the Court of Justice, but also the basis of all fundamental rights.[315] As noted by Advocate General Trstenjak, the question whether and how Article 1 can apply autonomously is not settled,[316] however, one can but notice the potentialities of the concept of human dignity in *non-refoulement* cases. The meaning and scope of the right to human dignity are yet to be developed by the Court of Justice.

(c) *Documents of the Human Rights Committee and UNHCR (and others): Additional Sources of Interpretation of EU Fundamental Rights*

Just like the European Court of Human Rights, the UN Human Rights Committee also interpreted the prohibition of torture, enshrined in Article 7 of the International Covenant on Civil and Political Rights (ICCPR), as carrying with it the prohibition of *refoulement*.[317] The decisions, concluding observations and General Comments issued by the Human Rights Committee are distinct from the judgments of the European Court of Human Rights in that, contrary to the latter, they are deprived of biding force.[318] This observation however falls short from casting doubts as to their relevance for the interpretation of EU fundamental rights that are also enshrined in the ICCPR.

Firstly, although they are non-binding in international law, the importance of Human Rights Committee acts is not negligible: decisions of the Human Rights Committee on individual communications are "generally complied with"[319] whereas concluding observations on country reports and General Comments, all adopted by consensus among all the Human Rights Committee

---

315 "Explanations to the Charter", [14/12/2007], *op. cit.*, Explanation on Article 1, p. 17.
316 Opinion AG Trstenjak in *NS*, notes 44 and 46.
317 The jurisprudential process through which the ECtHR and the HRC constructively deduced the prohibition of refoulement from the prohibition of torture is detailed in Part II hereinafter.
318 M. Nowak, *U.N. Covenant on Civil and Political Rights: CCPR Commentary* (2005), *op. cit.*, see e.g. Introduction, §§ 6 and 21, and Commentary on Article 40 ICCPR, p. 749, fn 188.
319 *Ibid.*, Introduction, § 6.

Members, are recognised as "authoritative and universal" interpretations of the Covenant.[320] The obligation to implement the ICCPR requires that EU institutions and Member States applying provisions of EU law that contain a right protected under the ICCPR take due account of the interpretation provided by the Human Rights Committee. The prohibition of torture, inhuman or degrading treatment or punishment enshrined in Article 7 of the Covenant must accordingly be interpreted as carrying with it the principle of *non-refoulement*. Secondly, the Charter of Fundamental Rights read together with Article 6 TEU make clear that the Union recognises, *inter alia*, the fundamental rights emanating from Member States' obligations under international treaties. Those obligations derive from the letter of the relevant treaty provision, as informed by its prevailing interpretation.[321] Where EU law recognises rights that are elsewhere enshrined in international treaties, the meaning and scope of those rights must provide at least the same level of protection as those treaties do, in their current interpretation. This is confirmed again by the Charter of Fundamental Rights: Article 53 provides that nothing in the Charter "shall be interpreted as restricting or adversely affecting human rights and fundamental freedoms as recognised, in their respective fields of application, by Union law and *international law* and by international agreements to which the Union or all the Member States are party".[322] The fact that Article 53 Charter refers to both "international law" and "international agreements…" indicates that international law for the purpose of the Charter is to be understood as being broader than merely treaty law. In like manner, the Explanation of Article 53 informs that the provision "is intended to maintain the level of protection currently afforded within their respective scope by Union law, national law and international law".[323] The Explanation reproduces the classical division of legal norms on the basis of the system in which they operate; the three levels traditionally identified are the national, regional, and international levels. It follows from the provision and its Explanation that the level of protection guaranteed by EU law must at least equivalent to that existing under international law, the term being understood in its broad sense: it encompasses not only treaty law but also the other sources of international law such as custom,[324] and the secondary sources that are treaty bodies' acts and case-law.

---

320 *Ibid.*, Introduction, § 21 and Commentary on Article 40, p. 749, § 66.
321 VCLT, Article 31(3) (a) and (b).
322 EU Charter, Article 53 [emphasis added].
323 "Explanations to the Charter", [14/12/2007], *op. cit.*
324 This will be discussed again below in (iv).

As a matter of fact, the case-law of the Court of Justice demonstrates that the Court has already accepted soft law emanating from the monitoring body of a treaty by which the Union is bound as a source of inspiration for the interpretation of the said treaty. In the context of EU external relations law, the Court indeed noted that "measures emanating from bodies which have been established by an international agreement [concluded by the EU], and which have been entrusted with responsibility for its implementation, are directly linked to the agreement which they implement", and concluded that therefore, "they form part of the Community legal order".[325] By analogy, the same could be argued concerning acts of other international treaty bodies, such as UNHCR. The Union is not a party to the Refugee Convention. However, Steve Peers argues that in light of the importance of the Refugee Convention within the EU legal order (it is repeatedly referred to in EU law)[326] and of the important operational role recognised to UNHCR under the Convention, it is logically possible to deduce that "'soft law' measures of the UNHCR" also form part of EU law.[327]

(d) *The Interpretation of EU Asylum Rights Must Also Conform with Customary International Law*

The broad reference made in Article 53 of the Charter of Fundamental Rights to "international law", *i.e.* not limited to treaty law, reflects the settled case-law of the Court of Justice who has indeed considered international law outside treaties. The Court has asserted that the European Union was bound by customary international law. In the *Poulsen and Diva* case concerning Council regulations on the conservation of the resources of the sea, the Court of Justice observes that "the European Community must respect international law in the exercise of its powers" and infers from this obligation, and in the specific context of the case, that EU law "must be interpreted, and its scope limited, in the light of the relevant rules of the international law of the sea".[328] The Court clarifies

---

325 See CJ, Case C-188/91, *Deutsche Shell Ag v. Hauptzollamt Hamburg-Harburg* ("*Deutsche Shell*") (21 January 1993) [1993] ECR I-00363, § 17; CJ, Case C-162/97, *Criminal Proceedings against Gunnar Nilsson, Per Olov Hagelgren and Solweig Arrborn* ("*Nilsson et al.*") (19 November 1998) [1998] ECR I-7477, § 49.

326 See for example Amsterdam Treaty, Declaration 17 to the Final Act; Qualification Directive, Recitals 3 and 4; Procedures Directive, Recitals 2, 13 and Articles 7(2)(b), 9(1)(c), 21 and 37(1)(c); Temporary Protection Directive, Recital 11 and Articles 3(3), 5(3)(d), 5(4)(c), 25(1) and 26(2); Reception Conditions Directive, Articles 14(2)(b) and 14(7).

327 S. Peers (2005), *op. cit.*, p. 29.

328 CJ, Case C-286/90, *Anklagemyndigheden v Peter Michael Poulsen and Diva Navigation Corp.* ("*Poulsen and Diva*") (24 November 1992) [1992] ECR I-06019, § 9.

that those rules of international law include customary international law.³²⁹ In the subsequent *Racke* case,³³⁰ the Court reiterates its statement in *Poulsen and Diva* that the European Union must respect international law in the exercise of its powers. As a consequence, the Court finds, the EU is "required to comply with the rules of customary international law".³³¹ In the particular circumstances of the case, the Court concluded specifically that the rules of customary international law concerning the termination and the suspension of treaty relations were binding upon the European Union in the exercise of its powers.³³²

It follows that EU fundamental rights must be interpreted in conformity with customary international law. The consequence of this on asylum rights can be better apprehended upon relevant rules of customary international law being identified (this will be done below in Chapter 3, II.) however, suffice to say at this juncture that the principle of *non-refoulement* is recognised as a principle of customary international law.³³³ This holds true in the context of risks to which entire populations are exposed: persons fleeing threats to their life or person may not be returned to their country of origin.

"General" European Union law enshrines a number of rights that are pertinent in the field of asylum, *a fortiori* since the entry into force of the Charter of fundamental rights. Among them, some can be invoked to justify the grant of protection to individuals who cannot be returned to their country or origin. European Union law further includes a *lex specialis*, a set of secondary legislation devising the common asylum policy of the Union. Among those acts, the Qualification Directive is of particular relevance to the present work as it concerns specifically the criteria conditioning asylum seekers' eligibility to an international protection status within EU Member States. It will be the main focus of following developments (III). The concept of temporary protection, which translated in EU law into the Temporary Protection Directive will be discussed first, albeit briefly, insofar as it provide some protection against return to certain groups of persons threatened by indiscriminate violence (II).

---

329 In the *Poulsen and Diva* case concerning Council regulations on the conservation of the resources of the sea, the Court of Justice referred specifically to "customary international maritime law". *Ibid.*, § 10.

330 CJ, Case C-162/96, *A. Racke Gmbh & Co. v Hauptzollamt Mainz* ("*Racke*") (16 June 1998) [1998] ECR I-03655.

331 *Ibid.*, § 45.

332 *Ibid.*, § 46.

333 *See* for instance: J. Allain (2001), *op. cit.*

II   The Temporary Protection Directive

As is apparent from the Preamble of the Temporary Protection Directive, EU institutions had in mind persons displaced by the conflict in the former Yugoslavia and by the Kosovo crisis when they drafted the text of the Temporary Protection Directive.[334] The absence of any formalised obligation of States to provide some form of international protection to persons fleeing armed conflicts or situations of generalised violence appeared all the more clearly during this period of time and it is with this protection gap in mind that the drafting process started.

Article 1 of the Temporary Protection Directive clarifies that:

> ... [t]he purpose of this Directive is to establish minimum standards for giving temporary protection in the event of a mass influx of displaced persons from third countries who are unable to return to their country of origin and to promote a balance of effort between Member States in receiving and bearing the consequences of receiving such persons.[335]

Two key criteria stand out as triggers for the activation of the Temporary Protection Directive: the concept of "mass influx" and the circumstance that return to the country of origin is impossible ("unable to return").

On the second point, Article 2(c) of the Directive clarifies that temporary protection can be triggered as a response to a situation of a mass influx or imminent mass influx of displaced persons who had to leave or have been evacuated from their country of origin and who cannot return "in safe and durable conditions" because of the situation prevailing in the country. Those persons are in particular:

> (i) persons who have fled areas of armed conflict or endemic violence;
> (ii) persons at serious risk of, or who have been the victims of, systematic or generalised violations of their human rights.[336]

---

334   Recital 6 in particular refers to conclusions adopted by the Council on 27 May 1999 whereby the Council called on the Commission and EU Member States "to learn the lessons of their response to the Kosovo crisis in order to establish the measures in accordance with the Treaty". Temporary Protection Directive, Preamble, recitals 3 and 6.
335   *Ibid.*, Article 1.
336   *Ibid.*

Armed conflicts, endemic violence and systematic or generalised violations of human rights are perceived by the drafters of the Directive as unsafe situations, precluding forcible return thereto.

As a prerequisite for the activation of the Temporary Protection Directive is the recognition by the Council that a given situation can be characterised as "mass influx" coming within the scope of the Directive. Article 5 of the Directive indicates that the Council adopts this decision by a qualified majority, on a proposal from the Commission. Member States may request the Commission to submit such proposal to the Council.[337]

The definition of what precisely is a "mass influx", in numerical terms for instance, is not provided by the Directive and given that, to date, the Temporary Protection has not yet been applied, it is only possible to speculate on what it actually encompasses. The only indication available, as to the size of a mass influx lies in Article 2(d) of the text: a mass influx is defined, rather circularly, as the arrival "of a large number of displaced persons".[338] UNHCR has called for the EU institutions to agree on what constitutes mass or large-scale displacement as "an essential first step in order to define the triggering factor for activating temporary protection".[339] UNHCR notes that what constitutes a "mass influx" is relative: it may differ from country to country, depending on the country's size and capacity.[340] There is no doubt indeed that the same group of migrants seeking asylum in Germany will not affect Germany's asylum system as it would affect Luxembourg's asylum system, were it to seek protection in the Grand Duchy.

Temporary protection is not *per se* a form of complementary protection but a tool for national asylum systems overwhelmed by massive flows of refugees, authorising them to postpone status determination until it becomes possible again to assess claims for international protection, on a case-by-case basis, through normal channels.

Under refugee law, the Geneva Convention and the Qualification Directive alike, States are obligated to process any asylum claim and determine whether the applicant meets the criteria conditioning the grant of an international

---

337   *Ibid.*, Article 5(1).
338   *Ibid.*, Article 2(d).
339   UNHCR, "Global Consultations on International Protection, Protection of Refugees in Mass Influx Situations: Overall Protection Framework" ("Protection of Refugees in Mass Influx Situations (Global Consultation)"), EC/GC/01/4, 19 February 2001, § 14.
340   *Ibid.*, § 14. I can be observed that, in UNHCR 2010 Statistical Yearbook, in the table on "major mass inflows" of refugees, UNHCR only includes arrivals of asylum of *50* refugees and more. T.A. Chabaké (Ed.) *UNHCR Statistical Yearbook 2010: Trends in Displacement, Protection and Solutions*, 10th ed. (Geneva: UNHCR, 2011), Annex, Table 18, p. 148.

protection status (refugee status or, under the Directive only, subsidiary protection). In mass influx situations however, national asylum systems might be unable to assess each and every application for international protection on an individual basis.[341] Under such circumstances, where the Council has established that a particular flow constitutes a "mass influx", EU Member States have the possibility to take exceptional measures to provide immediate and temporary protection to the displaced persons, without deciding on their individual claims yet.

In that respect, temporary protection is in full conformity with Geneva Convention Article 33 and the universal principle of *non-refoulement*: refugees, as individuals who meet the Geneva Convention definition, regardless of whether they have been recognised as such by State authorities, have a right not to be returned to a situation where their life or freedom would be under threat.

In brief, temporary protection is "a pragmatic response intended to clarify the application of the principle of *non-refoulement* in certain circumstances and to prioritise the granting of particular rights to persons arriving *en masse*".[342] Beneficiaries are indeed not merely allowed to stay on the territory of a receiving State; they have, during that time, a right to employment, housing, social welfare, emergency medical care and family unity.[343] For G.S. Goodwin-Gill and J. McAdam, the trigger mechanism for temporary protection – conditional upon a Decision of the Council[344] – carefully circumscribes temporary protection; this, the authors add, accounts for the relative generosity of temporary protection in terms of entitlements.[345]

---

341 The requirement that the assessments of applications for international protection be carried out "on an individual basis" appears explicitly in Article 4(3) of the Qualification Directive. Such requirement is however absent of the Geneva Convention. For the UNHCR, nothing in the Geneva Convention precludes it being applied in mass influx situations; it is States implementing the Convention that put in place the individualised assessment of the subjective element of fear. This individualised process has proven problematic, especially in cases of large flows of displaced persons, but the Office of the High Commissioner considers that it would generally be rendered unnecessary in large-scale situations "as being on its face self-evident from the event or situation which obviously precipitated the flight". UNHCR, "Protection of Refugees in Mass Influx Situations (Global Consultation)", *op. cit.*, §§ 17–18.

342 G.S. Goodwin-Gill and J. McAdam, *The Refugee in International Law* (2007), *op. cit.*, p. 341.

343 Temporary Protection Directive, Articles 8–16.

344 "The existence of a mass influx of displaced persons shall be established by a Council Decision adopted by a qualified majority on a proposal from the Commission, which shall also examine any request by a Member State that it submit a proposal to the Council". *Ibid.*, Article 5.

345 G.S. Goodwin-Gill and J. McAdam, *The Refugee in International Law* (2007), *op. cit.*, p. 342.

Moreover, individuals who are afforded temporary protection are left in limbo: they are safe from being returned but for a limited and unspecified period of time, until their claim is processed by the host State authorities. Article 4 of the Directive stipulates that the duration of temporary protection is one year, and can be brought to two years at a maximum, through six month period extensions.[346] In the event that the reasons for temporary protection persist, the Council may decide its extension by up to one year, by qualified majority, on a proposal by the Commission (which can be requested by a State to do so).[347] The Council can also end it at any time, under Article 6.[348]

The status enjoyed by temporary protection beneficiaries, albeit seemingly generous, appears precarious; by contrast, refugee status and subsidiary protection are granted on a permanent basis. Once it has granted refugee status or subsidiary protection, a State may revoke the corresponding status only in a limited number of situations. The Refugee Convention clarifies those reasons under an exhaustive list of cessation clauses, which were reproduced under the Qualification Directive.[349] There is a common understanding that the cessation clauses are to be interpreted restrictively;[350] the power of States to terminate refugee status or subsidiary protection is therefore regulated and rather limited.

---

346 Temporary Protection Directive, Article 4(1).
347 *Ibid.*, Article 4(2).
348 *Ibid.*, Article 6(1)(b).
349 The Refugee Convention provides that refugee status can be withdrawn when the circumstances under which status was granted have ceased to exist, unless the individual can invoke compelling reasons arising out of previous persecutions (Article 1C, paragraphs 5 and 6). As adopted in 2004, the Qualification Directive made no reference to this exception to the "ceased circumstances" cessation clauses. This lacuna was remedied with the adoption of the recast Qualification Directive providing that cessation clauses "shall not apply to a refugee who is able to invoke compelling reasons arising out of previous persecution for refusing to avail himself or herself of the protection of the country of nationality or, being a stateless person, of the country of former habitual residence". Qualification Directive, Article 11(3).
350 *See* and, for an assessment of temporary protection with regards to Convention refugee status, UNHCR, *Handbook and Guidelines on Procedures and Criteria for Determining Refugee Status under the 1951 Convention and the 1967 Protocol Relating to the Status of Refugees*, and Guidelines on Procedures and Criteria for Determining Refugee Status under the 1951 Convention and the 1967 Protocol Relating to the Status of Refugees ("*UNHCR Handbook on Procedures*"), HCR/IP/4/Eng/REV.3 (Geneva: UNHCR, 1979, reissued December 2011), § 180; S.M. Akram and T. Rempel, "Temporary Protection as an Instrument for Implementing the Right of Return for Palestinian Refugees", *Boston University International Law Journal*, Vol. 22, No. 1 (2004), pp. 1–162.

To date, the 2001 Temporary Protection Directive has not yet been activated. An analysis of when it is likely to be applied can therefore be only speculative.

At the national level, in 2009, a group of Members of Parliament in France called on the French *Assemblée Nationale* to request the European Commission to submit a proposal to the Council for the activation of the Temporary Protection Directive concerning Afghani asylum seekers. Their proposal was rejected by the *Assemblée Nationale* on the ground that "the three preconditions" for temporary protection were not met. The report indicates that the very large majority (96 percent) of persons displaced from Afghanistan lives in Pakistan and Iran. Proportionately, the report finds, the flow of Afghani asylum seekers in the EU is limited. There is therefore no "mass influx" in the EU for the purpose of the Directive.[351] Secondly, the inflows of Afghani asylum-seekers do not affect the functioning of any EU Member State.[352] Thirdly, neither the ECtHR nor the United Nations have acknowledged the existence of a situation of generalised violence of such a level of intensity in Afghanistan that it precludes returning Afghanis there.[353]

At the European level, activation of the Directive was sought in recent years, in the context of large and mixed flows of migrants reaching the external borders of the European Union, from Northern Africa and Syria especially. The "Arab Spring", that is the wave of democratic uprisings that took place in the Arab world, starting with Tunisia in December 2010, triggered governmental changes,[354] political unrest and conflicts, which have claimed many lives and led to the displacement of hundreds of thousands of people. The repercussions of the crisis in the Southern Mediterranean were soon – and are still – felt in Europe with a significant increase in the number of people seeking to enter the EU, especially from its southernmost borders. Malta and Italy, whose reception and asylum systems were particularly exposed and overwhelmed, repeatedly called for the activation of the temporary protection mechanism, including via formal exchanges of letters between their respective governments and the

---

351   C. Caresche and T. Mariani, Assemblée nationale Commission des affaires européennes, "Rapport fait au nom de la commission des affaires européennes sur la proposition de resolution (n° 2153) de Mme Sandrine Mazetier et plusieurs de ses collegues et les membres du groupe socialiste, radical, citoyen et divers gauche et apparentés, sur la Protection Temporaire", 19 janvier 2010, pp. 9–10.
352   *Ibid.*, p. 10.
353   *Ibid.*, p. 11.
354   Including the overthrow of Presidents Zine El Abidine Ben Ali in Tunisia, Mohamed Hosni Mubarak in Egypt, Ali Abdullah Saleh in Yemen and Muammar Al-Qadhafi in Libya.

Commission.³⁵⁵ In April 2011, during a debate in the presence of EU Commissioner Cecilia Malmström, Members of the European Parliament called on the European Commission to table a proposal for the EU Council to activate the solidarity mechanism envisaged by the Temporary Protection Directive, in order to give Southern Member States the means to respond to the migration flows.³⁵⁶ The European Parliament subsequently adopted a resolution in that sense, urging the EU Council to provide protection in Europe to persons displaced in the context of the humanitarian crisis in northern Africa, in accordance with the provision of the Temporary Protection Directive.³⁵⁷ None of these requests met with success insofar as the Commission did not submit a proposal to the Council. In May 2011, in response to the different calls for action, the European Commission committed to closely monitor the continuously evolving situation and stated that it "*may* decide, if the relevant conditions are met, to trigger the Temporary Protection Directive to provide immediate and temporary protection to displaced persons from third countries that are unable to return to their country of origin".³⁵⁸ In other words, at the time, the Commission did not find that the flow of migrants constituted a mass influx of displaced persons under the Directive.³⁵⁹

---

355 On the demarches undertaken by Malta and Italy before the European Commission, *see*: H. Beirens, *et al.*, *Study on the Temporary Protection Directive: Final Report* (Luxembourg: Publications Office of the European Union, 2016), pp. 126 and 131–132, retrieved from: <http://ec.europa.eu/dgs/home-affairs/e-library/documents/policies/asylum/temporary-protection/docs/final_report_evaluation_tpd_en.pdf> [10/11/2016].

356 The minutes of the debate are available on the European Parlimanent website: European Parliament, "EU Response to the Migration Flows in North Africa and the Southern Mediterranean, in Particular, in Lampedusa – Migration Flows Arising from Instability: Scope and Role of EU Foreign Policy (Debate)", Debates of the European Parliament, CRE 04/04/2011 – 19, 04/04/2011, at: <http://www.europarl.europa.eu/sides/getDoc.do?pubRef=-//EP//NONSGML+CRE+20110404+SIT+DOC+PDF+V0//EN&language=EN> [29/09/2016]. *See* also "Migrant Landings in Southern Europe: European Commission Should Activate Solidarity Mechanism – Simon Busuttil and Salvatore Iacolino (MEPs)", *Press Release* (EPP Group in the European Parliament, 2011), retrieved from: <http://arc.eppgroup.eu/press/showpr.asp?prcontroldoctypeid=1&prcontrolid=10235&prcontentid=17340&prcontentlg=en> [29/09/2016].

357 European Parliament, Resolution of 5 April 2011 on Migration Flows Arising from Instability: Scope and Role of EU Foreign Policy 2010/2269(INI), § 26.

358 European Commission, "Communication from the Commission to the European Parliament, the Council, the Economic and Social Committee and the Committee of the Regions on Migration", COM (2011) 248 final, 4 May 2011, p. 6 [emphasis added].

359 EU Commissionner Cecilia Malmström had already made this point clear after the debate in the European Parliament in April 2011: "At this point we cannot see a mass influx

A month before the European Commission, the Parliamentary Assembly of the Council of Europe had stated, in a resolution of April 2011, that:

> If a mass exodus of Libyan refugees occurs because of increasing terror by Colonel Gaddafi or the emergence of a civil war, the Assembly encourages the European Union member states to consider applying the temporary protection directive.[360]

It is possible to infer *a contrario* from the above resolution that the Parliamentary Assembly had made the same analysis of the situation as the EU institutions and found that the flow of migrants reaching the southernmost border of Europe from Libya did not constitute, at the time the Resolution was adopted, a "mass exodus" or, under EU law, a "mass influx", calling for the activation of the Temporary Protection Directive.

In November 2014, the question was raised in the context of Syrian refugee crisis. E. Gardini, Italian Member of the European Parliament, submitted a written question to the European Commission. Recalling that more than 3 million people had been displaced in the context of the armed conflict in Syria, E. Gardini enquired whether the arrival of displaced persons from Syria into the EU could constitute a "mass influx" and therefore justify that the Commission invoke Article 5 of the Temporary Protection Directive.[361] And indeed, in view of the scale of displacement triggered by the Syrian conflict, the question appeared legitimate. As mentioned above, in May 2011, the Commission rejected the qualification of "mass influx" concerning the arrivals of people (mostly Tunisians, Libyans, Somalis, Eritreans and Sudanese[362]) crossing the

---

of migrants to Europe even though some of our member states are under severe pressure. The temporary mechanism is one tool that could be used in the future, if necessary, but we have not yet reached that situation". C. Malmström, "Debate on Migration Flows", © European Union, 1995–2016, 06 April 2011, retrieved from the website of the European Commission at: <http://ec.europa.eu/archives/commission_2010-2014/blogs/malmstrom/page/26/index.html> [26/09/2016].

360 PACE, "Resolution 1805 (2011), the Large-Scale Arrival of Irregular Migrants, Asylum Seekers and Refugees on Europe's Southern Shores", 14 April 2011, § 14; PACE Committee on Migration, Refugees and Population, "Report to the Committee on Migration, Refugees and Population: The Large-Scale Arrival of Irregular Migrants, Asylum Seekers and Refugees on Europe's Southern Shores", Doc. 12581, 13 April 2011.

361 European Parliament, "Application of Directive 2001/55/EC: Question for Written Answer Submitted to the Commission by MEP Elisabetta Gardini under Rule 130", E-008507-14, 29/10/2014.

362 European Commission, "2011 Communication on Migration", *op. cit.*, p. 5.

Mediterranean, from Tunisia and Libya, and reaching the shores of Malta and Italy. According to Eurostat, taken together, these asylum applications amounted to 9 500 from January to April 2011.[363] On the other hand, the number of Syrians who had applied for asylum in 2014, at the time MEP E. Gardini submitted her question to the Commission, was about ten times more.[364] The Commission however replied in the negative to both aspects of the question:

> According to Eurostat statistics, almost 100 000 Syrians have applied for asylum in the EU between January and October 2014. In view of the scale of the influx and the manner in which these persons' asylum applications have been handled, the Commission considers that a proposal to trigger the EU-wide temporary protection regime provided by the TPD would not be justified in the present circumstances.[365]

With a view to understanding the reasons for the non-implementation of the Temporary Protection Directive and to assessing its actual relevance to contemporary issues, the European Commission commissioned a study on the Directive, published in January 2016. The authors analyse the lack of a clear-cut definition of what constitutes a "mass influx" under the Directive as both a strength – a flexible definition can potentially cover a broad array of situations – and a weakness – EU stakeholders may have diverging interpretations and fail to agree to activate the Directive in a given situation, whether it is due to the Commission denying a request by a State or to the lack of qualified majority within the Council.[366]

---

363 Calculation made on the basis of Eurostat statistics. A. Bitoulas, "Asylum Applicants and First Instance Decisions on Asylum Applications: Second Quarter 2011", 03 February 2012, © European Union, 1995–2012, *Eurostat: Statistics in focus*, Table 2, p. 5, retrieved from the website of the European Commission – Eurostat at: <http://ec.europa.eu/eurostat/documents/3433488/5584484/KS-SF-12-011-EN.PDF/f52d2b8c-a888-42eb-b9a3-a71b434125d1> [06/09/2016].

364 According to Eurostat data, 93 515 Syrian citizens have applied for asylum in the EU from January to October 2015. A. Bitoulas, "Asylum Applicants and First Instance Decisions on Asylum Applications: 2014" ("Eurostat: Data in focus 3/2015"), March 2015, © European Union, 2015, *Eurostat: Data in focus*, Table 2, p. 5, retrieved from the website of the European Commission – Eurostat at: <http://ec.europa.eu/eurostat/documents/4168041/6742650/KS-QA-15-003-EN-N.pdf/b7786ec9-1ad6-4720-8a1d-430fcfc55018> [01/10/2016].

365 European Parliament, "Answer Given by Mr Avramopoulos on Behalf of the Commission (Question E-008507/2014)", 28 January 2015.

366 For an analysis of the strenghts and weaknesses of the Temporary Protection Directive, *see*: H. Beirens, *et al.*, "Study on the Temporary Protection Directive: Final Report" (Luxembourg:

A number of reasons have been identified for the non-implementation of the Temporary Protection Directive. Firstly, the cumbersome activation procedure would make the mechanism unfit to provide emergency responses in crisis situations, including a swift relief to affected asylum systems.[367] Secondly, many Member States appear to fear that the grant of temporary protection under the Directive might constitute a pull factor for migration towards the EU.[368] Thirdly, the absence of an objective and clear definition of activation criteria gives way to varying interpretations, potentially imbued with political considerations. Member States who are not directly affected might fail to see the urgency of a given situation – if not be reluctant to share the burden with receiving States.[369] Achieving the required qualified majority in the Council might therefore prove difficult.[370] A fourth reason pertains to facts: according to the Commission, the EU has not yet been confronted with an inflow of displaced persons of such a scale that it reached the Directive's "mass influx" threshold.[371]

As of now, it is unclear how and to which situations the Directive may apply. In the hypothesis where it were to be activated, it should be borne in mind that the protection it will provide will be – quite obviously so – temporary only, until the examination of claims for international protection (refugee status and subsidiary protection) under standard asylum procedures becomes possible. The granting and content of refugee status and subsidiary protection, regulated under EU law in the Qualification Directive, are the focus of the following developments.

Publications Office of the European Union, 2016), retrieved from: <http://ec.europa.eu/dgs/home-affairs/e-library/documents/policies/asylum/temporary-protection/docs/final_report_evaluation_tpd_en.pdf> [10/11/2016].

367 *Ibid.*, pp. 19–23 and 126.
368 M. Ineli-Ciger (2015), *op. cit.*, pp. 233–235.
369 Malta, Italy and like-minded States and observers have deplored the lack of solidarity among EU Member States.
370 According to Maltese MEP Simon Busuttil, the Commission invoked the absence of majority among Member States to justify that it did not submit a proposal for the activation of the Directive to the Council. European Parliament, "Debate on the Conclusions of the European Council meeting (24–25 March 2011)", Debates of the European Parliament, 5 April 2011, p. 35 at: <http://www.europarl.europa.eu/sides/getDoc.do?pubRef=-//EP//NONSGML+CRE+20110405+SIT+DOC+PDF+V0//EN&language=EN> [20/09/2016].
371 H. Beirens, *et al.*, "Study on the Temporary Protection Directive: Final Report" (2016), *op. cit.*, p. 132; "Debate on the Conclusions of the European Council meeting (24–25 March 2011)", *op. cit.*, p. 35.

III The Qualification Directive

With the entry into force of the Treaty of Amsterdam,[372] the European Union became competent to adopt measures concerning refugees and asylum generally. The Tampere European Council Conclusions spelled out which measures the Union should adopt according to the timetable set in the Treaty of Amsterdam[373] to the end of creating a Common European Asylum System (CEAS).[374] The first stage of the creation of the CEAS involved the adoption of common minimum standards concerning the determination of the State responsible for examining an asylum application, asylum procedures, conditions of reception of asylum seekers, and the grant and content of refugee status and of subsidiary forms of protection.[375] It is on the latter of those so-called "first-phase instruments",[376] the Qualification Directive, that the present work will focus, insofar as it defined common criteria for the identification of persons in need of international protection within the European Union. Even more specifically, for this Part's purpose of identifying the forms of protection available within the EU for persons fleeing indiscriminate threats, Qualification Directive provisions establishing and spelling out a harmonised form of complementary protection ("subsidiary protection") are the most relevant and will therefore constitute the focus of the following developments. Since its adoption in 2004,[377] the Qualification Directive has been recast, as part of the second phase of the development of the CEAS, with the objective of achieving higher standards of protection and ensuring their consistent application

---

372 Amsterdam Treaty.
373 Article 63 of the TEC in its consolidated Amsterdam version provided for the adoption by the Council of measures in the field of asylum within a period of five years after the entry into force of the Treaty of Amsterdam. This timetable was globally respected with the exception of the Asylum Procedures Directive: after lengthy negotiations in the Council, the required unanimity of the Council's Members was eventually reached and the Asylum Procedures Directive adopted in December 2005. TEC (1997), Article 63; H. Ragheboom (2009), *op. cit.*, pp. 189–190.
374 "Tampere Conclusions", *op. cit.*, §§ 13–17.
375 *Ibid.*, § 14.
376 See for example European Commission, "Commission Staff Working Document Accompanying the Proposal for a Directive of the European Parliament and of the Council on Minimum Standards for the Qualification and Status of Third Country Nationals or Stateless Persons as Beneficiaries of International Protection and the Content of the Protection Granted: Impact Assessment" ("Commission Impact Assessment – Proposal for a Recast QD"), SEC (2009) 1373 final, 14863/09 ADD 1 ASILE 81 CODEC 1224, 21 October 2009.
377 Qualification Directive (2004).

across the EU.[378] To ensure that the revision of first-phase legislation be useful, the Hague Programme provided for a mandatory review of those instruments, as an intermediate step before the Commission prepares its proposals for recast, "second phase", instruments. On the basis of the information it had collected from various reports, studies, academic publications and commentaries by UNHCR and civil society stakeholders on the transposition and implementation of the Directive, the Commission proposed amendments to the first-phase Directive, intended to remedy the identified deficiencies of the text.[379] This specific, "experimentalist",[380] form of governance that includes *inter alia* the recursive revision of the legislative instrument concerned in the light of its results is an important feature of EU policy-making in the field of asylum (and of Justice and Home Affairs generally): it warrants (or has the potential to do so) the flexibility of EU asylum policy and the adaptability of its objectives and instruments to evolving challenges and circumstances.[381] The evolution of the Qualification Directive text indeed demonstrates that EU legislation can effectively evolve and take due account, in so doing, of the criticisms formulated against it and of the shortcomings identified through a review of its implementation. An example of the positive effect of this form of experimentalist governance on the Qualification Directive is the approximation of the contents of refugee and subsidiary protection statuses,[382] which was welcome

---

378 European Commission, "Report from the Commission to the European Parliament and the Council on the Application of Directive 2004/83/EC of 29 April 2004 on Minimum Standards for the Qualification and Status of Third Country Nationals or Stateless Persons as Refugees or as Persons Who Otherwise Need International Protection and the Content of the Protection" ("Commission Report on the application of QD (2004)"), COM (2010)314 final, 16/06/2010, p. 3.

379 *Ibid*; and "Commission Impact Assessment – Proposal for a Recast QD", *op. cit.*

380 For an analysis of EU governance in the field of Justice and Home Affairs in particular, see J. Monar, "Experimentalist Governance in Justice and Home Affairs", *in* C.F. Sabel and J. Zeitlin (Eds.), *Experimentalist Governance in the European Union: Towards a New Architecture* (Oxford: Oxford University Press, 2010).

381 J. Monar analyses EU governance in the field of Justice and Home Affairs (including asylum). He observes that its can be categorised as "functionally 'experimentalist'" insofar as it provides for "a higher degree of flexibility, a less hierarchical approach, and – above all – adaptability of targets and instruments". J. Monar clarifies the concept of experimentalist governance by pinpointing its key elements. Accordingly, there are four of them: "the establishment of framework objectives; strong input of 'lower-level' units (national and sub-national) into the way objectives are pursued; reporting, monitoring and peer review of results; and recursive revision of objectives in the light of these results". *Ibid.*

382 Qualification Directive, Recital 39 and Chapter VII: "Content of International Protection", Articles 20 to 35.

in international protection circles, who had advocated it. All beneficiaries of international protection under the recast Qualification Directive are entitled to the same rights and freedoms. It remains to be seen however whether the different amendment brought by the revision of the Directive will suffice to remedy the different shortcomings identified during the first five years of its operation.

These points will be developed below. After a presentation of the background of the Qualification Directive and, in particular, of the regime it creates of subsidiary protection, and an overview of the EU international protection system hence devised (A), developments will focus on those provisions of the Directive that describe the three categories of "serious harm" associated with the grant of subsidiary protection, namely Article 15 provisions. Article 15 (a) and (b), refer to the prohibitions of the death penalty and of torture and inhuman or degrading treatments and punishments. They broadly reflect Member States human rights obligations. *Non-refoulement* obligations under international human rights law will be the focus of the following chapter[383] and Article 15 (a) and (b) will therefore be discussed here briefly only and jointly (B). By contrast, Article 15 (c) reflects State practice of providing protection from return to persons fleeing conflict situations; it is more innovative but also controversial and will therefore be discussed in greater depth (C). To conclude this part, the impact of the Qualification Directive on Member States' asylum practices will be examined in the light of the Directive's initial objective of creating a level playing field[384] with respect, in particular, to the qualification of beneficiaries of international protection (D).

---

383   *See* Chapter 3 on "Relevant provisions of international human rights law", p. 174s.

384   In 2010, in the process of recasting the Qualification Directive, the Commission recalls in those terms (*i.e.* in full: "the creation of a level playing field with respect to the qualification and status of beneficiaries of international protection and to the content of the protection granted") the original objective pursued by the European Union creating the Common European Asylum System. At the time the Commission presented its initial proposal for the adoption of the first phase Qualification Directive, this objective was rather described as "harmonisation". *See* European Commission, "Commission Report on the application of QD (2004)", *op. cit.*, p. 15; compare with EU Commission, "Proposal for a Council Directive on Minimum Standards for the Qualification and Status of Third Country Nationals and Stateless Persons as Refugees or as Persons Who Otherwise Need International Protection, Explanatory Memorandum" ("Explanatory Memorandum – QD (2004)"), COM (2001) 510 final, 12 September 2001.

A Background and Overview of the Directive

The text of the Qualification Directive as it was eventually adopted and as it stands today – after it was recast[385] – is the fruit of discussions that had been ongoing in Europe since the 1970s, on the necessity to harmonise national asylum rules and practices for the protection of recognised refugees but also of other persons in need of international protection (1). An overview of the international protection regime devised by the Directive will follow (2).

Prior to entering the discussion on the subject matter, a remark needs be made. Hereinafter, regard will often be had to UNHCR comments or recommendations. UNHCR's interpretation and opinions on the Qualification Directive (or on EU asylum law in general) are not *per se* binding upon EU Member States however, they are of utmost relevance and importance. As highlighted by UNHCR itself, the Qualification Directive "goes to the heart of UNHCR's international protection mandate":[386] Article 8 of UNHCR's Statute indeed calls upon the High Commissioner to provide for the protection of refugees *inter alia* by "promoting the conclusion and ratification of international conventions for the protection of refugees, *supervising their application and proposing amendments thereto*".[387] European Union law too has long recognised the supervisory responsibility of UNHCR: Declaration 17 of the Treaty of Amsterdam provided that, for the purpose of the adoption by the Council of measures on asylum, "[c]onsultations shall be established with the United Nations High Commissioner for Refugees (...) on matters relating to asylum policy".[388] UNHCR's views were indeed taken into account by the drafters of the Qualification Directive. The European Commission explains that, in this context, besides the Refugee Convention itself, UNHCR's Handbook on Procedures[389] as well

---

385 The recast Qualification Directive was adopted by the European Parliament and the Council on 13 December 2011. Some important modifications were made, intended to remedy the deficiencies identified during the first years of operation of the Directive although, for the purpose of the present work, they are not major: the criteria for refugee status and subsidiary protection remained unaltered. Among other changes brought through the legislative amendment of the Qualification Directive, the most relevant to this work is perhaps the approximation of both international protection statuses (*see* Qualification Directive, Recital 39.) This will be briefly discussed again below in "4. Harmonisation: a long way ahead", p. 168.

386 UNHCR, *Asylum in the European Union: A Study of the Implementation of the Qualification Directive* (Geneva: UNHCR, November 2007), p. 7.

387 Statute of the Office of the United Nations High Commissionner for Refugees ("UNHCR Statute"), 14 December 1950 UNGA Res 428 (V), Article 8 [emphasis added].

388 Amsterdam Treaty, Declaration 17.

389 UNHCR, *Handbook on Procedures, op. cit.*

as conclusions issued by UNHCR Executive Committee served as "sources of reference".³⁹⁰ The Qualification Directive in facts also refers to the High Commissioner for Refugees: it encourages Member States to consult with UNHCR for valuable guidance when determining refugee status, and to turn to it – and to the European Asylum Support Office – for up-to-date information on asylum seekers' countries of origin.³⁹¹ For all the above reasons, it should come as no surprise that UNHCR comments and recommendations on the Qualification Directive are oft cited below. The Commission also consulted, in addition to Member States and UNHCR, "expert non-governmental organisations in the field such as the European Council on Refugees and Exiles (ECRE) and Amnesty International, specialised non-governmental organisations such as the European Women's Lobby and Save the Children, academic experts such as the ODYSSEUS academic network for legal studies on immigration and asylum in Europe, and representatives of the judiciary such as the International Association of Refugee Law Judges".³⁹² ECRE's studies and views in particular but also academic work will also be taken into consideration in the following developments. This clarification being made, let us now turn to addressing the background and substance of the Qualification Directive.

1   Background of the Qualification Directive and Impetus for the Harmonisation of National Asylum Rules and Practices

In 1976, more than two decades after the United Nations Convention Relating to the Status of Refugees entered into force,³⁹³ the Parliamentary Assembly of the Council of Europe acknowledged that there were, within its Member States, a "considerable number of persons" who, although they were not recognised as refugees under the Geneva Convention, were "unable or unwilling for political, racial, religious or other valid reasons to return to their countries of origin (*de facto* refugees)".³⁹⁴ In view of their number and of their often precarious situation, the Parliamentary Assembly therefore recommended States to draft an instrument that would ensure a uniform treatment of *de*

---

390   "Explanatory Memorandum – QD (2004)", *op. cit.*, p. 5. *See* also: EU Council, "Opinion of the Legal Service", 10560/02 ASILE 34 JUR 247, 10 July 2002, p. 7, endorsing UNHCR's view on the respective objects and purposes of temporary protection and subsidiary protection.

391   Qualification Directive, Recital 22 and Article 8(2).

392   "Explanatory Memorandum – QD (2004)", *op. cit.*, p. 3.

393   The Refugee Convention (*op. cit.*), adopted 28 July 1951, entered into force 22 April 1954.

394   PACE, "Recommendation 773 (1976) on the Situation of *de Facto* Refugees", 26 January 1976, § 1.

facto refugees in the Council of Europe Member States;[395] to this end, Member States were encourages to extend, as much as possible, the applicability of the Refugee Convention articles to *de facto* refugees who should be granted access to, among others, employment and vocational training, housing, and social security.[396] Their right to non-*refoulement* should additionally be affirmed.[397] This 1976 recommendation was the first of a long series of repeated calls by the Council of Europe for a harmonised approach to *de facto* refugee protection.[398] States' awareness of the necessity to define a common regime for failed refugee claimants rose, albeit slowly, and was reinforced by the growing realisation of the relevance of international human rights law in asylum cases. In that sense, in 1994, the Executive Committee of the United Nations High Commissioner for Refugees (ExCom), taking note of the fact that States generally perceived the grant of international protection to persons fleeing armed conflict situations, whether or not they qualify for refugee status under the Convention, as their "humanitarian responsibility",[399] pinpointed States' failure to fully implement their obligations under international law:

> The protection accorded in these countries to persons who are not deemed to be refugees under the 1951 Convention is normally granted as a sovereign humanitarian act, or as a duty under national law (including constitutional provisions), without reference to international legal obligations. It should be noted however that many of these countries are parties to other international instruments that could be invoked in certain circumstances against the return of some non-Convention refugees to a place where their lives, freedom or other fundamental rights would [be] in jeopardy.[400]

UNHCR Executive Committee hence indicated that rather than a mere possibility to discretionarily grant some form of protection to failed refugee claimants, States would actually have, in certain circumstances, an obligation under

---

395 *Ibid.*, §§ 2–4.
396 *Ibid.*, § 5.
397 *Ibid.*, §§ 5 (I.b.) and 5 (II.ii.).
398 See for instance: PACE, "Recommendation 1327 (1997) on the Protection and Reinforcement of the Human Rights of Refugees and Asylum-Seekers in Europe", 24 April 1997; PACE, "Recommendation 1525 (2001) on the United Nations High Commissioner for Refugees and the Fiftieth Anniversary of the Geneva Convention" ("PACE"), 27 June 2001.
399 UNHCR, "Note on International Protection (Submitted by the High Commissioner)" ("Note on International Protection (1994)"), A/AC.96/830, 7 September 1994, § 40.
400 *Ibid.*

relevant norms of international human rights law not to return those persons. The Executive Committee goes on and expressly refers to the principle of non-*refoulement* enshrined in Article 3 of the Convention Against Torture and Other Cruel, Inhuman or Degrading Treatment or Punishment (CAT), and in Article 3 of the European Convention for the Protection of Human Rights and Fundamental Freedoms (ECHR).[401] This observation made by UNHCR confirms and elaborates on the recommendation issued a few months earlier by the Parliamentary Assembly of the Council of Europe who had underlined that States' asylum obligations under international law did not solely emanate from the 1951 Geneva Convention but also from the Convention for the Protection of Human Rights and Fundamental Freedoms, and inferred from this in particular protection obligations towards persons who do not necessarily qualify as refugees under the Geneva Convention.[402]

The answer to the pleas voiced by the Council of Europe Parliamentary Assembly, UNHCR and in international protection literature[403] eventually came from the European Union in the form of a directive. The initiative falls to the Danish Delegation in the Council of the European Union (EU) who, in 1997, called for the harmonisation of "subsidiary protection" which it deemed both natural and necessary for considerations of "due process of law, of counteracting 'forum shopping' and of the derived effect in relation to the associated and candidate countries".[404] Soon after, a note was issued by the Netherlands Presidency, which stressed that Article 3 ECHR in particular

---

401 *Ibid.*
402 Parliamentary Assembly of the Council of Europe, Recommendation 1236 (1994) on the Right of Asylum, 12 April 1994, 8(iii).
403 A number of authors acknowledged the existence of "*de facto* refugees" and the necessity to address their genuine need of international protection. *See* for example: A. Paludan, "Refugees in Europe", *International Migration Review* (The Center for Migration Studies of New York, Inc.), Vol. 15, No. 1/2 (1981), pp. 69–73, pp. 71–72; J.F. Thomas, "Refugees: A New Approach", *International Migration Review* (The Center for Migration Studies of New York, Inc.), Vol. 15, No. 1/2 (1981), pp. 20–25, p. 22; A. Grahl-Madsen, "Identifying the World's Refugees", *Annals of the American Academy of Political and Social Science* (Sage Publications, Inc. in association with the American Academy of Political and Social Science), Vol. 467 (May 1983), pp. 11–23; G.S. Goodwin-Gill, "*Non-Refoulement* and the New Asylum Seekers", *in* D.A. Martin (Ed.), *The New Asylum Seekers: Refugee Law in the 1980's, the Ninth Sokol Colloquium on International Law* (Dodrecht: Martinus Nijhoff Publishers, 1988), pp. 103–122.
404 EU Council, "Note from the Danish Delegation to the Asylum and Migration Working Parties: Subsidiary Protection", 6764/97 ASIM 52, 17/03/1997; as cited in EU Council, "Note from the General Secretariat of the Council to Migration and Asylum Working Parties: Summary of Replies Concerning the National Instruments of Protection Falling Outside

provided a legal basis for the protection of people falling outside the scope of the Refugee Convention.[405] To follow up this Danish-Dutch initiative, the Council of the European Union invited Member States to respond to a questionnaire about their existing "national, alternative instruments of protection".[406] In so doing, the Council clearly undertook to apprehend and harmonise States' complementary protection practices. Precisely, discussions centred around the concept of "subsidiary protection", that was defined in a 1998 note from the Austrian Presidency as:

> ... protection for persons from third states who do not fall within the scope of the Geneva Convention but who still have need of some other form of international protection.[407]

It appears that the persons identified as worthy of subsidiary protection in the framework of the harmonisation process undertaken by the Council are also those whose distressing situation had caused international protection circles to call for a harmonised, binding regime of complementary protection in Europe. The Presidency further elaborates on the concept of subsidiary protection and clarifies the scope of the prospected instrument: it is intended to cover situations where applicants do not fulfil the criteria for refugee status as defined under the Refugee Convention but where the principle of *non-refoulement* should apply, either under the Refugee Convention (*i.e.* when a "[Refugee] Convention-like ground" exists), or on humanitarian grounds, in the light of the general situation in the country of origin.[408] The scope of subsidiary protection is defined even more clearly by contrasting it with that of temporary protection. The Presidency Note indicates that the two forms of protection should be distinguished for the following reason:

> Whilst subsidiary protection is granted to persons needing protection following an examination of individual circumstances, temporary

---

the Scope of the Geneva Convention – Subsidiary Protection" ("Summary of replies – subsidiary protection"), 13667/97 ASIM 267, 6 January 1998, p. 1.

405 EU Council, "Note from the Presidency to the Asylum and Migration Working Group: Implication of Article 3 of the European Convention on Human Rights for the Expulsion of Illegally Resident Third Country Nationals", 7779/97 ASIM 89, 28 April 1997; cited in EU Council, "Note from the Presidency to the Asylum Working Party: Subsidiary Protection" ("1999 Note from the Austrian Presidency"), 6246/99 ASILE 7, 23 Feburary 1999, at 2.
406 "Summary of replies – subsidiary protection", *op. cit.*, p. 1.
407 "1999 Note from the Austrian Presidency", *op. cit*; cited in *ibid.*, at 3.
408 *Ibid.*

protection is usually taken to mean any form of protection granted in the event of a mass refugee movement to members of a particular group of persons needing protection, independently of an examination of each individual case.[409]

The distinction is hence made clear between temporary protection, as an "emergency of provisional device",[410] whose application is triggered in mass influx situations[411] and subsidiary protection, as a "response by States to individual asylum seekers who cannot be removed by virtue of the extended principle of non-refoulement under international law".[412]

The replies to the aforementioned questionnaires were summarised by the General Secretariat of the Council who observed that all the (then) fifteen Member States provided "some kind of subsidiary protection for asylum seekers who do not fall within the scope of the Geneva Convention" and confirmed the absence of a uniform approach among them.[413] Commentators assessed European State practice as being characterised by "highly varied *ad hoc* responses, premised largely on executive discretions".[414] In France for instance, a 1998 law had created a new form of protection, additional to refugee status and Constitutional asylum (*asile constitutionnel*, granted to "freedom fighters"), on the basis, in particular, of Article 3 of the European Convention for Human Rights (ECHR). So-called "territorial asylum" (*asile territorial*) was devised to protect aliens who could establish that removal to their country of origin would expose them to threats to their life or freedom, or to treatments prohibited by Article 3 of the ECHR.[415] Broad as it may seem, the effectiveness of the provision is however substantially impaired in the following, one sentence long, paragraph of the Article providing that the decision, which belongs

---

409 "1999 Note from the Austrian Presidency", *op. cit*; cited in *ibid.*, at 3.
410 R. Mandal, *Protection Mechanisms Outside of the 1951 Convention ("Complementary Protection")* (June 2005), *op. cit.*, p. 3.
411 The concept of temporary protection was developed with the adoption in 2001 of the Temporary Protection Directive. Above pp. 93s.
412 J. McAdam, *Complementary Protection in International Refugee Law* (2007), *op. cit.*, p. 3.
413 "Summary of replies – subsidiary protection", *op. cit.*, p. 3.
414 H. Storey, "Complementary Protection: Should There Be a Common Approach to Providing Protection to Persons Who Are Not Covered by the 1951 Geneva Convention?", paper prepared for the Joint ILPA/IARLJ Symposium, 6 December 1999 (1999).
415 The Article entered into force on 12 May 1998 and was abrogated on 1 January 2004. France: Loi n° 52–893 relative au droit d'asile of 25 July 1952 [27 July 1952] *JORF*, p. 7642 amended by Loi no 98–349 relative à l'entrée et au séjour des étrangers en France et au droit d'asile of 11 May 1998 [12 May 1998] *JORF n°109*, p. 7087, Article 13.

not to an asylum administrative or judicial authority but to the Minister of the Interior, "needs not be motivated".[416] Territorial asylum was hence an "arbitrarily defined"[417] form of protection; additionally, the fact that its granting was entrusted with the Ministry of the Interior, rather than the OFPRA (already existing at the time), most likely accounts for it being a very residual only form of protection granted.[418] In the United Kingdom, as in most EU Member States, the Home Office has made it a practice not to return foreign nationals to regions or countries "where war is raging or uncontrolled violence is endemic".[419] A 2009 case reveals that for many years (and until 2008), a "departmental operational enforcement manual" was in force that provided that enforcement action "should not be taken against Nationals who originate from countries which are currently active war zones".[420] From a broader perspective, a 1999 report by the European Council on Refugees and Exiles (ECRE) showed that the then fifteen Member States of the European Union provided complementary protection to persons fleeing armed conflict and/or serious human rights violations.[421]

In October 1999, the drafting process was given impetus by the European Council who held in Tampere a special meeting on the creation, called for by the treaty of Amsterdam,[422] of an area of freedom, security and justice in the European Union. The Presidency Conclusions recalled that from its very beginning, European integration had been rooted in a "shared commitment to freedom based on human rights, democratic institutions and the rule of law", three values which are keys to securing peace and developing prosperity in

---

416   *Ibid.*, Article 13.
417   V. Zederman, "The French Reading of Subsidiary Protection", *in Convention Refugee Status and Subsidiary Protection Working Party: First Report*, IARLJ 7th World Conference, Held in Mexico City, November 2006, p. 30.
418   *Ibid.*, p. 18.
419   United Kingdom: EWCA (Civil Division), *Secretary of State for the Home Department v. HH (Iraq)* ("HH"), [2009] EWCA Civ 727, 14 July 2009, § 6. See also United Kingdom: EWCA, *QD (Iraq) v. Secretary of State for the Home Department; AH (Iraq) v. Secretary of State for the Home Department* ("QD & AH v Secretary of State for the Home Department"), [2009] EWCA Civ 620, 24 June 2009, § 21.
420   The operational enforcement manual is cited in EWCA, *HH*, 14 July 2009, *op. cit.*, § 1 (for the provision of paragraph 12.3 cited above) and § 4 (for § 12.3 of the manual in full).
421   For an overview of ECRE's 1999 findings, see the synoptic table provided by UNHCR in its submissions to the UK Court of Appeal in the *QD & AH* case cited above in note 504. EWCA, *QD & AH v Secretary of State for the Home Department*, 24 June 2009, *op. cit.*, Submissions by UNHCR, Annexure 1, pp. 640–642.
422   TEU (1997), Article 63.

the EU and fundamental for the enlarging of the Union.[423] The Conclusions observed with satisfaction that the "major ingredients of a shared area of prosperity and peace" had already been put in place for EU citizens but deplored that regarding this freedom "which includes the right to move freely throughout the Union" as the "exclusive preserve" of the Union's citizens thus denying it to those "whose circumstances lead them justifiably to seek access to the [EU] territory" would be "in contradiction with Europe's traditions". From this, the European Council inferred the obligation for the Union to develop common policies on asylum and immigration, based on principles which are clear to EU citizens and offer guarantees to those who seek protection in or access to the European Union.[424]

Of particular relevance for the present discussion is the intention expressed by the Tampere European Council to achieve "an open and secure European Union, fully committed to the obligations of the 1951 Refugee Convention and other relevant human rights instruments, and able to respond to humanitarian needs on the basis of solidarity"[425] in particular through the establishment of a Common European Asylum System (CEAS), based on the full and inclusive application of the Geneva Convention, thus ensuring that nobody is sent back to persecution, *i.e.* maintaining the principle of non-*refoulement*.[426] According to the Tampere Conclusions, the CEAS should include not only rules on the recognition and content of refugee status but also "measures on subsidiary forms of protection offering an appropriate status to any person in need of such protection", adopted by the Council on the basis of Commission proposals.[427]

In 2001, the Commission, integrating the continuous developments which had occurred in the European Union in relation to subsidiary forms of protection since the 1997 Danish Delegation Note, submitted to the Council a proposal for a directive on minimum standards for the qualification and status of third country nationals and stateless persons as refugees or as persons who otherwise need international protection.[428] In drafting its proposal, the Commission drew from the "disparate Member State systems" – which it found to be partly based on the case-law of the European Court of Human Rights

---

423 "Tampere Conclusions", *op. cit.*, § 1.
424 *Ibid.*, §§ 2–3.
425 *Ibid.*, § 4.
426 *Ibid.*, § 13.
427 *Ibid.*, § 14.
428 "Proposal for a Council Directive on Minimum Standards for the Qualification and Status of Third Country Nationals and Stateless Persons as Refugees or as Persons Who Otherwise Need International Protection" ("Commission Proposal QD (2004)"), COM (2001) 510 final, 12/09/2001.

and general principles of international humanitarian law – and attempted to "adopt and adapt the best ones".[429] The adopted text of the Qualification Directive is largely based on the Commission proposal and broadly reproduces the asylum regime the Commission had drafted.[430]

2 Overview of the International Protection Regime Devised by the Directive

The adopted Qualification Directive[431] elaborates on the two regimes of international protection available within the European Union that are refugee status and subsidiary protection. The Directive makes clear that its refugee definition is based on the Refugee Convention and Protocol[432] which "provide the cornerstone of the international legal regime for the protection of refugees".[433] As a matter of fact, the Qualification Directive refugee definition "broadly reflects"[434] the corresponding provision of the Refugee Convention.[435] One main distinction is however often put forward in literature: whereas the Refugee Convention applies to any person who is outside his or her country of origin and stateless persons,[436] the benefit of refugee status under the Qualification Directive is instead limited to third-country nationals only.[437] This is in direct line with Protocol 24 on asylum for nationals of Member States of the European Union, annexed to the Treaty on the Functioning of the EU. This

---

429 *Ibid.*, Explanatory Memorandum, p. 6.
430 More detailed comments on the *travaux préparatoires* and on the successive modifications of the text that preceded the adoption of the Qualification Directive will be made, if the need arises, when specific provisions are discussed.
431 Qualification Directive (2004). The Qualification Directive has since been recast. Unless otherwise indicated, reference will be made hereinafter to the text of the Qualification Directive in its current consolidated version of 20/12/2011.
432 Protocol Relating to the Status of RefugeesProtocol Relating to the Status of Refugees, 30 January 1967 [1967] *UNTS* Vol. 606, p. 267.
433 Qualification Directive, Recital 4 (ex Recital 3).
434 M.T. Gil-Bazo, "Refugee Status, Subsidiary Protection, and the Right to Be Granted Asylum under EC Law", *UNHCR Research Papers*, November 2006, No. 136 (2006), p. 9.
435 The same is not true of provisions concerning the content of the status granted. Hélène Lambert observes in that respect that "not one sentence from the Refugee Convention on the issue of the content of international protection has been reproduced in the Directive". The author cites among others the freedom to practise religion, on which the Directive is silent. H. Lambert, "The EU Asylum Qualification Directive, Its Impact on the Jurisprudence of the United Kingdom and International Law", *International & Comparative Law Quarterly*, Vol. 55 (January 2006), pp. 161–192, p. 178.
436 Refugee Convention, Article 1(A)2.
437 Qualification Directive, Articles 1 and 2.

Protocol, initially added by the Treaty of Amsterdam, contains a sole article to the effect that, within the European Union, the right to asylum is in principle for third-country nationals only.[438] The article states in particular:

> Given the level of protection of fundamental rights and freedoms by the Member States of the European Union, Member States shall be regarded as constituting safe countries of origin in respect of each other for all legal and practical purposes in relation to asylum matters.[439]

The provision has ever since attracted much criticism. Accordingly, a "certificate of democracy" and a presumption of respect of fundamental rights would be the unwarranted corollaries of EU Membership.[440] Protocol 24, commentators argued, was contrary to the principle of non-discrimination and incompatible with the Refugee Convention.[441] As logic would suggest, similar criticisms concern the limited personal scope of the Qualification Directive.

---

438   TFEU, Protocol (no 24) on asylum for nationals of Member States of the European Union.
439   *Ibid.*, Sole Article, § 1. Belgium is the only country within the European Union who has made a declaration in accordance with point (d) of the Protocol's sole Article, to the effect that it would carry out an individual examination of any asylum request made by a national of another Member State. This, Belgium stated, was in accordance with its obligations under the 1951 Refugee Convention and 1967 Protocol. *See* Amsterdam Treaty, Declaration by Belgium on the Protocol on asylum for nationals of Member States of the European Union.
440   Commenting of the interpretation of Protocol 24 by Member States' national courts, H. Labayle analyses the jurisprudence of the French *Conseil d'État* in three cases concerning the international protection claims submitted by Romanian nationals invoking their belonging to the Rom minority. Literally applying Protocol 24, the *Conseil d'État* rejected the claims in view of the fact that Romania had joined the European Union. The author critically observes: "*Le simple fait que la Roumanie ait, quelques mois plus tôt, rejoint l'Union européenne vaut donc brevet de démocratie et présomption de respect des droits fondamentaux*". H. Labayle (March-April 2011), *op. cit.*, p. 275.
441   UNHCR, "Position on the Proposal of the European Council Concerning the Treatment of Asylum Applications from Citizens of European Union Member States" (Geneva, January 1997); S. Peers and N. Rogers (Eds.), *EU Immigration and Asylum Law: Text and Commentary Immigration and Asylum Law and Policy in Europe*, Immigration and Asylum Law and Policy in Europe, Vol. 12 (Leiden: Brill Academic Publishers, 2006), pp. 515s; F. Julien-Laferrière, "La compatibilité de la politique d'asile de l'Union européenne avec la Convention de Genève du 28 juillet 1951 relative au statut des réfugiés", *in La Convention de Genève du 28 juillet 1951 relative au statut des réfugiés, 50 ans après : bilan et perspectives* (Bruxelles: Bruylant, 2001).

Commentators deplore the "unfortunate fact"[442] that EU nationals are excluded from the scope of the Directive and may not be granted international protection within the European Union.[443] This limited personal scope of refugee protection under the Qualification Directive is said to contravene States' obligation, enshrined in Article 3 of the Refugee Convention, not to discriminate on grounds of country of origin.[444] Other anticipated negative impacts of this limitation of the Directive's scope include: the incompatibility of the limitation with the fact that, under Article 42(1) of the Refugee Convention, States may not make any reservation to Article 1 of the Convention;[445] the risk that with the ongoing enlargement of the EU, the repercussions of such limitation appear even more dearly, and the bad precedent it sets for other regions of the world.[446] Observing that under international law the right to seek asylum is not limited either by nationality or geography,[447] UNHCR recommends[448]

---

442   ECRE, "Information Note on the Council Directive 2004/83/EC of 29 April 2004 on Minimum Standards for the Qualification of Third Country Nationals and Stateless Persons as Refugees or as Persons Who Otherwise Need International Protection and the Content of the Protection Granted" ("Information Note on QD (2004)") (October 2004), p. 5.
443   UNHCR, "UNHCR Comments on the European Commission's Proposal for a Directive of the European Parliament and of the Council on Minimum Standards for the Qualification and Status of Third Country Nationals or Stateless Persons as Beneficiaries of International Protection and the Content of the Protection Granted (Com(2009)551, 21 October 2009)" ("Comments on Proposal for Recast QD") (July 2010), Recommendation, p. 4; UNHCR, "UNHCR Annotated Comments on the EC Council Directive 2004/83/EC of 29 April 2004 on Minimum Standards for the Qualification and Status of Third Country Nationals or Stateless Persons as Refugees or as Persons Who Otherwise Need International Protection and the Content of the Protection Granted (OJ L 304/12 of 30.9.2004)" ("Annotated Comments on QD (2004)") [January 2005], Comment on Article 1, p. 10; ECRE (October 2004), "Information Note on QD (2004)", *op. cit.*, pp. 4–5.
444   H. Lambert (January 2006), *op. cit.*, p. 178; ECRE (October 2004), "Information Note on QD (2004)", *op. cit.*, p. 5.
445   A. Klug, "Harmonization of Asylum in the European Union: Emergence of an EU Refugee System?", *German Yearbook of International Law*, Vol. 47 (2004), pp. 594–628, p. 600.
446   ECRE (October 2004), "Information Note on QD (2004)", *op. cit.*, p. 5.
447   UNHCR (July 2010), "Comments on Proposal for Recast QD", *op. cit.*, Recommendation, p. 4.
448   Reference will often be made hereinafter to UNHCR comments or recommendations. UNHCR's interpretation and opinions on the Qualification Directive (or on EU asylum law in general) are not *per se* binding upon EU Member States however, they are of utmost relevance and importance. As highlighted by UNHCR itself, the Qualification Directive "goes to the heart of UNHCR's international protection mandate" (UNHCR, *Asylum in the European Union: A Study of the Implementation of the Qualification Directive* (November 2007), *op. cit.*, p. 7). Article 8 of UNHCR's Statute calls upon the High Commissioner to provide for the protection of refugees *inter alia* by "promoting the conclusion and ratification

States to make clear in their domestic legislation that the provision applies to all persons, third-country and EU nationals alike.[449] As mentioned above, in a case concerning a decision of Belgium asylum authorities to return an individual to Greece, the Court of Justice concluded that the presumption underpinning the Dublin system[450] that the same level of human rights protection was available across the European Union was necessarily rebuttable.[451] In other words, the Court acknowledged that Member States might not always be accurately construed as "safe countries of origin in respect of each other"[452] in relation to asylum matters. This fuels UNHCR's above-mentioned argument. Should all the consequences be drawn of the Court's finding, it would indeed imply that EU nationals whose country falls short from qualifying as "safe country of origin" should not be *refoulé* and should be entitled to the benefit of the Qualification Directive. This reasoning has not been followed yet and

---

of international conventions for the protection of refugees, *supervising their application and proposing amendments thereto*" [emphasis added]. European Union law itself has long recognised the supervisory responsibility of UNHCR: Declaration 17 of the Treaty of Amsterdam provided that, for the purpose of the adoption by the Council of measures on asylum, "[c]onsultations shall be established with the United Nations High Commissioner for Refugees (...) on matters relating to asylum policy". (Amsterdam Treaty, Declaration 17.) UNHCR's views were in fact taken into account by the drafters of the Qualification Directive. The European Commission explains that, in this context, besides the Refugee Convention itself, UNHCR's "Handbook on procedures and criteria for determining refugee status" as well as UNHCR ExCom conclusions served as "sources of reference" ("Explanatory Memorandum – QD (2004)", *op. cit.*, p. 5;, *op. cit.* p. 7, endorsing UNHCR's view on the respective objects and purposes of temporary protection and subsidiary protection) The Qualification Directive in facts also refers to UNHCR: Recital 22 encourages Member States to consult with UNHCR since such consultations may provide them with valuable guidance when determining refugee status. The Directive also refers to UNHCR as a source of up-to-date information on asylum seekers' countries of origin, next to the European Asylum Support Office (Qualification Directive, Recital 22 and Article 8(2)). For all the above reasons, UNHCR comments and recommendations on the Qualification Directive are of particular significance.

449 UNHCR (July 2010), "Comments on Proposal for Recast QD", *op. cit.*, Recommendation, p. 4; "Annotated Comments on QD (2004)", [January 2005], *op. cit.*, Comment on Article 1, p. 10.
450 The purpose of the Dublin system is to establish criteria and procedures for determining the EU Member State responsible for examining an asylum application lodged within the European Union by a third-country national. Dublin Regulation. (*op. cit.*).
451 *See* developments above on the judgment of the Court of Justice in the NS & ME case: pp. 81s.
452 This is the wording of the Protocol on asylum for nationals of Member States of the European Union. TFEU, Protocol 24, Sole Article.

international protection under the Qualification Directive is still a prerogative of third-country nationals.[453]

Whereas the clarifications introduced by the Qualification Directive on key concepts of refugee law are generally welcome in relevant literature,[454] the main added-value of the Directive pertains to the new regime it devises, of "subsidiary protection". As a matter of fact, the Directive is the first binding supranational instrument that elaborates a specific definition of and status for persons in need of international protection but who fall outside the scope of the 1951 Refugee Convention.[455] In particular, it is distinct from international treaties from which the principle of *non-refoulement* derives because it attaches to the operation of this principle the grant of a package of rights.[456]

Recital 33 of the Qualification Directive articulates the two international protection statuses in the following terms:

> … Subsidiary protection should be complementary and additional to the refugee protection enshrined in the Geneva Convention.[457]

It follows that refugee status should be maintained by States as the primary status for the protection of individuals who have a genuine need of international protection. Subsidiary protection is intended to be, as clear from its

---

[453] With the exception of Belgium that declared, in accordance with Protocol 24, that it would examine asylum claims submitted by EU nationals. See above note 524.

[454] ECRE/ELENA, "The Impact of the EU Qualification Directive on International Protection", October 2008, pp. 4–7; J. McAdam, "The European Union Qualification Directive: The Creation of a Subsidiary Protection Regime", *International Journal of Refugee Law*, Vol. 17, No. 3 (2005), pp. 461–516, p. 468.

[455] Jane McAdam distinguishes on this point the Qualification Directive from the AU Convention and the Cartagena Declaration: the latter two regional instruments do not create a distinct status for persons who fall outside the scope of the Refugee Convention refugee definition but instead apply the Refugee Convention status to a broader category of persons. J. McAdam, "Part I: Overview", *in Convention Refugee Status and Subsidiary Protection Working Party, First Report*, IARLJ 7th World Conference, Held in Mexico City, November 2006, p. 2, note 4; see also C. Reid, "Alternative Standards Specific to Refugees – the Regional Level", *in* C. Reid (Ed.) *International Law and Legal Instruments*, Expert Guides (n/a: © 2010 Forced Migration Online and Contributors, March 2005), p. 41, retrieved from: <http://www.forcedmigration.org/research-resources/expert-guides> [06/10/2010].

[456] J. McAdam, *Complementary Protection in International Refugee Law* (2007), *op. cit.*, pp. 11 and 45.

[457] Qualification Directive, Recital 33 (ex Recital 24).

name, complementary to refugee status:[458] it "should be seen as a residual status for people in need of protection who clearly fall outside a full and inclusive interpretation of the Refugee Convention, not as a substitute for refugee protection".[459] Studies on the implementation of the Qualification Directive confirm that Member States use a sequential procedure to assess asylum claims: an application for international protection is first assessed against refugee criteria and, if it fails to fulfil them, against subsidiary protection criteria.[460] As will be shown below, the sequential approach to the assessment of asylum claims does not always ensure that persons who fulfil the refugee definition criteria are indeed granted refugee status.[461]

As mentioned, the Directive bases its refugee definition on the 1951 Convention. On the other hand, in its proposal for a directive, the Commission indicated that the criteria for subsidiary protection had to be regarded as a clarification and codification of the disparate Member State subsidiary protection

---

458 "Annotated Comments on QD (2004)", [January 2005], *op. cit.*, Comment on Article 15, pp. 31–32. ECRE, "The Impact of the EU Qualification Directive on International Protection", October 2008.

459 ECRE/ELENA, *op. cit.*, p. 27, Recommendation 22; "Annotated Comments on QD (2004)", [January 2005], *op. cit.*, Comment on Article 2 (e)-(g), p. 11. *See* also for example the opinion expressed by the French national human rights institution (*Commission nationale consultative des droits de l'Homme* – CNCDH) stressing that subsidiary protection should not supersede refugee status. CNCDH, "Avis sur le projet de loi modifiant la loi n° 52–893 relative au droit d'asile" ("Avis 2003"), 24 avril 2003, p. 3. In particular, the CNCDH later warned, subsidiary protection should not jeopardise the progress made in the application of the uneasily-defined notion of "membership of a particular social group" as ground for refugee status under the Refugee Convention. CNCDH, "Avis sur les conditions d'exercice du droit d'asile en France" ("Avis 2006"), 29 juin 2006, §§ 30–31. On the notion of social group, its interpretations in literature and case-law and potential scope, *see* for example: F. Julien-Laferrière, "La Notion de 'Groupe Social'", *in* J. Gerkrath (Ed.), *Droit d'asile au Grand-Duché de Luxembourg et en Europe: développements récents* (Bruxelles: Larcier, 2009), pp. 218–234.

460 ECRE/ELENA, *op. cit.*, pp. 6, 25–28 and 184–186 (ECRE surveyed nineteen EU Member States but also Norway, whose asylum legislation was "broadly modelled on the Directive", *see* p. 9). *See* also the study conducted by UNHCR on the implementation of the Qualification Directive. UNHCR Study focused on practice in five EU Member States: France, Germany, Greece, the Slovak Republic and Sweden, which together received in 2006 close to half of all asylum applications lodged within the EU UNHCR, *Asylum in the European Union: A Study of the Implementation of the Qualification Directive* (November 2007), *op. cit.*, p. 82.

461 *See* below, "4. Harmonisation: a long way ahead", p. 168.

practices. The lack of any specific EU *acquis* related to subsidiary protection was noted by the Commission who pointed to the fact that the European Convention on Human Rights and the case law of the European Court of Human Rights nevertheless provided for a "legally binding framework, which informed the choice of categories of beneficiary in this Proposal".[462] In its adopted and now consolidated version, the text of the Qualification Directive reflects the views expressed by the Commission: Recital 34 of the Directive Preamble states that the eligibility criteria for subsidiary protection are, as the Council of Europe and UNHCR Executive Committee[463] had suggested, "drawn from international obligations under human rights instruments and practices existing in Member States".[464]

Article 2(f) of the Qualification Directive read together with Article 15 offers a definition of "person eligible for subsidiary protection status". Pursuant to Article 2(f), is eligible for subsidiary protection in the EU:

> ... a third country national or a stateless person who does not qualify as a refugee but in respect of whom substantial grounds have been shown for believing that the person concerned, if returned to his or her country of origin, or in the case of a stateless person, to his or her country of former habitual residence, would face a real risk of suffering serious harm as defined in Article 15 (...) and is unable, or, owing to such risk, unwilling to avail himself or herself of the protection of that country.[465]

The language of the provision confirms that prior instruments of international law form the foundations of the Qualification Directive. It is indeed reminiscent of the language used in the Refugee Convention and in *non-refoulement* case-law.

The definition of persons eligible for subsidiary protection is complemented by the cross-reference made to Article 15 of the Qualification Directive, where three categories of serious harm that may trigger the grant of subsidiary protection are identified. Under Article 15, serious harm consists of:

(a) the death penalty or execution; or
(b) torture or inhuman or degrading treatment or punishment of an applicant in the country of origin; or

---

462 "Explanatory Memorandum – QD (2004)", *op. cit.*, p. 26.
463 See above pp. 104s.
464 Qualification Directive, Recital 34 (ex Recital 25).
465 *Ibid.*, Article 2(f).

(c) serious and individual threat to a civilian's life or person by reason of indiscriminate violence in situations of international or internal armed conflict.⁴⁶⁶

According to the Commission, those three categories of "serious harm" constitute "three separate but potentially overlapping grounds to consider when establishing whether an applicant falls to be granted subsidiary protection status".⁴⁶⁷ The Directive provisions incorporating the prohibitions of the death penalty (Article 15(a)) and of torture and inhuman or degrading treatment or punishment (Article 15(b)) as grounds for the grant of subsidiary protection are relatively spared by interpretative uncertainties; the extension of subsidiary protection to individuals fleeing situations of armed conflict (Article 15(c)) on the other hand raises a number of concerns. The importance of disambiguating the terms of Article 15 appears all the more clearly since granting subsidiary protection to those eligible for it is not a mere possibility given to States but an obligation: the English version of the article states that States "shall grant" subsidiary protection in the given cases. The other language versions of the document confirm that it is indeed an obligation for States. To cite but a few examples:

– In French: "*Les États membres* octroient..."
– In Swedish: "*Medlemsstaterna* skall *bevilja*..."
– In German: "*Die Mitgliedstaaten* erkennen..."
– In Spanish: "*Los Estados miembros* concederán..." [Emphases added]⁴⁶⁸

Commentators, including UNHCR and the European Council on Refugees and Exiles, all welcome the creation of the express legal obligation for EU Member States to grant subsidiary protection to those at risk of serious harm and who do not qualify for refugee status.⁴⁶⁹

The Qualification Directive, insofar as it creates a status for persons in need of international protection who fall outside the scope of the Geneva Convention has the potential to significantly contribute to the harmonisation of Member

---

466   *Ibid.*, Article 15.
467   "Explanatory Memorandum – QD (2004)", *op. cit.*, p. 26.
468   The Qualification Directive is available in the different official languages of the EU. All the versions of the text are published by the Publications Office of the European Union on the EUR-Lex website: © European Union, at <http://eur-lex.europa.eu> [31/05/2012].
469   "Annotated Comments on QD (2004)", [January 2005], *op. cit.*, Comment on Article 15, p. 31; ECRE (October 2004), "Information Note on QD (2004)", *op. cit.*, p. 4.

States legislation and practices in that respect. "This is the most ambitious attempt to combine refugee law and human rights law in this way to date".[470] This noble and ambitious objective is however challenged by textual difficulties – be they mere infelicities of style or "ambiguities, deliberate 'gaps' or derogation possibilities"[471] – and the resulting diverging interpretations. Those however do not affect all the provisions of the Directive alike. This appears clearly with regards to Article 15 provisions: much literature and a number of judicial decisions have been produced on the interpretation of Article 15 (c) whereas the first two paragraphs of the article are by far less discussed because less contentious.[472] As mentioned, the first two paragraphs of Article 15 very much reflect States obligations under international human rights law; those obligations being examined in length in the following Chapter, the provisions of Article 15 (a) and (b) will be discussed only briefly (B). The third category on the other hand is more innovative: the protection it provides for people fleeing indiscriminate threats "cannot be traced to language found in a specific universal or regional

---

470   H. Lambert (January 2006), *op. cit.*, p. 162.
471   "Commission staff working document – Proposal for a Recast QD", *op. cit.*, pp. 10–11. Similarly, H. Labayle recalls how arduous it was for States to adopt common norms in the asylum field and notes: "*Ces négociations difficiles ont eu pour conséquence concrète un corpus juridique de faible valeur, fait d'ambiguïtés sinon de contradictions volontaires, seule méthode susceptible de forcer le consensus européen indispensable à l'époque*". H. Labayle (March-April 2011), *op. cit.*, p. 274. For an overall assessment of the Qualification Directive and a discussion of the main issues it raises in light of Member States obligations under international refugee law and human rights law, see M.T. Gil-Bazo (2006), *op. cit.*, pp. 28–30; for a critical assessment of the European immigration and asylum policy in its earlier stage, five years after the Treaty of Amsterdam, see F. Julien-Laferrière, *et al.* (Eds.), *La politique européenne d'immigration et d'asile : bilan critique cinq ans après le traité d'Amsterdam Précis de la faculté de droit de l'Université Libre de Bruxelles*, Précis de la faculté de droit de l'Université Libre de Bruxelles (Bruxelles: Bruylant, 06/2005).
472   "Annotated Comments on QD (2004)", [January 2005], *op. cit.*, Comments on Article 15 and 15(c), pp. 31–33; UNHCR, "Statement Subsidiary Protection under the EC Qualification Directive for People Threatened by Indiscriminate Viole", January 2008; VluchtelingenWerk, "Article 15(c): Qualification for Subsidiary Protection Status and the Definition of Serious Harm", © 2012 Qualification Directive, retrieved from the website of the project Networking on the Transposition of the Qualification Directive [01/07/2012]. Examples of case law include: United Kingdom: UKAIT, *KH (Article 15(c) Qualification Directive) Iraq v. Secretary of State for the Home Department ("KH")*, CG [2008] UKAIT 00023, 25 March 2008; EWCA, *QD & AH v Secretary of State for the Home Department*, 24 June 2009, *op. cit*; UNHCR, "Submission by UNHCR in the Case of *QD (Iraq) v. Secretary of State for the Home Department*", 31 May 2009; CJ, *Elgafaji*; J.-F. Durieux and University of Oxford. Refugee Studies Centre, "Salah Sheekh Is a Refugee: New Insights into Primary and Subsidiary Forms of Protection", *Working paper series / Refugee Studies Centre* (Refugee Studies Centre), No. 49 (2008).

human rights instrument",[473] it will therefore be analysed in more details below (C). Straying from those general considerations on the EU asylum regime, it is worth noting that additionally, Article 15(c), insofar as it provides for the protection of persons exposed to serious risks which are "situational" rather than individually targeted,[474] is of particular interest in the developments made in the following parts on the protection of persons fleeing risks for their life or persons threatening in situations of environmental disasters.[475]

B *A Reflection of the Classical Right to Life and Prohibition of Torture and Inhuman or Degrading Treatment or Punishment: Article 15(a) and (b)*

Paragraphs (a) and (b) will be discussed successively before a concluding remark is made.

1 Article 15(a)

Article 15(a) of the Directive protects people from being sent back to a real risk of being sentenced to death or executed in absolute terms. The *travaux préparatoires* in Council clarify that this provision was derived from Protocol 6 of the European Convention on Human Rights (ECHR)[476] which is binding upon all, now 27, EU Member States and prohibits the imposition of the death penalty in peace time, and from the related jurisprudence of the European Court of Human Rights.[477] The ECtHR indeed found[478] that where there were substantial grounds for believing that a person would, if returned to his or her

---

473 R. Mandal, *Protection Mechanisms Outside of the 1951 Convention ("Complementary Protection")* (June 2005), *op. cit.*, p. 18.

474 UNHCR, "Statement on Subsidiary Protection under the EC Qualification Directive for People Threatened by Indiscriminate Violence" ("Statement on Article 15(c) QD"), January 2008, p. 6.

475 The applicability or potential applicability of Article 15(c) of the Qualification Directive to persons displaced by environmental disasters will be discussed in Parts II and III.

476 Article 1 of the Protocol 6 of the ECHR states: "The death penalty shall be abolished. No-one shall be condemned to such penalty or executed". Protocol (No. 6) to the European Convention for the Protection of Human Rights and Fundamental Freedoms Concerning the Abolition of Death Penalty ("Protocol 6 ECHR"), 28 April 1983, entered into force 1 March 1985 ETS Vol. 114, Article 1.

477 EU Council, "Presidency Note to the Strategic Committee on Immigration, Frontiers and Asylum (ASILE 43)" ("Presidency Note (ASILE 43)"), 12148/02 ASILE 43, 20 September 2002, p. 5. J.-F. Durieux and University of Oxford. Refugee Studies Centre (2008), *op. cit.*, p. 15; H. Storey, "EU Refugee Qualification Directive: A Brave New World?", *International Journal of Refugee Law*, March 1, 2008, Vol. 20, No. 1 (2008), pp. 1–49, p. 14.

478 This will be further discussed at more length further below in "Chapter 3. Relevant provisions of international human rights law", p. 174s.

country, face a real risk of being subjected to death penalty contrary to Article 1 of the 6th Protocol, Article 1 carried with it the obligation for States not to return (*refouler*) the person concerned to that country.[479] Although the Council does not refer to Protocol 13 ECHR, it is clear from the drafting history of both instruments that Article 15(a) reflects it too. Contrary to Protocol 6, Article 15(a) is absolute; no exception is permissible, not even in war time. The abolition of the death penalty was however reaffirmed and broadened by Protocol 13 of the ECHR prohibits the death penalty in all circumstances, including war time, to which the vast majority of EU Member States are parties.[480] Protocol 13 was adopted in May 2002; the application of subsidiary protection to persons at risk of being sentenced to the death penalty or of being executed was proposed just a month later, in June 2002, by the German and Austrian delegations.[481] At that time, Protocol 13 had not yet entered into force (it did in July 2003), which certainly explains why the Council did not refer to it.[482]

Additionally, Article 15(a) reflects the jurisprudence of the European Court of Human Rights (ECtHR) in relation to Articles 2 and 3 of the ECHR. Extraditions exposing individuals to the risk of being sentenced to death have been condemned by the ECtHR relying on Articles 3 of the ECHR. In those cases, the Court highlights, it is not the death penalty *per se* which rises issues under ECHR Articles 2 or 3 but the circumstances (including time considerations) in which the sentence is being carried out.[483]

Lastly, even though neither the Commission nor the Council mentioned it in their successive explanations to the evolving provisions of the proposal, Article 15(a) is also compatible with the prohibition of the use of the death

---

479 In its decision, published in French only, the Court stated: "*Ainsi, lorsqu'il y a des motifs sérieux et avérés de croire que l'intéressé, si on le livre à l'État en question, y courra un risque réel d'être soumis à la peine de mort contraire à l'article 1 du Protocole n° 6, cette disposition implique-t-elle l'obligation de ne pas extrader la personne en question vers ce pays*". ECtHR, *Ismaili v. Germany*, Application No. 58128/00 (15 March 2001).

480 All EU Member States are parties to Protocol 13 with the exception of Poland who became signatory in 2002 but has not ratified it yet (according to the chart of signatures and ratifications provided by the Treaty Office of the Council of Europe and available at: <http://conventions.coe.int> [20/06/2012]). Protocol (No. 13) to the Convention for the Protection of Human Rights and Fundamental Freedoms, Concerning the Abolition of the Death Penalty in All Circumstances ("Protocol 13 ECHR"), 3 May 2002, entered into force 1 July 2003 ETS Vol. 187.

481 EU Council, "Asylum Working Party – Outcome of Proceedings of 4–5 June 2002" ("Outcome of Proceedings (ASILE 25)"), 9038/02 ASILE 25, 17 June 2002, p. 22, n. 3.

482 "Presidency Note (ASILE 43)", *op. cit.*

483 See below the *Soering* case: ECtHR (Plenary), *Soering v. The United Kingdom* ("*Soering*"), Application No. 14038/88, Series A Vol. 161 (7 July 1989); ruling discussed pp. 188s.

penalty in peace time enshrined in the 2nd Optional Protocol to the International Covenant on Civil and Political Rights, to which all EU Member States are now parties,[484] and is consistent with the jurisprudence of the Human Rights Committee.[485]

It can be concluded from the above observations that Article 15(a) of the Qualification Directive "reflects the myriad of death-penalty related legal obligations and the EU's abolitionist policy".[486] It is worth noting that the risk of facing the death penalty or of being executed was not included in the Commission's 2001 proposal but its inclusion resulted from a consensus among EU Member States.[487]

2   Article 15(b)

Article 15(b) protects individuals from being sent to a country where they risk suffering torture, inhuman or degrading treatment or punishment. It reflects Member States obligations under Article 3 of the European Convention of Human Rights and the jurisprudence of the ECtHR and was generally supported by Member States.[488] The wording is very similar to that of corresponding provisions in international human rights treaties such as the ECHR and International Covenant on Civil and Political Rights,[489] and broader than Article 3 of the UN Convention Against Torture which expressly covers torture

---

484   At the time the Qualification Directive was adopted, France had not yet acceded to the Second Optional Protocol to the ICCPR but has since done so, on 2 October 2007.

485   The Human Rights Committee stated that any State party to ICCPR OP 2, and, more broadly, any abolitionist State, would violate an individual's right to life under ICCPR article 6, paragraph 1, by deporting him or her to a country where he or she is under sentence of death, without ensuring that the death penalty would not be carried out. See HRC, *Judge v. Canada*, CCPR/C/78/D/829/1998, *Communication No. 829/1998 (5 August 2003)*, § 10.6.

486   R. Mandal, *Protection Mechanisms Outside of the 1951 Convention ("Complementary Protection")* (June 2005), op. cit., § 46.

487   See "Presidency Note (ASILE 43)", op. cit., p. 5. The various discussion papers then submitted confirm the consensus: Article 15(a) did not give rise to any subsequent discussion or comment (*see* for example EU Council, "Presidency Note to the Strategic Committee on Immigration, Frontiers and Asylum, on the Proposal for a Council Directive on Minimum Standards for the Qualification and Status of Third Country Nationals and Stateless Persons as Refugees or as Persons Who Otherwise Need International Protection" ("Presidency Note (ASILE 47)"), 12382/02 ASILE 47, 30 September 2002; EU Council, "Presidency Note to the Council (Justice, Home Affairs and Civil Protection)" ("Presidency Note (ASILE 53)"), 12619/02 ASILE 53, 9 October 2002).

488   "Presidency Note (ASILE 43)", op. cit., p. 5.

489   Battjes demonstrates that Article 15(b) of the Qualification Directive "could cover all acts of harm meant in Article 7 CCPR". H. Battjes, *European Asylum Law and International Law* (2006), op. cit., p. 235, § 295.

only.[490] In fact and as mentioned in the Directive's *travaux préparatoires*, it is "based on the obligations of Member States laid down in Article 3 of the ECHR and the jurisprudence of the ECtHR".[491] This was later confirmed by the Court of Justice who recalled that Article 15(b) of the Directive "corresponds, in essence, to Article 3 of the ECHR".[492]

According to the Council, Article 15(b) is however narrower than Article 3 ECHR: it is intended to exclude from its scope cases based on purely compassionate grounds, such as illness.[493] The Council refers to the decision of the European Court of Human Rights in *D. v. UK* [494] where, according to the Council, the Court found that although the lack of access to adequate treatment and support did not in itself constitute torture or inhuman or degrading treatment, *refoulement* to such situation did. Ill-treatment in such case stems from the "combination" of the country of origin's failure to assure its population access to an adequate health system with the termination of treatment in the host country as a consequence of its decision to expel the individual concerned.[495] It is analysed by the Council as a compassionate grounds case falling, as such, outside the intended scope of the Qualification Directive.[496] Recital 15 of the Directive indeed confirms that asylum seekers "who are allowed to remain in the territories of the Member States for reasons not due to a need for international protection but on a discretionary basis on compassionate or humanitarian grounds fall outside the scope of this Directive".[497]

To avoid that subsidiary protection extends to such cases where protection is sometimes granted by States on compassionate or humanitarian grounds, Article 15(b) clarifies that ill-treatment will be construed as serious harm for the purpose of the Directive if and only if it is inflicted "in the country of origin".[498] H. Battjes clarifies that the requirement should be read as limiting the scope of Article 15(b) to ill-treatment inflicted "by an actor in the territories of a receiving state upon expulsion to the country of origin".[499] J. McAdam

---

490   CAT, Article 3.
491   "Presidency Note (ASILE 43)", *op. cit.*, p. 5.
492   CJ, *Elgafaji*, § 28.
493   "Presidency Note (ASILE 43)", *op. cit.*, pp. 5–6.
494   ECtHR, *D. v. The United Kingdom* ("*D. v. UK*"), Application no. 30240/96, Reports 1997-III (02/05/1997).
495   J. McAdam, *Complementary Protection in International Refugee Law* (2007), *op. cit.*, p. 69.
496   "Presidency Note (ASILE 43)", *op. cit.*, p. 6.
497   Qualification Directive, Recital 15.
498   *Ibid.*, Article 15(b).
499   H. Battjes, *European Asylum Law and International Law* (2006), *op. cit.*, pp. 235–237, §§ 296–297.

observes that it remains to be seen whether or not asylum authorities will apply the "country of origin" requirement so strictly as to exclude "combination cases" but notes that, in the light of the recent case-law of the ECtHR and of the high threshold it set for the operation of the principle of *non-refoulement* in cases involving allegations of insufficient medical treatment,[500] it is unlikely that subsidiary protection will be granted in such cases.[501]

Key elements of the principle of *non-refoulement* and legal bases of most forms of complementary protection,[502] the rights protected under Article 3 ECHR also are at the core of the concept of persecution.[503] There exists however an essential distinction to be made between those violations of the prohibition of torture that can trigger the grant of subsidiary protection and those that entitle their (actual or putative) victims to refugee status. A constitutive element of persecution is the existence of a causal like between the ill-treatment and one or several immutable characteristics of the asylum seeker; on the other hand, the grounds for ill-treatment, if any, are not taken into

---

500 The jurisprudence of the European Court of Human Rights on the principle of *non-refoulement* in connection with risks to the applicant's health should he or she be returned to his or her country of origin will be further elaborated upon in Part II. See below pp. 361s.

501 J. McAdam, *Complementary Protection in International Refugee Law* (2007), *op. cit.*, p. 69.

502 Besides obligations under Article 3 ECHR, the impossibility in practice (due to the absence of interruption of transport for instance) to return failed asylum seekers to their country of origin can also justify the grant of a form of complementary protection by States (although generally, the protection is limited and consists chiefly in the temporary suspension of the transfer, without additional rights being attached to it). Under German law for example, the deportation of failed asylum seekers to their country of origin may be temporarily suspended, so long as there exist factual obstacles to it ("tolerance" or "*Duldung*"): "*Die Abschiebung eines Ausländers ist auszusetzen, solange die Abschiebung aus tatsächlichen (...) Gründen unmöglich ist und keine Aufenthaltserlaubnis erteilt wird*". Germany: Aufenthaltsgesetz of 30 July 2004 (hereafter "AufenthG") [25 February 2008] *BGBl. I*, p. 162, last amended by Article 1 and Article 6 paragraph 2 of the Act of 1 June 2012, *BGBl. I*, p. 1224, Article 60a (2). For an overview of the different forms of protection, complementary to refugee status and subsidiary protection, maintained by EU Member States after the transposition of the Qualification Directive in their national legislation, *see* the studies produced by the European Migration Network in 2010 (covering 23 EU Member States) and the European Council on Refugees and Exiles in 2009 (covering 9 EU Member States and Switzerland): EMN, "The Different National Practices Concerning Granting of Non-EU Harmonised Protection Statuses" (December 2010); ECRE, *Complementary Protection in Europe* (Brussels: European Council on Refugees and Exiles, July 2009).

503 On the definition of "acts of persecution", *see* Part II, Chapter 6. II. A.

consideration in international human rights law which prohibits *refoulement* in absolute terms.[504]

Subsidiary protection, insofar as it is intended to complement refugee status, should apply to cases where a risk of ill-treatment contrary to Article 3 ECHR exists but has no link to a Convention ground. UNHCR, commenting on the Qualification Directive as adopted in 2004, emphasised that the Directive's provisions on subsidiary protection comprised grounds "which would indicate a strong presumption for Convention refugee status in certain cases".[505] Referring to Article 15(b) specifically, UNHCR notes that "an act of torture perpetrated by State actors would normally be linked to a Convention ground". The scope of Article 15(b) is therefore limited to torture and inhuman or degrading treatment or punishment inflicted out of "purely criminal motivation". Cases where a nexus exists between the ill-treatment and a Convention ground are covered by refugee status, therefore, UNHCR stresses, subsidiary forms of protection are only needed where violations of Article 3 have no link to a Convention ground.[506]

3   Concluding Remark on Article 15 (a) and (b)

All EU Member States being Parties to the European Convention on Human Rights and to its sixth additional protocol, they are bound to safeguard and respect the rights they enshrine such as the right to life under Article 2 ECHR, the prohibition of the death penalty under Article 1 Protocol 6, and the prohibition of torture, inhuman and degrading treatment under Article 3 ECHR. Paragraphs (a) and (b) of Article 15 of the Qualification Directive, in that they correspond, in substance, to Article 1 of ECHR 6th Protocol and to Articles 2 and 3 of the ECHR, sanction the principle of *non-refoulement* in EU asylum law. They translate into European Union law obligations which Member States already bore under instruments of international human rights law that pre-date the adoption of the Qualification Directive (and are still binding upon Member States).[507] The scope and content of the principle of *non-refoulement*

---

504   *See* developments below on the operation of the principle of *non-refoulement* in general international human rights law, under "III. Relevant provisions of international human rights law", pp. 176s.

505   "Annotated Comments on QD (2004)", [January 2005], *op. cit.*, Comment on Article 15, pp. 31–32.

506   *Ibid.*

507   On the continued binding force of Member States' obligations under international human rights law, *see* above: "I. Preliminary remark: Member States' obligations under international human rights law are unaltered by EU membership", pp. 23s.

under international human rights law will be analysed below,[508] therefore, to avoid redundancy, the scope of Article 15 (a) and (b) will not be further elaborated upon here.

Suffice to stress, at this juncture, an essential distinction between the operation of the principle of *non-refoulement* in international human rights law and that in EU asylum law. *Non-refoulement* under human rights law, generous though it may be, does not exceed its intrinsic scope: it protects its beneficiaries from being returned to harmful situations. No less but, most importantly, no more: *non-refoulement* in human rights law "is separated from any direct attaching status".[509] By contrast, Article 15 of the Qualification Directive attaches to the operation of the principle of *non-refoulement* the grant of a package of rights: subsidiary protection beneficiaries are not only permitted to stay on the territory of the Member State concerned, they are also formally granted a number of political, economic, social and cultural rights.[510] Since the Qualification Directive was recast, in 2011, this package of rights is the same for subsidiary protection beneficiaries and recognised refugees.[511]

If Article 15(b) was the "least contentious element" of Article 15,[512] the wording of both paragraphs (a) and (b) in fact soon met a general consensus within the Council.[513] On the contrary, Article 15(c) was and still is subject to most discussions. Suffice to note that the first reference for preliminary ruling submitted by a national court to the Court of Justice of the European Union precisely concerned the interpretation of Article 15(c).[514]

C   *A Controversial Innovation in EU Law: Article 15(c)*

Paragraphs (a) and (b) take note of Member States' international human rights obligations and incorporate them, almost literally, into EU asylum law. The European legislator hence duly acknowledged the bearing of the prohibitions of the death penalty and of torture and inhuman or degrading treatment or punishment on international protection claims. Article 15(c) on the other hand is innovative. At the time the Qualification was drafted, African and Latin American States were familiar with the concepts used in Article 15(c) since

---

508   Below "Chapter 3. I. Treaty law enshrining the principle of non-refoulement", pp. 177s.
509   Jane McAdam defines *non-refoulement* under international human rights law as "*non-refoulement* 'without more'". J. McAdam, *Complementary Protection in International Refugee Law* (2007), *op. cit.*, pp. 11 and 45.
510   Qualification Directive, Articles 20 to 35.
511   *Ibid.*, Recital 39 and Articles 20 to 35.
512   J. McAdam, *Complementary Protection in International Refugee Law* (2007), *op. cit.*, p. 68.
513   "Presidency Note (ASILE 47)", *op. cit.*, p. 2.
514   CJ, *Elgafaji*.

the 1969 African Union Convention Governing the Specific Aspects of Refugee Problems in Africa and the 1984 Cartagena Declaration respectively already both provided for the protection of persons fleeing armed conflict situations in their country of origin.[515] No such provision however existed in any instrument of international law, either at the universal level or at the European level. Despite this gap, the protection existed in European State practice.

Surveys conducted by the Council of the European Union, UNHCR and ECRE all showed that, prior to the adoption of the Qualification Directive, EU Member States already had made provisions in their national legislation or practices for the protection of persons who could not qualify for refugee status under the Geneva Convention but who were nevertheless in an acknowledged need of international protection due to a situation of armed conflict or generalised violence in their country of origin. All commentators however highlighted the wide variations existing between those national measures: from discretionary measures merely protecting individuals from removal, to the granting of a status akin to refugee status, following a procedure for the examination of the claim similar to refugee status determination.[516]

According to the Commission, the categories of persons concerned by Article 15 "represent a clarification and codification of existing practice"; they are "drawn very much from the disparate Member States practices and are believed to encompass the best ones".[517] This is especially true of Article 15(c) for which, as mentioned, the drafters could not draw from any existing legal obligation binding upon EU Member States. Although, as noted by UNHCR, reference was made to the African Union Convention, the Cartagena Declaration and the evolution of the UNHCR Mandate during the drafting of the Directive to justify the inclusion of people fleeing indiscriminate violence and massive violations of human rights,[518] Article 15(c) is deemed to reflect European State

---

515 Cartagena Declaration on Refugees ("Cartagena Declaration"), 22 November 1984, Colloquium on the International Protection of Refugees in Central America, Mexico and Panama, § 3; AU Refugee Convention, Article 1(2).

516 *See*: EU Council, "Note from the General Secretariat of the Council to the Asylum Working Party: Compilation of Replies to Questionnaire on Complementary Forms of Protection", 8378/01 ASILE 27, 3 May 2001; UNHCR, "Complementary Forms of Protection: Their Nature and Relationship to the International Refugee Protection Regime" ("Complementary Forms of Protection"), EC/50/SC/CRP.18, 9 June 2000, §§ 10–11; UNHCR, "Statement on Article 15(c) QD", *op. cit.*, pp. 16s; ECRE, "Complementary/Subsidiary Forms of Protection in the EU Member States: An Overview" ("Complementary/Subsidiary Forms of Protection"), December 2003, updated in July 2004.

517 "Explanatory Memorandum – QD (2004)", *op. cit.*, p. 26.

518 UNHCR, "Statement on Article 15(c) QD", *op. cit.*, p. 14.

practice.[519] The Court of Justice confirmed the innovative nature of Article 15(c) in the welcome *Elgafaji* case. The Court, before clarifying the scope and meaning of Article 15(c), emphasised the originality of this provision which, unlike the preceding paragraphs of Article 15, does not derive from existing legal obligations of States (such as Article 3 ECHR). In the Court's words:

> Article 15(c) of the Directive is a provision, the content of which is different from that of Article 3 of the ECHR, and the interpretation of which must, therefore, be carried out independently, although with due regard for fundamental rights, as they are guaranteed under the ECHR.

Article 15 paragraph (c) constitutes an innovation within the European Union legal order; unlike paragraphs (a) and (b), it cannot be traced to the language of the European Convention of Human Rights. Instead, it reflects the practice[520] of EU Member States of granting some form of protection to individuals fleeing indiscriminate violence arising in armed conflict situations. The absence of any legal obligation however accounts for the wide variations observed in State practice in that respect. In view of the diversity of the forms of protection granted, the adoption of common standards appeared all the more crucial, and incidentally, consensus on their wording all the more uneasy to reach. The text of Article 15 paragraph (c) in fact underwent significant drafting changes[521] to eventually be unclear and, to some extent, potentially self-contradictory. In particular, scrutiny reservations were consistently raised during the discussions on the text of article 15(b) regarding the opportunity of a requirement that the alleged threat be *individualised* where the situation at hand is one of *indiscriminate* violence (1). Member States and commentators suggested a number of interpretation and amendments before the Court of Justice of the European Communities eventually clarified the meaning of the provision in the 2009 *Elgafaji* case[522] (2).

1   Individual Threat and Indiscriminate Violence: An Oxymoron?

As originally proposed, Article 15 (c) meant to provide subsidiary protection to any individual who feared:

---

519 R. Mandal, *Protection Mechanisms Outside of the 1951 Convention ("Complementary Protection")* (June 2005), op. cit., § 47.
520 Above note 601.
521 J. McAdam counts six chief amendments to the original wording proposed by the Commission. J. McAdam, *Complementary Protection in International Refugee Law* (2007), op. cit., p. 70, note 104 and references cited.
522 CJ, *Elgafaji*.

a threat to his or her life, safety or freedom as a result of indiscriminate violence arising in situations of armed conflict, or as a result of systematic or generalised violations of their human rights.[523]

The Commission drew this definition from Article 2(c) of the Council Directive on minimum standards for giving temporary protection in the event of a mass influx of displaced persons.[524] The Commission contended that since Member States were bound to cover persons falling into this category when they arrived in a "Council agreed 'mass influx'", it was only "consistent and appropriate" to include them also when they arrived individually, and did not qualify as a refugee.[525] UNHCR also supported this view.[526] This clear link between the scope of subsidiary protection and that of temporary protection was later blurred through the successive amendments[527] of Article 15(c). The language of the provision has strayed from that of Article 2(c) of the Temporary Directive, so much so that, as adopted in 2004 – and as it still stands today, Article 15(c) refers to:

> serious and individual threat to a civilian's life or person by reason of indiscriminate violence in situations of international or internal armed conflict.[528]

At a glance, it is unclear how individuals can show they are personally at risk in a situation of indiscriminate violence, the very nature of such situation being that it affects individuals randomly.[529] Much criticism arose and keeps arising in literature. For J.-F. Durieux, attempting to reconcile the two requirements is like "trying to untie the Gordian knot".[530] In that sense too, albeit less colourfully, the French national human rights institution (CNCDH) commenting on Article 15(c) as transposed in French law recommended that the provision be amended in order to remove the "paradoxical dual requirement" of an

---

523 "Commission Proposal QD (2004)", *op. cit.*, Article 15(c); the provision is identical in the recast Qualification Directive, see Qualification Directive, Article 15(c).
524 Temporary Protection Directive, Article 2(c).
525 "Explanatory Memorandum – QD (2004)", *op. cit.*, pp. 26–27.
526 "Annotated Comments on QD (2004)", [January 2005], *op. cit.*, Comment on Article 15, p. 32.
527 Above note 606.
528 Qualification Directive (2004), Article 15(c).
529 CNCDH, "Avis 2006", *op. cit.*, § 31.
530 J.-F. Durieux, "Of War, Flows, Laws and Flaws: A Reply to Hugo Storey", *Refugee Survey Quarterly*, September 1, 2012, Vol. 31, No. 3 (2012), pp. 161–176, p. 174.

individual threat and a situation of generalised violence (*"la double exigence paradoxale d'une menace individuelle et d'un climat de violence generalisée"*). Only then, the CNCDH argues, could subsidiary protection adequately cover the international protection need of persons fleeing countries where "chaos and generalised violence" prevail. In like manner, the United Kingdom Asylum and Immigration Tribunal observed that, "[m]ost conspicuously, if it is given an ordinary language reading then it would appear to contain a near contradiction in terms".[531] It follows that a constructive interpretation of the terms of Article 15(c) would be necessary in order to make the "academic hypothesis"[532] relevant in practice.

UNHCR deplored the changes operated in the course of the discussions and appears to favour the original wording the Commission had proposed. Specifically and firstly, UNHCR observes that, with the adoption of the Temporary Protection Directive, a harmonised understanding regarding beneficiaries of temporary protection was achieved across EU Member States. This common, accepted, definition could have served as basis for the identification of persons eligible for subsidiary protection. In accord with the Commission's initial suggestion, UNHCR notes that "it would be consistent if individuals fleeing for similar reasons (but outside the context of a mass influx) were to be granted protection" under the Qualification Directive.[533] Secondly, UNHCR visibly regrets the deletion of the terms "or as a result of systematic or generalised violations of their human right" from the wording of Article 15(c) and recommends States to use this broader language when transposing the Directive into their legislation:

> UNHCR further notes that the provision is restricted to cases where the threshold of an "internal or international armed conflict" is reached. Persons fleeing indiscriminate violence and gross human rights violations more generally would, however, similarly be in need of international protection. It hopes that States will recognize the need to grant protection broadly in transposing and applying this provision.[534]

The various amendments made to the Commission's Proposal have resulted in the provision being more narrowly circumscribed. In particular, the

---

531 UKAIT, *KH*, 25 March 2008, *op. cit.*, § 32.
532 CNCDH, "Avis 2003", *op. cit.*, p. 5.
533 "Annotated Comments on QD (2004)", [January 2005], *op. cit.*, Comment on Article 15(c), pp. 32-33.
534 *Ibid.*

requirement that individuals demonstrate a "serious and individual threat" promises to significantly narrow the scope of Article 15(c).

As a matter of fact, as revealed by the *travaux préparatoires*, narrowing of the scope of Article 15(c) was precisely the drafters' intention: a vast majority of States indeed supported the reference to "individual" in order "to avoid an undesired opening of the scope" of Article 15 (c).[535] The inclusion of the term nevertheless failed to convince all Member States.[536] Germany for example suggested replacing "serious and individual threat" by "significant real threat"[537] whereas Finland and the Netherlands explicitly warned against the potentially restrictive effect of the term "individual" on the scope of the provision. Article 15(c), the two delegations explain, should also cover situations where a person is not individually targeted.[538] Interestingly, as a response to Germany's call for clarifications on the intended scope of "serious and individual threat", the Chair suggested the addition of a recital in the preamble of the directive, reading: "whereas third country nationals or stateless persons fleeing due to a general sense of insecurity in situations of international or internal armed conflict fall outside the scope of this Directive". This proposal was well-received and eventually led to the adoption of Recital 35 (ex Recital 26): "risks to which a population of a country or a section of the population is generally exposed do normally not create in themselves an individual threat which would qualify as serious harm".[539] Incidentally, this recital brought about even more confusion as to the interpretation of Article 15(c). The text of Article 15(c), as adopted in 2004 disregarded the warning and maintained the requirement that the threat be individual. The recast Qualification Directive does not differ from the first-phase Qualification Directive on this point.[540]

Two main pitfalls brought about by the individualisation requirement will be discussed below. Firstly, it risks entangling the respective scopes of serious

---

535 "Presidency Note (ASILE 47)", *op. cit.*, § 4.
536 *See* for example the scrutiny reservations lodged by Belgium, Ireland and the UK on the expression "individual threat" and the repeated calls, by Germany, for a clarification of the scope of such threat. "Presidency Note (ASILE 43)", *op. cit.*, p. 10, note 4; "Presidency Note (ASILE 53)", *op. cit.*, p. 4, note 3; EU Council, "Presidency Note to the Permanent Representative Committee, on the Proposal for a Council Directive on Minimum Standards for the Qualification and Status of Third Country Nationals and Stateless Persons as Refugees or as Persons Who Otherwise Need International Protection" ("Presidency Note (ASILE 55)"), 23 October 2002, p. 3, note 4.
537 "Presidency Note (ASILE 43)", *op. cit.*, p. 10, note 4.
538 "Presidency Note (ASILE 47)", *op. cit.*, p. 4, note 3.
539 Qualification Directive, Recital 35.
540 Qualification Directive (2004).

harm and persecution (a). Secondly, it could be used by asylum authorities to deny subsidiary protection to individuals who fulfil the criteria but arrive as part of a mass influx (b). Despite UNHCR suggesting an interpretation of the term "individual" consistent with the original purpose of subsidiary protection (c), State practice bears witness to the confusion the requirement caused (d).

(a)   *Disentangling Individualised Threats to Life or Person and Acts of Persecution*

The requirement that applicants for subsidiary protection demonstrate the individual nature of the threat they invoke risks causing subsidiary protection and refugee status to overlap. As mentioned in Recital 33 of the Qualification Directive, as was already stated by the Commission in its Explanatory Memorandum accompanying its proposal for the Directive, and pursuant to the objectives defined by the Tampere European Council in October 1999, the subsidiary protection regime is not to affect the scope of refugee status but is meant to complement it.[541] Commentators, including UNHCR and ECRE, have consistently stressed that subsidiary protection should only be a residual status for categories of people in need of protection who clearly fall outside the Refugee Convention.[542] It should not undermine the existing global refugee protection regime and should therefore not be applicable in cases where refugee status can be granted.[543] In other words, the risks covered by Article 15(c) must be different from those covered by the Refugee Convention; it follows that the expression "individual threat" should not be construed as a requirement that the asylum seeker demonstrates that he or she is personally targeted, by reason of his or her personal circumstances. To better reflect this view, UNHCR suggested that the words "serious and individual threat" be replaced by "indiscriminate serious threats": linking "indiscriminate" to "threats" rather than "violence" would make clearer the difference between the respective scope of subsidiary protection and refugee status. Indiscriminate threats qualify for subsidiary

---

541   Qualification Directive Recital 35 (ex Recital 24) provides that "subsidiary protection should be complementary and additional to the refugee protection enshrined in the Geneva Convention". *See* also: "Explanatory Memorandum – QD (2004)", *op. cit.*, p. 26.

542   ECRE, "Comments from the European Council on Refugees and Exiles on the Proposal for a Council Directive on Minimum Standards for the Qualification and Status of Third Country Nationals and Stateless Persons as Refugees or as Persons Who Otherwise Need International Protection (Brussels, 12.9.2001, Com(2001) 510 Final)" ("Comments on QD (2004) Proposal"), March 2002, p. 9.

543   See for instance: "Annotated Comments on QD (2004)", [January 2005], *op. cit.*, Comment on Article 15, p. 31.

protection whereas discriminate threats (where discrimination is based on a Convention ground) qualify for refugee status.[544]

(b)   *Individual Risk vs. an Individual's Risk*

As shown above, Article 15(c) should not require that the threat be targeted at an individual on ground of his or her personal circumstances. It should not either require that the threat be targeted at one individual only.

UNHCR indeed stressed that "the clear wording as well as the spirit of Article 15(c)" demand that persons in danger of "serious and individualized threats" systematically be granted subsidiary protection, regardless of the fact that they might "form part of a larger segment of the population affected by the same risks". In UNHCR's opinion, interpreting Article 15(c) otherwise would result in an "unacceptable protection gap, at variance with international refugee law and human rights law".[545] The interpretation of Article 15(c) should encompass risks faced "more generally by people in situations of indiscriminate violence", risks which (potentially) threaten groups of people.[546] In other words, anyone and everyone affected by a given armed conflict situation should be entitled to subsidiary protection. UNHCR finds that the added value of Article 15(c) stems precisely from its ability to provide protection from serious risks which are "situational" rather than individually targeted.[547]

One could in fact wonder how States could justify, in legal terms, denying protection to a person, despite the existing real risk to his or her life or person, simply because he or she belongs to a larger segment of the population affected by the same risks. Such differentiation reveal Member States' fear that, should they recognise subsidiary protection to an individual fleeing a given armed conflict situation, they would have to grant it to all individuals fleeing the same situation.[548] According to Goodwin-Gill and McAdam, there is in fact no legal distinction between people fleeing individually and *en masse*.[549]

---

544   UNCHR, "Some Additional Observations and Recommendations on the European Commission 'Proposal for a Council Directive on Minimum Standards for the Qualification and Status of Third Country Nationals and Stateless Persons as Refugees or as Persons Who Otherwise Need International Protection' (Com(2001) 510 Final, 2001/0207(Cns) of 12 September 2001)" ("Some additional obsevations and recommendations on QD (2004) Proposal"), July 2002, p. 7.
545   "Annotated Comments on QD (2004)", [January 2005], *op. cit.*, Comment on Recital 26, p. 7.
546   UNHCR, "Statement on Article 15(c) QD", *op. cit.*, p. 6.
547   *Ibid.*, p. 6.
548   *See* for example the concerns expressed by France during the drafting of the Qualification Directive. EU Council, "Asylum Working Party, Outcomes of Proceedings of 5–6 and 17–18 September 2002", 12199/01 ASILE 43, 25 September 2002, p. 20, note 8.
549   G.S. Goodwin-Gill and J. McAdam, *The Refugee in International Law* (2007), *op. cit.*, p. 329.

The reference to "individual" threat was supported by the majority of Member States during the drafting of the Directive as a means of avoiding an "undesired opening of the scope" of paragraph (c).[550] Internal security, financial or political considerations States invoke to try and limit the number of persons entitled to subsidiary protection on their territory have no bearing in refugee law.[551] State practice relating to the grant of subsidiary protection nevertheless reveals that national authorities have used the "individual threat" requirement as a means of unduly denying subsidiary protection.

(c)   *A Convenient Ambiguity? State Practice under Consideration*

Studies and examples drawn from national case-law reveal that a number of EU Member States have adopted a restrictive interpretation of Article 15(c) of the Qualification Directive and therefor either denied subsidiary protection to individuals who were in fact eligible for it or granted subsidiary protection to individuals who could qualify for refugee status. After an overview (i) of Member States' restrictive interpretations of Article 15(c), an example drawn from French case-law will serve to illustrate the confusion made by some national asylum authorities between individualised threat and grounds for persecution (ii).

(i)   Member States' Restrictive Interpretations of Article 15(c)

Intuitively, one might think that a broad interpretation of Article 15(c) is favourable to asylum seekers. In fact, too broad an interpretation of Article 15(c) might turn out to be counterproductive: if the category of subsidiary protection beneficiaries is excessively broadened, Member States might seek to lower the level of rights granted.[552] In UNHCR's opinion, the term "individual" should thus serve to limit the scope of Article 15(c), not by imposing a higher threshold and heavier burden of proof on the applicant but by removing from the

---

550 "Presidency Note (ASILE 47)", *op. cit.*, p. 2.

551 In that sense, the Preamble of a 1998 European Parliament resolution on complementary protection notes that "the entry, residence and status of persons seeking international protection in the territory of the Member States cannot be treated merely as issues relating to the international security of those States and involve political and moral values which are underwritten by the international conventions to which those States are parties". European Parliament, Resolution on the Harmonisation of Forms of Protection Complementing Refugee Status in the European Union A4-0450/98 [28/05/1999] *OJ C150/203*, Recital G. On the applicability of the Refugee Convention to refugees arriving *en masse*, see also Part II, p. 312s.

552 Germany warns against such adverse effect of a broad interpretation of Article 15(c). The German warning is recounted by UNHCR in its "Note on UNHCR's main issues of concern regarding the Qualification Directive" (copy with the author).

scope of the provision persons for whom the alleged risk is merely a remote possibility.[553] This interpretation of the term "individual" in fact seems to be compatible with the original intent of the European Commission when it first submitted a proposal for the adoption of the Qualification Directive. The Commission's draft of Article 15(c) did not refer to "individual threat" but to "a threat to [the applicant's] life, safety or freedom as a result of indiscriminate violence". Despite the absence of reference to "individual" in the proposed text, the Commission explained that, in the case of subsidiary protection, "an applicant must still establish a well-founded fear for his or her life *on an individual basis*" [emphasis added]. The Commission adds that "although the reasons for the fear may not be specific to an individual he or she must still establish that the fear is well founded in their particular case".[554] The interpretation suggested by the UNHCR appears to be reflective of the object and purpose the Commission intended to give to Article 15(c): protecting any individual who shows that he or she has a well-founded fear of suffering serious harm if returned to their country or region of origin where a situation of indiscriminate violence prevails.

It is however not surprising that Member States have strayed from this interpretation originally given to the provision by the Commission. Firstly and as mentioned above, the requirement that people fleeing situations of "indiscriminate violence" demonstrate an "individual threat" is rather counterintuitive. Secondly, the inclusion of Recital 35 (ex Recital 26) in the Qualification Directive indeed achieved to further obfuscate the scope of subsidiary protection.[555]

Practice confirms that the wording of Article 15(c) is not entirely satisfactory. Firstly, in spite of the Directive's purpose to harmonise State legislation, the provision was not transposed in uniform manner in all EU Member States. In its report to the European Parliament and the Council on the application of the Qualification Directive, the European Commission indicates that eight Member States have chosen to omit the qualification "individual" when transposing the requirement of a "serious and individual threat" into their national

---

553   UNHCR, "Statement on Article 15(c) QD", *op. cit.*, p. 6. See also "Annotated Comments on QD (2004)", [January 2005], *op. cit.*, Comment on Article 15(c), p. 32.
554   "Explanatory Memorandum – QD (2004)", *op. cit.*, pp. 26–27.
555   Recital 35 reads as follows: "Risks to which a population of a country or a section of the population is generally exposed do normally not create in themselves an individual threat which would qualify as serious harm". Qualification Directive, Recital 35. *See* also above p. 132.

legislation.⁵⁵⁶ France on the other hand did transpose the reference to "individual" and added to it the requirement that the threat also be "direct".⁵⁵⁷

Secondly, Article 15(c) interpretation by national authorities is not uniform across the European Union. The provision's lack of clarity may well have occasionally served the interests of Member States who, relying on this – convenient it seems – ambiguity, used it to give the narrowest interpretation possible to Article 15(c). In a November 2007 study on the implementation of the Qualification Directive, UNHCR reviewed decisions taken in five EU Member States and observed that the reference to "individual", taken together with Recital 35 of the Directive, resulted in "denial of subsidiary protection to persons who clearly risk[ed] serious harm in their country of origin".⁵⁵⁸ UNHCR and, more recently, the European Commission observed that France, Germany and Sweden adopted a similar reasoning and interpreted the requirement of an individual threat in conjunction with the notion of "indiscriminate violence" and Recital 35 (ex Recital 26) as requiring that the applicant demonstrates that he or she is "at a greater risk of harm than the rest of the population, or sections of it, in his or her country of origin".⁵⁵⁹

French jurisprudence at the time was summarised as follows:

> The applicant is required to show a particular degree of individual harm, or at least, why he/she would be more concerned by the serious threat. The Court requires that the applicant be at greater risk of harm than the rest of the population.⁵⁶⁰

In like manner, German authorities have denied subsidiary protection in situations where the threats affected the entire population of the applicant's

---

556 European Union: European Commission, *Report on the application of Directive 2004/83/EC of 29 April 2004 on minimum standards for the qualification and status of third country nationals or stateless persons as refugees or as persons who otherwise need international protection and the content of the protection*, 16 June 2010, COM (2010)314 final, p. 9. The 8 Member States are: Austria, Belgium, the Czech Republic, EL (?), Germany, Spain, Hungary and Lithuania.

557 *Code de l'entrée et du séjour des étrangers et du droit d'asile*, Version consolidée au 12 février 2011, Article L712-1.

558 UNHCR, *Asylum in the European Union: A Study of the Implementation of the Qualification Directive* (November 2007), op. cit., pp. 71s.

559 European Commission, "Commission Report on the application of QD (2004)", op. cit., pp. 8–9; and UNHCR, *Asylum in the European Union: A Study of the Implementation of the Qualification Directive* (November 2007), op. cit.

560 ECRE/ELENA, op. cit., p. 202.

country of origin, or even, merely parts of the population: the applicant in such cases was found to be as exposed to risks as the rest of the population. UNHCR cites a case of Kassel Administrative Court concluding that Article 15 (c) had to be limited to "especially individual" threats; such is a threat "which does not exist at all or not to the same extent for the rest of the persons affected by the conflict".[561] German courts required that an applicant demonstrates "individual risk-enhancing features" (*Individuell-gefahrerhöhende Merkmale*),[562] which expose him or her to risks that "significantly" differ from those to which the rest of the population is "unfortunately" exposed.[563]

Similarly, Luxembourg's Administrative Tribunal and Court also repeatedly stated that the reference to "serious and individual threats" required that the applicant could show a high degree of individualisation of the alleged threat in a situation of indiscriminate violence: applicants were asked to demonstrate that they were "concretely and individually" exposed.[564]

Such interpretation by national courts was particularly problematic. Firstly, a requirement that an individual fleeing a situation of indiscriminate violence demonstrate that, in such situation which is "by definition random and haphazard",[565] he or she is more at risk than others, risks negating the adoption of Article 15(c). The Commission[566] had made clear by drawing from the Temporary Protection Directive that the purpose of Article 15(c) was to protect individuals who had to leave a specific country or geographical area by reason of the situation prevailing there.[567] Should any different approach be adopted, the added value of Article 15(c) in comparison to refugee status or subsidiary

---

561 The Kassel Administrative Court ruled Kassel Administrative Court, 1 E 1213/05 of 23 November 2006, cited in UNHCR, *Asylum in the European Union: A Study of the Implementation of the Qualification Directive* (November 2007), *op. cit.*, p. 73.

562 The High Administrative Court of Schleswig-Holstein found that being of Kurdish ethnicity in Iraq did not constitute "*Individuell-gefahrerhöhende Merkmale*" in view of the large number of persons (millions) and returnees specifically (thousands) sharing the same characteristics (including a common language). Germany: High Administrative Court (*Oberverwaltungsgericht*) of Schleswig-Holstein ("*1 Lb 17/08*"), 1 LB 17/08, 19 September 2008, p. 9.

563 In the court's words: "*Abgesehen davon werden mit diesen Aspekten Risiken angesprochen, die sich nicht 'significant' (…) von den allgemeinen Gefahren unterscheiden, die im Irak – leider – jedermann treffen können*". *Ibid.*, p. 8.

564 See for example Luxembourg: Administrative Tribunal, n° 23306, 18 February 2008, p. 8; Luxembourg: Cour Administrative, n° 23643C, 14 February 2008, pp. 6–7.

565 J. McAdam, *Complementary Protection in International Refugee Law* (2007), *op. cit.*, p. 72.

566 See above pp. 129s.

567 Temporary Protection Directive, Recitals (c) and (d).

protection under Article 15(a) and (b) would be only tenuous.[568] Secondly, it risked undermining refugee protection: the requirement that applicants establish that they are more at risk than the rest of the population by reason of their personal circumstances is not unreminiscent of the nexus criterion of the refugee definition. National courts have in fact occasionally referred to individualising risk factors which corresponded to Convention grounds for refugee status to instead grant subsidiary protection to the applicant, where the claim involved a reference to an armed conflict situation in the country of origin.[569]

Commentators insist that national courts ought to consider granting refugee status first, before subsidiary protection. If a nexus between the risk of ill-treatment and a Convention ground exists, the person concerned must be granted refugee status. It is only after this nexus is found to be missing that subsidiary protection can come into play.[570] The decision of the EU Court of Justice in the *Elgafaji* case clarified the meaning and scope of Article 15(c) of the Qualification Directive and, in so doing, significantly impacted national case-law. The influence of the case in Member States' jurisprudence is particularly clear in the French *Kona* case: the final decision taken in the case by the *Conseil d'État* draws on the *Elgafaji* judgment to quash a prior decision

---

568   See also UNHCR, who argues that Article 15(c) should cover risks which are "situational". This approach, UNHCR argues, would ensure the *effet utile* of Article 15(c). UNHCR, "Statement on Article 15(c) QD", *op. cit.*, pp. 5–6.

569   The case-law of Luxembourg Administrative Tribunal was for example criticised for that reason in a study conducted by UNHCR. In 2007, the Tribunal, UNHCR found, granted subsidiary protection to asylum seekers who in fact qualified for refugee status; in the cases cited by UNHCR, there existed a causal link between the feared ill-treatment and the applicants' political opinion or membership in a particular social group. UNHCR, "Etude de jurisprudence du tribunal administratif du Grand-Duché de Luxembourg en matière de protection internationale", *in* J. Gerkrath (Ed.), *Droit d'asile au Grand-Duché de Luxembourg et en Europe : développements récents*, Collection de la Faculté de Droit, d'Economie et de Finance de l'Université de Luxembourg (Bruxelles: Larcier, 2009), pp. 62–132, pp. 116–117. In France, in the Kona case, an applicant was granted subsidiary protection despite her being vulnerable on account, *inter alia*, of her religion. France: CRR (Sections réunies), *Mlle Bernadette Kona* ("*Kona*"), N°419162, 17 February 2006. See also the study conducted in 2007 by UNHCR on the implementation of the Qualification Directive: Sweden and France in particular are pointed at by UNHCR for failing to grant refugee status in cases where a causal link with a Convention ground had been demonstrated. UNHCR, *Asylum in the European Union: A Study of the Implementation of the Qualification Directive* (November 2007), *op. cit.*, pp. 74–75.

570   This is in conformity with UNHCR's understanding of the international protection regime devised by the Qualification Directive. See for example: "Annotated Comments on QD (2004)", [January 2005], *op. cit.*, Comment on Article 15, pp. 31–32.

of the *Cour nationale d'asile* which reflected the above-mentioned restrictive approach to Article 15(c). For that reason, the decision of the *Cour nationale d'asile* is discussed below.

(ii) France: The *Kona* Case, an Illustration of the Confusion between Individualised Threat and Grounds for Persecution

As mentioned, in practice, national asylum authorities have sometimes blurred the line between the respective ambits of refugee status and subsidiary protection. The French *Kona* case[571] is a clear illustration of the positive impact of the EU Court of Justice *Elgafji* judgment on the interpretation of Article 15(c) by national authorities.

The French National Court of Asylum (*Cour nationale du droit d'asile* or CNDA)[572] was asked to review a decision issued by the first instance asylum authority (OFPRA)[573] refusing refugee status but granting subsidiary protection to the applicant, Ms Kona. The applicant in the case is a woman, member of the Assyro-Chaldean Christian community in Iraq but not of the political party in power (Baas party), who fled Iraq by reason of the armed conflict situation prevailing in the country. She argues that in Iraq, she would be isolated (her mother and sister are recognised refugees in France) and rumoured to be wealthy, and would be subjected to persecution for all the above reasons. On 27 January 2006, the CNDA rejects the plaintiff's appeal. The Court finds that Ms Kona failed to established that the circumstances that caused her leaving from

---

571 France: CRR, *Kona*, 17 February 2006, *op. cit.* and France: Conseil d'Etat (Section du contentieux, 10ème et 9ème sous-sections réunies), *Mlle Kona* ("*Kona*"), N°292564, 25 March 2009.

572 The National Court of Asylum (*Cour nationale du droit d'asile* – CNDA; formerly Commission des recours des réfugiés – CRR) is a specialised administrative court competent to review appeals lodged against decisions made by the first instance asylum authority, the French Office for the Protection of Refugees and Stateless Persons (*Office français de protection des réfugiés et apatrides* – OFPRA). CNDA decisions can themselves be appealed before the Council of State (*Conseil d'État*), the highest French administrative court. The CNDA is a unique type of national jurisdiction: one of its members is nominated by the UN High Commissioner for Refugees (after assent of the *Conseil d'État*) and hence participates in the exercise of French national sovereignty. France: Code de l'entrée et du séjour des étrangers et du droit d'asile (hereafter "CESEDA"), Consolidated version of 20 June 2012, Articles 731–1 to 733–3. On the uniqueness of the CNDA, *see* F. Malvasio, "Étude : La famille et le droit d'asile en France", *in Contentieux des réfugiés: Jurisprudence du Conseil d'État et de la Cour nationale du droit d'asile, année 2010* (Montreuil: CNDA, Juin 2011), pp. 201–217, pp. 201–202, retrieved from: <http://www.cnda.fr/media/document/CNDA/recueil-2010.pdf> [28/08/2012].

573 French Office for the Protection of Refugees and Stateless Persons (*Office français de protection des réfugiés et apatrides* – OFPRA). Above note 657.

Iraq were linked to any of the Geneva Convention grounds, including religion or imputed political opinions. The CNDA concludes to the granting of subsidiary protection – rather than refugee status, thereby confirming the decision made by the first instance asylum authority.

The decision of the CNDA is two-fold. Firstly, the court finds that the risks to which the applicant is exposed in Iraq must be considered as originating from the climate of generalised violence created by the ongoing internal armed conflict situation prevailing in the country:

> ... les risques (...) auxquels elle est aujourd'hui exposée, doivent être regardés comme trouvant leur origine dans le climat de violence généralisée résultant de la situation de conflit armé interne qui prévaut aujourd'hui en Irak...[574]

Secondly, on account of the applicant's personal circumstances (a Christian, presumably wealthy, isolated woman), the court analyses those threats as serious direct and individual threats:

> ... ils constituent des menaces graves directes et individuelles, eu égard à son appartenance à la communauté assyro-chaldéenne chrétienne, à sa situation de femme isolée et à son aisance financière supposée...[575]

From those two observations – and in view of the absence of protection available in the country – the CNDA infers that subsidiary protection should be granted to the applicant.[576]

The court's conclusion appears on its face to be erroneous in law: religion being a Refugee Convention ground – acknowledged by the court[577] – and the CNDA having established that Ms Kona was exposed to serious, direct and individual threats by reason of, *inter alia*, her religion, the court should have concluded that Ms Kona qualified for refugee status. Such was in fact the conclusion eventually reached by the *Conseil d'État* on appeal. The latter decision being posterior to the EU Court of Justice judgment in *Elgafaji* and reflective of it, it will be addressed below.[578] The oral conclusions of the *rapporteur public* of the *Conseil d'État* can nevertheless already be cited here insofar as they

---

574   CRR, *Kona*, 17 February 2006, *op. cit.*, Considérant 8.
575   *Ibid.*, Considérant 8.
576   *Ibid.*
577   *Ibid.*, Considérant 7.
578   See below, in "(b) The Court of Justice reconciles 'individual threat' with 'indiscriminate violence': the Elgafaji case", pp. 140s. CE, *Kona*, 25 March 2009, *op. cit.*

interpret the decision of the CNDA. The CNDA decision, Ms Burguburu analysed, leads to believe that the applicant was not granted refugee status because the threats she invoked, albeit being linked to a Convention ground (religion), were "insufficiently individualised" to reach the Refugee Convention threshold of persecution:

> La décision de la Commission laisse, en effet, entendre que si Mlle Kona a obtenu la protection subsidiaire, et non conventionnelle, c'est parce que ses craintes, certes fondées sur un motif religieux, n'étaient pas suffisamment individualisées au regard des exigences conventionnelles alors qu'au contraire, la protection subsidiaire exigerait un moindre degré d'individualisation.[579]

Accordingly, the CNDA distinguished between cases where an applicant for international protection can be singled out and those where the applicant is merely more at risk than the rest of the population. If singled out, by reason of religion as in the case at hand, the applicant shall be granted refugee status. If she is at greater risks than the rest of the population, by reason of her personal circumstances (such as religion) but not personally targeted, she will instead be granted subsidiary protection under Article 15(c). As will be discussed below, the CNDA interpretation of the criteria for refugee status and subsidiary protection were found to be erroneous by the *rapporteur public* as well as the *Conseil d'État*. The Council did not endorse the CNDA approach, choosing instead to follow the interpretation given by the EU Court of Justice in the *Elgafaji* case.

Manifestly oblivious of the fact that refugee status is also applicable to people fleeing armed conflict situations, national asylum authorities and courts appeared to be blinded by the existence of an armed conflict context surrounding the case at hand: hurriedly discarding the examination of the claim under refugee status provisions, disregarding the fact that Convention grounds may be met, they proceeded to considering a grant of subsidiary protection instead. In that part of the examination, Convention grounds were not regarded as constitutive elements of persecution but as distinguishing factors meeting the individualisation requirement of Article 15(c) of the Qualification Directive (and of the corresponding provision in their national legislation).[580]

---

579 "Conclusions of *Rapporteur Public* Julie Burguburu" ("Conclusions J. Burguburu in Kona (CE)"), in CE (10ème et 9ème sous-sections réunies), *292564 Mlle Kona*, 25 mars 2009, p. 3.
580 On this last point, *see* in particular the above cited decision of the Administrative court of Luxembourg (case 23643C): in the court's view, the applicant's failure to demonstrate a

The ambiguous wording of Article 15(c) of the Qualification Directive has led some national asylum authorities to either grant subsidiary protection – and the often less generous status attached – to individuals who were entitled to refugee status; or to deny subsidiary protection in cases where they deemed the level of individualisation of the threat to be insufficient. Whether this was an "intentional mistake" on the part of national asylum authorities, concerned with avoiding an undesired opening of the scope of the provision cannot be asserted nor demonstrated but the fact that those States that appear to favour subsidiary protection in the unduly grey area of persecution occurring in situations of generalised violence are also States who chose to recognise lower sets of rights for subsidiary protection than for refugee status[581] does cast doubts on the genuineness of their error.

The preliminary ruling of the EU Court of Justice requested by the Netherlands Council of State in the *Elgafaji* case, concerning the interpretation of Articles 2(e) and 15(c) of the Qualification Directive, brought clarity on the subject matter.

2   The Court of Justice Reconciles "individual threat" with "indiscriminate violence": The *Elgafaji* Case

In the *Elgafaji* case,[582] the Court of Justice of the European Union clarified, though indirectly, the respective scope of subsidiary protection and refugee status. The ambiguous requirement of an individualisation of the threat in a context of indiscriminate violence was explained by the Court who, by the same token, could justify the existence of the just as obscure Recital 35

---

causal link between his misfortune ("*déboires*") and a Convention ground (in the case, his ethnicity) is also pertinent in the context of the examination of the claim under subsidiary protection provisions since the criteria for each form of protection are connected. In the court's words: "*La circonstance que ces deux premiers arguments de persécution, auxquels la Cour se rallie entièrement, ont été dégagés dans le cadre de l'analyse du bien-fondé ou mal-fondé de la demande d'asile proprement dite de Monsieur X ne sauraient affecter leur pertinence dans le contexte d'une mesure de protection subsidiaire, étant donné que les conditions d'octroi d'une mesure de protection subsidiaire ne sauraient être entrevues comme entièrement détachées ou détachables de la demande d'asile au sens de la Convention de Genève*". CA (Lux.), 14 February 2008, *op. cit.*, p. 6.

581   On the comparative contents of subsidiary protection and refugee status in the different EU Member States, see: European Commission, "Commission Report on the application of QD (2004)", *op. cit.*, pp. 11–15; ECRE/ELENA, *op. cit.*, pp. 239–243; and concerning the difference in the duration of residence permits granted to refugees and to beneficiaries of subsidiary protection (the latter receiving shorter residence permits that refugees), see "Commission Impact Assessment – Proposal for a Recast QD", *op. cit.*, p. 49.

582   CJ, *Elgafaji*.

(ex Recital 26) of the Qualification Directive. This decision of the Court of Justice provides a welcome interpretation of Article 15(c) of the Directive (a) which has since been followed by national courts (b).

(a)   *Summary and Assessment of the Leading Elgafaji Judgment*
The Court of Justice (CJ) was referred two questions for preliminary ruling by the Dutch State Secretary for Justice who, in brief, asked the Court to clarify the respective scopes of Article 15(c) of the Qualification Directive and of Article 3 of the European Convention of Human Rights (ECHR), and to elaborate on the criteria for the qualification of persons as beneficiaries of subsidiary protection.[583]

On the first question, the Court confirms that the fundamental right enshrined in Article 3 ECHR is a general principle of Community law[584] and confirms that, in interpreting the scope of this right, it takes into consideration the case-law of the European Court of Human Rights (ECtHR). However, the CJ adds, it is not Article 15(c) but Article 15(b) of the Directive that corresponds in essence to Article 3 ECHR.[585] The Court makes clear that Article 15(c) is an "autonomous concept"[586] devised to provide protection in cases not covered by Article 3 ECHR and whose interpretation should therefore be carried out independently but without prejudice to fundamental rights as they are guaranteed under the ECHR.[587]

On the second question, on the notion of "individual threat", Advocate General Poiares Maduro, basing his analysis on the notion of fundamental rights, observed that substantive breaches of fundamental rights undeniably also occur in the absence of any discrimination.[588] According to the Advocate General, in certain circumstances, armed conflict situations can expose entire populations to risks of serious harm as real as the risks run by applicants claiming refugee status or subsidiary protection under Article 15(a) or (b).[589] It is those situations that Article 15(c) should cover: that it is to say, situations in which individuals are not singled out but nevertheless victims of serious harms.

---

583   Ibid., § 26.
584   See the earlier case-law of the Court of Justice on this point above: "II.A.1. Fundamental Rights as General Principles of Community Law", pp. 35s.
585   CJ, *Elgafaji*, § 28.
586   K. Lenaerts, "The Contribution of the European Court of Justice to the Area of Freedom, Security and Justice", *International and Comparative Law Quarterly*, Vol. 59, No. 2, p. 295.
587   CJ, *Elgafaji*, § 28.
588   Opinion of Adv. Gen. Poiares Maduro, *Case C-465/07 Meki Elgafaji and Noor Elgafaji v. Staatssecretaris Van Justitie* ("AG Opinion in *Elgafaji*") (9 September 2008), §§ 34 and 38.
589   Ibid., § 34.

In like manner, the Court of Justice interprets paragraph (c) by setting it back in the broader context of Article 15. The Court analyses the respective scopes of the three paragraphs of Article 15 and concludes that paragraphs (a) and (b) cover situations in which applicants for subsidiary protection are "specifically exposed to the risk of a particular type of harm", whereas paragraph (c) covers "a more general risk of harm".[590] It follows that transposing the level of individualisation required in Article 15 (a) and (b) to situations covered by 15(c) would make Article 15 altogether redundant.[591] In that sense, the Court stresses that the term "indiscriminate" implies precisely that the threat may extend to people "irrespective of their personal circumstances".[592] The interpretation of "individual threat" shall not remove the substance of Article 15(c) by neglecting this key element of the provision.

A consideration of the French wording of Article 15(c) of the Qualification Directive could actually have supported the Advocate General and Court's view: where Article 15(c) refers in English to "*indiscriminate* violence", the French version mentions a "*violence aveugle*" (blind).[593] The type of violence covered by Article 15(c) appears clearly:[594] it is a form of violence which, as personified in the French version of the text, does not choose its victims but randomly, "blindly" hits.

The Court confirms that Article 15(c) cannot be interpreted as requiring a link between the threat and the applicant's personal circumstances:

> ... the existence of a serious and individual threat to the life or person of an applicant for subsidiary protection is not subject to the condition that

---

590   CJ, *Elgafaji.*, §§ 32–33.
591   K. Lenaerts, *op. cit.*, pp. 295–296.
592   CJ, *Elgafaji*, § 34.
593   The French version of the Qualification Directive defines serious harms ("*atteintes graves*") for the purpose of Article 15(c) as: "*des menaces graves et individuelles contre la vie ou la personne d'un civil en raison d'une violence aveugle en cas de conflit armé interne ou international*". Qualification Directive, French version, Article 15(c).
594   Clear as it may be, the wording of the French version of the Qualification Directive is however not reproduces *verbatim* in French legislation (possibly because the French Asylum act transposed the Qualification Directive "by anticipation", at a time when the final text of the Directive was not yet adopted). In particular, the notion of "*violence généralisée*" replaces the terms "*violence aveugle*". I believe the latter wording would have better reflected the intended purpose of Article 15(c). CESEDA, *op. cit.*, Article 712-1(c). On the anticipatory incorporation of the Directive in French law and the reasons behind it, *see* V. Chetail, "The Implementation of the Qualification Directive in France: One Step Forward and Two Steps Backwards", *in* K. Zwaan (Ed.), *The Qualification Directive: Central Themes, Problem Issues, and Implementation in Selected Member States* (Nijmegen: Wolf Legal Publishers, 2007), pp. 87–102, p. 87.

that applicant adduce evidence that he is specifically targeted by reason of factors particular to his personal circumstances[595]

Instead, the Court interprets the term individual as covering situations in which the degree of indiscriminate violence is so high that any individual would, "solely on account of his presence on the territory", face a real risk of being subject to a threat to his or her life or person.[596]

Prima facie, this interpretation appears to contradict the text of Recital 35 (ex 26) of the Directive, stating that "risks to which a population of a country or a section of a population is generally exposed do normally not create in themselves an individual threat which would qualify as serious harm".[597] Advocate General Poiares Maduro had however already proposed and justified such interpretation in the light of Recital 35 by stating that Article 15(c) would precisely cover those situations in which the level of indiscriminate violence exceeds the risks described in Recital 35: to wit, Article 15(c) must be interpreted as covering violence which "exceeds the risks to which the population of a country or a section of the population are generally exposed".[598] The Court of Justice, following a similar approach, reconciles Recital 35 with the scope it purports to give to Article 15(c): the Court relies on the use of the term "normally" in Recital 35 to infer *a contrario* that, exceptionally, risks to which a population is generally exposed is so high that they may qualify as serious harm.[599] In such exceptional situation, the Court finds that consideration of the high level of indiscriminate violence should prevail over the requirement of individualisation of the threat.[600]

The Court observes that the two notions are in fact linked, and clarifies that, as for the burden of proof, the level of indiscriminate violence and the level of individualisation which the applicant must establish as being inversely proportional:

> ... the more the applicant is able to show that he is specifically affected by reason of factors particular to his personal circumstances, the lower the level of indiscriminate violence required for him to be eligible for subsidiary protection.[601]

---

595   CJ, *Elgafaji*, § 43.
596   *Ibid.*, § 35.
597   Qualification Directive, Recital 35 (formerly Recital 26).
598   AG *Opinion in Elgafaji*, § 36.
599   CJ, *Elgafaji*, §§ 36–37.
600   H. Labayle (March-April 2011), *op. cit.*, p. 283.
601   CJ, *Elgafaji*, § 39.

The Court thereby elaborates the so-called concept of a "sliding scale".[602] It follows that, in extreme situation of generalised violence, applicants will be "presumed"[603] to be "subject individually"[604] to the risk in question. The Court confirms that such situation, for exceptional it may be, falls within the scope of Article 15(c) of the Directive. The statement is not unreminiscent of the approach adopted by the European Court of Human Rights in *NA v. UK*[605] (discussed below) to which the Court of Justice refers in this case. The Court of Justice states:

> ... the existence of such a threat can exceptionally be considered to be established where the degree of indiscriminate violence characterising the armed conflict taking place (...) reaches such a high level that substantial grounds are shown for believing that a civilian, returned to the relevant country or, as the case may be, to the relevant region, would, solely on account of his presence on the territory of that country or region, face a real risk of being subject to that threat.[606]

As mentioned, the Court clarifies the ostensibly paradoxical wording of Article 15(c) and demonstrates its compatibility with the infamous Recital 35 of the Directive. After asserting the originality of Article 15(c) *vis-à-vis* Article 3 of the European Convention of Human Rights, the Court endeavours and indeed achieves to secure its *effet utile* through a teleological interpretation of the provision. Through a systematic reading of Article 15,[607] the Court defines the intended scope of Article 15(c) by comparison with that of paragraphs (a) and (b), and deduces therefrom the meaning of the term "individual" for the purpose of 15(c). The internal logic of Article 15 thus identified by the Court reflects the views expressed by UNHCR on the matter and presented soon after

---

602 The term is used in literature to describe the relationship between the levels of individualisation and of indiscriminate violence. UNHCR, *et al.*, *Safe at Last? Law and Practice in Selected EU Member States with Respect to Asylum-Seekers Fleeing Indiscriminate Violence*, Law and Practice in Selected EU Member States with Respect to Asylum-Seekers Fleeing Indiscriminate Violence (Brussels: UNHCR, July 2011), pp. 49–54; J.-F. Durieux (2012), *op. cit.*, pp. 172–175.
603 AG *Opinion in Elgafaji*, § 36.
604 CJ, *Elgafaji*, § 37.
605 ECtHR, *N.A. v. The United Kingdom* ("*NA v. UK*"), Application no. 25904/07 (17 July 2008), § 115. Below pp. 226s.
606 *Ibid.*, § 43.
607 E. Broussy, *et al.*, "Chronique de jurisprudence communautaire", *AJDA*, No. 18 (18/05/2009), pp. 980–990, p. 980.

the *Elgafaji* case was submitted to the Court of Justice. Commenting on Article 15(c) insofar as it provides subsidiary protection to persons fleeing individual threats, UNHCR considered that the "added value" of Article 15(c) was "its ability to provide protection from serious risks which are situational, rather than individually targeted".[608] The Court's finding that the serious risks covered by Article 15(c) are those to which an individual is exposed "solely on account of his presence" on a given territory is indeed along the same lines.

As mentioned, the requirement that an applicant establishes that he or she is at greater risk than the rest of the population, by reason of his or her personal circumstances risked rendering the protection offered by Article 15(c) and had been amply criticised in literature. The clarifications given by the EU Court of Justice in the *Elgafaji* case should however be conducive to Member States granting subsidiary protection in a more uniform manner throughout the Union. This harmonisation could carry with it, for those States who had adopted the restrictive interpretation of the term "individual" in particular, a broadening of the scope of subsidiary protection and a correlative increase in positive decisions. It can also clarify the respective scope of refugee status and subsidiary protection: individualisation shall not be mistaken for a requirement that the applicant establish that he or she is personally at risk, targeted by reason of his or her personal characteristics. Such level of individualisation will indeed often connote eligibility for refugee status since, in armed conflict situations, people who are personally at risk will often be those who are targeted on religious, political, racial, nationalist or other discriminatory grounds. The circumstance of an armed conflict situation shall be incidental only and not, in any case, shift national authorities' focus away from granting refugee status if the applicant has a well-founded fear of being exposed to risks for his or her life or person, by reason of his or her religion, race, nationality, political opinion or membership in a particular social group.

The judgment of the Court of Justice was generally well received in relevant literature; it casts "a welcome light on the conditions stated in Article 15(c) and on the relationship between them".[609] In particular, by rejecting the requirement that an applicant adduce evidence that he or she is specifically targeted in a context of indiscriminate violence, by reason of his or her personal circumstances, the Court ensures that the provision of subsidiary protection for people fleeing armed conflict situations is effective. A finding of the contrary risked leading to the "absurd result" that individuals fleeing the most severe

---

608   UNHCR, "Statement on Article 15(c) QD", *op. cit.*, pp. 5–6.
609   R. Errera, "The CJEU and Subsidiary Protection: Reflections on Elgafaji – and After", *International Journal of Refugee Law*, March 1, 2011, Vol. 23, No. 1 (2011), pp. 93–112, pp. 104–105.

but also widespread situation of indiscriminate violence would fall short of Article 15(c) definition.[610]

Through its "constructive interpretation"[611] of Article 15(c), the Court of Justice secured the *effect utile* of Article 15(c). From the broader perspective of fundamental rights, the Court of Justice further entrenched their protection within the European Union legal order, not least by asserting the autonomy of EU fundamental rights protection from the European Convention of Human Rights.[612]

> Le juge communautaire (...) s'immerge toujours plus dans l'univers des droits fondamentaux en consolidant, espère par espèce, l'élaboration d'une Communauté de droit "effective et non pas théorique et illusoire"...[613]

The EU Court of Justice, as the European Court of Human Right, ensures that EU law guarantees "not rights that are theoretical or illusory but rights that are practical and effective".[614] Effectiveness can indeed be found to characterise the impact of the Court on Member States' decision-making: national asylum authorities were often found to refer, explicitly or not, to the *Elgafaji* judgment as guidance to rule on indiscriminate violence asylum cases.

(b)   *A Leading Judgment Followed by National Courts*

The clarifications brought by the Court of Justice in the *Elgafaji* case are reflected in EU Member States' asylum decisions[615] issued afterwards.[616]

For example, let us return to France and to the conspicuously erroneous decision issued by the *Cour nationale du droit d'asile* (CNDA) in the *Kona* case. As mentioned above, the CNDA had found that by reason of her belonging to a

---

610   K. Lenaerts, *op. cit.*, p. 296.
611   E. Broussy, *et al.* (18/05/2009), *op. cit.*, pp. 980 and 981.
612   CJ, *Elgafaji*, § 28; L. Burgorgue-Larsen, "De l'autonomie de la protection du droit communautaire par rapport à la Convention européenne des droits de l'homme ?", *AJDA*, No. 24 (06/07/2009), pp. 1321–1326, p. 1323.
613   The author cites the dictum of the European Court of Human Rights in the *Artico* case: The Court recalls that the Convention is intended to guarantee L. Burgorgue-Larsen (06/07/2009), *op. cit.*, p. 1323.
614   ECtHR, *Artico v. Italy* ("*Artico*"), No. 6694/74 (13 May 1980).
615   Germany: BVerwG ("*BVerwG 10 C 9.08*"), 10 C 9.08, 14 July 2009.
616   R. Errera for example surveys domestic cases decided since *Elgafaji* and based on it, in Bulgaria, the Czech Republic, France, Germany, the Netherlands and the United Kingdom. R. Errera (2011), *op. cit.*, pp. 105–112.

religious minority, Ms Kona was exposed to a greater risk of harm than the rest of the population in the context of the armed conflict situation prevailing in Iraq.[617] On the face it, this decision failed to fully implement the Qualification Directive. In 2009, the case was brought before the French highest administrative court (*Conseil d'état* – "Council"), who concluded that the CNDA decision was indeed erroneous in law. The Council found that the CNDA failed to draw "the appropriate legal conclusions from its own observations and had made an error in law in denying [the applicant] refugee status".[618]

The *Conseil d'État* followed the interpretation proposed by the *rapporteur public* in her oral conclusions ("the Conclusions"), which clearly described how refugee status and subsidiary protection articulate. In her conclusions, Ms Burguburu clarified that, if threats originate in both a situation of generalised violence linked to an armed conflict and in the applicant's membership in a particular social group, then, the latter criterion should prevail and refugee status be granted accordingly. The existence of any of the Convention grounds does not *de facto* exclude subsidiary protection but, the *rapporteur public* explains, either the threats are based on a Convention ground (such as religion) and refugee status should be granted or the circumstance invoked by the applicant is "non-decisive, quasi-incidental, and not sufficient to establish the existence of threats of persecutions" and only then is it appropriate to consider the potential eligibility of the applicant to subsidiary protection.[619] The Conclusions further clarify the meaning of the required "individualisation". Accordingly, the CNDA misinterpreted refugee law in assuming that subsidiary protection differed from refugee protection in that it merely required a lesser degree of individualisation. Firstly, the Geneva Convention does not mention that threats should be of a personal nature, and secondly, the notion of "individual threat" in subsidiary protection provisions should be construed in contrast with threats against political, social, religious or ethnic groups since, in the latter case, refugee status should prevail.[620] In substantiation of her argumentation on the respective scopes of refugee status and subsidiary

---

617 Above pp. 139s.
618 CE, *Kona*, 25 March 2009, *op. cit.*, Considérant 2.
619 In the words of the *rapporteur public* in the case: "*de deux choses, l'une, soit les craintes sont fondées sur un motif conventionnel, et le statut de réfugié doit être accordé, soit l'élément, religieux en l'espèce, est un élément de contexte non déterminant, quasi-incident, qui ne suffit pas à établir les menaces de persécution, auquel cas il convient – mais seulement dans un second temps – de s'interroger sur une éventuelle admission au bénéfice de la protection subsidiaire*"., "Conclusions J. Burguburu in Kona (CE)", *op. cit.*, pp. 2–3.
620 *Ibid.*, p. 3.

protection, the *rapporteur public* explicitly – albeit not by name – refers to the ruling of the Court of Justice in the *Elgafaji* case.[621]

The *Conseil d'État*, as said, ruled on the same lines. The CNDA, the Council's argument ran, had observed that Ms Kona was threatened on ground of her religion; this being a Refugee Convention ground, it should have examined Ms Kona's claim as an application for refugee status. In any case, the CNDA failed to demonstrate that the other criteria for refugee status were not met by the applicant.[622]

The main thrust of the Council's decision pertains to the sequential procedure which should govern the assessment of asylum claims. It is indeed well-established that national asylum authorities ought to first assess applications for international protection against the criteria for refugee status, before proceeding, if the refugee criteria are not met, to examine qualification for subsidiary protection.[623] The Council confirms this principle: the CNDA should have assessed Ms Kona's claim against refugee status criteria first and could not legally decide on the applicability of subsidiary protection before it had expressly ruled it out, as the case may be, refugee status. Incidentally it seems, the Council nevertheless confirmed, on the basis of the *Elgafaji* case, that were the CNDA to examine qualification for subsidiary protection in a context of generalised violence, it could, as it did in 2006, take account of the applicant's personal circumstances to justify the granting of subsidiary protection in the case.[624] The endorsement by the *Conseil d'État* of the approach taken by the Court of Justice in *Elgafaji* is manifest; the Council notes that:

> ... the serious, direct and individual threats enounced in (c) [CESEDA Article L.712-1(c)[625]] must be considered as concerning only civilians, regardless of their origins, social status and belief, when the degree of violence reached by a conflict in a country is such as to establish that they have substantial grounds for believing that their returning to their country would expose them to the risk of being exposed to the above-mentioned threats.[626]

---

621   Ibid.
622   CE, *Kona*, 25 March 2009, *op. cit.*, *Considérant* 2.
623   Above pp. 116–117 and footnotes 458–459.
624   CE, *Kona*, 25 March 2009, *op. cit.*, *Considérant* 2.
625   The type of serious harm defined in Article 15(c) of the Qualification Directive corresponds in essence to that covered by Article L.712-1(c) of the relevant legislation (*Code de l'entrée et du séjour des étrangers et du droit d'asile*). CESEDA, *op. cit.*, Article L.712-1(c).
626   CE, *Kona*, 25 March 2009, *op. cit.*, *Considérant* 2.

Less than two months later, in *OFPRA v. M. Baskarathas*,[627] the *Conseil d'État* had the opportunity to elaborate on its interpretation of Article L.712-1(c) CESEDA (transposing Article 15(c) QD) and to implement, more directly than in *Kona*, the *Elgafaji* judgment. In the *Baskarathas* case, the CNDA first carefully assessed Mr Baskarathas's (Mr B.) application against the criteria for refugee status.[628] The CNDA concluded that the applicant had failed to demonstrate a real risk of being persecuted, by reason of his ethnicity or political opinion specifically and subsequently only examined Mr B.'s qualification for subsidiary protection.[629] The CNDA hence abided by the sequential assessment required by the *Conseil d'État* in *Kona*. The CNDA then proceeded to adduce from available country information that the situation prevailing in Northern and Eastern Sri Lanka was one of generalised violence resulting from the internal armed conflict taking place in the country.[630] In particular, the CNDA had due regard to the applicant's personal circumstances: Mr B.'s region of origin and residence, the CNDA observed, was "particularly affected" by the on-going civil war. The Court inferred from these findings that Mr B. would be exposed in his region of origin to a grave, direct and individual threat against his life or person by reason of the high level of indiscriminate violence prevailing in that part of the country.[631] The *Office français de protection des réfugiés et apatrides* (OFPRA) lodged an appeal before the *Conseil d'état*, against the CNDA decision. The CNDA decision was however confirmed by the *Conseil d'État* and OFPRA's appeal rejected on all grounds.[632] The Council confirmed that neither the Qualification Directive nor French law required that the violence and the armed conflict situation coexist everywhere within the same geographical area.[633] The CNDA, the Council finds, gave a circumstantial account of the factual elements[634] that concurred to establish the existence of a situation of

---

627 France: CE (10ème et 9ème sous-sections réunies), *OFPRA C/Baskarathas* ("*Baskarathas*"), N° 320295, 3 July 2009.
628 France: CNDA (Sections réunies), *M B.* ("*Baskarathas*"), N° 581505, 27 June 2008.
629 *Ibid.*, *Considérants* 3 and 4.
630 *Ibid.*, *Considérant* 6.
631 *Ibid.*, *Considérants* 6 and 7.
632 CE, *Baskarathas*, 3 July 2009, *op. cit.*
633 *Ibid.*, *Considérant* 3.
634 As the *Conseil d'État* mentioned, among the different elements cited, the CNDA had mentioned that the belligerents were committing grave violations of international humanitarian law against civilian populations. This reference to international humanitarian law can be analysed as palliating, in part, the absence of definition in the Qualification Directive of the terms "international or internal armed conflict". *Ibid.*, § 4; CNDA, *Baskarathas*, 27 June 2008, *op. cit.*, § 6. See also R. Errera arguing that international humanitarian law,

indiscriminate and generalised violence in the applicant's region of origin.[635] The *rapporteur public* chiefly welcomed the fact that the CNDA did not only acknowledge the existence of a situation of generalised violence but also endeavoured to ascertain its particular intensity in the applicant's region of origin. In line with the *Elgafaji* judgment, the Conclusions presented by the *rapporteur public* make clear that an applicant for international protection is presumed to be individually targeted only in situations of exceptionally intense violence.[636] In all other cases, the *rapporteur public* adds, asylum authorities must look into the applicant's personal circumstances, such as his or her region of origin, which might be exposed to higher level of violence.[637] A different interpretation would be incompatible with the Qualification Directive (and transposing acts) and qualify for subsidiary protection in the EU any person fleeing from an area where an "ordinary" (as opposed to "exceptional") level of generalised violence prevails.[638] The *rapporteur public*'s reasoning appears compatible with the *Elgafaji* judgment and its interpretation of Article 15(c), in view of Recital 35 of the Directive. Generalised violence does not normally create threats of serious harm but can exceptionally do so, when the level of indiscriminate violence is so high that anyone is at risk, by their sole presence on the territory.[639] As to the burden of proof, the applicant's personal circumstances can be used to support the reality of the risks invoked.[640]

---

        among other legal sources, can cast light on the conditions for subsidiary protection stated in Article 15(c) of the Qualification Directive. R. Errera (2011), *op. cit.*, pp. 105s. See also on the "overwhelming reasons" for giving an international humanitarian law meaning to key terms in Article 15(c) of the Qualification Directive: UKAIT, KH, 25 March 2008, *op. cit.*, §§ 33–59 and *contra* EWCA, QD & AH v Secretary of State for the Home Department, 24 June 2009, *op. cit.*, §§ 34–37 and 40; United Kingdom: UKUT (Immigration and Asylum Chamber), *HM and Others (Article 15(c)) Iraq Cg ("HM and Others")*, [2010] UKUT 331 (IAC), 22 September 2010. In the latter case, the Upper Tribunal found that the Court of Appeal had made clear in QD (*op. cit.*) that "a misconception that international humanitarian law (IHL) should drive the construction of the kind of harm identified in Article 15 [Qualification Directive] had led [the Asylum Immigration Tribunal in KH] to read the terms 'indiscriminate violence' and 'life or person' too narrowly and to set the threshold of risk too high". *HM and Others*, § 66.

635   CE, *Baskarathas*, 3 July 2009, *op. cit.*, Considérant 4.
636   "Conclusions of *rapporteur public* Julien Boucher", in CE (10ème et 9ème sous-sections réunies), 320295 OFPRA c. Baskarathas, 3 July 2009, p. 9.
637   *Ibid.*, p. 9.
638   This is not an exact translation of the rapporteur public's statement but I believe it better conveys the thrust of the argument. *Ibid.*, p. 9.
639   Above pp. 140s.
640   In that sense, CJ, *Elgafaji*, § 39.

As said, the *Conseil d'état* confirms the ruling of the CNDA and reproduces *verbatim* the *Elgafaji* judgment.⁶⁴¹ The *Conseil d'État* has since again literally restated the *Elgafaji* interpretation of Article 15(c).⁶⁴²

In view of the case-law of the German Federal Administrative Court (*Bundesverwaltungsgericht – BVerwG*) predating the *Elgafaji*, it is not really surprising that the judgment of the Court of Justice was soon followed by German courts.⁶⁴³ The *BVerwG* had indeed in 2008 already formulated an interpretation of the scope of subsidiary protection in indiscriminate violence cases which is not unsimilar to that adopted by the Court of Justice in *Elgafaji*. In June 2008, the Federal Administrative Court had already observed that the adverb "normally" used in Recital 35 of the Directive prompted the inference that Recital 35 did not exclude the possibility that cases existed in which the risks to which a population is generally exposed may create, in themselves, individual threats tantamount to serious harm.⁶⁴⁴ Furthermore, the *BVerwG* found that a threat to which a large number of civilians are exposed by reason of an armed conflict may "concentrate" (*verdichten*) in the person of an applicant, so much so that it amounts, for the applicant, to a serious and individual threat to his or her life or person for the purpose of Article 15(c) of the Qualification Directive.⁶⁴⁵ The Federal Administrative Court called upon the EU Court of Justice, where the *Elgafaji* case was pending at the time, to clarify both questions.⁶⁴⁶ For that reason, it is possible to reiterate the comment made above: it is unsurprising that the Federal Administrative Court welcomed and endorsed the

---

641   CE, *Baskarathas*, 3 July 2009, *op. cit.*, Considérant 6. The same observation is made by D. Ritleng in D. Ritleng, *et al.*, "Jurisprudence administrative française intéressant le droit communautaire", *Revue trimestrielle de droit européen*, No. 2 (28/07/2010), pp. 453–492, p. 476.

642   France: Conseil d'Etat (10ème sous-section), *M. Athavan A.* ("*M. Athavan A.*"), N° 341270, 24 August 2011, Considérant 1.

643   BVerwG, *BVerwG 10 C 9.08*, 14 July 2009, *op. cit.*

644   The German Federal Administrative Court (*BVerwG*) observed: "*Ausgeschlossen wird eine solche Betroffenheit der gesamten Bevölkerung oder einer ganzen Bevölkerungsgruppe allerdings nicht, was schon durch die im 26. Erwägungsgrund gewählten Formulierung 'normalerweise' deutlich wird*". Germany: BVerwG ("*BVerwG 10 C 43.07*"), 10 C 43.07, 24 June 2008, § 35.

645   According to the *BVerwG*'s, it is left for courts to prove: "*... ob sich die von einem bewaffneten Konflikt für eine Vielzahl von Zivilpersonen ausgehende – und damit allgemeine – Gefahr in der Person der Kläger* so verdichtet hat, *dass sie eine erhebliche individuelle Gefahr im Sinne des § 60 Abs. 7 Satz 2 AufenthG darstellt*". [emphasis added]. The second sentence of Section 60(7) of the Residence Act to which the judgment refers transposes Article 15(c) of the Qualification Directive into German law. *Ibid.*, § 34.

646   *Ibid.*, § 34 and 36.

judgment of the EU Court of Justice in the *Elgafaji* case. In 2009, the *BVerwG* observes that the conclusions of the Court of Justice are "essentially the same" as the conclusions it had reached in the abovementioned 2008 judgment.[647]

(c)   *A Misleading Judgment?*

The *Elgafaji* ruling can be welcome in that it provides clarifications on the meaning and scope of Article 15(c) of the Qualification Directive and ensures that subsidiary protection effectively protects individuals who do not qualify as refugees but who nevertheless need international protection in view of the exceptional level of indiscriminate violence prevailing in their country of origin. As said, the Court succeeded in safeguarding the *effet utile* of a provision whose unclear wording failed to convince; one substantial reservation can nevertheless be made and one important shortcoming deplored. The first comment concerns the "sliding scale" developed by the Court between the level of individualisation and degree of indiscriminate violence (i). The second concerns the lack of guidance provided to national authorities on the definitions of decisive terms of Article 15(c) such as, in particular "international or internal armed conflict" (ii).

(i)   The "sliding scale": A Reminiscence of Article 15(c) Ambiguous Wording

Firstly, the judgment of the Court certainly ensures a broadened application of Article 15(c) in a number of Member States, including those who until then seemingly confused individualisation with grounds for persecution and required a high level of individualisation of the risk in armed conflict situations to justify the granting of subsidiary protection. The Court's judgment nevertheless cannot but disappoint insofar as it fails to fully discard the concept of individual risk in contexts of generalised violence. It is to be feared that the "sliding scale" elaborated by the Court of Justice, still leaves national authorities with a large leeway. In cases where asylum authorities assess the situation in the applicant's country or region of origin as falling short from the *Elgafaji* standard of "exceptionality", to wit when the degree of indiscriminate violence is deemed to be insufficiently high, excessive weight might be attached to the individualisation requirement in order to deny subsidiary protection. It can be deplored that the Court of Justice did not give Article 15(c) its full *effet utile*, that of offering protection to any individual coming from situations of

---

647   In the *BVerwG*'s words: "*Inzwischen hat der Gerichtshof diese Fragen mit [Elgafaji-]Urteil ... grundsätzlich geklärt und sie im Wesentlichen ebenso beurteilt wie der Senat in dem erwähnten Urteil vom 24. Juni 2008*". BVerwG, *BVerwG 10 C 9.08*, 14 July 2009, *op. cit.*, § 13.

indiscriminate violence. The *travaux préparatoires* of the Qualification Directive, discussed above, suggest that such was indeed the original object and purpose of Article 15(c).[648] The Commission drew the provision from the criteria for temporary protection in the event of a mass influx of displaced persons. The term "individual" was then absent in the provision but the notion was already somewhat present. It is worth recalling here that, contrasting subsidiary protection with temporary protection, the Commission explained:

> In the case of subsidiary protection though, an applicant must still establish a well-founded fear for his or her life *on an individual basis*. Although the reasons for the fear may not be specific to an individual he or she must still establish that the fear is well founded in their particular case.[649]

In other words, it seems that the Commission suggests, and this was possibly meant to secure States' adherence to the concept of subsidiary protection in armed conflict situations, that subsidiary protection (and, correlatively, the corresponding status) is intended to be granted on the basis of an individual examination of claims and not, like temporary protection, on the basis of group determination. The following sentence of the Commission's Explanatory Memorandum seems to buttress this interpretation. The Commission observes that:

> Member States are bound to cover persons falling into this category where they arrive in a Council agreed 'mass influx' so it is consistent and appropriate to include them also when they arrive individually, and do not qualify as a refugee.[650]

The Commission devised subsidiary protection as a form of protection available to *individuals* who flee situations where violence is indiscriminate. Subsidiary protection might be best described as the "individual counterpart"[651] of temporary protection, "extending protection to single or small group arrivals on the same humanitarian basis".[652] Claims being assessed on a case-by-case basis, it is required that applicants establish a well-founded fear for their life or

---

648   Above p. 126.
649   "Explanatory Memorandum – QD (2004)", *op. cit.*, explanation on Article 15(c), pp. 26–27 [emphasis added].
650   *Ibid.*, p. 27.
651   J. McAdam, *Complementary Protection in International Refugee Law* (2007), *op. cit.*, p. 43.
652   *Ibid.*, p. 43.

person. A 2007 judgment of the UK Asylum and Immigration Tribunal can actually support this view. The Tribunal granted subsidiary protection ("humanitarian protection" under UK's Immigration Rules[653]) to the applicant on the basis of the general situation prevailing in Iraq. On the notion of "individual threat", the judgment articulates that:

> ... whereas the threat may be individual it is, to borrow terminology from a separate jurisdiction, joint and several. Indiscriminate violence does not by its simple and logical definition, target individuals; it targets no one, but affects anyone and potentially everyone.[654]

Accordingly, in subsidiary protection cases, as soon as a situation of indiscriminate violence exists, it should not be expected from the applicant that he is able to demonstrate that "he is specifically affected by reason of factors particular to his personal circumstances"[655] in order for him to satisfy Article 15(c) criterion of "individual threat". Indiscriminate violence threatens the entire population of the area it concerns; it means that potentially, all individuals within this area run a similar risk of becoming victims of indiscriminate violence. In the same judgment of the UKAIT, Judge JFW Philips held:

> It would be ridiculous to suggest that if there were a real risk of serious harm to members of the civilian population in general by reason of indiscriminate violence that an individual Appellant would have to show a risk to himself over and above that general risk.[656]

The *Elgafaji* judgment provided some guarantee that national authorities shall not focus on the individualisation of the risk and shall even, though in certain exceptional circumstance only,[657] recognise that a well-founded fear is automatically established, in view of the scale and intensity of the violence. It seems however that the Court could have gone one step further and eliminated from the equation the requirement of a level of individualisation. The

---

653 United Kingdom: Immigration Rules – Part 11: Asylum, HC 395 [23 May 1994], last updated July 2012, § 339C.

654 United Kingdom: UKAIT, *Lukman Hameed Mohamed v. The Secretary of State for the Home Department* ("*Lukman*"), AA/14710/2006, 13 September 2007 (unreported case), § 19. Cited in UNHCR, "Statement on Article 15(c) QD", *op. cit.*, pp. 22–23.

655 CJ, *Elgafaji*, § 39.

656 UKAIT, *Lukman*, 13 September 2007 (unreported case), *op. cit.*, Judge JFW Phillips. Cited in UNHCR, "Statement on Article 15(c) QD", *op. cit.*, p. 6.

657 CJ, *Elgafaji*, § 43.

construct of a sliding scale, for helpful as it may be provided that the notion of "factors particular to [the applicant's] personal circumstances" is generously interpreted, perpetuates the paradox of Article 15(c): in cases where the level of indiscriminate violence is low (the Court does not provide guidance on the definition of those levels), applicants must be able to show that they are more affected than the rest of the population.[658] According to J.-F. Durieux, the *Elgafaji* ruling of the Court of Justice "has (...) not disentangled the nonsensical wording of Article 15(c)".[659] J.-F. Durieux, responding to H. Storey's enthusiasm towards the *Elgafaji* concept of a sliding scale, submits that it will benefit asylum seekers in only very limited cases. Assuming that "levels" of intensity of violence and "degrees" to which an individual is more affected than the rest of the population can ever be quantified, the author argues that, in order to "tilt" the scale in his favour, the applicant will have to show either that he or she is "especially exposed" (because he or she lives or works in areas prone to attacks) or that he or she is "especially vulnerable" (women, the elderly, children or disabled persons) to risk.[660]

Originally devised for the purpose of protecting individuals fleeing a "threat to their life, safety or freedom as a result of indiscriminate violence arising in situations of armed conflict",[661] Article 15(c) – and, by the same token, the harmonisation process of asylum law and practices within the EU – could instead have benefited from clarifications on its core element, to wit, on what constitutes "indiscriminate violence in situations of international or internal armed conflict".[662]

This leads to my second point.

(ii)   A Definitional Gap: "international or internal armed conflict"
The *Elgafaji* judgment provides no definition of what constitutes a situation of "international or internal armed conflict". The margin of appreciation reserved to States by the Qualification Directive and the Court of Justice might lead to States characterising differently similar situations. Before considering

---

658   *Ibid.*, § 39.
659   J.-F. Durieux (2012), *op. cit.*, p. 172.
660   J.-F. Durieux draws on situations described by H. Storey as examples of cases when the sliding scale would lean towards the applicant but analyses that those two examples are in fact the two "*only* examples" conceivable. *Ibid.*, p. 173; and H. Storey, "Armed Conflict in Asylum Law: The 'War-Flaw'", *Refugee Survey Quarterly*, Vol. 31, No. 2 (2012), pp. 1–32, p. 26.
661   In the Commission's original Proposal, the provision in fact read further "... or as a result of systematic and generalised violations of their human rights". "Commission Proposal QD (2004)", *op. cit.*, Article 15.
662   Qualification Directive, Article 15(c).

different approached to this definitional gap, a short detour will be made in Sweden, where the interpretation made by national asylum authorities of the concept of "internal armed conflict" in relation with Iraq and Somalia has been amply criticised.

After it had granted residence permits, on the ground of subsidiary protection, to a large population of Iraqi asylum-seekers, Sweden significantly changed its practice subsequent to a controversial precedent-setting decision of the Migration Court of Appeal in 2007.[663] On 26 February 2007, the Migration Court of Appeal delivered a judgement whereby it concluded that there was no internal armed conflict in Iraq.[664] To reach this conclusion, the Migration Court of Appeal assessed the situation prevailing in Iraq, allegedly against the standards of international law. The Court stated that, in order to qualify as "internal armed conflict" under international law, hostilities must oppose governmental armed forces and dissident armed groups, be more than civil unrest or merely sporadic or isolated acts of violence and imply, on the part of the armed groups, a certain measure of territorial control allowing them to carry out military activities.[665] Those criteria used by the Court were analysed as being a strict[666] or "narrow and erroneous interpretation"[667] of international law. Firstly, there is actually no conclusive definition of "internal armed conflict" in international humanitarian law or international criminal law.[668] Secondly, the criterion of "territorial control" mentioned by the Court cannot be drawn from available working definitions or authoritative interpretations of the concept of "internal armed conflict".[669] This definition of internal armed conflict

---

663 Sweden transposed the Qualification Directive in 2010 only however, prior to the adoption of the Directive, Swedish Aliens Act (*utlänningslagen*) already provided for the protection of persons fleeing, *inter alia*, internal armed conflicts (former Chapter 4, Section 2, Paragraph 1, Item 2).

664 Sweden: Migrationsöverdomstolen (Migration Court of Appeal), MIG 2007:9, 26 February 2007.

665 In the Migration Court of Appeal's words: "*Dessa stridigheter måste vara av sådan karaktär att de går utöver vad som kan klassas som inre oroligheter eller som endast utgör sporadiska eller isolerade våldshandlingar. Vidare måste de väpnade grupperna ha ett visst mått av territoriell kontroll vilket tillåter dem att utföra militära operationer*". Ibid.

666 UNHCR, et al., *Safe at Last?* (July 2011), *op. cit.*, p. 69.

667 R. Stern, "Complementary Protection in Sweden: More Alternatives but Fewer Possibilities?", *2011 Nordic Asylum Law Seminar: The State of International Refugee Law, EU Harmonization and the Nordic Legacy*, Copenhagen, 26–27 May 2011, p. 10.

668 UNHCR, et al., *Safe at Last?* (July 2011), *op. cit.*, p. 67.

669 The different definitions available in Article 3 common to the 1949 Geneva Conventions and relevant case-law of the ICTY in particular and in Article 8(2) of the Rome Statute of the International Criminal Court, instead require, in addition to a certain intensity of the

therefore appears to be particular to Sweden[670] rather than rooted in international law. This decision of the Migration Court of Appeal (intentionally?[671]) caused international protection recognition rates for Iraqis to substantially decline during 2008.[672] The decision was strongly criticised at the time: according

---

violence (for the assessment of which territorial control can be taken into account but is not as a precondition), that the armed groups are characterised by a certain level of organisation (the existence of a chain of command and internal rules, and the ability to recruit and train new combatants for example). Article 1(1) of Additional Protocol II to the 1949 Geneva Conventions on the other hand does mention territorial control as a criterion however, as made clear by the same Article 1(1), Protocol II "develops and supplements Article 3 common to the Geneva Conventions of 12 August 1949 without modifying its existing conditions of application". It follows that the definition of "internal armed conflict" laid down in Article 3 common to the 1949 Geneva Conventions is still valid and if, for the purpose of applying Additional Protocol II, it is necessary that dissident armed groups exercise a certain level of territorial control, the absence of such control does not however condition the applicability of common Article 3. Geneva Convention Relative to the Protection of Civilian Persons in Time of War ("Fourth Geneva Convention"), 12 August 1949, entered into force 21 October 1950 [1950] UNTS Vol. 75, p. 287; Protocol Additional to the Geneva Conventions of 12 August 1949, and Relating to the Protection of Victims of Non-International Armed Conflicts (Protocol II) ("AP II"), 8 June 1977, entered into force 7 December 1978 [1978] UNTS Vol. 1125, p. 609; Rome Statute of the International Criminal Court, 17 July 1998, last amended January 2002 A/CONF. 183/9; S. Vité, "Typology of Armed Conflicts in International Humanitarian Law: Legal Concepts and Actual Situations", *International Review of the Red Cross*, Vol. 91, No. 873 (March 2009), pp. 69–94, pp. 75–83; see also R. Stern, *op. cit.*, p. 9.

670 R. Stern, *op. cit.*, p. 11.

671 In January 2011, the Swedish newspaper *Svenska Dagbladet* reported the existence of US diplomatic telegrams (made available by *WikiLeaks*) recounting the efforts, including diplomatic negotiations with Iraq, undertaken in 2007 by Swedish ministers (the Ministers of Foreign Affairs and of Immigration) to curb the inflow of Iraqi asylum seekers in Sweden. According to *Svenska Dagbladet*, the increasing population of Iraqi asylum seekers was then described by the Swedish ministers as a matter of national concern, given the size of the incoming population, the fact that most Iraqis lacked resources, education and skills (including language skills) and after honour killings had taken place in Sweden. To my knowledge, the ministers concerned have neither infirmed nor confirmed these allegations. M. Åkerman, "Ministrar ville stoppa våg av irakier", *Svenska Dagbladet*, 21 januari 2011; O. Truc, "En 2007, les ministres suédois voulaient stopper les réfugiés irakiens", Le Monde.fr, 21 January 2011, retrieved from: <http://www.lemonde.fr/europe/article/2011/01/21/en-2007-les-ministres-suedois-voulaient-stopper-les-refugies-irakiens_1468991_3214.html> [03/09/2012].

672 EMN, "Sweden National Report", *in Annual Report on Asylum and Migration Statistics 2007* (n/a: EMN, November 2009), pp. 4–5, retrieved from: <http://emn.intrasoft-intl.com>; I. Karlsson, "Sweden Slammed over Iraqi Deportations" (Inter Press Service – IPS, 2012),

to observers and to the practice in most EU Member States,[673] the situation prevailing in Iraq then could only but be recognised as an armed conflict for the purpose of granting international protection and, in any case, there was a broad consensus in the international community, including within the EU, that Iraqi asylum seekers should be granted international protection, not least against *refoulement*.

The Swedish Court however corrected its position in 2009 on appeal on three judgments concerning Somalia[674] and confirmed this amended position in 2011.[675] In particular, the Court clearly discarded the requirement of "territorial control".[676] The new criteria are more in line with international law, which the Migration Court of Appeal indeed took into consideration, together with "international case law, legal writings, the Qualification Directive, the *Elgafaji* judgment and submissions by UNHCR and the Swedish Cross as well as Swedish law, case law and preparatory works".[677] The new criteria identified by the Court, albeit broader than the previous (the requirement of "territorial control" has disappeared), still fail to entirely convince.[678]

---

24 January 2011, retrieved from: <http://www.ipsnews.net/2011/01/sweden-slammed-over-iraqi-deportations/> [03/09/2012]; E. Mcgovern, et al., *Iraq's New Reality: The Impact of Conflict on Minorities, Refugees, and the Internally Displaced* (Washington, DC and Waterloo: The Stimson Center and the Centre for International Governance Innovation – CIGI, 2009), pp. 5–6, retrieved from: <http://www.cigionline.org/sites/default/files/Iraq_Report1.pdf> [01/09/2012].

673 UNHCR, et al., *Safe at Last?* (July 2011), op. cit., p. 69; UNHCR, *Asylum in the European Union: A Study of the Implementation of the Qualification Directive* (November 2007), op. cit., pp. 76–79.

674 Sweden: Migrationsöverdomstolen (Migration Court of Appeal), MIG 2009:27, 6 October 2009.

675 Sweden: Migrationsöverdomstolen (Migration Court of Appeal), MIG 2011:14, 22 June 2011.

676 The Migration Court of Appeal found that the absence of territorial control and subsequent non-applicability of the second Additional Protocol to the 1949 Geneva Conventions could not exclude the characterisation of a conflict as "internal armed conflict": "*Det är emellertid Migrationsöverdomstolens uppfattning att det inte går att dra slutsatsen att det inte skulle råda en inre väpnad konflikt i ett land enbart av det skälet att kravet på territoriell kontroll i Tilläggsprotokoll II till 1949 års Genèvekonventioner inte är uppfyllt och protokollet därför inte är tillämpligt*". MIG 2009:27, 6 October 2009, op. cit.

677 R. Stern, op. cit., p. 10.

678 R. Stern notes that the Migration Court of Appeal visibly confused criteria for defining the concept of internal armed conflict with the consequences such a conflict has on populations. In particular, the Court requires, and the formulation is not unreminiscent of the *Elgafaji* judgment, that "the violence initiated by the conflict is indiscriminate and sufficiently severe for substantial grounds to be shown for believing that a civilian, solely on

This case illustrates the risk that, in the absence of clear guidance for States on how to apply, in particular, Article 15(c) of the Qualification Directive, State practices remain varied and the Directive's purpose of reducing "asylum shopping" and secondary movements, a dead letter.

Different approaches compete in literature and national case-law on how to define international and internal armed conflicts under Article 15(c) of the Qualification Directive. Some argue that Article 15(c) should be read in international humanitarian law terms[679] whereas others plead for an autonomous reading of the provision.[680] The latter position appears to be the most effective from a protection perspective.

National asylum authorities adopting an approach to the interpretation of Article 15(c) based on international humanitarian law and international criminal law would hence use common standards to assess situations of violence; theoretically at least, this could warrant a (more) uniform application of the notions of "international and internal armed conflict". The difficulties faced by States in this regard are unquestionable: great disparities observed across the EU between recognition rates for a given nationality of asylum seekers are telling. This will be discussed below[681] but suffice is to notice that in 2014, among Syrian asylum-seekers who were granted international protection in Germany, 86 percent received refugee status and 14 percent, subsidiary protection whereas in Sweden, 11 percent received refugee status and 89 percent, subsidiary protection.[682] The desirability, for the sake of coherence of the EU asylum system, of the adoption of common criteria for the definition of key legal concepts of EU asylum law manifests itself in those statistics. For two reasons however, it seems that a solution based in international humanitarian law and international criminal law is not the best suited options.

---

account of his or her presence, would face a personal and serious threat to his or her life or person". *Ibid.*, pp. 11–12.

679   UNHCR notes that courts in Belgium, France, Germany, the Netherlands and Sweden interpret the concept of "internal armed conflict" with reference to international humanitarian law. UNHCR, *et al.*, *Safe at Last?* (July 2011), *op. cit.*, pp. 67–71; for arguments in favour of an international humanitarian law reading of Article 15(c), see H. Storey (2012), *op. cit*; R. Errera (2011), *op. cit.*

680   In the United Kingdom, the Court of Appeal concluded that, given that humanitarian law and refugee law have different objects and purposes, Article 15(c) of the Qualification Directive should be given "an autonomous meaning broad enough to capture any situation of indiscriminate violence". EWCA, *QD & AH v Secretary of State for the Home Department*, 24 June 2009, *op. cit.*, §§ 34–35 and 18. UNHCR, *et al.*, *Safe at Last?* (July 2011), *op. cit.*, p. 103; J.-F. Durieux (2012), *op. cit.*

681   Below, "4. Harmonisation: a long way ahead", pp. 168s.

682   *See* Table 1 below, p. 177.

As noted by UNHCR, if international humanitarian law and international criminal law can inform the interpretation of Article 15(c), nowhere in the Qualification Directive is it required that Article 15(c) be interpreted in conformity with those norms, nor is in fact any reference made to them.[683] Departing from an international humanitarian law to interpret the terms of the Directive therefore appears possible; it is also necessary, for two main reasons. Firstly, the nature of conflicts causing cross-border displacement of populations has significantly changed since the international refugee law system was devised. It has become clear that persecution, with discrimination on race, religion, political opinion, membership in a social group or nationality as underlying cause, is not the only reason causing people to flee.[684] Many people are forced out of their country of origin by internal conflicts, civil wars, or other forms of violence[685] (Somalia, Sri Lanka, Sudan and Libya are but a few illustrations) and the causes, parties to and evolution of the conflict are more often than not hardly identifiable.[686] Moreover, it is often a nexus of causes which eventually lead to population movements.[687] UNHCR finds for example that the protean internal conflict prevailing in Somalia, coupled with a severe drought, has led in 2011 to a sharp upsurge in the exodus of Somalis to neighbouring countries and beyond.[688] It follows that the *effet utile* of Article 15(c) can only be safeguarded provided the concepts of "international and internal armed conflict" are applied liberally:

> Persons may face a real risk of serious harm due to indiscriminate violence regardless of whether the context is classified as "armed conflict".[689]

---

683   UNHCR, *op. cit.*, § 20.

684   It appears that the drafters of the 1951 Refugee Convention had anticipated this evolution when, in Recommendation E to the Final Act of the Convention, they invited States to extend the treatment provided by the Convention to persons "who would not be covered by the terms of the Convention". Refugee Convention, Final Act, Recommendation E. The possible extension of the treatment provided by the Convention to environmentally-displaced persons as new categories of "refugees" under the Convention will be further discussed in Part III.

685   UNHCR, *The State of the World's Refugees 2012: In Search of Solidarity* (2012), *op. cit.*, pp. 11–33.

686   *Ibid.*

687   IOM, *Migration and Climate Change: A Complex Nexus*, retrieved from: <http://www.iom.int/jahia/Jahia/complex-nexus> [15/12/2011]; E. Piguet, *et al.*, "Migration and Climate Change: An Overview", *Refugee Survey Quarterly*, September 1, 2011, Vol. 30, No. 3 (2011), pp. 1–23.

688   UNHCR, *The State of the World's Refugees 2012: In Search of Solidarity* (2012), *op. cit.*, p. 6, Box 0.2.

689   UNHCR, *et al.*, *Safe at Last?* (July 2011), *op. cit.*, p. 103.

Secondly, with regards internal armed conflicts specifically, international humanitarian law would in fact provide little guidance since it does not conclusively define or regulate this type of conflicts.[690]

For the purpose of assessing a claim for subsidiary protection, the existence of generalised violence must be sufficient a circumstance for Article 15(c) to be applicable. The categorisation of this instance of violence under international humanitarian law as "international armed conflict", "internal armed conflict", or generalised violence below that level shall be immaterial; from the point of view of the persons exposed to an indiscriminate threat to their life or person, by reason of their sole presence on the territory, it is. As mentioned, it appears from the background and preparatory work of the Qualification Directive that subsidiary protection was originally intended as the "individual counterpart"[691] of temporary protection, devised to protect individuals fleeing indiscriminate threats to their life.[692] The Temporary Protection Directive[693] identifies as displaced persons in need of protection "persons who have fled areas of armed conflict or endemic violence" and "persons at serious risk of, or who have been the victims of, systematic or generalised violations of their human rights". Drawing on those provisions could in fact provide the desired interpretative guidance for the application of Article 15(c): worded in broader terms, descriptive of a situation (endemic violence, systematic or generalised violations of their human rights) rather than tied to a legal concept (international or internal armed conflict), they can, it seems, better adapt to the reality of today's conflicts and of their correlate, international displacement. It is argued that today's conflicts are characterised by increased exposure of civilian populations[694] – this is also confirmed by UNHCR who observes that civilians are sometimes deliberately targeted, and sexual and gender-based violence "widely encountered" as a weapon in conflict, as in the conflict raging in the Democratic Republic of Congo.[695] In this context, it appears that people do not flee the conflict itself, the "killings",[696] but the consequences and risks attached to them.

---

690   H. Storey (2012), *op. cit*; J.-F. Durieux (2012), *op. cit*; UNHCR, *op. cit.*
691   J. McAdam, *Complementary Protection in International Refugee Law* (2007), *op. cit.*, p. 43.
692   *See above* pp. 126s especially.
693   Temporary Protection Directive, *op. cit.*
694   H. Lambert and T. Farrell, "The Changing Character of Armed Conflict and the Implications for Refugee Protection Jurisprudence", *International Journal of Refugee Law*, Vol. 22, No. 2 (2010), pp. 237–273.
695   UNHCR, *et al.*, *Safe at Last?* (July 2011), *op. cit.*, pp. 13–15.
696   J.-F. Durieux (2012), *op. cit.*, p. 174.

It is not violence which is indiscriminate, but its effects: massive loss of livelihoods, collapse of public services, epidemics, etc., are by-products of generalised violence, and they affect civilians far beyond circumscribed zones of dense or intensive fighting to the point of endangering their lives or persons.[697]

Along the same lines, it is often noted that the causes of forced displacement are complex; human rights violations, armed conflict but also poverty, environmental degradation and poor governance can combine, mutually aggravate each other and eventually cause forced displacement without it being possible to disentangle them.[698] Against this backdrop, the inadequacy of a definition of indiscriminate violence based solely on international humanitarian law and international criminal law criteria appears all the more clearly: it would fail to address the new reality of forced displacement. H. Lambert and T. Farrell observe that alongside the changes in the nature of conflict, the concept of security has shifted its focus from securing the State to safeguarding people's physical integrity.[699]

The *Elgafaji* judgment entrusted competent national authorities with the task of identifying, on a case-by-case basis, those exceptional situations characterised with such a high degree of indiscriminate violence that anyone, solely on account of his or her presence on the territory, would be individually exposed to a serious threat to his or her life or freedom.[700] However, a shortcoming of the EU asylum system as it was devised by the Qualification Directive and construed by the Court of Justice in its *Elgafaji* judgment is that it does not provide Member States with any clear guidance on how to assess the situation in countries of origin. The formulation of the *Elgafaji* judgment indeed "leaves open a very large area of factual judgment"[701] and it can be anticipated that national authorities' assessments of the severity of a given armed conflict as well as its categorisation as an "armed conflict" may – and

---

697 *Ibid.*
698 E. Feller, "Asylum, Migration and Refugee Protection: Realities, Myths and the Promise of Things to Come", *International Journal of Refugee Law*, Vol. 18 (2006), pp. 509–536, p. 515; N. Myers and J. Kent, *Environmental Exodus: An Emergent Crisis in the Global Arena* (June 1995), *op. cit.*, pp. 29–32; IOM, "Migration and Climate Change: A Complex Nexus", retrieved from: <www.iom.int/jahia/Jahia/complex-nexus> [15/12/2011].
699 H. Lambert and T. Farrell (2010), *op. cit.*, pp. 257–260.
700 Drawn from CJ, *Elgafaji*, § 43.
701 EWCA, *QD & AH v Secretary of State for the Home Department*, 24 June 2009, *op. cit.*, § 26.

do – vary across the European Union. In a July 2011 research report, UNHCR in fact notes that, if the assessment of levels of indiscriminate violence and risk of harm "is not uniform or consistent across or within Member States", the appears to be some consensus however on the criteria to be used. They must be both quantitative and qualitative, and are actually not dissimilar to those suggested by H. Lambert and T. Ferrell.[702] According to UNHCR, the assessment made by national authorities generally include: the security situation, figures for casualties and security incidents, population displacement, foreseeable socio-economic, political and security-related developments, the capacity of actors of protection and indicators of state failure, and the humanitarian situation. As will be shown in the following section, a similar approach appears to guide the European Court of Human Rights' assessment of situations in an applicant's country of origin.[703]

In that respect, and as will be discussed below, the creation and development of the European Asylum Support Office insofar as it will facilitate the exchange of updated and detailed country of origin information but also best practices between Member States might effectively contribute to harmonising States' interpretations of the degree of indiscriminate violence required in order to trigger the application of Article 15(c).

D   *Harmonisation: A Long Way Ahead*

The Qualification Directive has been amply commented and criticised. A number of its provisions were found by commentators to be disappointing in view of the Directive's declared objectives, contradictory, ambiguous or even incompatible with Member States' obligations under human rights law and refugee law.[704] J. McAdam finds that the instruction in Article 63 of the

---

702   H. Lambert and T. Farrell already referred in 2010 to cases, in UK case-law especially, where the metrics they identified had been considered in courts. H. Lambert and T. Farrell (2010), *op. cit.*, p. 272.

703   This is particularly clear in the most recent ECtHR case-law, in the case of *Sufi and Elmi v. UK* or *Hirsi Jamaa and others v. Italy*. Below pp. 230s.

704   H. Lambert notes that on several points, the Qualification Directive is inconsistent with international law and in fact sets standards at a lower level than under international refugee law and human rights law. H. Lambert (January 2006), *op. cit.*, pp. 177–182. *See* generally: "Commission Impact Assessment – Proposal for a Recast QD", *op. cit*; J. McAdam (2005), *op. cit*; M.T. Gil-Bazo (2006), *op. cit.* as well as comments made by UNHCR and ECRE in particular on the Qualification Directive: UNHCR, "Statement on Article 15(c) QD", *op. cit*; UNHCR, "Some additional obsevations and recommendations on QD (2004) Proposal", *op. cit*; "Annotated Comments on QD (2004)", [January 2005], *op. cit*; UNHCR (July 2010),

Treaty establishing the European Community to adopt *minimum* standards on asylum has in fact been taken "very literally, with the asylum Directives frequently adopting lowest common denominator standards instead of aiming for the higher standards afforded by some Member States".[705] As a result, for some Member States, the obligation to transpose the Directive might be tantamount to giving them *carte blanche* to narrow the scope of their existing forms of complementary protection, to put them in line with the Directive's provisions on subsidiary protection.[706] Observers argue that those shortcomings follow from the Qualification Directive being an instrument of compromise, negotiated during more than two years and eventually hurriedly adopted just before the May 2004 enlargement of the European Union with the adhesion of ten new Member States, which risked rendering an agreement on the text even more difficult to reach.[707] R. Errera noted:

> The ambiguities and the implicit or apparent inconsistencies are the (usual) outcome of negotiation and compromise.[708]

Practice confirms the imperfection of the Qualification Directive. The various studies and comments made on the implementation of the Directive all concur and point to the fact that national legislation and practices still vary widely across EU Member States despite the adoption of the Directive and its declared

---

"Comments on Proposal for Recast QD", *op. cit*; and ECRE (October 2004), "Information Note on QD (2004)", *op. cit.*

[705] J. McAdam, "The Qualification Directive: An Overview", *in* K. Zwaan (Ed.), *The Qualification Directive: Central Themes, Problem Issues, and Implementation in Selected Member States* (Nijmegen: Wolf Legal Publishers, 2007), pp. 7–29, p. 9.

[706] During the 2011 Nordic Asylum Law Seminar, E. Nykänen showed that the scope of subsidiary protection under the Qualification Directive was narrower than that of complementary protection as it pre-existed in Finnish law. Danish Institute for International Studies (DIIS), *et al.*, 2011 Nordic Asylum Law Seminar: The State of International Refugee Law, EU Harmonization and the Nordic Legacy, organised in Copenhagen, on 26–27 May 2011; 27 May, Workshop 5, notes taken during Eeva Nykänen's presentation on the complementary protection categories entailed in the Finnish Aliens Act. H. Lambert for example observes five instances where the Qualification Directive appears to set standards below those existing in the United Kingdom. H. Lambert (January 2006), *op. cit.*, pp. 171–177.

[707] J. van Selm and E. Tsolakis, "The Enlargement of an 'Area of Freedom, Security and Justice': Managing Migration in a European Union of 25 Members", *Migration Policy Institute – Policy Brief*, No. 4 (May 2004), p. 2.

[708] R. Errera (2011), *op. cit.*, p. 104. Similarly, M.T. Gil-Bazo (2006), *op. cit.*, p. 30.

objective of harmonising the granting of international protection within the European Union.[709] In 2009, the European Commission acknowledged in the impact assessment accompanying its proposal for a recast Qualification Directive that "it [was] clear that the agreed common minimum standards [had] not created the desired level playing field".[710]

To illustrate the fact that the application of the Qualification Directive is not uniform in the EU, suffice is to look at the outcome of decisions taken by Member States asylum authorities in a year: the ratio of rejections to positive decisions (and within them, the proportions of refugee status, subsidiary protection and protection granted on humanitarian grounds) varies greatly from one State to another. The charts below illustrate those wide divergences. Based on data published by Eurostat in March 2015, they show the outcome of decisions issued in 2015 in the European Union globally as well as in six EU Member States: Belgium, France, Germany, Italy, the United Kingdom and Sweden. The selected States are those EU Member States who registered the highest numbers of asylum applicants in 2015.[711]

Those divergences illustrate Member States' varying interpretations of the Qualification Directive. Whereas in Belgium, France, Germany and the United Kingdom refugee status is the main form of protection granted, in Italy and Sweden, subsidiary protection prevails. It should be noted that, *a priori*, such distribution of statuses does not reflect the intention of the drafters of the Qualification Directive who repeatedly stressed and recalled in the Preamble

---

709   European Commission, "Commission Report on the application of QD (2004)", *op. cit*; UNHCR, *Asylum in the European Union: A Study of the Implementation of the Qualification Directive* (November 2007), *op. cit. See also*: G. Gyulai, *The Luxemburg Court: Conductor for a Disharmonious Orchestra?* (Budapest: Hungarian Helsinki Committee, 2012). In February 2009, at the time the EU Commission proposed setting up the European Asylum Support Office, Jacques Barrot, then European Commissioner responsible for Justice, Freedom and Security, deplored that whereas in Belgium, Italy and Sweden, every fourth asylum application was successful, in Greece, Slovakia and Slovenia only three out of a hundred were. M. Barrot insisted on the imperative of remedying such discrepancies. J. Barrot, *Bulletin quotidien Europe*, 19 février 2009, No. 9843 (2009), p. 8.

710   "Commission Impact Assessment – Proposal for a Recast QD", *op. cit.*, p. 4.

711   *See*: "Eurostat News Release: Asylum in the EU27, the Number of Asylum Applicants Registered in the EU27 Rose to 301 000 in 2011", STAT/12/46, © European Union, 1995–2012, 23 March 2012, retrieved from the website of the European Union at: <http://europa.eu/rapid/pressReleasesAction.do?reference=STAT/12/46&format=HTML&aged=1&language =EN&guiLanguage=en> [30/07/2012]; "Eurostat: Data in focus 3/2015", *op. cit.*

FIGURE 1   *First instance decisions by outcomes in selected EU Member States in 2014*

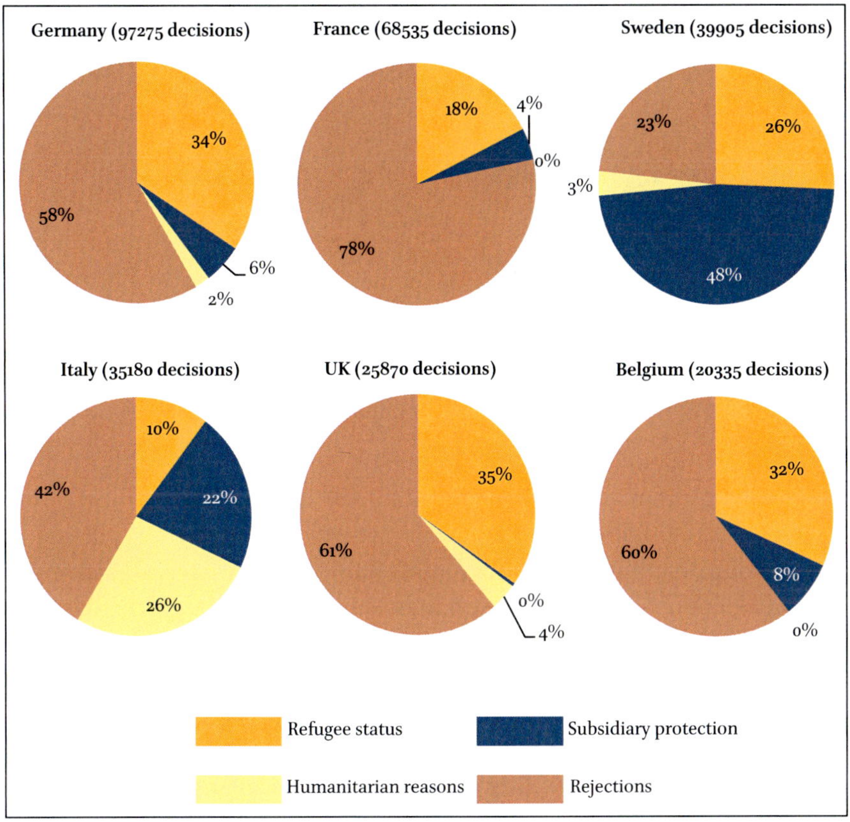

Germany (97275 decisions): Refugee status 34%, Subsidiary protection 6%, Humanitarian reasons 2%, Rejections 58%

France (68535 decisions): Refugee status 18%, Subsidiary protection 4%, Humanitarian reasons 0%, Rejections 78% (3%)

Sweden (39905 decisions): Refugee status 26%, Subsidiary protection 48%, Humanitarian reasons 3%, Rejections 23%

Italy (35180 decisions): Refugee status 10%, Subsidiary protection 22%, Humanitarian reasons 26%, Rejections 42%

UK (25870 decisions): Refugee status 35%, Subsidiary protection 0%, Humanitarian reasons 4%, Rejections 61%

Belgium (20335 decisions): Refugee status 32%, Subsidiary protection 8%, Humanitarian reasons 0%, Rejections 60%

SOURCE: EUROSTAT, DATA IN FOCUS – 3/2015.[712]

that "subsidiary protection should be complementary and additional to the refugee protection enshrined in the Geneva Convention".[713] Further evidence of the failure of the Qualification Directive to fully harmonise State practice is the sometimes large proportion of protection granted outside of the Directive: in Italy especially but also in Germany and Sweden, protection granted on humanitarian grounds is above EU average.

712   "Eurostat: Data in focus 3/2015", *op. cit.*, p. 11.
713   Qualification Directive, Recital 33.

FIGURE 2   *First instance decisions by outcomes in the EU-28 in 2014*

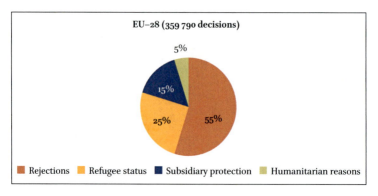

SOURCE: THE ABOVE CHART IS BASED ON THE SAME DATA USED IN THE PREVIOUS CHART, DATA PUBLISHED IN MARCH 2015 BY EUROSTAT.[714]

Those observations call for a comment on the content of each form of protection granted. Starting with the last observation: protection granted on compassionate or humanitarian grounds was left out of the Qualification Directive, intentionally so,[715] by the drafters. It follows that those forms of protection are left for Member State to regulate; States may at will choose to attach to their granting a more or less extensive set of rights, from *non-refoulement* only to a package of a broad range of fundamental rights.[716] Three factors come to mind which could explain the high proportion of complementary forms of protection granted in some Member States. A first explanation could be that subsidiary protection, as devised by the Qualification Directive, falls short of addressing all international protection needs:[717] Member States would need to resort to complementary forms of protection, to protect from removal to ill-treatment in a third country individuals who fall outside both refugee status and subsidiary protection. Alternatively, and this is a second explanation,

---

714   *Ibid.*, Table 8: First instance decisions by citizenship and outcome, selected Member States, 2014, p. 12.

715   *Ibid.*, Recital 15.

716   The variety of national forms of protection was already observed prior to the adoption of the Qualification Directive, for protection falling outside the scope of the Refugee Convention. It was the main trigger for the adoption of the Directive, intended to harmonise Member State practice and thereby limit secondary movements of asylum seekers within the European Union. Above note 601.

717   M.T. Gil-Bazo (2006), *op. cit.*

it might be that national asylum authorities are to "blame" in place of the Directive: the need to resort to complementary forms of protection would originate in the authorities' restrictive, if not erroneous, interpretation of the Directive. This explanation in turns points at the ambiguity and tortuous wording[718] of the Directive. Whichever, if any, of those first two explanations is valid, the fact remains: a significant number of persons within the EU are beneficiaries of non-harmonised forms of protection. In 2011 only, in total 12 040 persons were authorised to stay in the EU for humanitarian reasons. To wit, the fact that Member States still resort to national – and non-harmonised – forms of protection to complement the protection offered by refugee status and subsidiary protection reveals a flaw of the Qualification Directive: either its scope is too narrow or it is ambiguous enough for Member States to – mistakenly or intentionally – interpret it narrowly. A third possible explanation for the sometimes relatively high proportion of protection granted on humanitarian grounds pertains to the leeway States enjoy in this case: as mentioned, authorisations granted for humanitarian reasons fall outside the scope of the Qualification, Member States therefore have all liberty (within the safeguards of their international human rights obligations) to define their regime and the content of the protection granted. This fact might encourage national asylum authorities to favour the granting of such forms of non-harmonised protection.

As for the prevalence in some Member States of subsidiary protection over refugee status, it is worth highlighting that, as it was adopted in 2004, the Qualification Directive gave the possibility to Member State to attach to the granting of refugee status or subsidiary protection different entitlements for their beneficiaries. Refugee status was more generous when it comes to, for instance: residence permits (a three year permit for refugees against a one year permit for beneficiaries of subsidiary protection),[719] access to employment,[720] social welfare and healthcare.[721] Could the lesser level of protection Member States are bound to provide beneficiaries of subsidiary protection, as compared to refugee status, account, if only partially, for some States' seeming preferment of subsidiary protection before refugee status? Studies on the transposition

---

718   Article 15(c) of the Directive was in particular described as "tortuously worded" by the United Kingdom Asylum and Immigration Tribunal. UKAIT, *KH*, 25 March 2008, *op. cit.*, § 32.
719   Qualification Directive (2004), Article 24.
720   *Ibid.*, Article 26.
721   *Ibid.*, Articles 28(2) and 29(2) respectively.

and implementation of the Qualification Directive indicate that in practice, States often chose not to differentiate between the two statuses.[722] There is however one key element of the content international protection which States tend to grant more generously to recognised refugees than to beneficiaries of subsidiary protection: the right to stay on their territory. Studies indeed reveal that residence permit is often granted for a shorter duration under subsidiary protection status.[723] France for instance grants refugees a renewable ten-year permit but subsidiary protection beneficiaries a renewable one-year permit only.[724] Similar practices are observed in other EU Member States, including Belgium,[725] Italy,[726] Germany,[727] whereas in Sweden[728] and the UK[729] for example, the validity of the residence permit granted is the same for refugees and beneficiaries of subsidiary protection.

Member States' apparent preference for granting subsidiary protection could thus in part be explained by the lesser level of rights they were bound to grant to the beneficiaries of the attached status (under the Qualification Directive as it was adopted in 2004). This is nonetheless obviously not true in all cases: Sweden for example appears to favour subsidiary protection although

---

722 European Commission, "Commission Report on the application of QD (2004)", *op. cit.*, pp. 11–15; F. Mlati and M. Tardis (Eds.), "Asile, La protection subsidiaire en Europe: une mosaïque de droits", *France Terre d'Asile: Les cahiers du social*, No. 18 (September 2008), pp. 32–63; and ECRE/ELENA, *op. cit.*, pp. 225–243.

723 European Commission, "Commission Report on the application of QD (2004)", *op. cit.*, pp. 11–15; F. Mlati and M. Tardis (Eds.) (September 2008), *op. cit.*, pp. 32–63; and ECRE/ELENA, *op. cit.*, pp. 225–243; "Commission Impact Assessment – Proposal for a Recast QD", *op. cit.*, p. 49.

724 CESEDA, *op. cit.*, Articles 711–2 and L-311-9 (refugee status) and Article L-712-3 (subsidiary protection).

725 F. Mlati and M. Tardis (Eds.) (September 2008), *op. cit.*, p. 55.

726 See C. Boca, et al., *The Practices in Italy Concerning the Granting of Non-EU Harmonized Protection Statuses* (Rome: Centro Studi e Ricerche IDOS – Italian National Contact Point for the European Migration Network, 2009), p. 24; and the practical guide published by the Protection System fior Asylum Seekers and Refugees (SPRAR), affiliated to the Italian Ministry of Interior, *Guida Pratica Per I Titolari Di Protezione Internazionale* (n/a: SPRAR – Sistema di Protezione per Richiedenti Asilo e Rifugiati, 2009), pp. 168–169, retrieved from: <www.serviziocentrale.it> [08/08/2012].

727 ECRE/ELENA, *op. cit.*, pp. 239–240.

728 Sweden: Aliens Act (*Utlänningslag*) (hereafter "Utlänningslag"), SFS 2005:716, 29 September 2005, entered into force 31 March 2006, last amended by *Lag om ändring i utlänningslagen* of 11 June 2012, SFS 2012:322, Chapter 5.

729 UK: Immigration Rules (HC 395), made under Section 3(2) of the Immigration Act 1971, last updated in July 2012 (hereafter "Immigration Rules"), Part 11 – Asylum, 339Q(i) and (ii).

the statuses granted to refugees and beneficiaries of subsidiary protection are identical.

It is noteworthy that with the adoption of the recast Qualification Directive, refugee status and subsidiary protection entitlements have been approximated. The differentiation originally made by the Qualification Directive between refugee status and subsidiary protection status had been repeatedly criticised in relevant literature;[730] the European Commission eventually concluded that it was "not objectively justified from a fundamental rights perspective" since its underlying assumption that protection needs of subsidiary protection beneficiaries were of shorter duration than those of refugees turned out not to be accurate.[731] The approximation of the two statuses was therefore welcome, including by UNHCR for example who observed, citing the jurisprudence of the European Court of Human Rights, that differentiating rights according to type of residence permit amounted to discrimination.[732] As a consequence, it remains to be seen whether the discrepancy observed in State practice will persist in the years to come since, from an "asylum cost" point of view, there will be no benefit for States in granting subsidiary protection rather than refugee status (when the criteria for refugee status are met).

It could however not be expected that asylum statistics be strictly the same for all Member States. International protection is not hard science and the examination of an asylum claim does not come down to solving an equation with quantifiable variables. On the contrary, it is impregnated with subjectivity: a claim is lodged by an individual recounting his or her asylum story and invoking his or her fear. It is assessed by another (or several) individual(s), relying in part on the perceived credibility of the claimant. Typical refugee law notions of fear, unwillingness to return or belief (as in "substantial grounds for

---

730   H. Battjes argues that reduced rights for subsidiary protection beneficiaries as compared to refugees could be justified but only concerning Article 15(c) of the Qualification Directive, if it is applied to mass influxes of asylum seekers or if it can be anticipated that the need for subsidiary protection will exist for a limited period of time only. H. Battjes, "Subsidiary Protection and Reduced Rights", *in* K. Zwaan (Ed.), *The Qualification Directive: Central Themes, Problem Issues, and Implementation in Selected Member States* (Nijmegen: Wolf Legal Publishers, 2007), pp. 49–55. ECRE (October 2004), "Information Note on QD (2004)", *op. cit.*, pp. 4, 13–17 in particular. UNHCR, "Note on Key Issues of Concern to UNHCR on the Draft Qualification Directive", March 2004, p. 2; "Annotated Comments on QD (2004)", [January 2005], *op. cit.*, pp. 35–47.

731   "Commission Impact Assessment – Proposal for a Recast QD", *op. cit.*, pp. 12–13.

732   UNHCR (July 2010), "Comments on Proposal for Recast QD", *op. cit.*, pp. 9–10. See also the opinion of the French national human rights institution (Commission nationale consultative des droits de l'Homme – CNCDH), CNCDH, "Avis 2006", *op. cit.*, p. 14, § 68.

believing") clearly point to the subjectivity of asylum claim assessment. It is therefore unsurprising that variations may exist, from one authority or judge to another, or, for that matter, from one country to another. However, the objective pursued with the creation of the Common European Asylum System was precisely "a *level playing field*, where persons genuinely in need of protection are guaranteed access to a high level of protection under *equivalent conditions in all MS*"[733] [emphases added]. The definition of common criteria and procedures should logically reduce discrepancies between Member States' asylum practices: although interpretation of facts has its place and may account for some variance, the adoption of common, detailed, rules regulating all (or most) aspects of international protection status determination ought to reduce the role played by subjectivity. Assuming that this anticipated effect of the harmonisation of national asylum rules proves correct, the ratio of refugee status to subsidiary protection would and should still vary from on Member State to another on account of the varied composition of the population of asylum seekers received by each State.[734] Each Member State receives a different "blend of citizenships";[735] the main factors that triggered population movements vary accordingly. It could hence be argued that a State who predominantly grants subsidiary protection may very well do so legitimately, because the main population group it receives comes from a country affected by armed conflict. Statistics however speak otherwise: looking at recognition rates with regard to a given national group of asylum seeker reveals that the ratio of refugee status to subsidiary protection still varies widely across the EU. The table below shows 2014 recognition rates for international protection in Germany, the Netherlands and Sweden with regard to Syrian asylum seekers, those countries being then the three main destination countries (within the EU) for Syrian citizens that year. Specifically, it shows the ratio of refugee status to complementary forms of protection (subsidiary protection and authorisations to stay on humanitarian grounds) among positive decisions issued in first instance during 2014.[736]

The striking disparities observed between Member States (the comparative view of German practice on the one hand and Swedish and Dutch practices on the other is particularly telling) confirms the assumption made above:

---

733 "Commission Impact Assessment – Proposal for a Recast QD", *op. cit.*, p. 4.
734 Eurostat, *Asylum in the EU27: The number of asylum applicants registered in the EU27 rose to 301 000 in 2011*, News Release issue no. 46/2012, 23 March 2012, p. 1.
735 For an overview of the five main citizenships of asylum applicants for every EU Member State, see: "Eurostat: Data in focus 3/2015", *op. cit.*, Table 5, p. 8.
736 *See* also below Annex 1, Tables 1 and 2.

TABLE 1 *Proportion of refugee status, subsidiary protection and authorisations to stay for humanitarian reasons among positive decisions issued in selected EU Member States concerning Syrian asylum-seekers in 2014.*

Country of asylum	Refugee status	Subsidiary Protection	Humanitarian reasons	Total
Germany	86% (20 505)	14% (3 245)	<1% (105)	23 855
Netherlands	6% (349*)	82% (4 985)	13% (775)	6 109
Sweden	11% (1 760)	89% (14 535)	n/a	16 295
EU-28	54% (35 760)	45% (29 575)	1% (925)	66 260

* According to UNHCR Statistical Yearbook 2014 (data not provided by Eurostat).[737] Data provided by Eurostat and UNHCR occasionally differ however the disparities do not significantly affect the above calculations.
SOURCE: THE ABOVE TABLE IS BASED, ALMOST EXCLUSIVELY, ON DATA PUBLISHED BY EUROSTAT.[738]

harmonisation has not yet been achieved within the European Union. It is particularly worrying that asylum-seekers coming from similar situations are treated differently across the European Union; the principle of non-discrimination indeed calls for a different state of fact. In this context, Greece has often been cited as an example of bad State practice: in 2009, statistics published by UNHCR revealed – and the fact was often highlighted by commentators[739] – that the percentage of positive decisions issued by Greece concerning asylum seekers from Afghanistan and Iraq was zero.[740] Statistics published by UNHCR, on the state of asylum in the world in 2010, show that positive decisions issued by Greece concerning applications for international protection submitted by Afghans and Iraqis were still scarce and even non-existing concerning

---

737   T. A. Chabaké and J. Tenkorang (Eds.), *UNHCR Statistical Yearbook 2014*, 14th ed. (Geneva: UNHCR, 2014), Annex, Table 12.
738   "Eurostat: Data in focus 3/2015", *op. cit.*, Tables 8 and 10.
739   The observation was often made by UNHCR during seminars and conferences in 2008–2009. E. Guild observed it too, on the basis of the statistics published in *UNHCR Statistical Yearbook 2009* during a course organised by ECRE/ELENA in September 2010. E. Guild, "The Qualification Directive: Using the Protections in National and EU Law", *ELENA course: the Common European Asylum System*, Athens, 17–18 September 2010, notes taken during E. Guild's presentation.
740   K. Diallo and Tarek Abou Chabaké (Eds.), *UNHCR Statistical Yearbook 2009: Trends in Displacement, Protection and Solutions* (Geneva: UNHCR, 2009), Annex, Table 12.

Somalis[741]; and yet, those three national groups were the three largest groups granted protection status in the European Union in 2010.[742]

The example of the different treatment of international protection claims submitted by Afghan asylum seekers in 2010 or by Syrian asylum seekers in 2014 calls for a more general comment on subsidiary protection for people threatened by indiscriminate violence: it is important to note that the Qualification Directive does not define "international or internal armed conflict".[743] Moreover, the *Elgafaji* judgment, enlightening as it may be, did not exemplify, nor even specified what constituted, in practical terms, an exceptionally high level of indiscriminate violence supporting a positive decision on a claim for subsidiary protection under Article 15(c).[744] The Court of Justice instead deferred this assessment to competent national authorities, deciding on a case-by-case basis.[745] Just a day after the Court of Justice issued its ruling in the *Elgafaji* case, the European Commission submitted to the European Parliament and Council a proposal for the creation of the European Asylum Support Office (EASO).[746] One purpose of the EASO is to remedy "the great disparities between Member States in the granting of international protection and the forms that such international protection takes"[747] by strengthening cooperation between Member States, in particular, by fostering the exchange of good practices and country of origin information. The Commission made clear in its Explanatory Memorandum that disparities observed between the – then – 27 Member States did not "arise simply from the need for greater legislative harmonisation" but also from

---

741 *See* below, Annex 1, Table 1.
742 A. Albertinelli, "Asylum Applicants and First Instance Decisions on Asylum Applications in 2010" ("Eurostat: Data in focus 5/2011"), May 2011, © European Union, 2011, *Eurostat: Data in focus*, Table 6b, p. 11, retrieved from the website of the European Commission – Eurostat at: <http://www.emnbelgium.be/sites/default/files/publications/eurostat_2010_overzicht_asiel.pdf> [29/08/2012].
743 UNHCR, "Statement on Article 15(c) QD", *op. cit.*, p. 14.
744 CJ, *Elgafaji*, § 43. R. Errera deplores that the Advocate General – and the judgment of the Court of Justice – in the Elgafaji case make no reference to international humanitarian law to clarify the scope of subsidiary protection under Article 15(c) of the Qualification Directive. The author subsequently observes that some national jurisdictions do take international humanitarian law into account when applying 15(c). R. Errera (2011), *op. cit.*, pp. 101–112.
745 CJ, *Elgafaji*, § 43.
746 Regulation (EU) No 439/2010 of the European Parliament and of the Council of 19 May 2010 Establishing a European Asylum Support Office ("EASO Regulation"), 19/05/2010 entered into force 18/06/2010 [29/05/2010] *OJ L* Vol. 132, p. 11.
747 *Ibid.*, Recital 2.

"non-legislative factors", including, in particular, "from differences in the information on the country of origin of applicants for international protection".[748] According to the Commission:

> This is why strengthening practical cooperation on asylum between the Member States is very important for achieving convergence between them in the processing of applications for international protection.[749]

It is anticipated that improved cooperation between Member States and the pooling of country of origin information will contribute to harmonising Sate practice.

As mentioned above, significant disparities were observed among Member States in the assessment of Afghan asylum seekers' claims in 2010, *i.e.* before the European Asylum Support Office became fully operational, on 19 June 2011.[750] Four years later, the treatment of asylum applications submitted by Syrian asylum seekers met with similarly diverging responses to their asylum claims across the EU. In view of those persisting disparities, it remains to be seen whether the EASO fulfils the objectives set by the Commission, that is to say, whether the exchange of country of origin information between Member States contributes to harmonising State practice in the granting of international protection.

To conclude on the Qualification Directive, the following can be said. As mentioned, the shortcomings of the Convention definition of refugees had been remedied by many European States who, prior to the entry into force of the Directive, already granted some form of protection to the so called "*de facto* refugees". However, in the absence of a common binding instrument of European law defining complementary protection, European State practice was characterised by "highly varied *ad hoc* responses, premised largely on executive discretions".[751]

---

748 European Commission, "Proposal for a Regulation of the European Parliament and of the Council Establishing a European Asylum Support Office, Explanatory Memorandum" ("Explanatory Memorandum – EASO"), COM (2009) 66 final – COD 2009/0027, 18 February 2009, p. 2.

749 *Ibid.*, pp. 2–3.

750 "European Asylum Support Office", © European Union, 1995–2012, 17 February 2011, retrieved from the website of Europa – Summaries of EU legislation at: <http://europa.eu/legislation_summaries/justice_freedom_security/free_movement_of_persons_asylum_immigration/jl0022_en.htm> [10/08/2012].

751 H. Storey (1999), *op. cit.*

The question remains whether the problems (asylum shopping, secondary movements, lack of legal certainty[752]) the Directive sought to remedy have been, at least partly, corrected since the entry into force of the text and its transposition in Member States' domestic legal system. The subsidiary protection regime, created to this end by the Qualification Directive, is meant to provide protection – uniform at the European Union level – to those who fall outside the scope of the Geneva Convention but who are, nevertheless, in need of international protection.

It appears that, so far, the Qualification Directive has not fulfilled the objectives it was assigned. Statistics notably evidence the remaining large divergences existing between recognition rates within the European Union; this is all the more worrying in view of the fact that asylum seekers from a given country of origin might receive different forms of protection, if any, depending on the Member State where their claim is assessed. Moreover, the Commission noted in 2009 that the Directive "has not had any effect on secondary movements";[753] some Member States indeed continue to be "more 'attractive' destinations than others",[754] despite the adoption of common standards. The combination of the failure of the Qualification Directive to effectively harmonise national asylum laws and practices with the operation of the Dublin system in fact creates the decried phenomenon of "asylum lottery"[755] in which asylum seekers find themselves within the EU pending a final decision being taken on their application.

As will be discussed below,[756] some States retain some of their pre-existing complementary form of protection, in addition to transposing the subsidiary protection regime in their domestic legal system. This connotes that the Qualification Directive still fails to protect all persons in need of international protection.

The failure of the Qualification Directive to fully harmonise national asylum laws and practices is in fact somewhat surprising. As observed by H. Labayle, be it by the text of the Directive itself or by the EU institutions, the main sources of inspiration of the Directive are identified as the Refugee Convention – an

---

752   TEC (1997), Art 63(2)(a).
753   "Commission Impact Assessment – Proposal for a Recast QD", *op. cit.*, p. 14. The same observation is made by H. Labayle: "*La réalité est tenace et le constat juridique décevant. L'Union européenne ne parvient pas à une harmonisation suffisante des droits nationaux relatifs à l'asile, au point de mettre fin ou de réduire les mouvements secondaires de personnes demandeuses de protection...*" H. Labayle (March-April 2011), *op. cit.*, pp. 273–274.
754   "Commission Impact Assessment – Proposal for a Recast QD", *op. cit.*, p. 14.
755   *Ibid.*
756   Part IV.

international convention ratified by all EU Member States – and the jurisprudence on Article 3 of the ECHR.[757] The Qualification Directive being derived from legal sources common to EU Member States, it could have been expected that harmonisation would be feasible, as a compilation into one single instrument of pre-existing, pre-accepted international legal obligations of Member States.

It is necessary to ponder on whether, beyond European Union law, complementary forms of protection deriving from international human rights law have a more inclusive scope (Chapter 3) before looking at national forms of protection (Chapter 4), some of which are in part based on States' international human rights law obligations.

---

757 In H. Labayle's words: *"Cette harmonisation n'est pourtant que la mise en œuvre au plan communautaire d'un engagement international ratifié par l'ensemble des États membres, la Convention de Genève, le tout cimenté par la jurisprudence relative à l'article 3 de la CEDH..."* H. Labayle (March-April 2011), *op. cit.*, p. 274.

CHAPTER 3

Relevant Provisions of International Human Rights Law

As mentioned, European States were already bound to protect individuals from being sent back to a country where their life or person would be threatened before the adoption of the Qualification Directive. The 1951 Refugee Convention,[1] "general"[2] international human rights law treaties at the global level – such as the International Covenant on Civil and Political Rights (ICCPR)[3] and the UN Convention Against Torture (CAT)[4] – and at the regional level (the European Convention on Human Rights – ECHR[5]) but also customary international law already made it an obligation for European Union States not to return individuals to countries where their life or freedom would be threatened. As mentioned, EU Member States did not release themselves of their *non-refoulement* obligations deriving from those legal norms by joining the European Union and are, on the contrary, still bound to abide by them.[6]

Refugee law can be and indeed often is recognised to be part of human rights law.[7] Therefore, strictly speaking, a reference to human rights law includes a reference to refugee law. The present Chapter however focuses on those norms of international human rights law which apply "generally", to any individual, including but not limited to asylum seekers and beneficiaries of international

---

1   Refugee Convention, *op. cit.*
2   The use of the adjective will be justified in the following paragraph.
3   ICCPR, *op. cit.*
4   CAT, *op. cit.*
5   ECHR, *op. cit.*
6   See above "Chapter 1. Preliminary remark: Member States' obligations under international human rights law are unaltered by EU membership", pp. 23s.
7   H. Lambert, "Protection against Refoulement from Europe: Human Rights Law Comes to the Rescue", *The International and Comparative Law Quarterly* (Cambridge University Press on behalf of the British Institute of International and Comparative Law), Vol. 48, No. 3 (1999), pp. 515–544, p. 519. For a description of the Refugee Convention as a human rights treaty, *see* for example: J.C. Hathaway, "Reconceiving Refugee Law as Human Rights Protection", *Journal of Refugee Studies*, Vol. 5, No. 2 (1991), pp. 113–131; J. McAdam, *Complementary Protection in International Refugee Law* (2007), *op. cit.*, pp. 29–33; T. Einarsen, "Drafting History of the 1951 Convention and the 1967 Protocol", *in* A. Zimmermann (Ed.), *The 1951 Convention Relating to the Status of Refugees and Its 1967 Protocol: A Commentary* (New York: OUP, 2011), pp. 37–73, pp. 1–3.

protection. It would be possible to refer to "general human rights law" on the one hand, to designate those norms of human rights law that do not concern asylum specifically – although they have a bearing in asylum cases, by contrast with "refugee law", as a *lex specialis* of human rights law, intended precisely to address international protection needs. For the following developments though, mainly with a view to simplifying the text, "human rights law" will be favoured to "general human rights law".

The Qualification Directive (already addressed in the previous Chapter[8]) and the Refugee Convention are therefore not the focus of the following developments. Considerations of the scope of *non-refoulement* under refugee law will nevertheless be included. Typically, they will highlight the comparatively broader scope of human rights treaties.

Human rights treaties will be addressed first. Particular attention will be given to the progressive and constructive interpretation of the European Convention of Human Rights and the International Covenant on Civil and Political Rights as encompassing the prohibition of *refoulement* and to the application of the principle in international protection cases. More specifically, since this Part is intended to identify the forms of protection available within the European Union for people fleeing threats to which an entire population (of a region or country) is potentially exposed, the application of the principle of *non-refoulement* to persons fleeing armed conflict situations will be considered (I). Developments will then focus on pertinent aspects of customary international law and on the existence of a customary obligation for States not to remove individuals to situations of indiscriminate threats to their life or person (II).

I   Treaty Law Enshrining the Principle of Non-refoulement

International human rights law instruments and chiefly the European Convention on Human Rights (ECHR)[9] have long provided asylum seekers in Europe protection against *refoulement*. Although the European Convention on Human Rights (ECHR) and the International Covenant on Civil and Political Rights (ICCPR)[10] alike contain neither the principle of *non-refoulement*, which they are both commonly praised to safeguard, nor a right of asylum, they can and do play an important role in protecting individuals from being expulsed to a country where they risk facing human rights abuses, provided they are read together with their respective judicial interpretations. Explicit in the 1951

---

8   *See* above Chapter 2., "III. The Qualification Directive", pp. 99s.
9   ECHR, *op. cit.*
10 ICCPR, *op. cit.*

Refugee Convention and in the UN Convention Against Torture (CAT),[11] the prohibition of *refoulement* was indeed inferred from the ECHR and ICCPR by their monitoring bodies – the European Court of Human Rights and the Human Rights Committee respectively.

As mentioned above, the present Chapter focuses on international human rights law insofar as it can protect asylum seekers irrespective of refugee or subsidiary protection status determination.[12] The application of the principle of *non-refoulement* under the Refugee Convention and the Qualification Directive is therefore not the object of the following developments; refugee law will however be mentioned, typically to illustrate the comparative breadth of "general" human rights law.

In particular, this Chapter will focus on the ICCPR and, mostly, the ECHR. Although the UN Convention Against Torture was in fact the first instrument of international human rights law to endorse the principle of *non-refoulement*, it will be only mentioned incidentally, for two reasons. Firstly, as said, neither the ECHR nor the ICCPR contain a prohibition of *refoulement*; they have been interpreted to encompass it. The question of their applicability in asylum cases, to prevent removal to a risk of torture, inhuman or degrading treatment or punishment, is therefore crucial. Much case-law from the European Court of Human Rights especially as well as decisions, concluding observations and General Comments[13] by the Human Rights Committee centred around this question and were many an opportunity for the monitoring bodies to elaborate on the scope of the principle under the ECHR or ICCPR. This Chapter will give an account of those jurisprudential developments. Since Article 3 of the

---

11 CAT, *op. cit.*

12 This should however not be interpreted as a negation of the existence of close links between human rights law and refugee law. The adoption of the Qualification Directive, which translated Member States' *non-refoulement* obligations (and practices) into the subsidiary protection regime, has made it all the more clear (*see* above in "II.C.", pp. 99s.) Conversely – and the case will be analysed in more depth in the second Part of this book, in view of its potential implications for environmentally-displaced persons – the European Court of Human Rights (ECtHR) appears to occasionally draw on developments of European Union law to expand human rights protection under the ECHR. On this last point, the 2011 judgment of the ECtHR in the *Sufi & Elmi* case illustrates how the case-law of the CJ and that of the ECtHR can feed each other. In *Sufi & Elmi*, the European Court of Human Rights referred to and drew from the judgment of the Court of Justice in *Elgafaji*, judgment which itself bore striking similarities with the earlier judgment of the ECtHR in *NA v. UK*. ECtHR (Fourth Section), *Sufi and Elmi v. The United Kingdom* ("*Sufi & Elmi*"), Applications nos. 8319/07 and 11449/07 (28 June 2011), §§ 225–226 and 293 especially; CJ, *Elgafaji*, § 35; ECtHR, *NA v. UK*, § 115. Discussed below pp. 224s and Part II pp. 347s.

13 On the legal force of acts issued by the HRC, *see* above pp. 90s.

UNCAT on the other hand explicitly protects against *refoulement*, the question of the applicability of the UNCAT in asylum cases needed not be and indeed was not raised. Secondly, the UNCAT limits the scope of *non-refoulement* to cases of torture; its relevance in asylum case is therefore limited or in any case narrower than that of the ECHR and ICCPR where *non-refoulement* extends to inhuman and degrading treatment and punishment.

In sum, this first section will primarily address European States' protection obligations deriving from the ECHR and the ICCPR. Reference will be made, but secondarily only, to the UN Convention Against Torture as well as to refugee law (the Refugee Convention and the Qualification Directive) where useful to confirm or illustrate the relative generosity of the protection against *refoulement* under general human rights law in comparison with refugee law.

As repeatedly stated by the European Court of Human Rights and the Human Rights Committee, there is no provision in either the ECHR or the ICCPR respectively enshrining a right to asylum as such.[14] In fact, until the entry into force in December 2009 of the Treaty of Lisbon, by which the Charter of Fundamental Rights[15] became legally binding upon EU Member States, States

---

14 See for example ECtHR, *Case of Salah Sheekh v. The Netherlands* ("*Salah Sheekh*"), Application no. 1948/04 (11 January 2007), § 135; ECtHR, *Vilvarajah and Others v. The United Kingdom* ("*Vilvarajah*"), Application Nos. 13163/87, 13164/87, 13165/87, 13447/87 and 13448/87 (30 October 1991), § 102. As regards the ICCPR, Article 13 thereof enshrines the right of aliens to be protected against arbitrary expulsion. The *travaux préparatoires* reveal that at the time Article 13 was being discussed, some States supported the inclusion of a specific provision, in the same article or in a separate one, on the right of asylum. The Philippines delegation noted that "[a]sylum from persecution, which is recognised in the [Universal] Declaration of Human Rights, should not be forgotten in the Covenant". The same concern was visibly shared by the French delegation who submitted a proposal based on Article 14 of the Universal Declaration of Human Rights – although the French proposal referred to a right to *seek* asylum from persecution but omitted the second element of the right enshrined in the UDHR, that is the right to *enjoy* asylum from persecution. Some also advocated including a provision on extradition in Article 13. The various proposals for the inclusion of provisions covering the right of asylum and extradition in the ICCPR were however all rejected. M.J. Bossuyt, *Guide to the "Travaux Préparatoires" to the International Covenant on Civil and Political Rights* (Dordrecht: Martinus Nijhoff Publishers, 1987), §§ 267–276. According to Manfred Nowak, it is "the resistance of Western and other States in the HRC and the complexity of the problems associated with them" which explain that the right of asylum and the prohibition of extradition failed to be adopted in the Covenant. M. Nowak, *U.N. Covenant on Civil and Political Rights: CCPR Commentary* (2005), *op. cit.*, Commentary on Article 13, p. 291, §3.

15 Article 18 of the EU Charter of Fundamental Rights enshrines the right to asylum. It remains for national courts and, chiefly, the Court of Justice to define its scope and content

had never before accepted an obligation to recognise and respect such right to asylum in any international or regional legal instrument.[16] The European Court of Human Rights and the Human Rights Committee alike both derive the principle of *non-refoulement* mainly from the prohibition of torture, cruel, inhuman or degrading treatment or punishment which both instruments enshrine. The two monitoring bodies have also occasionally relied on the right to life,[17] and both have acknowledged that other rights might also be applicable to prohibit the removal of an individual to a situation where those rights would risk be violated.[18]

---

however, the recent judgment of the Court of Justice seems to confirm what a cursory reading of the provision suggested: Article 18 would correspond in essence to the protection from *refoulement* enshrined in Article 33 of the 1951 Refugee Convention. *See* above pp. 86s.

16 G.S. Goodwin-Gill and J. McAdam, *The Refugee in International Law* (2007), *op. cit.*, pp. 358–369.

17 ECtHR, *Bader v. Sweden*, Application no. 13284/04 (8 November 2005), § 42; HRC, *Judge v. Canada*.

18 Right to fair trial: ECtHR (Plenary), *Soering v. The United Kingdom* ("*Soering*"), Application No. 14038/88, Series A Vol. 161 (7 July 1989); ECtHR, *Case of Othman (Abu Qatada) v. The United Kingdom* ("*Othman*"), Application no. 8139/09 (09 May 2012), §§ 236–287, for the first time, the Court finds that the applicant's deportation gave rise to a violation of Article 6 of the Convention (the Court found that the admission of torture evidence constituted a flagrant denial of justice). Right to private and family life: ECtHR (Grand Chamber), *N. v. The United Kingdom* ("*N. v. UK*"), Application no. 26565/05 (27 May 2008); ECtHR, *Bensaid v. The United Kingdom* ("*Bensaid*"), Application no. 44599/98 (6 February 2001). Freedom of religion: ECtHR, *Z and T against the United Kingdom* ("*Z. & T. v. UK*"), Application no. 27034/05. Generally: H.R. Committee, "General Comment No 31: Nature of the General Legal Obligation Imposed on States Parties to the Covenant", CCPR/C/21/Rev.1/Add.13; HRC, *Kindler v. Canada*, CCPR/C/48/D/470/1991 Communication No. 470/1991 (11 November 1993), § 6.2; HRC, *Judge v. Canada*; HRC, *Sergio Euben Lopez Burgos v. Uruguay* ("*Burgos v. Uruguay*"), Supp. No. 40 (A/36/40), Communication No. R.12/52 (29 July 1981), p. 176 (1981). For analyses of the extraterritorial application of other ICCPR and ECHR rights, *see* for example: J. McAdam, *Complementary Protection in International Refugee Law* (2007), *op. cit.*, pp. 143–172; N. Mole and C. Meredith, *Asylum and the European Convention on Human Rights*, 4 ed. (Strasbourg: Council of Europe Publishing, 2007), pp. 87–102; R. Piotrowicz and C. van Eck, "Subsidiary Protection and Primary Rights", *International and Comparative Law Quarterly*, Vol. 53, No. 1 (2004), pp. 107–138, pp. 125–131; M. Foster, "*Non-Refoulement* on the Basis of Socio-Economic Deprivation: The Scope of Complementary Protection in International Human Rights Law", *New Zealand Law Review*, Part II (2009), pp. 257–310; G. Noll, "Delimiting and Justifying the Protection under the ECHR", *in Negotiating Asylum: The EU Acquis, Extraterritorial Protection, and the Common Market of Deflection* (The Hague: Kluwer Law International, 2000), pp. 453–474;

The European Court of Human Rights especially has had many occasions to decide on cases involving expulsions to countries where conflicts were taking place. In those cases, the Court assessed State Party decisions to expel applicants in light of the prohibition of cruel, inhuman or degrading treatment enshrined in Article 3 (discussed below, under C). The Court however could only do so after it had in its earlier case-law, asserted the "extraterritoriality"[19] of the ECHR thus affirming the principle of *non-refoulement* (A), and defined its scope (B). Through a survey of their respective jurisprudence, it appears that the Human Rights Committee and the ECtHR adopt similar approaches of the principle of *non-refoulement*. Material produced by the ECtHR being more substantial, focus will be put on this Court although, where relevant, reference will be made to the decisions and General Comments issued by the HRC.

A   *Recognition of the Principle of* Non-refoulement *under the* ECHR *and the* ICCPR

The recognition of the principle of *non-refoulement* by the European Court of Human Rights (ECtHR) and the Human Rights Committee (HRC) goes hand in hand with that of the extraterritoriality of the prohibition of torture, cruel, inhuman or degrading treatment or punishment. Its application or applicability to other rights (including socio-economic rights) will be discussed in the following parts of this book.

In order to apply the ECHR or the ICCPR in asylum cases, it is necessary to first clear the hurdle of the personal and territorial scope of those instrument's relevant provisions. Indeed, in such cases, not only is the person concerned not a national of the Contracting State (1) but, additionally, the constitutive element of the alleged violation of the treaty obligation is a treatment administered in a third State (2).

1   Nationality: An Immaterial Consideration

The wording of both the ECHR and the ICCPR is unequivocal: State Parties may not reserve the enjoyment of the rights to their own nationals only. On the contrary, both treaties expressly stipulate that the benefit of the rights therein enshrined is only dependant on the individual being subject to the jurisdiction of a State Party.[20]

M. Nowak, *U.N. Covenant on Civil and Political Rights: CCPR Commentary* (2005), *op. cit.*, Commentary on Article 6, p. 150, § 51.

19 The term will be nuanced and its understanding clarified below in "A.1(b)(i). Extraterritoriality: an understanding of the term", pp. 185s.

20 As highlighted by Manfred Nowak, this is actually true of all but one article of the Covenant and the ECHR: "In contrast to the ECHR, which in Article 16 expressly entitles States

Article 1 of the ECHR thus states:

> The High Contracting Parties shall secure to everyone within their jurisdiction the rights and freedoms defined in Section 1 of this Convention.[21]

This provision is strengthened by the prohibition of discrimination laid down in ECHR Article 14:

> The enjoyment of the rights and freedoms set forth in this Convention shall be secured without discrimination on any ground such as sex, race, colour, language, religion, political or other opinion, national or social origin, association with a national minority, property, birth or other status.[22]

A cross-reading of both ECHR articles makes clear the States Parties' obligation to grant ECHR rights to all individuals within their jurisdiction without discrimination based, *inter alia* on nationality. Whereas drafters of the European Convention on Human Rights chose to define the scope of the legal obligations undertaken by contracting States and to enshrine the prohibition of discrimination in two separate articles, Article 2 of the ICCPR alone clarifies the personal and territorial scope of the Covenant. Its first paragraph states:

> Each State Party to the present Covenant undertakes to respect and to ensure to all individuals within its territory and subject to its jurisdiction the rights recognized in the present Covenant, without distinction of any kind, such as race, colour, sex, language, religion, political or other opinion, national or social origin, property, birth or other status.[23]

Both the ICCPR and the ECHR contain a general jurisdictional clause: their provisions are clearly applicable to all persons who fall within the jurisdiction of a State Party, regardless of their personal innate or acquired characteristics

---

to generally place restrictions on the political activity of aliens, this is only true for the Covenant in the case of the political rights in Article 25". Interestingly, the author adds: "however, a right to enter and reside in a State party is not ensured to aliens". M. Nowak, *U.N. Covenant on Civil and Political Rights: CCPR Commentary* (2005), *op. cit.*, pp. 54–55, §47.

21 ECHR, Article 1.
22 *Ibid.*, Article 14.
23 ICCPR, Article 2, § 1.

or status. In other words, all rights in both instruments ought to be read in the light of the principle of non-discrimination. This prohibition is of "accessory character". As to the ICCPR, M. Nowak clarifies that the violation of the prohibition of discrimination can only occur "in conjunction with the concrete exercise (but not necessarily violation) of one of the substantive rights ensured by the Covenant".[24] The same is true of the ECHR: N. Mole explains that "Article 14 is not a free-standing right and the protection from discrimination may only be invoked in relation to the enjoyment of other Convention rights".[25] This has been amply confirmed by the Human Rights Committee and the European Court of Human Rights who have repeatedly stated that the principle of non-discrimination complemented and governed the implementation of all other substantive treaty provisions; discriminations based on nationality have often been condemned by both treaty bodies.[26]

---

24   As explained by M. Nowak in relation with the ICCPR specifically. M. Nowak, *U.N. Covenant on Civil and Political Rights: CCPR Commentary* (2005), *op. cit.*, p.29, § 3.

25   N. Mole and C. Meredith, *Asylum and the European Convention on Human Rights* (2007), *op. cit.*, p. 111. This is also made clear by the European Court of Human Rights itself, who for example stated in *Abdulaziz v. UK*: "According to the Court's established case-law, Article 14 (art. 14) complements the other substantive provisions of the Convention and the Protocols. It has no independent existence since it has effect solely in relation to "the enjoyment of the rights and freedoms" safeguarded by those provisions. Although the application of Article 14 (art. 14) does not necessarily presuppose a breach of those provisions – and to this extent it is autonomous -, there can be no room for its application unless the facts at issue fall within the ambit of one or more of the latter".

   See for example: ECtHR, *Rasmussen v. Denmark* ("*Rasmussen*"), Application no. 8777/79 (28 November 1984), § 29; ECtHR (Plenary), *Abdulaziz, Cabales and Balkandali v. The United Kingdom* ("*Abdulaziz v. UK*"), Application no. 9214/80, 9473/81 and 9474/81 (28 May 1985), § 71; ECtHR, *Sahin v. Germany*, Application no. 30943/96 (08 July 2003), § 85.

26   This is confirmed by the Human Rights Committee, who stated in its General Comment 15 on the position of aliens under the Covenant: "In general, the rights set forth in the Covenant apply to everyone, irrespective of reciprocity, and irrespective of his or her nationality or statelessness". HRC, "General Comment No. 15: The Position of Aliens under the Covenant" ("General Comment No. 15"), 11 April 1986, § 1. The obligation of States under the Covenant to grant the rights therein enshrined to nationals and aliens alike was reaffirmed in 2004 by the HRC in its 31st General Comment. HRC, "General Comment No. 31: The Nature of the General Legal Obligation Imposed on States Parties" ("General Comment No. 31"), CCPR/C/21/Rev.1/Add. 13, 26 May 2004, § 10. *See* also most recently the judgment of the European Court of Human Rights in *Kurić* where the Court elaborated on Article 14 ECHR and on its invocability in conjunction with Article 8 ECHR, in a case concerning the difference of treatment between two-groups of non-nationals, on the

Asylum cases brought before the European Court of Human Rights and the Human Rights Committee mainly concerned alleged violations of the prohibition of torture, in breach of Article 3 of the Convention or Article 7 of the Covenant respectively. In such cases, individuals who are not nationals of their host State challenge the said State's decision to expel them to a risk of ill-treatment proscribed by Article 3 ECHR or Article 7 ICCPR. Of particular relevance in this context is therefore the obligation for States Parties to the ECHR and the ICCPR to safeguard the rights therein enshrined without discrimination based on nationality (or absence thereof)[27] or "or other status":[28] it entails that any asylum seeker within the jurisdiction of an EU Member State, whichever his or her national origin and regardless of the fact that he may or may not be eligible for international protection,[29] is in principle entitled to every ECHR and ICCPR rights (all EU Member States being Parties to both legal instruments), including therefore the prohibition of torture, inhuman or degrading treatment or punishment. This was confirmed in 2004 by the Human Rights Committee who, drawing on its 1986 General Comment 15 on "the position of aliens under the Covenant",[30] expressly referred to asylum seekers and refugees, in General Comment 31, on the nature of State Parties' general legal obligations:

> ... the enjoyment of Covenant rights is not limited to citizens of States Parties but must also be available to all individuals, regardless of nationality or statelessness, such as asylum seekers, refugees, migrant workers and other persons, who may find themselves in the territory or subject to the jurisdiction of the State Party.[31]

The Human Rights Committee made clear that nationality – or statelessness – and immigration status were immaterial to the enjoyment of ICCPR rights. As will be shown below, this principle is confirmed in practice: both the Human Rights Committee and the European Court of Human Rights have heard numerous cases lodged by non-nationals of a defendant State Party, including asylum-seekers, who allegedly violated his or her fundamental rights.

---

ground of their national origin. ECtHR, *Kurić and Others v. Slovenia* ("*Kurić*"), Application no. 26828/06 (26 June 2012).

27 See above note 870: the Human Rights Committee stressed that ICCPR rights apply to everyone, "irrespective of his or her nationality of statelessness". "General Comment No. 15", *op. cit.*, § 1.
28 Article 14 ECHR and Article 2 ICCPR quoted above.
29 E. Lauterpacht and D. Bethlehem (2003), *op. cit.*, §§ 239–240.
30 "General Comment No. 15", *op. cit.*
31 HRC, "General Comment No. 31", *op. cit.*, § 10.

The applicability of the ICCPR and ECHR provisions to individuals who are not nationals of the Contracting States is thus established. All individuals within the jurisdiction of a State are entitled to ICCPR and ECHR protection, including the protection against torture, inhuman or degrading treatment or punishment. The obligation of State Parties to apply each instrument in a non-discriminatory manner implies that the benefit of the rights the ICCPR and ECHR enshrine must be guaranteed to all individuals within the States' jurisdiction, including aliens or, for that matter, asylum seekers.

In asylum cases however, the nationality of the complainant is not the only apparent obstacle to the applicability of human rights treaties. The question of the territoriality of the constitutive element of the violation must also be addressed.

2   Territoriality of the Ill-treatment: An Immaterial Consideration

The principle of *non-refoulement* protects individuals from being sent to a territory where they would be exposed to risks for their life or person. The ill-treatment justifying international protection hence takes place in a third country, outside the jurisdiction of the expelling State. The question therefore arose whether an extradition or an expulsion which would expose an individual to a risk of suffering a treatment proscribed under Article 3 ECHR or Article 7 ICCPR in the receiving State could trigger the expelling State's responsibility.

Both monitoring bodies replied in the affirmative.

(a)   *Extraterritoriality: An Understanding of the Term*

A semantic remark must be made as to the term "extraterritoriality". As mentioned by the ECtHR in the *Soering* case,[32] Article 1 of the ECHR which obliges Contracting States to secure to everyone within their jurisdiction the rights and freedoms enshrined in the Convention "sets a limit, notably territorial, on the reach of the Convention".[33] The Court further noted that "the Convention does not govern the actions of the States not Parties to it".[34]

Bearing in mind the rules governing the law of treaties, it could seem counter-intuitive that, after recalling those principles, both monitoring bodies nevertheless assert the applicability of the ECHR and ICCPR in asylum cases. Among other rules, the 1969 Vienna Convention on the Law of Treaties (VCLT) codifies the principles of free consent, good faith and *pacta sunt servanda*.[35]

---

32   ECtHR, *Soering*.
33   *Ibid.*, § 86.
34   *Ibid.*, § 86.
35   VCLT, Preamble recital 3.

For the purpose of the present discussion, it is noteworthy that the VCLT applies the principle of good faith not only to the performance of treaties[36] but specifically also to their interpretation.[37] The VCLT also elaborates on the territorial scope of treaties. Article 29 defines it as follows: "unless a different intention appears from the treaty or is otherwise established, a treaty is binding upon each party in respect of its entire territory". It can be inferred *a contrario* from Article 29 that a treaty is not to be binding upon a State Party to it in respect of another State's territory.

In asserting the so-called "extraterritoriality" of the treaty they each monitor, the ECtHR and HRC however did not disregard those rules governing the law of treaties. Indeed, the extraterritorial applicability of the ECHR and ICCPR, as it is construed by the ECtHR and the HRC, does not create obligations for States who are not parties to them; the principles governing the law of treaties are therefore not infringed. This applicability results from a legal construct which can be better explained through an analogy to the criminal law concept of complicity. As explained by M. Nowak, the responsibility of an extraditing or expelling State is comparable to the criminal responsibility of an individual who aids, abets or otherwise assists in the commission of a crime.[38] Although the crime (*i.e.* a treatment proscribed under international human rights law) is committed by a third person (*i.e.* individuals or groups falling under the jurisdiction of another State), its commission was only possible by the prior action of the "accomplice" (*i.e.* the expelling State taking the decision to remove the asylum seeker). In more concrete terms, this means that although the ill-treatment would in fact be administered to the failed asylum-seeker outside the jurisdiction of the expelling State, the HRC and the ECtHR find that it is the State's removal decision itself which constitutes a breach of the State's legal obligation under the Covenant or the ECHR.[39] To wit:

> ... the extraditing or expelling State, according to the principle of *non-refoulement*, commits human rights violations on its own territory by the very decision of expulsion or extradition and its practical implementation.[40]

---

36   *Ibid.*, Article 26.
37   *Ibid.*, Article 31 (1).
38   M. Nowak, *U.N. Covenant on Civil and Political Rights: CCPR Commentary* (2005), *op. cit.*, Commentary on Art. 3 First OP, p. 862, § 35.
39   The relevant decisions issued by the HRC and ECtHR will be discussed subsequently.
40   M. Nowak, *U.N. Covenant on Civil and Political Rights: CCPR Commentary* (2005), *op. cit.*, Commentary on Art. 3 First OP, pp. 861–862, § 35.

It could in fact be argued that should the HRC and the ECtHR have ruled otherwise, then the principle of good faith would be impaired. As mentioned by the Vienna Convention on the Law of Treaties[41] and the Human Rights Committee[42] notably, the principle of good faith is universally recognised and ought to govern States conventional relations. Already in 1981 did the Human Rights Committee state that "it would be *unconscionable* to so interpret the responsibility under article 2[43] of the Covenant as to permit a State party to perpetrate violations of the Covenant on the territory of another State, which violations it could not perpetrate on its own territory".[44] The abolition of the death penalty can serve as an example. In the ICCPR system, pursuant to Article 6, protecting the right to life and read together with the 2nd Optional Protocol,[45] States Parties to both instruments have the obligation to prohibit the death penalty within their jurisdiction.[46] This prohibition would risk be deprived of all meaning if an abolitionist State could in effect contribute to the execution of a death sentence in another State by lawfully returning the sentenced individual to that country; this would be tantamount to allowing the State to re-establish the death penalty "by proxy in respect of a certain category of persons under its jurisdiction".[47] Such was the reasoning followed by dissenting judges in the controversial *Kindler v. Canada*[48] and later endorsed by the Human Rights Committee. Indeed, in its landmark case of *Judge v. Canada*,[49] the HRC makes clear that no abolitionist State, irrespective of whether or not it has yet ratified the Second Optional Protocol, is allowed to extradite a person to another State where he or she faces a real risk of being sentenced to death or executed.[50]

---

41 VCLT, Preamble recital 3 and Article 26.
42 HRC, "General Comment No. 31", *op. cit.*, § 3.
43 Article 2 ICCPR, cited above p. 182, reads: "Each State Party to the present Covenant undertakes to respect and to ensure to all individuals within its territory and subject to its jurisdiction the rights recognized in the present Covenant, without distinction of any kind, such as race, colour, sex, language, religion, political or other opinion, national or social origin, property, birth or other status".
44 HRC, *Burgos v. Uruguay*, § 12.3.
45 Second Optional Protocol to the International Covenant on Civil and Political Rights, aiming at the abolition of the death penalty ("ICCPR 2nd OP"), 15 December 1989, entered into force 11 July 1991 A/RES/44/128.
46 M. Nowak, *U.N. Covenant on Civil and Political Rights: CCPR Commentary* (2005), *op. cit.*, §§ 26 and 29.
47 HRC, *Kindler v. Canada*, Dissenting opinion of Christine Chanet. See also *ibid.*, Dissenting opinions submitted by Bertil Wennergren, Francisco Jose Aguilar Urbina (§ 22 in particular), Rajsoomer Lallah (§ 3.4), Fausto Pocar.
48 *Ibid.*
49 HRC, *Judge v. Canada*.
50 *Ibid.*, § 10.6.

Similarly, the ECtHR stated that prohibiting Contracting States from subjected individuals within their jurisdiction to torture while allowing them knowingly to surrender an individual to a real risk of torture in another State would "plainly be contrary to the spirit and intendment" of the prohibition.[51]

A comprehensive reading of the Human Rights Committee General Comment 31, on the nature of State Parties' general legal obligation under the Covenant suggests that it is indeed the principle of good faith that calls for the extraterritorial applicability of ICCPR rights. Paragraph 3 stresses that "[p]ursuant to the principle articulated in article 26 of the Vienna Convention on the Law of Treaties, States Parties are required to give effect to the obligations under the Covenant in good faith". Clarifications on the meaning of Article 2 ICCPR (defining the scope of States' legal obligations under the Covenant) follow including, in paragraph 12, the assertion that Article 2 "entails" an obligation for State Parties "an obligation not to extradite, deport, expel or otherwise remove a person from their territory, where there are substantial grounds for believing that there is a real risk of irreparable harm, such as that contemplated by articles 6 and 7 of the Covenant".[52] A combined reading of the two paragraphs hence unambiguously reveals that the extraterritorial application of the ICCPR flows from an interpretation in good faith of the Covenant, and, in particular, of Article 2 read in conjunction with Articles 6 (right to life) and 7 (prohibition of torture or cruel, inhuman or degrading treatment or punishment).

J. McAdam notes that the mechanism which is sometimes referred to as "principle of extraterritoriality" would be better described as "State responsibility arising from the foreseeable consequences of a removal decision which exposes an individual to a 'real risk' of ill-treatment in a third State" (citations omitted).[53] For lack of better word though, the term "extraterritoriality"[54] is used here and after to describe the legal construct enabling the monitoring bodies to entertain claims of alleged violations of the Covenant or of the Convention in asylum cases. As mentioned, it is not to be understood as describing an extension of the scope of ECHR and ICCPR legal obligations either to States

---

51   ECtHR, *Soering*, § 88.
52   HRC, "General Comment No. 31", *op. cit.*, §§ 3 and 12.
53   J. McAdam, *Complementary Protection in International Refugee Law* (2007), *op. cit.*, p. 143.
54   The term is amply used in literature. H. King, "The Extraterritorial Human Rights Obligations of States", *Human Rights Law Review*, January 1, 2009, Vol. 9, No. 4 (2009), pp. 521–556; M. Scheinin, "Extraterritorial Effect of the International Covenant on Civil and Political Rights", *in* F. Coomans and M.T. Kamminga (Eds.), *Extraterritorial Application of Human Rights Treaties* (Antwerp: Intersentia, 2004), pp. 73–82; T. Meron, "Extraterritoriality of Human Rights Treaties", *The American Journal of International Law* (American Society of International Law), Vol. 89, No. 1 (1995), pp. 78–82.

who are not parties to them or to violations committed outside the jurisdiction of the Contracting States. Instead, it serves the purpose of illustrating how monitoring bodies could quite logically attract asylum cases under their scrutiny by deciding to examine States' decisions to expel and their adverse consequences by the yardstick of States' human rights treaty obligations and regardless of the fact that those consequences unfold beyond the State's borders.

(b)   *A Constructive Interpretation of the Prohibition of Torture by the ECtHR...*

The question of the extraterritoriality of the ECHR was first considered in detail by the European Court in 1989, concerning extradition, in the *Soering* case.[55] The case concerned the extradition of M. Soering from Great Britain to the United States. M. Soering was to stand trial on capital charges and risked be sentenced to death. Although Article 2 ECHR addresses the right to life and specifically the death penalty, the applicant instead invoked Article 3, arguing that the treatment he would be subjected to when remaining on death row would constitute inhuman and degrading treatment contrary to Article 3.

The United Kingdom government contended that Article 3 should not be interpreted "so as to impose responsibility on a Contracting State for acts which occur outside its jurisdiction". The government added that "extradition [did] not involve the responsibility of the extraditing State for inhuman or degrading treatment or punishment which the extradited person may suffer outside the State's jurisdiction".

The European Court of Human Rights differed. The United Kingdom pointed to the fact that whereas other instruments of international law expressly and specifically prohibit State Parties to them to remove individuals in certain circumstances,[56] the absence of any similar provision in the ECHR was to be interpreted as placing no such obligation on Contracting States. The Court however objected that the existence of a *lex specialis* specifically prohibiting the removal of aliens to a country where they risk be exposed to torture did not mean that "an essentially similar obligation [was] not already inherent in the general terms of Article 3".[57] The Court thus hints that the prohibition of torture in Article 3 does include, not expressly but inherently, an obligation for Contracting States not to remove individuals to a risk of torture.

---

55   ECtHR, *Soering*.
56   The UK Government referred to the 1951 Refugee Convention (Article 33), the 1957 European Convention on Extradition (Article 11) and the 1984 UN Convention Against Torture and Other Cruel, Inhuman and Degrading Treatment or Punishment (Article 3). *Ibid.*, § 86.
57   *Ibid.*, § 88.

To the United Kingdom Government arguments against the extraterritoriality of the Convention, the Court conceded that the rights and freedoms listed therein were indeed to be secured by a Contracting State, "within its own jurisdiction". It also answered the United Kingdom government's concern that the applicability of Article 3 in extradition cases would interfere with international treaty law. The UK government had stated that the suggested approach would lead to "a conflict with the norms of international judicial process, in that it in effect involves adjudication on the internal affairs of foreign States not Parties to the Convention or to the proceedings before the Convention institutions".[58] The Court confirmed that the Convention was not to apply to States who were not parties to it: "the Convention does not govern the actions of States not Parties to it, nor does it purport to be a means of requiring the Contracting States to impose Convention standards on other States".[59] The Court however concluded on this matter by underlining that the assessment of the situation in the receiving State against the standards of the Convention was necessarily called for to establish whether the feared treatment would indeed be in violation of the Convention. This assessment, the Court objected, was not tantamount to adjudicating on or establishing the responsibility of the receiving country, whether under general international law, under the Convention or otherwise.[60]

Before addressing the question whether Article 3 ECHR was applicable in the case, the Court set out a number of principles. The Court notes that the ECHR is a treaty "for the collective enforcement of human rights and fundamental freedoms" whose object and purpose require that its provisions be interpreted and applied so as to make its safeguards "practical and effective".[61] Those principles can be described as "interpretation principles": they are not specific to Article 3 but concern the Convention at large and suggest its "wide, inclusive interpretation".[62] As for Article 3 in particular, the Court notes that it prohibits torture in absolute terms and thus enshrines "one of the most fundamental values of the democratic societies making up the Council of Europe".[63] These characteristics "strengthen the call for an inclusive interpretation" of the provision.[64] On this premise, the Court, following a teleological and indeed

---

58   Ibid., § 83.
59   Ibid., § 86.
60   Ibid., § 91.
61   Ibid., § 90.
62   H. Battjes, "Landmarks: Soering's Legacy", *Amsterdam Law Forum*, Vol. 1, No. 1 (VU University of Amsterdam, 2008), retrieved from: <http://ojs.ubvu.vu.nl/alf/article/view/51/67> [03/09/2012].
63   ECtHR, *Soering.*, § 88.
64   H. Battjes, "Landmarks: Soering's Legacy" (2008).

inclusive interpretation of Article 3 ECHR, finds that extradition of an individual to another State where there are substantial grounds for believing that he or she would face a real risk of being subjected to torture or inhuman or degrading treatment "while not explicitly referred to in the brief and general wording of Article 3, would plainly be contrary to the spirit and intendment of the Article".[65]

In conclusion, the Court stated that:

> In sum, the decision by a Contracting State to extradite a fugitive may give rise to an issue under Article 3 (art. 3), and hence engage the responsibility of that State under the Convention, where substantial grounds have been shown for believing that the person concerned, if extradited, faces a real risk of being subjected to torture or to inhuman or degrading treatment or punishment in the requesting country.[66]

It clarified that Contracting States could indeed be liable under the Convention for treatments administered in other States; the Court explained that:

> In so far as any liability under the Convention is or may be incurred, it is liability incurred by the extraditing Contracting State by reason of its having taken action which has as a direct consequence the exposure of an individual to proscribed ill-treatment.[67]

The applicability of the Convention – and of Article 3 thereof in particular – to extradition cases was thus established and generally accepted and applied since by national authorities, persuaded by the Court's principled demonstration.[68] The Court later extended the extraterritoriality of Article 3 to expulsion cases. In *Cruz Varas v. Sweden*, the Court quotes *verbatim* its *Soering* judgement, recalling that Contracting States may incur liability by reason of their decision to extradite an individual and thereby expose him or her to proscribed ill-treatment.[69] The Court goes on to add:

---

65 ECtHR, *Soering.*, § 88.
66 *Ibid.*, § 91.
67 *Ibid.*, § 91.
68 H. Battjes notices a series of rhetorical effects in the language used by the Court (such as "the abhorrence of torture" and the Convention as "common heritage of political traditions, ideals, freedom and the rule of law") which served the purpose of justifying the inclusive interpretation of the Convention but also of convincing and persuading States of the validity if such interpretation. H. Battjes, 'Landmarks: Soering's Legacy" (2008).
69 ECtHR, *Cruz Varas and Others v. Sweden* ("*Cruz Varas*"), Application no. 15576/89 (20 March 1991), § 69.

> Although the present case concerns expulsion as opposed to a decision to extradite, the Court considers that the above principle also applies to expulsion decisions and a fortiori to cases of actual expulsion.[70]

The applicability of Article 3 ECHR in expulsion cases too was henceforth established.

In 2005, in the *Salah Sheekh* judgement, the Court reiterates and synthesises its *Soering* findings and the subsequent developments. The Court reiterates that, under international law, States have a right to control the entry, residence and expulsion of aliens. In parallel, the Court concedes, the European Convention of Human Rights does not contain a right to political asylum.[71] However, the Court stresses that States are nevertheless bound, when exercising their right to control the expulsion of aliens, to comply with Article 3 ECHR. The Court makes clear that Article 3 of the Convention:

> ... enshrines one of the fundamental values of democratic societies and prohibits in absolute terms torture or inhuman or degrading treatment or punishment, irrespective of the victim's conduct, however undesirable or dangerous.[72]

The Court confirms the link between Article 3 and the principle of *non-refoulement* in the following terms:

> The expulsion of an alien may give rise to an issue under this provision, and hence engage the responsibility of the expelling State under the Convention, where substantial grounds have been shown for believing that the person in question, if expelled, would face a real risk of being subjected to treatment contrary to Article 3 in the receiving country. In such circumstances, Article 3 implies an obligation not to expel the individual to that country.[73]

The reference to "an obligation not to expel" confirms that the territoriality of the breach of Article 3 by an expelling State is this State's own territory or jurisdiction. An obligation not to expel is violated by the antonymous decision to expel. It is true that the ill-treatment unfolds in a territory under the

---

70 Ibid., § 70.
71 ECtHR, *Salah Sheekh*, § 135.
72 Ibid., § 135.
73 Ibid., § 135.

jurisdiction of another State but the very decision to remove the individual to that territory[74] was taken by the authorities of the expelling State, within the expelling State's jurisdiction: the material element of the breach of Article 3 ECHR can therefore be located within the expelling State's jurisdiction.

The decision of the Court in *Salah Sheekh*, although it is on its face similar to that reached in *Soering* and subsequent cases, however represents a significant liberalisation of the Court's jurisprudence in many respects. As will be discussed below, it relaxed the test for demonstrating a "real risk" and reconsidered the requirement that the threat be individualised.[75]

As made clear in the jurisprudence of the European Court on Human Rights, and although neither the principle of *non-refoulement* nor the right to political asylum is contained in either the Convention or its Protocols,[76] the ECHR is nevertheless applicable to all asylum cases. M. Nowak encapsulates the mechanism as follows:

> ... the prohibition of torture gives rise to the (negative) duty on the State to refrain from expulsion or extradition when this would facilitate torture or inhuman treatment by a third State, which need not itself be a party to the Convention. If a State party to the ECHR disregards this duty, then it violates (albeit indirectly) the prohibition of torture.[77]

The European Court of Human Rights has made clear its position concerning the possible extraterritorial application of Article 3 ECHR. The prohibition, also enshrined in Article 7 of the International Covenant on Civil and Political Rights, was in fact applied in like manner by the Human Rights Committee through its case-law and general comments to expulsion cases.

(c) *... A Constructive Interpretation Endorsed by the Human Rights Committee*

The same extraterritoriality also applied to the International Covenant on Civil and Political Rights. The opinion of the Human Rights Committee (HRC) has however significantly evolved in time. In 1991, the Committee received a communication in an extradition case. The facts were similar to those of the

---

74 Or, in case of chain *refoulement*, to a third State which itself expelled the individual to the territory where ill-treatment occurred or risks occurring.

75 Below "3. Application to armed conflict situations", pp. 233s.

76 *See* for example ECtHR, *Salah Sheekh*, § 135; ECtHR, *Vilvarajah*, § 102.

77 M. Nowak, *U.N. Covenant on Civil and Political Rights: CCPR Commentary* (2005), *op. cit.*, p. 185, § 45.

ECtHR *Soering* case: M. Kindler had been sentenced to death in the United States, in Pennsylvania, but escaped and hid in Canada where he was later arrested.

In its decision on the admissibility of the case, the Human Rights Committee concisely establishes its competence *rationae materiae* before addressing at length its competence *rationae loci*. On the first point, the HRC conceded that extradition as such was outside the scope of the Covenant but noted that the consequences of extradition could raise issues under specific provisions of the Covenant.[78] In addressing the second point, the HRC emphatically affirmed the applicability of the Covenant in extradition cases. The reasoning and the language used by the Committee to find that States could be liable for the adverse consequences of extradition are echoes of the ECtHR judgment in the *Soering* case.

The Human Rights Committee first took note of Article 2 of the ICCPR, obligating States to guarantee the rights enshrined in the Covenant to all persons within their jurisdiction. The Committee adds that extradition *per se* is not prohibited under the Covenant and that human rights violations suffered by the individual concerned after his or her expulsion, within the jurisdiction of another State, will not generally trigger the expelling State's responsibility. In that sense, the Committee stresses: "a State party clearly is not required to guarantee the rights of persons within another jurisdiction".[79]

However, the Committee notes, and this is the essence of the so-called extraterritoriality of the ICCPR (and ECHR alike):

> ... if a State party takes a decision relating to a person within its jurisdiction, and the necessary and foreseeable consequence is that that person's rights under the Covenant will be violated in another jurisdiction, the State party itself may be in violation of the Covenant.[80]

The HRC finds that the Covenant cannot be interpreted as allowing a State Party to knowingly expel an individual to a situation where he or she will be subjected to ill-treatment prohibited under the ICCPR, including torture:

> ...a State party's duty under article 2 of the Covenant would be negated by the handing over of a person to another State (whether a State party to the Covenant or not) where treatment contrary to the Covenant is

---

78 HRC, *Kindler v. Canada.*, § 6.1.
79 *Ibid.*, § 6.2.
80 *Ibid.*, § 6.2.

certain or is the very purpose of the handing over. For example, a State party would itself be in violation of the Covenant if it handed over a person to another State in circumstances in which it was foreseeable that torture would take place.[81]

The extraterritoriality of the prohibition of Article 6 and Article 7 treatments is thereby established beyond a doubt; in other words, so is the principle of *non-refoulement* under the ICCPR.

However, on the merits, and despite its stating that it had had "careful regard" to the ECtHR *Soering* judgement,[82] the Committee found that the extradition of M. Kindler to the United States where he was to face capital punishment did not violate Article 6 (right to life) or 7 (prohibition of torture) of the Covenant. The Committee contended that "important facts leading to the judgment of the European Court" were "distinguishable on material points" from the facts in the *Kindler* case. In particular, the Committee cited the age and mental state of the offender, and the conditions on death row in the respective prison systems.[83] This 1993 *Kindler v. Canada* decision was highly controversial, not least because it was hardly conceivable how Canada, who had abolished the death penalty – even though it had not (yet[84]) ratified the Second Optional Protocol to the ICCPR, could lawfully under the ICCPR return someone to a real risk of execution.[85] The Human Rights Committee, drawing from the dissenting opinions expressed by judges in this case soon corrected its controversial decision: the HRC decision in the *Charles Chitat Ng v. Canada* ("*Ng*")[86] responded to the concerns expressed by dissenting judges and commentators.

---

81   *Ibid.*, § 6.2.
82   *Ibid.*, § 15.3.
83   *Ibid.*, § 15.3.
84   Canada acceded to the Second Optional Protocol to the ICCPR, aiming at the abolition of the death penalty, on 25 Nov 2005 (Source: website of the Treaty Section of the Office of Legal Affairs of the United Nations, available at <http://treaties.un.org> last accessed 08/06/2012.).
85   It is worth noting that seven of the Committee members submitted individual opinions in the *Kindler* case, two of which were dissenting on the admissibility yet concurring on the merits Kurt Herndl and Waleed Sadi jointly) and five were dissenting on the merits (Bertil Wennergren, Rajsoomer Lallah, Fausto Pocar – dissenting on the HRC finding of a non-violation of Article 6 ICCPR, Christine Chanet and Francisco Jose Aguilar Urbina). *See* also above note 187 and corresponding text.
86   HRC, *Charles Chitat Ng v. Canada* ("*Ng v. Canada*"), CCPR/C/49/D/469/1991 (7 January 1994).

The author of the communication to the Human Rights Committee was M. Ng, a British subject born in Hong Kong and a US resident. He was arrested, charged and convicted in 1985 in Canada following an attempted store theft and shooting of a security guard. In 1987, the United States requested and obtained his extradition to stand trial in California (on 19 criminal counts, including kidnapping and 12 murders) where, if convicted, M. Ng could face the death penalty and execution by gas asphyxiation.[87] Without seeking assurances from the United States that the death penalty would not be imposed, Canada, an abolitionist State since 1976, extradited M. Ng in 1991.[88] The Committee's admissibility decision is modelled on its decision in *Kindler*.[89] The developments concerning the HRC competence *rationae loci* in fact reproduce word for word the corresponding paragraphs of the *Kindler* decision.[90]

Although this is less pertinent to observe in the present discussion on the extraterritorial applicability of the ICCPR, it is nevertheless noticeable that on the merits, in the *Ng* case, the Human Rights Committee departed from its conclusions in the *Kindler* case and found a violation of Article 7 ICCPR. The HRC considered that execution by gas asphyxiation would not meet the test of "least possible physical and mental suffering"[91] and constituted cruel and inhuman treatment, in violation of article 7 of the Covenant. The Committee concluded that "accordingly, Canada, which could reasonably foresee that M. Ng, if sentenced to death, would be executed in a way that amounts to a violation of article 7, failed to comply with its obligations under the Covenant, by extraditing M. Ng without having sought and received assurances that he would not be executed".[92] The Committee however, as in *Kindler*, found no violation of the right to life (Article 6 ICCPR) which caused a number of judges to submit dissenting opinions, on this point of the decision at least. The Committee eventually overruled its jurisprudence in the 2003 case of *Judge v. Canada* and

---

87 *Ibid.*, §§ 1 and 2.1.
88 *Ibid.*, §§ 2.2 to 2.5.
89 HRC, *Kindler v. Canada*, §§ 6.1 – 7; HRC, *Ng v. Canada*, §§ 6.1 – 7. On the competence *rationae materiae*, compare: HRC, *Kindler v. Canada*, § 6.1; with HRC, *Ng v. Canada*, § 6.1.
90 Above p. 194.
91 Such is the standard established by the Committee in its General Comment on Article 7. Article 6 of the ICCPR, which protects the rights to life, allows State Parties to maintain the death penalty but only for the most serious crimes. When imposing the death penalty, the HRC urged "retentionist" States to ensure that the execution of the sentence be "carried out in such a way as to cause the least possible physical and mental suffering". *See* HRC, "General Comment No. 20 on Article 7 (Prohibition of Torture, or Other Cruel, Inhuman or Degrading Treatment or Punishment)" ("General Comment No. 20"), 10 March 1992, § 6.
92 HRC, *Ng v. Canada*, § 16.4.

concluded that Canada, as any abolitionist State, could not remove an individual from its jurisdiction if it could be "reasonably anticipated" that they will be sentenced to death, "without ensuring that the death sentence would not be carried out".[93]

As shown from the above decisions of the Human Rights Committee, the principle that State Party responsibility arises under the ICCPR from the foreseeable consequences of a removal decision is unquestionable. Additionally, a further confirmation of the validity of the principle came in 2004, in the HRC General Comment on the nature of the general legal obligation imposed on states parties to the Covenant. The Human Rights Committee reasserted the extraterritoriality of the ICCPR as follows:

> ... the article 2 obligation requiring that States Parties respect and ensure the Covenant rights for all persons in their territory and all persons under their control entails an obligation not to extradite, deport, expel or otherwise remove a person from their territory, where there are substantial grounds for believing that there is a real risk of irreparable harm, such as that contemplated by articles 6 and 7 of the Covenant, either in the country to which removal is to be effected or in any country to which the person may subsequently be removed. The relevant judicial and administrative authorities should be made aware of the need to ensure compliance with the Covenant obligations in such matters.[94]

The extraterritoriality of the ECHR and the ICCPR and the implied principle of *non-refoulement* having been established beyond dispute, it fell on the ECtHR and the HRC respectively to define the scope of the protection thus afforded to aliens faced with expulsion to prohibited ill-treatment.

B   Operating the Principle of Non-refoulement *in Asylum Cases*

Besides the recognition of the extraterritoriality of the ECHR, two additional elements are worth being highlighted in the leading *Soering* decision. Firstly, the Court established that a violation of the ECHR could be constituted already at a time the feared ill-treatment had not yet taken place and even regardless of whether it would eventually take place or not (1). Secondly, the Court pointed at the fact that although the ECHR and the Refugee Convention might both be applicable in a given situation, they however differ in scopes, that of the ECHR being the broadest (2).

---

93   HRC, *Judge v. Canada*, § 10.4.
94   HRC, "General Comment No. 31", *op. cit.*, § 12.

As noted before,[95] the European Court of Human Rights has often dealt with asylum cases. Comparatively, the Human Rights Committee has only received and decided on very few cases.[96] It should therefore not be surprising that the following developments will concern mainly the case-law of the European Court of Human Rights.

1   State Liability and Hypothetical Ill-treatment

In the *Soering* case[97] and although the United Kingdom Government had not raised the issue, the Court, anticipatorily it seems, addressed the question whether a State could be held liable for a treatment which had not yet been suffered by the applicant at the time the application was lodged. The Court observes that, as of principle, it is not for the Convention institutions to pronounce on the existence or otherwise of "potential violations" of the Convention but notes that:

> ... where an applicant claims that a decision to extradite him would, if implemented, be contrary to Article 3 by reason of its foreseeable consequences in the requesting country, a departure from this principle is necessary, in view of the serious and irreparable nature of the alleged suffering risked, in order to ensure the effectiveness of the safeguard provided by that Article 3.[98]

It could be argued that giving consideration to the unverified yet consequences of a State's actions, and the potential violations of the Convention they might constitute, risks weakening the decisions of the Court. The Court could indeed be perceived as placing too heavy a burden on State authorities deciding in asylum cases: States would risk be found in violation of the ECHR for the hypothetical treatment to be suffered by an individual outside the State's jurisdiction. However, the expediency of the Court's decision in extradition – and expulsion – cases is ensured by the requirement that the consequences be "foreseeable". The requirement was phrased by the Court in the *Soering* case:

> In sum, the decision by a Contracting State to extradite a fugitive may give rise to an issue under Article 3 (art. 3), and hence engage the responsibility of that State under the Convention, where *substantial grounds*

---

95   Above p. 180.
96   H. Lambert (1999), *op. cit.*, p. 523, n. 36.
97   ECtHR, *Soering*.
98   *Ibid.*, § 90.

have been shown *for believing* that the person concerned, if extradited, faces a *real risk* of being subjected to torture or to inhuman or degrading treatment or punishment in the requesting country [emphases added].[99]

The responsibility of the expelling Contracting State can be engaged under the ECHR if "substantial grounds" have been shown for believing that the person would face, upon return, a "real risk" of being ill-treated.

The jurisprudence of the Court illustrates that the reality of the risk is rigorously assessed by the Court who consistently found that a "mere possibility" of ill treatment was not in itself sufficient to give rise to a breach of Article 3.[100]

In like manner, the Human Rights Committee stated in *Kindler v. Canada* that no State Party can extradite an individual to a third State when it is "foreseeable" that he or she would be subjected to ill-treatment there. In particular, the HRC noted:

> The foreseeability of the consequence would mean that there was a present violation by the State party, even though the consequence would not occur until later on.[101]

The Committee in *Kindler* however found no violation of the ICCPR in Canada's decision to extradite the applicant to the United States where he had been sentenced to death.

The findings of the HRC in *Charles Chitat Ng v. Canada* show that the HRC adopted a similar approach to that of the ECtHR. The Committee indeed took into consideration the "foreseeability of the consequence" of an extradition to find that Canada should have refrained from expulsing M. Ng to the US.[102] The HRC, as the Court does, relies on the reality of the risk incurred by an individual upon removal. The committee thus observed that if a State Party deports a person who is present within its territory and subject to its jurisdiction "in such circumstances that as a result, there is a *real risk* that his or her rights under the Covenant will be violated in another jurisdiction, that State party itself may be in violation of the Covenant".[103] This position was succinctly put by the Committee in the 2003 *Judge v. Canada* case. In this case concerning

---

99   Ibid., § 91.
100 See for example ECtHR, *Vilvarajah*, § 111; ECtHR, *Salah Sheekh*, § 135.
101 HRC, *Kindler v. Canada*, § 6.2.
102 See HRC, *Ng v. Canada*, § 6.2.
103 HRC, *Mrs. G.T. v. Australia*, CCPR/C/61/D/706/1996 (4 November 1997), § 8.2 [emphasis added].

the deportation of a US citizen from Canada to the United States where he had been sentenced to death, the Committee stated that "the extradition itself would not amount to a violation by Canada unless there was a *real risk* that the author's rights under the Covenant would be violated in the United States".[104] The requirement was made clear again by the HRC in 2004 in General Comment 31:

> ... the article 2 obligation (...) entails an obligation not to extradite, deport, expel or otherwise remove a person from their territory, where there are *substantial grounds for believing* that there is a *real risk* of irreparable harm...[105]

To conclude that a State is in breach of its treaty obligation under the ECHR or the ICCPR in an asylum case, the European Court of Human Rights and the Human Rights Committee respectively and alike consider the "foreseeable consequences" of an expulsion; the risk allegedly incurred, both monitoring bodies find, must be "real".

The similarity between the two monitoring bodies' approaches is not surprising given that, as mentioned, the Human Rights Committee heavily relied on the *Soering* judgment to formulate its first decision in an extradition case, in *Kindler*.[106] Although they adopted similar approaches to the interpretation of the extraterritorial scope of, mainly, the prohibition of torture and inhuman or degrading treatment or punishment, the ECtHR and HRC nevertheless offer distinct possibilities of protection. H. Lambert, comparing the scope of the protection against *refoulement* in Europe under the different pertinent human rights law instruments, notes that beyond this resemblance in approaches, the practice of the HRC in fact seems to be less consistent than that of the ECtHR and its views, a "restrictive application" of the principles developed by the ECtHR.[107] Additionally, the jurisprudence of the Human Rights Committee is also characterised by the limited range of evidence it can use: Article 5(1) of the Optional Protocol stipulates that the HRC will consider communications

---

104 HRC, *Judge v. Canada*, § 10.2 [emphasis added]. Incidentally, the *Judge v. Canada* case is particularly interesting in relation to the abolition of death penalty. The HRC extended the principle of *non-refoulement* to the right to life (Article 6), finding that Article 6(1) prohibiting the death penalty implied the obligation for abolitionist States not to remove individuals to retentionist States – be they Parties to the Covenant or not – without ensuring first that the death sentence would not be carried out. *Ibid.*, § 10.4.
105 HRC, "General Comment No. 31", *op. cit.*, § 12 [emphasis added].
106 See above p. 193.
107 H. Lambert (1999), *op. cit.*, p. 532, n. 85 and p. 543.

received in the light only of written information submitted to it by the individual and by the State Party concerned.[108] It is particularly unfortunate in *refoulement* cases where accurate, up-to-date and comprehensive information on the situation in the country of origin or destination is of crucial importance. Practice of the ECtHR and of national courts in asylum cases is illustrative: much attention is paid to reports provided by humanitarian actors, including non-governmental organisations and United Nations agencies.[109] H. Lambert in fact concludes that, in spite of HRC proceedings having the advantage of being shorter and producing better intelligible views than the ECtHR, the ICCPR "stands out as the least suitable instrument".[110]

The case-law of the European Court of Human Rights clarifies that the assessment of the *reality* of the risk relies on a range of considerations: of time (the flight and application for asylum take place years after the events invoked to substantiate the claim took place[111]), of the severity of the invoked risk (psychological distress felt by prisoners on death row;[112] prolonged exposure to the sun,[113] adultery woman exposed to whipping, flogging and stoning,[114] deterioration of the applicant's ill health due to the interruption of healthcare[115]) and of the probability that the risk materialises (deterioration of the applicant's health status,[116] situations of generalised violence[117]).

In cases involving situations of indiscriminate violence caused by an armed conflict prevailing in the applicant's country of origin, the European Court of Human Rights assesses the reality of the risk (which includes the probability that the applicant become victim of the generalised violence) in view of the

---

108 Optional Protocol to the International Covenant on Civil and Political Rights, 16 December 1966, entry into force 23 March 1976 [1976] UNTS Vol. 999, p. 171.
109 For particularly telling examples, see: UK Court of Appeal, EWCA, *QD & AH v Secretary of State for the Home Department*, 24 June 2009, op. cit; ECtHR, *Sufi & Elmi*.
110 H. Lambert (1999), op. cit., p. 543.
111 ECtHR, *Thampibillai v. The Netherlands* ("*Thampibillai*"), Application No. 61350/00 (17 February 2004).
112 ECtHR, *Soering*.
113 ECtHR, *Said v. The Netherlands* ("*Said v. NL*"), Application No. 2345/02 (15 July 2005).
114 ECtHR, *Jabari v. Turkey* ("*Jabari*"), Application No. 40035/98 (11 July 2000).
115 Such treatment may reach the required severity threshold only in "exceptional" or "very exceptional" circumstances. AIDS: ECtHR, *N. v. UK*; and ECtHR, *D. v. UK*; Schizophrenic applicant with psychotic illness: ECtHR, *Bensaid*; Applicant infected with HIV opposing removal to Zambia: ECtHR, *S.C.C. v. Sweden* ("*S.C.C. v. Sweden*"), Application No. 46553/99 (15 February 2000).
116 See cases cited above.
117 ECtHR, *Salah Sheekh*; ECtHR, *Vilvarajah*.

level of violence and of the personal nature of the risk. Relevant cases will be analysed below.[118]

2 Non-refoulement: Absolute in Human Rights Law, Qualified in Refugee Law

The relative breadth of international human rights law[119] in comparison with international refugee law was already touched upon by the European Court of Human Rights in 1989 in *Soering* and clarified in 1996 in *Chahal*.[120] More precisely: in its judgment in the *Chahal* case, the Court underlines that the ECHR is broader than the Geneva Convention in that it protects individuals regardless of their conducts, including those conducts that could potentially be dangerous for the hosting State.[121] Regard – or disregard – for the conduct of individuals (a) is not the only element to be taken into consideration when comparing the scope of general human rights law and refugee law. The influence of the identity of the authors of and of the reasons for the impugned treatment also differs (b).

(a) *Prevalence of the Individual Need for International Protection over State National Security Concerns*

As observed in 2007 by the Parliamentary Assembly of the Council of Europe: "in human rights law, unlike in refugee law, the prohibition applies irrespective of any security considerations in the host state".[122] The influence of national security concerns on the assessment of protection needs under refugee law will be discussed (i), as a necessary preliminary to the appreciation of the relative breadth of human rights law. It will be concluded in view of the European Convention of Human Rights (ii) and of the ICCPR and Convention Against Torture (iii) that the EU Qualification Directive strikes as a missed opportunity to fully integrate human rights law into EU refugee law (iv).

---

118   Below "3. Application to armed conflict situations", pp. 233s.
119   As mentioned before, refugee law forms part of the larger *corpus* of human rights law. Here however and as mentioned above, "human rights law" refers to those norms of human rights law which are not aimed at the sole protection of the asylum seekers and beneficiaries of international protection but apply generally, to any individual. Above p. 176.
120   ECtHR, *Soering*; ECtHR, *Chahal v. The United Kingdom* ("*Chahal*"), Application no. 70/1995/576/662 (11 November 1996).
121   ECtHR, *Chahal*, § 80.
122   Council of Europe Commissioner for Human Rights, "Issue Paper: The Human Rights of Irregular Migrants in Europe", CommDH/IssuePaper (2007) 1, 17 December 2007, p. 17.

(i)   Preliminary Remark on Refugee Law

As known and as will be discussed below, under the Refugee Convention (and the Qualification Directive alike), individuals who fulfil the criteria for international protection might nevertheless be excluded from its benefit on certain specific grounds enumerated in so-called "exclusion clauses". One might expect that the prohibition of *refoulement*, enshrined in international refugee law come to the rescue of those failed asylum seekers, whose risk of being subjected to persecution or serious harm in their country of origin is otherwise unchallenged. More generally, *non-refoulement* should, it seems, protect anyone against removal to a life-threatening situation. It is however not the case in refugee law.

Although the prohibition of *refoulement* initially proposed by the Ad Hoc Committee on Statelessness and Related Problems was absolute, the Conference of Plenipotentiaries later qualified the principle by adding exceptions to it.[123] The first paragraph of Article 33 of the Refugee Convention proscribes *refoulement*; the second paragraph stipulates that, in exceptional circumstances, a States may return an individual to a life-threatening situation. Those exceptions are the alleged danger the individual poses to the community or to the security of the country[124] and appear in the national legislation of many States. Within the European Union, Article 21 of the Qualification Directive mirrors Article 33 of the Refugee Convention: its first paragraph enshrines the principle and its second paragraph, an optional provision, reflects the exceptions provided for in the Geneva Convention.[125] Even though the exception clause in the Qualification Directive is optional, the 2010 report of the European Commission on the application of the Directive documents that "all but a few" EU Member States had in 2010 chosen to incorporate in their national law the principle together with its exceptions.[126]

As a consequence, within the European Union, the benefit of *non-refoulement* may lawfully be denied to a refugee – including even a recognised

---

123 G.S. Goodwin-Gill, "Convention Relating to the Status of Refugees – Protocol Relating to the Status of Refugees" (United Nations Audiovisual Library of International Law, © United Nations, 2008), retrieved from: <http://untreaty.un.org/cod/avl/pdf/ha/prsr/prsr_e.pdf> [02/08/2011].

124 Refugee Convention, Article 33(2).

125 Qualification Directive (2004), Article 21(1) and (2).

126 European Commission, "Report on the Application of Directive 2004/83/EC of 29 April 2004 on Minimum Standards for the Qualification and Status of Third Country Nationals or Stateless Persons as Refugees or as Persons Who Otherwise Need International Protection and the Content of the Protection" ("Report on the application of the Qualification Directive"), COM(2010)314 final, 16 June 2010, at 5.5.4.

refugees or beneficiary of subsidiary protection[127] – whom there are "reasonable grounds for regarding as a danger to the security of the country in which he is, or who, having been convicted by a final judgement of a particularly serious crime, constitutes a danger to the community of that country".[128] G.S. Goodwin-Gill, commenting on the Refugee Convention, suggests that those permitted exceptions to the principle of *non-refoulement* do not significantly affect its force: "apart from such limited situations of exception, however, the drafters of the 1951 Convention made it clear that refugees should not be returned, either to their country of origin or to other countries in which they would be at risk".[129] Nevertheless, the fact remains that in practice, the exception laid down in Article 33(2) has – legitimately – been invoked by States to expel refugees (be they recognised as such or not) to life-threatening situations, on the ground that they constituted a danger to the community or security of the expelling State.

The Refugee Convention exceptions to the principle of *non-refoulement* have been used by States and, for example, the United States' Immigration and Nationality Act provides a blatant example of national asylum legislation mirroring Article 33(2) exceptions to the principle of *non-refoulement*.[130] US asylum act in fact goes one step further and incorporates the exceptions mentioned in Article 33(2) not merely as exceptions to the prohibition of *refoulement* but as bars preventing the individual concerned from applying for asylum.[131] The launch of the so-called "War on terror" by United States President G.W. Bush in 2001[132] translated in terms of legislation into amendments of the law with

---

127 Article 21(1) of the Qualification Directive refers to the principle of *non-refoulement* which Member States shall respect "in accordance with their international obligations". Commentators agree that it applies without distinction to both refugees and persons eligible for subsidiary protection. H. Battjes, *European Asylum Law and International Law* (2006), *op. cit.*, p. 490. P. Tiedemann, "Subsidiary Protection and the Function of Article 15(c) of the Qualification Directive", *Refugee Survey Quarterly*, Vol. 31, No. 1 (2012), pp. 123–138, pp. 126–127; "Annotated Comments on QD (2004)", [January 2005], *op. cit.*, Comment on Article 17(3), p. 34.
128 Refugee Convention, Article 33(2).
129 G.S. Goodwin-Gill, "Convention Relating to the Status of Refugees – Protocol Relating to the Status of Refugees" (2008), p. p. 5.
130 J.C. Hathaway and A.K. Cusick, "Refugee Rights Are Not Negotiable", *Georgetown Immigration Law Journal*, Vol. 14 (2000), pp. 481–537.
131 *Ibid.*, pp. 535–538.
132 G.W. Bush, "Presidential Address to the Nation (the Treaty Room)" (Office of the Press Secretary, 7 October 2001), retrieved from: <http://georgewbush-whitehouse.archives.gov/news/releases/2001/10/20011007-8.html> [14/07/2012].

RELEVANT PROVISIONS OF INTERNATIONAL HUMAN RIGHTS LAW   211

the enactment of the USA PATRIOT Act[133] that made the bars even stricter.[134] In Europe too, the fight against terrorism has impacted asylum law: it caused States as well as EU institutions to adopt counter-terrorism policies that damage human rights and refugee protection[135] but it also significantly influenced the text of the Qualification Directive.

As demonstrated by a commentator, the Qualification Directive:

> ... clearly bears the mark of a thorough "terrorist proofing" by the Commission and Council in a legislative attempts at closing off the asylum channel to alleged terrorists and other threats to the internal security of the EU.[136]

Coincidentally, it is the day after the United States was hit by unprecedented terrorist attacks that the European Commission adopted its proposal for the Qualification Directive, on 12 September 2011.[137] A comparison between the text of the original Commission proposal and the adopted Qualification Directive illustrates that the different amendments introduced by the Commission as well as by Member States within the Council were conducive to the scope of the Directive being narrower, sometimes at the expense of clarity or even, of conventionality. Among the various evolutions of the text, suffice is to note two[138] of them to confirm the above assertion. As originally drafted, the

---

133 An Act to Deter and Punish Terrorist Acts in the United States and around the World, to Enhance Law Enforcement Investigatory Tools, and for Other Purposes of 26 October 2001 (hereafter "PATRIOT Act").

134 For more details on the evolution and state of US asylum law through the prism of anti-terrorism measures, see: A. Farmer, "Non-Refoulment and Jus Cogens: Limiting Anti-Terror Measures That Threaten Refugee Protection", *Georgetown Immigration Law Journal*, Vol. 23 (2008–2009), pp. 1–38, pp. 16–21.

135 UNGA, "Protection of Human Rights and Fundamental Freedoms While Countering Terrorism: Note by the Secretary-General, Report of the Special Rapporteur on the Promotion and Protection of Human Rights and Fundamental Freedoms While Countering Terrorism" ("General Secretariat's Note on Human Rights and counter-terrorism"), A/62/263, 15 August 2007, § 51; J. Allain (2001), *op. cit.*, pp. 544–557; A. Farmer (2008–2009), *op. cit.*, p. 17.

136 N. Coleman, "From Gulf War to Gulf War: Years of Security Concern in Immigration and Asylum Policies at European Level", *in* E. Guild and A. Baldaccini (Eds.), *Terrorism and the Foreigner: A Decade of Tension around the Rule of Law in Europe* (Leiden: Martinus Nijhoff Publishers, 2007), p. 63.

137 "Commission Proposal QD (2004)", *op. cit.*

138 The two amendments cited below illustrate how the text of the Directive evolved to be less protective than it was initially. Other amendments specifically evidence the

Qualification Directive enshrined the principle of *non-refoulement* but did not explicitly include exceptions to it. The provision read:

> Member States shall respect the principle of non-refoulement and shall not expel persons enjoying international protection, otherwise than in accordance with their international obligations.[139]

The exceptions to the principle which are laid down in the Refugee Convention were introduced at a later stage so that, as said, the *non-refoulement* provision in the Qualification Directive mirrors that in the Refugee Convention. As a matter of fact, and this is additional evidence of the narrowing of the Directive's scope during the negotiation process, exceptions to the prohibition of *refoulement* were also introduced as grounds for excluding individuals from the scope of the Directive.

Although exclusion clauses and exceptions to the principle of *non-refoulement* serve different purposes, a comment on exclusion from international protection under the Qualification Directive is therefore called for at this point. In refugee law, the conduct of an individual is taken into consideration in the assessment of his or her claim for international protection. The 1951 Refugee Convention and the Qualification Directive both contain exclusion clauses to the effect of excluding certain sentenced or alleged criminals from their protective scopes. In the main, the Qualification Directive mirrors the Refugee Convention on this point. Article 1(F) of the Refugee Convention provides that

---

incursion of anti-terrorism in EU asylum law. Two recitals added to the Preamble of the Directive make it clear: Recital 31 (ex Recital 22) recalls that "acts, methods and practices of terrorism" as well as the "financing, planning and inciting" thereof are acts contrary to the purposes and principles of the United Nations. Recital 37 (ex Recital 28) further notes that "the notion of national security and public order also covers cases in which a third country national belongs to an association which supports international terrorism or supports such an association". The clarification is of importance since national security and public order may be invoked by Member States as exceptions to the prohibition of refoulement but also, and this will be discussed below, to exclude individuals from international protection under the Directive. Qualification Directive, Recitals 31 and 37. The concern prevailing at the time that EU asylum law should not cause EU Member States to become safe havens for terrorists also appears clearly in a Working Document of the Commission responding to the Council on the question of the "relationship between safeguarding internal security and complying with international protection obligations and instruments". EU Commission, "Commission Working Document: The Relationship between Safeguarding Internal Security and Complying with International Protection Obligations and Instruments", COM(2001) 743 final, 05 December 2001.

139 "Commission Proposal QD (2004)", *op. cit.*, Article 19.

the Convention shall not apply to any person with respect to whom there are serious reasons for considering that:

(a) He has committed a crime against peace, a war crime, or a crime against humanity, as defined in the international instruments drawn up to make provision in respect of such crimes;
(b) He has committed a serious non-political crime outside the country of refuge prior to his admission to that country as a refugee;
(c) He has been guilty of acts contrary to the purposes and principles of the United Nations.[140]

As analysed by J.C. Hathaway, two reasons account for the drafters' decision to exclude from international protection such criminals, who are otherwise genuinely at risk of persecution in their country of origin. Firstly, it is rooted in "a commitment to the promotion of an international morality".[141] During the discussions on Article 1(F) of the Refugee Convention, on 1(F)(b) specifically, M. Rochefort, the representative of France, recalled that excluding certain ordinary criminals from the refugee definition was in line with the Constitution of the International Refugee Organisation[142] and implicitly stressed that it was a guarantee of "the moral value attached to the name 'refugee'".[143] In other words, the purpose of exclusion clauses is to exclude from international protection persons who are deemed undeserving of it in view of the gravity

---

140 Refugee Convention, Article 1(D).
141 J.C. Hathaway, *The Law of Refugee Status* (London: Butterworths, 1991), p. 214.
142 Annex I to the IRO Constitution provided definitions relevant for the purpose of the Constitution. Part II (of Annex I) identified "persons who will not be the concern of the Organisation". Those persons included (in the context of the recent signing of the Second World War armistice): "war criminals, quislings and traitors" (§ 1), persons who have "assisted the enemy in persecuting civil populations of countries, Members of the United Nations" or who have "voluntarily assisted the enemy forces since the outbreak of the second world war in their operations against the United Nations" (§ 2) and "ordinary criminals who are extraditable by treaty" (§ 3). It is to the latter paragraph that M. Rochefort referred. Regard to the previous two paragraphs is however interesting insofar as it reveals that war criminals were already in the IRO Constitution considered not to be worthy of international protection. Constitution of the International Refugee Organisation ("Constitution of the IRO"), 15 December 1946, entered into force 20 August 1948 [1948] *UNTS* Vol. 18, p. 3, Annex I, Part II, §§ 1–3.
143 "Debate before the Economic and Social Council", E/AC.7/SR.166, 22 August 1950, p. 5. Cited in J.A. Donald, *Prosecution or Persecution? Political Offenders and the 1951 Convention Refugee Definition* (Ann Arbor: UMI Dissertation Services, 1997), § 35.

of the acts they perpetrated;[144] it is also intended to ensure that such persons do not seek to misuse the institution of asylum in order to escape liability for their criminal acts.[145] Exclusion clauses are "intended to protect the integrity of the institution of asylum".[146] Secondly, the insertion of exclusion clauses in the refugee definition also served the purpose of securing the adhesion of the largest possible number of States to the Refugee Convention. It is indeed rooted in "a pragmatic recognition that states are unlikely to agree to be bound by a regime which requires them to protect undesirable refugees".[147] Concerns were raised concerning exclusion clauses, and the exclusion of common law criminals (Article 1(F)(b)) in particular, at the time the Refugee Convention was adopted. As P. Weis warned:

> It is ... difficult to see why a person who before becoming a refugee, has been convicted of a serious crime and has served his sentence should forever be debarred from refugee status. Such a rule would seem to run counter to the generally accepted principle of penal law that a person who has been punished for an offence should suffer no further prejudice on account of the offence committed.[148]

It follows that it is only those criminals who are still liable to prosecution or punishment that may be excluded from international protection. On the other hand, applicants who have already served their sentence, have been granted a pardon or have benefited from an amnesty and who fulfil the criteria for international protection should be granted a protective status. This is in fact the interpretation provided by UNHCR[149] but also the approach adopted by States

---

144 "Annotated Comments on QD (2004)", [January 2005], *op. cit.*, Comment on Article 14(4)-6), p. 30.
145 See UNHCR, "Statement on Article 1F of the 1951 Convention: Issued in the Context of the Preliminary Ruling References to the Court of Justice of the European Communities from the German Federal Administrative Court Regarding the Interpretation of Articles 12(2)(B) and (C) of the Qualification Directive" ("Statement on Article 1F of the 1951 Convention"), July 2009, p. 6; and UN Conference of Plenipotentiaries on the Status of Refugees and Stateless Persons, "Conference of Plenipotentiaries on the Status of Refugees and Stateless Persons: Summary Record of the 24th Meeting", A/CONF.2/SR.24, 27 November 1951, statements by MM Herment (Belgium) and Hoare (UK) on extradition expecially.
146 UNHCR, "Statement on Article 1F of the 1951 Convention", *op. cit.*, p. 6.
147 J.C. Hathaway, *The Law of Refugee Status* (1991), *op. cit.*, p. 214.
148 P. Weis, "The Concept of the Refugee in International Law", *Journal du droit international*, Vol. 87 (1960), p. 928, pp. 984–986. Cited in J.C. Hathaway, *The Law of Refugee Status* (1991), *op. cit.*, p. 223.
149 UNHCR, *Handbook on Procedures*, *op. cit.*, § 157.

during the United Nations Conference on Territorial Asylum. Although the proposed Convention on Territorial Asylum never materialised, it is worth noting that delegations had agreed and provisionally adopted articles on the granting of asylum including a provision stating that asylum shall not be granted to any person "whom there are serious reasons for considering that *he is still liable to prosecution or punishment* for" certain grave crimes and acts.[150]

The Qualification Directive, which builds on Article 1(F) of the Refugee Convention concerning exclusion from international protection, did not content itself with reproducing Refugee Convention exclusion clauses but adds to them considerations of national security. In addition to the criteria mentioned in Article 1(F) of the Convention, Member States chose to include the exception to the principle of *non-refoulement* as additional exclusion clauses,[151] irrespective of the fact that this exception "was not, however, conceived as a ground for terminating refugee status".[152]

As far as subsidiary protection is concerned, the addition is patent: Article 17(1)(d) of the Qualification Directive allows any receiving EU Member State to invoke the danger a person would constitute to its public order or national security to exclude him or her from subsidiary protection.[153] On the other hand, the clause is absent of Article 12 enumerating grounds for exclusion from refugee status; it instead follows from a paragraph oddly inserted in Article 14 of the Directive (on revocation of, ending of or refusal to renew refugee status) that the same reasons can be invoked by States as grounds for refusal of refugee status where such a decision has not yet been taken.[154] How "refusal to grant" differs in effect from "exclusion from" refugee status is not self-explanatory, to say the least. As for individuals who have been granted international protection, the Qualification Directive is clear: relevant national authorities can invoke a danger to the State's security or to the community to revoke, end or

---

150 Draft UN Convention on Territorial Asylum: Report of the United Nations Conference on Territorial Asylum, 21 April 1977 UN doc. A/CONF.78/12, Article 2(2) [emphasis added]. The website of the International Law Commission provides further clarifications on the drafting history and content of the Draft Convention on Territorial Asylum. *See*: ILC Codification Division – Office of Legal Affairs, "Right of Asylum", last updated 30 June 2005, retrieved from: <http://untreaty.un.org/ilc/summaries/6_2.htm#_ftn5> [31/08/2012].
151 EU Council, "Presidency Note to the Strategic Committee on Immigration, Frontiers and Asylum (ASILE 59)" ("Presidency Note (ASILE 59)"), 13623/02 ASILE 59, 30 October 2002, p. 3.
152 "Annotated Comments on QD (2004)", [January 2005], *op. cit.*, pp. 30–31.
153 Qualification Directive, Article 17(1)(d).
154 Qualification Directive, Article 14(5).

refuse to renew refugee status and subsidiary protection status alike.[155] This has been described by commentators as confusion between Refugee Convention exclusion clauses and exceptions to the principle of *non-refoulement*.[156] Grounds for exclusion are "*exhaustively* enumerated in the 1951 Convention" and do not include national security grounds.[157]

It can be noted that the Refugee Convention does not address specifically the revocation of (ending of or refusal to renew) refugee status; it is however understood that exclusion clauses in the Convention serve this purpose:

> Where facts which would have led to exclusion only come to light after the grant of refugee status, this would justify cancellation of refugee status on the grounds of exclusion. (…) Where a refugee engages in conduct falling within Article 1F(a) or 1F(c), this would trigger the application of the exclusion clauses and the revocation of refugee status, provided all the criteria for the application of these clauses are met.[158]

In other words, pursuant to the Refugee Convention, refugee status may be revoked if the refugee concerned has committed a crime against peace, a war crime, or a crime against humanity or has been guilty of acts contrary to the purposes and principles of the United Nations.[159] The danger supposedly posed by an individual to the host State's national security or public order is an exception to the prohibition of *refoulement* but cannot be used to exclude from, or revoke, end or refuse to renew refugee status. As noted by UNHCR, "[g]iven the close linkages between refugee status and subsidiary forms of protection, in so far as they cover persons under UNHCR's mandate" the same approach is also pertinent for subsidiary protection.[160]

Consulted during the drafting process on the issue of the integration of public order and national security as additional grounds for exclusion from international protection, UNHCR had expressed reservations on the compatibility of such inclusion with the Refugee Convention.[161] UNHCR's concerns were

---

155 Qualification Directive, Article 14(4) and Article 19(3)(a).
156 "Annotated Comments on QD (2004)", [January 2005], *op. cit.*, on Article 14(4)-14(6), pp. 30–31.
157 *Ibid.*, Comment on Article 12(2), p. 27.
158 UNHCR, "Guidelines on International Protection, Application of the Exclusion Clauses: Article 1F of the 1951 Convention Relating to the Status of Refugees" ("Guidelines on the application of the exclusion clauses"), HCR/GIP/03/05, 4 September 2003.
159 Refugee Convention, Article 1F(a) and 1F(c).
160 "Annotated Comments on QD (2004)", [January 2005], *op. cit.*, Comment on Article 17(3), p. 34.
161 "Presidency Note (ASILE 59)", *op. cit.*, p. 3.

discarded on the grounds that "the difference in treatment of a third country national or a stateless person who is excluded and that of a refugee who is not given the benefit of *non-refoulement* is *insignificant*".[162]

The entanglement of Refugee Convention exclusion clauses and exceptions to *non-refoulement* in the Qualification Directive resulted in new grounds being added to exclude individuals from international protection: hence, under the Directive, considerations of national security and public order can justify that national asylum authorities refuse, revoke, end or refuse to renew refugee status or subsidiary protection status, in non-compliance with the Refugee Convention. It follows that Qualification Directive exclusion clauses risk become tools for States to deny international protection to individuals despite their fulfilling the criteria for refugee status or subsidiary protection, in cases where a proper application of the Refugee Convention would call for international protection being granted.

In such situations, should the person concerned lodge a case before the European Court of Human Rights (ECtHR), the Human Rights Committee (HRC) or the Committee Against Torture (CAT) against the Contracting State's decision to expel him or her, this State faces the risk of being found in breach of its international human rights obligations, even though its decision was in conformity with its obligations under the 1951 Refugee Convention or the Qualification Directive. As noted by the Council during the negotiation process and by Member States ever since, in some cases, a person who should be expelled pursuant to the exception to *non-refoulement* or who has been excluded from the scope of the Directive may nevertheless be protected from removal by Article 3 of the European Convention of Human Rights or of the CAT Convention.[163] The judgment of the ECtHR in the *Chahal* case and the decision of CAT in *Paez v. Sweden*[164] illustrate the seeming paradox. In *Chahal* for instance, the United Kingdom government invoked the refugee law exception to the

---

162   *Ibid.*, p. 3.
163   *Ibid.*, p. 4. On Member States' understanding of their obligations under the various instruments binding upon them, see the answers provided to the ECRE/ELENA questionnaire. States generally acknowledge that if the exceptions to *non-refoulement* or exclusions clauses apply, "a grant of asylum should be refused but this does not mean that removal will always be possible" (response on the United Kingdom). Information provided in the ECRE/ELENA study also evokes the precarious situation in which the persons concerned find themselves: excluded from international protection and expellable under the exception to *non-refoulement*, they receive no legal status and limited or no residence permit (*see* information on Belgium, France, the Netherlands or Norway in particular). ECRE/ELENA, *op. cit.*, pp. 143–149.
164   CAT Committee, *Gorki Ernesto Tapia Paez v. Sweden* ("*Paez v. Sweden*"), CAT/C/18/D/39/1996 (28 April 1997).

principle of *non-refoulement* to justify an exception to Article 3 ECHR.[165] Let us turn to what the ECHR has to say in this regard.

(ii)   Under the ECHR

The Court has repeatedly stressed that Article 3 prohibited, in absolute terms, expulsions to face torture or inhuman or degrading treatment or punishment. In particular, the absolute nature of the prohibition has led the Court to finding that the conduct of the applicant was immaterial. The European Court of Human Rights did so in the landmark case of *Soering v. the United Kingdom* where the applicant, M. Soering, was a suspected murderer who risked being sentenced to death in the United States, were the United Kingdom to extradite him. The case was already discussed above[166] so the following will focus on those parts of the judgment pertinent to illustrate the irrelevance of national security considerations for the application of *non-refoulement* under human rights law.

Concerning the national security of the expelling State, the European Court of Human Rights notes in the *Soering* judgement that "it would hardly be compatible with the underlying values of the Convention, that "common heritage of political traditions, ideals, freedom and the rule of law" to which the Preamble refers, were a Contracting State knowingly to surrender a fugitive to another State where there were substantial grounds for believing that he would be in danger of being subjected to torture, *however heinous the crime allegedly committed*".[167]

One paragraph of the *Soering* judgement indeed was ambiguous and risked be used by States to justify derogations to the otherwise absolute prohibition of *refoulement*. The tortuous and controversial paragraph read as follows:

> ... inherent in the whole of the Convention is a search for a fair balance between the demands of the general interest of the community and the requirements of the protection of the individual's fundamental rights.

The Court then notes that migration is an increasing phenomenon, with people moving about the work more easily, and adds that, in this context, "it is increasingly in the interest of all nations that suspected offenders who flee abroad should be brought to justice". Conversely, the Court adds:

---

165   ECtHR, *Chahal*.
166   Above pp. 188s.
167   ECtHR, *Soering*, § 88 [emphasis added].

... the establishment of safe havens for fugitives would not only result in danger for the State obliged to harbour the protected person but also tend to undermine the foundations of extradition. These considerations must also be included among the factors to be taken into account in the interpretation and application of the notions of inhuman and degrading treatment or punishment in extradition cases.[168]

After the Court had clearly and forcefully expressed the absolute nature of the prohibition of torture and of inhuman or degrading treatment or punishment, its mentioning of a "search for a fair balance" between the general interest of the community and the fundamental rights of an individual was surprising and likely to shatter if not negate the premise of the decision. As noted by N. mole, unfortunately, the Court did not give any further explanation on what this "search for a fair balance" should consist in. Perhaps the Court included this paragraph with the sole intention of easing States' concerns that, following *Soering*, they would have the obligation under the ECHR to harbour even the most dangerous criminals (the death penalty being generally imposed as a punishment for the worst crimes), with no lawful possibility to extradite them but, as noted, this is not clarified by the Court.[169] On its face, the *dictum* ambiguously and inappropriately it seems suggests that the real risk of suffering ill-treatment proscribed by Article 3 ECHR in the country of destination can be assessed against the expelling State's alleged own interests in expelling the individual. Such was in fact the interpretation put forward by the United Kingdom in the *Chahal* case before the ECtHR, which came down to a distinction between individuals who are worthy of protection and those who, because they "have done something that is injurious to human society or to other men" are not.[170] Fortunately though, in the *Chahal* judgment, the Court dispelled the ambiguity caused by the *Soering* dictum. This will be shown below.

The United Kingdom Government argued that in expulsion cases, the prohibition contained in Article 3 was not absolute. The fact that States were to take into consideration "an uncertain prediction of future events in the receiving State" in deciding whether or not to expel an individual called for the possibility for States to also have regard to the threat the individual could pose, if he were to be authorised to stay, to the hosting State's national security. According to the United Kingdom, there was an implied limitation to Article 3 entitling a

---

168   *Ibid.*, § 89.
169   N. Mole and C. Meredith, *Asylum and the European Convention on Human Rights* (2007), *op. cit.*, p. 33.
170   ECtHR, *Chahal*, § 98.

Contracting State to expel an individual to a receiving State even where a real risk of ill-treatment existed, if such removal was required on national security grounds". In support of its theory, the Government notably referred to the exception to the principle of *non-refoulement* laid down in the second paragraph of Article 33 of the Geneva Convention on the status of refugees.[171]

In response to the UK Government arguments, the Court however unambiguously asserted that a State Party who would take the decision to expel an individual to a real risk of ill-treatment would, in doing so, violate the Convention, regardless of whether such expulsion was compatible with the State's obligations under other instruments of international law to which it is party, such as the 1951 Geneva Convention.

The ECtHR made its position clear that whether an individual could constitute a danger to the national security of the hosting State or to its community was not a material consideration under international human rights law in expulsion cases. The Court, after recalling the well-established absolute nature of the prohibition of *refoulement* stated:

> The prohibition provided by Article 3 against ill-treatment is equally absolute in expulsion cases. Thus, whenever substantial grounds have been shown for believing that an individual would face a real risk of being subjected to treatment contrary to Article 3 if removed to another State, the responsibility of the Contracting State to safeguard him or her against such treatment is engaged in the event of expulsion (...)[172]

Exposure to a real risk of treatment in breach of Article 3 is sufficient a criterion to trigger the State's obligation not to return the individual to the destination country; national security concerns are, in any case, immaterial.[173]

As to host States' concerns for their own security, the Court plainly rejected the argument:

> In these circumstances, the activities of the individual in question, however undesirable or dangerous, cannot be a material consideration.[174]

---

171 *Ibid.*, § 76.
172 *Ibid.*, § 80.
173 *Ibid.*, § 102. Similarly, the Commission, in its report on the application submitted by the Chahal family had already stated it was "unable to accept the Government's submission that Article 3 of the Convention may have implied limitations entitling the State to expel a person because of the requirements of national security" (*Ibid.*).
174 *Ibid.*, § 80.

Aware of the uncertainties to which the controversial part of the *Soering* judgment led, the Court further noted:

> It should not be inferred from the Court's remarks concerning the risk of undermining the foundations of extradition, as set out in paragraph 89 of the same judgment, that there is any room for balancing the risk of ill-treatment against the reasons for expulsion in determining whether a State's responsibility under Article 3 is engaged.[175]

The ECtHR did not however clarify how then the *Soering* dictum should be interpreted.[176] The debate was eventually closed by the Court in the *Saadi v. Italy* case and reiterated since in numerous judgments. In *Saadi*, the Court refers to the "principle stated in the *Chahal* judgment" and reaffirms that, under the ECHR:

> ... it is not possible to weigh the risk of ill-treatment against the reasons put forward for the expulsion in order to determine whether the responsibility of a State is engaged under Article 3, even where such treatment is inflicted by another State. In that connection, the conduct of the person concerned, however undesirable or dangerous, cannot be taken into account...[177]

The principle is made clear: the expelling State's national security concerns have no bearing in asylum cases.

It can be noted that incidentally, in *Chahal* and similarly in *Saadi*, the Court took the opportunity it was given to explicitly state the greater scope of the ECHR in comparison with that of the Refugee Convention. After noting that an applicant's activities, including his or her criminal conduct, cannot be a material consideration in expulsion cases, the Court stated:

> The protection afforded by Article 3 is thus wider than that provided by Articles 32 and 33 of the United Nations 1951 Convention on the Status of Refugees.[178]

---

175 *Ibid.*, § 81.
176 N. Mole and C. Meredith, *Asylum and the European Convention on Human Rights* (2007), *op. cit.*, pp. 32–37.
177 ECtHR (Grand Chamber), *Case of Saadi v. Italy* ("*Saadi*"), Application no. 37201/06 (28 February 2008), § 138.
178 ECtHR, *Chahal*, § 80; ECtHR, *Saadi*, § 138.

The Court confirms the observation made above:[179] refugee law admits exceptions to the principle of *non-refoulement*, namely the perceived risk posed by the individual to the community or national security of the host State.

After some ambiguities and uncertainties, the position of the ECtHR is now clear: the conduct, be it criminal, of an individual is not a material consideration in asylum cases. The firm line taken in the *Chahal* case has been long maintained and reaffirmed.[180] This could be of particular relevance in today's world context of a rise in terrorist threats or attacks. In this regard, the recent *Khashiyev and Akayeva v. Russia* case is worth mentioning.[181] Although it does not concern expulsion or extradition (applicants alleged their deceased relatives were victims of torture committed in Russia in the context of counter-terrorism), the judgment is however noteworthy insofar as it reaffirms with increased strength the absolute nature of the prohibition of torture and inhuman or degrading treatment or punishment. The Court firmly stated that:

> Even in the most difficult circumstances, such as the fight against terrorism and organised crime, the Convention prohibits in absolute terms torture and inhuman or degrading treatment or punishment. Unlike most of the substantive clauses of the Convention and its Protocols, Article 3 makes no provision for exceptions and no derogation from it is permissible under Article 15 § 2 even in the event of a public emergency threatening the life of the nation.[182]

The absolute prohibition of Article 3 treatments carries with it the same "absoluteness" of the prohibition of *refoulement* under the ECHR since the latter

---

179   Above pp. 220s.
180   For an early confirmation of the *Chahal* judgment, *see* for example ECtHR, *Ahmed v. Austria*, Application no. 25964/94 (17 December 1996). The *Ahmed* case relied in large part on the Chahal case and confirmed that the applicant's conduct was not a material consideration in asylum cases. The *Ahmed* judgment was cited together with the *Chahal* case by the applicant in *M.A.R. v. UK* to emphasise the "absolute and non-derogable nature" of Articles 2 and 3 of the Convention. This argument was not challenged by the defendant Government and therefore appeared to be, already then (in 1997) beyond dispute. *See* ECtHR, *M.A.R. v. United Kingdom* ("*M.A.R. v. UK*"), 28038/95 (16 January 1997). *See* also: ECtHR, *Al-Nashif v. Bulgaria*, Application no. 50963/99 (20 June 2002), §§ 123–124; ECtHR, *Selmouni v. France* ("*Selmouni*"), Application no. 25803/94 (28 July 1999), § 95; ECtHR, *Assenov and Others v. Bulgaria*, Application no. 24760/94 (28 October 1998), § 93.
181   ECtHR, *Khashiyev and Akayeva v. Russia*, Applications nos. 57942/00 and 57945/00 (24 February 2005).
182   *Ibid.*, § 170.

derives from the former. It can be inferred from the *Khashiyev and Akayeva* that State Parties to the ECHR may not return an individual to a real risk of suffering treatment proscribed under Article 3, not even "in the most difficult circumstances", "in the event of a public emergency threatening the life of the nation". In anticipation of the second part, which will consider the applicability of existing norms and principles of the international human rights law to cover the international protection needs of persons fleeing environmental catastrophes, it is worth observing that such inference could be of particular weigh in cases where mass influx of asylum seekers reach the territory of a State Party to the ECHR, in the aftermath of an environmental disaster. The decision of the Court in *Khashiyev and Akayeva* suggests that host States could not invoke public emergency, such as that caused by the sudden influx of a large population of asylum seekers to justify the removal of the individuals concerned to their country of origin (provided substantial grounds have been shown for believing that they would be exposed there to a real risk of treatment proscribed under Article 3 ECHR). Incidentally, if national security and public emergency are no exceptions to the absolute prohibition of Article 3 treatments, let alone financial costs. Recent case-law however casts doubts on the accuracy of this last statement;[183] this will be discussed below in Part II.

(iii)   Under the ICCPR and UNCAT

As mentioned earlier, the absolute nature of the principle of *non-refoulement* has also been asserted by the Human Rights Committee. Similar to ECHR Article 3, Article 7 of the ICCPR prohibits torture, cruel, inhuman and degrading treatments and punishments. It is among the rights enumerated in Article 4 of the Covenant as rights to which no derogation is possible, even in time of public emergency threatening the life of the nation.[184] The absolute nature of the prohibition is confirmed by the Human Rights Committee in its General Comments on articles 2, 4 and 7. The text of the prohibition of torture, the

---

183   Reference is made here to the *N. v. UK* case, where the Court appeared to take host States' budgetary constraints into consideration to reject the application of the principle of *non-refoulement* in the case. The case concerned the return of an individual suffering from AIDS. The Court, after reasserting the "fundamental importance of Article 3" indeed controversially found that: "Article 3 does not place an obligation on the Contracting State to alleviate such disparities through the provision of free and unlimited health care to all aliens without a right to stay within its jurisdiction. A finding to the contrary would place too great a burden on the Contracting States". ECtHR, *N. v. UK*, § 44. This case-law will be further discussed in Part 1 and its potential implications on the protection of persons fleeing regions devastated by environmental catastrophes. See below Part 1, Chapter 7. II.

184   ICCPR, Article 4.

HRC states, "allows of no limitation", "even in situations of public emergency". The Committee further observes that "no justification or extenuating circumstances may be invoked to excuse a violation of article 7, for any reason".[185] However and as a commentator observed: "there has been little practice before the HRC on the "*non-refoulement*" principle. Instead, most of the jurisprudence has been before the UN Committee Against Torture".[186]

The UN Convention against Torture and Other Cruel, Inhuman or Degrading Treatment or Punishment (CAT Convention) also prohibits *refoulement* in absolute terms. It does so even more clearly than the ECHR and ICCPR since the prohibition to expel an individual to a risk of torture or other prohibited treatment is expressly enshrined in the Convention. Article 3 states that no State Party shall expel, return (*"refouler"*) or extradite a person to another State where there are substantial grounds for believing that he would be in danger of being subjected to torture. This provision is left unqualified. It is in fact deliberately that the drafters of the CAT Convention, who had drawn inspiration from Article 33 of the Refugee Convention, did not include any limitation to it.[187] The *a priori* non-derogability of the prohibition of *refoulement* under the CAT Convention was confirmed by the Committee Against Torture (CAT Committee) in the case of *Paez v. Sweden*.[188] The case concerned a Peruvian citizen, residing and claiming refugee status in Sweden. Swedish authorities stressed the asylum seeker's membership in a terrorist group and the crimes he had committed in that capacity. They invoked the exclusion clauses of Article 1(F) of the 1951 Refugee Convention to support their decision to deny protection to M. Paez and expel him to Peru. The Committee on the contrary considered that:

> ... the test of article 3 of the Convention is absolute. Whenever substantial grounds exist for believing that an individual would be in danger of being subjected to torture upon expulsion to another State, the State party

---

185   HRC, "General Comment No. 31", *op. cit.*, Article 2, §12; HRC, "General Comment No. 20", *op. cit.*, § 3; HRC, "General Comment No. 29: States of Emergency (Article 4)" ("General Comment No. 29"), CCPR/C/21/Rev.1/Add.11, 31 August 2001, § 7; HRC, "General Comment No. 24", *op. cit.*, § 8.
186   F. Piana, "The Principle of "Non-Refoulement" in the Fight against Terrorism", pp. 183–195, p. p. 188, retrieved from: <http://publikon.hu/application/essay/492_1.pdf> [04/09/2010].
187   D. Weissbrodt and I. Hortreiter, "The Principle of Non-Refoulement: Article 3 of the Convention against Torture and Other Cruel, Inhuman or Degrading Treatment or Punishment in Comparison with the Non-Refoulement Provisions of Other International Human Rights Treaties", *Buffalo Human Rights Law Review*, Vol. 5 (1999), pp. 1–74, p. 16.
188   CAT Committee, *Paez v. Sweden*.

is under obligation not to return the person concerned to that State. The nature of the activities in which the person concerned engaged cannot be a material consideration when making a determination under article 3 of the Convention.[189]

The CAT Committee added that Sweden's decision to expel M. Paez, albeit based on the exclusion clause of Article 1(F) of the 1951 Convention, did not meet the requirements of Article 3 of the CAT Convention. Sweden, the Committee concluded, had an obligation to refrain from forcibly returning M. Paez to Peru.[190] In so concluding, the CAT Committee implicitly highlighted that the protection afforded by the prohibition of *refoulement* in human rights law was wider than that provided in refugee law. This confirmed the similar but then explicit assessment made a year before by the ECtHR in the *Chahal* case. The discrepancy between *non-refoulement* under refugee law and under human rights law is clear; it is also regrettable.

(iv)   The Qualification Directive: A Missed Opportunity to Fully Integrate Human Rights Law into EU Refugee Law

In view of the above, one can but observe that, as far as EU Member States international obligations are concerned, Article 21 of the Qualification Directive appears to be inherently contradictory. The article, already discussed above,[191] is reproduced in full hereunder for the purpose of addressing its terms now that States' obligations under international human rights law have been clarified:

1. Member States shall respect the principle of *non-refoulement* in accordance with their international obligations.
2. Where not prohibited by the international obligations mentioned in paragraph 1, Member States may *refoule* a refugee, whether formally recognised or not, when:
   (a) there are reasonable grounds for considering him or her as a danger to the security of the Member State in which he or she is present; or

---

189   Ibid., § 14.5.
190   Ibid., §§ 14.6 and 15. A similar case had in fact been brought by M Paez's brother, also denied refugee status in Sweden on the basis of Article 1(F), before the European Commission of Human Rights. M. Paez winning his case before the CAT Committee, Sweden felt constrained to grant M. Paez's brother permanent residence in Sweden. The case before the ECnHR was consequently struck out of the list. ECnHR, *Case of Paez v. Sweden* ("*Paez v. Sweden*"), Reports 1997-VII (30 October 1997), §§ 24–31.
191   Above pp. 203s.

(b) he or she, having been convicted by a final judgement of a particularly serious crime, constitutes a danger to the community of that Member State.

3. Member States may revoke, end or refuse to renew or to grant the residence permit of (or to) a refugee to whom paragraph 2 applies.[192]

As said, the text of Article 21 mirrors Article 33(2) of the 1951 Geneva Convention. On the face of it, it follows that Member States, provided they are acting in conformity with the Qualification Directive, will, by the same token, respect the principle of *non-refoulement* in accordance with their international obligations under the Geneva Convention. However, if this might be true *vis-à-vis* Member States' obligations of *non-refoulement* under the Refugee Convention,[193] it appears from the above survey of *non-refoulement* under international human rights law that the same is not true of Member States' international obligations under human rights law. As mentioned, international human rights law – the ECHR, ICCPR and UNCAT in particular – do not allow for any exception to the prohibition of *refoulement*. The principle, as enshrined in international human rights law, is of absolute nature. As illustrated by the *Chahal* (ECtHR) and *Paez* (CAT) cases cited above, EU Member States risk therefore facing conflicting obligations under refugee law and human rights law: whereas a State may lawfully, under EU refugee law, invoke a danger to its security to expel a refugee to a country where he fears persecution, the ECtHR, the HRC or the CAT Committee may find this State liable under the ECHR, the ICCPR or the CAT Convention respectively since, as pointed out by the Court in *Chahal*, the scope of the prohibition of *refoulement* is wider under the ECHR than it is under the 1951 Refugee Convention or, for that matter, under the Qualification Directive.[194]

Discussions on the text of the Qualification Directive started with the submission by the Commission of a proposal, to the Council, in 2001, *i.e.* five years after the European Court of Human Rights had issued its judgement in the *Chahal* case. If the Commission did state, in the explanatory memorandum attached to its proposal, that it had had due regard to the ECHR and to the Court's case-law when drafting the proposal, concerning subsidiary protection

---

192 Qualification Directive, Article 21.
193 The question of compatibility of the Qualification Directive with the Refugee Convention on issues of qualification and exclusion from refugee status or subsidiary protection is more problematic. *See* above pp. 208s.
194 ECtHR, *Chahal*, § 80.

in particular,[195] it seems however that it did not fully integrate the jurisprudence of the Court when devising EU refugee law. This appears all the more clearly when exclusion clauses and exceptions to the principle of *non-refoulement* are under scrutiny.

The Qualification Directive could have been an opportunity for the European Union to disentangle the wording of the various applicable norms of international law – including refugee law and human rights law – relevant to solving the questions arising in cases of expulsions to indiscriminate threats to life or person, in situations of armed conflict or else. It seems though that the EU missed the opportunity to do so, yielding to political pressures. The interpretation of refugee law and of the principle of *non-refoulement* in particular should be informed by developments which have taken place (and continue to do so) in other fields of law as well as in practice since the adoption of the 1951 Refugee Convention.[196] *Non-refoulement* being absolute in human rights law, the drafters of the Qualification Directive should have taken cognisance of it and enshrined a similarly absolute prohibition of *refoulement* (at least to face torture, inhuman or degrading treatment or punishment) in the Directive. Their failure to do so, and the introduction of a clause similar to Article 33(2) of the Refugee Convention in the Directive, is compatible with a "literal wording of" the Refugee Convention but "does not reflect the broader international law obligations of Member States".[197] The risk of conflicting rights and obligations for States follows; Nuala Mole warns EU Member States:

> States need to be as aware of that overarching obligation [the absolute protection from expulsion under the ECHR] as they are of the exclusion clauses of the Geneva Convention and the Qualification Directive.[198]

Under the ECHR, the applicant's behaviour is immaterial. It is also clear from the Court's case-law that the identities of the authors of as well as the reasons for the impugned treatments are not influential.

---

195 The Commission noted: "Though no specific EU acquis on the issue of subsidiary protection exists, the ECHR and the case law of the European Court on Human Rights provide for a legally binding framework, informing the Commission's legislative work on this issue". "Explanatory Memorandum – QD (2004)", *op. cit.*, p. 5.
196 E. Lauterpacht and D. Bethlehem (2003), *op. cit.*, §§ 151–159.
197 M.T. Gil-Bazo (2006), *op. cit.*, p. 21.
198 N. Mole and C. Meredith, *Asylum and the European Convention on Human Rights* (2007), *op. cit.*, p. 29.

(b)   *Origin of the Threat: State and Non-State Actors Alike*

The precedent developments showed that the prohibition of *refoulement* under human rights law is more generous than that under refugee law insofar as it protects any individual exposed to a real risk of proscribed treatment upon being removed to his or her country of origin, regardless of the danger the individual represents for the host State. Can the same conclusion be reached here? Does human rights law set itself apart from refugee law by considering as "persecutors" a broader range of actors? Refugee law will be discussed first, before the ECHR and the ICCPR.

(i)   Preliminary Remark on Refugee Law

In respect of agents of persecution, at least the adoption of the EU Qualification Directive has achieved its harmonisation goal and brought a major improvement in EU refugee law. Prior to the entry into force of the Qualification Directive, EU Member States had adopted varying interpretations of the 1951 Geneva Convention. A survey of national cases reveals that national courts had identified four situations when dealing with alleged persecution by non-State agents. ECRE identified those four categories and analysed State practice for each category in the following terms:

(a) Persecution is carried out by quasi-States or *de facto* authorities who have gained control over the whole or part of the territory: there is uniform practice in acknowledging *de facto* authorities (their definition however varies) as relevant agents of persecution.
(b) Persecution is carried out by non-State agents and the State is unwilling to protect (whether it instigates, condones or tolerates the act of persecution): State practice is uniform in granting refugee status in such situations.
(c) Persecution is carried out by non-State agents, and the State is willing but unable to provide protection: in these situations, State practice lacks uniformity and opposes proponents of the "accountability-view" and those of the "protection-view".
(d) Persecution is carried out by non-State agents and there are no State authorities left that could provide protection against persecution (in civil war situations for example): some courts argue that there cannot be persecution without a functioning State (e.g. the German Administrative Court), whereas other courts grant refugee status also in these situations.[199]

---

199   ECRE/ELENA, "Research Paper on Non-State Agents of Persecution" (ECRE) (November 1998, updated in autumn 2000), p. 1.

In brief, EU Member States agreed on granting protection to individuals fleeing persecution imputable, directly or indirectly, to the State. Persecutions by non-State agents against which the State is unwilling to protect its nationals fall within the latter category. On the other hand, Member States long disagreed on whether or not to grant refugee protection in cases where the national State's accountability cannot be established, in view of its inability to act or of the absence of governmental power.[200] The approach taken by some of them, not to grant refugee status in such cases, where State authorities are unable to provide protection or unintentionally fail to provide protection, was in fact endorsed by EU Member States in a Joint Position on the harmonized application of the definition of the term refugee.[201]

Some States, the European Parliament, UNHCR and other commentators however pointed to the fact that no such restriction on the scope of the Refugee Convention could be deduced either from its *travaux préparatoires* or from its letter. Hence the opposition of Sweden and of the European Parliament to the above-mentioned Joint Position, which is (fortunately though) not legally-binding. It is observed that the Refugee Convention and its *travaux préparatoires* do not say much about the source of the persecution feared by the refugee; "no necessary linkage between persecution and government authority is formally required".[202]

In light of the above, it appears that it is not the Refugee Convention itself which limits the scope of *non-refoulement* to the sole cases where State actors

---

200 For a detailed overview of EU Member States national case-law, see *ibid.*, pp. 7 and 19S. See also for a detailed presentation of the German approach: ECRE, "Non-State Agents of Persecution and the Inability of the State to Protect – the German Interpretation" (September 2000).

201 Point 5.2 of the Joint Position reads: "Persecution by third parties will be considered to fall within the scope of the Geneva Convention where it is based on one of the grounds in Article 1A, is individual in nature and is encouraged or permitted by the authorities. Where the official authorities fail to act, such persecution should give rise to individual examination of each application for refugee status, in accordance with national judicial practice, in the light in particular of whether or not the failure to act was deliberate. The persons concerned may be eligible in any event for appropriate forms of protection under national law". EU Council, "Joint Position of 4 March 1996 Defined by the Council on the Basis of Article K.3 of the Treaty on European Union on the Harmonized Application of the Definition of the Term 'Refugee' in Article 1 of the Geneva Convention of 28 July 1951 Relating to the Status of Refugees" ("1996 EU Joint Position on the definition of the term 'refugee' under the Refugee Convention") [13/03/1996] *OJ L 063*, pp. 2–7.

202 G.S. Goodwin-Gill and J. McAdam, *The Refugee in International Law* (2007), *op. cit.*, p. 98. See also for instance: J.-Y. Carlier, "General Report", *in* J.-Y. Carlier, *et al.* (Eds.), *Who Is a Refugee? A Comparative Case Law Study* (The Hague: Kluwer Law International, 1997), pp. 683–718, pp. 705s.

of persecution (or States' willingness to protect against persecution) are involved[203] but the restrictive interpretation of the Convention by some States, anxious to limit the scope of their obligations. The observation of a relative breadth on this point of international human rights law as compared to refugee law is therefore to be nuanced. The assertion would only be true insofar as national refugee law or practice in some EU Member States, who chose to restrictively interpret the Refugee Convention, is concerned.

The EU Qualification Directive however closed the debate and, as mentioned earlier, defined – non-exhaustively ("include") – as actors of persecution or serious harm:

(a) the State;
(b) parties or organisations controlling the State or a substantial part of the territory of the State;
(c) non-State actors, if it can be demonstrated that the actors mentioned in (a) and (b), including international organisations, are unable or unwilling to provide protection against persecution or serious harm as defined in Article 7.[204]

As a consequence, EU Member States are required to consider persecution and serious harm perpetrated by non-State agents as justifying the grant of international protection, not only in situations where the State is unwilling to protect against persecution but also when it is unable to do so.

This approach reflects the well-established jurisprudence of the European Court of Human Rights and of the Human Rights Committee,[205] as well as State practice.[206]

(ii) Under the ECHR and ICCPR

The case-law of the European Court of Human Rights informs that the Court inferred the irrelevance of the source of ill-treatment from the absolute character of the prohibition of torture, cruel, inhuman or degrading treatments and punishments. The responsibility to protect an individual however

---

203 The interpretation of the Refugee Convention and potential applicability *de lege lata* to environmentally-displaced persons will be elaborated on in Part 1.
204 Qualification Directive, Article 6.
205 The UNCAT Committee on the other hand requires the feared ill-treatment to be inflicted by the State or with its acquiescence or, alternatively, by "groups exercising quasi-governmental authority". See *CAT Committee, Hmhi v. Australia*, UN Doc A/57/44, p.166 (2002), Communication 177/2001 (01/05/2002).
206 ECRE/ELENA, *op. cit.*, pp. 15–16 and 84–86.

primarily rests with his or her State of nationality; the Court therefore requires that where an applicant alleges he or she will face ill-treatment administered by non-State actors, he or she establish the inability of his or her national State authorities to protect him or her. The principle was established by the Court in the case of *HLR v. France*[207] and subsequently reaffirmed as follows:

> Owing to the absolute character of the right guaranteed, Article 3 of the Convention may also apply where the danger emanates from persons or groups of persons who are not public officials. However, it must be shown that the risk is real and that the authorities of the receiving State are not able to obviate the risk by providing appropriate protection.[208]

In the recent case of *N. v. Sweden*, the Court had to decide whether the Swedish authorities' decision to return Ms N. to Afghanistan would give rise to a violation of Article 3. The Court observed that Ms N. would not be granted protection by Afghan authorities given that the latter saw "violence against women as legitimate", and took into account "various cumulative risks of reprisals" falling under Article 3 of the Convention to conclude that the implementation of the deportation order would give rise to a violation of the Convention. Specifically, the Court referred to risks of ill-treatments from the applicant's husband and in-laws, from her own family and from the Afghan society.[209]

(c) *The Five Refugee Convention Grounds for Persecution: Inoperative in International Human Rights Law (and, Incidentally, in Subsidiary Protection Cases)*

An element that fundamentally narrows the scope of the principle of *non-refoulement* under Article 33 of the Refugee Convention and under the corresponding Qualification Directive provision (Article 21) pertains to the definition of the threat, which corresponds to the definition of an act of persecution. The provision protects a person from being expelled or returned "to the frontiers of territories where his life or freedom would be threatened *on account of* his race, religion, nationality, membership of a particular social group or political opinion".[210]

It is well-established, the Refugee Convention protection against *refoulement* does not avail only those who have been recognised as refugees but any

---

207 ECtHR, *H.L.R. v. France*, Application No. 24573/94 (29 April 1997), § 40.
208 *See* for example: ECtHR, *Salah Sheekh*, § 137; ECtHR, *NA v. UK*, § 110.
209 ECtHR, *N v. Sweden*, Application no. 23505/09 (20 July 2010), § 62.
210 Refugee Convention, Article 33(1) [emphasis added].

individual who fulfils the refugee definition criteria.[211] To wit, the principle, as it appears in Article 33 of the 1951 Convention, "applies clearly and categorically to refugees within the meaning of article 1".[212] Goodwin-Gill and McAdam confirm that a refugee needs not be formally recognised as such under Article 1 of the Convention before he or she can enjoy the protection of Article 33 of the Convention. Asylum seekers awaiting a decision, *prima facie* refugees and those with a presumptive claim to refugee status, regardless of the legality of their entry or presence on the territory of the State, are entitled to *non-refoulement* protection,[213] at least until and unless their asylum claims are formally rejected. It is clear; refugees need not be recognised as such to benefit from the prohibition of *refoulement*. They must nevertheless be refugees pursuant to the Refugee Convention definition. Only those individuals for whom a causal link exists between the threats invoked and factors personal to him or her can therefore seek to invoke a right to *non-refoulement* under the refugee Convention. In other words, to "attract" the protection of the Refugee Convention, the threat to the person's life or freedom must be linked with at least one of the grounds for persecution set out in Article 1A(2) of the Convention[214] and reproduced in Article 33(1) of the Convention: race, religion, nationality, membership of a particular social group or political opinion.

Under human rights law on the contrary, the principle of *non-refoulement* applies to protect any individual from being returned to a territory where his or her life, person or freedom would be threatened, irrespective of whether the harm would be inflicted upon him or her for any particular reason, pertaining to his or her personal circumstances or characteristics inclusive. The judgment of the Court in *D. v. UK* illustrates this fact. The Court has applied the principle of *non-refoulement* to protect individuals against risks of proscribed treatments inflicted on them regardless of the reasons, if any, motivating those treatments.[215] The *D. v. UK* is in fact a landmark case: it extends the applicability of Article 3 ECHR to cases where no responsibility can be attributed to the State, either directly or indirectly and, therefore, no intention either. The

---

211   UNHCR ExCom, "Conclusion No. 6 (XXVIII) *Non-Refoulement* (1977)" ("Conclusion No 6 on *Non-refoulement* (1977)"); P. Weis, *The Refugee Convention, 1951: The Travaux Préparatoires Analysed* (Cambridge: Cambridge University Press, 1995), pp. 233s; UNHCR, *Handbook* (1979, reissued December 2011), *op. cit.*, § 28; E. Lauterpacht and D. Bethlehem (2003), *op. cit.*, §§ 89–99.
212   G.S. Goodwin-Gill and J. McAdam, *The Refugee in International Law* (2007), *op. cit.*, p. 232.
213   See *ibid.*, pp. 232–233 and references cited.
214   N. Mole and C. Meredith, *Asylum and the European Convention on Human Rights* (2007), *op. cit.*, p. 25.
215   *See* for example: ECtHR, *H.L.R. v. France*.

judgment will be discussed in length in the second part of this work, however, suffice to say at this point that the Court found that the expulsion by the United Kingdom of an applicant living with AIDS and whose life expectancy would be significantly reduced upon being sent back to St Kitts, would constitute a violation of Article 3 of the ECHR.[216] The risk for the applicant to suffer a treatment proscribed by Article 3 ECHR emanates from an illness and not from any intentionally inflicted act. The judgment stresses that the Court is not prevented from:

> ... scrutinising an applicant's claim under Article 3 (art. 3) where the source of the risk of proscribed treatment in the receiving country stems from factors which cannot engage either directly or indirectly the responsibility of the public authorities of that country...[217]

The fact that the harm invoked does not emanate from an intentionally-inflicted act, and therefore that no causal link can be established between the harm and the applicant's personal characteristics (such as the Convention grounds for persecution), does not exclude the individual from the benefit of *non-refoulement*. This has been confirmed since by the Court who has recognised the invocability of Article 3 ECHR in expulsion cases where the applicant's "ill-treatment" originates in a "naturally-occurring illness and the lack of sufficient to deal with it in the receiving country".[218]

It follows from the above that the principle of *non-refoulement* applies under human rights law to asylum seekers, irrespective of their status under refugee law, of the origin of the threat, and of the reasons, if any, for the threat. This broad understanding of the principle of *non-refoulement* will be assessed against its applicability in cases of indiscriminate threats and specifically, in armed conflict situations. Does the principle of *non-refoulement* offer as broad a protection as could be expected, in view of the above?

C Application to Armed Conflict Situations

The previous developments concluded that *non-refoulement* under human rights law was broader than under refugee law.

In the context of armed conflict, and within the framework of the Qualification Directive, it appears that the scope of the prohibition of cruel inhuman or degrading treatment or punishment is more broadly interpreted by the

---

216   ECtHR, *D. v. UK*.
217   ECtHR, *H.L.R. v. France*, § 49.
218   ECtHR, *N. v. UK*; ECtHR, *Sufi & Elmi*, §§ 281–282.

institutions of the Council of Europe than by the EU. When the European Court of Human Rights has analysed whether returning an individual to a situation of generalised violence could constitute a breach of ECHR, it did so under Article 3 of the Convention which, the Court found, was applicable in conflict situations. This will be shown below but it can be noted already that in most cases the Court found it necessary for a violation of Article 3 to be constituted that the applicant establish that he was at greater risk than the general population.[219] On the other hand, the Qualification Directive is based on a different approach: the protection against return to armed conflict situations is not rooted in the prohibition of torture and inhuman or degrading treatment or punishment. As made clear by the EU Court of Justice in *Elgafaji*:[220] subsidiary protection granted in cases of armed conflict situations in the applicant's country of origin (Article 15(c) of the Qualification Directive) is different from the protection granted by Article 3 ECHR.[221] The Qualification Directive indeed defines as two separate categories of acts likely to constitute serious harm: cruel, inhuman or degrading treatment or punishment on the one hand (Article 15(b)), and serious and individual threat to a civilian's life or person by reason of indiscriminate violence in situations of armed conflict on the other hand (Article 15(c)). A 2002 Presidency Note in fact elaborated on this distinction as follows:

> Sub-paragraphs (a) and (b) would in all cases appear to cover applicants facing a serious threat to life or physical integrity. However, threats arising in situations of indiscriminate violence, would not be covered since such situations can not be described as treatment or punishment or suffering the death penalty.[222]

The Council thus justifies the inclusion of a separate paragraph 15(c), to ensure that persons whose need of international protection originates in a situation of indiscriminate violence can receive protection under the EU Qualification Directive. It is worth noting that, although it just stated that threats arising in situations of indiscriminate violence could not be described as, in particular, "treatment or punishment", the Council subsequently seems to contradict

---

219   See for example ECtHR, *Salah Sheekh*; ECtHR, *Müslim v. Turkey*, Application no. 53566/99 (26 April 2005); ECtHR, *N v. Sweden*; ECtHR, *NA v. UK*; ECtHR, *Vilvarajah*; ECtHR, *Gashi and Others v. Sweden* ("*Gashi v. Sweden*"), Application no. 61167/08 (4 May 2010).

220   Above pp. 140s.

221   CJ, *Elgafaji*, § 28.

222   "Presidency Note (ASILE 43)", *op. cit.*, p. 6.

itself when, in the following paragraph, it highlights that the inclusion of 15(c) would bring EU law in line with the jurisprudence of the European Court of Human Rights on Article 3 of the ECHR (that is, on the very prohibition of cruel, inhuman or degrading treatments) according to which "an expulsion as such to a situation with a high level of danger and insecurity/indiscriminate violence *could be considered an inhuman or degrading treatment*".[223]

Regardless of the Council's ambiguous statement, where returns of aliens to situations of generalised violence are concerned, the relevant provision of the ECHR under which the European Court of Human Rights has appreciated such situations is indeed Article 3. It appears that situations of generalised violence, if they do not themselves constitutes a "treatment" – as argued by the EU Council, could nevertheless expose individuals to a real risk of suffering such treatment, so that return to those situations may constitute a violation of ECHR Article 3.

The jurisprudence of the Court has significantly evolved over the past decades concerning the personal nature of the risk and situations of indiscriminate violence.

1 Early Developments in the Case-law of the ECtHR in Relation with Armed Conflict Situations

The ECtHR long required under its infamous and now revisited *Vilvarajah* jurisprudence that the applicant should demonstrate the personal nature of the alleged risk by showing that there existed special distinguishing features, concerning him personally.[224] The Court revisited its position in *Salah Sheekh v. the Netherlands* which has been repeatedly confirmed since. Where it is established that a certain group is the target of ill-treatment, and that the applicant is a member of this group, then, the Court found, it might render the protection offered by ECHR Article 3 illusory if, in addition to the fact that he belongs to the given targeted group, the applicant be required to show the existence of further special distinguishing features.[225] The Court thus lowered the degree of individualisation that the applicant needs to demonstrate: membership of a targeted group is sufficient to activate the protection of Article 3 against refoulement. It is not necessary that the applicant demonstrates further distinguishing features which would place him or her personally at higher risk than other members of the same minority. As noted by N. Mole though, ECtHR case law does oblige the applicant to "substantiate through the relevant

---

223 *Ibid.*, p. 7 [emphasis added].
224 ECtHR, *Vilvarajah*, § 112.
225 ECtHR, *Salah Sheekh*, § 148.

documentation, membership of the group in question and the treatment meted out as a result".²²⁶

In *N.A. v. the United Kingdom*, the Court left open the possibility that returning an individual to a situation of indiscriminate violence can constitute in itself a violation of Article 3, if the level of violence reaches a certain threshold.

> ... the Court has never excluded the possibility that a general situation of violence in a country of destination will be of a sufficient level of intensity as to entail that any removal to it would necessarily breach Article 3 of the Convention. Nevertheless, the Court would adopt such an approach only in the most extreme cases of general violence, where there was a real risk of ill-treatment simply by virtue of an individual being exposed to such violence on return.²²⁷

A situation of general violation subjecting any individual entering the territory to a risk of ill-treatment appears to correspond to, if not actually to describe, the impact of armed conflicts on territories and populations. It could therefore be expected that the Court, when transmitted a case concerning the return of a displaced person to a country affected by a war, especially one that is recognised as such by the international community, would conclude to a violation of Article 3. The Court has been asked to rule on a number of cases concerning armed conflict situations. The Court consistently held that a prevailing general context of violence was in itself not sufficient to bar *refoulement*.²²⁸

In 2010, the Court confirmed the approach it had adopted in *N.A. v. the United Kingdom* in its judgment in the *Gashi v. Sweden*²²⁹ case, concerning a risk of exposure to violations of Article 3 upon return to Kosovo. The situation prevailing in Kosovo at the time was described in 2009 by UNHCR in the following terms: "incidents of targeted ethnic violence on a large scale have decreased since the last major outbreaks in March 2004. Nevertheless,

---

226   Nuala MOLE, *Asylum and the European Convention on Human Rights*, Human Rights Files, No.9 (revised), Strasbourg: Council of Europe, 2010), p. 44.
227   ECtHR, *NA v. UK*, § 116.
228   See for example Afghanistan: ECtHR, *Sultani c. France*, Application no. 45223/05 (20 September 2007); ECtHR, *N v. Sweden*. Irak: ECtHR, *Müslim v. Turkey*; ECtHR, *Ahmed Samir Said Al Khadumi c. Roumanie*, Application no. 35380/03 (18 October 2005). *See also*: ECtHR, *Aoulmi c. France*, Application no. 50278/99 (17 January 2006); ECtHR, *Kavak v. Germany*, Application no. 46089/99 (18 May 1999).
229   ECtHR, *Gashi v. Sweden*.

ethnically-motivated security incidents and threats reportedly continue".[230] The Court relied on this country information provided by UNHCR to reach a decision in the case but concluded that the applicants had failed to substantiate that they would face a real risk of being subjected to treatment contrary to Article 3 of the Convention if deported to Kosovo. Their claim was therefore declared manifestly ill-founded:

> There is no indication (...) that the situation is so serious that return of the applicants to Kosovo would constitute, in itself, a violation of Article 3 of the Convention. The Court reiterates in this respect that it has never excluded the possibility that a general situation of violence in a country of destination will be of sufficient level of intensity as to entail that a removal to it would necessarily breach Article 3 of the Convention. Nevertheless, the Court would adopt such an approach only in the most extreme cases of general violence, where there is a real risk of ill-treatment simply by virtue of an individual being exposed to such violence on return.[231]

It appears from the above: the Court is not inclined to finding a violation of Article 3 of the Convention by reason of the removal of an individual to an armed conflict situation when the risk is purely indiscriminate. The Court has found a violation of Article 3 in cases where the applicant was a member of a group or minority, affected in the context of an armed conflict. The applicant must then adduce evidence of his or her membership in this group; he or she however needs not demonstrate that, within this group, he or she is at higher risk.

Although, as mentioned in the case cited above, the Court never excluded that a general situation of violence in a country of destination could reach such a high level of intensity that removal to this situation would necessarily entail a breach Article 3 of the Convention, it has however long refused to find such "sufficient level". Many cases illustrate that such situation would be exceptional.[232]

---

230 UNHCR, "UNHCR's Eligibility Guidelines for Assessing the International Protection Needs of Individuals from Kosovo", HCR/EG/09/01, 9 November 2009.
231 ECtHR, *Gashi v. Sweden*, p. 6.
232 General context in Afghanistan: ECtHR, *Sultani c. France*; ECtHR, *N v. Sweden*. General context in Irak: ECtHR, *Müslim v. Turkey*; ECtHR. General situation in Sri Lanka: ECtHR, *Thampibillai*; ECtHR, *Venkadajalasarma v. The Netherlands* ("*Venkadajalasarma*"), Application no. 58510/00 (17 February 2004). General situation in Turkey or "*conjuncture instable*": ECtHR, *Emine Akyüz and Other v. Germany*, Application no. 58388/00 (28 September 2000); ECtHR, *Kavak v. Germany*. Georgia, applicant's situation not worse than that of

Against this background, the judgment of the Court in the *Sufi and Elmi v. UK* case is of crucial importance.

2 A "most extreme case of general violence": An Analysis of the Situation in Mogadishu by the ECtHR in *Sufi and Elmi v. the United Kingdom*

Restating its earlier case-law[233] and its decision in the *NA v. UK* case[234] in particular, the European Court of Human Rights recalls the meaning of the principle of *non-refoulement* under its interpretation of Article 3 ECHR. In essence the Court notes, the "*sole* question"[235] the Court shall answer in expulsion cases is whether substantial grounds have been shown for believing that return to his or her country of origin would expose the person concerned to "a real risk of being subjected to treatment contrary to Article 3 of the Convention". In the affirmative, removal is proscribed under Article 3 ECHR, "regardless of whether the risk emanates from a general situation of violence, a personal characteristic of the applicant, or a combination of the two".[236] However, until the *Sufi & Elmi* judgment, the Court had found a breach of Article 3 only in "combination cases" but never when risks emanated solely from the general situation of violence prevailing in the country of origin.[237] It is indeed settled case-law: not every situation of general violence gives rise to a real risk of exposure to treatment proscribed under Article 3 ECHR. On the contrary, according to the Court, it is only in "the most extreme cases" that a general situation of violence would be of such intensity that an individual would be exposed to a real risk of ill-treatment "simply by virtue of [him or her] being exposed to such violence on return".[238]

On 28 June 2011 however, in its judgment in the *Sufi and Elmi v. the United Kingdom* case, the ECtHR considers that the situation of general violence prevailing in Mogadishu was one such most extreme case of violence. To reach this conclusion, the Court conducted a thorough assessment of the situation in the capital city of Somalia, on the basis of four criteria, drawn from the practice

---

other members of the minority to which he belongs, maybe not even than that of the rest of the population: ECtHR, *Fatgan Katani Et Autres c. Allemagne* ("*Katani v. Germany*"), Application no. 67679/01 (31 May 2001).

233 ECtHR, *Sufi & Elmi*, §§ 212–219.
234 ECtHR, *NA v. UK*.
235 ECtHR, *Sufi & Elmi*, § 218.
236 *Ibid.*, § 218.
237 Above pp. 228s.
238 ECtHR, *NA v. UK*, § 115.

of the United Kingdom Asylum and Immigration Tribunal.[239] According to the ECtHR, the level of a situation of general violence should be assessed by the yardstick of the following indicators:

- 1: "whether the parties to the conflict were either employing methods and tactics of warfare which increased the risk of civilian casualties or directly targeting civilians";
- 2: "whether the use of such methods and/or tactics was widespread among the parties to the conflict";
- 3: "whether the fighting was localised or widespread"; and
- 4: "the number of civilians killed, injured and displaced as a result of the fighting".[240]

The Court endorsed the approach of the UK Asylum and Immigration Tribunal, thereby providing guidance to its State Parties on how to assess the intensity of a conflict and remedying its earlier case-law which, precisely, fell short of identifying such criteria.

The ECtHR took account of various reports produced by national and international organisations and institutions to apply the above mentioned indicators to the situation prevailing in Mogadishu.[241] On this basis, the Court reached the following conclusion:

> [The] large quantity of objective information overwhelmingly indicates that the level of violence in Mogadishu is of sufficient intensity to pose a real risk of treatment reaching the Article 3 threshold to anyone in the capital. In reaching this conclusion the Court has had regard to the indiscriminate bombardments and military offensives carried out by all parties to the conflict, the unacceptable number of civilian casualties, the substantial number of persons displaced within and from the city, and the unpredictable and widespread nature of the conflict.[242]

The *Sufi & Elmi* judgment is significant for several reasons. Firstly, it is the first judgment of the Court which concludes to the existence of a situation of general conflict of such intensity that it exposes every individual, solely on account

---

239 UK: UKAIT, *AM & AM (Armed Conflict: Risk Categories) Somalia v. Secretary of State for the Home Department* ("*AM & AM (Somalia)*"), CG [2008] UKAIT 00091.
240 ECtHR, *Sufi & Elmi*, § 241.
241 Ibid., §§ 241–248.
242 Ibid., § 248.

of his or her being present in the region or country, to a real risk of torture or inhuman or degrading treatment or punishment. As such it is a "lead case" insofar as it established the principles to be applied in all the other 214 similar cases pending at the time before the ECtHR;[243] the same was observed in the United Kingdom, albeit apprehensively sometimes, in view of M Sufi's lengthy criminal records in particular.[244] As a matter of fact, the Court has since confirmed the interpretation and assessment made in *Sufi & Elmi*, in a recent judgment concerning eleven Somali nationals and thirteen Eritrean nationals who had left Libya with the aim of reaching Italy but whose vessel was intercepted at sea by Italian authorities.[245]

Secondly, the Court provides useful guidance to national authorities by establishing, for the first time, specific criteria for assessing the severity of a situation of general violence in the applicant's country of origin.[246]

Lastly, the potential impact of the *Sufi & Elmi* judgement on European Union asylum law cannot be ignored. In what could be perceived as an intimation of vexation on its part, the European Court of Human Rights went back over the appreciation made by the Court of Justice in *Elgafaji* of the respective scopes of Article 3 ECHR and Article 15(c) of the Qualification Directive[247] in the following terms:

> The jurisdiction of this Court is limited to the interpretation of the Convention and it would not, therefore, be appropriate for it to express any

---

243   Registrar of the ECtHR, "Press Release: The United Kingdom Would Violate Human Rights of Two Somali Nationals If It Returned Them to Mogadishu", ECHR 076 (2011), 28 June 2011, p. 1 and n. 1.

244   S. James reports – and visibly shares – the concerns of a Member of the British Parliament and of a spokesman of the UK Border Agency that the decision of the Court in *Sufi & Elmi* disappointedly conduces to Europe (and the UK in the case) becoming a safe haven for criminals. S. James, "Locked up Again, Somali Crook We Can't Send Home", *Daily Mail* (Solo Syndication Ltd.) (2011), p. 12.

245   The Court referred to the *Sufi & Elmi* case to conclude that repatriation to Somalia or Eritrea would violate Article 3 ECHR in view of the situation prevailing in those countries, which "posed and continues to pose widespread serious problems of insecurity". The Court also concluded, as a consequence, that Italy transferring of the applicants to Libya, where they risked repatriation to Somalia and Eritrea, was in breach of Article 3 ECHR. ECtHR (Grand Chamber), *Case of Hirsi Jamaa and Others v. Italy* ("*Hirsi Jamaa et al. v. Italy*"), Application no. 27765/09 (23 February 2012), §§ 150–152 and 158.

246   UNHCR, et al., *Safe at Last?* (July 2011), *op. cit.*, p. 13.

247   The Court of Justice found that the situations covered by Article 15(c) of the Qualification Directive, *i.e.* indiscriminate violence in armed conflict situations, were not covered by Article 3 ECHR which, the CJ found, had a different content. CJ, *Elgafaji*, §§ 27–28.

views on the ambit or scope of article 15(c) of the Qualification Direction. However, based on the ECJ's interpretation in *Elgafaji*, the Court is not persuaded that Article 3 of the Convention, as interpreted in *NA*, does not offer comparable protection to that afforded under the Directive. In particular, it notes that the threshold set by both provisions may, in exceptional circumstances, be attained in consequence of a situation of general violence of such intensity that any person being returned to the region in question would be at risk simply on account of their presence there.[248]

As mentioned earlier, as interpreted, not least by the Court of Justice in *Elgafaji*, it is Article 15(b) of the Qualification Directive which corresponds in essence to Article 3 ECHR.[249] It follows that the conclusion of the ECtHR in *Sufi & Elmi*, that returning an individual to a situation of "extreme violence" (as the one identified in Mogadishu) constitutes a breach of Article 3 ECHR, might be conducive of EU Member States granting subsidiary protection to individuals fleeing such situation under Article 15(b) – instead of 15(c) – of the Qualification Directive. Quite circularly, it would mean that the Court of Justice, in attempting to clarify the scope of Article 15(c) QD, by contrasting it with the scope of Article 3 ECHR, might in fact have hollowed Article 15(c) out by diverting subsidiary protection claims in cases of extreme general violence onto Article 15(b). Indeed, a combined reading of *Elgafaji* (CJ) and *Sufi & Elmi* (ECtHR) would logically lead national authorities to grant subsidiary protection under Article 15(b) in cases where the threats to which individuals are exposed in situations of extreme violence reach the Article 3 ECHR threshold. As a matter of fact, it emerges from a survey conducted by UNHCR in six EU Member States that in 2010, most of them had granted subsidiary protection to Afghans, Iraqis and Somalis on the basis of Article 15(b).[250] This observation raises additional questions as to the actual added value of Article 15(c). With a view to safeguarding the *effet utile* of the provision, a possible approach could be to interpret Article 15(c) as covering risks of harm which originate in situations of indiscriminate violence but do not reach the threshold of Article 3 ECHR.

In conclusion, the comparative overview of the scope of *non-refoulement* under international human rights law and under refugee law reveals that each of the two bodies of norms presents both advantages and shortcomings.

---

248 ECtHR, *Sufi & Elmi*, § 226.
249 CJ, *Elgafaji*, § 28.
250 UNHCR, et al., *Safe at Last?* (July 2011), *op. cit.*, pp. 24–28.

It appears that human rights law might often be more generous than refugee law in covering individuals regardless of their status, of the origin of the alleged threat, and of the reason for it. However, the adoption of the Qualification Directive tempers the finding in relation to armed conflict situations, which might be covered in broader terms under EU refugee law than under the ECHR.

A difference remains between human rights law on the one hand and refugee law on the other, and it is of significant importance: refugee law, unlike human rights law, confers upon the beneficiary of protection a legal status, a formal "package" of opposable rights and entitlements. Human rights law on the other hand can be described as granting individuals a right to *"non-refoulement* without more".[251]

II Customary International Law

The obligation to protect individuals exposed to indiscriminate threats is a norm of customary international law. Besides the general negative obligation for States not to expel individuals to a situation where they risk being subjected to ill-treatment threatening their life or person (A), there also exists under customary international law a positive obligation to provide statutory protection to persons fleeing indiscriminate threats, at least when such risk originates in an armed conflict situation (B).

A *A Negative Obligation for States:* Non-refoulement, Its Existence and Nature in Customary International Law

Asylum is an ancestral practice. Moral and religious precepts, humane and humanitarian considerations, followed by legally binding norms have long justified the practice of granting asylum to individuals fleeing threats to their lives or freedoms. Texts written more than three millennia ago reveal that the practice already existed then, in Mesopotamia (Assyrians) and ancient Egypt for instance. Historians find that asylum also existed in Classical Greece as well as in the Roman Empire, partly under the influence of the Christian Church, who long maintained the practice.[252] Throughout history, the practice developed

---

[251] Jane McAdam, *Complementary Protection in International Refugee Law* (New York: Oxford, 2007), pp.11 and 45.

[252] On some church buildings, "sanctuary rings" still bear witness of the right of asylum which fugitives could claim under certain circumstances (in Paris for example, one such door knocker can be observed on a door of the Cathedral of Notre-Dame).

but its purpose remained relatively constant: it carried an obligation for authorities granting asylum to protect beneficiaries and not to return them to a risk of death or mutilation.[253]

From being essentially rooted in morals, the practice of granting refuge or safe haven to persons in need of protection progressively developed into a legal obligation: the principle of *non-refoulement*.[254] It is well rehearsed in relevant literature: the principle of *non-refoulement* forms part of customary international law (a). Academic debate now centres instead on the nature of the obligation under customary international law: is it absolute? Is it *jus cogens*? It is not the purpose of the present part to solve the question however a few arguments are worth being recounted (b).

1   A Glance beyond Europe's Borders to Confirm the Obvious

The principle of *non-refoulement* has been analysed at length and the fact is now undisputed: *non-refoulement* forms part of customary international law.[255] There is ample literature on the customary international law nature of *non-refoulement* and it is not the object of the following developments to review it. Nevertheless, in order to give some account of the obvious, let us cast a glance beyond European borders.

It is well-known: treaties can be used as evidence of international custom. Accordingly, UNHCR Executive Committee finds evidence of the prohibition

---

253   See also: D. Chotouras, *Le statut juridique en droit international du réfugié écologique : une nécessité !* (*Le phénomène migratoire du fait des modifications environnementales*), 9 February 2012, Doctoral Thesis, Université de Lorraine (not yet published: 2012), §§ 111s; UNHCR, "Refugees" (© UNHCR, 2001–2012), retrieved from: <http://www.unhcr.org/pages/49c3646c125.html> [07/09/2012].

254   G.S. Goodwin-Gill (1988), *op. cit.*

255   In the opinion of G.S. Goodwin-Gill and J. McAdam, State practice before the adoption of the Geneva Convention was equivocal as to whether Article 33 of the Refugee Convention reflected or crystallised an existing rule of customary international law. No such doubt is however permissible, in the authors' opinion, as to the existence of such a rule nowadays. According to the two commentators, State practice since the adoption of the 1951 Convention "is persuasive evidence of the concretization of a customary rule, even in the absence of any formal pronouncement". G.S. Goodwin-Gill and J. McAdam, *The Refugee in International Law* (2007), *op. cit.*, pp. 346–347. Other examples of assertions of the customary international law prohibition of *refoulement* include: E. Lauterpacht and D. Bethlehem (2003), *op. cit.*, §§ 193–253; J. Allain (2001), *op. cit.*, pp. 538–541. Respect for the principle of *non-refoulement* has gained increased topicality in the context of anti-terrorism. The following report is an example: International Helsinki Federation for Human Rights (IHF), *Anti-Terrorism Measures, Security and Human Rights Developments in Europe, Central Asia and North America in the Aftermath of September 11* (Vienna: IHF, April 2003).

of *refoulement* as customary international law in the fact that "the fundamental humanitarian principle of *non-refoulement* has found expression in various international instruments adopted at the universal and regional levels and is generally accepted by States".[256] In this work, in this Chapter as well as in the previous one, reference has been made to a number of international treaties, both at the regional and global levels, which protect individuals against *refoulement*, be it explicitly, as in the Refugee Convention, the EU Qualification Directive or the Convention Against Torture, or through the interpretation of their provisions including, chiefly, those provisions concerning the prohibition of torture or inhuman or degrading treatment or punishment (as is the case for the ECHR and ICCPR).[257]

The focus of this work being international protection available in European Union Member States, the principle of *non-refoulement* has so far been discussed from a European perspective and the legal instruments of universal scope enumerated above were therefore mainly considered from a European point of view (although reference has been occasionally made to State practice outside the European Union, in the discussion of the scope of non-refoulement under the ICCPR for instance[258]). Discussing customary international law is an opportunity to look beyond Europe and observe that other regions of the world also acknowledge the need to protect individuals against return to situations where the life or person of the returnee would be under threat.

In the context of human rights generally, the Arab Charter on Human Rights adopted by the League of Arab States ("Arab League"), in its revised version, in 2005 and in force since 2008 enshrines the right not to be subjected to "physical or psychological torture or to cruel, degrading, humiliating or inhuman treatment".[259] The Charter was criticised for failing to include, following the example of the UN Convention Against Torture,[260] an express prohibition of extradition or return to countries where persons may face serious human rights violations, including torture or inhuman treatment or punishment.[261] The consequences in practice of this lacuna can however be put into

---

256 ExCom, "Conclusion No 6 on *Non-refoulement* (1977)", *op. cit.*, (a).
257 Above, Chapter 2, Section II., pp. 93s and Chapter 3, Section I, pp. 181s in particular.
258 See above pp. 193s on Canadian extradition decisions and their appreciation by the Human Rights Committee by the yardstick of State Parties' *non-refoulement* obligations under the ICCPR.
259 League of Arab States, Arab Charter on Human Rights ("Arab Charter"), adopted 15 September 1994, entered into force 15 March 2008 *reprinted in International Human Rights Report* Vol. 12, p. 893 [2005], Article 8.
260 CAT, Article 3.
261 M. Rishmawi, "The Revised Arab Charter on Human Rights: A Step Forward", *Human Rights Law Review*, Vol. 5, No. 2 (2005), pp. 361–376, 372–373 and 376.

perspective. Firstly, many of the twenty-two current Arab League Members are parties to at least the ICCPR, the Refugee Convention or the CAT Convention.[262] Among the State Parties to the CAT Convention that are also Members of the Arab League, none has issued reservations to Article 3, which prohibits *refoulement*.[263] Secondly, the Preamble of the Arab Charter through an express reference to a number of international treaties including, chiefly, the International Covenant on Civil and Political Rights, reaffirms the principles therein enshrined.[264] As we know, Article 7 of the ICCPR, in the interpretation that prevails, carries with it the principle of *non-refoulement*. It can be concluded from those two observations that State Parties to the Arab Charter must in any case interpret its Article 8 in conformity with international human rights law and hence respect the principle of *non-refoulement* as an essential and traditional correlate to the prohibition of torture.

The same approach spurs the conclusion that *non-refoulement* is also enshrined in African and American human rights law. Commentators point to the fact that the absolute prohibition of torture, cruel, inhuman or degrading treatments and punishments included in Article 5 of the African Charter on Human and Peoples' Rights (the "African Charter")[265] and in Article 5(2) of the American Convention on Human Rights[266] must be interpreted, in the African and American contexts too, as implicitly carrying with it the absolute prohibition of *refoulement*.[267] Recent developments[268] of the law in the

---

262   Eleven out of the twenty-two Arab League Members (including the "State of Palestine") are not parties to the Refugee Convention but only five are not parties to the ICCPR and four, to the CAT Convention, with Sudan being however a signatory since 1986. Observations based on the data provided by the Secretary-General of the United Nations. See, "Depositary Notifications Issued by the Secretary-General" (United Nations, 2012), last updated 08/07/2012, retrieved from: <http://treaties.un.org/Pages/CNs.aspx> [08/07/2012].

263   Observations based on the data provided by the Secretary-General of the United Nations. See, *ibid.*

264   *Arab Charter*, Preamble, Recital 5.

265   African Charter on Human and Peoples' Rights – "Banjul Charter" ("ACHPR"), 27 June 1981, entered into force 21 October 1986 CAB/LEG/67/3 rev. 5, 21 I.L.M. 58 (1982).

266   American Convention on Human Rights – "Pact of San Jose, Costa Rica" ("ACHR"), 22 November 1969, entered into force 18 July 1978.

267   E. Lauterpacht and D. Bethlehem (2003), *op. cit.*, § 236; C.A. Odinkalu and M. Zard, "African Regional Mechanisms That Can Be Utilized on Behalf of the Forcibly Displaced", *in* J.F. Fitzpatrick (Ed.), *Human Rights Protection for Refugees, Asylum-Seekers, and Internally Displaced Persons: A Guide to International Mechanisms and Procedures* (New York: Transnational Publishers, 2002), pp. 264–265.

268   R. Murray gives an overview of recent human rights developments in the African Union and the African Charter. The article refers to developments which are relevant in asylum and migration contexts but has a more encompassing scope. R. Murray, "Recent

African human rights system reinforce the contention. In 2000, the African Commission on Human and Peoples' Rights "signalled its endorsement of the underlying principle"[269] of *non-refoulement* when it concluded that Botswana had acted is breach of Article 5 of the African Charter (among other rights): the deportation of the applicant, the Commission found, "exposed him to personal suffering and indignity in violation of the right to freedom from cruel, inhuman or degrading treatment".[270] More recently, in 2007, two resolutions of the African Commission further support the theory of an implicit prohibition of *refoulement* in the African human rights system. In its Resolution 105, the Commission "calls on *all*[271] States Parties to the African Charter to ratify the Convention against Torture and other Cruel, Inhuman or Degrading Treatment or Punishment, and the Optional Protocol thereto, of 18 December 2002, without reservations".[272] By ratifying the CAT Convention, States are automatically bound by the prohibition of *refoulement* (to face a risk of torture). Resolution 114 on Migration and Human Rights recommends State Parties to the African Charter to "respect the principle of customary international law of non-refoulement".[273] It follows that, should the African Commission be called to interpret Article 5 of the African Charter in the context of expulsion or extradition, it would certainly deduce from it the prohibition of *refoulement*.[274]

Developments in the African Human Rights System 2007", *Human Rights Law Review*, Vol. 8, No. 2 (2008), pp. 356–376.

269   E. Lauterpacht and D. Bethlehem (2003), *op. cit.*, § 236.

270   ACnHPR, *John K. Modise v. Botswana* ("*Modise v. Botswana*"), Communication No. 97/93 (6 November 2000), § 92.

271   Either intentional or not, it can be noted that, of the four recommendations made by the African Commission, only the first one, urging States to ratify the CAT Convention is explicitly addressed to "*all* States Parties" [emphasis added] to the African Charter whereas the other paragraphs refer simply to "States Parties". The word could be interpreted as a reflection of the endorsement by the ACnHPR of the customary international law nature of the principles enshrined in the CAT Convention (prohibition of torture and principle of *non-refoulement*). As principles of international custom, they are binding upon all States and should therefore be unanimously adhered to within the African region. ACnHPR, "Resolution 105 on the Prevention and Prohibition of Torture and Other Cruel, Inhuman or Degrading Treatment or Punishment" ("Resolution 105"), ACHPR/Res.105 (XXXXI), 30 May 2007, § 2 [emphasis added].

272   *Ibid.*, § 2.

273   *Ibid.*

274   E. Lauterpacht and D. Bethlehem found in 2003 that the African Commission (and the Inter-American Court of Human Rights alike) had not yet had to address the issue whether the prohibition of torture, inhuman or degrading treatment and punishment was to be interpreted as prohibiting *refoulement*. I conclude from the survey of decisions issued

As noted above, there is "no reason to believe" that the Inter-American Court of Human Rights would adopt a different approach.[275]

In the context of refugees on the other hand, the prohibition of *refoulement* is explicit in the American Convention on Human Rights. Article 22(8) states that "[in] no case may an alien be deported or returned to a country, regardless of whether or not it is his country of origin, if in that country his right to life or personal freedom is in danger of being violated because of his race, nationality, religion, social status, or political opinions".[276] The Convention, adopted by American States in 1969 hence clearly draws on the principle of *non-refoulement* as it is enshrined in the 1951 Refugee Convention: deportation and return of an individual to a risk of persecution is prohibited in the Inter-American system. The principle was reaffirmed in 1984 in the Cartagena Declaration.[277] Unlike *non-refoulement* in the Refugee Convention though, the prohibition spelled out in Article 22(8) ACHR and in the Cartagena Declaration is not subject to any exception. The same is true of *non-refoulement* under the African Union Convention Governing the Specific Aspects of Refugee Problems in Africa[278] which was in fact the first binding instruments of international law to enshrine the principle in absolute terms. States in Asia and the Middle East have also agreed, together with some African States, to include the principle of *non-refoulement* in an international instrument, although a non-binding one. The final text of the 1966 Bangkok Principles on Status and Treatment of Refugees[279] was adopted by the Asian-African Legal Consultative Organisation on 24 June 2001. Forty-four States,[280] mainly Asian, Middle East and East African States, signed the Bangkok Principles and none expressed reservations on Article 3, which prohibits *refoulement* in line with Article 33 of

---

since by the African Commission that the observation is still valid to date (I examined the decisions issued by the African Commission on communications it received and published on the webpage of the African Commission on Human and Peoples' Rights: African Commission on Human and Peoples' Rights, *Latest Decisions on Communications,* <www.achpr.org/communications> [05/09/2012].).

275   E. Lauterpacht and D. Bethlehem (2003), *op. cit.*, § 236.
276   ACHR, Article 22(8).
277   Cartagena Declaration, Conclusion 5.
278   AU Refugee Convention, Article 2(3).
279   Bangkok Principles.
280   The Asian-African Legal Consultative Organisation (AALCO) has forty-seven Member States but three of them joined the AALCO after the final text of the Bangkok Principles was adopted: Brunei Darussalam (2003), South Africa (2004) and Cameroon (2006). The list Member States and year of joining the AALCO is available on the website of the Asian-African Legal Consultative Organisation (AALCO), <www.aalco.int> [05/09/2012].

the Refugee Convention and actually even more with the 1967 Declaration on Territorial Asylum.[281]

In view of the nearly universal recognition in instruments of international law of the principle of *non-refoulement*, it comes with no surprise that the customary international law nature of the prohibition of *refoulement* does not spark controversy (anymore).[282] If the existence of the rule is now undisputed, commentators, both institutional and academic, however discuss whether it may or not be subject to exceptions.

2 The Controversial *Jus Cogens* Nature of the Principle of Non-refoulement

As mentioned, *non-refoulement* has been broadly accepted as a norm of customary international law. On the other hand, exceptions to the principle "have not garnered similar status".[283] Accordingly, it is unsure whether the principle of *non-refoulement* does or does not accept derogations. As known and shown above, the Refugee Convention provides for exceptions to the principle of *non-refoulement*, for reasons of national security or public order.[284] This however did not stop the Executive Committee of the UN High Commissioner for Refugees – whose very duty is to supervise the application of the Refugee Convention[285] – from asserting the absolute nature of the prohibition of *refoulement*:

> Distressed at the widespread violations of the principle of non-refoulement and of the rights of refugees, in some cases resulting in loss of refugee lives, and seriously disturbed at reports indicating that large numbers of refugees and asylum-seekers have been refouled and expelled in highly dangerous situations; [the Executive Committee] recalls that *the principle of non-refoulement is not subject to derogation*.[286]

---

281 The Declaration on Territorial Asylum will be mentioned again below, when exceptions to the principle of *non-refoulement* are considered. "Declaration on Territorial Asylum" [14 December 1967], *op. cit.*

282 The existence of international treaties adopted at regional and global levels is only one piece of evidence of the existence of the *non-refoulement* principle in customary international law; it is not my contention that it suffices to establish the rule. As mentioned in the onset, in view of the ample literature and consensus on the matter, I chose to focus on this aspect only.

283 A. Farmer (2008–2009), *op. cit.*, p.9.

284 Refugee Convention, Article 33(2).

285 UNHCR Statute; and Refugee Convention, Preamble, Recital 6.

286 UNHCR, "General Conclusion on International Protection" ("General Conclusion No. 79 on International Protection"), No. 79 (XLVII), 11 October 1996, (i) [emphasis added].

This assertion of the absolute nature of the prohibition of *refoulement* in fact follows a series of conclusions adopted earlier by the Executive Committee (ExCom) since the early 1980s, which laid the bases of this approach.[287] J. Allain in fact deduces from certain Conclusions adopted by ExCom but also from State practice in Latin America (which has emerged on the basis of the Cartagena Declaration[288]) evidence that the principle of *non-refoulement* has acquired the level of a norm of *jus cogens*.[289] To counter this interpretation, some however point at the numerous instances in State practice of exceptions to *non-refoulement*, not least in the context of counter-terrorism:

> Notwithstanding the clear prohibition on *refoulement* that exists within human rights instruments, the existence of "terrorist" exceptions to the prohibition on *refoulement*, either through the use of a balancing test in some jurisdictions or the current practice of "rendition", alongside Refugee Convention exceptions, indicates that the goal of acquiring peremptory status for the principle of *non-refoulement* in international law has yet to be reached.[290]

J. Allain acknowledges the existence of cases where States or international organisation have adopted or adopt measures with the effect of returning an individual to a risk of proscribed treatment, often on the ground of his or her participation in terrorist activities, but contends that these so-called

---

287   E. Lauterpacht and D. Bethlehem observe that the Executive Committee has reasserted the application of *non-refoulement* in extradition cases (Conclusion No. 17), *i.e.* in cases where States could seek to invoke an Article 33(2) exception to *non-refoulement*, on the ground that an individual convicted of a serious crime can reasonably be regarded as a danger to the community of the host State. Similarly, although a large influx of asylum seekers could be said to pose a danger to the security of the host country, Conclusion 22 urges States to "scrupulously observe" the "fundamental principle of *non-refoulement*". As for Conclusion 25, it noted that the principle of *non-refoulement* "was progressively acquiring the character of a peremptory rule of international law". UNHCR ExCom, "Conclusion No. 17 (XXXI) Problems of Extradition Affecting Refugees (1980)" ("Conclusion No 17 on Extradition (1980)"), (c); UNHCR ExCom, "Conclusion No. 22 (XXXII) Protection of Asylum-Seekers in Situations of Large-Scale Influx (1981)" ("Conclusion No 22 on Large-Scale Influx (1981)"), II(A)(2); UNHCR ExCom, "Conclusion No. 25 (XXXIII) General (1982)" ("Conclusion No 25 "*General*" (1982)"), (b). *See* also E. Lauterpacht and D. Bethlehem (2003), *op. cit.*, § 155.
288   Cartagena Declaration.
289   J. Allain (2001), *op. cit.*, p. 539.
290   A. Duffy, "Expulsion to Face Torture? *Non-Refoulement* in International Law", *International Journal of Refugee Law*, Vol. 20 (2008), p. 390.

exceptions to *non-refoulement* in fact ought to be analysed as breaches of the principle[291] and, as such, do not affect the *jus cogens* nature of the principle[292] since, as expressed by the International Court of Justice (ICJ), the existence of a customary rule is not conditional upon it being absolutely complied with at all times.[293] Drawing on the ruling of the ICJ in the *Nicaragua* case, it is actually possible to go one step further and suggest that because States endeavour to defend their conduct "by appealing to exceptions or justifications within the rule itself",[294] measures taken by States in contravention of the absolute prohibition of *refoulement* might in fact paradoxically reinforce the existence of the rule.[295] As a matter of fact, derogations from the principle of *non-refoulement* do not go unnoticed and decision-makers do not spare efforts to justify their actions in such cases. States invoke national security concerns to justify the adoption of counter-terrorism measures; the European Court of Human Rights – and the decision is controversial – invokes the additional budgetary constraints which caring for an alien suffering from AIDS would put on a State to invalidate the State's decision to expel the individual to a life-threatening situation.[296] It seems indeed that the fact that States and courts find it necessary to provide such justifications for their seemingly rule-breaking application of non-refoulement "can reasonably be regarded as an implicit confirmation of their acceptance of the principle".[297] Lastly, it can be noted that pursuant to the law of treaties, once the peremptory nature of *non-refoulement* has been accepted, only by a subsequent norm of same character can it be modified.[298] As a consequence, mere inconsistent State practice could not affect the *jus cogens* nature of the principle of *non-refoulement*.

E. Lauterpacht and D. Bethlehem distinguish between *non-refoulement* in a refugee context and in a human rights context and combine the two to clarify the content of the principle of *non-refoulement* under customary international law along the following lines: it is indeed absolute when return exposes the individual to a risk of torture, inhuman or degrading treatment or punishment but can be derogated from, for overriding reasons of national security of public

---

[291] J. Allain draws on the judgement of the International Court of Justice in the *Nicaragua* case where the Court found that "instances of State conduct inconsistent with a given rule should generally have been treated as breaches of that rule, not as indications of the recognition of a new rule". ICJ, *Nicaragua (Merits)*, § 98.

[292] J. Allain (2001), *op. cit.*, pp. 540–541.

[293] ICJ, *Nicaragua (Merits)*, § 98.

[294] *Ibid.*, § 98.

[295] J. Allain (2001), *op. cit.*, pp. 540–541; and A. Duffy (2008), *op. cit.*, pp. 386–387 and 388–389.

[296] The case will be analysed below in Part 1, Chapter 8. ECtHR, *N. v. UK*, § 44.

[297] UNHCR, *op. cit.*, § 5.

[298] VCLT, Article 53.

order when the act of persecution does not reach such level of severity.[299] In the latter case, should exceptions be applied, their international legality is conditional on compliance with "principles of due process of law and the requirement that all reasonable steps must first be taken to secure the admission of the individual concerned to a safe third country".[300] The requirements that due process of law be respected and steps taken to grant the expellee the opportunity of going to a third State bear witness to the evolution of the concept in international (refugee) law since it was first enshrined, in the Refugee Convention. The 1966 Bangkok Principles (eventually adopted in 2001)[301] and the 1967 United Nations General Assembly Declaration on Territorial Asylum[302] both draw on Article 33 of the Refugee Convention but narrow its exceptions by adding a new paragraph to the provision. Article 3, paragraph 3 of the Declaration on Territorial Asylum stipulates that:

> ... [s]hould a State decide in any case that exception to the principle (...) would be justified, it shall consider the possibility of granting to the person concerned, under such conditions as it may deem appropriate, an opportunity, whether by way of provisional asylum or otherwise, of going to another State.[303]

Later developments in the field of refugee law went even further and enshrined the prohibition of *refoulement* in absolute terms: under Article 2(3) of the AU Refugee Convention,[304] Article 22(8) of the American Convention on Human Rights[305] and Principle 5 of the Cartagena Declaration,[306] *non-refoulement* is

---

299 E. Lauterpacht and D. Bethlehem (2003), *op. cit.*, § 253.
300 *Ibid.*, §§ 253 and 151–159.
301 Bangkok Principles, Article 3.
302 "Declaration on Territorial Asylum" [14 December 1967], *op. cit.*, Article 3.
303 *Ibid.*, Article 3(3). The text corresponds in essence to the previously drafted fourth paragraph (renumbered 3) of Article 3 of the Bangkok Principles.
304 "No person shall be subjected by a Member State to measures such as rejection at the frontier, return or expulsion, which would compel him to return to or remain in a territory where his life, physical integrity or liberty would be threatened for the reasons set out in Article I, paragraphs 1 and 2 [on the definition of the term "refugee"]". AU Refugee Convention, Article 2(3).
305 "In no case may an alien be deported or returned to a country, regardless of whether or not it is his country of origin, if in that country his right to life or personal freedom is in danger of being violated because of his race, nationality, religion, social status, or political opinions". ACHR, Article 22(8).
306 Conclusion 5 reflects the drafters' objective to "reiterate the importance and meaning of the principle of non-refoulement (including the prohibition of rejection at the frontier) as a corner-stone of the international protection of refugees. This principle is imperative

subject to no exception. In international human rights law too, the prohibition of *refoulement* is absolute.[307]

Notwithstanding this distinct trend against exceptions to the principle of *non-refoulement*, it does not appear possible to conclude that the principle is absolute in customary international law: a number of States, including national asylum authorities as well as institutional and academic commentators still appeal to the derogations mentioned in Article 33(2) of the 1951 Refugee Convention to justify, in exceptional circumstances, their decision to expel a refugee (in the broad sense of the term). At EU level, suffice is to recall that the drafters of the Qualification Directive, instead of integrating the above-mentioned developments of international refugee and human rights law, chose to resort to the 1951 Refugee Convention and include in EU asylum law the principle of *non-refoulement* together with its exceptions.[308] In turn, the vast majority of EU Member States, although the Qualification Directive empowers them to introduce or maintain more favourable standards,[309] also chose to include exceptions to the principle of *non-refoulement*.[310] As noted by M.-T. Gil-Bazo:

> In relation to *non-refoulement*, the Council [of the EU] (admittedly, after having consulted with UNHCR), seems to have ignored the evolution of international law regarding this norm over the past 50 years by introducing a clause similar to Article 33(2) of the Geneva Convention in a legally binding instrument of EC law. While this provision may not be at odds with the literal wording of the Geneva Convention, it does not reflect the broader international law obligations of Member States.[311]

From all the above, it can be concluded that in circumstances in which the threat invoked reaches the threshold of torture or inhuman or degrading treatment or punishment, the prohibition of such treatments, as a peremptory norm of international law, carries with it the *jus cogens* nature of the prohibition of *refoulement*. In circumstances however in which the threat of ill-treatment is not or may not be regarded as being on par with a danger of torture, inhuman or degrading treatment or punishment, national authorities

---

in regard to refugees and in the present state of international law should be acknowledged and observed as a rule of *jus cogens*". Cartagena Declaration, Conclusion 5.
307 Above pp. 177s.
308 Qualification Directive, Article 21.
309 *Ibid.*, Preamble, Recital 8.
310 Commission, "Commission Report on the application of QD (2004)", *op. cit.*, p. 12, at 5.5.4.
311 M.T. Gil-Bazo (2006), *op. cit.*, p. 21.

may expel the individual concerned but only in strictly exceptional cases, when the national security or public safety of the host State is jeopardised and provided due process safeguards have been respected and reasonable steps have been taken to ensure the individual will be admitted to a safe third country.

The circumstance that the threat concerns everyone and anyone within a territory is immaterial as long as the criteria set above (the severity of the risk) are met. Protection against *refoulement* is indeed not conditional upon the threat being individually targeted: "the precise identification of the cause of that threat is not material".[312] The extended definitions of refugees enshrined in the AU Convention, in the Cartagena Declaration and, albeit under the name of "beneficiary of subsidiary protection", in the Qualification Directive as well as the equivalent extension of UNHCR Mandate to cover persons who have fled situations of generalised or indiscriminate violence are evidence of the fact that no one can be returned to a life-threatening situation, including when such risk also threatens any other individual removed to the same territory.[313]

Indiscriminate threats are often associated with the notion of "mass influx". Indeed, if anyone within a territory is exposed to a danger for his or her life or person, it can be expected that everyone within that territory will endeavour to escape from such danger, including presumably by leaving this territory, sometimes crossing the international border of the State. It could be argued that the impact of the arrival of a large number of asylum seekers can be regarded as a danger to the security or community of the receiving State. As revealed by the *travaux préparatoires* of the Refugee Convention, the argument was made by Switzerland and supported by the Netherlands, Belgium, Italy, Germany and Sweden during the discussion of the *non-refoulement* provision. It is of some interest to note that of the six countries mentioned, the majority are characterised by their relatively small territory and / or population.[314] Nevertheless, the absence from the text of the Refugee Convention as adopted of any specific provision for the purpose of relieving State Parties to the Convention of their *non-refoulement* obligations in circumstances of mass influx of asylum seekers on their territory suggests that no such exception exists. Additionally, UNHCR Executive Committee has made clear that in all cases of situations of large-scale influx:

---

312   E. Lauterpacht and D. Bethlehem (2003), *op. cit.*, § 139.
313   *Ibid.*, §§ 136–144.
314   Whereas Swedish territory is vast, only a comparatively minor proportion of it is inhabited and its population small in comparison with that of other States involved in the negotiations at the time.

... the fundamental principle of non-refoulement including non-rejection at the frontier must be scrupulously observed.[315]

Further evidence of the applicability of the principle of *non-refoulement* in situations of large influx of asylum seekers in a receiving country include State practice and, at the European Union level, the adoption of the Temporary Protection Directive,[316] which devised a form of protection precisely to ensure that people arriving *en masse* are not returned to life threatening situations.[317] Element of a temporary protection policy, group determination of refugee status on a *prima facie* basis has been analysed by UNHCR as a means of ensuring "admission to safety, protection from *refoulement* and basic humanitarian treatment to those patently in need of it".[318] UNHCR observes the wide application of this practice in Africa and in Latin America.[319]

In conclusion, under customary international law, the principle of *non-refoulement* protects individuals fleeing situations of indiscriminate threat to their life or person, including when those individuals arrive in large groups ("mass influx").

In addition to being protected from *refoulement*, it appears that persons exposed to indiscriminate also receive protection on other grounds. More than the mere negative obligation for States not to expel individuals faced with a risk of proscribed ill-treatment, customary international law also creates a positive obligation to protect individuals confronted with situations of indiscriminate threats to their life or person.

B   *A Positive Obligation to Provide Protection to Persons Exposed to Indiscriminate Threats*

International protection and assistance is traditionally provided to persons exposed to indiscriminate threats in situations of conflicts or generalised violence but also of gross violations of human rights, famine, economic insecurity

---

315   ExCom, "Conclusion No 22 on Large-Scale Influx (1981)", *op. cit.*, § II. A. 2.
316   Temporary Protection Directive.
317   For a detailed account of the appliation and applicability of the principle of *non-refoulement* in cases of mass influx, *see*: E. Lauterpacht and D. Bethlehem (2003), *op. cit.*, §§ 103–111; and J. Rodger, "Defining the Parameters of the Non-Refoulement Principle" (Faculty of Law of Victoria University of Wellington, 2001), retrieved from: <http://www.refugee.org.nz/JessicaR.htm#2> [05/09/2012].
318   UNHCR, "Protection of Refugees in Mass Influx Situations (Global Consultation)", *op. cit.*, § 6.
319   *Ibid.*, § 8.

and poverty.[320] UNHCR, through the extension of its original mandate, is responsible for providing this protection to refugees and displaced persons (a) however it is argued that States also share this obligation under customary international law (b).

1   Evidence of a Consensus: The Broad Support to UNHCR's Protection Activities

Over the years since its creation in 1950, the United Nations High Commissioner for Refugees has seen a gradual extension of its mandate[321] formalised by UN General Assembly resolutions.[322] Originally devised to protect persons falling under the Refugee Convention definition, the category of "people of concern to UNHCR" has grown, sometimes in anticipation of UNGA resolutions,[323]

---

320   UNGA, "Resolution 56/166: Human rights and mass exoduses", A/RES/56/166, 26 February 2002, Preamble Recital 2.
321   I.C. Jackson gives an account of the evolution of UNHCR's Mandate, before and after the adoption of the AU Refugee Convention and Cartagena Declaration, and elaborates on the notions of "good offices" and "broader refugee concept". I.C. Jackson, "The 1951 Convention Relating to the Status of Refugees: A Universal Basis for Protection", *International Journal of Refugee Law*, Vol. 3, No. 3, pp. 403–413, pp. 409–411.
322   In 1968, at a time the African Union (former "Organisation of African Unity" – OAU) has already started working on the adoption of a regional refugee Convention, and similarly in 1969, following the adoption of the Convention Governing the Specific Aspects of Refugee Problems in Africa (which expanded the definition of the term "refugee"), the UN General Assembly requested UNHCR "to continue to provide protection and assistance to refugees who are his concern, while giving special attention to *new groups of refugees*, particularly in Africa". UNGA, "Report of the United Nations High Commissioner for Refugees (1968)" ("1968 Report of UNHCR"), A/RES/2399 (XXIII), 6 December 1968, 1; UNGA, "Report of the United Nations High Commissioner for Refugees (1969)" ("1969 Report of UNHCR"), A/RES/2594 (XXIV), 16 December 1969, 1. A review of some of the resolutions adopted by the General Assembly inform that in many instances, rather than attributing new competences to UNHCR, the General Assembly in fact acknowledges to commend them measures already taken by UNHCR towards persons who do not fall within the 1951 Refugee Convention but whom UNHCR considers in need of protection and/or assistance. See for example: UNGA, "Report of the United Nations High Commissioner for Refugees (1976)" ("1976 Report of UNHCR"), A/RES/31/35 (XXXI), 30 November 1976; UNGA, "Report of the United Nations High Commissioner for Refugees (1975)" ("1975 Report of UNHCR"), A/RES/3454 (XXX), 9 December 1975; UNGA, "Humanitarian assistance to the Indo-Chinese displaced persons", A/RES/3455 (XXX), 9 December 1975.
323   In Latin American States, it is observed that UNHCR occasionally exceeded its mandate, anticipating its extension, and "verged on the provision of international protection within the country of origin". UNHCR's acting "off-mandate" was however either called for or acquiesced in by all concerned parties. R. Cuéllar, *et al.*, "Refugee and Related Developments

to include refugees, asylum-seekers, returned refugees, internally-displaced persons (IDPs),[324] returned IDPs, stateless people and other individuals who do not necessarily fall directly into any of the other categories but to whom UNHCR provide protection or assistance.[325] The sub-category of refugees itself also significantly evolved. It originally corresponded to the definition laid down in the 1951 Refugee Convention but later it expanded, parallel to and as a reflexion of the adoption in Africa then Latin America[326] of broader definitions of the term refugee. As part of its "statutory responsibility for the progressive development of international refugee law and standards",[327] UNHCR must not only promote the adoption and ratification of instruments of international refugee law but also supervise their application.[328] UNHCR, who was closely involved in the drafting process of the various regional instruments, became competent to supervise their application; to wit, it became competent to supervise the provision of protection by African and Latin American to persons fleeing risks of persecution (as defined in the 1951 Refugee Convention) but also to "non-targeted"[329] asylum seekers, who flee "external aggression, occupation, foreign domination or events seriously disturbing public order"[330]

---

in Latin America: Challenges Ahead", *International Journal of Refugee Law*, 1 July 1991, Vol. 3, No. 3 (1991), pp. 482–498, p. 490.

324   Internally-displaced persons (IDPs) are not yet protected under any binding instrument of international law at the global level (at the regional level however, within the framework of the African Union, African States have agreed and adopted in Kampala in October 2009, the African Union Convention for the Protection and Assistance of Internally Displaced Persons in Africa. AU Convention on IDPs.

325   As mentioned, the protection and assistance needs of internally-displaced persons, whose often distressing situation is however repeatedly brought to the fore by humanitarian actors (both institutional and civil society), have not yet garnered the full attention of the international community so that, to date, there exists no binding instrument of international law adopted at the global level and providing for the protection of IDPs. This notwithstanding, in 2011, this category represented the largest group of persons of concern to UNHCR, before refugees. The size of each group of people of concerns to UNHCR (as of 1st January 2011) is available in: UNHCR, *The State of the World's Refugees 2012: In Search of Solidarity* (2012), *op. cit.*, p. 2.

326   It is often observed, although the Cartagena Declaration is not binding in law, it has been "transposed" in national law by most States in the region and is therefore a key indication of the state of international refugee law in the world. The large support manifested by Latin American States to the Cartagena Declaration is mentioned in passing by UNHCR in *The State of the World's Refugees 2012* (*op. cit.*), p. 41.

327   UNHCR, *The State of the World's Refugees 2012: In Search of Solidarity* (2012), *op. cit.*, p. 37.

328   UNHCR Statute, 8(a).

329   T. Einarsen (2011), *op. cit.*, § 80.

330   AU Refugee Convention, Article 1(2); and similarly Cartagena Declaration, Conclusion 3.

or "massive violation of human".³³¹ The adoption of the AU Refugee Convention and of the Cartagena Declaration thus contributed to the extension of UNHCR's mandate;³³² this is confirmed by UNHCR itself who observed in 1994 that the Office of the High Commissioner for Refugees had, for some years already then:

> ... adopted the usage of regional instruments such as the OAU [AU] Refugee Convention and the Cartagena Declaration, using the term "refugee" in the broader sense, to denote persons outside their countries who are in need of international protection because of a serious threat to their life, liberty or security of person in their country of origin as a result of persecution or armed conflict, or serious public disorder.³³³

Over the years, States have "repeatedly reaffirmed their support for UNHCR's mandate activities undertaken to secure international protection for persons fleeing the indiscriminate effects of violence associated with armed conflicts and serious public disorder".³³⁴ States' expression of support to UNHCR's extended mandate – as well as their financial contribution to UNHCR's protection activities³³⁵ – can be viewed as evidence of States' belief that the provision of international protection and, or assistance to persons fleeing situations of armed conflict and serious public disorder is a necessity.

Further evidence that, as a rule, people fleeing indiscriminate threats to their life or person must be granted international protection or assistance emanates from the above-mentioned formal broadening of the scope of UNHCR's mandate. This evolution of UNHCR's responsibilities is the result of a continuing series of UN General Assembly Resolutions.³³⁶ As recalled by UNHCR Executive Committee:

---

331 Cartagena Declaration, Conclusion 3.
332 J.-F. Durieux (2012), *op. cit.*, p. 171. See also above note 1166.
333 UNHCR, "Note on International Protection (1994)", *op. cit.*, § 32.
334 "Annotated Comments on QD (2004)", [January 2005], *op. cit.*, Comment on Article 15(c), p. 32.
335 UNHCR indicates that its budget consists "almost entirely" in voluntary contributions, with 93 percent coming from national governments, 4 percent from inter-governmental organisation and pooled funding mechanisms and 3 from the private sector. UNHCR, "Financial Figures" (© UNHCR, 2001–2012), retrieved from: <http://www.unhcr.org/pages/49c3646c1a.html> [07/09/2012].
336 For an overview of the successive extensions of the UNHCR's Mandate, *see*: D. Lanz, "Subversion or Reinvention? Dilemmas and Debates in the Context of UNHCR's Increasing Involvement with IDPs", *Journal of Refugee Studies*, Vol. 21, No. 2 (2008), pp. 192–209.

UNHCR has often been requested by the United Nations General Assembly to extend protection and assistance to persons who have been forced to seek refuge outside their countries of origin as a result of situations of conflict, and encourages the High Commissioner to continue to provide international protection to such persons, and to seek solutions to the problems arising from their forced displacement, in accordance with relevant General Assembly resolutions[337]

It can be noted that although General Assembly resolutions are not formally legally binding, their legal effect is not insignificant. They may contain rules of law, be declaratory of pre-existing rules of customary international law or play a role in the formation of new customary rules.[338] UNGA resolutions which have progressively led to the extension of UNHCR Mandate do not provide any detailed definition of who is identified under the broad terms "refugees" or "displaced persons". It is therefore for UNHCR to interpret them and extend, if need be, its protection and assistance to groups perceived as falling under any of those terms. The wording of those UNGA resolutions that are relevant to the definition of the High Commissioner's mandate suggests that the General Assembly, who commends UNHCR's work and requests it to pursue its actions, endorses UNHCR's interpretation of its mandate;[339] the resolution often appear to be mere validation, *a posteriori*, of the tasks undertaken by UNHCR.[340] In that sense, the General Assembly refrains from exhaustively listing UNHCR mandate refugees and instead refers to "the various groups of refugees within [UNHCR] competence"[341] or to "those of concern to his Office",[342] thus using UNHCR's own wording.

The breadth of the category of people considered being in need of international protection or assistance is patent in a 2002 resolution of the UN General

---

337 UNHCR ExCom, "Conclusion No. 74 (Vlv) General (1994)" ("Conclusion No. 74 "General" (1994)").
338 D. Akande, "International Organizations", *in* M.D. Evans (Ed.), *International Law* (New York: Oxford, 2003), pp. 269–297, p. 284.
339 See for example: UNGA, "1976 Report of UNHCR", *op. cit*; UNGA, "Resolution 56/166: Human rights and mass exoduses", *op. cit.*
340 In its Resolution on human rights and mass exoduses, the UNGA for instance called upon the UNHCR to "continue to respond to the assistance and protection needs of refugees and other displaced persons worldwide". UNGA, "Resolution 56/166: Human rights and mass exoduses", *op. cit.*, § 7.
341 UNGA, "Report of the United Nations High Commissioner for Refugees (1965)" ("1965 Report of UNHCR"), A/RES/2039 (XX), 7 December 1965.
342 UNGA, "1975 Report of UNHCR", *op. cit.*

Assembly, on "Human rights and mass exoduses". A cross-referenced reading of its Preamble and paragraph 7 informs that the General Assembly calls for the protection of refugees and persons displaced worldwide by "gross violations of human rights, persecution, political and ethnic conflicts, famine and economic insecurity, poverty and generalized violence".[343] The series of resolutions adopted by the United Nations General Assembly, which identify the different categories of persons (including refugees) who are in need of international protection and assistance as well as States' repeated expressions of support and financial contributions to UNHCR activities are evidence of a consensus within the international community that individuals fleeing such harsh situations ought to be internationally protected. This consensus in turns might point at the existence of a rule of customary international law although resolutions adopted by the UN General Assembly identify UNHCR as the main duty-bearer in that context. This notwithstanding, the question remains as to whether any State obligation can be deduced from the observed consensus.

2   States' Obligation to Provide Protection for Individuals Exposed to Indiscriminate Threats

In the specific context of indiscriminate threats, the practice of protecting people arriving in large groups has developed, but on a temporary basis. As observed by G. Goodwin-Gill:

> [Whereas the] conditions which generate a well-founded fear of persecution within an individual are commonly no more compelling than those which cause the flight of thousands from violence and civil unrest (...) States are generally reluctant to grant permanent asylum to the latter, while they are more receptive towards the former.[344]

As a response to situations of large-scale influx, States hence developed the concept of "temporary refuge".[345] On the basis of an analysis of "State practice, expressions of the norm in international bodies, and statements by regional and expert groups", D. Perluss and J.F. Hartman concluded in 1986 that temporary refuge had merged as "a binding principle of customary international law",[346]

---

343   UNGA, "Resolution 56/166: Human rights and mass exoduses", *op. cit.*, 7 read together with Preamble Recital 2.
344   G.S. Goodwin-Gill (1988), *op. cit.*, p. 108.
345   J.F.H. Deborah Perluss, "Temporary Refuge: Emergence of a Customary Norm", *Virginia Journal of International Law*, Vol. 26, No. 3 (1986), pp. 551–626.
346   *Ibid.*, p. 624.

protecting individuals who flee "not from individualised persecution" but from life-threatening situations caused by generalised violence prevailing in their country or origin.[347] The existence of such a legal obligation under international law to grant temporary protection has been amply confirmed since. Continued State practice[348] as well as, at the European Union level for example, the adoption of the Temporary Protection Directive[349] are further evidence of the rule of temporary refuge granted to large-scale groups of people fleeing indiscriminate threats.

It can be argued that beyond a mere prohibition to expel or return individuals exposed to indiscriminate threats in their country of origin, States actually have the obligation to grant those people, whether they come individually, in small groups or in large groups, a protective status. Under EU law, beneficiaries of temporary protection shall be granted at a minimum certain rights including a residence permit for the duration of the temporary protection,[350] the right to be informed in a language they are likely to understand,[351] the right to work (although States may give priority to other categories of non-nationals such as EU citizens or legally resident third-country nationals),[352] access to housing, education (for minors),[353] at least emergency care and essential treatment,[354] and, in certain circumstances, a right to family reunification.[355] State practice and the adoption at the regional level of norms of international law which extend the 1951 Refugee Convention definition or create new regimes of complementary forms of protection and which all grant a status (a more or less extensive catalogue or rights), buttress the contention.

In Europe, discussions were initiated at institutional level within the Council of Europe and European Union on the adoption of common standards of protection for persons who did not qualify for refugee status after it had been

---

347   *Ibid.*, p. 597.
348   Ivor C. Jackson gives a thorough analysis of the evolution of the refugee concept in group situations (prima facie status determination and temporary protection) in law and State practice in Africa, Asia, Central America and Europe, from the 1940s (with the creation of the International Refugee Organisation) until the 1990s. I.C. Jackson, *The Refugee Concept in Group Situations* (The Hague: Kluwer Law International, 1999).
349   Temporary Protection Directive, *op. cit.*
350   *Ibid.*, Article 8.
351   *Ibid.*, Article 9.
352   *Ibid.*, Article 12.
353   *Ibid.*, Article 14.
354   *Ibid.*, Article 13, (1), (2) and (4).
355   *Ibid.*, Article 15.

acknowledged that most Member States had already adopted such forms of protection, intended to fill in the gaps of refugee law, by providing protection to persons fleeing non-targeted threats in particular. At the EU level, the aim pursued by the institutions was to harmonise the widely varying State practice in that respect, in order to avoid secondary movements within the territory of the Union[356] among other reasons. In 2005, commenting on the Qualification Directive, UNHCR confirmed the observation made by European institutions and noted the existence of a consistent State pattern of granting international protection "to persons risking indiscriminate but serious threats as a result of armed conflict or generalized violence".[357] The State practice of providing some form of protection to individuals fleeing indiscriminate threats therefore preceded the adoption of the EU Qualification Directive and the creation of the subsidiary protection. Prior to the adoption of the Directive however, European Union States were not legally bound to grant any protective status to persons to whom refugee status did not apply. Where States did grant a status, it was often on a discretionary basis or pursuant to their national law. It is therefore not possible to affirm that States did so out of the belief that they had the legal obligation to grant protection in such cases; some States have in fact sought to characterise the protection they granted in such cases as "a sovereign humanitarian act or a duty under national (including constitutional) law, rather than deriving from any international obligation".[358] Some other States, on the other hand, invoked compliance with their obligations under international human rights law.[359]

---

356 Qualification Directive, Preamble Recital 13.

357 "Annotated Comments on QD (2004)", [January 2005], op. cit., p. 32.

358 J. McAdam, Complementary Protection in International Refugee Law (2007), op. cit., p. 42.

359 In the Netherlands, admission for "compelling humanitarian reasons", to which attached the granting of a package of rights and benefits identical to refugee status, could be granted in cases in which return to his or her country of origin would be in breach of the ECHR or of the CAT Convention. See EU Council, "Note from the General Secretariat of the Council to the Asylum Working Party: Compilation of Replies to Questionnaire on Complementary Forms of Protection", 8378/01 ASILE 27, 3 May 2001, op. cit., Replies of the Netherlands, p. 28. In the United Kingdom, the Home Secretary had to grant "exceptional leave to remain" to any persons who did not meet the requirements of the Refugee Convention but whom return would expose to treatments proscribed under Article 3 or 8 ECHR. It conferred upon its beneficiaries a package of rights, albeit less favourable than refugee status. Ibid., Replies of the United Kingdom, pp. 39–40. In France, the legislator introduced in 1998 a form of protection, complementary to refugee status: "territorial asylum". It could be granted by the Minister of the Interior to individuals exposed in their country of origin to threats to their life or freedom, or to treatments proscribed under Article 3 ECHR. France: Loi no 98-349 du 11 mai 1998 relative à l'entrée et au séjour des

A second element strengthening the existence of a State obligation to provide protection to individuals exposed to indiscriminate threats refers back to the above-mentioned UNGA resolutions, reaffirming or extending UNHCR's mandate. The expansion of UNHR's mandate placed upon it the duty to provide protection and assistance to, *inter alia*, persons fleeing indiscriminate threats to their life or person. Although those resolutions are chiefly addressed to UNHCR, it is noticeable that they are also, to some extent, addressed to States: the General Assembly indeed often also calls upon national governments to cooperate with each other and with humanitarian actors (including UNHCR) and to, for example, "respond to the assistance and protection needs of refugees and other displaced persons worldwide".[360] As mentioned, it is not one but a series of UNGA resolutions that have empowered UNHCR to act pursuant to a growing mandate. In the Nuclear Weapons Advisory Opinion, the ICJ noted that "a series of resolutions may show the gradual evolution of the *opinio juris* required for the establishment of a new rule".[361] Accordingly, the repeated adoption by the UNGA of resolutions encouraging or requesting UNHCR and, often also States, to effectively address the protection needs of persons fleeing indiscriminate violence might be the manifestation of an *opinio juris*. This approach must however be nuanced, at least in the present case, given the fact that most (if not all?) of those General Assembly resolutions, pertinent to define people of concerns to UNHCR, were adopted without a vote and hence, without States expressing their view on the matter. As a consequence, there is no voting pattern to analyse, which could cast a light on the existence or emergence of an *opinio juris*.[362] The consistency with which those resolutions have been adopted for nearly five decades nevertheless prompts one to attach importance to them. To this end, the following appreciation of the relation between resolutions and custom appears relevant: a resolution or, *a fortiori*, a series of consistent resolutions, "may more or less passively evidence (…) the existence of rules of customary international law or they may contribute actively to the formation of customary law".[363] Whether the successive General

---

étrangers en France et au droit d'asile of 11 May 1998 (hereafter "Loi no 98–349") [12 mai 1998] *JORF*, 109, p. 7087, Article 36.

360 UNGA, "Resolution 56/166: Human rights and mass exoduses", *op. cit.*, §§ 3–7.

361 ICJ, *Legality of the Threat or Use of Nuclear Weapons, Advisory Opinion* ("*Nuclear Weapons case*"), I.C.J. Reports 1996 (8 July 1996), p. 226, § 70.

362 M.D. Öberg, "The Legal Effects of Resolutions of the UN Security Council and General Assembly in the Jurisprudence of the ICJ", *European Journal of International Law*, November 2005, Vol. 16, No. 5 (2005), pp. 879–906, pp. 900–904.

363 R.A. Müllerson, *Ordering Anarchy: International Law in International Society* (The Hague: Martinus Nijhoff Publishers, 2000), p. 234.

Assembly resolutions which contributed to the progressive expansion of UNHCR mandate are evidence of the existence of a rule of customary international law or participated in its formation, or both may not be easy to establish[364] (partly due to their adoption without vote) – nor is it actually essential, for the main argument here is that the rule now is in existence. However, should doubts persist on the value of General Assembly's repeated calls for action by UNHCR and States for the protection of persons exposed to indiscriminate threats, it seems possible to read the resolutions not in isolation but against a backdrop of congruent State practice and of instruments of international law adopted at the regional levels of Africa, Latin America, the European Union as well as in Asia and in the Arab States. In this light, it is possible to assert that the development of UNHCR mandate should indeed not be overlooked. G.S. Goodwin-Gill in fact reaches the same conclusion and observes:

> This development might be described as purely functional, enabling the UNHCR to provide limited protection and assistance, but not otherwise entailing legally binding obligations. State practice and conventional international law, however, suggest otherwise.[365]

Let us now turn to those instruments of international law which were adopted at the regional level and buttress the conclusion of the existence in customary international law of a positive obligation for States to provide protection to persons fleeing indiscriminate threats to their life or person.

In some regions of the world, instruments of international law have come to the rescue of State practice and formally broadened the Geneva Convention refugee definition to bring victims of indiscriminate violence into its ambit. Such is the case in Africa and Latin America. The Organisation of African Unity (replaced in 2002 by the "African Union" – hereinafter "AU") adopted in 1969 the Convention Governing the Specific Aspects of Refugee Problems in Africa. It reproduces Article 1(A)2 of the 1951 Refugee Convention but complements its refugee definition by adding the following paragraph:

> The term "refugee" shall also apply to every person who, owing to external aggression, occupation, foreign domination or events seriously disturbing public order in either part or the whole of his country of origin

---

364 R.A. Müllerson notes that those two functions performed by General Assembly resolutions "may often be almost indistinguishable". *Ibid.*, p. 234.
365 G.S. Goodwin-Gill (1988), *op. cit.*, p. 104.

or nationality, is compelled to leave his place of habitual residence in order to seek refuge in another place outside his country of origin or nationality.[366]

It is noteworthy that, whereas the requirement exists in the 1951 Geneva Convention, the African Union Convention does not require the refugee to show that he or she is personally at risk: under the AU Refugee Convention, refugee status is not conditioned upon the demonstration of a direct link between the refugee and the future harm invoked.[367] By moving away from the Refugee Convention requirement of a "well-founded fear of persecution", the AU Refugee Convention "explicitly gave credence to the fact that a refuge exodus could be the result of factors of a more general nature, intrinsic to the particular country in question, rather than to the individual subjective status or fears of the refugee".[368]

Following the precedent in Africa, where the AU legislator was "able to translate into a regional instrument progress achieved in State and international practice in addressing the concrete issues presented by massive refugee flows, even as these were still taking place", Latin America States agreed on a similar approach.[369] In a lengthy but explicit paragraph, the 1984 Cartagena Declaration on Refugees details and justifies the refugee definition it recommends Latin American states to adopt:

> ... in view of the experience gained from the massive flows of refugees in the Central American area, it is necessary to consider enlarging the concept of a refugee, bearing in mind, as far as appropriate and in the light of the situation prevailing in the region, the precedent of the OAU Convention (article 1, paragraph 2) and the doctrine employed in the reports of the Inter-American Commission on Human Rights. Hence the definition or concept of a refugee to be recommended for use in the region is one which, in addition to containing the elements of the 1951 Convention and the 1967 Protocol, includes among refugees persons who have fled their country because their lives, safety or freedom have been threatened by generalized violence, foreign aggression, internal conflicts, massive

---

366 AU Refugee Convention, Article 1 (2).
367 Human Rights Education Associates – HREA, "Study Guide: Refugees and Displaced Persons" (© HREA, 1997–2007), retrieved from: <http://www.hrea.org/index.php?doc_id=418> [06/06/2012].
368 J. Oloka-Onyango, "Human Rights, the Oau Convention and the Refugee Crisis in Africa: Forty Years after Geneva", *International Journal of Refugee Law*, Vol. 3, No. 3 (1991), p. 455.
369 R. Cuéllar, et al. (1991), *op. cit.*, p. 484.

violation of human rights or other circumstances which have seriously disturbed public order.³⁷⁰

Their existence however bears witness of the acknowledgement in both Africa and Latin America of States' obligation to provide protection to individuals fleeing indiscriminate threats to their lives, safety or freedom.

The AU instrument is a convention therefore its provisions are binding upon all its Contacting States. Fifty-three African States are Members of the African Union out of which a vast majority (forty-five) are parties to the AU Convention. In practice, the provision is often applied in African countries: refugee status is "widely provided, often on a *prima facie* basis, for persons fleeing [situations of indiscriminate threats]".³⁷¹ The 1984 Cartagena Declaration on the other hand is not legally binding. It was not drafted by a regional organisation but emerged out of a colloquium gathering an *ad hoc* group of experts and representatives from Central-American governments; its original scope was that of an "academic reflection and recommendation of principle".³⁷² Despite the Cartagena Declaration lacking formal legal binding force, many Latin American States have relied on its definition to grant refugee status,³⁷³ some having directly transposed its provision into their national legislation.³⁷⁴ Moreover, the Cartagena Declaration has been consistently endorsed by the General Assembly of the Organisation of American States who encouraged States who had not done it already to also endorse it too³⁷⁵ and has gained recognition and support outside Latin America too, including in the United Nations General Assembly.³⁷⁶

Following on the path paved by African and Latin American law, the European legislator adopted the Qualification Directive. The creation of a regime of "subsidiary protection" serves a similar purpose: it extends States' obligation

---

370 Cartagena Declaration, Conclusion 3.
371 UNHCR, "Providing International Protection Including Through Complementary Forms of Protection", EC/55/SC/CRP.16, 2 June 2005, § 9.
372 R. Cuéllar, *et al.* (1991), *op. cit.*, p. 484.
373 UNHCR, "Providing International Protection Including Through Complementary Forms of Protection", *op. cit.*, § 9.
374 It is the case of Mexico for example. Mexico: Ley de Refugiados Y Protección Complementaria of 9 December 2010, entered into force 28 January 2011 [27 January 2011] *Diário Oficial de la Federación*, Article 13 (II) and (III).
375 *See* for instance OAS General Assembly, "Resolution on the Legal Situation of Refugees, Returnees and Displaced Persons in the American Hemisphere", AG/RES.1170 (XXII-0/92), 23 May 1992, Resolution 3.
376 R. Cuéllar, *et al.* (1991), *op. cit.*, p. 487.

to provide protection beyond refugee status to cases where an individual's life or person are threatened by reason of indiscriminate violence in situations of armed conflict.[377] The adoption of the Qualification Directive in fact brings coherence in the international refugee law system: it ensures that individuals coming from an African or Latin American country where they risk be exposed to indiscriminate threats to life or person and seeking protection in Europe are eligible to international protection as they would have been, had they stayed in their region of origin – provided European States do not adopt an overly restrictive interpretation of the terms of the Directive (such as Article 15(c) "armed conflict").[378] Although the scope of subsidiary protection in situations of indiscriminate threats is essentially equivalent to that of the protection provided in Africa and Latin America in similar circumstances pursuant to the extended refugee definition, it can nevertheless be noted that, from the point of view of UNHCR in particular:

> The co-existence within the world-wide regime of both "refugee" and "non-refugee/subsidiary" definitions, covering in essence the same situations, induces a sort of institutional schizophrenia.[379]

Perhaps from a UNHCR institutional point of view, the adoption of an extended definition of refugee rather than the creation of a complementary form or protection would have been preferable.[380] This notwithstanding, the co-existence of international protection regimes designed to protect persons fall outside the traditional scope of refugee protection under the 1951 Convention reinforces the contention that the positive obligation for States to provide protection to individuals fleeing indiscriminate threats forms part of customary international law. Turning to the Asia region further confirms it.

In the Asia region, the text of the 1966 Bangkok Principles on the Status and Treatment of Refugees was revised and adopted in June 2001 by the Asian-African Legal Consultative Organization (AALCO) in New Delhi. The

---

377   Above pp. 124s and Qualification Directive, Article 15(c).
378   In that sense, UNHCR in fact recommends EU Member States to adopt a "humanitarian and protection-oriented approach" to the interpretation of Article 15(c), in line with its object and purpose, rather than a "restrictive and extremely technical" one having the unfortunate result that "the same people the international community seeks to protect and assist when they flee to countries in their region of origin are regularly found not to be in need of protection when they reach Europe". UNHCR, et al., *Safe at Last?* (July 2011), *op. cit.*, p. 102.
379   J.-F. Durieux (2012), *op. cit.*, p. 171.
380   See UNHCR's call for a "humanitarian and protection-oriented" interpretation of Article 15(c). Above note 1222.

refugee definition therein laid is similar to that in the AU Refugee Convention. According to the members of the AALCO, the Bangkok Principles aim in particular at "inspiring Member States for enacting national legislation for the Status and Treatment of Refugees and as a guide to deal with the refugee problems".[381] Accordingly, and as described by the Bangkok Principles themselves, the definition is declaratory and non-binding.[382] This notwithstanding, the "notes, comments and reservations" made by the Member States of AALCO at the time of signature are informative. As made clear by the Bangkok Principles, those notes, comments and reservations "are an integral part" of the Principles. Among the forty-four AALCO States who participated in the drafting process, twenty-three of whom are not parties either to the Refugee Convention or to its Protocol,[383] only three expressed concerns or reservations on the adoption of the expanded refugee definition.[384]

From this survey of existing law, practices and endorsed principles, it appears that the need to protect individual fleeing indiscriminate threats to their life or person has been acknowledged by a vast majority of States in Africa, Europe, Latin America, the Middle East and Asia. If follows that the granting of protection to persons exposed in their country of origin to indiscriminate threats is, under customary international law, a positive obligation for States. It applies in situations where indiscriminate threats originate in armed conflicts as well as in events or circumstances seriously disturbing public order. The latter notion is found within both the AU Convention, the Cartagena Declaration and the Bangkok Principles is particularly appealing to who seeks to identify environmentally-displaced persons as refugees under any of the two instruments or under customary international law for that matter. Its relevance will be discussed in the following part.

---

381   Bangkok Principles, Introductory remarks, p. 6.
382   *Ibid.*
383   The figure is based on the status of ratification of the Refugee Convention and 1967 Protocol relating to the Status of Refugees, as compared with the list of AALCO Member States. *Status of Multilateral Treaties Deposited with the Secretary-General* © United Nations, 2012, retrieved from: <http://treaties.un.org> [08/09/2012].
384   Bahrain proposed the deletion of the phrase "disturbing public order in either part or the whole of his country of origin or nationality". Singapore and India opposed the adoption of the expanded definition of refugees altogether, in fear that this may result in "undue pressures on receiving states in dealing with large number of refugees" (Singapore). India noted that the "universally accepted criteria of "well-founded fear of persecution" should remain the core of the definition" and warned that the proposed expansion of the definition risked jeopardise the adoption of durable solutions for refugees and weaken refugee protection. Bangkok Principles, Notes, Comments and reservations made by the Member States of AALCO, on Article 1, §§ 1, 3 and 5, p. 6.

CHAPTER 4

Member States' Non-harmonised Protection Responses

In 2012, on the basis of data provided by the Ministries of Interior, Justice or immigration agencies of the Member States, Eurostat – statistical office of the EU – observed the repartition of first instance decisions made by Member States in 2011 on asylum applications. Among the positive decisions, the proportion of authorisation to stay granted for humanitarian reasons, *i.e.* reasons other than those that trigger refugee status or subsidiary protection, is significant.

> In 2011 in the EU27, 237 400 first instance decisions were made on asylum applications. There were 177 900 rejections (75% of decisions), 29 000 applicants (12%) were granted refugee status, 21 400 (9%) subsidiary protection and 9 100 (4%) authorisation to stay for humanitarian reasons. It should be noted that first instance decisions made in 2011 may refer to applications registered in previous years.[1]

The Qualification Directive makes it clear that it does not apply to "third-country nationals or stateless persons who are allowed to remain in the territories of the Member States for reasons not due to a need for international protection but on a discretionary basis on compassionate or humanitarian grounds".[2] The above figures illustrate that the 9 100 authorisations to stay "for humanitarian reasons" granted by Member States are protection granted outside the scope of the Directive. It follows that Member States recognise certain protection needs outside the existing protection scheme devised by the Qualification Directive. It should be added that, in some countries, subsidiary protection may be granted on grounds not covered by the Qualification Directive[3] – which does

---

1 Eurostat, *Asylum in the EU27: The number of asylum applicants registered in the EU27 rose to 301 000 in 2011*, News Release issue no. 46/2012, 23 March 2012, p. 1.
2 Qualification Directive, Preamble, Recital 15.
3 In Portugal, subsidiary protection may be granted for "humanitarian reasons" and in Germany, when deportation would be in breach of the ECHR or would expose the individual concerned to "a substantial concrete danger to his or her life and limb or liberty", as summarised in European Migration Network – EMN, *The Different Practices Concerning Granting of Non-EU Harmonised Protection Statuses* (n/a: EMN, December 2010), p. 21 and ANNEXES, Table 1, retrieved from: <http://emn.intrasoft-intl.com/Downloads/prepareShowFiles.do?directoryID=122> [01/06/2011]; and Serviço de estrangeiros e fronteiras – SEF, "Portugal

not appear in the above figures but reinforce the view that subsidiary protection as it is devised in the Qualification Directive does not cover effectively all international protection needs falling outside the scope of refugee protection. Two conclusions could be drawn from this observation. Firstly, refugee status together with subsidiary protection, as they are currently construed under EU law, fails to address the international protection needs of every internationally displaced person. Secondly, uninterrupted by the adoption of the Qualification Directive and the creation thereby of "subsidiary protection" as a complement to refugee status, the continued practice of national asylum authorities to occasionally grant complementary protection on humanitarian grounds demonstrates that, *de lege lata*, EU asylum law fails to meet every international protection needs. It could also be argued that States choose to (mis)interpret the Qualification Directive in such a way as to deny its protection and instead grant national forms of protection, given the often less generous status (if any) which attaches to such non-harmonised protection. However, the present Chapter will only focus on those grounds for complementary protection which appear to genuinely apply in cases not covered by subsidiary protection under the Directive. In such cases, States acknowledge that there exist scenarios where a person who qualifies for neither of the two protective statuses nevertheless has a valid claim for international protection given the impossibility of his or her returning to his or her country of origin. Subsidiary protection was intended to remedy the inadequacies of refugee status protection whose grant was too narrowly circumscribed by the requirement of a discriminatory ground for persecution to effectively protect all persons in need of international protection. The above suggests it does not.

Authorisations to stay accorded on humanitarian grounds represent a significant part (4%) of first instance decisions and, by deduction from Eurostat figures cited above, to more than 15% of positive decisions. In order to have an accurate global picture of what international protection means within the European Union, it is therefore necessary that we identify the factual or personal elements of an asylum claim that States analyse as so-called "humanitarian reasons"[4] for granting some form of protection to the applicant.

Should a common pattern appear in Member States' practice, concerning certain categories of asylum seekers who are not currently protected de *lege*

National Report (November 2009) Protection Statuses Complementing EU Legislation Regarding Immigration and Asylum in Portugal", *in* EMN *Study on The Different Practices Concerning Granting of Non-EU Harmonised Protection Statuses* (n/a: EMN, December 2010), p. 12, retrieved from: <http://emn.intrasoft-intl.com/Downloads/download.do;jsessionid=48CB45 E0CA5EB4C57AD0BB871285B576?fileID=852> [06/06/2011].

4 Qualification Directive, Preamble Recital 15.

lata in EU law, it might be evidence of or develop into a norm of customary law, if only regional. Additionally, the drafting history of subsidiary protection illustrates that State practice can impact on EU law. Subsidiary protection was incorporated into EU asylum law in order to harmonise the existing widespread State practice to protect asylum seekers who failed to fulfil the criteria for refugee status but were found to be nevertheless in need of international protection. It is reasonable to think that a similar bottom-up legislative process could unfold again if a common practice of protecting environmentally-displaced persons were to develop among Member States. For this reason too, and by anticipation of the second part where the rules and practices identified in this part will be tested in the context of displacement triggered by environmental change, the following will examine what EU law analyses as humanitarian reasons for protection and whether those include environmental degradation.

As mentioned, States had already prior to the adoption of the Qualification Directive felt the need to fill in the gaps of international law and made provisions for the protection of persons falling outside the scope of the Geneva Convention. Those forms of protection, complementary to refugee status, often corresponded to obligations that were (and are still[5]) incumbent on States under international human rights law. They generally reflected the prohibition of *refoulement* enshrined, explicitly or implicitly, in the conventions EU Member States were and are Parties to (the ECHR, the ICCPR and the CAT Convention). Indeed, national asylum authorities commonly considered risks of death penalty, execution or torture as reasons to grant some form of protection to the individual concerned.[6]

Beyond those "clear-cut" cases, whose reality was acknowledged by the European legislator adopting the Qualification Directive (Article 15), some States have also recognised other grounds of protection, also based on their obligations under international human rights law, but which were not reproduced in the Qualification Directive (I). Such grounds include the right to health, the right to private and family life, and the rights of the child. Lastly, some States also chose to provide protection in cases which did not – at least not explicitly – fall within the ambit of international human rights law requirements. For example, some States have chosen to grant a residence permit to individuals who have achieved a significant level of social integration in the host country. Other examples include poor conditions of living in the destination country and environmental disaster (II). This part does not purport to give a comprehensive

---

5   See Part 1, introductory remarks on the prevalence of international obligations of States despite their joining the European Union.
6   ECRE, *Complementary Protection in Europe* (July 2009), *op. cit.*, p. 5.

overview of all complementary forms of protection existing at the national level within the European Union. It will provide examples of forms of protection, bearing in mind the purpose of this work, to wit, the identification, if possible, of forms of protection applicable in cases of indiscriminate threats resulting from the degradation of the environment in the applicant's country of origin.

In comparison with the broad range of protection grounds listed above, the complementary form of protection introduced in Community law by Qualification Directive Article 15, *i.e.* subsidiary protection, appears to be of narrower scope. More accurately maybe, it could be described as inadequate in view of the fact that many EU Member States who have transposed the Qualification Directive in their national legal system have maintained additional forms of complementary protection.

1   Protection Grounds Based on International Obligations

Within this category, two sub-categories appear: some provisions of national asylum legislation reflect certain specific obligations of States deriving from human rights treaties they are parties to while some others are worded in general terms (so-called "blanket clauses"[7]). As regards the first group, of grounds for complementary protection based on specific provisions of international human rights law, several human rights are commonly invoked. Those rights include typically the right to life and prohibition of torture, the right to private and family life (including family unity), the right to health, and the rights of the child. In all such cases, national legislation and authorities may or may not refer explicitly to the corresponding provision of the ECHR in particular or of another instrument of international law (such as the UN Convention Against Torture in Luxembourg[8]).

Developments below will focus on the United Kingdom and Germany where such protection clauses exist and refer in large part to the ECHR. Albeit not

---

7 *Ibid.*, p. 6.
8 In Luxembourg for example, authorities may not return an individual to a country where his or her life or freedom are threatened or if he or she risks be exposed there to treatments proscribed under Article 3 ECHR or Articles 1 and 3 of the Convention Against Torture. Grand-Duché de Luxembourg: Loi du 29 août 2008 portant sur la libre circulation des personnes et l'immigration (hereafter "Loi sur la libre circulation des personnes et l'immigration") [10 September 2008] *Mémorial A*, n° 138, last amended by Loi du 1er juillet 2011 modifiant la loi modifiée du 29 août 2008 sur la libre circulation des personnes et l'immigration et la loi modifiée du 5 mai 2006 relative au droit d'asile et à des formes complémentaires de protection of 1 July 2011, [25 July 2011] *Mémorial A n° 151*, p. 2179, Article 129.

designed specifically to address situations where threats are indiscriminate (such as threats originating in situations of armed conflicts can be), they can apply in such cases. In the United Kingdom for instance Discretionary Leave (a form of protection complementary to refugee status and subsidiary protection) can be granted in cases of "severe humanitarian conditions meeting the Article 3 threshold".[9]

In the United Kingdom, three protection regimes exist after the transposition of the Qualification Directive in the national legal system. Those regimes are to be envisaged following a sequential procedure. Individuals seeking protection may be granted refugee status,[10] Humanitarian Protection (which corresponds to subsidiary protection as defined by the Qualification Directive)[11] or Discretionary Leave.[12] Discretionary Leave[13] is considered to be an authorisation to stay rather than a protection status.[14]

Subsidiary protection (*i.e.* in the UK "Humanitarian Protection") is granted in cases involving a real risk of serious harm proscribed under Article 2 (right to life), Protocol 13 (prohibition of the death penalty) or, mainly, Article 3 of the European Convention for Human Rights. Discretionary Leave on the other hand covers "other Article 3 cases"[15] but also cases in which applicants invoke a breach of another article of the ECHR.[16]

---

9   Home Office UK Border Agency, "Asylum Process Guidance: Considering Human Rights Claims" ("APG Human Rights Claims"), last updated 10 August 2012, p. 21 at: <www.ukba.homeoffice.gov.uk/sitecontent/documents/policyandlaw/asylumprocessguidance/consideringanddecidingtheclaim/guidance/consideringhrclaims.pdf?view=Binary>.

10 UK: Immigration Rules, Part 11b – Asylum, Last Updated October 2012 (hereafter "Immigration Rules"), §§ 334–339BA.

11 *Ibid.*, §§ 339C–339H.

12 Humanitarian Protection and Discretionary Leave replace the former Exceptional Leave to Remain.

13 Discretionary Leave is granted outside the Immigration Rules. Home Office UK Border Agency, "Asylum Policy Instructions: Discretionary Leave", Last updated 13 July 2012, at: <www.ukba.homeoffice.gov.uk/sitecontent/documents/policyandlaw/asylumpolicyinstructions/apis/discretionaryleave.pdf?view=Binary>.

14 L. Rice and Kiren Vadher for the Home Office UK Border Agency, "UK National Report (March 2010): Practices in the UK Concerning the Granting of Non-EU Harmonised Protection Statuses and Leave to Remain", *in EMN Study on The Different Practices Concerning Granting of Non-EU Harmonised Protection Statuses* (n/a: EMN, December 2010), p. 8, retrieved from: <http://emn.intrasoft-intl.com/Downloads/download.do;jsessionid=48CB45E0CA5EB4C57AD0BB871285B576?fileID=1001> [01/06/2011].

15 The UK Border Agency clarifies that whereas "Humanitarian Protection overlaps considerably with Articles 2 and 3 of the ECHR (plus Protocol 13) (…) there may be some cases where a person who does not qualify for Humanitarian Protection will still have a successful Article 3 claim and may get Discretionary Leave". "APG Human Rights Claims", *op. cit.*, p. 5.

16 *Ibid.*, pp. 13–14.

In the UK Border Agency's analysis, United Kingdom's obligations under Article 3 ECHR may apply in cases which do not fall under the Qualification Directive. This includes cases where an applicant's reprehensible or criminal conduct excludes him or her from subsidiary protection[17] (*i.e.* "Humanitarian Protection").[18] This interpretation is indeed in compliance with Article 3 of the ECHR which prohibits *refoulement* regardless of the applicant's behaviour and of the danger he or she may pose to the host country's national security.[19] Other examples of cases where individuals may not qualify for subsidiary protection but be granted Discretionary Leave in accordance with UK's perceived obligations under Article 3 ECHR include medical cases.[20] When a person claims that return would expose him or her to a risk of Article 3 ill-treatment because of his or her medical condition, this risk arises because of a lesser level of healthcare available in the country of origin and of the applicant's personal circumstances. According to the Border Agency, those persons are therefore "not in need of international protection"[21] and hence not eligible for Humanitarian Protection. In such cases, the threshold of Article 3 will be reached only "in rare and extreme circumstances", where applicants can show "exceptional circumstances that prevent return, namely that there are compelling humanitarian considerations such as the applicant being in the final stages of a terminal illness without prospect of medical care or family support on return".[22]

Additionally, Discretionary Leave may be granted in "extreme cases" where the applicant would face upon return such "severe humanitarian conditions" (including for example absence of water, food or basic shelter) that removal in itself would result in a breach of Article 3.[23] Because the harm invoked originates in poor general conditions in the country, those cases, like medical cases, are construed as "not protection-related cases", hence the applicant's qualification for Discretionary Leave rather than subsidiary protection.[24]

---

17 Exclusion clauses are enumerated in the UK Immigration Rules. Immigration Rules, *op. cit.*, paragraph 339 D.
18 "APG Human Rights Claims", *op. cit.*, p. 17.
19 Above pp. 202s.
20 "APG Human Rights Claims", *op. cit.*, p. 19.
21 Home Office UK Border Agency, "Asylum Policy Instructions: Humanitarian Protection" ("API Humanitarian Conditions"), Last updated 13 July 2012, p. 11 at: <www.ukba.home office.gov.uk/sitecontent/documents/policyandlaw/asylumpolicyinstructions/apis/humanitarian-protection.pdf?view=Binary>.
22 "APG Human Rights Claims", *op. cit.*
23 *Ibid.*, p. 21.
24 "API Humanitarian Conditions", *op. cit.*, p. 11.

In cases where applicants invoke other ECHR rights to oppose their being returned to their country of origin, the threshold is high. It is required that substantial grounds exist for believing that there is a real risk that return will expose the applicant to a "flagrant violation of the very essence of the right" invoked[25] and the relevant threshold is high. The House of Lords emphasised the high threshold of "flagrant violation" in the *Ullah and Do* judgment: a "flagrant violation" was defined as a case "where the right will be completely denied or nullified in the destination country".[26] The Border Agency notes that given this very high threshold, it is only in exceptional cases that treatment in the country of return will engage the UK's obligations under ECHR, other than Article 3.[27] The Border Agency notes that those other ECHR rights invoked by applicants in the UK are mainly the right to liberty and security (Article 5 ECHR), right to a fair trial (Article 6 ECHR), freedom of thought, conscience and religion (Article 9 ECHR) and freedom of expression (Article 10 ECHR). The high threshold set for the engagement of those rights is justified in view of their derogability under the Convention.[28] Medical cases may also fall under this category of cases where rights other than Article 3 ECHR are invoked: the right to private life (Article 8) may indeed be raised in the context of a medical claim.[29] The "flagrant violation" test then applies, however, as observed by the House of Lords, "it is not easy to think of a foreign health care case which would fail under Article 3 but succeed under Article 8".[30] In other words, the complete denial or nullification of the right to private life would generally amount to inhuman or degrading treatment proscribed under Article 3 ECHR.

In Germany, subsidiary protection may be granted on grounds not covered by the Qualification Directive. These include cases in which deportation would be inadmissible under the terms of the European Convention for Human Rights,[31] or when deportation would expose the individual concerned to

---

25 UK: UKHL, *Regina v. Special Adjudicator (Respondent) Ex Parte Ullah (Fc) (Appellant); Do (Fc) (Appellant) v. Secretary of State for the Home Department (Respondent)* ("*Ullah and Do*"), [2004] UKHL 26, 17 June 2004, § 50.
26 *Ibid.*, § 69.
27 "APG Human Rights Claims", *op. cit.*, p. 14.
28 *Ibid.*, p. 14. *See* also: "UK National Report (March 2010): Practices in the UK Concerning the Granting of Non-EU Harmonised Protection Statuses and Leave to Remain", *op. cit.*, pp. 8–9.
29 "APG Human Rights Claims", *op. cit.*, p. 19.
30 UK, *Regina v. Secretary of State for the Home Department Ex Parte Razgar* ("*Regina v. Secretary of State for the Home Department Ex Parte Razgar*"), 17 June 2004 [2004] UKHL 27, § 59.
31 Section 60(5) of German's "Residence Act" reads: "*Ein Ausländer darf nicht abgeschoben werden, soweit sich aus der Anwendung der Konvention vom 4. November 1950 zum Schutze*

"a substantial concrete danger to his or her life and limb or liberty".[32] It is noted that where inadmissibility under the ECHR is invoked, applicants must establish that the danger emanates from the state or from a quasi-state organisation, or can be attributed to the state due to its inability to protect the individual concerned. The same is however not required where danger to life and limb or liberty is invoked.[33] The latter ground includes significant or life-threatening deterioration of the applicant's health in the absence of treatment in the country of origin.[34] It can be noted that this national form of subsidiary protection in Germany accounts for a large part of positive decisions: in 2009, half the decisions to grant subsidiary protection were based on the latter ground.[35]

Besides such protection grounds, anchored in States' international obligations, national law and practice may grant some form of protection without reference to any obligation of the State under international law. States then choose to grant protection on a discretionary basis. In such cases, national law and practice vary greatly from one State to another. These cases are referred to below as forms of protection granted on discretionary grounds.

II   Discretionary Grounds for Complementary Protection

National law and practice is characterised by its heterogeneity when it comes to protection statuses granted on non-harmonised grounds, in particular where States do not explicitly refer to their obligations under international law.

---

der Menschenrechte und Grundfreiheiten (...) ergibt, dass die Abschiebung unzulässig ist". Germany: Gesetz über den Aufenthalt, die Erwerbstätigkeit und die Integration von Ausländern im Bundesgebiet of 30 July 2004, in the version published of 25 February 2008 (hereafter "AufenthG") *BGBl. I*, p. 162, last amended by Article 1 and Article 6, § 2 of the Law of 1 June 2012, *BGBl. I*, p. 1224, Section 60(5).

[32]   "*Von der Abschiebung eines Ausländers in einen anderen Staat soll abgesehen werden, wenn dort für diesen Ausländer eine erhebliche konkrete Gefahr für Leib, Leben oder Freiheit besteht*". *Ibid.*, Section 60(7), first sentence.

[33]   Bernd Parusel for German Federal Office for Migration and Refugees, "Germany National Report (March 2010): The Granting of Non-EU Harmonised Protection Statuses in Germany, Research Study II/2009 in the Framework of the European Migration Network (EMN)", in *EMN Study on The Different Practices Concerning Granting of Non-EU Harmonised Protection Statuses* (n/a: EMN, Februay 2010), p. 22, retrieved from: <http://emn.intrasoft-intl.com/Downloads/download.do;jsessionid=48CB45E0CA5EB4C57AD0BB871285B576?fileID=960> [04/06/2011].

[34]   *Ibid.*, p. 31.

[35]   *Ibid.*, p. 48.

Without elaborating further on all national forms of protection, and on the basis of the various studies conducted on complementary forms of protection, by the European Migration Network, the European Council on Refugees and Exiles, and UNHCR in particular, it is possible to highlight some of those national, non-harmonised forms of protection. Clauses may be worded in general terms such as humanitarian reasons (Germany, Ireland), compassionate grounds (Finland) or considerations of humanitarian nature (Denmark). They may refer to conflicts which do not reach the threshold of Article 15(c) of the Qualification Directive (Sweden, Spain, Finland), to the practical impossibility of returning a person (Denmark and Germany), or to the level of social integration of the person within the country (Sweden, Switzerland, Belgium and Germany for example) as reasons to grant him or her protection. Lastly, other, more isolated grounds include: freedom fighters (France), victims or witnesses of human trafficking (Austria, Portugal, Spain), and specifically, persons fleeing environmental or natural disaster (Finland, Sweden).[36] The last mentioned provisions of Finnish and Swedish law being directly applicable to environmentally-displaced persons, whom they are specifically and explicitly intended to protect, they will be discussed in Part 2, on the possibility for persons displaced by environmental disasters to be protected in Europe, under existing law.

The scarcity of national law providing explicitly for the protection of environmentally-displaced persons, the fact that, where they exists, those provisions have never led to the grant of protective status and the possibility that might actually be abrogated does not bode well for the future legal protection of environmentally-displaced persons within the European Union. The conclusion is however premature; let us first consider the various options in Part 2.

---

36 Summary based on information provided available in ECRE, *Complementary Protection in Europe* (July 2009), *op. cit*; EMN (December 2010), *op. cit*; and *ibid.*, ANNEXES.

CHAPTER 5

Conclusions of Part 1

The present Part sought to give a comprehensive overview of the norms applicable within the European Union for the protection of persons fleeing indiscriminate threats to their life or person in their country or origin. EU's growing concern for human rights, patent in the evolution of the Court of Justice's case-law, also translated in the field of international protection. The adoption of the Qualification Directive, intended to harmonise national asylum legislation, is evidence of this trend. On the basis of State practice and of the sometimes corresponding States' obligations under international human rights law, the European legislator devised a new form of protection applicable in Europe, alongside with refugee status: subsidiary protection.

Promising as it may have seemed, the newly devised subsidiary protection regime has been heavily criticised for failing to achieve its stated objectives. Evidence of the various lacuna of the resulting protection is the observation of great discrepancies among EU Member States, in terms of positive decisions granted in asylum cases. Commentators often point to the Qualification Directive reflecting European States marked preference for harmonisation, through the European Union, "towards the lowest common denominator in terms of human rights and refugee protection standards".[1]

Notwithstanding criticisms and shortcomings, the Qualification Directive truly constitutes a major step in the development of EU asylum law, not least because it provides a harmonised protective status to persons who do not fulfil the criteria for refugee status but who would risk be subjected to "serious harm"[2] in their country of origin. The EU Court of Justice and national measures adopted subsequently appear to be in line with the approach UNHCR had long advocated: subsidiary protection, as it was introduced in the EU legal order by the Qualification Directive, is *inter alia* meant to provide protection from serious risks which are "situational rather than individually targeted".[3]

---

1 Human Rights Watch, 50 Years On: What Future for Refugee Protection?, p. 3 at: <http://www.hrw.org/sites/default/files/reports/pdf1.pdf> [06/12/2011].
2 Qualification Directive, Article 15.
3 UN High Commissioner for Refugees, UNHCR Statement on Subsidiary Protection Under the EC Qualification Directive for People Threatened by Indiscriminate Violence, January 2008, available at: <http://www.unhcr.org/refworld/docid/479df7472.html> [accessed 12 March 2011], p. 6.

It is the sole presence of an individual on a given territory where the situation have deteriorated to such an extent as to expose anyone present to a serious risk against his or her life or person which justifies that international protection be granted him or her.

Along the same lines, the European Court of Human Rights has applied the principle of *non-refoulement* deriving from Article 3 ECHR to conclude in the leading case *Sufi & Elmi* case that the situation of violence in the Somali capital was of such a level of intensity that anyone in the city would be at real risk of treatment prohibited by Article 3 ECHR;[4] returns to Mogadishu were accordingly prohibited under Article 3 ECHR.

Customary international protection confirms that "situational threats" have indeed been long acknowledged and protection and assistance granted to individuals fleeing such situation. If armed conflicts are indeed of those factors which create situations where anybody's life or person is under threat, other events can arguably have similar effects. Large-scale catastrophes, be they man-made (industrial accidents), natural (tsunami, earthquake) or both (climate change, infrastructure damages caused by *e.g.* an earthquake), can arguably affect the living conditions in a country in such a way as to jeopardise the essential human rights of the population, if not people's life itself.

On the basis of the norms identified in the present Part, applicable to situations where people flee indiscriminate threats to their life or freedoms, Part 2 will seek to identify whether, *de lege lata*, as the law stands and is currently interpreted, environmentally-displaced persons could claim protection within the European Union. The present Part focused on complementary forms of protection, based on the premise of a parallel between the impacts of armed conflict situations on the civilian population and those of environmental degradation. A person fleeing by reason of the risks associated with indiscriminate violence in situations of armed conflict is generally exposed to the same risks as the rest of the population and can therefore not claim refugee status in Europe. The assumption followed that the same would logically be true of environmentally-displaced persons, exposed to the indiscriminate effects of environmental degradation. Part 2, concerned with the applicability of existing norms of international law to situations of environmentally-triggered displacement will necessarily test the premise. It will then seek to identify which are the human rights at stake in situations of natural catastrophes and consider whether human rights law and refugee law as they stand can effectively provide protection to individuals fleeing such catastrophes.

---

4   ECtHR, *Sufi & Elmi*, § 248.

PART 2

Testing Existing Refugee Law, Human Rights Law and Practices through the Prism of Environmental Disasters

∴

Introduction to Part 2

The 1951 Refugee Convention, main instrument and foundation of modern refugee law, makes no reference to the environment. A cursory look at the Refugee Convention suggests that environmentally-displaced persons cannot be protected as refugees under the Convention definition, which is premised on the concept of persecution. As observed in the first Part, developments in the field of international refugee law and international human rights demonstrate that the 1951 Convention refugee status is however not the only protection available for persons fleeing threats to life or freedom. Authorities and decision-makers at the national, regional and international levels acknowledge that the 1951 Convention is insufficient to provide protection to all those who need it. In particular, and as was shown in Part 1, persons fleeing indiscriminate threats to their life or person, notably in the context of an armed conflict situation prevailing in their country of origin, have long been granted some form of protection. Principles of humanity and the legal principle of *non-refoulement* have traditionally protected people from being sent back to a life-threatening situation, including where such threats originate in indiscriminate violence. On this ground and by reason of the perceived inadequacy of the Refugee Convention, so-called "complementary protection" regimes (based in large part on the principles cited above) have developed to protect persons who need international protection but who do not qualify as conventional refugees, in particular because they flee indiscriminate, non-targeted, threats. The present part will analyse the existing protection mechanisms identified in Part 1 through the prism of environmental displacement and assess whether, as they are currently interpreted and implemented, they may apply to protect, not least from return, environmentally-displaced persons. Protection mechanisms under refugee law will be examined first (Chapter 7), before relevant norms of international human rights law (Chapter 8).

It should be noted that the question of environmental displacement in fact raises issues that call for consideration of further norms of international law, which were not considered in the first Part because they are not – and this is stating the obvious concerning the Refugee Convention – complementary protection mechanisms.

On the premise that armed conflict situations and environmental disasters were similar insofar as they both create non-targeted, situational risks,[1] it was assumed that environmentally-displaced persons would be excluded from the

---

[1] The terms are drawn from UNHCR comments on the proposal for a recast Qualification Directive. UNHCR (July 2010), "Comments on Proposal for Recast QD", *op. cit.*, p. 16.

scope of the Refugee Convention but might qualify for a complementary form of protection, as is the case for people fleeing the indiscriminate impacts of armed conflicts. As a consequence, the previous part sought to identify the rules, principles and practices which govern the protection of persons displaced by indiscriminate, non-targeted threats. The present Part seeks to determine whether, *de lege lata*, persons displaced by the impacts of an environmental change can seek and obtain protection within the European Union. Therefore, with a view to comprehensively answer the question, it appeared necessary to test the above-mentioned premise. The possibility that the Refugee Convention applies to so-called "environmental refugees" will therefore be discussed first, in the section on refugee law (Chapter 6, Section 1).

Drawing a parallel between the impacts of environmental disaster and armed conflict automatically suggests that international humanitarian law might be pertinent. Including considerations of international humanitarian law in the present part was in fact envisaged; however, it was eventually excluded for several reasons. Before elaborating on those reasons, it is necessary to acknowledge that humanitarian law may have some bearing on the question.

It seems that international humanitarian law can indeed be of relevance to situations of environmental degradations, not least where such degradations occur in times of armed conflict, be it as a consequence of the hostilities or instead as a catalyst for conflicts, over depleted natural resources in particular. The link between environmental degradation and displacement on the one hand and armed conflict on the other is amply evidenced and commented upon in literature. It is multiple.

Firstly, as mentioned at the onset of this work and recalled here above, armed conflicts and environmental degradations strike as similar in terms of impact on populations: the risks they each create are "situational rather than individually targeted".[2] This statement was made by UNHCR concerning indiscriminate violence for the purpose of the application of Article 15(c) of the Qualification Directive. There is no reason to conclude, and this follows logic as well as information relayed by the media coverage of environmental catastrophes and reports produced by humanitarian aid actors involved in providing assistance to persons concerned, that the same statement is not also pertinent in the context of environmental disasters. Suffice is to look at images of the 2011 tsunami wave implacably progressing across Japanese territory, traveling several kilometres inland, and sweeping away entire cities[3] to realise how

---

2   UNHCR, "Statement on Article 15(c) QD", *op. cit.*, p. 6.
3   B. Delouis, *et al.*, "Le Séisme", *in Séisme de Tohoku-Oki (Japon 11 mars 2011)* (n/a: Institut national des sciences de l'univers du Centre national de la recherche scientifique – INSU-CNRS,

indiscriminate environmental disasters can be. The massive displacements of population both situations can trigger is also clear evidence of their indiscriminate effects; it is in fact of some interest to notice that environmental disasters are often reported to displace even larger groups than armed conflicts.[4]

Secondly, a causal link may exist between the two circumstances. The link can be direct: the use of certain means of warfare is particularly damaging for the environment (nuclear and chemical weapons, bombardments, scorched earth policy, burning of oil wells, etc.).[5] This is unchallenged. International humanitarian law acknowledges this direct link too as made clear by the Convention on the prohibition of military or any hostile use of environmental modification techniques and the first protocol additional to the four 1949 Geneva Conventions.[6] To cite but one example of environmental degradation caused by armed conflict (or by the use of illegal means of warfare more specifically), the US military spraying of herbicides during the Vietnam war caused, on the US Air Force's own admission, severe damage in the country.[7] From 1961 to 1971, the US military reportedly sprayed tens of millions of heavily dioxin-contaminated herbicides over Vietnam. Estimates vary, from 72 million litres (including 44 million litres of infamous Agent Orange and 170 kilograms of dioxin) according to US Defence Department data to approximately 100 million litres

---

2011), retrieved from: <http://www.insu.cnrs.fr/terre-solide/catastrophes-et-risques/seismes/le-seisme> [14/09/2012].

4   Examples of displacement caused by natural disasters and by armed conflicts are legion. Though it concerns internal displacement only, a report indicates of the Norwegian Refugee Council indicates that between 2007 and 2012, natural disasters have displaced 19 million people in Pakistan and armed conflicts, over five million. IDMC, "Pakistan: Displacement Caused by Conflict and Natural Disasters, Achievements and Challenges" (Norwegian Refugee Council, 2012), 10 January 2012, retrieved from: <www.internal-displacement.org> [12/02/2012].

5   UNEP, *Protecting the Environment During Armed Conflict: An Inventory and Analysis of International Law* (Nairobi: UNEP, 2009); L. Low and D. Hodgkinson, "Compensation for Wartime Environmental Damage: Challenges to International Law after the Gulf War", *Virginia Journal of International Law*, Vol. 35, No. 2 (Winter 1995), pp. 405–484.

6   Convention on the Prohibition of Military or Any Hostile Use of Environmental Modification Techniques, 10 December 1976, entered into force 5 October 1976 [1976] *UNTS* Vol. 1108, p. 151; Protocol Additional to the Geneva Conventions of 12 August 1949, and Relating to the Protection of Victims of International Armed Conflicts (Protocol I), 8 June 1977, entered into force 7 December 1979 [1979] *UNTS* Vol. 1125, p. 3, Articles 35 and 55 (on methods and means of warfare and the protection of the natural environment).

7   W.A. Buckingham, Jr., *Operation Ranch Hand: The Air Force and Herbicides in Southeast Asia 1961–1971* (Washington, D.C.: Office of Air Force History, 1982), retrieved from: <http://www.dtic.mil/cgi-bin/GetTRDoc?Location=U2&doc=GetTRDoc.pdf&AD=ADA121709>.

(including 366 kilograms of dioxin) according to academic studies. Used to defoliate complex roads and footpaths, forests and plains, and to destroy crops as a tactic of war, they exceeded their goals and also destroyed clean water resources and likely caused long-term impoverishment of soils.[8]

The causal link can also be indirect. Although some are skeptic[9] or reject the argument altogether,[10] the majority in relevant literature argues that environmental degradation may create or exacerbate tensions within the population competing for depleting or depleted resources,[11] and eventually spark off violence and conflicts.[12] In the latter case, skeptics generally concur with the

---

8   Information displayed in the War Remnants Museum, Ho Chi Minh City, Vietnam (visited in July 2011) and corroborated: *ibid*; W.A. Buckingham, Jr., "Operation Ranch Hand: Herbicides in Southeast Asia", *Air University Review* (July–August 1983), retrieved from: <http://www.airpower.maxwell.af.mil/airchronicles/aureview/1983/jul-aug/buckingham.html>; J.M. Stellman, *et al.*, "The Extent and Patterns of Usage of Agent Orange and Other Herbicides in Vietnam", *Nature*, 17 April 2003, Vol. 422, pp. 681–687; S.D. Stellman and J.M. Stellman, "Exposure Opportunity Models for Agent Orange, Dioxin, and Other Military Herbicides Used in Vietnam, 1961–1971", *Journal of Exposure Analysis & Environmental Epidemiology* (Nature Publishing Group), Vol. 14, No. 4 (2004), pp. 354–362; L.W. Dwernychuk, *et al.*, "Dioxin Reservoirs in Southern Viet Nam: A Legacy of Agent Orange", *Chemosphere*, Vol. 47, No. 2 (April 2002), pp. 117–137.

9   I. Salehyan, "From Climate Change to Conflict? No Consensus Yet", *Journal of Peace Research*, May 1, 2008, Vol. 45, No. 3 (2008), pp. 315–326.

10 E. Gartzke argues that industrialisation and economic development, which contribute to climate change, also contribute to reducing conflicts between the States concerned. The author concludes: "[in] a somewhat ironic twist, the same forces that are polluting our planet and altering the climate also have beneficial effects on international conflict". E. Gartzke, "Could Climate Change Precipitate Peace?", *Journal of Peace Research*, January 1, 2012, Vol. 49, No. 1 (2012), pp. 177–192, p. 189; O.M. Theisen, *et al.*, "Climate Wars?: Assessing the Claim That Drought Breeds Conflict", *International Security*, Vol. 36, No. 3 (Winter 2011/12), pp. 79–106.

11 The Parliamentary Assembly of the Council of Europe (PACE) affirmed in particular the importance of water, it being "essential for human survival". The Parliamentary Assembly deplores that "[u]nfortunately, population growth, the contrasting but increasing needs of the developing countries and the industrialised countries, as well as climatic vagaries, exacerbate the crucial nature of water, making it a political issue which often gives rise to conflict situations". PACE, "Resolution 1809 (2011): Water: A Source of Conflict", 15 April 2011, § 1 and 7.

12 Most recently, the Intergovernmental Panel on Climate Change voiced concerns about the influence of climate factors on violence and conflicts in its Fifth Assessment Report (Chapters 12 and 19 in particular). IPCC: W.N. Adger, *et al.*, Chapter 12: "Human security" and IPCC: M. Oppenheimer, *et al.*, Chapter 19: "Emergent risks and key vulnerabilities", in: C.B. Field, *et al.* (eds.), *Climate Change 2014: Impacts, Adaptation, and Vulnerability, Part A: Global and Sectoral Aspect,. Contribution of Working Group II to the Fifth Assessment*

other side in the debate: it is not environmental or climate change which itself and alone causes conflicts but a combination of factors ("interaction effects"[13]) among which is the transformation of the environment.[14] In 2006, Kofi Annan, in his capacity as UN Secretary-General, warned about the destabilising effect of environmental change:

> Environmental degradation has the potential to destabilize already conflict-prone regions, especially when compounded by inequitable access or politicization of access to scarce resources.[15]

Lastly, the massive displacement of population which accompanies the occurrence or persistence of armed conflict situations or of environmental

---

Report of the Intergovernmental Panel on Climate Change (Cambridge and New York: Cambridge University Press, 2014), pp. 771–775 and pp. 1060–1061 respectively. See also UNGA, "A More Secure World: Our Shared Responsibility, Report of the High-Level Panel on Threats, Challenges and Change" ("A More Secure World"), A/59/565, 2 December 2004, also available, pp. 25s at: <http://www.un.org/secureworld/report2.pdf>; A. Mayoral, "Climate Change as a Conflict Multiplier", *Peace Brief*, No. 120 (United States Institute of Peace, 2012), 1 February 2012, retrieved from: <http://www.usip.org/files/resources/PB%20120.pdf>; N. Myers, "Environment and Security", *Foreign Policy* (Washingtonpost. Newsweek Interactive, LLC), No. 74 (1989), pp. 23–41; CNA Corporation, *National Security and the Threat of Climate Change* (Alexandria, VA: CNA Corporation, 2007), pp. 13–18; C. Raleigh and D. Kniveton, "Come Rain or Shine: An Analysis of Conflict and Climate Variability in East Africa", *Journal of Peace Research*, Vol. 49, No. 1 (2012), pp. 51–64; C.S. Hendrix and I. Salehyan, "Climate Change, Rainfall, and Social Conflict in Africa", *Journal of Peace Research*, Vol. 49, No. 1 (2012), pp. 35–50; B. Saul, "Climate Change and Resource Scarcity: Towards an International Law of Distributive Justice", *in* R. Lyster (Ed.), *In the Wilds of Climate Law* (Bowen Hills, QLD: Australian Academic Press, 2010), pp. 71–94.

13 N.P. Gleditsch, "Whither the Weather? Climate Change and Conflict", *Journal of Peace Research*, Vol. 49, No. 3 (2012), pp. 3–9, p. 6.

14 T.F. Homer-Dixon formulates and illustrates a "combined model" showing the linkages between various sources and consequences of environmental degradation and how the interaction between different social, economic and environmental factors can trigger conflicts. T.F. Homer-Dixon, "Environmental Scarcities and Violent Conflict: Evidence from Cases", *International Security*, Vol. 19, No. 1 (Summer 1994), pp. 5–40, pp. 31–35; A. Warnecke, *et al.*, "Climate Change, Migration and Conflict: Receiving Communities under Pressure?" (The German Marshall Fund of the United States, June 2010); N.P. Gleditsch, *et al.*, "Climate Change and Conflict: The Migration Link", *Working Paper Series – Coping with Crisis* (International Peace Academy, 2007).

15 UN Secretary-General, "Report of the Secretary-General: Progress Report on the Prevention of Armed Conflict" ("Progress report on the prevention of armed conflict"), A/60/891, 18 July 2006.

degradations risks affecting the environment of the region of destination[16] (be it within the same country or beyond national borders), possibly leading there too to conflict, between the host population and the migrant population.[17]

Addressing the hypotheses mentioned above of environmental degradations and their effects on societies triggering conflicts, including where population displacement is involved, T.F. Homer-Dixon has argued that severe environmental degradation can produce three principal types of conflicts: "Simple Scarcity Conflicts", triggered by resource scarcity, "Group-identity Conflicts", arising from large-scale movements of populations shifting ethnic balance in regions of destination especially and propelling together different ethnic and cultural groups under circumstances of deprivation and stress, and "Relative-deprivation Conflicts", caused by the increasing gap between lower-status groups and elites, the latter having more means and power to maintain their standard of living, in spite of the environmental problems and correlative decrease in wealth production experienced in the country.[18] It emerges from this categorisation (its author clarifies that each category is porous and protean) that environmental degradation does not alone cause conflict but contributes, in certain circumstances, to exacerbate existing social, economic, inter-ethnic, inter-religious, political, etc. disparities and tensions. As observed by the UN Secretary General's High-level Panel on Threats, Challenges and Change:

> Poverty, infectious disease, environmental degradation and war feed one another in a deadly cycle.[19]

---

16 M. Keita, *Impacts des migrations forcées sur les pays hôtes*, November 2007, Doctoral Thesis, Faculté des études supérieures de l'Université de Montréal (Montréal: Université de Montréal, 1 May 2008), in particular Chapter 3, "Les afflux massifs de réfugiés ont-ils affecté le bien-être des populations hôtes en Guinée?".

17 For the demonstration of a link between patterns of environmental migration and conflict in the host region (with environmental migration having a contributing role in the escalation of tensions or conflicts) on the basis of case studies, *see*: R. Reuveny, "Climate Change-Induced Migration and Violent Conflict", *Political Geography*, Vol. 26, No. 6 (2007), pp. 656–673. D. Smith and J. Vivekananda, *A Climate of Conflict: The Link between Climate Change, Peace and War* (London: International Alert, 2007); CNA Corporation, *National Security and the Threat of Climate Change* (2007), *op. cit.*, pp. 16–18; V.O. Kolmannskog, *Future Floods of Refugees: A Comment on Climate Change, Conflict and Forced Migration* (Oslo: Norwegian Refugee Council, April 2008).

18 T.F. Homer-Dixon, "On the Threshold: Environmental Changes as Causes of Acute Conflict", *International Security*, Vol. 16, No. 2 (Fall 1991), pp. 76–116, pp. 106–111.

19 UNGA, "A More Secure World", *op. cit.*, p. 15, § 22.

Some argue that it necessarily follows from the interconnection between environmental changes and armed conflicts that humanitarian law is relevant in the discussion on the international protection of persons displaced by environmental disasters. As said, it will not be envisaged in the present part, for the following reasons.

Firstly, humanitarian law is only binding between the parties in conflict[20] and applies in precisely defined situations ("international armed conflicts" and, albeit to a less extent, "non-international armed conflicts"),[21] which exclude a number of situations generalised violence with indiscriminate effects.[22] It appears therefore that, insofar as the question of the protection of displaced persons is concerned, its pertinence is only limited to those environmental displacements which occur in the context of an armed conflict situation, across State borders possibly but in any case between the territories of belligerent States. Secondly, its application is limited in time. Should an armed conflict occur, triggered by environmental degradation, or should conversely the environment be devastated by an ongoing conflict, international humanitarian law would apply, activated by the existence of an armed conflict. Once the hostilities de-escalate below the humanitarian law threshold of international or non-international armed conflict or cease, humanitarian law ceases to be applicable.[23] In other words, international humanitarian law is *lex specialis*, and shall apply in all situations of armed conflict. Along the same lines, Members of the International Law Commission (ILC), currently involved in the process

---

20   J.-F. Durieux (2012), *op. cit.*, p. 176.

21   Generally, on the preconditions for the application of international humanitarian law: "Basic Concepts of International Humanitarian Law", *in* W. Kälin and J. Künzli (Eds.), *The Law of International Human Rights Protection* (New York: Oxford University Press, 2009), pp. 150–182, pp. 150–159.

22   An overview was made above of the different arguments in favour and against the interpretation of Article 15(c) of the Qualification Directive in humanitarian law terms. The criticism formulated then against such interpretation are, in the main, also valid here. Above pp. 155s.

23   See for example paragraph 3 of common Article 2 of the 1949 Geneva Conventions which makes clear that the four Geneva Conventions apply between belligerents: "Although one of the Powers in conflict may not be a party to the present Convention, the Powers who are parties thereto shall remain bound by it in their mutual relations. They shall furthermore be bound by the Convention in relation to the said Power, if the latter accepts and applies the provisions thereof". The same is true in situations of internal armed conflicts; common Article 3 enumerates a number of principles which "each Party to the conflict shall be bound to apply, as a minimum". Fourth Geneva Convention, common Article 2, § 3 and Article 3.

of drafting articles on the Protection of persons in the event of disasters,[24] conceded that there might be cases where it is "difficult to separate a situation of an armed conflict from a pure disaster" but insisted that "the most important matter was to ensure that the *lex specialis* of international humanitarian law continue to apply in situations of armed conflict".[25] This view was endorsed by the ILC: in its current version, draft Article 4 clarifies that the draft articles on the Protection of persons in the event of disasters "do not apply to situations to which the rules of international humanitarian law are applicable".[26]

Similarly N. Schrepfer and W. Kälin also exclude international humanitarian law from the scope of their 2012 paper on the international protection of persons fleeing the impacts of climate change. The authors compendiously state:

> International humanitarian law governs situations of international and non-international armed conflict and is therefore of no practical relevance in the protection of persons moving across borders in the context of climate change.[27]

The authors add that international humanitarian law will not be relevant either in situations of unrest seriously disturbing public order, violence or even armed conflict, triggered, at least partially, by a decrease in essential resources caused by environmental degradation (or climate change), "unless the country of refuge is a party to the conflict".[28]

---

[24] The ILC draft articles on the Protection of persons in the event of disasters do not address the issue of cross-border forced displacement of populations triggered by environmental disasters but focuses on the protection of persons "internally" (that is, on the territory of the affected State but including in cases where internal displacement has occurred) and the provision of disaster relief and assistance, including in cases where external assistance is involved. For the draft articles, as provisionally adopted, *see* ILC, "Report of the International Law Commission on the work of its 63rd session" [2011] *GAOR, 66th Session, Supplement No. 10 (A/66/10 and Add.1)*, §§ 288s. For the most recent developments, *see* also the information provided on the International Law Commission website.

[25] ILC, "Report of the International Law Commission on the work of its 61st session" [2009] *GAOR, 64th session, Supplement No. 10 (A/64/10)*, § 172.

[26] ILC, "Report of the International Law Commission on the work of its 63rd session" [2011], *op. cit.*, Text of the draft articles on the Protection of persons in the event of disasters provisionally adopted so far by the Commission, § 288, Draft Article 4.

[27] W. Kälin and N. Schrepfer, *Protecting People Crossing Borders in the Context of Climate Change Normative Gaps and Possible Approaches* (February 2012), *op. cit.*, pp. 27–28.

[28] *Ibid.*, pp. 27–28 and 16 (where the "scenario 5" referred to is described).

For all these reasons, in search of a general solution for the protection of environmentally-displaced persons and in view of the fact that, according to estimates, the impacts of environmental change, magnified by climate change, are and will be the principal trigger for displacement, even in the absence of any simultaneous or resulting armed conflict situation, the present Part will focus on the possible applications of refugee law and human rights law since those two bodies of norms apply at all times and to all States (provided they are bound by them, by treaty or custom), no matter how geopolitically or geographically involved they may be in the root cause of the environmental displacement.

Lastly, this Part will briefly turn to recent environmental disasters and observe if and, if so, how States in Europe and beyond have responded to the protection claims of affected populations (Chapter 9).

Throughout this Part, reference will be made to recent New Zealand case-law. Between 2013 and 2015 in particular, New Zealand courts issued a series of decisions[29] in cases concerning claims for asylum, complementary protection (*i.e.*, under New Zealand law, status of "protected person"[30]), or authorisation to stay on humanitarian grounds, submitted by citizens of low-lying Pacific Islands, who invoked, among other arguments, changes to their living environment in their country of origin associated with climate change. Two cases strike as particularly relevant. For ease of reference, the facts and conclusions of each case are presented here; the following Chapters will refer to specific elements of the courts' reasoning, as appropriate. The first case concerns an

---

29 *See* for instance the series of decisions issued in the case of M. Teitiota (and his family), a citizen of Kiribati who had been declined refugee status and protected person status by asylum authorities. New Zealand Immigration and Protection Tribunal, *AF (Kiribati)* [2013] NZIPT 800413, 25 June 2013; New Zealand High Court, *Teitiota v. The Chief Executive of the Ministry of Business Innovation and Employment* [2013] NZHC 3125, 26 November 2013; New Zealand Court of Appeal, *Teitiota v. Chief Executive of Ministry of Business, Innovation and Employment* [2014] NZCA 173, 8 May 2014 and New Zealand Supreme Court, *Ioane Teitiota v. The Chief Executive of the Ministry of Business, Innovation and Employment* [2015] NZSC 107, 20 July 2015. Similarly, New Zealand Immigration and Protection Tribunal found that a group of appellants, citizens of Tuvalu, were neither refugees nor protected persons but, on a decision issued on the same day, that they were entitled to resident visas on humanitarian grounds. New Zealand Immigration and Protection Tribunal, *AC (Tuvalu)* [2014] NZIPT 800517–520, 4 June 2014 and *AD (Tuvalu)* [2014] NZIPT 501370–371, 4 June 2014 respectively.

30 New Zealand: Immigration Act 2009, 2009 No 51, 16 November 2009, Sections 130 (protected person under the 1984 Convention Against Torture) and 131 (protected person under the 1966 International Covenant on Civil and Political Rights).

applicant from Kiribati, I. Teitiota,[31] and the second, applicants from Tuvalu. I. Teitiota and his wife, both citizens of Kiribati, moved to New Zealand in 2007, after they were granted work visas. In 2011, I. Teitiota was found to have overstayed his visa. After his application for refugee status[32] was denied, he appealed against this decision before the Immigration and Protection Tribunal, claiming, as he did in his asylum application, that he was entitled to refugee status on the basis of the adverse impacts of climate change on his environment (including sea-level rise and its consequences).[33] The first instance judgement provides detailed information about the situation in Kribati[34] and about the applicant's living conditions[35] before assessing them against the criteria for refugee status and for "protected person" status. The judgment is particularly instructive in that New Zealand Immigration and Protection Tribunal conducted a thorough analysis of the potential eligibility of environmentally-displaced persons to refugee status (within the meaning of the 1951 Refugee Convention) or to complementary protection (as defined in New Zealand law, *i.e.* status of "protected persons" under Articles 6 and 7 of the ICCPR or under the CAT Convention[36]). The Tribunal indicated that it did not rule out the applicability of the Refugee Convention to cases concerning environmental disasters, including in the context of climate change, but stressed that applicants invoking such circumstances had to fulfil the standard Refugee Convention criteria,[37] as they are construed in New Zealand law and case-law: applicants must demonstrate "a real chance of a sustained or systemic violation of a core

---

31 Normally, to minimise risks of retaliation or reprisal against an applicant or his family in the country of origin, a refugee claimant's name is not published (the appellant was identified as "*AF (Kiribati)*" in first instance), however, the High Court clarified that in the present case the applicant, who invokes neither persecution by Kiribati authorities nor by non-state actors in Kiribati, did not seek anonymity. [2013] NZHC 3125, §12.

32 It appears that procedural imperatives guided, at least partly, the attorney's decision to invoke entitlement to refugee status: because I. Teitiota had overstayed his work visa and hence stayed illegally in New Zealand, he was precluded from applying for an immigration permit on humanitarian grounds. [2013] NZHC 3125, *Teitiota*, § 43. For a thorough coverage and analysis of M. Teitiota case before New Zealand authorities and courts, *see*: K.R. Weiss, "The Making of a Climate Refugee", *Foreign Policy*, 28/01/2015, available at: <http://foreignpolicy.com/2015/01/28/the-making-of-a-climate-refugee-kiribati-tarawa-teitiota/> [last accessed on 06/11/2016].

33 New Zealand: Immigration and Protection Tribunal, *AF (Kiribati)*, [2013] NZIPT 800413, 25 June 2013, § 2.

34 NZIPT, *AF (Kiribati), op. cit.*, §§ 5–21.

35 *Ibid.*, §§ 23–33.

36 *See* above, footnote 30.

37 *Ibid.*, § 64–65.

human right demonstrative of a failure of state protection which has sufficient nexus to a Convention ground".[38] In the case, the Tribunal found that none of those criteria was fulfilled. Firstly, the decline in I. Teitiota's standard of living, albeit unchallenged, was not such as to amount to serious harm for the purpose of the Convention.[39] Secondly, there was no nexus between the alleged harm and a Convention ground, the impacts of climate change being felt indiscriminately by the entire population of Kiribati.[40] Lastly, there was no evidence of a failure of state protection.[41] I. Teitiota was also declined poteced person status under the ICCPR on the grounds that he had failed to establish an omission of the state (Kiribati government is taking active steps to protect the citizens' right to life)[42] and the imminence of the risk.[43] Both the High Court (2013) and the Court of Appeal (2014) subsequently declined I. Teitiota leave to appeal the Tribunal's decision, and upheld the Tribunal's decision. So did the Supreme Court in 2015.[44]

In the case concerning applicants from Tuvalu, a family of four, all citizens of Tuvalu residing in New Zealand, lodged two types of appeals contemporaneously:[45] on the one hand, they appealed against the authorities' decision to deny them refugee or protected person status, and on the other, they submitted humanitarian appeals, *i.e.* they requested authorisations to stay on humanitarian grounds. The Tribunal issued both decisions on the same date. In respect of the first claims, the Tribunal referred to and endorsed the decision taken in the case of I. Teitiota and observed that, in like manner, the harm the applicants faced and would face again in Tuvalu could not be linked to any of the five Convention grounds. The applicants, the Tribunal found, were therefore not refugees within the meaning of the Refugee Convention.[46]

---

38   *Ibid.*, § 65.
39   *Ibid.*, § 74.
40   *Ibid.*, § 75.
41   *Ibid.*
42   *Ibid.*, § 88.
43   *Ibid.*, § 89.
44   New Zealand High Court, *Teitiota v. The Chief Executive of the Ministry of Business Innovation and Employment* [2013] NZHC 3125, 26 November 2013; New Zealand Court of Appeal, *Teitiota v. Chief Executive of Ministry of Business, Innovation and Employment* [2014] NZCA 173, 8 May 2014 and New Zealand Supreme Court, *Ioane Teitiota v. The Chief Executive of the Ministry of Business, Innovation and Employment* [2015] NZSC 107, 20 July 2015.
45   New Zealand Immigration Act 2009, Sections 194(6) and 195(7) require that the two appeals be lodged simultaneously.
46   New Zealand Immigration and Protection Tribunal, [2014] NZIPT 800517–520 AC (*Tuvalu*), 4 June 2014, §§ 45–46.

The appellants were also denied the qualification of "protected persons" under the ICCPR.[47] According to the Tribunal, there was no evidence that the appellants would be in danger of being arbitrarily deprived of their lives[48] or subjected to cruel treatment[49] in Tuvalu, nor that the government of Tuvalu was failing to take appropriate measures to protect its citizens from the adverse impacts of climate change.[50] In a separate decision however, the Tribunal considered that, when considered in combination, the same appellants' circumstances, including the detrimental impact of climate change on their living environment, amounted to exceptional circumstances of a humanitarian nature that would make it unjust or unduly harsh for them to be deported to Tuvalu. The Tribunal allowed the appellants' humanitarian appeals against liability for deportation and granted them resident visas in New Zealand.[51]

Decisions issued in those cases will be particularly relevant under Chapters 6 and 8 as they assess environmentally-displaced persons' claims against criteria for refugee status and complementary protection (Chapter 6) and on the basis of humanitarian and discretionary grounds (Chaper 8, 11).

Let us now turn to the subject matter of the present Part, to wit, the applicability of existing norms of refugee law (on refugee status and complementary forms of protection) and human rights law to the protection needs of persons displaced by environmental disasters ("environmentally-displaced persons").

---

47   Under New Zealand Immigration Act, an applicant can be granted complementary protection on two grounds: as "protected person" either under the 1984 Convention Against Torture (Immigration Act 2009, Section 130) or under Articles 6 and 7 of the 1966 International Covenant on Civil and Political Rights (Immigration Act 2009, Section 131). The appellants in this case hwever did not make any allegation of a risk of torture. The Tribunal therefore did not elaborate on the potential applicability of this provision to the case of environmentally-displaced persons. NZIPT, AC (Tuvalu), §§ 47–50.

48   NZIPT, AC (Tuvalu), §§ 99–100.

49   Ibid., §§ 109–114.

50   Ibid., §§ 101–108 concerning steps taken by the State to protect the citizen's right to life and §§ 109–114 regarding cruel treatment.

51   NZIPT, AD (Tuvalu), op. cit., §§ 2, 30 and 37.

CHAPTER 6

Environmentally-Displaced Persons as Beneficiaries of International Protection under Refugee Law?

As mentioned in the introduction of the present part, this Chapter will first consider whether, *de lege lata*, environmentally-displaced persons can or could be recognised as refugees (I) before considering their qualification as beneficiaries of subsidiary protection or of other forms of complementary protection (II).

I   Environmental "refugees"?

This first section focuses on the question whether individuals who fled from their country of origin by reason of an environmental disaster may be granted refugee status under the Refugee Convention or, within the European Union specifically, under the Qualification Directive,[1] as they currently read and are interpreted and implemented. Reference will often be made to UNHCR Handbook and Guidelines on Procedures and Criteria for Determining Refugee Status under the 1951 Convention and the 1967 Protocol Relating to the Status of Refugees,[2] for it is an authoritative (if not the most authoritative[3]) interpretation of the Refugee Convention and Protocol.

Refugee protection under EU law, that is, under the Qualification Directive, is governed by the application of the Refugee Convention. The Preamble of the Directive recall that the Common European Asylum System is based on "the full and inclusive application" of the Refugee Convention (as supplemented by its 1967 Protocol), which provides "the cornerstone of the international legal regime for the protection of refugees".[4] Many occurrences of the Refugee Convention appear in the operative parts of the Directive (Article 9 for instance

---

1   Article 2(d) of the Qualification Directive scrupulously reproduces the criteria of the refugee definition provided by the Refugee Convention in Article 1A(2).
2   UNHCR, *Handbook and Guidelines on Procedures and Criteria for Determining Refugee Status under the 1951 Convention and the 1967 Protocol Relating to the Status of Refugees* ("UNHCR Handbook on Procedures"), HCR/IP/4/Eng/REV.3 (Geneva: UNHCR, 1979, reissued December 2011).
3   J. Hong, "Refugees of the 21st Century: Environmental Injustice", *Cornell Journal of Law and Public Policy*, Vol. 10 (2001), pp. 323–348, p. 338; A. Lopez (2007), *op. cit.*, p. 378.
4   Qualification Directive, Recitals 3 and 4.

defines the criteria for an act to be regarded as an act of persecution "within the meaning of Article 1(A) of the [Refugee] Convention"[5]) and, most significantly, the refugee definition adopted in the Qualification Directive replicates the definition provided in Article 1A of the Refugee Convention. In practice, the application of the Qualification Directive by Member States in fact integrates the developments made in international refugee law on the interpretation of the 1951 Refugee Convention. In the present section, reference will therefore be found to both the Refugee Convention and the Qualification Directive.

For the sake of clarity, the refugee definition adopted in the Refugee Convention, supplemented in 1967 by the Protocol adopted under its authority,[6] and replicated in the Qualification Directive is hereafter recalled. In the Convention framework, a refugee is any person who:

> ... owing to well-founded fear of being persecuted for reasons of race, religion, nationality, membership of a particular social group or political opinion, is outside the country of his nationality and is unable or, owing to such fear, is unwilling to avail himself of the protection of that country; or who, not having a nationality and being outside the country of his former habitual residence as a result of such events, is unable or, owing to such fear, is unwilling to return to it.[7]

There are three essential elements in the refugee definition. The first one, the requirement that the applicant is outside is or her country of origin, is obviously fulfilled in the present work which focuses specifically on cross-border displacement triggered by environmental disasters and will therefore not be further discussed. The two other key elements are the "persecution" requirement, and the requirement of a causal link between persecution and any of the five grounds identified in the definition ("for reasons of"). As will be discussed below, the latter two prerequisites, reflective of the underlying intention of States to reject the universalistic approach to refugee protection and instead retain a control of the refugee determination process,[8] significantly limit the scope of the refugee definition. The prevailing interpretation and application

---

5 *Ibid.*, Article 9(1).
6 Protocol Relating to the Status of Refugees, *op. cit.*
7 Refugee Convention, Article 1A(2). The limitations in time and space originally included in the Geneva Convention were raised by the 1967 Protocol.
8 *See* in that sense and, more generally, on the evolution in time of the underlying premise of refugee law, from humanitarianism to a "self-interested control": J.C. Hathaway, "A Reconsideration of the Underlying Premise of Refugee Law", *Harvard International Law Journal*, Vol. 31, No. 1 (Winter 1990), pp. 129–183, pp. 143–144.

of the two requirements ought to be considered with the special features of environmentally induced migrations in mind, in order to determine whether environmentally displaced persons can be eligible to refugee status under the Convention definition (B and C). Prior to the discussion of those two definitional elements, the developments below will linger on the notion of "well-founded fear" (A).

A *Preliminary Remark: On the Well-Foundedness of the Fear of "Environmental Refugees"*

The general rules concerning the assessment of the well-foundedness of an applicant's fear will be reminded (1) before considering their implications in cases where the fear emanates in a context of environmental degradation (2); the shorthand term "environmental persecution" is used in such cases. Lastly, in the context of environmental disasters, which can severely destabilise States and limit their capacity to effectively respond to the disaster and to the needs of their population, the notion of absence of State protection might play a pivotal role (3).

1 Evidence of Well-Foundedness and the Clarifications Brought by the Qualification Directive

It appears from a cursory reading of the phrase, "well-founded fear" of persecution encompasses both a subjective and an objective dimension.[9] If fear, defined as a "state of mind and a subjective condition",[10] cannot be quantified,[11] it is however qualified by the term "well-founded", which implies that the fear must be supported by objective elements.[12] This bipartite approach developed by UNHCR in its Handbook and Guidelines on Procedures and Criteria for Determining Refugee Status under the 1951 Convention and the 1967 Protocol Relating to the Status of Refugees (hereinafter "UNHCR Handbook on

---

9   The term "objective" and "subjective" commonly used could possibly be appropriately replaced by "general" and "personal". As noted by Goodwin-Gill and McAdam: "What seems to be intended, however, is not so much evidence of subjective fear, as evidence of the subjective aspects of an individual's life, including beliefs and commitments". G.S. Goodwin-Gill and J. McAdam, *The Refugee in International Law* (2007), *op. cit.*, p. 64; see also J.C. Hathaway and W.S. Hicks, "Is There a Subjective Element in the Refugee Convention's Requirement of 'Well-Founded Fear'?" *Michigan Journal of International Law*, Vol. 26 (Winter 2005), p. 550, pp. 508–509 in particular.

10 UNHCR, *Handbook on Procedures, op. cit.*, § 38.

11 G.S. Goodwin-Gill and J. McAdam, *The Refugee in International Law* (2007), *op. cit.*, pp. 63–64.

12 UNHCR, *Handbook on Procedures, op. cit.*, § 38.

Procedures")[13] has been broadly adopted in practice by asylum courts around the world.[14]

In the European Union, this appears clearly in the Qualification Directive, which endorses the refugee definition provided by the Refugee Convention[15] but also develops its terms. In particular, Article 4 of the Directive elaborates on the facts and circumstances which national authorities must take into consideration when assessing claims for international protection. The list of relevant facts or circumstances includes country of origin data (including information on national legislation and its implementation, and on ongoing situations) as well as statements and documentation informing the authorities on the applicant's position and personal circumstances and on past episodes or threats of persecution.[16] Those clarifications brought by the Qualification Directive were broadly welcome. In particular, they are in line with UNHCR Handbook on Procedures insofar as they include both objective and subjective facts and circumstances in the examination of a claim for international protection and make it clear that the duty to ascertain and evaluate all the relevant facts is a joint responsibility[17] of the applicant and the examiner.[18] Commentators in particular welcomed the recognition of the importance of individual statements,[19] of previous occurrences or threats of persecution, serious harms as serious indication of the applicant's well-founded fear of persecution or real risk of suffering serious harm,[20] and of non-documentary evidence.[21]

In order for the fear to be analysed as well-founded, the claimant must establish "to a reasonable degree" that his or her staying in or returning to his country of origin would be "intolerable" to him.[22] This will be assessed by national authorities on the basis of facts and information available on the situation in the applicant's country of origin and in light of all the relevant personal

---

13 *Ibid.*, §§ 37–38 and 37–50.
14 J.C. Hathaway and W.S. Hicks (Winter 2005), *op. cit.*
15 Refugee Convention, Article 1A(2); Qualification Directive, Article 2(d).
16 Qualification Directive, Article 4.
17 Article 4(a) of the Qualification Directive clarifies that Member States have the duty to assess the relevant elements of the application "[i]n cooperation with the applicant". *Ibid.*, Article 4(1).
18 "Annotated Comments on QD (2004)", [January 2005], *op. cit.*, Comment on Article 4(1), pp. 13–14.
19 ECRE (October 2004), "Information Note on QD (2004)", *op. cit.*, p. 6.
20 *Ibid.*, p. 6; "Annotated Comments on QD (2004)", [January 2005], *op. cit.*
21 "Annotated Comments on QD (2004)", [January 2005], *op. cit.*, Comment on Article 4(5)(e), p. 16.
22 UNHCR, *Handbook on Procedures, op. cit.*, § 42.

circumstances of the applicant,[23] including his or her "own interpretation of the situation";[24] in cases where documentary evidence is missing, the credibility of the applicant plays a crucial rule.[25] To reach the threshold of well-foundedness, the applicant needs not establish the certainty of the alleged persecution, nor even that persecution is more probably than not, but a reasonable possibility, likelihood or chance.[26]

2   The Well-Foundedness of a Fear of "Environmental Persecution"
In the discussion on whether or not to recognise persons fleeing environmental degradation as refugees, the risk invoked can be described as twofold; it includes firstly, the risk that severe environmental degradation occurs and secondly, the risk that its consequences for the applicant reach the level of persecution.

When displacement takes place in the aftermath of a sudden environmental catastrophe (an earthquake for example), the first of the two components of the risk of "environmental persecution" is satisfied. It is for the applicant to adduce evidence, as in a standard refugee procedure, that in this context and in view of his or her personal circumstances, he or she has a well-founded fear of being persecuted in his or her country of origin.

When displacement takes place in the context of the slow deterioration of environment, the well-foundedness of the fear might be questioned by those challenging the notion of "environmental refugees" on the ground that, in such situations where environmental degradation has not yet occurred or is progressive only, the threshold of likelihood of the threat is not met.

An appreciation of the risks that environmental degradation occurs will not be made in the present work for this appreciation is beyond the scope of this study and the competences of its author. Numerous scientific publications[27] however substantiate the prevailing concern, among the community of experts, that climate change will have and, in fact already has, an undeniable impact on the environment.[28] Some of the existing (and continuously

---

23   G.S. Goodwin-Gill and J. McAdam, *The Refugee in International Law* (2007), *op. cit.*, pp. 63–64; J.C. Hathaway and W.S. Hicks (Winter 2005), *op. cit.*, pp. 508–509.
24   UNHCR, *Handbook on Procedures, op. cit.*, § 41.
25   *Ibid.*, § 41.
26   P. Weis, *The Refugee Convention, 1951: The Travaux Préparatoires Analysed* (1995), *op. cit.*, p. 8. UNHCR, "Note on Burden and Standard of Proof in Refugee Claims", 16 December 1998, § 17; J.C. Hathaway and W.S. Hicks (Winter 2005), *op. cit.*, p. 508.
27   IPCC (2014), *Synthesis Report, op. cit.*, SPM, pp. 8–16; IPCC (2007), *op. cit.*, p. 8 (Table SPM 2); IPCC (2001), *op. cit.*, p. 9; D.A. Randall, *et al.* (2007), *op. cit.*, pp. 591–596 in particular.
28   United Nations Secretary-General Ban Ki-Moon described climate change as "the major, overriding environmental issue of our time, and the single greatest challenge facing

developing) climate models developed by scientists have already demonstrated their performance, which strengthens the level of scientific confidence[29] in the ability of those models to provide useful projections of future climate.[30] In particular, studies reveal that certain regions and countries are more prone to natural disasters than others.[31] Additionally, numerous statements by environmentalists and humanitarian actors alike already bear witness of a growing number of persons displaced by environmental degradation, be it related to climate change or not.[32]

For nationals of countries or region identified as prone to disasters and, or, from which patterns of displacement are observed, it could therefore be argued that there is a reasonable likelihood that environmental degradation will occur and trigger displacement.

Nevertheless, although the refugee law assessment of a risk of persecution is essentially prospective, there are implicit "limits on how pre-emptive flight may be".[33] As said, an asylum-seeker needs not establish that persecution is

---

environmental regulators". It is, the Secretary General added, "a growing crisis with economic, health and safety, food production, security, and other dimensions". The statement is cited in the material produced by the United Nations Environment Programme (UNEP), sub-programme on Climate Change. In particular UNEP, *UNEP Year Book 2010: New Science and Developments in Our Changing Environment* (Nairobi: UNEP, 2010); UNEP, *Factsheet: Climate Change* (Paris: UNEP, July 2000). *See* also, at the European Union level: material produced by the European Commission Directorate-General for Climate Action, <http://ec.europa.eu/clima/news/index_en.htm> [05/05/2012]. D. Chotouras, *Le statut juridique en droit international du réfugié écologique : une nécessité !* (*Le phénomène migratoire du fait des modifications environnementales*), Thesis, *op. cit.*, §§ 25–34.

29 IPCC (2007), *op. cit.*, p. 8 (Table SPM 2).
30 IPCC (2001), *op. cit.*, p. 9; D.A. Randall, *et al.* (2007), *op. cit.*, pp. 591–596 in particular.
31 M.L. Parry, *et al.*, "2007: Technical Summary", *in* M.L. Parry, *et al.* (Eds.), *Climate Change 2007: Impacts, Adaptation and Vulnerability. Contribution of Working Group II to the Fourth Assessment Report of the Intergovernmental Panel on Climate Change* (Cambridge: Cambridge University Press, 2007), TS.4.5.
32 N. Myers, "Environmental Refugees", *Population and Environment*, Vol. 19, No. 2 (1997), pp. 167–182; E. El-Hinnawi, *Environmental Refugees* (Nairobi: United Nations Environment Programme, 1985); P. Matlou, "Upsetting the Cart: Forced Migration and Gender Issues, the African Experience", *in* D. Indra (Ed.), *Engendering Forced Migration* (New York and Oxford: Berghahn Books, 1999); S. Leiderman and R. Black, "Environmental Refugees: Myth or Reality?" *New Issues in Refugee Research* (UNHCR), No. 34 (2001); S. Castles, "Environmental Change and Forced Migration: Making Sense of the Debate", *New Issues in Refugee Research* (UNHCR), No. 70 (2002).
33 J. McAdam, *Climate Change, Forced Migration, and International Law* (Oxford, New York: Oxford University Press, 2012), p. 49.

more probably than not; a reasonable possibility, likelihood or chance[34] can be sufficient to establish a well-founded fear. On the other hand, "a mere chance or remote possibility of being persecuted" is insufficient.[35] It remains to be seen whether asylum authorities would be prepared to consider, on the basis of growing evidence of on-going, worsening and mostly ineluctable degradation of the environment in a number of regions and countries, that asylum-seekers' fear is well-founded. Even if asylum authorities were to accept that it is likely that environmental degradation will occur, they might find that such degradation will not necessarily be such as to force people to move: references to societies' resilience or capacity to adapt to environment changes might come into play and justify a conclusion that the degree of likelihood of the alleged risk's happening is not sufficient.

As concerns the second element of the risk, that environmental degradation when it occurs causes harm to populations, ample literature, part of the topical discussion on the impacts of climate change in particular, substantiates the claim that environmental change affects the enjoyment of human rights by the populations concerned.[36] Whether this can reach the threshold of persecution will be the subject of the following subsection. The link between environmental disaster and harm appears less clearly in situations of slow-onset degradation of the environment. Individuals are not overnight deprived of their means of subsistence; rather, fresh water sources, food stocks, surfaces of agricultural land, etc. are progressively decreasing. The impact on populations may not be immediate, it is nevertheless undoubted. It is arguable that the fact that environmental harm is *chronic* does not preclude it from reaching the severity threshold of persecution.

Firstly, persecution can consist of an accumulation of measures or factors which, taken together "produce an effect on the mind of the applicant that can reasonably justify a claim to well-founded fear of persecution on 'cumulative grounds'".[37] The notion of time elapsing is not unrelated to the terms *accumulation* or *cumulative*. To accumulate means "to make or become greater in quantity or size, especially over a long period of time" or "to collect or grow

---

34 P. Weis, *The Refugee Convention, 1951: The Travaux Préparatoires Analysed* (1995), *op. cit.*, p. 8. UNHCR, *op. cit.*, § 17; J.C. Hathaway and W.S. Hicks (Winter 2005), *op. cit.*, p. 508.

35 "The Michigan Guidelines on Well-Founded Fear", *Michigan Journal of International Law*, Vol. 26 (March 2004), pp. 491–503, no. 6.

36 In like manner, New Zealand Immigration and Protection Tribunal unequivocally stated that it was "indubitably correct that natural disasters and environmental degradation can involve significant human rights issues". NZIPT, *AD (Tuvalu)*, *op. cit.*, § 65.

37 UNHCR, *Handbook on Procedures*, *op. cit.*, § 53. Similarly: Qualification Directive, Article 9(1)(b).

into a mass";[38] accumulation is defined as the product of this action but also as the process itself.[39] Accordingly, the worsening of the situation over time and increasing risk and level of harm could cumulate to constitute persecution under the accepted definition of acts of persecution.

A second argument can be derived from case-law. In a case concerning an alleged risk of "physical persecution" resulting from deprivation of the right to work on discriminatory ground (the applicant's religion), the US Court of Appeals for the Third Circuit clarified that the terms "physical persecution" do not require or even connote "the use of intense physical force applied to the body with all the dramatics of the rack and wheel". Most significant at this point is the Court's suggestion that the time element in the materialisation of harm was immaterial. Although the case did not concern slow-onset environmental disaster, the reasoning of the US Court is interesting and could be pertinent. The US Court explained:

> The denial of an opportunity to earn livelihood (...) is the equivalent of a sentence to death by means of slow starvation and none the less final because it is gradual. The result of both is the same (...).[40]

The link between, on the one hand, progressive environmental degradation and worsening conditions of living and, on the other, a risk of persecution can hence be established. Gradual deprivation of one's means of subsistence exposes to a real risk of harm and eventually of death; this unquestionably reaches the severity threshold of persecution.[41]

---

38 *Longman Dictionary of English Language and Culture*, 1st ed. (Harlow: Longman Group UK Ltd, 1992), "accumulate".

39 "Accumulation" (Centre National de Ressources Textuelles et Lexicales – CNRTL, 2012), retrieved from: <www.cnrtl.fr/definition/accumulation> [02/07/2012]; "Accumulation", *in Macmillan Dictionary* (n/a: Macmillan Publishers Limited, 2009–2012), retrieved from: <www.macmillandictionary.com/dictionary/british/accumulation>; "Accumulation", *in Dictionnaire de français* (n/a: Larousse, 2012), retrieved from: <http://www.larousse.fr/dictionnaires/francais/accumulation>.

40 USA: (Court of Appeals Third Circuit), *Chris Dunat, Appellant, v. L.W. Hurney, District Director of Immigration, Philadelphia* ("*Dunat v. Hurney*"), 297 F.2d 744, 24 January 1962, § 6. The case is cited by M. Foster and A. Grahl-Madsen earlier. A. Grahl-Madsen, *The Status of Refugees in International Law* (Leiden: A.W. Sijthoff, 1966), p. 208; M. Foster, *International Refugee Law and Socio-Economic Rights: Refuge from Deprivation*, Vol. 51 (Cambridge, New York: Cambridge University Press, 2007), p. 92. Qualification Directive, Article 9(1)(b). The case is cited by M. Foster and A. Grahl-Madsen earlier. *Dunat v. Hurney*, 24 January 1962, *op. cit.*, § 6.

41 *A contrario*, in the case of I. Teitiota, a refugee claimant from Kiribati, New Zealand Immigration and Protection Tribunal acknowledged that, were the appellant to be returned

It is of interest to notice that those States and regions identified as being more at risk of suffering from the detrimental impacts of climate change are located in the less developed parts of the world.[42] The capacity of those States to take the appropriate measures to mitigate the effects of environmental disasters and, in this context, to assure their populations the basic means of subsistence will be particularly challenged by reason of their often limited adaptive capacity and high costs relative to those countries' Gross Domestic Product (GDP). This in turn makes the risk for populations more real.[43]

It follows from the above that, although the possibility is rather tenuous for those displaced by slow-onset disasters due to the difficulty authorities may have to accepting the foreseeability of environmental degradation capable of harming populations, it might be possible for environmentally-displaced persons to invoke a well-founded fear that their continued stay in or return to their country of origin would be intolerable[44] (subject to the categorisation of the risks invoked as acts of persecution). The assumption is buttressed by the notion of "inability of the State to protect".

3 Absence of State Protection, Likelihood of Persecution and Well-Foundedness of the Fear

Traditionally, persecution was perceived as an act of State: either State agents engaged in acts of persecution or they deliberately denied protection against persecution. The emergence of non-State agents of persecution[45] however led to increased awareness that, in certain cases, States are genuinely incapable of protecting individuals against acts of persecution committed by non-State

---

from New Zealand to Kiribati, his "standard of living" would decrease, but concluded that the environmental conditions the appellant would face there were not "so parlous that his *life* [would] be placed in jeopardy, or that he and his family [would] not be able to resume their prior subsistence life with *dignity*". NZIPT, AF (*Kiribati*), *op. cit.*, §§ 73–74.

42 In its fourth Assessment Report (published in 2007), the Intergovernmental Panel on Climate Change (IPCC) identified in particular the Arctic, Africa and especially the sub-Saharan region, small islands, and Asian megadeltas, such as the Ganges-Brahmaputra and the Zhujiang deltas. IPCC, "2007: Summary for Policymakers", *in* M.L. Parry, *et al.* (Eds.), *Climate Change 2007: Impacts, Adaptation and Vulnerability. Contribution of Working Group II to the Fourth Assessment Report of the Intergovernmental Panel on Climate Change* (Cambridge: Cambridge University Press, 2007), pp. 13–15; M.L. Parry, *et al.* (2007), *op. cit.*, TS.4.5.

43 D. Chotouras, *Le statut juridique en droit international du réfugié écologique : une nécessité ! (Le phénomène migratoire du fait des modifications environnementales)*, Thesis, *op. cit.*, § 130.

44 UNHCR, *Handbook on Procedures, op. cit.*, § 42.

45 W. Kälin, "Non-State Agents of Persecution and the Inability of the State to Protect", *Georgetown Immigration Law Journal*, Vol. 15 (2000–2001), pp. 415–431, p. 415.

actors (or State actors they fail to control). The link between lack of State protection and well-foundedness of the fear can be articulated as follows:

> The persecuted clearly do not enjoy the protection of their country of origin, while evidence of the lack of protection (...) may create a presumption as to the likelihood of persecution and to the well-foundedness of any fear.[46]

Well-foundedness of the fear can be reinforced by the circumstance that State protection is lacking in the applicant's country of origin. On the basis of the above cited passage from Guy S. Goodwin-Gill's work, the Supreme Court of Canada, having accepted the existence of a fear on the part of the applicant, clarified that decision-makers are "entitled to presume that persecution will be likely and the fear well-founded if there is an absence of state protection". The well-foundedness of the fear, the court added, "can be established through the use of such a presumption".[47] As a matter of fact, UNHCR has always maintained the same approach: persecution is normally related to action by State authorities of a country but may also emanate from non-State actors if those acts are "knowingly tolerated by the authorities, or if the authorities refuse, or *prove unable*, to offer effective protection".[48] It is precisely the object and purpose of refugee law to protect those individuals who do not enjoy the protection of (or are persecuted by) their own State. As confirmed by W. Kälin: "the unwillingness of refugees to avail themselves of the protection of their country of origin is well founded if this country is unable to provide the minimum of safety and security that serves as the very foundation of the legitimacy of State power".[49]

In a situation of environmental disaster, it is conceivable if not presumable that the affected State's capacity to offer effective protection to its population will often be overwhelmed. The State risks be unable to secure basic needs (water, food, health, and shelter chiefly) to its population. Moreover, people might be exposed to increased insecurity and confronted with the incapacity of national authorities to effectively contain it. This case confirms that amid the disorder caused by environmental disasters, governments might be unable

---

46 G.S. Goodwin-Gill, *The Refugee in International Law*, First ed. (Oxford, New York: Oxford University Press, 1984), p. 67.

47 Canada: Supreme Court, *Canada (Attorney General) v. Ward* ("*Canada (Attorney General) v. Ward*"), 30 June 1993, [1993] 2 SCR. 689, § 708. The decision is cited in G.S. Goodwin-Gill and J. McAdam, *The Refugee in International Law* (2007), *op. cit.*, p. 92.

48 UNHCR, *Handbook on Procedures*, § 65 [emphasis added].

49 W. Kälin (2000–2001), *op. cit.*, p. 431.

to provide effective protection to its population. In such situation, the fear invoked by the asylum seeker appears all the more reasonable and well-founded.

At this stage of the discussion, it seems that there is no obstacle to applying refugee status to environmentally-displaced persons, insofar as the existence of a well-founded fear is concerned. The main question remains though: is the treatment invoked by persons claiming a need of international protection arising from the degradation of their environment in their country of origin constitutive of persecution under the Geneva Convention?

The developments below will assess the validity of the concept of "environmental persecution" against each criterion separately and successively although the analysis might seem somewhat artificial since persecution and the existence of a causal link are inseparable for the purpose of identifying refugees. An individual may well be exposed to threats of such severity that they reach the level of persecution but if the threats are not linked to one or more of the five Refugee Convention grounds, he or she is not a refugee under the Convention.[50] Conversely, differences in treatment would not amount to persecution if they do not reach a certain threshold of severity, that is if they neither lead to consequences "of a substantially prejudicial nature" nor produce in the mind of the person concerned, "a feeling of apprehension and insecurity as regards" his or her future existence.[51] Bearing in mind that the two criteria are cumulative, let us first turn to the act of persecution, the treatment itself (B), leaving aside the reasons for it, before addressing the requirement of a causal link (nexus) between persecution and one or several of the five Refugee Convention grounds (C).

B Environmental Persecution?

At the time the Refugee Convention was adopted, the environment and climate change in particular were not topical issues. The possibility that the harm caused by environmental disaster qualify as persecution under the Refugee Convention should therefore be considered. At the outset, it should be noted that if "environmental persecution" is not explicitly mentioned in refugee law, conversely, "[n]othing in either international or national standards explicitly disavows the idea that one may be persecuted through environmental harm".[52]

---

50   "The Michigan Guidelines on Nexus to a Convention Ground", *Michigan Journal of International Law*, Vol. 23 (Winter 2002), pp. 211–221.
51   UNHCR, *Handbook on Procedures, op. cit.*, §§ 54–55.
52   C.M. Kozoll, "Poisoning the Well: Persecution, the Environment, and Refugee Status", *Colorado Journal of International Environmental Law and Policy*, Vol. 15, No. 2 (2004), pp. 271–307, p. 274.

"Persecution" is not defined in the 1951 Convention[53] nor does it have any universally accepted definition.[54] Some authors interpret this lack of definition of the term as intentional on the drafters' part, who presumably meant, in so doing, to leave the definition open to future, yet unpredictable, protection needs. In the words of Atle Grahl-Madsen:

> The term "persecution" has nowhere been defined and this was probably deliberate. It seems as if the drafters have wanted to introduce a flexible concept which might be applied to circumstances as they might arise; in other words, that they capitulated before the inventiveness of humanity to think up new ways of persecuting fellow men.[55]

Definitions of the terms have emerged with the Convention being implemented. They focus on two main aspects: what constitutes an act of persecution (1), and who are actors of persecution (2).

1   Acts of Persecution: Is the Notion Broad Enough?

In an attempt to concretise the notion of "persecution", UNHCR highlights that the prohibition of *refoulement* enshrined in Article 33 of the refugee Convention is designed to protect refugees (whether or not they have been recognised as such) from being returned to threats to their "life or freedom". Through a cross-referenced reading of the Refugee Convention, UNHCR infers that the threats referred to in Article 33 – that is threats to life or freedom, but also other "serious violations of human rights" – are to be construed as acts of persecution.[56] Across relevant literature, the link between Article 1A(2), on the definition of the term "refugee" centred on the notion of persecution, and Article 33 proscribing the *refoulement* of refugees is likewise widely accepted. So is the corollary compatibility between the concept of persecution, cornerstone of the refugee definition, and the notion of threat to life or freedom underlying the prohibition of *refoulement*.

E. Lauterpacht and D. Bethlehem infer from the definition of refugee the scope of the protection against *refoulement* enshrined in Article 33 of the

---

53 Guy S. Goodwin-Gill and J. McAdam, *The refugee in international law*, 3rd ed. (New York: Oxford University Press, 2007), p. 90; J.C. Hathaway, *The Law of Refugee Status* (London: Butterworths, 1991), pp. 99–134.

54 UNHCR, *Handbook on Procedures, op. cit.*, §51.

55 Atle Grahl-Madsen, *The Status of Refugees in International Law*, vol. I (Leiden: A.W. Sijthoff, 1966), p. 193.

56 UNHCR, *Handbook on Procedures, op. cit.*, §§ 51–53.

Convention. They argue that the phrase "where his life or freedom would be threatened" must be construed as incorporating the "well-founded fear of persecution", central to the definition of refugee. They further elaborate on the respective scope of the two phrases to conclude that the notion of threat central to the prohibition of *non-refoulement* is broader than that of persecution.[57] Conversely, the UNHCR Handbook infers from Article 33 of the Refugee Convention that "a threat to life or freedom on account of race, religion, nationality, political opinion or membership of a particular social group is always persecution".[58] Similarly, G.S. Goodwin-Gill deduces from the letter of Articles 31 and 33 of the Refugee Convention that "persecution" includes the threat of death or of torture, or cruel, inhuman or degrading treatment or punishment. The author adds that a comprehensive analysis of the notion of persecution would in fact require the general notion "to be related to developments within the broad field of human rights" and refers in particular to Article 7 of the CAT Convention (on the prosecution of persons alleged to have committed torture), Article 3 ICCPR (equality between men and women), Article 6 ECHR (right to fair trial), Article 5 of the American Convention on Human Rights (right to humane treatment) and to the African Charter of Human and Peoples' Rights.[59]

It appears clearly that threats to life or freedom are at the core of refugee protection. The notion of "protected interests",[60] underlying the concept of persecution, can also shed light on the matter: "race, religion, nationality, membership of a particular social group, or political opinion" and the resulting rights can indeed help grasp the concept of persecution, and the sufferings against which it is intended to protect.

Civil and political rights are however not the only ones at stake in the aftermath of an environmental disaster. J. McAdam notes quite on the contrary that "the impacts of climate change are felt predominantly in the enjoyment of socioeconomic rights".[61] In this context, it is therefore important to note that the protection of basic civil and political rights was actually not the sole

---

57 Sir Elihu Lauterpacht and Daniel Bethlehem, "Avis sur la portée et le contenu du principe du non-refoulement", in Erika Feller, Frances Nicholson and Volker Türk (Eds.), *La protection des réfugiés en droit international* (Bruxelles : Larcier, 2010).
58 UNHCR, *Handbook on Procedures, op. cit.*, § 51.
59 G.S. Goodwin-Gill, "Convention Relating to the Status of Refugees – Protocol Relating to the Status of Refugees" (2008), *op. cit.*, p. 3; G.S. Goodwin-Gill and J. McAdam, *The Refugee in International Law* (2007), *op. cit.*, p. 91. Similarly, A. Grahl-Madsen, *The Status of Refugees in International Law* (1966), *op. cit.*, p. 196–197.
60 G.S. Goodwin-Gill and J. McAdam, *The Refugee in International Law* (2007), *op. cit.*, pp. 92s.
61 J. McAdam, "From Economic Refugees to Climate Refugees?" *Melbourne Journal of International Law*, Vol. 10, No. 2 (2009), pp. 579–595, p. 588.

concern of the drafters of the Convention, who had acknowledged that social or economic factors could also force people out of their country.[62] The absence of a definition of persecution in the Refugee Convention is interpreted as a deliberate omission by the drafters who intended to leave the meaning undefined in order to allow for its evolution and its continued pertinence in a world where persecution might assume myriad of unpredictable new forms.[63] It is well established that "other *serious* violations of human rights",[64] themselves or in combination with other factors,[65] can also constitute persecution. M. Foster contributes to the discussion on the respective or correlative scopes of Article 1A and Article 33 of the Refugee Convention by noticing that courts have generally rejected the argument formulated by some States, on the basis of Article 33 (*non-refoulement*), that persecution encompassed only threats to "life or freedom"; hence the recognition by courts of harms to other civil and political rights or to economic and social rights as acts of persecution.[66]

This appears to be the approach adopted at the European Union level too.

The adoption of the Qualification Directive provides useful guidance on the meaning of persecution. Member States have committed to base the nascent Common European Asylum System "on the full and inclusive application of the Geneva Convention".[67] Adopted to this end, the Qualification Directive replicates the Convention refugee definition and further clarifies its terms. In particular, Article 9(1) of the Directive describes an act of persecution, within the meaning of Article 1A of the Geneva Convention, as an act which is *sufficiently serious* by its nature or repetition as to constitute a severe violation of basic human rights, in particular the right to life and the prohibitions of torture, slavery and forced labour,[68] or which is an accumulation of various measures, including violations of human rights, which is *sufficiently severe* as

---

62 J.C. Hathaway refers to statements made by the representative of the American Federation of Labor and the delegate of France during the drafting of the Refugee Convention (Summary Record of the meeting of 6 February 1950, UN Doc. E/AC.32/SR.17, at 3–4) in J.C. Hathaway, *The Law of Refugee Status* (1991), *op. cit.*, p. 103.

63 B.S. Chimni (Ed.) *International Refugee Law: A Reader*, First ed. (New Delhi: Sage Publications, 2000), pp. 3–4.

64 UNHCR, *Handbook on Procedures, op. cit.*, § 51.

65 *Ibid.*, § 53.

66 M. Foster, *International Refugee Law and Socio-Economic Rights: Refuge from Deprivation* (2007), *op. cit.*, pp. 92–93.

67 European Union: Council of the European Union, *Presidency Conclusions, Tampere European Council, 15–16 October 1999*, 16 October 1999, §13.

68 The Qualification Directive refers to "the rights from which derogation cannot be made under Article 15(2) of the European Convention for the Protection of Human Rights and

to affect an individual in a similar manner.[69] This definition of acts of persecution was transposed in their national legislation by most EU Member States.[70] Persecution potentially includes any human rights violation (or accumulation of violations), provided they reach a certain level of severity or seriousness.

Besides defining acts of persecution, the Directive also provides a list of examples of such acts. It can be noted that although environmental degradations or their impacts are – obviously – not mentioned, the provision however makes it clear that the list is not exhaustive (*"inter alia"*) and, in transposing the article in full, Member States have therefore agreed to take other forms of persecution into account. In its 2010 Report on the application of the Directive, the European Commission in fact observed that among the Member States that had already transposed the Directive, only Slovenia had transposed the list as an exhaustive one.[71] The *travaux préparatoires* of the Qualification Directive inform that it was the intention of the Commission to allow a leeway for interpretation and extension of the list of acts constitutive of persecution. In its Explanatory Memorandum to the proposal, the European Commission clarified the nature of persecution in the following terms:

Fundamental Freedoms" which also include the right not to be punished without law. Qualification Directive, Article 9(1)(a) [emphasis added].

69 *Ibid.*, Article 9(1)(b) [emphasis added].

70 In its report to the European Parliament and Council on the application of the Qualification Directive, the Commission notes that France did not transpose Article 9 of the Directive. French legislation indeed does not provide for an extensive definition of a refugee but instead lists three categories of refugees: freedom fighters, Mandate refugees and "refugees who fulfil the criteria of the Geneva Convention definition" (indicative translation). The Convention criteria themselves are not listed and, *a fortiori*, not detailed. The Commission's Report also highlights that Czech Republic uses a different definition of the term persecution. Albeit different, the Czech definition is nevertheless similar in that it is anchored in human rights: "persecution means serious violation of human rights as well as measures which result in psychological pressure or any other similar treatment". European Commission, "Report on the application of the Qualification Directive", *op. cit.*, pp. 7–8; CESEDA, *op. cit.*, Article L711-1; Czech Republic: Act of 11 November 1999 on Asylum and Amendment to Act No. 283/1991 Coll., on the Police of the Czech Republic, as Amended (the Asylum Act), 325/1999 Coll., consolidated version of 31 January 2008, Section 2(8) [English translation of the Act available on the website of the Ministry of the Interior of the Czech Republic: <www.mvrc.cz>]; Qualification Directive, Article 9(1)(b) [emphasis added].

71 European Union: European Commission, *Report on the application of Directive 2004/83/EC of 29 April 2004 on minimum standards for the qualification and status of third country nationals or stateless persons as refugees or as persons who otherwise need international protection and the content of the protection*, 16 June 2010, COM(2010)314 final, p. 7.

As the concept of persecution is not grounded in time, the interpretation of persecution outlined in this Article is intended to be flexible, adaptable and sufficiently open, in order to reflect ever-changing forms of persecution, which may constitute a basis for refugee status.[72]

Persecution, the European Commission confirms, is intended to cover not certain forms of harm but rather any harm of a certain severity.

Although this was not made explicit in the 1951 Convention, acts of persecution have long been construed as human rights violations.[73] Arguably, such interpretation is in line with the spirit of the Refugee Convention: its Preamble refers explicitly to the principle, enshrined in the UN Charter[74] and the Universal Declaration of Human Rights (UDHR[75]), that human beings shall all enjoy fundamental rights and freedoms without discrimination.[76]

In 1991, J.C. Hathaway proposed a definition of acts constitutive of persecution, entrenched in human rights law, on the basis of a categorisation of human rights in four groups. Three of them are types of harm encompassed in the notion of persecution under refugee law: first, those rights enshrined in the Universal Declaration of Human Rights which are binding and non-derogable under the International Covenant on Civil (ICCPR), second, other civil and political rights, also enshrined in both the UDHR and ICCPR and from which States may derogate only in exceptional circumstances, and third, rights contained in the UDHR and codified in the International Covenant on Economic, Social and Cultural Rights (ICESCR), which States must progressively realise, to the maximum of their available resources. Violations of rights of the fourth category, to wit those rights which are enshrined in the UDHR but were codified in neither of the two Covenants, would not ordinarily suffice "in and of themselves" to claim international protection on their basis.[77]

---

72 European Union: European Commission, *Explanatory Memorandum to the Commission Proposal for a Council Directive on Minimum Standards for the Qualification and Status of Third Country Nationals and Stateless Persons as Refugees or as Persons Who Otherwise Need International Protection*, COM (2001)510 final, 12 September 2001, Commentary on Article 11 (*i.e.* now Article 9 of the Qualification Directive), p. 19.

73 UNHCR Handbook refers to threat to life or freedom and other "serious violations of human rights". UNHCR, *Handbook on Procedures, op. cit.*, § 51.

74 UN Charter, *op. cit.*

75 UDHR, *op. cit.*

76 D. Lobry, "Pour une définition juridique des réfugiés écologiques : réflexion autour de la qualification juridique de l'atteinte à l'environnement", *REVUE Asylon(s)*, No. 6: Exodes écologiques, November 2008, retrieved from: <http://www.reseauterra.eu/article846.html> [16/07/2012].

77 J.C. Hathaway, *The Law of Refugee Status* (1991), *op. cit.*, pp. 108–112.

This dynamic reading of the Refugee Convention, along a human-rights based approach, has in fact gained momentum in recent years, in literature and in asylum case-law.[78] On the basis of a thorough analysis of case law from various jurisdictions, M. Foster found that asylum authorities have expressed and demonstrated increased willingness to consider claims based on the deprivation of economic and social rights.[79] This notwithstanding, M. Foster deplores that this willingness has not often translated into positive decisions, granting refugee status to the applicant.[80] It appears that the persistent tendency of asylum authorities to rely on a hierarchical approach to human rights[81] or on an overly categorical approach, instead of recognising the indivisibility or "interconnectedness" of human rights, accounts in large part for the limited positive outcome of socio-economic claims.[82] Additionally, decision-makers have shown a tendency to be distracted by the existence of socio-economic factors and overlook, in such cases, the existence of other, non-economic factors, thereby reducing the applicant's displacement to a mere search for a better life.[83] Nevertheless, the fact remains that socio-economic rights are broadly acknowledged as constitutive of persecution – albeit in certain circumstances only.

New Zealand courts appear to endorse the same approach. A 2012 decision issued by the Immigration and Protection Tribunal clearly states that:

---

78   Michelle Foster, on the basis of a systematic analysis of international, regional and national decisions (mainly in Australia, Canada, New Zealand, South Africa, the United Kingdom and the United States), notes that the human rights approach to interpreting the Refugee Convention "is now dominant in the common law world, and increasingly accepted in many civil law jurisdictions as well". M. Foster, *International Refugee Law and Socio-Economic Rights: Refuge from Deprivation* (2007), *op. cit.*, pp. 87–88 and evidenced throughout the book; J.C. Hathaway, *The Law of Refugee Status* (1991), *op. cit.*, pp. 108–112.
79   M. Foster, *International Refugee Law and Socio-Economic Rights: Refuge from Deprivation* (2007), *op. cit.*, pp. 91–111.
80   In contrast though, M. Foster notes that "it is now almost indisputable that cases involving a complete denial of the right to work are considered sufficiently serious to warrant characterisation as 'persecution'". For M. Foster, the impacts that denial of all means to earn a living has on a person's subsistence might account for the recognition of such denial as persecution. *Ibid.*, pp. 94; *ibid.*, pp. 91–111.
81   M. Foster notes that "in undertaking the task of weighing the gravity of the harm in a particular case, decision-makers must abandon notions of a hierarchy as between starkly defined categories, and recognize that violations of a range of socio-economic rights are capable of constituting persecution". *Ibid.*, p. 213; *ibid.*, pp. 94.
82   *Ibid.*, pp. 123–155.
83   *Ibid.*, pp. 238–247.

[the Immigration and Protection Tribunal] accepts that breaches of rights under the ICESCR may, in principle, be relied on to found a refugee claim as rights *in themselves*.[84]

Through its case-law, New Zealand Immigration and Protection Tribunal has confirmed that breaches of socio-economic rights might trigger the applicability of the Refugee Convention in the context of environmental changes and disasters.[85] Decisions analysed whether the harm invoked by the refugee claimant in a given case was constitutive of a breach at the core of several human rights,[86] including for example the right to work,[87] the right to safe drinking water,[88] the right to an adequate standard of living,[89] or the right to adequate food.[90]

From the different elements of definition cited above, it can be inferred that the main criterion is not one of the type of harm invoked but one of "severity" or "seriousness"[91] of the acts, "because of their inherent nature or because of their repetition",[92] or due to their combination with other factors and circumstances such as the geographical, historical and ethnological context (persecution on "cumulative grounds").[93] The question of the existence of persecution indeed remains one "of degree and proportion".[94] In order to determine whether measures or treatments amount to persecution, it is necessary to conduct:

---

84   New Zealand: Immigration and Protection Tribunal, BG (*Fiji*), [2012] NZIPT 800091, 20 January 2012, § 90.

85   [2015] NZIPT 800859, AF (*Tuvalu*), 20 October 2015, § 51; NZIPT, AF (*Kiribati*), § 63.

86   In the case concerning I. Teitiota, New Zealand High Court found that the appellant was not entitled to refugee status because the alleged harm did not amount to persecution. The appellant, the Court stated, failed to establish that he would suffer "a sustained and systemic violation of his basic human rights such as the right to life under Article 6 of the ICCPR or *the right to adequate food, clothing and housing under Article 11 of ICESCR*". NZHC, *Teitiota, op. cit.*, § 54 [emphasis added].

87   NZIPT, AF (*Tuvalu*), §§ 50–71.

88   *Ibid.*, §§ 72–75 and NZIPT, AF (*Kiribati*), § 73.

89   AF (*Kiribati*), §§ 73–74.

90   *Ibid.*

91   Such are the terms used in the Qualification Directive, in the definition of acts of persecution. Qualification Directive, Article 9(1).

92   *Ibid.*, Article 9(1).

93   UNHCR, UNHCR, *Handbook on Procedures, op. cit.*, § 53.

94   G.S. Goodwin-Gill and J. McAdam, *The Refugee in International Law* (2007), *op. cit.*, p. 92.

... an assessment of a complex of factors, including (1) the nature of the freedom threatened, (2) the nature and severity of the restriction, and (3) the likelihood of the restriction eventuating in the individual case.[95]

As mentioned above, the concept of persecution is broad and a wide variety of harms may be considered as persecutory. Concerning claims based on economic, social and cultural rights, it can be argued that deprivation of a one such right can be on a par with deprivation of a civil or political right;[96] in particular, J.C. Hathaway argues that:

... the deprivation of certain of the socio-economic rights, such as the ability to earn a living, or the entitlement to food, shelter, or health care will at an extreme level be tantamount to the deprivation of life or cruel, inhuman or degrading treatment, and hence unquestionably constitute persecution.[97]

M. Foster notes that decision-makers (in the UK and USA in particular) have indeed recognised that economic or social harm and civil or political harm can each produce an impact of similar gravity on an individual.[98]

Deprivation of a social or economic right can also on its own constitute persecution when the measure leads to the right being completely "nullified",[99]

---

95 Ibid., p. 92; also C.M. Kozoll (2004), op. cit., pp. 282–283.
96 NZIPT, AF (Kiribati), §§ 68 (the Tribunal envisages a breach of the right to food in connection with the right to life).
97 J.C. Hathaway, The Law of Refugee Status (1991), op. cit., p. 111.
98 M. Foster, International Refugee Law and Socio-Economic Rights: Refuge from Deprivation (2007), op. cit., pp. 91–92.
99 The term was used by the House of Lords in the Ullah & Do case, albeit not to assess whether a measure constituted persecution but in the context of UK's non-refoulement obligations. The House of Lords stated that any ECHR right could be invoked to substantiate a claim against refoulement however, it must be demonstrated that return would expose the individual to a "flagrant violation" of the right invoked, to a situation where the right would be "completely denied or nullified" in the destination country. UKHL, Ullah and Do, 17 June 2004, op. cit., § 69; M. Foster, International Refugee Law and Socio-Economic Rights: Refuge from Deprivation (2007), op. cit., pp. 91–92.

when the violation concerns the core,[100] the essence of the right,[101] or when it is "tantamount to destitution or otherwise of a serious nature".[102]

The broad and open concept of persecution therefore appears to allow for the inclusion of threats such as those resulting from environmental disasters under the notion of persecution.[103] Situations of sudden or slow-onset environmental degradation, in which dwellings and infrastructures are destroyed or threaten to be, resources are reduced or scarce, and State authorities weakened, unquestionably hamper, or possibly prevent, people's enjoyment of their human rights. Environmental disasters affect populations as well as, by nature, their conditions or standard of living.[104] As observed by N. Schrepfer and W. Kälin in the specific context of climate change:

> ... similar to persecution, climate change-related disasters and the unavailability of adequate food, drinking water or health services in their aftermath may constitute serious threats to life, limb and health.[105]

---

100   Under New Zealand case-law: "the claimant's predicament must establish a real chance of a sustained or systemic *violation of a core human right* demonstrative of a failure of state protection which has sufficient nexus to a Convention ground". NZIPT, *AF (Kiribati)*, § 65 [emphasis added].

101   M. Foster, *International Refugee Law and Socio-Economic Rights: Refuge from Deprivation* (2007), *op. cit.*, §§ 195–214. The Qualification Directive, which defines persecution as a "severe violation" of human rights can also be interpreted in that sense. It is not a matter of hierarchy of rights, based on their nature (social, cultural and economic *versus* civil and political), but rather a matter of gravity of the breach itself. Qualification Directive, Article 9(1)(a) and (b).

102   G. Jaeger, "The Definition of 'Refugee': Restrictive Versus Expanding Trends", *in* R.E. Tripp and United States Committee for Refugees – Uscr (Eds.), *World Refugee Survey, 1983* (Washington DC: USCR, 1984), pp. 5–9, p. 7.

103   C. Marcs refers to threats to life and deprivation of economic, social and cultural rights. C. Marcs, "Spoiling Movi's River: Towards Recognition of Persecutory Environmental Harm within the Meaning of the Refugee Convention ", *American University International Law Review*, Vol. 24, No. 1 (2008), pp. 31–71, pp. 47–52.

104   Groupe de Travail du Comité de Gestion Interagence sur le Risque l'Urgence et le Sinistre pour l'Amérique et les Caraïbes (REDLAC), *Méthodologie d'évaluation rapide pour l'assistance humanitaire* (n/a: REDLAC, December 2006), p. 9. In this context, Article 25 of the Universal Declaration of Human Rights is of relevance insofar as it identifies elements of what constitutes "a standard of living adequate for the health and well-being"; these include food, clothing, housing and medical care and necessary social services. UDHR, Article 25.

105   W. Kälin and N. Schrepfer, *Protecting People Crossing Borders in the Context of Climate Change Normative Gaps and Possible Approaches* (February 2012), *op. cit.*, p. 32.

Other rights can also be severely threatened if not nullified: the possibility to work and earn a living when office buildings have been destroyed or fields devastated, to acquire education when school buildings have collapsed, to receive medical treatment when hospitals are overloaded, medical equipment damaged, or supplies of medicines exhausted, or the right to own and reclaim one's property are but examples of effects environmental disasters may have on populations. It can be added that this holds true for slow-onset disasters and is particularly visible in communities where lifestyles and livelihoods are highly dependent on the environment, such as indigenous people but not only. In Alaska, the village of Shishmaref, on Sarichef Island, and its population are facing the effects of the increase in global average temperature: the village, built on permafrost, is shrinking with the thawing of permafrost. Major erosions have already occurred and swept away dwellings and infrastructures. Moreover, the population relies heavily on subsistence lifestyle, including hunting, fishing and handicrafts.[106] The rise in temperature threatens their homes, traditions and culture, and subsistence. The changes occurring in the Sundarbans, a specific type of mangrove forest in south Bangladesh (and in India), are also significant. Increasing soil salination, in part triggered by a tsunami in 1988, has led to the transformation of rice paddies and pasturelands for cattle into shrimp farms, depriving many of their work, as well as to the depletion of fresh-water sources.[107] Similarly, climate change threatens to reduce the surface of habitable land on the low-lying Pacific islands of Tuvalu and Kiribati, increasing the overcrowding of the islands and pressure on the already labour market, and affecting agricultural capacity, itself worsened by increasing soil salination.[108]

Degraded environmental conditions can be of such severity that they threaten individuals' life or person, or expose them to risks of severe violations of other human rights. In view of the above and, in particular, of the definition of persecution provided in the Qualification Directive, it is possible to state that the effects of environmental degradation or their accumulation can expose individuals to serious threats which would qualify as persecution if in the context of "standard" refugee cases. As noted by UNHCR in 2012:

> Even where the cause of displacement – whether internal or across borders – is purely environmental, the affected populations may have

---

106   Collectif Argos, *Climate Refugees* (Cambridge, MA: Massachusetts Institute of Technology Press, 2010), pp. 18–51.
107   *Ibid.*, pp. 58–59 in particular.
108   J. McAdam, *Climate Change, Forced Migration, and International Law* (2012), *op. cit.*, pp. 43–44.

protection needs and vulnerabilities similar to those of people whose flight is provoked by violence or human rights abuses.[109]

The apparent potential for inclusion of the threats caused by environmental disasters in the seemingly broad and adaptable definition of persecution must however be nuanced. The identity of actors of persecution must be discussed (2). The second – and possibly most challenging – caveat, which will be analysed subsequently, pertains to the reasons of persecution (3).

2 Actors of Persecution: From the "Accountability Theory" to the (Absolute?) "Protection Theory"

The notion of "persecution" intimates that there is a "persecutor". A problem which manifests itself clearly in a context of damage caused and migration triggered by environmental disaster is that of the identity of this persecutor. As it was originally conceived – and implemented, the legal notion of "refugee" was meant to protect individuals against persecution by their own State.[110] In many cases however, persecution emanates not from the State but from non-State actors against which State authorities cannot or will not protect. Following the debate which opposed proponents of the "accountability theory" to those of the "protection theory" (a), asylum authorities and the EU legislator in particular have chosen to focus not (entirely) on the identity of the agent of persecution but rather on the existence or absence of State protection against persecution (b). A further development which follows on naturally from this shift in focus, from the identity of actors of persecution to the existence or absence of protection against persecution, is the recognition that persons who flee persecution, *whichever its source*, deserve international protection as soon and as long as they do not receive effective protection in their country of origin (c).

(a) *The Arguments in the Debate about Non-state Actors of Persecution*

Proponents of the "accountability theory" were typically States presumably anxious to limit their obligations under refugee law and dissuade refugees from seeking asylum on their territories.[111] National authorities endorsing this

---

109 UNHCR, *The State of the World's Refugees 2012: In Search of Solidarity* (2012), *op. cit.*, p. 169.
110 W. Kälin (2000–2001), *op. cit.*, p. 430.
111 The idea of a dissuasive impact anticipated by States adopting such restrictive interpretation of the notion of actors of persecution is formulated by Daphné Bouteillet-Paquet in *L'Europe et le droit d'asile* (Paris: L'Harmattan, 2001), p. 243. The author presents the various interpretations of the notion prevailing at the turn of the millennium, both in literature (including the position of the UNHCR) and in European states' case-law (pp. 240–249).

view restrictively interpreted Article 1A of the Geneva Convention as requiring that the alleged persecution emanate either from State authorities themselves or from non-State agents whose actions are supported or at least tolerated by State authorities. They described persecution within the meaning of the refugee definition as "an act of government against individuals".[112]

In Europe, French courts[113] first considered that persecution could only emanate from public authorities; were for example designated under this label the government[114] and its administration,[115] the military[116] and public hospital authorities.[117] Their position evolved under the influence of the *Conseil d'état* who held that persecution could emanate from non-State agents and lead to recognition where "the facts [were] in fact voluntarily tolerated or encouraged by the public authorities, effectively making it impossible for the interested party to claim the protection of these authorities".[118] The notions of "voluntary tolerance" and "encouragement", criticised for being vague and open to interpretation,[119] were subsequently abundantly elaborated upon by courts, who drew a blurred line between what could and could not be recognised as persecution. According to F. Tiberghien, French Councillor of State, ensuing case-law became "exuberant, complicated and protean" in spite of the Convention refugee definition being obvious.[120] In light of the meaning of the word persecution and of the object and purposes of the Convention, F. Tiberghien argues, Article 1A(2) very clearly implies that the sole impossibility for an individual to claim the protection of his or her State is sufficient to identify a refugee.[121]

---

112   Astri Suhrkem, "Global Refugee Movements and Strategies of Response", in Mary M. Kritz (ed.), *US Immigration Policy: Global and Domestic Issues* (Mass.: Lexington Books, 1983), 157–159.

113   For a critical survey and analysis of earlier French jurisprudence on agents of persecution, see in particular Frédéric Tiberghien, "Statut de réfugié et persecution par des agents non publics", RFDA No.2, 1998 p. 244s.

114   France: Commission des Recours des Réfugiés (hereinafter "CRR"), 2 March 1956, *Pritsch*, 1389.

115   France: CRR, 01 February 1977, *Zaoude*, 8637.

116   France: CRR, 25 Sept. 1986, *Melle Lambert*, 43599.

117   France: CRR, 18 Sept. 1991, *Melle X*, 164078. In this case, female circumcision carried out by public hospital authorities was seen as constitutive of an act of persecution.

118   France: Conseil d'Etat, 27 mai 1983, *Dankha*, 42074. The ruling is cited in European Council on Refugees and Exiles, ELENA *Research Paper on Non-State Agents of Persecution*, 1 September 2000, p. 31. [Translation by ECRE].

119   F. Tiberghien, "Statut de réfugié et persécution par des agents non publics", RFDA No.2, 1998 p. 244s, at IV.B.

120   *Ibid.*, at IV.C.3 and VIII. [My translation].

121   *Ibid.*, at I.

This is the position steadily held by UNHCR[122] and other partisans of the "protection theory":[123] persecution can emanate from non-State agents and qualify asylum seekers as refugees if the authorities of the State of origin proved *unwilling or unable*[124] to provide an effective protection to victims.[125] The formulation echoes the text of Article 1A(2): a Convention refugee, by definition, is "unable or unwilling" to avail himself of the protection of his country of origin. In the words of Goodwin-Gill:

> [T]he notion of inability to secure the protection of the State is broad enough to include a situation where the authorities cannot or will not provide protection, for example, against the persecution of non-State actors.[126]

This "protection theory" reflects the fundamental function of refugee protection: it is a form of "surrogate protection",[127] a substitute for the protection which is lacking from the state.[128] The approach was eventually adopted by French courts but also at EU level with the adoption of the Qualification Directive.

(b) *Non-state Actors of Persecution: A Reality Acknowledged by the Qualification Directive*

The EU Qualification Directive eventually closed the debate – in Europe – when, embracing the more liberal views of UNHCR and of the majority of European States, it made it mandatory for all EU Member States to adhere to the "protection theory". Under Article 6 of the Qualification Directive, actors of persecution (or serious harm, where subsidiary protection is at stake) include:

(a) the State;
(b) parties or organisations controlling the State or a substantial part of the territory of the State;

---

122   UNHCR, *Handbook on Procedures, op. cit.*, § 65.
123   J.C. Hathaway, *The Law of Refugee Status* (1991), *op. cit.*, pp. 125–133; W. Kälin (2000–2001), *op. cit.*
124   J.C. Hathaway observes that "there is a failure of protection where a government is *unwilling* to defend citizens against private harm, as well as in situations of objective *inability* to provide meaningful protection". J.C. Hathaway, *The Law of Refugee Status* (1991), *op. cit.*, p. 127.
125   *See* for example Andrew E. Schacknove, "Who is a Refugee?" *Ethics, vol. 95, No.2* (1985), p. 277; and UNHCR, *Handbook on Procedures, op. cit.*, § 65.
126   Guy S. Goodwin-Gil, *Introductory Note, Convention relating to the Status of Refugees & Protocol relating to the Status of Refugees* (New York: Audiovisual Library of International Law), p. 3.
127   W. Kälin (2000–2001), *op. cit.*, p. 431.
128   J.-Y. Carlier (1997), *op. cit.*, pp. 705–707.

(c) non-State actors, if it can be demonstrated that the actors mentioned in (a) and (b), including international organisations, are *unable or unwilling* to provide protection against persecution or serious harm.[129]

Studies on the implementation of the Qualification Directive show that a large majority of Member States chose to transpose this provision literally in their national legislation and accepted, in practice, non-State actors as actors of persecution.[130] At the time ECRE completed its study, although some Member States could not yet produce examples of relevant jurisprudence, the majority stated that no non-State actor of persecution had not been recognised as such (that is, all non-State actors of persecution were recognised as persecutors).[131] In other words, Member States consider that persecution, if it is inflicted by a non-State agent, should nevertheless be recognised as such and its author therefore as an "actor of persecution".

In such cases, where persecution emanates from non-State actors, applicants must demonstrate that it is coupled with the absence of protection by their country's national authorities against such acts. In Luxembourg[132] and

---

129   Qualification Directive, Article 6.
130   European Union: European Commission, *Report on the application of Directive 2004/83/EC of 29 April 2004 on minimum standards for the qualification and status of third country nationals or stateless persons as refugees or as persons who otherwise need international protection and the content of the protection*, 16 June 2010, COM(2010)314 final, at 5.1.3.; European Council on Refugees and Exiles, *The Impact of the EU Qualification Directive on International Protection*, October 2008, pp. 84–93; Academic Network for Legal Studies on Immigration and Asylum in Europe: Study on "Conformity Checking of the Transposition by Member States of 10 Directives in the Sector of Asylum and Immigration", Directive 2004/83 Qualification Directive, Synthesis Report, 2007, at 3.2.3.
131   European Council on Refugees and Exiles, *The Impact of the EU Qualification Directive on International Protection*, October 2008, p. 90.
132   In Luxembourg, the reasoning is the following: "cependant, il échet de rappeler que les actes de persécution émanant de personnes étrangères aux autorités publiques s'analysent en une persécution émanant non pas de l'Etat, mais d'un groupe de la population et ne sauraient dès lors être reconnus comme motif d'octroi du statut de réfugié que si la personne en cause ne bénéficie pas de la protection des autorités de son pays d'origine pour l'une des cinq causes visées à l'article 1er de la Convention de Genève ou si elles sont incapables de fournir une telle protection. Il convient d'ajouter que la notion de protection de la part du pays d'origine n'implique pas une sécurité physique absolue des habitants contre la commission de tout acte de violence et qu'une persécution ne saurait être admise dès la commission matérielle d'un acte criminel. Il ne saurait en être autrement qu'en cas de défaut de protection, dont l'existence doit être mise suffisamment en évidence par le demandeur d'asile. Il faut en plus que le demander d'asile ait

the United Kingdom,[133] individuals invoking persecution by non-State actors have been denied protection in cases where national asylum authorities have found that the claimants had failed to establish that state protection was not available in their country of origin. In France, the *Commission de Recours des Réfugiés* found that a Somali national was to be granted refugee status due to the persecutions she would be exposed to upon return to Somalia and to the incapacity of the government then in place to effectively control the Somali territory and protect persecuted minorities.[134]

The "protection theory", long advocated by UNHCR and by the majority of commentators, prevailed in European Union asylum law with the adoption of the Qualification Directive. Its actual reach in cases where displacement is triggered by environmental change must be clarified.

(c)   *Environmental Persecution and Protection: By Whom?*
The "protection theory", as it prevails under EU law, must be put to the test of environmental persecution. To contextualise the notions of "agent of persecution" and "protection against persecution" issues of agent of persecution, four scenarios can be put forward.

– The degradation of the environment is deliberately caused by State or non-State agents (1) (discussed below, in (ii))
  ○ and targets the applicant or the group he or she belongs to (1a).
  ○ and causes unintended collateral damage to the applicant (1b).
– The degradation is accidental (technological or industrial accident) or natural (weather-related or geophysical[135]) (discussed below, in (iii))
  ○ but State authorities are *unwilling* to protect the applicant (2a).
  ○ and State authorities are *unable* to protect the applicant (2b).

---

concrètement recherché cette protection, de sorte que ce n'est qu'en cas de défaut de protection, dont l'existence doit être mise suffisamment en exergue par le demandeur d'asile, qu'il y a lieu de prendre en compte une persécution commise par des tiers (cf. Jean-Yves Carlier : *Qu'est-ce qu'un réfugié ?*, p. 113, n° 73 et suivants)". Tribunal administratif du Grand-Duché de Luxembourg, N° 21505, 9 June 2006.

133   European Council on Refugees and Exiles, *The Impact of the EU Qualification Directive on International Protection*, October 2008, pp. 91–92.

134   France: Commission des Recours des Réfugiés (hereinafter "CRR"), Sections réunies, 29 July 2005, *Melle A.*, 4487336. French law had in fact been amended to transpose the Qualification Directive already in 2003, *i.e.* prior to the adoption of the Directive (*LOI n° 2003-1176 du 10 décembre 2003 modifiant la loi n° 52-893 du 25 juillet 1952 relative au droit d'asile*, Article 1, now *Code de l'entrée et du séjour des étrangers et du droit d'asile*, Article L 713-2).

135   For a typology of natural hazard-related disasters, *see* Annex 3.

Before turning to consider each scenario, regard must be had to the notion of "actors of protection" and its controversial definition by the Qualification Directive (i).

(i) State and Non-state Actors of Protection

The EU Qualification Directive in fact broadens the notion of "actor of protection": pursuant to Article 7 of the Directive, actors of protection in the country of origin can be the State but also "parties or organisations, including international organisations, controlling the State or a substantial part of the territory of the State".[136] The possibility that protection be provided by non-State actors was maintained in the recast Qualification Directive, despite UNHCR's objections that non-State actors do not have the attributes of a State, nor the same obligations as States under international law.[137] The provision was however amended. In particular, and in line with the judgment of the EU Court of Justice in *Abdulla*,[138] the Directive clarifies that protection must always be "effective and durable" and actors of protection not only be *willing* to offer protection but also *able* to. As a guarantee that protection is indeed effective, the Directive further stipulates that protection is conditional upon applicants having *access* to it and actors of protection taking "reasonable steps to prevent the persecution". Article 7 clarifies the vague requirement of "reasonable steps" by indicating that such step can consist in, *inter alia*, the operation of "an effective legal system for the detection, prosecution and punishment of acts constituting persecution (...) and when the applicant has access to such protection". This controversial approach to protection against persecution appears as a "pragmatic response to the political reality that states are not the exclusive repositories of power in the modern world".[139]

In the aftermath of a sudden large-scale environmental disaster, protection and assistance is brought to affected population by a variety of actors. National authorities, civil society, aid agencies, foreign governments, international

---

136 Qualification Directive, Article 7.
137 UNHCR (July 2010), "Comments on Proposal for Recast QD", *op. cit.*, Comment on Article 7, pp. 4–5.
138 The *Abdulla* case concerned the cessation of refugee status by reason of a change of circumstances. The Court of Justice noted that pursuant to the Directive, the "change of circumstances will be of a 'significant and non-temporary' nature, within the terms of Article 11(2) of the Directive, when the factors which formed the basis of the refugee's fear of persecution may be regarded as having been permanently eradicated". CJ, *Salahadin*, § 73; UNHCR (July 2010), "Comments on Proposal for Recast QD", *op. cit.*, Comment on Article 7, pp. 4–5.
139 P. Mathew, et al., "The Role of State Protection in Refugee Analysis", *International Journal of Refugee Law* (Oxford University Press / USA), Vol. 15, No. 3 (2003), pp. 444–460, § 35.

governmental and non-governmental organisation mobilise to support the affected country and population, albeit in more or less coordinated manner. Only those who can be held responsible under international law can qualify as "actor of protection" under the Qualification Directive; this includes States, including the affected State, but also international agencies with legal personality (such as United Nations agencies) and who are mandated under international law to provide assistance and protection. In any case and pursuant to the principle of State sovereignty, the consent of the State affected by a disaster is a prerequisite.[140]

It follows that an EU Member State may return an environmentally-displaced person under the pretext of the presence of governmental and non-governmental national or international organisations in the applicant's country of origin, delivering assistance and protection to the population, but only under the cumulative conditions that the State of origin has consented to this presence, that these non-governmental actors of protection are willing and able to provide effective and non-temporary protection to which the applicant has access, that they demonstrate this ability and willingness by taking reasonable steps to the end of providing such protection and, lastly, that they can be held responsible under international law for their actions. This holds true both in situations of slow-onset disasters and of sudden-onset disasters. In the former case, the protection provided to the population confronted to depleting resources due to a progressive deterioration of the environment can be devised to avoid tensions in the country, fostered for instance by competition over scarce resources or over property of arable lands. It can also be in the form of technical assistance to development projects meant to mitigate the effects of environmental degradation, such as the construction of seawalls, wells, antiseismic buildings, etc. In the case of sudden-onset disasters, protection may comprise international peace-keeping forces, medical personnel, the provision of food, water and medicine supplies, technical assistance for the reconstruction, etc.[141]

Three final observations can temper the otherwise persuasive criticisms formulated against an extended definition of "actors of protection". Firstly, as noted by the European Commission in 2010, a number of EU Member States choose to set additional criteria for the recognition of an entity as an "actor of

---

140 *Ibid.*, §§ 34–39.
141 The United Nations' humanitarian response to the earthquake which struck Haiti in 2010, organised in clusters (discussed in Part 3), is detailed in: R. Margesson and M. Taft-Morales, *Haiti Earthquake: Crisis and Response* (Washington, DC: Congressional Research Service, 19 February 2010), pp. 9–12.

protection". Some States consider that only States and international organisations can be actors of protection, other States consider that the entity must have the attributes of a state, or lastly, it may be required by national law or asylum authorities that the protection provided by non-State entities be accessible, durable and effective.[142] The Commission deplored that some other States chose to view clans, tribes or non-governmental organisations as capable of providing protection against persecution.[143] A second point follows: the Commission endeavoured to limit the risks of excessive expansion of the notion of actors of protection in its proposal for a recast Qualification Directive. As mentioned above, the amendments brought in the text place important safeguards. Lastly, it is possible to wonder whether the provision might not after all have some positive impacts. Under the Qualification Directive, States can legally return an applicant to a country where a risk of persecution exists but is deviated by the presence and efficiency of national authorities or international organisation (fulfilling the requirement mentioned above) who have the demonstrated willingness and ability to protect the applicant against persecution. Would it not be in States' best interest[144] then to further develop international cooperation and ensure that international organisations with legal personality are equipped with sufficient means (human, material and financial) to provide effective protection *in situ* to populations affected by "displacement-triggering disasters"?

(ii)   Scenario 1: The Degradation of the Environment is Deliberately Caused

A healthy environment is essential to human life. Man has long acknowledged and made "good" use of this obvious connection, altering a village, region or country's environment to harm its inhabitants. Environmental degradation can either directly harm populations (chemical weapons or construction of a dam) or indirectly and force them to flee in search of an inhabitable environment (soil or water contamination for instance). When governments knowingly inflict such "environmental harm" on individuals, provided it reaches a

---

142   European Commission, "Commission Report on the application of QD (2004)", *op. cit.*, p. 6.
143   *Ibid.*
144   That is, assuming that States' demonstrated preference (often portrayed in Europe as the construction of "fortress Europe") for reducing inflows of migrants on their territory is indeed in States' best interests. Norman Myers observed this tendency in 1997 already in N. Myers (1997), *op. cit*; European Commission, "Commission Report on the application of QD (2004)", *op. cit.*

certain level of severity, it could constitute persecution ("environmental persecution") under the Refugee Convention,[145] regardless of whether the direct harm is on the environment or on the individual.[146] In a word, "environmental harm is as capable of being a *means* of persecution as any other form of harm".[147]

This can correspond to the situation where a party in a conflict uses means or methods of warfare which severely alter the environment, in order to gain a military advantage or harm populations. Such practice causes the populations concerned to flee and seek protection in a country of refuge which is not a party to the conflict.[148] A similar case is the deliberate destruction of the environment by the government intended to persecute the local population, in retaliation for its supposed or confirmed opposition to the party in power.[149] The poisoning of water wells or burning of crops or draining of marshlands[150] and the scorched earth policy are but examples of environmental destructions inflicted as methods to "persecute, intimidate or displace a particular population".[151] Concrete examples include the use of herbicides sprayed over Vietnam by US forces to defoliate landing strip or roads and to destroy "enemy crops" as part of a food denial program[152] and the deliberate draining and desiccation of Southern Iraq marshlands by Saddam Hussein's regime, in retaliation of the Marsh Arabs' support to the Shiites during the so-called "First Gulf War".

---

145 J.B. Cooper, "Environmental Refugees: Meeting the Requirements of the Refugee Definition", *New York University Environmental Law Journal*, Vol. 6 (1998), pp. 480–529, p. 520; also V.O. Kolmannskog, *Future Floods of Refugees: A Comment on Climate Change, Conflict and Forced Migration* (April 2008), op. cit., p. 27.
146 C.M. Kozoll (2004), op. cit., p. 273.
147 Ibid., p. 297 [emphasis added].
148 If the party of refuge is a party to the conflict, it is bound by the rules of international humanitarian law relevant to the protection of civilian populations. Also above, pp. 286s.
149 W. Kälin and N. Schrepfer, *Protecting People Crossing Borders in the Context of Climate Change Normative Gaps and Possible Approaches* (February 2012), op. cit., pp. 32–33; M. Vinez and S. Leonard, "The Iraq Marshlands: The Loss of the Garden of Eden and Its People", 19th Annual Illinois State University Conference for Students of Political Science, organised in Illinois, in 8 April 2011 p. 4, retrieved from: <http://pol.illinoisstate.edu/current/conferences/2011/LeonardIraqMarshes.pdf> [06/12/2011]; W. Kälin, "Keynote Address on Internal Displacement and the Marsh Arabs of Iraq", Panel on IDP Issues and the Marsh Arabs, the AMAR Foundation Conference, organised in London, in 1 March 2006, retrieved from: <www.brookings.edu/events/2006/03/01-iraq> [06/12/2011].
150 UNHCR (1997), op. cit., p. 28, Box 1.2.
151 Ibid., p. 28, Box 1.2.
152 W.A. Buckingham, Jr., "Operation Ranch Hand: Herbicides in Southeast Asia" (July-August 1983). Also above note 1275 and corresponding text.

Development projects can also have deleterious consequences on the environment, affecting natural resources and forcing people to move (extractive industries,[153] dam projects[154]). According to estimates, 4 million people are displaced by dam projects every year and 6 million by urbanisation and transport infrastructure.[155] The realisation of large-scale development projects indeed sometimes necessitates the destruction of entire villages and hence the forced displacement of their former inhabitants, whose resettlement is not always assisted by national authorities.[156] Moreover, displacement caused by such projects is found to expose individuals concerned to a risk of impoverishment due to their losing their lands, dwellings or work, to marginalisation in their host society, food insecurity, increase in morbidity and mortality, impaired access to shared resources and social disorganisation.[157]

In view of the risks to which populations affected by the deliberate alteration of their living environment by their State, or by non-State actors supported or tolerated by the State, or against the acts of which the State is unable to protect, it is possible to infer that such situations may place the individuals concerned in refugee-like situations. A central element of the refugee definition which can no longer be ignored at this point is the discriminatory element of the definition: threat to life or limb, or a severe violation of other human rights can only be construed as persecution if the applicant is exposed to it "for reasons of race, religion, nationality, membership of a particular social group or political opinion".[158] Two variations of scenario 1 must therefore considered: either the voluntary alteration of the environment exposes the applicant to a differential risk of harm as against the rest of society for one of the five reasons

---

153 See for examples the cases cited in L. Westra, *Environmental Justice and the Rights of Ecological Refugees* (London, Sterling, VA: Earthscan, 2009), pp. 57–60; and C.M. Kozoll (2004), *op. cit.*, pp. 299 307; C. Marcs (2008), *op. cit.*

154 China building its Three Gorges dam is home to the world's largest hydropower project. The giant dam and powerful dam had however been highly controversial ever since the inception of the project. It has already forced the relocation of over a million persons and may cause more; scientists fear it will trigger landslides, severe earthquakes, and alter ecosystems. L. Westra, *Environmental Justice and the Rights of Ecological Refugees* (2009), *op. cit.*, pp. 57–60; and C.M. Kozoll (2004), *op. cit.*, pp. 299–307; C. Marcs (2008), *op. cit.*

155 M.M. Cernea, "Déplacement forcé et réinstallation de populations : recherche, politiques d'intervention et planification", *in* M.M. Cernea (Ed.), *La dimension humaine dans les projets de développement: les variables sociologiques et culturelles* Karthala Editions (1999), p. 207s, pp. 212–214.

156 D. Chotouras, *Le statut juridique en droit international du réfugié écologique : une nécessité ! (Le phénomène migratoire du fait des modifications environnementales)*, Thesis, *op. cit.*, §§ 141–146.

157 M.M. Cernea (1999), *op. cit.*, pp. 218–221.

158 Refugee Convention, Article 1A(2); Qualification Directive, Article 2(d).

cited (scenario 1a) or exposure to harm is an unintended collateral damage of the voluntary alteration of the environment (scenario 1b). The discriminatory element of the refugee definition is the focus of the next Subsection (C); the final assessment of the chances that environmentally-displaced persons in a "scenario 1" situation are refugees under the Refugee Convention will therefore be made then.

The two scenarios below concern this other, larger, group of persons displaced by environmental change which governments did not – or not deliberately at least – trigger.

(III)   Scenario 2: The Degradation of the Environment is Caused by Technological Accident or Natural Hazard

The link between environmental disasters and forced displacement is unquestionable. The Norwegian Refugee Council's Internal Displacement Monitoring Body (IDMC) reports numerous hazard-related disasters each year and provides estimates of the numbers of persons displaced by such disasters.[159] ReliefWeb publishes a continuously updated list of natural hazard-related disasters; those reports often note the population movements those events trigger.[160] UNHCR also acknowledges the correlation between environmental change and displacement and frequently engages in natural disasters by providing support or being operationally involved.[161] Soil salination, desertification, thawing permafrost, tsunami, or earthquakes are just so many examples of severe disruption of the environment induced by natural hazard likely to displace large populations. Recent decades provide numerous illustrations: Hurricane Mitch in Honduras and Nicaragua in 1998, series of earthquakes in El Salvador in 2001, 2004 Indian Ocean earthquake and ensuing tsunami, 2008 Cyclone Nargis in Burma, 2010 earthquake in Haiti and 2011 earthquake and tsunami in Japan.[162] The impact of slow-onset disasters is also visible and acknowledged: thawing permafrost in Alaska, desertification of the Sahel, salination of Bangladesh Sundarbans, and the shrinking or "sinking" of Pacific island States (Tuvalu and Kiribati being typically mentioned) are frequently evoked.

As illustrated in scenario 1, large development projects can also transform and alter the environment. Voluntarily launched by State authorities, their

---

159   M. Yonetani and IDMC, *Global Estimates 2011: People Displaced by Natural Hazard-Induced Disasters* (Geneva: IDMC – NRC, June 2012). An overview of recent reports published by the IDMC can be found in annex.
160   See Annex 4.
161   UNHCR, *et al.*, *Safe at Last?* (July 2011), *op. cit.*, pp. 169 and 181.
162   *See* also above note 176.

development or operation may incidentally harm the environment and local populations, although such is typically not their intended effect. In some cases, it is less their realisation than accidents affecting them, their faults or their un-anticipated effects that cause environmental harm. Dams can serve as an illustration. Men have long acknowledged that the forces of nature were powerful and developed technology to use those forces to their benefit. Dams are a patent example of this exploitation of nature by men, using hydropower to produce electricity. However, as mentioned above in the example of China's Three Gorges dam, they can cause unplanned or unintended collateral damage such as landslides or earthquakes. The extreme case of dam break, confirming the adage that nature is the ultimate authority, has dramatic consequences for both the environment and populations situated downstream of the breaking dam. Nuclear accidents, such as the Chernobyl and Fukushima Dai-ichi disasters are further examples of potentially severe anthropogenic but involuntary harm to the environment and populations (hereinafter "environmental harm").

The scenarios considered here take place in such situations, where environmental degradation (or threat of degradation) is not voluntarily inflicted by a State or non-State agent. The origin of the harm may be purely natural or partly anthropogenic (technological accidents). The impact on populations will largely depend on governments' response to the disaster. States have the obligation under international law to respect human rights and ensure them to all individuals within their territory and subject to their jurisdiction without distinction of any kind.[163] It follows that, in the aftermath of a natural disaster, the primary duty and responsibility to provide protection and assistance to the affected populations is incumbent on the national authorities of the affected State.[164] It can nevertheless happen that authorities are unable to provide

---

163   The promotion of respect for human rights and for fundamental freedoms for all without distinction as to race, sex, language, or religion appears among the purposes of the Charter of the United Nations United Nations, *Charter of the United Nations*, 24 October 1945, 1 UNTS XVI, Article 1. *See* also UN General Assembly, *International Covenant on Civil and Political Rights*, 16 December 1966, United Nations, Treaty Series, vol. 999, p. 171, Article 2 and Council of Europe, *European Convention for the Protection of Human Rights and Fundamental Freedoms*, 4 November 1950, ETS 5, Article 1.

164   The IASC Operational Guidelines on Human Rights and Natural Disasters stress the responsibility of national authorities and governments in situations of natural disasters affecting their territories. The Guidelines provide valuable information and guidance on the impact of natural disasters on affected populations. It is worth noting that, although they acknowledge that natural disasters are a cause of displacement, they only deal with internal displacement. Inter-Agency Standing Committee, *Human Rights and Natural*

assistance and protection to the affected population (2a); they might also be unwilling to do so (2b).

From the standpoint of refugee protection, the nuance between the two situations is essential, even though, individuals in both situations are exposed to the same risks. The refugee definition, built on the central notion of persecution, and rooted in the condemnation of discrimination, implies that some degree of volition or decision-making is required, either in the infliction of harm or in the refusal to protect. This interpretation of the nexus clause can be summarised as follows:

> Persecution has two elements – the infliction of serious harm, and failure of the state to provide protection – and it is sufficient for one of those elements to connect to a Convention ground for a successful claim to be established.[165]

It follows that in a situation where infliction of serious harm is indiscriminate – as it is when nature alone[166] caused the disaster – the required discriminatory element must be found in States' response to disasters. This response can be described as twofold: it can be anticipatory and consist in the adoption of policies and measures devised to reduce the vulnerability of populations in regions identified as prone to disasters. It can also be reactive and consist in aid provision to affected populations. If protection is willingly denied prior[167] or after the disaster to a certain group, the serious harm inflicted by reason of the discriminatory provision of aid and protection can constitute persecution.

As mentioned in scenario 1 already, an essential element of the definition of refugee as it was conceived by the drafters of the Refugee Convention and implemented since is the discriminatory element. It was argued above that harms suffered by environmentally-displaced persons can reach the threshold of persecution. But harm will constitute persecution only if it can be shown that the applicant is exposed to it "for reasons of race, religion, nationality, membership of a particular social group or political opinion".[168]

Disasters. Operational Guidelines and Field Manual on Human Rights Protection in Situations of Natural Disaster, January 2011, p. 12, General Principles II.1.

165 M. Foster, *International Refugee Law and Socio-Economic Rights: Refuge from Deprivation* (2007), *op. cit.*, pp. 268–269.

166 Climate change – which is partly anthropogenic – as well as the adoption and implementation of disaster detection mechanisms and of anticipatory measures to reduce the vulnerability of regions and communities increase their resilience and adaptability to disasters can however play a role in the impact of the disaster.

167 Below note 201.

168 Refugee Convention, Article 1A(2); Qualification Directive, Article 2(d).

Scenarios 1 and 2 must be put to this final and challenging test, that of the requirement of a causal link, a nexus, between persecution or absence of protection against persecution and one of the five Convention grounds.

C Environmental Persecution Possibly, but for What (Conventional) Reason?

To begin with, it is pertinent to notice, in view of the large number of people displaced by environmental disasters, that although it requires the individualisation of the threat of persecution, the Refugee Convention cannot be interpreted as opposing the grant of refugee status in mass influx situations. The historical framework of the Convention in fact reveals that refugee protection was devised to protect not merely persons who can demonstrate a particularised risk of persecution but persons within large groups, "whose fear of persecution is generalized".[169] If the harm is sufficiently serious to constitute persecution and if it has a differential impact on a specific group, identifiable by the race, religion, nationality, political opinion or "social" characteristic of its members, then any member of that group may individually qualify for refugee status, irrespective of how many other persons are exposed to the same risk and, as such, also qualify for refugee protection.[170] The same conclusion was reached by G. Jaeger who in 1984, anticipating the findings of M. Foster's 2007 study, stated that economic oppression and deprivation, although they affect entire populations, could qualify their victims for refugee status provided they are of a sufficiently severe nature and directed at a particular group protected under the Refugee Convention.[171] It follows that the circumstance that environmental disasters affect large groups or entire populations does not *per se* exclude the application of the Refugee Convention.[172] Rather to the contrary, a larger

---

169 J.C. Hathaway, *The Law of Refugee Status* (1991), op. cit., p. 95. Similarly, M. Foster observes that the Refugee Convention was in fact initially designed "to accommodate extremely large groups of refugees such as Jews fleeing Nazi Germany". M. Foster, *International Refugee Law and Socio-Economic Rights: Refuge from Deprivation* (2007), op. cit., p. 11.

170 J.C. Hathaway, *The Law of Refugee Status* (1991), op. cit., p. 95; A. Grahl-Madsen, *The Status of Refugees in International Law* (1966), op. cit., p. 213.

171 G. Jaeger (1984), op. cit., p. 7.

172 International law, relevant to addressing specifically the protection needs of population fleeing in mass will be discussed in a subsequent section. Under the following section, other forms or mechanisms of protection available within the European Union will be analysed under the prism of claims formulated by environmentally displaced persons. Relevant law includes the Qualification Directive and the Directive providing for the grant of temporary protection in situations of mass influx as well as certain national forms of protection. Qualification Directive; Temporary Protection Directive; G. Jaeger (1984), op. cit., p. 7. UNHCR, Conclusion No. 19 (XXXI) of 1980 concerning Temporary Refuge,

number of persons exposed to harm could in fact be an indication of the gravity of the situation in the country of origin.

UNHCR Handbook on Procedures and Criteria for Determining Refugee Status was quoted above to clarify what could constitute an act of persecution. The Handbook makes clear that the rights to life and freedom are not the only rights protected: "serious violations of human rights" could also constitute acts of persecution. In full, the provision in fact further qualifies the term persecution:

> ... a threat to life or freedom on account of race, religion, nationality, political opinion or membership of a particular social group is always persecution. Other serious violations of human rights – *for the same reasons* – would also constitute persecution.[173]

The Convention requires a causal link between the act of persecution and the grounds for persecution Article 1A enumerates (race, religion, nationality, membership of a particular social group and political opinion). Like threats to life or freedom, other serious violations of human rights can constitute acts of persecution but provided they are linked to a Convention ground.

Let us turn back to the scenarios identified above which potentially cause refugee movements.

(a)   Scenario 1: The Degradation of the Environment is Deliberately Caused

As mentioned above, if a State or non-State actors voluntarily causes the environment to deteriorate in order to harm a particular group, this harm might constitute "environmental persecution". It follows from the nexus requirement that it may do so only if exposure to this "environmental harm" is linked to any of the five grounds enumerated in the Convention (scenario 1a). As mentioned, environmental degradation is sometimes used by governments as an instrument of war or as a weapon against a particular section of the population. In those cases, where an act of such gravity as depriving an individual

---

Conclusion No. 22 (XXXII) of 1981 concerning Protection of Asylum-seekers in Situations of Large-scale Influx.

173   UN High Commissioner for Refugees, *Handbook on Procedures and Criteria for Determining Refugee Status under the 1951 Convention and the 1967 Protocol relating to the Status of Refugees*, reissued December 2011, §51 [emphasis added].

of his or her means of subsistence through the destruction or degradation of their environment is deliberately used against an individual (or group) by reason of his or her race or any other Convention ground, refugee status should be granted under the Convention, the definitional criteria being met. S. Castles, opposing the term "environmental refugee" argues that in such situations, refugee claims "would be based on persecution itself rather than the form of it, making the term environmental refugee redundant".[174] Persecution and refugeehood could be established when environmental harm is deliberately inflicted by the State (or non-State agents in the absence of protection) to harm a specific group, such as an ethnic and, or political group (Marsh Arabs, see below) or religious (possibly Tibetans[175]), national or social groups.

In comparison with the observed and expected numbers of persons displaced by natural hazard-related disasters, such cases will however most likely represent only but a limited subset of displacement triggered by environmental degradations. The deliberate desiccation of the Marsh Arabs' marshlands in retaliation of their perceived treason of the government in power illustrates this scenario. Similarly, governments might use starvation as a political tool to weaken insurgency groups.[176]

If however a State or non-State actor deliberately or knowingly deteriorates the environment and, in so doing, causes unintended or indiscriminate harm to populations (scenario 1b), a claim for refugee protection on this ground is not substantiated. The construction of a dam can correspond to this scenario. Typically in this case, the builder or government's choice is guided by technical considerations pertaining to the geography of the land rather than by discriminatory motives. It follows that displacement caused by large development is more likely to occur within the border of the State: large development projects

---

174 S. Castles (2002), *op. cit.*, pp. 8-9.
175 China's massive deforestation and policy of forced collectivisation of agriculture on the Tibetan plateau as well as nuclear proliferation and testing have exposed Tibetans to severe human rights violations caused by environmental degradations. L.S. Ziemer, "Application in Tibet of the Principles on Human Rights and the Environment", *Harvard Human Rights Journal*, Vol. 14 (2001), pp. 233-275, pp. 236 and 246-275; S. Castles (2002), *op. cit.*, pp. 8-9.
176 M. Foster cites S. Schmeidl, who argued that Nigeria during the Biafra conflict and Ethiopia during its conflict with Eritrea induced famine "by destroying crops or poisoning water to break the will of insurgency groups". S. Schmeidl, "Conflict and Forced Migration: A Quantitative Review, 1964-1995", in A.R. Zolberg and P.M. Benda (Eds.), *Global Migrants, Global Refugees: Problems and Solutions* (New York: Berghahn Books, 2001); cited in: M. Foster, *International Refugee Law and Socio-Economic Rights: Refuge from Deprivation* (2007), *op. cit.*, p. 10; L.S. Ziemer (2001), *op. cit.*, pp. 236 and 246-275.

are coupled with relocation programs for the populations displaced[177] and in any case, even if assistance for their relocation is not provided to displaced persons (except when it is denied on discriminatory grounds and exposes individuals to risks of persecution), there is generally no reason to believe that they cannot or would not prefer to move locally. The "environmental harm" they suffer is "situational" insofar as it is directly linked to them residing, so to speak, at the wrong place, at the wrong moment but is not meant to affect them specifically. It is therefore conceivable that they will be able to relocate elsewhere in the country and, should they be exposed to a risk of harm amounting to persecution (either by non-State agents or caused by the environmental degradation), can turn to the authorities for protection. The question in scenario 1b can however become a question of protection: should the authorities deny protection to the affected populations on a discriminatory ground, persecution could be constituted.

This first scenario corresponds to only a small subset of the much larger group of persons displaced across international borders by environmental disasters which includes for the most part persons displaced by events the induction of which States hardly have any leverage on:[178]

> For the most part, ecological disasters and – in general – environmental conditions that might render a territory unsafe and unliveable are not the direct result of deliberate persecution by governments.[179]

Scenario 2 below concerns this other, larger, group of persons displaced by environmental change which governments did not – or not deliberately at least – trigger.

---

177 D. Chotouras, *Le statut juridique en droit international du réfugié écologique : une nécessité !* (*Le phénomène migratoire du fait des modifications environnementales*), Thesis, op. cit., §§ 141–146.

178 State policies and actions can impact the environment (there is growing scientific evidence and consensus that climate change is partly anthropogenic); hence the growing literature on State responsibility or liability for climate-change damages. States are however not responsible for directly triggering any specific climate-related disaster. On the notion of State responsibility for climate change damages: R.S.J. Tol and R. Verheyen, "State Responsibility and Compensation for Climate Change Damages – a Legal and Economic Assessment", *Energy Policy*, Vol. 32 (2004), pp. 1109–1130; M.G. Faure and A. Nollkaemper, "International Liability as an Instrument to Prevent and Compensate for Climate Change", *Stanford Environmental Law Journal*, Vol. 23A (June 2007); D. Chotouras, *Le statut juridique en droit international du réfugié écologique : une nécessité ! (Le phénomène migratoire du fait des modifications environnementales)*, Thesis, op. cit., §§ 141–146.

179 L. Westra, *Environmental Justice and the Rights of Ecological Refugees* (2009), op. cit., p. 29.

(b) Scenario 2: The Degradation of the Environment is Caused by Technological Accident or Natural Hazard

In situations where environmental threat emanates from a natural hazard or technological accident, threats to life or limb, or the complete denial or nullification of rights, although they amount to persecution in terms of their severity, will only be stamped as persecution if they affect certain individuals more than the rest of society at large and that this differential risk is linked to the individuals' capacity as members of any of the five protected groups identified in the Convention.[180] This was also the findings made by M. Foster upon studying case law on asylum claims based on socio-economic deprivation: violation of socio-economic rights may constitute persecution but provided it consists in severe discrimination (in education, healthcare and rights related to an adequate standard of living) based on the race, religion, nationality, political opinion or particular social group of the people concerned.[181] Although it considerably reduces the prospect of having environmentally-displaced persons recognised as victims of persecution, in view of the essentially indiscriminate effects of environmental disasters, it does not necessarily and automatically excludes them from refugee protection. UNHCR Handbook notes that this requirement:

> ... rules out such persons as victims of famine or natural disaster, *unless* they also have well-founded fear of persecution for one of the reasons stated.[182]

In cases where harm emanates from hazard-related or accidental environmental disasters, it must be shown that the threats to life or limb or threats of serious impairment of their economic, social and cultural rights affect the applicants specifically, as members of a group identifiable by the race, religion, nationality, political opinion or distinct social characteristic of its members.

---

180 In that sense, J. McAdam notes that "[in] refugee law, for deprivation to move beyond the 'mere' non-realization of a right to a violation of a right in a manner that amounts to persecution, a discriminatory element is required". J. McAdam, *Climate Change, Forced Migration, and International Law* (2012), *op. cit.*, p. 44. J.C. Hathaway also noted in 1991 that persecution could constitute, *inter alia*, in the State's failure to guarantee any economic, social or cultural right notwithstanding available financial resources to do so or if it safeguards such right but discriminatorily, to certain groups only. J.C. Hathaway, *The Law of Refugee Status* (1991), *op. cit.*, pp. 110–112.

181 M. Foster, *International Refugee Law and Socio-Economic Rights: Refuge from Deprivation* (2007), *op. cit.*, pp. 110 and 103–111 for the review and analysis of cases.

182 UNHCR, *Handbook on Procedures, op. cit.*, § 39 [emphasis added].

In other words, for a claim of environmentally-displaced persons to succeed, it is necessary that the disaster exposes individuals to a harm which is so severe that it reaches the level of persecution and, cumulatively, that it exposes the applicants to a greater risk of harm as against the rest of the population because the racial, religious, national, political, or social group they belong to is marginalised.[183]

It is clear that persecution can emanate either from actions by the State or non-State actors or from the inability or unwillingness of, typically, governments to prevent persecution from occurring.[184] In situations of environmental disasters, the source of the harm is neither the State nor a non-State entity but the environment, which can obviously not be "accused" of discriminating among its victims. It is therefore rather at the level of protection against persecution that the discriminatory element might come into play; indeed, in certain circumstances, it does.

In principle, victims of natural hazard-related disasters (such as floods or earthquakes) or, to a lesser extent, of technological accidents, who have to flee to another country because their government is unable or unwilling to provide them with relief assistance, are not *per se* Convention refugees in that they are exposed to the same indiscriminate risks as the rest of the population.[185] New

---

183   J. McAdam, *Climate Change, Forced Migration, and International Law* (2012), *op. cit.*, p. 44; A. Lopez (2007), *op. cit.*, p. 176.

184   UNHCR, *Handbook on Procedures, op. cit.*, § 65; B. Mayer, "The International Legal Challenges of Climate-Induced Migration: Proposal for an International Legal Framework", *Colorado Journal of International Environmental Law and Policy*, Vol. 22 (Summer 2011), pp. 357–417, p. 382.

185   Such was the conclusion reached by courts in Australia and New Zealand. The Refugee Review Tribunal of Australia, referring to the "non-discriminatory nature of the risk" to which victims of natural disasters are exposed, found that "the environmental problem of the rise in the sea level around Tuvalu is not [Refugee] Convention related". Refugee Review Tribunal of Australia, N95/09386 [1996] RRTA 3191, 7 November 1996. Similarly, in 2010, the same Tribunal concluded in a case concerning an applicant from Tuvalu that there was "no evidence or suggestion that the harm the applicant fears is in any way consciously directed by any individual or group, against the applicant or anyone else, or that it is motivated by any of the Convention reasons". Refugee Review Tribunal of Australia, N99/30231 [2000] RRTA 17, 10 January 2000. Pacific Island citizens claiming refugee status in New Zealand on the basis of climate change induced environmental changes in their country of origin met with the same hindrance before New Zealand courts. Their claims were dismissed because "the *indiscriminate nature* of these events and processes gave rise to *no nexus to a Convention ground*". NZIPT, *AF (Kiribati), op. cit.*, § 67 (and references cited) and § 75. *See also* NZHC, *Teitiota, op. cit.*, § 54 and Refugee Status Appeals Authority, Refugee Appeal No. 72189/2000, 17 August 2000, §§ 13–15.

Zealand Refugee Status Appeals Authority hence denied refugee status to applicants from Tuvalu on the ground that they could not be said to be "differentially at risk of harm amounting to persecution" due to any of the five Refugee Convention grounds. Instead, the Authority found that the applicants:

> ...were unfortunate victims, *like all other Tuvaluan citizens*, of the forces of nature leading to the erosion of coastland and the family property being partially submerged at high tide.[186]

However, it can be the case that some individuals or groups within the affected population are exposed to higher risks than the rest of the population, notably because they receive a lower level of assistance and protection, if any. As noted by New Zealand Immigration and Protection Tribunal Judge B.L. Burson, "the provision of post-disaster humanitarian relief may become politicised".[187] Those individuals who are denied protection by reason of their membership in a minority group and who, as a consequence, have to flee to another country in order to avoid starvation or exposure should be granted refugee status[188] "because the harm feared is serious and connected to the state, and the requisite element of civil or political differentiation is present".[189]

It is the case when governments or, in the EU context, other actors of protection deliver aid on a discriminatory basis or consciously obstruct the provision of international humanitarian assistance to certain groups;[190] aid is reserved for sections of the population which are identified as "worthier" of protection, chiefly in cases where resources are scarce and State's capacities limited

---

186 New Zealand: Refugee Status Appeals Authority, Refugee Appeal No. 72189/2000, *op. cit.*, § 13 (emphasis added).

187 Among other sources, Judge B.L. Burson refers to studies conducted in the aftermath of natural disasters, which "provide evidence of a political weighting of state response in which the recovery needs of marginalised groups are sometimes not met". NZIPT, *AF (Kiribati)*, *op. cit.*, § 58.

188 In the above-cited case, New Zealand Refugee Status Appeals Authority denied refugee status to the applicants because the shortage of drinkable water and other deficiencies in the social services of Tuvalu affected all citizens of Tuvalu "indiscriminately", and could not be said to be "forms of harm directed at the appellants for reason of their civil or political status". *Ibid.*, §13.

189 J.C. Hathaway, *The Law of Refugee Status* (1991), *op. cit.*, p. 94.

190 B. Mayer (Summer 2011), *op. cit.*, pp. 382–383; W. Kälin and N. Schrepfer, *Protecting People Crossing Borders in the Context of Climate Change Normative Gaps and Possible Approaches* (February 2012), *op. cit.*, pp. 32–33; UNHCR, "Climate Change, Natural Disasters and Human Displacement: A UNHCR Perspective" [23 October 2009], p. 7.

or supplies and assistance received insufficient to cover the needs of all the population – although, obviously, whereas such circumstances might explain discrimination in aid provision, neither of them can legitimate such practice. Such can also be the case where the power and authority is not in the hands of the official government anymore but of some rebel or other groups controlling how assistance (including international aid) is distributed. Similarly, persecution must be considered established when governments voluntarily increased or refused to reduce the known vulnerability of a certain religious, national, political, racial or social group to environmental disasters.[191]

Discrimination in aid provision is in fact mentioned as a "problem often encountered by persons affected by the consequences of natural disasters" in the Inter-Agency Standing Committee Operational Guidelines on Human Rights and Natural Disasters.[192] UNHCR confirms that where it occurs, persons must be granted refugee protection under the Refugee Convention:

> Individuals who cannot return to their country of origin because of natural or ecological disasters do not generally fall under the protection regime of the 1951 Convention, unless access to national protection is denied on the basis of a Convention ground.[193]

However, as mentioned, in the majority of environmental disaster situations, environmental degradation is not voluntarily caused by the State just as the

---

191 B. Mayer (Summer 2011), *op. cit.*, pp. 382–383. *A contrario*, D.Z. Falstrom argues that in cases where a government does nothing to prevent environmental disasters from occurring, for its environmental policies or inactions to rise to the level of persecution, "the government would have to state, for example, that it is not going to ensure the safe operation of a state-owned nuclear power plant because it hopes the plant explodes and kills the people living within a two-mile radius". D.Z. Falstrom, "Stemming the Flow of Environmental Displacement: Creating a Convention to Protect Persons and Preserve the Environment", *Colorado Journal of International Environmental Law and Policy*, Vol. 13 (2002), pp. 1–29, p. 13.

192 IASC, *Protecting Persons Affected by Natural Disasters: IASC Operational Guidelines on Human Rights and Natural Disasters* (Washington, DC: Brookings-Bern Project on Internal Displacement, June 2006), p. 8.

193 UNHCR, "Complementary Forms of Protection", *op. cit.*, § 10. A year earlier, C.M. Kozoll had already concluded that "[a]lthough the mere existence of naturally or accidentally occurring environmental harm alone is not enough to establish one's status as a refugee, a government's policies regarding these harms may be prosecutorial if they demonstrate a judgment about the relative merits of protecting individuals from environmental harm because of the individuals' race, religion, nationality, membership in a particular social group, or political opinion, and represent a deliberate attempt to inflict harm or refuse aid". C.M. Kozoll (2004), *op. cit.*, p. 274.

absence of State protection is generally not deliberate but instead flows from authorities' genuine inability to provide assistance and protection to its population.[194] The catastrophic weakening of governments in countries affected by environmental disaster was – and can still be – observed in Haiti after the 2010 earthquake. Haiti's capacity to provide assistance and basic social services to its population, not to mention to rebuild the country, was extremely limited, not least due to the earthquake claiming the lives of many government officials and civil servants, and to the collapse of official buildings and infrastructures.[195]

In other words, for the most part, environmental displacement cannot fall under the Refugee Convention because there is no identifiable "persecutor", which in turn points to the absence of discriminatory reasons for the harm invoked.[196]

Some authors seek to argue that environmentally-displaced persons fulfil the criteria of the Conventional refugee definition: to this end, they rely on the notions of "environmental persecution"[197] and on a conceptualisation of environmentally-displaced persons as a social group defined by its "political disempowerment".[198] On the first point, as argued above, the detrimental

---

[194] J. McAdam notes the case of the Pacific island States of Kiribati and Tuvalu where the governments endeavour to protect their citizens. J. McAdam, *Climate Change, Forced Migration, and International Law* (2012), *op. cit.*, p. 45.

[195] UN SC, "Report of the Secretary-General on the United Nations Stabilization Mission in Haiti", S/2010/200, 22 February 2010; C. Forelle and J.D. Córdoba, "Among Quake's Victims: Haiti's Government", *The Wall Street Journal*, 17 January 2010; S. Lawry, "Paul Farmer's Call for a New Conversation on Aid to Haiti", *Humanitarian & Development NGOs Domain of Practice Blog* (Hauser Center for Nonprofit Oganizations at Harvard University, 2011), 9 December 2011, retrieved from: <http://hausercenter.org/iha/2011/12/09/paul-farmer%e2%80%99s-call-for-a-new-conversation-on-aid-to-haiti/> [02/02/2012]; "Haiti: Capacity Building Is Key to Recovery, Says Progressio", *Progressio*, 12 January 2012, retrieved from: <http://www.progressio.org.uk/blog/news/haiti-capacity-building-key> [16/01/2012].

[196] UNSC, *op. cit*; C. Forelle and J.D. Córdoba, 17 January 2010, *op. cit*; S. Lawry, "Paul Farmer's Call for a New Conversation on Aid to Haiti" (2011); "Haiti: Capacity Building Is Key to Recovery, Says Progressio".

[197] Andrew Simms and Molly Conisbee, *Environmental Refugees: The Case for Recognition* (London: New Economic Foundation, 2003), p. 26 and pp. 30–35.

[198] Jessica B. Cooper, "Environmental Refugees: Meeting the Requirements of the Refugee Definition", *New York University Environmental Law Journal*, No.6 (1982), 522. A similar argument was invoked before the Refugee Review Tribunal of Australia by a Kiribati citizen who had applied for a "protection visa" in Australia, on the ground that he was a refugee under the 1951 Refugee Convention (Migration Act 1958, Section 36(2)(a)). The appellant

effects of environmental disruption on the life and standards of living of the affected populations can indeed potentially be labelled as acts of persecution or "environmental persecution". The second point is however more problematic: the construction appears to be inappropriate and to some extent erroneous.[199] The argument that environmentally-displaced persons are a social group defined by its political disempowerment fails to convince as its premise is flawed: it presupposes the existence of "environmental refugees" to demonstrate it. Accordingly, "environmental refugees" are a particular social group and are persecuted for that reason, hence their qualification for refugee status. In other words, the theory is based on the premise of the existence of a particular social group of "environmental refugees" and thus reasons in a circle: the conclusion is the premise. As a consequence, this interpretation of the concept of particular social group being "manifestly absurd or unreasonable",[200] it is legally untenable. The theory is formulated as a proposal towards a constructive interpretation of the Convention; it will be elaborated upon in Part 3, where avenues are explored towards the formulation of an instrument for the international protection of environmentally-displaced persons. Suffice is to notice that to date, the theory has not been endorsed by many in literature, nor by national authorities, including national courts. The *Conseil d'état* in France explicitly ruled out the qualification of Chernobyl nuclear disaster victims as members of a particular social group in 2000:

> ... les victimes de la catastrophe nucléaire de Tchernobyl ne constituaient pas un "groupe social" au sens des stipulations précitées de la convention de Genève.[201]

The Refugee Review Tribunal of Australia also rejected the argument:[202] while the Tribunal acknowledged that the applicant could be identified as a member

---

in the case sought to resort to the notion of "particular social group" albeit in slightly different terms. The appellant claimed that he had "a well-founded fear of persecution in Kiribati for reasons of membership of a particular social group: namely, people from Kirabati and / or from the Island of Kiribati who have lost the capacity to earn a livelihood as a result of climate change". Refugee Review Tribunal of Australia, 0907346 [2009] RRTA 1168, 10 December 2009, § 22.

199   This will be further developed in Part 3.
200   United Nations, *Vienna Convention on the Law of Treaties*, 23 May 1969, United Nations, Treaty Series, vol. 1155, p. 331, Article 32(b).
201   France: Conseil d'Etat (Section du Contentieux), N° 185837, 15 March 2000, 6th Considérant.
202   Case cited above in footnote 226.

of several particular social groups (*e.g.* citizen of Kiribiati, citizen of Kiribati who has lost his ability to learn a living or who has been displaced in the context of environmental degradation), it found that the causal link between this characteristic and the risk of persecution was lacking.

> ... the Tribunal does not believe that it is possible to identify any agent of persecution who or which can be said to be undertaking actions which harm the applicant *for reasons of* membership of any particular social group. (...) the *absence of the element of motivation* means that persecution cannot be said to be occurring for reasons of membership of any such group.[203]

In other words, environmentally-displaced persons may not invoke the environmental disaster situation they escape as a specific ground for protection under the Refugee Convention. They must instead demonstrate a causal link between their fear of persecution (triggered as it may be by environmental factors) and at least one of the five grounds enumerated in the Convention, as they are traditionally construed.

The inadequacy of existing refugee law to address disaster-related displacement was – seemingly regretfully – conceded by the Refugee Review Tribunal of Australia in what can be interpreted as an *obiter dictum*, expressing a moral judgement against an irresponsible behaviour on the part of States who maintain their high levels of greenhouse gas emissions, despite their having knowledge of the contributing factors and impacts of global warming, on low-lying island States among others. The Refugee Review Tribunal of Australia hence noted:

> [H]istorically high emitters of carbon dioxide or other greenhouse gases (...) who continue to contribute to global warming may be accused of having an indifference to the plight of those affected by it once the consequences of their actions are known, but this does not overcome the problem that there exists no evidence that any harms which flow are motivated by one of more of the Convention grounds.[204]

It follows from the above that the Refuge Convention nexus requirement is the main obstacle hindering environmentally-displaced persons' entitlement to refugee status.

---

[203] Refugee Review Tribunal of Australia, 0907346 [2009] RRTA 1168, 10 December 2009, § 52.
[204] Refugee Review Tribunal of Australia, 0907346 [2009], *op. cit.*, §§ 51.

D Concluding Remark: Many Displaced but Few Refugees

Scenarios 1a and 2a,[205] each of which implies an element of discrimination, can therefore fulfil the refugee definition provided by the Refugee Convention and endorsed, at the EU level, by the Qualification Directive – and by Member States at the latest upon transposing the Directive, provided discrimination is linked to one or several of the Convention grounds. Individuals may qualify for refugee status under the Convention where they risk be subjected to persecution, as a consequence of the disastrous impact of a degradation of their living environment, where, although the degradation affects the whole population indiscriminately, their life or freedoms are specifically jeopardised due to the selective distribution of aid by actors of protection in their country of origin, denying them relief assistance or protection for any of the Convention reasons.

The Parliamentary Assembly of the Council of Europe reached the same conclusion in December 2008 and summarised these findings in the following terms:

> Although the case may be weak for extending the 1951 Convention and 1967 Protocol to include socalled "environmental refugees", they may nevertheless qualify as refugees in the legal sense in cases of "environmental persecution", *i.e.* if their own governments are intentionally destroying their environment, are discriminating against them in the provision of assistance and/or are using the consequences of the disaster in ways that amount to persecution for one or more of the reasons of the 1951 Refugee convention. The environmental degradation or disaster cannot be considered as a persecution ground, but it could be considered as a form of persecution.[206]

The above does not bode well for the application of the Refugee Convention to environmentally-displaced persons. In the vast majority of cases, to wit, in cases where environmental harm emanates from natural hazard-related disasters and States are unable to cope with the impact of the disaster, asylum seekers fleeing such harm and seeking protection in the European Union will not be recognised as refugees. The principle obstacle to their recognition as refugees is the conundrum of meeting the Refugee Convention requirement of a causal

---

205   Above p. 305.
206   PACE, "Report of the Committee on Migration, Refugees and Population on Environmentally Induced Migration and Displacement: A 21st Century Challenge" ("Report of the Committee on Migration: a 21st century challenge"), Rapporteur: Tina Acketoft, Doc. 11785, 23 December 2008, p. 18, § 82.

link, the impacts of natural hazards being fundamentally indiscriminate. The premise of this work is hence, in the main, confirmed; it is however nuanced since, as mentioned, in certain circumstances, refugee status could be granted.

Under the interpretation which prevails in literature and courts, environmentally-displaced persons do not constitute a "special category" protected *per se* under the Convention but must meet the same criteria as traditional refugees. In that sense, the term "environmental refugees" is misleading. Just as the term "political refugee" indicates that the person was discriminated against by reason of his or her political opinion, the term "environmental refugees" would suggest that persons protected in this capacity are defined by a common immutable characteristic, that environmental disaster is a Convention ground. As mentioned, this would be confusing the nature of the harm and the reason for persecution.

Depending on the features of the disaster (technological accident or natural hazard, of sudden- or slow-onset, etc.), individuals will be exposed to various types of harm: threats to life, limb or health, deprivation of other civil and political rights or of social, economic and cultural rights, at shorter- or longer-term. The multitude of harms an environmental disaster may expose individuals to (threat to life or limb and deprivation of various, potentially all, other human rights) was referred to above under the umbrella term of "environmental harm". As argued above, environmental degradation can expose individuals to harm of such severity that it is tantamount to persecution. Environmental harm reaching persecution's threshold of severity is however not sufficient for an applicant to qualify as refugee; he or she must also fulfil the other criteria for refugeehood, including, chiefly, the requirement of a causal link. Just as the Refugee Convention does not automatically apply to any person fleeing the indiscriminate threats posed by an armed conflict situation, it does not either automatically protect individuals exposed to the indiscriminate threats posed by environmental disasters. In other words, an environmentally-displaced person who would receive refugee status would not become an "environmental refugee" but, simply, a "refugee" (or Convention refugee), who has met the standard criteria for refugee status, and whose risk of persecution merely "happens" to originate in a situation of environmental disaster. In a word:

> Climate change, disasters and degradation may not be a Convention ground, but could constitute a form of persecution.[207]

---

207   V.O. Kolmannskog, "To What Extent Can Existing Forms of Legal Protection Apply in Climate Change-Related Cross-Border Displacement?" *Workshop on Environmental Change and Migration*, Oxford University, 8–9 January 2009, p. 5.

The actuality of the problem of environmentally-triggered displacement and the portent that the phenomenon may increase with climate change impacting on the Earth's environment call for a consideration of the application of other norms of international protection to the persons concerned. The presumed pertinence of the norms identified in the first Part, applicable in situations of indiscriminate or non-targeted threats, must now be tested.

II   Subsidiary Protection and Other Forms of Complementary Protection

As argued above, in the majority of cases, environmentally-displaced persons will not receive refugee status in Europe. As was shown in Part 1, additional forms of protection have developed in refugee law, besides refugee status, to palliate the protection gap in which people fleeing indiscriminate threats for life or person were falling, not least where the threats originated in armed conflict situations. It is time to consider whether any of the forms of complementary protection developed within the European Union, at EU and national levels, foremost among which is subsidiary protection (A), can be successfully invoked by environmentally-displaced persons. The idiosyncratic forms of protection created under Finnish and Swedish law will then be addressed (B). Lastly, recent New Zealand cases, envisioning the eligibility of Pacific Island citizens to complementary protection (*i.e.* status of "protected person" under the Convention Against Torture or the ICCPR[208]) on the basis of alleged breaches of their human rights in the context of environmental degradation linked to climate change will be succinctly discussed (C).

A   *Subsidiary Protection*

The discussion below focuses on the subsidiary protection regime created by the Directive, as it was transposed and is implemented in EU Member States.

As mentioned in Part 1, throughout the drafting history of the Directive, many debates surrounded the adoption of the terms of Article 15. The European Commission initially devised subsidiary protection as a true codification of the principle of *non-refoulement* and relevant State practice into a harmonised, statutory form of complementary protection. Originally, the definition of "serious and unjustified[209] harm" included not only torture,

---

208   New Zealand, Immigration Act 2009, *op. cit.*, Sections 130 and 131.
209   The awkward epithet, which suggested *a contrario* that certain serious harms could be "justified", was soon erased from Article 15. *See* the comments made by the Swedish

inhuman or degrading treatment or punishment but also any "violation of a human right, sufficiently severe to engage the Member State's international obligations". Article 15(c) was also broader: the provision covered not only threats resulting from indiscriminate violence in situations of armed conflict but also those resulting from "systematic or generalised violations of human rights".[210] Certainly, as proposed initially by the European Commission, the grounds for subsidiary protection were significantly broader than they are now, after a series of amendments carved the original text, until Member States eventually agreed on a "minimum common denominator".[211] Nevertheless, subsidiary protection markedly advances international protection in Europe; it formally acknowledges that certain persons who do not qualify for refugee status should nevertheless receive international protection. Can environmentally-displaced persons fall under one of those protected categories?

Under Articles 2 and 15 of the Directive read together, Member States must grant subsidiary protection to persons in respect of whom substantial grounds have been shown for believing that the person concerned would face, upon return in his or her country of origin, a real risk of suffering death penalty or execution (Article 15a), torture or inhuman or degrading treatment or punishment (Article 15b), or serious and individual threat to his or her life or person by reason of indiscriminate violence in situations of international or internal armed conflict (Article 15c).[212] The language of the Directive (the indicative "serious harm *consists of*" and the conjunction "or"[213]) and the *travaux préparatoires* indicate that the three categories of serious harm identified in Article 15 constitute an exhaustive list. Can the risks threatening populations affected by natural disasters be construed as constitutive of "serious harm" under Article 15 of the Qualification Directive? The three paragraphs of Article 15 will be considered successively.

1 Article 15(a)

A cursory glance at Article 15 paragraph (a) suffices to exclude it from the subsequent discussion. Under this provision, persons who would be exposed to

---

delegation on Article 2 and Article 15. EU Council, "Asylum Working Party – Outcome of Proceedings of 3–4 and 16–17 October 2002" ("Outcome of Proceedings (ASILE 54)"), 12620/02 ASILE 54, 23 October 2002, p. 3, n. 3 and p. 21, n. 1.

210 "Explanatory Memorandum – QD (2004)", *op. cit.*, Article 15.
211 M.T. Gil-Bazo (2006), *op. cit.*, p. 30.
212 Qualification Directive, Article 2(e) and Article 15.
213 *Ibid.*, Article 15 [emphasis added].

a real risk of being sentenced to the death penalty or of being executed shall be granted subsidiary protection.[214] The preparatory work of the Qualification Directive reveals that this absolute obligation for States to protect asylum-seekers facing a real risk of death penalty or execution (provided applicants are not otherwise excluded from subsidiary protection) is derived from EU Member States' obligations under Protocol 6[215] and Protocol 13[216] of the European Convention on Human Rights (ECHR) and from the related case-law of the European Court of Human Rights.[217]

Whereas the prohibition of the death penalty derives from the right to life, it is not a general obligation to protect life but "merely" an obligation to abolish and protect against the death penalty and execution. If Article 15(a) is interpreted, as it should be, in accordance with the ordinary meaning to be given to its terms and in light of the *travaux préparatoires*,[218] it is clear that the provision is of little pertinence for persons fleeing environmental disasters. Whereas its application cannot be excluded in situations of environmental disasters, it would however not apply in the very vast majority of cases where the serious harm emanates not from a risk of being sentenced to the death penalty executed but from the impacts of the disaster on the environment. A hypothetical, fictional, case where Article 15(a) would apply is one where a person who has been sentenced to the death penalty escapes in a context of environmental disaster (did the walls of the main Haitian prison not collapse in the earthquake striking the country in 2010?[219]) and seeks asylum abroad on the ground that return would expose him or her to the death row or execution.

Some might want to argue that returning an individual to a situation where they will be deprived of the most basic means of subsistence (water resources and food stocks wearing down or depleted, overwhelmed health system capacity, etc.) because their country was struck by a major earthquake or tsunami, their land is progressively and inexorably shrinking (by submersion or erosion) or due to desertification for example, is tantamount to returning him or her to a life-threatening situation and, therefore, to sentencing this individual to death. This is however not the ordinary meaning of the legal terms "death penalty" and "execution" which refer to capital punishment imposed by a judicial

---

214   The provision refers to "death penalty or execution" as a form of serious harm. *Ibid.*, Article 15(a).
215   Protocol 6 ECHR.
216   Protocol 13 ECHR.
217   Above Part 1, pp. 118s.
218   VCLT, Article 31.
219   "Haïti: la police pointe de nouvelles formes de violence après le séisme" (AFP, 2010), retrieved from: <http://www.reliefweb.int/rw/rwb.nsf/db900SID/RMOI-8264EH?OpenDocument> [28 January 2010].

authority typically for what is perceived under national law as a most serious offence.²²⁰

On the other hand, seeking the application Article 15 paragraphs (b) or (c) to environmentally-displaced persons appears more pertinent (or less far-fetched) but is it actually?

2   Living Conditions in a Degraded Environment: Inhuman and Degrading Treatment under Article 15(b)?

Under Article 15(b), EU Member States have the obligation to protect asylum seekers from a serious risk of torture, inhuman or degrading treatment or punishment awaiting them in their country of origin. The language of Article 15(b) clearly mirrors that of the prohibition of torture, inhuman or degrading treatment or punishment laid down in Article 3 of the European Convention on Human Rights. The EU Court of Justice in fact made it clear in the *Elgafaji* judgment: Article 15(b) of the Qualification Directive "corresponds, in essence, to Article 3 of the ECHR".²²¹ It follows that Article 15(b) should be interpreted in line with Article 3 of the ECHR.

The EU Charter of Fundamental Rights confirms it: insofar as the Charter contains rights which correspond to rights guaranteed by the ECHR, the meaning and scope of those rights shall be the same as those laid down by the ECHR.²²² The prohibition of torture and inhuman or degrading treatment or punishment is among those rights which are enshrined in both the ECHR (Article 3) and the Charter (Article 4). A final confirmation comes from the Explanations provided by the *Praesidium* of the Convention which drafted the Charter. The Explanation on Article 4 clarifies that, by virtue of the above-mentioned rule of conformity of Charter rights with ECHR rights, the Charter prohibition of torture and inhuman or degrading treatment or punishment therefore has the same meaning and the same scope as ECHR Article 3.²²³

Lastly, the judgment of the Court of Justice in the *NS & ME* case, reflecting the ECtHR judgment in *M.S.S. v. Greece*, exemplifies how the Court of Justice interprets the prohibition of torture, inhuman or degrading treatment or punishment and the principle of *non-refoulement* in line with the case-law of the ECtHR.²²⁴

---

220   See for example: UNGA, "Resolution 62/149: Moratorium on the Use of the Death Penalty" ("Moratorium on the use of the death penalty"), A/RES/62/149, 26 February 2008.
221   CJ, *Elgafaji*, § 28. The *Elgafaji* judgment was discussed in Part 1; *see* above pp. 138s.
222   EU Charter, Article 52(3).
223   "Explanations to the Charter", [14/12/2007], *op. cit.*, Explanation on Article 4.
224   CJ, *NS & ME*; ECtHR, *M.S.S.* This point is made above in Part 1, pp. 81s.

In other words, the prohibition has, within the EU legal system, the same meaning and scope as within the ECHR framework. Advocate General Poiares Maduro reached a similar conclusion in his opinion in the *Elgafaji* case; he observed that:

> ... although the case-law of the Strasbourg court is not a binding source of interpretation of Community fundamental rights, it constitutes none the less a starting point for determining the content and scope of those rights within the European Union.[225]

For that reason, in order to determine whether environmentally-displaced persons fall under the scope of subsidiary protection under Article 15(b), it is necessary to "start" with an assessment of the living conditions of victims of environmental disasters against the standards identified in the ECHR and relevant case-law of the ECtHR. The question of the pertinence of the notion of "torture, inhuman or degrading treatment or punishment" to assess the situation faced by victims of environmental disasters will be discussed in the following Chapter (Chapter 7). It will therefore not be dealt with here since, in the main, this would anticipate on the findings of Chapter 7. For the same reason, the developments made in Chapter 7 on this subject matter will be applicable here. In any case, it might be worth keeping in mind that the EU Charter of Fundamental Rights adds to the requirement that Charter rights are interpreted in conformity with ECHR rights that this requirement "shall not prevent Union law providing more extensive protection".[226]

As mentioned in Part 1, the European Court of Human Rights (ECtHR), in the *Sufi & Elmi* case, blurred the line the EU Court of Justice (CJ) had attempted to draw between Article 15(b) and Article 15(c) of the Directive.[227] In particular, the ECtHR compared the scope of Article 15(c) (as interpreted in *Elgafaji*) and Article 3 ECHR and found that:

> ... the threshold set by both provisions may, in exceptional circumstances, be attained in consequence of a situation of general violence of such intensity that any person being returned to the region in question would be at risk simply on account of their presence there.[228]

---

225 AG *Opinion in Elgafaji*, § 23.
226 EU Charter, Article 52(3).
227 Above pp. 140s. and pp. 143s.
228 ECtHR, *Sufi & Elmi*, § 226.

By approximating the scope of Article 15(c) QD and Article 3 ECHR, the Court in fact incidentally narrows the difference between Article 15(c) and Article 15(b) QD.

And indeed, in *Sufi & Elmi*, for the first time, the ECtHR concluded to the existence in the applicants' country of origin of a level of violence of such intensity that any person returned to the region in question would be at risk "simply on account of their presence there".[229] In the case, concerning Somali applicants, the Court stated that "the level of violence in Mogadishu is of sufficient intensity to pose a real risk of treatment reaching the Article 3 threshold to anyone in the capital".[230]

The lack of clarity regarding the distinct scopes of paragraphs (b) and (c) of Article 15 of the Directive was observed by UNHCR who, after investigating 2010 first instance international protection rates for Afghan, Iraqi and Somali applicants in the six principal EU Member States of destination,[231] concluded that many (and in some countries, by far, most) of the decisions to grant subsidiary protection to those applicants, who fled a situation of protracted conflict, were based not on Article 15(c) but on Article 15(b).[232] It is to be expected that the yet unclear difference in scope between the two provisions will only become apparent through the evolving case law of the Court of Justice and of the European Court of Human Rights.[233] National decisions might also bring light on the issue.

The practice in France is worth mentioning here, all the more since it pertains to environmental disaster. Subsidiary protection was granted under Article 15(b) to Haitian applicants who fled in the aftermath of the earthquake for the reasons explained below. A number of reports reveal that the earthquake which struck Haiti in January 2010 severely affected Haitian police. In 2010, in response to information requests, the Immigration and Refugee Board of Canada compiled and the various reports and information available on the security situation in Haiti and revealing the failure of the police to protect the population; shortages of police personnel (worsened by the earthquake), of equipment and training reduce the effectiveness of the police force.[234] Several

---

229 *Ibid.*, § 226.
230 *Ibid.*, § 248.
231 Belgium, France, Germany, the Netherlands, Sweden and the United Kingdom.
232 UNHCR, *et al.*, *Safe at Last?* (July 2011), *op. cit.*, pp. 24–28.
233 Opinion of the German Ministry of the Interior expressed in an interview with UNHCR in November 2010 and reported in UNHCR, *et al.*, *Safe at Last?* (July 2011), p. 56.
234 Immigration and Refugee Board of Canada Research Directorate, "Haiti: Overview of Police Reform Efforts; the Effectiveness of the Police; Existence of a Police Complaints Authority and Recourse Available to Individuals Who File Complaints against the Police;

police officers were reported killed in the earthquake, police headquarters in Port-au-Prince and many local police stations collapsed, documents and archives were destroyed and, to make the situation worse, the partial destruction of the main prison of the country incidentally released some seven thousands criminals.[235] According to information available, the national police force can hardly fulfil its tasks and is overwhelmed by the increase in crime the country is now facing. In several cases, the *Cour national du droit d'asile* (CNDA) relied on the above-mentioned report by the Immigration and Refugee Board of Canada, as updated in March 2012, to support its assessment of a claim for international protection. The French Court observed that, by reason of its lack of training, of professionalism and of efficiency, amplified by the earthquake, the Haitian police was unable to protect the population – especially the most vulnerable persons[236] – in the context of a very high level of general violence (the CNDA noted that one hundred and fifty persons had been killed between January and March 2012).[237] As a consequence and despite the context of insecurity, the French Court granted subsidiary protection to the applicants, not under Article 15(c) but under Article 15(b). In other words, a very high level of general violence combined with the inability of national authorities to provide protection and the personal circumstances of the applicants justified the grant of subsidiary protection. It is of importance to notice that the applicants were not protected as victims of an environmental disaster but as vulnerable persons exposed to a risk of inhuman or degrading treatment against which national authorities could not protect them.

It is not possible to draw firm conclusions from the above, partly because it only concerns one of the EU Member States, partly also because I did not have a direct access to the decisions referred to above[238] however, it is possible to suggest on the basis of this case-law a possible interpretation of Article 15(b) as against Article 15(c).

To reconcile the judgment of the Court of Justice in *Elgafaji* with that of the European Court of Human Rights in *Sufi & Elmi* it could be proposed that,

---

Initial Impact of 12 January 2010 Earthquake" ("Haitian police in the aftermath of the 2010 earthquake"), HTI103346.E, 16 February 2010.

235 "Haïti: la police pointe de nouvelles formes de violence après le séisme" (2010). Immigration and Refugee Board of Canada, "Haitian police in the aftermath of the 2010 earthquake", *op. cit.*

236 Isolated women exposed to a risk of domestic violence and the elderly for example.

237 Information kindly provided by Barbara Derain, senior legal officer at the *Office français de protection des réfugiés et apatrides* – OFPRA. B. Derain (OFPRA), Personal Communication, 28 August 2012.

238 OFPRA decisions are confidential and not all CNDA decisions are published.

beside cases where individuals are personally at risk, Article 15(b) applies in cases where the test formulated by the ECtHR in *NA v. UK* is pertinent: that is, in cases where "an applicant alleges that he or she is a member of a group systematically exposed to a practice of ill-treatment".[239] On the other hand, Article 15(c) would apply when the *Sufi & Elmi* test is pertinent: in cases where applicants invoke a situation of general violence which exposes them to a "real risk of Article 3 ill-treatment solely on account of [their] presence"[240] in the region concerned, that is, in cases of purely indiscriminate threats.

In any case, the above example of French case-law concerning Haitian applicants illustrates that environmentally-displaced persons are not automatically excluded from the scope of subsidiary protection under Article 15(b). However, in cases where they are granted protection, it is after fulfilling the standard criteria for subsidiary protection; environmental disaster may play a role in that it is an amplifying factor of vulnerabilities but is not *per se* included in the scope of Article 15(b).

The applicability of Article 15(c) is the object of the following discussion.

3   Indiscriminate Violence, Armed Conflicts and Environmental Disasters

Subsidiary protection protects certain individuals who, although they do not fulfil the criteria for refugee status, are in need of international protection.[241] In the majority of cases, environmentally-displaced persons will not be recognised as refugees[242] and the main impediment to their recognition is the Refugee Convention (and Qualification Directive) requirement of a causal link between persecution and the applicant's race, religion, nationality, membership in a particular social group political opinion. Indeed, environmental disasters of slow- and sudden-onset alike do not target their victims; their effects are indiscriminate. Like armed conflict, they potentially affect anyone and everyone present on a given territory; they both create generalised, non-targeted or indiscriminate,[243] situational risks and to that extent, they are similar. Article 15(c) addresses specifically threats to life or person caused by indiscriminate

---

239   ECtHR, *NA v. UK*, § 116.
240   ECtHR, *Sufi & Elmi*, § 293.
241   Part 1, pp. 99s.
242   *See* the concluding remark above pp. 322s. and, for more details, the develoments leading to it.
243   As noted in 2010 by the Immigration and Asylum Chamber of the United Kingdom Upper Tribunal in *HM and Others*, in the context of the armed conflict situation prevailing in Iraq at the time, "[s]uch violence is indiscriminate in effect even if not necessarily in aim". UKUT, *HM and Others*, 22 September 2010, *op. cit.*, § 80; ECtHR, *Sufi & Elmi*, § 293.

violence in situations of international or internal armed conflict. In view of the similarity of the risks caused by environmental disasters as against those caused by armed conflicts, Article 15(c) is at first glance appealing to one who seeks to include environmentally-displaced persons in the scope of subsidiary protection. *De lege lata*, can "environmental harm" constitute a serious harm for the purpose of Article 15(c) of the Qualification Directive?

Besides the hopeful reference to "indiscriminate", the language of Article 15(c) in fact does not kindle much hope that environmentally-displaced persons can fall under its scope. Serious harm under Article 15(c) is described as "serious and individual threat to a civilian's life or person *by reason of* indiscriminate violence *in situations of* international or internal armed conflict".[244] Article 15(c) is devised to apply in a specific context, doubly qualified. Firstly, the threat to life or person must originate in indiscriminate violence and secondly, this indiscriminate violence must be linked to an armed conflict situation.

Some courts interpret the notion of indiscriminate violence broadly: it needs not necessarily be caused by the parties to the conflict but can be an indirect consequence of it. In France, in a case concerning Sri Lanka, the *Conseil d'état* stated that it was possible to conclude to the existence of generalised (or indiscriminate) violence in an area even though instances of violence were not all caused by the parties in conflict.[245] Drawing on this decision, the Immigration and Asylum Chamber of the UK Upper Tribunal found that "it is not necessary for the threat to life or person to derive from protagonists in the armed conflict in question: it can simply be a product of the breakdown of law and order".[246] Insecurity or criminal acts[247] that result from a situation of armed conflict can cause serious harm for the purpose of 15(c) although they are not directly caused by the conflict. Furthermore, other indirect consequences of the armed conflict can be taken into account: UNHCR notes that threats to life or person can result from the destruction of basic means of subsistence (food, water, shelter and healthcare), be it deliberately caused by a party to the conflict as a tactic to weaken the enemy or a consequence of the

---

244 Qualification Directive, Article 15(c) [emphases added].
245 The *Conseil d'état* notes that under the Qualification Directive, the grant of subsidiary protection is not conditional upon violence and the armed conflict situation coexisting at all times within the applicant's region of origin. A requirement that they do coexist (that *"la violence et la situation de conflit armé coexistent en tout point sur la même zone géographique"*) would not be in conformity with the Directive. CE, *Baskarathas*, 3 July 2009, *op. cit.*, 3rd Considérant; Qualification Directive, Article 15(c) [emphases added].
246 UKUT, *HM and Others*, 22 September 2010, *op. cit.*, § 80.
247 *Ibid.*, § 80; CE, *Baskarathas*, 3 July 2009, *op. cit.*, 3rd Considérant.

conflict.[248] This approach was adopted in the Netherlands, Sweden and the United Kingdom.[249] In summary, for the purpose of Article 15(c), serious harm can encompass threats to life or person which are a direct consequence of violence perpetrated by parties in a conflict or which are caused by anarchy and criminality reigning in the country affected by armed conflict or, lastly, which result from the destruction of basis means of subsistence.

A different approach to the interpretation of what constitute "threats to life or person" might in fact be incompatible with States' obligation to protect the "right to life" enshrined in various instruments of international human rights law. Increasingly, the interpretation of the right to life "looks far beyond issues of killing"[250] to derive a number of positive obligations for States. The right not to be deprived of one's own means of subsistence[251] and the rights to safe and clean drinking water and sanitation,[252] to a healthy environment,[253] to food, to adequate housing,[254] to health[255] are examples of rights perceived as components of the right to life or at least as essential to it realisation.

In any case, whether the threat emanates directly or indirectly from the violence, it is necessary that a causal link exists ("by reason of"[256]) between

---

248   UNHCR, et al., *Safe at Last?* (July 2011), op. cit., p. 62.
249   Ibid., pp. 62-63.
250   E. Wicks, "The Meaning of 'Life': Dignity and the Right to Life in International Human Rights Treaties", *Human Rights Law Review*, June 1, 2012, Vol. 12, No. 2 (2012), pp. 199-219.
251   ICCPR, Article 1(2); ICESCR, Article 1(2).
252   CESCR, "General Comment No. 15: The Right to Water" ("GC 15: Right to Water"), E/C.12/2002/11, 2003; UNHRC, "Human Rights and Access to Safe Drinking Water and Sanitation", A/HRC/RES/15/9, 30 September 2010, §§ 2–3; UNGA, "Resolution 64/292: The human right to water and sanitation", A/RES/64/292, 3 August 2010.
253   PACE, "Recommendation 1885 (2009): Drafting an Additional Protocol to the European Convention on Human Rights Concerning the Right to a Healthy Environment" ("Recommendation 1885 (2009)"), 30 September 2009; UN Conference on the Human Environment, Declaration of the United Nations Conference on the Human Environment ("Stockholm Declaration"), 16 June 1972 UN Doc. A/CONF.48/14/Rev. 1(1973); India: Rajasthan High Court, *L.K. Koolwal v. State of Rajasthan and Others* ("*L.K. Koolwal v. State of Rajasthan and Others*"), Writ petition No. 121, 19 September 1986, *AIR* 1988 Raj 2; India: Supreme Court, *Construction of Park at Noida near Okhla Bird Sanctuary, Anand Arya & Anr. (Applicants) T.N. Godavarman Thirumulpad (Petitioner) v. Union of India & Ors.* ("*Construction of Park at Noida near Okhla Bird Sanctuary*"), Writ petition (civil) No.202 of 1995, 3 December 2010, § 66.
254   Inter-American Court of Human Rights, *Yakye Axa Indigenous Community v. Paraguay*, Series C No. 125 (17 June 2005).
255   Legal Response Initiative, "Human Rights and Climate Change", 19 July 2010, §§ 8–9.
256   Qualification Directive, Article 15(c).

the threats and the armed conflict. UNHCR confirms the requirement: "there is nothing in Article 15(c) that limits its application according to the source of the violence *as long as it arises in the context of an armed conflict*";[257] so does State practice. The French *Conseil d'état* repeatedly reaffirmed that for a threat to constitute serious harm under Article 15(c) it must originate in generalised violence which is inherent to and characterises a situation of armed conflict.[258] As a result, the *Conseil d'état* found that the *Cour nationale du droit d'asile* has erred in law when it granted subsidiary protection to an applicant without considering whether the situation of insecurity or violence invoked by the applicant indeed resulted from an internal or international armed conflict; the Council quashed the Court's decision in the case.[259] Germany further requires that the threat to the applicant's life or person is a direct consequence of the indiscriminate violence exerted by the parties in the conflict.[260] UNHCR notes that in like manner, Belgium, the Netherlands, Sweden and the United Kingdom apply Article 15(c) only in cases where armed conflict is involved, even though all do not require a direct link between the threat to life or person and the conflict.[261] In view of the 2010 European Commission report on the application of the Directive, there is no reason to conclude that any EU Member State omitted the requirement of a link with armed conflict upon transposing the provision in their national legislation.[262]

It follows that people forced to leave their home and country due to an environmental disaster may only qualify for subsidiary protection under Article 15(c) of the Qualification Directive if they also flee a situation of armed

---

257 UNHCR, et al., *Safe at Last?* (July 2011), *op. cit.*, p. 60.

258 The Conseil d'état states: "*la violence généralisée à l'origine de la menace justifiant la demande de protection subsidiaire est inhérente à une situation de conflit armé et la caractérise*". CE, *Baskarathas*, 3 July 2009, *op. cit*; France: Conseil d'Etat (10ème sous-section jugeant seule), *OFPRA C/Manivasagam* ("*Manivasagam*"), N° 323667, 7 mai 2012.

259 In a case concerning an applicant from Congo to whom the *Cour nationale du droit d'asile* had granted subsidiary protection on the basis of CESEDA Article L. 712-1(c) – transposing Article 15(c), the Conseil d'état found that: "*en s'abstenant de rechercher si la situation d'insécurité générale qui régnait alors au Congo résultait d'une situation de conflit armé interne ou international, la cour a commis une erreur de droit et a insuffisamment motivé sa decision*" and therefore quashed the Court's decision. France: Conseil d'Etat, *OFPRA C/Mme M.* ("*OFPRA C/Mme M*."), N° 328420, 15 December 2010; CE, *Baskarathas*, 3 July 2009, *op. cit*; CE, *Manivasagam*, 7 mai 2012, *op. cit.*

260 UNHCR, et al., *Safe at Last?* (July 2011), *op. cit.*, p. 61, n. 321 and decisions cited.

261 *Ibid.*, pp. 61–63.

262 Euroopean Commission, "Report on the application of the Qualification Directive", *op. cit.*, pp. 8–9.

conflict. As mentioned, environmental change can exacerbate tensions or even trigger conflicts, due to competition over depleting resources for instance. Conversely, conflicts can also deteriorate the environment to such an extent that life in the area becomes unbearable and forces people to move. Irrespective of the chronology – which can sometimes hardly be established, as long as there is an armed conflict, it is possible to consider the application of Article 15(c). The criteria used are the standard criteria described in Part 1 for the grant of subsidiary protection to persons fleeing armed conflict situations, under Article 15(c) of the Qualification Directive.[263] If conflict does occur, the sliding scale defined by the Court of Justice in its judgment in the *Elgafaji* case applies: beside exceptional cases when the degree of indiscriminate violence reaches such a high level that any person returned to the area would be exposed to a real risk of threat to life or person solely on account of his or her presence in the area, when the degree of violence does not reach this threshold of gravity, applicants will need to be able to invoke their personal circumstances to show they are specifically affected.[264] It seems that people displaced in the aftermath of a natural hazard-related disaster or technological accident would in general be excluded from subsidiary protection: they flee the immediate consequences of the disaster rather than a conflict.

To conclude, it appears that subsidiary protection offers only limited possibilities for the protection of environmentally-displaced persons. In view of the preparatory work for the Qualification Directive, this finding comes as no real surprise. In a 1999 discussion paper on subsidiary protection submitted by the Presidency, Member States were asked to clarify which situations they believed should come in the purview of subsidiary protection. The discussion paper enumerated sixteen different situations including armed conflicts, gender-specific problems, compulsory humanitarian reasons, practical impossibility of repatriation, but also environmental disasters.[265] Reference to environmentally-displaced persons did not reappear in later documents; this clearly indicates that, if their protection had been envisaged, the idea was however soon discarded.

The question whether environmental harm can constitute inhuman or degrading treatment and hence trigger the application of Article 15(b) remains

---

263 Above Part 1, Chapter 2., III. C., pp. 124s.
264 CJ, *Elgafaji*, §§ 43 and 39.
265 EU Council, "Note from the Presidency to the Asylum Working Party: Discussion Paper on Subsidiary Protection" ("Discussion Paper (ASILE 41)"), 13167/99 ASILE 41, 19 November 1999, p. 3.

to be addressed though; as mentioned, it will be so in the following Chapter (Chapter 7), when Article 3 ECHR is analysed under the prism of environmental harm.

Against this rather pessimistic assessment, a glance at Finnish and Swedish legislation might rekindle some hope.

B   The Protection of Environmentally-Displaced Persons in Finnish and Swedish Law: A Nordic Legacy or Mere Aberration?

In Sweden, protection can be granted to asylum seekers provided they fall within any of the three categories identified under Swedish asylum legislation: they can be refugees,[266] persons in need of subsidiary protection ("*alternativt skyddsbehövande*", in line with the EU Qualification Directive)[267] or persons "otherwise in need of protection" ("*övrig skyddsbehövande*").[268]

Persons "otherwise in need of protection" include persons who need protection because they have a well-founded fear of being subjected to serious abuses by reason of an external or internal armed conflict, or other severe conflicts in their country of origin as well as persons who are unable to return to the country of origin because of an environmental disaster.[269]

It can be noted that, in Sweden, a Member of Parliament of the ecologist party in fact sought to have persons fleeing environmental disasters protected under an extended refugee definition. The proposal was however rejected by the Swedish Parliament.[270]

To date, this provision on complementary protection for persons displaced by environmental disasters has never been used.[271] The preparatory work informs that the provision is intended to apply only in cases of sudden-onset disasters and provided there is no internal protection alternative.[272] Its scope

---

266   Utlänningslag, *op. cit.*, Chapter 4, Section 1.
267   *Ibid.*, Chapter 4, Section 2.
268   *Ibid.*, Chapter 4, Section 2a.
269   *Ibid.*, Chapter 4, Section 2a.
270   Riksdag (Swedish Parliament) Socialförsäkringsutskottet (Social Committee), "2009/10:Sfu14 Migration Och Asylpolitik – Riksdagen" [2010], Bodil Ceballos, p. 78.
271   Swedish Migration Board, "Sweden National Report (April 2010): The Practices in Sweden Concerning the Granting of Non-EU Harmonised Protection Statuses", *in EMN Study on The Different Practices Concerning Granting of Non-EU Harmonised Protection Statuses* (n/a: EMN, December 2010), p. 4, retrieved from: <http://emn.intrasoft-intl.com/Downloads/download.do;jsessionid=48CB45E0CA5EB4C57AD0BB871285B576?fileID=1005> [06/06/2011].
272   V.O. Kolmannskog and F. Myrstad, "Environmental Displacement in European Asylum Law", *European Journal of Migration and Law*, Vol. 11 (2009), pp. 313–326, p. 323.

is thereby limited. Additionally, the Aliens Act provides that in a situation where Sweden's asylum reception capacity is stretched to its limits, the Swedish Government can decide that residence permits shall not be granted to "persons otherwise in need of protection". Furthermore, according to commentators in Sweden,[273] it is likely that the provision will be withdrawn from Swedish law after the legislator has realised what implications such a provision could potentially have on Sweden's migrant intake.

In Finland, if the requirements for granting refugee status or subsidiary protection are not met, a person applying for international protection shall[274] be granted humanitarian protection[275] if he or she "cannot return to his or her country of origin or country of former habitual residence as a result of an environmental catastrophe or a bad security situation which may be due to an international or internal armed conflict or a poor human rights situation".[276] It appears however that protection has not yet been granted under this provision to persons fleeing environmental catastrophe,[277] in great part due to the fact that its application is strictly regulated.[278]

Although Swedish and Finnish law offer promising regimes of protection for persons displaced by environmental disasters, practice reveals that they have not been used yet. The impetus for the adoption of a regime of protection for environmentally-displaced persons, harmonised at the European level, will apparently not (yet) come from the North.

In view of the above, we can conclude that States will generally not recognise a need of international protection to persons internationally displaced

---

273   This observation emerged from various conversations I had in Sweden in March 2010 and April 2016, with different interlocutors (professors and members of the Migration courts of Malmö and Göteborg).

274   V.O. Kolmannskog and F. Myrstad indeed observe that humanitarian protection is not discretionary under Finnish law. V.O. Kolmannskog and F. Myrstad (2009), *op. cit.*, p. 322.

275   EMN, "Finland National Report (February 2010): The Different National Practises Concerning Granting of Non-EU Harmonised Protection Statuses", *in* EMN *Study on The Different Practices Concerning Granting of Non-EU Harmonised Protection Statuses* (n/a: EMN, December 2010), p. 11, retrieved from: <http://emn.intrasoft-intl.com/Downloads/download.do;jsessionid=48CB45E0CA5EB4C57AD0BB871285B576?fileID=965>.

276   Finland: Aliens Act (301/2004, Amendments up to 1152/2010 Included) (hereafter "Finnish Aliens Act") [Unofficial translation published by the Finnish Minitry of the Interior], Section 88a: Humanitarian protection.

277   J. McAdam, *Climate Change, Forced Migration, and International Law* (2012), *op. cit.*, p. 104.

278   Conversation with Eeva Nykänen during the 2011 Nordic Asylum Law Seminar: The State of International Refugee Law, EU Harmonization and the Nordic Legacy, Copenhagen, 26–27 May 2011.

by environmental degradation. However, at this stage of the analysis, it would be premature to say that their case is lost. Human rights instruments and the prohibition of *refoulement* therein enshrined, be it explicitly or implicitly, might provide them with a safeguard against removal.

C   The Status of "Protected Person" under New Zealand Law

New Zealand law derives the country's protection obligations from treaties to which New Zealand is a State Party. As it is the case within the European Union, asylum seekers in New Zealand may be granted either refugee status or a form of complementary protection.[279] Under the Immigration Act, beneficiaries of the latter receive the status of "protected persons". This form of complementary protection is based on New Zealand's obligations under the Convention against Torture and Other Cruel, Inhuman or Degrading Treatment or Punishment and under the International Covenant on Civil and Political Rights.[280]

As was mentioned in the outset of Part 2, New Zealand courts recently envisioned the qualification of low-lying Pacific island citizens, claiming international protection in New Zealand, as "protected persons" under the Immigration Act. Decisions focus in particular on the potential recognition of these appellants as protected persons under the ICCPR.

Section 131 of New Zealand Immigration Act provides that:

> [a] person must be recognised as a protected person in New Zealand under the Covenant on Civil and Political Rights if there are substantial grounds for believing that he or she would be in danger of being subjected to arbitrary deprivation of life or cruel treatment if deported from New Zealand.[281]

In other words, protection status under New Zealand law is intended to reflect New Zealand's obligations under Articles 6 and 7 of the ICCPR. In recent cases, concerning citizens of Kiribati and Tuvalu invoking adverse changes in their standards of living under the influence of climate change, New Zealand

---

279   As it is the case under the EU Qualification Directive, New Zealand Immigration Act provides for a sequential procedure: asylum authorities ("refugee and protection officers") should first determine whether the applicant qualifies as refugee and, in the negative, consider recognition as a protected person. New Zealand: Immigration Act 2009, 2009 No 51, 16 November 2009, Section 137. The same sequential procedure applies in courts, on an appeal against a decision by a refugee and protection officer declining to grant refugee or protected person status. *Ibid.*, Section 198.
280   *Ibid.*, Part 5: Refugee and protection status determinations, Sections 124–152.
281   *Ibid.*, Section 131(1).

courts thoroughly assessed the appellants' claims against the criteria set in Section 131. The claims were dismissed.²⁸²

According to New Zealand Immigration and Protection Tribunal, the possibility that disaster-displaced persons be recognised as protected person under the ICCPR in New Zealand derives from the growing recognition of States' positive obligations to protect the rights enshrined in the human rights treaties they are parties too against risks arising from natural disasters:²⁸³

> It provides a protection-oriented contour law around which claims for recognition as a protected person under Section 131 of the Act [in the context of natural disasters] may in principle wrap, both in the context of claims based on a danger of being subjected to arbitrary deprivation of life, and of suffering cruel, inhuman or degrading treatment.²⁸⁴

With regard to the right to life, the Tribunal finds that States have positive obligations to protect life against risks arising from natural disasters and that failure to do so may, in principle, constitute an omission constitutive of a breach of this right.²⁸⁵ In other words, "arbitrary deprivation" of life may result from either an act or an omission of the State.

In *AC (Tuvalu)*, the Tribunal instead finds that the government of Tuvalu is taking active steps to try and protect the lives of its citizens from the adverse impacts of known environmental hazards.²⁸⁶ The circumstance that those efforts may fall short of preventing environmental hazards from occurring is not to be construed as State failure but pertains to the special and partly insurmountable vulnerability of the islands to natural hazards such as droughts, hurricanes, inundations and storm surges.²⁸⁷

> While the Government of Tuvalu certainly has both obligations and capacity to take steps to reduce the risks from known environmental hazards, (...) it is simply not within the power of the Government of Tuvalu to mitigate the underlying environmental drivers of these hazards.

---

282   New Zealand: Immigration and Protection Tribunal, *AC (Tuvalu)*, [2014] NZIPT 800517-520, 4 June 2014, §§ 51–114; and *AF (Kiribati)*, [2013] NZIPT 800413, 25 June 2013, §§ 80–96.
283   NZIPT, *AC (Tuvalu)*, op. cit., § 68.
284   Ibid.
285   NZIPT, AF (Kiribati), §§ 85–87.
286   Ibid., §§ 101–108.
287   Ibid., § 75.

> To equate such inability with a failure of state protection goes too far. It places *an impossible burden on a state*.[288]

In other words, the Tribunal found that the alleged risk to life could not be attributed to any act or omission by the government of Kiribati. Furthermore, as it did in *AF (Kiribati)*,[289] the Tribunal considered that the degree of risk to life invoked by the appellants did not meet the severity requirement of ICCPR Article 6. The Tribunal acknowledged that the appellants would be faced with poverty-related challenges,[290] particularly in relation to food and water security in Tuvalu.[291] However, the Tribunal found that the appellants had failed to establish that, if returned to Tuvalu, "their lives would be so precarious *as a result of any act or omission by the state* that they are in danger of being arbitrarily deprived of their lives".[292] For those reason, the Tribunal dismissed the claims on this limb.

The same is true of the appellants' claims based on the prohibition of cruel, inhuman and degrading treatment. Central to the assessment was the definition of the notion of "treatment". The Immigration and Protection Tribunal clarified the acceptance of the term under New Zealand law in the *Fiji* case.[293] By contrast with the position adopted by the European Court of Human Rights (ECtHR), New Zealand courts require, for the purpose of assessing a breach of the prohibition of cruel, inhuman or degrading treatment, that the alleged harm arise from a "qualifying treatment in the receiving state".[294] The Tribunal thereby declines to follow the "unorthodox"[295] ECtHR approach whereby the alleged future harm emanates not from the receiving State's acts or omissions "but from a naturally occurring illness and the lack of sufficient resources to deal with it"[296] in the receiving country. In *Fiji*, the Tribunal observes:

---

288 *Ibid.*, § 75 (emphasis added).
289 NZIPT, *AF (Kiribati)*, § 89.
290 NZIPT, *AC (Tuvalu)*, § 101.
291 *Ibid.*, § 108.
292 *Ibid.*, § 100.
293 Immigration and Protection Tribunal, *BG (Fiji)*, [2012] NZIPT 800091, 20 January 2012.
294 *Ibid.*, § 181 (*a contrario*). See also NZIPT, *AC (Tuvalu)*, § 77.
295 The New Zealand Immigration and Protection Tribunal opposes the "orthodox approach" it endorses – requiring that the alleged harm emerges from a "qualifying treatment" in the receiving State, to the ECtHR's "modified approach", regarding expulsion itself as qualifying treatment. The Tribunal elaborates on the two respective approaches in NZIPT, *Fiji*, §§ 180–196.
296 ECtHR, *Sufi & Elmi*, § 281.

As a general rule, socio-economic deprivation arising from general policy and conditions in the receiving state is not to be regarded as a breach of Article 7 of the ICCPR as there is no relevant treatment.[297]

In *AC (Tuvalu)* and *AF (Kiribati)*, the Tribunal concluded that there was no evidence of a danger for the appellants to be subjected to cruel, inhuman or degrading treatment in their country of origin by reason of some act or omission by the State, failing to discharge its obligation to protect its population and territory against the adverse impacts of natural disasters and climate change.[298] On the contrary, the Tribunal highlighted for instance that the Government of Tuvalu was "actively engaged in seeking to reduce the impacts of climate change on its territory and population".[299]

The Tribunal's interpretation of the concept of "treatment" under ICCPR Article 7 delineates the scope of complementary protection under New Zeland law. The choice for a restrictive, literal interpretation of ICCPR Article 7 is allegedly intended to preserve the coherence of New Zealand Immigration Act and reflect the drafters' intention. The Tribunal indeed relies on the existence of a "free-standing humanitarian jurisdiction" in the Immigration Act, separate from provisions on complementary protection (protected person), to justify that humanitarian conditions be analysed not as "a treatment" by the receiving State but merely as discretionary grounds for possibly granting humanitarian visas.[300] As noted by J. McAdam: "context is everything" and had New Zeland law not provided for the possibility to grant authorisations to stay on discretionary humanitarian grounds, decision-makers might have interpreted the scope of complementary protection granted under ICCPR prohibition of cruel, inhuman and degrading treatment more broadly.[301]

The next Chapter will elaborate on the capacity of international human rights law and the principle of *non-refoulement* in particular to protect environmentally-displaced persons against forcible return to their country of origin, where they would risk be exposed to human rights violations.

---

297 NZIPT, *Fiji*, § 197.
298 NZIPT, AF (Kiribati), §§ 93–95; NZIPT, *AC (Tuvalu)*, §§ 109–114.
299 NZIPT, *AC (Tuvalu)*, § 113.
300 *Ibid.*, § 82.
301 J. McAdam, "The emerging New Zealand jurisprudence on climate change, disasters and displacement", *Migration Studies*, Volume 3, Number 1 (2015), pp. 131–142, p. 138.

CHAPTER 7

Under International Human Rights Law

De lege lata, Member States of the European Union are under no explicit obligation to protect and grant an international protection status to "environmental refugees", whose needs for protection are otherwise often stated.

"The refugee question (...) is in its essence a human rights question".[1] This statement made by E. Feller appears to be all the more pertinent in the context of environmental displacement: can international human rights law come to the rescue of environmentally-displaced persons, whose claims for international protection will generally fail?

With a view to assessing the likelihood that those norms of international human rights law, forming part of the international protection regime, be also applicable in the specific situation of environmentally-displaced persons, regards must be had to their interpretation and application by courts and asylum authorities. At the time of writing, no case involving an environmentally displaced person had been brought before any of the monitoring bodies. Some decisions are nevertheless worth taking into consideration where the personal situation of an environmentally-displaced person can be construed as similar or, at least comparable, to that of the claimant in the case. The European Court of Human Rights, insofar as it issued a myriad decisions pertaining to expulsion, return and extradition, will be the main focus of this Chapter.

The principle of *non-refoulement* was elaborated upon in the first Part. It finds expression in or derives from a number of international instruments; it provides that no person may be returned in any manner whatsoever to a country where his or her life or person would be at risk, regardless of his or her status or conduct. It is in particular a considerable safeguard against removal for individuals who have been denied international protection status. For the purpose of considering whether human rights law could protect environmentally displaced persons against return to their country of origin, affected by an environmental disaster, it is necessary to first clarify in what manner and to what extent disasters affect populations and, in so doing, identify the human rights the enjoyment of which is jeopardised in such circumstances (I).

The first Part showed that the principle of *non-refoulement* was derived by treaty-monitoring bodies from the prohibition of torture and inhuman or

---

1 E. Feller (2006), *op. cit.*, p. 514.

degrading treatment or punishment. Whereas the application of the principle to violations of other rights was never excluded by the European Court of Human Rights and has already occurred in some cases, the risk of ill-treatments proscribed under Article 3 ECHR remains the main trigger for States' obligation under the principle of *non-refoulement*. This should not be interpreted as disregard for other human rights. To the contrary, the Court increasingly had regard to other rights, including other civil and political rights but also socio-economic rights, upon considering alleged violations of Article 3. The Court relied on notions such as access to medical treatment, shelter or the applicant's ability to provide for his or her most basic needs (including food, water and hygiene) to conclude, in certain cases, that return to a situation of deprivation of any or several of them constitutes a violation of Article 3 ECHR. As observed by J. McAdam, for the European Court of Human Rights to consider socio-economic rights, "such rights must first pass through the doorway of the protected civil and political rights".

Two recent judgments issued by the European Court of Human Rights are particularly relevant to the discussion on whether environmentally-displaced persons are protected from *refoulement*. The *N. v. UK* case and the *Sufi & Elmi* case will be the focus of the second sub-section; the situation of environmentally-displaced person will be put to the test elaborated (or confirmed) by the Court in those two cases (II).

I   The Impact of Environmental Disasters on the Enjoyment of Human Rights

Environmental disasters, of slow- and of sudden-onset, significantly alter conditions of living. Two main aspects of their impact on populations will be highlighted below: they affect one's enjoyment of most, if not all, human rights (A) and they affect populations in an indiscriminate manner (B).

A   *Human Rights at Stake in Situations of Environmental Disaster*
As mentioned, growing awareness of the phenomenon of climate change gave considerable impetus to the discussion on the international protection of environmentally-displaced persons. Observations of current trends and numerous projections concur in finding that global warming already has and will have impacts on human populations and mobility. It is not the increase in temperature itself as much as "the associated changes in, and combined effects of, precipitation patterns (drought and flooding), storms, and sea level rise; loss of biodiversity, and ecosystem services; and resulting health risk, food

and livelihood insecurity".[2] The link between climate change or, more generally, the environment and human rights is well-established.[3]

In a consensus resolution adopted in 2008, its first concerning human rights and climate change, the UN Human Rights Council recognised that climate change "poses an immediate and far-reaching threat to people and communities around the world and has implications for the full enjoyment of human rights".[4] Subsequent, annual, UN Human Rights Council resolutions clarified the rights, the effective enjoyment of which will be jeopardised in environments affected by the impacts of climate change. Those rights include:

> ... the right to life, the right to adequate food, the right to the enjoyment of highest attainable standard of physical and mental health, the right to adequate housing, the right to self-determination, the right to safe drinking water and sanitation and the right to development...[5]

The UN Human Rights Council further recalled that "in no case may a people be deprived of its own means of subsistence".[6] The Human Rights Council

---

2   M. Wahlström (6–7 June 2011).
3   S.A. Mcinerney-Lankford, *et al.*, *Human Rights and Climate Change: A Review of the International Legal Dimensions* (Washington, D.C.: World Bank, 2011), pp. 11–19 especially; Stand up for Your Rights, "The Human Side of Climate Change: Human Rights Violations and Climate Change Refugees" (December 2009), pp. 17–23; S. Humphreys and R. Archer (Eds.), *Climate Change and Human Rights: A Rough Guide* (Versoix: International Council on Human Rights Policy, 2008), pp. 21–27; J. Neumann, *Human Rights and Climate Change: International Human Rights as an Instrument for Measures of Equalization?*, Master Thesis, University of Auckland (Norderstedt: GRIN, September 2010), pp. 16–19.
4   UNHRC, "Resolution 7/23 on Human Rights and Climate Change" ("Resolution 7/23"), A/HRC/RES/7/23, 28 March 2008, Preamble Recital 1.
5   UNHRC, "Resolution 32/33 on Human Rights and Climate Change" ("Resolution 32/33"), Resolution A/HRC/RES/32/33, 18 July 2016, Preamble Recital 10. Resolution 32/33 confirms in that respect the position expressed by the Human Rights Council in its previous resolutions on the same subject matter. See for instance UNHRC, "Resolution 29/15 on Human Rights and Climate Change" ("Resolution 29/15"), A/HRC/RES/29/15, 22 July 2015; UNHRC, "Resolution 26/27 on Human Rights and Climate Change" ("Resolution 26/27"), A/HRC/RES/26/27, 15 July 2014, Preamble Recital 17; UNHRC, "Resolution 18/22 on Human Rights and Climate Change" ("Resolution 18/22"), A/HRC/RES/18/22, 17 October 2011, Preamble Recital 12; and UNHRC, "Resolution 10/4 on Human Rights and Climate Change" ("Resolution 10/4"), A/HRC/RES/10/4, 25 March 2009, Preamble Recital 7.
6   UNHRC, "Resolution 32/33", *op. cit.*, Preamble Recital 10; UNHRC, "Resolution 10/4", *op. cit.*, Preamble Recital 7; UNHRC, "Resolution 18/22", *op. cit.*, Preamble Recital 12.

reiterated these statements, made in relation to climate change specifically, in the broader context of the interaction between human rights and the environment generally. The language of the resolution itself is broader: "environmental damage can have negative implications, both direct and indirect, for the effective enjoyment of *all* human rights".[7] The Office of the High Commissioner for Human Rights (OHCHR) has also repeadtedly highlighted the links between human rights and disasters, including in the context of climate change.[8] A number of States have also expressed the importance of addressing the human rights implications of climate change and the necessity to integrate human rights in climate responses.[9]

Environmental degradation, including that caused by the effects of climate change or armed conflicts, affects primarily a territory and, but, one might say, incidentally only, populations who happen to be present or live on that territory. In that sense, they affect people in an indiscriminate manner. Two observations must however be made that nuance this assumption. Firstly, all regions of the world are in reality not equal when it comes to environmental disasters: some are more affected than others by extreme weather events, earthquakes or volcano eruption for instance. Some regions or areas within a country may also be more prone than others to severe pollution. Lastly, armed conflicts also tend

---

7   UNHRC, "Resolution 28/11 on Human Rights and the Environment" ("Resolution 28/11"), A/HRC/RES/28/11, 7 April 2015, Preamble Recital 8. Similarly: UNHRC, "Resolution 16/11 on Human Rights and the Environment" ("Resolution 16/11"), A/HRC/RES/16/11, 12 April 2011, Preamble Recital 14.

8   *See* for instance the Submission of the Office of the High Commissioner for Human Rights to the 21st Conference of the Parties to the United Nations Framework Convention on Climate Change (COP21): OHCHR, "Understanding Human Rights and Climate Change", submission of the OHCHR to the 21st COP to the UNFCCC, 2015, available at: <http://www.ohchr.org/Documents/Issues/ClimateChange/COP21.pdf> [accessed 10/04/2016]. In a 2015 opinion piece, the High Commissioner for Human Rights, Zeid Ra'ad Al Hussein, recalling that "climate change is having a devastating impact on a wide range of internationally-guaranteed human rights", calls for "solutions rooted in climate justice". UN High Commissioner for Human Rights: Zeid Ra'ad Al Hussein, "Opinion piece: Burning down the house", 3 December 2015, available at: <http://www.ohchr.org/EN/NewsEvents/Pages/BurningDowntheHouse.aspx> [accessed 08/05/2016].

9   In February 2015, 18 States signed "The Geneva Pledge on Human Rights in Climate Action" (initially launched by Costa Rica). More than 30 States thereby committed to "facilitate the exchange of expertise and best practice" between human rights and climate experts to build their "collective capacity to deliver responses to climate change that are good for people and the planet". The Geneva Pledge on Human Rights in Climate Action, available at: < http://www.rree.go.cr/files/includes/files.php?id=453&tipo=contenido> [19/09/2016].

to occur in certain regions more than in others.[10] Secondly, humanitarian actors have repeatedly put forward that within populations affected by disasters (including natural disasters and armed conflicts), certain categories of people are often more vulnerable than the rest of the population. Such groups include children, women, and the elderly, persons with disabilities or HIV/AIDS, and minorities (including indigenous people). Stakeholders involved in providing assistance and protection to disaster-hit populations must recognise the differing needs of those vulnerable groups and thus enable them to clear the physical, cultural and social hurdles that may otherwise hinder their access to services, relief assistance and support.[11] The Human Rights Council too acknowledges those vulnerabilities and recognises that while all individuals and communities around the world will be affected, "the effects of climate change will be felt most acutely by those segments of the population who are already in vulnerable situations owing to factors such as geography, poverty, gender, age, indigenous or minority status and disability".[12] In other words, environmental degradations, including the impacts of climate change, also jeopardise among other rights minority rights, women's rights, the rights of the child, of indigenous people and of persons with disabilities.

The Inter-Agency Standing Committee (IASC), "a unique inter-agency forum for coordination, policy development and decision-making involving the key UN and non-UN humanitarian partners"[13] whose role as primary mechanism

---

10   According to the World Bank, "conflicts often are not one-off events, but are ongoing and repeated: 90 percent of the last decade's civil wars occurred in countries that had already had a civil war in the last 30 years". Core Writing Team, *et al.* (Eds.), *World Development Report 2011: Conflict, Security, and Development* (Washington, DC: The World Bank, 2011), p. 2 and Table F1.1, p. 3; UNHRC, "Resolution 16/11", *op. cit.*, Preamble Recital 14.

11   In that sense, see The Sphere Project, *Humanitarian Charter and Minimum Standards in Disaster Response*, Third edition, (Geneva: The Sphere Project, 2004), pp. 9–10 in particular; Michel Prieur, *Ethical Principles on Disaster Risk Reduction and People's Resilience* (Strasbourg: Council of Europe, 2009): p. 29; Inter-Agency Standing Committee, *Pilot Manual Accompanying the IASC Operational Guidelines on Human Rights and Natural Disasters*, (Washington DC: Brookings-Bern Project on Internal Displacement, March 2008), pp. 63–77 especially; Rozan (Non-governmental organisation), *Checklist to facilitate Gender Sensitivity of Relief and Reconstruction efforts for Survivors of the Earthquake in Pakistan* (Geneva: World Health Organisation, January 2006); Erica Harper, *Manual on international law and standards applicable in natural disaster situations* (Rome: International Development Law Organization, March 2009), pp. 71–136.

12   UNHRC, "Resolution 18/22", *op. cit.*, Preamble Recital 13; UNHRC, "Resolution 10/4", *op. cit.*, Preamble Recital 8.

13   More information about the IASC's members, mandate and actions, are available on the website of the Standing Committee: <http://www.humanitarianinfo.org/iasc/> [10/09/2011].

for inter-agency coordination of humanitarian assistance was affirmed by the UN General Assembly,[14] has developed operational guidelines and a field manual on human rights protection in situations of natural disaster.[15] They are intended to ensure that States, intergovernmental and non-governmental humanitarian actors conduct disaster relief and reconstruction efforts within a framework that protects and furthers human rights. Specifically, the IASC guidelines deal with *in situ* assistance: they address the protection needs of communities affected by a natural disaster and possibly displaced by it but internally only (Internally Displaced Persons, or IDPs). These guidelines are nevertheless relevant in the present discussion on the protection of victims of environmental disasters who were forced to leave their home and move across State borders insofar as they identify the effects of environmental disasters on populations. The fact is that whether people move within or beyond the borders of their State, in both cases, an environmental disaster exposed them to risks of such gravity that they felt they had no choice but to move. Displacement beyond State borders can have many explanations; it can also be evidence of the absence of protection available in the country of origin against threats to life or person originating in the disaster, or be symptomatic of a particularly large-scale disaster.

The IASC Guidelines on Human Rights and Natural Disasters groups human rights into the four following categories:

- Rights related to protection of life; security and physical integrity; and the protection of family ties in the context of evacuations;
- Rights related to food; health; shelter; and education;
- Rights related to housing, land and property; and livelihoods; and
- Rights related to documentation, free movement in the context of durable solutions for internally displaced persons; re-establishment of family ties, expression and opinion; and elections.[16]

It appears clearly from this enumeration that environmental disasters impact all aspects of life. The Guidelines clarify that this categorisation does not suggest any hierarchy among rights. IASC indicates that "only the full respect of *all*

---

14   UNGA, *Strengthening of the coordination of humanitarian emergency assistance of the United Nations*, Resolution 48/57, A/RES/48/57, 14/12/1993, §6.
15   IASC, *Operational Guidelines On the Protection of Persons in Situations of Natural Disasters*, On the Protection of Persons in Situations of Natural Disasters (Washington, DC: The Brookings – Bern Project on Internal Displacement, January 2011).
16   Those four categories of rights are enumerated in *ibid.*, p. 9.

rights mentioned [in the Guidelines] can ensure adequate protection of the human rights of those affected by natural disasters".[17] In particular, the Guidelines refer to the Vienna Declaration and Programme of Action, which was approved by 171 States at the World Conference on Human Rights in Vienna, in 1993, and which asserts that "all human rights are universal, indivisible and interdependent and interrelated".[18]

Environmental disasters affect all aspects of human life. Another essential feature is that they affect population in indiscriminate manner (with the nuance made above pertaining to regional and, or individual vulnerabilities). The evolution of the ECtHR case-law on the application of *non-refoulement* when threats are indiscriminate was described in the first Part. It will be briefly traced again below but this time with environmental displacement in mind.

B   *Environmental Disaster as a Source of Indiscriminate Threats*

One essential characteristic of environmental disasters is that their effects on the population are indiscriminate by nature. Individuals and groups of individuals are victims on the sole ground of their being present on the affected territory. This partly accounts for the complexity of the question whether affected populations should be granted a form of international protection and, if so, on which grounds and from whom.

For decades, individuals displaced by the indiscriminate effects of armed conflicts were confronted with the same legal vacuum. The nexus requirement of the Refugee Convention excludes from the refugee definition victims of purely indiscriminate threats. Under human rights law instruments, protection from *refoulement* was long conditional upon the applicant adducing evidence that he or she would be more at risk than the rest of the population.[19] The ECtHR long required under its infamous and now revisited *Vilvarajah* jurisprudence that the applicant should demonstrate the personal nature of the alleged risk by showing that there existed special distinguishing features, concerning him personally.[20] The Court revisited its position in *Salah Sheekh v. the Netherlands* which has been repeatedly confirmed since. In situations where it is established that a certain group is the target of ill-treatment, and that the applicant is a member of this group, then, the Court found, it might render

---

17   Ibid., p. 10.
18   World Conference on Human Rights, "Vienna Declaration and Programme of Action", UN Doc A/CONF.157/23, 12 July 1993, § 5.
19   Above Part 1, Chapter 3, I. C. 1., pp. 228s.
20   Council of Europe: European Court of Human Rights, *Vilvarajah and Others v. The United Kingdom*, Appl. No. 45/1990/236/302-306, 26/09/1991, §112.

the protection offered by ECHR Article 3 illusory if, in addition to the fact that he belongs to the given targeted group, the applicant were required to show the existence of further special distinguishing features.[21] The Court thus lowered the degree of individualisation that the applicant needed to demonstrate: membership of a targeted group is sufficient to activate the protection of Article 3 against *refoulement*. It is not necessary that the applicant demonstrates further distinguishing features which would place him or her personally at higher risk than other members of the same minority. As noted by Nuala Mole though, ECtHR case law does oblige the applicant to "substantiate through the relevant documentation, membership of the group in question and the treatment meted out as a result".[22] Accordingly, environmentally-displaced persons may be protected from *refoulement* but provided they can establish their membership in a group at risk.

UNHCR in fact suggested that the protection needs of persons fleeing armed conflicts and of those fleeing natural disaster might in certain circumstances be equated.[23] In a Note issued in 2005, UNHCR analysed State practice and the case-law of monitoring bodies applying the *non-refoulement* principle to persons fleeing armed conflicts or serious public order. The findings of UNHCR were based on the now outdated 1991 *Vilvarajah* jurisprudence. The date is noteworthy: at the time the UNHCR Note was drafted (2005), the European Court of Human Rights had not yet ruled in the *Salah Sheekh* case (2007) which, as described above, extended the scope of *non-refoulement* by making way for the requirement for individualisation. In 2005, UNHCR thus rightly observed that the existence of an armed conflict situation was generally not sufficient in itself. To trigger the host State's obligation of *non-refoulement*, applicants had to demonstrate that their returning to their country of origin would reach the threshold of torture, cruel, inhuman or degrading treatment due to their personal risk of suffering serious violations of fundamental rights there;[24] as mentioned, the position of the ECtHR has since evolved on this point. The UNHCR Note then moves to address *refoulement* in cases of environmental disaster. The UN High Commissioner notes:

> Similarly, it could be argued that the return of individuals who have fled natural or ecological disaster to their country of origin might in

---

21 ECtHR, *Salah Sheekh*, § 148.
22 N. Mole and C. Meredith, *Asylum and the European Convention on Human Rights*, 5 ed., No. 9 (Strasbourg: Council of Europe Publishing, 2010), p. 44.
23 UNHCR, "Complementary Forms of Protection", *op. cit.*
24 *Ibid.*

exceptional circumstances reach a level of severity amounting to inhuman treatment and consequently give rise to protection from refoulement under human rights instruments.[25]

The position of human rights monitoring bodies on the prohibition of *refoulement* in the context of an armed conflict has evolved, as evidenced by the European Court of Human Rights decision in *Salah Sheekh*[26] and *NA v. UK*.[27] In light of this evolution and of the parallel made by UNHCR in 2005, it can be argued that, like people fleeing armed conflicts, persons who flee environmental disasters should be protected from *refoulement* if the group to which they belong is more exposed to threats of inhuman or degrading treatment as against the rest of the population. It could be the case where the provision of humanitarian assistance and support for example would be discriminatory: access to social services including healthcare and housing or food, would be ensured in priority for the members of the dominant group of the population, whereas members of certain minorities (ethnic, religious or else) in the country would only receive residual assistance. As seen in the previous Chapter (Chapter 6), this would most likely be a case for recognition of the applicant as a refugee. International human rights law might nevertheless play a role, not least because a refugee might be excluded from refugee protection pursuant to the exclusion clauses and because the principle of *non-refoulement* under refugee law contains exceptions to it.

Under this case-law, it seems that a number of persons fleeing armed conflicts or natural disasters would not have successful claims. In many cases indeed, given the indiscriminate effects of both situations, it is very likely that individuals fleeing the affected areas or countries cannot invoke that it is their belonging to a particular group that exposes them to ill-treatment. The evolution of the principle of *non-refoulement* under Article 3 of the ECHR is nonetheless significant: the protection it provides can now be triggered "prima facie", on the presumption that the applicant's membership of a certain group necessarily exposes her to ill-treatment, should she be returned.

The recent judgment of the ECtHR in the *Sufi & Elmi* case, analysed in Part 1,[28] brought two major developments in the scope of *non-refoulement* under Article 3 ECHR. Firstly, it shed light on what constitutes the "most extreme cases"[29] of generalised violence, in which the Court can find a violation of

---

25   Ibid., § 19.
26   ECtHR, *Salah Sheekh*. See Part 1, Chapter 3, I. C., pp. 224s.
27   ECtHR, *NA v. UK*. See Part 1, Chapter 3, I. C., pp. 224s.
28   Above pp. 228s.
29   ECtHR, *NA v. UK*, § 116.

Article 3, without there being a need for the applicant to show any element of individualisation of the risk (neither a personalisation of the risk nor the applicant's belonging in a group at risk). For the first time, the Court concluded that the degree of general violence in the case at hand was so high that any returnee would be exposed to a real risk of Article 3 ill-treatment, "solely on account of his presence there".[30] Secondly, it clarified what criteria authorities should use to assess risks of harm emanating from naturally-occurring phenomena.[31]

Presumably, should the European Court of Human Rights be submitted a claim of violation of Article 3 in a situation of involuntary return of an environmentally-displaced person to his or her country of origin, it would apply the tests it has already developed to assess the situation of individuals who invoke risks of torture or inhuman or degrading treatment or punishment in their country of origin. The Court has in fact alluded to the possibility that Article 3 ECHR, as it is interpreted in case-law, applies to persons displaced by environmental disasters. In *Sufi & Elmi*, the Court noted that the test formulated in *N. v. the United Kingdom*[32] might be the appropriate one to deal with a "naturally occurring phenomenon"[33] rather than the test adopted in *MSS v. Belgium and Greece*,[34] which applies when the source of ill-treatment stems, in some part at least, from factors that can engage, directly or indirectly, responsibility of the public authorities in the country of origin.[35] Both tests will be applied to environmental disaster situations in the following Section (II).

II   Environmental Harm and the Principle of *Non-refoulement* in the Case-Law of the ECtHR

A preliminary remark pertains to the relevance and applicability of the prohibition of *refoulement* in mass influx situations. It is made clear under international human rights law and customary law:[36] the circumstance that applicants form part of a large group of persons displaced cannot preclude the

---

30   ECtHR, *Sufi & Elmi*, § 293.
31   Ibid., § 282.
32   The case concerned an HIV-positive applicant from Uganda where her lifespan would be reduced by reason of the fact that treatment facilities available in Uganda were inferior to those available in the UK. It is discussed below. ECtHR, *N. v. UK*; ECtHR, *Sufi & Elmi*, § 282.
33   ECtHR, *Sufi & Elmi*, § 282.
34   ECtHR, *M.S.S.*
35   ECtHR, *N. v. UK*, § 32, a contrario.
36   As mentioned in Part 1, the same is also true under refugee law. See E. Lauterpacht and D. Bethlehem (2003), *op. cit.*, §§ 103–111; ExCom, "Conclusion No 22 on Large-Scale Influx (1981)", *op. cit.*, I.3 and II.A.1 and 2.

application of the principle.[37] The Court thus made clear in the *M.S.S.* case that the fact that a large number of persons find themselves exposed to the same risks in their country of origin "does not make the risk concerned any less individual where it is sufficiently real and probable".[38]

As stated in Part 1, if there is a real risk of threat to life or freedom upon removal, States cannot invoke the applicant's status or conduct to justify a decision to return him or her; what is more, in principle, States cannot invoke their own circumstances and the challenges posed to their asylum systems to return asylum seekers to life-threatening situations.[39] In a word, the reality of the alleged risk should be the only decisive factor.[40]

This is particularly relevant in the context of environmentally-induced displacement: environmental disasters of such a severity that they will trigger displacement typically trigger – or will trigger – large-scale movements of population. This applies to both sudden- as well as to slow-onset disasters.

It is often stressed in response to States' sometimes express concern that relaxing asylum regulations might expose them to unmanageable flows of migrants seeking protection: humanitarian actors observe that the preferred option of individuals coerced to flee their habitual residence is by far to settle in an alternative location within their home country. In general, cross-border displacement indeed presupposes an impossibility to relocate internally. Inductively, it is possible to assume that environmental degradations causing individuals to seek protection in a third country are those which are of such a magnitude that populations could not resettle in another part of their country of origin. If an environmental degradation is in fact of such magnitude, the affected population will be correspondingly sizeable. As a consequence, it is to be expected that where the trigger for displacement is environmental degradation, neighbouring – mainly – and other States will encounter large flows of asylum seekers.

The principle of *non-refoulement* being absolute, the challenge posed by a mass influx of asylum seekers to the host State's asylum capacities is however immaterial:

---

37   Above Part 1, Chapter 3, I. C. 1., pp. 226s. and Chapter 3. II., pp. 232s.
38   ECtHR, *M.S.S.*, § 359.
39   Chapter I, pp. 223s.
40   H. Labayle and F. Sudre, "Jurisprudence de la Cour européenne des droits de l'homme et droit administratif (2009)", *RFDA*, Vol. 4 (July-August 2009), p. 707.

As a matter of international law, refoulement is not justifiable no matter how debilitating a sudden influx of refugees might be on a State's resources, economy, or political situation.[41]

The recent judgment of the European Court of Human Rights in the *N. v. UK* case actually questions the accuracy of the statement as well as, more generally, the absolute nature of the principle of *non-refoulement*. The Court indeed took into consideration the host State's budgetary constraints to conclude that the expulsion of a person with an HIV and AIDS-related condition to a country where she could not benefit from the same treatment as in the UK and where, as a result, the quality of her life and her life expectancy would be affected, would not give rise to a violation of Article 3.[42]

In fact, and rather inauspiciously for environmentally-displaced persons, the Court stated in *Sufi & Elmi* that the test in *N. v. UK* may well be the appropriate test to assess alleged violations of Article 3 when threats originate in dire humanitarian conditions prevailing in the country of origin and which cannot engage the direct or indirect responsibility of the public authorities there.[43]

The case is discussed below (A). After considering whether environmental disasters meet the test in *N. v. UK*, the second subsection turns to the test in the *M.S.S.* and *Sufi & Elmi* cases to assess whether environmental disasters, together with the direct or indirect action of the affected country's authorities, can place individuals in such "particularly serious" conditions that they are unable to cater for their most basic needs and therefore justify protection against *refoulement* (B).

A   *Environmental Disasters as "Compelling Humanitarian Considerations" against Removal?*

An example of application of the *non-refoulement* principle as deduced from article 3 of the ECHR is the case-law of the European Court of Human Rights concerning cases of removal of HIV positive people. The *N. v. UK*[44] case offers little hope of seeing the protection against *refoulement* offered by Article 3 ECHR apply to environmentally-displaced persons (2). The Court's case-law had yet given some measure of hope in that respect (1).

---

41   G.S. Goodwin-Gill and J. McAdam, *The refugee in international law*, 3rd ed., (New York: Oxford, 2007), p. 335.
42   ECtHR, *N. v. UK*, §§ 44, 50–51.
43   ECtHR, *Sufi & Elmi*, § 282.
44   ECtHR, *N. v. UK*.

1   *Non-refoulement* and "Naturally-Occurring" Phenomena: Some Promising First Steps

In its judgment in the *H.L.R v. France*[45] case, the Court had announced that, due to the absolute nature of the prohibition of torture and inhuman or degrading treatment and punishment, it did not rule out that Article 3 of the ECHR may apply when the danger emanates from persons or groups who are not public officials, provided that the claimant demonstrates that the risk is real and that the authorities of the receiving country[46] are unable to obviate this risk by providing appropriate protection.[47]

In *D. v. UK*,[48] the Court went one step further. The Court observed that the principle of *non-refoulement* had until then been applied by the Court only in contexts in which the alleged risk awaiting the applicant in the receiving country emanated from acts intentionally inflicted either by State authorities or by non-State agents when authorities were unable to afford appropriate protection against them.[49] This notwithstanding, in view of the fundamental importance of Article 3 ECHR, the Court considers itself competent to scrutinise an applicant's claim under Article 3 also when the source of the risk of proscribed treatment in the receiving country "stems from factors which cannot engage either directly or indirectly the responsibility of the public authorities of that country"[50] – or which, taken alone, did not in themselves infringe the standards of Article 3.[51]

The *D. v. UK* case concerned a national of St Kitts, who had been convicted and sentenced in the United Kingdom and whom UK authorities sought to deport to St Kitts after he had completed his sentence of imprisonment in the UK. The applicant was suffering from AIDS; by the time deportation was considered, he presented signs of critical immunosuppression and appeared to be close to death. The Court observed that the "conditions of adversity" awaiting him in St Kitts, including the absence of support from family or close relatives, "his lack of shelter and of a proper diet as well as exposure to the health and sanitation problems which beset the population of St Kitts",

---

45   ECtHR, *H.L.R. v. France*.
46   In the human rights law context, *non-refoulement* prohibits removal to a so-called "receiving country". This country will also often be what refugee law refers to as the applicant's "country of origin" or "country of habitual residence". The terms will therefore be used interchangeably.
47   ECtHR, *H.L.R. v. France*, § 40.
48   ECtHR, *D. v. UK*.
49   *Ibid.*, § 49.
50   *Ibid.*, § 49.
51   *Ibid.*, § 49.

as well as the incapacity of St Kitts to provide him with appropriate medical treatment, risked further reducing the applicant's "already limited life expectancy".[52] As a consequence, the Court found that "the implementation of the decision to remove him to St Kitts would amount to inhuman treatment by the respondent State in violation of Article 3".[53] In conclusion, the Court stated that:

> ... in the very exceptional circumstances of this case and given the compelling humanitarian considerations at stake, it must be concluded that the implementation of the decision to remove the applicant would be a violation of Article 3 (art. 3).[54]

Illness, limited medical facilities and conditions of adversity (lack of shelter, proper diet and exposure to generalised health and sanitation problems[55]) were analysed by the Court as factors which "cannot engage either directly or indirectly the responsibility of the public authorities"[56] and indeed, the Court further stressed that those conditions could not be said to themselves be a breach of the standards of Article 3 ECHR.[57]

It follows that the responsibility of the country of origin[58] in the risk of ill-treatment is not necessary for the expelling State's obligation under Article 3 ECHR to apply; that is to say that the State obligation not to return individuals to a risk of ill-treatment in their country of origin is not conditional upon the risk being attributable, directly or indirectly, to the authorities of the country of origin. Environmental degradations, for which in most cases national authorities of the country concerned cannot be, directly or indirectly, held responsible thus seemed to be within the purview of Article 3 of the Convention.

Concerning the types of treatments falling under Article 3, there again the interpretation given by the Court seemed broad enough to allow for the impact of environmental disaster on populations to be construed as inhuman or degrading treatment. The Court clarified the notion through its case-law. It considered as "ill-treatments" for the purpose of Article 3 treatments

---

52 Ibid., § 52.
53 Ibid., § 53.
54 Ibid., § 54.
55 Ibid., § 52.
56 Ibid., § 49.
57 Ibid., § 43.
58 Above note 1599.

reaching a minimum level of severity and causing "if not actual bodily injury, at least intense physical and mental suffering to the persons subjected thereto".[59] The Court also ruled that a treatment was "degrading" in the purview of Article 3 if it "humiliates or debases an individual, showing a lack of respect for, or diminishing, his or her human dignity, or arouses feelings of fear, anguish or inferiority capable of breaking an individual's moral and physical resistance".[60]

In the *BB v. France* case,[61] which was struck out of the list after France issued not a residence permit but a compulsory residence order against the applicant and undertook not to deport him,[62] the European Commission of Human Rights (ECnHR) had even invoked environmental factors in its opinion in the case. The Commission concluded that there was a violation of Article 3 of the ECHR in case of deportation by France of the claimant, who was suffering from AIDS and presented signs of acute immunosuppression, to the Republic of Congo. The Court, affirming that the object and purpose of the Convention, "as an instrument for the protection of individual human beings, require that its provisions be interpreted and applied so as to make its safeguards practical and effective", considered that "exposing a person to a real and substantiated risk to his health which is so serious as to amount to a violation of Article 3 on account of other factors in the receiving country, such as the lack of medical care and services, as well as social and *environmental* factors, are capable of engaging the responsibility of the State intending to expel the person".[63] Therefore, it appeared conceivable that a State who would expel an individual to a destination country laid waste by environmental disaster in spite of him or her showing a real and substantiated risk of bodily injury or intense physical and mental suffering, could be held responsible under Article 3 of the Convention.

However, that possibility now seems rather tenuous in view of the judgment of the Court in the *N. v. UK* case.

---

59   ECtHR, § 167. Also ECtHR, *Case of V. v. The United Kingdom* ("*V. v. UK*"), Application no. 24888/94 (16 December 1999), § 71.
60   ECtHR, *Case of Pretty v. The United Kingdom* ("*Pretty v. UK*"), Application no. 2346/02 (29/07/2002), § 52.
61   ECnHR, *B.B. Contre La France* ("*BB v. France*"), Application N° 30930/96 (9 March 1998).
62   ECtHR, *Case of B.B. v. France* ("*BB v. France*"), Application no. 30930/96 (7 September 1998).
63   ECnHR, *BB v. France*, § 54 [emphasis added]. The opinion of the Commission, originally in French, appears in a translated English version in joint dissenting opinion of Judges Tulkens, Bonello and Spielman in ECtHR, *N. v. UK*, Joint dissenting opinion of Judges Tulkens, Bonello and Spielmann, § 16.

2 A Retrograde Step? The N. v. UK Case

In this judgment, the Court first reasserted its earlier case-law, citing in particular the principles formulated in *D. v. UK* and applied since, although never in favour of the applicant;[64] to wit, in very exceptional cases, "compelling humanitarian considerations" might prevent removal. The Court reiterates that this threshold is high and necessarily so:

> ... given that in such cases the alleged future harm would emanate not from the intentional acts or omissions of public authorities or non-State bodies, but instead from a naturally occurring illness and the lack of sufficient resources to deal with it in the receiving country.[65]

The *N. v. UK* case bears striking similarities with the *D. v. UK* case: it concerned an HIV-positive applicant from Uganda, whose quality of life and life expectancy would be reduced if she were to be returned to her country of origin on account of the fact that she would not have the possibility to receive there the same level of treatment as in the United Kingdom. The Court accepted those facts but noticed that, unlike M D., Ms N was not "critically ill".[66] In particular, the Court – being overly optimistic perhaps? – stated that:

> ... the rapidity of the deterioration which she would suffer and the extent to which she would be able to obtain access to medical treatment, support and care, including help from relatives, must involve a certain degree of speculation, particularly in view of the constantly evolving situation as regards the treatment of HIV and AIDS worldwide.[67]

The Court concludes that:

> ... the applicant's case (...) does not disclose very exceptional circumstances, such as in *D. v. the United Kingdom* (...), and the implementation of the decision to remove the applicant to Uganda would not give rise to a violation of Article 3 of the Convention.[68]

This decision of the Court clarifies what constitutes "compelling humanitarian considerations". The Court warned in *D. v. UK*: the removal of an individual to

---

64 ECtHR, *N. v. UK*, Joint dissenting opinion of Judges Tulkens, Bonello and Spielmann, § 15.
65 Ibid., § 43.
66 Ibid., § 50.
67 Ibid., § 50.
68 Ibid., § 51.

a risk of harm emanating from a naturally-occurring phenomenon might give rise to a breach of Article 3 ECHR only in "very exceptional circumstances".[69]

In view of the Court's case-law, to be protected against *refoulement*, persons who left their home by reason of an environmental disaster would need to demonstrate more than the "mere" risk that their life and life expectancy will be affected upon being returned to their country of origin. This appears clearly in *N. v. UK*:

> The fact that the applicant's circumstances, including his life expectancy, would be significantly reduced if he were to be removed from the Contracting State is not sufficient in itself to give rise to breach of Article 3.[70]

This decision is questionable and was criticised on a number of points, not least by judges Tulkens, Bonello and Spielmann in their dissenting opinion. It is discussed below.

(a) *Compelling Humanitarian Reasons: A Very High a Threshold*

The comparison between *D. v. UK*, where *non-refoulement* prohibited the applicant's removal to his country of origin on the ground of "compelling humanitarian considerations", and *N. v. UK*, where it did not, reveals that what was decisive in *D. v. UK* was that the applicant "was critically ill and appeared to be close to death, could not be guaranteed any nursing or medical care in his country of origin and had no family there willing or able to care for him or provide him with even a basic level of food, shelter or social support".[71]

The threshold is indeed very high.

Looking more closely at the different circumstances confirms the assertion. Ms N. was not considered critically ill or close to death despite evidence submitted before national courts and acknowledged by the ECtHR indicating that, were she to be deprived of her medication, "her condition would rapidly deteriorate and she would suffer ill-heath, discomfort, pain and death *within a few years*".[72] Earlier case-law cited by the Court also indicated that the fact that removal and its correlate, the interruption of treatment, would cause "development of AIDS within one to two years and death within three to four years" does not indicate an advanced or terminal stage in the applicant's illness.[73]

---

69   ECtHR, *D. v. UK*, § 54.
70   ECtHR, *N. v. UK*, § 42.
71   Ibid., § 42.
72   Ibid., § 47 [emphasis added].
73   ECtHR, *Ndangoya v. Sweden*, Application no. 17868/03 (22 June 2004). The case is cited by the Court in *N. v. UK*, § 40.

In other words, it is a matter of severity but also of imminence of the threat. J. McAdam observes that the requirement of imminence appears regularly in the case-law of the Court[74] and is a hallmark of Article 3 cases.[75] Such degree of imminence appears exceptional and, in any case, will most likely not been met by people fleeing slow-onset environmental disasters.

The other circumstances are just as restrictively analysed by the Court. Be it the support of family or close relatives or medical treatment, for both, the Court appears to consider that their sole existence suffices to dismiss a need for protection against removal. Ms N. claimed that, although she did have some family members in Uganda, they would not be willing or able to care for her if she were seriously ill.[76] The Court appears to have discarded the applicant's concerns and presumed that the applicant could obtain some level of family support.[77] Similarly, the Court disregarded the fact that due to a lack of resources in Uganda, antiretroviral medication was received by only half of those in need,[78] and then again concluded that the applicant would be able to obtain access to medical treatment, albeit to an unknown extent.[79] Reliance on the availability of treatment, support and care rather than on their accessibility[80] does not seem appropriate in this context. Availability of medical treatment without a possibility to access it evidently[81] renders the protection illusory.

---

74   The Court for instance rejected the application of Article 6(1) ECHR (applicants argued that they had not been able to secure a ruling by a tribunal on their objections to the extension of a nuclear power plant) noting that applicants had failed to show that the operation of the power station "exposed them personally to a danger that was not only serious but also specific and, *above all, imminent*". ECtHR (Grand Chamber), *Case of Balmer-Schafroth and Others v. Switzerland* ("*Balmer-Schafroth*"), Application no. 22110/93 (26 August 1997), § 40.

75   J. McAdam, *Climate Change, Forced Migration, and International Law* (2012), op. cit., pp. 84–87.

76   ECtHR, *N. v. UK*, § 48.

77   *Ibid.*, § 50.

78   *Ibid.*, § 48.

79   *Ibid.*, § 50.

80   The view was in fact endorsed by the French legislator who, following the *N. v. UK* amended the CESEDA to limit the grant of residence permit on medical grounds to cases where no treatment exists in the country of origin. This will be discussed below.

81   In that sense, *see* V. Tchen (Ed.) "Droit Des Étrangers", *Constitutions – Revue de droit constitutionnel appliqué*, No. 3 (July-September 2010), p. 437, p. 438. The author welcomed the decision of the *Conseil d'état* to overturn its earlier case-law and conclude, in cases where applicants suffer from a serious illness, that the mere availability of treatment in their country of origin was not sufficient. French authorities must ensure that the treatment is effectively accessible to anyone in the country; in particular, its cost should not

This further thins out the chances for environmentally-displaced persons to be protected against *refoulement*: by analogy, it can be anticipated that the mere fact that fresh water, food and medical supplies are available in the country, even though they might be depleted and cannot cover the needs of all the population, will likely be sufficient to discard a risk of ill-treatment on this ground.

(b) *The Search for a Fair Balance: An Unfortunate Legacy of the Soering Case*

Lastly, particularly worrisome is the reference made by the court to the "search for a fair balance between the demands of the general interest of the community and the requirements of the protection of the individual's fundamental rights".[82] The dissenting judges note that such "proportionalist errings",[83] once suggested by the Court in the *Soering* case,[84] had since been clearly rejected by the Court. Hence the *Saadi* judgment where the Court, after reiterating that in order to assess the reality of a risk of ill-treatment, it had to "examine the foreseeable consequences of sending the applicant to the receiving country, bearing in mind the general situation there and his personal circumstances",[85] made clear that protection against *refoulement* to Article 3 ill-treatment being absolute, "Article 3 imposes an obligation not to (...) expel any person who, in the receiving country, would run the real risk of being subjected to such treatment".[86] The Court adds that "there can be no derogation from that rule".[87]

It thus seems both contradictory and regrettable that, after having accepted that "the quality of the applicant's life, and her life expectancy, would be affected if she were returned to Uganda",[88] the Court did not conclude that the UK decision to return the applicant to Uganda constituted a violation of Article 3.

As was recalled above, according to the well-established case-law of the Court on the absolute nature of the protection against Article 3 ill-treatments, the general interest of the host country should be immaterial. That interpretation is corroborated when one refers to other instruments of international human rights law who guarantee rights similar to those enshrined in Article

---

be so high as to deter or bar access to it. This approach has however since be changed, as will be discussed in Chapter 8 on authorisations to stay granted by Member States on a discretionary basis.

82   ECtHR, *N. v. UK*, § 44.
83   *Ibid.*, Joint dissenting opinion of Judges Tulkens, Bonello and Spielmann, § 7.
84   Above Chapter 1, pp. 223s.
85   ECtHR, *Saadi*, § 130.
86   *Ibid.*, § 138.
87   *Ibid.*, § 138.
88   ECtHR, *N. v. UK*, § 50.

3 of the ECHR. The International Covenant on Civil and Political Rights (IC-CPR), as is well-known, is interpreted as containing a similar protection against *refoulement* in its Article 7. That right is, there again, absolute. It accepts no restriction. While the International Covenant on Economic, Social and Cultural Rights (ICESCR) imposes on States an obligation to take steps, to the maximum of their available resources, for the "progressive realisation" of the rights it enshrines,[89] the State Parties to the ICCPR are not allowed such leeway. The prohibition derived from Article 7 ICCPR, just like that derived from Article 3 ECHR, is absolute and States cannot, without breaching their obligations under either instrument, invoke their "available resources" or general interest to limit their responsibility and justify the removal of an individual to a destination country where he or she is at risk of being subjected to any of the proscribed treatments.

As mentioned, such was not however the conclusion reached by the Court, in *N. v. UK*. As noted by judges Tulkens, Bonello and Spielmann, it is to be feared that the real motivation of the Court is a refusal to impose an overly heavy burden on contracting States. Contracting States, the Court said, rather cynically,[90] are under no obligation to alleviate disparities between levels of treatment available in different countries "through the provision of free and unlimited health care to all aliens without a right to stay within its jurisdiction".[91] The dissenting judges suggest that this reflects the real concern of the majority of the Court in the present case that "if the applicant were allowed to remain in the United Kingdom to benefit from the care that her survival requires, then the resources of the State would be overstretched".[92] Implicitly, it reveals the fear that the finding of a breach of Article 3 would open up the "floodgates" to medical immigration and make Europe "the 'sick-bay' of the world".[93] As observed by J.-P. Marguénaud, three months only after the *Saadi* judgment

---

89 Article 2 of the ICESCR provides that each State Party to the Covenant "undertakes to take steps, individually and through international assistance and co-operation, especially economic and technical, to the maximum of its available resources, with a view to achieving progressively the full realization of the rights recognized in the present Covenant by all appropriate means, including particularly the adoption of legislative measures to achieving progressively the full realization of the rights". ICESCR, Article 2(1); ECtHR, *N. v. UK*, § 50.

90 H. Labayle and F. Sudre, "Jurisprudence de la Cour européenne des droits de l'homme et droit administratif (2012)", *RFDA*, No. 3 (May-June 2012), pp. 455–460, p. 456; H. Labayle (March-April 2011), *op. cit.*, p. 938.

91 ECtHR, *N. v. UK*, § 44.

92 *Ibid.*, Joint dissenting opinion of Judges Tulkens, Bonello and Spielmann, § 8.

93 *Ibid.*, Joint dissenting opinion of Judges Tulkens, Bonello and Spielmann, § 8.

forcefully asserted the non-derogability of the prohibition of inhuman and degrading treatments, the majority in the Court gave in to the misconceived[94] "floodgate" argument, and "let the worm of proportionality eat into the fruit of Article 3's non-derogability".[95]

By taking into consideration the resources of the expelling State, the Court appears to be considering the right at stake not as a fundamental civil right, from which no derogation is possible, but as a socio-economic right, which States would have the obligation to respect but "to the maximum of its available resources"[96] only. This difference between the two "categories" of rights is reminded by the Court who, selectively and in fact inaccurately quoting its earlier judgment in the case of *Airey v. Ireland*,[97] notes:

> Although many of the rights it contains have implications of a social or economic nature, the Convention is essentially directed at the protection of civil and political rights.[98]

In *Airey v. Ireland*, the thrust of the Court's argument was in fact the reverse; the Court had then observed that:

> ... [w]hilst the Convention sets forth what are essentially civil and political rights, many of them have implications of a social or economic nature.[99]

The indivisibility of human rights was then clearly asserted by the Court who stated that:

> ... the mere fact that an interpretation of the Convention may extend into the sphere of social and economic rights should not be a decisive factor

---

94 *Ibid.*
95 "*A trois mois de distance, la volonté farouche de protéger l'Europe contre l'invasion de hordes de malades du sida venu chercher le traitement salutaire qu'il ne peuvent pas se procurer dans leur Afrique déshéritée a donc poussé la Cour de Strasbourg à introduire le ver de la proportionnalité dans le fruit de l'intangibilité de l'article 3*". J.-P. Marguénaud, "La Trahison Des Étrangers Sidéens", *RTD Civ.* (2008), p. 643.
96 ICESCR, Article 2(1).
97 ECtHR, *Case of Airey v. Ireland* ("*Airey*"), Application no. 6289/73 (9 October 1979), § 26.
98 ECtHR, *N. v. UK*, § 44.
99 ECtHR, *Airey*, § 26.

against such an interpretation; there is no water-tight division separating that sphere from the field covered by the Convention.[100]

In other words, the fact that an alleged risk of Article 3 ill-treatment originates in the applicant's being deprived of certain socio-economic rights does not make the risk any less real or, as applied to facts in *N. v. UK*, the fact that the alleged ill-treatment originates in the absence of medical treatment should not divert the Court from the fact that this absence of medicines and care[101] exposes the applicant to a risk of inhuman and degrading treatment. Similarly, Judges Tulkens, Bonello and Spielmann state that the case is not about social and economic rights but instead "about one of the core fundamental civil rights guaranteed under the Convention, namely that of Article 3".[102]

The idea of a "water-tight" division between the two spheres of human rights, explicitly rejected by the Court in *Airey v. Ireland* has long been opposed and it is well-established that the two spheres indeed permeate each other.[103] The contemporary understanding of the relationship between human rights is summarised by the 1993 Vienna Declaration and Programme of Action, approved by the large majority of UN Member States, making clear that all human rights are "universal, indivisible and interdependent and interrelated".[104] This "integrated" or "holistic" approach to human rights is "primarily based on the idea that civil and political rights have inherent socio-economic elements".[105] The *N. v. UK* judgment however attempts to rebuild the partition which the *Airey* judgment, anxious to ensure a more effective protection of human rights, had brought down.[106]

The *N. v. UK* decision, taking into consideration the host State' resources, appears to ignore the absolute nature of the principle of *non-refoulement* albeit in a case of alleged Article 3 ECHR ill-treatment, and instead focus on the right to health dimension of the case, a right States must guarantee to the maximum

---

100   *Ibid.*, § 26.
101   The right to health is enshrined in Article 12 of the ICESCR.
102   ECtHR, *N. v. UK*, Joint dissenting opinion of Judges Tulkens, Bonello and Spielmann, § 6.
103   M. Foster elaborates on the relationship between civil and political rights and economic and social rights. M. Foster, *International Refugee Law and Socio-Economic Rights: Refuge from Deprivation* (2007), *op. cit.*, pp. 157–201.
104   "Vienna Declaration and Programme of Action", *op. cit.*, § 5.
105   V. Mantouvalou, "Work and Private Life: Sidabras and Dziautas v. Lithuania", *European Law Review*, Vol. 30 (2005), pp. 573–585, p. 574.
106   In the words of J.-P. Marguénaud: "*Sans oser l'affirmer ouvertement, l'arrêt* N. c/ Royaume-Uni *a donc reconstruit la cloison que l'arrêt* Airey *avait abattue dans le but de rendre les droits de l'Homme plus concrets et effectifs*". J.-P. Marguénaud (2008), *op. cit.*

of their available resources.[107] This approach was suggested by the UK Government, defendant in the case.[108]

As noted by J. McAdam:

> ... breaches of socio-economic rights are often "re-characterized" as violations of Article 3 of the ECHR, since this is an absolute right containing a clear *non-refoulement* obligation whose breach cannot be justified on the grounds of insufficient resources.[109]

In *N. v. UK*, it seems that the Court proceeded the other way around and "re-characterised" the breach of the prohibition of inhuman or degrading treatment as a violation of the right the health, which is not an absolute right and whose breach can be justified on the grounds of insufficient resources.

To conclude on *N. v. UK*, the decision contradicts the absolute nature of the principle of *non-refoulement*, which has been reaffirmed time and again by the European Court of Human Right and confirmed in other instruments of international human rights law.

It also hinders the cause of environmentally-displaced persons. States' reluctance to extend the scope of their *non-refoulement* obligations in general and to people displaced by environmental disasters in particular is in no small part motivated by their fear that it would lead to an obligation to accept too many people. The judgment of the European Court of Human Rights in *N. v. UK* seems to provide those States with the necessary argument to oppose an extension of the scope of *non-refoulement*: the principle does not apply to environmentally-displaced persons because it would place "too great a burden" on States.

Assessed through the *N. v. UK* test of "compelling humanitarian considerations", it is unlikely that environmentally-displaced persons can be protected

---

107   The concept of progressive realisation of economic, social and cultural rights was elaborated in the International Covenant on Economic, Social and Cultural Rights. ICESCR, Article 2(1); V. Mantouvalou (2005), *op. cit.*, p. 574. This is not to say that the Court applies the ICESCR, however and increasingly, the Court resorts to international instruments of social law, such as the ICESCR, International Labour Organisation conventions or the European Social Charter for instance, in order to formulate constructive interpretations of the European Convention on Human Rights, so much so that it could be labelled a "European court of social rights". J.-P. Marguénaud and J. Mouly, "L'avènement d'une Cour européenne des droits sociaux (à propos de CEDH 12 novembre 2008", "Demir et Baykara c. Turquie"), *Recueil Dalloz*, No. 11 (2009), pp. 739–744; ICESCR, Article 2(1).
108   ECtHR, *N. v. UK*, § 24.
109   J. McAdam, *Climate Change, Forced Migration, and International Law* (2012), *op. cit.*, p. 65.

against *refoulement* to a risk of Article 3 ill-treatment. This test however, elaborated by the European Court of Human Rights to assess risks originating in naturally occurring phenomena, might not be always appropriate: the influence of State and non-State actors in the occurrence of environmental disasters and on how disasters impact on populations cannot be ignored. As a consequence, it is necessary to consider also the approach adopted by the Court in *MSS v. Belgium and Greece*[110] and developed in *Sufi & Elmi*.[111]

B   National Authorities' Actions and Inactions, Environmental Disasters and Applicants' Ability to Cater for Their Most Basic Needs

The *MSS v. Belgium and Greece* case was mentioned in Part 1 because it illustrates the influence of ECtHR case-law on the case-law of the EU Court of Justice. Following the ECtHR judgment, the Court of Justice indeed ordered the suspension of Dublin transfers to Greece, in view of the conditions of detention and living conditions awaiting asylum-seekers in the country, thus admitting that the presumption underlying the Dublin system that all EU Member States were to be considered as "safe countries" was rebuttable.[112]

The following developments focus instead on those living conditions which the European Court of Human Rights construed as inhuman treatments for the purpose of Article 3 ECHR. The doctrine developed by the Court in *MSS* and *Sufi & Elmi* will first be detailed, keeping environmental harm in mind (1) before its relevance in situations of environmental disasters is suggested (2).

1   Humanitarian Crises and the Protection of Vulnerable Persons Unable to Cater for Their Most Basic Needs

In *MSS v. Belgium and Greece*, the ECtHR concluded that the conditions of detention which the applicant had experienced in Greece were "unacceptable"[113] and constituted degrading treatments. Specifically, the Court stated that:

> ... the feeling of arbitrariness and the feeling of inferiority and anxiety often associated with it, as well as the profound effect such conditions of detention indubitably have on a person's dignity, constitute degrading treatment contrary to Article 3 of the Convention. In addition, the applicant's distress was accentuated by the vulnerability inherent in his situation as an asylum seeker.[114]

---

110 ECtHR, *M.S.S.*
111 ECtHR, *Sufi & Elmi*.
112 Above Part 1, Chapter 2, I. C., 3(b), pp. 80s.
113 ECtHR, *M.S.S.*, § 233.
114 *Ibid.*, § 233.

The Court therefore found that Greece had violated its obligations under Article 3 ECHR.

Furthermore, the Court considered that the living conditions the applicant experienced in Greece, outside detention centres, and which amounted to "a situation of extreme material poverty",[115] also constituted inhuman and degrading treatment resulting from the inaction of Greek authorities in disregard of the applicant's vulnerability as an asylum seeker.[116] Specifically, the Court had regard to the fact that the applicant had found himself "for several months, living in the street, with no resources or access to sanitary facilities, and without any means of providing for his essential needs".[117] In conclusion, the Court states that:

> ... the applicant has been the victim of humiliating treatment showing a lack of respect for his dignity and that this situation has, without doubt, aroused in him feelings of fear, anguish or inferiority capable of inducing desperation. [The Court] considers that such living conditions, combined with the prolonged uncertainty in which he has remained and the total lack of any prospects of his situation improving, have attained the level of severity required to fall within the scope of Article 3 of the Convention.[118]

The Court further found that because the applicant faced such real and "individual enough" risk to be exposed to Article 3 ill-treatment upon being removed to Greece, a risk which Belgium knew or ought to have known,[119] Belgium's decision to transfer the applicant to Greece gave rise to a violation of Article 3 of the Convention.[120]

As mentioned, the Court applied the same test in *Sufi & Elmi* concerning the removal of Somali nationals from the United Kingdom to their country of origin, in the grip of a dire humanitarian crisis, attributable predominantly to the ongoing conflict in the country and in part too to drought.[121]

---

115 *Ibid.*, § 252.
116 *Ibid.*, § 263.
117 *Ibid.*, § 263.
118 *Ibid.*, § 263.
119 The Court mentions in particular that Belgian authorities could not "merely to assume that the applicant would be treated in conformity with the Convention standards" but should have verified how Greece applied its legislation in practice. Had they done so, the Court notes, Belgium authorities "would have seen that the risks the applicant faced were real and individual enough to fall within the scope of Article 3". *Ibid.*, § 359.
120 *Ibid.*, § 360.
121 ECtHR, *Sufi & Elmi*, § 282.

A distinction between the circumstances of *MSS* and of *Sufi & Elmi* is of interest: in *MSS*, the Court focused on the situation awaiting the applicant in Greece, where being an asylum-seeker, he would be particularly vulnerable, and found on this ground a violation of Article 3 ECHR by Belgium and Greece.[122] The Court made clear that it attached "considerable importance" to the applicant's status "as an asylum seeker and, as such, a member of a particularly underprivileged and vulnerable population group in need of special protection".[123] The Court "individualises" the situation of asylum seekers, whom it identifies as a vulnerable group.[124] In *Sufi & Elmi*, the vulnerability of the applicants was also referred to by the Court however it is significant that the group they belong to is markedly broader: the applicants would belong in Somalia to the large group of "persons facing a humanitarian crisis".[125] The group includes people depending on food aid (half of Somalia's population) and displaced persons, including both internally-displaced persons (IDPs) and persons seeking asylum in refugee camps in neighbouring countries. The latter group was estimated at 2,4 million persons (nearly a third of the country's

---

[122] In the assessment of the applicant's claim of an alleged violation by Greece of Article 13, taken in conjunction with Articles 2 and 3 of the Convention, because of the shortcomings in Greek asylum procedures which exposed the applicant to a risk of *refoulement* to Afghanistan, the Court noted that, in view of the situation of insecurity prevailing in Afghanistan and of the applicant's belonging to a category of persons particularly exposed to reprisals (he worked as an interpreter for international air force troops stationed in Kabul – § 31), the applicant had an arguable claim under Article 2 or 3 of the Convention. On this point, the Court concluded that there had been a violation of Article 13 of the Convention taken in conjunction with Article 3 "because of the deficiencies in the Greek authorities' examination of the applicant's asylum request and the risk he faces of being returned directly or indirectly to his country of origin without any serious examination of the merits of his asylum application and without having access to an effective remedy". ECtHR, *M.S.S.*, §§ 294–297; ECtHR, *Sufi & Elmi*, § 282.

[123] ECtHR, *M.S.S.*, § 251.

[124] In his partly concurring and partly dissenting opinion on the case, Judge Sajó objects to the Court's unconditional appreciation of asylum-seekers in general as a particularly vulnerable group. *Ibid.*, Partly concurring and partly dissenting opinion of Judge Sajó, pp. 101–107 in particular.

[125] This is not an expression used by the Court however the Court, referring to various reports by non-governmental organisations (NGOs) and UN agencies, accepts that "half of Somalia's population was dependent on food aid", a quarter of the country's population in 2010 and a third in 2011 "faced a humanitarian crisis" and that this figure would keep increasing if rains continued to fail in the country. ECtHR, *Sufi & Elmi*, § 284; H. Labayle and F. Sudre (May-June 2012), *op. cit.*, p. 456.

population) in February 2011 and expected to further grow if drought persisted in the country.¹²⁶

Read in the context of environmental displacement, the *Sufi & Elmi* judgment suggests that the Court stressing the particular "vulnerability" of an applicant does not equate a requirement of personalisation of the risk. The group of vulnerable persons can be as large as, as in *Sufi & Elmi*, half the population – and possibly more: it is indeed conceivable that dependency on food aid, which is considered by the Court in this case, may very well concern the majority of a country's population. In that sense, vulnerability could be better construed as evidence of the reality of the alleged risk¹²⁷ rather than as a requirement that the applicant, as an individual or as a member of a group, be more at risk than the rest of the population.

As mentioned above, in the *Sufi & Elmi* case, the Court analysed the situation in Mogadishu as a situation of general violence of such intensity that any returnee would be at real risk of Article 3 ill-treatment solely on account of his or her presence there. Only those who have powerful connections in the city could be expected to stay there.¹²⁸ Such was not the case of the applicants and the Court therefore sought whether they could safely relocate to and settle in any other part of the country, that is, without being exposed to a risk of Article 3 ill-treatment. Such possibility being tenuous in view of the insecurity prevailing in some regions or in regions through which access can be gained to safer areas, the Court considers that the applicants would most likely have to have recourse to either an IDP or refugee camp.¹²⁹ The Court therefore analysed the humanitarian conditions in those camps. To do so, the Court drew from the circumstances of the MSS case and had regard to:

> ... [the] applicant's ability to cater for his most basic needs, such as food, hygiene and shelter, his vulnerability to ill-treatment and the prospect of his situation improving within a reasonable time-frame.¹³⁰

---

126   ECtHR, *Sufi & Elmi*, § 284.
127   Support for this interpretation of the term can be found in the MSS case. The Belgian Government argued that the applicant had not sufficiently "individualised", before the Belgian authorities, the risks he alleged. In response the Court indicated that Belgian authorities should have verified how asylum legislation was applied in practice in Greece; had they done so, the Court stated, "they would have seen that the risks the applicant faced were real and *individual enough* to fall within the scope of Article 3" [emphasis added]. ECtHR, *M.S.S.*, § 359.
128   ECtHR, *Sufi & Elmi*, § 293.
129   *Ibid.*, § 294.
130   *Ibid.*, § 283.

In view of the insecurity inside and outside the camps, of the fact that camps are overcrowded, of the very limited access to food, water, and shelter and of the very little prospect of displaced persons' situation improving within a reasonable timeframe,[131] the Court concluded that:

> ... any returnee forced to seek refuge in either camp would be at real risk of Article 3 ill-treatment on account of the dire humanitarian conditions.[132]

The Court thus concluded that people returned to Somalia who would need to seek refuge in a camp – that is, in view of the Court's assessment of the situation prevailing in the country, the majority of returnees – would be exposed to a risk of inhuman or degrading treatment on account of the dire humanitarian conditions there. It is conceivable that the risks originating in environmental disasters – which are not dissimilar to those identified in the *Sufi & Elmi* case – could, in like manner, be characterised as inhuman or degrading treatment under Article 3 ECHR. In the case, an environmental disaster (drought) was in fact identified by the Court as a contributing factor to the dire humanitarian conditions prevailing in Somalia.[133]

But to pass the *Sufi & Elmi* test and access protection from *refoulement* in Europe, environmentally-displaced persons would have to clear one main hurdle: the environmental harm they allege must be linked to an act or omission attributable, either directly or indirectly, to their State of origin.

2   Environmental Disasters vs "Naturally Occurring" Phenomena

The main obstacle to a conclusion that persons displaced by environmental disaster, who would be unable to cater for their most basic needs upon being returned to their country of origin, could be protected from *refoulement* under the MSS and *Sufi & Elmi* doctrine appears to be the absence of any direct or indirect "responsibility"[134] of the home country's authorities in the risk of ill-treatment. As mentioned by the Court in *Sufi & Elmi*:

> If the dire humanitarian conditions in Somalia were solely or even predominantly attributable to poverty or to the State's lack of resources to deal with a naturally occurring phenomenon, such as a drought, the test in *N. v. the United Kingdom* may well have been considered to be the

---

131   Ibid., §§ 284–291.
132   Ibid., § 292.
133   Ibid., §§ 282–284.
134   ECtHR, *N. v. UK*, § 32.

appropriate one. However, it is clear that while drought has contributed to the humanitarian crisis, that crisis is predominantly due to the direct and indirect actions of the parties to the conflict.[135]

As observed by J. McAdam, "in cases concerning the deliberate action or inaction by a State, it seems that a breach of Article 3 may be more readily established".[136] Indeed, by contrast, the *N. v. UK* threshold is much higher: it triggers *non-refoulement* "only in a very exceptional case, where the humanitarian grounds against the removal are compelling".[137] Compelling was for instance the circumstance in the *D. v. UK* case that the applicant was close to death.

It follows that environmentally-displaced persons have more chances to be protected from *refoulement* under the *Sufi & Elmi* test than under the *N. v. UK* test, which the Court unfortunately considers more appropriate.

It is arguable though that the clear-cut distinction the Court draws between cases where harm emanates from the acts or omissions of State- or non-State actors in the country of origin and cases where harm originates in a naturally occurring phenomenon and the lack of sufficient resources to deal with it in the country is not necessarily an obstacle to the protection of environmentally-displaced persons pursuant to the *Sufi & Elmi* doctrine or, alternatively, that it is not pertinent in environmental-disaster cases.

Firstly, dire humanitarian conditions originating in environmental disasters caused by technological accidents could, following the Court's logic, prevent removal to the affected country since the source of the risk of ill-treatment in the country would stem "from factors which could (...) engage either directly or indirectly the responsibility of the public authorities of that country".[138]

Secondly, it was recalled in the introduction to this Part, numerous reports and articles inform of a causal link between environmental disasters and conflicts. The link is not necessarily direct and it is often uneasy to identify which of the two (disasters or conflict) triggered the other. Nonetheless, in all cases where environmental disaster is coupled with armed conflict, irrespective of the chronology between the two, environmentally-displaced persons facing dire humanitarian conditions upon return should be protected against *refoulement* under the *Sufi & Elmi* test.

---

135   ECtHR, *Sufi & Elmi*, § 282.
136   J. McAdam, *Climate Change, Forced Migration, and International Law* (2012), *op. cit.*, p. 70.
137   ECtHR, *N. v. UK*, § 42.
138   *Ibid.*, § 32.

Thirdly, it is well-established, a drought, tsunami or other such "naturally-occurring phenomenon" alone does not expose populations to risks of harm; the authorities' lack of preparedness and, or an insufficient response to the disaster are decisive.[139] This is observed notably in the context of discussion on the impact of climate change[140] and on the possibility to mitigate it; the better prepared – and often, the more developed[141] – the countries, the less assistance needs and forced displacement caused by environmental disaster. As observed by UNHCR:

> Natural hazards do not in themselves constitute disasters; rather human actions exacerbate the effects of natural phenomena to create disasters.[142]

UNHCR adds that "the impact of natural disasters is a function of both the severity of the natural hazard and the capacity of a population to deal with it",[143] which was translated by N. Schrepfer and W. Kälin as follows:

> Impact of the disaster = (hazard + vulnerability) / capacities[144]

As a result, dire humanitarian conditions which can exist in the aftermath of a natural hazard disaster or due to the progressive degradation of the environment can be partly attributed to the authorities of the State. The requirement

---

139 G. Hugo, "Lessons from Past Forced Resettlements for Climate Change Migration", *in* E. Piguet, *et al.* (Eds.), (Cambridge, New York: Cambridge University Press, UNESCO Publishing, 2011), pp. 260–288.

140 UNGA, "Climate Change and Its Possible Security Implications: Report of the Secretary-General" ("Climate change and its possible security implications"), A/64/350, 11 September 2009, § 27. The IPCC in particular stresses the importance that both mitigation and adaptation measures be adopted: "Even the most stringent mitigation efforts cannot avoid further impacts of climate change in the next few decades, which makes adaptation essential, particularly in addressing near-term impacts. Unmitigated climate change would, in the long term, be likely to exceed the capacity of natural, managed and human systems to adapt". IPCC (2007), *op. cit.*, pp. 19–20.

141 L. Westra finds that the statistics published by the United Nations Development Programme (UNDP) on the impacts of natural disasters in the Asia-Pacific region (from 1972 to 2000) indicate "the strong correlation between the level of development of a country and the level of mortality following disaster". L. Westra, *Environmental Justice and the Rights of Ecological Refugees* (2009), *op. cit.*, p. 80; IPCC (2007), *op. cit.*, pp. 19–20.

142 UNHCR, *The State of the World's Refugees 2012: In Search of Solidarity* (2012), *op. cit.*, p. 178.

143 *Ibid.*, p. 178.

144 W. Kälin and N. Schrepfer, *Protecting People Crossing Borders in the Context of Climate Change Normative Gaps and Possible Approaches* (February 2012), *op. cit.*, p. 6.

that an "act or omission" of the State be involved in the causation of the alleged harm should therefore be considered fulfilled.

This is reinforced by recent developments concerning the right to life, protected under Article 2 of the ECHR. In *Budayeva v. Russia*, the Court recalled that Article 2 of the Convention "lays down a positive obligation on States to *take appropriate steps* to safeguard the lives of those within their jurisdiction", including legislative and administrative measures.[145] The Court notes that this duty extends to prevention of and protection from environmental disasters (mudslides in the case), which could engage the State's responsibility "for positive preventive action".[146]

A further observation buttresses this assertion. The conclusion reached by the Court in *MSS* and *Sufi & Elmi* but also, albeit reluctantly, in *D. v. UK*,[147] appears to reflect the integrated approach to human rights which the Court had already embraced in the *Airey v. Ireland* judgment.[148] That "civil and political rights have inherent socio-economic elements"[149] is manifestly unchallenged by the Court who finds deprivation of socio-economic rights constitutive of inhuman and degrading treatment proscribed under Article 3 ECHR.

As observed by M. Foster, all rights contained in the International Covenant on Economic, Social and Cultural rights contain "two key duties of an immediate nature":[150] firstly, States must guarantee them to all without discrimination and secondly, States must take steps to realise each right to the maximum of their available resources.[151] According to the UN Committee on Economic, Social and Cultural Rights (CESCR), in any case, State Parties have a "minimum core obligation to ensure the satisfaction of, at the very least, minimum essential levels of each of the rights".[152] It follows that if a State affected by environmental disaster fails to adopt measures or fails to do it to the maximum of its capacity to the end of safeguarding a minimum essential level of, *inter alia*, the right to an adequate standard of living, including *adequate food, clothing and*

---

145   ECtHR, *Case of Budayeva and Others v. Russia* ("*Budayeva v. Russia*"), Applications nos. 15339/02, 21166/02, 20058/02, 11673/02 and 15343/02 (29 September 2008), § 128.
146   *Ibid.*, § 142.
147   Above Chapter 2, II.B., 1(a), pp. 352s.
148   ECtHR, *Airey*. And above pp. 360s.
149   V. Mantouvalou (2005), *op. cit.*, p. 574.
150   M. Foster, *International Refugee Law and Socio-Economic Rights: Refuge from Deprivation* (2007), *op. cit.*, pp. 171–172.
151   ICESCR, Article 2(1).
152   CESCR, "General Comment No. 3: The Nature of States Parties Obligations (Art. 2, Para. 1, of the Covenant)" ("GC 3: The Nature of State Parties' Obligations"), UN Doc. E/1991/23, 14 December 1990, § 10.

housing, and to the *continuous improvement of living conditions*,[153] or the right to highest attainable standard of physical and mental health,[154] or if it guarantees the enjoyment of those rights (or others) in a discriminatory manner within the population, then the harm invoked by displaced persons to oppose their return to their country of origin is partly caused by an "act or omission" of their State of origin.

In *D. v. UK*, the Court notes that expulsion might give rise to a violation of Article 3 ECHR "where the source of the risk of proscribed treatment in the receiving country stems from factors which cannot engage either directly or indirectly the responsibility of the public authorities of that country, *or which, taken alone, do not in themselves infringe the standards of that Article 3*".[155] As a consequence, limited access to healthcare for instance might not on its own constitute inhuman treatment but, if it is in a context where the enjoyment of other rights is also limited, then the combination of those factors might constitute inhuman or degrading treatment for the purpose of Article 3 ECHR. In direct application of *MSS* and *Sufi & Elmi*, an environmentally-displaced person should not be returned to a country where, by reason of actions or omissions of the authorities, he or she would be exposed to humanitarian conditions reaching the threshold of inhuman or degrading treatment.

Closely related to the previous point is the principle, contained in international humanitarian law as well as international human rights law and confirmed by the Guiding Principles on Internal Displacement, that States, confronted with humanitarian problems, have the responsibility to seek international assistance[156] and cannot impede access by international humanitarian organisations to those in need of assistance in the country.[157] If a State denies or impedes the provision of international assistance to its population,[158]

---

153   ICESCR, Article 11 [emphasis added].
154   *Ibid.*, Article 12.
155   ECtHR, *N. v. UK*, § 32; ECtHR, *D. v. UK*, § 49 [emphases added].
156   UNHCR, *The State of the World's Refugees 2012: In Search of Solidarity* (2012), *op. cit.*, p. 176.
157   UN Commission on Human Rights, "Report of the Representative of the Secretary-General, Mr. Francis M. Deng, Submitted Pursuant to Commission Resolution 1997/39. Addendum: Guiding Principles on Internal Displacement " ("Guiding Principles on Internal Displacement"), E/CN.4/1998/53/Add.2, 11 February 1998, Principle 25; W. Kälin, *Annotations to the Guiding Principles on Internal Displacement*, No. 38 (Washington, DC: The American Society of International Law and The Brookings Institution, 2008), pp. 116–122.
158   In 2008, in the aftermath of cyclone Nargis, Burma was heavily criticised for opposing the provision of international assistance to affected populations on its territory. G. Evans, "Facing up to Our Responsibilities", *The Guardian*, 12 May 2008, retrieved from: <www.guardian.co.uk/commentisfree/2008/may/12/facinguptoourresponsbilities>

the dire humanitarian conditions faced by the population are partly attributable to the State. The requirement of a "fault"[159] by the authorities of the country of origin would undoubtedly be met. It follows that then again, the *Sufi & Elmi* test should apply and protection against *refoulement* be granted to an applicant who is, by reason of the humanitarian situation, unable to cater for his or her most basic needs.[160] Furthermore, the State's denial of assistance would suggest that populations have "very little prospect of their situation improving within a reasonable timeframe".[161]

Lastly, scientists project that climate change impacts and will continue to impact on the frequency and intensity of most environmental disasters. Moreover, it is established that climate change is partly anthropogenic.[162] It could therefore also be argued that the dire conditions caused by climate-related environmental disaster are partly attributable to the authorities in the country of origin and, therefore, return proscribed under Article 3 ECHR as applied in *Sufi & Elmi*. It is however unlikely that such an approach would succeed. As will be discussed in Part 3, the question of State responsibility for climate change is far from settled. In particular, attributing responsibility to a State for a particular disaster triggering displacement is not possible in the present state of science and data available. Furthermore, it is observed that States that will be most affected by the impacts of climate change are also those who – until now – emitted the lowest levels of heat-trapping greenhouse gases[163] and will most likely endeavour to protect their populations. As a consequence, a suggestion that any country affected by disasters is partly responsible for its fate would

---

[01/06/2012]; R. Cohen, "The Burma Cyclone and the Responsibility to Protect" (The Brookings Institution, 2012), 21 July 2008, retrieved from: <www.brookings.edu/research/speeches/2008/07/21-myanmar-cohen> [01/06/2012].

159   ECtHR, *M.S.S.*, § 264.
160   As said though, in case where assistance is denied on the ground of the applicant's race, religion, nationality, political opinion or membership of a particular social group, refugee status should be granted. Above Chapter 6.
161   ECtHR, *Sufi & Elmi*, § 291.
162   J. Kilinski, "International Climate Change Liability: A Myth or Reality?" *Journal of Transnational Law and Policy*, Vol. 18 (Spring 2009), p. 377, p. 387. *See also* IPCC: Core Writing Team, *et al.* (Eds.), *Climate Change 2007: Synthesis Report Contribution of Working Groups I, II and III to the Fourth Assessment Report of the Intergovernmental Panel on Climate Change*, Contribution of Working Groups I, II and III to the Fourth Assessment Report of the Intergovernmental Panel on Climate Change (Geneva: IPCC, 2007).
163   In Bangladesh, Atiq Rhaman, founder of the Bangladesh Centre for Advanced Studies (BCAS) notes that "[although Bangladesh] produces only 0,3 to 0,4% of total worldwide greenhouse gas emissions – less than the city of New York – we must work to reduce them". Cited in Collectif Argos, *Climate Refugees* (2010), *op. cit.*, p. 65.

certainly not receive much support, even if it were to the end of securing *non-refoulement* for its displaced population.

C Other ECHR Rights Proscribing Refoulement

Theoretically, any ECHR right could give rise to an obligation of *non-refoulement*. In practice though, as mentioned, the very vast majority of claims, and hence successful claims too, relied on breached of Article 3 ECHR.

The right to life, enshrined in Article 2 ECHR, appears to be particularly pertinent in situations of environmental disasters exposing the individual to depleted resources and impeded satisfaction of other essential needs. All the more so in view of recent developments in human rights law, that tend to include in the right to life a broad range of entitlements. There is a marked tendency to derive from the right to life, traditionally construed as the right not to be killed,[164] a number of positive obligations for States such as the obligations to guarantee the right not to be deprived of one's own means of subsistence[165] and the rights to safe and clean drinking water and sanitation,[166] to a healthy environment,[167] to food, to adequate housing,[168] to health.[169] In the European Convention on Human Rights framework however, even when Article 2 was invoked by applicants in expulsion cases, and the case declared admissible under this provision, the Court generally found it unnecessary to examine the case on the merits under Article 2 and instead preferred examining it under Article 3.[170] As shown above, this does not prevent the Court from having regard to socio-economic factors such as those considered to form part of the right to life. As illustrated by the cases cited above (chiefly *N. v. UK*, *M.S.S.* and *Sufi & Elmi*), the Court has occasionally analysed living conditions in the country of origin as inhuman and degrading treatment proscribing *refoulement*, and

---

164 E. Wicks (2012), *op. cit*; J. McAdam, *Complementary Protection in International Refugee Law* (2007), *op. cit.*, p. 147.
165 ICCPR, Article 1(2); ICESCR, Article 1(2).
166 CESCR, "GC 15: Right to Water", *op. cit*; UNHRC, *op. cit.*, §§ 2–3; UNGA, "Resolution 64/292: The human right to water and sanitation", *op. cit.*
167 PACE, "Recommendation 1885 (2009)", *op. cit*; Stockholm Declaration; *L.K. Koolwal v. State of Rajasthan and Others*, 19 September 1986, *op. cit*; Supreme Court, *Construction of Park at Noida near Okhla Bird Sanctuary*, 3 December 2010, *op. cit.*, § 66.
168 IACHR, *Yakye Axa Indigenous Community v. Paraguay*.
169 Legal Response Initiative, *op. cit.*, §§ 8–9.
170 N. Mole and C. Meredith, *Asylum and the European Convention on Human Rights* (2010), *op. cit.*, p. 89; ECtHR, *M.S.S.*, § 361. Typically, the judgment of the ECtHR in *MSS* states: "[h]aving regard to that conclusion and to the circumstances of the case, the Court finds that there is no need to examine the applicant's complaints under Article 2".

indeed, given the absolute nature of the prohibition of torture and inhuman or degrading treatment or punishment:

> ... claims based on a lack of access to resources in the country to which removal is proposed have typically relied on Article 3 ECHR, on the grounds that return to those conditions constitutes "inhuman or degrading treatment".[171]

The Court hence found that the premeditated destruction of the applicants' home and property by security forces, "carried out contemptuously and without respect for the feelings of the applicants", deprived the applicants of their livelihoods and forced them to leave their village and constituted ill-treatment proscribed under Article 3 ECHR.[172] In that sense too, in *Z. and T. v. the United Kingdom*, the Court did not rule out the possibility that expulsion might in exceptional circumstances give rise to a violation of Article 9 ECHR (right to freedom of thought, conscience and religion) but found "it would be difficult to visualise a case in which a sufficiently flagrant violation of Article 9 would not also involve treatment in violation of Article 3 of the Convention".[173] Recently though, in the *Othman* case, the Court found that the right to a fair trial (Article 6 ECHR) could on its own prohibit *refoulement*.[174]

If the flagrant violation of any ECHR right can potentially give rise to State responsibility and prohibit *refoulement*, and although there have been significant progress made in that field (the *Othman* case being particularly exemplary of such progress), it appears clearly from case-law surveyed that it does in very limited circumstances only. In reality, the Court has made little use of the flexibility it reserved to itself to address the application of other articles of the Convention in expulsion cases, to prevent *refoulement*.

Article 3, and the absolute prohibitions it enshrines, remains the main tool for the protection of displaced persons against *refoulement* to a risk of inhuman or degrading treatment.

D   A Final Analysis: The Requirement of Imminence of the Risk

A final concern pertains to the long-standing requirement that the risk be "real". Again, this does not appear as problematic for people displaced by

---

171   J. McAdam, *Complementary Protection in International Refugee Law* (2007), op. cit., p. 164.
172   ECtHR, *Case of Selçuk and Asker v. Turkey* ("*Selçuk v. Turkey*"), Applications No. 23184/94 and 23185/94 (24 April 1998) *Reports 1998-II*, §§ 76–80.
173   ECtHR, *Z. & T. v. UK*, p. 7.
174   ECtHR, *Othman*.

sudden-onset disasters as for people forced to move by reason of the progressive deterioration of the environment and hence of their conditions of living. Nonetheless, it will be argued below that it is not necessarily an obstacle to *non-refoulement* in slow-onset disaster cases.

1   Occurrence of the Requirement in Medical and Environmental Cases

It was evoked above, in cases concerning applicants suffering from serious illness, the "imminence" of the threat carried much weight in the Court's assessment of the reality of the alleged risk. In *N. v. UK*, the "development of AIDS within one to two years and death within three to four years"[175] was not perceived as imminent enough to justify *non-refoulement*. It appears from human rights case-law that this requirement of imminence is generalised. J. McAdam hence observes that, in cases concerning nuclear power (both nuclear weapons and power plants) and the potential threats it poses to life, human rights treaty bodies typically acknowledge the general risk posed by nuclear power but consider that applicants have not sufficiently established the imminence and, or directness of the alleged threat.[176]

In the Netherlands, applicants submitted a claim to the Human Rights Committee that they were victims of a violation of their right to life (Article 6 ICCPR) because of the Netherlands' recognition of the lawfulness of potential use of nuclear weapons which put "many lives at risk, including their own". The Committee found no violation. Specifically, the decision clarifies that, for a person to claim to be a victim of a violation of an ICCPR right, he or she must show:

> ... either that an act or an omission of a State party has already adversely affected his or her enjoyment of such right, or that such an effect is imminent.[177]

Similarly, in *Balmer-Schafroth v. Switzerland*, where applicants alleged a violation of their right to a fair hearing by a tribunal (Article 6(1) ECHR) because they had not been able to secure a ruling by a tribunal on their objections to the extension of a nuclear power plant, the European Court of Human Rights

---

175   ECtHR, *N. v. UK*, § 47. The case is cited by the Court in *N. v. UK*, § 40.
176   J. McAdam, *Climate Change, Forced Migration, and International Law* (2012), op. cit., pp. 84–85.
177   HRC, *G. Aalbersberg and 2,084 Other Dutch Citizens v. The Netherlands* ("*Aalbersberg v. The Netherlands*"), Communication No. 1440/2005 (12 July 2006), § 6.3.

rejected the claim noting that the applicants had failed to show that the operation of the power station "exposed them personally to a danger that was not only serious but also specific and, above all, imminent".[178] In a later case concerning also the potential danger posed by a nuclear power plant, the Court relied on its *Balmer-Schafroth* judgment and similarly indicated that a "general danger" was not sufficient; applicant must establish a "specific and imminent danger in their personal regard".[179]

Incidentally, it is worth stressing that it is not the Court's reference to a "danger in [the applicant's] personal regard", as opposed to "general danger", as much as the requirement of imminence that would be problematic for the application of *non-refoulement* to persons displaced by a progressive deterioration of the environment. Recent ECtHR case-law illustrates that a risk needs not be personalised for it to be "real". Hence, in *Sufi & Elmi*, the Court found a real risk of Article 3 ill-treatments in a situation of general violence; in the same case, it also found that anyone living in an internally-displaced person camp in Somalia or a refugee camp in Kenya would live in dire humanitarian conditions reaching the threshold of Article 3 ill-treatments.[180]

The European Court of Human Rights has not yet ruled on a case concerning the removal of persons displaced where environmental disaster was the principal source of harm. In *Sufi & Elmi*, the Court referred to the drought affecting Somalia and noted its impact on populations but analysed it as an aggravating factor for the dire humanitarian conditions caused by the armed conflict rather than as the predominant source of the crisis.[181] One can therefore only speculate but possibly temper the finding that the Court's "nuclear power" jurisprudence does not bode well for the protection of environmentally-displaced persons.

2   Conceptualising Slow-Onset Disasters as Imminent Threats

The consequences of the use of nuclear weapons and of nuclear power plant catastrophes are environmental disasters likely to trigger displacement. As mentioned though, in situations where such sudden-onset disaster occurs, *non-refoulement* should apply since the disaster and resulting humanitarian conditions are, at least partly, attributable to the State and the MSS – *Sufi & Elmi* test hence pertinent. It is not on this aspect that nuclear power cases

---

178 ECtHR, *Balmer-Schafroth*, § 40.
179 ECtHR, *Case of Athanassoglou and Others v. Switzerland* ("*Athanassoglou*"), Application no. 27644/95 (6 April 2000), § 52.
180 ECtHR, *Sufi & Elmi*, §§ 293–296 and above in 2.
181 *Ibid.*, §§ 282 and 284.

appear relevant. Nuclear attacks and accidents, besides being disasters in and of themselves, also cause long-term degradations of the environment (soil, surface air, water, fauna and flora contamination[182]) and, in that sense they bear similarities with climate-change related disasters.

It is however possible to distinguish between nuclear disasters and other slow-onset disasters (including climate-related disasters). In principle at least, nuclear weapons should not be used: one hundred and ninety States have become parties to the Treaty on the Non-Proliferation of Nuclear Weapons (NPT), thereby committing to advance nuclear disarmament and non-proliferation, and to use atomic energy for peaceful purposes only.[183] As for disasters caused by radiation leaks from or reactor explosion in nuclear power plants, they are technological accidents which States have the obligation to prevent and anticipate.[184] Nuclear activities are "hazardous activities"[185] and potentially pose a high risk to human lives. The ECtHR infers from the right to life enshrined in Article 2 of the Convention and from States' "positive obligation to take all appropriate steps to safeguard life", the obligation for States to adopt appropriate regulations governing "the licensing, setting up, operation, security and supervision of the activity" and making it compulsory for all those concerned "to take practical measures to ensure the effective protection of citizens whose lives might be endangered by the inherent risks".[186] In other words, in principle – or in theory, nuclear power plants and possession by one's State of nuclear weapons do not *per se* constitute a risk for populations. In that sense, the risks involved by the applicants in the cases cited above were only hypothetical.

---

182   A.V. Yablokov, et al., "Atmospheric, Water, and Soil Contamination after Chernobyl", *Annals of the New York Academy of Sciences*, Vol. 1181, No. 1 (November 2009), pp. 223–236.

183   Treaty on the Non-Proliferation of Nuclear Weapons ("Non-Proliferation Treaty"), 01 July 1968, entered into force 5 March 1970 [1970] *UNTS* Vol. 729, p. 161.

184   Among other obligations, States engaging in hazardous activities have a positive obligation, under Article 8 ECHR, to establish an "effective and accessible procedure" which enables populations to access "relevant and appropriate information". ECtHR, *Mcginley and Egan v. The United Kingdom* ("*McGinley and Egan v. UK*"), Applications nos. 21825/93 and 23414/94 (9 June 1998), § 101.

185   ILC, Articles on the Prevention of Transboundary Harm from Hazardous Activities, Report of the 53rd Session ("Articles on the Prevention of Transboundary Harm from Hazardous Activities") UN Doc. A/56/10 (2001) *GAOR, 56th session, Supplement No. 10, at 370*.

186   ECtHR, *Case of Öneryıldız v. Turkey* ("*Öneryıldız*"), Application no. 48939/99 (30 November 2004), § 90. The ILC Articles on the Prevention of Transboundary Harm from Hazardous Activities mention similarly that States engaging in activities which involve "a risk of causing significant transboundary harm" have the obligations to *inter alia* prevent, inform, develop contingency plans for responding to emergencies and notify emergencies. ILC Articles on the Prevention of Transboundary Harm from Hazardous Activities.

Such was perhaps the meaning of the Court's requirement that applicants demonstrate a "specific and imminent danger".

On the other hand, in cases where pollution *is* occurring, the Court has found violations of ECHR rights by States. In 1994, the Court found that the nuisance and health problems caused by a waste treatment plant adversely affected the applicant's private and family life.[187] The Court concluded that the State had failed to take all necessary measures for protecting the applicant's right to respect for her home and for her private and family life under Article 8 and had therefore acted in breach of the Convention.[188] The Court also found that, in cases where harm indeed occurred, States violated their obligations under Article 2 ECHR if they failed to inform populations of the known risks associated hazardous activities they had engaged in[189] or to take measures to prevent the harm from occurring when they knew or ought to have known of the risks caused by technical shortcomings of the installations.[190]

Arguably, this interpretation is not undermined by the Court's decisions in nuclear test cases. In *Tauira v. France*, applicants were residents of French Polynesia who had worked on or who lived near the Mururoa Atol, where France had conducted and was to resume underground nuclear weapon testing. They claimed they were victims of a continuing violation of their rights (Article 2, 3 and 8 ECHR and Article 1 of Protocol 1) by France given the consequences which nuclear tests had already had and would have in the future, due to the persistent risk of radioactivity leakage.[191] The Commission rejected the claim on the basis that the applicants invoking a future risk had to produce "reasonable and convincing evidence of the likelihood" of the violation; "mere suspicion or conjecture", the Commission added, "is insufficient in this respect".[192] The Commission did not actually reject the ideas of a continuing violation of human rights or of long-term harm (applicants invoked persisting radioactivity). Instead, it appears that the "controversy surrounding a number of points",

---

187 ECtHR, *Case of López Ostra v. Spain* ("*Lopez Ostra*"), Application no. 16798/90 (9 December 1994), § 51.
188 *Ibid.*, §§ 56 and 58.
189 *A contrario*, in LCB v. UK the Court considered that, the risks associated with nuclear testing and with exposure to radiations being unknown at the time, UK authorities could not have been expected to notify the applicants' parents of these matters; there was therefore no violation of Article 2 ECHR. ECtHR, *Case of L.C.B. v. The United Kingdom* ("*LCB v. UK*"), Application no. 23413/94 (9 June 1998), § 41.
190 ECtHR, *Öneryıldız*, § 101.
191 ECnHR, *Tauira and 18 Others v. France* ("*Tauira v. France*"), Application N° 28204/95 (4 December 1995).
192 *Ibid.*, p. 131.

the lack of scientific knowledge and consensus on the impact of underground nuclear tests on the environment and populations were decisive in the Court's decision. The Court also blamed (so it seems) the applicants for failing to provide "the slightest evidence" as to their state of health, the cause of their health problems, or "at the very least, that they do suffer from health problems".[193] Similarly, in *LCB v. UK*, the Court considered that the risks associated with nuclear testing and with exposure to radiations being unknown at the time the applicant's father was exposed, authorities could not have been expected to notify the applicant's parents of these matters. The Court therefore concluded that there was no violation of Article 2 ECHR in the case.[194]

Against this background and to justify that the "imminence" requirement which appears in environment-related domestic cases as well as in medical cases[195] is not pertinent in slow-onset disaster cases, climate change could be analysed as a form of pollution which already affects the environment and populations' enjoyment of their human rights, and the reality and impacts of which the scientific community agrees on. Whereas the risks of nuclear attack and of nuclear accident are relatively remote, climate change is already occurring and impacting the environment and populations. Moreover, the risks associated with climate change and slow-onset disasters such as soil salination or desertification are amply documented and highly topical so that it is reasonable to say that States know or ought to know[196] of them. Protection against *refoulement* for persons displaced by slow-onset disasters should therefore not be automatically excluded. "A degree of speculation about future risk does not preclude a protection need from being recognized".[197]

To conclude on the possibility that human rights law, as it is currently applied, protects environmentally-displaced persons from *refoulement* to their country of origin in a word: if it appears possible in theory, much will depend on the willingness of asylum authorities and courts, including the European Court of Human Rights, to ensure that the principle of *non-refoulement* fully serves its original purpose of protecting persons who would face ill-treatment in their country of origin.

A remark pertains to situations of generalised violence. As said in Part 1, in the *Sufi & Elmi* case, before assessing the living conditions awaiting the

---

193 *Ibid.*, pp. 132–133.
194 ECtHR, *LCB v. UK*, § 41.
195 Such as *D. v. UK* and *N. v. UK* cited above.
196 The classical "knew or should have known" standard was used by the Court for example in ECtHR, *Öneryıldız*, § 101.
197 J. McAdam, *Climate Change, Forced Migration, and International Law* (2012), *op. cit.*, p. 86.

applicants upon their being removed to Somali, the Court first assessed the situation of generalised violence in Mogadishu and concluded, for the first time, to the existence of a situation of general violence of sufficient intensity to expose any returnee to a real risk of Article 3 ill-treatment solely on account of her or his presence in the city.[198] The same conclusion as that reached on the applicability of Article 15(c) of the Qualification Directive applies here too: in a case where the context in the applicant's country of origin is one of environmental disaster coupled with an armed conflict causing a situation of generalised violence of the intensity described above, then, environmentally-displaced persons can be protected against return, not specifically as persons fleeing environmental disaster but as persons fleeing the indiscriminate threats of an exceptionally high level of violence. In other cases, the two tests discussed above apply.

In conclusion, it appears that the test developed by the ECtHR in MSS and elaborated upon in *Sufi & Elmi* is the appropriate test to consider most claims submitted by environmentally-displaced persons. It appears also that, operating the MSS – *Sufi & Elmi* test could protect from *refoulement* people displaced by environmental disasters provided the situation in their country of origin exposes them to risks of inhuman or degrading treatment. Whether courts would be willing to disregard the (accommodating) indication by the ECtHR that the appropriate test is the "compelling humanitarian considerations" test (*N. v. UK*) to instead accept the above argument, that environmental disasters and their impacts on populations are hardly ever purely "naturally occurring" but always, if only partly, attributable to the State, remains to be seen. The observed trend in State practice is however not toward the broadening of protection grounds.

Recent State practice in response to environmental disasters suggests that States may be ready to refrain from returning environmentally-displaced persons, on a temporary and discretionary basis, but rarely ever otherwise.

---

198 ECtHR, *Sufi & Elmi*, § 293.

CHAPTER 8

State Practice in Response to Disasters and Other Humanitarian Crises

It was mentioned in Part 1, States have developed a number of instruments and mechanisms intended to apply in cases where other existing forms of protection failed or would fail. In view of the limited prospect that refugee law and international human rights law effectively protect all environmentally-displaced persons, it is necessary to consider the application of those different forms of protection to environmentally-displaced persons, be it temporary protection, the concept of which EU law has endorsed (I), authorisations to stay granted on a discretionary basis (II) or *ad hoc* responses to humanitarian crises, including, environmental disasters (III).

I   Temporary Protection Directive: Dealing with Mass Influx of Displaced Persons

Temporary protection[1] has been used by States, prior to the adoption of the Qualification Directive and is being applied by States outside the European Union. An example is the temporary protection afforded by the United States to Haitians in the aftermath of the earthquake which devastated the "Pearl of the Antilles" in January 2010. Two particularities of the United States' Temporary Protected Status are worth noticing: firstly, the provision explicitly includes environmental disasters resulting in a substantial but temporary disruption of living conditions as a ground for temporary protection.[2] Secondly, its benefit is however limited to persons who are already present on US territory.

In Europe, since 2001, temporary protection is regulated under EU law by a Directive.[3] It is therefore under this Directive that the relevance of temporary protection for environmentally displaced persons will be considered hereafter.

---

1   ExCom, "Conclusion No 22 on Large-Scale Influx (1981)", *op. cit*; UNHCR ExCom, "Conclusion No. 19 (XXXI) Temporary Refuge (1980)" ("Conclusion No 19 on Temporary Refuge (1980)").
2   United States: Immigration and Nationality Act (hereafter "INA"), as amended 4 March 2010, Act 244: Temporary Proteced Status, Section 244.1(b)(1)(B).
3   European Union: Council of the European Union, *Council Directive 2001/55/EC of 20 July 2001 on Minimum Standards for Giving Temporary Protection in the Event of a Mass Influx of Displaced Persons and on Measures Promoting a Balance of Efforts Between Member States*

It should be reminded at the onset that temporary protection is not a "third form of protection, alongside refugee status and subsidiary protection";[4] it is distinct in that it only lasts as long as it is not possible for national asylum authorities to examine temporary protection beneficiaries' claims for international protection on an individual basis. It can be described as an emergency relief for national asylum systems overwhelmed by large flows of asylum seekers although, under EU law, the inability of the State's asylum system to absorb the mass influx is not a precondition.[5] Most importantly, it protects individuals again return to an "unsafe" situation.[6]

It is granted for a maximum of two years, with a possibility, if the reasons for temporary protection persist, that the Council decides (by qualified majority) its extension by up to one year. It is revocable at any time by Council Decision, and does not prejudge of the recognition of refugee status or subsidiary protection. In fact, it seems that temporary protection might be able to respond to the main concerns of States opposing the creation of a protective status for environmentally-displaced persons.

At first glance, circumstances in which temporary protection applies bear similarities with the features of environmentally-induced migrations ("mass influx", impossibility to return "in safe and durable conditions", serious risk of "systematic or generalised [human rights] violations").[7] In view of the finding that the two more permanent forms of international protection (*i.e.* refugee status and subsidiary protection) will hardly cover the protection needs of populations forced to move due to natural disasters, examining the possibility that the latter be granted some formalised protection, albeit on a temporary basis, manifests itself as opportune.

---

in Receiving such Persons and Bearing the Consequences Thereof, 7 August 2001, OJ L.212–223 7.8.2001, 2001/55/EC.

4 "Proposal for a Council Directive on Minimum Standards for Giving Temporary Protection in the Event of a Mass Influx of Displaced Persons and on Measures Promoting a Balance of Efforts between Member States in Receiving Such Persons and Bearing the Consequences Thereof" ("Proposal for Temporary Protection Directive"), COM (2000) 303 final, 24 May 2000 [31/10/2000] *OJ C 311 E*, § 1.4.

5 European Union: Council of the European Union, *Council Directive 2001/55/EC of 20 July 2001 on Minimum Standards for Giving Temporary Protection in the Event of a Mass Influx of Displaced Persons and on Measures Promoting a Balance of Efforts Between Member States in Receiving such Persons and Bearing the Consequences Thereof*, 7 August 2001, OJ L.212–223 7.8.2001, 2001/55/EC, Art.2(a).

6 Temporary protection applies when, *inter alia*, people are "unable to return in *safe* and durable conditions". Temporary Protection Directive, Article 2(c) [emphasis added].

7 *Ibid.*, Article 2(c).

It must be born in mind that this protection was devised to apply to situations of mass influx only; it follows that persons seeking protection from the consequences of an environmental disaster may only benefit from it if they form part of a larger group of displaced persons reaching the territory of an EU Member State.

Under Article 2(c), the Directive is meant to provide some emergency and temporary relief to persons displaced by armed conflict or endemic violence as well as to victims of persons at serious risk of systematic or generalised violations of their human rights. In the event of a natural disaster affecting the territory of a State and, as a consequence, the population of that State, one could seek to argue that temporary protection should be triggered under Article 2(c) of the Directive. To wit, it could be argued that environmentally-displaced communities are at serious risk of, or who have been victims of, systematic or generalised violations of their human rights.[8] In view of the interconnection which can exist between natural disaster and generalised violence, one might even attempt to describe communities affected by natural disasters as persons who have fled zones of endemic violence.[9]

Due to the partial imprecision of the terms and to the fact that there has been no example of the use of Directive so far,[10] the meaning of "temporary protection" under EU law is somewhat mysterious. It can be tempting to conclude that the lack of precision was intended to allow for a flexible interpretation of the Directive, to accommodate the protection needs of communities displaced by factors that could either not be anticipated or not yet meet the consensus of States, at the time the Directive was adopted. A look into the *Travaux préparatoires* to the Directive is instructive. It is made clear in the Opinion of

---

8   *Ibid.*, Article 2(c)(ii).
9   *Ibid.*, Article 2(c)(i).
10 Strikingly, and as mentioned in the first Part, the Temporary Protection Directive was not activated in the context of the Syrian refugee crisis. The armed conflict which broke out in Syria in March 2011 has displaced millions of people, both internally and across borders. Displaced persons fled initially and mainly still to neighbouring countries but an ever growing number of them has also been entering or seeking to enter EU territory. Despite repeated calls formulated by observers (including UNHCR) and human rights groups especially, the European Union has chosen not to resort to temporary protection as a response to the so-called "Syrian refugee crisis". *See* for instance: UNHCR, "UN-HCR's Proposals in Light of the EU Response to the Refugee Crisis and the EU Package of 9 September 2015", 10 September 2015, retrieved from: <http://www.unhcr.org/55f28c4c9.pdf> [22/10/2016]; Human Rights Watch, "EU: Provide Protection for Syrian Refugees", 23 December 2012, retrieved from: <https://www.hrw.org/news/2012/12/23/eu-provide-protection-syrian-refugees> [22/10/2016]. *See* also above, Part 1.Chapter 2.11, pp. 92s.

the Economic and Social Committee of the European Union on the proposal for the Directive that temporary protection was not designed to apply to persons displaced by natural disasters:

> Although the Committee notes and understands that the proposal only applies to people fleeing from political situations, it thinks there might also be a case for a directive providing temporary reception and protection mechanisms for persons displaced by natural disasters.[11]

In one paragraph, the Economic and Social Committee almost simultaneously annihilates and revives hopes that the international protection needs of environmentally-displaced persons can be addressed, at least temporarily, in EU law.

At the national level, Finland again extended the scope of EU law to include persons displaced by environmental disaster:

> Temporary protection may be given to aliens who need international protection and who cannot return safely to their home country or country of permanent residence, because there has been a massive displacement of people in the country or its neighbouring areas as a result of an armed conflict, some other violent situation or an environmental disaster. Providing temporary protection requires that the need for protection may be considered to be of short duration. Temporary protection lasts for a maximum of three years in total.[12]

Temporary protection status for environmentally displaced persons has however never been applied in Finland. It was claimed by Sri Lankan victims of the tsunami which hit South-East Asia in 2004 but not granted. Commentators blamed the procedure for being "too stiff":[13] paragraph 2 of the above-cited Section 109 provides that temporary protection is activated by the prior decision of the Government, adopted in plenary session, which identifies the group of beneficiaries and the duration of the temporary residence permits

---

11 European Union: Economic and Social Committee, *Opinion of the Economic and Social Committee on the "Proposal for a Council Directive on minimum standards for giving temporary protection in the event of a mass influx of displaced persons and on measures promoting a balance of efforts between Member States in receiving such persons and bearing the consequences thereof"* (2001/C 155/06), 29/05/2001, §2.3.

12 Finnish Aliens Act, *op. cit.*, Section 109, § 1.

13 "Finland National Report (February 2010): The Different National Practises Concerning Granting of Non-EU Harmonised Protection Statuses", *op. cit.*, p. 11.

granted. Observers deplore the complexity and length of this activation mechanism. Beside the mentioned procedural aspects, the Tsunami was in fact not regarded as an environmental disaster for the purpose of Section 109 of the Finnish Aliens Act.[14]

To date, it is uneasy to assess whether temporary protection can ever be triggered to apply to large influx of persons displaced by an environmental disaster in their country of origin. Were it to apply, it seems that special safeguards should be set to ensure that individuals are not returned, when the temporary status elapses, to situations of insecurity or severe violations of human rights. In other words, "temporary" protection might in certain cases not be sufficient: it is granted for a maximum of two years, with a possibility if the reasons for temporary protection persist, that the Council decides by qualified majority its extension by up to one year but, depending on the disaster, its nature, pace, and intensity, it can take many more years before return is effectively possible. Suffice is to mention the example of Haiti: two years precisely after the earthquake which Haiti in January 2010, the situation is described to be precarious for a number of persons. Violence, criminality, the outbreak of cholera, the insufficient number of housing rebuilt in two years expose populations to grave risks.

Other forms of protection exist at the national level, which have not been harmonised yet.

II   Authorisations to Stay Granted on a Discretionary Basis

As observed in Part 1, State practice in this area is varied. The following will focus only on a few discretionary grounds for protection, perceived as most likely to apply to claims by environmentally-displaced persons. The first Subsection (A) will briefly turn to the New Zealand Immigration and Protection Tribunal decision whereby citizens of Tuvalu who had been denied refugee status and complementary protection were however granted, in a contemporaneous decision, authorisations to stay in New Zealand on humanitarian grounds.[15] The grant of Discretionary Leave, in the United Kingdom (B), to applicants claiming that their return would expose them to Article 3 ECHR ill-treatment as well as the protection granted in some States on medical grounds seem particularly

---

14   *Ibid.*, p. 11. It is noted that Section 51 of the Aliens Act (temporary residence permit) was instead used in such case.
15   New Zealand Immigration and Protection Tribunal, *AD (Tuvalu)* [2014] NZIPT 501370–371, 4 June 2014.

relevant in a context of environmental disaster. Focus will be had to authorisations to stay granted on medical grounds in Finland (C), Sweden (C), France (E) and Luxembourg (F).

A   *New Zealand*

It was mentioned in Part 1, under the Qualification Directive, EU Member States must assess asylum claims against, first, the criteria for refugee status and then, if those criteria are not met, against the criteria for subsidiary protection.[16] In like manner, asylum authorities in New Zealand must determine whether to recognise the applicant as a refugee under the 1951 Refugee Convention, or, in the negative, as a protected person (under the Convention Against Torture or the ICCPR).[17] On an appeal against a decision by asylum authorities declining international protection status, New Zealand courts must follow the same sequential procedure.[18] Should the applicants' claim fail under both limbs, and provided the applicants have lodged a contemporaneous humanitarian appeal, they may nonetheless be authorised to stay in New Zealand, not on the basis of any national or international protection obligation but on purely discretionary humanitarian grounds.

New Zealand Immigration Act provides the possibility for persons who appeal against a decision of asylum authorities declining to grant them refugee status or "protected person" status to simultaneously lodge a humanitarian appeal,[19] that is a claim to be granted residence visa (*i.e.* not to be deported) on humanitarian grounds, in case their claim for international protection is dismissed. To substantiate their claims, the appellants must demonstrate that:

(a) there are exceptional circumstances of a humanitarian nature that would make it unjust or unduly harsh for the appellant to be deported from New Zealand; and
(b) it would not in all the circumstances be contrary to the public interest to allow the appellant to remain in New Zealand.[20]

In several decisions concerning applicants who had invoked the adverse impacts of climate change in their claims for refugee or protected person

---

16   Above Part 1.Chapter 2.III.A.2. "Overview of the international protection regime devised by the Directive", pp. 116s.
17   New Zealand: Immigration Act 2009, *op. cit.*, Section 137.
18   New Zealand Immigration Act 2009, Section 198. *See* also: NZIPT, *AF (Kiribati)*, *op. cit.*, § 36.
19   New Zealand Immigration Act 2009, Sections 194(5) and (6), and 195(6) and (7).
20   New Zealand Immigration Act 2009, Section 207(1).

status, New Zealand courts, who rejected the argument as a matter of law but acknowledged and sometimes expressed empathy for the applicants' predicament,[21] have pointed to the provisions on authorisations to stay based on humanitarian grounds[22] as being the most relevant in such cases. Following the courts' cue, appellants in the case of AD (*Tuvalu*)[23] submitted not only appeals against the authorities' decision declining to grant them refugee status or protected person status[24] but also, contemporaneously, appeals on humanitarian grounds, claiming that they "would be deprived of their ability to have 'a safe and fulfilling life' if forced back to Tuvalu because of the effects of climate change".[25] The case was mentioned above (Chapter 6): a family of four citizens of Tuvalu sought to be granted "protected person" status in New Zealand, on the ground that the adverse effects of climate change in Tuvalu exposed them to a risk of being arbitrarily deprived of their lives or subjected to cruel treatment.[26] While the Immigration and Protection Tribunal acknowledged that the applicants would be faced with poverty-related challenges,[27] particularly in relation to food and water security in Tuvalu,[28] the applicants' appeal was dismissed: the applicants, the Tribunal found, did not fulfil the criteria to be granted either refugee status or protected person status.[29]

The Immigration and Protection Tribunal therefore turned to consider their appeals based on humanitarian grounds and assess whether the applicants' circumstances could constitute "exceptional circumstances of a humanitarian nature" under Section 207(1) of the Immigration Act.[30] The appeals were granted and reference was made in the Tribunal's decision to climate change however not as a decisive ground for granting a humanitarian visa in the case. The Tribunal found that the appellants' family ties[31] and integration[32] in

---

21 See for instance: NZHC, *Teitiota, op. cit.*, § 60; NZIPT, AF (Kiribati), *op. cit.*, § 94 and Refugee Review Tribunal of Australia, 0907346, *op. cit.*, §51.
22 See for instance: NZHC, *Teitiota*, §§ 42–44, 59; NZIPT, BG (*Fiji*), *op. cit.*, "Humanitarian Appeals under the Act Provide Further Scope for Relief", §§ 198–201.
23 NZIPT, AD (*Tuvalu*), *op. cit.*
24 NZIPT, AC (*Tuvalu*), *op. cit.*
25 NZIPT, AD (*Tuvalu*), § 14.
26 NZIPT, AC (*Tuvalu*), *op. cit.*
27 *Ibid.*, § 101.
28 *Ibid.*, § 108.
29 Above, pp. 351s.
30 Cited above.
31 NZIPT, AD (*Tuvalu*), §§ 19–20 and 31.
32 *Ibid.*, §§ 21–22.

New Zealand, together with the best interest of the children appellants[33] (including their heightened vulnerability to natural disasters and to the adverse impacts of climate change[34]) constituted, "on a cumulative basis", exceptional humanitarian circumstances that would make it unjust or unduly harsh for the family to be removed to Tuvalu.[35]

The Tribunal acknowledged the adverse impacts of climate change on the enjoyment of human rights[36] as well as the special vulnerability of children in the context of natural disasters and climate change.[37] Moreover, the Tribunal noted that exposure to the impacts of natural disasters could "in general terms, be a humanitarian circumstance"[38] however, because other factors in the appellants' case already justified granting them resident visas, the Tribunal felt it needed not reach a conclusion on this point.[39]

It appears that although the risk of exposure to the adverse impacts of climate change did, to some extent, weigh in the decision to grant Tuvaluan citizens authorisations to stay in New Zealand, on humanitarian grounds, it was clearly not the decisive factor. Furthermore, as noted by J. McAdam, the Tribunal's decision being based on discretionary ground – rather than on national or international protection obligations, it does not set any precedent.[40] Nonetheless, the decision can be viewed as a positive development. It supplements New Zealand courts' comprehensive assessment of environmentally-displaced persons' circumstances against relevant provisions of New Zealand legislation, thereby helping clarify the potential applications but also – and mainly – the shortcomings of existing law. By explicitly referring to and acknowledging the adverse and differential impacts of climate change and disasters, notably on one's enjoyment of his or her human rights, but also as a context in which displacement takes place, this decision contributes to the broader discussion and growing awareness of the issue and incidentally confirm that triggers for displacement are multiple and often interlinked.

B   *United Kingdom*

In the United Kingdom, as known, a person whose claim for refugee status or subsidiary protection (so-called "Humanitarian Protection") has failed may

---

33   *Ibid.*, §§ 23–26.
34   *Ibid.*, § 25.
35   *Ibid.*, § 30.
36   *Ibid.*, §§ 28–29.
37   *Ibid.*, § 25.
38   *Ibid.*, § 32. Similarly also: § 27.
39   *Ibid.*, § 33.
40   J. McAdam, "The emerging New Zealand jurisprudence on climate change, disasters and displacement", *Migration Studies*, Volume 3, Number 1 (2015), pp. 131–142, p. 137.

nevertheless be authorised to stay in the UK, upon being granted Discretionary Leave. As a reminder, according to the UK Border Agency:

> ... [t]here may be some cases (although any such cases are likely to be rare) where the general conditions in the country – for example, absence of water, food or basic shelter – are so poor that return in itself could, in extreme cases, constitute ill treatment under the Immigration Rules. Decision makers need to consider how those conditions would impact upon the individual if they were returned. Any such cases, if granted, would qualify for Discretionary Leave rather than Humanitarian Protection (because they are not protection-related cases) (...)[41]

Case-law clarifies what can be considered humanitarian conditions meeting the Article 3 ECHR threshold.[42] Removal was considered to be in breach of Article 3 where the applicant would be returned to "a camp where conditions are described as "sub-human" and [he or she would] face medical conditions described as some of the worst in the world".[43] Were also protected against return "an amputee who had serious mental problems who would not receive either financial or medical support in the Gambia, and would only have recourse to begging for his support"[44] and a 16-year-old boy whose return "would leave him destitute and without any protection".[45] Harsh conditions of living, including deprivation of healthcare and other socio-economic rights can reach the threshold of inhuman or degrading treatment, proscribed under Article 3 of the Convention.

The judgment of the Asylum and Immigration Tribunal in *AM & AM* is of utmost importance in this context. The Asylum and Immigration Tribunal (AIT) ruling in a case concerning removal to Somalia where conflict was ongoing and humanitarian conditions were poor rejected the Secretary of State submission that "in and of themselves, poor humanitarian conditions in Somalia, even if in an IDP camp, would not establish an Article 3 breach". The Tribunal instead found that the European Court of Human Rights had never excluded that living conditions could attain such a level of severity as to amount to Article 3

---

41   "API Humanitarian Conditions", *op. cit.*, p. 11.
42   The three examples are those cited by M. Foster in M. Foster, *International Refugee Law and Socio-Economic Rights: Refuge from Deprivation* (2007), *op. cit.*, pp. 188–189.
43   UK: UKIAT, *Paul Owen v. Secretary of State for the Home Department* ("*Owen*") [2002] UKIAT 3285, § 27 [as cited by M. Foster].
44   UK: High Court (Queen's Bench Division), *R v. Secretary of State for the Home Department, Ex Parte Kebbeh* ("*Kebbeh*"), CO/1269/98, 30 April 1999, *Crown Office List*, § 8.
45   UK: UKIAT, *Korca v. Secretary of State for the Home Department* ("*Korca v. Secretary of State for the Home Department*"), Appeal No. HX-360001-2001, 29 May 2002, *Unreported*, § 9.

ill-treatment.[46] Most significantly – and partly so because it is in direct line with the premise of the present work, the AIT, citing the European Court of Human Rights' jurisprudence on (non-)refoulement to situations of general violence, asserted that:

> ... the approach taken by the Court in *NA v UK*, para 116,[47] when dealing with "situations of general violence" is one which would be equally applicable if one substitutes the words "poor humanitarian conditions".[48]

If one combines the suggestion made by the Asylum and Immigration Tribunal, with the paragraph of the *NA v. UK* case the Tribunal refers to, it is possible to infer that the Tribunal leaves open the possibility that:

> ... [poor humanitarian conditions] in a country ... will be of a sufficient level of intensity to breach Article 3. Nevertheless the [Tribunal] would only adopt such an approach in the most extreme case of [poor humanitarian conditions], where there was a real risk of ill-treatment simply by virtue of an individual being exposed to such violence on return.[49]

Such reasoning nurses the hope that environmentally-displaced persons can be protected from being returned to their country of origin, under existing norms of international human rights law – even though the finding of the Tribunal in the case may call for some temperance. The Tribunal concluded in the case that "whilst the humanitarian situation is dire, it does not appear that civilians *per se* face a real risk of denial of basic food and shelter and other bare necessities of life". In particular, the AIT took note of UN estimates that forty-three percent of the population of Somalia was in need of assistance but to deduce with implacable logic that "over a half of the population" was therefore "not in need of humanitarian assistance".[50] The Tribunal further considered that, despite obstruction and dangers aid agencies could meet in delivering

---

46   Inferred from the *Pancenko v. Latvia* to which the Tribunal refers. ECtHR, *Pancenko v. Latvia*, Application no. 40772/98 (28 October 1999), 2; UKAIT, *AM & AM (Somalia), op. cit.*, § 87.
47   In the official version of the *NA v. UK* judgment, published on the website of the European Court of Human Rights, the paragraph the Tribunal appears to allude to is in fact paragraph 115.
48   UKAIT, *AM & AM (Somalia), op. cit.*, § 87.
49   This paragraph does not appear in the *AM & AM* judgment but is deduced from the combined reading of UKAIT, *AM & AM*, § 87 and ECtHR, *NA v. UK*, § 115.
50   UKAIT, *AM & AM (Somalia), op. cit.*, § 157.

aid, a significant percentage of those in need were reached; others, the AIT found, often received assistance from clans and the Somali diaspora. This can be put into perspective with the ECtHR judgment in the *Sufi & Elmi* case. To conclude that return to Somalia would expose individuals to risks of Article 3 ill-treatments, the Court inferred from the numerous reports it considered that chances of receiving appropriate humanitarian assistance in Somalia were, in reality, slim.[51]

It was mentioned in Chapter 6, Finland and Sweden have adopted additional grounds for protection under their respective asylum legislation, including environmental disasters, and grant an "asylum-like" status to persons "otherwise in need of protection". As it happens, the two countries also have provisions in their national law for the grant of residence permits to persons who do cannot benefit either refugee status or complementary protection status.

C Finland

Under Finnish law an alternative exists for persons who are not granted refugee or complementary protection: they may be granted a temporary residence permit, on a discretionary basis, if they cannot be returned to their country of origin "for temporary reasons of health or if they cannot actually be removed from the country".[52]

They may also be issued a permanent residence permit "on compassionate grounds", if refusing them a residence permit "would be manifestly unreasonable with regard to their health, ties to Finland or on other compassionate grounds, particularly in consideration of the circumstances they would face in their home country or of their vulnerable position".[53]

D Sweden

In Sweden too, there is an additional ground for protection, sitting outside Swedish refugee-subsidiary-complementary protection framework. An applicant who was not granted protection under any of the above provisions may nevertheless receive "humanitarian protection": he or she may be permitted

---

51   It can be mentioned that the AM & AM precedes the *Sufi & Elmi* case however, among the reports cited by the ECtHR, some provide information on the situation as it already was in Somalia at the time the AM & AM judgement was issued. ECtHR, *Sufi & Elmi*, §§ 163, 182, 284, 291 and 292.

52   Finnish Aliens Act, *op. cit.*, Section 51. "Finland National Report (February 2010): The Different National Practises Concerning Granting of Non-EU Harmonised Protection Statuses", *op. cit.*

53   Finnish Aliens Act, *op. cit.*, Section 52.

to stay in Sweden on compassionate grounds.[54] Under Chapter 5 Section 6 of the Swedish Aliens' Act, a residence permit may be granted to an alien if, on an overall assessment of his or her situation, "there are found to be such exceptionally distressing circumstances that he or she should be allowed to stay in Sweden".[55] The provision urges asylum decision-makers in assessing the overall situation of the claimant to pay particular attention "to the alien's state of health".[56]

Looking at the proposal submitted by the Swedish government to the Parliament clarifies that the provision was intended to grant residence permit, inter alia, to persons suffering from a serious illness and whose condition may be improved in Sweden if a medical treatment is not available in their country of origin[57] and in cases where there is a risk of social exclusion, trauma caused by torture or other painful experiences in the country of origin or as a result of trafficking.[58] The provision is also meant to protect the development and best interest of the child.[59]

Swedish case-law provides examples of cases where the applicant's affliction by chronicle disease has been considered by migration courts upon deciding whether to allow the applicant to stay in Sweden.

Under Chapter 5 Section 6 of Swedish Aliens Act,[60] an individual who does not qualify for refugee status or subsidiary protection and does not fall within the category of "persons otherwise in need of protection" may nevertheless be awarded a residence permit, due to "exceptionally distressing circumstances" (*"synnerligen ömmande omständigheter"*), including the person's health.

The preparatory work to this section of the Aliens' Act[61] suggests that, in examining the claim, authorities should give special consideration to, *inter alia*, the alien's health status. In particular, "life-threatening physical or mental illness for which no treatment can be given in the alien's home country could constitute a reason for the grant of a residence permit".[62]

The Appeal court for Migration rejected the claim of a Cameroon national infected with HIV who had applied for protection in Sweden. The Court notes

---

54 UNHCR, et al., *Safe at Last?* (July 2011), op. cit., p. 94.
55 Utlänningslag, *op. cit.*, Chapter 4, Section 2a.
56 *Ibid.*, Chapter 5, Section 6.
57 "Regeringens Proposition 2004/05:170: Ny Instans- Och Processordning I Utlännings- Och Medborgarskapsärenden" ("Regeringens proposition 2004/05:170"), 26 May 2005, p. 190.
58 *Ibid.*, p. 192.
59 *Ibid.*, pp. 193–195.
60 Sweden: *Aliens Act ("Utlänningslagen")*, 2005:716.
61 Government Bill 2004/05:170, 189–195, at pp. 190–191.
62 Preparatory Report, Government Bill 2004/05:170, pp. 190–191.

that HIV is a chronic disease and is life-threatening if no treatment is provided to the infected person.[63] The Court also notes that, in Cameroon, the applicant may be incapable of bearing the costs of the treatment he has been receiving in Sweden and which has given good results.[64] The Court however concludes that the conditions for granting a residence permit on the basis of "particularly distressing circumstances" to an applicant suffering from HIV (or other health condition) are not met when health care and medicines are available in the home country, regardless of their cost,[65] and, therefore, regardless of whether the applicant will actually be able to gain access to the care his condition requires. The decision is also in line with a governmental guiding decision which makes clear that financial impediments to getting care in the home country cannot alone justify that applicants be allowed to stay in Sweden.[66] The Migration Court of Appeal observed:

> ... the legislative history and past practice says that the financial implications for Sweden must be considered in the assessment of whether a residence permit should be granted and that economic difficulties to obtain care in the home country should not lead to granting a residence permit...[67]

As a consequence, the Migration Court of Appeal concluded that a residence permit due to medical reasons could not be granted in the case.[68] In a series of guiding decisions, the Swedish Government made its position clear: economic difficulties hindering effective access to costly medical care cannot form the basis for the grant of a residence permit on humanitarian grounds.[69]

This interpretation of the principle of *non-refoulement* is comparable to that given by the European Court of human Rights in the above cited case-law in

---

63   Sweden: Migrationsöverdomstolen (Migration Court of Appeal), MIG 2007:48, UM1344-06, 27/11/2007, pp. 9–10.
64   *Ibid.*, p. 10.
65   *Ibid.*, p. 10.
66   Sweden: Aliens Act – Guiding Decision, Reg. 23–94.
67   MIG 2007:48, UM1344-06, 27/11/2007, *op. cit.*, p. 10. English translation available: Sweden – Migration Court of Appeal, 27 November 2007, Um 1344-06, retrieved from the EDAL – European Database of Asylum Law website at: <http://www.asylumlawdatabase.eu/en/case-law/sweden-migration-court-appeal-27-november-2007-um-1344-06> [05/08/2012].
68   MIG 2007:48, UM1344-06, 27/11/2007, *op. cit.*, p. 10. English translation available: *see* previous footnote.
69   Rebecca Stern, *Ny utlänningslag under lupp* (Stockholm: Svenska Röda Korset, April 2008), p. 61.

N. v. UK. Accordingly, States should not bear the burden of the inadequacy of third countries' healthcare systems. This consideration appears to prevail over the otherwise unchallenged risk of severe health deterioration the applicant will face upon being returned to his country of origin. Incidentally, this interpretation gives much leeway to States in HIV/AIDS cases since, as a matter of fact, treatment is available in most countries. The essential question however is: how many persons can access and afford it? Availability should not be the decisive criterion for the mere existence of treatment in the country does not necessarily carry with it that all persons in need of it, without discrimination, will be able to benefit from it. In other words, "availability" is an informative but insufficient indicator; it must be coupled with considerations pertaining to "accessibility".[70]

A relaxing of Swedish case-law in that sense might in fact have occurred in a recent judgment of the Migration Court of Appeal.[71] In 2010, a woman who had been diagnosed with blood cancer and who risked developing acute leukaemia if she were not to receive appropriate treatment was granted permanent residence permit in Sweden. The Court took into consideration the fact that, although medicines were available in the applicant's country of origin (Mongolia), they were however not accessible through legal channels. The Court considered that it would be unreasonable to expect from the applicant that she uses unofficial, or even illegal, channels in order to acquire the medicines and therefore considered that care being both irregular and uncertain, was not *available*[72] and the applicant should therefore not be returned. In reaching this conclusion, the Court noted that the continued provision of

---

70 On "human rights indicators" as tools used for measuring the degree of implementation of human rights in a particular country, see UN Commission on Human Rights, *Preliminary report of the Special Rapporteur on the right to education Ms. Katarina Tomaševski*, submitted in accordance with Commission on Human Rights Resolution 1998/33, 13/01/1999, E/CN.4/1999/49, at 42–74. See also UNDP, *Indicators for Human Rights and Human Rights Based Approaches to Development in UNDP Programming: A Users Guide* (Final Draft Version March 2006); K. Tomasevski, *Human Rights Obligations in Education – The 4-A Scheme* (Wolf Legal Publishers, 2006); C. Johnsson, J. Grimheden, K. Nowak, J. Svedberg and A. Algård, *A Study on Methods and Tools for Analysis in the Work on Human Rights* (Lund: Raoul Wallenberg Institute for Human Rights and Humanitarian Law, 2005); and M. Green, "What We Talk About When We Talk About Indicators: Current Approaches to Human Rights Measurement", *Human Rights Quarterly*, Vol.23 (2001): p. 1065.

71 Sweden: Migration Court of Appeal (*"Migrationsöverdomstolen"*), MIG 2010:23, UM7664-09, 25/10/2010.

72 Sweden: Migration Court of Appeal (*"Migrationsöverdomstolen"*), MIG 2010:23, UM7664-09, 25/10/2010.

treatment to the applicant in Sweden would not result in unreasonable economic consequences.

E   France

In France, aliens whose health requires medical treatment, the absence of which can have consequences of an exceptional gravity, may receive a temporary residence permit (*carte de séjour temporaire "vie privée et familiale"*) if medical treatment is not available in their country of origin.[73] For the same reasons, they may not be issued an "obligation to leave French territory" (*obligation de quitter le territoire français* – OQTF)[74] nor expelled.[75] This right to stay in France on medical grounds has been depicted as one of the few exceptions to France closing its doors to "unwanted" migrants, which palliated the increasingly restrictive interpretation of asylum law.[76] The recent amendment of French asylum law, in June 2011, significantly narrowed its scope of application.

The evolution of legislation and case-law on this ground for protection against return has not been linear.

Initially, the law referred to the "absence" of treatment in the country of origin;[77] an implementing circular however clarified that the finding of a possibility of appropriate treatment and hence return of the person to his or her country of origin required that the treatment not merely existed in the country but also that the applicant had the capacity to access it.[78]

Despite the implementing circular, the *Conseil d'état* long confined its assessment to one of the existence or "theoretical availability" of an appropriate treatment,[79] even after the law had been amended to integrate the notion of

---

73   CESEDA, *op. cit.*, Article L313-11-11°.

74   *Ibid.*, L511-4-10°.

75   *Ibid.*, Article L512-3 and L523-4.

76   D. Turpin, "La loi n°2017-672 du 16 juin 2011 relative à l'immigration, à l'intégration et à la nationalité (1) : de l'art de profiter de la transposition des directives pour durcir les prescriptions nationales", *Revue critique de droit international privé*, No. 3 (July-September 2011), pp. 499–520, pp. 518–519.

77   The provisions initially referred to: "*L'étranger résidant habituellement en France dont l'état de santé nécessite une prise en charge médicale dont le défaut pourrait entraîner pour lui des conséquences d'une exceptionnelle gravité, sous réserve de l'absence d'un traitement approprié dans le pays de renvoi...*". 11 May 1998 Loi no 98–349, *op. cit.*, [emphasis added].

78   "*La possibilité pour l'intéressé de bénéficier ou non du traitement approprié à son état dans son pays d'origine dépend non seulement de l'existence des moyens sanitaires adéquats, mais encore des capacité d'accès du patient à ces moyens*". "Circulaire D'application de la Loi N° 98–349 Du 11 Mai 1998 Relative À L'entrée Et Au Séjour Des Étrangers En France Et Au Droit D'asile", n° NOR/INT/D/98/00108/C, 12 May 1998, p. 21.

79   D. Turpin (July-September 2011), *op. cit.*, p. 519 and references cited in note 58.

"effective access"[80] to appropriate medical treatment. Eventually, acknowledging the fact that "availability" often failed to grasp the reality of the situation in that it was not synonymous with the possibility for the applicant to effectively access the treatment, the *Conseil d'état*, eventually endorsing the approach maintained since 2006 by the Paris Administrative Court of Appeal,[81] clarified that the criterion should be that of the effective accessibility of the treatment for the applicant. In particular, authorities should have regard to the relative cost of the treatment and possibility for the applicant, in view of his or her personal circumstances, to effectively access it.[82] In so doing, the *Conseil d'état* distanced itself from the judgment of the European Court of Human Rights in *N. v. UK*[83] in which the assessment by the Court was limited to observing the availability of treatment, irrespective of the quasi-impossibility for the applicant to access it. After the *Conseil d'état* had adopted a series of decisions in that sense,[84] the legislator however chose to reverse this trend. The same

---

80 As of 1 March 2005, the relevant provisions of the CESEDA refer to "[*l*]*'étranger résidant habituellement en France dont l'état de santé nécessite une prise en charge médicale dont le défaut pourrait entraîner pour lui des conséquences d'une exceptionnelle gravité, sous réserve qu'il ne puisse effectivement bénéficier d'un traitement approprié dans le pays de renvoi*". CESEDA, Version en vigueur du 1 mars 2005 au 25 juillet 2006. The different versions of the text can be accessed on the Légifrance website: <www.legifrance.gouv.fr>.

81 France: Cour administrative d'appel ("CAA") de Paris, *Préfet de Police c. Okba Ben Belcacem X* ("*Préfet de Police c. Okba Ben Belcacem X*"), 06PA00482, 15 December 2006, *AJDA* 2007.749, note D. Lecucq.

82 "*Considérant que (...) l'autorité administrative ne peut légalement décider l'éloignement de l'étranger que s'il existe des possibilités de traitement approprié de l'affection en cause dans le pays de renvoi ; que si de telles possibilités existent mais que l'étranger fait valoir qu'il ne peut en bénéficier, soit parce qu'elles ne sont* pas accessibles à la généralité de la population, eu égard notamment aux *coûts du traitement ou à l'absence de modes de prise en charge adaptés, soit parce qu'en dépit de leur accessibilité, des circonstances exceptionnelles tirées des particularités de sa* situation personnelle *l'empêcheraient d'y accéder effectivement, il appartient à cette même autorité, au vu de l'ensemble des informations dont elle dispose, d'apprécier si l'intéressé peut ou non bénéficier effectivement d'un traitement approprié dans le pays de renvoi*". France: Conseil d'Etat, *Ministre d'Etat, Ministre de l'Intérieur et de l'Aménagement du Territoire* ("*Ministre d'Etat, Ministre de l'Intérieur et de l'Aménagement du Territoire*"), 301640, 7 April 2010, 2nd Considérant [emphases added]. *See* also V. Tchen (Ed.) (July-September 2010), *op. cit.*, p. 438.

83 O. Boskovic, *et al.*, "Panorama: Droit des étrangers et de la nationalité, septembre 2009–août 2010", *Recueil Dalloz*, No. 43 (9 December 2010), p. 2868, p. 2875.

84 France: Conseil d'Etat, *Mme Amina A.*, N° 329450, 16 February 2011, (surgery cost impeding access to required treatment in the country of origin); France: Conseil d'Etat, *Ministre de l'immigration, de l'intégration, de l'identité nationale et du développement solidaire* (*M. Samba A*), N° 319960, 16 July 2010, (impossibility for a person with no income to

"relativisation" of the absolute nature of Article 3 ECHR protection, which was a marked flaw of the judgment of the ECtHR in *N. v. UK*,[85] appears to have inspired the French legislator:[86] the "absence" of treatment (in place of the impossibility to benefit from it) has made its way back into the CESEDA.[87] The legislator nonetheless included a safeguard against return in situation of "exceptional humanitarian circumstance".[88]

F Luxembourg

In Luxembourg too, possibilities to obtain an authorisation to stay in the country on medical grounds appear to have narrowed under the influence – and in direct application of – the case-law of the European Court of Human Rights in medical cases.

In 2009, the Administrative Tribunal concluded that an applicant could not be returned to her country of origin (Bosnia and Herzegovina) in view of her acute mental weakness including chronic depression and anxiety symptomatic of a post-traumatic stress disorder, of the apparent absence of appropriate medical facilities financially accessible to her in her country or origin and of the risk that her condition would deteriorate in the absence of treatment.[89]

In 2011 however, the Administrative Court of Appeal, in line with the relevant appealed judgment of the Administrative Tribunal, extensively cited the case-law of the ECtHR and deduced from it that an applicant could be returned to his or her country of origin if the three following criteria were met: the applicant is not in the advanced or final stages of a terminal illness, he or she has the possibility to find appropriate treatment in his or her country of origin, even if it is at high cost or in limited amount, and he or she has family members with whom he or she maintained some connections and who could help.

---

receive necessary treatment against Hepatitis B in his country of origin). See also "Droit des étrangers malades : de la condition d'accès effectif aux soins dans le pays d'origine ou de renvoi", *AJDA*, No. 16 (3 May 2010), p. 881, pp. 883–885.

85   Above Chapter 7, II. A. 2(b) "The search for a fair balance: an unfortunate legacy of the Soering case", pp. 357s.

86   H. Labayle, "Etude: La loi relative à l'immigration, l'intégration et la nationalité du 16 juin 2011 réformant le droit des étrangers : le fruit de l'arbre empoisonné", *RFDA*, No. 5 (September-October 2011), p. 934s, p. 938.

87   CESEDA, *op. cit.*, Articles L313-11-11°, L511-4-10°, L512-3 and L523-4 ; 11 May 1998 Loi no 98-349, *op. cit.*

88   CESEDA, *op. cit.*, Articles L313-11-11°, L511-4-10°, L512-3 and L523-4.

89   Luxembourg: Tribunal administratif (2e chambre), n° 24212a, 4 June 2009, available at: <http://www.clae.lu/pdf/migrations/desicions_judiciares/police/juin2009/24212a.pdf>.

The applicant in the case had invoked two provisions of Luxembourg immigration law: Article 129, proscribing return to a risk of ill-treatment proscribed by Article 3 ECHR[90] and Article 130, proscribing the removal on medical grounds.[91]

The Administrative Court observed that the situation of the applicant in the case at hand was comparable to that of the applicant in *N. v. UK*. Whereas the Tribunal had found that deprivation of treatment would have consequences of an exceptional gravity on the applicant's health,[92] the Administrative Court found that, although the applicant suffered chronic liver disease and although his infection with HIV and type 2 diabetes required medical therapy, his grave illnesses were not in an advanced or final stage and a more or less rapid deterioration of his health would occur only in case of interruption of treatment.[93] Moreover, in light of a UNGASS[94] country report indicating that sixty-seven percent of the HIV-positive Guinean population received antiretroviral treatment and noting the steady increase in treatment availability in the country, the Court saw fit to infer that treatment was, in principle, available (*"disponibilité de principe"*) and hence, accessible.[95] The Court further observed that the applicant had siblings in the country who could help him if needed (although the applicant had argued otherwise).

In conclusion, the appeal was rejected on both grounds: the "exceptional circumstance" threshold set by the ECtHR in Article 3 medical cases was not met[96] and the applicant had not demonstrated that he could not access treatment in his country of origin.[97]

---

90   Article 129 also prohibits return to a threat to life or person and to ill-treatments proscribed by Articles 1 and 3 of the UN Convention Against Torture. Loi sur la libre circulation des personnes et l'immigration, *op. cit.*, Article 129.

91   The applicant must show that the medical conditions he or she invokes requires a medical treatment, the absence of which would have exceptionally grave consequences on his or her health, and that he or she will not be able to effectively have access to any appropriate treatment in his or her country of origin. *"Sous réserve qu'il ne constitue pas une menace pour l'ordre public ou la sécurité publique, l'étranger ne peut être éloigné du territoire s'il établit au moyen de certificats médicaux que son état de santé nécessite une prise en charge médicale dont le défaut entraînerait pour lui des conséquences d'une exceptionnelle gravité, et s'il rapporte la preuve qu'il ne peut effectivement bénéficier d'un traitement approprié dans le pays vers lequel il est susceptible d'être éloigné". Ibid.*, Article 130.

92   Luxembourg: Tribunal administratif, n° 27296, 12 January 2011, pp. 5–6.

93   Luxembourg: Cour administrative, n° 27943C, 5 May 2011, p. 6.

94   United Nations General Assembly Special Session on AIDS.

95   CA (Lux.), n° 27943C, 5 May 2011, *op. cit.*, p. 7.

96   *Ibid.*, p. 7.

97   *Ibid.*, p. 8.

The tendency observed in national as well as European case-law to consider the mere existence of humanitarian assistance, support or healthcare in the country of origin as sufficient a guaranty that the alleged and often real risk of ill-treatment will not materialise does not augur well for environmentally-displaced persons. In the aftermath of a disaster and, even more so, in the course of slow-onset environmental degradation, State capacities are reduced but certainly not fully annihilated. Despite the outbreak of diseases, shortage of personnel and medicines or collapse of hospitals (with other facilities being incapable of accommodating all those in needs), some level of healthcare can still be *available* (that is, observable) in the country. The same goes for water resources and food stocks – to mention but the most basic necessities of life. It is all the more true when humanitarian relief efforts are underway.

Paradoxically under this approach, the existence of humanitarian assistance in a country, irrespective of the practical difficulties it faces in effectively accessing populations in need, can be invoked by national authorities to deny an authorisation to stay to persons otherwise in need of protection. It seems on the contrary that the presence of international aid agencies in a country could be valuable indicators of an ongoing humanitarian crisis, calling for international cooperation if not solidarity.

III State Practice in Response to Recent Environmental Disasters

After the earthquake which struck Haiti on 12 January 2010, the UN High Commissioner for Refugees (UNHCR) and the High Commissioner for Human Rights (OHCHR) issued a joint emergency appeal, urging governments to suspend all involuntary returns to Haiti, in view of the humanitarian crisis triggered by the earthquake.[98] UNHCR and OHCHR mentioned in particular that despite the international response to the earthquake, many people were still lacking "basic amenities such as shelter, food, water and medical assistance" and therefore called on all States not to return Haitians "and to continue granting interim protection measures on humanitarian grounds", at least "pending stabilization

---

98   UNHCR / M. Fleming, "Briefing Notes: OHCHR / UNHCR Urge Extending Suspension of Returns to Haiti" ("OHCHR / UNHCR urge extending suspension of returns to Haiti"), 12 February 2010, at: <http://www.unhcr.org/4b7543026.html> [10/08/2012]; OHCHR-UNHCR, "Joint UNHCR-OHCHR Return Advisory Update on Haiti", 9 June 2011, at: <www.unhcr.org/4e0305666.html> [10/08/2012].

and until such time as people can return safely and sustainably".[99] UNHCR and OHCHR renewed their appeal in June 2011, in view of the situation still prevailing in the country.[100]

France announced it suspended removals to Haiti just a day after the earthquake, on 13 January 2010. In Martinique and Guadeloupe, deportations resumed in June 2011,[101] despite UNHCR-OHCHR reiterating their appeal the same month; in French Guyana on the other hand, the stay on deportation was still in effect in January 2012.[102]

The earthquake was also taken into consideration by French courts in cases concerning children. Some Haitian nationals working in France and whose children were still living in Haiti at the time the earthquake struck invoked their right to family reunification (*"regroupement familial"*) and sought to have long term visas delivered to their children. Given the "tragic events" in Haiti, the separation of children from their parents was considered to justify the grant of a visa.[103] In several cases, the implementation of French administrative authorities' decisions to refuse to grant visas or to deny the right to family reunification was suspended by administrative courts. It was the case notably when the applicants invoked the precarious situation in which children found themselves in Haiti in the aftermath of the disaster; reference was occasionally made to Article 8 ECHR and to the Convention on the Rights of the Child.[104] Tribunals had regard to the personal circumstances of the children including their age, their precarious situation following the earthquake, their being internally-displaced and living in a camp, the death of their relatives or flight to other countries, or the outbreak of cholera for instance.[105] It was noted that

---

99 "OHCHR / UNHCR urge extending suspension of returns to Haiti", *op. cit*; "Joint UNHCR-OHCHR Return Advisory Update on Haiti", *op. cit.*
100 "Joint UNHCR-OHCHR Return Advisory Update on Haiti", *op. cit.*
101 A. Bertin, *et al.*, *Appui aux migrants haïtiens: sensibiliser, accompagner, plaider – Carnet de route d'une année d'expérience* (Paris: Collectif Haïti de France, March 2012), p. 18; UNHRC, "Report of the Independent Expert on the Situation of Human Rights in Haiti, Michel Forst, Addendum: Forced Returns of Haitians from Third States", A/HRC/20/35/Add.1, 4 June 2012, p. 10.
102 A. Virassamy, "Les expulsions vers Haïti toujours suspendues", *France-Guyane*, 17 January 2012.
103 France: Conseil d'Etat, *Mme Anne-Rose A* ("*Mme Anne-Rose A*"), n° 333870, 18 January 2010; CE, *Mme Léone A* ("*Mme Léone A*"), n° 334522, 2 February 2010.
104 France: Tribunal administratif de Montreuil, n° 1011709, 9 December 2010, p. 1; France: Tribunal administratif de Montreuil, n° 1012197, 6 January 2011, p. 3.
105 France: Tribunal administratif de Montreuil, n° 1012197, 6 January 2011, *op. cit.*, p. 3; TA Montreuil, n° 1011709, 9 December 2010, *op. cit.*, pp. 2–3; Conseil d'Etat, *M.A.* ("*M.A.*"),

administrative authorities upon deciding on a request for family reunification should appreciate the information at hand with due regard to the right to private and family life as it is enshrined in Article 8 ECHR.[106] Family reunification was also granted to a man living in France and whose wife and four children were in Haiti, "in view of the very specific circumstances of the case".[107] A 2010 decision of the Paris Administrative Court of Appeal is also of some interest: the applicant, Ms A, a Haitian national, did not qualify for refugee status or subsidiary protection. However, the Administrative Court explicitly advised the applicant to apply for temporary residence permit on humanitarian or exceptional grounds.[108]

By contrast, it can be noted that a series of decision issued in 2004 concerning Algerian nationals, considered that the circumstance that the applicants' house had collapsed during an earthquake could not in itself oppose a removal decision.[109]

J. McAdam details a number of group-based "*ad hoc* humanitarian schemes" devised to protect victims of environmental disasters,[110] such as the suspension of involuntary returns to countries affected by the 2004 Asian Tsunami (the United Kingdom, Germany and the Netherlands) or use of an accelerated procedure to consider applications for permanent or temporary visas.[111] Moreover, Denmark reportedly granted humanitarian asylum to single women and families with young children when return would expose them to living conditions "considered to be extremely difficult, for example due to famine" (so-called "survival criterion");[112] it applied from 2001 to 2006 to returns to Afghanistan by reason of the drought there.

Outside Europe, it should be noted that Brazilian National Immigration Council adopted in January 2012 a resolution to regularise Haitians already living in Brazil at the time the resolution was adopted and to devise a special

---

n° 336018, 26 February 2010; France: Conseil d'Etat, *M. Jean Yvon a Et Mme Modiana B Épouse A* ("*M. Jean Yvon a Et Mme Modiana B Épouse A*"), n° 335698, 16 April 2010.

106   France: Tribunal administratif de Versailles, *n° 1004754*, 3 August 2010, pp. 3–4.
107   Tribunal administratif de Melun, n° 1006486/1, 17 December 2010.
108   France: Cour administrative d'appel (CAA) de Paris, *Mme Antonide A.*, N° 09PA02362, 8 February 2010; CESEDA, *op. cit.*, Article L313-14.
109   France: Conseil d'Etat, *M Mourad X* ("*M Mourad X*"), n° 263960, 28 July 2004; France: Conseil d'Etat, *Préfet Du Val-D'oise* ("*Préfet Du Val-D'oise*"), n° 273072, 27 july 2005; France: Conseil d'Etat, *M. Kamel X* ("*M. Kamel X*"), n° 258742, 26 May 2004.
110   J. McAdam, *Climate Change, Forced Migration, and International Law* (2012), *op. cit.*, pp. 106–112.
111   *Ibid.*, pp. 109–110.
112   V.O. Kolmannskog and F. Myrstad (2009), *op. cit.*, p. 324.

work visa program for Haitians willing to move to Brazil. The visas are to be applied for at the Brazilian embassy in Haiti; one thousand two hundred visas are to be issued per year. The Brazilian Government notes that for this special type of visas, "proof of labor skills and employment relationship will not be required".[113] The measure was praised by the High Commissioner for Refugees, António Guterres who, reiterating that Haitians, as persons displaced by an environmental disaster, were not refugees under the Refugee Convention, stated that Brazil had hence found "a pragmatic approach to recognize their need for protection".[114]

UNHCR reports additional examples and analyses that:

> ... there are many examples of states granting permission to remain, or at the very least granting a stay of deportation, to persons whose country of origin has been hit by a natural disaster or another extreme such event.[115]

To conclude, although they are often limited, in time in particular,[116] and dependent on States' good will, some measures were and are adopted, on a

---

113   Brazil: Resolução Normativa N° 97: Dispõe Sobre a Concessão Do Visto Permanente Previsto No Art. 16 Da Lei N° 6.815, de 19 de Agostode 1980, a Nacionais Do Haiti of 12 January 2012; Secretariat for Social Communications of the Federative Republic of Brazil, "Brazilian Government Establishes Special Haiti Work Visa Program" (Portal Brasil, 2012), press release, 13 January 2012, retrieved from: <www.brasil.gov.br/para/press/press-releases/january-2012/brazilian-government-establishes-special-haiti-work-visa-program/br_model1?set_language=en> [25/06/2012].

114   UNHCR / L.F. Godinho, "Rio+20 summit: UN refugee chief calls for joint approach to urban refugees, displaced", 21 June 2012, retrieved from the UNHCR website at: <http://www.unhcr.org/news/latest/2012/6/4fe2e7d76/rio20-summit-un-refugee-chief-calls-joint-approach-urban-refugees-displaced.html> [29/06/2012].

115   UNHCR, *The State of the World's Refugees 2012: In Search of Solidarity* (2012), op. cit., p. 186.

116   In that sense, the non-governmental organisation Migrants d'Outre-Mer notes that courts do not find it illegal to issue an expulsion order against Haitians but, "to the most", call upon authorities not to implement it "immediately". "L'expulsion d'un Haïtien est légale.... mais à exécuter un peu plus tard" (Migrants Outre-Mer, 1950–2012), 5 March 2010, retrieved from: <www.migrantsoutremer.org/Mesures-d-eloignement-vers-Haiti> [12/03/2011]. The article refers in particular to the decision of a Cour administrative d'appel which concludes that administrative authorities should indeed refrain from "immediately" implementing their decision, in view of the extremely precarious living conditions in the country caused by the earthquake, this "major natural catastrophe". "*Considérant que s'il appartient à l'administration, eu égard au séisme d'une gravité exceptionnelle survenu en Haïti le 12 janvier 2010, de veiller à ne pas mettre immédiatement à exécution l'obligation faite au requérant de quitter le territoire français à destination de ce pays, compte tenu de la*

case-by-case basis to alleviate the dire humanitarian situation in which victims of environmental disasters found themselves. As a matter of fact, the Nansen Initiative found, through the consultations it conducted from 2012 to 2015, that at least fifty countries in the world had agreed to receive or had refrained from returning disaster-displaced persons.[117]

---

situation d'extrême précarité des conditions de vie qui y prévaut actuellement du fait de cette catastrophe naturelle majeure, il résulte de ce qui précède que l'arrêté attaqué n'est entaché d'aucune illégalité" France: Cour administrative d'appel de Versailles, *M. Michelet A* ("*M. Michelet A*"), 09VE00667, 9 February 2010.

117 N. Initiative, *Fleeing Floods, Earthquakes, Droughts and Rising Sea Levels: 12 Lessons Learned About Protecting People Displaced by Disasters and the Effects of Climate Change* (*Fleeing Floods, Earthquakes, Droughts and Rising Sea Levels*) (Geneva: Nansen Initiative, October 2015), p. 20.

CHAPTER 9

Conclusions of Part 2

From the examination of existing norms, of their current interpretation, and of practices, it can be concluded that, as law and practice stand, it is unlikely that European States grant protection to persons who were forced to leave their home and country by reason of a sudden or slow degradation of the environment there. It should be borne in mind that the circumstance that flight is partly or predominantly triggered by environmental disaster does not in and of itself exclude international protection. If claimants fulfil the standard requirements for protection, they should be granted protection, irrespective of the existence of other factors or circumstances surrounding their claim. If an applicant demonstrates a well-founded fear of being persecuted (due to State and non-State actors' actions or due to the unwillingness or inability of actors of protection to fulfil their role) by reason of his or her belonging to a Refugee Convention-protected group, or a real risk of serious harm (Article 15 QD), of Article 3 ECHR ill-treatment or of complete denial or nullification of any of his or her right, he or she should be granted the corresponding status or protection.

The assessment of a claim for international protection – at large, that is, refugee status, subsidiary protection and other forms of complementary protection including *non-refoulement* broadly and temporary protection – could be conceived as the assemblage of a clockwork. As long as the required pieces are put together, the existence of spare parts does not affect the functioning of the clockwork; to the most, they can replace a defective part. In like manner, the circumstance of an environmental disaster does not make a claim for international protection on the ground of a well-founded fear of persecution or of real risk of serious harm or ill-treatment less valid. A context of environmental disaster can however substantiate a claim, not least by establishing the existence of dire humanitarian conditions despite the non-existence of an armed conflict.

There could be two possible ways to look at State practice. Firstly, States have not adopted (yet) any legal instrument at either regional or global level whereby they would bind themselves to grant protection to persons displaced in the event of an environmental disaster. They instead choose to act, on a discretionary, *ad hoc* basis. On the other hand, a number of States do adopt measures, temporary for the most part, to protect individuals fleeing dire humanitarian conditions, including in the aftermath of an environmental disaster. This is a sign that they indeed recognise the seriousness of the threats populations are exposed to, by reason of environmental degradation or the general deterioration of conditions of living in a country. It is armed with the latter perception of State practice that Part 3 will undertake to explore ways of addressing the question of the international protection of environmentally-displaced persons.

PART 3

Exploring Means of Protecting "environmental refugees" in International Law

∵

Introduction to Part 3

> Migration is not just a failure of adaptation; it is also one of the possible adaptation strategies to climate and environmental change.[1]

As concluded in Part 2, it is very unlikely that existing instruments of international law can or will be implemented to protect persons who are forced to cross a State international border due to the detrimental effects of an environmental disaster. On the other hand, although estimates vary widely, the reality of the phenomenon is unchallenged: environmental change always did and will cause populations to move in search of inhabitable or less inhospitable places. The other certainty is that, under the influence of global warming, the environment will change in every region of the world. In 2008, the Under-Secretary-General for Humanitarian Affairs and Emergency Relief Coordinator hence warned:

> What we are witnessing is not an aberration, but rather a "curtain raiser" on the future. These events are not abnormal; they're what I call the "new normal".[2]

A number of mechanisms, laws and policies, although they might not be directly applicable to the case of environmentally-induced migrations, are nevertheless worth elaborating upon as they can provide interesting angles of inquiry.

An obvious remedy would be the adoption of a new international convention relating specifically to environmentally-displaced persons. But prior to discussing such an eventuality, we will need to ponder on existing norms of international law and their eventual potentialities. As shown in the previous Part, the Refugee Convention is neither directly applicable nor is it applied to address the protection needs of environmentally-displaced persons. It is nevertheless the subject of heated discussions in literature. Some claim it is underestimated whereas others find it obsolete. The former call for the constructive interpretation of the text; this, they argue, would be in line with the original object and purpose of the Convention and would ensure that any situation

---

1 IOM, "Migration and Climate Change: A Complex Nexus", *op. cit.*
2 S.J. Holmes, "Opening Remarks by Sir John Holmes, USG for Humanitarian Affairs and ERC at the DIHAD 2008 Conference", *News and Press Release*, 08/04/2008 (New York: UN Office for the Coordination of Humanitarian Affairs), 3.

that may arise in which international protection is called for fall within the scope of the Refugee Convention. The latter advocate instead for the revision of the contemporary refugee definition.

Coming back to the argument that solution are to be extracted, through a constructive interpretation of their terms, from existing instruments of international law, some authors also recommend national policy makers to interpret the relevant human rights provisions in a progressive manner. Some others seek for answer in environmental law and the rules on State responsibility.

The present Part will give a critical overview of the different protection alternatives currently discussed and suggest other, possibly new, angles of inquiry. The first protection options considered below rely on existing norms of the international protection regime enshrined in refugee law and human rights law (Chapter 10). The question whether State responsibility should play a role in devising a form of protection for environmentally-displaced persons will then be addressed (Chapter 11). Lastly, this Part will take on to formulate elements of a *sui generis* regime for environmentally-displaced persons, which borrows from and articulates some of the various instruments, rules and principles identified throughout this work. Chapter 12 will indeed envisage the creation of a framework, where the problem of environmental displacement is addressed with due regard to its complexity: its causes, modalities and implications are indeed varied and all need to be dealt with. Different mechanisms can be envisaged, which would develop within the framework of existing fora (such as the UN Framework Convention on Climate Change – UNFCCC) and borrow from various areas of law and policy to address environmentally-induced displacements with a holistic approach. Notions pertaining to State responsibility at large or for environmental harm in particular, to environmental law, migration law, humanitarian and human rights law but also to taxation and insurance must, *inter alia*, be used.

CHAPTER 10

Solutions Based on Existing Asylum Law and Relevant Norms International Human Rights Law

It was concluded in the previous Part that under existing norms of refugee and human rights law, in their current reading and interpretation, environmentally-displaced persons had little chances to receive international protection. As a consequence, the present Chapter will turn to envisage various possible interpretations of or amendments to existing norms of asylum law (I) and human rights law (II) likely to bring environmentally-displaced persons within the ambit of protection of either of these bodies of norms.

I   Drawing Upon Existing Asylum Law

Existing asylum law applies to and protects millions of people around the world. Since the Refugee Convention was adopted, in 1951, the content and scope of refugee law has experienced a number of developments, so that its relevance to address contemporary needs of international protection be safeguarded. In today's world, instances of environmentally-triggered displacement of populations raise concerns as to the means to protect those persons who are compelled to leave their homes due to the degradation of their living environment, and sometimes seek refuge across the border of their home State. It comes with no surprise that solutions to address their legal status and protection needs are sought within the body of norms and principles of refugee law. The Refugee Convention, as the cornerstone of international refugee law will be considerd first: can it be re-interpreted or recast so as to protect environmentally-displaced persons (A)? Alternatively, the relevance of subsidiary protection should be considered. Originally designed to provide protection to those whom the Refugee Convention failed to protect, could subsidiary protection apply to environmentally-displaced persons (B)? Within the European Union, another instrument to be taken into consideration, as an element of the EU acquis on asylum, is the Temporary Protection Directive. Could it be triggered in the event of an environmental disaster and hence protect, albeit temporarily, persons from being sent back to such situation (C)?

An additional avenue to explore is the concept of "internal protection alternative". We will argue that this aspect of status determination, when it is read together with States' human rights obligations and the principle of non-discrimination, points towards a broadening of the scope of *non-refoulement*, which would benefit environmentally-displaced persons (D).

A   *The Refugee Convention: Obsolete or Underestimated?*

Some stigmatise the 1951 Refugee Convention as a "product of its time",[1] not anymore "fit for its purpose".[2] Possibly aimed as a criticism, this is but a fact; the adoption of the Convention was triggered by the Second World War and the atrocities which affected targeted communities, defined by their (perceived or actual) common race, religion, nationality, political opinion or belonging to a particular social group. The wording of the refugee definition adopted at that time is reflective of the contemporary concerns of the international community.[3] Building on this observation, two proposals are made in literature. Firstly, the Refugee Convention is outdated but not obsolete: it could cover the needs of environmentally-displaced persons, among other persons in need of international protection, provided that a constructive interpretation of the text is adopted. Secondly, the Refugee Convention is indeed obsolete and must be "amended": the refugee definition should be reformulated or complemented by means of an amendment to the text or through the adoption of a new Protocol[4] so that environmentally-displaced persons enter the scope of Convention.

Although the Convention is criticised by some for being of too narrow a scope, not suited to address the needs of all persons in need of protection, the authors of the Convention could actually be praised for having opted for a refugee definition by categories for it made clear, by excluding them, that more categories of persons were in fact worthy of international protection. "Practice shows that focusing for decision purposes on a rather narrow set of issues in fact permits States to identify other categories of persons who should

---

1   J.B. Cooper (1998), *op. cit.*, p. 482.
2   E. West, "It's Not the Home Office's Fault: The UN Convention on Refugees Is Not Fit for Purpose", *The Telegraph*, 11 January 2011.
3   In that sense, *see* for example S.M. Akram and T. Rempel (2004), *op. cit.*, p. 7 and references cited.
4   For example, Republic of the Maldives, Ministry of Environment, Energy and Water, Report on the First Meeting on Protocol on Environmental Refugees: Recognition of Environmental Refugees in the 1951 Convention and 1967 Protocol Relating to the Status of Refugees (Male, Maldives, 14–15 August 2006), cited in F. Biermann and I. Boas, "Protecting Climate Refugees: The Case for a Global Protocol", *Environment*, November-December 2008, retrieved from: <www.environmentmagazine.org/Archives/Back%20Issues/November-December%202008/Biermann-Boas-full.html> [21/04/2012]. *See* also: H. Grant, *et al.*, "UK Should Open Borders to Climate Refugees, Says Bangladeshi Minister", *The Guardian*, 4 December 2009.

be protected".[5] Can the 1951 Refugee Convention take account of its limits and allow under its scope additional categories of persons in need of international protection? Two means to this end will be considered: a constructive interpretation of the Convention and its amendment (formally or by means of an additional protocol).

1   A Constructive Interpretation of the Refugee Convention: Unconvincing and Unlikely

To include environmentally-displaced persons in the scope of the Refugee Convention, in the absence of any formal modification of the original provisions, requires a constructive interpretation of the text. Prior to considering how to interpret the Convention so as to provide protection to any person displaced by the detrimental alteration of their living environment (b and c), it is worth recalling the prevailing rules on the interpretation of international treaties and looking at the drafting history of the Convention (a).

(a)   *Preparatory Work of the Refugee Convention: Did States Foresee the Expansion of the Refugee Definition?*

Pursuant to the VCLT,[6] any treaty must be interpreted "in good faith in accordance with the ordinary meaning to be given to the terms of the treaty in their context and in the light of its object and purpose".[7] The object and purpose of the Refugee Convention are clear, unambiguously informed by the context of its adoption, and confirmed by the Preamble of the Convention – which, as indicated by the VCLT, is to be considered as part of the text of a treaty.[8] The Preamble explains that the Refugee Convention aims at assuring refugees the widest possible exercise of the fundamental rights and freedoms enshrined in the Charter of the United Nations and the Universal Declaration of Human Rights.[9] It further clarifies the humanitarian purpose of the Convention.[10]

Key to this discussion, Article 31(2)(a) of the Vienna Convention on the Law of Treaties deserves to be reproduced here. It provides as follows:

---

5   G.S. Goodwin-Gill, "Asylum 2001: A Convention and a Purpose", *International Journal of Refugee Law*, Vol. 13, No. 1–2 (2001), Editorial, p. 7.
6   United Nations, *Vienna Convention on the Law of Treaties*, 23 May 1969, United Nations, Treaty Series, vol. 1155, p. 331.
7   VCLT, Article 31(1).
8   *Ibid.*, Article 31(2).
9   Refugee Convention, Preamble, §§ 1–2.
10   "Expressing the wish that all States, recognizing the social and humanitarian nature of the problem of refugees, will do everything within their power to prevent this problem from becoming a cause of tension between States". *Ibid.*, Preamble, § 5.

> The context for the purpose of the interpretation of a treaty shall comprise, in addition to the text (...) any agreement relating to the treaty which was made between all the parties in connexion with the conclusion of the treaty.[11]

Important as it is, this provision invites commentators to take into consideration those acts which were agreed upon by the drafters, at the time the Refugee Convention was signed. On the day the Refugee Convention was concluded, the Conference of Plenipotentiaries also adopted the "Final Act", carrying five recommendations. Those recommendations were adopted unanimously – which fulfils article 31(1)(b) requirement that the instrument resorted to for the purpose of the interpretation of the treaty be made "between all parties".

Recommendation E of the Final Act in particular could turn out to be a powerful tool for a constructive interpretation of the 1951 Convention. It reads as follows:

> The Conference expresses the hope that the Convention relating to the Status of Refugees will have value as an example exceeding its contractual scope and that all nations will be guided by it in granting so far as possible to persons in their territory as refugees and who would not be covered by the terms of the Convention, the treatment for which it provides.[12]

This suggests that the drafters of the Convention had envisaged its expansion to new categories of refugees but let us explore the Convention's *travaux préparatoires* before we draw the potential consequences of Recommendation E on the interpretation of the Convention as an instrument capable of protecting environmental refugees.

During the numerous meetings that preceded the adoption of the Convention, heated discussions took place on the formulation of the refugee definition. Many proposals were made, justified by varying theories and considerations. In particular, States participating in the drafting process[13] were split

---

11   VCLT, Article 31(2)(a).
12   Refugee Convention, Final Act, Recommendation E.
13   At the earliest stage, 13 States constituted the Ad Hoc Committee on Statelessness and Related Problems (New York, 16/01/1950 to 16/02/1950): Belgium, Brazil, Canada, China, Denmark, France, Israel, Poland, Turkey, the Union of Soviet Socialist Republics, the United Kingdom, the United States and Venezuela. The Soviet Union and Poland however resigned on the first day in protest against the representation of China in the Committee by the Nationalist government on Taiwan, which they did not consider as a legitimate UN member (UN Ad Hoc Committee on Refugees and Stateless Persons, "Report of the Ad

over whether to adopt a broad-encompassing refugee definition, phrased in general terms, or to identify in advance categories of persons in need of protection. The leading Western powers at the time, namely France, the United Kingdom, and the United States were in fact divided in this debate. The United Kingdom[14] was in favour of a universal refugee definition; the United States on the other hand supported the adoption of a definition by categories. The French position was somewhat hybrid: its delegation first appeared, in the draft Convention it initially submitted, as a strong proponent of universalism but later sided with the other party and insisted on maintaining a geographical limitation ("events occurring *in Europe*"[15]) in the refugee definition.

In the earlier stages of the drafting process however, the French delegation advocated conceiving the definition of refugees "in the most generous spirit".[16] To justify this approach, France invoked the then recently adopted Universal Declaration of Human Rights[17]: when adopting the Declaration, the Member State of the United Nations undertook "to ensure universal and effective respect for human rights and fundamental freedoms". States proclaimed that every individual, without discrimination was entitled to the rights enshrined in the UNDHR. Accordingly, whether as national States *vis-à-vis* their citizens, or as host States vis-à-vis refugees (or migrants one could add), the UN Member States shall endeavour to safeguard those rights to all.[18] In other words,

---

Hoc Committee on Statelessness and Related Persons (Lake Success, New York, 16 January to 16 February 1950)" ("E/AC.35/5"), E/1618, E/AC.35/5, 17 February 1950, §§ 2 and 10.) During the following discussions in the Social Committee of the ECOSOC (31/07/1950 to 10/08/1950), the representatives of 15 States convened to discuss the Ad Hoc Committee report. The issue was then brought to the General Assembly where 56 States voted on the proposal submitted by the UNGA Third Committee (41 in favour, 5 against, 10 blank). Despite the large participation observed in the vote in the General Assembly, only 25 States (23 initially) showed their interest in entering a "refugee convention" and appeared in the Conference of Plenipotentiaries, where the 1951 Refugee Convention was eventually adopted and ratified by most (the United States signed but did not ratify).

14   UN Ad Hoc Committee on Refugees and Stateless Persons, Ad Hoc Committee on Statelessness and Related Problems, "United Kingdom: Revised Draft Proposal for Article 1 (E/AC.32/2)", E/AC.32/L.2/Rev.1, 19 January 1950.
15   Refugee Convention, Article 1B.
16   UN Conference of Plenipotentiaries on the Status of Refugees and Stateless Persons, "Summary Record of the Nineteenth Meeting" ("A/CONF.2/SR.19"), 26 November 1951, statement by M. Rochefort on behalf of the French government.
17   UDHR, op. cit.
18   UN Ad Hoc Committee on Refugees and Stateless Persons, Ad Hoc Committee on Statelessness and Related Problems, "France: Proposal for a Draft Convention Preamble", E/AC.32/L.3, 17 January 1950, Preamble, para. 2.

every person, without discrimination, must be able to claim the protection of a State: the protection of his or her country of origin or, in the absence thereof, the protection of a host country. Accordingly, the definition proposed by the French delegation was broad-encompassing and identified as refugees any person who:

(a) seeking asylum or having been granted asylum under the conditions specified in Article 14 of the Universal Declaration of Human Rights; or
(b) having left his country of origin and refusing to return thereto owing to a justifiable fear of persecution, or having been unable to obtain from that country permission to return,
(c) for either of the reasons indicated in sub-paragraph (b) above, is unwilling or unable to claim the protection of the said country;

Proponent of the opposite theory, the United States suggested following the pre-existing practice of identifying the different categories of refugees on the basis of nationality or origin, or by referring to specific events (temporal and geographical constraints). As the United States representative later clarified,[19] the proposal submitted by the US delegation[20] encompassed four categories of persons. The first was clearly defined and comprised the "so-called refugees of the First World War: Russians, Armenians, Assyrians and assimilated, the fate of whom had already been settled by previous conventions".[21] The second group was just as narrowly defined: the German, Austrian, Czechoslovak, Italian and Spanish victims of Nazism, Fascism (or allied regimes) and Falangism who were outside their country of origin because of persecution or fear of persecution on account of race, nationality, religion or political belief.[22] In the third group were protected the "neo-refugees",[23] a category that will be further elaborated upon below. Lastly, the fourth group covered displaced persons

---

19 UN Ad Hoc Committee on Refugees and Stateless Persons, Ad Hoc Committee on Statelessness and Related Problems, "First Session: Summary Record of the Third Meeting Held at Lake Success, New York, on Tuesday, 17 January 1950, at 3 P.M." ("E/AC.32/SR.3"), E/AC.32/SR.3, 26 January 1950, §§ 42–50.
20 UN Ad Hoc Committee on Refugees and Stateless Persons, Ad Hoc Committee on Statelessness and Related Problems, "United States of America: Memorandum on the Definition Article of the Preliminary Draft Convention Relating to the Status of Refugees (and Stateless Persons) (E/AC.32.2)" ("E/AC.32/L.4"), E/AC.32/L.4, 18 January 1950.
21 *Ibid.*, Article 1A(1).
22 *Ibid.*, Article 1A(2)(a) and (b).
23 *Ibid.*, Article 1A(2)(c).

and unaccompanied children.[24] As an aside, it should be noted that the term "displaced persons" used in the US proposal is not to be mistaken as describing "internally displaced persons" (IDPs). In the US draft definition, the group of "displaced persons" is essentially similar to the first group, but with no criterion of nationality: it covers any person who has been deported or displaced from his or her country of origin by Nazism or Fascism or a sympathiser regime.[25]

The third group is particularly worth commenting on. A "neo-refugees" was defined as any person who was not a refugee under any of the three other categories and who:

> ... as a result of events subsequent to the outbreak of the Second World War, is unable or unwilling to avail himself of the protection of the government of his country of nationality or former nationality, and who has not acquired another nationality.[26]

Formulated in broader terms than the other three, according to the French delegate, this category could and should cover "[n]ew categories of refuges not explicitly covered by the convention, and which might come into existence as a result of later events".[27] Such was however not the scope the United States intended to give to this category. Firmly opposed to signing a "blank check" whereby they would undertake to protect unknown numbers of refugees, the US delegate clarified that if the provisions indeed aimed at permitting the inclusion of new groups in the convention, such an inclusion would in any case not be automatic but would require the adoption of "protocols, addenda or later agreements".[28]

Considerable discussions continued to oppose States within the Ad Hoc Committee until it was agreed by consensus that the refugee definition would identify categories of beneficiaries. Similar debates took place within the Economic and Social Council and lead, for the same reasons, to the same decision of principle: the refugee definition would be a definition by categories. In favour of this conclusion, one key argument, raised within both the Ad Hoc Committee and the Economic and Social Council, was that more States would be inclined to adhere to a convention which clearly defined, in a foreseeable

---

24   Ibid., Article 1A(3).
25   Ibid., Article 1A(3)(a).
26   Ibid., Article 1A(2)(c).
27   "E/AC.32/SR.3", op. cit., § 50.
28   Ibid. § 54.

manner, the scope of their obligations under it.²⁹ The Ad Hoc Committee submitted a draft to the Economic and Social Council (ECOSOC), who considered it together with other drafts: the Belgian and British proposals were in favour of a general definition, whereas the French delegation had drafted a definition by categories. The Economic and Social Council, taking into account the different arguments put forward before it, amended the Committee's draft refugee definition relying on the French new proposal. In so doing, the Economic and Social Council adopted a broadened refugee definition. The categories of beneficiaries were expanded: no specific nationality or origin was mentioned. The main criteria for identifying the different groups of persons in need of protection were temporal and geographical elements: the Council's definition covered any persons outside their country of origin with a well-founded fear of being persecuted for reasons of race, religion, nationality or political opinion, "as a result of events in Europe before 1 January 1951, or circumstances directly resulting from such events" and who are unable or unwilling to avail himself or herself of the protection of their government.³⁰

The revised draft, adopted by the Economic and Social Council, was submitted by the Ad Hoc Committee to the United Nations General Assembly. Several other drafts, proposed by Belgium, Canada, Turkey and the UK, as advocates of the universalistic definition, and a Venezuelan draft, representing the adverse view, were also submitted to the UNGA. The definition eventually adopted by the UNGA was largely based on the ECOSOC draft and included those persons who had been identified as refugees in previous treaties as well as any person who:

> As a result of events occurring before 1 January 1951, and owing to well-founded fear of being persecuted for reason of race, religion, nationality or political opinion is outside the country of his nationality, or, owing to such fear or for reasons other than personal convenience, is unwilling to avail himself of the protection of that country; or who, not having a nationality and being outside the country of his former habitual residence,

---

29   See in that sense: "E/AC.35/5", *op. cit.*, p. 38; and UN Economic and Social Council, "UN ESCOR, 11th Session, 158th Meeting"; summarised in "Background Paper Submitted by the Office of the UNHCR", *Colloquium on the development in the law of refugees with particular reference to the 1951 Convention and the Statute of the Office of the United Nations High Commissioner for Refugees, Villa Serbelloni Bellagio (Italy), 21–28 April 1965*, MHCR/23/65; 67-1809, 28 April 1965, note 53.

30   UN ECOSOC, "Resolutions 319 (XI): Refugees and Stateless Persons" ("Resolutions 319 (XI)"), E/RES/319 (XI), 11 and 16 August 1950, pp. 52–59, Resolution B: Draft Convention relating to the status of refugees, pp. 56–59, Article 1A(3).

is unable or owing to such fear or for reasons other than personal convenience, is unwilling to return to it.[31]

This definition, very similar to the one eventually adopted in the 1951 Refugee Convention, nevertheless differs from it on one key element: the geographical limitation is absent. It was only on the insistence of France that the terms "in Europe" were reintroduced in the text prior to its final adoption. Again, proponents and opponents of universalism opposed on this issue and eventually agreed that States would be given the choice to decide whether they wanted to reserve refugee protection for victims of events that had occurred – before 1 January 1951 – in Europe only or to undertake broader obligations under the Convention by considering refugee situations caused by events occurring "in Europe and elsewhere".[32] Only seven of the 19 signatories at the time adopted the first of the two alternatives. In other words, the majority of Contracting States (nearly three out of four) favoured universalism.

Throughout the drafting process of the Refugee Convention, the United Kingdom maintained its position as proponent of universalism. It is therefore not surprising that the proposal to adopt what is known as "Recommendation E" emanated from the British delegation.[33] As already mentioned, the possibility that the scope of the Convention be subsequently expanded had been anticipated by the United States. A similar provision was incorporated in the majority of the drafts submitted by the various governments and committees, either in the form of an additional paragraph to Article 1,[34] or of a recital in the preamble.[35] Two methods were foreseen for the inclusion of new categories

---

31 UNGA, "Draft Convention Relating to the Status of Refugees" ("UNGA"), A/RES/429, 14 December 1950, Annex, Article 1A(2).

32 *Ibid.*, Article 1B(1).

33 The recommendation, as it was originally phrased by the UK, referred to "refugees (...) who would not be covered by the terms of paragraph A of Article 1". The UK delegation proposed to delete the reference to Article 1A after the French representative had expressed his fear that the initially proposed wording would stigmatise those States who had introduced a geographical limitation in the definition of refugees under Article 1A, *i.e.* in particular, France. All States, including France, agreed to this modified version of the recommendation and adopted Recommendation E unanimously. UN Conference of Plenipotentiaries on the Status of Refugees and Stateless Persons, "Draft Convention Relating to the Status of Refugees, United Kingdom: Recommendation for Inclusion in the Final Act", A/CONF.2/107, 25 July 1951.

34 UN ECOSOC, "France: Amendment to the Draft Convention Relating to the Status of Refugees", UN Doc. E/L.82, 29 July 1950, Article 1B.

35 "Resolutions 319 (XI)", *op. cit.*, Resolution B, Preamble, recital 7.

of persons in need of protection: it was necessarily recommended by the UN General Assembly or additionally, States could freely undertake it. To briefly summarise the lengthy discussions concerning such provision, one can observe that the vast majority of States believed that the Convention should provide for the possibility of its extension. States however failed to agree on technical and procedural aspects: in which part of the text does the provision belong? Who can define additional categories of refugees and following which procedure? The British proposal settled the dispute. The UK delegate, M Hoare, stressed that "it was right that the Conference should express a sentiment such as that contained in the paragraph" but suggested that, instead of a paragraph in the Preamble of the Convention, and more than a mere declaration, the possible future expansion of the scope of the Convention to cover new categories of refugees should be a recommendation, supplementing the text of the Convention.[36] After France's initial concerns were dispelled by means of a modification of the draft, Recommendation E was adopted unanimously by the 23 member States of the Conference of Plenipotentiaries.[37] In other words, the drafters of the Convention agreed that the Convention could apply on an "ever-widening scale".[38]

The lengthy developments above, on the preparatory work of the Convention meant to illustrate that, by and large, the international community of States that were involved in the Convention's drafting process were in favour of a broad refugee definition. The pre-existing practice of adopting *ad hoc* instruments of international law, devised to address the needs of newly emerged categories of refugees has been abandoned.[39] The Refugee Convention defines in broader terms persons who qualify for the status of refugee. The geographical limitation reintroduced at the insistence of France was not adopted by many and, in any case, soon "deleted" by the 1967 Protocol. With the Protocol, the temporal limitation also was omitted from the refugee definition.

The United States and France (at the Conference of Plenipotentiaries especially) manifested themselves as opponents of the universalistic approach.

---

36   UN Conference of Plenipotentiaries on the Status of Refugees and Stateless Persons, "Summary Record of the 31st Meeting", 20 July 1951, p. 24.

37   Twenty-four States were members of the Conference of Plenipotentiaries however, the United Kingdom being at the initiative of the proposed recommendation, it could not take part in the vote.

38   The term was used by the Representative of France to describe the original draft Article 1 of the Convention; it is however pertinent to describe Recommendation E also. "A/CONF.2/SR.19", *op. cit.*, Statement by M. Rochefort.

39   The same conclusion is reached by Jane McAdam in J. McAdam, *Complementary Protection in International Refugee Law* (2007), *op. cit.*, p. 31.

It is nonetheless possible to nuance the observation. France explained its position in the Conference of Plenipotentiaries. Accordingly, the delegation urged the Conference to limit the scope of the Convention to Europe after it had noticed that some States, who initially showed their interest in securing a refugee definition drafted in general terms, were not anymore taking part in the negotiations. France questioned their genuine interest in the adoption of a refugee convention and in fact suspected those States had participated in the earlier discussions in order to foster the adoption of the universalistic definition as this would serve their cause best: States parties to the Convention would undertake to protect any refugee, regardless of his or her nationality and origin. Those States had been willing to place the burden of asylum on European States (sic) but did not manifest their readiness to themselves undertake to grant refugee status as defined under the Convention. "One problem was ready to form the subject of an international convention, namely, the problem of the European refugees".[40] The fact that those States did not take part in the final negotiations, in the Conference of Plenipotentiaries, demonstrated, in the French delegate's opinion, that they in fact had no intention to themselves adhere to the Convention. France switching side and seemingly abandoning the view that international protection should be "conceived in the most generous spirit" and applied "on an ever-widening scale" might actually be pragmatism, possibly tinged with bitterness, rather than a shift away from its initial position.

As for the United States' position, pragmatism might also be underlying. Hence M Warren, representative of the United States, urging the Conference of Plenipotentiaries that "one constructive step should be taken at a time": a convention drafted to meet European requirements was, accordingly, the first step. This seems to be confirmed by the following sentence of his statement:

> ... the development of an unrestricted charter for refugees would involve a certain amount of duplication of effort between the preparation of the draft International Covenant on Human Rights and the drafting of the Refugee Convention, and would represent a very much larger undertaking, in which the United States Government would be only too willing to participate if and when it was clearly understood that such was the objective.[41]

The US delegation thus expresses its willingness to take part, in the future, in further developments of international refugee law.

---

40   "A/CONF.2/SR.19", *op. cit.*, Statement by M Rochefort, § 10.
41   *Ibid.*, Statement by M Warren, § 3.

For these reasons, in view of the humanitarian object and purpose of the Convention, apparent in the preparatory work, in the various opinions expressed by its drafters and eventually in the Convention Preamble,[42] it seems that the 1951 Refugee Convention could be interpreted in a constructive way so as to extend the protection it provide to additional categories. Will this however be sufficient to include environmental refugees in its scope?

(b)   *A Possible Re-interpretation of Article 1A to Include "Environmental Refugees"?*

The previous Part addressed the question whether environmentally-displaced persons fitted in the scope of the Convention as it is currently interpreted and implemented. The conclusion was negative. Whether a "renewed" interpretation of the Convention is conceivable is discussed below. Then again, the conclusion is mainly negative.

Article 1A(2) provides that alleged acts of persecution will only be considered as such if they are related to one of the five enumerated grounds; the language of the provision is clear, only when this causal link with any of the five Convention grounds exists is the person concerned a refugee.

> [T]he definition does not leave open for interpretation the reasons for persecution, but instead it includes an exhaustive list of "race, religion, nationality, membership of a particular social group or political opinion", clearly setting the boundaries of the legal application of the Refugee Convention.[43]

Race, religion, nationality and political opinion are clear-cut notions which necessitate no or little interpretation. The notion of "particular social group" is in turn more ambiguous and has produced much literature. It is open to interpretation and the reason for its inclusion in the Convention in the first place is unclear. As noted by G.S. Goodwin-Gill and J. McAdam, the *travaux préparatoires* do not clarify whether the notion "was expected or intended to apply generally to then unrecognized groups facing new forms of protection".[44] The authors further note that there is no reason why this ground, "should not be progressively developed".[45] Proponents of the inclusion of environmentally-displaced

---

42   Refugee Convention, Preamble Recital 5.
43   A. Williams, "Turning the Tide: Recognizing Climate Change Refugees in International Law", *Law & Policy*, Vol. 30, No. 4 (October 2008), p. 508.
44   G.S. Goodwin-Gill and J. McAdam, *The Refugee in International Law* (2007), *op. cit.*, p. 74.
45   *Ibid.*, p. 74.

persons under the umbrella of the Convention, as refugees, therefore rightly sought to propose an interpretation of the concept of social group to accommodate their theory.

Those arguing that "environmental refugees" meet the requirements of the Refugee Convention refugee definition have in fact demonstrated commendable interpretative creativity when attempting to fulfil this criterion. The five grounds for persecution are central to the refugee definition. Accused by some of being a "product of its time",[46] not anymore "fit for its purpose", the Refugee Convention is undoubtedly reflective of the context in which it was adopted: the aftermath of the Second World War. The five relevant grounds of persecution the Convention unmistakably bear witness of the personal characteristics of the groups persecuted in the context of the War.[47] To constitute an act of persecution, the alleged harmful treatment must be justified, in the mind of the persecutor, by the victim's race, religion, nationality, membership in a particular social group or political opinion, be it presumed or real. In order to be recognised as a Convention refugee, a person fleeing an environmental disaster would need to link the threat they allege to at least one of those grounds. "Membership of a particular social group" being the broadest of the five grounds, authors have resorted to it.

Jessica B. Cooper in particular argued that "environmental refugees" were persecuted for reasons of their membership in a group of persons lacking political power to protect their own environment. It would be "on account of their political disempowerment that these people become victims of their environmental degradation".[48] The group in question, she argues, exists independently of the persecution. The author provides examples of such groups. Populations displaced by the desertification of the Sahel would constitute a social group: it would be because they lack the political power to protect their environment that African governments continue to subject them to environmental degradation.[49] Likewise, J. Cooper continues, Soviet citizens' lack of political power

---

46   J.B. Cooper (1998), *op. cit.*, p. 482.
47   *See* for example S.M. Akram and T. Rempel (2004), *op. cit.*, p. 7 and references cited.
48   Jessica B. Cooper cites a ruling by the Federal Court of Australia in *Denissenko v Hasket and Minister for Immigration & Ethnic Affairs* to support her view: the Australian Court ruled that "the phrase, 'particular social group', in the fourth Convention reason, means 'a recognisable or cognisable group within a society that shares some interest or experience in common'". J.B. Cooper (1998), *op. cit.*, p. 522; Australia: Federal Court of Australia, *Olga Denissenko v. Christine Haskett and Minister for Immigration, Local Government and Ethnic Affairs*, unreported (Federal Court, Foster J, 9 May 1996), NG 509 of 1995 FED No. 404/96. On the notion of particular social group: F. Julien-Laferrière (2009), *op. cit.*
49   J.B. Cooper (1998), *op. cit.*, pp. 504–507.

made it possible for the Soviet government to recklessly exploit nuclear power plants near populated but voiceless areas, and subject local populations to the environmental degradation caused by the Chernobyl disaster.[50] The same reasoning is held concerning "climate change refugees": countries which will be confronted to the most severe environmental damage from climate change are predominantly "developing countries with little political power in the global arena", who "do not have the political leverage to halt the global warming that threatens them".[51] Again, populations of developing countries would be environmentally persecuted by reason of their political disempowerment:

> It is precisely because the citizens of the nations to be most severely affected by global warming are members of a "social group" without political power to protect their environment that the governments of the developed world continue to expose them to the risks of environmental degradation.[52]

The argument, albeit innovative, fails to convince. As noted by V.O. Kolmannskog commenting on the proposed interpretation of the "social group" ground: "persecution itself cannot define the social group".[53] In fact, the causal link between so-called "environmental persecution" and the Convention ground of "membership of a particular social group" seems to be misinterpreted.

The historical context of the adoption of the Convention assists in explaining the causal link. Persecutions suffered by the victims of the Second World War (Jews, gypsies, opponents to the 3rd Reich) were the manifestation of the authoritarian regimes' intention to neutralise if not annihilate the targeted groups. When it comes to environmental disasters, it is true that certain groups of victims can be identified such as populations of developed countries, primarily endangered by climate change. It can also be true that the most severely affected by natural disasters are the poorest and less politically empowered:[54] the dire consequences of earthquakes will generally carry more weight on slums than on antiseismic constructions. Observers noted for instance that

---

50   *Ibid.*, pp. 514–519.
51   *Ibid.*, pp. 525s.
52   *Ibid.*, pp. 525s.
53   V.O. Kolmannskog, *Future Floods of Refugees: A Comment on Climate Change, Conflict and Forced Migration* (April 2008), *op. cit.*, p. 27.
54   "… *les victimes font souvent partie des couches sociales les plus démunies*". P. Gonin and V. Lassailly-Jacob, "Les Réfugiés de L'environnement : Une Nouvelle Catégorie de Migrants Forcés ?" *Revue européenne des migrations internationales*, Vol. 18, No. 2 (2002).

after the Bhopal (India) gas leak catastrophe, the most affected population was that living in the vicinity of the pesticide plant, *i.e.* the workers, whereas wealthier families, residing in the upper neighbourhoods, were spared.[55] However, for the purpose of refugee law, the notion of persecution is intrinsically linked with that of discrimination.[56] Female genital mutilation is carried out on women by reason of their gender; homosexuals are threatened by reason of their allegedly reprehensible lifestyle; and Christians in Iran or independent Muslims in Uzbekistan[57] are persecuted by reason of their religion. Those examples illustrate that actions of the persecutor are directed against individuals by reasons of a reproved individual characteristics. Governments however do not willingly inflict harm on or deny protection to populations by reason of their political disempowerment. States contributing – actively or passively – to the occurrence of natural disasters affecting certain populations do not persecute those populations because they reprove of their political disempowerment; instead, the political disempowerment of victimised populations enabled States to act recklessly. It is not the reason for State damageable action but it is the reason why State damageable action could carry through.

This proposed approach to the inclusion of environmentally-displaced persons in the purview of the Refugee Convention through a (re)interpretation of the notion of particular social group therefore fails to convince.

It appears that the only way for it to succeed in protecting environmentally-displaced persons would be to combine it with the adoption of the "predicament" approach advocated by M. Foster.[58] In brief, the reference in the Refugee Convention of a fear of being persecuted "for reasons of" membership of a protected group should not be interpreted as a requirement of an "intentional identification" of the asylum-seeker. Instead, focus should be on "why the person is in the predicament of fearing persecution".[59] An analogy with armed conflict can illustrate the approach: children, the elderly or disabled persons are disproportionately affected in situations of generalised or *indiscriminate* violence however they are not intentionally targeted. This also bears an analogy to indirect discrimination: a measure which is not discriminatory at face value can be discriminatory in effect because by applying the same rule to all,

---

55   *Ibid.*
56   G.S. Goodwin-Gill and J. McAdam, *The Refugee in International Law* (2007), *op. cit.*, p. 70.
57   A. Shields and Human Rights Watch, *Creating Enemies of the State: Religious Persecution in Uzbekistan* (n/a: Human Rights Watch, 2004).
58   M. Foster, *International Refugee Law and Socio-Economic Rights: Refuge from Deprivation* (2007), *op. cit.*, pp. 270–286.
59   *Ibid.*, p. 270.

it disregards the particular needs or vulnerabilities of some groups within the population and hence affects them disproportionately.[60]

Under this approach, members of vulnerable groups (such as children) forced to leave their homes due to the severe deterioration of their living conditions caused by an environmental disaster could be recognised as refugees: they face a disproportionate risk of harm by reason of their particular vulnerability.

Going one step further, drawing on J.C. Cooper's suggestion to define environmentally-displaced persons as one identifiable group: it is not only those vulnerable people within the larger group of environmentally-displaced persons who could be refugees but the group at large. Persons who are displaced by reason of environmental disasters are those who have no means of coping with the disaster; moving is a last resort solution. Displacement would therefore be an indicator of disempowerment and environmentally-displaced persons could be construed as a homogenous group of disempowered people. Assuming for now that this analysis is correct, and following the predicament approach, it would be possible to conclude that the Refugee Convention is applicable to "environmental refugees": States do not contribute to global warming with the intention of harming disempowered populations but those populations, being disempowered, are disproportionately affected by environmental disasters. Environmentally-displaced persons would be individuals who fled from their home because they had a well-founded fear of suffering harm there for reason of their being disempowered. Accordingly, they would be "environmental refugees".

The expansion of the scope of the Refugee Convention on the basis of a constructive interpretation of its terms appears to be overly interpretative for at least three reasons. For one, the predicament approach is far from being predominant; the approach to the causal link ("for reasons of") "undoubtedly remains one of requiring intent".[61] This does mean that in a situation where threats are indiscriminate, persons facing a disproportionate risk of harm cannot receive protection. This however appears to be rather a matter of complementary protection (or expanded refugee definition); under EU law, personal circumstances are taken into consideration to identify a risk of serious harms in situations of indiscriminate threats.[62]

---

60   The analogy is also made by M. Foster. *Ibid.*, p. 271.
61   *Ibid.*, p. 280.
62   As made clear by the Court of Justice in the *Elgafaji* judgment and the sliding scale devised then. CJ, *Elgafaji*.

Secondly, conceiving environmentally-displaced persons as disempowered people who had no choice but to move could have the adverse effect of suggesting that those who stay in affected areas are not in need of protection; it might well be that those who stay are in fact in higher need of protection or assistance.[63]

Thirdly, the same criterion of disempowerment could be used to describe any displaced person, whichever the root cause (or causes) for his or her displacement, rendering the other Convention grounds irrelevant. In other words, such an interpretation of the Refugee Convention definition and of a "particular social group" specifically, rather than constructive, would in fact be "destructive".

What then can be the purpose of Recommendation E?

(c) *Expanding Not the Definition but the Status*

In Europe, the inability of the Refugee Convention to provide protection to all the persons in need of it has already been declared. The EU Qualification Directive creates a new form of protection – subsidiary protection – for persons fleeing threats to their life or person for reasons not pertaining to any Conventional grounds or indiscriminate threats in situations of generalised violence originating in an armed conflict. During the discussions preceding the adoption of the text, States, EU institutions and other stakeholders confronted their views on the necessity or not to adopt such a text, supplementing the existing regime created by the Refugee Convention. The European Commission clarified the reasons for and aims of the Directive in its Explanatory Memorandum to the Directive.

> Although the Geneva Convention is thought to be sufficiently broad and inclusive to provide protection for a significant number of those in need of it, international human rights instruments and Member State practice in this area have extended the scope of international protection still further. The Directive's aim is to provide that a minimum standard of

---

63 The International Organisation for Migration (IOM) observed that "the people most vulnerable to climate change are not necessarily the ones most likely to migrate" since "the ability to migrate is a function of mobility and resources (both financial and social)". O. Brown, *Migration and Climate Change* (2008), op. cit., p. 9. The impacts of climate change on ecosystems and human societies might not only lead to displacement but also to populations being "trapped", by reason of the financial and social barriers they may face which limit their ability to migrate. C. Gray and E. Wise, "Country-Specific Effects of Climate Variability on Human Migration", *Climatic Change*, Vol. 135, No. 3 (2016), pp. 555–568.

subsidiary protection is available to complement the Geneva Convention in all Member States to reflect what has been existing practice at Member State level and as a step towards harmonisation.[64]

The European Commission implicitly stated the inability of the Refugee Convention, even interpreted in a progressive way, to assure international protection to all in need of it. The very fact that the Qualification Directive was adopted confirms that the majority of EU Member States, most of whom had already developed complementary forms of protection supplementing Conventional refugee status, share this view. One can therefore anticipate that European States, who have already objected to applying the Refugee Convention in cases of indiscriminate violence due to armed conflicts, will likewise reject its application to cases of indiscriminate threats linked with an environmental degradation.

Let us now finally turn back to Recommendation E. It expresses:

> ... the hope that the Convention relating to the Status of Refugees will have value as an example exceeding its contractual scope and that all nations will be guided by it in granting so far as possible to persons in their territory as refugees and who would not be covered by the terms of the Convention, the treatment for which it provides.[65]

Some authors argue that this Recommendation justifies that new categories of persons in need of protection be considered as refugees under the Convention. The contention does not appear to be in line with the meaning of the Recommendation though. On its face but also in due consideration of the drafting history of the provision, Recommendation E invites Contracting States to grant the *treatment* for which the Convention provides to persons present on their respective territory as refugees. In other words, States should endeavour to grant refugee status, as a "package" of rights and entitlements, to persons have left their country of origin and are in need of protection. The provision does not invite State Parties to reinterpret the terms of Article 1 nor, *a fortiori*, to amend Article 1 if the need arises; it instead invites States to apply the protection devised in the Convention liberally and respect the rights it enshrines *vis-à-vis* individuals who fall outside the scope of the classical refugee definition but who are nevertheless in need of international protection ("persons in their territory as *refugees*").

---

64 "Commission Proposal QD (2004)", *op. cit.*, p. 13.
65 Refugee Convention, Final Act, Recommendation E.

Such is in fact the interpretation that the High Commissioner for Refugees appears to adopt. UNHCR indicates that:

> ... the dynamic nature of the 1951 Convention, informed by its objective and purpose as well as by developments in related areas of law (human rights law, humanitarian law and international criminal law), offers the possibility for States to extend its application to persons who are in need of international protection beyond the scope of the "classical" refugee definition.[66]

The High Commissioner cites as an example the African Union Refugee Convention[67] and the Cartagena Declaration.[68] Both instruments endorse the Refugee Convention refugee definition and broaden the concept of refugee to encompass further categories of persons in need of protection. As a consequence, in the corresponding regions, refugee status is granted not only to "Convention refugees" but also to persons who flee "external aggression, occupation, foreign domination or events seriously disturbing public order"[69] or "generalized violence, foreign aggression, internal conflicts, massive violation of human rights or other circumstances which have seriously disturbed public order"[70] respectively. Hence, Contracting African States and Signatory Latin American States, while recognising the 1951 Refugee Convention (together with its 1967 Protocol) as the "basic and universal instrument relating to the status of refugees"[71] and urging States to accede to it,[72] chose to reinterpret the term "refugee" in order to adapt the concept of refugee to the reality of their respective regions.[73]

UNHCR but also the Council of Europe in fact long recommended European States to implement an extended refugee definition.[74] The Council of Europe and the Working Group both call upon States to recognise in law the

---

66   UNHCR, "Statement on Article 15(c) QD", *op. cit.*, p. 8.
67   AU Refugee Convention, *op. cit.*
68   Cartagena Declaration, *op. cit.*
69   AU Refugee Convention, Art. I(2).
70   Cartagena Declaration, III(3).
71   AU Refugee Convention, Preamble, Recital 9.
72   *Ibid.*, Preamble, Recital 10; Cartagena Declaration, (a).
73   The Preamble of the African Union Convention confirms what is already apparent in the Convention's title itself: "all the problems of our continent must be solved (...) in the African context". AU Refugee Convention, Preamble, Recital 8. Likewise, the Cartagena Declaration refers to "situation prevailing in the region". Cartagena Declaration, III(3).
74   UNHCR, "Statement on Article 15(c) QD", *op. cit.*, p. 9.

existence of additional categories of persons in need of international protection. In 1976 already, the Parliamentary Assemble of the Council of Europe (PACE) recommended that States "apply liberally" the Convention's refugee definition and make applicable to "*de facto* refugees" within their jurisdiction "as many articles as possible"[75] of the Refugee Convention.[76] A 1991 Working Group, established at the request of UNHCR's Executive Committee, also urged States who had not yet adopted complementary protection schemes aimed at supplementing the classical refugee definition (including, therefore, European States), to do so.[77] Unlike the 1976 PACE Recommendation, the Working Group Report does not expressly mention the Refugee Convention but instead refers to the African Union Convention and the Cartagena Declaration "as examples on which States elsewhere might wish to draw in developing their own national legislation".[78] J. McAdam observes that since those two regional protection models revert to the Refugee Convention as "the blueprint for legal status", an implicit reference to the Refugee Convention should be read between the Report's lines.[79] Hence, consistent with UNHCR's position, both sets of recommendations are premised on the conviction that the Refugee Convention provides "the appropriate *legal status* for extra-Convention refugees" too.[80] It is in that sense that Recommendation E of the Final Act of the UN Conference of Plenipotentiaries on the Status of Refugees and Stateless Persons must be construed.

It can be concluded from the above that the drafters of the Convention made clear in unanimously adopting Recommendation E that, in their minds, the key element of the Refugee Convention was not the refugee definition itself but rather the guarantee it created that persons in genuine need of international protection would be granted a certain status within receiving countries, a package of rights receiving Contracting States would have the obligation to respect and safeguard.

---

75   Recommendation 773 explicitly refers to public relief, social security, a range of labour rights, housing, education, travel documents and the prohibition of expulsion or return as elements of the treatment *de facto* refugees should benefit from. PACE, Recommendation 1976 (2011), *op. cit.*, 5 (1), §§ a–f.
76   *Ibid.*, at 5(II)(i) and 5(I)(b).
77   UNHCR, "Report of the Working Group on Solutions and Protection to the Forty-Second Session of the Executive Committee of the High Commissioner's Programme" ("EC/SCP/64"), EC/SCP/64, 12 August 1991.
78   *Ibid.*, 55(b).
79   J. McAdam, *Complementary Protection in International Refugee Law* (2007), *op. cit.*, p. 45.
80   *Ibid.*, p. 45 [emphasis added].

The grant of refugee status entitlements to additional categories of persons in need of protection is therefore fully compatible with the Refugee Convention. There might however be conceptual or political objections to such an extension, on the part of EU Member States at least. Already in 1976, the Rapporteur of the Netherlands, co-author of the Report of the Committee on Population and Refugees that preceded the adoption of PACE Recommendation 773, rather bluntly observed:

> The problem of the *de facto* refugees would not exist, at least for the overwhelming majority of them, if our governments were interpreting liberally the Convention of 1951 and the Protocol of 1967.
>
> However, there is hardly a government in Europe which can lay claim to such liberalism. Most think only of keeping the number of accepted refugees as limited as the amount of money that they have available for their refugee schemes.[81]

Blunt as it may be, the statement might still be accurate; after all, it is only some thirty years after the Parliamentary Assembly of the Council of Europe recommended States to extend the benefit of refugee status to categories of persons falling outside the refugee definition that EU Member States agreed on a – still limited – definition of a complementary form of protection. Even with the Directive being adopted, EU legislation was not fully in line the suggested expansion of refugee entitlements: as adopted in 2004, the Qualification Directive distinguished between status granted to refugees and that granted to subsidiary protection beneficiaries. The 2011 recast Directive however corrected this inequity and approximated the two statuses – while maintaining distinct labels ("refugees" and "beneficiaries of subsidiary protection" where Africa and Latin America only refer to "refugees", defined in broader terms)[82] so that the Qualification Directive is now in line with Recommendation E and with the PACE Recommendation for it grants the same rights to refugees and beneficiaries of subsidiary protection. It could be added that granting a refugee-like

---

81   PACE, "Situation of de Facto Refugees (Debate on the Report of the Committee on Population and Refugees, Doc. 3642, Addendum and Amendments, and Votes on the Draft Recommendation and Draft Resolution)", 26 january 1976 [1976] *Official Report of Debates* Vol. III, pp. 733–1084, p. 741.

82   "Commission Impact Assessment – Proposal for a Recast QD", *op. cit.*, pp. 12–13. Qualification Directive (2004).

status to all beneficiaries of international protection also follows on naturally from the principle that human rights are universal and inalienable.

It was concluded in Part 2 (Chapter 6), environmentally-displaced persons may qualify as refugees only if they meet "standard" refugee definition criteria: people with a well-founded fear of persecution on a Convention ground "fall squarely within the 1951 Convention definition".[83] They cannot however be protected as "environmental refugees". As argued above, a *de lege lata* interpretation of the Convention's refugee definition, constructive as it may be, does not make a difference. Nonetheless, legislative and State practice in Africa, Latin America and Europe demonstrates that, in direct line with the Convention drafters' recommendation, the package of rights attached to one's recognition of refugeehood by asylum authorities can be extended to additional categories of beneficiaries, besides Conventional refugees.

The inadequacy of the existing refugee definition to address environmental displacement led some to suggest instead that it be recast by way of either an amendment to the text, or the adoption of a second protocol to the Convention.

2 Recasting the Conventional Definition of Refugee: An Improbable Consensus for an Unfit Solution

As mentioned, among those who describe the Refugee Convention as outdated, some argue it can nevertheless be interpreted in a progressive way so as to cover new international protection needs. Some others find that the Refugee Convention is in fact obsolete and must be extended: the refugee definition should be reformulated or complemented by means of a revision of the Convention, of an amendment to the text or through the adoption of a new Protocol so that environmentally-displaced persons enter the scope of the Convention.

(a) The Law of Treaties Considered: Procedural Aspects

Before environmentally-displaced persons can enter the scope of the 1951 Refugee Convention, a recast of the Convention's refugee definition is needed. Three possibilities exist under the law of treaties: the Convention could be amended or revised, or an additional protocol could be adopted.

Any formal change in the text of a treaty touches upon States' freedom of consent. The balance of interests and rules that was agreed upon at the time the treaty was concluded is necessarily altered in the process;[84] the law of treaties,

---

83   UNHCR, "Statement on Article 15(c) QD", *op. cit.*, p. 8.
84   J. Combacau and S. Sur, *Droit International Public* (2004), *op. cit.*, p. 138.

as codified by the 1969 Vienna Convention on the Law of Treaties[85] ("VCLT"), therefore requires that the State parties to the original treaty renew their consent to be bound before the amended treaty can be applicable to them. The Final Clauses of the Refugee Convention contain no specific provision relating to amendments to the Convention; hence the principles of the VCLT apply.[86] Article 39 clarifies that amending a treaty is tantamount to concluding a treaty anew: the agreement of States is a precondition to the existence and entry into force of the treaty as an instrument of international law binding upon its parties.[87] Article 40 elaborates on the specific rules governing amendments to multilateral treaties: only those States that have consented to be bound by the amending agreement become parties to it. Others remain bound by the unamended treaty, which will prevail in their relations to any party of the treaty, including those who adopted the amending agreement.[88]

Silent on the possibility to amend it, the Refugee Convention instead expressly addresses its revision. Article 45 of the Refugee Convention provides that any Contracting State may request revision of the Convention by a notification to the United Nations Secretary-General. It would then be for the UN General Assembly to recommend the steps, if any, to be taken in respect of the State's request.[89] The 1969 Vienna Convention on the Law of Treaties did not devise any revision procedure and in fact does not expressly mention treaty revision. Looking at the United Nations Charter however offers some guidance. Revision of the Charter is addressed under Chapter XVIII (on amendments), which contains two articles. The first of the two, Article 108, describes the procedure for amending the Charter. Revision is dealt with in the second article, Article 109.[90] An amendment to a treaty is a change of a specific provision of the treaty. Revision on the other hand can be construed as multiple simultaneous amendments: "a revised treaty is a new treaty".[91] It therefore comes with no surprise that the Charter devises a procedure for its revision that is stricter than a single amendment procedure.[92] In particular, in view of the

---

85   VCLT, *op. cit.*
86   M. Fitzmaurice, "The Practical Working of the Law of Treaties", *in* M.D. Evans (Ed.), *International Law*, First Edition ed. (New York: Oxford, 2003), p. 176, 1.
87   VCLT, Article 39.
88   *Ibid.*, Article 40.
89   Refugee Convention, Article 45.
90   UN Charter, Articles 108 and 109.
91   L. Mcnair, *Law of Treaties*, 2nd ed. (New York: Oxford University Press, 1986), 534.
92   Article 109 requires that, for the purpose of reviewing the Charter, a General Conference of the Members of the United Nations be held at a date and place to be fixed by a two-thirds vote of the members of the General Assembly and by a vote of any nine members of

fundamental change a revision would bring in the Refugee Convention, it can be presumed that the procedure would be just as strict. As it is the case for the UN Charter, a revision of the 1951 Refugee Convention could be conditioned upon its State Parties initially agreeing to the idea of a revision. In other words, not only should States reach an agreement on the content of the new convention, they should also and beforehand agree to undertake a revision.

It can be noted that the VCLT also deals with the "modification" of multilateral treaties between certain of the parties only.[93] A precondition for such modification is however that the treaty provides for this possibility. The Refugee Convention contains no such provision and it is therefore needless to consider the option.

The third option available to the proponents of a recast of the Convention's refugee definition is the adoption of a new protocol to the 1951 Convention. The procedure is not unknown: as mentioned, the scope of the refugee definition was already corrected once with the adoption of the 1967 Protocol which lifted the Convention's temporal and geographical limitations.

To conclude on the different options at hand, it can be observed that if the extension of the refugee definition by means of a constructive interpretation was improbable, treaty modification procedures are such that the inclusion of environmental refugees in the Refugee Convention by means of a formal change in the text is close to inconceivable. The adoption of a protocol, unlikely though it may be, is more realistic an option than a revision or amendment. An important distinguishing factor between amendments and revision on the one hand, and protocols on the other hand justifies the assertion. As highlighted above, in both mechanisms, State consent is a prerequisite. A protocol though may come into existence as soon as it is signed and ratified by, at a minimum, two states. Its entry into force is conditioned upon it being ratified by a given number of states; this number is specified in the text of the protocol. The 1967 Protocol for instance provided that it would enter into force on the day of deposit of the sixth instrument of ratification.[94]

The three solutions (amendment, revision, additional protocol) are similar to the extent that they will only create obligations on the part of those States who will have expressed their consent to be bound by the newly adopted

---

the Security Council. It further requires that the revised Charter be adopted by two thirds of the Members of the United Nations including all the permanent members of the Security Council. United Nations, *Charter of the United Nations*, 24 October 1945, 1 UNTS XVI.

93   VCLT, Article 41.
94   UN General Assembly, *Protocol Relating to the Status of Refugees*, 31 January 1967, United Nations, Treaty Series, vol. 606, p. 267, Article VIII.

refugee definition. Only States who formally agree to view environmentally-displaced persons as refugees under the Convention will have an obligation to protect them as such. The three solutions are also equivalent on the substance: the wording of the extended refugee definition will be the same, whichever the solution chosen. In the hypothesis of a revision or of an amendment to Article 1(A) of the 1951 Convention, the amended treaty will expressly apply to environmental displacement. The same status will apply to environmental refugees if States choose instead to adopt an additional protocol to the 1951 Convention only in this case, the extended refugee definition will flow from the combined reading of Article 1(A) of the 1951 Convention, Article I of the 1967 Protocol and the relevant article of the second additional protocol in question. On account of these similarities, in the discussion below concerning the inclusion of environmental refugees in the scope of the Refugee Convention, the three solutions will not be distinguished – unless otherwise stated of course.

(b)   *A Preliminary Objection to a Broadening of the Refugee Definition*
Before the substance of the proposals is even touched upon, fundamental objections to any expansion of the scope of the Refugee Convention are worth considering. One reason to argue against approaching environmentally-induced displacement as an asylum issue is the risk of dilution of international protection. In particular, the already limited budget allocated to UNHCR would soon be exhausted if the mandate of the UN refugee agency were to be further extended to yet additional categories of persons of concern to UNHCR.[95]

The argument is not new: it was already invoked during the discussions on the original text of the Refugee Convention by the representative of the United States among others who objected to the adoption of an "unduly broad" refugee definition in the following terms:

> Such an influx of new refugees who would be enabled by an unduly broad definition to place themselves automatically under the protection of the United Nations would give rise to administrative and financial problems

---

[95] PACE, "Report of the Committee on Migration: a 21st century challenge", *op. cit.*, Explanatory Memorandum, §§ 49 and 56; O. Brown, *Migration and Climate Change* (2008), *op. cit.*, p. 14. Similarly, UN Under Secretary-General Hans van Ginkel observes that "global organizations [were] already overwhelmed by the demands of conventionally-recognized refugees, as originally defined in 1951". Cited in "As Ranks of "Environmental Refugees" Swell Worldwide, Calls Grow for Better Definition, Recognition, Support", *Press Release* (United Nations University – Institute for Environment and Human Security, UNU-EHS 2005), 11 October 2005, retrieved from: <www.ehs.unu.edu/file/get/3916> [01/12/2010].

of so great an extent that the High Commissioner would be overwhelmed and wholly unable to meet them.[96]

The US delegation insisted that a refugee definition worded in broad terms would entail an uncontrolled extension of the mandate of the High Commissioner, which would hamper its activities.[97] As it turned out however, it is interesting to note that the Mandate of UNHCR has been repeatedly extended by United Nations General Assembly resolutions so that it nowadays covers many more categories of persons than those described as refugees in the 1951 Refugee Convention.

States' concerns at the time the drafting of Refugee Convention was underway did not relate only to UN capacities but also, their own. In the same statement, the US delegate added:

> The definition should simply be precise, so that the United Nations and the Governments concerned would know exactly to whom the benefits of the convention would be extended.[98]

The concerns expressed by States prior to the adoption of the 1951 Refugee Convention were alleviated by the possibility that was given to them to opt for a narrow interpretation of the geographic scope of the Convention.[99] Additionally, the time limit set in the original text also constricted States' obligations: only those claiming asylum as a result of events occurring before 1 January 1951 were entitled to protection under the Convention. Satisfied that the proposed limitations clearly enumerated the categories of refugees to which States were bound grant protection, States eventually adopted the Convention.

Legal history however shows that extending the scope of the Convention may prove to be desirable in time. State Parties[100] to the Convention formally agreed, through the 1967 Protocol – a binding instrument of international law, to virtually delete the temporal and geographical references criteria from the refugee definition.

It follows that the Refugee Convention framework has already been expanded to accommodate the needs of new categories of refugees.

---

96   "E/AC.32/SR.3", *op. cit.*, §39.
97   *Ibid.*, §§35–41.
98   *Ibid.*, §40.
99   This option was however favoured by a limited number of States only. *See* above: pp. 406 and 412 in particular.
100 With the exception of Madagascar.

A principled objection to a broadening of the scope of the Convention intended to address new refugee situations therefore appears untenable. One should look deeper into the reasons for and terms of the proposed recasts to determine whether protecting environmentally-displaced persons under an extended Refugee Convention could be a suitable approach.

(c)   *The 1951 Refugee Convention Framework Corrected (again) to Protect Environmental Refugees*

Expanding the refugee definition to include "environmental refugees" is advocated by reference to the drafting history of the 1967 Protocol to the Convention. As said, the scope of the 1951 Refugee Convention was limited both in time and space : were entitled to protection under the Convention mainly persons who had become refugees by reason of events occurring before 1 January 1951, in Europe. These temporal and geographical limitations were the results of a legal compromise: States had expressed their reluctance to signing a "blank cheque" and to undertaking "obligations toward future refugees, the origin and number of which would be unknown".[101] The preparatory work of the Refugee Convention was mentioned above to determine what the object and purpose of the Convention were, and how to interpret Recommendation E of the Final Act. The drafting history will again be considered below but to clarify how the 1967 Protocol came into existence.

France among others strongly advocated the limitation of the geographical scope of the Convention to refugee situations resulting from events occurring in Europe. This limitation, its proponents argued, was necessary: States were concerned they might have to assume "unduly onerous commitments" in undertaking to grant the rights and benefits provided in the Convention to all refugees irrespective of their country of origin.[102] The representative of France, M. Rochefort, cited as an example the hypothetical case of a State which would

---

101   "E/AC.35/5", *op. cit.*, Annex II, Comments of the Committee on the Draft Convention, Article 1, p. 38. *See* in that sense the statement made by the representative of China, insisting that the different categories of refugees to which the convention should apply "be clearly indicated". UN Ad Hoc Committee on Refugees and Stateless Persons, Ad Hoc Committee on Statelessness and Related Problems, "First Session: Summary Record of the Fifth Meeting Held at Lake Success, New York, on Wednesday, 18 January 1950, at 2.15 P.M." ("E/AC.32/SR.5"), E/AC.32/SR.5, 30 January 1950, at 4.

102   The view was summarised in those terms – albeit not shared – by the representative of the government of the United Kingdom, M. Hoare, self-described as "proponent of the universalistic theory". UN Conference of Plenipotentiaries on the Status of Refugees and Stateless Persons, "Conference of Plenipotentiaries on the Status of Refugees and Stateless Persons: Summary Record of the Thirty-Third Meeting", A/CONF.2/SR.33, 30 November 1951.

have refugees of various origins in its territory: "Such a State might wish to bind itself in respect of some, but might experience difficulty in binding itself in respect of others, if, for example, the latter were so numerous that application of the Convention in their case would create problems with which the State in question was not at that moment able to deal".[103] It is worth noting here that this position appears to be hardly sustainable; its compatibility with the principle of non-discrimination is in particular highly questionable. As for the economic considerations (or "problems[104]") France had invoked as necessarily allowing States a leeway in identifying the populations worthy of refugee status within their territory, they were disregarded.

As a consequence of States' concerns and dissenting views on the matter, the Contracting Parties were given two options: they could choose at the time of signature (or ratification or accession) to construe the words "events occurring before 1 January 1951" as meaning "events occurring in Europe" prior to that date or "events occurring in Europe *or elsewhere* [emphasis added]" prior to that date. Only seven of the 19 signatories at the time adopted alternative (a) of article 1 Section B (1) of the Convention, thus limiting the scope of the Convention to refugee situations caused by events occurring in Europe. In other words, the majority of Contracting States in fact disapproved of the French position and, defending a universalistic approach of the definition of refugee, considered that "a refugee was a refugee, wherever he was".[105]

As noted by UNHCR, the global crisis affecting the world in the 1960's outgrew parts of the 1951 Refugee Convention.[106] Because of the geographical and temporal limitations set in the original document, numerous refugees were not recognised as such and were therefore "unable to take advantage of the minimum standards of treatment for which the Convention provides".[107] Besides, the limited scope of the 1951 Convention conflicted with the universal and unlimited competence of UNHCR under its Statute. Those issues were addressed at a colloquium of legal experts in 1965:

103　*Ibid.*
104　*Ibid.*
105　In M. Hoare's words (representative of the United Kingdom during the discussions). *Ibid.*
106　UNHCR, "The Wall Behind Which Refugees can Shelter: The 1951 Geneva Convention", *Refugees*, Vol. 2, No. 123 (2001), p. 2.
107　UN High Commissioner for Refugees, *Colloquium on the development in the law of refugees with particular reference to the 1951 Convention and the Statute of the Office of the United Nations High Commissioner for Refugees held at Villa Serbelloni Bellagio (Italy) from 21–28 April 1965: Background paper submitted by the Office of the United Nations High Commissioner for Refugees, Palais des Nations, Geneva, Switzerland, 1965*, 28 April 1965, MHCR/23/65; 67-1809, §§7–8.

> The Colloquium had regard to the fact that it was increasingly recognized that the refugee problem has now become universal in nature and of indefinite duration, and that the Convention is therefore no longer adequate; an increasing number of refugees are not covered by the Convention, particularly as it is limited to persons who have become refugees as a result of events before 1 January 1951. The members of the Colloquium were of the opinion that it was urgent for humanitarian reasons that refugees not at present covered by the Convention should be granted similar benefits by means of an international instrument.[108]

The opinions of the Colloquium were endorsed by UNHCR Executive Committee and the Protocol eventually adopted. It entered into force on 4 October 1967 to "amend"[109] the Refugee Convention by removing, for its State Parties, the geographical and temporal limitations to the scope of the Convention, so that the Convention regime become truly universal and adapt to the new reality of refugee movements at the time.[110]

To date, 144 States are parties to the 1951 Refugee Convention of which only one – Madagascar – has neither ratified the 1967 Protocol nor chosen to extend its obligations under the Convention by adopting alternative (b) of Section B (1) of article 1 of the Convention. Additionally, three Sates – Cape Verde, the USA and Venezuela – are parties to the 1967 Protocol but not to the Convention. In light of those figures, one can conclude that the large majority of States (146 out of the 192 Member States of the United Nations, and including France since 1971) have committed to protect refugees, regardless of their country of origin.

---

108   UN High Commissioner for Refugees, *Colloquium on the legal aspects of refugee problems (Note by the High Commissioner)*, 5 May 1965, A/AC.96/INF.40, at 3, available at: http://www.unhcr.org/refworld/docid/3ae68bea8.html [accessed 30 April 2012].

109   The Protocol is often referred to as amending the Convention although technically it is not an amendment to the text but a separate instrument of conventional law, which State Parties to the Refugee Convention are free to adopt or not.

110   Additionally, UNHCR was reportedly concerned with preserving the supremacy the Refugee Convention and of its own Mandate. At the time the adoption of a Protocol was considered, the adoption of a refugee convention was already underway in Africa. UNHCR's interest in fostering the Protocol was thus partly also to ensure that the Convention, being made universal, would attract more State Parties while at the same time to "prevent or forestall the proliferation of regional refugee instruments", such as the one envisaged then in Africa, "which could take precedence over the UNHCR and create a system of differential regional refugee protection". S.E. Davies, "Redundant or Essential? How Politics Shaped the Outcome of the 1967 Protocol", *International Journal of Refugee Law*, Vol. 19, No. 4 (2007), pp. 703–728, pp. 715–716.

In other words, the large majority of States already have in the past taken cognisance and sought to remedy the shortcomings of the 1951 Convention definition of a refugee.

Lastly, it is of interest to notice that the United States, who had, as mentioned, introduced the idea of a more casuistic refugee definition – as opposed to a universal one, in fact never excluded the possible future expansion of the definition. As said, the group of "neo-refugees" they proposed was intended to allow the inclusion, by means of "protocols, addenda or later agreements",[111] of new categories of persons forced to flee from their countries "in the future".[112]

The statement made at the time by UNHCR to justify the adoption of the 1967 Protocol resonates today as the international protection of environmentally-displaced persons is debated.

> In view of the time which has elapsed since the adoption of the basic legal instruments relating to the status of refugees, it was felt necessary that there should be a re-examination of refugee problems in their legal aspects. In particular, it was deemed desirable to consider adapting the Convention relating to the Status of Refugees of 1951 to meet new refugee situations which have arisen...[113]

It is nowadays argued that, just as its scope was extended by the adoption of the 1967 Protocol, the Refugee Convention definition should again be corrected to address the needs of the growing group of persons forced to move because of environmental disasters.[114]

Proponents of an extended refugee definition, capable of including environmental refugees invoke four main reasons in support of their claim. These arguments however appear to yield to the more convincing arguments against such expansion of the refugee definition. Both categories will be discussed below.

---

111 "E/AC.32/SR.3", *op. cit.*, § 54.
112 *Ibid.*, § 45.
113 UN High Commissioner for Refugees, *Colloquium on the legal aspects of refugee problems (Note by the High Commissioner)*, 5 May 1965, A/AC.96/INF.40, at 2, available at: http://www.unhcr.org/refworld/docid/3ae68bea8.html [accessed 30 April 2012].
114 Arguing in favour of a revision of the Convention: M. Conisbee and A. Simms, "Environmental Refugees: The Case for Recognition" (New Economics Foundation) (2003), pp. 32–33 and 37; J. Hong (2001), *op. cit.*, pp. 340–341. Likewise, the Bangladeshi Finance Minister observed that the Refugee Convention could be revised to protect environmentally-displaced since it "has been through other revisions, so this should be possible". Cited in: A. Kraler, *et al.*, "Climate Refugees: Legal and Policy Responses to Environmentally Induced Migration" (European Parliament – Directorate General for Internal Policies), PE 462.422 (2011), p. 40.

(d)   *Few Pros, More Cons: The Improbable and Unfit Recast Definition*
Arguments for both sides will be discussed successively, starting with those in favour of a recast refugee definition, before the more convincing arguments against it are considered.

(i)   In Favour of a Recast Refugee Definition to Include "Environmental Refugees"

Besides the elapse of time since the refugee definition was adopted and the necessity that refugee law responds to existing international protection needs, three main types of arguments can be invoked to justify the expansion of the refugee definition.

Firstly, the humanitarian[115] purpose of refugee law can be emphasised. Refugee law should act as "surrogate protection" for all those for whom there is no likelihood of "meaningful protection of basic human rights".[116] Thus, the notion of protection – or absence thereof – is central to the refugee definition and is emphasised by UNHCR who notes that "whether unable or unwilling to avail himself of the protection of his government, a refugee is always a person who does not enjoy such protection".[117] It follows that environmental refugees, as persons who seek protection outside their country of origin because their State is unable (or unwilling) to protect them from the disastrous consequences of environmental degradation occurring on their territory, should accordingly be protected.

Secondly, the nature of the Refugee Convention as a human rights treaty,[118] as a "Bill of Rights" for refugees[119] is mentioned: as such, it ought to evolve

---

115   The 1951 Refugee Convention stresses the humanitarian and social nature of refugee law in its Preamble. UN General Assembly, *Convention Relating to the Status of Refugees*, 28 July 1951, United Nations, Treaty Series, vol. 189, p. 137, Preamble, Recital 5.
116   J.C. Hathaway (1991), *op. cit.*, pp. 123 and 124.
117   UNHCR, *Handbook on Procedures, op. cit.*, § 97. This interpretation of the Handbook is proposed by J. Hong in J. Hong (2001), *op. cit.*, p. 339.
118   See in particular, J. McAdam, "The Refugee Convention as a Rights Blueprint for People in Need of International Protection", *in* J. McAdam (Ed.), *Forced Migration, Human Rights and Security* (Oxford: Hart Publishing, 2008), pp. 263–282. M. Foster also argues for an evolutionary approach to the interpretation of the Refugee Convention so that it takes into account evolving developments in human rights law. She however advocates this approach not in the context of environmentally-displaced persons specifically but to justify that deprivation of economic and social rights can constitute persecution for the purpose of the Refugee Convention. M. Foster, *International Refugee Law and Socio-Economic Rights: Refuge from Deprivation* (2007), *op. cit.*, pp. 59–63. See also below note 2008 and references cited.
119   B. Gorlick, "Human Rights and Refugees: Enhancing Protection through International Human Rights Law", *Nordic Journal of International Law*, Vol. 69 (2000), pp. 117–177, p. 122.

in line with the developments of human rights law.[120] An expanded refugee definition, based on international human rights law would, theoretically, reconcile "the vast discrepancy between the Convention definition of a refugee and the mounting numbers of [environmentally-displaced persons]".[121] Notably, the two Covenants (ICCPR and ICESCR) adopted fifteen years after the Refugee Convention proclaim that "[i]n no case may a people be deprived of its own means of subsistence"[122] and enshrine the rights of all peoples to "enjoy and utilize fully and freely their natural wealth and resources".[123] Additionally, the right to life has grown to include for example a right to water[124] and sanitation.[125] The right to a healthy environment has also been enshrined in international law,[126] the Parliamentary Assembly of the Council of Europe suggested drafting an additional protocol to the ECHR concerning this right[127] and more recently recommended that it be included in a new protocol to the revised European Social Charter on the right to health and was recently confirmed by the European Court of Human Rights who, on the ground that the collection, treatment and disposal of waste – at hand in the case – were hazardous activities, found that the State had a positive obligation to adopt

---

120 D. Keane, "The Environmental Causes and Consequences of Migration: A Search for the Meaning of 'Environmental Refugees'", *Georgetown International Environmental Law Review*, Vol. 16 (2003–2004), pp. 209–223, p. 125; J.B. Cooper (1998), *op. cit.*, pp. 494–495.

121 B. Havard, "Seeking Protection: Recognition of Environmentally Displaced Persons under International Human Rights Law", *Villanova Environmental Law Journal*, Vol. 18, No. 1 (2007), pp. 65–82, p. 79. A. Michelot, "Vers un statut de réfugié écologique ?" *in Les catastrophes écologiques et le droit : échecs du droit, appels au droit* (Bruxelles: Bruylant, 2012), pp. 517–541, p. 528.

122 ICCPR, Article 1(2); ICESCR, Article 1(2); Directive 2000/60/EC of the European Parliament and of the Council of 23 October 2000 Establishing a Framework for Community Action in the Field of Water Policy [22/12/2000] *OJ L 327* pp. 1–73.

123 ICCPR, Article 47; ICESCR, Article 25.

124 CESCR, "GC 15: Right to Water", *op. cit.*

125 UNGA, "Resolution 64/292: The human right to water and sanitation", *op. cit.*

126 Article 1 of the Aarhus Convention enshrines "the right of every person of present and future generations to live in an environment adequate to his or her health and well-being". Convention on Access to Information, Public Participation in Decision-Making and Access to Justice in Environmental Matters, 25 June 1998, entered into force 30 October 2001 [2001] *UNTS* Vol. 2161, p. 447.

127 PACE Committee on the Environment, Agriculture and Local and Regional Affairs, "Drafting an Additional Protocol to the European Convention on Human Rights Concerning the Right to a Healthy Environment", Doc. 12003, 11 September 2009; PACE, "Recommendation 1976 (2011): The Role of Parliaments in the Consolidation and Development of Social Rights in Europe" ("Recommendation 1976 (2011)"), 23 June 2011, § 2.

reasonable and appropriate measures to protect the rights of the persons concerned and in particular, their right to respect for private life and home "and more generally, their right to enjoy a healthy and protected environment".[128]

In view of such developments of human rights law, some hence argue for the corresponding expansion of the Refugee Convention definition, "along human rights lines".[129] J.C. Cooper for instance suggests the inclusion of a new paragraph in the refugee definition, to the effect of including any internationally displaced person who is unwilling or unable to return to his country of origin owing "to degraded environmental conditions threatening his life, health, means of subsistence, or use of natural resources".[130]

Lastly, it is by virtue of a principle of humanity that environmentally displaced persons should be protected, because they are victims of "environmental injustice".[131] J. Hong uses the term by reference specifically to the issue of "environmental justice", particularly discussed in US literature, which emphasises equal enforcement of environmental laws among all communities,[132] in a non-discriminatory manner as well as a right to participation in environmental decision-making.[133] Referring specifically to technological disasters, the author finds that victims of environmental catastrophes are often "politically disempowered". However, unlike J.C. Cooper, J. Hong does not consider that they can, as a result, be identified as a "social group", political disempowerment being not an immutable characteristic;[134] this "environmental injustice" calls instead for a "revision of the language" of the Convention.[135]

Several arguments have been formulated in favour of the expansion of the Refugee Convention definition, by means of an amendment or of a new

---

128 The case is to date only available in French: "... *il pesait sur l'Etat l'obligation positive d'adopter des mesures raisonnables et adéquates capables de protéger les droits des intéressés au respect de leur vie privée et de leur domicile et, plus généralement, à la jouissance d'un environnement sain et protégé*". ECtHR, *Affaire Di Sarno et autres c. Italie* ("*Di Sarno*"), Requête no 30765/08 (10 January 2012, final 10 April 2012), § 110.
129 J.B. Cooper (1998), *op. cit.*, p. 494.
130 *Ibid.*, p. 494; J. Hong (2001), *op. cit.*, pp. 344–345.
131 J. Hong (2001), *op. cit.*, p. 343.
132 L. Westra notes that literature on the issue establishes a link between environmental causes to health effects and racial discrimination. This is "particularly evident as hazardous operations are routinely sited in areas inhabited by African Americans and Hispanics". L. Westra, *Environmental Justice and the Rights of Ecological Refugees* (2009), *op. cit.*, p. 187.
133 J. Hong (2001), *op. cit.*, p. 343, note 134.
134 *Ibid.*, p. 343.
135 *Ibid.*, p. 345.

protocol, but in view of the many more arguments against it, this option must be dismissed.

(ii)   The Overriding Arguments against an Expanded Refugee Definition

The main argument is pragmatic. It is common knowledge that states are anxious to maintain control over the number of persons entering their territories to settle there, be they migrants or refugees. This appeared forthrightly during the debates preceding the adoption of the 1951 Refugee Convention where some States vigorously opposed the adoption of a refugee definition couched in general terms as this would entail their committing to grant asylum to yet unknown numbers[136] of refugees.[137] The trend being more towards restrictive asylum policies[138] than the other way around, and in view of the absence of consensus on the necessity or suitability of extending the existing refugee definition, it is unlikely that States would agree to a legally-binding expansion of their obligations under the Convention.[139] It is indeed hardly conceivable that States, who have been demonstrating an increasingly restrictive approach to asylum,[140] would bind themselves to recognising and protecting an additional category of refugees,[141] all the more so when scientific projections forecast this population to come to hundreds of millions. At the European level, States agreed on the adoption of a harmonised complementary form of protection about three decades after African States did and after having been recommended to do so, by the Council of Europe among others, and twenty years after Latin America proclaimed its Cartagena Declaration.[142] What is more, the

---

136   Note: reality is different. The vast majority of the world's refugees are hosted by countries in the "South". United Nations, Department of Economic and Social Affairs, Population Division, "Migrants by origin and destination: The role of South-South migration", *Population Facts*, No. 2012/3 (June 2012): at 9.

137   *See* developments above on the *travaux préparatoires* of the Convention, pp. 406s.

138   F. Biermann and I. Boas (2008), *op. cit.*

139   T. King, "Environmental Displacement: Coordinating Efforts to Find Solutions", *Georgetown Immigration Law Journal*, Vol. 18 (2005–2006), pp. 543–565, p. 554; F. Biermann and I. Boas (2008), *op. cit.*, p. 2; S. Castles (2002), *op. cit.*, p. 12.

140   In the context of asylum and immigration discussion, Europe is often referred to as "Fortress Europe". Norman Myers observed this tendency in 1997 already in N. Myers (1997), *op. cit.* Cf. also Canada, UK, France in 2010–2011.

141   Gregory McCue, "Environmental Refugees: Applying International Environmental Law to Involuntary Migration", *Georgetown International Environmental Law Review*, Vol. 6, Issue 1 (1993–1994): 151–190, pp. 176–177.

142   Similarly, referring to G.S. Goodwin-Gil and J. McAdam, I. Millar observes that just as States were reluctant in the 1980s to negotiating a new protocol to the Refugee Convention to address complementary protection, they would likely be just as reluctant now – if

inclusion of persons displaced by environmental disasters had been considered but, as it turned out and as is apparent in the text of the Qualification Directive, was deliberately excluded. Chances are European States will not agree to a further expansion of their international protection obligations, not in the short-run at least. Data available on displacement indicate that more people are already now displaced each year by environmental disasters than by armed conflict;[143] this makes it even less likely that European States who were cautious in extending refugee-like protection to people displaced by generalised violence would choose to commit to protect an even larger population.

Secondly, the broadening of the refugee definition carries the risk that existing refugee protection standards and organisational mandates be diluted or overshadowed.[144] The adoption of an expanded definition would necessarily imply that higher numbers of persons apply for refugee status. The capacities of national asylum systems risk be overstretched and arguably, as a consequence, asylum authorities and courts "will have to narrow who can receive protection by redefining 'persecution' and 'well-founded fear'" and existing asylum systems will moreover be incapable of assimilating all environmentally displaced persons.[145] Additionally, should States agree to amend the Refugee Convention (rather than adopt a protocol to it), it is feared, not least by UNCHR, that re-opening the refugee definition adversely lead to a lowering of existing protection standards.[146] In fact, although some draw a parallel between the adoption of the 1967 Protocol and the proposed broadening of the refugee definition, the two expansions would significantly differ. The Protocol removed

---

not more one may add – to negotiate a protocol on environmental displacement. I. Millar, "There's Not Place Like Home: Human Displacement and Climate Change", *Australian International Law Journal*, Vol. 14 (2007), pp. 71–98, p. 85.

143   UNHCR, *The State of the World's Refugees 2012: In Search of Solidarity* (2012), *op. cit.*, p. 169.

144   J. McAdam and B. Saul, "An Insecure Climate for Human Security? Climate-Induced Displacement and International Law", *Legal Studies Research Paper* (Sydney Law School), No. 08/131 (October 2008), p. 1.

145   K.K. Moberg, "Extending Refugee Definitions to Cover Environmentally Displaced Persons Displaces Necessary Protection", *Iowa Law Review*, Vol. 94, No. 3 (2009), pp. 1107–1137, p. 1129.

146   See for example: the statement made by Andreas Kamm, ECRE Chair and Secretary General of the Danish Refugee: "If we re-open the Geneva Convention, we'll end up with less protection for refugees". A. Kamm, "ECRE Interview with ECRE Chair, Andreas Kamm", *ECRE Weekly Bulletin*, 26 February 2010. PACE, "Report of the Committee on Migration: a 21st century challenge", *op. cit.*, § 55. Similarly: D. Corlett, *Stormy Weather: The Challenge of Climate Change and Displacement* (Sydney, NSW: University of New South Wales, 2008), pp. 47–48.

the geographical and temporal constraints which restricted the applicability of the Convention but left the substance of the refugee definition unchanged. Including "environmental refugees" in the purview of the Convention would in turn require substantial changes in the definition: the refugee definition, based on the notion of discrimination, would need to be adjusted to include victims of non-discriminatory threats such as most environment-related threats.

Thirdly, the nature of environmental displacement comes into play. The protection devised by the Refugee Convention was intended to be temporary: it was expected that refugees would return to their home countries once the threatening situation has ceased.[147] In many cases however, in the context of global warming, it is anticipated that environmentally-displaced persons will not be able to return to their home country for a long period of time, or not at all.[148] Moreover, the Refugee Convention protects only those who are outside their country of origin, in the majority of cases though, it is anticipated that environmental disasters will displace persons within their own country. Addressing environmental displacement from a refugee law point of view would therefore provide only a very limited solution to the existing legal vacuum.[149] Additionally, J. McAdam notes, "this may encourage spontaneous arrivals rather than planned, gradual movements".[150] Furthermore, it seems that the Convention's individualistic approach to the root cause of persecution and hence of displacement and to refugee status determination in general is not suitable to address environmental displacement.[151] According to C. Cournil, the emergency situation in which most persons affected by environmental disasters will find themselves calls instead for a *prima facie* approach to status

---

147 Article 1C of the Refugee Convention hence lists a number of cicrumstances in which the Convention ceases to apply to a person recognised as refugee under Article 1A. Those cessation clauses include situations in which the circumstances in connexion with which he had been recognised as a refugee have ceased to exist.

148 M. Doevenspeck, "The Thin Line between Choice and Flight: Environment and Migration in Rural Benin", *International Migration* (IOM), Vol. 49 (S1) (2011), p. 390.

149 C. Mcdowell and G. Morrell, *Displacement Beyond Conflict: Challenges for the 21st Century* (Oxford, New York: Berghahn Books, 2010), p. 83; C. Cournil, "Quelle protection juridique pour les 'réfugiés écologiques'?" *in* Gisti (Ed.), *Quel Statut Pour Les Réfugiés Environnementaux ? Actes de La Journée Du 14 Décembre 2007* (Paris: Gisti, Juin 2008), pp. 18–23, p. 19; A. Michelot (2012), *op. cit.*, pp. 529–530.

150 J. McAdam, "Refusing 'Refuge' in the Pacific: (de)Constructing Climate-Induced Displacement in International Law", *in* E. Piguet, *et al.* (Eds.), *Migration and Climate Change* (Cambridge, New York: Cambridge University Press, UNESCO Publishing, 2011), p. 118.

151 *Ibid.*, pp. 118–119; L. Westra, *Environmental Justice and the Rights of Ecological Refugees* (2009), *op. cit.*, pp. 5 and 12.

determination.¹⁵² Lastly on this aspect, environmental displacement will generally concern large groups of displaced persons; as a consequence, in the unlikely hypothesis where States accept to extend the refugee definition, courts will "have to narrow who can receive protection by redefining 'persecution' and 'well-founded fear'"¹⁵³ and asylum programs will operate (even¹⁵⁴) more slowly.

Fourthly, creating an additional category of, specifically, "environmental refugees" would fail to encapsulate the multiple causes for migration: environmental and natural factors "are part of a complex pattern of multiple causality, in which [they] are closely linked to economic, social and political ones".¹⁵⁵

Fifthly, it would be conceptually uneasy and, to some extent, inaccurate to describe environmental displacement as a refugee flow. Whereas refugees leave their countries because they fear persecution from their State or non-State actors against which authorities fail to protect them, no one pushes environmentally-displaced persons out of the country; to the contrary, in the majority of cases, national authorities and individuals alike will endeavour to avoid that it become necessary for the population to move.¹⁵⁶ It would not take a mere adjustment of the text but fundamentally affect the Convention, requiring that its underlying premise (the protection of individuals against human rights violations orchestrated by the State,¹⁵⁷ or which the State fails to prevent) be "rewritten", "undermining completely the original intent of the Convention and rendering it meaningless".¹⁵⁸ Perniciously even, in the context of climate

---

152 C. Cournil (Juin 2008), *op. cit.*, p. 19. In like manner, J. McAdam finds that *prima facie* status determination would be "a more efficient process". It would be based on receiving States identifying, on an *ad hoc* basis, which countries demonstrate "sufficient, objective characteristics that 'justify' movement". J. McAdam (2011), *op. cit.*, pp. 119–120.

153 K.K. Moberg (2009), *op. cit.*, p. 1129.

154 *Ibid.*

155 S. Castles (2002), *op. cit.*, p. 5.

156 D. Corlett, *Stormy Weather: The Challenge of Climate Change and Displacement* (2008), *op. cit.*, pp. 46–47. In cases concerning citizens of low-lying Pacific island States applying for refugee status or complementary protection in New Zealand, courts repeatedly acknowledged – often together with the applicants – that the governments were taking active steps, including by requesting international assistance, to mitigate the impacts of climate change on their populations. *See* for instance: New Zealand Supreme Court, *Teitiota*, [2015] NZSC 107, *op. cit.*, § 12; Immigration and Protection Tribunal, *AF (Kiribati)*, [2013] NZIPT 800413, *op. cit.*, § 75; and Immigration and Protection Tribunal, *AF (Tuvalu)*, [2015] NZIPT 800859, 20 October 2015, § 69.

157 In that sense, I. Millar observes that the question goes to the core of the Convention this would fundamentally affect the Convention, the underlying premise of the Convention would have to be rewritten. I. Millar (2007), *op. cit.*, p. 86.

158 *Ibid.*

change-related displacement, affected countries being typically those who contributed less to global warming, displaced persons seeking protection abroad would in fact often be seeking protection from those States which contributed most by their greenhouse gas emissions to causing their flight.[159] Such approach "completely reverses the traditional refugee paradigm".[160]

Last but not least, the persons the most concerned themselves reject the qualifier "refugee".[161] As it turns out, inhabitants of Pacific island States have voiced their firm opposition to the term which, they perceive, connotes persecution by one's own government and victimhood[162] (based in particular on the image of refugee camps, where individuals are perceived as having little prospects for the future). They instead want to raise awareness at the responsibility of the international community and industrialised States in particular in causing climate change and at the necessity to take actions to reduce greenhouse gas emission, and seek to formulate solutions to their own situation capable of securing their future.[163] Also directly concerned, UNHCR has consistently opposed the term "environmental refugee" and correlative expansion of the refugee definition.[164]

---

159   In that sense, J. McAdam (2009), *op. cit.*, p. 592; PACE, "Report of the Committee on Migration: a 21st century challenge", *op. cit.*, § 56. This was the case before the Refugee Review Tribunal of Australia when a citizen of Kiribati applying for a "protection visa" (Australia Migration Act 1958, Sections 65 and 36(2)(a)) claimed to be a refugee as a member of a particular social group (that of environmentally-displaced persons) in respect of whom Australia, whose historically high emissions of greenhouse gases continued unabated despite it being aware of the causes and impacts of climate change, had protection obligations. The applicant claimed that "in light of scientific knowledge of the impact of carbon dioxide emissions, Australia's continued production of high levels of such pollution, in complete disregard for people on low lying islands, *constitutes the relevant motivation to characterise climate change as persecution*". The Tribunal, albeit seemingly ready to concede Australia's guilty indifference, rejected the argument on the basis that the nexus requirement between Australia's behaviour (and the resulting harm for low lying islands' citizens) and a Convention ground for persecution was not fulfilled. Refugee Review Tribunal of Australia, 0907346 [2009] RRTA 1168, 10 December 2009, *op. cit.*, §§ 45 and 51.
160   New Zealand Hight Court, *Teitiota*, [2013] NZHC 3125, *op. cit.*, § 55.
161   C. Farbotko and H. Lazrus, "The First Climate Refugees? Contesting Global Narratives of Climate Change in Tuvalu", *Global Environmental Change*, Vol. 22 (2012), pp. 382–390.
162   C. Farbotko and H. Lazrus refer for example to a statement made by President Tong, of Kiribati, indicating that the people of Kiribati did not want to leave their country as "environmental refugees" but instead as "skilled migrants". *Ibid.*, p. 383.
163   J. McAdam and M. Loughry, "We Aren't Refugees", *Essays & reportage* (Inside Story, 2009), 30 June 2009, retrieved from: <http://inside.org.au/we-arent-refugees/> [03/02/2010].
164   On the basis of interviews she conducted with UN High Commissioner for Refugees diplomats in 2004 K.E. McNamara concludes that UNHCR views "environmental refugees"

Additional arguments can be invoked not only to oppose redefining refugees to include "environmental refugees" but to counter the adoption of a solution to environmental displacement based on refugee law only. They will be briefly mentioned.

3   Final Objections to Addressing Environmental Displacement under the Refugee Convention

All the objections formulated above, against a constructive interpretation of the refugee definition and against a recast refugee definition are also valid here. Additionally, other reasons can be mentioned against a solution based in refugee law.

The object of refugee law is to cover "what ought to be a situation of exception".[165] Environmental degradations however can hardly be labelled as exceptional: those caused by climate change in particular will not be exceptions but are instead bound to become the rule for the populations concerned. Science shows that the effects of climate change on the environment will challenge populations and their access to natural resources including water. In some areas, the consequences can be dire. The same is true with the impact of nuclear catastrophes on populations and the environment. In such circumstances, the situation that triggered displacement in the refugee's country of origin will not improve in human lifespan; it is instead bound to persist and, in fact, to worsen. Hence the imperative that States take action to prevent catastrophes from happening, to adapt to the inevitable environmental changes and, to mitigate their effects on populations and territories. Such is note the purpose of refugee law.

Protecting incoming "environmental refugees" without attempting to remedy the ongoing environmental degradation which triggered their movement would be illusory: if adaptation and, or mitigation measures are not taken and implemented to restore bearable – at a minimum – living conditions in the region of origin, environmental emigration from the affected area can only be incremental. Refugee law however being fundamentally palliative,[166] the 1951

"as a non-legitimate category of movers/mobile populations", who exist outside its mandate and "hence [do] not automatically qualify for formal assistance and protection". K.E. Mcnamara, "Conceptualizing Discourses on Environmental Refugees at the United Nations", *Population and Environment*, Vol. 29 (2007), pp. 12–24, pp. 18–19 especially.

165   G.S. Goodwin-Gill and J. McAdam, *The refugee in international law*, 3rd ed., (New York: Oxford, 2007), p. 1.

166   James C. Hathaway, *The Rights of Refugees under International Law* (Cambridge: Cambridge University Press, 2005), p. 5. J.C. Hathaway also notes elsewhere: "Refugee law's palliative focus is a healthy counterweight to the international legal system's predilection to

Convention – and other refugee law instruments alike[167] – does not equip its Contracting States with means to take action, in the refugee's country of origin, to improve the local situation. Moreover, the Convention's purpose being fundamentally humanitarian,[168] States do not have any interest on their own.[169] In that sense, asylum may be described as a "service" rendered by States[170] to persons in need of international protection, to the States and generally, to the international community's "public order".[171] The Refugee Convention thus

---

dwell comfortable in the macro-political sphere, and should not be sacrificed". J.C. Hathaway, "On the Virtues of Modesty: Why the Refugee Regime Ought Not to Lose Its Focus", *The Growth of Forced Migration: New Directions in Research, Policy and Practice*, University of Oxford, Refugee Studies Programme, 25–27 March 1998.

167 In that sense, the African Union Convention stresses that the grant of asylum to refugees is a humanitarian act. African Union, *Convention Governing the Specific Aspects of Refugee Problems in Africa ("AU Convention")*, 10 September 1969, 1001 U.N.T.S. 45, Article II (2). As to the humanitarian purpose of the 1951 Refugee Convention, it appears clearly in the Preamble of the Convention and has been repeatedly confirmed since, in relevant literature and case-law. *See infra* notes: 169 and 213.

168 Moreover, the Refugee Convention is analysed as a human rights treaty. As such, its primary objective is to serve the interests of the subjects of states rather than the states themselves. Hence the non-applicability to human rights treaties of the principle of reciprocity that normally governs the application of any bilateral or multilateral treaties: contracting States cannot invoke a material breach of a human rights treaty by another party to suspend the operation of the treaty (VCLT, Article 60(5).) On the peculiar nature of state obligations arising from international human rights law treaties, *see*: J. Combacau and S. Sur, *Droit International Public* (2004), *op. cit.*, p. 389. On the observation that the Refugee Convention is a human rights treaty, *see* for example: J.C. Hathaway (1991), *op. cit.*, pp. 113–131; J. McAdam, *Complementary Protection in International Refugee Law* (2007), *op. cit.*, pp. 29–33; T. Einarsen (2011), *op. cit.*, pp. 1–3.

169 ICJ, *Advisory Opinion Concerning Reservations to the Convention on the Prevention and Punishment of the Crime of Genocide ("Reservations to the Genocide Convention")* (28 May 1951) *ICJ Reports 1951*, p. 15.

170 The notion of "service" is borrowed from a statement made by M Rochefort, representative of the French delegation in the discussions that lead to the adoption of the 1951 Refugee Convention. In full, the French representative stated that "[t]he hospitality offered by the countries of Europe was a service they rendered on behalf of all the United Nations to the cause of freedom and civilization". UN Ad Hoc Committee on Refugees and Stateless Persons, *Ad Hoc Committee on Refugees and Stateless Persons, Second Session: Summary Record of the Thirty-Third Meeting Held at the Palais des Nations, Geneva, on Monday, 14 August, 1950, at 11 a.m.*, 20 September 1950, E/AC.32/SR.33.

171 On the notion of common public order, *see* the admissibility decision of the European Commission on Human Rights in the 1961 case of *Austria v. Italy*, where the Commission, relying on the Preamble to the ECHR noted that "the purpose of the High Contracting Parties in concluding the Convention was not to concede to each other reciprocal rights and

creates rights for refugees and the corresponding obligation for States to respect those rights; it does not however create a right for Contracting States to intervene in third countries, be it to alleviate a distressing human rights situation prevailing in the country.

For this reason too, environmental displacement will not be appropriately tackled if the solution put forward is framed in refugee law terms only. *Quid* of other existing norms of international protection?

B   Environmentally-Displaced Persons as Beneficiaries of Subsidiary Protection

At the time the Qualification Directive was being drafted, the European Commission justified the adoption of a new regime of protection, complementary to refugee status, in view of the changing nature of causes of forced displacement. The Commission noticed specifically "a growing mismatch between the nature of demand and the criteria of the Refugee Convention".[172] The Commission attributed this "mismatch" mainly to:

> ... the proliferation of armed conflicts generating situations of widespread insecurity and human rights violations that are difficult to fit within the definition of persecution as traditionally interpreted for the purposes of the Geneva Convention in Europe.[173]

Just like the European Union addressed this gap in refugee law applicable at the EU level, by devising the regime of subsidiary protection, it could again endeavour to achieve the adequacy of EU asylum law with the reality of present forms of harms threatening populations to the point of forcing them to leave their homes.

Besides growing concerns in international protection circles that existing asylum law fails to protect those populations displaced by environmental disasters, there is also growing evidence of the current and future impacts of climate

---

obligations in pursuance of their individual national interests but to realize the aims and ideals of the Council of Europe (...) and to establish a common public order of the free democracies of Europe with the object of safeguarding their common heritage of political traditions, ideas, freedom and the rule of law". Council of Europe: European Commission on Human Rights, *Austria vs Italy*, Application No.788/60, *European Yearbook of Human Rights*, Vol.4, No.116 (1961), at 140.

172   European Commission, "Communication from the Commission to the Council and the European Parliament: Towards a Common Asylum Procedure and a Uniform Status, Valid Throughout the Union, for Persons Granted Asylum", COM(2000) 755 final, 22 November 2000, p. 5.

173   *Ibid.*, p. 5.

change on the environment and, henceforth, on populations. It is undisputed that environmental change is and has always been a powerful trigger for population movements; climate change is in turn described as an amplifier of the frequency and intensity of both slow- and sudden-onset disasters and as "an accelerator of other global trends that create or affect" displaced persons, such as urbanisation, economic inequalities and conflict.[174] It follows logically that population movements can be expected to increase under the influence of climate change.

Confronted with a new "mismatch" between existing criteria for international protection and the nature of protection claims, the EU should again adapt norms so that they address this new evolution; so that they adapt for the new reality.[175]

As a matter of fact, such extension of subsidiary protection to persons who, suffering from the severe degradation of the environment and confronted with the absence of protection against resulting threats to their life or person, are forced to live their home and seek protection in the EU, appears to be in direct line with the broad objective pursued with the creation of the Common European Asylum System of "progressively establishing an area of freedom, security and justice open to those who, forced by circumstances, legitimately seek protection in the Union".[176] How to amend the Qualification Directive (1) and why (2) will be discussed below.

1   A Proposal

Returning to the initial premise of this work, the proposed amendment to the criteria for subsidiary protection under the Qualification Directive would draw on Article 15(c) which appears to be best equipped for such expansion, notably in that it refers to "indiscriminate" threat (violence). Part 2 argued that Article 15(c) is, as it stands, applicable to individuals who escape environmental degradation *and* armed conflict, be it because tensions and disputes over depleting resources triggered the conflict or because the conflict deteriorates the environment or because conflict and environmental degradation feed each other. It is argued here that the definition of serious harm laid down in Article 15(c) could be expanded to include also serious "environmental harm", even in cases where no armed conflict is taking place.

As mentioned in Part 2, some States consider that, for the purpose of Article 15(c) of the Qualification Directive, serious harm consists not only of those

---

174   UNHCR, *The State of the World's Refugees 2012: In Search of Solidarity* (2012), *op. cit.*, pp. 169 and 171.
175   Or, in the words of the Under-Secretary General for Humanitarian affairs, Sir John Holmes, the "new normal". S.J. Holmes, 08/04/2008, *op. cit.*, *supra* note 2 (p. 423).
176   Qualification Directive, Preamble Recital 2.

threats to life or person directly caused by an armed conflict but also of those linked with criminal behaviours and insecurity in a society destabilised by conflicts, where law enforcement and public order are seriously disturbed, and of those threats resulting from the destruction of basic means of subsistence (such as water, food, health and shelter).[177] It was mentioned throughout this work, environmental change can expose individuals to risks which are tantamount to those created by armed conflict situations. This appears again clearly in view of the three categories of risks associated with armed conflicts, identified above. Environmental disasters too can directly threaten individuals' life or person; they can similarly cause a breakdown of law and order resulting in increased criminality and insecurity;[178] and they can also deplete fresh water resources and food stocks, exhaust healthcare systems and deprive individuals of shelter.

The proposed broadening of the scope of subsidiary protection under Article 15(c) would ensure that, by virtue of the principle of non-discrimination, persons exposed to similar risks are treated similarly. This should not be perceived by States as a potential threat to their national asylum systems; just as not every situation of violence triggers qualification for subsidiary protection, not all environmental disasters would justify that persons displaced be recognised as persons in need of international protection. To be sure, the same criteria could actually be used.

In Part 1, in the criticism of the *Elgafaji* judgment, notably insofar as it fails to define what constitutes "indiscriminate violence in situations of international or internal armed conflicts" for the purpose of Article 15(c), reference was made to H. Lambert and T. Farrell's proposal to resort to indicators ("metrics"[179]), rather than to a set definition, to assess the severity of a conflict. The four indicators proposed by the authors are: battle casualties, civilian casualties, state failure[180] and population displacement.[181] In the context of armed conflicts,

---

177 UNHCR, et al., *Safe at Last?* (July 2011), op. cit., pp. 62–63.
178 The example of Haiti was mentioned earlier, where the national police force, substantially weakened by the 2010 earthquake, does not have the capacity to protect the population against growing insecurity and criminality.
179 Above, pp. 155s.
180 State failure here is assessed on the basis of a series of social, economic and political indicators, such as "demographic pressures, mass population movement and displacement, uneven economic development, sharp economic decline, deterioration of public services, widespread violation of human rights, and intervention by external states and other actors". H. Lambert and T. Farrell refer here to some of the indicators applied by the non-governmental organisation "Fund for Peace", who created a Failed State Index for assessing state failure. H. Lambert and T. Farrell (2010), op. cit., pp. 263–264; The Fund for Peace, *Failed States Index*, <http://www.fundforpeace.org/global/?q=fsi> [21/08/2012].
181 H. Lambert and T. Farrell (2010), op. cit., pp. 257–273 especially.

courts have used some of those criteria or similar ones. Hence the European Court of Human Rights (ECtHR), referring to the case-law of the UK Asylum and Immigration Tribunal (UKAIT), took into consideration and among other criteria "the number of civilians killed, injured and displaced as a result of the fighting".[182] Forced displacement of population was also taken into account by French courts for the assessment of a situation of generalised violence.[183] In the context of environmental disasters and in the absence of armed conflict, the first two indicators could be merged into one ("casualties") but in fact also extended to include, in line with the UKAIT and ECtHR case-law, the number of persons injured as a result of the disaster; the other two indicators – state failure and population displacement – would be fully pertinent.

In brief, Article 15(c) could be amended to include "environmental harm"; under paragraph c, serious harm could then consist of:

> ... serious and individual threat to a civilian's life or person by reason of indiscriminate violence in situations of international or internal armed conflict *or by reason of the indiscriminate impacts of an environmental disaster*.[184]

In view of the fact that armed conflicts and environmental disasters can feed each other so that they coexist and, or that it is uneasy to identify which one of the two caused the other, a broader wording could be preferred, which would draw from the language used by the European Court of Human Rights in *Sufi & Elmi*. Reference to "environmental disaster" would not be included to avoid the conundrum of defining what constitutes a disaster. Under Article 15(c), serious harm would consist of:

> ... serious and individual threat to a civilian's life or person by reason of indiscriminate violence or dire humanitarian conditions in the country of origin.

As for the definition of "dire humanitarian conditions", the case-law of the ECtHR and chiefly the *Sufi & Elmi* case can provide useful guidance.[185]

---

182 ECtHR, *Sufi & Elmi*, §§ 241s; UKAIT, *AM & AM (Somalia)*, *op. cit.*
183 CE, *Baskarathas*, 3 July 2009, *op. cit*; CNDA, *Baskarathas*, 27 June 2008, *op. cit.*
184 The terms in italics are a proposed addition to the current text of Article 15(c) of the Qualification Directive.
185 *See* the discussion above pp. 349s. and pp. 366s more specifically.

Support for this interpretation can be found in the judgment of the UK Asylum and Immigration Tribunal in *AM & AM*. The Tribunal indeed observed that the principle of *non-refoulement* could apply in like manner in situations of general violence and of poor humanitarian conditions.[186]

2   Reasons for the Expansion of Subsidiary Protection Grounds

Several reasons can be invoked to support this amendment to Article 15(c). Firstly, as it is suggested above, expanding the grounds for subsidiary protection to include environmentally-displaced persons within the purview of Article 15 QD would not require a major recast of the Qualification Directive but solely an addition, such as the one proposed, to paragraph c of the article.

Secondly, it would ensure the conformity of EU asylum law with the principle of *non-refoulement* as it is enshrined in human rights law and customary international law: States have the absolute obligation not to return individuals to a real risk of torture, inhuman or degrading treatment or punishment, irrespective of its source.

It would additionally reflect the ongoing evolution of migration flows: observers agree that environmental degradation is, in combination with other factors, an increasingly powerful driver for displacement.[187]

Lastly, just like the African Union – then Organisation of African Unity – and, in Latin America, the Cartagena Declaration paved the way to the grant of international protection to persons fleeing indiscriminate threats to their life or person by reasons of conflicts or other events seriously disturbing public order, the European Union could take the leadership[188] and address the claims of environmentally-displaced persons in an instrument of binding law.

---

186   UKAIT, *AM & AM (Somalia)*, op. cit., § 87.
187   UNHCR, *The State of the World's Refugees 2012: In Search of Solidarity* (2012), op. cit., p. 169; IOM, *Climate Change, Environmental Degradation and Migration*, No. 18 (Geneva: IOM, 2012), p. 10.
188   This is not to forget that the Arab Refugee Convention already contains an expanded refugee definition which includes environmentally-displaced persons but the Convention, adopted in 1994, has not yet been ratified by any State. The definition includes refugees as defined in the 1951 Refugee Convention as well as "[a]ny person who unwillingly takes refuge in a country other than his country of origin or his habitual place of residence because of sustained aggression against, occupation and foreign domination of such country or *because of the occurrence of natural disasters* or grave events resulting in major disruption of public order in the whole country or any part thereof". League of Arab States, Arab Convention on Regulating Status of Refugees in the Arab Countries ("Arab Refugee Convention"), adopted in 1994, not ratified, Article 1.

This could constitute an exemplary legislative practice, which other regions in the world could subsequently adopt too.

At the crossing between status determination and *non-refoulement*, the concept of internal protection alternative, elaborated upon in Article 8 of the Qualification Directive will be addressed below (D). But let us first briefly turn to yet another instrument of EU law, relevant to asylum: temporary protection (C).

C   *Temporary Protection*

Under EU law, temporary protection can be triggered by a mass influx of asylum seekers on the territory of the European Union. Displacement caused by slow-onset degradation of the environment will most likely not fulfil this precondition. In such cases, it is anticipated that displacement is or will be progressive rather than sudden. J. McAdam observes that movement away from "disappearing States" or island States such as Tuvalu and Kiribati, "like the nature of the climate process itself, is likely to be slow and gradual".[189] It would therefore be applicable mainly (or only?) to mass influx of people displaced by sudden environmental disasters.

As said, the Temporary Protection Directive has never yet been activated and it is therefore uncertain how it will apply and whether environmentally-displaced persons could or could not be beneficiaries.

It can nevertheless be recommended that, in situations of mass influx of environmentally-displaced persons, who cannot return in safe and durable conditions to their country of origin because of the dire humanitarian situation prevailing there in the aftermath of a disaster, the Temporary Protection Directive should be activated.

Temporary protection is granted for a maximum of two years, with a possibility that the Council extends it by up to one more year if the reasons for temporary protection persist. As the Haiti example illustrates however, in certain situations, the passing of two (or three) years might not be sufficient to guarantee the return of persons concerned in "safe and durable conditions".[190]

As a consequence, it is necessary that the time limits for temporary protection be applied with flexibility, in view of the actual situation prevailing in the country of origin,[191] and with due regard to States' obligations under international human rights law and the principle of *non-refoulement* in particular.

---

189   J. McAdam, "Disappearing States", *in* J. McAdam (Ed.), *Climate Change and Displacement: Multidisciplinary Perspectives* (Oxford: Hart, 2010), pp. 105–129, 109.

190   Temporary Protection Directive, Article 2(c).

191   The Temporary Protection Directive indicates that States should make possible the voluntary return of persons enjoying temporary protection. In this context, States have the

It can be a suitable emergency response to large-scale displacement caused by sudden environmental disasters. In particular, it can provide both the persons concerned and the authorities with sufficient time to find resettlement solutions if need be.

Though it is – potentially at least – a non-negligible protection against return to unsafe situation, temporary protection (under the Directive) remains above all an administrative tool: it ceases to apply as soon as authorities are able to process the applicant's claim under standard asylum procedures. As a consequence, if it is not accompanied with an extension of the grounds for subsidiary protection, temporary protection alone will neither solve nor markedly improve the situation of environmentally-displaced persons.

So far, in the discussion on whether a solution to protect environmentally-displaced persons can be found in existing asylum law, only limited possibilities have appeared. However, before we turn to consider solutions based on human rights law, it is worth reflecting upon the concept of internal protection alternative. It is an aspect of protection status determination closely related to human rights and to the principle of *non-refoulement*.

D   *Drawing Upon the Concept of Internal Protection Alternative: Towards a Broader-Encompassing Reading of the Principle of Non-refoulement?*

The concept of "internal protection", developed under Article 8 of the Qualification Directive, is at the crossing between status determination and the principle of *non-refoulement*. As will be shown below, when assessing whether an alternative location within the applicant's country of origin would be safe, some Member States have carried out a review of the situation of certain civil, political, social, economic and cultural rights. Such a review suggests a "human rights threshold" for returnability higher than the one traditionally deduced from the prohibition of torture, cruel, inhuman or degrading treatment and punishment.

In the prospective analysis of an internal flight alternative, the key element is the situation awaiting the applicant in the relocation area rather than his or her possible qualification as beneficiary of international protection: internal

---

obligation to provide persons who wish to return with information on the situation prevailing in their country of origin: "Member State shall ensure that the decision of those persons to return is taken in full knowledge of the facts". Moreover, the Directive adds, Member States "may provide for exploratory visits". Similarly, it could be not a possibility but an obligation for States and EU institutions to provide for such visit when temporary protection ends, to ensure that return can indeed be safe and durable. *Ibid.*, Article 21(1).

flight alternative can indeed be imposed on applicants who otherwise fulfil the criteria for refugee status or subsidiary protection. In a claim for international protection, applicants have to demonstrate a real risk of persecution or serious harm.[192] Conversely, when considering the applicability of the concept of internal protection, it is States who have to demonstrate that returning the asylum seeker to a given area would not be unsafe and, what is more, that the returned person would enjoy a certain standard of living. A finding of the contrary by the State leads them to conclude to the "non-returnability" of the applicant.

The concept of "internal protection" or "internal flight alternative" might provide some guidance to identify which rights, besides those traditionally protected under the principle of *non-refoulement* (*i.e.* especially the right not to be subjected to torture), are likely to protect asylum seekers from being returned to their home country.

Under international law, the primary responsibility to protect individuals lies on the State under the jurisdiction of which those individuals are, *i.e.* the State of nationality or habitual residence. International protection must come into play only as a remedy to the failure of that State to effectively protect persons under its jurisdiction. With this in mind, States have developed the idea of an "internal flight alternative". Even though an applicant has demonstrated a real risk of ill-treatment upon return to his country of origin, asylum authorities can conclude that the applicant is not in need of international protection if they find that he can be safe in an alternative location in the country. Under the Qualification Directive, States are allowed to refuse protection to an individual and return him to an alternative part of his country of origin if they find that he would be safe there, be it because he would not be exposed to ill-treatment or because he would be effectively protected against it. Article 8 of the Directive states:

1. As part of the assessment of the application for international protection, Member States may determine that an applicant is not in need of international protection if in a part of the country of origin, he or she:
    (a) has no well-founded fear of being persecuted or is not at real risk of suffering serious harm; or
    (b) has access to protection against persecution or serious harm as defined in Article 7; and he or she can safely and legally travel to and gain admittance to that part of the country and can reasonably be expected to settle there.[193]

---

192   Qualification Directive, Article 4.
193   *Ibid.*, Article 8(1).

Before returning an asylum seeker to an allegedly safe part of his country of origin, Article 8 requires that asylum authorities assess the risk of persecution or serious harm in that region, with regard to the general situation there and the personal circumstances of the applicant. An applicant might, after assessment of his claim, fulfil the refugee definition but invoking an "internal protection alternative" gives States the possibility of denying her international protection if they find that she would be safe in a given location within the country of origin. The construct of "internal protection" provides States with a magnifying lens through which they are allowed to scrutinize countries of origin and map what they deem to be safe havens.

In a way, the assessment of an application for international protection would, as a result, be two-fold: the application is considered at country-scale before it is considered again at regional scale. As a consequence, only those asylum seekers who would be at risk of ill-treatment, not merely in their country of origin but in every part of it, would be recognised to be in need of international protection. Commentators have raised concerns about this. A first argument is legal: nowhere does the Refugee Convention require that asylum seekers show a well-founded fear of persecution in all areas of the country.[194] One can also fear that too high a burden of proof be imposed on asylum-seekers and too broad a margin of interpretation given to States.

In this context, UNHCR, reiterating the usual rule that the burden of proving an allegation rests on the one who asserts it, stresses that it must be the decision-maker who "bears the burden of proof of establishing that an analysis of relocation is relevant to the particular case".[195] Another concern relates to the country of origin information and their examination. Errors of appreciation cannot be ruled out. If States might welcome the leeway which the internal flight alternative construct gives them, and be eager to identify safe havens in applicants' countries of origin, they might also genuinely misappreciate the country information available to them and identify safe havens where there are, in fact, none. Additionally, the actual reliability of the identified alternative is questionable. Assuming that State asylum authorities rightly identify a safe area in an applicant's country of origin, the limits of this area being, more likely than not, immaterial, how can the expelling State be satisfied that

---

194   N. Mole and C. Meredith, *Asylum and the European Convention on Human Rights* (2010), *op. cit.*, p. 69.

195   UNHCR, "Guidelines on International Protection No. 4: 'Internal Flight or Relocation Alternative' within the Context of Article 1a(2) of the 1951 Convention and/or 1967 Protocol Relating to the Status of Refugees" ("Guidelines on International Protection No. 4"), HCR/GIP/03/04, 23 July 2003, §§ 33–34.

the threat will remain outside the area, that the solution is durable?[196] Lastly, accessibility of the safe area identified by the asylum authorities has to be considered. UNHCR has repeatedly warned that the internal relocation will only be a conceivable alternative if the returnee can "practically, safely and legally"[197] gain access to it.

Possibly as a safeguard for asylum seekers against receiving States' unquestioned inclination to limit the number of displaced persons settling on their territory, the Qualification Directive adds an additional criterion. Return in the designated area must not expose the individual to persecution and serious harm and, additionally, it must be reasonable to expect from the returned person that she stays in the given area. In the author's view, this additional precondition to activating an internal flight alternative might in fact lead to an enlargement of the *non-refoulement* obligation of States, at least theoretically if not in practice.

A survey of State practice shows that the two preconditions combined have led the national asylum authorities of a number of Member States to conduct a thorough evaluation of the situation awaiting the applicant in the relocation area. This evaluation includes human rights considerations.[198] Violations of social and economic rights are not unanimously construed as ill-treatments qualifying for an international protection status nor do they systematically trigger the principle of *non-refoulement*; national decisions and case-law illustrate that they however impact on States' assessments of the "reasonableness" of an internal flight alternative in a given case.

France for example finds that internal relocation of the applicant is a reasonable option only if the authorities have ascertained that the applicant can safely access the alternative area, settle, and "lead a normal life" there.[199] What

---

196 By way of example, the UNHCR warns that, in countries in the grip of armed conflict, shifting armed fronts render internal flight alternative unworkable. UN High Commissioner for Refugees, *Guidelines on International Protection No. 4: "Internal Flight or Relocation Alternative" Within the Context of Article 1A(2) of the 1951 Convention and/or 1967 Protocol Relating to the Status of Refugees*, 23 July 2003, HCR/GIP/03/04, §27.

197 UN High Commissioner for Refugees, *Guidelines on International Protection No. 4: "Internal Flight or Relocation Alternative" Within the Context of Article 1A(2) of the 1951 Convention and/or 1967 Protocol Relating to the Status of Refugees*, 23 July 2003, HCR/GIP/03/04, §§10–12.

198 H. Lambert (January 2006), *op. cit.*, pp. 166–167.

199 According to the French Constitutional court: *"il appartiendra à l'Office, sous le contrôle de la Commission des recours des réfugiés, de ne refuser l'asile pour le motif énoncé au troisième alinéa du III du nouvel article 2 de la loi du 25 juillet 1952 qu'après s'être assuré que l'intéressé peut, en toute sûreté, accéder à une partie substantielle de son pays d'origine, s'y établir et*

constitutes a "normal" life is informed by the decisions issued by asylum authorities. "Living conditions", "a constant threat of being subjected to police harassment", the possibility to find a job, access to housing, and the existence of family ties in the region were but some of elements which had a bearing in the decision to relocate or not an applicant.[200]

Belgium asylum authorities have had due regard to the existence of family, ethnic or other connections in the region,[201] and, in the case of a single woman with children, to very harsh conditions of living.[202]

A study conducted by ECRE on the implementation of the Qualification Directive reveals that national asylum authorities also make references to, among other notions: the possibility to earn the subsistence minimum (Germany), the real possibility to survive economically or the economic viability (UK), the general respect for human rights (Luxembourg), the absence of threat to life or person (Germany) or, on the contrary, economic annihilation, utter destitution or existence below an adequate level of subsistence (UK).[203] The German response to ECRE's questionnaire indicates that some decisions apply the internal protection alternative as a blanket measure for certain categories of applicants but stresses that "a considerable number" of administrative and court decisions consider the applicant's personal circumstances when evaluating the internal protection alternative including his or her age, disability, health and sex, as well as his ethnic, cultural, religious, political or social connections, language skills, and ability to access a job and housing.[204]

To sum things up, if an applicant cannot demonstrate a well-founded fear of persecution or serious harm, receiving States are allowed to withhold their international protection and, provided that return is not prescribed under the principle of *non-refoulement*, they can return the failed applicant to his or her country of origin. If on the contrary the applicant can establish the well-foundedness of

---

   y mener une existence normale". France : Conseil Constitutionnel, *Décision n° 2003-485 DC du 04 décembre 2003 relative à la Loi modifiant la loi n° 52-893 du 25 juillet 1952 relative au droit d'asile*, §17.

200 France: CRR, Sections réunies, *M.B.*, 446177, 25/06/2004; CRR, *M. IH.*, 487151, 25/01/2005; CRR, Melle N., 542469, 30/03/2006.

201 Belgium: CPRR, 03-2282/F1654, 23/11/2004; CPRR, 04-2344/F2189, 26/10/2005; Conseil du contentieux des étrangers (CCE), 1968, 26/09/2007, RDE 2007, n°144, p. 341.

202 The Belgian asylum authorities (*Commission permanente de recours des réfugiés*) refer to "*conditions d'existence très pénibles*" awaiting the applicant upon relocation in the given area to reject the application of the internal flight alternative in the case. CPRR, 20 octobre 2004, n° 04-0511/F1652, *RDE*, 2004, n° 130, p. 630.

203 ECRE/ELENA, *op. cit.*, pp. 119–135.

204 *Ibid.*, p. 128.

his fear, he should, in principle, be afforded international protection. That said, the receiving State may still withhold international protection if it can invoke the existence of an "internal protection alternative".

This power of States is however circumscribed: asylum authorities must demonstrate that the applicant, who has shown a "general" well-founded fear of persecution or serious harm, would have no such fear if returned to a specific region of his country of origin. Given the risk to which States might expose individuals returned under such conditions, additional safeguards were provided by the Qualification Directive: internal relocation must be reasonable in view of the general circumstances prevailing in the region and of the personal circumstances of the applicant.[205] Whereas the assessment of an applicant's claim for international protection is based on security considerations, internal relocation on the other hand requires that national asylum authorities should establish that the applicant will be safe in the relocation area and, in addition, that he will enjoy a certain quality of life there, including the benefit of certain social, economic and cultural rights in particular.[206] *A contrario*, it means that EU Member States are not allowed to relocate an applicant in areas where the human rights situation is not good enough. In that sense, internal protection, especially as it is implemented by the above-mentioned Member States, carries with it a broadening of the scope of *non-refoulement* State obligations. For example, as mentioned above, French asylum authorities have found incompatible with France's obligations under the Directive a relocation alternative which would infringe on the applicant's right to work. In other words, France recognises the extraterritoriality of the right to work, enshrined in particular in Article 7 of the International Covenant on Economic, Social and Cultural Rights, at least insofar as internal flight alternative is at stake.

The principle of *non-refoulement* under human rights law here appears to be informed by developments of European Union refugee law – which itself in the first place meant to integrate in EU law the human rights obligations of EU Member States deriving from international treaties to which they are parties. More accurately, more than the provisions of EU refugee law themselves it is mainly their transposition and implementation by States that is suggestive of an evolution in States' perception of their obligations towards displaced persons.

---

205   Qualification Directive, Article 8(2).
206   The Qualification Directive requires that States willing to return an individual to a allegedly safe area within his or her country of origin ensure that he or she "can reasonably be expected to settle there" (Qualification Directive, Article 8(1)(b), *in fine*). As mentioned above, States' assessment of the situation in the designated area against this yardstick include human rights considerations. *See* above pp. 476s.

It is worth noting that the Netherlands and the UK clarified that a simple lowering of living standards or deterioration of economic status would not be deemed "unreasonable". The worsening of the economic and social status of the applicant must reach a certain threshold of severity for the Dutch and British authorities to find it unreasonable to apply the internal flight alternative in the case.[207]

In view of the specific context in which such broadened application of the principle of *non-refoulement* occurs, and of the spectrum of State practices, the importance to be awarded to the perceived broadening of State obligations must be put into perspective. Should State practice be constant over time (the entry into force of the Qualification Directive is, after all, still very recent) and uniform among EU Member States, it might attest to the recognition by States of the extraterritoriality of an increased number of human rights. A few words follow to clarify this point.

In principle, failed asylum seekers can be returned to their country of origin, unless return would be contrary to Article 3 of the European Convention of Human Rights. On the other hand, the concept of internal protection alternative, as it is devised in Article 8 of the Qualification Directive and operated by States suggests that other rights should be taken into consideration before removing an individual to his or her country of origin. The additional safeguards to return are intended to apply only when return concerns persons who otherwise qualify for refugee status or subsidiary protection. It was mentioned in Part 1, State Parties to the ECHR and ICCPR have the obligation to assure the rights enshrined in those instruments to all individuals within their jurisdiction.[208] Similarly, Article 2 of the International Covenant on Economic, Social and Cultural Rights (ICESCR) provides that States Parties' obligation to guarantee that the rights it enunciates "will be exercised without discrimination of any kind as to race, colour, sex, language, religion, political or other opinion, national or social origin, property, birth or other status". As a result, EU Member States, who are all parties to all three instruments, have the legal obligation to safeguard civil, political, economic, social and cultural rights to all individuals within their jurisdiction without discrimination of any kind; the status of refugee or beneficiary of subsidiary protection or the absence of any such status should therefore be immaterial. As a consequence of the principle of non-discrimination enunciated above and for the sake of coherence of the EU asylum system, every individual should be protected against *refoulement* under the same conditions. There is no justification in human rights law for a

---

207   ECRE/ELENA, *op. cit.*, p. 123.
208   Above Part 1. Chapter 3.1.A.1, pp. 185s.

differentiation based on international protection status. It should follow that no one should be returned to a country or region where he or she cannot "reasonably be expected to settle"[209] in view of the human rights situation prevailing in the area.

The interpretation would obviously benefit environmentally-displaced persons. It was argued above, in the majority of cases, persons displaced by environmental disasters will not qualify for refugee status or subsidiary protection. It will therefore often be necessary that the principle of *non-refoulement* come to the rescue. An assessment of the feasibility of returning an individual to his or her country of origin, or to a specific area within this country, based on the human rights situation prevailing in the destination area and on whether it can be reasonably expected from the returnee that he or she settles there would certainly benefit people fleeing environmental disasters, confronted in their country of origin with depleted natural resources, impeded access to healthcare and deprivation of numerous economic, social and cultural rights.

II   Possible Developments in International Human Rights Law

Two aspects will be discussed below. Firstly, the absolute nature of the principle of *non-refoulement* must be respected (A). Secondly, on the basis of the conclusions reached in Part 2, it will be recalled that an individual's "ability to cater for his [or her] most basic needs" must be the principal indicator in environmental-disaster cases (B).

A   *Reaffirming the Absolute Nature of the Principle of* Non-refoulement

As shown in Part 2, existing instruments of international human rights law have not yet been applied to protect environmentally-displaced persons from being sent back to their country of origin. It was argued though that, *de lege lata*, the principle of *non-refoulement* is applicable to environmentally-displaced persons. Before courts and treaty-bodies at the regional and global level take a stand on the issue, EU Member States could be recommended to adopt policies and implement the principle in a "progressive way"[210] in order to, at a minimum, authorise environmentally-displaced persons to stay on their territory.

---

209   Qualification Directive, Article 8(1).
210   The same policy option was recommended by the participants in the 2011 UNU-EHS Summer Academy. The findings of the Summer Academy were compiled by M. Morel in M. Morel, "Protecting Environmental Migrants: Findings from the UNU-EHS Summer Academy", 11 November 2011, retrieved from: <www.internationallawobserver.eu/2010/11/11/

It would in fact be counterintuitive to talk here, with a view to encourage it, of a "constructive" or "progressive" interpretation of the principle of *non-refoulement* as a precondition to its applicability to environmentally-displaced persons. It would be more accurate to encourage decision-makers, authorities and courts to make *full use* of the principle and, in legal terms, to implement it pursuant to the general principle of good faith.[211] The absolute prohibition to return individuals to a real risk of inhuman or degrading treatment must be respected at all times, regardless of the source of the harm and regardless also of the receiving State's own perceived interest. In that respect, the humanitarian nature of *non-refoulement* cannot be ignored.[212] The International Court of Justice (ICJ) in a case concerning reservations to the Genocide Convention clearly defined what the obligations of States are under norms of humanitarian purpose. The ICJ notes that the Genocide Convention was adopted for a "purely humanitarian" purpose, "to safeguard the very existence of certain human groups", and adds that:

> ... [i]n such a convention the contracting States do not have any interests of their own; they merely have, one and all, a common interest, namely, the accomplishment of those high purposes which are the *raison d'être* of the convention.[213]

Similarly, the *raison d'être* of the humanitarian principle of *non-refoulement* is to safeguard the existence and human dignity of persons.

It would only be logical and coherent in view of the "absolute nature"[214] of the principle of *non-refoulement*, consistently reasserted, that it be applied to prohibit returns to any life-threatening situations, whichever its source or cause.

The judgment of the Court in *N. v. UK* and its "proportionalist errings"[215] could be analysed as an accidental drift away by the Court (by the majority at least) from its long-standing, always reaffirmed, absolute principle of *non-refoulement*. The Court might perhaps want to reconsider its case-law

---

protecting-environmental-migrants-findings-from-the-unu-ehs-summer-academy/> [02/12/2012].
211   VCLT, Article 31.
212   UNHCR, "The Principle of Non-Refoulement as a Norm of Customary International Law", *op. cit.*, § 15.
213   ICJ, *Reservations to the Genocide Convention*.
214   See above, Part 1. Chapter 3. I., pp. 181s.
215   ECtHR, *N. v. UK*, Joint dissenting opinion of Judges Tulkens, Bonello and Spielmann, § 7.

to retrieve from the *Chahal* jurisprudence the essence of the principle: *non-refoulement* is absolute, irrespective of the behaviour of the individual concerned. Many questions arise. Why then take into consideration elements that should be even less pertinent in the appreciation of the individual's genuine need for protection? If criminal conduct of the individual[216] and danger he or she may represent to the host State's security and community are irrelevant and do not affect his or her protection-"worthiness", how then can the host State's allegedly overstretched healthcare system, a failure of the State against which the individual is powerless, be taken into consideration to deny him or her protection, *a fortiori* against deterioration of his or her health and decrease in life expectancy? How can States validly invoke their own interest to deny protection to a person with an otherwise valid claim? How can States lawfully invoke the financial burden an asylum seeker would impose on their economy to return the individual to a situation they acknowledge to be life-threatening? How can the fact that the threat to the applicant's life emanates from his State's inability rather than unwillingness to secure the most basic needs of its population justify that a receiving State denies protection to the individual?

At a time when poverty alleviation, development and international solidarity are recurrent in the international discourse,[217] it seems that Europe is not sending a positive signal. Again, the very purpose of the principle of *non-refoulement* is not the pursuit by States of their own interests but the protection of individuals – or so it should be. It is in that sense that *non-refoulement* should be interpreted.

It can be noted that, whereas States have no interest on their own in implementing *non-refoulement*, it is nonetheless possible that the operation of the principle of *non-refoulement* in practice benefits States. In particular, it can be beneficent to the State of origin, insofar as it can relieve it of its responsibility towards individuals it is unable to protect within its jurisdiction. It is also worth mentioning at this juncture that migration at large, including displacements of populations in need of protection, should not be perceived as automatically negative for and by receiving States. This is common knowledge – albeit seemingly forgotten at times – societies are the product of centuries of migratory

---

216 As mentioned, an individual's involvement in terrorist activities is not an exception to the principle of *non-refoulement*.

217 For instance, the Rio+20 United Nations Conference on Sustainable Development was the occasion for States and Governments to reaffirm their commitment "to freeing humanity from poverty and hunger as a matter of urgency". UN Conference on Sustainable Development, "Outcome of the Conference: The Future We Want", A/CONF.216/L.1 [19 June 2012], § 2.

flows. Suffice is to have a glance at modern history: European settlement and colonisation in the Americas, in Oceania or Africa, the two World Wars, or the large scale migration flows after 1945, mainly from Southern Europe, North Africa and Turkey to Western European countries who needed labour force for post-war reconstruction, and the economic growth and expansion that followed, are but examples of population movements that contributed to shaping contemporary European societies.

B   Returnability to Environmental Disasters Situations Assessed by the Standard of "Ability to Cater for One's Most Basic Needs"

Part 2 concluded that, *de lege lata*, international human rights law could protect individuals displaced by environmental disasters from being returned to their country of origin. To reiterate but the main conclusion, it was argued that the test formulated by the European Court of Human Rights in *MSS v. Belgium and Greece* and developed in *Sufi & Elmi* was applicable. Under this approach, the Court has regard to:

> ... an applicant's ability to cater for his most basic needs, such as food, hygiene and shelter, his vulnerability to ill-treatment and the prospect of his situation improving within a reasonable time-frame.[218]

On the basis of those indicators, the Court concluded in the case that returning the applicant to a displaced person camp where humanitarian conditions are dire would expose him to a real risk of Article 3 ECHR ill-treatment.

This approach has two main assets for the purpose of protecting environmentally-displaced persons: firstly, the threshold is less high than in *D. v. UK* and *N. v. UK* where only "compelling humanitarian considerations" can justify *non-refoulement*. Secondly, the indicator used by the Court to assess the reality of the risk in *MSS – Sufi & Elmi* is of utmost relevance in situations of environmental disaster (ability to cater for one's most basic needs). Due consideration of the applicant's vulnerability is essential: the IASC Guidelines underline that certain groups of persons are indeed "particularly vulnerable and/or have particular needs in the event of a disaster".[219] Particularly promising is the reference to the applicant's "prospect of his situation improving within a reasonable time-frame". Its potential for application in the context of slow-onset disasters and long-term environmental degradation as well as in post-disaster (and, or post-conflict) situations is evident.

---

218   ECtHR, *Sufi & Elmi*, § 283.
219   IASC, *Operational Guidelines* (January 2011), *op. cit.*, p. 61, Annex II.

According to the Court, this test is intended to apply in cases where the risk engages "either directly or indirectly the responsibility of the public authorities of that country".[220] This precondition is met in environmental disaster cases since, as also shown in Part 2, not only disasters can be caused, directly or indirectly by State action or inaction, but their impact on population also varies greatly depending on national authorities' preparedness and response to the disaster.

A final remark concerns the possible development of a right to a healthy environment. Within the Council of Europe, in 2008, the Committee on Migration, Refugees and Population of the Parliamentary Assembly published a report on environmentally-induced migration and displacement. It considered means of "enhancing the human rights protection mechanisms *vis-à-vis* the challenges of climate change and environmental degradation processes" and to that end, invited States to consider "adding an additional protocol to the European Convention on Human Rights, concerning the right to a healthy and safe environment".[221] So far, that proposal has not been pursued.[222] It could be argued however that, should the protocol be implemented, it might be of limited use to trigger the prohibition of *refoulement*. It is mainly on the ground of Article 3 ECHR that the Court developed and has applied since the principle of *non-refoulement*. Where other rights are invoked, in most cases, it is in conjunction with Article 3 that they apply, if at all. For that reason, the proposed Protocol could make clear that violation of the right to a healthy

---

220 ECtHR, *N. v. UK*, § 32 read a contrario; ECtHR, *Sufi & Elmi*, § 282.

221 Council of Europe, Parliamentary Assembly, Committee on Migration, Refugees and Population, *Environmentally Induced Migration and Displacement: A 21st Century Challenge*, COE Doc 11785 (23 December 2008), para 121 and 6.3 respectively.

222 In 2009, the Parliamentary Assembly of the Council of Europe reiterated its recommendation to the Committee of Ministers that it draws up an additional protocol to the European Convention on Human Rights, recognising the right to a healthy and viable environment. PACE, "Recommendation 1885 (2009)", *op. cit.* In the meantime, the European Court of Human Rights has had opportunities to assert the existence of such a right. 2012, the ECtHR, citing its earlier case-law (its 2009 judgement in the *Tătar* case) referred to the "right to a healthy and protected environment". In the case *di Sarbo and others v. Italy*, concerning the state of emergency in relation to waste collection, treatment and disposal in a region of Italy, the Court found that the collection, treatment and disposal of waste being hazardous activities, Italy was "under a duty to adopt reasonable and appropriate measures capable of safeguarding the right of those concerned to respect for their private life and for their home, and, more generally, their *right to enjoy a healthy and protected environment*". ECtHR, *Affaire Di Sarno et autres c. Italie* ("*Di Sarno*"), Requête n°0765/08 (10 January 2012), § 110; ECtHR, *Affaire Tătar c. Roumanie* ("*Tătar*"), Requête n° 67021/01 (27 January 2009, final 6 July 2009), § 107.

and safe environment can be tantamount to exposing individuals to torture, inhuman or degrading treatment or punishment. Alternatively, L. Westra advocates the recognition of the right not to be exposed to "environmental harms" as a *jus cogens* norm, "given the gross human rights violations that ensue".[223]

C *Why* Non-refoulement *Will Not Adequately Protect Environmentally-Displaced Persons*

There are several reasons why a response to environmental displacement based solely on international human rights law would fail to effectively and fully tackle the issue. Three main arguments will be considered.

Undeniably, *non-refoulement* is a fundamental guarantee for individuals who left their country of origin, where they risk be exposed to inhuman or degrading treatment, that they shall not be returned. As argued, it is applicable to environmental displacement. However, in view of existing case-law, it will most certainly protect persons displaced by sudden disasters while persons who move due to slow-onset environmental degradation risk be excluded. One of the key characteristics of environmental displacement is its timespan. Displacement can – and should – take place at different paces, starting at different stages of the environmental degradation. It would be counterproductive, not to mention questionable on a legal, moral, and ethical point of view, to expect populations affected or likely to be affected by severe alterations of their living environmental that they stay, as long as possible in the affected area, until their conditions of living become unbearable. Under the case-law of the two European courts however, it appears that it is typically when the living conditions have become unbearable and expose populations to a risk of death or inhuman or degrading treatment that persons on the move can be protected from *refoulement*. Another time-related limitation pertains not to the activation of the principle of *non-refoulement* but to its duration. It is not a permanent form of protection; "[a]t most, *non-refoulement* creates an obligation for temporary refuge".[224]

Secondly, States have the obligation to grant to all within their jurisdiction, without discrimination, the rights enshrined in the human rights treaties they are parties to. Unlike refugee law though, international human rights law does not confer any formal status to individuals so that their situation is often

---

223 L. Westra, *Environmental Justice and the Rights of Ecological Refugees* (2009), op. cit., p. 187.
224 R.L. Newmark, "Non-Refoulement Run Afoul: The Questionable Legality of Extraterritorial Repatriation Programs", *Washington University Law Review*, Vol. 71, No. 3 (1993), pp. 833–870, p. 863.

characterised by much uncertainty.[225] *Non-refoulement* can be salutary and the absence of status acceptable but for a limited period of time only. In cases where the reasons for the flight persist – as in cases where the disasters are particularly severe and reconstruction lengthy or when the environment progressively deteriorates, sustainable solutions will be called for. *Non-refoulement* alone does not provide such longer-term protection. Nonetheless, it is worth recalling that, in a European context, developments in international human rights law may have a direct impact on the grant of subsidiary protection status. As stated in Part 1, subsidiary protection was developed by the European legislator in order to cover situations where applicants are not entitled to refugee status but to whom the principle of *non-refoulement* should apply.[226] It follows that if subsidiary protection is to fulfil its stated aim to reflect Member States' obligation under international human rights law instruments (including, in particular, ECHR Article 3), the recognition of the right of environmentally-displaced persons, as such, to *non-refoulement* ought to be reflected in the grant of subsidiary protection to individuals in similar situations.[227]

Lastly, a solution based solely on the extension of the protection provided under existing human rights law, although it would surely be a progress, would merely be a "lesser evil". The criticism also applies to Convention-based solutions: it would fail to address the causes of environmental displacement. In other words, legislators and policymakers opting for a solution based solely on refugee law or human rights law would be burying their head in the sand.

Part 2 concluded by stating that solutions in existing law were few to protect environmentally-displaced persons. The first Chapter of the present Part concludes with another rather pessimistic observation: drawing on existing norms of international protection might not be appropriate either to effectively tackle the issue of displacement triggered by environmental disasters. It is therefore necessary to consider alternatives. A first alternative is also based on existing law but on the law of State responsibility. Can and should States be held responsible for environmental displacement (Chapter 11)? The second alternative will be dealt with subsequently: the adoption of a *sui generis* framework to address environmental displacement (Chapter 12).

---

225 J. McAdam for example refers to *non-refoulement* "without more". J. McAdam, *Complementary Protection in International Refugee Law* (2007), *op. cit.*, p. 45.
226 *See* above Part 1. Chapter 2.III.A.1, pp. 106s.
227 *See* also previous developments on environmentally-displaced persons as beneficiaries of subsidiary protection, pp. 444s.

CHAPTER 11

Can (and Should) States be Held Responsible for Environmental Displacement?

As concluded from the two previous parts, neither refugee law nor international human rights law can offer fully appropriate solutions to the problem of environmental displacement. It is therefore necessary to turn to broader international law and analyse whether States bear any obligation to prevent or else react to environmental displacement. According to M. Fitzmaurice, the question whether States are legally responsible for climate change should be examined within the broader context of State responsibility for environmental damage.[1]

It is commonly stated: it is not environmental degradation *per se* that alone triggers displacement. Instead, the causes are multiple and interrelated,[2] so much so that disentangling them may prove challenging if not impossible and drawing the line between voluntary and forced migration a conundrum.[3] Likewise, literature indicates that environmental degradation itself often has a plurality of causative sources; it also has a variety of short-term and long-term impacts. This has been made particularly clear in the context of a growing interest for the actual and projected impacts of climate change. Climate science shows that, if certain regions are at higher risk of experiencing the

---

1 M. Fitzmaurice, "Responsibility and Climate Change", *German Yearbook of International Law*, Vol. 53 (2010), p. 89.
2 A. Suhrke (1994), *op. cit.*, The complexity of causes was notably evidenced in a joint report by the United Nations University and UNHCR who, on the basis of interviews with refugees from the East and Horn of Africa and with actors involved and field visits examined the perceptions and experiences of displaced persons. Drivers for migration can include external and personal circumstances such as environmental factors, violence, financial resources, social networks in the destination area or education and skills. T. Afifi, *et al.*, *Climate Change, Vulnerability and Human Mobility: Perspectives of Refugees from the East and Horn of Africa* (June 2012), *op. cit.*
3 C. Bates and G. Hugo hence depicted population mobility as a continuum, ranging from purely or principally voluntary migration to forced or last resort migration. D.C. Bates, "Environmental Refugees? Classifying Human Migrations Caused by Environmental Change", *Population and Environment*, Vol. 23, No. 5 (May 2002), pp. 467–469; G. Hugo, "Migration, Development and Environment – Draft Paper", *Research Workshop on Migration and the Environment: Developing a global research agenda*, held in Munich on 16–18 April 2008, p. 11, retrieved from: <www.ciesin.columbia.edu/repository/pern/papers/hugo_statement.pdf> [05/05/2012].

harmful impacts of climate change for reasons pertaining to their geographical situation, the effects of global warming on a region's environment will also be in large part determined by a series of factor, ranging from political or economic to demographic circumstances.[4] The same is true of any environmental degradation, be it connected with climate change or not. The severity of its impacts on affected population and territory will be of varying intensity, scale and duration depending on the region's level of preparedness to environmental degradations, its technological advancement, its ability (including financial) to react and adapt, its resilience capacity,[5] the density of its population and the possible availability of international assistance and support. Some of those factors entail elements of State responsibility; some others do not, or hardly so. In fact, M. Fitzmaurice warned that the question of whether States were legally responsible for climate change was "one of the most complicated and debated issues".[6]

In short, the sources and consequences of environmental degradation are often multiple. The same goes for the drivers of migration. Therefore, the question of the attributability of environmental displacement takes shape as a complex problem, involving many variables. The purpose of this Chapter is to determine whether the benefits of a responsibility-based approach to environmental displacement are worth the endeavour.

An approach based on State responsibility in fact soon manifests itself as inappropriate to effectively address the issue of environmental displacement. For that reason, only the main aspects of the question which are also the main obstacles to the responsibility-based approach will be discussed below.

The responsibility of States for internationally wrongful act is regulated under customary international law. Those rules have been codified[7] and are presently formulated in the Articles on the Responsibility of States for internationally wrongful acts, adopted by the International Law Commission in 2001[8]

---

4   M.L. Parry, *et al.* (2007), *op. cit.*, pp. 26s.
5   For a definition of "resilience capacity", *see* for example the "resilience capacity index" developed by Kathryn Foster (University at Buffalo Regional Institute, State University of New York) and described at: <http://brr.berkeley.edu/rci/> [accessed 10/06/2012].
6   Malgosia Fitzmaurice, "Responsibility and Climate Change", *German Yearbook of International Law*, Vol.53 (2010), p. 89.
7   Although not every ILC Article on State Responsibility reflects custom, for some of them, this status is undisputed. It includes in particular Article 2.
8   ILC, Articles on Responsibility of States for Internationally Wrongful Acts, Report of the 53rd Session ("ILC Articles on State Responsibility") UN Doc. A/56/10 (2001) *GAOR, 56th session, Supplement No. 10, at 43*.

and endorsed by the UN General Assembly in 2008.[9] Article 2 states that internationally wrongful acts consist of an action or omission which is "attributable to the State under international law" (I) and which constitutes "a breach of an international obligation of the State" (II). The two aspects of the question will be addressed before a conclusion is reached (III).

I Attributability

Besides the plurality of causes of disasters and of migration, another obstacle to addressing environmental displacement from the perspective of State responsibility appears: as mentioned, to hold a State responsible for environmental displacement, one must establish this State's responsibility in triggering the displacement. In a context where most environmental disruptions are caused by climate change, the prerequisite will oft be tantamount to establishing the State's contribution to climate change.

Negotiations, debates and the disappointing outcomes[10] of the recent meetings of the Conference of the Parties to the Framework Convention on Climate Change (UNFCCC) are striking evidence: States are not all[11] and jointly ready to rise to the challenge of climate change. States' reluctance to recognise their respective contributions to global warming accounts in large part for their

---

[9] UNGA, "Responsibility of States for Internationally Wrongful Acts: Resolution/Adopted by the General Assembly", A/RES/62/61, 8 January 2008.

[10] It was amply reported in the press: "negotiations were difficult and the conclusions vague". D. Shukman, "Rio+20 Summit Criticised as 'Disappointing'", BBC News, 22 June 2012, video, at 00:20; J. Watts and L. Ford, "Rio+20 Earth Summit: Campaigners Decry Final Document", 23 June 2012; J. Egeland and J. Evans, "Rio+20 Missed an Opportunity to Bolster Human Rights", The Guardian – Poverty Matters Blog, 27 June 2012. A more balanced view is expressed by John Vidal who, together with environmental activist Richard Sandbrook, notes that international targets and timetables were already in place before the 2012 Earth Summit and are still afterwards. A positive outcome of the 2012 Conference was in particular, that developed countries, including the United States, renewed their commitment in that regard. The reporter however observes that the implementation and achievement of the measures and objectives set require stronger institutions. J. Vidal, "Rio+20: Reasons to Be Cheerful", The Guardian – Poverty Matters Blog, 27 June 2012, points 1 and 2 in particular. Similarly, UN Secretary General Ban Ki-Moon considers the Outcome Document as a "solid package" where Member States endorsed the idea of "sustainable development" and stresses that action and implementation will be determining. D. Shukman, 22 June 2012, op. cit., Interview with UN Secretary General Ban Ki-Moon, at 00:30.

[11] Some criticisms are formulated against developing or emerging countries in particular. L. Gray, "Rio+20: Nick Clegg Blames China for 'Disappointing Text'", The Telegraph, 21 June 2012.

timid commitment to undertake greenhouse gas emissions cuts but also for their unwillingness to address the question of the protection and assistance of environmentally-displaced persons.[12] The question of the attributability of climate change-related disasters and displacement is therefore not only a legal question but also a highly political and sensitive one.

A   Causality: Some (Insurmountable) Hurdles Pertaining to the Source of Harm being Environmental

Succinctly, States are responsible for the actions or omissions which, being attributable to them under international law, constitute breaches of an international obligation of the State and cause an injury to another State.[13]

The State may be held responsible if the act results from the conduct of organs of the State[14] or of persons or entities exercising elements of governmental authority.[15] In the leading *Nicaragua Case*,[16] the International Court of Justice (ICJ) found that State responsibility may also result, *inter alia*, from acts that were carried out on its "instruction", or under its "direction or control".[17] The International Law Commission codified the rule.[18]

The provision can be of particular relevance in the case of environmental degradation as these may be the consequence of activities conducted by public or private companies for instance. In the *Nicaragua case*, the ICJ considered that a State should have "effective control"[19] over the conduct of the person or group of persons committing the act. The test was lowered by the International Criminal Tribunal for the Former Yugoslavia (ICTY) in the *Tadic case*: there, the ICTY distinguished between the acts of individuals or unorganised groups, and the acts of organised and structured groups.[20] The Tribunal considered that the degree of control required to trigger State responsibility for the conduct of private persons may vary according to the factual circumstances of the case;[21] an "overall control" may be sufficient.[22]

---

12   K.E. Mcnamara (2007), *op. cit.*, pp. 20–21.
13   ILC Articles on State Responsibility, Articles 1 and 2.
14   *Ibid.*, Article 4.
15   *Ibid.*, Article 5.
16   ICJ, *Nicaragua (Merits)*.
17   See ICTY (Appeals Chamber), *Prosecutor v. Tadic* ("*Tadic*"), Case IT-94-1 (15 July 1999) 38 I.L.M. 1518.
18   ILC Articles on State Responsibility., Article 8.
19   ICJ, *Nicaragua (Merits)*, § 115.
20   ICTY, *Tadic*, § 120.
21   ICTY, *Tadic*, § 117.
22   ICTY, *Tadic*, § 131.

In the hypothesis of environmental degradation caused by industrial accident (Bhopal) or technological accident (including development projects such as the Three Gorges dam project in China), responsibility for the environmental harm caused by the catastrophe, and subsequent population movement, may be attributed to the companies' national State by reason of the control States necessarily have over the activities concerned. In relation to industrial accidents causing pollution with chemicals or radioactive material: the activity being hazardous, States have a duty under international law to regulate and control such activity.[23] In addition to adopting and implementing appropriate legislation in that sense, governments also have the obligation to protect their citizens from damaging acts that may be perpetrated by private parties.[24] States' responsibility will be triggered by its failure to prevent[25] the accident, to cooperate, and to notify and warn[26] of the accident.

The rule was formulated by the arbitrary tribunal in the Trail Smelter case: "no State has the right to use or permit the use of its territory in such a manner as to cause injury by fumes in or to the territory of another or the properties or persons therein".[27]

It follows that State's responsibility for environmental degradation can be seen as nearly automatic. The State's failure to effectively control the activities of the companies can generally be invoked.

Recently, more than a year after the nuclear accident that hit Japan in March 2011 following a 9.0 magnitude earthquake and towering tsunami, an independent investigation commission, mandated by the Japanese parliament, released a report on Fukushima nuclear accident. Its findings are unequivocal: the nuclear accident was a "man-made disaster". The panel, composed of a seismologist, professors, lawyers, doctors and a journalist,[28] points to the

---

23   See in that sense: ICJ, *Nuclear Weapons case*, pp. 241–242, § 29; ILC Articles on the Prevention of Transboundary Harm from Hazardous Activities; UN Conference on Environment and Development, Rio Declaration on Environment and Development ("Rio Declaration"), 13 June 1992 UN Doc. A/CONF.151/26 (vol. I), Principle 15.

24   African Commission on Human and Peoples' Rights, *Social and Economic Rights Action Centre for Economic and Social Rights v. Nigeria*, Comm. No. 155/96 (27 October 2001).

25   ICJ, *Case Concerning United States Diplomatic and Consular Staff in Tehran, Judgment* ("*United States of America v. Iran*") (24 May 1980) *ICJ Reports 1980*, p. 3.

26   ICJ, *Corfu Channel (United Kingdom of Great Britain and Northern Ireland v. Albania)* ("*Corfu Channel Case*") (9 April 1949) *ICJ Reports 1949*, p. 4, pp. 22–23.

27   Arbitrary Tribunal, *Trail Smelter Case (USA, Canada)* ("*Trail Smelter*") UNRIAA Vol. III, pp. 1906–1982, p. 1965.

28   H. Hiyama, "Fukushima: un 'désastre créé par l'homme', selon un rapport officiel", *TV5 Monde* (AFP, 2012), 5 July 2012, retrieved from: <http://www.tv5.org/cms/chaine-francophone/info> [05/07/2012].

responsibilities of the Japanese government (especially the Prime Minister at the time, Naoto Kan), regulatory agencies and the nuclear plant operator (Tokyo Electric Power Co., "TEPCO"). The Fukushima accident was, accordingly, the result of "collusion between" and "lack of governance by" those actors.[29] The report mentions that the Fukushima Daiichi nuclear plant was particularly vulnerable due to delays in anti-seismic reinforcement works and in the adoption of tsunami measures, and highlights that TEPCO management as well as the national Nuclear Industrial Safety Agency were aware of this vulnerability.[30] The investigator further blame TEPCO, the government and its administration for not acting promptly in the aftermath of the accident, in part due to miscommunications between them, and for failing to properly inform the population (sometimes deliberately).[31] Heard by the parliamentary investigation commission in May 2012, former Prime Minister Nato Kan in fact recognised the Japanese State's responsibility in causing the catastrophe.[32]

It appears therefore that the first obstacle of attributability can be cleared.

A second obstacle which appears much more problematic is that of establishing a causal link between a given action or omission of the allegedly responsible State with the alleged injury. The repeated references made in the present work to scientific studies intimate the technicality of the subject matter. A responsibility-based approach to environmental displacement would necessarily imply giving due consideration to the technical data available, essential to establishing causality and to identifying the actor(s) of the environmentally-damaging act. Affected States would have to provide "clear and convincing evidence"[33] that the injury they allegedly suffered and the displacement of population were caused by a certain act or omission of the defending State. This precondition for State responsibility will disqualify a significant part of environmental displacement: in cases where no causal link exists (purely natural disasters such as earthquakes and volcanic eruptions) or where no causal link can be "convincingly" demonstrated, the affected State (and populations) cannot validly claim reparation for the injury suffered.

---

29   H. Hiyama, "Fukushima Was 'Man-Made' Disaster: Japanese Probe", *Phys.Org* (AFP, 2012), 04 July 2012, retrieved from: <http://phys.org/news/2012-07-japan-diet-publish-fukushima-disaster.html> [05/07/2012].
30   *Ibid.*
31   A. Westlake, "Japanese Parliament's Fukushima Disaster Report to Be Published", *The Japan Daily Press*, 5 July 2012, retrieved from: <http://japandailypress.com/japanese-parliaments-fukushima-disaster-report-to-be-published-055941> [05/07/2012].
32   H. Hiyama, "Fukushima: un 'désastre créé par l'homme', selon un rapport officiel" (2012).
33   Arbitrary Tribunal, *Trail Smelter*.

As a consequence, protection based on responsibility might often be difficult to invoke. Given the complexity of environmental and climate mechanisms, the causal link between State's conduct and environmental degradation will often be extremely difficult to prove,[34] if not impossible in cases where the catastrophe is "purely natural".[35] The complexity and technical character of environmental problems can be described as only but two of the imputed "disadvantages to enforcing international environmental law in this way"; other impediments include the adverse effect of international litigation on inter-State relations, the length and expense of international litigation and the unsettled character of some of the law.[36]

Even assuming that this second difficulty can be overcome and that it can be possible to establish such causal link between the injury and the behaviour of another State, the question of the identity of the State responsible remains.

B   An "Act of State" but of Which State?

Two sub-questions arise in this context. Firstly, in the context of climate change-related displacement, the environmental degradation is the result of climate change and thus, in part, of the accumulation of greenhouse emissions by all States (some more than others) and over time. Which of those States could be held responsible for a specific displacement of populations? Additionally, it could also be argued that States affected by climate change and whose nationals are forced to move across international borders also are in part responsible since they failed to protect persons within their jurisdiction: they failed to implement appropriate prevention, mitigation and adaptation measures and thus contributed to triggering population displacement. The question was formulated by V.O. Kolmannskog in the following terms:

> It may be stretching the term too much to talk of climate change persecution. Who would in that case be the persecutor(s)? The state that directly fails to protect its citizens from the impacts, and/or the states that are the most responsible for the climate change?[37]

---

[34] P.W. Birnie, A. Boyle and C. Redgwell, *International Law and the Environment*, Third Ed. (New York: Oxford University Press, 2009), p. 211.

[35] W. Kälin and N. Schrepfer, "Protecting People Crossing Borders in the Context of Climate Change: Normative Gaps and Possible Approaches", UN *High Commissioner for Refugees Legal and Protection Policy Research Series*, PPLA/2012/01, February 2012, p. 8.

[36] P.W. Birnie, *et. al.* (2009), *op. cit.*, p. 211; V.O. Kolmannskog (2008), *op. cit.*

[37] V.O. Kolmannskog (2008), *op. cit.*, p. 27.

In the case of environmental displacement related to climate change in particular, Article 47 of the ILC Articles on State Responsibility is all the more topical. The Article addresses the hypothesis of a plurality of responsible States:

> Where several States are responsible for the same internationally wrongful act, the responsibility of each State may be invoked in relation to that act.[38]

The notion of "for the same internationally wrongful act" is problematic. The Article "only addresses the situation of a plurality of responsible States in relation to the *same* internationally wrongful act" hence excluding cases "where several States by separate internationally wrongful conduct have contributed to causing the same damage".[39] In such cases, the International Law Commission clarifies that the responsibility of each of the States who contributed to the injury "is determined individually, on the basis of its own conduct and by reference to its own international obligations". This again goes back to the question of causality: injured States would have to demonstrate the causal link between the environmental degradation and population displacement and a given State's contribution to climate change (assuming that a figure can indeed be put on this contribution[40]).

Where the link between the effects of climate change and the environmental degradation causing displacement is established, the affected State may invoke the responsibility of several States, who allegedly contributed to causing global warming, due to their greenhouse gas emissions. All States in the world contribute, albeit to widely varying proportions to the increase in atmospheric greenhouse gas concentrations. Accordingly, it is virtually the responsibility of all States within the international community that could be invoked. The question of attribution of responsibility is the next challenge facing affected States (and, primarily, the judicial institution dealing with the complaint) who chose to initiate international litigation in that regard (the question of reparation will be further developed below).

---

38   UN General Assembly, *Responsibility of States for internationally wrongful acts: resolution/ adopted by the General Assembly*, 8 January 2008, A/RES/62/61, Article 47.

39   ILC, "Report on the work of its 53rd session", A/CN.4/SER.A/2001/Add.1 (Part 2), 2001 *Yearbook of the International Law Commission* Vol. II, Part Two, p. 125.

40   G.C. Hegerl, *et al.*, "2007: Understanding and Attributing Climate Change", *in* S. Solomon, *et al.* (Eds.), *Contribution of Working Group 1 to the Fourth Assessment Report of the Intergovernmental Panel on Climate Change* (Cambridge, New York: Cambridge University Press, 2007).

II A Breach of an International Obligation

The duty of States to ensure that the activities within their jurisdiction or control do not cause damage to the environment of other States or of areas beyond the limits of national jurisdiction, expressed in the *Trail Smelter* arbitration case, was formulated in non-binding instruments of international law, in 1972, in the Stockholm Declaration (Principle 21) and reiterated in 1992 in the Rio Declaration (Principle 2).

The International Court of Justice later construed the principle of preservation of the environment as a legal obligation for States:

> The Court also recognizes that the environment is not an abstraction but represents the living space, the quality of life and the very health of human beings, including generations unborn. The existence of the general obligation of States to ensure that activities within their jurisdiction and control respect the environment of other States or of areas beyond national control is now part of the corpus of international law relating to the environment.[41]

The responsibility of States "to ensure that activities within their jurisdiction or control do not cause damage to the environment of other States or of areas beyond the limits of national jurisdiction" was also recalled in the Preamble of the UN Framework Convention on Climate Change.[42] This obligation is however an obligation of due diligence[43] but not an absolute prohibition to cause environmental damage.[44] In the context of hazardous activities, the International Law Commission made it clear that States indeed have the obligation to "take all appropriate measures to prevent significant transboundary harm or at any event to minimize the risk thereof".[45]

The obligation is well-established and could potentially apply when a disaster has a "dual" cause; when it originates in the combination of natural hazard

---

41 International Court of Justice, *Legality of the Threat or Use of Nuclear Weapons, Advisory Opinion*, I.C.J. Reports 1996, p. 226, at 29.

42 United Nations Framework Convention on Climate Change, 9 May 1992 [1992] UNTS Vol. 1771, p. 107, Preamble, Recital 8.

43 This is mentioned by the International Law Commission in its commentaries on the Draft Articles on the prevention of transboundary harm from hazardous activities. ILC, "Report on the work of its 53rd session", *op. cit.*, pp. 148 and 154–155.

44 P.W. Birnie, *et al.*, *International Law and the Environment*, 3rd ed. (Oxford, New York: Oxford University Press, 2009), p. 146.

45 ILC Articles on the Prevention of Transboundary Harm from Hazardous Activities, Article 3.

and technological accident for instance. The 2011 nuclear accident in Japan, although it affected principally Japanese population and territory can illustrate such case. In 2012, Diet's Fukushima Nuclear Accident Independent Investigation Commission, pointing to the government, the regulators and plant operator (TEPCO) concluded that they failed to adopt and implement appropriate preventive measures and response mechanisms. In so doing, the Investigation Commission finds, they disregarded "the nation's right to be safe from nuclear accidents".[46] As mentioned above, the Japanese Prime Minister at the time also recognised Japan's responsibility in the disaster.[47]

When there is a causal link between the omission by a State to take appropriate measures[48] and the occurrence of the harm on the territory of another State, its responsibility can be invoked for the damage caused. In cases of pollution, the principle is well-established.

In the context of climate change however, the "no significant harm" rule is more controversial.[49] A main obstacle is the unwillingness by some States to recognise climate change as a "common concern of mankind", "which can easily be interpreted as an unwillingness to make the same obligations apply to the climate as to the global commons".[50]

Turning to States' obligation under treaty law, States can only be held responsible for acts in breach of existing obligations. An action or omission by a State, which is not in conformity with what is required by international law only constitutes a breach of that obligation "if the act was performed at the time when the obligation was in force for that State".[51] It follows that States can only be held responsible for breaches of their obligation to reduce their emissions of heat-trapping gases regarding emissions post-dating the entry into force of the Kyoto Protocol.[52] Ratified to date by 192 States and the European

---

46 H. Hiyama, "Fukushima: un 'désastre créé par l'homme', selon un rapport officiel" (2012), *op. cit.*

47 *Ibid.*

48 ILC, "Report on the work of its 53rd session", *op. cit.*, p. 154.

49 For an argument that customary international law and the no harm rule in particular provide a solid basis for responsibility for climate change impacts, *see*: R.S.J. Tol and R. Verheyen (2004), *op. cit.*

50 A.-C. Rosenblom, *Claiming State Responsibility for Climate Change Damages*, Master Thesis, Faculty of Law (Lund: University of Lund, Spring 2009), p. 47.

51 ILC Articles on State Responsibility, Article 18(1).

52 Kyoto Protocol to the United Nations Framework Convention on Climate Change ("Kyoto Protocol"), 11 December 1997, entered into force 16 February 2005 U.N. Doc FCCC/CP/1997/7/Add.1 [1998] *ILM* Vol. 37, p. 22. As noted by W. Kälin and N. Schrepfer, the UN Framework Convention on Climate Change does not contain a specific obligation for

Union,[53] the Protocol however entered into force in 2005 only, which means the responsibility of State Parties could only be invoked for greenhouse gases emitted since February 2005;[54] compared with the total of anthropogenic greenhouse gas emissions which have contributed and will continue to contribute to climate change,[55] this constitutes "only a rather small part".[56]

III   Conclusion

It must be concluded from the above that an approach to environmental displacement based on State responsibility risks be counterproductive and would anyway fail to provide a comprehensive response to the complex issue. Seeking to identify the State or States responsible for the detrimental impacts of climate change on a given territory in order to obtain from them that they provide protection or, alternatively, assistance to the displaced population concerned appears to be counterproductive.

A first obstacle derives from the natural fact that no State wishes to take the blame for climate change or, for that matter, for environmental displacement.

State Parties to reduce their greenhouse gas emissions. W. Kälin and N. Schrepfer, *Protecting People Crossing Borders in the Context of Climate Change Normative Gaps and Possible Approaches* (February 2012), *op. cit.*, p. 9.

53   "Status of Ratification of the Kyoto Protocol", retrieved from: <http://unfccc.int/kyoto_protocol/status_of_ratification/items/2613.php> [07/11/2016].

54   In view of scientific evidence available today, States would however certainly not be able to invoke the "unforeseen" consequences of an increase in greenhouse gas concentrations in the atmosphere to excuse their behaviour since then. ILC Articles on State Responsibility, Article 23. The point is made by Roda Verheyen and Richard S.J. Tol in R.S.J. Tol and R. Verheyen (2004), *op. cit.*, pp. 1117–1118 and 1127.

55   On the finding that, even if emissions were to stop overnight, global warming would still continue, *see* for example: Susan Solomon, G.K. Platter, R. Knutti, and P. Friedlingstein, "Irreversible climate change due to carbon dioxide emissions", *Proceedings of the National Academy of Sciences*, No.106 (2009), pp. 1704–1709; G.H. Roe and K.C. Armour, "How sensitive is climate sensitivity?", *Geophysical Research Letters*, 38, L14708 (2011); and Marcia B. Baker, Gerard H. Roe, "The Shape of Things to Come: Why Is Climate Change So Predictable?", *Journal of Climate*, Vol. 22, Issue 17 (2009), pp. 4574–4589. For a popularised version of the findings of G.H. Roe and K.C. Armour, *see*: University of Washington, "If greenhouse gas emissions stopped now, Earth would still likely get warmer, new research shows", *ScienceDaily*, 15 February 2011, available at: <http://www.sciencedaily.com/releases/2011/02/110215150845.htm> [accessed 30/04/2012].

56   W. Kälin and N. Schrepfer, *Protecting People Crossing Borders in the Context of Climate Change Normative Gaps and Possible Approaches* (February 2012), *op. cit.*, p. 9.

K.E. McNamara reported the statement made by a senior diplomat, member of one of the Pacific missions to the UN explaining the little progress made on the recognition of the phenomenon of environmental displacement in the following terms:

> ... if you have an environmental refugee, you normally have a cause for that and somebody has produced that cause. And, not a lot of countries would be happy to admit guilt on that part.[57]

Secondly, such an endeavour to systemise States' responsibility for climate change, the success of which is uncertain, risks deviating attention and resources from instead formulating solutions to its effects. In other words, governments, international organisations and other stakeholders would be well-advised to rather use the time, energy and resources (both intellectual and financial) it would take to identify which State is more responsible than another for disasters occurring around the globe on working up adequate solutions to prevent, mitigate and respond to environmental degradations and consequential population movements.[58] It appears that issues of causality have so far contributed to braking the process of recognition of environmental displacement:

> ... Les tensions et obstacles qui freinent l'inscription des migrations environnementales à l'agenda politique international font de la scène politique une véritable arène au sein de laquelle les acteurs ne cessent de s'opposer, ne sachant à qui imputer la responsabilité causale et politique du problème.[59]

If ensuring the protection of environmentally-displaced persons is the main concern of States in invoking the rules of State responsibility in that context,

---

57   K.E. Mcnamara (2007), *op. cit.*, p. 21.
58   Recent literature on the topic reinforce this view and confirm that such an approach, that focuses attention on "very difficult-to-establish matters of causation and divert attention from the protection needs of the displaced" (J. McAdam) would not be "fruitful" (N. Schrepfer and W. Kälin). J. McAdam, *Climate Change, Forced Migration, and International Law* (2012), *op. cit.*, p. 96; W. Kälin and N. Schrepfer, *Protecting People Crossing Borders in the Context of Climate Change Normative Gaps and Possible Approaches* (February 2012), *op. cit.*, p. 8.
59   A. Baillat, *Les migrations environnementales : Logiques d'investissement des acteurs et obstacles relatifs à la construction d'un nouveau problème public*, Masters Thesis Recueil Alexandries, (September 2010), pp. 17–18.

then an approach that focuses on causality and attribution of responsibility is misguided. The complexity of the matter renders illusory the protection sought under it. Inherent to any litigation is the question of the burden of proof. The burden of proving the allegation lies on the applicant, that is, in the case at hand, the affected State; as shown above, proving the causal link between the alleged injury and a State's breach of its international law obligation would indeed be burdensome. The risk being that, if no State can be held responsible or if it is impossible to identify which State is responsible, environmentally-displaced persons will be left with no protection.[60] Although in such cases, States would still be bound to comply with their obligations under international human rights law in particular.[61]

Moreover, international litigation places States in an adversary situation – in which States generally do not wish to find themselves:[62] the affected State has the uneasy task to provide convincing evidence of the responsibility of the defending State in causing the environmental degradation causing populations to move. In a world where climate is changing and increasingly affecting the environment, this will often be tantamount to proving the State's contribution to global warming. On the other hand, defending States will have to adduce evidence to the contrary. In other words, defending States will endeavour to negate their contribution to climate change in order to obviate responsibility under international law. Firstly, this might lead to a tendency among States, especially among those of the developed world, to deny or minimise their contribution to climate change and, potentially reject

---

60   G.S. Goodwin-Gill and J. McAdam's analysis of the responsibility of agents of persecution within the framework of the Refugee Convention appears pertinent here: "[t]he purpose is not to attribute responsibility, in the sense of state responsibility, for the persecution. If it were, then qualifying as a refugee would be conditional on the rules of attribution, and protection would be denied in cases where, for any reason, the actions of the persecutors were not such as to involve the responsibility of the State". G.S. Goodwin-Gill and J. McAdam, *The Refugee in International Law* (2007), op. cit., p. 99.

61   OHCHR, "Report on the relationship between climate change and human rights", op. cit., §§ 72s.

62   It was notably observed by Theodor Meron, during a seminar he had convened in 1989. Commenting on a remark by Professor Grossman, T. Meron highlighted the small number of intestate complaints submitted to the European Commission and European Court of Human Rights, and concluded, together with Professor Grossman, that "States are reluctant to pay the political price involved in utilizing the existing complaint procedures against other states". T. Meron, "State Responsibility for Violations of Human Rights: Remarks", *in Proceedings of the 101st Annual Meeting*, Vol. 83 (Washington, DC: American Society of International Law, April 1989), pp. 372–385, p. 382.

any further commitment to reduce their greenhouse gas emissions (based on the allegation that their historical contribution being inferior to the estimates put forward by injured States). Secondly, by concentrating on their self-centred interest in "winning" this conflict over their alleged respective historical contributions to global warming, States would risk "losing the forest for the trees".

Resorting to the rules of international State responsibility to address environmental displacement would be counterproductive. Originally intended to support and protect environmentally-displaced persons and regions affected by environmental degradations, this approach would lead to fostered individualism on the part of States, to wit, to the negation or antithesis of international cooperation; in the context of climate change, cooperation is perceived to be essential.[63] As noticed by Brazilian president Dilma Rousseff during the Rio+20, United Nations Conference on Sustainable Development:

> All countries must take responsibility. Nobody can point the finger.[64]

Adding further to the list of arguments against a State responsibility based approach to environmental displacement is the observation that the traditional model of State responsibility becomes relevant mainly once the damage has already occurred. Its purpose is to afford reparation to the victim rather than to prevent the damage from occurring.[65] In the context of environmental displacement however, it is necessary that States do not confine their action to being merely reactive in nature.

In fact, if global warming could teach States but one lesson, perhaps is it precisely that reparation is not always possible. Scientific projections and data issued in recent years concur and find that global warming has now become irreversible. Considering the high concentrations of heat-trapping greenhouse gases already accumulated in the atmosphere and in light of their long atmospheric retention time, studies show that the Earth mean temperature will

---

63 "Climate change can only be effectively addressed through cooperation of all members of the international community". OHCHR, "Report on the relationship between climate change and human rights", *op. cit.*, § 84.

64 The statement made by Brazilian president Dilma Rousseff during the Rio+20 United Nations Conference on sustainable development was reported in J. Watts and L. Ford, 23 June 2012, *op. cit.*

65 Patricia W. Birnie, Alan Boyle and Catherine Redgwell, *International Law and the Environment*, Third Ed. (New York: Oxford University Press, 2009), p. 211.

keep increasing, even if greenhouse gas emissions were to stop overnight.⁶⁶ Although States cannot abate climate change, they can and indeed should nevertheless endeavour to not further fuel it with entrammelled greenhouse gas emissions.

As said, on a human life scale, the damage caused by anthropogenic emissions to the Earth atmosphere and climate cannot be repaired, nevertheless, science demonstrates that by reaching a sustained decrease of or at least a *status quo* in their greenhouse gas emissions, States could contribute to curbing the increase in surface temperature on the (very) long run. Additionally and in the shorter term, well-aware of the fact that global warming will have unavoidable impacts on the environment, States must prepare and adopt measures aimed at mitigating their consequences, at adapting to them, and, if at all possible, at remedying them. It is agreed that in most regions of the world, the impact of climate change on the environment will be detrimental. It is also well-established that environmental degradations cause populations concerned to change their habits, infrastructures, etc. to adapt to the new circumstances or force those populations to move when the degradation reaches a certain threshold of severity.⁶⁷

The State responsibility approach in fact contributes to formulating a response to environmental displacement insofar as it brings to light the numerous aspects of the question, which all need to be addressed in order for the response to be as efficient as possible. It seems that to tackle the issue of environment and climate induced displacement, a specific framework must be conceived, which places the needs of individuals and populations at the centre, and builds on them to identify appropriate policies and laws capable of addressing both the challenge of climate change, of its various causes and impacts, and the sensitive issue of migration.

---

66 See for example: Susan Solomon, G.K. Platter, R. Knutti, and P. Friedlingstein, "Irreversible climate change due to carbon dioxide emissions", *Proceedings of the National Academy of Sciences*, No.106 (2009), pp. 1704–1709; G.H. Roe and K.C. Armour, "How sensitive is climate sensitivity?", *Geophysical Research Letters*, *38*, L14708 (2011); and Marcia B. Baker, Gerard H. Roe, "The Shape of Things to Come: Why Is Climate Change So Predictable?", *Journal of Climate*, Vol.22, Issue 17 (2009), pp. 4574–4589. For a popularised version of the findings of G.H. Roe and K.C. Armour, *see*: University of Washington, "If greenhouse gas emissions stopped now, Earth would still likely get warmer, new research shows", *ScienceDaily*, 15 February 2011, available at: <http://www.sciencedaily.com/releases/2011/02/110215150845.htm> [accessed 30/04/2012].

67 J.R. Smith (2011).

A number of proposals have been formulated in literature. Below is neither a summary of existing proposals nor a new fully-fledged framework; it is rather a circumstantial inventory, based on the findings made until now in this work, of elements which I believe should be included in such *ad hoc* framework.

CHAPTER 12

A *Sui Generis* Framework to Address Environmental Displacement and Migration

There is a divide in literature between authors who suggest the adoption of a new convention drawn specifically to tackle environmental displacement, and addressing either internal or cross-border displacement or both simultaneously,[1] and those who oppose it.[2] In brief, three tendencies appear: proposed options are based on elements of the existing international protection regime and/or on (labour) migration law[3] or on international environmental law,[4] or draw on a combination of elements of different fields of law.[5] Whereas the

---

1   V. Magnigny, *Les réfugiés de l'environnement: Hypothèse juridique à propos d'une menace écologique*, 25 May 1999, Doctoral Thesis, Université de Droit – Paris I Panthéon Sorbonne (n/a: Recueil Alexandries, Collections Etudes, 1999); B. Docherty and T. Giannini, "Confronting a Rising Tide: A Proposal for a Convention on Climate Change Refugees", *Harvard Environmental Law Review*, Vol. 33 (2009), pp. 349–403.
2   J. McAdam, "Swimming against the Tide: Why a Climate Change Displacement Treaty Is Not the Answer", *International Journal of Refugee Law*, Vol. 23, No. 1 (2011), pp. 2–27.
3   M. Morel (2011), *op. cit*; B. Glahn, "'Climate Refugees'? Addressing the International Legal Gaps", *International Bar Association*, retrieved from: <www.ibanet.org/Article/Detail.aspx?ArticleUid=B51C02C1-3C27-4AE3-B4C4-7E350EB0F442> [02/05/2010]; D.Z. Falstrom (2002), *op. cit*; A. Michelot (2012), *op. cit*; A. Lopez (2007), *op. cit*.
4   A. Williams (October 2008), *op. cit*; F. Biermann and I. Boas (2008), *op. cit*; A. Michelot (2012), *op. cit*; G.S. McCue, "Environmental Refugees: Applying International Environmental Law to Involuntary Migration", *Georgetown International Environmental Law Review*, Vol. 6 (1993–1994), pp. 151–190.
5   M. Prieur, *et al.*, "Projet de convention relative au statut international des déplacés environnementaux", *Revue Européene de Droit de l'Environnement*, Vol. 4 (2008), pp. 81–93, original French version translated into English, Spanish, Portuguese and Italian; the Limoges proposal was also published by the RDUS, preceded with a report, providing explanations on the project and terminology used, M. Prieur, *et al.*, "Projet de convention relative au statut international des déplacés environnementaux", *Revue de droit de l'Université de Sherbrooke – RDUS*, Vol. 39 (2008–09), pp. 451–505; B. Mayer (Summer 2011), *op. cit*; B. Docherty and T. Giannini (2009), *op. cit*; D.Z. Falstrom (2002), *op. cit*. B. Mayer proposes the adoption of an international legal framework on climate-induced migration. A Security Council resolution recognising the "security challenge" posed by climate change and calling for international action would give impetus to the creation of this framework which would be established by

majority of instruments proposed are meant to apply at the global level, some authors suggest regional[6] or bilateral[7] solutions instead.

The attempts made in the two previous chapters to try and tackle the issue of environmental displacement under each of the relevant branches of international law showed that, when singly considered, the different normative bodies all fail to comprehensively address environmental displacement. At the same time, each normative body proved to be suitable to address certain specific aspects of the issue. Persons displaced by environmental degradation do not automatically fall within the ambit of the existing regime of international protection however the principle of *non-refoulement* is but one element of this regime that can be relevant to address their claims. The rules of State responsibility for environmental damage and its consequences do not account for the specificities of the root causes of environmental damage and of migration, and risk undermining efforts towards a necessary international cooperation. Nonetheless, principles derived from it such as States' obligation of due diligence can be relevant. It is therefore not unreasonable to suggest that an effective means of comprehensively addressing environmental displacement might lay in the combination of relevant rules, mechanisms and principles borrowed from the different branches of international law.

Elements to import from the different areas of law considered above as against those to leave out of a new framework devised to protect environmentally-displaced persons can be presented in the form of a table, as follows.

---

a UN General Assembly resolution, containing guidelines – recalling States' human rights obligations and their common and shared responsibility for climate change – and institutional provisions. A Fund on Climate-Induced Migration would be established, distinct but coordinated within the UNFCCC as well as a UN Agency on Climate Change Migration and an Expert Panel. Within the framework of the proposed UNGA resolution, negotiations should be organised at the regional level.

6 A. Williams (October 2008), *op. cit.*
7 C. Cournil mentions the option of developing "bilateral" protection: States whose territory is threatened by climate change (such as Pacific island States) could negotiate in advance bilateral agreements on the protection of their displaced population. C. Cournil notes that, though it would certainly be the most pragmatic of solutions, incentives for potentially receiving States to enter into such agreement are few – unless the international community takes on to redistribute the financial burden such agreements would otherwise impose on receiving States. Additionally, from the point of view of the persons displaced, this solution might not be suitable as it deprives them of their choice as to their destination. C. Cournil (Juin 2008), *op. cit.*

TABLE 2   *Selectively drawing from existing frameworks to devise a sui generis framework for the protection of environmentally-displaced persons.*

Area of law	"In"	"Out"
Refugee law	· Humanitarian nature · Anticipatory assessment of risk · Legal status granted	· "for reason of" (the notion of protected groups) · Exceptions to *non-refoulement* · Short-sightedness[8]
Human rights law[9]	· Absolute prohibition of *refoulement* · Anticipatory assessment of risk · Protection from indiscriminate threats · Indivisibility, universality and inalienability of human rights · Protection of vulnerable persons · Human rights indicators	· No formal status granted · (Balance of interests[10]) · Short-sightedness

---

8   The term is used in its literal meaning. In refugee cases like in human rights cases, the assessment of claims relies on the likelihood or reality of the risk invoked; it is based on conditions prevailing in the destination country at the time the decision is made. K. Röhl, "Fleeing Violence and Poverty: Non-Refoulement Obligations under the European Convention of Human Rights", *New Issues in Refugee Research* (UNHCR), No. 111 (2005), pp. 27–28.

9   The particular relevance and potential of human rights law to protect environmentally-displaced persons has been highlighted on several occasions by Jane McAdam, who stated for instance that: "[s]olutions need to be developed within a human rights framework, underscored by broader humanitarian norms such as the fundamental principles of humanity, human dignity, human rights and international cooperation". J. McAdam, "Legal solutions: if a treaty is not the answer, then what is?", speech delivered during the ClimMig Conference on Human Rights, Environmental Change, Migration and Displacement held in Vienna on 20–21 September 2012, available at: <http://www.humanrights.at/climmig/wp-content/uploads/McAdam-Jane_speech-20-Sept-2012.pdf> [accessed 02/04/2015].

10 This element is mentioned however it is not and should not be a feature of human rights law but mainly a "jurisprudential accident". Reference is made to the judgment of the European Court of Human Rights in *N. v. UK* where the Court took into consideration budgetary constraints in the defendant's State to conclude that the removal of the applicant to her country of origin was not in breach of Article 3 ECHR, even though her life expectancy would be reduced there. ECtHR, *N. v. UK*, §§ 44, 49–50 in particular. The case was discussed in Part II.

TABLE 2 *Selectively drawing from existing frameworks to devise a sui generis framework for the protection of environmentally-displaced persons.* (cont.)

Area of law	"In"	"Out"
Temporary protection (EU)	· Emergency device · Some legal status granted · Group-based	· *Per se*, temporary only · Reactive · Cumbersome activation procedure · Only theoretical thus far
State responsibility for environmental damage	· Due diligence · Duty to notify and warn[11] · (Very) forward-looking · Protection of the environment · Common but differentiated responsibilities	· "Adversarial"

In view of the capacity of each of the areas of law considered above to address but certain aspects of environmental displacement, it appears that it is only through the formulation of a response based on a combination of relevant principles, mechanisms and norms borrowed from different areas of law that environmental displacement can be comprehensively addressed. On the basis of the elements highlighted in the above table and drawing from relevant literature and recent events, the following developments will highlight some essential components of a *sui generis* framework to address environmental displacement and mobility, in terms of practical legal solutions, policies and implementation measures. In other words, the proposed framework was conceived as a set of recommended principles, measures and practices which could – or should – form part of the responses to the multitude of challenges posed by environmental displacement. A similar "toolbox" approach was adopted by the Nansen Initiative upon developing, in greater lentgth, its comprehensive Agenda for the Protection of Cross-Border Displaced Persons in the Context of Disasters and Climate Change.[12]

---

11   ICJ, *Corfu Channel Case*, pp. 22–23.
12   The Nansen Initiative, *Agenda for the Protection of Cross-Border Displaced Persons in the Context of Disasters and Climate Change* ("*Protection Agenda*") (Geneva: The Nansen Initiative, 2015), retrieved from: <https://nanseninitiative.org/wp-content/uploads/2015/02/PROTECTION-AGENDA-VOLUME-1.pdf> [28/03/2016]. *See* below pp. 524s.

The object, scope and purpose of such framework must first be specified (I) before key elements of a solution to address the situation of persons who (will) move from regions affected by environmental degradation are formulated (II).

I   Adopting a *Sui Generis* Framework for "Environmentally-Displaced Persons": Initial Stumbling Blocks

The primary aspect which needs to be addressed is the unsettled question of the term by which persons who leave their home or country where environmental change affects their living conditions should be identified (A). In large part related to this first question is that of the scope of the proposed framework (B). Lastly, the very existence of any such framework being conditional upon States' willingness to devise and take part in it, the last part will highlight some of the incentives for States to commit (C).

A   "What's in a Name..?"[13]

In literature, persons who move due to the degradation of their living environment are alternatively termed "refugees" or "displaced persons" or "migrants". It is noteworthy that the reference made in international protection literature to the term "refugee" is not necessarily meant to call for the extension of the Refugee Convention regime. Quite to the contrary, it is precisely the contention of those arguing in favour of the recognition of a category of "environmental refugees" that the use of the term refugee is not the prerogative of the 1951 Refugee Convention. Nonetheless, a drawback of the adoption of a new instrument on "environmental refugee" is precisely the risk of confusion with the existing regime of the Refugee Convention. According to Goodwin-Gill and McAdam, the term refugee is "a term of art, that is, a term with a content verifiable according to principles of general international law".[14] For the purpose of creating a new category of protected persons, with specific needs and rights, it would be preferable to choose another terminology, so as to avoid undermining either the Refugee Convention or the anticipated regime, or both.

An obstacle to the adoption of a new legal instrument specifically developed to protect environmentally-displaced persons is the lack of a broadly accepted

---

13   W. Shakespeare, *Romeo and Juliet* (London: John Danter, 1597), II, ii, 1–2.
14   G.S. Goodwin-Gill and J. McAdam, *The refugee in international law*, 3rd ed., (New York: Oxford, 2007), p. 1.

definition of who these migrants actually are. The lack of consensus on the terminology is revealing of a more profound dissension among commentators. Those who favour the term environmental or climate "refugees" advocate for the recognition of the international protection needs of the persons concerned and the correlative duty of States to address them. As mentioned in the first Chapter of this Part (*i.e.* Chapter 10), those authors often formulate solutions based on existing refugee law; they might call for a constructive interpretation of the Refugee Convention, the adoption of an amendment to the text or of a new protocol to the Convention for example. In choosing this meaningful term, they can also aim at raising awareness on the potentially disastrous effects of climate change and at urging States to take action to mitigate those effects.[15]

On the other hand, "environmental migrants" suggests that the cross-border movement is voluntary and relieves States of any international protection obligation they might otherwise bear. In this hypothesis, persons who move for environmental reasons are perceived as voluntary migrants who seek to improve their quality of life, aspiring for better work conditions for example, and should arguably be dealt with as economic migrants.

On this notion too, that environmentally-displaced persons are but "economic migrants", opinions diverge. Norman Myers and Jennifer Kent – derisively – observe that:

> ... [t]he factor of economic attraction may not be so attractive as is sometimes represented. If it were, much of the population of southern Italy would have relocated to northern Italy, and of Spain and Portugal to France – and many more Mexicans would have made their way to the United States.[16]

In a similar vein, one could cite the case of Haiti, whose population has been enduring a broad range of sufferings including the experience of dictatorship and correlate violence of paramilitary groups, deforestation, pummelling tropical storms and hurricanes and, most recently, a devastating earthquake followed by a cholera outbreak, all against a backdrop of poverty. The observation might help allaying developed States concerns that environmental degradations will cause massive flows of protection seekers

---

[15] "The significance of the term ["environmental refugees"] lies in its application to environmentalist literature rather than asylum literature – highlighting the environment as a sole cause or consequence of large migration movements will increase interest in its protection". D. Keane (2003–2004), *op. cit.*, p. 223.

[16] Norman Myers and Jennifer Kent, *Environmental Exodus: An Emergent Crisis in the Global Arena* (Washington DC: Climate Institute, June 1995), p. 27.

on their territories: despite the numerous and seemingly uninterrupted crises Haiti has been facing throughout its comparatively young history, the country nevertheless retain a population, and a growing one too.[17] The notion of resilience, which will be elaborated upon later, emerges in this observation.[18]

The terminology and the categorisation suggested are themselves dependant on the authors' understanding of the notion of environmental disruption (natural, man-made or climatic, of slow or acute onset, permanent or reversible, etc.) and on the characteristics of the migration (voluntary or forced, temporary or permanent, etc.).

UNHCR however warns against the watertight line some claim exists between voluntary and involuntary migration:

> It is generally accepted that almost all migration involves some kind of compulsion; labour migration for example, while usually regarded as "voluntary", is often prompted by poverty.[19]

Another conceptual difficulty, closely related to this first distinction and particularly relevant in the discussion on environmental displacement, is that of differentiating between spontaneous and planned migration. Whereas the first ones are more often perceived as forced, the latter can easily be mistaken for being necessarily voluntary movements.

UNHCR in fact stresses that categorisations in general might be of little relevance in some contexts: different "categories" of displaced persons may very well be "living alongside each other in equally difficult circumstances"[20] so that a differentiation would be meaningless or, at worst, unfair.

Finally, the identity of the author is noteworthy: international organisations, political actors, academics, experts, NGOs and the general public have

---

17 Data retrieved from the website of the Statistic Division of the United Nations Food and Agriculture Organisation indicates that the population of Haiti continuously increased between 1962 and 2012. To illustrate this, here are some the estimates provided for the following dates (in millions): 1962: 4,024; 1972: 4,878; 1982: 5,958; 1992: 7,423; 2002: 8,935; 2012: 10,256. Data available at: <http://faostat.fao.org> [accessed 10/06/2012].

18 "Secretary-General Praises Faith, Resilience of Haitian People Amid Tragedy", UN News Centre, 21 January 2010.

19 UNHCR also stresses in the same publication that "[a]s a rule, people do not abandon their homes and flee from their own country or community unless they are confronted with serious threats to their life or liberty". UNHCR (1997), op. cit., pp. 1 and 13–14.

20 Ibid., p. 14.

different views on the issue. In the specific context of climate change, this is partly explained by the divide between environmentalists, who tend to be rather alarmist, and migration experts, who typically adopt a more sceptical approach to climate change-related displacement.[21] All stakeholders use terms "based on their aims regarding expertise, 'academic theorisation', activism or political actions, and depending on the forms of protection they wish to see emerging".[22] The solutions they put forward are accordingly varied. In that sense, the use of the term "refugee" appears not to be innocent: resorting to this meaningful term serves the purpose of raising awareness about the reality of climate change and of its anticipated impacts. The term "climate refugee" suggests a "catastrophic human impact of climate change" and "a failure to cope with environmental disruptions",[23] although it might not accurately encapsulate the complex causes and patterns of migration triggered by environmental change.[24]

Conversely though, those most directly concerned by the impacts of climate change, the populations and governments of Pacific small island states firmly oppose the sanctioning of the term "climate refugees".[25] In particular, they fear accepting the term would be resigning themselves to a life of helplessness.[26]

To conclude on this variety of understandings and perceptions of how to qualify persons displaced by environmental change, it can be highlighted that the controversy on the name – dear to lawyers – should not serve as an excuse to postpone decision-making:

---

21 The parallel evolution of the discourse on climate change and displacement in environmental policies and in migration policies is well documented and convincingly analysed by F. Gemenne. F. Gemenne, "How They Became the Human Face of Climate Change. Research and Policy Interactions in the Birth of the 'Environmental Migration' Concept", *in* E. Piguet, *et al.* (Eds.), *Migration and Climate Change* (Cambridge, New York: Cambridge University Press, UNESCO Publishing, 2011), pp. 225–259.

22 C. Cournil, "The Protection of 'Environmental Refugees' in International Law", *in* E. Piguet, *et al.* (Eds.), *Migration and Climate Change* (Cambridge, New YorkCambridge, New York: Cambridge University Press, UNESCO Publishing, 2011), pp. 359–387, p. 359.

23 F. Gemenne (2011), *op. cit.*, pp. 253–254.

24 In that sense also: J. McAdam, *Climate Change, Forced Migration, and International Law* (2012), *op. cit.*, p. 40.

25 K.E. McNamara, C. Gibson "'We do not want to leave our land': Pacific ambassadors at the United Nations resist the category of 'climate refugees'", *Geoforum* 40 (2009), pp. 475–483.

26 C. Farbotko and H. Lazrus (2012), *op. cit.*, p. 383.

It is time now to stop debating about precise definitions and bureaucratic reasons why a refugee flees and start deciding what we can do to return these people to a decent life in their own countries and prevent others from fleeing in future.[27]

Imperfect though it may be, the term "environmentally-displaced person" appears as rather self-explanatory and hence a good basis on which to build a protection framework. Its use will be justified below, when the personal scope of the suggested framework is detailed.

B Scope of the Proposed Framework

The two main elements of the term "environmentally-displaced persons" will be successively addressed.

1 Environment vs. Climate

In view of the ongoing discussions on climate change and growing evidence of its reality, increasing attention has been given to its actual and potential impacts on human populations. Many of the proposals for the adoption of an instrument, devised to tackle the issue of environmental displacement were formulated in this context. As a consequence, some of them focus on those environmentally-induced displacements that are linked to climate change;[28] some authors hence suggest addressing the matter within the framework of the UNFCCC.[29] While this would have the potential to significantly improve the situation of those displaced by environmental degradation caused by climate change (the number of which might be significant and increasingly so), it would leave those fleeing environmental degradations unrelated to climate change or whose causal link with climate change cannot be established in a normative gap, even though their claims for protection would be just as valid.

In concrete terms, under such instrument, an individual fleeing an environment devastated by a nuclear catastrophe or an earthquake would risk being

---

27   R.K.L. Panjabi, "International Politics in the 1990s: Some Implications for Human Rights and the Refugee Crisis", *Dickinson Journal of Int'l Law*, Vol. 10, No. 1 (1991–1992), pp. 1–23, pp. 12–13.
28   A. Williams (October 2008), *op. cit*; B. Docherty and T. Giannini (2009), *op. cit*; D. Hodgkinson and L. Young, "'In the Face of Looming Catastrophe': A Convention for Climate Change Displaced Persons" January 2012), retrieved from: <www.ccdpconvention.com> [12/04/2012]; B. Mayer (Summer 2011), *op. cit*; S. Byravan and R.S. Chella, "Providing New Homes for Climate Change Exiles", *Climate Policy*, No. 6 (2006), pp. 246–252.
29   F. Biermann and I. Boas (2008), *op. cit*.

returned to the affected territory whereas an individual moving from an area hit by floods or drought would be allowed to relocate. Such differentiation makes little, not to say, no sense, both in legal terms and in moral terms. For that reason, the scope of the proposed instrument should be broad enough to encompass all persons displaced by a degradation of their living environment, regardless of its causes, as long and as soon as it is of such intensity that life circumstances there have become unbearable.[30]

A broad-encompassing definition of environmental degradations causing displacement would additionally facilitate the assessment of protection claims for it would dispense with the requirement that causality be shown between the environmental degradation invoked and climate change – an assessment which, as mentioned in Chapter 11, borders on impossible. Although climate scientists' understanding of the observed changes in the environment is improving, uncertainties remain as to the precise trigger mechanism. Their assessment is essentially probabilistic.[31] The following example, albeit pertaining to climate change litigation specifically, can illustrate it:

> Climate change litigation (...) depends on scientists' ability to prove a causal link between individual natural disasters and a slowly changing climate. Such attribution is possible only in a probabilistic sense. For example, it is very likely that the flood risk was raised by more than 20% in England and Wales in 2000 because of human-made greenhouse gas emissions.[32]

---

30   The same conclusion was reached by the participants of the Nansen Conference on Climate Change and Displacement held in Oslo, in June 2011. See M. Wahlström, "Chairperson's Summary", *Nansen Conference: Climate Change and Displacement in the 21st Century*, Oslo, 5–7 June 2011 (2011): §5; and J. McAdam, "How to Address the Protection Gaps – Ways Forward", *Nansen Conference: Climate Change and Displacement in the 21st Century*, Oslo, 5–7 June 2011 (2011): 2. The authors of the Draft Convention on the International Status of Environmentally-Displaced Persons – the proposal of the Faculty of Law of Limoges (France) – also reached the same conclusion. They similarly excluded the terms "ecological" and "climatic" and preferred the broader-encompassing reference to the "environment". M. Prieur, et al. (2008–09), *op. cit.*, pp. 462–463.

31   Martin Manning, Michel Petit, David Easterling at al. (eds.), *Report of the IPCC Workshop on Describing Scientific Uncertainties in Climate Change to Support Analysis of Risk and of Options held at the National University of Ireland, 11–13 May 2004* (Boulder: IPCC Working Group I Technical Support Unit, 2004).

32   Nature Geoscience, "The challenge of extremes", *Nature Geoscience*, Vol.4, Editorial (2011): 129.

Conditioning international cooperation, assistance to and protection of persons whose very subsistence is ineluctably threatened by untrammelled climate change on probabilistic attribution of State responsibility strikes as inappropriate. The international protection framework for environmental displacement shall not be limited to address only those environmental degradations that have a causal link with climate change, partly because in certain cases, strong evidence of the said causality might prove impossible to provide and partly to obviate the absurdity of reaching antagonistic conclusions on similar claims (earthquake and tsunami as against nuclear catastrophe and floods).

A justification for the limited scope of international protection to the sole cases of displacement caused by climate change based on the consideration that an element of State responsibility must be identifiable within the causes of displacement in order to trigger State obligation to protect (just as international refugee law and human rights law refer to *actors* of harm or persecution), fails to convince since, as mentioned, it can be argued that an element of State responsibility can be established in most hypotheses of environmental degradations:

> Natural hazards do not in themselves constitute disasters; rather human actions exacerbate the effects of natural phenomena to create disasters.[33]

Where an earthquake hits, the home State could be held responsible for their companies' failure to include seismic studies into the planning of their projects (anti-seismic constructions in Japan significantly reduce the impacts of earthquake on infrastructures whereas developing countries faced with comparable or weaker earthquakes suffer more damage[34]). If the degradation is caused by

---

33   UNHCR, *The State of the World's Refugees 2012: In Search of Solidarity* (2012), *op. cit.*, p. 178. In that sense also, N. Dolsak and A. Prakash stress: "[c]limate change is often going to be the domino that falls. But that does not mean we can ignore the rest of the dominos in the row". N. Dolsak and A. Prakash, "'Climate Change Did It!' Is a Convenient Excuse", Slate, 21 October 2016, accessible at: <http://www.slate.com/articles/health_and_science/science/2016/10/blaming_natural_disasters_on_climate_change_will_backfire.html> [21/10/2016].

34   Similarly, Norman Myers provides comparative examples of natural disasters that recently took place in different parts of the world: the damages caused by those disasters of comparable scale varied greatly depending on their localisation. Myers cites the example of an earthquake which killed more than 10,000 persons in India (1993) whereas a similar Richter-scale strength earthquake in Los Angeles killed 'only' about 50 persons. Norman

a company, the injury will generally be attributed to the State because it failed to control and regulate the activities. Likewise, where volcano eruptions occur, the damage caused by lava flows or fallouts can be attributed to the State, who failed to act with due diligence (for example in delineating a safety perimeter inside which human activity and settlement is not allowed[35]) or to notify then warn populations presumably concerned.[36] The case of famines, in countries suffering from drought is also illustrative of the mixed root causes of environmental displacement: exogenous factors (drought) combine with social, economic and political factors to cause the environment to severely deteriorate and eventually force populations to move in search for food and other basic means of subsistence.[37] N. Myers and J. Kent cite the example of famine in Sub-Saharan Africa, hit by recurrent drought, and find that climate cannot always be blamed for famines. The authors argue:

> These famines have stemmed from droughts that have been neither a necessary nor sufficient cause [[38]]. Often enough, drought has merely triggered famines by disrupting the social economic and political processes that would normally ensure sufficient access or entitlement to food.[39]

It follows that, all disasters being in part triggered by some degree of State responsibility, a distinction along these lines cannot be justified. States' obligation under international human rights law not to discriminate between persons in similar situations confirms it.

All environment-related displacement should for those reasons be addressed in a single instrument. Although the majority of protection options

---

Myers and Jennifer Kent, *Environmental Exodus: An Emergent Crisis in the Global Arena* (Washington DC: Climate Institute, June 1995), p. 25. Essam El-Hinnawi, *Environmental Refugees* (Nairobi: United Nations Environment Programme, 1985), p. 6.

35   For example: ECtHR, *Budayeva v. Russia*.
36   ICJ, *Corfu Channel Case*.
37   T. Afifi, et al., *Climate Change, Vulnerability and Human Mobility: Perspectives of Refugees from the East and Horn of Africa* (June 2012), *op. cit.*, pp. 39–47 in particular.
38   N. Myers and J. Kent cite: Downing et al., *Coping with Drought in Kenya: National and Local Strategies* (Boulder: L. Reinner Publications, 1989); Berry and Downing, "Drought and Famine in Africa: 1981–1986" *in* I.O. Field (ed.), *The Challenge of Famine* (Hartford: Kumarian Press, 1993), pp. 35–58.; and Bohle et al., "Climate Change and Social Vulnerability", *Global Environmental Change*, Vol.4 (1994): 37–48.
39   N. Myers and J. Kent, *Environmental Exodus: An Emergent Crisis in the Global Arena* (June 1995), *op. cit.*, pp. 29–32.

formulated thus far focus on climate change related displacement, some authors also reach the same conclusion. Noteworthy is the draft convention published by a group of legal scholars within the French University of Limoges[40] which devises an international legal stauts for "environmentally-displaced persons";[41] climate change is perceived as but one cause of environmental degradation forcing people to move.[42]

Who would be the persons protected?

2   Personal Scope

The Refugee Convention framework only protects those individuals who have left their country of origin and crossed the international border of the State.[43] It was evoked when solutions based on refugee law were considered: this precondition to refugee protection makes refugee law little relevant only in the context of environmental displacement since, according to projections, the vast majority of displacement triggered by environmental factors is and will be internal.

The alienage requirement of refugee law implies that internally-displaced persons (IDPs) are automatically excluded from the protection it provides and IDPs are dependent upon their home State authorities' protection and assistance. Internal displacement however is a significant aspect of the issue of environmentally-induced displacement. Recent natural disasters inform that "all too often the human rights of disaster victims are not sufficiently taken into account".[44] In other words, although it is for the home State authorities to protect IDPs, violations of the human rights of IDPs are observed and well-documented and indicate that those authorities often fail to protect IDPs in

---

40   M. Prieur, et al. (2008), op. cit.

41   Such broad scope was already called for by the authors of the draft convention in 2005 in their "Appel de Limoges". Crideau and CIDCE, "Appel de Limoges sur les réfugiés écologiques", 23 juin 2005, retrieved from: <http://www.cidce.org/pdf/Appel%20de%20 Limoges.pdf> [02/06/2012].

42   Under the Draft Convention, causes of environmental degradation include "in particular climate change and/or the loss of biological diversity, drought, desertification, deforestation, soil erosion, epidemics, armed conflict, major infrastructure and more generally, natural and technological hazards". M. Prieur, et al. (2008), op. cit., Preamble, recital 2.

43   J.C. Hathaway argues that the "alienage requirement" of refugee law is essential to refugee law because it "denies states the possibility of inaction grounded in respect for sovereign boundaries, the alienage requirement of refugee law should be maintained". J.C. Hathaway, op. cit.

44   Inter-Agency Standing Committee, Pilot Manual Accompanying the IASC Operational Guidelines on Human Rights and Natural Disasters, (Washington DC: Brookings-Bern Project on Internal Displacement, March 2008): p. 1.

reality. The consequences for the internally-displaced are oft dire and include unequal access to assistance and aid provision, unsafe and involuntary return or resettlement, sexual and gender-based violence, recruitment of child-soldiers, and loss of property and possessions.[45] They are more vulnerable than the rest of the population of the country. The automatic application of "classical" human rights law to IDPs has proven to be insufficient to effectively address their distressing situation. Displacement, be it triggered by armed conflicts or environmental disasters, not only jeopardises the full and effective enjoyment of their rights by internally-displaced persons; it also prompts issues that are specific to them.

Developments of the law have already occurred at the national, regional[46] and international[47] levels. In addition to internal displacement, environmental degradation, caused by climate change in particular, already causes and will continue causing cross-border population movements. In both scenarios, solutions can be reached (including curbing displacement) and the situation of the persons concerned will improve only if the root causes of the displacement are addressed.

Endeavours to tackle environmental displacement that integrate measures intended to prevent, mitigate and adapt to environmental degradation will necessarily bear on both types of displacement. Additionally, internal and cross-border displacements are not exclusive of each other: persons who have sought protection in third countries in the aftermath of a natural disaster may choose to return to their home country (in their region of origin or not) after the situation has improved. Upon return, they might encounter some of the problems typically faced by internally-displaced persons such as property

---

45 Inter-Agency Standing Committee, *Pilot Manual Accompanying the IASC Operational Guidelines on Human Rights and Natural Disasters*, (Washington DC: Brookings-Bern Project on Internal Displacement, March 2008); and Inter-Agency Standing Committee, *Protecting Persons Affected by Natural Disasters. IASC Operational Guidelines on Human Rights and Natural Disasters*, June 2006.

46 African Union, *African Union Convention for the Protection and Assistance of Internally Displaced Persons in Africa ("Kampala Convention")*, 22 October 2009.

47 Inter-Agency Standing Committee, *Handbook for the Protection of Internally Displaced Persons*, June 2010; Inter-Agency Standing Committee, *Pilot Manual Accompanying the IASC Operational Guidelines on Human Rights and Natural Disasters*, (Washington DC: Brookings-Bern Project on Internal Displacement, March 2008); and Inter-Agency Standing Committee, *Protecting Persons Affected by Natural Disasters. IASC Operational Guidelines on Human Rights and Natural Disasters*, June 2006; UN Commission on Human Rights, *Guiding Principles on Internal Displacement*, 11 February 1998, E/CN.4/1998/53/Add.2.

restitution[48] or access to housing and work. They might in fact become internally-displaced persons if they are unable or unwilling to move back to their region of origin and might for that reason settle elsewhere within the country. Conversely, in the hypothesis where the environment further deteriorates and that deterioration increasingly expands within the State's territory, populations who were initially "only" internally-displaced may be forced beyond the State's borders and thus become internationally-displaced.

On account of the permeability of the two categories of environmentally-displaced persons and of the similarity or even identity of their respective root causes, it is an all-encompassing system, wherein both categories would be taken into consideration, which must be called into existence.

C   *Why Should States Consent to be Bound?*

It appears as a necessity: to secure States' participation in such legally-binding instrument, a number of incentives must be conceived.

> Designing a convention with the self-interests of the participants in mind makes adoption much more likely than if policymakers attempt to force developed nations to give humanitarian aid on an *ad hoc* basis.[49]

The preparatory work of the 1951 Refugee Convention bears witness of the fact that States are concerned and jealous of protecting their national borders; at the same time, the reality of international displacement shows that:

> … [i]n any case, no wall will be high enough to prevent people from coming…[50]

---

48   Inter-Agency Standing Committee, *Pilot Manual Accompanying the IASC Operational Guidelines on Human Rights and Natural Disasters*, (Washington DC: Brookings-Bern Project on Internal Displacement, March 2008, p. 1.

49   Gregory McCue, "Environmental Refugees: Applying International Environmental Law to Involuntary Migration", *Georgetown International Environmental Law Review*, Vol. 6, Issue 1 (1993–1994): 151–190, pp. 178–179.

50   R. Lubbers, "Statement by Mr. Ruud Lubbers, United Nations High Commissioner for Refugees", *High Commissionner Statements*, Informal Meeting of the European Union Ministers for Justice and Ministers for Home Affairs, organised in Stockholm, on 8 February 2001. Similarly, the Parliamentary Assembly of the Council of Europe invites States to recognise that "there will always be a number of irregular migrants present in Europe, regardless of the policies adopted by governments to prevent their entry or to return them speedily". PACE, "Resolution 1509 (2006): Human Rights of Irregular Migrants", Adopted on 27 June 2006, § 4.

Already in 1949, in his Study on Statelessness, the UN Secretary General insisted that the issue of the status of refugees ought not to be tackled by States individually, through their respective national legislation, but in an international convention. Among the reasons given by the Secretary-General, the first one was the following:

> No Government will be willing to take the first step in this direction for fear of being the only one to improve the status of [*de jure* or *de facto*][51] stateless persons, thus causing an influx of them into its territory.[52]

The same is undoubtedly still true in present time and is confirmed in practice: no State has taken upon to accept environmentally-displaced persons on its territory. Part 2 mentioned the Swedish and Finnish Aliens' Act provisions on the protection of nationals of third States who were forced to flee to escape natural disasters.[53] To date however, none of these provisions has ever been applied by Swedish or Finnish asylum authorities or courts.[54] It is therefore possible to conclude that, within the European Union, no State has taken a meaningful step in the direction of granting international protection to environmentally-displaced persons.

---

51 The concept of statelessness in the present context has to be understood broadly. This is made clear by the Secretary-General who explains that the contemplated convention should concern "refugees who fled from their country of origin, and who have thus become stateless *de jure* or *de facto*" (UN Ad Hoc Committee on Refugees and Stateless Persons, *A Study of Statelessness*, United Nations, August 1949, Lake Success – New York, 1 August 1949, E/1112; E/1112/Add.1, p. 52, a). The term thus encompasses not only stateless persons *per se*, as persons deprived of their or any nationality, but also '*de facto*' stateless persons, as "persons who do not enjoy the protection of any government" (Economic and Social Council, *Resolution 116 (VI) D* of 1–2 March 1948 (Report of the Second Session of the Commission on Human Rights, Stateless persons)(E/777), p. 18, at 46, cited in the Study of the Secretary-General, p. 2). *See* also clarifications provided in UN High Commissioner for Refugees, *Colloquium on the development in the law of refugees with particular reference to the 1951 Convention and the Statute of the Office of the United Nations High Commissioner for Refugees held at Villa Serbelloni Bellagio (Italy) from 21–28 April 1965: Background paper submitted by the Office of the United Nations High Commissioner for Refugees, Palais des Nations, Geneva, Switzerland*, 1965, 28 April 1965, MHCR/23/65; 67–1809, at 34.

52 UN Ad Hoc Committee on Refugees and Stateless Persons, *A Study of Statelessness*, United Nations, August 1949, Lake Success – New York, 1 August 1949, E/1112; E/1112/Add.1, p. 52, a.

53 Respectively: Sweden: Aliens Act 2005:716, Chapter 4, Section 2(3) and Finland: Aliens' Act (301/2004, amendments up to 1152/2010 included), Section 88(a).

54 Information provided by Liv Feijen, UNHCR (email conversation, 27/05/2012).

The fear of being the only State to do so and to, in so doing, create an influx of (environmentally-)displaced persons on its own territory is as topical as it was in 1949. The conclusion reached by UNHCR then therefore seems just as valid: the issue, that requires international cooperation, must be addressed at the international level in a binding instrument offering each Contracting State guarantees that other States undertake the same commitment. A similar argument is used in India to justify India's reluctance *vis-à-vis* the ratification of the 1951 Refugee Convention: none of its neighbouring States being party to the Refugee Convention, it would "make India the only *de jure* 'refugee-friendly' country in the region" and incidentally prompt refugees to seek asylum there rather than in another country where their chances of success are more limited.[55]

> With no cooperation from its neighbours or from richer countries, India would bear the entire burden for the subcontinent.[56]

This reasoning reveals the importance of seeking a broad participation of States in the drafting of a new instrument of international law binding States to provide assistance to third country nationals.

International cooperation, quite tautologically, can only be achieved through international cooperation itself: States – the above Indian example confirms it – will be more inclined to undertake additional obligations if other States do too. This is particularly obvious in the context of asylum where States, by fear of becoming the main or sole safe haven of a region and of attracting therefore large number of refugees to their territories, lie in wait of their neighbouring States to express their readiness to accept a share of the region's incoming asylum seekers before they themselves do. Again, the statement made by India is illustrative:

> India needs more commitment from other countries before it can accede to the Convention or any other international commitment to refugee rights.[57]

---

55   O. Chaudhary, "Turning Back: An Assessment of Non-Refoulement under Indian Law", *Economic and Political Weekly* (17 July 2004), pp. 3257–3264, p. 3263. In the same way: H.K. Thames, "India's Failure to Adequately Protect Refugees", *Human Rights Brief*, Vol. 7, No. 1 (1999), pp. 20–23, p. 21.
56   O. Chaudhary (17 July 2004), *op. cit.*, p. 3263.
57   *Ibid.*, p. 3263.

It follows that not only should arguments be formulated to convince States to undertake new obligations under international law, *vis-à-vis* environmentally-displaced persons, but these arguments should be capable of winning the support of as large a number of States as possible.

A first reason why States should consent to be bound pertains to pragmatism and realism: climate change and environmental disasters *are* occurring and already impacting on the environment and populations. States' growing awareness of the reality of climate change and its impacts on human mobility calls for international law and the international community to address these phenomena, their rootcauses and consequences (1).

A key element emerges from States' concerns: it appears that, in order to secure States' commitment, the proposed framework must carry with it an insurance of burden-sharing (2). Lastly, States' apprehension towards additional migratory pressure must be taken into account and answered: anticipating displacement and adopting measures ahead of it, within the proposed framework, can help reduce migratory pressure (3).

1   A New Reality, Slowly Acknowledged by States

The reluctance of States to accept further international legal obligations is patent where migration and asylum are concerned[58] – this is, after all, perceived as one major attribute of sovereignty. A consideration of the outcomes of ongoing discussions on climate change informs that States are likewise reluctant to restrict their freedom under environmental law. The issue of environmentally-induced human displacement is a hybrid one. It is not only a matter of asylum or migration; it also pertains to States' environmental behaviour. It is little wonder States have not yet fully tackled this pressing issue.

States' timid progress and commitment with regard to reducing their contribution to climate change is oft decried. In an interesting article on the United States press coverage of global warming from 1988 to 2002, M.T. and J.M. Boykoff show that the US press adherence to the norm of "journalistic balance" significantly contributed to the mistranslation of the generally agreed-upon scientific discourse on global warming into the popular arena.[59] Media's persistence in presenting information on climate change in a balanced manner adversely led to casting doubts on the reality of the threat. Climate-change sceptics were given a platform to express their views on an equal footing with scientists.

---

58   V.O. Kolmannskog, *Future Floods of Refugees: A Comment on Climate Change, Conflict and Forced Migration* (April 2008), *op. cit.*, p. 25.
59   M.T. Boykoff and J.M. Boykoff, "Balance as Bias: Global Warming and the US Prestige Press", *Global Environmental Change*, Vol. 14 (2004), pp. 125–136.

They presented people with a choice, and the alternative theory they defended seduced, precisely because it was non-conformist.⁶⁰ According to the authors, doubt,⁶¹ instigated deliberately or not,⁶² served the cause of oil conglomerates⁶³ and corporate industry lobby groups.⁶⁴ It is in fact well-known of all negationists, in the broad sense of the term (*i.e.* including Holocaust deniers, creationists and, at large, liars), that "the grossly impudent lie always leaves traces behind it, even after it has been nailed down".⁶⁵ Repeated warnings of the scientific community on the reality of anthropogenic global warming were therefore partly overshadowed by opposing theories, groundless though they may have been. The statement made by United States President Barack Obama in his 2009 Nobel Peace Prize acceptance speech, was particularly noteworthy insofar as it markedly put forward the change in the US official position on the issue of climate change:

> ... the world must come together to confront climate change. There is little scientific dispute that if we do nothing, we will face more drought, more famine, more mass displacement – all of which will fuel more conflict for decades.⁶⁶

---

60   In the context of Holocaust denial, Patrice Loraux analyses negationist discourse and ascribes part of its success to the fact that, when being presented two different arguments, people are more likely to be impressed by that which contradicts the being (*"l'être"*) than by that which confirms it. P. Loraux, "Consentir", *Le genre humain*, No. 22 (Autumn 1990).

61   The same term is used in negotionist speech analyses. According to P. Loraux, sowing doubt in people's mind is easy, as though people were in fact enclined to doubting: *"le doute est très aisé à produire avec les moyens "sceptiques" les plus élémentaires, comme si, en nous tous, quelque chose n'attendait que cela"*. *Ibid.*

62   M.T. Boykoff and J.M. Boykoff (2004), *op. cit.*, p. 133. *See* also N. Oreskes and E.M. Conway, *Merchants of Doubt: How a Handful of Scientists Obscured the Truth on Issues from Tobacco Smoke to Global Warming* (New York: Bloomsbury Press, 2010).

63   Gordon and Suzuki observed in 1991 that the then new Bush administration budget asked for access to more wilderness areas for oil exploration. A. Gordon and D. Suzuki, *It's a Matter of Survival* (Cambridge: Harvard University Press, 1991), p. 212.

64   M.T. Boykoff and J.M. Boykoff (2004), *op. cit.*, p. 133. *See* also N. Oreskes and E.M. Conway, *Merchants of Doubt: How a Handful of Scientists Obscured the Truth on Issues from Tobacco Smoke to Global Warming* (2010), *op. cit.*

65   A. Hitler, *Mein Kampf*, Translated by J. Murphy (London: Hurst And Blackett Ltd., 1939), "Chapter 10: Why the Second Reich collapsed", p. 131.

66   Barack Obama, "Remarks by the President at the Acceptance of the Nobel Peace Prize", Oslo, 10 December 2009 (released by the White House Office of the Press Secretary).

Already in the First Assessment Report, the international scientific community stated their common certitude that the Earth global mean surface air temperature had already increased[67] and that anthropogenic emissions of greenhouse gases would contribute to additional global warming:[68]

> ... analysing 928 abstracts, published in refereed scientific journals between 1993 and 2003. The 928 papers were divided into six categories: explicit endorsement of the consensus position, evaluation of impacts, mitigation proposals, methods, paleoclimate analysis, and rejection of the consensus position. Of all the papers, 75% fell into the first three categories, either explicitly or implicitly accepting the consensus view; 25% dealt with methods or paleoclimate, taking no position on current anthropogenic climate change. Remarkably, none of the papers disagreed with the consensus position.[69]

Despite the alarming forecasts which are regularly published by a variety of sources on the future consequences of climate change on the environment and on migration, States' commitments to take action are timid. If States do perceive climate change as a serious threat to the environment requiring immediate action, their concerns do not eventually translate into sufficient actions. Negotiations are in fact often lengthy and arduous but hardly end in any strong commitment by States – as was demonstrated by the Copenhagen Summit. The 2011 Durban Agreement however rekindles some hope. It confirms that:

> [It] opens the way to bring all of the world's major greenhouse gas emitters – including the United States, China, India and Brazil – into a new international legal framework for reducing carbon pollution.
>
> In addition, the 194 countries represented at the United Nations conference adopted a package of measures which will consolidate and build on the extensive actions already under way around the world to reduce emissions.[70]

---

67 J.T. Houghton, et al., *First Assessment Report, Climate Change: The IPCC Scientific Assessment, Report Prepared for Intergovernmental Panel on Climate Change by Working Group I: Policymakers Summary*, IPCC AR1 – WG 1: SPM (1990), op. cit., p. xii.

68 *Ibid.*, p. xi.

69 N. Oreskes, "Beyond the Ivory Tower: The Scientific Consensus on Climate Change", *Science*, 3 December 2004, Vol. 306, No. 5702, pp. 1686s.

70 Greg Combet (Australian Minister for Climate Change and Energy Efficiency), "Breakthrough at Durban Climate Change Conference", *Department of Climate Change and*

The Durban Agreement reaffirmed States' awareness and willingness to act to reduce climate change by cutting their greenhouse gas emissions.

Science shows that the effects of climate change on the environment will challenge populations and their access to natural resources, including water. In some areas, the consequences can be dire. In such circumstances, the situation that triggered displacement in the refugee's country of origin will not improve in human lifespan; it is instead bound to persist or, in fact, to worsen. The same is true of the impact of technological accidents such as nuclear catastrophes on populations and the environment. Hence the imperative that States take action to prevent catastrophes from happening, to adapt to the inevitable environmental changes, and to mitigate their effects.

States' acknowledgement of a linkage between climate change and migration is nonetheless cautious: the 2010 Cancun Agreements mention the correlation between mobility, at large, and climate change, from an adaptation perspective. They do not create any obligation for States to achieve any particular result in terms of the international protection of the persons displaced by climate change. Paragraph 14 of the Decision on Long-term Cooperative Action under the Convention "merely":

> Invites all Parties to enhance action on adaptation under the Cancun Adaptation Framework, taking into account their common but differentiated responsibilities and respective capabilities, and specific national and regional development priorities, objectives and circumstances, by undertaking, inter alia (...) [m]easures to enhance understanding, coordination and cooperation with regard to climate change induced displacement, migration and planned relocation, where appropriate, at the national, regional and international levels.[71]

Nonetheless, Paragraph 14 of the Cancun Outcome Agreement is a landmark provision in that climate change induced displacement is thereby and for the first time referred to within an international instrument, a decision adopted by the international community of States within the framework of the United Nations Convention on Climate Change (UNFCCC). But the resulting

---

Energy of the Australian Government, Media release, GC343/11 (11 December 2011), available at: <http://www.climatechange.gov.au/~/media/Files/minister/combet/2011/media/december/MR20111211.pdf> [accessed 17/12/2011].

71 United Nations Framework Convention on Climate Change, *Report of the Conference of the Parties on its Sixteenth Session, held in Cancun from 29 November to 10 December 2010*, FCCC/CP/2010/7/Add.1, 15/03/2011, Decision 1/CP.16, §14(f).

consequences for States are only limited.[72] The actions States are "invited" to take are defined in broad and vague terms, leaving States with a large leeway as to the measures they should adopt. Commentators anticipated that, by reason of its abstract language, it was unlikely that the provision would lead to any concrete international action in the short term.[73] The outcome of the negotiations which took place in Durban in November-December 2011 confirmed this apparent nonchalance: although a year had passed since the Cancun Agreements, only little progress was observed with regards to the consequences of climate change on human mobility.[74]

Despite advocacy work by international organisations (including the United Nations Environment Programme (UNEP), the UN Office of the Coordination and Humanitarian Affairs (OCHA), the UN University (UNU), the UN Population Fund (UNFPA), the International Organization for Migration (IOM)[75] and the UN High Commissionner for Refugees (UNHCR)[76]), States have been slow in recognising the correlation between climate change and displacement, and in integrating the consequences of this correlation in their policies and actions (not to mention legislation). At the close of the 2011 Durban Climate Change Conference (29 November – 9 December 2011), IOM urged States to take rapid and effective actions to address the consequences of climate change on human mobility. The organisation's Director General William Lacy Swing, addressing the High Level Panel of the Durban Climate Change Conference, deplored that the little tangible progress made in a year did not come up to the expectations the Cancun agreements,[77] which called on governments to adopt measures on climate change-induced displacement, had given rise to.

> Whilst we find encouragement in the 2010 Cancun agreement that includes migration in the context of climate change vulnerability, the

---

72 IOM, *Climate Change, Environmental Degradation and Migration* (2012), op. cit., pp. 18–19.
73 B. Mayer, "Climate Migrants and the IOM at Cancun Conference on Climate Change", *McGill Editorials*, 21 January 2011.
74 International Organization for Migration (IOM), Press Briefing Note published on the IOM website on 9 December 2011 and available at: <http://www.iom.int/jahia/Jahia/media/press-briefing-notes/pbnAM/cache/offonce/lang/en?entryId=31024> [accessed 17/12/2011].
75 IOM and the United Nations Population Fund (UNFPA) co-sponsored a two-day Expert Seminar on Migration and the Environment in Bangkok, Thailand on 22–23 February 2007.
76 See below.
77 United Nations Framework Convention on Climate Change, *Report of the Conference of the Parties on its Sixteenth Session, held in Cancun from 29 November to 10 December 2010*, FCCC/CP/2010/7/Add.1, 15/03/2011.

international community is slow off the blocks to address this major phenomenon.[78]

States' careful commitment to act in the field of climate change induced displacement together with the observed lack of tangible progress made in the space of a year confirm our assumption: reaching a consensus among States to adopt a binding international instrument on climate change-induced displacement or, more broadly, on environmentally displaced persons, promises to come close to being impossible, in the short run at least.

With this in mind, the collaborative approach adopted and progresses achieved or fostered by the Nansen Initiative appear all the more valuable and expedient. Already in 2010, ahead of the High Commissioner's Dialogue on Protection Challenges on the theme "Protection Gaps and Responses", UNHCR acknowledged natural disasters and climate change as new drivers of displacement and identified the institutional and legal gap those displaced in such contexts would be confronted with.[79] Throughout 2011, as part of UNHCR commemorations for the 60th anniversary of the 1951 Refugee Convention and 50th anniversary of the 1961 Convention on the Reduction of Statelessness, UNHCR sustained its awareness-raising and thought-provoking efforts.[80] In a background note to an intergovernmental ministerial-level meeting held at the end of the year, UNHCR sought to trigger States' reflections and engagement by first reiterating the existence of gaps in the

---

[78] International Organization for Migration (IOM), Press Briefing Note published on the IOM website on 9 December 2011 and available at: <http://www.iom.int/jahia/Jahia/media/press-briefing-notes/pbnAM/cache/offonce/lang/en?entryId=31024> [accessed 17/12/2011].

[79] UNHCR, "Background paper to the 2010 High Commissioner's Dialogue on Protection Challenges: Protection Gaps and Responses", 30 November 2010, available at: UNHCR <http://www.unhcr.org/4cebeeee9.html>, pp. 2–4 [accessed 10/12/2015].

[80] The topic was addressed in a series of commemorative events organised by UNHCR in 2010–2011, under the theme "new forms of displacement", starting with the abovementioned High Commissioner's Dialogue on Protection Challenges (held in Geneva, on 8–9 December 2010), followed by the Expert meeting on climate change and displacement (Bellagio, Italy, 22–26 February 2011), the Nansen Conference on Climate Change and Displacement (Oslo, Norway, 6–7 June 2011), and the Intergovernmental Event mentioned hereafter (Geneva, 7–8 December 2011). For an overview of UNHCR Commemorations, see: UNHCR, "UNHCR Commemorations in 2011", available at: <http://www.unhcr.org/4d1c9a409.html> [accessed 10/12/2015].

international protection regime[81] and then asking, among other questions, the following ones:

> Would it be useful for States, UNHCR and other relevant actors to develop a *global guiding framework or instrument*[82] to apply to situations of displacement across borders other than those covered by the 1951 Convention? If so, should this be limited to displacement relating to climate change and natural disasters, or could it be broader? Could temporary or interim protection arrangements be useful? If so, in which situations?[83]

Speaking at the outset of the high-level meeting, the High Commissioner for Refugees at the time, António Guterres, stressed the urgency of filling the "serious protection gaps" people forcibly displaced in the context of mixed movements, large-scale complex emergencies and environmental disasters (whose number is expected to grow under the influence of climate change) are confronted with: "while the nature of forced displacement is rapidly evolving, the responses available to the international community have not kept pace".[84]

---

81   UNHCR referred to the absence of any "coherent international normative framework for protecting the rights of persons who are displaced across borders owing to forces other than persecution, serious human rights violations and ongoing conflict". UNHCR, Intergovernmental Event at the Ministerial Level of Member States of the United Nations on the Occasion of the 60th Anniversary of the 1951 Convention relating to the Status of Refugees and the 50th Anniversary of the 1961 Convention on the Reduction of Statelessness (7–8 December 2011), "Background Note for the Roundtables", HCR/MINCOMMS/2011/08, 18 November 2011, p. 3, § 7(viii).

82   The need to develop "a global guiding framework or instrument" to apply to situations of cross-border displacement that fall outside the scope of the 1951 Refugee Convention (including especially displacement resulting from sudden- and slow-onset disasters linked to climate change) was identified by the above-mentioned Expert meeting on Climate change and Displacement. UNHCR, Expert meeting on climate change and displacement (Bellagio, Italy, 22–26 February 2011), "Summary of Deliberations on Climate Change and Displacement", available at: <http://www.unhcr.org/4da2b5e19.pdf> [accessed 19/10/2016].

83   UNHCR, "Background Note for the Roundtables" (2011 Commemorations), *op. cit.*, p. 3, § 7(viii) (emphasis added).

84   A. Guterres, "Statement by Mr. António Guterres, United Nations High Commissioner for Refugees", delivered during the UNHCR Intergovernmental Meeting at Ministerial Level to mark the 60th anniversary of the 1951 Convention relating to the Status of Refugees and the 50th anniversary of the 1961 Convention on the Reduction of Statelessness (held in Geneva, on 7–8 December 2011), available at: <http://www.unhcr.org/4ecdocde9.html> [accessed 08/10/2016].

The outcome of the Ministerial event however made no reference to cross-border disaster-related displacement. According to Walter Kälin (Envoy of the Chairmanship of the Nansen Initiative), this reflected States' reluctance to addressing the issue, arising from "reasons of sovereignty, competing priorities or the lead role of UNHCR in the process".[85]

A few States nonetheless answered UNHCR's call and pledged to explore initiatives at regional and sub-regional levels "to assess the protection gaps created by new forms of forced displacement, especially environmentally-related cross-border displacement".[86] In October 2012, Norway and Switzerland hence launched the Nansen Initiative, a state-led, bottom-up, consultative process aimed at building consensus among interested states on definitions and on effective means to address cross-border displacement in the context of sudden- and slow-onset disasters. Between 2012 and 2015, through a series of regional- and sub-regional consultations (involving government, experts, and representatives of affected populations), in regions particularly affected or at particular risk of being affected by disaster-induced cross-border displacements and in close cooperation with academics and relevant organisations dealing with humanitarian issues, development and climate change, the Nansen Initiative developed a unique, invaluable and comprehensive understanding and knowledge of the phenomenon of disaster-displacement and its multiple causes, triggers, patterns as well as of the existing or possible means to address it. The Nansen Initiative compiled its work and findings in the Agenda for the Protection of Cross-Border Displaced Persons in the Context of Disasters and Climate Change ("Protection Agenda"), which was endorsed by 109 States of all regions of the world, and supported by relevant international organisations during the Global Consultation held in October 2015 in Geneva.[87] Bearing in mind States' demonstrated reluctance to engaging with the issue of disaster

---

85   W. Kälin, "From the Nansen Principles to the Nansen Initiative", *Forced Migration Review*, Vol. 41 (December 2012), pp. 48–49. See also Jane McAdam's account of the international developments on climate change and displacement, and attempts to develop a normative framework which took place between 2010 and 2013.

86   A. Guterres, "Closing remarks by the United Nations High Commissioner for Refugees", delivered in closing of the UNHCR Intergovernmental meeting at Ministerial level (held in Geneva, on 7–8 December 2011), available at: <http://www.unhcr.org/4ef094a89.html> [accessed 10/10/2016].

87   The Nansen Initiative, *Agenda for the Protection of Cross-Border Displaced Persons in the Context of Disasters and Climate Change ("Protection Agenda")* (Geneva: The Nansen Initiative, 2015), retrieved from: <https://nanseninitiative.org/wp-content/uploads/2015/02/PROTECTION-AGENDA-VOLUME-1.pdf> [28/03/2016].

displacement in previous years, the broad support for the Protection Agenda and participation in the Global Consultation[88] appear as validation of the Nansen Initiative's sensible and judicious choice for a collaborative bottom-up approach aimed at gathering knowledge and at formulating a set (a "toolbox"[89]) of – non-binding – recommendations and examples of good practices, at the disposal of States and other stakeholders. Besides the Protection Agenda, the Nansen Initiative's findings and advocacy were also instrumental in fostering progress in relevant international fora,[90] including the inclusion of disaster displacement within instruments such as the Sendai Framework for Disaster Risk Reduction 2015–2030[91] and the 2015 Paris Climate Change Agreement.[92]

---

88 The Conference report indicates that 361 participants representing governments, international organisations, academic institutions and civil society attending the Global Consultation. The Nansen Initiative, "The Nansen Initiative Global Consultation, organised in Geneva, on 12–13 October 2015: Conference Report" (hereinafter "Conference Report") (Geneva: The Nansen Initiative, December 2015), available at: <https://www.nanseninitiative.org/wp-content/uploads/2015/02/GLOBAL-CONSULTATION-REPORT.pdf> [accessed 06/06/2016], p. 8.

89 D. Burkhalter, Federal Councillor and Head of the Federal Department of Foreign Affairs, Government of Switzerland, "Opening address" delivered on the occasion of the Nansen Initiative Global Consultation, organised in Geneva, on 12–13 October 2015. All statements are annexed to the conference report. The Nansen Initiative, "Conference Report", *op. cit.*, p. 9.

90 The Nansen Initiative actively participated for instance in the 8th annual High Commissioner's Dialogue on Protection Challenges, which took place in December 2015 in Geneva, and in the 2016 World Humanitarian Summit consultative process. UNHCR, "Background Paper" issued ahead of the High Commissioner's Dialogue on Protection Challenges on the theme "Understanding and addressing root causes of displacement" (held in Geneva on 16–17 December 2015), 17 November 2015, available at: <http://www.unhcr.org/564c53429.html> [accessed 01/06/2016], pp. 6–8; W. Kälin, "The Nansen Initiative: building consensus on displacement in disaster contexts, Disasters and displacement in a changing climate", *Forced Migration Review*, Vol. 49 (May 2015), pp. 6–7.

91 UNGA, "Resolution 69/283: Sendai Framework for Disaster Risk Reduction 2015–2030", A/RES/69/283, 23 June 2015, Preamble § 4 and Priorities for Action §§ 28(d), 33(h) and (j). Walter Kälin, Envoy of the Chairmanship of the Nansen Initiative elaborates on the Nansen Initiative and its participating States' role in securing references to disaster displacement in the Sendai Framework as well as on the Framework's relevance for "more effectively tackling the multiple challenges of disaster-related displacement" in W. Kälin, "Sendai Framework: An important step forward for people displaced by disasters", *Up Front*, published on Brookings website, 20 March 2015, available at: <http://www.brookings.edu/blogs/up-front/posts/2015/03/20-sendai-disasters-displaced-kalin> [accessed 20/06/2016].

92 The "Paris Agreement" was signed in Paris on 12 December 2015 under the United Nations Framework Convention on Climate Change and entered into force on 4 November

The Paris Agreement is a long-awaited international climate agreement which set a limit to global average temperature rise and established a framework to measure, review and verify States' commitments to adopt measures and policies intended to reduce their greenhouse gas emissions.[93] Most significantly in the context of discussions on disaster-displacement, among other decisions adopted to give effect to the Agreement, it was decided that a task force on displacement would be created under the UNFCCC Warsaw International Mechanism for Loss and Damage associated with Climate Change Impacts.[94] The Conference of Parties requests the Executive Committee of the Warsaw Mechanism to establish a task force:

> ... to complement, draw upon the work of and involve, as appropriate, existing bodies and expert groups under the Convention (...) as well as relevant organizations and expert bodies outside the Convention, to develop recommendations for integrated approaches to avert, minimize and address displacement related to the adverse impacts of climate change[95]

Initially, there had been pushes, including by the Nansen Initiative, to have disaster displacement mentioned under "Adaptation", to reflect the fact and

---

2016. United Nations Framework Convention on Climate Change (UNFCCC), *Report of the Conference of the Parties on its twenty-first session, held in Paris from 30 November to 13 December 2015*, FCCC/CP/2015/10/Add.1, 29 January 2016, Addendum, Part two: Action taken by the Conference of the Parties at its twenty-first session, "Decision 1/CP.21: Adoption of the Paris Agreement", pp. 2–36.

93 The Paris Agreement aims to strengthen the global response to the threat of climate change by, inter alia, holding the increase in the global average temperature to "well below 2°C" and pursuing efforts to limit it to 1,5°C. Paris Agreement, *op. cit.*, Article 2(a).

94 The Warsaw International Mechanism was established in 2013 by the 19th Conference of Parties "to address loss and damage associated with impacts of climate change, including extreme events and slow onset events, in developing countries that are particularly vulnerable to the adverse effects of climate change". United Nations Framework Convention on Climate Change (UNFCCC), Report of the Conference of the Parties on its nineteenth session, held in Warsaw from 11 to 23 November 2013, FCCC/CP/2013/10/Add.1, 31 January 2014, Addendum, Part two: Action taken by the Conference of the Parties at its twenty-first session, FCCC/CP/2013/10/Add.1, "Decision 2/CP.19 Warsaw international mechanism for loss and damage associated with climate change impacts", § 1.

95 Paris Agreement, *op. cit.*, § 49.

acknowledgement that migration and relocation can be means to adapt to the adverse effects of climate change. The creation of the task force, under provisions on loss and damages, is nevertheless a progress not only in that disaster displacement is now expressly addressed in an international agreement on climate change but also because it has a strong operational potential: it provides a platform for competent and relevant bodies and expert groups both under and outside the Convention to formulate coordinated recommendations, aimed at taking effective actions to avert, minimise and address disaster-displacement. Incidentally, the possibility for organisations outside the Convention to participate in the task force may leave the door open for the Nansen Initiative's successor, the Platform on Disaster Displacement, to contribute its expertise to the work of the task force.

At the EU level, in November 2015, under and at the initiative of the Luxembourg Presidency of the Council of the European Union, Member States addressed the existing and anticipated impacts of climate change on human rights and mobility during an informal meeting of the Working Party on Human Rights (COHOM[96]), held in Luxembourg. The discussions, in which a representative of the Nansen Initiative participated and provided an overview of the Protection Agenda, were all the more timely as they took place after the Nansen Initiative Global Consultation, ahead of the Paris Conference of the Parties to the United Nations Framework Convention on Climate Change ("COP21") and in the context of the Syrian refugee crisis.

The obligation of States under international refugee and human rights law to grant a protection to individuals whose life or person is threatened in their country of origin and who cannot receive protection from their home or national State, might actually account, if only partly, for States' reticence to recognise the humanitarian situation of environmentally-displaced persons. Should a new category of "persons in need of international protection" be brought to conceptual existence, States would have no choice but to draw the legal consequences of this and extend their protection – be it refugee status or complementary form of protection – to them.

Apart from ensuring the adequacy of international with the new world order, further incentives are needed. The insurance of burden-sharing (2) and the perspective that the proposed framework might help reducing migratory pressure by anticipating it (3) will be developed below.

---

96 COHOM is the EU Council working group which deals with the human rights aspects of the external relations of the EU and supports the Council's decision-making process in this area.

2 Burden-sharing: Common but Differentiated Responsibility

The system devised must ensure that the "burden" of environmental displacement is evenly or fairly distributed within the international community.

The environment and, for that reason, environmental displacement being the concern of all States, all States should contribute to tackling the problem, albeit in different ways. Some will contribute by hosting environmentally-displaced persons (EDPs) where the case may be, some others will assist affected States and those exposed to an increased risk by way of financial support or technological guidance, whereas the latter States will take measures to prevent environmental degradations – be they of slow or sudden onset, and implement adaptation and mitigation projects.

Regional and international organisations also have a considerable role to play; they can coordinate State action. The United Nations and the European Union for instance have experience in providing humanitarian assistance *sur place* to countries affected by natural disasters or armed conflicts. They are also both involved in development projects, all around the world.

The recent judgment of the European Court of Human Rights in the *N. v. UK* case illustrates that account must be taken, not in law but visibly in practice, of the burdens of receiving States. Despite advocacy work to convince States of the positive impact immigration at large can have on their society and economy, States have been and manifestly remain convinced that refugee protection is a burden: examples of States' endeavours to close their borders to incoming refugees are numerous. Already in 1997, J.C. Hathaway warned that a system that fails to pay attention to receiving States' preoccupations pertaining to excessive burdens posed by asylum on their economies incurs the risk of being counterproductive:

> Refusal to balance the claims of refugees with those of receiving states simply invites a continuation of present trends toward *en bloc* denials of access.[97]

The author additionally promoted the development of a robust system of temporary protection that addresses not only repatriation but also development assistance. Temporary protection, J.C. Hathaway finds, can benefit the whole asylum system insofar as it would "regularly regenerate the asylum capacity of host states".[98]

---

[97] J.C. Hathaway, "Preface: Can International Refugee Law Be Made Relevant Again?" *in* J.C. Hathaway (Ed.), *Reconceiving International Refugee Law* (The Hague: Kluwer Law International, 1997), pp. xvii–xxix, p. xxii.

[98] *Ibid.*, p. xxiii.

The system suggested by J.C. Hathaway, criticised at the time, in fact appears to be adaptable to the question of environmental displacement. The system was one of "common but differentiated responsibility toward refugees" in which States would play different roles. Some would be or remain long-term or permanent resettlement countries, some other could undertake to provide temporary protection in certain circumstances, still other States would contribute to the international protection system chiefly financial, technical or logistical support.[99] In anticipation of criticisms that the proposed system would weaken international refugee law by undermining its humanitarian premise, Hathaway objects that existing (at the time) norms of international refugee law obviously failed to prevent States from adopting excessively restrictive policies towards refugees. The author therefore pragmatically observed:

> If the international protection of refugees is to be meaningfully regulated, then we must temper the demands of moral criticality to meet the constraints of practical feasibility.[100]

When environmental displacement is concerned, two main reasons justify an approach where States would have differentiated responsibility towards not only displaced persons but displacement at large.

Firstly, it is anticipated that under the influence of climate change, States and regions of the world will not all be affected to a similar degree by environmental disasters. It follows that population displacement will occur more in certain regions than in some others. As a consequence, States in those regions would *de facto* be host countries for persons displaced, both internally and internationally, because of the alteration of their living environment (the unbalance is already visible now with Europe receiving only a small share of the world's refugee in comparison with Asia and Africa[101]). States in other regions of the world could then contribute financially or provide assistance (human, humanitarian or expertise for instance) to affected countries or regions. Secondly, it is obvious that States do not all have the same resources (human, financial or technical), experience and expertise; they also differ when it comes to culture, geography, religion, etc. States' respective contributions would reflect their respective capacities and features, and would reckon with the possible similarities or compatibilities between the culture,

---

99 *Ibid.*, p. xxiv.
100 *Ibid.*, p. xxiv.
101 UNHCR, *The State of the World's Refugees 2012: In Search of Solidarity* (2012), *op. cit.*, p. 2.

traditions, language or living environment of the contributing State and that of the displaced population.¹⁰²

In any event, it is worth stressing that the expression "burden-sharing" should not be misleading: rather than burdensome, addressing environmental displacement and anticipating its occurrence and impact is in States' best interest, be they home States, host States or third States.

3   Reducing Migratory Pressure by Anticipating it

It is observed by D.Z. Falstrom:

> Merely allowing environmentally-displaced individuals to move does not solve the problem. Not only is their homeland continually decimated, but also the massive influx of environmental refugees to other areas creates a vicious cycle of environmental problems in these areas.¹⁰³

It follows – and confirms the finding made above – that a solution based solely on international protection would not suffice to effectively tackle environmental displacement. Additional measures must be taken.

Under the proposed framework, all States parties would undertake to acknowledge the protection needs of environmentally-displaced persons, to address them by assisting affected populations *in situ* or by granting a protective status to those who cross the international border of their country of origin and seek protection abroad. As said however, in practice, the degree to which each State fulfils its "share" will vary, in large part depending on its geographical location but also – and it is partly related – to its development.

All States could in fact benefit from the resulting framework.

Firstly, measures would be implemented in anticipation of environmental degradations, especially in regions identified as being particularly prone to disasters. Actions and programmes will be launched to reduce the impact of environmental degradations on the environment itself and on populations. As observed, environmental displacement is not purely environmental but partly man-made; the impact of disasters on population indeed varies greatly

---

102   Inhabitants of Shishmaref (Sarichef Island, Alaska) and of Tuvalu alike seek to relocate under conditions that will enable them to safeguard, to the largest extent possible, their traditions and culture. To this end, they search for alternative territories with similar living environments. See for example: G.-P. Chomette, "United States: Alaska, the Kigiqtaamiut in Jeopardy", *in* Collectif Argos (Ed.), *Climate Refugees* (Cambridge, MA: Massachusetts Institute of Technology Press, 2010), pp. 22–23.

103   D.Z. Falstrom (2002), *op. cit.*, p. 1.

depending on national authorities' preparedness and response to the disaster. As a consequence, it is anticipated that fostering the adoption and implementation of anticipatory measures in countries can curb forced displacement. Those countries that fear they might become destination countries could see in this mechanism an assurance that the influx of displaced persons from affected regions will be contained.

Nonetheless, despite mitigation and preparedness actions, disasters will occur and migration must be developed as a response to them. Therefore and this is a second point, as part of the anticipatory measures, States can adopt resettlement programs so that population movements, when they occur, are planned and, inasmuch as it is possible, organised. It is often noted that displaced people, if they cannot stay within their country of origin, generally move in neighbouring countries, *i.e.* they stay within the same region. Disasters will affect mainly those countries that are currently less developed. It could therefore be an incentive for developed States to adhere to an instrument that would favour infra-regional resettlement for populations displaced by environmental factors. The problem would thus remain a distant one.

Thirdly, Erika Feller notes that developed States could in fact benefit from influxes of displaced persons on their territories. She notes that "as populations age, birth rates decline and economies start to suffer, the potential benefits of migration, rather than only the threats, are beginning to receive more serious attention".[104] Addressing more specifically asylum, she adds:

> Host States need to be encouraged to appreciate more directly the potential of refugees as a positive factor able to contribute to their development, not only as a recipient of aid and a long term liability.[105]

As for countries of origin, they would benefit from the support of the international community to increase their resilience and minimise injuries, damages and losses when disasters occur. The anticipatory migration schemes could moreover contribute to alleviating the pressure States, and within the State, regions hosting internally-displaced persons, would face in situations of disasters. This decrease in demographic pressure, could arguably facilitate the reconstruction process, in the aftermath of sudden-onset disasters, or, in situations of slow-onset environmental degradation, bolster the country's adaptive capacity. On this last point and this will be developed below, the contribution of diaspora to the economy of their country of origin is often non-negligible.

---

104 E. Feller (2006), *op. cit.*, p. 517.
105 *Ibid.*, p. 517.

This specificity of the root causes of environmental displacement, among other considerations, calls for a customised framework. If it is to effectively tackle the issue, the anticipated framework will have to be two-fold: it shall provide protection to those already displaced but also make provision for the adoption of prevention, adaptation and mitigation measures. In other words and as announced, it must borrow from the existing international protection regime as well as from environmental law.

II A Necessarily Holistic Answer to a Complex Problem: A Proposal (Norms, Principles and Mechanisms Involved)

The proposed framework does not only consider environmental displacement as an established fact, a reality States will have – and to a certain extent already have – to deal with. Instead, it considers it as one element of a broader picture: environmental degradation including climate change at large. Seen through this wide-angle lens, environmental displacement appears as a phenomenon with a *before*, a *during* and an *after*. It encourages and empowers States and other stakeholders to act not only in a palliative manner, once the catastrophe has occurred (or begun) and populations are on the move, but also pre-emptively, to prepare the environment, infrastructures as well as populations both in countries of origin and in destination countries. Additionally, it allows for a longer-term solution to the different problems and envisages measures to adopt at a later stage, to address the consequences of the disaster and of the correlate population movement (including return to their once devastated region of origin). The inadequacy of existing law, the complexity of the issue of climate change and the truly global nature of the issue call for a multidisciplinary and multi-pronged approach to environmental displacement and migration.[106]

---

106 I can only but again agree with Jane McAdam who concluded a presentation on possible legal solutions to the issue of environmental displacement and migration in the following terms: "Crucially, policy responses to climate-related movement must not operate in a vacuum. To be effective, interventions must be attuned to and complement policies relating to development, housing, family planning, and the 'carrying capacity' of particular environments. We need much greater emphasis on the non-sexy issues, like urban planning and improved infrastructure. This requires sustained dialogue between actors from each of these policy and disciplinary spheres to ensure that responses are appropriately targeted". MCADAM, JANE, "Legal solutions: if a treaty is not the answer, then what is?", speech delivered during the ClimMig Conference on Human Rights, Environmental Change, Migration and Displacement held in Vienna on 20–21 September 2012, available

A global framework should be devised, for all environmental displacement, irrespective of the root causes of the disaster and displacement, in the sense that the "decision" to leave one's home results from an accumulation of factors and considerations which should not – and often cannot – be considered in isolation.[107]

The proposed framework can be read together with existing draft conventions on environmental displacement. Among them, the Draft Convention on the International Status of Environmentally-Displaced Persons published by legal scholars within the University of Limoges (France)[108] strikes as particularly promising and elaborate: it applies to environmental displacement at large,[109] formulates a set of principles and rights relevant for the protection of the persons concerned both before and after displacement takes place,[110] defines their international legal status,[111] and devises a specialised institutional framework.[112]

Finally, before elaborating further on the proposed framework, it is necessary to refer again to the invaluable work conducted by the Nansen Initiative,[113] from its launch in October 2012 by the governments of Norway and Switzerland until October 2015. During those three years, the Nansen Initiative – self-described as a "state-led, bottom-up consultative process" – held a series of intergovernmental regional and sub-regional consultations, civil society meetings, and country visits in regions which are or are expected to be particularly affected by disaster-related cross-border displacement. Relevant international organisations (such as the United Nations High Commissioner for Refugees and the International Organization for Migration), academic experts, representatives of civil society and of affected populations were involved in the process. The Nansen Initiative compiled the lessons learned and conclusions reached through this consultative process in a non-legally binding instrument, the

---

at: <http://www.humanrights.at/climmig/wp-content/uploads/McAdam-Jane_speech-20-Sept-2012.pdf> [accessed 02/04/2015].
107 V. Magnigny, "Des victimes de l'environnement aux réfugiés de l'environnement", REVUE Asylon(s), No. 6, Exodes écologiquesNovember 2008), retrieved from: <www.reseau-terra.eu/article845.html> [02/02/2012].
108 M. Prieur, et al. (2008), op. cit.
109 Supra note 40 (p. 517).
110 M. Prieur, et al. (2008), op. cit., Chapters 2, 3 and 4.
111 Ibid., Chapter 5.
112 Ibid., Chapter 6.
113 See also above pp. 527s.

Agenda for the Protection of Cross-Border Displaced Persons in the Context of Disasters and Climate Change,[114] which was endorsed by 109 governmental delegations during a global intergovernmental consultation in October 2015 in Geneva. The Agenda is described as a "toolbox"[115] providing affected countries and other relevant actors with examples of effective practices. It also highlights remaining normative, institutional, operational and knowledge gaps to be addressed.[116] Together with its Annexes, it compiles invaluable material on cross-border disaster-displacement and human mobility dynamics, and illustrates effective practices to address them. Although the Nansen Initiative process differs from the present work in terms of methodology and means employed (the present work being essentially academic rather than empirical), its findings and conclusions corroborate the approach detailed below. For that reason, the following developments can also be read together with the Nansen Initiative Protection Agenda.

Necessarily cross-sectoral,[117] a *sui generis* framework would have three essential and interrelated components, each corresponding to a different aspect of environmental displacement. They can be summarised in three terms: Anticipate (A), Protect (B), Mitigate (C). Developments below will consist in practical legal solutions and implementation measures which could be developed independently of the possible drafting a convention on the legal status of environmentally-displaced persons (such as the one formulated by the University of Limoges), or, should such a convention be adopted, which could translate its provisions into reality and add to them, so that the complex and multifaceted issue of environmental displacement be comprehensively addressed.

---

114 The Nansen Initiative. *Agenda for the Protection of Cross-Border Displaced Persons in the Context of Disasters and Climate Change* (Geneva: The Nansen Initiative, 2015), retrieved from: <https://nanseninitiative.org/wp-content/uploads/2015/02/PROTECTION-AGENDA-VOLUME-1.pdf> [28/03/2016].

115 Didier Burkhalter, Federal Councillor and Head of the Federal Department of Foreign Affairs, Government of Switzerland, "Opening address" delivered on the occasion of the Nansen Initiative Global Consultation, organised in Geneva, on 12–13 October 2015. All statements are annexed to the conference report. The Nansen Initiative, "The Nansen Initiative Global Consultation, organised in Geneva, on 12–13 October 2015: Conference Report" (Geneva: The Nansen Initiative, December 2015), available at: <https://www.nanseninitiative.org/wp-content/uploads/2015/02/GLOBAL-CONSULTATION-REPORT.pdf> [accessed 06/06/2016], p. 9.

116 The Nansen Initiative, "Conference Report" (Geneva: The Nansen Initiative, December 2015), *op. cit.*

117 *See* also above p. 507, Table 2.

A *Anticipate*

The measures concern not only catastrophes but migration itself. In other words, measures must be adopted and implemented in States, which aim at preventing environmental catastrophes from occurring (anti-seismic constructions, control of hazardous activities,[118] greenhouse gas emissions reduction commitments, etc.) but also at preventing migration from occurring (resilience and capacity-building). In that it addresses measures to adopt in order to prevent environmental catastrophes, the framework proposed is connected or possibly overlaps with UNFCCC. Measures adopted under this framework should however be broader since they are concerned with preventing not only climate change-related environmental degradations but all environmental disasters at large (including technological and "purely" natural such as tsunamis). Two aspects must be addressed. It is necessary to anticipate the impacts of environmental disasters and of climate change on countries and populations. This includes both prevention and resilience building (1). IPCC notes that the impacts of climate change are ineluctable, even if States were to completely interrupt greenhouse gas emissions (which is anyway not realistic). Disasters will nevertheless occur and severely affect populations who will have to move, at least temporarily but possibly permanently. It is therefore also necessary to anticipate the need of populations to move and resettle elsewhere, be it within their State or abroad (2).

1 Prevention and Resilience Building

In its Firfth Assessment Report, the Intergovernmental Panel on Climate Change (IPCC) highlighted the link between climate-related extreme events (*e.g.* drought, floods, heat waves, cyclones and wildfires), their impacts ("alteration of ecosystems, disruption of food production and water supply, damage to infrastructure and settlements, human morbidity and mortality and consequences for mental health and human well-being"), and the country's level of preparedness. In affected countries, regardless of their level of development, the harmful impacts of climate-related extremes occur where ecosystems and human systems are particularly vulnerable or exposed. According to IPCC, increased vulnerability and exposure to climate-related extremes correlate with a significant lack of preparedness.[119]

---

118 See ILC Draft Articles in that respect.
119 IPCC: Core Writing Team, et al. (Eds.), *Climate Change 2014: Synthesis Report* (2014), *op. cit.*, p. 53.

It is a well-established principle of State responsibility: States should, to the best of their abilities and knowledge, endeavour to prevent disasters from occurring and to warn and protect their population against them. In the context of natural disasters, UNHCR Working Group on Solutions and Protection added, in its 1991 report to the Forty-second Session of the Executive Committee of the High Commissioner's Programme, that:

> ... it is the responsibility of States to implement national disaster preparedness management programmes, which are essential for the effective planning of responses and mitigation of the effects of natural disasters.[120]

Under international human rights law, States' obligations under the International Covenant on Economic, Social and Cultural Rights bears particular significance. Pursuant to its Article 2, State Parties have the obligation "to take steps, individually and through international assistance and co-operation, especially economic and technical, to the maximum of its available resources, with a view to achieving progressively the full realization of the rights recognized in the present Covenant by all appropriate means, including particularly the adoption of legislative measures". Two elements appear essential and pertinent: firstly, States must cooperate and secondly, they must adopt measures for the progressive realisation of rights.

It follows that States, aware of the projected impacts of environmental disasters on their population and territory must adopt necessary measures to ensure that the human rights of the population are safeguarded at all times.

Moreover, in cases where a State does not have the financial or technological capacity to adopt such appropriate measures, it is clear from Article 2 ICESCR that other States Parties have an obligation to cooperate and assist[121] the State in realising rights.[122]

---

120   UNHCR, "EC/SCP/64", op. cit., §33.
121   This appears all the more clearly in General Comment 3 to the International Covenant on Economic Social and Cultural Rights, which states that "in accordance with Articles 55 and 56 of the Charter of the United Nations, with well-established principles of international law, and with the provisions of the Covenant itself, international cooperation for development and thus for the realization of economic, social and cultural rights is an obligation of all States". The Committee adds that international cooperation "is particularly incumbent upon those States which are in a position to assist others in this regard". CESCR, "GC 3: The Nature of State Parties' Obligations", op. cit., § 14.
122   In human rights law still, the development of the right to a healthy and safe living environment further reinforces States' obligations towards populations.

Whether projects and programs are financed by the State, vulnerable to environmental disaster, alone or in cooperation with other actors,[123] local communities should as much as possible be empowered to contribute to them.[124]

In concrete terms, those measures can include:[125]

- Building codes[126] and, where appropriate, antiseismic constructions
  - priority should be given to hospitals, infrastructures, potentially hazardous installations, designated shelters and official buildings to limit risks and ensure that, in case of disaster, relief and assistance can be effectively provided to the population.
- zoning policies,[127] environmental regulations,[128] water management;[129]
- urban planning to anticipate movements of population from affected areas to cities;
- designation of high-risk zones;[130]

---

123   In this context, the operation of the recentlty-established Green Climate Fund may provide useful guidance. United Nations Framework Convention on Climate Change (UNFCCC), *Report of the Conference of the Parties on its seventeenth session, held in Durban from 28 November to 11 December 2011*, "Decision 3/CP.17: Launching the Green Climate Fund" ("Decision 3/CP.17"), FCCC/CP/2011/9/Add.1, 15 March 2012.

124   Such a claim is repeatedly expressed by indigenous peoples in particular. *See* for instance: the Representatives of Indigenous Peoples Attending the World Summit on Sustainable Development, *Indigenous Peoples' Plan of Implementation on Sustainable Development*, issued during the 2002 World Summit on Sustainable Development held in Johannesburg, South Africa, retrieved from the website of the International Work Group for Indigenous Affairs (IWGIA) at: <http://www.iwgia.org/images/stories/sections/envir-and-devel/sust-development/docs/WSSDIPPlanofImplem.doc> [12/11/2016].

125   Similar and other examples of measures are included in C.D. Perthuis, *et al.*, *Économie de l'adaptation au changement climatique* (n/a: Conseil Economique pour le Développement Durable, February 2010).

126   J. Hyndman, *Dual Disasters: Humanitarian Aid after the 2004 Tsunami* (Sterling, VA: Kumarian Press, 2011), p. 5.

127   *Ibid.*, p. 5.

128   *Ibid.*, p. 5.

129   M.L. Parry, *et al.* (2007), *op. cit.*, p. 65.

130   W. Kälin, "Conceptualising Climate-Induced Displacement", *in* J. McAdam (Ed.), *Climate Change and Displacement: Multidisciplinary Perspectives* (Oxford: Hart, 2010), pp. 81–103, p. 85.

- reforestation,[131] coastal defence;[132]
- awareness-raising and information campaigns;[133]
- contingency plans;
- accessible and publicised environmental change reporting mechanism and Ombudsman
  - populations should have the possibility to report observed changes in their living environment to facilitate timely and appropriate decision-making.
  - the "Ombudsman" could mediate between populations concerned by a relocation scheme and the authorities to ensure that the best fit solution is adopted.[134]

The IPCC suggests that measures taken in reaction to climate change are costly; this reinforces the need to adopt preventive measures as a means of anticipating not only disasters but also costs.[135]

Whereas such measures can contribute to limiting the need for populations to migrate,[136] they will however not be sufficient if not accompanied by

---

131 N. Myers describes reforestation as "a prime way to tackle desertification, salinization [and] in fact several sorts of land degradation". He highlights in particular reforestation as a means for shelter belts to "retain soil moisture, and to resist soil erosion". N. Myers, "Environmental Refugees: An Emergent Security Issue", 13th Economic Forum, organised in Prague, in 23–27 May 2005, on 22 May 2005, EF.NGO/4/05 p. 5. In that sense, the Vietnam Red Cross's Mangrove Plantation/Disaster Risk Reduction project, initially focused on coastal environmental protection through the re-establishment of mangrove forests on deserted mudflats, appears as a good example. Red Cross Red Crescent, *RCRC: Périr en quête d'une vie meilleure*, Numero 3 (2015), p. 21 (the following two pages also include examples of prevention and resilience building measures).
132 IPCC (2007), *op. cit.*, p. 19.
133 It was observed by H.G. Wells in 1921: "Human history becomes more and more a race between education and catastrophe". H.G. Wells, *The Outline of History: Being a Plain History of Life and Mankind* (New York: Macmillan Company, 1921), p. 594.
134 Collectif Argos, *Climate Refugees* (2010), *op. cit.*
135 M.L. Parry, *et al.* (2007), *op. cit.*, p. 19.
136 In 2012, the *Groupe d'Appui aux Rapatriés et Réfugiés* (GARR), concerned about the number of Haitian boat people who died in 2011 urged Haitian authorities to strive to combat trafficking in persons and to give their citizens "reasons to hope" and hence stay in Haiti. The GARR "exhorte les autorités haïtiennes à redoubler d'efforts pour combattre le trafic de personnes et offrir aux citoyens et citoyennes haïtiens des raisons d'espérer dans leur propre pays au lieu de risquer leurs vie sur de frêles embarcations qui vont les conduire à la mort en haute mer". C. Lespinasse and GARR, "Plus de 75 boat people noyés en un

anticipatory measures for population movements. As noted by the UN Office for the Coordination of Humanitarian Affairs in its plan and budget for 2012 and 2013, even where early-warning systems, technology, policies and measures are in place to anticipate disasters, these might not be sufficient to prevent human and material loss from occurring in the event a disaster occurs. Japan and the consequences of the 2011 earthquake and tsunami on its population, territory and infrastructures is a telling illustration of it:

> An earthquake in Japan showed that even high-income countries with sophisticated preparedness mechanisms in place can still fall victim to disaster.[137]

Migration and relocation schemes should therefore be anticipated.

2 Migration and Relocation Schemes

There are only two possible scenarios: either people move within their country or to another country. Solutions will be discussed below accordingly.

(a) *Internal Migration*

The possibility for people affected by environmental disasters (including sudden-onset and slow-onset) to remain on the territory of their home State will depend on this State's capacity, in terms of territory and financial means. The case of disappearing island States is one extreme case where relocation within the State is not sustainable. Let us assume for now that internal relocation is possible. Two sets of measures can be distinguished: States should adopt contingency plans, to be implemented in the event of a sudden-onset disaster (i). They should also devise and implement relocation programs, which can be implemented progressively (ii).

(i) Contingency Plans

According to E. Brown Weiss, States have a number of duties in international environmental law in relation to disasters. Besides the general duty of preventing disasters, they also have a duty to minimise damage and provide emergency assistance, which includes "obligations to notify promptly and to provide

---

seul mois, c'est trop !", 30 December 2011, retrieved from: <http://www.garr-haiti.org/index.php/nouvelles/actualite/migrants/item/897-spip897> [01/09/2012].

137 T. de Mul (Ed.) *OCHA in 2012 & 2013: Plan and Budget* (New York: UN OCHA, 2012), p. 2, retrieved from: <OCHA in 2012 & 2013: Plan and Budget> [01/09/2012].

information, to develop contingency plans, and to cooperate in minimizing damage".[138] It could be added that those contingency plans should include emergency relocation plans.

Contingency plans, including emergency relocation plans, should be devised by national authorities in anticipation of disasters, and ready to be implemented in situations of sudden catastrophe requiring the population to relocate. Typically, relocation would be organised internally, on a temporary or permanent basis, depending on the nature, scale and anticipated impacts of the disaster.

A number of States, aware of the risks to which their territory and population are or might be exposed engage in various preparedness activities.

A United States government agency for example sponsored a research on the anticipated impacts of the explosion of an improvised nuclear device (as opposed to strategic nuclear weapons) intended to provide advanced modelling and technical assessment to assist authorities devising response planning activities. To contextualise and illustrate its findings, the report, published in November 2011, takes as working hypothesis a nuclear terrorist attack in downtown Washington, DC. The report evaluates the impacts (principally the immediate and short-term effects but also some long-term consequences) of such a detonation on the population, territory and infrastructures and formulates recommendations. The report notes that pre-planning is essential to mitigate the impacts and, in particular, reduce casualties; it should include the training of personnel (including in hospitals), pre-incident preparedness activities at community level, sheltering and evacuation strategies and the elaboration of public information plans to be activated in the aftermath of the incident. As concluded by the report:

> A prepared emergency management agency and an informed citizenry can prevent hundreds of thousands of casualties.[139]

---

138   E. Brown Weiss adds that States also have the general duty of compensating for injuries from disasters. E. Brown Weiss, "Environmental Disasters in International Law", *Anuario Jurídico Interamericano* (1986), pp. 141–169. As cited in: A.A. Cançado Trindade, "The Contribution of International Human Rights Law to Environmental Protection, with Special Reference to Global Environmental Change", in E. Brown Weiss (Ed.), *Environmental Change and International Law: New Challenges and Dimensions* (Tokyo: The United Nations University, 1992), note 187.

139   B.R. Buddemeier, et al., *Key Response Planning Factors for the Aftermath of Nuclear Terrorism* (Livermore: Lawrence Livermore National Laboratory, November 2011), p. 49.

The report adds:

> Pre-incident preparedness is essential to saving lives. After a nuclear detonation, public safety will depend on the ability to quickly make appropriate safety decisions. Empowering people with knowledge can save thousands of lives.[140]

The same awareness of the virtue of anticipation and preparedness is well recognised in Japan. While Japan is still recovering from the earthquake, tsunami and nuclear power plant accident which occurred in March 2011, a Japanese governmental agency (the Cabinet Office) published in August 2012 estimates of the human impacts of a magnitude 9-class quake and subsequent massive tsunami hitting the central and western parts of the country. The Cabinet Office predicted that up to 323,000 persons could be killed (with the tsunami accounting for 70 per cent of the victims) and 623,000 across Japan could suffer injuries.[141] Albeit noting the extremely low probability that an earthquake of such magnitude occurs, the Cabinet Office undertook to plan for the worse and adopt new countermeasures against natural disasters within a year. The working hypothesis is intended to foster the improvement by national authorities, the private sector and the population of early-warning systems, evacuation strategies, mitigation measures and emergency responses.[142]

It appears that lessons were learned from 2011 Fukushima Daiichi nuclear plant accident. The French nuclear safety agency (*Autorité de sûreté nucléaire – ASN*) at the occasion of the launch of its report on nuclear safety in France noted that Fukushima nuclear accident marked a turning point in nuclear safety and radioprotection monitoring.[143] The weak operational response to and disastrous consequences of the 2011 Japanese nuclear accident prompt the strengthening of measures for controlling and regulating the exploitation of nuclear plants. Not only should infrastructures be reinforced to effectively

---

140   *Ibid.*, p. 48.
141   "Huge Nankai Quake Could Kill 320,000 in Japan: Gov't", *The Mainichi*, 29 August 2012.
142   "Scénario du pire: 323 000 Japonais morts dans un tsunami", *L'essentiel Online* (AFP, 2012), 29 August 2012, retrieved from: <http://www.lessentiel.lu/fr/news/monde/story/323-000-Japonais-morts-dans-un-tsunami-28595146> [29/08/2012].
143   The ASN Report analyses: "*il y a un avant et un après Fukushima*" (i.e.: "there is a before and an after Fukushima"). Autorité de Sûreté Nucléaire, "Rapport sur l'état de la sûreté nucléaire et de la radioprotection en France en 2011", J.-J. Dumont, *et al.* (Eds.) (Paris: 2012), p. 5.

resist enduring situations, it is also essential that personnel be trained and procedures be devised[144] to respond to catastrophes should they occur.

(ii)   Relocation Programs

For those States that have the capacity to relocate the parts of their population victims of disaster, they should also adopt such relocation programs, in due consultation with the communities concerned.[145] The importance of the right of the persons concerned by the relocation to participate in the decisions and measures affected them is clearly emphasised in the Guidance on Protection People from Disasters and Environmental Change Through Planned Relocation, published by Brookings, Georgetown University and UNHCR in October 2015.[146] The "Guidance on Planned Relocation" is a comprehensive guidance on planned relocation, providing States, communities and other relevant actors with a set of definitions, overarching principles, and elements of the legal,

---

144   *Ibid.*, 16–28. The ASN report clarifies what measures have already been or can be adopted to reinforce the resistance of nuclear plant infrastructures. It also stresses, based on its observations of the handling of Fukushima nuclear crisis, that in the aftermath of a nuclear accident, the ability of the plant operator personnel, and subcontractors if any, to adapt and cooperate is crucial (*see* pp. 19–21 in particular).

145   In concrete terms, the situation of the population of Shishmaref is indicative. Located on the Alaskan Sarichef island, the village is threatened by the erosion of the island, heightened by the continuing thawing of permafrost. Significant losses of land have already occurred; the subsistence of the community is also threatened due to changing environmental conditions which affect their traditional way of life (dependent in large part on hunting and fishing). The majority of the community is in favour of moving. The State of Alaska proposed their relocation in small towns, in two different areas, some three hundred kilometres away from their island. Another alternative would be to relocate the village in a single location on the mainland, twenty kilometres from the island. The first alternative, favoured by authorities, is less expensive and take advantage of existing urban infrastructures. The second alternative, is more expensive, the destination area being uninhabited yet; it is however favoured by the Shishmaref community since it would enable to it to maintain its subsistence lifestyle and preserve its culture and integrity. Members of the community anticipate that, if the State maintains its favoured option, they will have to themselves organise their relocating to the mainland. Collectif Argos, *Climate Refugees* (2010), *op. cit.*, pp. 22–28; Shishmaref Alaska Erosion & Relocation Coalition, *Shishmaref: We Are Worth Saving!*, <www.shishmarefrelocation.com> [20/09/2012].

146   Brookings, Georgetown University and United Nations High Commissioner for Refugees, *Guidance on Protecting People from Disasters and Environmental Change through Planned Relocation* ("*Guidance on Planned Relocation*"), 7 October 2015, also available online at: <http://www.unhcr.org/protection/environment/562f798d9/planned-relocation-guidance-october-2015.html> [accessed 27/10/2016].

policy and institutional frameworks necessary for carrying out planned relocation. It also provides tools for assessing a need for planned relocation but also for planning, implementing and evaluating it once the need has been identified.[147] Planned relocation is defined as:

> a planned process in which persons or groups of persons move or are assisted to move away from their homes or places of temporary residence, are settled in a new location, and provided with the conditions for rebuilding their lives. Planned Relocation is carried out under the authority of the State, takes place within national borders, and is undertaken to protect people from risks and impacts related to disasters and environmental change, including the effects of climate change. Such Planned Relocation may be carried out at the individual, household, and/or community levels.[148]

A typical example is the situation of Arctic communities whose territory is shrinking due to thawing permafrost. Canada, the United States and Nordic States have the legal obligation to protect their own populations; in particular, States must respect and ensure to those individuals as to any other individual within their jurisdiction any obligation arising out of the international human rights treaties they are parties to.

Moreover, in cases where the populations displaced are indigenous, particular consideration must be had to the special connection those peoples have with the land. In any case, the relocation planned by the State must respect to the best of the country's ability (including in terms of geography) the culture and traditions of the populations displaced.[149] This can be particularly true, as said, of indigenous people[150] but also of large countries, where traditions may considerably vary from one region within it to another.

---

147 *Ibid.*
148 *Ibid.*, p. 4.
149 In its Fifth Assessment Report, on the basis of existing studies, IPCC highlights that relevant authorities must take into account that there are psychological and cultural dimensions to moving and settling people in new location in order to secure the legitimacy and success of the planned relocation. IPCC: W.N. Adger, J.M. Pulhin, J. Barnett, *et. al.*, "Human security", in: C.B. Field, V.R. Barros, D.J. Dokken, *et. al.* (eds.), *Climate Change 2014: Impacts, Adaptation, and Vulnerability, Part A: Global and Sectoral Aspects, Contribution of Working Group II to the Fifth Assessment Report of the Intergovernmental Panel on Climate Change* (Cambridge, New York: Cambridge University Press, 2014), pp. 755–791, p. 771.
150 E. Marino studies the case of Shishmaref (Alaska) and difficulties faced by the populations to adapt but also to plan their relocation, in part due to the non-existence of any

During the Rio+20 "Earth Summit", indigenous people claimed their right to "full and effective participation at all stages and levels of decision making in programmes, policy and institutions promoting sustainable development".[151]

In this case too, the Ombudsman for environmental displacement suggested above could play a significant role in assisting the formulation of relocation alternatives satisfactory for both State authorities and displaced persons.

As acknowledged throughout this work, environmental disasters will mainly cause people to move within the borders of their home State but not only. International migrations occur and will continue to occur, both at the regional and global level. They too need be addressed.

(b)   *International Migration*

Here too, two types of anticipatory measures can be envisaged. governments, who have the primary responsibility to protect individuals within the jurisdiction of the State, in States at risk of "losing" parts or the entirety of their territory, rendered uninhabitable by environmental change should consider migration options for the populations concerned (ii). Additionally, contingency plans of an international dimension could also be put in place (i).

(i)   Contingency Plans

It was observed at the national level, some States do adopt contingency plans including sheltering and evacuation strategies to be activated in cases of disasters. Similarly, sheltering and evacuation strategies could be developed, in cooperation with neighbouring States, for cases where it is anticipated that internal relocation will not be suitable. G.S. McCue, in his proposal for a convention addressing environmental migration, based, not on refugee law but on international environmental law, also insists on this aspect.[152]

---

overarching agency with the capacity to relocate communities pre-emptively and to the long-standing complicated relationship that exist between these communities and State authorities. E. Marino notes that, for indigenous communities in particular, "this threatens not only life and home, but also cultural stability". E. Marino, "The Long History of Environmental Migration: Assessing Vulnerability Construction and Obstacles to Successful Relocation in Shishmaref, Alaska", *Global Environmental Change*, Vol. 22 (2012), pp. 374–381, p. 380.

151   *Indigenous Peoples' Plan of Implementation on Sustainable Development*, op. cit., § 90.
152   G.S. McCue (1993–1994), *op. cit.*, pp. 180–182 and specifically 184.

The contingency plan could include in particular:

- an estimate of the size of the population the receiving State accepts to host;
- the identification of the destination area;[153]
- the anticipated costs for the receiving State;
- planning of reception facilities which should, at a minimum, allow persons to provide for their most basic needs (shelter, food, water, sanitation and healthcare);[154]
- the identification of national, regional or international organisations including non-governmental organisations, governmental agencies, and members of the civil society in charge of providing assistance and protection to the displaced population;[155] and
- awareness-raising and information campaigns for both potentially-displaced populations in the country of origin and local populations in the receiving State.

Although it is conceivable that such plans can develop at a bilateral level, it seems that G.S. McCue's proposal to include them in the broader framework of a convention would indeed be preferable and in fact more realistic. Apart from otherwise valid humanitarian considerations, it is uneasy to think of any reason which could motivate States to enter into such agreement[156] whereby they commit to host possibly large groups of persons suddenly, temporarily and sometimes repeatedly displaced by environmental disasters. The destabilising effect of groups of migrant suddenly crossing borders, the possible hostility of local populations towards these groups, the risk of environmental degradation caused in the host country by a large influx of displaced persons, obligations host States would automatically have, notably under international human rights law, towards those individuals once they are on their territory and hence within their jurisdictions but also correlative associated costs are just so many

---

153 The IASC Guidelines could be used as reference to identify an appropriate evacuation area within the host country. IASC, *Operational Guidelines* (January 2011), *op. cit.*, pp. 17–18.

154 There too, the IASC Guidelines which provide detailed guidance on the provision on essential goods and services to persons displaced by natural disasters could be used as a reference guide. *Ibid.*, pp. 31–38.

155 Related to this point is the suggestion made by G.S. McCue that contingency plans be communicated to the Office of the Under-Secretary-General who could begin coordinating assistance whenever environmental migration is triggered. G.S. McCue (1993–1994), *op. cit.*, p. 187.

156 A similar analysis is made by C. Cournil in C. Cournil (Juin 2008), *op. cit.*, p. 22.

factors which could dissuade States to enter such agreement. Such arguments have in fact already been invoked by States as excuses, particularly in cases of large influxes of asylum-seekers, to deny entry or forcibly return the persons concerned.[157]

Promoting the conclusion of such bilateral agreements in the broader context of a regional or international framework could offer incentives to receiving States. Such framework would, as suggested above, include contribution to a fund. On the basis of the data provided in the contingency plan, it could be possible to assess the cost incurred by the receiving State and budget it in the fund.

(ii) Resettlement Programs

In other cases, such as the obvious case of disappearing island States, migration will most likely be progressive. Migration schemes should be put in place, to allow populations concerned to move abroad, "pre-emptively", before the conditions in their country become uninhabitable.

Then again, the culture and traditions of the persons should be maintained as far as possible. For that reason, regional solutions are often sought – although one might wonder whether Pacific islander lifestyle would not bear more similarities with that on, for instance, Indian ocean islands than with Australian mainland lifestyle.[158] Preferable options would also include maintaining the cohesion of the nations or, at least, communities within them. In other words, the migration schemes devised should endeavour to allow for the relocation of large groups of migrants.

---

157 G.S. Goodwin-Gill and J. McAdam refer specifically to "lack of resources, threats to national security, and fears of political destabilization". G.S. Goodwin-Gill and J. McAdam, *The Refugee in International Law* (2007), *op. cit.*, p. 232. It can be noted that the construction of a "wall" by India along its border with Bangladesh to stop immigration suggests that indeed, in the absence of incentives, States will not voluntarily undertake to host environmentally-displaced persons. On the "Indian wall", see for example: S. Carney, *et al.*, "Fortress India: Why Is Delhi Building a New Berlin Wall to Keep out Its Bangladeshi Neighbors?" July/August 2011 ; P.R. Ghosh, "India-Bangladesh Border: The ?Berlin Wall? Of Asia", *International Business Times*, 12 June 2012; "Bangladesh: Border Killings Mount Despite No-Shooting Decree" (UN News Service), 6 December 2011.

158 The concern of displaced population to preserve as far as possible their cultures and traditions appears clearly in Nauru's rejection of Australia's resettlement offers lest the loss of their identity. J. McAdam, "'Disappearing States', Statelessness, and Relocation", in *Climate Change, Forced Migration, and International Law* (Oxford, New York: Oxford University Press, 2012), pp. 151–152.

It is necessary to plan the relocation of the populations concerned as early as possible, in consultation with those populations.[159] The duty of States to consult with populations concerned was derived by indigenous people groups participating in the 2012 Rio+20 Earth Summit from their right to self-determination.[160]

> We demand the creation of an Ad Hoc Open-Ended Inter-Sessional Working Group on Indigenous Peoples and Local Communities and Climate Change with the objective of studying and proposing timely, effective and adequate solutions to respond to the emergency situations caused by climate change affecting Indigenous Peoples and local communities.[161]

B   Protect (and Minimise Damage)

States' duty to protect and minimise damage includes the obligation, derived from the rules on State responsibility, for affected States to notify other States (and competent international organisation) of a risk of transnational migration and to provide relevant information on the root cause situation.

Where environmental degradation and correlate displacement occur, in spite of the preventive measures adopted, the international community has the obligation to acknowledge and address the protection needs of the populations displaced, be it internally or internationally.

Clear evidence that a form of international protection is warranted flows from the fact that people fleeing degrading or devastated environments actually reach another State's territory. UNHCR often underlines that one does not take the decision to flee his or her country of origin lightly.[162] The decision to leave one's home, family and region often is a last resort solution, when the different attempts made to adapt to the disruption have failed.[163]

It could in fact be presumed that a person who leaves his or her home (and hence his or her relationships, work, education, cultural ties, etc.) does not do so unless compelled to. Moreover, the journey displaced persons embark on is of uncertain outcome, to say the least, and more often than not perilous. What,

---

159   G.-P. Chomette, "United States: Alaska, the Kigiqtaamiut in jeopardy", in Collectif Argos, *Climate Refugees* (Paris: Massachusettes Institute of Technology, 2010), pp. 18–51.
160   *Indigenous Peoples' Plan of Implementation on Sustainable Development*, op. cit., §§ 4–12.
161   *Ibid.*, § 65.
162   UNHCR (1997), op. cit., p. 1.
163   T. Afifi, et al., *Climate Change, Vulnerability and Human Mobility: Perspectives of Refugees from the East and Horn of Africa* (June 2012), op. cit., pp. 12, 39–40 and 46.

if not desperation can push individuals to abandon their homes and undertake an uncertain journey at the risk of their life? In other words, over-simplistically perhaps but logically it seems: what threat can cause an individual to risk his or her life in order to escape it if not a threat to life itself?[164]

1   Definition of Persons in Need of Protection (Internal or International)

Two aspects of the question will be focused on. Firstly, it is necessary to identify a threshold of habitability or "returnability" (a). Secondly, it is necessary to distinguish between slow-onset and sudden environmental disasters (b).

(a)   *Sustainable Conditions for Return: Safety and Dignity*

· Should be protected persons who cannot return in safety and dignity.[165]

An important difficulty confronting decision makers in international protection claims is that of distinguishing between those who migrate voluntarily and those who are forced to do so, all the more in a context of progressive degradation of the environment.[166]

D.C. Bates conceptualised the decision to migrate as a continuum, thereby illustrating that there is no clear-cut divide between voluntary and forced migration but instead a multitude of shades of grey: based on the level of control

---

164   The life-threatening situation in which boat people find themselves is telling. S. Shabazz, "Haitians Again Risking Lives to Escape Poverty", *The Final Call – World News*, last updated 3 August 2012, retrieved from: <http://www.finalcall.com/artman/publish/World_News_3/article_9090.shtml> [01/09/2012].

165   M. Bradley elaborates on the notion of "return in safety and dignity" and notably traces the history of the notion in international law. In particular, M. Bradley cites as the first major instrument to include such notion the 1989 Declaration and Concerted Plan of Action in favour of Central American Refugees, Returnees and Displaced Persons (CIREFCA), adopted by the International Conference on Central American Refugees. Article 3 expresses the signatories' commitment to the return of refugees "under conditions of personal security and dignity that would allow them to resume a normal life". M. Bradley, "Return in Dignity: A Neglected Protection Challenge", RSC *Working Paper Series* (University of Oxford, Refugee Studies Centre), No. 40 (June 2007), the CIREFCA is mentioned p. 3. UNHCR Handbook on Voluntary Repatriation indicates that part of UNHCR Mandate for voluntary repatriation is "to promote the creation of conditions that are conducive to voluntary return in safety and with dignity". UNHCR, *Handbook on Voluntary Repatriation: International Protection* (Geneva: UNHCR, 1996), § 1.6.

166   W. Kälin, "Displacement Caused by the Effects of Climate Change: Who Will Be Affected and What Are the Gaps in the Normative Framework for Their Protection?" *in* S. Leckie,

people have over their migration decisions, migration ranges from being involuntary to being compelled or, at the other end of the spectrum, voluntary. D.C. Bates (referring to G. Hugo's earlier work[167]) proposes to classify environmentally-displaced persons along the same continuum of agency in migration, from environmental refugees, on the involuntary end of the continuum, to "environmental emigrants" and to migrants on the other end.[168]

It seems that, instead of seeking to identify drivers for displacement, focusing on the situation awaiting individuals upon return would be more appropriate and avoid a complex if not impossible assessment of the applicant's motives.

In view of the complexity and variety of environmental disasters and of the impacts may have on populations, adopting a detailed definition of the threats to which individuals should not be returned would run the risk of being incomplete. It appears that the notion of dignity in particular is sufficiently clear yet broad to adapt to the complexity of the impacts of environmental disasters on human life. In that sense, the vagueness of the concept is its main virtue.[169]

It could be added that the principle of *non-refoulement* shall be respected at all time.

Reference to notions such as of "human rights violations" or, *a fortiori*, "persecution" should in any case be avoided: they prompt considerations of State responsibility which often have little relevance in cases of environmental displacement. As said, the majority of environmental displacement originates (and will increasingly so) in natural hazard-related disasters[170] against the effects of which national authorities are unable to shield their populations.[171]

---

    et al. (Eds.), *Climate Change and Displacement Reader* (New York, NY: Earthscan, 10 October 2008), pp. 135–143, p. 137.

167   G. Hugo, "Environmental concerns and international migration", *International Migration Review* (The Center for Migration Studies of New York, Inc.), Vol. 30, No. 1, Special Issue: Ethics, Migration, and Global Stewardship(Spring, 1996), pp. 105–131.

168   D.C. Bates (May 2002), *op. cit.*, p. 468, Figure 1: Continuum of control over migration decisions in situations of environmental change.

169   M. Bradley (June 2007), *op. cit.*, pp. 10–11. M. Bradley observes that the concept of return in safety and dignity has gained much resonance amongst international actors, especially since the 1980s, not least in the context of internal displacement (the concept is enshrined in the Guiding Principles on Internal Displacement). *Ibid.*, pp. 1–7.

170   *See* Annex 3.

171   The numerous actions undertaken by the governments of the Pacific island States of Tuvalu and Kiribati or of the Maldives for example is illustrative of those States' willingness to formulate appropriate responses to the needs of their populations, confronted with

Environmental disaster affects peoples' enjoyment of their human rights, including the most basic ones. Enumerating rights, such as the right to life, including the right to water and sanitation or the right to food, the right to housing, the right not to be subjected to inhuman or degrading treatment and the right to private and family life could be tempting. However, this would be disregarding the indivisibility of human rights and the doctrine of "flagrant violation"[172] or "fundamental breach"[173] of rights. Hence, returning an individual to a territory where he or she has no possibility to practice his or her religion can constitute a flagrant violation of the right to freedom of religion and engage, in and of itself or because it amounts to inhuman or degrading treatment, the responsibility of the returning State.[174] Other examples can include cases where children but also adults have no access to education:[175] the right to education is analysed as a fundamental right of "vital importance",[176] which empowers adults and children to "lift themselves out of poverty".[177] It is

---

the ineluctable deterioration of their environment. Some consider relocation as an option (Kiribati), some other officially reject it to concentrate instead on the fight against climate change and its impacts. Hence the following statement by the Tuvaluan Prime Minister: "We will fight to keep our country, our culture and our way of living". The Australian Professor Jane McAdam has extensively researched the question of disappearing States and possible solutions for displaced populations, including the proposals made by those most directly concerned, *i.e.* the governments of those "drowning" States. J. McAdam (Ed.) *Climate Change and Displacement: Multidisciplinary Perspectives* (Oxford: Hart, 2010), pp. 143–153; J. McAdam, *Climate Change, Forced Migration, and International Law* (2012), *op. cit.*, pp. 143–158; J. McAdam (2011), *op. cit.*, pp. 110–111 and 121–131 especially. See also: D. Corlett, *Stormy Weather: The Challenge of Climate Change and Displacement* (2008), *op. cit.*, pp. 39–42.

172 In *Ullah and Do*, the House of Lords finds that the approach adopted by the Immigration Appeal Tribunal is the correct one and cites the Tribunal's decision. In cases involving qualified rights, the Tribunal stated, "[t]he reason why *flagrant denial or gross violation* is to be taken into account is that it is only in such a case – where the right will be *completely denied or nullified* in the destination country – that it can be said that removal will breach the treaty obligations of the signatory state however those obligations might be interpreted or whatever might be said by or on behalf of the destination state". UKIAT, *Owen, op. cit.*, § 111. Cited in UKHL, *Ullah and Do*, 17 June 2004, *op. cit.*, § 24.

173 UKHL, *Ullah and Do*, 17 June 2004, *op. cit.*, § 69.

174 ECtHR, *Z. & T. v. UK*, p. 7; UKHL, *Ullah and Do*, 17 June 2004, *op. cit.*, § 67.

175 On deprivation of the right to education as a form of persecution, see: M. Foster, *International Refugee Law and Socio-Economic Rights: Refuge from Deprivation* (2007), *op. cit.*, pp. 214–226.

176 CESCR, "General Comment 11: Plans of Action for Primary Education" ("GC 11: primary education"), E/C.12/1999/4, 10 May 1999, § 2.

moreover essential to the "full development of the human personality".[178] The situation of indigenous people is also a manifest example of a case where violation of economic, social and cultural rights can fundamentally affect and threaten an individual's and community's life not least by depriving them of their means of subsistence.[179] Returning indigenous peoples to areas where adaptation is not possible or would lead to the nullification of a people's culture and traditions, and jeopardise their subsistence is incompatible with the principle of *non-refoulement*.

It is necessary to stress the indivisibility and universality of all human rights. As said in Part 2, just like civil and political rights,[180] economic, social and cultural rights are essential to a person's life and their deprivation can trigger the principle of *non-refoulement*.

The International Law Commission, working on the adoption of articles on the protection of persons in the event of disasters, considers that the principle of human dignity must inspire the protection of persons in the event of disasters. The ILC observed that "dignity" is present "as an inspiration of all major universal human rights instruments", is included in the preamble of most regional human rights instruments and is widely applied by courts.[181] The European Court of Human Rights is indeed particularly familiar with the concept.[182]

---

177   The Committee on Economic, Social and Cultural Rights describes the right to education as an "empowerment right". CESCR, "General Comment No. 13: The Right to Education" ("GC 13 (right to education)"), E/C.12/1999/10, 8 December 1999, § 1.

178   *Ibid.*, § 4.

179   On the particular vulnerability of indigenous peoples to the impacts of climate change, the necessity to integrate their special relationship to the land, to acknowledge and value their traditions and to adapt international law (including refugee law) so that it can effectively respond to their plight, *see*: L. Westra, *Environmental Justice and the Rights of Ecological Refugees* (2009), *op. cit.*, pp. 117–126. On indigenous in the Arctic region and specifically in Alaska: Collectif Argos, *Climate Refugees* (2010), *op. cit.*, pp. 18–51. More case studies are included in: M. Macchi, *et al.*, *Indigenous and Traditional Peoples and Climate Change* (n/a: International Union for Conservation of Nature – IUCN, March 2008), pp. 29–62, retrieved from: <http://cmsdata.iucn.org/downloads/indigenous_peoples_climate_change.pdf> [accessed 19/10/2016].

180   Not limited to the right to life and the prohibition of torture, inhuman or degrading treatment and punishment. Most recently, the right to fair trial has been successfully invoked before the European Court of Human Rights who concluded in the cases that expulsion of the applicant was in violation of Article 6 ECHR. ECtHR, *Othman*.

181   ILC, "Third report on the protection of persons in the event of disasters by Eduardo Valencia-Ospina, Special Rapporteur", A/CN.4/629, 31 March 2010, §§ 51–62.

182   In *Pretty v. UK* for instance, the European Court of Human Rights asserted that "the very essence of the Convention is respect for human dignity in freedom"; the Court has regularly resorted to the concept in Article 3 cases (notably concerning conditions of detention)

Whereas it is not a human right *per se*, it is "posited as a fundamental principle that gave rise to all human rights"[183] or, often too, as the source of all rights.

In the broader context of the environment, the very first principle of the Stockholm Declaration adopted by the UN Conference on the Human Environment proclaims that "Man has the fundamental right to freedom, equality and adequate conditions of life, in an environment of a quality that permits a life of dignity and well-being".[184]

The notion of human dignity can hence encapsulate all human rights while intimating a certain minimum level of attainment of those rights. For that reason, grounding the definition of environmentally-displaced persons in need of international protection in the notion of human dignity appears appropriate.

The choice for such definition is also justified by reference to the Guiding Principles on Internal Displacement[185] and to the IASC Operational Guidelines on the protection of persons in situations of natural disasters.[186]

---

or in Article 8 cases. On the conditions of detention of a person with severe mental illness, the Court concluded in the case that "[e]ven though there was no intention to humiliate or debase him, the Court finds that the conditions which the applicant was required to endure were *an affront to human dignity* and reached the threshold of degrading treatment for the purposes of Article 3". ECtHR, *Case of M.S. v. The United Kingdom* ("*MS v. UK*"), Application no. 24527/08 (3 May 2012, final 3 August 2012), § 45. The Court for example stated that "access to properly equipped and hygienic sanitary facilities is of paramount importance for maintaining the inmates' sense of personal dignity". ECtHR, *Ananyev and Others v. Russia* ("*Ananyev*"), Applications Nos. 42525/07 and 60800/08 (10 January 2012), § 156. In Article 8 ECHR cases, the Court found that the right to private life included "respect for human dignity and the quality of life in certain respects". ECtHR, *Pretty v. UK*, § 65; ECtHR, *Case of L. v. Lithuania*, Application no. 27527/03 (11 September 2007, final 31 March 2008), § 56.

183   ILC, "Report of the International Law Commission on the work of its 62nd session" [2010] *GAOR, 65th session, Supplement No. 10 (A/65/10)*, § 305. Also: E. Wicks (2012), *op. cit.*, pp. 206–208 and 212–216; O. Schachter, "Human Dignity as a Normative Concept", *The American Journal of International Law* (American Society of International Law), Vol. 77, No. 4 (1983), pp. 848–854, p. 852 in particular, where O. Schatcher proposes a list of examples of conducts and ideas "antithetical or incompatible with respect for inherent dignity".

184   Stockholm Declaration, Principle 1.

185   Principle 28 states that "Competent authorities have the primary duty and responsibility to establish conditions, as well as provide the means, to allow internally displaced persons to return voluntarily, in safety and with dignity, to their homes or places of habitual residence, or to resettle voluntarily in another part of the country". UN Commission on Human Rights, "Guiding Principles on Internal Displacement", *op. cit.*, Principle 28.

186   IASC, *Operational Guidelines* (January 2011), *op. cit.*

In particular, the IASC Operational Guidelines clarify that in situations of internal displacement caused by natural disasters, conditions conducive to making displaced persons' return, local integration or settlement elsewhere in the country sustainable should be established as soon as possible. In particular, conditions are considered sustainable if internally displaced persons:

(a) Are and feel safe and secure, free from harassment and intimidation, as well as from unmitigated risks of further natural disasters;
(b) Have been able to access adequate housing, including, in the case of return, to repossession of and adequate reconstruction or rehabilitation of their homes; and
(c) Can return to their lives as normally as possible, with access to water, basic services, schools, livelihoods, employment, markets, etc. without discrimination.[187]

In like manner, if such sustainable conditions are not established in the person's country or origin, a State cannot remove an individual there. This was already argued above in the context of the Qualification Directive (Article 8) and the internal flight alternative it provides: there is no reason to distinguish between those conditions which are considered conducive of sustainable return when displaced persons return from within the country or from another country.

The IPCC Fifth Assessment Report provides policymakers with valuable tools for the assessment of this "returnability" threshold. The Report, indeed addresses the question of the impact of climate change on human security including on migration and population displacement.[188]

(b)   *Sudden Disaster or Progressive Degradation of the Environment*
The main distinction in the present case would be between persons displaced by slow-onset disasters and those displaced by sudden disasters.

For the latter, under European Union law, the displaced's claims for international protection must be assessed through standard asylum procedures. In the majority of cases, refugee status will not apply (unless aid is distributed discriminatorily). Applicants will then be eligible for subsidiary protection, in

---

187   *Ibid.*, D.2.3., p. 47.
188   IPCC: C.B. FIELD, *et. al.* (eds.), *Climate Change 2014: Impacts, Adaptation, and Vulnerability, Part A: Global and Sectoral Aspects, Contribution of Working Group II to the Fifth Assessment Report of the Intergovernmental Panel on Climate Change* (Cambridge, New York: Cambridge University Press, 2014), pp. 755–791.

the amended version proposed above. Applicant's particular vulnerabilities (children, disabled persons or the elderly for instance) should be taken into consideration to assess the reality of the alleged threat to their life or person.

In situations of slow-onset disasters, the assessment of the claim will necessarily be more complex. It was mentioned in the previous constituent of this proposed answer, migration schemes must put in place, regionally especially but also internationally, to allow persons who move by reason of the progressive degradation of their living environment to permanently (if they so desire) resettle. On the other hand, are considered to be in need of protection those who are forced to move because their area is becoming uninhabitable.

It seems that science can greatly contribute to the assessment of the well-foundedness of the claim in the context of alleged environmental degradation: scientific measurements and observations as well as projections can assist decision-makers by providing them with key information on the actual or future circumstances in the country of origin. Such information could ensure that, in the context of displacement allegedly triggered by progressive environmental change, assessing the genuineness of the applicant's fear and the reality of the risk incurred upon return to the affected territory be subject to less uncertainty and subjectivity (than an assessment of credibility for instance). Available scientific data and, if need be, projections will provide objective evidentiary elements of the applicant's situation. Just as above, reference was made to "returnability" threshold, one could think of formulating "habitability thresholds" (temperature, frequency and intensity of extreme weather events, number of days of rain or drought, sea level) beyond which it would be presumed that life becomes unbearable. The degradation of the environment would be of such severity that populations would have no other choice but to flee to other regions or countries. The practice would in fact not be completely unknown of environmentalists:

> In many environmental fields, there are thought to be thresholds below which only minor effects occur. Critical levels in acid rain are one example (Brodin and Kuylenstierna, 1992). These kinds of thresholds also are possible in climate change and are incorporated into some models as "tolerable" levels that must be exceeded before significant impacts occur.[189]

---

189   IPCC, *Contribution of Working Group II to the Third Assessment Report of the Intergovernmental Panel on Climate Change, Climate Change 2001: Impacts, Adaptation, and Vulnerability*, James J. McCarthy, Osvaldo F. Canziani, Neil A. Leary, David J. Dokken Kasey S. White (eds.) (Cambridge: Cambridge University Press, 2001), pp. 92–93.

2 Examination of the Need for International and Humanitarian Protection

To assess the reality of the risk, it might be necessary again to distinguish between sudden-onset and slow-onset disasters.

- Sudden-onset disasters: receiving States can base their decision on available reports by international and national agencies, non-governmental organisation, scientific observatories, media report, etc. on the situation and inhabitability of the country or region of origin.
- Slow-onset disasters: the same sources can be used, read together with scientific projections. The assessment of the risk could rely on statistics, climate and environmental models, the nature of the environmental degradation, and other cumulative risk factors such as: conflicts, demographic pressure, health situation, functioning of institutions and infrastructures, etc.

It could be recommended that in view of the interest at stake (the life or person or the applicant) and of the fact that the prejudice caused would risk be irreparable[190] (as in cases where individuals' health deteriorates upon being returned to their country or if they die – cf refoulement death penalty), the benefit of the doubt or, in environmental terms, a precautionary principle should prevail. Instead, it appears that, in cases of doubt, the Court chooses to presume the absence of risk. In the medical cases cited, the ECtHR relied on the existence (rather than accessibility) of treatment or on the presence of relatives (rather than evidence of their ability or willingness to support) to "authorise" the removal of applicants to their country of origin. Similarly, in the *Di Sarno* case (otherwise noteworthy in that it reasserts a right to healthy and protected environment[191]), the Court deduced from the scientific controversy on the existence of a causal link between exposure to waste (garbage) and an increased risk of pathologies such as cancer or congenital malformation that it could not conclude that the applicants' life had been threatened in the case.[192]

Earlier, in the *Tătar* case, the Court first stated that in the absence of evidence of a causal link between the pollution invoked and a risk for health and in view of the fact that modern diseased are characterised by their plurality of causes, it could engage in "probabilistic reasoning". This would be possible, the Court added, in cases of "scientific uncertainty accompanied by sufficient and

---

190 HRC, "General Comment No. 31", *op. cit.*, §§ 3 and 12. ECtHR, *Soering*, § 90.
191 ECtHR, *Di Sarno*, § 110.
192 *Ibid.*, § 108.

convincing statistical elements".¹⁹³ The Court in the case however found that there were no such statistical elements – the increase in diseases following the pollution was not sufficient to establish a "causal probability". The Court found a violation of Article 8 ECHR because the State had failed to adopt the necessary measures to ensure the applicant's right to enjoy a healthy environment¹⁹⁴ however, the Court concluded, there was no causal link between the deterioration of the applicant's health and the breach of the Convention.¹⁹⁵ The amount of statistical information required by the Court appears to be high¹⁹⁶ and, again, when in doubt, it appears to conclude to the absence of causal link. Reference can also be made to the European Commission of Human Rights who, in the 1995 nuclear test case of *Tauira v. France*, relied in large part on the absence of scientific consensus on whether underground nuclear testing could harm the environment and the health of local populations, to reject the applicants' claim of their rights under Article 2, 3 and 8 ECHR and Article 1 Protocol 1.¹⁹⁷ The Court has consistently held that *non-refoulement* should apply when there is a real *risk* of ill-treatment; never did it require an absolute certainty. In that context and in view of the gravity of the risk at hand, a precautionary principle should be applied and protection against removal granted rather than not.

The precautionary principle is well-known of environmental law including European Union environmental law. Once a philosophical concept, it has evolved into a legal norm¹⁹⁸ of primary EU law: it is enshrined in Article 191 of the Treaty on the Functioning of the European Union.¹⁹⁹ The EU Court of Justice has applied it, mainly in health-related cases.²⁰⁰

---

193   ECtHR, *Tătar*, § 105.
194   Ibid., § 112.
195   Ibid., §§ 105–106.
196   N. Hervieu, "Droit à un environnement sain (Art. 8 CEDH) : Catastrophe écologique, obligations de protection de l'Etat et lien de causalité entre une maladie et la catastrophe" (CREDOF Université Paris Ouest Nanterre La Défense, retrieved from: <www.droits-libertes.org> [01/08/2011].
197   ECnHR, *Tauira v. France*.
198   ECtHR, *Tătar*, § 69 (h).
199   Consolidated version of the Treaty on the Functioning of the European Union ("TFEU") [2010] OJ C 83/47, Article 191.
200   The precautionary principle was for instance formulated as follows by the Court of Justice: "[lorsque] des incertitudes subsistent quant à l'existence où à la portée des risques pour la santé des personnes, les institutions peuvent prendre des mesures sans avoir à attendre que la réalité et la gravité ce ces risques soient pleinement démontrées". CJ, *National Farmer's Union*, C-157/96 (5 May 1998) Rec. I-2211; CJ, *Royaume Uni/Commission*, C-180/96 (5 May 1998) Rec. I-2265.

3 Form of Protection Granted

The principle of *non-refoulement* should in any case be respected.

It could be recommended that European Union institutions activate the Temporary Protection Directive in all instances of influx of persons displaced by environmental disasters.

The duration of the protection granted will be dependent on the assessment of the claim. In cases of irreversible degradation of the environment, and if no relocation within the applicant's country of origin is conceivable, long-term solutions should be sought, including granting permanent residence status or resettlement in a third country. When voluntary repatriation becomes possible again, UNHCR could provide assistance.[201]

C *Mitigate*

Two elements will be addressed. Firstly, in view of States restrictive asylum and immigration policies and among the different measures which can be envisaged as "mitigation" measures, focus will be had on planned relocation and migration (1) and humanitarian assistance (2). Secondly, financial support will be considered (3).

1 Planned Relocation and Migration

The Guidance on Planned Relocation highlights the relevance of planned relocation not only as an anticipatory measure but as also a reactive measure States may take in response to disaster and environmental change, in order to protect people from future harm.[202]

Migration can also contribute to rebuilding a country affected by a disaster. The situation of the Haitian diaspora is illustrative. World Bank statistics evaluate that financial transfers from the Haitian diaspora to Haiti represent about 35 per cent of the country's gross domestic product (GDP).

> C'est une évidence, l'aide financière de la diaspora est une planche de survie pour les familles haïtiennes. Cependant, aussi importante que cette contribution puisse paraître, elle n'a pas permis la création d'investissements productifs dans le pays. L'argent est souvent utilisé pour les dépenses immédiates : achat de nourriture, paiement de loyers ou de quelques mois de scolarité, cérémonies religieuses et funéraires, etc. Si pour l'heure, les

---

[201] UNHCR, *Handbook on Voluntary Repatriation: International Protection* (1996), op. cit., p. 42.
[202] Brookings, Georgetown University and UNHCR, *Guidance on Planned Relocation*, op. cit., p. 3 and § 9.

transferts financiers ne sont pas encore coordonnés au point de financer le développement d'Haïti, cela ne signifie pas que la diaspora, elle, ne s'organise pas pour s'approprier les droits humains et pour accomplir ses devoirs de citoyen.[203]

Migration can hence be a pragmatic solution for populations affected by a disaster but also benefit the affected country and, to some extent, destination countries too. The diaspora contributes to the betterment of the living conditions of their relatives who stayed in the affected country by providing them with financial means to sustain themselves. As alluded to in the article cited above, members of the diaspora can also get organised within existing or *ad hoc* non-governmental organisations, collectives or action groups[204] and raise awareness about the situation in their country of origin or gather support (legal, financial or material) within their host population. In Haiti, the importance, influence and value of the diaspora and of its contribution to the country's social and economic life are well-known and even institutionalised: the *Ministère des Haïtiens vivant à l'étranger* ("Minister for Haitians Living Abroad") provides information to Haitians abroad, contributes to their integration in their host society, and facilitates cooperation between different Haitians communities abroad, or between those communities and the local Haitian population. It seeks to foster the implication of the diaspora in the process of Haiti's sustainable development (described as "co-development") and to facilitate its political, economic and social reintegration in the country's affairs.[205]

A number of European States are also aware of the contribution diaspora can make to the development of their country of origin. The European Migration Network highlights measures taken in nine EU Member States supporting the involvement of diaspora groups in their country of origin. Those measures included participation in networks, dialogues and remittance projects, initiated

---

203   C. Drogue and A. Bertin, "Même après le séisme, la France terre d'écueils", *Nouvelles Images d'Haiti* (NIH) (Collectif Haïti de France) (January 2012).

204   See for example the various civil society initiatives launched at the local or national level in France by, *inter alia* the Collectif Haïti de France (CHF), the Groupe d'appui aux rapatriés et réfugiés (GARR) and the Groupe d'information et de soutien des immigrés (GISTI), the Comité inter mouvements auprès des évacués (CIMADE) or the Association nationale d'assistance aux frontières pour les étrangers (Anafé), to cite only a few. See A. Bertin, *et al.*, *Appui aux migrants haïtiens: sensibiliser, accompagner, plaider – Carnet de route d'une année d'expérience* (March 2012), *op. cit.*

205   Information retrieved from the website of the Ministère des Haïtiens vivant à l'étranger (MHAVE), <www.mhave.gouv.ht> [01/09/2012].

locally or at a regional or global level, by international organisation such as the IOM or the Global Forum for Migration and Development for example.[206] Luxembourg for example, who hosts a large Cap-Verdean community,[207] has developed a micro-finance project aimed at promoting savings mobilisation for investment purposes in Cape Verde and facilitating remittance transfers between Luxembourg and Cape Verde.[208]

2   Humanitarian Assistance

This model is not an alternative but a complement to the adoption of programs and policies aimed at preventing environmental degradations, adapting to the changing environment, and remedying the harmful consequences of degradations when they occur. The mechanism created to coordinate those programs and policies would rely on inter-institutional cooperation. Intergovernmental organisations would join their forces, capitalising on their resources – human and material, experiences and good practices in order to adequately and efficiently address the causes and consequences of environmental displacement.

United Nations agencies are well-equiped to provide humanitarian assistance in the event of environmental disaster and indeed have experience in that field. The position of UNHCR on the notion of so-called "environmental refugees" is well-known. On the basis of interviews she conducted with UN High Commissioner for Refugees diplomats in 2004, K.E. McNamara concludes that UNHCR views "environmental refugees" "as a non-legitimate category of movers/mobile

---

206   EMN, *EMN Synthesis Report – Annual Policy Report 2010*, September 2011), p. 84, retrieved from: <http://www.emn.europa.eu> [03/09/2012].

207   In Luxembourg, in a population of approximately 509,000 (CIA estimate of July 2012), 10,000 to 12,000 belong to the Cape Verdean community and among them, 4,000 to 5,000 hold a Cape Verdean passport. Central Intelligence Agency, *The World Factbook*, <https://www.cia.gov/library/publications/the-world-factbook/index.html> [03/09/2012]; J.-F. Colin, "M. Juncker est un grand ami du Cap-Vert", *Luxemburger Wort*, 25 April 2012, retrieved from: <http://www.wort.lu/fr/view/m-juncker-est-un-grand-ami-du-cap-vert-4f980bdce4bod08d36c040f9> [02/05/2012].

208   "EU Accountability Report on Financing for Development: Luxembourg's Replies to the Questionnaire for Preparing the 2012 Report" (© European Union, 1995–2012), retrieved from: <http://ec.europa.eu/europeaid/how/finance/documents/lu-eu-2012-monitoring-questionnaire-final-sanitized_en.pdf> [03/09/2012]. *See* also the study published by the *Agence de Transfert de Technologie Financière* in 2005, calling for the development of a microfinance project between Luxembourg and Cape Verde. J.-L. Guarniero, *Le transfert d'argent des migrants : le cas Luxembourg – Cap Vert* (Luxembourg: Agence de Transfert de Technologie Financière – ATTF, December 2005), retrieved from: <www.microfinance2005.lu> [03/09/2012].

populations", who exist outside its mandate and "hence [do] not automatically qualify for formal assistance and protection".[209] Nevertheless, UNHCR recognises the *de facto* needs for assistance of populations affected by disaster:

> ... all persons who are involuntary migrants as a result of natural or man-made causes may claim the institutional support of UNHCR by way of material assistance, aid in voluntary repatriation or resettlement, and in some cases legal protection.[210]

UNHCR is not the sole UN agency involved in providing assistance and support to environmentally-displaced persons. In 1986, the Group of Governmental Experts on International Co-operation to Avert New Flows of Refugees, in its report to the UN General Assembly, highlighted the necessity to improve international cooperation[211] in order to avert massive flows of environmentally-displaced persons. In this context, the Group of Governmental Experts noted that a number of States and international organisation already recognised "the significance of force majeure as a cause of refuge flows"[212] and had agreed to some form of cooperation:

> For instance, and agreement exists between the Office of the United Nations High Commissioner for Refugees (UNHCR) and the Office of the United Nations Disaster Relief Co-ordinator (UNDRO) making the latter responsible for relief measures for persons displaced by natural disasters. UNDRO also helps to avert such flows of refugees with its disaster-preparedness and disaster-prevention programmes. The Food and Agriculture Organization of the United Nations (FAO) and the World Food Programme (WFP) build-up of food reserves for the victims of drought must also be seen in this context.[213]

The multitude of organisations whose mandate is relevant to address environmental displacement appears clearly from the above. So does the correlate

---

209 Karen Elizabeth McNamara, "Conceptualizing discourses on environmental refugees at the United Nations", *Population and Environment*, Vol. 29 (2007), pp. 18–19.
210 J.C. Hathaway, *The Law of Refugee Status* (London: Butterworths, 1991), p. 27.
211 See also: UNHCR, "EC/SCP/64", *op. cit.*, §35.
212 UNGA, "International Co-Operation to Avert New Flows of Refugees: Note by the Secretary-General" ("International Co-operation to Avert New Flows of Refugees"), A/41/324, 13 May 1986, §41.
213 *Ibid.*

risk that inadequate cooperation and communication among them lead to confusion and, eventually, inefficiency. Concerned with the weak operational response to the Darfur humanitarian crisis in 2004,[214] Jen Egeland, United Nations Under-Secretary-General for Humanitarian Affairs and Emergency Relief Coordinator at the time, introduced the "cluster approach" in the United Nations machinery.

This approach is based on the assumption that better results can be achieved in response to humanitarian emergencies if the division of labour among the organisations involved is clear and their respective roles and responsibilities better defined.[215] Humanitarian assistance in response to crisis has many facets.[216] The cluster approach organises the provision of humanitarian assistance into nine key thematic sectors ("clusters"),[217] whose actions are coordinated by the UN Humanitarian Coordinator. For each cluster, one of the UN agencies involved in the response is designated as leader of the operations on the field. This cluster approach has already demonstrated its efficiency. With regards to environmental degradations of such magnitude that their aftermath calls for international humanitarian assistance, the coordinated work of UN agencies such as the International Organization for Migration, the UN High Commissioner for Refugees, the International Federation of Red Cross and Red Crescent Societies and the UN Development Program among others is essential.

Albeit efficient, it is still to be perfected:

> The response to the Haiti earthquake and Pakistan floods in 2010 exposed a number of weaknesses and inefficiencies in the international humanitarian response: gaps in humanitarian leadership and deployment

---

214   Jan Egeland, "Towards a Stronger Humanitarian Response System", *Forced Migration Review*, Supplement (October 2005), pp. 4–5.

215   For a schematic vision of the cluster approach, see: UN OCHA, "How are disaster relief efforts organised? Cluster Approach", accessible at: <http://business.un.org/en/assets/39c87a78-fec9-402e-a434-2c355f24e4f4.pdf> [last accessed on 18/09/2013].

216   *See also:* UN High Commissioner for Refugees, *Report of the Working Group on Solutions and Protection to the Forty-second Session of the Executive Committee of the High Commissioner's Programme*, 12 August 1991, EC/SCP/64, §35: "The Group recognized the need for increased mobilization of resources and greater coordination among agencies to respond systematically and promptly to victims of disasters world-wide".

217   The nine clusters are Nutrition, Health, Water and Sanitation, Emergency Shelter, Camp Coordination and Management, Protection, Early Recovery, Logistics, and Emergency Telecommunications. More information available at: <http://business.un.org/en/documents/249> [accessed on 18/12/2011].

of senior managers, in coordination structures, and in the practices of assessment, planning, monitoring and accountability.[218]

It is worth noting that the creation of this cluster approach was inspired by the reported lack of cooperation between UN agencies working on the field in situations of humanitarian crisis. The very fact that those agencies were simultaneously intervening, albeit in a disorderly manner, reveals the interconnectedness of their respected tasks. In times of crisis situations such as armed conflicts but also, the two being closely linked, (severe) environmental degradation, populations and countries need broadly-defined assistance. This gives credit to the hypothesis that environmental disruptions and their impacts on human displacement should be addressed in an interdisciplinary manner, even when they are of slow-onset. The crisis situation addressed by humanitarian assistance under the cluster approach abruptly and acutely brings to light the various facets of the work which need to be conducted to prevent, adapt to and respond to environmental degradation and, therefore, environmentally-induced displacement.

3   Financial Support

As mentioned at the outset, the framework would partly rely on the notion of common but differentiated responsibility. What is meant is that States should all contribute to addressing the issue of environmental displacement but according to their specific assets, circumstances and capacities.

Two prior observations that will be developed below can be made. Firstly, environmental degradations caused or aggravated by climate change will not hit the world uniformly: some countries and regions are more prone do disasters than some others. Secondly, the intensity of the impacts of climate change will vary greatly from one country to another depending on each country's level of development.

A mapping of the regions of the world at higher risk of environmental degradation shows that climate change will affect the developing world more that developed countries (although the developed world will not be spared[219]).

---

218   UN OCHA, *Overview of the Consolidated Appeals and Similar Concerted Humanitarian Action Plans at Mid-Year 2012* (Geneva, New York: OCHA, 23 July 2012), p. 8.

219   M.L. Parry, O.F. Canziani, J.P. Palutikof et al., "2007: Technical Summary" *in* M.L. Parry, O.F. Canziani, J.P. Palutikof, et al. (eds.), *Climate Change 2007: Impacts, Adaptation and Vulnerability. Contribution of Working Group II to the Fourth Assessment Report of the Intergovernmental Panel on Climate Change* (Cambridge: Cambridge University Press, 2007), at TS.4.5; and IPCC, "2007: Summary for Policymakers" *in* M.L. Parry, O.F. Canziani, J.P.

The Fourth Assessment Report of the Intergovernmental Panel on Climate Change mentions in particular Africa, at large, Asian and African megadeltas as regions likely to be especially affected by climate change (the list also includes small low-lying islands and the Arctic).[220] This will create a vicious circle: developing countries, precisely because of their low level of development, have limited capacities and means to prevent and mitigate environmental degradations, and to rebuild in their aftermath. The impacts of climate change (in terms of human casualties and damage to infrastructures) on those countries which are often overpopulated will therefore be all the more dramatic, most likely long-lasting, and require their governments to allocate significant parts of the State's economy to the reconstruction of the affected region or entire territory, which will further hinder those countries' development.

Environmental displacement is perceived by most States (and societies) as a threat.[221] They fear that recognising environmentally displaced persons as "refugees" in the broad sense of the term, as persons in need of international protection, would carry with it the obligation for States to open their borders and asylum systems to excessively large number of persons,[222] at the expense of their respective national economy, social system and, potentially, national security. Addressing the alleged financial burden of environmental displacement for host States could therefore alleviate States' reluctance to addressing the genuine protection needs of environmental migrants. In regions particularly

---

Palutikof et al. (eds.), *Climate Change 2007: Impacts, Adaptation and Vulnerability. Contribution of Working Group II to the Fourth Assessment Report of the Intergovernmental Panel on Climate Change* (Cambridge: Cambridge University Press, 2007), pp. 13–15.

[220] IPCC: Core Writing Team, R.K. Pachauri and A. Reisinger (eds.), *Climate Change 2007: Synthesis Report. Contribution of Working Groups I, II and III to the Fourth Assessment Report of the Intergovernmental Panel on Climate Change* (Geneva: IPCC, 2007), p. 72.

[221] Karen Elizabeth McNamara, "Conceptualizing discourses on environmental refugees at the United Nations", *Popul Environ*, Vol. 29 (2007), pp. 20–21.

[222] Judge Priestley actually referred to this argument in the New Zealand High Court decision in the case concerning M. Teitiota, a citizen of Kiribati who had claimed an entitlement to be recognised as a refugee or a "protected person" (*i.e.* a form of protection derived from the ICCPR under New Zealand law) on the basis of environmental degradation associated with climate change affecting Kiribati. Judge Priestley noted that, were the applicant's arguments to succeed "(...) *at a stroke, millions of people who are facing medium-term economic deprivation, or the immediate consequences of natural disasters or warfare, or indeed presumptive hardships caused by climate change, would be entitled to protection under the Refugee Convention or under the ICCPR*". New Zealand: Hight Court, *Teitiota v the Chief Executive of the Ministry of Business Innovation and Employment* ("*Teitiota*"), [2013] NZHC 3125, 26 November 2013, § 51.

affected – or at risk of being particularly affected – by climate extremes, potential host States could receive financial aid earmarked for supporting their asylum system and capacities. To ensure that the aid be adequately distributed among receiving countries, in proportion of their needs, each of them would be asked to put an approximate figure on the cost – direct as well as in services and infrastructure – of hosting a refugee on its territory and granting him or her a protective status. On the basis of this estimate cost, host countries' budget for asylum can be anticipated. In the event of flows of environmentally displaced persons crossing or foreseen to cross the international border of their State to seek protection in another State, the receiving State could call for financial aid from the international community (*e.g.*: EU Refugee Fund, Budget Support[223] or within UN framework).

Thresholds could be defined per country, based on its national capacities, beyond which financial support could be claimed. When the number of persons displaced by the severe worsening of the environment in their home and, typically neighbouring, country who cross the State border reaches the relevant threshold, financial aid could be allocated to the host country, in proportion of the number of persons incoming and the aforementioned estimate cost. This aid would be repeated, in tranches, if needs be. The budget thus allocated would be earmarking for pre-identified asylum-related expenses: this would ensure donor States that the aid they contribute to providing would not be misused.

Such scheme could be used at different levels and scales:

- By a single country, on a bilateral basis. This is conceivable in the case of existing cultural links between the donor country and the receiving country. Former colonial powers could come to the rescue of their former colonies. Countries with religious ties could likewise support each other.
- By a member state of a regional organisation, to a country affected outside the region. For example, EU Member States could, through the European Refugee Fund (or Budget Support for instance) contribute to development projects in Bangladesh or to the asylum expenses of India when receiving environmental migrants from Bangladesh.

---

[223] European Commission, EuropeAid Cooperation Office, *Budget Support: the Effective Way to Finance Development?*, brochure published in 2008 and available at: <http://ec.europa.eu/europeaid/infopoint/publications/europeaid/documents/budgetsupport08_en.pdf> [accessed 01/05/2012].

The European Union is in fact already involved in a number of climate change related projects. For example, it contributes 85% of the budget of the African, Caribbean and Pacific Observatory on Migration. The Observatory is a consortium of African, Caribbean, Pacific as well as European research institutions, implemented by the International Organization for Migration (IOM) and designed to produce data on South-South migration. The Observatory does not itself run capacity-building projects but "fosters the inclusion of migration into pilot countries' development strategies". Among other research angles, it studies patterns of migration linked to the effects of climate change.[224]

- By the international community, through the UNFCCC for instance: the Bangladeshi NGO EquityBD presented a petition in that sense by during the 16th Conference of the Parties (COP16) to the United Nations Framework Convention on Climate Change (UNFCCC) held in Cancun late 2010.[225]

The feasibility of such fund would however require expertise in this area and above were principally suggestions.

---

224 African, Caribbean and Pacific Observatory on Migration, *Leaflet*, available at: <www.acpmigration.org> [accessed 01/05/2012].

225 Equity and Justice Working Group Bangladesh (EquityBD), *Climate Change Induced Forced Migrants: in need of dignified recognition under a new Protocol*, December 2009, accessible at <http://www.mediaterre.org/docactu,QoRJLUwtMy9kb2NzL2NsaW1hdGUtbWlncmFudC1wcmludGVkLXBvc2loaW9uLWRlYyowOQ==,1.pdf> [accessed 08/10/2016]. Jane McAdam notes that EquityBd no longer uses the 'refugee' terminology but instead calls for the recognition of the persons concerned as "Universal Natural Persons". See J. McAdam, "Refusing 'refuge' in the Pacific: (de)constructing climate-induced displacement in international law", in E. Piguet, A. Pécoud and P. de Guchteneire (Eds.), *Migration and Climate Change* (Cambridge and Paris: Cambridge University Press and UNESCO jointly, 2011), p. 103, fn. 8.

CHAPTER 13

Conclusion of Part 3

The various alternatives existing for the protection of environmentally-displaced persons on the basis of one or another area of existing law all appear to fail to comprehensively address the issue, its multiple causes, forms and consequences. Devising a *sui generis* framework therefore manifests itself as a preferable alternative. If there are valid reasons for States to enter such agreement, it seems however that States' still timid commitments to reduce their contributions to climate change and recognise their responsibility in this respect, together with States' increasingly restrictive approach to migration and asylum do not bode well for a protection of environmentally-displaced persons in the short term.

Some possibilities exist, which could be implemented before a global consensus is reached. The absolute nature of the principle of *non-refoulement* should first be reasserted and respected at all times. A proposal to amend the EU Qualification Directive to apply subsidiary protection to serious harm consisting of threat to life or person originating in dire humanitarian conditions appears to be a possible solution: it would ensure the conformity of EU law with human rights law jurisprudence, it would also ensure the principle of non-discrimination is respected and, lastly and mainly, would give European Union asylum law the human rights dimension the Court of Justice has endeavoured to develop over the years.

General Conclusion

> We cannot continue ignore environmental refugees simply because there is no established mode of dealing with the problem they represent[1]

A new framework is called into existence to empower the international community as a whole, regions, individual States and populations to rise to the challenge of environmental displacement. Legal, moral and ethical considerations command that a broad-encompassing definition of environmental degradation be adopted so that the needs of all environmentally-displaced persons without discrimination are addressed. On account of the reality and inexorability of climate change and of its harmful impacts on the environment worldwide, an environmental displacement framework should hurriedly be called into existence. Environmental displacement and the impacts of global warming alike are already observed around the world; both require a general response, not only reactive in nature but also proactive. For the proactive measures to be effective, it is necessary to adopt and implement them as early as possible so that capacity-building including through awareness-raising, prevention, resilience and adaptation does not remain a dead letter.

Objectively, the adoption of a *sui generis* framework is ambitious, but in view of the reality and universality of the issue of environmental displacement, it is a necessity, if not a legal obligation for States.[2]

Two main and general recommendations can be made: States must develop, at the regional and international levels as appropriate, in due consultation with all stakeholders, a new *ad hoc* framework intended to effectively address environmental displacement, its root causes and consequences and the protection needs of affected persons. In the meantime, States should liberally apply existing norms of international refugee law and international human rights law to ensure that no one is returned to a territory where his or her life or freedom would be threatened as a consequence of the degradation of the local environment. The unprecedented media coverage that the growing body

---

1 Norman Myers and Jennifer Kent, *Environmental Exodus: An Emergent Crisis in the Global Arena* (Washington DC: Climate Institute, June 1995), p. 154.
2 Under the UN Charter, States have an obligation to take joint and separate action in cooperation with the United Nations to support the achievement of higher standards of living, full employment, and conditions of economic and social progress and development, as well as solutions of international economic, social, health, and related problems. Charter of the United Nations, 24 October 1945, UNTS Vol. 1 p. XVI, Articles 55–56.

of case-law issued in Australian and New Zealand courts concerning Pacific island asylum applicants further illustrate the topicality of the issue as well as the role litigation and courts could play in securing the broadest possible application of existing norms.

A *sui generis* framework for the protection of environmentally-displaced persons may be amibitious but utopic, it is not. A consideration of States' own best interests comes into play and leads to suggest the ambition is realistic. In a nutshell, a State typically perceives its best interest lies in maintaining contained international flows of migrants on its territory. The contemporary discourse on the impacts of environmental disasters (including in particular climate change related disasters) and environmental displacement often lingers on the risk that both will exacerbate tensions and possibly foster conflicts both within and between countries. The securitisation of climate and environmental issues, for accurate it may be, risks however diverting national and international authorities' focus from what it ought to be: the protection of the lives and rights of individuals. Incidentally, such discourse could have a constructive counterpart: it could possibly motivate States to adopt measures to mitigate, anticipate, and adapt to environmental change, in a spirit of international cooperation and respect for individuals, which, by alleviating environmental and climate change pressure on countries and populations could limit migration and hence reduce alleged national and international security risks. Looking at developed States specifically, the incentive may appear all the more clearly. Pragmatically or cynically perhaps, by addressing the root causes of displacement and promoting the elaboration of migration schemes at the regional level (that is, within the developing world mainly), developed States could ensure that the problem of environmental displacement remains but a distant one. These two considerations point to the feasibility of a truly universal instrument, where the interests of all States (developing and developed, countries of origin and of destination) could meet.

In any case, it should be highlighted that environment and climate change are primarily a threat to people and communities: they are "human security issues", not international security concerns.[3] Additionally, States and societies cannot be oblivious of the fact that migration is part of human history and has always shaped societies. As observed by J.R. Smith, archaeology demonstrates this reality:

---

3 L. Elliott, "Climate Migration and Climate Migrants: What Threat, Whose Security?" *in* J. McAdam (Ed.), *Climate Change and Displacement: Multidisciplinary Perspectives* (Oxford, Portland OR: Hart Publishing, 2010), pp. 176–190.

> One thing that certainly comes out of any examination of the archeological records and the recent past in terms of adaptation to climate change is just how critically important migration is and always has been as an adaptive response. And that's something which clearly raises challenges for today because the opportunities for migration are somewhat more limited now than they would have been 125000 years ago.[4]

Migration has long been a coping mechanism; it still is and there is every reason to believe that it will remain an essential response to disasters. Reports by international organisations inform that people seek entry into another country every day, sometimes to the point of risking their lives. Devising a framework capable of organising and managing migration therefore appears as a more realistic approach than obstinate – and hopeless – endeavours to impede migration. A 2013 communication from the European Commission, auspiciously titled "Maximising the Development Impact of Migration", in fact appears as a positive first step taken by the European Union on that path. The Commission called on the EU, within its policies and programmes, to:

> Further exploring and addressing the links between climate change, environmental degradation and migration, including the importance of climate change adaptation and Disaster Risk Reduction (DRR) in reducing displacement, and the role of migration as a strategy to strengthening adaptation and DRR.[5]

A number of developments, mentioned in this work, are auspicious evidence of the growing awareness of the challenges posed by the impacts of disasters and climate change on environments and populations and of the necessity to address them. Progress was achieved in that regard in diverse fora, such as the United Nations Framework on Climate Change (in particular through the adoption of the 2015 Paris Agreement and the express reference made therein to displacement related to climate change) and the Sendai Framework for Disaster Risk Reduction, and patent in the frequency of related discussions

---

4 J.R. Smith (2011).
5 European Commission, "Communication from the Commission to the European Parliament, the Council, the European Economic and Social Committee and the Committee of the Regions, 'Maximising the Development Impact of Migration: The EU Contribution for the UN High-Level Dialogue and Next Steps Towards Broadening the Development-Migration Nexus'", COM(2013) 292 final, 21 May 2013, p. 12.

and events taking place at the international level.[6] The large support received by the Nansen Initiative and broad endorsement of its Protection Agenda confirm that a large number of States acknowledge the necessity to take action.

Perhaps the challenge of environmental displacement raises in fact an even greater challenge: that of reconsidering the premise of international law and building a new legal order founded not on national sovereignty but of which human beings, all equal in Law, would be the core. Along those lines, reviving a notion of global citizenship could be called for. If this would remain but a philosophical concept, it should perhaps inspire governments in cooperating to devise a new framework for the protection of environmentally-displaced persons.

---

6   Human rights, climate change and displacement are recurrent items on the agendas of UNHCR High Commissioner Dialogues and of the Human Rights Council.

Annex

Annex 1: International Protection Recognition Rates Per Status by Country of Origin and Country of Asylum in Selected European Countries

TABLE 1   *International protection recognition rates by country of origin (Afghanistan, Iraq and Somalia) and of asylum (main EU receiving countries, Norway and Switzerland) in 2010*

Country of origin	Country of asylum		Refugee status % (number)	Complementary protection status % (number)	Total number of decisions taken
Afghanistan	Austria	FA	25 (584)	28 (669)	2380
Afghanistan	Belgium	FI	35 (387)	26 (292)	1106
Afghanistan	Belgium	RA	–	–	–
Afghanistan	Denmark	FI	2 (16)	39 (397)	1010
Afghanistan	Finland	FI	6 (28)	36 (168)	462
Afghanistan	France	FI	31 (142)	3 (14)	453
Afghanistan	Germany	NA	11 (525)	33 (1597)	4847
Afghanistan	Germany	RA	26 (42)	19 (31)	160
Afghanistan	Greece	FI	3 (9)	2 (7)	330
Afghanistan	Greece	AR	*	–	*
Afghanistan	Hungary	FI	1 (10)	13 (108)	846
Afghanistan	Italy	FI	24 (176)	66 (480)	724
Afghanistan	Netherlands	FI	3 (49)	32 (617)	1907
Afghanistan	Netherlands	RA	–	–	–
Afghanistan	Norway	FI	9 (247)	27 (785)	2867
Afghanistan	Norway	AR	4 (54)	1 (15)	1504
Afghanistan	Romania	FA	11 (13)	19 (22)	114
Afghanistan	Sweden	FI	11 (162)	59 (884)	1510
Afghanistan	Sweden	JR	6 (36)	12 (71)	596
Afghanistan	Switzerland	FI	5 (40)	48 (385)	799
Afghanistan	UK	FI	8 (215)	22 (615)	2840
Afghanistan	UK	RA	–	–	20
Iraq	Austria	FA	21 (81)	39 (154)	391
Iraq	Belgium	FI	31 (303)	43 (424)	981

TABLE 1   *International protection recognition rates* (cont.)

Country of origin	Country of asylum	Refugee status % (number)		Complementary protection status % (number)	Total number of decisions taken
Iraq	Belgium	RA	–	–	–
Iraq	Bulgaria	FI	–	37 (86)	233
Iraq	Cyprus	FI	–	36 (63)	175
Iraq	Cyprus	AR	–	–	62
Iraq	Denmark	FI	6 (6)	17 (16)	93
Iraq	Finland	FI	6 (71)	44 (536)	1209
Iraq	France	FI	73 (244)	1 (5)	336
Iraq	Germany	NA	52 (3151)	1 (90)	6035
Iraq	Germany	RA	29 (154)	7 (39)	529
Iraq	Greece	FI	5 (12)	*	227
Iraq	Greece	AR	–	–	–
Iraq	Italy	FI	32 (105)	47 (154)	328
Iraq	Netherlands	FI	6 (132)	48 (1091)	2253
Iraq	Netherlands	RA	–	–	–
Iraq	Norway	AR	3 (28)	2 (17)	1098
Iraq	Norway	FI	10 (137)	17 (245)	1417
Iraq	Sweden	FI	31 (569)	18 (324)	1846
Iraq	Sweden	JR	1 (60)	4 (147)	4048
Iraq	Switzerland	FI	13 (148)	27 (305)	1112
Iraq	Switzerland	RA	–	–	–
Iraq	UK	FI	8 (80)	9 (90)	990
Iraq	UK	RA	–	–	20
Somalia	Austria	FA	52 (189)	23 (84)	365
Somalia	Belgium	FI	24 (44)	23 (42)	180
Somalia	Denmark	FI	*	29 (20)	70
Somalia	Finland	FI	1 (6)	62 (647)	1047
Somalia	France	FI	38 (103)	32 (86)	273
Somalia	Germany	NA	41 (372)	9 (80)	897
Somalia	Greece	FI	*	*	38
Somalia	Netherlands	FI	2 (97)	64 (3391)	5329
Somalia	Netherlands	RA	–	–	–
Somalia	Norway	FI	35 (705)	27 (541)	2002
Somalia	Norway	AR	*	1 (5)	895
Somalia	Sweden	FI	9 (464)	77 (4141)	5357

ANNEX

Country of origin	Country of asylum	Refugee status % (number)		Complementary protection status % (number)	Total number of decisions taken
Somalia	Sweden	JR	*	33 (377)	1137
Somalia	Switzerland	FI	9 (148)	73 (1141)	1572
Somalia	UK	FI	40 (435)	9 (95)	1090

Source: The numbers of decisions (refugee status, complementary protection and total) reproduced in the table are those published by UNHCR in its 2010 Statistical Yearbook.[1] The proportions indicated are calculated on the basis of the total number of decisions taken during the year of 2010. Those decisions encompass: decisions to grant an international protection status, rejections and decisions to otherwise close a case. Afghanistan, Iraq and Somalia were the three main countries of origin af asylum applicants in Europe in 2010.

FI: First Instance decisions
AR: Administrative Review decisions
RA: Repeat/reopened applications
NA: New Applications
*:   values between 1 and 4
–:   the value is zero or not available

---

[1] T.A. Chabaké (Ed.), *UNHCR Statistical Yearbook 2010: Trends in Displacement, Protection and Solutions* (2011), *op. cit.*, Annex, Table 12.

TABLE 2 *International protection recognition rates by country of origin (Afghanistan, Eritrea and Syria) and country of asylum (main EU receiving countries) in 2014*

Country of origin	Country of asylum		Refugee status % (number)	Complementary protection status % (number)	Total number of decisions taken
Afghanistan	Austria	FA	56 (883)	42 (651)	1564
Afghanistan	Germany	NA	27 (1830)	19 (1307)	6876
Afghanistan	Germany	RA	48 (196)	17 (70)	411
Afghanistan	Greece	FI	6 (219)	8 (288)	3470
Afghanistan	Greece	AR	9 (145)	11 (175)	1670
Afghanistan	Hungary	FI	>0 (17)	1 (58)	6875
Afghanistan	Hungary	RA	–	–	–
Afghanistan	Italy	FI	10 (255)	85 (2143)	2520
Afghanistan	Sweden	FI	25 (621)	35 (877)	2503
Afghanistan	Sweden	AR	8 (86)	12 (135)	1094
Afghanistan	Sweden	RA	9 (7)	51 (39)	77
Eritrea	Denmark	FI	88 (193)	8 (17)	219
Eritrea	Germany	NA	42 (738)	13 (230)	1757
Eritrea	Netherlands	FI	1 (33)	90 (3455)	3845
Eritrea	Sweden	FI	78 (5131)	2 (125)	6579
Eritrea	Sweden	RA	*	–	9
Eritrea	Sweden	AR	3 (6)	*	219
Eritrea	United Kingdom	FI	86 (2185)	1 (12)	2542
Eritrea	United Kingdom	AR	44 (50)	–	114
Syria	Austria	FA	91 (3334)	9 (319)	3657
Syria	Denmark	FI	76 (3122)	21 (864)	4123
Syria	Denmark	AR	13 (7)	17 (9)	54
Syria	Germany	NA	78 (19560)	12 (2998)	25027
Syria	Germany	RA	57 (947)	21 (354)	1676
Syria	Netherlands	FI	6 (349)	86 (5090)	5952
Syria	Sweden	FI	10 (1759)	80 (14627)	18204

ANNEX

Country of origin	Country of asylum	Refugee status % (number)	Complementary protection status % (number)	Total number of decisions taken
Syria	Sweden	AR *	1 (6)	842
Syria	Sweden	RA *	55 (12)	22

Source: The numbers of decisions (refugee status, complementary protection and total) reproduced in the table are those published by UNHCR in its 2014 Statistical Yearbook.[2] The proportions indicated are calculated on the basis of the total number of decisions taken during the year of 2010. Those decisions encompass: decisions to grant an international protection status, rejections and decisions to otherwise close a case. Afghanistan, Eritrea and Syria were the three main countries of origin of asylum applicants in Europe in 2014.

FI: First Instance decisions
AR: Administrative Review decisions
RA: Repeat/reopened applications
NA: New Applications
*: values between 1 and 4
–: the value is zero or not available

---

2   T.A. Chabaké and J. Tenkorang (Eds.), *UNHCR Statistical Yearbook 2014* (2014), *op. cit.*, Table 12.

Annex 2: The Impacts of Climate Change and the Human Rights Affected

Climate Impact	Human Impact	Rights Implicated
Sea Level Rise • Flooding • Sea Surges • Erosion • Salination of land and water	• Loss of land • Drowning, injury • Lack of clean water, disease • Damage to coastal infrastructure, homes, and property • Loss of agricultural lands • Threat to tourism, lost beaches	• Self-determination [ICCPR;ICESCR,1] • Life [ICCPR, 6] • Health [ICESCR, 12] • Water [CEDAW,14; ICRC 24] • Means of subsistence [ICESCR,1] • Standard of living [ICESCR, 12] • Adequate housing [ICESCR,12] • Culture [ICCPR, 27] • Property [UDHR,17]
Temperature Increase • Change in disease vectors • Coral bleaching • Impact on Fisheries	• Spread of disease • Changes in traditional fishing livelihood and commercial fishing • Threat to tourism, lost coral and fish diversity	• Life [ICCPR, 6] • Health [ICESCR, 12] • Means of subsistence [ICESCR, 1] • Adequate standard of living [ICESCR, 12]
Extreme Weather Events • Higher intensity storms • Sea Surges	• Dislocation of populations • Contamination of water supply • Damage to infrastructure: delays in medical treatment, food crisis • Psychological distress • Increased transmission of disease • Damage to agricultural lands • Disruption of educational services • Damage to tourism sector • Massive property damage	• Life [ICCPR,6] • Health [ICESCR,12] • Water [CEDAW,14; ICRC 24] • Means of subsistence [ICESCR,1] • Adequate standard of living [ICESCR, 12] • Adequate and secure housing [ICESCR,12] • Education [ICESCR,13] • Property [UDHR,17]
Changes in Precipitation • Change in disease vectors • Erosion	• Outbreak of disease • Depletion of agricultural soils	• Life [ICCPR,6] • Health [ICESCR,12] • Means of subsistence [ICESCR,1]

SOURCE: M. LIMON.[3]

---

[3] M. Limon, "Human Rights and Climate Change: Constructing a Case for Political Action", *Harvard Environmental Law Review*, Vol. 33 (2009), pp. 439–476, Annex. Please note that the copyright in the Environmental Law Review is held by the President and Fellows of Harvard College, and that the copyright in the article is held by the author.

Annex 3: A Typology of Natural Hazard-related Disasters

■ Highlighted hazards are those included in the IDMC Disaster Induced Displacement Dataset (DiDD) underlying this study

	Weather-related disasters		
	Meteorological	**Hydrological**	**Climatological**
Sudden onset	Tropical storms, winter storms, tornados, snow and sand storms	Floods (flash, coastal/storm) surges, riverine), wet mass movements (landslides, avalanches, sudden subsidence)	Extreme winter conditions, heat waves, wild fires
Slow onset		Long-lasting subsidence	Drought
	Geophysical and biological disasters		
	Geophysical	**Biological**	
Sudden onset	Earthquakes, volcanic eruptions, dry mass movements (rockfalls, snow and debris avalanches, landslides, sudden subsidence)	Epidemics, insect infestations, animal stampedes	
Slow onset	Long-lasting subsidence	Epidemics, insect infestations	

SOURCE: IDMC, GLOBAL ESTIMATES 2011.[4]

---

4 M. Yonetani and IDMC, *Global Estimates 2011: People Displaced by Natural Hazard-Induced Disasters* (June 2012), *op. cit.*, p. 8, Table 1. The report clarifies in a footnote that this typology was adapted from the general classification of natural hazard events developed by CRED in agreement with the reinsurance company Munich Re. Below R., Wirtz A., Guha-Sapir D., *Disaster Category Classification and Peril Terminology For Operational Purposes*, 2009.

Annex 4: Latest Fifteen Disaster Reports Published by ReliefWeb, on 15 October 2016[5]

ReliefWeb website was launched by the United Nations Office for the Coordination of Humanitarian Affairs (OCHA) and provides, *inter alia*, a continuously updated list of natural hazard-related disasters.[6] For the first nine months of 2016 (from January to September 2016[7]), ReliefWeb reported fify-seven disasters worldwide, mainly in Africa, the Middle East and Southeast Asia. The latest fifteen reports relayed by ReliefWeb are reproduced below for information:

Typhoon Sarika – Oct 2016
Affected countries: China, Philippines, Viet Nam
A weather disturbance which formed earlier this week, in the sea, east of Philippines has intensified to Typhoon Sarika (local name Karen). The national meteorological agency estimates that Sarika will make landfall in the Aurora Quezon area as an equivalent of Category 2 cyclone early Sunday, 16 October. (IFRC, 15 Oct 2016).

Yemen: Cholera Outbreak – Oct 2016
Affected countries: Yemen
Health authorities in Yemen confirmed a cholera outbreak on 6 October 2016, posing an increased health risk to the population especially children. The Ministry of Public Health and Population (MoPHP) announced that a total of 11 out of 25 suspected diarrhea cases have been confirmed as Cholera cases in the capital, Sana'a. As per the Inter-Agency joint response plan, UNICEF additional fund requirements for the cholera outbreak response stands at US$3.2 million. (UNICEF, 11 Oct 2016).

---

5   Apart from some minor formatting, this is the exact copy of the information retrieved from ReliefWeb on 15 October 2016. Reliefweb, "Disasters" (© ReliefWeb, 2016), retrieved from: <http://reliefweb.int/disasters> [15/10/2016].
6   Disasters included in ReliefWeb's list are those defined by the Internal Displacement Monitoring Body as "natural hazard-related disasters". It includes weather-related disasters (meteorological, hydrological and climatological) as well as geophysical and biological disasters, of both sudden-onset and slow-onset. M. Yonetani and IDMC, *Global Estimates 2011: People Displaced by Natural Hazard-Induced Disasters* (June 2012), *op. cit.*, p. 8. IDMC Typology was reproduced above in the previous annex, *see* Annex 3, p. 542.
7   As of 17 September 2012, when the ReliefWeb webpage was last accessed.

Hurricane Matthew – Sep 2016
Affected countries: Aruba (The Netherlands), Bahamas, Barbados, Belize, Bonaire, Saint Eustatius and Saba (The Netherlands), Colombia, Cuba, Curaçao (The Netherlands), Dominican Republic, Haiti, Jamaica, Puerto Rico (The United States of America), Saint Lucia, Saint Vincent and the Grenadines, United States of America, Venezuela (Bolivarian Republic of).
As of 1100 EST on 3 October, Category 4 Hurricane Matthew was some 330 km south-east from Kingston (Jamaica) and 440 km south-west from Port-au-Prince (Haiti) in the Caribbean Sea, moving north-west at 9 km/h, with maximum sustained winds of 220 km/h, according to the National Hurricane Center (NOAA). Hurricane-force winds extend outwards up to 55 km from the centre and tropical-storm-force winds extend outwards up to 295 km. (OCHA, 3 Oct 2016).

Niger: Rift Valley Fever Outbreak – Sep 2016
Affected countries: Niger
The Ministry of Health, which officially declared the outbreak on 20 September, says 23 people have died from the virus and 60 people have been infected. Nearly all of those infected are pastoralists. There are also reports of significant livestock deaths from the virus, particularly cattle, sheep and camels. (IFRC, 23 Sep 2016).

Benin: Cholera Outbreak – Sep 2016
Affected countries: Benin
An initial three cholera cases were reported in So-Ava and an outbreak was declared on 16 August by local government authorities. Reported and verified cases were few in the early weeks and considered manageable by local authorities, but a sharp and heightened spike in the number of confirmed cases between 25–30 August in the three main areas of Cotonou, Savalou and So-Ava resulted in a request from Benin Red Cross Society to IFRC for support through DREF to respond. As of 4 September 2016, a total of 281 cases and 9 deaths were recorded with a 3.20% case fatality rate, with Cotonou the most affected area to date. (IFRC, 12 Sept 2016).

Tanzania: Earthquake – Sept 2016
Affected countries: Uganda, United Republic of Tanzania
At least 13 people were killed and 203 injured in northwest Tanzania when a 5.7 magnitude earthquake hit the country Saturday, local authorities told AFP. "The toll has climbed from 11 people dead to 13 and from

192 injured to 203," said Deodatus Kinawilo, District Commissioner for Bukoba, the town close to the epicentre of the quake. (AFP, 10 Sep 2016).

Senegal: Floods – Sep 2016
Affected countries: Senegal
On the nights of September 4 and 5, 2016, a heavy rain accompanied by strong winds caused significant material and human damage with a large number of affected people. In the area of St. Louis, it was estimated that there were about 1,313 affected families; especially in the department of Dagana that recorded 5 deaths and 106 injured, and destroyed houses, fields, schools, sleeping materials, household goods (chair, clothing, etc.) and walls. In addition, food stock reserves, poultry and livestock were lost in 4 towns and in the 40 villages mentioned below. (IFRC, 21 Sep 2016).

DPR Korea: Floods – Aug 2016
Affected countries: Democratic People's Republic of Korea
From 29 August to 31 August 2016, heavy rains fell in North Hamgyong Province, Democratic People's Republic of Korea (DPRK). More than 300mm of rain were reported in just two days, causing flooding of the Tumen River and its branches in this region around the Chinese-DPRK border. (IFRC, 3 Sep 2016).

Nigeria: Polio Outbreak – Aug 2016
Affected countries: Cameroon, Central African Republic, Chad, Niger, Nigeria
Following the recent detection of wild poliovirus in Nigeria, Ministers of Health from Cameroon, Central African Republic, Chad, Niger and Nigeria have declared the polio outbreak in Nigeria as a public health emergency for countries of the Lake Chad basin. The declaration, coming out of the 66th session of the World Health Organization Regional Committee for the African Region, demonstrates commitment from governments across the region to bolster momentum in the fight against the virus. (Global Polio Eradication Initiative, 29 Aug 2016).

Peru: Earthquake – Aug 2016
Affected countries: Peru
On 14 August, a 5.4 earthquake shook department of Arequipa, killing four people. Some 1,564 families are affected, 1,074 houses are inhabitable and 383 houses have collapsed. National and regional authorities are assisting affected people. The Government declared a 60-day state

of emergency for seven districts in the province Arequipean province of Caylloma. (OCHA, 15 Aug 2016).

Lao PDR: Floods – Aug 2016
Affected countries: Lao People's Democratic Republic (the)
Torrential rain from 11 to 12 August has triggered flood and flash flood in the northern provinces of Lao PDR. As reported by the Social Welfare Department (SWD), Ministry of Labour and Social Welfare, the flood has submerged several villages in Xayabuly, Oudomxay and Luangprabang Provinces (ASEAN, 18 Aug 2016).

Central African Republic: Cholera Outbreak – Aug 2016
Affected countries: Central African Republic
The CAR Government declared a cholera epidemic in the country on 10 August after samples had tested positive for the disease. At least 66 cases have been identified and 16 people have died. The disease was detected in Mourou-Fleuve village, Djoukou sub-province in the central region on 27 July. In response to this emergency, the humanitarian community has activated a crisis committee and is actively supporting the Government's efforts.

Philippines: Floods and Landslides – Aug 2016
Affected countries: Philippines
Heavy rains and flooding caused by the southwest monsoon combined with a low-pressure weather front, forced over 260,000 people to flee their homes in the Philippines last weekend August 13–14. The intense monsoon rains affected six regions of the country, mostly in Luzon, triggering flooding as landslides in some parts of Rizal province and Northern Luzon…Days after the torrential rains, close to 18,000 people remain housed in 77 designated evacuation centres across the country. On August 17, Dagupan, a city 200 km north of Manila declared a state of calamity, following a city-wide flooding. (IFRC, 18 Aug 2016).

FYR Macedonia: Flash Floods – Aug 2016
Affected countries: the former Yugoslav Republic of Macedonia
In the afternoon of 6 August 2016, torrential rains caused flash floods in the former Yugoslav Republic of Macedonia, severely affecting the populated areas and agricultural regions in Skopje and Tetovo. This led to loss of human lives and great material damage such as destroyed ring-roads, streets, demolished vehicles and infrastructure, including water channels. The most affected areas are located in the northern part of Skopje,

where more than 70 per cent of the houses have been flooded. (IFRC, 18 Aug 2016).

Viet Nam: Floods and Landslides – Aug 2016
Affected countries: Viet Nam
The Tropical Storm Nida affected many areas in the norhtern provinces in Viet Nam. According to the Department of Natural Disaster Prevention and Control, the storm has damaged around 3,600 houses and submerged 500 houses. At least six people died and 19 were missing because of the incident (ASEAN, 7 Aug 2016).

Hurricane Earl – Aug 2016
Affected countries: Belize, Dominican Republic, Guatemala, Honduras, Mexico
Tropical Storm Earl formed Tuesday August 2 in the Caribbean, prompting at least three countries (Belize, Honduras, Mexico) to issue warnings over potentially heavy rains and a big storm surge. (AFP, 2 Aug 2016).

Bibliography

International Case-Law

UN Committee Against Torture, *J.H.A. v. Spain* ("1d8a0d242ee0b7f6f718ea8f186651ba"), CAT/C/41/D/323/2007 (21 November 2008).

Court of First Instance, *Yassin Abdullah Kadi v. Council and Commission*, Case T-315/01 (21 September 2005).

GC, Case T-315/01, *Yassin Abdullah Kadi v. Council and Commission* ("*Kadi*") (21 September 2005) [2005] ECR II-3649.

GC, Case T-306/01 *Ahmed Ali Yusuf and Al Barakaat International Foundation v. Council and Commission* ("*Yusuf*") (21 September 2005) [2005] ECR II-03533.

CJ (Grand Chamber), Joined cases C-402/05 P and C-415/05 P, *Kadi and Al Barakaat International Foundation v. Council and Commission* ("*Kadi*") (3 September 2008) [2008] ECR I-06351.

CJ, Joined cases 21 to 24–72, *International Fruit Company Case v. Produktschap Voor Groenten En Fruit* ("*International Fruit Company*") (12 December 1972) [1972] ECR 1219.

CJ (Grand Chamber), Case C-540/03, *European Parliament v. Council* ("*Parliament v. Council*") (27 June 2006) [2006] ECR I-5769.

CJ, Case C-222/84, *Johnston v. Chief Constable of the Royal Ulster Constabulary* (15 May 1986) [1986] ECR 1651.

CJ, Case C-260/89, *Elliniki Radiophonia Tiléorassi Ae and Panellinia Omospondia Syllogon Prossopikou v. Dimotiki Etairia Pliroforissis and Sotirios Kouvelas and Nicolaos Avdellas and Others* ("*ERT v. DEP*") (18 June 1991) [1991] ECR I-2925.

CJ, Case C-112/00, *Eugen Schmidberger, Internationale Transporte Und Planzüge v. Republik Österreich* ("*Schmidberger*") (12 June 2003) [2003] ECR I-05659.

CJ (First Chamber), Case C-36/02, *Omega Spielhallen- Und Automatenaufstellungs-Gmbh v. Oberbürgermeisterin Der Bundesstadt Bonn* ("*Omega*") (14 October 2004) [2004] ECR I-09609.

CJ, Case 4–73, *J. Nold, Kohlen- Und Baustoffgroßhandlung v. Commission* ("*Nold*") (14 May 1974) [1974] ECR 491.

CJ, Case 374/87, *Orkem v. Commission* ("*Orkem*") (18 October 1989) [1989] ECR 3283.

CJ, Joined Cases C-297/88 and C-197/89, *Massam Dzodzi v. Belgian State* ("*Dzodzi*") (18 October 1990) [1990] ECR I-3763.

CJ, Case C-249/96, *Lisa Jacqueline Grant v. South-West Trains Ltd.* ("*Grant*") (17 February 1998) [1998] ECR I-621.

ECtHR, *Case of Bosphorus Hava Yollari Turizm Ve Ticaret Anonim Sirketi v Ireland* ("*Bosphorus*"), No. 45036/98 (30 June 2005).

ECtHR, *Case of Capital Bank Ad v. Bulgaria*, No. 49429/99 (24 November 2005).

CJ, Case C–158/91, *Criminal Proceedings against Jean-Claude Levy (Levy)* (*"Levy"*) (2 August 1993) [1993] ECR I–4287.

ECtHR (Plenary), *Ireland v. The United Kingdom*, Application no. 5310/71, Series A Vol. 25 (18 January 1978).

CJ, Case 812/79, *Attorney General v Juan C. Burgoa* (*"Burgoa"*) (14 October 1980) [1980] ECR 2787.

CJ, Case C-84/98, *Commission of the European Communities v. Portuguese Republic* (*"Commision v. Portugal"*) (4 July 2000) [2000] ECR I-05215.

European Commission of Human Rights, *Decision of 10 June 1958*, no. 235/56 Yearbook 2, p. 256.

European Commission of Human Rights, *Austria v. Italy* (*"Austria v. Italy"*), no. 788/60 (11 January 1961) Yearbook 4, p. 116.

Human Rights Committee, *Sayadi v. Belgium*, Communication No. 1472/2006 (22 October 2008).

CJ, Case C-216/01, *Budějovický Budvar National Corporation v Rudolf Ammersin Gmbh* (*"Budějovický Budvar"*) (18 November 2003) [2003] ECR I-13617.

CJ (Grand Chamber), Case C-205/06, *Commission of the European Communities v. Republic of Austria* (*"Commission v Austria"*) (3 March 2009) [2009] ECR I-01301.

CJ, Case C-118/07, *Commission of the European Communities v. Republic of Finland* (19 November 2009) [2009] ECR I–10889.

ECtHR (Grand Chamber), *N. v. The United Kingdom* (*"N. v. UK"*), Application no. 26565/05 (27 May 2008).

UN Committee Against Torture, *Hajrizi Dzemajl et al. v. Yugoslavia*, CAT/C/29/D/161/2000, No 161/2000 (21 November 2002).

ECtHR, *Case of Selçuk and Asker v. Turkey* (*"Selçuk v. Turkey"*), Applications No. 23184/94 and 23185/94 (24 April 1998) *Reports 1998-II*.

Opinion of Adv. Gen. Poiares Maduro, *Case C-402/05 P Yassin Abdullah Kadi v. Council of the European Union and Commission of the European Communities* (16 January 2008).

Court of Justice, Case C-112/00, *Eugen Schmidberger Internationale Transporte Planzuge v. Austria* [2003] ECR I-5659.

CJ, Case C-124/95, *R. v. H.M. Treasury and Bank of England, Ex Parte. Centro-Com Srl* (*"Centro-COM"*) (14 January 1997) [1997] ECR I-00081.

CJ, Case 2/74, *Reyners v Belgium* (21 June 1974) [1974] ECR 631.

CJ, Case 33/74, *Van Binsbergen v Bestuur Van de Bedrijfsvereniging Voor de Metaalnijverheid* (*"Van Binsbergen"*) (3 December 1974) [1974] ECR 1299.

CJ, Case 106/77, *Amministrazione Delle Finanze Dello Stato v. Simmenthal Spa* (*"Simmenthal"*) [1978] ECR 629.

CJ, Case 11–70, *Internationale Handelsgesellschaft Mbh v Einfuhr- Und Vorratsstelle Für Getreide Und Futtermittel* (*"Internationale Handelsgesellschaft"*) (17 December 1970) [1970] ECR 1125.

CJ, Case 29/69, *Erich Stauder v. City of Ulm* (*"Stauder"*) (12 November 1969) [1969] ECR 419.

Opinion of Adv. Gen. Karl Roemer, CMLR 112, delivered on 12 November 1969, *Case 29/69 Stauder v. City of Ulm* [1970] CMLR 112.

CJ, Case 4–73, *J. Nold, Kohlen- Und Baustoffgroßhandlung v Commission of the European Communities* (*"Nold"*) (14 May 1974) [1974] ECR 491.

CJ, Case C-215/03, *Salah Oulane v Minister Voor Vreemdelingenzaken En Integratie* (*"Oulane"*) (17 February 2005) ECR I-1215.

CJ, Case 48–75, *Jean Noël Royer* (*"Royer"*) (8 April 1976) [1976] ECR 497.

CJ, Case C-376/89, *Panagiotis Giagounidis v Stadt Reutlingen* (5 March 1991) [1991] ECR I-1069.

CJ, Case 26–62, *Nv Algemene Transport- En Expeditie Onderneming Van Gend & Loos v. Netherlands Inland Revenue Administration* (*"Van Gend en Loos"*) (5 February 1963) [1963] ECR 1.

CJ, Case 2/74, *Gabrielle Defrenne v. Société Anonyme Belge de Navigation Aérienne Sabena* (8 April 1976) [1974] ECR 631.

CJ, Case 6/64, *Flaminio Costa v. Enel* (15 July 1964) [1964] ECR 585.

CJ, Case 5/88, *Wachauf v. Bundesamt Für Ernährung Und Forstwirtschaft* (13 July 1989) [1989] ECR 2609.

ECtHR (Grand Chamber), *Agim Behrami and Bekir Behrami v. France, Ruzhdi Saramati v. France, Germany and Norway* (*"Behrami"*), Nos. 71412/01 and 78166/01 (2 May 2007).

ICJ, *Case Concerning the Military and Paramilitary Activities in and against Nicaragua (Nicaragua v. United States of America), Merits, Judgment* (*"Nicaragua (Merits)"*) (27 June 1986) *ICJ Reports 1986*, p. 14.

CJ, Opinion 2/94, *Accession by the Community to the European Convention for the Protection of Human Rights and Fundamental Freedoms* (*"Opinion 2/94"*) (28 March 1996) [1996] ECR I-1759.

Opinion of Adv. Gen. Kokott, delivered on 29 April 2010, *Case C-550/07 P Akzo Nobel Chemicals Ltd and Akcros Chemicals Ltd v. European Commission*.

CJ (Grand Chamber), Case C-236/09, *Association Belge Des Consommateurs Test-Achats Asbl and Others v Conseil Des Ministres* (*"Test-Achats"*) (1 March 2011) [2011].

Opinion of Adv. Gen. Trstenjak, delivered on 22 September 2011, *Case C-411/10 N. S. v. Secretary of State for the Home Department* ("Opinion AG Trstenjak in *NS*").

CJ (Grand Chamber), Joined Cases C-411/10 and C-493/10, *N.S. v. Secretary of State for the Home Department and M.E., A.S.M., M.T., K.P., E.H. v. Refugee Applications Commissioner, Minister for Justice, Equality and Law Reform* (*"NS & ME"*) (21 December 2011).

CJ, Joined Cases C-175/08, C-176/08, C-178/08 & C-179/08, *Salahadin Abdulla and Others v. Bundesrepublik Deutschland* (*"Salahadin"*) (2 March 2010).

CJ, Case C-31/09, *Bolbol v. Bevándorlási És Állampolgársági Hivatal* (*"Bolbol"*) (17 June 2010).

CJ, Joined cases C-57/09 and C-101/09, *Bundesrepublik Deutschland v. B and D* ("*B and D*") (9 November 2010).
CJ, Case C-112/00, *Eugen Schmidberger, Internationale Transporte Und Planzüge v. Republik Österreich* ("*Schmidberger*") (12 June 2003) [2003] ECR I-05659.
CJ, Case C-548/09 P, *Bank Melli Iran v Council* (16 November 2011) [2011].
GC (Second Chamber), Case T-527/09, *Ayadi v. Commission* ("*Ayadi*") (31 January 2012).
CJ, Case C-400/10 PPU, *J. Mcb. v. L. E.* ("*J. McB. v. L. E.*") (5 October 2010) [2010] *OJC 328/10*.
CJ, Case C-286/90, *Anklagemyndigheden v Peter Michael Poulsen and Diva Navigation Corp.* ("*Poulsen and Diva*") (24 November 1992) [1992] ECR I-06019.
CJ, Case C-162/96, *A. Racke Gmbh & Co. v Hauptzollamt Mainz* ("*Racke*") (16 June 1998) [1998] ECR I-03655.
CJ, Case C-188/91, *Deutsche Shell Ag v. Hauptzollamt Hamburg-Harburg* ("*Deutsche Shell*") (21 January 1993) [1993] ECR I-00363.
CJ, C-465/07, *Meki Elgafaji and Noor Elgafaji v. Staatssecretaris Van Justitie* ("*Elgafaji*") (17 February 2009) ECR I-921.
ECtHR, *D. v. The United Kingdom* ("*D. v. UK*"), Application no. 30240/96, Reports 1997-III (02/05/1997).
ECtHR (Plenary), *Soering v. The United Kingdom* ("*Soering*"), Application No. 14038/88, Series A Vol. 161 (7 July 1989).
HRC, *Judge v. Canada*, CCPR/C/78/D/829/1998, Communication No. 829/1998 (5 August 2003).
ECtHR (Grand Chamber), *M.S.S. v. Belgium and Greece* ("*M.S.S.*"), Application No. 30696/09 (21 January 2011) *Reports of Judgments and Decisions 2011*.
Opinion of Adv. Gen. Trstenjak, delivered on 22 September 2011, *Case C-493/10 M. E. And Others v. Refugee Applications Commissioner and Minister for Justice, Equality and Law Reform* ("Opinion AG Trstenjak in *ME*").
Opinion of Adv. Gen. Poiares Maduro, *Case C-465/07 Meki Elgafaji and Noor Elgafaji v. Staatssecretaris Van Justitie* ("*AG Opinion in Elgafaji*") (9 September 2008).
ECtHR, *Artico v. Italy* ("*Artico*"), No. 6694/74 (13 May 1980).
ECtHR (Fourth Section), *Sufi and Elmi v. The United Kingdom* ("*Sufi & Elmi*"), Applications nos. 8319/07 and 11449/07 (28 June 2011).
ECtHR, *Bader v. Sweden*, Application no. 13284/04 (8 November 2005).
ECtHR, *Bensaid v. The United Kingdom* ("*Bensaid*"), Application no. 44599/98 (6 February 2001).
ECtHR, *Rasmussen v. Denmark* ("*Rasmussen*"), Application no. 8777/79 (28 November 1984).
ECtHR (Plenary), *Abdulaziz, Cabales and Balkandali v. The United Kingdom* ("*Abdulaziz v. UK*"), Application no. 9214/80, 9473/81 and 9474/81 (28 May 1985).
ECtHR, *Sahin v. Germany*, Application no. 30943/96 (08 July 2003).
ECtHR, *Kurić and Others v. Slovenia* ("*Kurić*"), Application no. 26828/06 (26 June 2012).

HRC, *Kindler v. Canada*, CCPR/C/48/D/470/1991 Communication No. 470/1991 (11 November 1993).

ECtHR, *Cruz Varas and Others v. Sweden* ("*Cruz Varas*"), Application no. 15576/89 (20 March 1991).

ECtHR, *Case of Salah Sheekh v. The Netherlands* ("*Salah Sheekh*"), Application no. 1948/04 (11 January 2007).

HRC, *Sergio Euben Lopez Burgos v. Uruguay* ("*Burgos v. Uruguay*"), Supp. No. 40 (A/36/40), Communication No. R.12/52 (29 July 1981), p. 176 (1981).

ECtHR, *Vilvarajah and Others v. The United Kingdom* ("*Vilvarajah*"), Application Nos. 13163/87, 13164/87, 13165/87, 13447/87 and 13448/87 (30 October 1991).

HRC, *Charles Chitat Ng v. Canada* ("*Ng v. Canada*"), CCPR/C/49/D/469/1991 (7 January 1994).

ECtHR, *Chahal v. The United Kingdom* ("*Chahal*"), Application no. 70/1995/576/662 (11 November 1996).

ECtHR, *Thampibillai v. The Netherlands* ("*Thampibillai*"), Application No. 61350/00 (17 February 2004).

ECtHR, *Said v. The Netherlands* ("*Said v. NL*"), Application No. 2345/02 (15 July 2005).

ECtHR, *Jabari v. Turkey* ("*Jabari*"), Application No. 40035/98 (11 July 2000).

ECtHR, *S.C.C. v. Sweden* ("*S.C.C. v. Sweden*"), Application No. 46553/99 (15 February 2000).

ECtHR (Grand Chamber), *Case of Saadi v. Italy* ("*Saadi*"), Application no. 37201/06 (28 February 2008).

ECtHR, *Ahmed v. Austria*, Application no. 25964/94 (17 December 1996).

ECtHR, *M.A.R. v. United Kingdom* ("*M.A.R. v. UK*"), 28038/95 (16 January 1997).

ECtHR, *H.L.R. v. France*, Application No. 24573/94 (29 April 1997).

GC, Joined Cases T-213/95 and T-18/96, *Stichting Certificatie Kraanverhuurbedrijf (Sck) and Federatie Van Nederlandse Kraanverhuurbedrijven (Fnk) v. Commission of the European Communities* ("*SCK and FNK v. Commission*") (22 October 1997) [1997] ECR II-01739.

CJ, Case C-162/97, *Criminal Proceedings against Gunnar Nilsson, Per Olov Hagelgren and Solweig Arrborn* ("*Nilsson et al.*") (19 November 1998) [1998] ECR I-7477.

ECtHR, *T.I. v. the United Kingdom* ("*T.I. v. UK*"), Application no. 43844/98 (07 March 2000) *Reports of Judgments and Decisions 2000-III*.

ECtHR, *Case of Waite and Kennedy v. Germany*, Application no. 26083/94 (18 February 1999) *Reports of Judgments and Decisions 1999-I*.

HRC, *Mrs. G. T. v. Australia*, CCPR/C/61/D/706/1996 (4 November 1997).

ECtHR, *Al-Nashif v. Bulgaria*, Application no. 50963/99 (20 June 2002).

ECtHR, *Selmouni v. France* ("*Selmouni*"), Application no. 25803/94 (28 July 1999).

ECtHR, *Assenov and Others v. Bulgaria*, Application no. 24760/94 (28 October 1998).

ECtHR, *Khashiyev and Akayeva v. Russia*, Applications nos. 57942/00 and 57945/00 (24 February 2005).

CAT Committee, *Gorki Ernesto Tapia Paez v. Sweden* (*"Paez v. Sweden"*), CAT/C/18/D/39/1996 (28 April 1997).

CAT Committee, *Hmhi v. Australia*, UN Doc A/57/44, p.166 (2002), Communication 177/2001 (01/05/2002).

ECtHR, *N.A. v. The United Kingdom* (*"NA v. UK"*), Application no. 25904/07 (17 July 2008).

ECtHR, *N v. Sweden*, Application no. 23505/09 (20 July 2010).

ECtHR, *Müslim v. Turkey*, Application no. 53566/99 (26 April 2005).

ECtHR, *Gashi and Others v. Sweden* (*"Gashi v. Sweden"*), Application no. 61167/08 (4 May 2010).

ECtHR, *Sultani c. France*, Application no. 45223/05 (20 September 2007).

ECtHR, *Aoulmi c. France*, Application no. 50278/99 (17 January 2006).

ECtHR, *Ahmed Samir Said Al Khadumi c. Roumanie*, Application no. 35380/03 (18 October 2005).

ECtHR, *Venkadajalasarma v. The Netherlands* (*"Venkadajalasarma"*), Application no. 58510/00 (17 February 2004).

ECtHR, *Kavak v. Germany*, Application no. 46089/99 (18 May 1999).

ECtHR, *Fatgan Katani Et Autres c. Allemagne* (*"Katani v. Germany"*), Application no. 67679/01 (31 May 2001).

ECtHR, *Emine Akyüz and Other v. Germany*, Application no. 58388/00 (28 September 2000).

ACnHPR, *John K. Modise v. Botswana* (*"Modise v. Botswana"*), Communication No. 97/93 (6 November 2000).

ICJ, *Legality of the Threat or Use of Nuclear Weapons, Advisory Opinion*, I.C.J. Reports 1996 (8 July 1996), p. 226.

ECnHR, *Case of Paez v. Sweden* (*"Paez v. Sweden"*), Reports 1997-VII (30 October 1997).

ECtHR (Grand Chamber), *Case of Hirsi Jamaa and Others v. Italy* (*"Hirsi Jamaa et al. v. Italy"*), Application no. 27765/09 (23 February 2012).

CJ (Grand Chamber), C-175/08, C-176/08, C-178/08 and C-179/08, *Salahadin Abdulla and Others v. Bundesrepublik Deutschland* (*"Abdulla"*) (2 March 2010) [2010] ECR I-01493.

ECtHR, *Ismaili v. Germany*, Application No. 58128/00 (15 March 2001).

ECtHR, *Case of Airey v. Ireland* (*"Airey"*), Application no. 6289/73 (9 October 1979).

ECtHR, *Case of V. v. The United Kingdom* (*"V. v. UK"*), Application no. 24888/94 (16 December 1999).

ECtHR, *Case of Pretty v. The United Kingdom* (*"Pretty v. UK"*), Application no. 2346/02 (29/07/2002).

ECnHR, *B.B. Contre La France* (*"BB v. France"*), Application No 30930/96 (9 March 1998).

ECtHR, *Case of B.B. v. France* (*"BB v. France"*), Application no. 30930/96 (7 September 1998).

Inter-American Court of Human Rights, *Yakye Axa Indigenous Community v. Paraguay*, Series C No. 125 (17 June 2005).

ECtHR, *Ndangoya v. Sweden*, Application no. 17868/03 (22 June 2004).

ECtHR (Grand Chamber), *Case of Balmer-Schafroth and Others v. Switzerland* (*"Balmer-Schafroth"*), Application no. 22110/93 (26 August 1997).

ECtHR, *Case of Othman (Abu Qatada) v. The United Kingdom* (*"Othman"*), Application no. 8139/09 (09 May 2012).

ECtHR, *Case of Budayeva and Others v. Russia* (*"Budayeva v. Russia"*), Applications nos. 15339/02, 21166/02, 20058/02, 11673/02 and 15343/02 (29 September 2008).

HRC, *G. Aalbersberg and 2,084 Other Dutch Citizens v. The Netherlands* (*"Aalbersberg v. The Netherlands"*), Communication No. 1440/2005 (12 July 2006).

ECtHR (Grand Chamber), *Case of Balmer-Schafroth and Others v. Switzerland* (*"Balmer-Schafroth"*), Application No. 22110/93 (26 August 1997).

ECtHR, *Case of Athanassoglou and Others v. Switzerland* (*"Athanassoglou"*), Application no. 27644/95 (6 April 2000).

ECtHR, *Mcginley and Egan v. The United Kingdom* (*"McGinley and Egan v. UK"*), Applications nos. 21825/93 and 23414/94 (9 June 1998).

ECtHR, *Case of Öneryıldız v. Turkey* (*"Öneryıldız"*), Application no. 48939/99 (30 November 2004).

ECtHR, *Case of López Ostra v. Spain* (*"Lopez Ostra"*), Application no. 16798/90 (9 December 1994).

ECtHR, *Case of L.C.B. v. The United Kingdom* (*"LCB v. UK"*), Application no. 23413/94 (9 June 1998).

ECnHR, *Tauira and 18 Others v. France* (*"Tauira v. France"*), Application no 28204/95 (4 December 1995).

ECtHR, *Pancenko v. Latvia*, Application no. 40772/98 (28 October 1999).

ECtHR, *Affaire Di Sarno et autres c. Italie* (*"Di Sarno"*), Requête no 30765/08 (10 January 2012, final 10 April 2012).

ECtHR, *Affaire Tătar c. Roumanie* (*"Tătar"*), Requête no 67021/01 (27 January 2009, final 6 July 2009).

ECtHR, *Case of L. v. Lithuania*, Application no. 27527/03 (11 September 2007, final 31 March 2008).

ECtHR, *Ananyev and Others v. Russia* (*"Ananyev"*), Applications Nos. 42525/07 and 60800/08 (10 January 2012).

ECtHR, *Case of M.S. v. The United Kingdom* (*"MS v. UK"*), Application no. 24527/08 (3 May 2012, final 3 August 2012).

ICJ, *Advisory Opinion Concerning Reservations to the Convention on the Prevention and Punishment of the Crime of Genocide* (*"Reservations to the Genocide Convention"*) (28 May 1951) *ICJ Reports 1951*, p. 15.

ICTY (Appeals Chamber), *Prosecutor v. Tadic* (*"Tadic"*), Case IT-94-1 *38 I.L.M. 1518*.

Arbitrary Tribunal, *Trail Smelter Case (USA, Canada)* (*"Trail Smelter"*) *UNRIAA Vol. III*, pp. 1906–1982.

ICJ, *Corfu Channel (United Kingdom of Great Britain and Northern Ireland v. Albania) ("Corfu Channel Case")* (9 April 1949) *ICJ Reports 1949*, p. 4.

CJ, *National Farmer's Union*, C-157/96 (5 May 1998) *Rec. I-2211*.

CJ, *Royaume Uni/Commission*, C-180/96 (5 May 1998) *Rec. I-2265*.

ECtHR, *Z and T against the United Kingdom ("Z. & T. v. UK")*, Application no. 27034/05.

National Case-Law

Australia

Refugee Review Tribunal of Australia, 0907346 [2009] RRTA 1168, 10 December 2009.

Refugee Review Tribunal of Australia, N99/30231 [2000] RRTA 17, 10 January 2000.

Federal Court of Australia, *Olga Denissenko v. Christine Haskett and Minister for Immigration, Local Government and Ethnic Affairs*, unreported (Federal Court, Foster J, 9 May 1996), NG 509 of 1995 FED No. 404/96.

Refugee Review Tribunal of Australia, N95/09386 [1996] RRTA 3191, 7 November 1996.

Canada

Supreme Court, *Canada (Attorney General) v. Ward ("Canada (Attorney General) v. Ward")*, 30 June 1993, [1993] 2 SCR. 689,.

France

Conseil d'Etat ("CE") (10ème sous-section jugeant seule), *OFPRA C/ Manivasagam ("Manivasagam")*, No 323667, 7 mai 2012.

CE (10ème sous-section), *M. Athavan A. ("M. Athavan A.")*, No 341270, 24 August 2011.

CE, *Mme Amina A.*, No 329450, 16 February 2011.

CE, *OFPRA C/ Mme M. ("OFPRA C/ Mme M.")*, No 328420, 15 December 2010.

Tribunal administratif de Versailles, no 1004754, 3 August 2010.

CE, *Ministre de l'immigration, de l'intégration, de l'identité nationale et du développement solidaire (M. Samba A)*, No 319960, 16 July 2010.

CE, *M. Jean Yvon a Et Mme Modiana B Épouse A ("M. Jean Yvon a Et Mme Modiana B Épouse A")*, no 335698, 16 April 2010.

CE, *Ministre d'Etat, Ministre de l'Intérieur et de l'Aménagement du Territoire ("Ministre d'Etat, Ministre de l'Intérieur et de l'Aménagement du Territoire")*, 301640, 7 April 2010.

CE, *M. A. ("M. A.")*, no 336018, 26 February 2010.

CE, *Mme Léone A ("Mme Léone A")*, no 334522, 2 February 2010.

CE, *Mme Anne-Rose A ("Mme Anne-Rose A")*, no 333870, 18 January 2010.

CE (10ème et 9ème sous-sections réunies), *OFPRA C/ Baskarathas ("Baskarathas")*, No 320295, 3 July 2009.

CE (Section du contentieux, 10ème et 9ème sous-sections réunies), *Mlle Kona* (*"Kona"*), No 292564, 25 March 2009.
CE, *Préfet Du Val-D'oise* (*"Préfet Du Val-D'oise"*), no 273072, 27 july 2005.
CE, *M Mourad X* (*"M Mourad X"*), no 263960, 28 July 2004.
CE, *M. Kamel X* (*"M. Kamel X"*), no 258742, 26 May 2004.
CE (Section du Contentieux), No 185837, 15 March 2000.
CE, *Bereciuarta-Echarri* (*"Bereciuarta-Echarri"*), 85234, 25 mars 1988.
Cour nationale du droit d'asile ("CNDA" – formerly *"Commission des recours des réfugiés"*) (Sections réunies), *M B.* (*"Baskarathas"*), No 581505, 27 June 2008.
Commission des recours des réfugiés ("CRR") (Sections réunies), *Mlle Bernadette Kona* (*"Kona"*), No 419162, 17 February 2006.
Cour administrative d'appel ("CAA") de Versailles, *M. Michelet A* (*"M. Michelet A"*), 09VE00667, 9 February 2010.
CAA Paris, *Mme Antonide A.*, No 09PA02362, 8 February 2010.
CAA Paris, *Préfet de Police c. Okba Ben Belcacem X* (*"Préfet de Police c. Okba Ben Belcacem X"*), 06PA00482, 15 December 2006, *AJDA 2007.749*, note D. Lecucq.
Tribunal administratif de Montreuil, no 1011709, 9 December 2010.
Tribunal administratif de Montreuil, no 1012197, 6 January 2011.
Tribunal administratif de Melun, no 1006486/1, 17 December 2010.

Germany
BVerwG (*"BVerwG 10 C 9.08"*), 10 C 9.08, 14 July 2009.
High Administrative Court (*Oberverwaltungsgericht*) of Schleswig-Holstein (*"1 Lb 17/08"*), 1 LB 17/08, 19 September 2008.
BVerwG (*"BVerwG 10 C 43.07"*), 10 C 43.07, 24 June 2008.

India
Supreme Court, *Construction of Park at Noida near Okhla Bird Sanctuary, Anand Arya & Anr. (Applicants) T.N. Godavarman Thirumulpad (Petitioner) v. Union of India & Ors.* (*"Construction of Park at Noida near Okhla Bird Sanctuary"*), Writ petition (civil) No.202 of 1995, 3 December 2010.
Rajasthan High Court, *L.K. Koolwal v. State of Rajasthan and Others* (*"L.K. Koolwal v. State of Rajasthan and Others"*), Writ petition No. 121, 19 September 1986, *AIR 1988 Raj 2*.

Luxembourg
Cour administrative, n° 27943C, 5 May 2011.
Cour Administrative, n° 23643C, 14 February 2008.
Tribunal administratif, n° 29464, 7 mars 2012.
Tribunal administratif, n° 27296, 12 January 2011.
Tribunal administratif (2e chambre), n° 24212a, 4 June 2009.
Administrative Tribunal, n° 23306, 18 February 2008.

New Zealand

Supreme Court, *Ioane Teitiota v. The Chief Executive of the Ministry of Business, Innovation and Employment*, [2015] NZSC 107, 20 July 2015.

Court of Appeal, *Teitiota v. Chief Executive of Ministry of Business, Innovation and Employment*, [2014] NZCA 173, 8 May 2014.

Hight Court, *Teitiota v the Chief Executive of the Ministry of Business Innovation and Employment ("Teitiota")*, [2013] NZHC 3125, 26 November 2013.

Immigration and Protection Tribunal, *AF (Tuvalu)*, [2015] NZIPT 800859, 20 October 2015.

Immigration and Protection Tribunal, *AC (Tuvalu)*, [2014] NZIPT 800517–520, 4 June 2014.

Immigration and Protection Tribunal, *AD (Tuvalu)*, [2014] NZIPT 501370–371, 4 June 2014.

Immigration and Protection Tribunal, *AF (Kiribati)*, [2013] NZIPT 800413, 25 June 2013 [the applicant, I. Teitiota, is identified by his name in subsequent appeals before the High Court, Court of Appeal and Supreme Court].

Immigration and Protection Tribunal, *BG (Fiji)*, [2012] NZIPT 800091, 20 January 2012.

Refugee Status Appeals Authority, Refugee Appeal No. 72189/2000, 17 August 2000.

Sweden

Migrationsöverdomstolen (Migration Court of Appeal), MIG 2011:14, 22 June 2011.
Migrationsöverdomstolen (Migration Court of Appeal), MIG 2009:27, 6 October 2009.
Migrationsöverdomstolen (Migration Court of Appeal), MIG 2007:48, UM1344-06, 27 November 2007.
Migrationsöverdomstolen (Migration Court of Appeal), MIG 2007:9, 26 February 2007.

United Kingdom

United Kingdom House of Lords ("UKHL"), *Regina v. Secretary of State for the Home Department (Appellant) Ex Parte Adam ("Regina v. Secretary of State for the Home Department (Appellant) Ex Parte Adam")*, [2005] UKHL 66, 3 November 2005.

UKHL, *Regina v. Special Adjudicator (Respondent) Ex Parte Ullah (Fc) (Appellant); Do (Fc) (Appellant) v. Secretary of State for the Home Department (Respondent) ("Ullah and Do")*, [2004] UKHL 26, 17 June 2004.

UKHL, *Regina v. Secretary of State for the Home Department Ex Parte Razgar ("Regina v. Secretary of State for the Home Department Ex Parte Razgar")*, [2004] UKHL 27, 17 June 2004.

High Court (Queen's Bench Division), *R v. Secretary of State for the Home Department, Ex Parte Kebbeh ("Kebbeh")*, CO/1269/98, *Crown Office List*, 30 April 1999.

England and Wales Court of Appeal ("EWCA") (Civil Division), *Secretary of State for the Home Department v. HH (Iraq) ("HH")*, [2009] EWCA Civ 727, 14 July 2009.

EWCA, *QD (Iraq) v. Secretary of State for the Home Department; AH (Iraq) v. Secretary of State for the Home Department ("QD & AH v Secretary of State for the Home Department")*, [2009] EWCA Civ 620, 24 June 2009.

United Kingdom Upper Tribunal ("UKUT") (Immigration and Asylum Chamber), *HM and Others (Article 15(c)) Iraq Cg ("HM and Others")*, [2010] UKUT 331 (IAC), 22 September 2010.

United Kingdom Immigration Appeal Tribunal ("UKIAT"), *Paul Owen v. Secretary of State for the Home Department ("Owen")* [2002] UKIAT 3285, 30 July 2002.

UKIAT, *Korca v. Secretary of State for the Home Department ("Korca v. Secretary of State for the Home Department")*, Appeal No. HX-360001-2001, 29 May 2002, *Unreported*.

UKIAT, *Devaseelan v Secretary of State for the Home Department ("Devaseelan")*, Appeal No.: HR/03442/01, 13 March 2002, [2002] *UKIAT 702*.

United Kingdom Asylum and Immigration Tribunal ("UKAIT"), *AM & AM (Armed Conflict: Risk Categories) Somalia v. Secretary of State for the Home Department ("AM & AM (Somalia)")*, CG [2008] UKAIT 00091, 27 January 2009.

UKAIT, *KH (Article 15(c) Qualification Directive) Iraq v. Secretary of State for the Home Department ("KH")*, CG [2008] UKAIT 00023, 25 March 2008.

UKAIT, *Lukman Hameed Mohamed v. The Secretary of State for the Home Department ("Lukman")*, AA/14710/2006, 13 September 2007 (unreported case).

USA

Court of Appeals (Second Circuit), *Gabriel Ashanga Jota v. Texaco Inc. ("Gabriel Ashanga Jota v. Texaco Inc.")*, Nos.97-9102, 97–9104, 97–9108 157 F.3d 153,.

Court of Appeals (Ninth Circuit), *Sarei Et. Al. v. Rio Tinto, Plc and Rio Tinto, Ltd. ("Sarei v. Rio Tinto")*, 221 F.Supp.2d at 1116, 7 August 2006.

Court of Appeals Third Circuit, *Chris Dunat, Appellant, v. L. W. Hurney, District Director of Immigration, Philadelphia ("Dunat v. Hurney")*, 297 F.2d 744, 24 January 1962.

United States Supreme Court, *Sale v. Haitian Centers Council, Inc. Et Al ("Sale v. Haitian Centers Council, Inc. Et Al")*, No. 92–343, 1993 113 S.Ct 2549,.

Treaties and Other International Instruments

Council of Europe

European Convention for the Protection of Human Rights and Fundamental Freedoms ("ECHR"), 4 November 1950, in force 3 September 1953 *ETS* Vol. 5.

Protocol (No. 13) to the Convention for the Protection of Human Rights and Fundamental Freedoms, Concerning the Abolition of the Death Penalty in All Circumstances ("Protocol 13 ECHR"), 3 May 2002, entered into force 1 July 2003 *ETS* Vol. 187.

Protocol (No. 6) to the European Convention for the Protection of Human Rights and Fundamental Freedoms Concerning the Abolition of Death Penalty ("Protocol 6 ECHR"), 28 April 1983, entered into force 1 March 1985 *ETS* Vol. 114.

European Union

Charter of Fundamental Rights of the European Union ("EU Charter"), 12 December 2007, entered into force 1 December 2009 [14/12/2007] *OJ C 303/01*.

Consolidated version of the Treaty on European Union ("TEU") [2010] *OJ C 83/13*.

Consolidated version of the Treaty on the Functioning of the European Union ("TFEU") [2010] *OJ C 83/47*.

Commission Regulation (EC) No 1560/2003 of 2 September 2003 Laying Down Detailed Rules for the Application of Council Regulation (EC) No 343/2003 Establishing the Criteria and Mechanisms for Determining the Member State Responsible for Examining an Asylum Application Lodged in One of the Member States by a Third-Country National ("Regulation – Dublin detailed rules") [05/09/2003] *OJ L 222/3*.

Commission Regulation (EC) No 2062/2001 of 19 October 2001 Amending, for the Third Time, Council Regulation (EC) No 467/2001 Prohibiting the Export of Certain Goods and Services to Afghanistan, Strengthening the Flight Ban and Extending the Freeze of Funds Andother Financial Resources in Respect of the Taliban of Afghanistan and Repealing Regulation (EC) No 337/2000 [20/10/2001] *OJ* Vol. L 277, p. 25.

Council Common Position of 27 May 2002 Concerning Restrictive Measures against Usama Bin Laden, Members of the Al-Qaida Organisation and the Taliban and Other Individuals, Groups, Undertakings and Entities Associated with Them and Repealing Common Positions 96/746/CFSP, 1999/727/CFSP, 2001/154/CFSP and 2001/771/CFSP [29/05/2002] *OJ* Vol. L 139, pp. 4–5.

Council Common Position of 26 February 2001 Concerning Additional Restrictive Measures against the Taliban and Amending Common Position 96/746/CFSP, 27/02/2001 *OJ L* Vol. 57, pp. 1–2.

Council Common Position of 15 November 1999 Concerning Restrictive Measures against the Taliban, 1999/727/CFSP [16/11/1999] *OJ* Vol. L 294, p. 1.

Council Directive 2001/55/EC of 20 July 2001 on Minimum Standards for Giving Temporary Protection in the Event of a Mass Influx of Displaced Persons ("Temporary Protection Directive"), 2001/55/EC [7 August 2001] *OJ L 212/12*.

Council Directive 2005/85/EC of 1 December 2005 on Minimum Standards on Procedures in Member States for Granting and Withdrawing Refugee Status ("Procedures Directive") [13/12/2005] *OJ L 326/13*.

Council Directive 2004/83/EC of 29 April 2004 on Minimum Standards for the Qualification and Status of Third Country Nationals or Stateless Persons as Refugees or as Persons Who Otherwise Need International Protection and the Content of the

Protection Granted ("Qualification Directive (2004)"), 2004/83/EC [30 September 2004] *OJ L 304/12*.

Council Directive 2003/9/EC of 27 January 2003 Laying Down Minimum Standards for the Reception of Asylum Seeker ("Reception Conditions Directive") [06/02/2003] *OJ L 31/18*.

Council Regulation (EC) No 561/2003 of 27 March 2003 Amending, as Regards Exceptions to the Freezing of Funds and Economic Resources, Regulation (EC) No 881/2002 Imposing Certain Specific Restrictive Measures Directed against Certain Persons and Entities Associated with Usama Bin Laden, the Al-Qaida Network and the Taliban [29/03/2003] *OJ* Vol. L 82, p. 1.

Council Regulation (EC) No 343/2003 of 18 February 2003 Establishing the Criteria and Mechanisms for Determining the Member State Responsible for Examining an Asylum Application Lodged in One of the Member States by a Third-Country National ("Dublin Regulation") [25/02/2003] *OJ L 50/1*, pp. 1–10, consolidated version of 04/12/2008.

Council Regulation (EC) No 881/2002 of 27 May 2002 Imposing Certain Specific Restrictive Measures Directed against Certain Persons and Entities Associated with Usama Bin Laden, the Al-Qaida Network and the Taliban, and Repealing Council Regulation (EC) No 467/2001 Prohibiting the Export of Certain Goods and Services to Afghanistan, Strengthening the Flight Ban and Extending the Freeze of Funds and Other Financial Resources in Respect of the Taliban of Afghanistan [29/05/2002] *OJ* Vol. L 139, p. 9.

Council Regulation (EC) No 407/2002 of 28 February 2002 Laying Down Certain Rules to Implement Regulation (EC) No 2725/2000 Concerning the Establishment of 'Eurodac' for the Comparison of Fingerprints for the Effective Application of the Dublin Convention [05/03/2002] *OJ L 62/1*.

Council Regulation (EC) No 467/2001 of 6 March 2001 Prohibiting the Export of Certain Goods and Services to Afghanistan, Strengthening the Flight Ban and Extending the Freeze of Funds and Other Financial Resources in Respect of the Taliban of Afghanistan, and Repealing Regulation (EC) No 337/2000 [09/03/2001] *OJ L* Vol. 67, p. 1.

Council Regulation (EC) No 2725/2000 of 11 December 2000 Concerning the Establishment of 'Eurodac' for the Comparison of Fingerprints for the Effective Application of the Dublin Convention ("Eurodac Regulation") [15/12/2000] *OJ L 316/1*.

Council Regulation (EC) No 337/2000 of 14 February 2000 Concerning a Flight Ban and a Freeze of Funds and Other Financial Resources in Respect of the Taliban of Afghanistan, 16/02/2000 *OJ L* Vol. 43, p. 1.

Décision de la Commission du 12 Février 1969, Relative aux mesures permettant à certaines catégories de consommateurs d'acheter du beurre à prix réduit, 12 February 1969 [03/03/1969] *JO L 52*.

Directive 2011/95/EU of the European Parliament and of the Council of 13 December 2011 on Standards for the Qualification of Third-Country Nationals or Stateless Persons as Beneficiaries of International Protection, for a Uniform Status for Refugees or for Persons Eligible for Subsidiary Protection, and for the Content of the Protection Granted ("Qualification Directive") [20/12/2011] *OJ L 337/09*, pp. 9–26.

Directive 2000/60/EC of the European Parliament and of the Council of 23 October 2000 Establishing a Framework for Community Action in the Field of Water Policy [22/12/2000] *OJ L 327* pp. 1–73.

EU Parliament, Resolution on the Harmonisation of Forms of Protection Complementing Refugee Status in the European Union, A4-0450/98 [28/05/1999] *OJ C150/203*.

Protocol (No. 8) Relating to Article 6(2) of the Treaty on European Union on the Accession of the Union to the European Convention on the Protection of Human Rights and Fundamental Freedoms ("Protocol 8 – Accession of the Union to the ECHR") [2010] *OJ C 83/273*.

Regulation (EU) No 439/2010 of the European Parliament and of the Council of 19 May 2010 Establishing a European Asylum Support Office ("EASO Regulation"), 19/05/2010 entered into force 18/06/2010 [29/05/2010] *OJ L* Vol. 132, p. 11.

Single European Act, 17 February 1986 [29/06/1987] *OJ L* Vol. 169/1.

Treaty of Amsterdam Amending the Treaty on European Union, the Treaties Establishing the European Communities and Related Acts ("Amsterdam Treaty") [10 November 1997] *OJ C 340/1*.

Treaty Establishing the European Atomic Energy Community ("Euratom"), 25 March 1957 [1958] *UNTS* Vol. 298, p. 167.

Treaty Establishing the European Economic Community ("Treaty of Rome (EEC)"), 25 March 1957 [1958] *UNTS* Vol. 298, p. 3.

Treaties Establishing the European Community, Consolidated Amsterdam version ("TEC (1997)") [10 November 1997] *OJ C 340/03*.

Treaty Establishing the European Coal and Steel Community, 18 April 1951, expired 23 July 2002 [1957] *UNTS* Vol. 261, p. 140.

Treaty of Lisbon Amending the Treaty on European Union and the Treaty Establishing the European Community ("Lisbon Treaty"), 13 December 2007, entered into force 1 December 2009 [17 December 2007] *OJ C 306/50*.

Treaty of Lisbon Amending the Treaty on European Union and the Treaty Establishing the European Community, 13 December 2007 *OJ* [2007] Vol. C 306/01.

Treaty on European Union, Consolidated Amsterdam version ("TEU (1997)") [10 November 1997] *OJ C 340/02*.

Treaty on European Union ("TEU (1992)"), signed in Maastricht, 29 July 1992 [*1992*] *OJ C 191/01*.

United Nations

Charter of the United Nations ("UN Charter"), 24 October 1945 [1946–1947] *UNTS* Vol. 1 p. XVI.

Constitution of the International Refugee Organisation ("Constitution of the IRO"), 15 December 1946, entered into force 20 August 1948 [1948] *UNTS* Vol. 18, p. 3.

Convention against Torture and Other Cruel, Inhuman or Degrading Treatment or Punishment ("CAT"), 10 December 1984, in force 26 June 1987 [1987] *UNTS* Vol. 1465, p. 85.

Convention on Access to Information, Public Participation in Decision-Making and Access to Justice in Environmental Matters, 25 June 1998, entered into force 30 October 2001 [2001] *UNTS* Vol. 2161, p. 447.

Convention on the Prohibition of Military or Any Hostile Use of Environmental Modification Techniques, 10 December 1976, entered into force 5 October 1976 [1976] *UNTS* Vol. 1108, p. 151.

Convention Relating to the Status of Refugees ("Refugee Convention"), 28 July 1951, entered into force 22 April 1954 [1954] *UNTS* Vol. 189, p. 137.

Convention Relating to the Status of Stateless Persons, 28 September 1954 *Treaty Series* Vol. vol. 360, p. 117.

Draft UN Convention on Territorial Asylum: Report of the United Nations Conference on Territorial Asylum, 21 April 1977, UN doc. A/CONF.78/12.

Geneva Convention Relative to the Protection of Civilian Persons in Time of War (Fourth Geneva Convention), 12 August 1949, entered into force 21 October 1950 [1950] *UNTS* Vol. 75, p. 287.

ILC, Articles on the Responsibility of International Organizations, with Commentaries ("ILC Articles RIO"), adopted by the ILC at its sixty-third session, in 2011, [2011] *Yearbook of the International Law Commission* Vol. II, Part Two.

ILC, Articles on the Prevention of Transboundary Harm from Hazardous Activities, Report of the 53rd Session ("Articles on the Prevention of Transboundary Harm from Hazardous Activities"), UN Doc. A/56/10 (2001) GAOR, 56th session, Supplement No. 10, at 370.

International Covenant on Civil and Political Rights ("ICCPR"), 16 December 1966, in force 23 September 1976 [1976] *UNTS* Vol. 999, p. 171.

International Covenant on Economic, Social and Cultural Rights ("ICESCR"), 16 December 1966, in force 23 March 1976 [1976] *UNTS* Vol. 993, p. 3.

Kyoto Protocol to the United Nations Framework Convention on Climate Change ("Kyoto Protocol"), 11 December 1997, entered into force 16 February 2005, U.N. Doc FCCC/CP/1997/7/Add.1 [1998] *ILM* Vol. 37, p. 22.

Optional Protocol to the International Covenant on Civil and Political Rights, 16 December 1966, entry into force 23 March 1976 [1976] *UNTS* Vol. 999, p. 171.

Protocol Relating to the Status of Refugees, 30 January 1967 [1967] *UNTS* Vol. 606, p. 267.

Protocol Additional to the Geneva Conventions of 12 August 1949, and Relating to the Protection of Victims of International Armed Conflicts (Protocol I), 8 June 1977, entered into force 7 December 1979 [1979] *UNTS* Vol. 1125, p. 3Protocol Additional to the Geneva Conventions of 12 August 1949, and Relating to the Protection of Victims of Non-International Armed Conflicts (Protocol II) ("AP II"), 8 June 1977, entered into force 7 December 1978 [1978] *UNTS* Vol. 1125, p. 609.

Rome Statute of the International Criminal Court, 17 July 1998, last amended January 2002, A/CONF. 183/9.

Second Optional Protocol to the International Covenant on Civil and Political Rights, aiming at the abolition of the death penalty ("ICCPR 2nd OP"), 15 December 1989, entered into force 11 July 1991, A/RES/44/128.

Statute of the Office of the United Nations High Commissionner for Refugees ("UNHCR Statute"), 14 December 1950, UNGA Res 428 (V).

UN Conference on the Human Environment, Declaration of the United Nations Conference on the Human Environment ("Stockholm Declaration"), 16 June 1972, UN Doc. A/CONF.48/14/Rev. 1(1973).

UN Conference on Environment and Development, Rio Declaration on Environment and Development ("Rio Declaration"), 13 June 1992, UN Doc. A/CONF.151/26 (vol. I) United Nations Framework Convention on Climate Change ("UNFCCC"), 9 May 1992 [1992] *UNTS* Vol. 1771, p. 107.

UN Framework Convention on Climate Change (UNFCCC), Paris Agreement, signed 12 December 2015, entered into force 4 November 2016, *Report of the Conference of the Parties on its twenty-first session, held in Paris from 30 November to 13 December 2015*, FCCC/CP/2015/10/Add.1, 29 January 2016, Addendum, Part two: Action taken by the Conference of the Parties at its twenty-first session, "Decision 1/CP.21: Adoption of the Paris Agreement".

UN Security Council, Resolution 1452 (2002): Threats to International Peace and Security Caused by Terrorist Acts, 20 December 2002, S/RES/1452 (2002).

UN Security Council, Resolution 1390 (2002): Modifies the Sanctions Regime Originally Imposed in Resolutions 1267 (1999) and 1333 (2000), 16 January 2002, S/RES/1390 (2002).

UN Security Council, Resolution 1333 (2000): Air and Arms Embargo, Restricted Travel Sanctions, Freezing of Funds of Usama Bin Laden and Associates, 19 December 2000, S/RES/1333 (2000).

UN Security Council, Resolution 1267 (1999): Establishes Security Council Committee; Imposes Limited Air Embargo and Funds and Financial Assets Embargo on the Taliban, 15 October 1999, S/RES/1267 (1999).

Treaty on the Non-Proliferation of Nuclear Weapons ("Non-Proliferation Treaty"), 01 July 1968, entered into force 5 March 1970 [1970] *UNTS* Vol. 729, p. 161.

Universal Declaration of Human Rights ("UDHR"), 10 December 1948, UNGA Res. 217 A (III).
Vienna Convention on the Law of Treaties ("VCLT"), 23 May 1969, entered into force 27 January 1980 [1980] *UNTS* Vol. 1155, p. 331.
World Health Organization, Constitution of the World Health Organization, 22 July 1946, entered into force 7 April 1948 [1946] *Official Records of the World Health Organization* Vol. 2, p. 100.

Others

African Charter on Human and Peoples' Rights – "Banjul Charter" ("ACHPR"), 27 June 1981, entered into force 21 October 1986, CAB/LEG/67/3 rev. 5, 21 I.L.M. 58 (1982).
African Union Convention for the Protection and Assistance of Internally Displaced Persons in Africa – Kampala Convention ("AU Convention on IDPs"), 22 October 2009, not yet entered into force.
American Convention on Human Rights – "Pact of San Jose, Costa Rica" ("ACHR"), 22 November 1969, entered into force 18 July 1978.
Asian-African Legal Consultative Organization (AALCO) Bangkok Principles on the Status and Treatment of Refugees ("Bangkok Principles"), 31 December 1966.
Cairo Declaration on Human Rights in Islam ("Cairo Declaration"), World Conference on Human Rights, 4th Sess., Agenda Item 5, UN Doc A/CONF.157/PC/62/Add.18 [9 June 1993] *UN GAOR*.
Cartagena Declaration on Refugees ("Cartagena Declaration"), 22 November 1984, Colloquium on the International Protection of Refugees in Central America, Mexico and Panama.
Convention Governing the Specific Aspects of Refugee Problems in Africa ("AU Refugee Convention"), 10 September 1969 [1976] *UNTS* Vol. 1001, p. 45.
League of Arab States, Arab Charter on Human Rights ("Arab Charter"), adopted 15 September 1994, entered into force 15 March 2008 *reprinted in International Human Rights Report* Vol. 12, p. 893 [2005].
League of Arab States, Arab Convention on Regulating Status of Refugees in the Arab Countries ("Arab Refugee Convention"), adopted in 1994, not ratified.

Documents from International Organisations

Council of Europe

Commissioner for Human Rights, "Issue Paper: The Human Rights of Irregular Migrants in Europe", CommDH/IssuePaper (2007) 1, 17 December 2007.
"Explanations Relating to the Charter of Fundamental Rights" ("Explanations to the Charter") [14/12/2007] *OJ C 303/17*.

PACE, "Resolution 1509 (2006): Human Rights of Irregular Migrants", Adopted on 27 June 2006.
PACE, "Recommendation 1976 (2011): The Role of Parliaments in the Consolidation and Development of Social Rights in Europe" ("Recommendation 1976 (2011)"), 23 June 2011.
PACE, "Resolution 1809 (2011): Water: A Source of Conflict", 15 April 2011.
PACE, "Resolution 1805 (2011), the Large-Scale Arrival of Irregular Migrants, Asylum Seekers and Refugees on Europe's Southern Shores", 14 April 2011.
PACE, "Recommendation 1885 (2009): Drafting an Additional Protocol to the European Convention on Human Rights Concerning the Right to a Healthy Environment" ("Recommendation 1885 (2009)"), 30 September 2009.
PACE, "Recommendation 1525 (2001) on the United Nations High Commissioner for Refugees and the Fiftieth Anniversary of the Geneva Convention" ("PACE"), 27 June 2001.
PACE, "Recommendation 1327 (1997) on the Protection and Reinforcement of the Human Rights of Refugees and Asylum-Seekers in Europe", 24 April 1997.
PACE, "Situation of de Facto Refugees (Debate on the Report of the Committee on Population and Refugees, Doc. 3642, Addendum and Amendments, and Votes on the Draft Recommendation and Draft Resolution)", 26 january 1976 [1976] *Official Report of Debates* Vol. III, pp. 733–1084.
PACE, "Recommendation 773 (1976) on the Situation of *de Facto* Refugees", 26 January 1976.
PACE Committee on Migration, Refugees and Population, "Report to the Committee on Migration, Refugees and Population: The Large-Scale Arrival of Irregular Migrants, Asylum Seekers and Refugees on Europe's Southern Shores", Doc. 12581, 13 April 2011.
PACE, Committee on Migration, Refugees and Population, "Report of the Committee on Migration, Refugees and Population on Environmentally Induced Migration and Displacement: A 21st Century Challenge" ("Report of the Committee on Migration: a 21st century challenge"), Rapporteur: Tina Acketoft, Doc. 11785, 23 December 2008.
PACE Committee on the Environment, Agriculture and Local and Regional Affairs, "Water: A Source of Conflict", Doc. 12538, 17 March 2011.
PACE Committee on the Environment, Agriculture and Local and Regional Affairs, "Drafting an Additional Protocol to the European Convention on Human Rights Concerning the Right to a Healthy Environment", Doc. 12003, 11 September 2009.
Steering Committee for Human Rights, "Draft Legal Instruments on the Accession of the European Union to the European Convention on Human Rights, Appendix I to the Report to the Committee of Ministers on the Elaboration of Legal Instruments for the Accession of the European Union to the European Convention on Human Rights", CDDH(2011)009 [14 October 2011].

Registrar of the ECTHR, "Press Release: The United Kingdom Would Violate Human Rights of Two Somali Nationals If It Returned Them to Mogadishu", ECHR 076 (2011), 28 June 2011.

European Union

EU Agency for Fundamental Rights (FRA), "The Stockholm Programme: A Chance to Put Fundamental Rights Protection Right in the Centre of the European Agenda", 14 July 2009.

European Commission, "Report from the Commission to the European Parliament, the Council, the European Economic and Social Committee and the Committee of the Regions: 2013 Report on the Application of the EU Charter of Fundamental Rights", SWD(2014) 224 final, 14 April 2014.

European Commission: Beirens, Hanne, Sheila Maas, Salvatore Petronella and Maurice Van Der Velden, *Study on the Temporary Protection Directive: Final Report* (Luxembourg: Publications Office of the European Union, 2016), retrieved from: <http://ec.europa.eu/dgs/home-affairs/e-library/documents/policies/asylum/temporary-protection/docs/final_report_evaluation_tpd_en.pdf> [10/11/2016].

European Commission, "Communication from the Commission to the European Parliament, the Council, the European Economic and Social Committee and the Committee of the Regions, 'Maximising the Development Impact of Migration: The EU Contribution for the UN High-Level Dialogue and Next Steps Towards Broadening the Development-Migration Nexus'", COM(2013) 292 final, 21 May 2013.

European Commission, "Communication from the Commission to the European Parliament, the Council, the European Economic and Social Committee and the Committee of the Regions the Future Approach to EU Budget Support to Third Countries", COM(2011) 638 final, 13 October October 2011.

European Commission, "Communication from the Commission to the European Parliament, the Council, the Economic and Social Committee and the Committee of the Regions on Migration", COM(2011) 248 final, 4 May 2011.

European Commission, "Communication from the Commission: Strategy for the Effective Implementation of the Charter of Fundamental Rights by the European Union", COM(2010) 573 final, 19/10/2010.

European Commission, "Report on the Application of Directive 2004/83/EC of 29 April 2004 on Minimum Standards for the Qualification and Status of Third Country Nationals or Stateless Persons as Refugees or as Persons Who Otherwise Need International Protection and the Content of the Protection" ("Report on the application of the Qualification Directive"), COM(2010)314 final, 16 June 2010.

EU Commission, "Report from the Commission to the European Parliament and the Council on the Application of Directive 2004/83/EC of 29 April 2004 on Minimum Standards for the Qualification and Status of Third Country Nationals or Stateless

Persons as Refugees or as Persons Who Otherwise Need International Protection and the Content of the Protection" ("Commission Report on the application of QD (2004)"), COM(2010)314 final, 16/06/2010.

European Commission, "Commission Staff Working Document Accompanying the Proposal for a Directive of the European Parliament and of the Council on Minimum Standards for the Qualification and Status of Third Country Nationals or Stateless Persons as Beneficiaries of International Protection and the Content of the Protection Granted: Impact Assessment" ("Commission Impact Assessment – Proposal for a Recast QD"), SEC(2009) 1373 final, 14863/09 ADD 1 ASILE 81 CODEC 1224, 21 October 2009.

European Commission, "Annexes Accompanying the Impact Assessment for the Proposal for a Directive of the European Parliament and of the Council on Minimum Standards for the Qualification and Status of Third Country Nationals or Stateless Persons as Beneficiaries of International Protection and the Content of the Protection Granted" ("Annexes to Impact Assessment – Proposal for a Recast QD"), SEC(2009) 1373 final (II part), 14863/09 ADD 4 ASILE 81 CODEC 1224, 21 October 2009.

European Commission, "Proposal for a Regulation of the European Parliament and of the Council Establishing a European Asylum Support Office, Explanatory Memorandum" ("Explanatory Memorandum – EASO"), COM(2009) 66 final – COD 2009/0027, 18 February 2009.

European Commission, "Commission Working Document: The Relationship between Safeguarding Internal Security and Complying with International Protection Obligations and Instruments", COM(2001) 743 final, 05 December 2001.

European Commission, "Proposal for a Council Directive on Minimum Standards for the Qualification and Status of Third Country Nationals and Stateless Persons as Refugees or as Persons Who Otherwise Need International Protection" ("Commission Proposal QD (2004)"), COM(2001) 510 final, 12/09/2001.

European Commission, "Proposal for a Council Directive on Minimum Standards for the Qualification and Status of Third Country Nationals and Stateless Persons as Refugees or as Persons Who Otherwise Need International Protection, Explanatory Memorandum" ("Explanatory Memorandum – QD (2004)"), COM(2001) 510 final, 12 September 2001.

European Commission, "Communication from the Commission to the Council and the European Parliament: Towards a Common Asylum Procedure and a Uniform Status, Valid Throughout the Union, for Persons Granted Asylum", COM(2000) 755 final, 22 November 2000.

European Commission, "Proposal for a Council Directive on Minimum Standards for Giving Temporary Protection in the Event of a Mass Influx of Displaced Persons and on Measures Promoting a Balance of Efforts between Member States in Receiving

Such Persons and Bearing the Consequences Thereof" ("Proposal for Temporary Protection Directive"), COM (2000) 303 final, 24 May 2000 [31/10/2000] *OJ C 311 E*.

European Commission, "Communication from the Commission on the Inclusion of Respect for Democratic Principles and Human Rights in Agreements between the Community and Third Countries", COM (95) 216 final, 23 May 1995.

EU Council, "Presidency Note to the Strategic Committe on Immigration, Frontiers and Asylum (ASILE 59)" ("Presidency Note (ASILE 59)"), 13623/02 ASILE 59, 30 October 2002.

EU Council, "Presidency Note to the Permanent Representative Committee, on the Proposal for a Council Directive on Minimum Standards for the Qualification and Status of Third Country Nationals and Stateless Persons as Refugees or as Persons Who Otherwise Need International Protection" ("Presidency Note (ASILE 55)"), 23 October 2002.

EU Council, "Asylum Working Party – Outcome of Proceedings of 3–4 and 16–17 October 2002" ("Outcome of Proceedings (ASILE 54)"), 12620/02 ASILE 54, 23 October 2002.

EU Council, "Presidency Note to the Council (Justice, Home Affairs and Civil Protection)" ("Presidency Note (ASILE 53)"), 12619/02 ASILE 53, 9 October 2002.

EU Council, "Presidency Note to the Strategic Committee on Immigration, Frontiers and Asylum, on the Proposal for a Council Directive on Minimum Standards for the Qualification and Status of Third Country Nationals and Stateless Persons as Refugees or as Persons Who Otherwise Need International Protection" ("Presidency Note (ASILE 47)"), 12382/02 ASILE 47, 30 September 2002.

EU Council, "Asylum Working Party, Outcomes of Proceedings of 5–6 and 17–18 September 2002", 12199/01 ASILE 43, 25 September 2002.

EU Council, "Presidency Note to the Strategic Committe on Immigration, Frontiers and Asylum (ASILE 43)" ("Presidency Note (ASILE 43)"), 12148/02 ASILE 43, 20 September 2002.

EU Council, "Opinion of the Legal Service", 10560/02 ASILE 34 JUR 247, 10 July 2002.

EU Council, "Asylum Working Party – Outcome of Proceedings of 4–5 June 2002" ("Outcome of Proceedings (ASILE 25)"), 9038/02 ASILE 25, 17 June 2002.

EU Council, "Note from the General Secretariat of the Council to the Asylum Working Party: Compilation of Replies to Questionnaire on Complementary Forms of Protection", 8378/01 ASILE 27, 3 May 2001.

EU Council, "Note from the Presidency to the Asylum Working Party: Discussion Paper on Subsidiary Protection" ("Discussion Paper (ASILE 41)"), 13167/99 ASILE 41, 19 November 1999.

EU Council, "Presidency Conclusions: Tampere European Council, 15 and 16 October 1999" ("Tampere Conclusions"), 16 October 1999, SN 200/99.

EU Council, "Note from the Presidency to the Asylum Working Party: Subsidiary Protection" ("1999 Note from the Austrian Presidency"), 6246/99 ASILE 7, 23 Feburary 1999.

EU Council, "Note from the Presidency to the Asylum Working Party: Subsidiary Protection" ("1998 Note from the Austrian Presidency"), 10811/98 ASIM 193 ASILE 9 MIGR 13, 05 August 1998.

EU Council, "Note from the General Secretariat of the Council to Migration and Asylum Working Parties: Summary of Replies Concerning the National Instruments of Protection Falling Outside the Scope of the Geneva Convention – Subsidiary Protection" ("Summary of replies – subsidiary protection"), 13667/97 ASIM 267, 6 January 1998.

EU Council, "Note from the Presidency to the Asylum and Migration Working Group: Implication of Article 3 of the European Convention on Human Rights for the Expulsion of Illegally Resident Third Country Nationals", 7779/97 ASIM 89, 28 April 1997.

EU Council, "Note from the Danish Delegation to the Asylum and Migration Working Parties: Subsidiary Protection", 6764/97 ASIM 52, 17/03/1997.

EU Council, "Joint Position of 4 March 1996 Defined by the Council on the Basis of Article K.3 of the Treaty on European Union on the Harmonized Application of the Definition of the Term 'Refugee' in Article 1 of the Geneva Convention of 28 July 1951 Relating to the Status of Refugees" ("1996 EU Joint Position on the definition of the term 'refugee' under the Refugee Convention") [13/03/1996] *OJ L 063*, pp. 2–7.

EU Economic and Social Committee, "Opinion of the Economic and Social Committee on the 'Proposal for a Council Directive on Minimum Standards for Giving Temporary Protection in the Event of a Mass Influx of Displaced Persons and on Measures Promoting a Balance of Efforts between Member States in Receiving Such Persons and Bearing the Consequences Thereof'", 2001/C 155/06 [29/05/2001] *OJ C 155/21*.

European Parliament, "Answer Given by Mr Avramopoulos on Behalf of the Commission (Question E-008507/2014)", 28 January 2015.

European Parliament, Question for written answer to the Commission – Rule 130 – Elisabetta Gardini (PPE), "Application of Directive 2001/55/EC", E-008507-14, 29 October 2014.

European Parliament, "EU Accession to the European Convention on Human Rights (Debate)", 19 April 2012, © European Union [2012], retrieved from the website of European Parliament at: <www.europarl.europa.eu> [23/07/2012].

EU: Bitoulas, Alexandros, "Asylum Applicants and First Instance Decisions on Asylum Applications: Second Quarter 2011", 03 February 2012, © European Union, 1995–2012, *Eurostat: Statistics in focus*, retrieved from the website of the European Commission-Eurostat at: <http://epp.eurostat.ec.europa.eu/cache/ITY_OFFPUB/KS-SF-12-011/EN/KS-SF-12-011-EN.PDF> [06/08/2012].

EU: Bitoulas, Alexandros, "Asylum Applicants and First Instance Decisions on Asylum Applications: 2014", March 2015, © European Union, 2015, *Eurostat: Data in focus*, retrieved from the website of the European Commission – Eurostat at: <http://

ec.europa.eu/eurostat/documents/4168041/6742650/KS-QA-15-003-EN-N.pdf/b7786ec9-1ad6-4720-8a1d-430fcfc55018> [01/10/2016].

EU: Albertinelli, Anthony, "Asylum Applicants and First Instance Decisions on Asylum Applications in 2010", May 2011, © European Union, 2011, *Eurostat: Data in focus*, retrieved from the website of the European Commission – Eurostat at: <http://www.emnbelgium.be/sites/default/files/publications/eurostat_2010_overzicht_asiel.pdf> [29/08/2012].

United Nations

CESCR, "General Comment No. 15: The Right to Water" ("GC 15: Right to Water"), E/C.12/2002/11, 2003.

CESCR, "General Comment No. 13: The Right to Education" ("GC 13 (right to education)"), E/C.12/1999/10, 8 December 1999.

CESCR, "General Comment 11: Plans of Action for Primary Education" ("GC 11: primary education"), E/C.12/1999/4, 10 May 1999.

CESCR, "General Comment No. 3: The Nature of States Parties Obligations (Art. 2, Para. 1, of the Covenant)" ("GC 3: The Nature of State Parties' Obligations"), UN Doc. E/1991/23, 14 December 1990.

HRC, "Resolution 16/24: Situation of Human Rights in Myanmar", A/HRC/RES/16/24, 12 April 2011.

HRC, "General Comment No. 31: The Nature of the General Legal Obligation Imposed on States Parties" ("General Comment No. 31"), CCPR/C/21/Rev.1/Add. 13, 26 May 2004.

HRC, "General Comment No. 29: States of Emergency (Article 4)" ("General Comment No. 29"), CCPR/C/21/Rev.1/Add.11, 31 August 2001.

HRC, "General Comment No. 24: Issues Relating to Reservations Made Upon Ratification or Accession to the Covenant or the Optional Protocols Thereto, or in Relation to Declarations under Article 41 of the Covenant" ("General Comment No. 24"), CCPR/C/21/Rev.1/Add.6, 04/11/1994.

HRC, "General Comment No. 20 on Article 7 (Prohibition of Torture, or Other Cruel, Inhuman or Degrading Treatment or Punishment)" ("General Comment No. 20"), 10 March 1992.

HRC, "General Comment No. 15: The Position of Aliens under the Covenant" ("General Comment No. 15"), 11 April 1986.

ILC, Articles on the Prevention of Transboundary Harm from Hazardous Activities, Report of the 53rd Session ("Articles on the Prevention of Transboundary Harm from Hazardous Activities"), UN Doc. A/56/10 (2001) *GAOR, 56th session, Supplement No. 10, at 370.*

ILC, Articles on Responsibility of States for Internationally Wrongful Acts, Report of the 53rd Session ("ILC Articles on State Responsibility"), UN Doc. A/56/10 (2001) *GAOR, 56th session, Supplement No. 10, at 43.*

ILC, "Report of the 63rd session", A/66/10 [2011] *GAOR, 66th session, Supplement No. 10.*

ILC, "Report of the 62nd session", A/65/10 [2010] *GAOR, 65th session, Supplement No. 10.*

ILC, "Report of the 61st session", A/64/10 [2009] *GAOR, 64th session, Supplement No. 10.*

ILC, "Report of the 53rd session", A/CN.4/SER.A/2001/Add.1 (Part 2), 2001 *Yearbook of the International Law Commission* Vol. II, Part Two.

ILC, "Third report on the protection of persons in the event of disasters by Eduardo Valencia-Ospina, Special Rapporteur", A/CN.4/629, 31 March 2010.

ILC, Martti Koskenniemi "Fragmentation of International Law: Difficulties Arising from the Diversification and Expansion of International Law, Report of the Study Group of the International Law Commission", A/CN.4/L.682, 13 April 2006.

OHCHR, Zeid Ra'ad Al Hussein (UN High Commissioner for Human Rights), "Opinion piece: Burning down the house", 3 December 2015, available at: <http://www.ohchr.org/EN/NewsEvents/Pages/BurningDowntheHouse.aspx> [accessed 08/05/2016].

OHCHR, "Annual Report of the United Nations High Commissioner for Human Rights and Reports of the Office of the High Commissioner and the Secretary-General: Report of the Office of the United Nations High Commissioner for Human Rights on the Relationship between Climate Change and Human Rights" ("Report on the relationship between climate change and human rights"), A/HRC/10/61, 15 January 2009.

UN Ad Hoc Committee on Refugees and Stateless Persons, "Report of the Ad Hoc Committee on Statelessness and Related Persons (Lake Success, New York, 16 January to 16 February 1950)" ("E/AC.35/5"), E/1618, E/AC.35/5, 17 February 1950.

UN Ad Hoc Committee on Refugees and Stateless Persons, Ad Hoc Committee on Statelessness and Related Problems, "First Session: Summary Record of the Third Meeting Held at Lake Success, New York, on Tuesday, 17 January 1950, at 3 P.M." ("E/AC.32/SR.3"), E/AC.32/SR.3, 26 January 1950.

UN Ad Hoc Committee on Refugees and Stateless Persons, Ad Hoc Committee on Statelessness and Related Problems, "United States of America: Memorandum on the Definition Article of the Preliminary Draft Convention Relating to the Status of Refugees (and Stateless Persons) (E/AC.32.2)" ("E/AC.32/L.4"), E/AC.32/L.4, 18 January 1950.

UN Ad Hoc Committee on Refugees and Stateless Persons, Ad Hoc Committee on Statelessness and Related Problems, "United Kingdom: Revised Draft Proposal for Article 1 (E/AC.32/2)", E/AC.32/L.2/Rev.1, 19 January 1950.

UN Ad Hoc Committee on Refugees and Stateless Persons, Ad Hoc Committee on Statelessness and Related Problems, "France: Proposal for a Draft Convention Preamble", E/AC.32/L.3, 17 January 1950.

UN Commission on Human Rights, Report of the Representative of the Secretary-General, Mr. Francis M. Deng, submitted pursuant to Commission resolution 1997/39. Addendum: Guiding Principles on Internal Displacement ("Guiding Principles on Internal Displacement"), E/CN.4/1998/53/Add.2, 11 February 1998.

UN Conference of Plenipotentiaries on the Status of Refugees and Stateless Persons, "Conference of Plenipotentiaries on the Status of Refugees and Stateless Persons: Summary Record of the Thirty-Third Meeting", A/CONF.2/SR.33, 30 November 1951.

UN Conference of Plenipotentiaries on the Status of Refugees and Stateless Persons, "Conference of Plenipotentiaries on the Status of Refugees and Stateless Persons: Summary Record of the 24th Meeting", A/CONF.2/SR.24, 27 November 1951.

UN Conference of Plenipotentiaries on the Status of Refugees and Stateless Persons, "Summary Record of the Nineteenth Meeting" ("A/CONF.2/SR.19"), 26 November 1951.

UN Conference of Plenipotentiaries on the Status of Refugees and Stateless Persons, "Draft Convention Relating to the Status of Refugees, United Kingdom: Recommendation for Inclusion in the Final Act", A/CONF.2/107, 25 July 1951.

UN Conference of Plenipotentiaries on the Status of Refugees and Stateless Persons, "Summary Record of the 31st Meeting", 20 July 1951.

UN Conference on Sustainable Development, "Outcome of the Conference: The Future We Want", A/CONF.216/L.1 [19 June 2012].

UN ECOSOC, "UN ESCOR, 11th Session, 158th Meeting".

UN ECOSOC, "Resolutions 319 (XI): Refugees and Stateless Persons" ("Resolutions 319 (XI)"), E/RES/319 (XI), 11 and 16 August 1950, pp. 52–59.

UN ECOSOC, "France: Amendment to the Draft Convention Relating to the Status of Refugees", UN Doc. E/L.82, 29 July 1950.

United Nations Framework Convention on Climate Change (UNFCCC), *Report of the Conference of the Parties on its twenty-first session, held in Paris from 30 November to 13 December 2015*, FCCC/CP/2015/10/Add.1, 29 January 2016, Addendum, Part two: Action taken by the Conference of the Parties at its twenty-first session, "Decision 1/CP.21: Adoption of the Paris Agreement", pp. 2–36.

United Nations Framework Convention on Climate Change (UNFCCC), *Report of the Conference of the Parties on its nineteenth session, held in Warsaw from 11 to 23 November 2013*, FCCC/CP/2013/10/Add.1, 31 January 2014, Addendum, Part two: Action taken by the Conference of the Parties at its twenty-first session, FCCC/CP/2013/10/Add.1, "Decision 2/CP.19 Warsaw international mechanism for loss and damage associated with climate change impacts".

United Nations Framework Convention on Climate Change (UNFCCC), *Report of the Conference of the Parties on its seventeenth session, held in Durban from 28 November to 11 December 2011*, "Decision 3/CP.17: Launching the Green Climate Fund" ("Decision 3/CP.17"), FCCC/CP/2011/9/Add.1, 15 March 2012.

United Nations Framework Convention on Climate Change (UNFCCC), *Report of the Conference of the Parties on its Sixteenth Session*, held in Cancun from 29 November to 10 December 2010, FCCC/CP/2010/7/Add.1, 15/03/2011.

United Nations Framework Convention on Climate Change (UNFCCC), *Report of the Conference of the Parties on its Sixteenth Session, held in Cancun from 29 November to*

10 December 2010, FCCC/CP/2010/7/Add.1, 15/03/2011, "Decision 1/CP.16: The Cancun Agreements: Outcome of the work of the Ad Hoc Working Group on Long-term Cooperative Action under the Convention".

UN, "Debate before the Economic and Social Council", E/AC.7/SR.166, 22 August 1950.

UNGA, "A More Secure World: Our Shared Responsibility, Report of the High-Level Panel on Threats, Challenges and Change" ("A More Secure World"), A/59/565, 2 December 2004, also available at: <http://www.un.org/secureworld/report2.pdf>.

UNGA, "Climate Change and Its Possible Security Implications: Report of the Secretary-General" ("Climate change and its possible security implications"), A/64/350, 11 September 2009.

UNGA, "Declaration on Territorial Asylum", A/RES/2312(XXII) [14 December 1967].

UNGA, "Draft Convention Relating to the Status of Refugees" ("UNGA"), A/RES/429, 14 December 1950.

UNGA, "International Co-Operation to Avert New Flows of Refugees: Note by the Secretary-General" ("International Co-operation to Avert New Flows of Refugees"), A/41/324, 13 May 1986.

UNGA, "Protection of Human Rights and Fundamental Freedoms While Countering Terrorism: Note by the Secretary-General, Report of the Special Rapporteur on the Promotion and Protection of Human Rights and Fundamental Freedoms While Countering Terrorism" ("General Secretariat's Note on Human Rights and counter-terrorism"), A/62/263, 15 August 2007.

UNGA, "Resolution 69/283: Sendai Framework for Disaster Risk Reduction 2015-2030", A/RES/69/283, 23 June 2015.

UNGA, "Resolution 66/100 on the Responsibility of International Organizations", A/RES/66/100, 9 December 2011.

UNGA, "Resolution 64/292: The human right to water and sanitation", A/RES/64/292, 3 August 2010.

UNGA, "Resolution 64/292 on the human right to water and sanitation", A/RES/64/292, 28 July 2010.

UNGA, "Resolution 62/149: Moratorium on the Use of the Death Penalty" ("Moratorium on the use of the death penalty"), A/RES/62/149, 26 February 2008.

UNGA, "Responsibility of States for Internationally Wrongful Acts: Resolution / Adopted by the General Assembly", A/RES/62/61, 8 January 2008.

UNGA, "Resolution 60/251: Human Rights Council", A/RES/60/251, 3 April 2006.

UNGA, "Resolution 56/166: Human rights and mass exoduses", A/RES/56/166, 26 February 2002.

UNGA, "Resolution 43/53: Protection of Global Climate for Present and Future Generations of Mankind", A/RES/43/53, 6 December 1988.

UNGA, "Resolution 51/113 on the Situation of Human Rights in Cuba", A/RES/51/113, 7 March 1997.

UNGA, "Report of the United Nations High Commissioner for Refugees (1976)" ("1976 Report of UNHCR"), A/RES/31/35 (XXXI), 30 November 1976.

UNGA, "Report of the United Nations High Commissioner for Refugees (1975)" ("1975 Report of UNHCR"), A/RES/3454 (XXX), 9 December 1975.

UNGA, "Humanitarian assistance to the Indo-Chinese displaced persons", A/RES/3455 (XXX), 9 December 1975.

UNGA, "Report of the United Nations High Commissioner for Refugees (1969)" ("1969 Report of UNHCR"), A/RES/2594 (XXIV), 16 December 1969.

UNGA, "Report of the United Nations High Commissioner for Refugees (1968)" ("1968 Report of UNHCR"), A/RES/2399 (XXIII), 6 December 1968.

UNGA, "Report of the United Nations High Commissioner for Refugees (1965)" ("1965 Report of UNHCR"), A/RES/2039 (XX), 7 December 1965.

UNHCR, "Background Paper" issued ahead of the High Commissioner's Dialogue on Protection Challenges on the theme "Understanding and addressing root causes of displacement" (held in Geneva on 16–17 December 2015), 17 November 2015, available at: < http://www.unhcr.org/564c53429.html> [accessed 01/06/2016], pp. 6–8;.

UNHCR, António Guterres, "Closing remarks by the United Nations High Commissioner for Refugees", delivered in closing of the UNHCR Intergovernmental Meeting at Ministerial level to mark the 60th anniversary of the 1951 Convention relating to the Status of Refugees and the 50th anniversary of the 1961 Convention on the Reduction of Statelessness (held in Geneva, on 7–8 December 2011), available at: <http://www.unhcr.org/4ef094a89.html> [accessed 10/10/2016].

UNHCR, António Guterres, "Statement by Mr. António Guterres, United Nations High Commissioner for Refugees", delivered during the UNHCR Intergovernmental Meeting at Ministerial Level to mark the 60th anniversary of the 1951 Convention relating to the Status of Refugees and the 50th anniversary of the 1961 Convention on the Reduction of Statelessness (held in Geneva, on 7–8 December 2011), avialbale at: <http://www.unhcr.org/4ecd0cde9.html> [accessed 08/10/2016].

By: António Guterres | 7 December 2011 UNHCR, Intergovernmental Event at the Ministerial Level of Member States of the United Nations on the Occasion of the 60th Anniversary of the 1951 Convention relating to the Status of Refugees and the 50th Anniversary of the 1961 Convention on the Reduction of Statelessness (7–8 December 2011), "Background Note for the Roundtables", HCR/MINCOM-MS/2011/08, 18 November 2011.

UNHCR, Expert meeting on climate change and displacement (Bellagio, Italy, 22–26 February 2011), "Summary of Deliberations on Climate Change and Displacement", available at: <http://www.unhcr.org/4da2b5e19.pdf> [accessed 19/10/2016].

UNHCR, "Updated UNHCR Information Note on National Practice in the Application of Article 3(2) of the Dublin II Regulation in Particular in the Context of Intended Transfers to Greece", 31 January 2011.

UNHCR, "Background paper to the 2010 High Commissioner's Dialogue on Protection Challenges: Protection Gaps and Responses", 30 November 2010, available at: UNHCR <http://www.unhcr.org/4cebeeee9.html>, pp. 2–4 [accessed 10/12/2015].

UNHCR, "Background paper to the 2010 High Commissioner's Dialogue on Protection Challenges: Protection Gaps and Responses", 30 November 2010, available at: UNHCR <http://www.unhcr.org/4cebeeee9.html>, pp. 2–4 [accessed 10/12/2015].

UNHCR, "UNHCR's Eligibility Guidelines for Assessing the International Protection Needs of Individuals from Kosovo", HCR/EG/09/01, 9 November 2009.

UNHCR, "Climate Change, Natural Disasters and Human Displacement: A UNHCR Perspective", 23 October 2009.

UNHCR, "UNHCR Comments on the European Commission's Proposal for a Directive of the European Parliament and of the Council on Minimum Standards for the Qualification and Status of Third Country Nationals or Stateless Persons as Beneficiaries of International Protection and the Content of the Protection Granted (Com(2009)551, 21 October 2009)" ("Comments on Proposal for Recast QD") (July 2010).

UNHCR, "Revised Note on the Applicability of Article 1D of the 1951 Convention Relating to the Status of Refugees to Palestinian Refugees", October 2009.

UNHCR, "Statement on Article 1F of the 1951 Convention: Issued in the Context of the Preliminary Ruling References to the Court of Justice of the European Communities from the German Federal Administrative Court Regarding the Interpretation of Articles 12(2)(B) and (C) of the Qualification Directive" ("Statement on Article 1F of the 1951 Convention"), July 2009.

UNHCR, "Submission by UNHCR in the Case of *QD (Iraq) v. Secretary of State for the Home Department*", 31 May 2009.

UNHRC, "Resolution 10/4 on Human Rights and Climate Change" ("Resolution 10/4"), A/HRC/RES/10/4, 25 March 2009.

UNHRC, "Resolution 7/23 on Human Rights and Climate Change" ("Resolution 7/23"), A/HRC/RES/7/23, 28 March 2008.

UNHCR, "Statement Subsidiary Protection under the EC Qualification Directive for People Threatened by Indiscriminate Viole", January 2008.

UNHCR, "Statement on Subsidiary Protection under the EC Qualification Directive for People Threatened by Indiscriminate Violence" ("Statement on Article 15(c) QD"), January 2008.

UNHCR, "Advisory Opinion on the Extraterritorial Application of Non-Refoulement Obligations under the 1951 Convention Relating to the Status of Refugees and Its 1967 Protocol", 26 January 2007.

UNHCR, "Providing International Protection Including Through Complementary Forms of Protection", EC/55/SC/CRP.16, 2 June 2005.

UNHCR, "Providing International Protection Including through Complementary Forms of Protection" ("Complementary Forms of Protection"), EC/55/SC/CRP.16, 2 June 2005.

UNHCR, "UNHCR Annotated Comments on the EC Council Directive 2004/83/EC of 29 April 2004 on Minimum Standards for the Qualification and Status of Third Country Nationals or Stateless Persons as Refugees or as Persons Who Otherwise Need International Protection and the Content of the Protection Granted (OJ L 304/12 of 30.9.2004)" ("Annotated Comments on QD (2004)") [January 2005].

UNHCR, "Ensuring International Protection and Enhancing International Cooperation in Mass Influx Situations", EC/54/SC/CRP.11, 7 June 2004.

UNHCR, "Note on Key Issues of Concern to UNHCR on the Draft Qualification Directive", March 2004.

UNHCR, "Guidelines on International Protection, Application of the Exclusion Clauses: Article 1F of the 1951 Convention Relating to the Status of Refugees" ("Guidelines on the application of the exclusion clauses"), HCR/GIP/03/05, 4 September 2003.

UNCHR, "Some Additional Observations and Recommendations on the European Commission 'Proposal for a Council Directive on Minimum Standards for the Qualification and Status of Third Country Nationals and Stateless Persons as Refugees or as Persons Who Otherwise Need International Protection' (Com(2001) 510 Final, 2001/0207(Cns) of 12 September 2001)" ("Some additional obsevations and recommendations on QD (2004) Proposal"), July 2002.

UNHCR, "Global Consultations on International Protection, Protection of Refugees in Mass Influx Situations: Overall Protection Framework" ("Protection of Refugees in Mass Influx Situations (Global Consultation)"), EC/GC/01/4, 19 February 2001.

UNHCR, "Complementary Forms of Protection: Their Nature and Relationship to the International Refugee Protection Regime" ("Complementary Forms of Protection"), EC/50/SC/CRP.18, 9 June 2000.

UNHCR, "Note on Burden and Standard of Proof in Refugee Claims", 16 December 1998.

UNHCR, "Position on the Proposal of the European Council Concerning the Treatment of Asylum Applications from Citizens of European Union Member States" (Geneva, January 1997).

UNHCR, "General Conclusion on International Protection" ("General Conclusion No. 79 on International Protection"), No. 79 (XLVII), 11 October 1996.

UNHCR ExCom, "Conclusion No. 74 (Vlv) General (1994)" ("Conclusion No. 74 'General' (1994)").

UNHCR, "Note on International Protection (Submitted by the High Commissioner)" ("Note on International Protection (1994)"), A/AC.96/830, 7 September 1994.

UNHCR, "The Principle of Non-Refoulement as a Norm of Customary International Law: Response to the Questions Posed to UNHCR by the Federal Constitutional Court of the Federal Republic of Germany in Cases 2 Bvr 1938/93, 2 Bvr 1953/93, 2 Bvr 1954/93", 31 January 1994.

UNHCR, "Report of the Working Group on Solutions and Protection to the Forty-Second Session of the Executive Committee of the High Commissioner's Programme", EC/SCP/64, 12 August 1991.

UNHCR ExCom, "Conclusion No. 25 (XXXIII) General (1982)" ("Conclusion No 25 'General' (1982)").

UNHCR ExCom, "Conclusion No. 22 (XXXII) Protection of Asylum-Seekers in Situations of Large- Scale Influx (1981)" ("Conclusion No 22 on Large-Scale Influx (1981)").

UNHCR ExCom, "Conclusion No. 19 (XXXI) Temporary Refuge (1980)" ("Conclusion No 19 on Temporary Refuge (1980)").

UNHCR ExCom, "Conclusion No. 17 (XXXI) Problems of Extradition Affecting Refugees (1980)" ("Conclusion No 17 on Extradition (1980)").

UNHCR ExCom, "Conclusion No. 6 (XXVIII) *Non-Refoulement* (1977)" ("Conclusion No 6 on *Non-refoulement* (1977)").

UNHCR, "Colloquium on the Development in the Law of Refugees with Particular Reference to the 1951 Convention and the Statute of the Office of the United Nations High Commissioner for Refugees Held at Villa Serbelloni Bellagio (Italy) from 21–28 April 1965: Background Paper Submitted by the Office of the United Nations High Commissioner for Refugees, Palais Des Nations, Geneva, Switzerland, 1965, 28 April 1965, Mhcr/23/65; 67-1809".

OHCHR, "Understanding Human Rights and Climate Change", submission of the Office of the High Commissioner for Human Rights to the 21st Conference of the Parties to the UNFCCC, 2015, available at: <http://www.ohchr.org/Documents/Issues/ClimateChange/COP21.pdf> [accessed 10/04/2016].

UNHRC, "Report of the Independent Expert on the Situation of Human Rights in Haiti, Michel Forst, Addendum: Forced Returns of Haitians from Third States", A/HRC/20/35/Add.1, 4 June 2012.

UNHRC, "Resolution 18/22 on Human Rights and Climate Change" ("Resolution 18/22"), A/HRC/RES/18/22, 17 October 2011.

UNHRC, "Resolution 16/31: Israeli Settlements in the Occupied Palestinian Territory, Including East Jerusalem, and in the Occupied Syrian Golan", A/HRC/RES/16/31, 13 April 2011.

UNHRC, "Resolution 16/11 on Human Rights and the Environment" ("Resolution 16/11"), A/HRC/RES/16/11, 12 April 2011.

UNHRC, "Human Rights and Access to Safe Drinking Water and Sanitation", A/HRC/RES/15/9, 30 September 2010.

UN Secretary-General, "Report of the Secretary-General on the United Nations Stabilization Mission in Haiti", S/2010/200, 22 February 2010.

UN Secretary-General, "Protection of Human Rights and Fundamental Freedoms While Countering Terrorism: Note by the Secretary General", UN Doc. A/ 62/263, UN GAOR, 62nd Session [2007].

UN Secretary-General, "Report of the Secretary-General: Progress Report on the Prevention of Armed Conflict" ("Progress report on the prevention of armed conflict"), A/60/891, 18 July 2006.

World Conference on Human Rights, "Vienna Declaration and Programme of Action", UN Doc A/CONF.157/23, 12 July 1993.

Others

ACnHPR, "Resolution 105 on the Prevention and Prohibition of Torture and Other Cruel, Inhuman or Degrading Treatment or Punishment" ("Resolution 105"), ACHPR/Res.105 (XXXXI), 30 May 2007.

CNCDH, "Avis sur les conditions d'exercice du droit d'asile en France" ("Avis 2006"), 29 juin 2006.

ECRE, "Complementary/Subsidiary Forms of Protection in the EU Member States: An Overview" ("Complementary/Subsidiary Forms of Protection"), December 2003, updated in July 2004.

ECRE, "Comments from the European Council on Refugees and Exiles on the Proposal for a Council Directive on Minimum Standards for the Qualification and Status of Third Country Nationals and Stateless Persons as Refugees or as Persons Who Otherwise Need International Protection (Brussels, 12.9.2001, Com(2001) 510 Final)" ("Comments on QD (2004) Proposal"), March 2002.

NATO, Statement by Mr Mendes-France, Chairman of the North Atlantic Council, at the Meeting of the North Atlantic Council Held on 9th September 1954, C-M(54)71 (unclassified an public disclosed) ⌊10 September 1954⌋ *NATO Secret doc.*

NATO, "Verbatim Record of the 22nd Meeting of the Council Held on Friday, 24th April, 1953 at 11 a.m. at the Palais de Chaillot, Paris XVIe". *NATO Secret Verbatim Record C-VR(53)2 (unclassified and public disclosed).*

OAS General Assembly, "Resolution on the Legal Situation of Refugees, Returnees and Displaced Persons in the American Hemisphere", AG/RES.1170 (XXII-0/92), 23 May 1992.

VluchtelingenWerk, "Article 15(c): Qualification for Subsidiary Protection Status and the Definition of Serious Harm", © 2012 Qualification Directive, retrieved from the website of the project Networking on the Transposition of the Qualification Directive [01/07/2012].

WMO, World Meteorological Organization, "40th Session of the Wmo Executive Council: Intergovernmental Panel on Climate Change", Res. 4 (EC-XL), 1988.

National law

Australia
Migration Act 1958: An Act relating to the entry into, and presence in, Australia of aliens, and the departure or deportation from Australia of aliens and certain other persons of 8 Oct 1958, C1958A00062 No. 62, 1958.

Migration Amendment (Complementary Protection) Act 2011: An Act to Amend the Migration Act 1958, and for Related Purposes of 14 Oct 2011, in force 24 March 2012 [24 Oct 2011], C2011A00121 No. 121, 2011.

Belgium
Loi du 15 décembre 1980 sur l'accès au territoire, le séjour, l'établissement et l'éloignement des étrangers of 15 December 1980 [Version of 22 September 2011].

Brazil
Resolução Normativa No 97: Dispõe Sobre a Concessão Do Visto Permanente Previsto No Art. 16 Da Lei No 6.815, de 19 de Agostode 1980, a Nacionais Do Haiti of 12 January 2012.

Czech Republic
Act of 11 November 1999 on Asylum and Amendment to Act No. 283/1991 Coll., on the Police of the Czech Republic, as Amended (the Asylum Act), 325/1999 Coll., consolidated version of 31 January 2008.

Finland
Aliens Act (301/2004, Amendments up to 1152/2010 Included) (hereafter "Finnish Aliens Act") [Unofficial translation published by the Finnish Minitry of the Interior].

France
Caresche, Christophe and Thierry Mariani, Assemblée nationale Commission des affaires européennes, "Rapport fait au nom de la commission des affaires européennes sur la proposition de resolution (n° 2153) de Mme Sandrine Mazetier et plusieurs de ses collegues et les membres du groupe socialiste, radical, citoyen et divers gauche et apparentés, sur la Protection Temporaire", 19 janvier 2010.

Circulaire d'application de la loi N° 98–349 Du 11 Mai 1998 relative à l'entree et au sejour des étrangers en France et au droit d'asile, n° NOR/INT/D/98/00108/C, 12 May 1998.

Code de l'entrée et du séjour des étrangers et du droit d'asile (hereafter "CESEDA"), Consolidated version of 20 June 2012.

Loi no 98–349 du 11 mai 1998 relative à l'entrée et au séjour des étrangers en France et au droit d'asile of 11 May 1998 (hereafter "Loi no 98-349") [12 mai 1998] *JORF*, 109, p. 7087.

Loi n° 52–893 relative au droit d'asile of 25 July 1952 [27 July 1952] *JORF*, p. 7642 amended by Loi no 98–349 relative à l'entrée et au séjour des étrangers en France et au droit d'asile of 11 May 1998 [12 May 1998] *JORF n° 109*, p. 7087.

Germany
Aufenthaltsgesetz of 30 July 2004 (hereafter "AufenthG") [25 February 2008] *BGBl. I*, p. 162, last amended by Article 1 and Article 6 paragraph 2 of the Act of 1 June 2012, *BGBl. I*, p. 1224.

Gesetz über den Aufenthalt, die Erwerbstätigkeit und die Integration von Ausländern im Bundesgebiet of 30 July 2004, in the version published of 25 February 2008 (hereafter "AufenthG") *BGBl. I*, p. 162, last amended by Article 1 and Article 6, § 2 of the Law of 1 June 2012, *BGBl. I*, p. 1224.

Luxembourg
Loi du 29 août 2008 portant sur la libre circulation des personnes et l'immigration (hereafter "Loi sur la libre circulation des personnes et l'immigration") [10 September 2008] *Mémorial A*, no 138, last amended by Loi du 1er juillet 2011 modifiant la loi modifiée du 29 août 2008 sur la libre circulation des personnes et l'immigration et la loi modifiée du 5 mai 2006 relative au droit d'asile et à des formes complémentaires de protection of 1 July 2011, [25 July 2011] *Mémorial A no 151*, p. 2179.

Loi du 5 mai 2006 relative au droit d'asile et à des formes complémentaires de protection of 5 May 2006 (hereafter "Loi sur le droit d'asile et les formes complémentaires de protection"), 78 [9 May 2006] *Mémorial A*, p. 1402 of 25 July 2011, last amended by Loi du 1er juillet 2011 modifiant la loi modifiée du 29 août 2008 sur la libre circulation des personnes et l'immigration et la loi modifiée du 5 mai 2006 relative au droit d'asile et à des formes complémentaires de protection of 1 July 2011, *Memorial A no 151*, p. 2179.

Texte coordonné du 27 décembre 2006 de la loi du 28 mars 1972 concernant l'entrée et le séjour des étrangers [27/12/2006] *Mémorial A*, no 230, pp. 4104–4116.

Mexico
Ley de Refugiados Y Protección Complementaria of 9 December 2010, entered into force 28 January 2011 [27 January 2011] *Diário Oficial de la Federación*.

New Zealand
New Zealand: Immigration Act 2009, 2009 No 51, 16 November 2009.

Sweden
Act Amending the Aliens Act (2005:716) of 31 March 2006, Issued on 17 December 2009.

Aliens Act (*Utlänningslag*) (hereafter "Utlänningslag"), SFS 2005:716, 29 September 2005, entered into force 31 March 2006, last amended by *Lag om ändring i utlänningslagen* of 11 June 2012, SFS 2012:322.

Aliens Act – Guiding Decision, Reg. 23–94.

"Regeringens Proposition 2004/05:170: Ny Instans- Och Processordning I Utlännings- Och Medborgarskapsärenden" ("Regeringens proposition 2004/05:170"), 26 May 2005.

Riksdag (Swedish Parliament) Socialförsäkringsutskottet (Social Committee), "2009/10:Sfu14 Migration Och Asylpolitik – Riksdagen" [2010].

Switzerland

Loi fédérale sur les étrangers ("LEtr") du 16 décembre 2005 of 16 December 2005 [Version of 11 October 2011] *RO 2007 5437*, 142.20.

Loi sur l'asile (LAsi) of 26 June 1998 [Version of 1 avril 2011] *RO 1999 2262*, 142.31.

United Kingdom

Immigration Rules, Part 11b – Asylum, Last Updated October 2012 (hereafter "Immigration Rules").

Home Office UK Border Agency, "Asylum Process Guidance: Considering Human Rights Claims" ("APG Human Rights Claims"), last updated 10 August 2012 at: <www.ukba.homeoffice.gov.uk/sitecontent/documents/policyandlaw/asylumprocessguidance/consideringanddecidingtheclaim/guidance/consideringhrclaims.pdf?view=Binary>.

Home Office UK Border Agency, "Asylum Policy Instructions: Discretionary Leave", Last updated 13 July 2012 at: <www.ukba.homeoffice.gov.uk/sitecontent/documents/policyandlaw/asylumpolicyinstructions/apis/discretionaryleave.pdf?view=Binary>.

Home Office UK Border Agency, "Asylum Policy Instructions: Humanitarian Protection" ("API Humanitarian Conditions"), Last updated 13 July 2012 at: <www.ukba.homeoffice.gov.uk/sitecontent/documents/policyandlaw/asylumpolicyinstructions/apis/humanitarian-protection.pdf?view=Binary>.

Home Office UK Border Agency, "Casework Instruction on Humanitarian Protection: Article 15 (C) of Qualification Directive" ("Casework Instruction: Article 15(c) QD"), September 2010.

Immigration Rules – Part 11: Asylum, HC 395 [23 May 1994], last updated July 2012.

Immigration Rules (HC 395), made under section 3(2) of the Immigration Act 1971, last updated in July 2012 (hereafter "Immigration Rules").

United States

Immigration and Nationality Act (hereafter "INA"), as amended 4 March 2010.

An Act to Deter and Punish Terrorist Acts in the United States and around the World, to Enhance Law Enforcement Investigatory Tools, and for Other Purposes of 26 October 2001 (hereafter "PATRIOT Act").

Literature

Books

Afifi, Tamer, Radha Govil, Patrick Sakdapolrak and Koko Warner, *Climate Change, Vulnerability and Human Mobility: Perspectives of Refugees from the East and Horn of Africa*, Report No. 1, Partnership between UNU and UNHCR (Bonn: United Nations University Institute for Environment and Human Security – UNU-EHS, June 2012).

Akande, Dapo, "International Organizations", *in* Evans, Malcolm D. (Ed.), *International Law* (New York: Oxford, 2003), pp. 269–297.

Baldaccini, Anneliese (Eds.), *Terrorism and the Foreigner: A Decade of Tension around the Rule of Law in Europe* (Leiden: Martinus Nijhoff Publishers, 2007).

Battjes, Hemme, *European Asylum Law and International Law*, Collection Immigration and Asylum Law and Policy in Europe (Leiden: Brill Academic Publishers, 2006).

Battjes, Hemme, "Subsidiary Protection and Reduced Rights", *in* Zwaan, Karin (Ed.), *The Qualification Directive: Central Themes, Problem Issues, and Implementation in Selected Member States* (Nijmegen: Wolf Legal Publishers, 2007), pp. 49–55.

Beirens, Hanne, Sheila Maas, Salvatore Petronella and Maurice van Der Velden, *Study on the Temporary Protection Directive: Final Report* (Luxembourg: Publications Office of the European Union, 2016).

Bertin, Anne, CHF, GARR and GISTI, *Appui aux migrants haïtiens: sensibiliser, accompagner, plaider – Carnet de route d'une année d'expérience* (Paris: Collectif Haïti de France, March 2012).

Beyani, Chaloka, "The Legal Premises for the International Protection of Human Rights", *in The Reality of International Law: Essays in Honour of Ian Brownlie* (New York: Oxford University Press, 1999).

Birnie, Patricia W., Alan E. Boyle and Catherine Redgwell, *International Law and the Environment*, 3rd ed. (Oxford, New York: Oxford University Press, 2009).

Birnie, Patricia, Alan Boyle and Caterine Redgwell, *International Law and the Environment*, 3rd ed. (Oxford: OUP, 2009).

Boca, Caterina, Franco Pittau, Antonio Ricci and Dossier Statistico Immigrazione Caritas/Migrantes, *The Practices in Italy Concerning the Granting of Non-EU Harmonized Protection Statuses* (Rome: Centro Studi e Ricerche IDOS – Italian National Contact Point for the European Migration Network, 2009).

Bossuyt, Marc J., *Guide to the "Travaux Préparatoires" to the International Covenant on Civil and Political Rights* (Dordrecht: Martinus Nijhoff Publishers, 1987).

Brown, Oli, *Migration and Climate Change*, IOM Migration Research Series, No. 31 (Geneva: IOM, 2008).

Brown, Oli and International Organization for Migration., *Migration and Climate Change*, IOM migration research series, Vol. 31 (Geneva: International Organization for Migration, 2008).

Brown Weiss, Edith (Ed.) *Environmental Change and International Law: New Challenges and Dimensions* (Tokyo: The United Nations University, 1992).

Brownlie, Ian and Guy S. Goodwin-Gill (Eds.), *Basic Documents on Human Rights*, 6th ed. (New York: Oxford University Press, 2010).

Brownlie, Ian, "State Responsibility: The Problem of Delegation", *in* Ginther, Konrad, Gerhard Hafner, Winfried Lang, Hanspeter Neuhold and Lilly Sucharipa-Behrmann (Eds.), *Völkerrecht Zwischen Normativem Anspruch Und Politischer Realität: Festschrift Für Karl Zemanek Zum 65. Geburtstag* (Berlin: Duncker & Humblot GmbH, 1994).

Buddemeier, Brooke R., Larry D. Brandt, Kyle K. Millage and Joshua E. Valentine, *Key Response Planning Factors for the Aftermath of Nuclear Terrorism* (Livermore: Lawrence Livermore National Laboratory, November 2011).

Cançado Trindade, Antônio Augusto, "The Contribution of International Human Rights Law to Environmental Protection, with Special Reference to Global Environmental Change", *in* Brown Weiss, Edith (Ed.), *Environmental Change and International Law: New Challenges and Dimensions* (Tokyo: The United Nations University, 1992).

Carlier, Jean-Yves, "General Report", *in* Carlier, Jean-Yves, Dirk Vanheule, Klaus Hullmann and Carlos Peña Galiano (Eds.), *Who Is a Refugee? A Comparative Case Law Study* (The Hague: Kluwer Law International, 1997), pp. 683–718.

Carlier, Jean-Yves, "General Report", *in* Carlier, Jean-Yves, Dirk Vanheule, Klaus Hullmann and Carlos Peña Galiano (Eds.), *Who Is a Refugee? A Comparative Case Law Study* (The Hague: Kluwer Law International, 1997).

Carlier, Jean-Yves, "The Geneva Refugee Definition and the 'Theory of the Three Scales'", *in* Nicholson, Frances and Patrick Twomey (Eds.), *Refugee Rights and Realities: Evolving International Concepts and Regimes* (Cambridge: Cambridge University Press, 1999).

Cernea, Michael M., "Déplacement forcé et réinstallation de populations : recherche, politiques d'intervention et planification", *in* Cernea, Michael M. (Ed.), *La Dimension Humaine Dans Les Projets de Développement: Les Variables Sociologiques Et Culturelles* (Karthala Editions 1999), pp. 207s.

Chabaké, Tarek Abou (Ed.) *UNHCR Statistical Yearbook 2010: Trends in Displacement, Protection and Solutions*, 10th ed. (Geneva: UNHCR, 2011).

Chaskalson, Arthur, "Human Dignity as a Constitutional Value", *in* Kretzmer, David and Eckart Klein (Eds.), *The Concept of Human Dignity in Human Rights Discourse* (The Hague: Kluwer Law International, 2002), pp. 133–144.

Chetail, Vincent, "The Implementation of the Qualification Directive in France: One Step Forward and Two Steps Backwards", *in* Zwaan, Karin (Ed.), *The Qualification Directive: Central Themes, Problem Issues, and Implementation in Selected Member States* (Nijmegen: Wolf Legal Publishers, 2007), pp. 87–102.

Chimni, B.S. (Ed.) *International Refugee Law: A Reader*, First ed. (New Delhi: Sage Publications, 2000).

CNA Corporation, *National Security and the Threat of Climate Change* (Alexandria, VA: CNA Corporation, 2007).

Colard-Fabregoule, Catherine and Christel Cournil (Eds.), *Changements climatiques et défis du droit, Actes de la journée d'études du 24 mars 2009* (Bruxelles: Bruylant, 2010).

Coleman, Nils, "From Gulf War to Gulf War: Years of Security Concern in Immigration and Asylum Policies at European Level", *in* Guild, Elspeth and Collectif Argos, *Climate Refugees* (Cambridge, MA: Massachusetts Institute of Technology Press, 2010).

Collins, M., R. Knutti, J. Arblaster, J.-L. Dufresne, T. Fichefet, P. Friedlingstein, X. Gao, W.J. Gutowski, T. Johns, G. Krinner, M. Shongwe, C. Tebaldi, A.J. Weaver and M. Wehner, "2013: Long-Term Climate Change: Projections, Commitments and Irreversibility", *in* Stocker, T.F., D. Qin, G.-K. Plattner, M. Tignor, S.K. Allen, J. Boschung, A. Nauels, Y. Xia, V. Bex and P.M. Midgley (Eds.), *Climate Change 2013: The Physical Science Basis. Contribution of Working Group I to the Fifth Assessment Report of the Intergovernmental Panel on Climate Change* (Cambridge, New York: Cambridge University Press, 2013).

Combacau, Jean and Serge Sur, *Droit International Public*, 6th ed. (Paris: Montchrestien, 2004).

Core Writing Team, Sarah Cliffe and Nigel Roberts (Eds.), *World Development Report 2011: Conflict, Security, and Development* (Washington, DC: The World Bank, 2011).

Corlett, David, *Stormy Weather: The Challenge of Climate Change and Displacement* (Sydney, NSW: University of New South Wales, 2008).

Cournil, Christel, "The Protection of 'Environmental Refugees' in International Law", *in* Piguet, Etienne, Paul de Guchteneire and Antoine Pécoud (Eds.), *Migration and Climate Change* (Cambridge, New York: Cambridge University Press, UNESCO Publishing, 2011), pp. 359–387.

Cournil, Christel, "Quelle protection juridique pour les 'réfugiés écologiques' ?", *in* GISTI (Ed.), *Quel Statut Pour Les Réfugiés Environnementaux ? Actes de La Journée Du 14 Décembre 2007* (Paris: Gisti, Juin 2008), pp. 18–23.

Craig, Paul and Gráinne de Búrca, *EU Law: Text, Cases, and Materials*, 3rd ed. (Oxford: Oxford University Press, 2003).

Craig, Paul and Gráinne de Búrca, *EU Law: Text, Cases, and Materials*, 4th ed. (Oxford: Oxford University Press, 2008).

Craig, Paul and Gráinne de Búrca, *EU Law: Text, Cases, and Materials*, 5th ed. (Oxford: Oxford University Press, 2011).

Diallo, Khassoum and Tarek Abou Chabaké (Eds.), *UNHCR Statistical Yearbook 2009: Trends in Displacement, Protection and Solutions* (Geneva: UNHCR, 2009).

Da Lomba, Sylvie, *The Right to Seek Refugee Status in the European Union* (Antwerp, Oxford, New York: Intersentia, 2004).

Donald, Jeanne Ann, *Prosecution or Persecution? Political Offenders and the 1951 Convention Refugee Definition* (Ann Arbor: UMI Dissertation Services, 1997).

Autorité de Sûreté Nucléaire, "Rapport sur l'état de la sûreté nucléaire et de la radioprotection en France en 2011", Dumont, Jean-Jacques, Michel Bourguignon, Andre-Claude Lacoste, Marie-Pierre Comets and Philippe Jamet (Eds.) (Paris: 2012).

Dyer, Gwynne, *Climate Wars: The Fight for Survival as the World Overheats* (Oxford: Oneworld, 2011).

ECRE, *Complementary Protection in Europe* (Brussels: European Council on Refugees and Exiles, July 2009).

Einarsen, Terje, "Drafting History of the 1951 Convention and the 1967 Protocol", *in* Zimmermann, Andreas (Ed.), *The 1951 Convention Relating to the Status of Refugees and Its 1967 Protocol: A Commentary* (New York: OUP, 2011), pp. 37–73.

El-Hinnawi, Essam, *Environmental Refugees* (Nairobi: United Nations Environment Programme, 1985).

Elliott, Lorraine, "Climate Migration and Climate Migrants: What Threat, Whose Security?", *in* Mcadam, Jane (Ed.), *Climate Change and Displacement: Multidisciplinary Perspectives* (Oxford, Portland OR: Hart Publishing, 2010), pp. 176–190.

Eschelbach, Katherine, Anna K. Schwab and David J. Brower, *Hazard Mitigation and Preparedness: Building Resilient Communities* (Hoboken, NJ: John Wiley & Sons Inc., 2006).

Ferris, Elizabeth, *Protection and Planned Relocations in the Context of Climate Change*, Legal and Protection Policy Research Series, No. PPLA/2012/04 (Geneva: UNHCR, August 2012).

Fitzmaurice, Malgosia, *Contemporary Issues in International Environmental Law* (Cheltenham, UK; Northampton, MA: Edward Elgar, 2009).

Foster, Michelle, *International Refugee Law and Socio-Economic Rights: Refuge from Deprivation*, Cambridge studies in international and comparative law, Vol. 51 (Cambridge, New York: Cambridge University Press, 2007).

Frowein, Jochen Abr., "Human Dignity in International Law", *in* Kretzmer, David and Eckart Klein (Eds.), *The Concept of Human Dignity in Human Rights Discourse* (The Hague: Kluwer Law International, 2002), pp. 121–132.

Gemenne, François, "How They Became the Human Face of Climate Change. Research and Policy Interactions in the Birth of the 'Environmental Migration' Concept", *in* Piguet, Etienne, Paul De Guchteneire and Antoine Pécoud (Eds.), *Migration and Climate Change* (Cambridge, New York: Cambridge University Press, UNESCO Publishing, 2011), pp. 225–259.

Gemenne, François, "Migrations et environnement : État des savoirs sur une relation méconnue", *in* GISTI (Ed.), *Quel Statut Pour Les Réfugiés Environnementaux ? Actes de La Journée Du 14 Décembre 2007* (Paris: Gisti, Juin 2008).

Goodwin-Gill, Guy S., *The Refugee in International Law*, First ed. (Oxford, New York: Oxford University Press, 1984).

Goodwin-Gill, Guy S., *"Non-Refoulement* and the New Asylum Seekers", *in* Martin, David A. (Ed.), *The New Asylum Seekers: Refugee Law in the 1980's, the Ninth Sokol Colloquium on International Law* (Dodrecht: Martinus Nijhoff Publishers, 1988), pp. 103–122.

Goodwin-Gill, Guy S. and Jane Mcadam, *The Refugee in International Law*, 3rd ed. (New York: Oxford University Press, 2007).

Gordon, Anita and David Suzuki, *It's a Matter of Survival* (Cambridge: Harvard University Press, 1991).

Government of the Republic of Haiti, "Annex: Haiti Earthquake Post-Disaster Needs Assessment: Assessment of Damage, Losses, General and Sectoral Needs", *in Action Plan for National Recovery and Development of Haiti: Immediate Key Initiatives for the Future* (n/a: Government of the Republic of Haiti, March 2010).

Grahl-Madsen, Atle, *The Status of Refugees in International Law* (Leiden: A.W. Sijthoff, 1966).

Groupe de Travail du Comité de Gestion Interagence sur le Risque l'Urgence et le Sinistre Pour l'Amérique et les Caraïbes (REDLAC), *Méthodologie d'évaluation rapide pour l'assistance humanitaire* (n/a: REDLAC, December 2006).

Gyulai, Gábor, *The Luxemburg Court: Conductor for a Disharmonious Orchestra?* (Budapest: Hungarian Helsinki Committee, 2012).

Hathaway, James C., *The Law of Refugee Status* (London: Butterworths, 1991).

Hathaway, James C., "Preface: Can International Refugee Law Be Made Relevant Again?", *in* Hathaway, James C. (Ed.), *Reconceiving International Refugee Law* (The Hague: Kluwer Law International, 1997), pp. xvii–xxix.

Hegerl, Gabriele C., Francis W. Zwiers, Pascale Braconnot, Nathan P. Gillett, Yong Luo, Jose A. Marengo Orsini, Neville Nicholls, Joyce E. Penner and Peter A. Stott, "2007: Understanding and Attributing Climate Change", *in* Solomon, Susan, Dahe Qin Co-Chair, Martin Manning Head, Melinda Marquis, Kristen Averyt, Melinda M.B. Tignor, Henry LeRoy MillerJr. and Zhenlin Chen (Eds.), *Contribution of Working Group I to the Fourth Assessment Report of the Intergovernmental Panel on Climate Change* (Cambridge, New York: Cambridge University Press, Cambridge, 2007).

Heinrigs, Philipp, *Incidences Sécuritaires Du Changement Climatique Au Sahel* (Paris: Club du Sahel et de l'Afrique de l'Ouest, CSAO/OCDE, 2010).

Hitler, Adolf, *Mein Kampf*, Translated by Murphy, James (London: Hurst And Blackett Ltd., 1939).

House of Lords – European Union Committee, *The Workload of the Court of Justice of the European Union: 14th Report of Session 2010–11*, HL Papers 128 (London: The Stationery Office, 2011).

Hugo, Graeme, "Lessons from Past Forced Resettlements for Climate Change Migration", *in* Piguet, Etienne, Paul De Guchteneire and Antoine Pécoud (Eds.), (Cambridge, New York: Cambridge University Press, UNESCO Publishing, 2011), pp. 260–288.

Human Rights Watch, "European Union", *in World Report 2012: Events of 2011* (New York: January 2012), pp. 441–458.

Humphreys, Stephen, *Human Rights and Climate Change* (Cambridge; New York: Cambridge University Press, 2010).

Humphreys, Stephen and Robert Archer (Eds.), *Climate Change and Human Rights: A Rough Guide* (Versoix: International Council on Human Rights Policy, 2008).

Hunt, Jo, "Fair and Just Working Conditions", *in* Hervey, Tamara K. and Jeff Kenner (Eds.), *Economic and Social Rights under the EU Charter of Fundamental Rights: A Legal Perspective* (Portland: Hart Publishing, 2003), pp. 45–66.

Hurwitz, Agnès, *The Collective Responsibility of States to Protect Refugees* (Oxford: Oxford University Press, 2009).

Hyndman, Jennifer, *Dual Disasters: Humanitarian Aid after the 2004 Tsunami* (Sterling, VA: Kumarian Press, 2011).

IASC *Operational Guidelines On the Protection of Persons in Situations of Natural Disasters* (Washington, DC: The Brookings – Bern Project on Internal Displacement, January 2011).

IASC, *Protecting Persons Affected by Natural Disasters: IASC Operational Guidelines on Human Rights and Natural Disasters* (Washington, DC: Brookings-Bern Project on Internal Displacement, June 2006).

Ineli-Ciger, Meltem, "Has the Temporary Protection Directive Become Obsolete? An Examination of the Directive and Its Lack of Implementation in View of the Recent Asylum Crisis in the Mediterranean", in Bauloz, Celine, Meltem Ineli-Ciger, Sarah Singer and Vladislava Stoyanova (Eds.), *Seeking Asylum in the European Union* (Leiden: Brill, 2015), pp. 225–246.

International Helsinki Federation for Human Rights (IHF), *Anti-Terrorism Measures, Security and Human Rights Developments in Europe, Central Asia and North America in the Aftermath of September 11* (Vienna: IHF, April 2003).

IOM, *Climate Change, Environmental Degradation and Migration*, International Dialogue on Migration, No. 18 (Geneva: IOM, 2012).

IPCC: W.N. Adger, J.M. Pulhin, J. Barnett, *et. al.*, "Human security", in: C.B. Field, V.R. Barros, D.J. Dokken, *et. al.* (eds.), *Climate Change 2014: Impacts, Adaptation, and Vulnerability, Part A: Global and Sectoral Aspects, Contribution of Working Group II to the Fifth Assessment Report of the Intergovernmental Panel on Climate Change* (Cambridge, New York: Cambridge University Press, 2014), pp. 755–791.

IPCC: Core Writing team, R.K. Pachauri and L.A. Meyer (Eds.), *Climate Change 2014: Synthesis Report, Contribution of Working Groups I, II and III to the Fifth Assessment Report of the Intergovernmental Panel on Climate Change* (Geneva: IPCC, 2014).

IPCC: M. Oppenheimer, M. Campos, R. Warren, *et. al.*, "Emergent risks and key vulnerabilities", in: C.B. Field, V.R. Barros, D.J. Dokken, *et. al.* (eds.), *Climate Change 2014: Impacts, Adaptation, and Vulnerability, Part A: Global and Sectoral Aspects, Contribution of Working Group II to the Fifth Assessment Report of the Intergovernmental Panel on Climate Change* (Cambridge, New York: Cambridge University Press, 2014), pp. 1039–1099.

IPCC, "Outline of the Working Group II Contribution to the Fifth Assessment Report Climate Change 2014: Impacts, Adaptation, and Vulnerability", IPCC-XXXI/Doc. 20, Rev.1, 28 October 2009.

IPCC, "2007: Summary for Policymakers", *in* Solomon, S., D. Qin and M. Manning (Eds.), *Climate Change 2007: The Physical Science Basis. Contribution of Working Group I to the Fourth Assessment Report of the Intergovernmental Panel on Climate Change* (New York: Cambridge University Press, 2007).

IPCC, "2007: Summary for Policymakers", *in* Parry, M.L., O.F. Canziani, J.P. Palutikof, P.J. Van Der Linden and C.E. Hanson (Eds.), *Climate Change 2007: Impacts, Adaptation and Vulnerability. Contribution of Working Group II to the Fourth Assessment Report of the Intergovernmental Panel on Climate Change* (Cambridge: Cambridge University Press, 2007).

IPCC: Core Writing Team, R.K. Pachauri and A. Reisinger (Eds.), *Climate Change 2007: Synthesis Report Contribution of Working Groups I, II and III to the Fourth Assessment Report of the Intergovernmental Panel on Climate Change* (Geneva: IPCC, 2007).

IPCC, "Summary for Policymakers", *in* Houghton, J.T., Y. Ding and D.J. Griggs (Eds.), *Climate Change 2001: The Scientific Basis. Contribution of Working Group I to the Third Assessment Report of the Intergovernmental Panel on Climate Change* (Cambridge: Cambridge University Press, 2001).

IPCC: Houghton, J.T., G.J. Jenkins and J.J. Ephraums, *First Assessment Report, Climate Change: The IPCC Scientific Assessment, Report Prepared for Intergovernmental Panel on Climate Change by Working Group I: Policymakers Summary* (*IPCC AR1 – WG 1: SPM*) (Cambridge: Cambridge University Press, 1990).

Jackson, Ivor C., *The Refugee Concept in Group Situations* (The Hague: Kluwer Law International, 1999).

Jacobs, Francis, "Remarks on Human Rights Protection in Europe", *in* Lefeber, René (Ed.), *Contemporary International Law Issues: Opportunities at a Time of Momentous Change, Proceedings of the Second Joint Conference of the American Society of International Law and the Nederlandse Vereniging Voor Internationaal Recht Held in the Hague, the Netherlands, 22–24 July 1993* (Dordrecht: Martinus Nijhoff Publishers, 1994), pp. 26–29.

Jaeger, Gilbert, "The Definition of 'Refugee': Restrictive Versus Expanding Trends", *in* Tripp, Rosemary E. and United States Committee For Refugees – USCR (Eds.), *World Refugee Survey, 1983* (Washington DC: USCR, 1984), pp. 5–9.

Jens Vedsted-Hansen, "The Borderline between Questions of Fact and Questions of Law", *in* Noll, Gregor (Ed.), *Proof, Evidentiary Assessment and Credibility in Asylum Law* (Leiden: Martinus Nijhof, 2005).

Julien-Laferrière, François, "La compatibilité de la politique d'asile de l'Union européenne avec la Convention de Genève du 28 juillet 1951 relative au statut des réfugiés", *in La Convention de Genève du 28 juillet 1951 relative au statut des réfugiés, 50 ans après : bilan et perspectives* (Bruxelles: Bruylant, 2001).

Julien-Laferrière, François, "La Notion de 'Groupe Social'", *in* Gerkrath, Jörg (Ed.), *Droit d'asile au Grand-Duché de Luxembourg et en Europe : développements récents* (Bruxelles: Larcier, 2009), pp. 218–234.

Julien-Laferrière, François, Henri Labayle and Örjan Edström (Odysseus Network) (Eds.), *La politique européenne d'immigration et d'asile : bilan critique cinq ans après le traité d'Amsterdam Précis de la faculté de droit de l'Université Libre de Bruxelles* (Bruylant, 06/2005).

Kaczorowska, Alina, *European Union Law*, 2nd ed. (Oxon, New York: Routledge-Cavendish, 2010).

Kälin, Walter and Nina Schrepfer, *Protecting People Crossing Borders in the Context of Climate Change Normative Gaps and Possible Approaches*, Legal and Protection Policy Research Series, No. PPLA/2012/01 (Geneva: UNHCR, February 2012).

Kälin, Walter, "Conceptualising Climate-Induced Displacement", *in* Mcadam, Jane (Ed.), *Climate Change and Displacement: Multidisciplinary Perspectives* (Oxford: Hart, 2010), pp. 81–103.

"Basic Concepts of International Humanitarian Law", *in* Kälin, Walter and Jörg Künzli (Eds.), *The Law of International Human Rights Protection* (New York: Oxford University Press, 2009), pp. 150–182.

Kälin, Walter, *Annotations to the Guiding Principles on Internal Displacement*, Studies in Transnational Legal Policy, No. 38 (Washington, DC: The American Society of International Law and The Brookings Institution, 2008).

Kälin, Walter, "Displacement Caused by the Effects of Climate Change: Who Will Be Affected and What Are the Gaps in the Normative Framework for Their Protection?", *in* Leckie, Scott, Ezekiel Simperingham and Jordan Bakker (Eds.), *Climate Change and Displacement Reader* (New York, NY: Earthscan, 10 October 2008), pp. 135–143.

Kelsen, Hans, *Pure Theory of Law*, 2nd ed., Translated by Knight, Max (Berkeley, Los Angeles: University of California Press, 1967).

Kenner, Jeff, "Economic and Social Rights in the EU Legal Order: The Mirage of Indivisibility", *in* Hervey, Tamara K. and Jeff Kenner (Eds.), *Economic and Social Rights under the EU Charter of Fundamental Rights: A Legal Perspective* (Portland: Hart Publishing, 2003), pp. 1–24.

Kiss, Alexandre, "Environmental and Consumer Protection", *in* Peers, Steve and Angela Ward (Eds.), *The European Union Charter of Fundamental Rights: Politics, Law and Policy* (Portland: Hart Publishing, 2004), pp. 247–268.

Kolmannskog, Vikram Odedra, *Future Floods of Refugees: A Comment on Climate Change, Conflict and Forced Migration* (Oslo: Norwegian Refugee Council, April 2008).

Kolmannskog, Vikram Odedra and Office of the UNHCR. Evaluation and Policy Analysis Unit, *Climate Change, Disaster, Displacement and Migration : Initial Evidence from Africa*, New issues in refugee research, no 180 (Geneva: UNHCR, 2009).

Laczko, Frank, Christine Aghazarm, International Organization for Migration., Intergovernmental Committee for Migration. and United Nations University. Institute For Environment and Human Security., *Migration, Environment and Climate Change : Assessing the Evidence* (Geneva: International Organization for Migration, 2009).

Lauterpacht, Elihu and Daniel Bethlehem, "The Scope and Content of the Principle of Non-Refoulement: Opinion", *in* Feller, Erika, Volker Türk and Frances Nicholson (Eds.), *Refugee Protection in International Law: UNHCR's Global Consultations on International Protection* (Cambridge: Cambridge University Press, 2003), pp. 87–177.

"Bereciartua-Echarri", *in* Lauterpacht, Elihu and C.J. Greenwood (Eds.), *International Law Reports*, Vol. 111 (Cambridge: Cambridge University Press, 1998), pp. 511–524.

Lavieille, Jean-Marc, Julien Bétaille and Michel Prieur (Eds.), *Les catastrophes écologiques et le droit : échecs du droit, appels au droit* (Bruxelles: Bruylant, 2012).

Leckie, Scott, Ezekiel Simperingham and Jordan Bakker, *Climate Change and Displacement Reader* (New York, NY: Earthscan, 2012).

Leino, Päivi, "When Every Picture Tells a Story: The European Court of Justice and the Jigsaw Puzzle of External Human Rights Competence", *in* Petman, Jarna and Jan Klabbers (Eds.), *Nordic Cosmopolitanism: Essays in International Law for Martti Koskenniemi* (Leiden: Brill Academic Publishers, 2003), pp. 261–290.

Longman Dictionary of English Language and Culture, 1st ed. (Harlow: Longman Group UK Ltd, 1992),.

Mcadam, Jane (Ed.) *Climate Change and Displacement: Multidisciplinary Perspectives* (Oxford: Hart, 2010).

Mandal, Ruma, *Protection Mechanisms Outside of the 1951 Convention ("Complementary Protection")*, Legal and Protection Policy Research Series, No. PPLA/2005/02 (Geneva: UNHCR, June 2005).

Margesson, Rhoda and Maureen Taft-Morales, *Haiti Earthquake: Crisis and Response*, CRS Report for Congress (Washington, DC: Congressional Research Service, 19 February 2010).

Matlou, Patrick, "Upsetting the Cart: Forced Migration and Gender Issues, the African Experience", *in* Indra, D. (Ed.), *Engendering Forced Migration* (New York and Oxford: Berghahn Books, 1999).

Mcadam, Jane, "Part I: Overview", *in Convention Refugee Status and Subsidiary Protection Working Party, First Report*, IARLJ 7th World Conference, Held in Mexico City, November 2006.

Mcadam, Jane, *Complementary Protection in International Refugee Law* (New York: Oxford University Press Inc., 2007).

Mcadam, Jane, "The Qualification Directive: An Overview", *in* Zwaan, Karin (Ed.), *The Qualification Directive: Central Themes, Problem Issues, and Implementation in Selected Member States* (Nijmegen: Wolf Legal Publishers, 2007), pp. 7–29.

Mcadam, Jane, "The Refugee Convention as a Rights Blueprint for People in Need of International Protection", *in* Mcadam, Jane (Ed.), *Forced Migration, Human Rights and Security* (Oxford: Hart Publishing, 2008), pp. 263–282.

Mcadam, Jane, "Disappearing States", *in* Mcadam, Jane (Ed.), *Climate Change and Displacement: Multidisciplinary Perspectives* (Oxford: Hart, 2010), pp. 105–129.

Mcadam, Jane, "Refusing 'Refuge' in the Pacific: (de)Constructing Climate-Induced Displacement in International Law", *in* Piguet, Etienne, Paul De Guchteneire and Antoine Pécoud (Eds.), *Migration and Climate Change* (Cambridge, New York: Cambridge University Press, UNESCO Publishing, 2011).

Mcadam, Jane, *Climate Change, Forced Migration, and International Law* (Oxford, New York: Oxford University Press, 2012).

Mcadam, Jane, "'Disappearing States', Statelessness, and Relocation", *in Climate Change, Forced Migration, and International Law* (Oxford, New York: Oxford University Press, 2012).

Mcdowell, Chris and Gareth Morrell, *Displacement Beyond Conflict: Challenges for the 21st Century* (Oxford, New York: Berghahn Books, 2010).

Mcinerney-Lankford, Siobhán Alice, Mac Darrow, Lavanya Rajamani and World Bank, *Human Rights and Climate Change: A Review of the International Legal Dimensions* (Washington, D.C.: World Bank, 2011).

Meron, Theodor, "State Responsibility for Violations of Human Rights: Remarks", *in Proceedings of the 101st Annual Meeting*, Vol. 83 (Washington, DC: American Society of International Law, April 1989), pp. 372–385.

Michelot, Agnès, "Vers un statut de réfugié écologique ?", *in Les catastrophes écologiques et le droit : échecs du droit, appels au droit* (Bruxelles: Bruylant, 2012), pp. 517–541.

Moderne, Franck, *Le droit constitutionnel d'asile dans les Etats de l'Union européenne*, Collection droit public positif (Paris, Aix-en-Provence: Economica, Presses Universitaires d'Aix-Marseille, 1997).

Mole, Nuala and Meredith Catherine, *Asylum and the European Convention on Human Rights*, 4 ed. (Strasbourg: Council of Europe Publishing, 2007).

Mole, Nuala and Catherine Meredith, *Asylum and the European Convention on Human Rights*, 5 ed., Human rights files, No. 9 (Strasbourg: Council of Europe Publishing, 2010).

Monar, Jörg, "Experimentalist Governance in Justice and Home Affairs", *in* Sabel, Charles F. and Jonathan Zeitlin (Eds.), *Experimentalist Governance in the European Union: Towards a New Architecture* (Oxford: Oxford University Press, 2010).

Müllerson, Rein A., *Ordering Anarchy: International Law in International Society* (The Hague: Martinus Nijhoff Publishers, 2000).

Myers, Norman and Jennifer Kent, *Environmental Exodus: An Emergent Crisis in the Global Arena* (Washington DC: Climate Institute, June 1995).

Network, European Migration, *Sweden: Annual Report on Asylum and Migration Statistics, 2007* (28 October 2008).

Noll, Gregor (Ed.) *Proof, Evidentiary Assessment and Credibility in Asylum Law* (Leiden: Martinus Nijhof, 2005).

Noll, Gregor, "Evidentiary Assessment under the Refugee Convention: Risk, Pain and the Intersubjectivity of Fear", *in* Noll, Gregor (Ed.), *Proof, Evidentiary Assessment and Credibility in Asylum Law* (Leiden: Martinus Nijhof, 2005).

Noll, Gregor, "Delimiting and Justifying the Protection under the Echr", *in Negotiating Asylum: The EU Acquis, Extraterritorial Protection, and the Common Market of Deflection* (The Hague: Kluwer Law International, 2000), pp. 453–474.

Nowak, Manfred, *U.N. Covenant on Civil and Political Rights: CCPR Commentary*, 2nd ed. (Kehl: N.P. Engel, Publisher, 2005).

Nykänen, Eeva, "How Absolute Is Absolute? – on the Limits of Article 3 of the European Convention on Human Rights in the Context of Immigration Control", *in* Hyttinen, Tatu and Katja Weckström (Eds.), *Turun Yliopiston Oikeustieteellinen Tiedekunta 50 Vuotta*, Publications of the Faculty of Law of the University of Turku (*Turun Yliopiston Oikeustieteellisen Tiedekunnan Julkaisuja A. Juhlajulkaisut*), No. 22 (Porvoo: WS Bookwell Oy, 2011), pp. 445–459.

Odinkalu, Chidi Anselm and Monette Zard, "African Regional Mechanisms That Can Be Utilized on Behalf of the Forcibly Displaced", *in* Fitzpatrick, Joan F. (Ed.), *Human Rights Protection for Refugees, Asylum-Seekers, and Internally Displaced Persons: A Guide to International Mechanisms and Procedures* (New York: Transnational Publishers, 2002).

Oreskes, Naomi and Erik M. Conway, *Merchants of Doubt: How a Handful of Scientists Obscured the Truth on Issues from Tobacco Smoke to Global Warming* (New York: Bloomsbury Press, 2010).

Parry, M.L., O.F. Canziani and J.P. Palutikof, "2007: Technical Summary", *in* Parry, M.L., O.F. Canziani and J.P. Palutikof (Eds.), *Climate Change 2007: Impacts, Adaptation and Vulnerability. Contribution of Working Group II to the Fourth Assessment Report of the Intergovernmental Panel on Climate Change* (Cambridge: Cambridge University Press, 2007).

Peers, Steve, "Chapter 5: Human Rights in the EU Legal Order: Practical Relevance for EC Immigration and Asylum Law", *in* Peers, Steve and Nicola Rogers (Eds.), *EU Immigration and Asylum Law: Text and Commentary*, Series: Immigration and Asylum Law and Policy in Europe, Vol. 12 (Leiden: Koninklijke Brill Nv, 2006), pp. 115–137.

Peers, Steve, "Human Rights in the EU Legal Order: Practical Relevance for Ec Immigration and Asylum Law", *in* Peers, Steve and Nicola Rogers (Eds.), *EU Immigration and Asylum Law: Text and Commentary*, Immigration and Asylum Law and Policy in Europe (Leiden: Brill Academic Publishers, 2006), pp. 115–137.

Peers, Steve and Nicola Rogers (Eds.), *EU Immigration and Asylum Law: Text and Commentary Immigration and Asylum Law and Policy in Europe*, Vol. 12 (Leiden: Brill Academic Publishers, 2006).

Pernice, Ingolf, "The Treaty of Lisbon and Fundamental Rights", *in* Griller, Stefan and Jaques Ziller (Eds.), *The Lisbon Treaty: EU Constitutionalism without a Constitutional Treaty?* (Wien, New York: Springer, 2008).

Pernice, Ingolf, "The Treaty of Lisbon and Fundamental Rights", *in* Griller, Stefan and Jacques Ziller (Eds.), *The Lisbon Treaty: EU Constitutionalism without a Constitutional Treaty?*, Schriftenreihe Der Österreichischen Gesellschaft Für Europaforschung (Ecsa Austria), Vol. 11 (Wien, New York: Springer, 2008), pp. 235–256.

Perthuis, Christian De, Stéphane Hallegatte and Franck Lecocq, *Économie de l'adaptation au changement climatique* (n/a: Conseil Economique pour le Développement Durable, February 2010).

Piguet, Etienne, Paul De Guchteneire and Antoine Pécoud, *Migration and Climate Change* (Cambridge, New York: Cambridge University Press, UNESCO Publishing, 2011).

Ragheboom, Hélène, "Le paquet asile", *in* Gerkrath, Jörg (Ed.), *Droit d'asile au Grand-Duché de Luxembourg et en Europe : développements récents*, Collection de la Faculté de Droit, d'Economie et de Finance de l'Université de Luxembourg (Bruxelles: Larcier, 2009).

Randall, D.A., R.A. Wood and S. Bony, "2007: Climate Models and Their Evaluation", *in* Solomon, S., D. Qin and M. Manning (Eds.), *Climate Change 2007: The Physical Science Basis. Contribution of Working Group I to the Fourth Assessment Report of the Intergovernmental Panel on Climate Change* (New York: Cambridge University Press, 2007).

Roca, Javier García, "El Preámbulo Contexto Hermenéutico Del Convenioun Instrumento Constitucional Del Orden Público Europeo", *in* Roca, Javier García and Pablo Santolaya Machetti (Eds.), *La Europa de Los Derechos: El Convenio Europeo de Derechos Humanos* (Madrid: CEPC, 2005).

Rosas, Allan, "Human Rights and the External Relations of the European Community: A Conceptual Perspective", *in* Weiler, Joseph H.H. and Martina Kocjan (Eds.), *Principles of Constitutions Law: The Protection of Human Rights*, The Law of the

European Union: Teaching Material, Unit 7 (New York, Florence: NYU School of Law, EUI, 2004/05).

Saul, Ben, "Climate Change and Resource Scarcity: Towards an International Law of Distributive Justice", *in* Lyster, Rosemary (Ed.), *In the Wilds of Climate Law* (Bowen Hills,QLD: Australian Academic Press, 2010), pp. 71–94.

Scheinin, Martin, "Extraterritorial Effect of the International Covenant on Civil and Political Rights", *in* Coomans, Fons and Menno T. Kamminga (Eds.), *Extraterritorial Application of Human Rights Treaties* (Antwerp: Intersentia, 2004), pp. 73–82.

Schermers, Henry, "Remarks on Human Rights Protection in Europe", *in* Lefeber, René (Ed.), *Contemporary International Law Issues: Opportunities at a Time of Momentous Change, Proceedings of the Second Joint Conference of the American Society of International Law and the Nederlandse Vereniging Voor Internationaal Recht Held in the Hague, the Netherlands, 22–24 July 1993* (Dordrecht: Martinus Nijhoff Publishers, 1994), pp. 22–24.

Schmeidl, Susanne, "Conflict and Forced Migration: A Quantitative Review, 1964–1995", *in* Zolberg, Aristife R. and Peter M. Benda (Eds.), *Global Migrants, Global Refugees: Problems and Solutions* (New York: Berghahn Books, 2001).

Shields, Acacia and Human Rights Watch, *Creating Enemies of the State: Religious Persecution in Uzbekistan* (n/a: Human Rights Watch, 2004).

Smith, D. and J. Vivekananda, *A Climate of Conflict: The Link between Climate Change, Peace and War* (London: International Alert, 2007).

Stern, Nicholas, *The Economics of Climate Change: The Stern Review* (Cambridge: Cambridge University Press, January 2007).

UN OCHA, *Overview of the Consolidated Appeals and Similar Concerted Humanitarian Action Plans at Mid-Year 2012* (Geneva, New York: OCHA, 23 July 2012).

UNEP, *Protecting the Environment During Armed Conflict: An Inventory and Analysis of International Law* (Nairobi: UNEP, 2009).

UNEP, *UNEP Year Book 2010: New Science and Developments in Our Changing Environment* (Nairobi: UNEP, 2010).

UNEP, *Factsheet: Climate Change* (Paris: UNEP, July 2000).

UNHCR, *Handbook and Guidelines on Procedures and Criteria for Determining Refugee Status under the 1951 Convention and the 1967 Protocol Relating to the Status of Refugees*, HCR/IP/4/Eng/REV.3 (Geneva: UNHCR, 1979, reissued December 2011).

UNHCR, *Handbook on Voluntary Repatriation: International Protection* (Geneva: UNHCR, 1996).

UNHCR, "Chapter 1: Safeguarding Human Security", *in The State of the World's Refugees: A Humanitarian Agenda* (Geneva: UNHCR, 1997).

UNHCR, "Etude de jurisprudence du tribunal administratif du Grand-Duché de Luxembourg en matière de protection internationale", *in* Gerkrath, Jörg (Ed.), *Droit d'asile au Grand-Duché de Luxembourg et en Europe : développements récents*,

Collection de la Faculté de Droit, d'Economie et de Finance de l'Université de Luxembourg (Bruxelles: Larcier, 2009), pp. 62–132.

UNHCR, *The State of the World's Refugees 2012: In Search of Solidarity* (Oxford, New York: Oxford University Press, 2012).

UNHCR, *The Dublin II Regulation: A UNHCR Discussion Paper* (Brussels: UNHCR, April 2006).

UNHCR, *Asylum in the European Union: A Study of the Implementation of the Qualification Directive* (Geneva: UNHCR, November 2007).

UNHCR, Clara Odofin, Daphne Bouteillet and Geertrui Daem, *Safe at Last? Law and Practice in Selected EU Member States with Respect to Asylum-Seekers Fleeing Indiscriminate Violence* (Brussels: UNHCR, July 2011).

Van Der Harst, Jan, "The European Defence Community and Nato: A Classic Case of Franco-Dutch Controversy", *in* Drent, Margriet, Arjan Van Den Assem and Jaap De Wilde (Eds.), *Nato's Retirement? Essays in Honour of Peter Volten*, Greenwood Paper 26 (Groningen: Centre of European Security Studies, 2011), pp. 83–94.

Verheyen, Roda, *Climate Change Damage and International Law: Prevention Duties and State Responsibility Developments in International Law*, No. 54 (Leiden, Boston: Martinus Nijhoff Publishers, 2005).

Weiler, Joseph H.H., "Fundamental Rights and Fundamental Boundaries: On Standards and Values in the Protection of Human Rights", *in* Neuwahl, Nanette A. and Allan Rosas (Eds.), *The European Union and Human Rights* (The Hague: Kluwer Law International, 1995), pp. 51–76.

Weiler, Joseph H.H. and Sybilla C. Fries, "A Human Rights Policy for the European Community and Union: The Question of Competences", *in* Alston, Philip (Ed.), *The EU and Human Rights* (Oxford, New York: OUP, 1999), pp. 147–166.

Weis, Paul, *The Refugee Convention, 1951: The Travaux Préparatoires Analysed* (Cambridge: Cambridge University Press, 1995).

Wells, H.G., *The Outline of History: Being a Plain History of Life and Mankind* (New York: Macmillan Company, 1921).

Wessel, Ramses A., "The Constitutional Relationship between the European Union and the European Community: Consequences for the Relationship with the Member States", *in* Weiler, J.J.H. and A. Von Bogdandy (Eds.), *European Integration: The New German Scholarship*, Jean Monnet Working Papers, 9/03 (Heidelberg: Max Planck Institute for Comparative Public Law and International Law, 2003).

Westra, Laura, *Environmental Justice and the Rights of Ecological Refugees* (London, Sterling, VA: Earthscan, 2009).

White, Gregory, *Climate Change and Migration: Security and Borders in a Warming World* (Oxford, New York: Oxford University Press, 2011).

WHO, *25 Questions & Answers on, Health & Human Rights* Health & Human Rights Publication Series, No. 1 (Geneva: World Health Organization, July 2002).

Yonetani, Michelle and IDMC, *People Displaced by Natural Hazard-Induced Disasters* (Geneva: IDMC – NRC, June 2012).

Zederman, Vera, "The French Reading of Subsidiary Protection", *in Convention Refugee Status and Subsidiary Protection Working Party: First Report*, IARLJ 7th World Conference, Held in Mexico City, November 2006.

Journals

Afifi, Tamer, "Economic or Environmental Migration? The Push Factors in Niger", *International Migration* (Blackwell Publishing Ltd), Vol. 49 (2011), pp. e95–e124.

Ahmed, Tawhida and Israel De Jesús Butler, "The European Union and Human Rights: An International Law Perspective", *The European Journal of International Law*, Vol. 17, No. 4 (2006).

Åkerman, Mikaela, "Ministrar ville stoppa våg av irakier", *Svenska Dagbladet*, 21 januari 2011.

Akram, Susan M. and Terry Rempel, "Temporary Protection as an Instrument for Implementing the Right of Return for Palestinian Refugees", *Boston University International Law Journal*, Vol. 22, No. 1 (2004), pp. 1–162.

Allain, Jean, "The Jus Cogens Nature of Non-Refoulement", *International Journal of Refugee Law*, Vol. 13, No. 4 (2001), pp. 533–558.

Allain, Jean, "The Jus Cogens Nature of Non-Refoulement", *International Journal of Refugee Law*, Vol. 13 (2001), pp. 533–558.

Alscher, Stefan, "Environmental Degradation and Migration on Hispaniola Island", *International Migration* (Blackwell Publishing Ltd), Vol. 49 (2011), pp. e164–e188.

Alston, Philip and J.H.H. Weiler, "An 'Ever Closer Union' in Need of a Human Rights Policy", *European Journal of International Law* (Oxford University Press / USA), Vol. 9, No. 4 (1998), p. 658s.

Anagnostakis, Ilias and Anna Lambropoulou, "An Instance of the Implementation of the Byzantine Institution of Asylum in the Peloponnese: The Slavs Seek Sanctuary in the Church of St Andrew of Patrai", *Byzantina Symmeikta*, Vol. 14 (2008), pp. 29–47.

Andrew, E. Shacknove, "Who Is a Refugee?", *Ethics*, Vol. 95, No. 2 (1985), pp. 274–284.

Arboleda, Eduardo, "Refugee Definition in Africa and Latin America: The Lessons of Pragmatism", *International Journal of Refugee Law*, April 1, 1991, Vol. 3, No. 2 (1991), pp. 185–207.

Ashworth, Andrew, "Sufi and Elmi v United Kingdom", *Criminal Law Review*, No. 11 (2011), pp. 882–883.

Atapattu, Sumudu, "Climate Change and Forced Migration: Implications for International Law", *Wisconsin International Law Journal*, Vol. 27, No. 3 (2009), pp. 607–636.

Aubert, Michel, Emmanuelle Broussy and Francis Donnat, "Chronique de jurisprudence de la CJUE", *AJDA*, No. 6 (20/02/2012), pp. 306–316.

Baker, Marcia B. and Gerard H. Roe, "The Shape of Things to Come: Why Is Climate Change So Predictable?", *Journal of Climate*, Vol. 22, No. 17 (2009), p. 4587.

Barbier, Marie, "Haïti: La France refuse d'accueillir nos enfants", *L'Humanité*, 24 August 2010.

Barrot, Jacques, *Bulletin quotidien Europe*, 19 février 2009, No. 9843 (2009).

Bates, Diane C., "Environmental Refugees? Classifying Human Migrations Caused by Environmental Change", *Population and Environment*, Vol. 23, No. 5 (May 2002).

Battjes, Hemme, "In Search of a Fair Balance: The Absolute Character of the Prohibition of Refoulement under Article 3 ECHR Reassessed", *Leiden Journal of International Law* (Cambridge University Press), Vol. 22, No. 3 (2009), pp. 583–621.

Beck, Roger B., "Book Review: It's a Matter of Survival by Anita Gordon; David Suzuki", *Politics and the Life Sciences*, Vol. 11, No. 2 (1992), pp. 285–286.

Bernauer, Thomas and Tobias Siegfried, "Climate Change and International Water Conflict in Central Asia", *Journal of Peace Research*, January 1, 2012, Vol. 49, No. 1, pp. 227–239.

Bétaille, Julien, "Des "réfugiés écologiques" à la protection des "déplacés environnementaux": Eléments du débat juridique en France", *Revue Hommes et migrations*, No. 1284: "Migrations et environnement" (March-April 2010).

Boskovic, Olivera, Sabine Corneloup, Fabienne Jault-Seseke, Natalie Joubert and Karine Parrot, "Panorama: Droit des étrangers et de la nationalité, septembre 2009 – août 2010", *Recueil Dalloz*, No. 43 (9 December 2010), p. 2868.

Boucher, Julien, "Conclusions of *rapporteur public* Julien Boucher", in CE (10ème et 9ème sous-sections réunies), 320295 OFPRA c. Baskarathas, 3 July 2009.

Boykoff, Maxwell T. and Jules M. Boykoff, "Balance as Bias: Global Warming and the Us Prestige Press", *Global Environmental Change*, Vol. 14 (2004), pp. 125–136.

Bradley, Megan, "Return in Dignity: A Neglected Protection Challenge", *RSC Working Paper Series* (University of Oxford, Refugee Studies Centre), No. 40 (June 2007).

Brandtner, Barbara and Allan Rosas, "Article. Human Rights and the External Relations of the European Community: An Analysis of Doctrine and Practice", *European Journal of International Law* (Oxford University Press / USA), Vol. 9, No. 3 (1998), p. 468.

Broussy, Emmanuelle, Francis Donnat and Christian Lambert, "Chronique de jurisprudence communautaire", *AJDA*, No. 18 (18/05/2009), pp. 980–990.

Brown Weiss, Edith, "Environmental Disasters in International Law", *Anuario Juridico Interamericano* (1986), pp. 141–169.

Burgorgue-Larsen, Laurence, "De l'autonomie de la protection du droit communautaire par rapport à la Convention européenne des droits de l'homme ?", *AJDA*, No. 24 (06/07/2009), pp. 1321–1326.

Burguburu, Julie, "Conclusions of *Rapporteur Public* Julie Burguburu" ("Conclusions J. Burguburu in Kona (CE)"), in CE (10ème et 9ème sous-sections réunies), *292564 Mlle Kona*, 25 mars 2009.

Byravan, S. and R.S. Chella, "Providing New Homes for Climate Change Exiles", *Climate Policy*, No. 6 (2006), pp. 246–252.

Byrne, Rosemary, "Harmonization and Burden Redistribution in the Two Europes", *Journal of Refugee Studies*, Vol. 16, No. 3 (2003), pp. 336–358.

Castles, Stephen, "Environmental Change and Forced Migration: Making Sense of the Debate", *New Issues in Refugee Research* (UNHCR), No. 70 (2002).

Chaudhary, Omar, "Turning Back: An Assessment of Non-Refoulement under Indian Law", *Economic and Political Weekly* (17 July 2004), pp. 3257–3264.

Chomette, Guy-Pierre, Donatien Garnier and Aude Raux, "Les déplacés environnementaux", *Accueillir*, No. 246, *Les déplacés environnementaux* (June 2008), pp. 14–16.

CNCDH, "Avis sur le projet de loi modifiant la loi no 52–893 relative au droit d'asile" ("Avis 2003"), 24 avril 2003.

Colloquium on Challenges in International Refugee Law and James C. Hathaway, "The Michigan Guidelines on Nexus to a Convention Ground", *Michigan Journal of International Law*, Vol. 23 (Winter 2002), pp. 211–221.

Colloquium on Challenges in International Refugee Law and James C. Hathaway, "The Michigan Guidelines on Protection Elsewhere", *Michigan Journal of International Law*, 10–12 November 2006, Vol. 28 (Winter 2007), pp. 207–221.

Colloquium on Challenges in International Refugee Law and James C. Hathaway, "The Michigan Guidelines on Well-Founded Fear", *Michigan Journal of International Law*, Vol. 26 (March 2004), pp. 491–503.

Conisbee, Molly and Andrew Simms, "Environmental Refugees: The Case for Recognition" (New Economics Foundation) (2003).

Cooper, Jessica B., "Environmental Refugees: Meeting the Requirements of the Refugee Definition", *New York University Environmental Law Journal*, Vol. 6 (1998), pp. 480–529.

Cournil, Christel, "Les Réfugiés Écologiques : Quelle(S) Protection(S), Quel(S) Statut(S) ?", *Revue de droit public*, No. 4 (2006), pp. 1035–1066.

Cournil, Christel, "A la recherche d'une protection pour les « réfugiés environnementaux » : actions, obstacles, enjeux et protections", *REVUE Asylon(s)*, Vol. No 6: Exodes écologiques (November 2008).

Crock, Mary, "Book Review: 'Seeking Asylum in Australia, Yearning to Breathe Free', D Lusher and N Haslam (Eds)", *Australian Year Book of International Law*, Vol. 27 (2008), pp. 257–262.

Cuéllar, Roberto, Diego García-Say'n, Jorge Montaño, Margarita Diegues and Leo Valladares Lanza, "Refugee and Related Developments in Latin America: Challenges Ahead", *International Journal of Refugee Law*, 1 July 1991, Vol. 3, No. 3 (1991), pp. 482–498.

Cunliffe, Alex, "The Refugee Crises: A Study of the United Nations High Commission for Refugees", *Political Studies* (Wiley-Blackwell), Vol. 43, No. 2 (1995), pp. 278–290.

Danwitz, Thomas Von, "The Charter of Fundamental Rights of the European Union between Political Symbolism and Legal Realism", *Denver Journal of International Law and Policy*, Vol. 29 (Summer/Fall 2001), pp. 289–304.

Davies, Sara E., "Redundant or Essential? How Politics Shaped the Outcome of the 1967 Protocol", *International Journal of Refugee Law*, Vol. 19, No. 4 (2007), pp. 703–728.

De Búrca, Gráinne, "The European Court of Justice and the International Legal Order after *Kadi*", *Harvard International Law Journal*, Vol. 51, No. 1 (Winter 2010), pp. 1–49.

Deborah Perluss, Joan F. Hartman, "Temporary Refuge: Emergence of a Customary Norm", *Virginia Journal of International Law*, Vol. 26, No. 3 (1986), pp. 551–626.

Decrop, Geneviève, "Un Statut de Réfugié Environnemental Est-Il Une Réponse Pertinente Aux Effets Sociaux Du Réchauffement Climatique ?", *REVUE Asylon(s)*, Vol. 6: Exodes écologiques (November 2008).

Derckx, Veelke, "Expulsion of Illegal Residents (Aliens) with Medical Problems and Article 3 of the European Convention on Human Rights", *European Journal of Health Law* (Martinus Nijhoff), Vol. 13, No. 4 (2006), pp. 313–319.

Devitt, Conor and Richard SJ Tol, "Civil War, Climate Change, and Development: A Scenario Study for Sub-Saharan Africa", *Journal of Peace Research*, January 1, 2012, Vol. 49, No. 1, pp. 129–145.

Docherty, Bonnie and Tyler Giannini, "Confronting a Rising Tide: A Proposal for a Convention on Climate Change Refugees", *Harvard Environmental Law Review*, Vol. 33 (2009), pp. 349–403.

Doevenspeck, Martin, "The Thin Line between Choice and Flight: Environment and Migration in Rural Benin", *International Migration* (Blackwell Publishing Ltd), Vol. 49 (2011), pp. e50–e68.

Doevenspeck, Martin, "The Thin Line between Choice and Flight: Environment and Migration in Rural Benin", *International Migration* (IOM), Vol. 49 (S1) (2011).

Drake, Nick A., Roger M. Blench, Simon J. Armitage, Charlie S. Bristow and Kevin H. White, "Ancient Watercourses and Biogeography of the Sahara Explain the Peopling of the Desert", *Proceedings of the National Academy of Sciences*, 11 January 2011, Vol. 108, No. 2 (2011), pp. 458–462.

Drogue, Cindy and Anne Bertin, "Même après le séisme, la France terre d'écueils", *Nouvelles Images d'Haiti (NIH)* (Collectif Haïti de France) (January 2012).

Duffy, Aoif, "Expulsion to Face Torture? *Non-Refoulement* in International Law", *International Journal of Refugee Law*, Vol. 20 (2008).

Dun, Olivia, "Migration and Displacement Triggered by Floods in the Mekong Delta", *International Migration* (Blackwell Publishing Ltd), Vol. 49 (2011), pp. e200–e223.

Durieux, Jean-Francois, "Of War, Flows, Laws and Flaws: A Reply to Hugo Storey", *Refugee Survey Quarterly*, September 1, 2012, Vol. 31, No. 3 (2012), pp. 161–176.

Durieux, Jean-François and University Of Oxford. Refugee Studies Centre, "Salah Sheekh Is a Refugee: New Insights into Primary and Subsidiary Forms of Protection",

Working paper series / Refugee Studies Centre (Refugee Studies Centre), No. 49 (2008).

Dwernychuk, L. Wayne, Hoang Dinh Cau, Christopher T. Hatfield, Thomas G. Boivin, Tran Manh Hung, Phung Tri Dung and Nguyen Dinh Thai, "Dioxin Reservoirs in Southern Viet Nam: A Legacy of Agent Orange", *Chemosphere*, Vol. 47, No. 2 (April 2002), pp. 117–137.

ECRE, "Five Years On: Europe Is Still Ignoring Its Responsibilities Towards Iraqi Refugees" (March 2008).

ECRE, "Sharing Responsibility for Refugee Protection in Europe: Dublin Reconsidered" (March 2008).

ECRE, "Information Note on the Council Directive 2004/83/EC of 29 April 2004 on Minimum Standards for the Qualification of Third Country Nationals and Stateless Persons as Refugees or as Persons Who Otherwise Need International Protection and the Content of the Protection Granted" ("Information Note on QD (2004)") (October 2004).

ECRE, "Non-State Agents of Persecution and the Inability of the State to Protect – the German Interpretation" (September 2000).

ECRE/ELENA, "The Impact of the EU Qualification Directive on International Protection", October 2008.

ECRE/ELENA, "Research Paper on Non-State Agents of Persecution" (ECRE) (November 1998, updated in autumn 2000).

Elmadmad, Khadija, "An Arab Convention on Forced Migration: Desirability and Possibilities", *International Journal of Refugee Law*, Vol. 3, No. 3 (1991), pp. 461–481.

Elmadmad, Khadija, "Asylum in the Arab World: Some Recent Instruments", *Journal of Peace Studies*, Vol. 6, No. 1 (January–February 1999).

EMN, "The Different National Practices Concerning Granting of Non-EU Harmonised Protection Statuses" (December 2010).

Errera, Roger, "The CJEU and Subsidiary Protection: Reflections on Elgafaji – and After", *International Journal of Refugee Law*, March 1, 2011, Vol. 23, No. 1 (2011), pp. 93–112.

Escalona, A.N.A. and Richard Black, "Refugees in Western Europe: Bibliographic Review and State of the Art", *Journal of Refugee Studies*, Vol. 8, No. 4 (1995), pp. 364–389.

Falstrom, Dana Zartner, "Stemming the Flow of Environmental Displacement: Creating a Convention to Protect Persons and Preserve the Environment", *Colorado Journal of International Environmental Law and Policy*, Vol. 13 (2002), pp. 1–29.

Farbotko, Carol and Heather Lazrus, "The First Climate Refugees? Contesting Global Narratives of Climate Change in Tuvalu", *Global Environmental Change*, Vol. 22 (2012), pp. 382–390.

Farmer, Alice, "Non-Refoulment and Jus Cogens: Limiting Anti-Terror Measures That Threaten Refugee Protection", *Georgetown Immigration Law Journal*, Vol. 23 (2008–2009), pp. 1–38.

Faure, Michael G. and Nollkaemper Andre, "International Liability as an Instrument to Prevent and Compensate for Climate Change", *Stanford Environmental Law Journal*, Vol. 23A (June 2007).

Feller, Erika, "Asylum, Migration and Refugee Protection: Realities, Myths and the Promise of Things to Come", *International Journal of Refugee Law*, Vol. 18 (2006), pp. 509–536.

Felli, Romain, "Justice globale pour les réfugié-e-s climatiques ?", *REVUE Asylon(s)*, Vol. No 6: Exodes écologiques (November 2008).

Fennelly, Nial, "The Area of" Freedom, Security and Justice "and the European Court of Justice: A Personal View", *The International and Comparative Law Quarterly* (Cambridge University Press on behalf of the British Institute of International and Comparative Law), Vol. 49, No. 1 (2000), pp. 1–14.

Fitzmaurice, Malgosia, "The International Court of Justice and the Environment", *Non-State Actors & International Law* (Martinus Nijhoff), Vol. 4, No. 3 (2004), pp. 173–197.

Fitzmaurice, Malgosia, "Responsibility and Climate Change", *German Yearbook of International Law*, Vol. 53 (2010).

Fitzpatrick, Joan, "Temporary Protection of Refugees: Elements of a Formalized Regime", *The American Journal of International Law*, Vol. 94, No. 2 (April 2000), pp. 279–306.

Fontanelli, Filippo, "The European Union's Charter of Fundamental Rights Two Years Later", *Perspectives on Federalism*, Vol. 3, No. 3 (2011), pp. 22–47.

Forman, Lisa, "Environmental Justice and the Rights of Unborn and Future Generations: Law, Environmental Harm and the Right to Health", *Global Public Health* (Routledge), Vol. 3, No. 4 (2008), pp. 455–458.

Foster, Michelle, "*Non-Refoulement* on the Basis of Socio-Economic Deprivation: The Scope of Complementary Protection in International Human Rights Law", *New Zealand Law Review*, Part II (2009), pp. 257–310.

Fouda, Lauren, "Compulsory Voluntary Repatriation: Why Temporary Protection for Sudanese Asylum-Seekers in Cairo Amounts to Refoulement", *Georgetown Journal on Poverty Law & Policy*, Vol. 14, No. 3 (2007), pp. 511–538.

Fullerton, Maryellen, "A Tale of Two Decades: War Refugees and Asylum Policy in the European Union", *Washington University Global Studies Law Review*, Vol. 10 (2011), pp. 87–132.

Gartzke, Erik, "Could Climate Change Precipitate Peace?", *Journal of Peace Research*, January 1, 2012, Vol. 49, No. 1, pp. 177–192.

Gartzke, Erik, "Could Climate Change Precipitate Peace?", *Journal of Peace Research*, January 1, 2012, Vol. 49, No. 1 (2012), pp. 177–192.

Gila, Oscar Alvarez, Ana Ugalde Zaratiegui and Virginia López De Maturana Diéguez, "Western Sahara: Migration, Exile and Environment", *International Migration* (Blackwell Publishing Ltd), Vol. 49 (2011), pp. e146–e163.

Gil-Bazo, Maria Teresa, "The Role of Spain as a Gateway to the Schengen Area: Changes in the Asylum Law and Their Implications for Human Rights", *International Journal of Refugee Law*, Vol. 10, No. 1 (1998), pp. 214–229.

Gil-Bazo, Maria Teresa, "The Practice of Mediterranean States in the Context of the European Union's Justice and Home Affairs External Dimension. The Safe Third Country Concept Revisited", *International journal of refugee law*, Vol. 18, No. 3–4 (2006), pp. 571–600.

Gil-Bazo, Maria Teresa, "Refugee Status, Subsidiary Protection, and the Right to Be Granted Asylum under EC Law", *UNHCR Research Papers*, November 2006, No. 136 (2006).

Gil-Bazo, Maria-Teresa, "The Charter of Fundamental Rights of the European Union and the Right to Be Granted Asylum in the Union's Law", *Refugee Survey Quarterly*, January 1, 2008, Vol. 27, No. 3 (2008), pp. 33–52.

Gilbert, Geoff, "Spread Too Thin?", *Harvard International Review* (Harvard International Review), Fall 2009, Vol. 31, No. 3 (2009), pp. 56–59.

Gleditsch, Nils Petter, "Whither the Weather? Climate Change and Conflict", *Journal of Peace Research*, Vol. 49, No. 3 (2012), pp. 3–9.

Gleditsch, Nils Petter, Ragnhild Nordås and Idean Salehyan, "Climate Change and Conflict: The Migration Link", *Working Paper Series – Coping with Crisis* (International Peace Academy, 2007).

Goddard, Brenda, "UNHCR and the International Protection of Palestinian Refugees", *Refugee Survey Quarterly*, Vol. 28, No. 2–3, pp. 475–510.

Goddard, Brenda, "UNHCR and the International Protection of Palestinian Refugees", *Refugee Survey Quarterly*, January 1, 2009, Vol. 28, No. 2–3 (2009), pp. 475–510.

Gonin, P. and V. Lassailly-Jacob, "Les Réfugiés de L'environnement : Une Nouvelle Catégorie de Migrants Forcés ?", *Revue européenne des migrations internationales*, Vol. 18, No. 2 (2002).

Goodwin-Gill, Guy S., "The Language of Protection", *International journal of refugee law.*, Vol. 1, No. 1 (1989), pp. 6–19.

Goodwin-Gill, Guy S., "Cases and Comment: The Haitian *Refoulement* Case", *International Journal of Refugee Law*, Vol. 6, No. 1 (1994), pp. 68–109.

Goodwin-Gill, Guy S., "The Politics of Refugee Protection", *Refugee Survey Quarterly*, January 1, 2008, Vol. 27, No. 1 (2008), pp. 8–23.

Gordon, Anita and David Suzuki, "It's a Matter of Survival", *Bulletin of Science, Technology & Society*, 1 April 1992, Vol. 12, No. 2 (1992), p. 114s.

Gorlick, Brian, "Human Rights and Refugees: Enhancing Protection through International Human Rights Law", *Nordic Journal of International Law*, Vol. 69 (2000), pp. 117–177.

Grahl-Madsen, Atle, "Identifying the World's Refugees", *Annals of the American Academy of Political and Social Science* (Sage Publications, Inc. in association with the American Academy of Political and Social Science), Vol. 467 (May 1983), pp. 11–23.

Groussot, Xavier and Laurent Pech, "Fundamental Rights Protection in the European Union Post Lisbon Treaty", *Fondation Robert Schuman, European Issues*, No. 173 (14 June 2010).

Groussot, Xavier, Tobias Lock and Laurent Pech, "EU Accession to the European Convention on Human rights: A Legal Assessment Of the Draft Accession Agreement of 14th October 2011", *Fondation Robert Schuman, European Issues*, No. 218 (7 November 2011).

Haddad, Emma, "The External Dimension of EU Refugee Policy: A New Approach to Asylum?", *Government and Opposition*, Vol. 43, No. 2 (2008), pp. 190–205.

Harper, Andrew, "Iraq's Refugees: Ignored and Unwanted", *International Review of the Red Cross*, Vol. 90, No. 869 (2008), pp. 169–190.

Hathaway, James C., "Leveraging Asylum", *Texas International Law Journal*, Vol. 45, No. 3, pp. 503–535.

Hathaway, James C., "Reconceiving Refugee Law as Human Rights Protection", *Journal of Refugee Studies*, Vol. 5, No. 2 (1991).

Hathaway, James C., "A Reconsideration of the Underlying Premise of Refugee Law", *Harvard International Law Journal*, Vol. 31, No. 1 (Winter 1990), pp. 129–183.

Hathaway, James C. and Anne K. Cusick, "Refugee Rights Are Not Negotiable", *Georgetown Immigration Law Journal*, Vol. 14 (2000), pp. 481–537.

Hathaway, James C. and Michelle Foster, "Membership of a Particular Social Group", *International Journal of Refugee Law*, Vol. 15, No. 3 (2003), pp. 477–491.

Hathaway, James C. and William S. Hicks, "Is There a Subjective Element in the Refugee Convention's Requirement of "Well-Founded Fear"?", *Michigan Journal of International Law*, Vol. 26 (Winter 2005), p. 550.

Havard, Brooke, "Seeking Protection: Recognition of Environmentally Displaced Persons under International Human Rights Law", *Villanova Environmental Law Journal*, Vol. 18, No. 1 (2007), pp. 65–82.

Heinz, Wolfgang S., "The Law of International Human Rights Protection", *European Journal of International Law*, Vol. 21, No. 1, pp. 245–247.

Hendrix, Cullen S and Idean Salehyan, "Climate Change, Rainfall, and Social Conflict in Africa", *Journal of Peace Research*, January 1, 2012, Vol. 49, No. 1, pp. 35–50.

Hendrix, Cullen S and Idean Salehyan, "Climate Change, Rainfall, and Social Conflict in Africa", *Journal of Peace Research*, January 1, 2012, Vol. 49, No. 1, pp. 35–50.

Hendrix, Cullen S. and Idean Salehyan, "Climate Change, Rainfall, and Social Conflict in Africa", *Journal of Peace Research*, Vol. 49, No. 1 (2012), pp. 35–50.

Homer-Dixon, Thomas F., "On the Threshold: Environmental Changes as Causes of Acute Conflict", *International Security*, Vol. 16, No. 2 (Fall 1991), pp. 76–116.

Homer-Dixon, Thomas F., "Environmental Scarcities and Violent Conflict: Evidence from Cases", *International Security*, Vol. 19, No. 1 (Summer 1994), pp. 5–40.

Hong, Jeanhee, "Refugees of the 21st Century: Environmental Injustice", *Cornell Journal of Law and Public Policy*, Vol. 10 (2001), pp. 323–348.

Hugo, Graeme, "Environmental concerns and international migration", *International Migration Review* (The Center for Migration Studies of New York, Inc.), Vol. 30, No. 1, Special Issue: Ethics, Migration, and Global Stewardship(Spring, 1996), pp. 105–131.

Hyndman, Jennifer and Alison Mountz, "Another Brick in the Wall? Neo-Refoulement and the Externalization of Asylum by Australia and Europe<LinkRid="Fn1">¹</Link>", *Government and Opposition*, Vol. 43, No. 2 (2008), pp. 249–269.

Iogna-Prat, Michel, "L'affaire Bereciartua-Echarri", *International Journal of Refugee Law*, Vol. 1, No. 3 (1989), pp. 403–408; also Note sous arrêt, Conseil d'État – 1er Avril 1988, Aff.: Jose Maria Bereciartua-Echarri, Req. No 85.234 (25 March 1988).

Isiksel, N.Türküler , "Fundamental Rights in the EU after Kadi and Al Barakaat", *European Law Journal*, Vol. 16, No. 5 (September 2010), pp. 551–577.

Jackson, Ivor C., "The 1951 Convention Relating to the Status of Refugees: A Universal Basis for Protection", *International Journal of Refugee Law*, Vol. 3, No. 3, pp. 403–413.

Jakab, András, "Problèmes de la Stufenbaulehre: L'échec de l'idée d'inférence et les perspectives de la théorie pure du droit", *Droit et société*, Vol. 2, No. 66 (2007), pp. 411–447.

James, Slack, "Locked up Again, Somali Crook We Can't Send Home", *Daily Mail* (Solo Syndication Ltd.) (2011), p. 12.

Jones, Oliver, "Customary Non-Refoulement of Refugees and Automatic Incorporation into the Common Law: A Hong Kong Perspective", *International & Comparative Law Quarterly* (Cambridge University Press), Vol. 58, No. 2 (2009), pp. 443–468.

Jones, Thomas David, "Sale v. Haitian Centers Council, Inc", *The American Journal of International Law* (American Society of International Law), Vol. 88, No. 1 (1994), pp. 114–126.

Julca, Alex, "Multidimensional Re-Creation of Vulnerabilities and Potential for Resilience in International Migration", *International Migration* (Blackwell Publishing Ltd), Vol. 49 (2011), pp. e30–e49.

Jülich, Sebastian, "Drought Triggered Temporary Migration in an East Indian Village", *International Migration* (Blackwell Publishing Ltd), Vol. 49 (2011), pp. e189–e199.

Julien-Laferrière, François, "L'éloignement Des Étrangers Malades : Faut-Il Préférer Les Réalités Budgétaires Aux Préoccupations Humanitaires?", *RevueTrimestrielle des Droits de l'Homme*, Vol. 77 (2009).

Jurasz, Olga, "The Law of International Human Rights Protection", *International Journal of Refugee Law*, Vol. 22, No. 1, pp. 153–155.

Kälin, Walter, "The Nansen Initiative: building consensus on displacement in disaster contexts, Disasters and displacement in a changing climate", *Forced Migration Review*, Vol. 49 (May 2015), pp. 6–7.

Kälin, Walter, "From the Nansen Principles to the Nansen Initiative", *Forced Migration Review*, Vol. 41 (December 2012), pp. 48–49.

Kälin, Walter, "Non-State Agents of Persecution and the Inability of the State to Protect", *Georgetown Immigration Law Journal*, Vol. 15 (2000–2001), pp. 415–431.

Kamm, Andreas, "ECRE Interview with ECRE Chair, Andreas Kamm", *ECRE Weekly Bulletin*, 26 February 2010.

Keane, David, "The Environmental Causes and Consequences of Migration: A Search for the Meaning of 'Environmental Refugees'", *Georgetown International Environmental Law Review*, Vol. 16 (2003–2004), pp. 209–223.

Kilinski, J., "International Climate Change Liability: A Myth or Reality?", *Journal of Transnational Law and Policy*, Vol. 18 (Spring 2009), p. 377.

King, Tracey, "Environmental Displacement: Coordinating Efforts to Find Solutions", *Georgetown Immigration Law Journal*, Vol. 18 (2005–2006), pp. 543–565.

King, Hugh, "The Extraterritorial Human Rights Obligations of States", *Human Rights Law Review*, January 1, 2009, Vol. 9, No. 4 (2009), pp. 521–556.

Kittrie, Orde F., "Averting Catastrophe: Why the Nuclear Nonproliferation Treaty Is Losing Its Deterrence Capacity and How to Restore It", *Michigan Journal of International Law*, Vol. 28 (2006–2007), pp. 337–430.

Klabbers, Jan, "Moribund on the Fourth of July? The Court of Justice on Prior Agreements of the Member States", *European law review* (Sweet & Maxwell), Vol. 26, No. 2 (2001), pp. 187–197.

Klabbers, Jan, "Safeguarding the Organizational Acquis: The Eu's External Practice", *International Organizations Law Review*, Vol. 4, No. 1 (2007), pp. 57–89.

Kline, Carol L., "EU Inconsistencies Regarding Human Rights Treatment: Can the EU Require Czech Action as a Criterion for Accession", *Boston College International and Comparative Law Review*, Vol. 23 (1999–2000), pp. 35–55.

Klug, Anja, "Harmonization of Asylum in the European Union: Emergence of an EU Refugee System?", *German Yearbook of International Law*, Vol. 47 (2004), pp. 594–628.

Kolmannskog, Vikram Odedra and Finn Myrstad, "Environmental Displacement in European Asylum Law", *European Journal of Migration and Law*, Vol. 11 (2009), pp. 313–326.

Koskenniemi, Martti, P Leino, Auml and IVI, "Fragmentation of International Law? Postmodern Anxieties", *Leiden Journal of International Law*, Vol. 15, No. 03 (2002), pp. 553–579.

Koubi, Vally, Thomas Bernauer, Anna Kalbhenn and Gabriele Spilker, "Climate Variability, Economic Growth, and Civil Conflict", *Journal of Peace Research*, 1 January 2012, Vol. 49, No. 1, pp. 113–127.

Kozoll, Christopher M., "Poisoning the Well: Persecution, the Environment, and Refugee Status", *Colorado Journal of International Environmental Law and Policy*, Vol. 15, No. 2 (2004), pp. 271–307.

Kraler, Albert, Tatiana Cernei and Marion Noack, "Climate Refugees: Legal and Policy Responses to Environmentally Induced Migration" (European Parliament – Directorate General for Internal Policies), PE 462.422 (2011).

Labayle, Henri, "Le droit européen de l'asile devant ses juges : précisions ou remise en question ?", *RFDA*, No. 2 (March–April 2011), pp. 273–290.

Labayle, Henri, "Etude: La loi relative à l'immigration, l'intégration et la nationalité du 16 juin 2011 réformant le droit des étrangers : le fruit de l'arbre empoisonné", *RFDA*, No. 5 (September–October 2011), p. 934s.

Labayle, Henri and Frédéric Sudre, "Jurisprudence de la Cour européenne des droits de l'homme et droit administratif (2009)", *RFDA*, Vol. 4 (July–August 2009).

Labayle, Henri and Frédéric Sudre, "Jurisprudence de la Cour européenne des droits de l'homme et droit administratif (2012)", *RFDA*, No. 3 (May–June 2012), pp. 455–460.

Labayle, Henri, Frédéric Sudre, Xavier Dupré De Boulois and Laure Milano, "Droit administratif et Convention européenne des droits de l'homme", *RFDA*, 06/07/2012, No. 3 (2012), pp. 455–470.

Lallemant, Hervé Raimana, "L`Apatride Climatique et la disparition d`Etat dans le Pacifique Sud", *Revue juridique polynésienne*, Vol. 15 (2009), pp. 77–94.

Lambert, Helene, "Protection against Refoulement from Europe: Human Rights Law Comes to the Rescue", *The International and Comparative Law Quarterly* (Cambridge University Press on behalf of the British Institute of International and Comparative Law), Vol. 48, No. 3 (1999), pp. 515–544.

Lambert, Hélène, "The EU Asylum Qualification Directive, Its Impact on the Jurisprudence of the United Kingdom and International Law", *International & Comparative Law Quarterly*, Vol. 55 (January 2006), pp. 161–192.

Lambert, Hélène and Farrell Theo, "The Changing Character of Armed Conflict and the Implications for Refugee Protection Jurisprudence", *International Journal of Refugee Law*, Vol. 22, No. 2 (2010), pp. 237–273.

Lambert, Hélène, Francesco Messineo and Paul Tiedemann, "Comparative Perspectives of Constitutional Asylum in France, Italy, and Germany: Requiescat in Pace?", *Refugee Survey Quarterly* (Oxford University Press / UK), Vol. 27, No. 3 (2008), pp. 16–32.

Lanz, David, "Subversion or Reinvention? Dilemmas and Debates in the Context of UNHCR's Increasing Involvement with IDPs", *Journal of Refugee Studies*, Vol. 21, No. 2 (2008), pp. 192–209.

Lavergne, Marc, "Le réchauffement climatique à l'origine de la crise du Darfour? La recherche scientifique menacée par le déni de la complexité", *Revue Tiers-Monde*, No. 204 (2010), pp. 220–250.

Leenders, Reinoud, "Refugee Warriors or War Refugees? Iraqi Refugees' Predicament in Syria, Jordan and Lebanon", *Mediterranean Politics*, Vol. 14, No. 3 (2009), pp. 343–363.

Legal Response Initiative, "Human Rights and Climate Change", 19 July 2010.

Leiderman, Stuart and Black Richard, "Environmental Refugees: Myth or Reality?", *New Issues in Refugee Research* (UNHCR), No. 34 (2001).

Lenaerts, Koen, "The Contribution of the European Court of Justice to the Area of Freedom, Security and Justice", *International and Comparative Law Quarterly*, Vol. 59, No. 2.

Liéber, Sophie-Justine and Damien Botteghi, "Droit des étrangers malades : de la condition d'accès effectif aux soins dans le pays d'origine ou de renvoi", *AJDA*, No. 16 (3 May 2010), p. 881.

Limon, Marc, "Human Rights and Climate Change: Constructing a Case for Political Action", *Harvard Environmental Law Review*, Vol. 33 (2009), pp. 439–476.

Lobry, Dorothée, "Pour une définition juridique des réfugiés écologiques : réflexion autour de la qualification juridique de l'atteinte à l'environnement", *REVUE Asylon(s)*, Vol. No 6: Exodes écologiques (November 2008).

Long, Katy, "The Refugee in International Society: Between Sovereigns. By Emma Haddad", *Journal of Refugee Studies*, Vol. 23, No. 1, pp. 99–101.

Lopez, Aurelie, "The Protection of Environmentally-Displaced Persons in International Law", *Environmental Law Review*, Vol. 37, No. 2 (2007), pp. 365–409.

Loraux, Parice, "Consentir", *Le genre humain*, No. 22 (Autumn 1990).

Low, Luan and David Hodgkinson, "Compensation for Wartime Environmental Damage: Challenges to International Law after the Gulf War", *Virginia Journal of International Law*, Vol. 35, No. 2 (Winter 1995), pp. 405–484.

Mancebo, François, "Katrina : Un Aller-Simple Pour Ailleurs. De L'exode À La Migration", *REVUE Asylon(s)*, Vol. No 6: Exodes écologiques (November 2008).

Mantouvalou, Virginia, "Work and Private Life: Sidabras and Dziautas v. Lithuania", *European Law Review*, Vol. 30 (2005), pp. 573–585.

Marat, Kengerlinsky, "Restrictions in EU Immigration and Asylum Policies in the Light of International Human Rights Standards", *Essex Human Rights Review*, Vol. 4, No. 2 (2007).

Marcelle, Reneman, "Access to an Effective Remedy in European Asylum Procedures", *Amsterdam Law Forum*, Vol. 1, No. 1 (2008), pp. 65–98.

Marcs, Carly, "Spoiling Movi's River: Towards Recognition of Persecutory Environmental Harm within the Meaning of the Refugee Convention ", *American University International Law Review*, Vol. 24, No. 1 (2008), pp. 31–71.

Marguénaud, Jean-Pierre, "La Trahison Des Étrangers Sidéens", *RTD Civ.* (2008), p. 643.

Marguénaud, Jean-Pierre and Jean Mouly, "L'avènement d'une Cour européenne des droits sociaux (à propos de CEDH 12 novembre 2008, 'Demir et Baykara c. Turquie')", *Recueil Dalloz*, No. 11 (2009), pp. 739–744.

Marino, Elizabeth, "The Long History of Environmental Migration: Assessing Vulnerability Construction and Obstacles to Successful Relocation in Shishmaref, Alaska", *Global Environmental Change*, Vol. 22 (2012), pp. 374–381.

Mathew, Penelope, James C. Hathaway and Michelle Foster, "The Role of State Protection in Refugee Analysis", *International Journal of Refugee Law* (Oxford University Press / USA), Vol. 15, No. 3 (2003), pp. 444–460.

Mayer, Benoît, "The International Legal Challenges of Climate-Induced Migration: Proposal for an International Legal Framework", *Colorado Journal of International Environmental Law and Policy*, Vol. 22 (Summer 2011), pp. 357–417.

Mayer Benoît, "Climate Migrants and the IOM at Cancun Conference on Climate Change", *McGill Editorials*, 21 January 2011.

Mcadam, Jane, "The emerging New Zealand jurisprudence on climate change, disasters and displacement", *Migration Studies*, Volume 3, Number 1 (2015), pp. 131–142.

Mcadam, Jane, "The European Union Qualification Directive: The Creation of a Subsidiary Protection Regime", *International Journal of Refugee Law*, Vol. 17, No. 3 (2005), pp. 461–516.

Mcadam, Jane, "The Standard of Proof in Complementary Protection Cases: Comparative Approaches in North America and Europe", *University of New South Wales Faculty of Law Research Series*, August 2008, Vol. 50 Working Paper (2008).

Mcadam, Jane, "From Economic Refugees to Climate Refugees?", *Melbourne Journal of International Law*, Vol. 10, No. 2 (2009), pp. 579–595.

Mcadam, Jane, "Swimming against the Tide: Why a Climate Change Displacement Treaty Is Not the Answer", *International Journal of Refugee Law*, Vol. 23, No. 1 (2011), pp. 2–27.

Mcadam, Jane and Ben Saul, "An Insecure Climate for Human Security? Climate-Induced Displacement and International Law", *Legal Studies Research Paper* (Sydney Law School), No. 08/131 (October 2008).

Mccrudden, Christopher, "Human Dignity and Judicial Interpretation of Human Rights", *European Journal of International Law*, September 1, 2008, Vol. 19, No. 4 (2008), pp. 655–724.

Mccue, Gregory S., "Environmental Refugees: Applying International Environmental Law to Involuntary Migration", *Georgetown International Environmental Law Review*, Vol. 6, pp. 151–190.

Mccue, Gregory S., "Environmental Refugees: Applying International Environmental Law to Involuntary Migration", *Georgetown International Environmental Law Review*, Vol. 6 (1993–1994), pp. 151–190.

Mcnamara, Karen Elizabeth, "Conceptualizing Discourses on Environmental Refugees at the United Nations", *Population and Environment*, Vol. 29 (2007), pp. 12–24.

Mercure, Pierre-François, "À la recherche d'un statut juridique pour les migrants environnementaux transfrontaliers: La problématique de la notion de réfugié", *Revue de droit de l'Université de Sherbrooke*, Vol. 37 (2006), pp. 1–39.

Merkl, Adolf, "Das Doppelte Rechtsantlitz", *Juristische Blätter*, Vol. 47 (1918).

Meron, Theodor, "Extraterritoriality of Human Rights Treaties", *The American Journal of International Law* (American Society of International Law), Vol. 89, No. 1 (1995), pp. 78–82.

Millar, Ilona, "There's Not Place Like Home: Human Displacement and Climate Change", *Australian International Law Journal*, Vol. 14 (2007), pp. 71–98.

Mlati, Fatiha and Matthieu Tardis (Eds.), "Asile, La protection subsidiaire en Europe: une mosaïque de droits", *France Terre d'Asile: Les cahiers du social*, No. 18 (September 2008).

Moberg, Kara K., "Extending Refugee Definitions to Cover Environmentally Displaced Persons Displaces Necessary Protection", *Iowa Law Review*, Vol. 94, No. 3 (2009), pp. 1107–1137.

Murray, Rachel, "Recent Developments in the African Human Rights System 2007", *Human Rights Law Review*, Vol. 8, No. 2 (2008), pp. 356–376.

Myers, Norman, "Environment and Security", *Foreign Policy* (Washingtonpost. Newsweek Interactive, LLC), No. 74 (1989), pp. 23–41.

Myers, Norman, "Environmental Refugees", *Population and Environment*, Vol. 19, No. 2 (1997), pp. 167–182.

Newmark, Robert L., "Non-Refoulement Run Afoul: The Questionable Legality of Extraterritorial Repatriation Programs", *Washington University Law Review*, Vol. 71, No. 3 (1993), pp. 833–870.

Nine, Cara, "Ecological Refugees, States Borders, and the Lockean Proviso Cara Nine Ecological Refugees, States Borders, and the Lockean Proviso", *Journal of Applied Philosophy*, Vol. 27, No. 4 (2010), pp. 359–375.

Öberg, Marko Divac, "The Legal Effects of Resolutions of the UN Security Council and General Assembly in the Jurisprudence of the ICJ", *European Journal of International Law*, November 2005, Vol. 16, No. 5 (2005), pp. 879–906.

Oloka-Onyango, Joe, "Human Rights, the Oau Convention and the Refugee Crisis in Africa: Forty Years after Geneva", *International Journal of Refugee Law*, Vol. 3, No. 3 (1991).

Oreskes Naomi, "Beyond the Ivory Tower: the Scientific Consensus on Climate Change", *Science* (3 December 2004), Vol. 306, No. 5702, pp. 1686s.

Pallis, Mark, "Obligations of States Towards Asylum Seekers at Sea: Interactions and Conflicts between Legal Regimes", *International Journal of Refugee Law*, April 1, 2002, Vol. 14, No. 2 and 3 (2002), pp. 329–364.

Paludan, Anne, "Refugees in Europe", *International Migration Review* (The Center for Migration Studies of New York, Inc.), Vol. 15, No. 1/2 (1981), pp. 69–73.

Panjabi, Ranee K.L., "International Politics in the 1990s: Some Implications for Human Rights and the Refugee Crisis", *Dickinson Journal of Int'l Law*, Vol. 10, No. 1 (1991–1992), pp. 1–23.

Peers, Steve, "Immigration, Asylum and the European Union Charter of Fundamental Rights", *European Journal of Migration and Law*, Vol. 3 (2001), pp. 141–169.

Peers, Steve, "Human Rights, Asylum and European Community Law", *UNHCR Refugee Survey Quarterly*, Vol. 24, No. 2 (2005).

Pestana, Inês Máximo, "'Tolerated Stay': What Protection Does It Give?", *Forced Migration Review*, Vol. 40 (August 2012), pp. 38–39.

Piguet, Etienne, "Climate Change and Forced Migration", *New Issues in Refugee Research* (UNHCR), No. 153 (2008).

Piguet, Etienne, Antoine Pécoud and Paul De Guchteneire, "Migration and Climate Change: An Overview", *Refugee Survey Quarterly*, September 1, 2011, Vol. 30, No. 3 (2011), pp. 1–23.

Piotrowicz, Ryszard and Carina Van Eck, "Subsidiary Protection and Primary Rights", *International and Comparative Law Quarterly*, Vol. 53, No. 1 (2004), pp. 107–138.

Piotrowicz, Ryszard and Carina Van Eck, "Subsidiary Protection and Primary Rights", *International and Comparative Law Quarterly*, Vol. 53, No. 1 (2004), pp. 107–138.

Posch, Albert, "The Kadi Case: Rethinking the Relationship between EU Law and International Law?", *Columbia Journal of European Law Online*, Vol. 15 (2009), pp. 1–5.

Prieur, Michel, Jean-Pierre Marguénaud, Gérard Monédiaire, Julien Bétaille, Bernard Drobenko, Jean-Jacques Gouguet, Jean-Marc Lavieille, Séverine Nadaud and Damien Roets, "Projet de convention relative au statut international des déplacés environnementaux", *Revue Européene de Droit de l'Environnement*, Vol. 4 (2008), pp. 81–93.

Prieur, Michel, Jean-Pierre Marguénaud, Gérard Monédiaire Julien Bétaille, Bernard Drobenko, Jean-Jacques Gouguet, Jean-Marc Lavieille, Séverine Nadaud and Damien Roets, "Projet de convention relative au statut international des déplacés environnementaux", *Revue de droit de l'Université de Sherbrooke – RDUS*, Vol. 39 (2008–09), pp. 451–505.

Raleigh, Clionadh and Dominic Kniveton, "Come Rain or Shine: An Analysis of Conflict and Climate Variability in East Africa", *Journal of Peace Research*, January 1, 2012, Vol. 49, No. 1, pp. 51–64.

Raleigh, Clionadh and Dominic Kniveton, "Come Rain or Shine: An Analysis of Conflict and Climate Variability in East Africa", *Journal of Peace Research*, January 1, 2012, Vol. 49, No. 1, pp. 51–64.

Raleigh, Clionadh and Dominic Kniveton, "Come Rain or Shine: An Analysis of Conflict and Climate Variability in East Africa", *Journal of Peace Research*, Vol. 49, No. 1 (2012), pp. 51–64.

Renaud, Fabrice G., Olivia Dun, Koko Warner and Janos Bogardi, "A Decision Framework for Environmentally Induced Migration", *International Migration* (Blackwell Publishing Ltd), Vol. 49 (2011), pp. e5–e29.

Reuveny, Rafael, "Climate Change-Induced Migration and Violent Conflict", *Political Geography*, Vol. 26, No. 6 (2007), pp. 656–673.

Rishmawi, Mervat, "The Revised Arab Charter on Human Rights: A Step Forward", *Human Rights Law Review*, Vol. 5, No. 2 (2005), pp. 361–376.

Ritleng, Dominique, Aude Bouveresse and Jean-Philippe Kovar, "Jurisprudence administrative française intéressant le droit communautaire", *Revue trimestrielle de droit européen*, No. 2 (28/07/2010), pp. 453–492.

Röhl, Katharina, "Fleeing Violence and Poverty: Non-Refoulement Obligations under the European Convention of Human Rights", *New Issues in Refugee Research* (UNHCR), No. 111 (2005).

Salehyan, Idean, "From Climate Change to Conflict? No Consensus Yet", *Journal of Peace Research*, May 1, 2008, Vol. 45, No. 3 (2008), pp. 315–326.

Schachter, Oscar, "Human Dignity as a Normative Concept", *The American Journal of International Law* (American Society of International Law), Vol. 77, No. 4 (1983), pp. 848–854.

Schermers, Henry G. and "The European Communities Bound by Fundamental Human Rights", *Common Market Law Review*, Vol. 27, No. 2 (1990).

Seatzu, Francesco, "On Some General Theoretical and Practical Questions Arising from the Application of the European Convention on Human Rights in Asylum Cases", *Anuario de Derecho Internacional*, Vol. 25 (2009), pp. 469–500.

Sgro, Aurélie, "Towards Recognition of Environmental Refugees by the European Union", *REVUE Asylon(s)*, Vol. No 6: Exodes écologiques (November 2008).

Shen, Shawn and François Gemenne, "Contrasted Views on Environmental Change and Migration: The Case of Tuvaluan Migration to New Zealand", *International Migration* (Blackwell Publishing Ltd), Vol. 49 (2011), pp. e224–e242.

Simeon, James C., "A Comparative Analysis of the Response of the UNHCR and Industrialized States to Rapidly Fluctuating Refugee Status and Asylum Applications: Lessons and Best Practices for Rsd Systems Design and Administration", *International Journal of Refugee Law*, Vol. 22, No. 1, pp. 72–103.

Simeon, James C., "A Comparative Analysis of the Response of the UNHCR and Industrialized States to Rapidly Fluctuating Refugee Status and Asylum Applications: Lessons and Best Practices for Rsd Systems Design and Administration", *International Journal of Refugee Law*, Vol. 22, No. 1 (2010), pp. 72–103.

Simsarian, James, "Draft International Covenant on Human Rights Revised at 1950 Session of the United Nations Commission on Human Rights", *The American Journal of International Law* (American Society of International Law), Vol. 45, No. 1 (1951), pp. 170–177.

Skouris, Vassilios, "Fundamental Rights and Fundamental Freedoms: The Challenge of Striking a Delicate Balance", *European business law review*, Vol. 17, No. 2 (2006), pp. 225–239.

Slettebak, Rune T, "Don't Blame the Weather! Climate-Related Natural Disasters and Civil Conflict", *Journal of Peace Research*, January 1, 2012, Vol. 49, No. 1, pp. 163–176.

Smith, Martin, "Book Reviews", *Journal of Social Work Practice* (Routledge), 03, Vol. 21, No. 1 (2007), pp. 119–126.

Stal, Marc, "Flooding and Relocation: The Zambezi River Valley in Mozambique", *International Migration* (Blackwell Publishing Ltd), Vol. 49 (2011), pp. e125–e145.

Stand up for Your Rights, "The Human Side of Climate Change: Human Rights Violations and Climate Change Refugees" (December 2009), pp. 17–23.

Stellman, Steven D. and Jeanne M. Stellman, "Exposure Opportunity Models for Agent Orange, Dioxin, and Other Military Herbicides Used in Vietnam, 1961–1971", *Journal of Exposure Analysis & Environmental Epidemiology* (Nature Publishing Group), Vol. 14, No. 4 (2004), pp. 354–362.

Stellman, Jeanne Mager, Steven D. Stellman, Richard Christian, Tracy Weber and Carrie Tomasallo, "The Extent and Patterns of Usage of Agent Orange and Other Herbicides in Vietnam", *Nature*, 17 April 2003, Vol. 422, pp. 681–687.

Storey, Hugo, "The Internal Flight Alternative Test: The Furisprudence Re-Examined", *International Journal of Refugee Law*, July 1, 1998, Vol. 10, No. 3 (1998), pp. 499–532.

Storey, Hugo, "Complementary Protection: Should There Be a Common Approach to Providing Protection to Persons Who Are Not Covered by the 1951 Geneva Convention?", paper prepared for the Joint ILPA/IARLJ Symposium, 6 December 1999 (1999).

Storey, Hugo, "EU Refugee Qualification Directive: A Brave New World?", *International Journal of Refugee Law*, March 1, 2008, Vol. 20, No. 1 (2008), pp. 1–49.

Storey, Hugo, "Armed Conflict in Asylum Law: The 'War-Flaw'", *Refugee Survey Quarterly*, Vol. 31, No. 2 (2012), pp. 1–32.

Suhrke, Astri, "Environmental Degradation and Population flows", *Journal of International Affairs*, Vol. 47 (1994), pp. 473–496.

Tchen, Vincent (Ed.) "Droit Des Étrangers", *Constitutions – Revue de droit constitutionnel appliqué*, No. 3 (July–September 2010), p. 437.

Teitgen-Colly, Catherine, "The European Union and Asylum: An Illusion of Protection", *Common Market Law Review* (Kluwer Law International), Vol. 43, No. 6 (2006), p. 1503.

Thames, H. Knox, "India's Failure to Adequately Protect Refugees", *Human Rights Brief*, Vol. 7, No. 1 (1999), pp. 20–23.

Theisen, Ole Magnus, Helge Holtermann and Halvard Buhaug, "Climate Wars?: Assessing the Claim That Drought Breeds Conflict", *International Security*, Vol. 36, No. 3 (Winter 2011/12), pp. 79–106.

Thomas, John F., "Refugees: A New Approach", *International Migration Review* (The Center for Migration Studies of New York, Inc.), Vol. 15, No. 1/2 (1981), pp. 20–25.

Tiedemann, Paul, "Subsidiary Protection and the Function of Article 15(c) of the Qualification Directive", *Refugee Survey Quarterly*, March 1, 2012, Vol. 31, No. 1 (2012), pp. 123–138.

Tiedemann, Paul, "Subsidiary Protection and the Function of Article 15(c) of the Qualification Directive", *Refugee Survey Quarterly*, Vol. 31, No. 1 (2012), pp. 123–138.

Tol, Richard S.J. and Roda Verheyen, "State Responsibility and Compensation for Climate Change Damages – a Legal and Economic Assessment", *Energy Policy*, Vol. 32 (2004), pp. 1109–1130.

Turpin, Dominique, "La loi no 2017-672 du 16 juin 2011 relative à l'immigration, à l'intégration et à la nationalité (1) : de l'art de profiter de la transposition des directives pour durcir les prescriptions nationales", *Revue critique de droit international privé*, No. 3 (July–September 2011), pp. 499–520.

Van Der Geest, Kees, "North–south Migration in Ghana: What Role for the Environment?", *International Migration* (Blackwell Publishing Ltd), Vol. 49 (2011), pp. e69–e94.

Van Selm, Joanne and Eleni Tsolakis, "The Enlargement of an 'Area of Freedom, Security and Justice': Managing Migration in a European Union of 25 Members", *Migration Policy Institute – Policy Brief*, No. 4 (May 2004).

Verhaeghe, Laure, "Quels droits pour les réfugiés environnementaux qui perdront leur Etat ? Le cas de Tuvalu", *REVUE Asylon(s)*, Vol. No 6: Exodes écologiques (November 2008).

Vité, Sylvain, "Typology of Armed Conflicts in International Humanitarian Law: Legal Concepts and Actual Situations", *International Review of the Red Cross*, Vol. 91, No. 873 (March 2009), pp. 69–94.

Walter Anthony, Katey M., Peter Anthony, Guido Grosse and Jeffrey Chanton, "Geologic Methane Seeps Along Boundaries of Arctic Permafrost Thaw and Melting Glaciers", *Nature Geosci* (Nature Publishing Group), Vol. advance online publication (2012).

Warnecke, Andrea, Dennis Tänzler and Ruth Vollmer, "Climate Change, Migration and Conflict: Receiving Communities under Pressure?" (The German Marshall Fund of the United States, June 2010).

Warner, Koko and Tamer Afifi, "Introduction", *International Migration* (Blackwell Publishing Ltd), Vol. 49 (2011), pp. e1–e4.

Weiler, J.H.H., "The Transformation of Europe", *The Yale Law Journal* (The Yale Law Journal Company, Inc.), Vol. 100, No. 8 (1991), pp. 2403–2483.

Weis, Paul, "The Concept of the Refugee in International Law", *Journal du droit international*, Vol. 87 (1960), p. 928.

Weissbrodt, David and Isabel Hortreiter, "The Principle of Non-Refoulement: Article 3 of the Convention against Torture and Other Cruel, Inhuman or Degrading Treatment or Punishment in Comparison with the Non-Refoulement Provisions of Other International Human Rights Treaties", *Buffalo Human Rights Law Review*, Vol. 5 (1999), pp. 1–74.

Wicks, Elizabeth, "The Meaning of 'Life': Dignity and the Right to Life in International Human Rights Treaties", *Human Rights Law Review*, June 1, 2012, Vol. 12, No. 2 (2012), pp. 199–219.

Williams, Angela, "Turning the Tide: Recognizing Climate Change Refugees in International Law", *Law & Policy*, Vol. 30, No. 4 (October 2008).

Yablokov, Alexey V., Vassily B. Nesterenko and Alexey V. Nesterenko, "Atmospheric, Water, and Soil Contamination after Chernobyl", *Annals of the New York Academy of Sciences*, Vol. 1181, No. 1 (November 2009), pp. 223–236.

Ziemer, Laura S., "Application in Tibet of the Principles on Human Rights and the Environment", *Harvard Human Rights Journal*, Vol. 14 (2001), pp. 233–275.

Newspaper Articles, Internet Resources, Conference Material prescriptions nationales", Revue critique and Others

Afifi, Tamer and Jäger Jill, *Environment, Forced Migration and Social Vulnerability* (New York: Springer, 2010), retrieved from: <http://myaccess.library.utoronto.ca/login?url=http://site.ebrary.com/lib/utoronto/Top?id=10408102>.

African, Caribbean and Pacific Observatory on Migration, *Leaflet*, available at: <www.acpmigration.org> [accessed 01/05/2012].

Araneta, Lina, "The Vision of Planetary Citizenship", *Manila Standard*, 11 January 1996, available at: <http://news.google.com/newspapers?nid=1370&dat=19960111&id=BP4tAAAAIBAJ&sjid=YwsEAAAAIBAJ&pg=6539,1635332> [11/07/2012].

Baillat, Alice, *Les migrations environnementales : Logiques d'investissement des acteurs et obstacles relatifs à la construction d'un nouveau problème public*, Masters Thesis Recueil Alexandries, (September 2010) available at: <www.reseau-terra.eu/article1078.html>.

Battjes, Hemme, "Landmarks: Soering's Legacy", *Amsterdam Law Forum*, Vol. 1, No. 1 (VU University of Amsterdam, 2008), retrieved from: <http://ojs.ubvu.vu.nl/alf/article/view/51/67>.

BBC News Online, "Haiti Cholera: UN Peacekeepers to Blame, Report Says", *BBC News, Latin America & Caribbean* (BBC, 2012), 8 December 2010, retrieved from: <http://www.bbc.co.uk/news/world-latin-america-11943902>.

BBC, "MEPs Clash over EU Accession to ECHR", *Democracy Live* (BBC, 2012), last updated 19 April 2012, retrieved from: <http://news.bbc.co.uk/democracylive/hi/europe/newsid_9709000/9709051.stm>.

Bernd Parusel for German Federal Office For Migration and Refugees, "Germany National Report (March 2010): The Granting of Non-EU Harmonised Protection Statuses in Germany, Research Study II/2009 in the Framework of the European Migration Network (EMN)", *in EMN Study on The Different Practices Concerning Granting of Non-EU Harmonised Protection Statuses* (n/a: EMN, Februay 2010), retrieved from: <http://emn.intrasoft-intl.com/Downloads/download.do;jsessionid=48CB45E0CA5EB4C57AD0BB871285B576?fileID=960> [04/06/2011].

Biermann, Frank and Boas Ingrid, "Protecting Climate Refugees: The Case for a Global Protocol", *Environment*, November–December 2008, retrieved from: <www.environmentmagazine.org/Archives/Back%20Issues/November-December%202008/Biermann-Boas-full.html>.

Bosshard, Peter, "Chinese Government Acknowledges Problems of Three Gorges Dam", *International Rivers*, 19 May 2011, retrieved from: <http://www.internationalrivers.org/blogs/227/chinese-government-acknowledges-problems-of-three-gorges-dam>.

Brookings, Georgetown University and United Nations High Commissioner for Refugees (UNHCR), *Guidance on Protecting People from Disasters and Environmental Change through Planned Relocation ("Guidance on Planned Relocation")*, 7 October 2015, also available online at: <http://www.unhcr.org/protection/environment/562f798d9/planned-relocation-guidance-october-2015.html> [accessed 27/10/2016].

Brown, Oli, *Climate Change and Forced Migration Observations, Projections and Implications* (Geneva: International Institute for Sustainable Development, 2007), retrieved from: <http://myaccess.library.utoronto.ca/login?url=http://site.ebrary.com/lib/utoronto/Top?id=10204295>.

Brown, Oli and International Organization for Migration., *Migration and Climate Change* (Geneva: International Organization for Migration, 2008), retrieved from: <http://myaccess.library.utoronto.ca/login?url=http://site.ebrary.com/lib/utoronto/Top?id=10222405>.

Buckingham, William A. Jr., *Operation Ranch Hand: The Air Force and Herbicides in Southeast Asia 1961–1971* (Washington, D.C.: Office of Air Force History, 1982), retrieved from: <http://www.dtic.mil/cgi-bin/GetTRDoc?Location=U2&doc=GetTRDoc.pdf&AD=ADA121709>.

Buckingham, William A. Jr., "Operation Ranch Hand: Herbicides in Southeast Asia", *Air University Review* (July–August 1983), retrieved from: <http://www.airpower.maxwell.af.mil/airchronicles/aureview/1983/jul-aug/buckingham.html>.

Bush, George W., "Presidential Address to the Nation (the Treaty Room)" (Office of the Press Secretary, 7 October 2001), retrieved from: <http://georgewbush-whitehouse.archives.gov/news/releases/2001/10/20011007-8.html>.

Butler, Israel De Jesús, "The EU and International Human Rights Law", *in* (Geneva: OHCHR, Regional Office for Europe, date unknown), retrieved from: <http://www.europe.ohchr.org/EN/Publications/Pages/publications.aspx> [10/07/2012].

Carney, Scott, Jason Miklian and Kristian Hoelscher, "Fortress India: Why Is Delhi Building a New Berlin Wall to Keep out Its Bangladeshi Neighbors?", July/August 2011 available at: <www.foreignpolicy.com/articles/2011/06/20/fortress_india> [11/05/2012].

Chotouras, Dimitrios, *Le statut juridique en droit international du réfugié écologique : une nécessité ! (Le phénomène migratoire du fait des modifications environnementales)*, 9 February 2012, Doctoral Thesis, Université de Lorraine (not yet published: 2012).

Colin, Jean-François, "M. Juncker est un grand ami du Cap-Vert", *Luxemburger Wort*, 25 April 2012, retrieved from: <http://www.wort.lu/fr/view/m-juncker-est-un-grand-ami-du-cap-vert-4f980bdce4bod08d36c040f9>.

CVCE, "The European Political Community" (Centre Virtuel de la Connaissance sur l'Europe – CVCE, 2004–2012), 11 August 2011, retrieved from: <www.cvce.eu>.

Danish Institute for International Studies (DIIS), Danish Institute For Human Rights (DIHR), Danish Ministry of Refugee; Immigration and Integration Affairs, Danish Refugee Council (DRC) and Aarhus University School Of Law, 2011 Nordic Asylum Law Seminar: The State of International Refugee Law, EU Harmonization and the Nordic Legacy, organised in Copenhagen, on 26–27 May 2011.

Delouis, B., R. Lacassin, J. Van Der Woerd and S. Lallemand, "Le Séisme", *in Séisme de Tohoku-Oki (Japon 11 mars 2011)*, 18 March 2011, last updated 24 March 2011 (n/a: Institut national des sciences de l'univers du Centre national de la recherche scientifique – INSU-CNRS, 2011), retrieved from: <http://www.insu.cnrs.fr/terre-solide/catastrophes-et-risques/seismes/le-seisme> [14/09/2012].

Derain, Barbara (OFPRA), Personal Communication, 28 August 2012.

Dolsak, Nives and Aseem Prakash, "'Climate Change Did It!' Is a Convenient Excuse", *Slate*, 21 October 2016, accessible at: <http://www.slate.com/articles/health_and_science/science/2016/10/blaming_natural_disasters_on_climate_change_will_backfire.html> [21/10/2016].

Doyle, Mark, "UN 'Should Take Blame for Haiti Cholera' – Us House Members", *BBC News, Latin America & Caribbean* (BBC, 2012), 20 July 2012, retrieved from: <http://www.bbc.co.uk/news/world-africa-18928405>.

Dun, Olivia and François Gemenne, "Defining Environmental Migration : Why It Matters So Much, Why It Is Controversial and Some Practical Processes Which May Help Move Forward", *REVUE Asylon(s)*, No. 6 (November 2008), retrieved from: <http://www.reseau-terra.eu/article847.html>.

Egeland, Jan and Jessica Evans, "Rio+20 Missed an Opportunity to Bolster Human Rights", *The Guardian – Poverty Matters Blog*, 27 June 2012, available at: <www.guardian.co.uk/global-development/poverty-matters/2012/jun/27/rio20-missed-opportunity-human-rights>.

EMN, "Finland National Report (February 2010): The Different National Practises Concerning Granting of Non-EU Harmonised Protection Statuses", *in EMN Study on The Different Practices Concerning Granting of Non-EU Harmonised Protection Statuses* (n/a: EMN, December 2010), retrieved from: <http://emn.intrasoft-intl.com/Downloads/download.do;jsessionid=48CB45E0CA5EB4C57AD0BB871285B576?fileID=965>.

EMN, "Sweden National Report", *in Annual Report on Asylum and Migration Statistics 2007* (n/a: EMN, November 2009), retrieved from: <http://emn.intrasoft-intl.com>.

EMN, *EMN Synthesis Report – Annual Policy Report 2010*, (September 2011), retrieved from: <http://www.emn.europa.eu> [03/09/2012].

Equity and Justice Working Group Bangladesh (EquityBD), "Climate Change Induced Forced Migrants: in need of dignified recognition under a new Protocol", December 2009, accessible at: <http://www.mediaterre.org/docactu,Q0RJLUwtMy9kb2Nz

L2NsaW1hdGUtbWlncmFudC1wcmludGVkLXBvc2loaW9uLWRlYyowOQ==,1.pdf> [accessed 08/10/2016].

L'Essentiel Online/Afp, "Scénario du pire: 323 000 Japonais morts dans un tsunami", *L'essentiel Online* (AFP, 2012), 29 August 2012, retrieved from: <http://www.lessentiel.lu/fr/news/monde/story/323-000-Japonais-morts-dans-un-tsunami-28595146>.

EUROPA, "European Asylum Support Office", © European Union, 1995–2012, 17 February 2011, retrieved from the website of Europa-Summaries of EU legislation at: <http://europa.eu/legislation_summaries/justice_freedom_security/free_movement_of_persons_asylum_immigration/jl0022_en.htm> [10/08/2012].

EUROPA, "EU Accountability Report on Financing for Development: Luxembourg's Replies to the Questionnaire for Preparing the 2012 Report" (© European Union, 1995–2012), retrieved from: <http://ec.europa.eu/europeaid/how/finance/documents/lu-eu-2012-monitoring-questionnaire-final-sanitized_en.pdf>.

EUROPA, "Fundamental Rights and Non-Discrimination", *in The Amsterdam treaty: a comprehensive guide* (n/a: European Union, 1995–2012), retrieved from: <http://europa.eu/legislation_summaries/institutional_affairs/treaties/amsterdam_treaty/index_en.htm> [03/08/2010].

Europa, European Commission, EuropeAid Cooperation Office, *"Budget Support: the Effective Way to Finance Development?"*, brochure published in 2008 and available at:<http://ec.europa.eu/europeaid/infopoint/publications/europeaid/documents/budgetsupport08_en.pdf> [accessed 01/05/2012].

European Migration Network – EMN, *The Different Practices Concerning Granting of Non-EU Harmonised Protection Statuses* (n/a: EMN, December 2010), retrieved from: <http://emn.intrasoft-intl.com/Downloads/prepareShowFiles.do?directory ID=122> [01/06/2011].

EUROSTAT, "Eurostat News Release: Asylum in the EU27, the Number of Asylum Applicants Registered in the EU27 Rose to 301 000 in 2011", STAT/12/46, © European Union, 1995–2012, 23 March 2012, retrieved from the website of the European Union at: <http://europa.eu/rapid/pressReleasesAction.do?reference=STAT/12/46&format=HTML&aged=1&language=EN&guiLanguage=en> [30/07/2012].

EUROSTAT, "Eurostat News Release: Asylum Decisions in the EU27: EU Member States Granted Protection to 84 100 Asylum Seekers in 2011", STAT/12/96, © European Union, 1995–2012, 19 June 2012, retrieved from the website of the European Union at: <http://europa.eu/rapid/pressReleasesAction.do?reference=STAT/12/96&format=HTML&aged=0&language=EN&guiLanguage=en> [30/07/2012].

Evans, Gareth, "Facing up to Our Responsibilities", *The Guardian*, 12 May 2008, retrieved from: <www.guardian.co.uk/commentisfree/2008/may/12/faciguptoour responsbilities>.

Ferris, Elizabeth, *Making Sense of Climate Change, Natural Disasters, and Displacement: A Work in Progress*, retrieved from: <http://link.library.utoronto.ca/eir/EIRdetail.cfm?Resources__ID=988671&T=F>.

Forelle, Charles and José De Córdoba, "Among Quake's Victims: Haiti's Government", *The Wall Street Journal*, 17 January 2010.

Frelick, Bill, "Sharing Greece's Asylum Shame", *The European Voice*, 29 September 2011, available at: <www.hrw.org/news/2011/09/29/sharing-greeces-asylum-shame> [04/08/2012].

Gamito, Philippe, Le Statut International Des Personnes Victimes de Catastrophes Naturelles : Être Ou Ne Pas Être Un Réfugié ? (Student Paper), retrieved from the Instituto de Ciências Jurídico-Políticas website at: <http://icjp.pt/sites/default/files/media/869-1384.pdf> [16/07/2012].

Ghosh, Palash R., "India-Bangladesh Border: The ?Berlin Wall? Of Asia", *International Business Times*, 12 June 2012, available at: <www.ibtimes.com/india-bangladesh-border-berlin-wall-asia-702454> [02/09/2012].

Glahn, Ben, "'Climate Refugees'? Addressing the International Legal Gaps", *International Bar Association*, retrieved from: <www.ibanet.org/Article/Detail.aspx?ArticleUid=B51C02C1-3C27-4AE3-B4C4-7E350EB0F442>.

Godinho, Luiz Fernando, "Rio+20 Summit: UN Refugee Chief Calls for Joint Approach to Urban Refugees, Displaced" (UNHCR, 2012), 21 June 2012, retrieved from: <http://www.unhcr.org/4fe2e7d76.html>.

Goodwin-Gill, Guy S., "Convention Relating to the Status of Refugees – Protocol Relating to the Status of Refugees" (United Nations Audiovisual Library of International Law, © United Nations, 2008), retrieved from: <http://untreaty.un.org/cod/avl/pdf/ha/prsr/prsr_e.pdf>.

Gray, Louise, "Rio+20: Nick Clegg Blames China for 'Disappointing Text'", *The Telegraph*, 21 June 2012, available at: <www.telegraph.co.uk/earth/environment/9347888/Rio20-Nick-Clegg-blames-China-for-disappointing-text.html> [25/06/2012]Cohen, Roberta, "The Burma Cyclone and the Responsibility to Protect" (The Brookings Institution, 2012), 21 July 2008, retrieved from: <www.brookings.edu/research/speeches/2008/07/21-myanmar-cohen>.

Guarniero, Jean-Louis, *Le transfert d'argent des migrants : le cas Luxembourg – Cap Vert* (Luxembourg: Agence de Transfert de Technologie Financière – ATTF, December 2005), retrieved from: <www.microfinance2005.lu> [03/09/2012].

Hervieu, Nicolas, "Droit à un environnement sain (Art. 8 CEDH) : Catastrophe écologique, obligations de protection de l'Etat et lien de causalité entre une maladie et la catastrophe" (CREDOF Université Paris Ouest Nanterre La Défense, retrieved from: <www.droits-libertes.org>).

Hiyama, Hiroshi, "Fukushima: un 'désastre créé par l'homme', selon un rapport officiel", *TV5 Monde* (AFP, 2012), 5 July 2012, retrieved from: <http://www.tv5.org/cms/chaine-francophone/info>.

Hiyama, Hiroshi, "Fukushima Was 'Man-Made' Disaster: Japanese Probe", *Phys.Org* (AFP, 2012), 04 July 2012, retrieved from: <http://phys.org/news/2012-07-japan-diet-publish-fukushima-disaster.html>.

Hodgkinson, David and Young Lucy, "'In the Face of Looming Catastrophe': A Convention for Climate Change Displaced Persons" (January 2012), retrieved from: <www.ccdpconvention.com>.

Hugo Graeme, "Migration, Development and Environment – Draft Paper", *Research Workshop on Migration and the Environment: Developing a global research agenda*, held in Munich on 16–18 April 2008, p. 11, retrieved from: <www.ciesin.columbia.edu/repository/pern/papers/hugo_statement.pdf> [05/05/2012].

Human Rights Education Associates – HREA, "Study Guide: Refugees and Displaced Persons" (© HREA, 1997–2007), retrieved from: <http://www.hrea.org/index.php?doc_id=418>.

Human Rights Watch, 50 Years On: What Future for Refugee Protection? at: <http://www.hrw.org/sites/default/files/reports/pdf1.pdf> [06/12/2011].

Humphreys, Stephen, *Human Rights and Climate Change* (Cambridge, New York: Cambridge University Press, 2010), retrieved from: <http://myaccess.library.utoronto.ca/login?url=http://dx.doi.org/10.1017/CBO9780511770722>.

Hvistendahl, Mara, "China's Three Gorges Dam: An Environmental Catastrophe?", *Scientific American*, 25 March 2008, retrieved from: <http://www.scientificamerican.com/article.cfm?id=chinas-three-gorges-dam-disaster>.

IDMC, "Pakistan: Displacement Caused by Conflict and Natural Disasters, Achievements and Challenges" (Norwegian Refugee Council, 2012), 10 January 2012, retrieved from: <www.internal-displacement.org>.

ILC Codification Division – Office of Legal Affairs, "Right of Asylum", last updated 30 June 2005, retrieved from: <http://untreaty.un.org/ilc/summaries/6_2.htm#_ftn5>.

Immigration and Refugee Board of Canada Research Directorate, "Haiti: Overview of Police Reform Efforts; the Effectiveness of the Police; Existence of a Police Complaints Authority and Recourse Available to Individuals Who File Complaints against the Police; Initial Impact of 12 January 2010 Earthquake" ("Haitian police in the aftermath of the 2010 earthquake"), HTI103346.E, 16 February 2010.

IOM, *Migration and Climate Change: A Complex Nexus*, retrieved from: <http://www.iom.int/jahia/Jahia/complex-nexus> [15/12/2011].

IOM, "Migration and Climate Change: A Complex Nexus", retrieved from: <www.iom.int/jahia/Jahia/complex-nexus>.

Kälin, Walter, "Sendai Framework: An important step forward for people displaced by disasters", *Up Front*, blog published on Brookings website, 20 March 2015, available at: <http://www.brookings.edu/blogs/up-front/posts/2015/03/20-sendai-disasters-displaced-kalin> [accessed 20/06/2016].

Kälin, Walter, "Keynote Address on Internal Displacement and the Marsh Arabs of Iraq", Panel on IDP Issues and the Marsh Arabs, the AMAR Foundation Conference, organised in London, in 1 March 2006, retrieved from: <www.brookings.edu/events/2006/03/01-iraq> [06/12/2011].

Karlsson, Ida, "Sweden Slammed over Iraqi Deportations" (Inter Press Service – IPS, 2012), 24 January 2011, retrieved from: <http://www.ipsnews.net/2011/01/sweden-slammed-over-iraqi-deportations/>.

Keita, Mama, *Impacts des migrations forcées sur les pays hôtes*, November 2007, Doctoral Thesis, Faculté des études supérieures de l'Université de Montréal (Montréal: Université de Montréal, 1 May 2008) available at: <http://hdl.handle.net/1866/2254>.

Lawson, Rick A., *Het EVRM en de Europese Gemeenschappen: Bouwstenen voor een aansprakelijkheidsregime voor het optreden van internationale organisaties*, 1999, Doctoral thesis (Leiden: Kluwer – Europese Monografieën, 1999).

Lawry, Steven, "Paul Farmer's Call for a New Conversation on Aid to Haiti", *Humanitarian & Development NGOs Domain of Practice Blog* (Hauser Center for Nonprofit Oganizations at Harvard University, 2011), 9 December 2011, retrieved from: <http://hausercenter.org/iha/2011/12/09/paul-farmer%e2%80%99s-call-for-a-new-conversation-on-aid-to-haiti/>.

Lespinasse, Colette and GARR, "Plus de 75 boat people noyés en un seul mois, c'est trop !", 30 December 2011, retrieved from: <http://www.garr-haiti.org/index.php/nouvelles/actualite/migrants/item/897-spip897>.

Lobry, Dorothée, "Pour une définition juridique des réfugiés écologiques : réflexion autour de la qualification juridique de l'atteinte à l'environnement", *REVUE Asylon(s)*, No. 6: Exodes écologiques, November 2008, retrieved from: <http://www.reseauterra.eu/article846.html>.

Lubbers, Ruud, "Statement by Mr. Ruud Lubbers, United Nations High Commissioner for Refugees", *High Commissionner Statements*, Informal Meeting of the European Union Ministers for Justice and Ministers for Home Affairs, organised in Stockholm, on 8 February 2001.

Macchi, Mirjam, Gonzalo Oviedo, Sarah Gotheil, Katharine Cross, Agni Boedhihartono, Caterina Wolfangel and Matthew Howell, *Indigenous and Traditional Peoples and Climate Change* (n/a: International Union for Conservation of Nature – IUCN, March 2008), retrieved from: <http://cmsdata.iucn.org/downloads/indigenous_peoples_climate_change.pdf>.

Magnigny, Véronique, "Des Victimes de L'environnement Aux Réfugiés de L'environnement", *REVUE Asylon(s)*, No. 6, *Exodes écologiques* (November 2008), retrieved from: <www.reseau-terra.eu/article845.html>.

Magnigny, Véronique, *Les réfugiés de l'environnement: Hypothèse juridique à propos d'une menace écologique*, 25 May 1999, Doctoral Thesis, Université de Droit – Paris I Panthéon Sorbonne (n/a: Recueil Alexandries, Collections Etudes, 1999) available at: <http://www.reseau-terra.eu/article689.html>.

Malvasio, Florence, "Étude : La famille et le droit d'asile en France", *in Contentieux des réfugiés: Jurisprudence du Conseil d'État et de la Cour nationale du droit d'asile, année*

2010 (Montreuil: CNDA, Juin 2011), pp.201–217, retrieved from: <http://www.cnda.fr/media/document/CNDA/recueil-2010.pdf> [28/08/2012].

The Mainichi, "Huge Nankai Quake Could Kill 320,000 in Japan: Gov't", *The Mainichi Newspapers*, 29 August 2012, available at: <http://mainichi.jp/english/english/newsselect/news/20120829p2g00m0dm089000c.html> [29/08/2012].

Mayoral, Amanda, "Climate Change as a Conflict Multiplier", *Peace Brief*, No. 120 (United States Institute of Peace, 2012), 1 February 2012, retrieved from: <http://www.usip.org/files/resources/PB%20120.pdf>.

Mcadam, Jane and Loughry Maryanne, "We Aren't Refugees", *Essays & reportage* (Inside Story, 2009), 30 June 2009, retrieved from: <http://inside.org.au/we-arent-refugees/>.

Mcadam, Jane, "Legal solutions: if a treaty is not the answer, then what is?", speech delivered during the ClimMig Conference on Human Rights, Environmental Change, Migration and Displacement held in Vienna on 20–21 September 2012, available at: <http://www.humanrights.at/climmig/wp-content/uploads/McAdam-Jane_speech-20-Sept-2012.pdf> [accessed 02/04/2015].

Migrants Outre-Merts, "L'expulsion d'un Haïtien est légale.... mais à exécuter un peu plus tard" (Migrants Outre-Mer, 1950–2012), 5 March 2010, retrieved from: <www.migrantsoutremer.org/Mesures-d-eloignement-vers-Haiti>.

Mcgovern, Elena, Matt Eason and Breanne Carter, *Iraq's New Reality: The Impact of Conflict on Minorities, Refugees, and the Internally Displaced* (Washington, DC and Waterloo: The Stimson Center and the Centre for International Governance Innovation – CIGI, 2009), retrieved from: <http://www.cigionline.org/sites/default/files/Iraq_Report1.pdf> [01/09/2012].

Morel, Michèle, "Protecting Environmental Migrants: Findings from the UNU-EHS Summer Academy", 11 November 2011, retrieved from: <www.internationallawobserver.eu/2010/11/11/protecting-environmental-migrants-findings-from-the-unu-ehs-summer-academy/>.

De Mul, Tomas (Ed.) *OCHA in 2012 & 2013: Plan and Budget* (New York: UN OCHA, 2012), retrieved from: <OCHA in 2012 & 2013: Plan and Budget> [01/09/2012].

Myers, Norman, "Environmental Refugees: An Emergent Security Issue", 13th Economic Forum, organised in Prague, in 23–27 May 2005, on 22 May 2005, EF.NGO/4/05.

The Nansen Initiative, "The Nansen Initiative Global Consultation, organised in Geneva, on 12–13 October 2015: Conference Report" (Geneva: The Nansen Initiative, December 2015), available at: <https://www.nanseninitiative.org/wp-content/uploads/2015/02/GLOBAL-CONSULTATION-REPORT.pdf> [accessed 06/06/2016].

Neumann, Julia, *Human Rights and Climate Change: International Human Rights as an Instrument for Measures of Equalization?*, Master Thesis, University of Auckland (Norderstedt: GRIN, September 2010).

Nykänen, Eeva, "How Absolute Is Absolute? – on the Limits of Article 3 of the European Convention on Human Rights in the Context of Immigration Control", *EDILEX*, 19 January 2012, retrieved from: <www.edilex.fi/lakikirjasto/8547.pdf>.

OHCHR-UNHCR, "Joint UNHCR-OHCHR Return Advisory Update on Haiti", 9 June 2011 at: <www.unhcr.org/4e0305666.html> [10/08/2012].

Piana, Fabio, "The Principle of 'Non-Refoulement' in the Fight against Terrorism", pp. 183–195, retrieved from: <http://publikon.hu/application/essay/492_1.pdf>.

Progressio, "Haiti: Capacity Building Is Key to Recovery, Says Progressio", *Progressio*, 12 January 2012, retrieved from: <http://www.progressio.org.uk/blog/news/haiti-capacity-building-key>.

Raworth, Kate, *Climate Wrongs and Human Rights: Putting People at the Heart of Climate-Change Policy*, Oxfam Briefing Paper 117 (Oxford: Oxfam International, September 2008), retrieved from: <http://link.library.utoronto.ca/eir/EIRdetail.cfm?Resources__ID=991274&T=F> [01/07/2012].

Red Cross Red Crescent, *RCRC: Périr en quête d'une vie meilleure*, Numero 3 (2015).

Reid, Claire, "Alternative Standards Specific to Refugees – the Regional Level", *in* Reid, Claire (Ed.) *International Law and Legal Instruments*, Expert Guides (n/a: © 2010 Forced Migration Online and Contributors, March 2005), retrieved from: <http://www.forcedmigration.org/research-resources/expert-guides> [06/10/2010].

Reliefweb, "Disasters" (© ReliefWeb, 2012), retrieved from: <http://reliefweb.int/disasters>.

Reliefweb, "Haïti: la police pointe de nouvelles formes de violence après le séisme" (AFP, 2010), retrieved from: <http://www.reliefweb.int/rw/rwb.nsf/db900SID/RMOI-8264EH?OpenDocument>.

The Representatives of Indigenous Peoples attending the World Summit on Sustainable Development, *Indigenous Peoples' Plan of Implementation on Sustainable Development*, issued during the 2002 World Summit on Sustainable Development held in Johannesburg, South Africa, retrieved from the website of the International Work Group for Indigenous Affairs (IWGIA) at: <http://www.iwgia.org/images/stories/sections/envir-and-devel/sust-development/docs/WSSDIPPlanofImplem.doc> [12/11/2016].

Rice, Linda and Kiren Vadher for The Home Office UK Border Agency, "UK National Report (March 2010): Practices in the UK Concerning the Granting of Non-EU Harmonised Protection Statuses and Leave to Remain", *in EMN Study on The Different Practices Concerning Granting of Non-EU Harmonised Protection Statuses* (n/a: EMN, December 2010), retrieved from: <http://emn.intrasoft-intl.com/Downloads/download.do;jsessionid=48CB45E0CA5EB4C57AD0BB871285B576?fileID=1001> [01/06/2011].

Rodger, Jessica, "Defining the Parameters of the Non-Refoulement Principle" (Faculty of Law of Victoria University of Wellington, 2001), retrieved from: <http://www.refugee.org.nz/JessicaR.htm#2>.

Rosenblom, Ann-Charlotte, *Claiming State Responsibility for Climate Change Damages*, Master Thesis, Faculty of Law (Lund: University of Lund, Spring 2009).

Secretariat for Social Communications of the Federative Republic of Brazil, "Brazilian Government Establishes Special Haiti Work Visa Program" (Portal Brasil, 2012), 13 January 2012, press release retrieved from: <www.brasil.gov.br/para/press/press-releases/january-2012/brazilian-government-establishes-special-haiti-work-visa-program/br_model1?set_language=en> [25/06/2012].

Servizio Centrale, *Guida Pratica Per I Titolari Di Protezione Internazionale* (n/a: SPRAR – Sistema di Protezione per Richiedenti Asilo e Rifugiati, 2009), retrieved from: <www.serviziocentrale.it> [08/08/2012].

Serviço de Estrangeiros E Fronteiras – SEF, "Portugal National Report (November 2009) Protection Statuses Complementing EU Legislation Regarding Immigration and Asylum in Portugal", *in EMN Study on The Different Practices Concerning Granting of Non-EU Harmonised Protection Statuses* (n/a: EMN, December 2010), retrieved from: <http://emn.intrasoft-intl.com/Downloads/download.do;jsessionid=48CB45E0CA5EB4C57AD0BB871285B576?fileID=852> [06/06/2011].

Shabazz, Saeed, "Haitians Again Risking Lives to Escape Poverty", *The Final Call – World News*, last updated 3 August 2012, retrieved from: <http://www.finalcall.com/artman/publish/World_News_3/article_9090.shtml>.

Shukman, David, "Rio+20 Summit Criticised as 'Disappointing'", *BBC News*, 22 June 2012, available at: <www.bbc.co.uk/news/science-environment-18560734> [30/06/2012].

Schuman, Robert, Déclaration du 9 mai 1950, issued in Paris (translation available on the website of the European Union) at: <http://europa.eu/about-eu/basic-information/symbols/europe-day/schuman-declaration/index_en.htm> [09/07/2012].

Smith, Jennifer R., "Human Adaptation to Climate Change in the Archaeological Past", presentation made during the 9th annual Radcliffe Institute for Advanced Study's science symposium, "Something in the Air: Climate Change, Science and Policy", Harvard University, Cambridge, 15 April 2011.

Solomon, Susan, "Understanding Climate Change, Irreversibility, and the Societal Challenge", presentation made during the 9th annual Radcliffe Institute for Advanced Study science symposium, "Something in the Air: Climate Change, Science and Policy", Harvard University, Cambridge, 15 April 2011.

Swedish Migration Board, "Sweden National Report (April 2010): The Practices in Sweden Concerning the Granting of Non-EU Harmonised Protection Statuses", *in EMN Study on The Different Practices Concerning Granting of Non-EU Harmonised Protection Statuses* (n/a: EMN, December 2010), retrieved from: <http://emn.intrasoft-intl.com/Downloads/download.do;jsessionid=48CB45E0CA5EB4C57AD0BB871285B576?fileID=1005> [06/06/2011].

Tiberghien, Frédéric, "« Réfugiés » écologiques ou climatiques : de Nombreuses Questions Juridiques En Suspens", *Accueillir*, No. 246, *Les déplacés environnementaux* (June 2008), pp. 17–22, retrieved from: <http://www.revues-plurielles.org/_uploads/pdf/47/246/deplaces_environnementaux.pdf>.

BIBLIOGRAPHY 665

Treves, Tullio, "Customary International Law" (Max Planck Institute for Comparative Public Law and International Law Heidelberg and Oxford University Press, 2012), last updated November 2006, retrieved from: <http://www.mpepil.com/sample_article?id=/epil/entries/law-9780199231690-e1393&recno=29&>.

Truc, Olivier, "En 2007, les ministres suédois voulaient stopper les réfugiés irakiens", *Le Monde.fr*, 21 January 2011, retrieved from: <http://www.lemonde.fr/europe/article/2011/01/21/en-2007-les-ministres-suedois-voulaient-stopper-les-refugies-irakiens_1468991_3214.html>.

UN News Service, "Bangladesh: Border Killings Mount Despite No-Shooting Decree", 6 December 2011, retrieved from: <http://www.refworld.org/docid/4ee1e0ae2.html> [06/06/2012].

UN News Centre, "Secretary-General Praises Faith, Resilience of Haitian People Amid Tragedy", 21 January 2010, retrieved from: <http://www.un.org/apps/news/story.asp/story.asp?NewsID=33542&Cr=haiti&Cr1=#.UouoU7Q9CZR> [23/01/2010].

UNFCCC, "Status of Ratification of the UNFCCC", retrieved from: <http://unfccc.int/essential_background/convention/status_of_ratification/items/2631.php> [07/11/2016].

UNFCCC, "Status of Ratification of the Kyoto Protocol", retrieved from: <http://unfccc.int/kyoto_protocol/status_of_ratification/items/2613.php> [07/11/2016].

UNHCR, "Financial Figures" (©UNHCR, 2001–2012), retrieved from: <http://www.unhcr.org/pages/49c3646c1a.html>.

UNHCR, "Refugees" (© UNHCR, 2001–2012), retrieved from: <http://www.unhcr.org/pages/49c3646c125.html>.

UNHCR, "UNHCR Commemorations in 2011", available at: <http://www.unhcr.org/4d1c9a409.html> [accessed 10/12/2015].

UNHCR / Luiz Fernando Godinho, "Rio+20 summit: UN refugee chief calls for joint approach to urban refugees, displaced", 21 June 2012, retrieved from the UNHCR website at: <http://www.unhcr.org/news/latest/2012/6/4fe2e7d76/rio20-summit-un-refugee-chief-calls-joint-approach-urban-refugees-displaced.html> [29/06/2012].

UNHCR / Melissa Fleming, "Briefing Notes: OHCHR / UNHCR Urge Extending Suspension of Returns to Haiti", 12 February 2010 at: <http://www.unhcr.org/4b7543026.html> [10/08/2012].

UN OCHA, "How are disaster relief efforts organised? Cluster Approach", accessible at: <http://business.un.org/en/assets/39c87a78-fec9-402e-a434-2c355f24e4f4.pdf> [last accessed on 18/09/2013].

UNU-EHS, "As Ranks of "Environmental Refugees" Swell Worldwide, Calls Grow for Better Definition, Recognition, Support", *Press Release* (United Nations University – Institute for Environment and Human Security, UNU-EHS 2005), 11 October 2005, retrieved from: <www.ehs.unu.edu/file/get/3916>.

Verhaeghe, Laure, "Quels droits pour les réfugiés environnementaux qui perdront leur Etat ? Le cas de Tuvalu", *REVUE Asylon(s)*, No. 6, *Exodes écologiques* (November 2008), retrieved from: <www.reseau-terra.eu/article853.html>.

Vidal, John, "Rio+20: Reasons to Be Cheerful", *The Guardian – Poverty Matters Blog*, 27 June 2012, available at: <www.guardian.co.uk/global-development/poverty-matters/2012/jun/27/rio20-reasons-cheerful> [30/06/2012].

Vinez, Meredith and Sarah Leonard, "The Iraq Marshlands: The Loss of the Garden of Eden and Its People", 19th Annual Illinois State University Conference for Students of Political Science, organised in Illinois, in 8 April 2011, retrieved from: <http://pol.illinoisstate.edu/current/conferences/2011/LeonardIraqMarshes.pdf> [06/12/2011].

Virassamy, Audrey, "Les expulsions vers Haïti toujours suspendues", *France-Guyane*, 17 January 2012.

Vogel, Toby, "Greek Asylum System in Disarray", *European Voice*, available at: <http://www.europeanvoice.com/article/imported/greek-asylum-system-in-disarray/70044.aspx> [04/08/2012].

Wahlström, Margareta, "Chairperson's Summary", Nansen Conference on Climate Change and Displacement in the 21st Century, organised in Oslo, on 6–7 June 2011.

Watts, Jonathan, "China Warns of 'Urgent Problems' Facing Three Gorges Dam", *The Guardian*, 20 May 2011, retrieved from: <http://www.guardian.co.uk/world/2011/may/20/three-gorges-dam-china-warning?INTCMP=SRCH>.

Watts, Jonathan and Liz Ford, "Rio+20 Earth Summit: Campaigners Decry Final Document", 23 June 2012, available at: <www.guardian.co.uk/environment/2012/jun/23/rio-20-earth-summit-document> [25/06/2012].

Wee, Sui-Lee, "Thousands Being Moved from China's Three Gorges – Again", *Scientific American* (Reuters, 2012), 22 August 2012, retrieved from: <http://www.scientificamerican.com/article.cfm?id=thousands-being-moved-from-chinas-t>.

Weiss, K.R., "The Making of a Climate Refugee", *Foreign Policy*, 28/01/2015, available at: <http://foreignpolicy.com/2015/01/28/the-making-of-a-climate-refugee-kiribati-tarawa-teitiota/> [last accessed on 06/11/2016].

Westlake, Adam, "Japanese Parliament's Fukushima Disaster Report to Be Published", *The Japan Daily Press*, 5 July 2012, retrieved from: <http://japandailypress.com/japanese-parliaments-fukushima-disaster-report-to-be-published-055941>.

Dictionaries and Encyclopedia Articles

CNRTL, "Accumulation" (Centre National de Ressources Textuelles et Lexicales – CNRTL, 2012), retrieved from: <www.cnrtl.fr/definition/accumulation>.

Larousse, Dictionnaire de Français, "Accumulation" (Larousse, 2012), retrieved from: <http://www.larousse.fr/dictionnaires/francais/accumulation>.

Macmillan Dictionary, "Accumulation" (Macmillan Publishers Limited, 2009–2012), retrieved from: <www.macmillandictionary.com/dictionary/british/accumulation>.

Wikipedia, "2011 Tōhoku Earthquake and Tsunami" (Wikipedia, 2012), last updated 11 September 2012, retrieved from: <http://en.wikipedia.org/wiki/2011_T%C5%8Dhoku_earthquake_and_tsunami#cite_note-21>.

Websites

UN Treaty Collection, *Depositary Notifications Issued by the Secretary-General* (© United Nations, 2012), last updated 08/07/2012, retrieved from: <http://treaties.un.org/Pages/CNs.aspx>.

UN Treaty Collection, *Status of Multilateral Treaties Deposited with the Secretary-General* (© United Nations, 2012), retrieved from: <http://treaties.un.org> [08/09/2012].

African Commission on Human and Peoples' Rights, *Latest Decisions on Communications* <www.achpr.org/communications>.

Asian-African Legal Consultative Organisation (AALCO), <www.aalco.int>.

Central Intelligence Agency, *The World Factbook* <https://www.cia.gov/library/publications/the-world-factbook/index.html>.

European Commission Directorate-General for Climate Action, <http://ec.europa.eu/clima/news/index_en.htm>.

The Fund for Peace, *Failed States Index* <http://www.fundforpeace.org/global/?q-fsi>.

Ministère des Haïtiens Vivant à l'étranger (MHAVE), <www.mhave.gouv.ht>.

Shishmaref Alaska Erosion & Relocation Coalition, *Shishmaref: We Are Worth Saving!* <www.shishmarefrelocation.com>.

Other

"The Geneva Pledge on Human Rights in Climate Action", available at: < http://www.rree.go.cr/files/includes/files.php?id=453&tipo=contenido> [19/09/2016].

War Remnants Museum, Ho Chi Minh City, Vietnam.

Index

'Ability to Cater for One's Most Basic Needs'. *See* European Court of Human Rights
Ad hoc Committee on Statelessness and Related Problems   209, 432–434n, 455n
Ad hoc responses to disaster-related movement. *See also* State practice   417–421
Adaptation. *See also* Burden-sharing, Disasters   5, 537
  to climate change/disasters   301, 301n, 387, 467
  migration as (*see also* Paris Agreement   13n, 14, 427, 525, 531, 533, 536, 574)
Affected communities
  Alaska   313, 535n, 547n, 548n, 552
  Bangladesh   313, 324, 390n, 458n, 551n, 570
  culture/identity   286, 534–535, 548, 551, 555–556
  importance of consultation   547, 548, 551–552
  indigenous people   313, 548–549, 552, 555–556
  Ombudsman   543, 549
  vulnerabilities   362
African Union (AU). *See also* Regional refugee instruments   3, 245n
  AU Convention Governing the Specific Aspects of Refugee Problems in Africa   130, 247, 255n, 263–265, 447–448, 468n
  AU Convention for the Protection and Assistance of Internally Displaced Persons in Africa ("Kampala Convention")   3, 518n
Agenda for the Protection of Cross-Border Displaced Persons in the Context of Disasters and Climate Change. *See* Nansen Initiative
Airey v. Ireland. *See* European Court of Human Rights (ECtHR)
Alaska. *See* Affected Communities
Alleviation of population//resource pressures. *See also* Migration as adaptation   536, 573
Armed conflict. *See also* Complementary protection; Generalised violence; Humanitarian law; Indiscriminate threats; International and internal armed conflicts; *Non-refoulement*; Subsidiary protection; Temporary protection   1, 8, 94, 108, 112
Asylum. *See* Refugee law
  as a humanitarian act   261, 431, 468, 534
Asylum seekers
  vulnerability (*see* MSS *v. Belgium and Greece*)
AU Convention Governing the Specific Aspects of Refugee Problems in Africa. *See* African Union
Australia. *See also* Authorisation to stay (discretionary), Australia; Complementary protection, Australia; Kiribati; New Zealand; Tuvalu
  Refugee Review Tribunal of Australia   332n, 335n
    climate change as indiscriminate threat   332n
    climate change refugee rejected   332n
Authorisation to stay (discretionary). *See also* Complementary protection   171–172, 268–269, 273–274, 403–417
  based on discretionary grounds   275–276
  based on international obligation grounds   271–275
  compelling humanitarian considerations (*see below* United Kingdom)
  'Discretionary Leave' (*see below* United Kingdom)
  distinguished from complementary protection   21–22
  Finland   409
  France   413–415, 417–419
  Germany   274–275
  Luxembourg   415–417
  New Zealand ('Humanitarian appeal') (*see also* Complementary protection, New Zealand ('Protected persons'))   289, 291, 357, 403–406)
  rates//statistics   171–172, 268
  Sweden   409–413
  United Kingdom   272, 273, 406–409

INDEX   669

Bangladesh. *See also* Affected communities 313, 324, 390n, 458n, 551n, 569n, 570

Bangkok Principles on Status and Treatment of Refugees. *See Non-refoulement*

Best interests of the child   406, 410

Bhopal disaster. *See* Disasters; State responsibility, for technological/industrial accidents

Burden-sharing   102, 522, 533–535

Cancun Adaptation Framework. *See* Cancun Agreements

Cancun Agreements. *See* UN Framework Convention on Climate Change (UNFCCC)

Carbon dioxide emissions   14, 16, 337, 466, 499n, 503n

Cartagena Declaration. *See also* Regional refugee instruments   72n, 130, 265, 447–448, 462, 473

Catastrophe. *See also* Disasters; Disasters, Sudden-onset/Nuclear/Technological   7

Chernobyl *see* Disasters; State responsibility, for technological/industrial accidents

Climate change. *See also* Climate change 'refugee'; Disasters; Indiscriminate threats; Intergovernmental Panel on Climate Change (IPCC); State responsibility
 adaptation (*see* Adaptation)
 analogy with nuclear disasters   395–396
 anthropogenic bases   9, 11, 12, 15, 326n, 330n, 390, 503
 attribution of displacement to (*see also* State responsibility   491–496)
 common and shared responsibility for 505–506n
 differential impacts   13–14, 301, 406, 536
 driver of migration, as (*see also* Migration, Drivers of-; Migration as adaptation 489, 527)
 human rights and-(*see also* UN Office of the High Commissioner for Human Rights   349n, 359, 360, 363, 582)
  Geneva Pledge on Human Rights in Climate Action   9n
  UN Human Rights Council   360–361
 impacts (*see also* Climate change, Differential impacts/Human rights and-/Science/Threat multiplier   13, 359, 387)

 indiscriminate threat, as an (*see* indiscriminate threats; new zealand; kiribati)
 persecution, as   339, 466n
 pollution, as   396–397
 science   14–16, 502–503, 523–525
 security   248, 284n, 297n, 298, 345–346, 505n, 573
 threat multiplier   284–286

Climate change 'refugee'. *See also* Environmental 'refugee'; Persecution
 Australian case-law (*see* Australia)
 New Zealand case-law (*see* New Zealand)
 term rejected by affected communities 466, 512

Committee against Torture (CAT)   72, 217, 224–226, 230

Common but differentiated responsibilities. *See also* Burden-sharing   508, 525, 533–535, 567

Common European Asylum System. *See also* Harmonization   24, 84, 103, 105n, 113, 176, 293, 306, 470

Community consultation. *See* Affected communities

Compelling humanitarian considerations. *See* European Court of Human Rights, *D. v. UK*; *Non-refoulement*

Compelling Humanitarian Reasons. *See also* Complementary protection   261n

Complementary forms of protection   172–181, 268, 270–271, 276, 278, 292, 422, 446

Complementary protection. *See also* Cartagena Declaration; Complementary forms of protection; Convention against Torture; Convention on the Rights of the Child; European Convention on Human Rights; International Covenant on Civil and Political Rights; *Non-refoulement*; Qualification Directive; Subsidiary protection   6, 7
 armed conflicts (*see also Non-refoulement*, Application to armed conflict situations 107–108, 112, 129–168)
 'Discretionary Leave' (*see* Authorisation to stay (discretionary))
 distinguished from discretionary forms of protection (*see also* Authorisation to stay (discretionary)   21–22)

Complementary protection. (cont.)
  distinguished from temporary protection 95
  'Humanitarian protection' status (see below In domestic law and practice, United Kingdom)
  in domestic law and practice
    Finland 352–354
    France 261n, 348, 350, 375
    Germany 274–275
    history 112, 179, 261n, 270
    Netherlands 261n
    New Zealand ('Protected persons') (see also Authorisation to stay (discretionary), New Zealand ('Humanitarian appeal') 354–357)
    relation to ECHR articles 2 and 3 272n
    Sweden 352–354
    United Kingdom ('Humanitarian Protection' status) (see also Subsidiary protection 261n, 272, 348, 406)
  meaning 21–22, 422
  'protected person' status (New Zealand)
Conflicts. See also Climate change (Threat multiplier); Resources
  identity 286
  resource scarcity 282, 285n, 286, 351, 470
Convention against Torture. See also Complementary protection; New Zealand; Non-refoulement; 'Protected person' status 24, 30, 72, 109, 125, 182–187, 195n, 223–225, 244, 246, 271, 289, 292n, 340, 354, 404, 416n
Convention on the Rights of the Child 74, 418
COP21. See UN Framework Convention on Climate Change (UNFCCC)
Copenhagen Accord. See UN Framework Convention on Climate Change (UNFCCC)
Credibility 175, 297, 559
Crime against humanity. See Refugee status, Exclusion clauses
Cruel, inhuman or degrading treatment. See also Complementary protection; Medical cases; Non-Refoulement; Socio-economic harm/rights

  impacts of climate change as-(see also New Zealand 355–357)
  non-refoulement 186, 187, 194, 230, 234, 235, 245–246, 365, 475
  as persecution 305, 311
  severity threshold 207, 356, 366, 372, 375, 382, 387, 407
  socio-economic deprivation 356–357
Culture/Identity. See Affected communities
Customary international law. See also Non-refoulement; Temporary refuge 22, 25, 71, 92–93, 182, 242–267, 270, 278, 367, 473, 490, 498n

De facto refugees. See also Non-refoulement 107–108, 109n, 179, 448–449
Death penalty. See Non-refoulement; Subsidiary protection
Degrading treatment. See Cruel, inhuman or degrading treatment
Demographic pressure. See Alleviation of population/resource pressures; Pacific island States; Kiribati; Tuvalu
Destitution. See also Economic, social and cultural rights, Deprivation of-as persecution 312, 479
Development projects. See also Disasters 324
Diaspora communities. See also Remittances 409, 536–537, 562–563
Dignity 58, 66, 89, 246, 301n, 483. See also Human dignity
  autonomous application 90
  conditions of detention (see also MSS v. Belgium and Greece 381)
  definition of persons in need of protection 553–558
  in the case-law of the ECtHR (non-refoulement) 89, 372, 381, 382
  living conditions (see also MSS v. Belgium and Greece 382)
  return in safety and- 553–558
'Disappearing States'. See also Pacific island States; Statelessness 474, 544, 551, 554, 555n
Disaster risk reduction 530, 543n, 574
  Sendai Framework for- 530, 574

INDEX 671

Disasters. *See also* Catastrophes; Environmental degradation; Indiscriminate threats; Migration, Drivers of-; State responsibility
definition   7–8
differential impacts   442–443, 515, 535
duty to prevent and protect from-(*see also* State responsibility   388)
human rights, and   359–364
impact of–(*see also* Adaptation; Climate change, Impacts   387, 495, 515–517, 535–536)
over time   403, 417, 474
partly attributable to States (*see also* ECtHR, *Sufi & Elmi v. UK*   387)
man-made (*see also* development projects 324, 325, 334n)
'man-made' *vs.* 'natural' disasters (*see also* Environmentally-displaced persons, Definition   10, 325, 494, 495, 513–517, 535–536, 540)
natural hazards (*see also* Climate change, Impacts   324)
nuclear
chernobyl (*see also* Persecution 325, 336)
Fukushima Daiichi nuclear plant accident   325, 493, 546
as persecution   339
preparedness   442–443, 515, 535–536
slow-onset Disasters   2, 7, 8, 10, 299–301, 312, 313, 320, 324, 339, 347, 359, 368, 375, 393, 470, 533, 536, 544, 560, 567, 583, 584n
conceptualised as imminent threats 394–398
state responsibility   355, 388
sudden-onset (*see also* Catastrophe   7, 8, 10, 312, 320, 339, 347, 352, 359, 368, 393, 394, 470, 533, 536, 544, 560, 583, 584n)
technological   324–327, 493
typology   8, 583
Discretionary leave (UK). *See* Authorisation to stay
Discrimination. *See also* Non-discrimination 64, 136, 146, 165, 175, 188–189, 331, 433–434, 558
as an 'act or omission' of the State (*see also* ECtHR, *MSS v. Belgium and Greece* and *Sufi & Elmi v. UK*   389)

in aid provision   326, 330, 332–334, 366
under the refugee convention   308, 323–324, 326, 331, 334, 338, 464
and persecution   269, 300, 331, 334, 338, 443
Displacement. *See* Environmentally-displaced persons; Internally-displaced persons; Migration
triggers   165, 167, 286, 406, 489, 529
environmental degradation/disasters as-   489
Drought. *See also* Climate change, Impacts; ECtHR, *Sufi & Elmi v. UK*   13n, 16, 165, 355, 359, 382, 384–387, 394, 419
Durban Agreement. *See* UN Framework Convention on Climate Change (UNFCCC)

Earthquake. *See also* Geophysical disasters; Haiti, Fukushima Daiichi nuclear plant accident   324, 325, 332, 335, 345–346, 361, 403, 417, 442, 493–494, 510, 513, 515, 544, 566, 583
collateral damage-Three Gorges dam (China)   325
ECHR. *See* European Convention on Human Rights
ECtHR. *See* European Court of Human Rights
Economic migrants   510
Economic, social and cultural rights. *See also* Disaster; Internal Protection; *Non-refoulement*
breaches/deprivation of-as persecution 305–314
New Zealand Immigration and Protection Tribunal   309–310
protection via civil and political rights 359, 388–389, 486
Emergency responses. *See* Mass influx; Temporary protection   34, 102, 475, 546
Environmental catastrophe. *See* Environmental disaster
Environmental degradation. *See also* Catastrophe; Disasters; Environmental disaster; Environmental harm; Environmental persecution; Environmental 'refugee'; Environmentally-displaced persons 7, 286

672 INDEX

Environmental degradation. (cont.)
  as a form of persecution (*see also* environmental harm; environmentally-displaced persons   338–339)
  as a source of 'serious threats' constitutive of persecution   312–314
  security (*see also* Climate change (Security)   285–286, 353)
Environmental disaster. *See also* Disasters; Environmentally-displaced persons), 7
  as a ground for complementary protection
    Finland   353–354
    Sweden   352–354
  as persecution (*see also* Environmentally-displaced persons   339)
  security (*see also* Climate change, Security; Environmental degradation, Security   353)
Environmental displacement. *See also* Displacement; Environmentally-displaced persons; Migration   324
  Holistic answer   537–570
Environmental harm. *See also* Environmental degradation; Environmentally-displaced persons   339
  as persecution   299, 323, 326, 329
    Contra-Review Tribunal of Australia   332n
Environmental migrant. *See also* Environmentally-displaced persons   510, 568–569
Environmental migration. *See also* Displacement; Migration, Drivers of-,   286n, 512, 549, 550n
Environmental persecution. *See also* Environmental 'refugee'; Persecution   303–327, 338
Environmental 'refugee'. *See also* Climate change 'refugee'; Environmentally-displaced persons   281–282, 293–340, 509
  many displaced, few 'refugees'   338–339
  refugee status applies   338–339
  term rejected by affected communities   466n
Environmentally-displaced persons. *See also* Human dignity; Refugee Convention
  'Ability to Cater for One's Most Basic Needs' (*see also* European Court of Human Rights; *Non-refoulement and below Non-refoulement*   381–391, 483, 485–487)
  as persons in need of protection, definition   553–559
  common but differentiated responsibility   533–534, 567
  complementary protection, as beneficiaries of   340–357
  definition   509–519, 553–558
  dignity (*see* Sustainable conditions for return)
  draft convention on the international status of environmentally-displaced persons   505n, 514n, 517, 538, 539
  environment *vs.* climate change   513–517
  incentives for States to protect   519–537
  non-refoulement, and the principle of (*see also* Internal protection   358, 367–398, 475–482–488)
    shortcomings of a solution based on human rights law   487–488
  refugees under the Refugee Convention (not) (*see also* Australia; Persecution   293–340, 332n, 445, 462n, 509)
    as a particular social group   353–354
  return in safety and dignity   553–558
    shortcomings of a solution based on human rights law (*see above Non-refoulement*)
  states' reluctance to expand refugee protection   520–521
  state responsibility   515–517
  subsidiary protection, as beneficiaries of   340–352
  sustainable conditions for return   553–558
  temporary protection, as beneficiaries of   474–475
  terminology   509–517
European Convention on Human Rights (ECHR). *See also* European Court of Human Rights; *Non-refoulement*
  EU accession to-   60–61
  extraterritoriality   186n, 187, 191–203
  invocation of article 3 with other rights   359, 407
  nationality   187–191

prohibition of torture, cruel, inhuman or degrading treatment or punishment (*see* Cruel, inhuman or degrading treatment; *Non-refoulement*)
European Court of Human Rights. *See also* Economic, social and cultural rights; Medical cases; *Non-refoulement*
  'Ability to Cater for One's Most Basic Needs' (*see also MSS v. Belgium and Greece* 381–391, 482, 485–487)
  Airey v. Ireland 377–379
  Budayeva v. Russia (*see also* Disasters, Duty to prevent and protect from-; Right to life; State responsibility 388, 516n)
  'compelling humanitarian considerations' (*see below D. v. UK*)
  D. v. UK 273, 371, 373, 374, 376, 380, 398, 485
  'Fair balance' (*see Airey v. Ireland*; *Soering* case)
  indivisibility of human rights (*see Airey v. Ireland*)
  MSS v. Belgium and Greece 79, 367, 381–385, 388–391, 394, 398, 485
  N. v. UK (*see also* Medical cases 186n, 207n, 223n, 233n, 250, 359, 367n, 369, 372–381, 416, 483)
  N.A. v. the United Kingdom 236
  'naturally occurring phenomenon' (*see Sufi & Elmi v. UK*)
  Soering case 124n, 186n, 191, 194n, 195–201, 203–204, 206–208, 218–219, 221, 376–381, 415n, 560n
  Sufi & Elmi v. UK 168n, 184n, 207n, 233n, 238–242, 278, 344–347, 356n, 359, 366, 367n, 369, 381–386, 388–391, 394, 397–398, 409, 472, 485–486
European Union. *See also* Complementary protection; Qualification Directive; Subsidiary Protection
  Accession to the European Convention on Human Rights 60–61
  Charter of Fundamental Rights of the- 61–70
  European Union Law 33–181
    fundamental rights and- 34–93
Exclusion clauses. *See* Refugee status; Subsidiary protection exclusion clauses

and exception to *non-refoulement* 209, 212
Execution. *See* Death penalty
Extradition. *See also* Extraterritoriality of human rights; *Non-refoulement* 88n, 124, 185n, 191–206, 213n, 214n, 218–219, 221–222, 224, 244, 246, 249n, 358
  constitutive of a human right violation 192, 200
Extraterritoriality of human rights. *See also* European Convention of Human Rights; *Non-refoulement* 480, 481
Extreme weather events. *See also* Climate change, Impacts 13n, 355, 359

Female genital mutilation 443
Fiji. *See* Authorisation to stay (discretionary), New Zealand; Economic, social and cultural rights, Medical cases
Final Act of the Conference of Plenipotentiaries. *See* Refugee Convention
Finland. *See* Complementary protection
First World War 434
Flooding. *See also* Disasters; Climate change, Impacts 16, 359, 586–587
France. *See also* Authorisation to stay (discretionary); Complementary protection; State practice
  response to Haiti earthquake 345–346, 418
Freedom of expression 274
Freedom of religion 186n, 274, 555
Fukushima Daiichi nuclear plant accident. *See also* Disasters; State responsibility (for technological/industrial accidents) 325, 493, 546
Future harm. *See also* Imminence of harm

Geneva Pledge on Human Rights in Climate Action 361n
General principles of EU/Community law 63–64, 74, 146
  human/fundamental rights as- 34–59
Generalised violence. *See* Armed conflict
Geophysical disasters. *See also* Disasters; Earthquakes 318, 583, 584n
Global warming. *See* Climate change
'Good offices' refugees 255n

Greece (return to). *See* MSS *v. Belgium and Greece*
Greenhouse gas emissions
Guiding Principles on Internal Displacement. *See* UN Guiding Principles on Internal Displacement

Haiti   10, 320, 324, 399, 403, 417, 471n, 474, 510–511, 543n, 566, 585
  diaspora (*see also* Diaspora; Migration, Beneficial to countries of origin   562–563)
  security situation   342, 345–346, 471n
  'Temporary Protected Status' (United States)   399–400
Harmonisation   105
Hazardous activities (*see also* Disasters, Nuclear, Technological; International Law Commission (ILC), Articles on the Prevention of Transboundary Harm from Hazardous Activities; Nuclear weapons; State responsibility)   395–396, 460, 461n, 486n, 493, 497, 540, 542
Health/healthcare. *See also* European Court of Human Rights, *N. v. UK*; Medical cases
Lack of access to-   389, 407, 411, 482–412
Human dignity. *See also* Dignity
  and the principle of *non-refoulement*   483
  protection of environmentally-displaced persons   507n, 557
    International Law Commission (ILC)   556
    sustainable conditions for return   553–558
  Under the Charter of Fundamental Rights of the European Union   66, 89–90
Human rights. *See also* Climate change; Cruel, inhuman or degrading treatment; Disasters; Economic, social and cultural rights; European Union, European Union Law, Fundamental rights and- extraterritoriality (*see also* European Convention on Human Rights; *Non-refoulement*   480, 481)
  fair balance (*see* Soering Case (ECtHR))
  hierarchy   309, 312n, 363
  indicators   412

indivisibility (*see also Airey v. Ireland*   378)
Human Rights Committee (HRC). *See also* International Covenant on Civil and Political Rights (ICCPR); *Non-refoulement*)   27, 72, 79, 90, 125, 184–190, 193–194, 199–206, 217, 223, 230, 393
Human rights violations. *See also* Cruel, inhuman or degrading treatment; Discrimination; Human Rights; *Non-refoulement*; Subsidiary protection, serious harm   112, 133, 167, 192, 200, 244, 307, 313, 357, 360n, 400, 554
  as drivers of migration   112, 133, 167, 528n
  as persecution (*see also* Persecution   307–308, 329n, 465, 469)
Humanitarian assistance   564–567
Humanitarian law   2, 6, 114, 154n, 155n, 161–162, 164, 282–283, 287–288, 322n, 389, 447
  International and internal armed conflicts, definition of-   161, 164–167, 178n
Exceptional Leave to Remain. *See also* 'Humanitarian Protection'; Discretionary Leave   272n
'Humanitarian protection' status. *See* Complementary protection, United Kingdom

IASC Guidelines on Human Rights and Natural Disasters. *See* UN Inter-Agency Standing Committee (IASC)
Identity/Culture. *See* Affected communities
IDP. *See* Internally-displaced persons
Illness. *See* Medical cases
Ill-treatment. *See* Cruel, inhuman or degrading treatment or punishment; Health/healthcare, Lack of access to-; Serious harm
Indigenous peoples. *See* Affected communities; 'Disappearing States'
Indiscriminate threats. *See also* Australia, Review Tribunal of-; Complementary protection; New Zealand; *Non-refoulement*; Subsidiary protection; Temporary protection   183, 227, 233, 253, 259–271, 277, 281, 332n, 339, 340, 347, 398, 444–446, 470, 473, 507

armed conflicts and disasters as 278, 347, 365
environmental disaster as a source of indiscriminate threats 364–367
expansion of subsidiary protection grounds to- 470–474
non-discriminatory risk v. persecution 332n
Prima facie refugees (*see Prima facie* refugees, Temporary protection)
situational risks 123, 136, 141n, 150, 277, 281–282, 330, 347
Indiscriminate violence. *See also* Armed conflict; Generalised violence; Indiscriminate threats; Subsidiary protection 85, 121, 130, 178, 207, 253, 262–263, 266, 278, 282, 443, 446
and *non-refoulement* (*see also* European Court of Human Rights, *N.A. v. the United Kingdom* 236, 241, 281)
under the Qualification Directive (Subsidiary protection) 129–160, 165–168, 234–235, 241, 341, 347–352, 471–472
Inhuman or degrading treatment. *See* Cruel, inhuman or degrading treatment
Institutional actors. *See also* UN agencies (listed under UN-) 527, 538–539, 548, 564, 565
clusters 320n, 566–567
Intergovernmental Panel on Climate Change (IPCC). *See also* Climate change, Science 11–16, 284–285, 298n, 301n, 390n, 496, 524n, 540, 548n, 558n, 559n, 567n, 568
Internal displacement. *See also* Bangladesh; Guiding Principles on Internal Displacement; Internally-displaced persons 517–519
Internal Displacement Monitoring Centre (IDMC) 4, 283n, 324
Internal flight alternative. *See* Internal protection
Internal protection/Internal flight alternative (under the EU Qualification Directive) 475–482
broadening the scope of states' *non-refoulement* obligations 478–482
economic, social and cultural rights 478–482

Internal relocation. *See also* Relocation/resettlement; Internal displacement; Internal flight alternative
Internally-displaced persons (IDP). *See also* African Union Convention for the Protection and Assistance of Internally Displaced Persons in Africa; Guiding Principles on Internal Displacement 256, 363, 383, 435, 517–519
UNHCR's mandate 256n
International and internal armed conflicts. *See* Humanitarian law; International criminal law; Subsidiary protection
International assistance. *See also* Humanitarian assistance 377n, 389, 465n, 490, 541
International Covenant on Civil and Political Rights (ICCPR). *See also* Non-Refoulement 199–203
International Covenant on Economic, Social and Cultural Rights (ICESCR). *See also* Economic, social and cultural rights 24, 67, 308, 310, 349n, 377, 378n, 379n, 380n, 388n, 389n, 391n, 460, 481, 541
International Criminal Court (ICC) 161n
International criminal law. *See also* International and internal armed conflicts 161, 164–165, 167, 447
International Criminal Tribunal for the Former Yugoslavia (ICTY) 161n, 492
International environmental law. *See also* UN Framework Convention on Climate Change; Precautionary principle
International law
fragmentation of- 8–9
International Law Commission (ILC) 215n
Articles on the Prevention of Transboundary Harm from Hazardous Activities 497n, 540n
Articles on the Responsibility of International Organizations 31
Articles on the Responsibility of States for internationally wrongful acts 490–492, 496
Protection of persons in the event of disasters 7, 287–288, 556–557
International Organisation for Migration (IOM)
calls for action 526–527

International organisations. *See* Institutional actors
International protection. *See* Refugee; Refugee Convention; Subsidiary protection
  humanitarian nature   431n, 459n, 507
  meaning in the qualification directive   114–123, 141n
  recognition rates   577–581
  regime, sources   6, 24, 31, 33, 266–267, 358, 428, 505, 528, 537
International refugee law. *See also* Environmental 'refugee'; International protection; Refugee Convention; Refugees; Regional refugee instruments; UN High Commissioner for Refugees (UNHCR)
  humanitarian nature   431n, 459n, 507
  non-refoulement (*see* Non-refoulement)
  persecution (*see* Persecution)
International Refugee Organisation   213, 260n

Jus cogens. See Non-refoulement

Kampala Convention. *See* African Union
Kiribati. *See also* adaptation; Affected communities, Climate change; Culture/Identity; Australia, Refugee Review Tribunal; 'Disappearing States'; New Zealand, Immigration and Protection Tribunal   289n, 290–291, 300n, 310n, 311n, 312n, 313, 324, 332n, 333n, 335n, 336n, 337, 354–357, 404n, 405n, 465n, 466n, 474, 554–555n, 568n
  climate change impacts (*see also* New Zealand, Teitiota case   2, 289, 290, 313, 324, 337, 568)
  climate change refugees (not) (*see* Australia; Climate change 'refugees'; New Zealand)
  demographic pressure   313
  'disappearing State'   474, 554–555n
  government, role of-   291, 335n, 355–357, 465n
    reversal of traditional refugee paradigm (*see also* Climate change 'refugee'   466)
  labour market   313
  migration, as a last resort   555n
  rejection of 'refugee' label   466, 512
  skilled migrants, people of Kiribati as   466n
  relocation   551–552, 555n
  resettlement programs   551–552
  right to life   356
  slow-onset environmental degradation   474

Labour Migration. *See also* Kiribati; Migration   290, 466, 505, 511
Legal status. *See* Environmentally-displaced persons, Shortcomings of a solution based on human rights law; Refugee; Subsidiary protection

Man-made disasters. *See* Disasters
Mandate refugees. *See* UN High Commissioner for Refugees (UNHCR)
Mass influx. *See also* Temporary Protection Directive   111, 133, 135, 158, 175n, 223, 253, 254, 327, 367–369, 399–403, 474–475
Media, role of
Medical treatment, lack of. *See also* Climate change, Human rights and-; Disasters, Human rights and-; *European Court of Human Rights, N. v. UK*   313, 320, 359, 411–412, 414
Medical cases. *See also* Economic, social and cultural rights; European Court of Human Rights, *N.v. UK*   127, 273, 207n, 274, 371–379, 393–394, 397, 407, 410–411, 413–416, 560
  New Zealand case-law
    illness *vs.* qualifying treatment under human rights law (*Fiji* case)   356–357
Migrant. *See also* Climate change 'refugee'; Environmental migrant; Environmental 'refugee'; Environmentally-displaced persons; Migration; Refugee
  environmentally-displaced persons, terminology   509
  skilled migrants, Kiribati migrants as-   466n
Migration. *See also* Environmentally-displaced persons; Internally-displaced persons; Pacific island States; Relocation/resettlement; Vulnerability

INDEX 677

alleviation of population/resource pressures   535–536
as adaptation   13n, 14, 427, 525, 531, 533, 574
as last resort   5, 444, 489n, 552
beneficial to countries of origin (*see also* diaspora communities; Haiti; remittances   536, 562–563)
bilateral or regional agreements   506, 550–551, 569
causes (*see below* Drivers of-)
continuum   511
decision to migrate   14
drivers of-   14, 165, 167, 406, 489, 490, 553–554
forced (*see also* Voluntary   511)
internal (*see also* Internal displacement 544–549)
international   549–552
labour migration   505, 511
work visas (*see also* New Zealand 290, 420)
multicausality, (*see above* Drivers of-)
planned   13n, 464, 511, 525, 536, 547–548, 562–564
relocation (*see also above* Planned   525, 547–548, 562–564)
remittances (*see* Remittances)
temporary (*see also* Temporary Protection) as a survival strategy
triggers (*see above* Drivers of-)
voluntary (*see also* Forced   511)
Minors. *See* 'Family'; Children
Mitigation   14, 16, 301, 320, 355, 387, 465n, 467, 495, 500, 510, 518, 524–525, 533, 536–537, 539, 541, 545, 546, 562–570, 573
More favourable standards. *See also* Qualification Directive, minimum standards   74n, 252
MSS v. Belgium and Greece. *See* European Court of Human Rights (ECtHR)

National Asylum Support Service (NASS)
Multifaceted approaches. *See* Holistic responses, importance of
Nansen Conference on Climate Change and Displacement in the 21st Century

Nansen Principles. *See* Nansen Conference on Climate Change and Displacement in the 21st Century
Nansen Initiative. *See also* Platform on Disaster Displacement   421, 508, 527–532, 538–539, 575
National security
and the principle of *non-refoulement* 208–223, 248, 250, 253, 273
as a ground for denying entry or protection   157n, 568, 573
Natural disasters. *See* Disasters
'Naturally occurring phenomenon'. *See* ECtHR, Sufi & *Elmi v. UK*; Medical cases
New Zealand. *See also* Australia; Authorisation to stay (discretionary), New Zealand; Complementary protection, New Zealand; Kiribati; Medical cases; Tuvalu
Court of Appeal (*see below* Immigration and Protection Tribunal (NZIPT))
High Court (*see below* Immigration and Protection Tribunal (NZIPT))
'humanitarian appeal' (*see also* Authorisation to stay (discretionary)   289, 291, 357, 403–406)
Immigration and Protection Tribunal (NZIPT) (*see also above and below*
'Humanitarian appeal' and 'Protected person' status   289–292, 354–357)
'protected person' status (*see also* Complementary protection 354–357)
refugee status denied to Pacific Island applicants   289–292, 332–333
Supreme Court (*see above* Immigration and Protection Tribunal (NZIPT))
'Teitiota case' (*see also above* New Zealand Immigration and Protection Tribunal (NZIPT)   289–291)
Nexus requirement. *See* Persecution
Non derogable rights   48, 78, 222, 223, 274, 306n, 376, 378
Non-discrimination. *See also* Discrimination 59, 64, 70, 115, 177, 189, 430, 456, 471, 571
operation of the principle of-under human rights treaties (ECHR, ICCPR, ICESCR)   187–191, 388, 481

Non-refoulement. See also Cruel, inhuman or degrading treatment; Environmentally-displaced persons; European Court of Human Rights, Extraterritoriality
  1966 Bangkok Principles on the Status and Treatment of Refugees   266–267
  1984 Cartagena Declaration on Refugees   264–265
  absolute nature   208–233, 249, 369, 370, 376–377, 379–380, 392, 415, 482–483, 507, 571
  application to armed conflicts situations   233–242
  AU Convention Governing the Specific Aspects of Refugee Problems in Africa   247
  Bangkok Principles on Status and Treatment of Refugees   247–248
  Convention against Torture (CAT)   223–225, 230–231
  Convention Governing the Specific Aspects of Refugee Problems in Africa   263–264
  customary international law, as   242–267
  derogable rights   186, 383n
  economic, social and cultural rights protected via civil and political rights   359, 486
  European Convention on Human Rights (ECHR), under the   218–223, 230–231
  Human Rights Committee (HRC)   199–203
  human rights law vs. refugee law (*see also above* Absolute nature   208–233, 507)
  humanitarian nature   483
  imminent risk   392–398
  indiscriminate threats   259–267
  International Covenant on Civil and Political Rights (ICCPR)   199–203, 223–225, 230–231
  Jus Cogens, as   248–254
  mass influx   367–369
  National Security Concerns   208–218
  Qualification Directive   225–226
  reality of the risk   155, 205, 207, 485, 507n, 559, 560
  under the Refugee Convention   208–233, 507
Non-State actors. *See also* Non-refoulement (Absolute nature)   228–231

Nuclear accident. *See* Disasters, Man-made, Nuclear
Nuclear power plant. *See* Disasters, Man-made, Nuclear
Nuclear weapons
  analogy with disasters regarding timing of harm   393, 394
  contingency plans   545
  ICJ Nuclear Weapons Advisory Opinion   262, 493n
  imminence of the threat   393, 394
  right to life   393, 395, 396
  State obligation to preserve the environment   497
  State responsibility (hazardous activity)   395, 493n

OAU Convention. *See also* African Union (AU Convention Governing the Specific Aspects of Refugee Problems in Africa)   255, 263, 473

Pacific island States. *See* Kiribati; Tuvalu
Paris Agreement. *See* UN Framework Convention on Climate Change (UNFCCC)
Participation by affected communities. *See also* Affected communities, views and participation
Particular social group. *See* Persecution
Persecution. *See also* Economic, social and cultural rights, Deprivation of-as persecution; Environmental 'refugee'; Human rights violations; Refugee; Refugee Convention
  effects of disasters as-   312–314
  environmental persecution   295, 297, 303–340
    deliberate infliction of environmental harm   329
    'particular social group'   335–337, 441–444
    France, nuclear disaster victims (excluded)   336
  nexus requirement/convention ground (*see also above* 'Particular social group')
    carbon dioxide emissions (*see also* Refugee Review Tribunal of Australia   330, 337, 466n)

non-State actors 316–321, 324–327, 331–340
severity threshold 299–300, 303, 307–308, 310, 322, 331, 339
serious harm 326
serious threats caused by disasters as- 312, 313
Persons in need of international protection. *See* B status refugees; *de facto* refugees; Extra-Convention refugees; 'Human rights refugees'; 'Humanitarian refugees'; Non-removable persons
Persons "otherwise in need of protection". *See* Sweden
Planned migration. *See* Migration
Platform on Disaster Displacement. *See also* Nansen Initiative 532
Pollution. *See also* Climate change, as Pollution 361, 396–397, 466n, 493, 498, 524, 560–561
Poverty. *See* Destitution
  as inhuman and degrading treatment (*see* MSS *v. Belgium and Greece*)
Precautionary principle. *See also* International environmental law 560, 561
Pre-emptive movement. *See also* Migration, planned; Migration, as adaptation; Relocation/resettlement;
Resilience 299–300, 537, 549n, 551
Preparedness. *See also* Disasters; Environmentally-displaced persons 387, 486, 490, 536, 540, 541, 544–546, 565
Prima facie refugees. *See also* Non-*refoulement*, Temporary protection 232, 254, 260n, 265, 366, 464, 465
Private life, right to. *See* Right to private life
Progressive realisation. *See* Economic, social and cultural rights; International Covenant on Economic, Social and Cultural Rights (ICESCR) 377, 380n, 541
Prohibition of torture, cruel, inhuman or degrading treatment or punishment. *See also* Cruel, inhuman or degrading treatment; *Non-refoulement*
Proportionality. *See also* European Convention on Human Rights, qualified rights; Balancing rights 41n, 78, 378, 483
'Protected person' status. *See* New Zealand

'Protection Agenda'. *See* Nansen Initiative
Protection gaps 268–269
Public emergency threatening the life of the nation. *See also* Non-*refoulement*, absolute nature 222–223
Public order 171

Qualification Directive. *See also* Refugee Convention; Subsidiary protection; Temporary Protection Directive 6, 103–181
  complementary protection *vs.* discretionary forms of protection 22n
  exclusion clauses 215
  harmonisation 168–171, 181
  history 106–123
  international protection regime 114–123
  Relationship to the Refugee Convention 114–118
  status (*see* Legal status, subsidiary protection)
  travaux préparatoires 107–114

Rapid-onset. *See* Sudden-onset events
Real risk 86, 89, 120, 123–124, 148, 149, 154, 159, 165, 193, 194, 197–199, 201, 203, 205–206, 219–220, 223, 228, 235–240, 272, 274, 278, 296, 300, 341–342, 345, 347, 351, 367–368, 376, 384–385, 394, 398, 408, 417, 422, 473, 476, 483, 485, 561
Refoulement. *See Non-refoulement*
Refugee. *See also* Climate change 'refugee'; Environmental 'refugee'; Environmentally-displaced persons; International refugee law; Refugee Convention
  'A term of art' 509
  additional categories 509
  claims based on climate change/environmental degradation (*see* Australia; New Zealand)
  credibility 175, 297, 559
  definition (*see also* Climate change 'refugee'; Environmental 'refugee'; Environmentally-displaced persons; Persecution 21, 87–88, 141, 294–295, 304, 338, 430)
    broadened in regional instruments 263–267
    discriminatory element 323–324, 326

Refugee. (cont.)
  revision (*see* Refugee Convention, Expansion, Extension of status to other categories of protected persons)
  under the Qualification Directive   114, 119, 293n, 294, 296, 306
  discriminatory denial of protection/humanitarian assistance   333–335
  exclusion clauses   212–215
    crime against humanity   213, 216
  persecution (*see* Persecution)
  rates/statistics   171–172, 268
  status   448, 450, 463
  temporary situations covered   467
Refugee Convention. *See also* Complementary protection; Qualification Directive; Refugee; Regional refugee instruments
  application to additional categories of refugees (*see* Climate change 'refugee'; Environmental 'refugee'; Environmentally-displaced persons;Scope As a human rights instrument   468n)
  climate change-related claims (*see* Australia; New Zealand)
  constructive interpretation   430, 431, 440–450
  environmental persecution   299, 323, 326, 329
  exclusion clauses   209, 212–217, 224–225, 227, 366
  expansion   431–469
  extension of status to other categories of protected persons   445–450, 520–521
  Final Act (of the Conference of Plenipotentiaries)   165n, 432, 437–438, 445–446, 448–449, 455
  grounds for persecution (*see* Persecution)
  history   213n, 431–440
  humanitarian purpose   431, 440, 459, 468, 483, 507
  1967 Protocol   73–75, 87, 97n, 114, 115n, 264, 267n, 293–295, 328n, 338, 430, 438, 447, 452–455, 457–458, 463
  recast   450–469
  Recommendation E of the Final Act   165n, 432, 437–438, 445–446, 448–449, 455
  Second World War   213n, 430, 435, 441–442
  States' reluctance to ratify or expand   520–521
  travaux préparatoires   431–440
Refugee law. *See* International refugee law; connection to other branches of international law; Human rights law, relationship to refugee law; Convention on the Rights of the Child, relationship to refugee law; Best interests of the child, relationship to refugee law; International law, holistic interpretation; Treaties, holistic relationship   507, 534
Refugee Review Tribunal (Australia). *See also* Australia   332n, 335n, 336–337, 405n, 466n, 572–573
Refugee Status Appeals Authority. *See* New Zealand
Regional refugee instruments. *See* African Union (AU); Cartagena Declaration; Qualification Directive
Religion, freedom of   186n, 555
Relocation/resettlement. *See also* Affected communities, Importance of consultation, Culture/Identity; Host communities; Kiribati; Tuvalu   547–549
  contingency plans   544–547
  internal (*see also* Internal flight alternative   544–549)
  International   549–552
  large groups/population (*see also* Pacific island States   551)
  resettlement programs   536, 551–552
Remittances. *See also* Diaspora communities   563–564
Resettlement. *See* Relocation/resettlement
Residence permits. *See* Authorisations to stay (discretionary); Refugee, Status; Subsidiary protection, Status
Resilience. *See also* Migration, as adaptation
Resources, lack of access to. *See also* Conflicts; Protection, for socio-economic reasons
  conflicts over   286
Responsibility to protect individuals within jurisdiction   230, 390n, 476, 549
Returnability. *See also*   475, 476, 485, 553, 558, 559
Rights (Human rights). *See* Climate change, Human rights and-; Disasters, Human

INDEX 681

rights and-; Economic, social and cultural rights; Internal protection/Internal flight alternative (under the EU Qualification Directive)
Right to a fair trial   44, 90, 186n, 274, 305, 392, 556n
Right to an adequate standard of living   310, 331, 388
Right to an effective remedy   89, 90, 383n
Right to development   360
Right to education   555, 556n
Right to employment   96
Right to food   310, 311n, 388, 555
Right to health. *See also* Medical cases; Right to life   270, 271, 379, 389, 460
Right to a healthy and safe environment   460, 486, 541n, 560
Right to (adequate) housing   96, 360, 555
Right to liberty and security of the person   274
Right to life. *See also* Climate change, Human rights and-; Disasters, Human rights and-, 72, 76–78, 123, 271, 342, 360, 555
  in connection with other rights   311n
  New Zealand case law (*see also* New Zealand, Immigration and Protection Tribunal   291, 292n, 310n, 355)
  non derogable right (*see also* Non derogable rights   78, 222n, 306n, 308)
  non-refoulement   124, 125n, 128, 186, 193–195, 201, 202, 206n, 222n, 247, 251n, 272n, 383n
  nuclear weapons and-   393
  other rights derived from the-   391, 460
  scope   349, 391, 460
  State's obligation to take steps to protect   291, 292n, 355, 388, 395
  violation of-as persecution   306
  violation of-as serious harm (*see also* Subsidiary protection   128, 272)
Right to private life. *See also* Medical cases   81, 186n, 270, 271, 274, 419, 555, 557n
Right to sanitation. *See* Right to life   291, 360, 460, 555
Right to self-determination   360
Right to water. *See also* Right to life   360, 391, 460, 555
Right to work   260, 300, 309n, 310, 480

Rio+20 "Earth Summit". *See* Affected communities (Indigenous people)

Safe country of origin   117
Safe third country   251, 253
Salination   313, 324, 397
Saltwater intrusion. *See* Salination
Sea-level rise. *See* Climate change, Impacts   359
Security. *See also* Conflicts   284, 386, 505n
'Serious and individual threat'. *See* Subsidiary protection
Serious harm. *See* Persecution; Subsidiary protection
Serious threat. *See also* Persecution; Subsidiary protection   257
  as trigger for displacement   511n
'Sinking islands'. *See* 'Disappearing States'
Slow-Onset Disasters. *See* Disasters
Small island States. *See also* 'Disappearing States'; Kiribati; Tuvalu
Socio-economic harm. *See* Economic, social and cultural rights; *Non-refoulement*; Persecution
Soering case (ECtHR). *See* European Court of Human Rights (ECtHR)
Somalia (return to). *See Sufi & Elmi v. UK*
State practice. *See also* Authorisation to stay on discretionary basis; *Non-refoulement*
  ad hoc responses   417–421
    Brazil   419–420
    France   417–419
    Germany   419
    Netherlands   419
    UK   419
    United States   399–400
  Haiti   417–420
  humanitarian protection (*see* Authorisation to stay on discretionary basis)
  temporary protection (*see* Temporary protection)
State responsibility. *See also* International Law Commission
  for climate change   330n
  for disasters   387
  for environmental displacement   489–503, 515–517

682 INDEX

State responsibility. (cont.)
  for industrial/technological accidents 493
Subsidiary protection. *See also* Complementary forms of protection; Complementary protection; Qualification Directive; Refugee status; Temporary protection
  amendment (*see below* Extension to environmentally-displaced persons (a proposal))
  armed conflicts (*see below* Indiscriminate violence)
  and international human rights law 123–129
  and residual forms of protection 270–271
  as an instrument of compromise 169
  as codification of existing practices 169, 270–271
  death penalty and execution 341–343
  definition 118–121
  distinguished from temporary protection 95, 111, 158
  exclusion clauses 209, 212, 215–217, 227
  Discretionary Leave (UK) (*see also* Authorisation to stay (discretionary)) 273
  extension to environmentally-displaced persons (a proposal) 469–474
  granted in cases not covered by the Qualification Directive 268–269, 274–275
  harmonisation 103, 110, 168–181
  history (*see also* Ad hoc responses to refugees 106–114, 270)
  'humanitarian protection' (United Kingdom) 272, 348, 406
  indiscriminate violence 112, 129–168, 233, 347–352, 469–474
  indiscriminate threats 166, 469–474
  individual threat 121, 131–159, 234, 341, 348, 472
  international or internal armed conflict 160–168, 178n
  rates/statistics 171–172, 268
  relationship to refugee status 127–128
  serious harm (*see also above* Indiscriminate violence, Individual threat 105, 112, 120–121, 126, 134, 138, 139, 234, 272, 277, 340)
    actors of- 230, 316–317

  extended definition (a proposal) 472, 571
  impacts of environmental degradations/disasters as- 341–352, 422, 444, 470–474
  previous occurrences as indication of real risk of future- 296
  relevant provisions of the ECHR 272
  serious threat (*see also below* Threat to life or person 135, 139, 164n, 167, 234, 261)
  status (*see also* Legal status, subsidiary protection 118, 129, 261n, 448, 450, 175n, 449)
  threat to life or person (*see also above* Serious threat 135, 164n, 234, 261, 348, 350, 351, 571)

Torture, inhuman or degrading treatment or punishment 343–347
Sudden-onset events. *See also* Disasters
Sufi & Elmi v. UK. See European Court of Human Rights (ECtHR)
Sweden. *See* Complementary protection
Syria. *See* Temporary Protection Directive
Technological accident. *See* Disasters, Man-made, Nuclear, Technological
'Temporary Protected Status' (United States). *See* Haiti; State practice, *Ad hoc* responses
Temporary protection. *See also* Indiscriminate threats; *Prima facie* refugees, Temporary Protection Directive
  and the principle of *non-refoulement* 96
  definition 95–96
  distinguished from complementary protection 95, 111
Temporary Protection Directive. *See also* Qualification Directive; Temporary protection 94–102, 111, 132, 399–403, 474–475
  not yet activated
    Afghanistan asylum-sekers 98
    Syrian conflict 98, 100–101
Terminology 509–513
Threat to life or freedom/person
  as persecution 305, 308n, 313, 323, 328, 339
  as a driver for displacement 511n, 553
  internal protection alternative 479

INDEX 683

non-refoulement under the Refugee Convention   304
non-refoulement under the ECHR   368
subsidiary protection   234, 348, 350, 351, 571

Torture. *See also* Complementary protection; Convention against Torture; Cruel, inhuman or degrading treatment; European Convention on Human Rights; International Covenant on Civil and Political Rights; *Non-Refoulement*; Prohibition of Torture, cruel, inhuman or degrading treatment or punishment; Socio-economic harm/rights; Subsidiary protection

Treaty on the Non-Proliferation of Nuclear Weapons (NPT). *See also* Nuclear weapons   395

Tuvalu. *See also* Adaptation; Affected communities, Culture/Identity, Importance of consultation; Australia; 'Disappearing States'; Indiscriminate threats; Migration, Alleviation of population/resource pressures; New Zealand; Remittances
    289n, 290–292, 299n, 310n, 332n, 333, 335n, 354–357, 403, 455–456, 465n, 466, 474, 535n, 554n
    buying land   535n
    climate change impacts (*see also* Kiribati, Climate change impacts   2, 289, 313, 324, 337, 568)
    climate change refugees (not) (*see* Australia; Climate change 'refugees'; New Zealand)
    demographic pressure   313
    'disappearing State'   474, 554–555n
    government, role of-   335n, 355, 357, 465n, 535n, 554–555n
        reversal of traditional refugee paradigm (*see also* Climate change 'refugee',   466)
    migration, as a last resort   555n
    labour market   313
    rejection of 'refugee' label   466, 512
    relocation   534–535
    right to life   355
    slow-onset environmental degradation   474

UN Commission on Human Rights   2n, 264, 389n, 412n, 518n, 557n
UN Development Programme (UNDP)   387n, 412n
UN Emergency Relief Coordinator   427, 566
UN Environment Programme   11, 298n, 516n, 526
UN Framework Convention on Climate Change (UNFCCC). *See also* Climate change; Environmentally-displaced persons   14
    addressing the causes of climate change   14
    Cancun agreements   525–526
    Copenhagen Summit   524
    COP   21 (*see below* Paris Agreement)
    displacement and-   513, 525, 531
    Durban Agreement   524–525
    environmentally-displaced persons (*see below* Warsaw International Mechanism)
    Green Climate Fund   542n
    loss and damages (*see below* Warsaw International Mechanism)
    migration   506n
    Paris Agreement (*see also* Adaptation   530–532)
    States' reluctance to commit (*see also above* Copenhagen Summit   15, 491–492, 524)
    Warsaw International Mechanism for loss and damage associated with climate change impacts (*see also* Migration, As adaptation; Nansen Initiative   531)
UN Guiding Principles on Internal Displacement   2–3, 389, 518n, 554n, 557
UN High Commissioner for Refugees (UNHCR)
    guidelines on international protection
        exclusion clauses   216n
        internal flight   477n, 478n
    High Commissioner's Dialogue on Protection Challenges   6n, 24n, 527, 530n
    Human rights, climate change and displacement   527, 575n
    internally-displaced persons (IDP) (*see also* Internally-displaced persons (IDP)   256)

UN High Commissioner for Refugees. (cont.)
mandate   130, 253, 255–259, 263, 457n, 553n
natural disasters and climate change as drivers if displacement   527
new challenges   6n, 24n, 527, 530n
UN Human Rights Council   47, 575n
climate change and human rights   8n
resolutions on climate change and human rights   360, 362
UN Inter-Agency Standing Committee (IASC)   325n, 334n, 362–363, 485, 517n, 518n, 519n, 550n, 557, 558
UN Office for the Coordination of Humanitarian Affairs (OCHA)   526, 544n, 566n, 567n, 584, 585, 587
UN Office of the High Commissioner for Human Rights (OHCHR)
climate change and human rights   8, 361n, 501n, 502n
environmental disasters, call for suspension of returns   417
human rights and disasters   361
UN Population Fund   526
UN University Institute for Environment and Human Security (UNU-EHS)   5, 453n, 482n, 526
United Kingdom. *See also* Complementary protection; Discretionary Leave (UK); Humanitarian protection
Urbanisation, as a cause of displacement   323, 470

Vulnerability   362, 381–385, 387
inability to move   445
movement as a sign of   445, 552–553

War crime. *See* Exclusions clauses   213, 216
Warsaw International Mechanism for Loss and Damage associated with Climate Change Impacts. *See* UN Framework Convention on Climate Change (UNFCCC)
Water   15, 273, 284, 299, 302, 310, 312–313, 320–322, 329, 333n, 342n, 348, 349, 356, 359–360, 376, 385, 391, 395, 405, 407, 417, 460, 467, 471, 525, 540, 542, 550, 555, 558, 566, 587
Well-founded fear (of persecution). *See* Persecution
Women   59, 64, 107, 160, 231, 305, 346n, 362, 419, 443
World Food Programme   565
World War One. *See* First World War
World War Two. *See* Second World War